THE ATLAS OF
PIDGIN AND CREOLE
LANGUAGE STRUCTURES

The Atlas and Survey of Pidgin and Creole Languages

These books represent the most comprehensive guide ever published to the world's pidgins and creoles, designed, edited, and written by the world's leading experts in the field. The *Atlas* examines the distribution among pidgins and creoles of one hundred and thirty linguistic features, covering their phonology, syntax, morphology, and lexicons. The *Survey* consists of the socio-historical and linguistic profiles of each of the languages. It is divided into three volumes reflecting the languages from which the pidgins and creoles originated.

The Atlas of Pidgin and Creole Language Structures

Edited by
Susanne Maria Michaelis, Philippe Maurer,
Martin Haspelmath, and Magnus Huber

in collaboration with
Melanie Revis, Bradley Taylor, and the
APiCS Consortium

The Survey of Pidgin and Creole Languages

Edited by
Susanne Maria Michaelis, Philippe Maurer,
Martin Haspelmath, and Magnus Huber

in collaboration with
Melanie Revis

VOLUME I

English-based and Dutch-based Languages

VOLUME II

Portuguese-based, Spanish-based, and
French-based Languages

VOLUME III

Contact Languages Based on Languages from Africa,
Asia, Australia, and the Americas

The Atlas of Pidgin and Creole Language Structures

Susanne Maria Michaelis, Philippe Maurer,
Martin Haspelmath, and Magnus Huber

IN COLLABORATION WITH

Melanie Revis, Bradley Taylor,
and the *APiCS* Consortium

UNIVERSITY PRESS

Great Clarendon Street, OX2 6DP,
United Kingdom

Oxford University Press is a department of the University of Oxford.
It furthers the University's objective of excellence in research, scholarship,
and education by publishing worldwide. Oxford is a registered trademark of
Oxford University Press in the UK and in certain other countries

© Susanne Maria Michaelis, Philippe Maurer,
Martin Haspelmath, and Magnus Huber 2013

The moral rights of the authors have been asserted

First edition published in 2013

Impression: 1

All rights reserved. No part of this publication may be reproduced, stored in
a retrieval system, or transmitted, in any form or by any means, without the
prior permission in writing of Oxford University Press, or as expressly permitted
by law, by licence or under terms agreed with the appropriate reprographics
rights organization. Enquiries concerning reproduction outside the scope of the
above should be sent to the Rights Department, Oxford University Press, at the
address above

You must not circulate this work in any other form
and you must impose this same condition on any acquirer

British Library Cataloguing in Publication Data

Data available

ISBN 978–0–19–969139–5 (Atlas)
ISBN 978–0–19–967770–2 (Atlas and Set)

Typeset in Ehrhardt
by Peter Kahrel Ltd, Lancaster

Printed and bound at Grafos, Barcelona

Links to third party websites are provided by Oxford in good faith and
for information only. Oxford disclaims any responsibility for the materials
contained in any third party website referenced in this work.

THE *APiCS* CONSORTIUM

Enoch O. Aboh
Denise Angelo
Umberto Ansaldo
Philip Baker
Peter Bakker
Marlyse Baptista
Angela Bartens
Alan N. Baxter
Noël Bernard Biagui
Theresa Biberauer
Annegret Bollée
Adrienne Bruyn
Hugo C. Cardoso
J. Clancy Clements
Serge Colot
Hans den Besten
Hubert Devonish
Sabine Ehrhart
Geneviève Escure
Nicholas Faraclas
Joseph T. Farquharson
Dominique Fattier
Malcolm Awadajin Finney
William A. Foley
Anthony P. Grant
Lisa Green
Stephanie Hackert
Tjerk Hagemeijer
John Holm
Magnus Huber

Incanha Intumbo
Liliana Inverno
Khin Khin Aye
Thomas B. Klein
Thomas A. Klingler
Silvia Kouwenberg
Sibylle Kriegel
Jürgen Lang
Michelle Li
Lisa Lim
Ralph Ludwig
Xavier Luffin
Stefano Manfredi
Stephen Matthews
Philippe Maurer
Felicity Meakins
Michael Meeuwis
Rajend Mesthrie
Miriam Meyerhoff
Susanne Maria Michaelis
Bettina Migge
Maarten Mous
Salikoko S. Mufwene
Susanne Mühleisen
Peter Mühlhäusler
Pieter Muysken
Ingrid Neumann-Holzschuh
Scott Paauw
Elena Perekhvalskaya
Sara Petrollino

Stefan Pfänder
Ingo Plag
Marike Post
Paula Prescod
Nicolas Quint
Melanie Revis
Sarah J. Roberts
Marcel Rosalie
William J. Samarin
Anne Schröder
Eva Schultze-Berndt
Armin Schwegler
Jeff Siegel
Eeva Sippola
Peter Slomanson
Geoff P. Smith
Ian R. Smith
Norval S. H. Smith
Patrick O. Steinkrüger
Dominika Swolkien
Dahlia Thompson
Margot C. van den Berg
Hein van der Voort
Robbert van Sluijs
Tonjes Veenstra
Viveka Velupillai
Donald Winford
Kofi Yakpo

CONTENTS

The APiCS Consortium — v
List of Abbreviations — xiv
Acknowledgements — xvii
About the authors — xviii
Introduction — xxxi

Word order — 1

1. Order of subject, object, and verb — 2
   Magnus Huber
2. Order of possessor and possessum — 6
   Magnus Huber
3. Order of adjective and noun — 10
   Magnus Huber
4. Order of adposition and noun phrase — 14
   Magnus Huber
5. Order of demonstrative and noun — 18
   Philippe Maurer
6. Order of cardinal numeral and noun — 22
   Martin Haspelmath and Susanne Maria Michaelis
7. Order of relative clause and noun — 26
   Martin Haspelmath and Susanne Maria Michaelis
8. Order of degree word and adjective — 30
   Martin Haspelmath
9. Position of definite article in the noun phrase — 34
   Martin Haspelmath
10. Position of indefinite article in the noun phrase — 38
    Martin Haspelmath
11. Order of frequency adverb, verb, and object — 40
    Martin Haspelmath
12. Position of interrogative phrases in content questions — 44
    Martin Haspelmath

Nominal categories — 49

13. Gender distinctions in personal pronouns — 50
    Philippe Maurer
14. Dual in independent personal pronouns — 54
    Martin Haspelmath
15. Inclusive/exclusive distinction in independent personal pronouns — 58
    Martin Haspelmath and Susanne Maria Michaelis

Contents

16	Person syncretism in independent personal pronouns *Martin Haspelmath*	60
17	Special dependent person forms for subject and object *Martin Haspelmath*	64
18	Politeness distinctions in second-person pronouns *Martin Haspelmath*	68
19	Interrogative pronouns *Martin Haspelmath*	72
20	Pronoun conjunction *Martin Haspelmath*	76
21	Indefinite pronouns *Martin Haspelmath*	80
22	Occurrence of nominal plural markers *Martin Haspelmath*	84
23	Expression of nominal plural meaning *Martin Haspelmath*	88
24	The associative plural *Susanne Maria Michaelis and Martin Haspelmath*	92
25	Nominal plural marker and third-person-plural pronoun *Philippe Maurer*	96
26	Functions of reduplication *Martin Haspelmath*	100
27	Antidual of paired body-part terms *Susanne Maria Michaelis*	104
28	Definite articles *Martin Haspelmath*	106
29	Indefinite articles *Martin Haspelmath*	110
30	Generic noun phrases in subject function *Philippe Maurer*	114
31	Co-occurrence of demonstrative and definite article *Martin Haspelmath*	118
32	Pronominal and adnominal demonstratives *Philippe Maurer*	122
33	Distance contrasts in demonstratives *Philippe Maurer*	126
34	Adnominal distributive numerals *Philippe Maurer*	130
35	Ordinal numerals *Philippe Maurer*	134
36	Sortal numeral classifiers *Philippe Maurer*	138

Nominal syntax — 141

37	Marking of pronominal possessors *Martin Haspelmath*	142
38	Marking of possessor noun phrases *Martin Haspelmath*	146
39	Independent pronominal possessors *Martin Haspelmath*	150
40	Gender agreement of adnominal adjectives *Philippe Maurer*	154
41	Comparative adjective marking *Susanne Maria Michaelis*	158
42	Comparative standard marking *Susanne Maria Michaelis*	162

Verbal categories — 167

43	Position of tense, aspect, and mood markers in relation to the verb *Philippe Maurer*	168
44	Internal order of tense, aspect, and mood markers *Philippe Maurer*	172
45	Tightness of the link between the past marker and the verb *Philippe Maurer*	176
46	Tightness of the link between the progressive marker and the verb *Philippe Maurer*	180
47	Uses of the progressive marker *Philippe Maurer*	184
48	Uses of the habitual marker *Philippe Maurer*	188
49	Tense–aspect systems *Philippe Maurer*	192
50	Negation and tense, aspect, and mood marking *Philippe Maurer*	196
51	Present reference of stative verbs and past perfective reference of dynamic verbs *Philippe Maurer*	200
52	Aspect markers and inchoative meaning *Martin Haspelmath and Susanne Maria Michaelis*	204
53	Aspect change in verb chains *Philippe Maurer*	208
54	Suppletion according to tense and aspect *Philippe Maurer*	212
55	Ability verb and epistemic possibility *Philippe Maurer*	216
56	The prohibitive *Philippe Maurer*	220

Contents

Argument marking — 225

57	Marking of patient noun phrases *Martin Haspelmath*	226
58	Alignment of case marking of full noun phrases *Martin Haspelmath*	230
59	Alignment of case marking of personal pronouns *Martin Haspelmath*	232
60	Ditransitive constructions with 'give' *Martin Haspelmath and Susanne Maria Michaelis*	236
61	Order of recipient and theme in ditransitive constructions *Martin Haspelmath*	240
62	Expression of pronominal subjects *Martin Haspelmath*	244
63	Expletive subject in 'seem' constructions *Susanne Maria Michaelis*	248
64	Expletive subject of existential verb *Martin Haspelmath*	252
65	Raining constructions *Susanne Maria Michaelis*	256
66	Experiencer constructions with 'headache' *Susanne Maria Michaelis*	260
67	Experiencer constructions with 'like' *Susanne Maria Michaelis*	264
68	Experiencer constructions with 'fear' *Susanne Maria Michaelis*	268
69	Instrumental expressions *Philippe Maurer*	272
70	Comitatives and instrumentals *Philippe Maurer*	276
71	Noun phrase conjunction and comitative *Philippe Maurer*	280
72	Nominal and verbal conjunction *Martin Haspelmath*	284

Clausal syntax — 289

73	Predicative noun phrases *Susanne Maria Michaelis*	290
74	Predicative adjectives *Susanne Maria Michaelis*	294
75	Predicative locative phrases *Susanne Maria Michaelis*	298
76	Predicative noun phrases and predicative locative phrases *Susanne Maria Michaelis*	302

77	Predicative possession *Susanne Maria Michaelis*	306
78	Existential verb and transitive possession verb *Susanne Maria Michaelis*	310
79	Going to named places *Susanne Maria Michaelis*	314
80	Coming from named places *Susanne Maria Michaelis*	318
81	Motion-to and motion-from *Susanne Maria Michaelis*	322
82	Transitive motion verbs: 'push' *Susanne Maria Michaelis*	326
83	Transitive motion verbs: 'pull' *Susanne Maria Michaelis*	330
84	Directional serial verb constructions with 'come' and 'go' *Philippe Maurer and Susanne Maria Michaelis*	334
85	'Take' serial verb constructions *Philippe Maurer*	338
86	'Give' serial verb constructions *Philippe Maurer*	342
87	Reflexive constructions *Martin Haspelmath*	346
88	Intensifiers and reflexive pronouns *Martin Haspelmath*	350
89	Reciprocal constructions *Martin Haspelmath*	354
90	Passive constructions *Martin Haspelmath*	358
91	Applicative constructions *Martin Haspelmath and Susanne Maria Michaelis*	362

Complex sentences   365

92	Subject relative clauses *Susanne Maria Michaelis and Martin Haspelmath*	366
93	Object relative clauses *Susanne Maria Michaelis and Martin Haspelmath*	370
94	Instrument relative clauses *Martin Haspelmath and Susanne Maria Michaelis*	374
95	Complementizer with verbs of speaking *Susanne Maria Michaelis*	378
96	Complementizer with verbs of knowing *Susanne Maria Michaelis*	382
97	'Want' complement subjects *Susanne Maria Michaelis and Martin Haspelmath*	386

Contents

98	Complements of 'think' and 'want' *Susanne Maria Michaelis*	390
99	Verb doubling in temporal clauses *Susanne Maria Michaelis and Martin Haspelmath*	394

Negation, questions, and focusing — 397

100	Negative morpheme types *Martin Haspelmath and Susanne Maria Michaelis*	398
101	Position of standard negation *Martin Haspelmath*	402
102	Negation and indefinite pronouns *Martin Haspelmath*	406
103	Polar questions *Martin Haspelmath*	410
104	Focusing of the noun phrase *Philippe Maurer*	414
105	Verb doubling and focus *Philippe Maurer*	418
106	Focus particle 'also' *Martin Haspelmath and Susanne Maria Michaelis*	422

Lexicon — 427

107	Vocative markers *Susanne Maria Michaelis and Martin Haspelmath*	428
108	Para-linguistic usages of clicks *Martin Haspelmath*	432
109	*Pequenino* *Magnus Huber*	436
110	*Savvy* *Magnus Huber*	440
111	'Tears' *Magnus Huber*	444
112	'Hand' and 'arm' *Magnus Huber*	448
113	'Finger' and 'toe' *Magnus Huber*	452
114	'Body hair' and 'feather' *Magnus Huber*	456
115	'Hear' and 'smell' *Magnus Huber*	460
116	'Green' and 'blue' *Magnus Huber*	464
117	Female and male animals *Magnus Huber*	468

Phonology — 473

118	Syllable onsets *Philippe Maurer*	474
119	Syllable codas *Philippe Maurer*	475
120	Tone *Philippe Maurer*	480
	Introduction to the segment chapters	484
121	Vowel height distinctions *Martin Haspelmath*	486
122	Nasal vowels *Martin Haspelmath*	487
123	The schwa vowel *Martin Haspelmath*	488
124	Labiodental fricatives *Martin Haspelmath*	489
125	Palato-alveolar sibilants *Martin Haspelmath*	490
126	The voiced sibilant [z] *Martin Haspelmath*	491
127	Interdental fricatives *Martin Haspelmath*	492
128	The palatal nasal *Martin Haspelmath*	493
129	Prenasalized consonants *Martin Haspelmath*	494
130	The segment [h] *Martin Haspelmath*	495

References — 497
Subject index — 507
Author index — 514
Language index — 518

LIST OF ABBREVIATIONS

Abbreviation	Meaning
1	first person
2	second person
3	third person
A	agent-like argument of canonical transitive verb
ABIL	ability (verb), abilitive mood
ABL	ablative, movement away from something
ABS	absolutive
ACC	accusative
ACCID	accidental
ACT	action marker
ADD	additive
ADJ	adjective, adjectival suffix
ADJ2	second adjective marker
ADJ3	third adjective marker
ADJZ	adjectivalizer
ADMON	admonitive
ADR	addressive
ADV	adverb, adverbial
ADVERS	adversative
ADVZ	adverbializer
AFF	affirmative
AG	agent, agentive
AGR	agreement
ALL	allative
ANAPH	anaphoric
ANIM	animate
ANT	anterior
ANTIP	antipassive
APPL	applicative
ART	article
ASP	aspect (marker, particle)
ASS	associative (plural)
ASSOBL	associative (obligation)
ASSOC	associative (preposition)
ATT	attenuative
ATTR	attributive marker
AUX	auxiliary
BE	identity copula, locative-existential copula
BEN	benefactive
BGND	background
CAUS	causative
CIS	cislocative, movement towards speaker
CL	class
CLF	classifier
CNS	consuetudinal
CNTRFAC	counterfactual
COLL	collocative, associative plural
COM	comitative
COMP	complementizer
COMPAR	comparative affix/marker
COMPL	accomplished, completive
COMPL1, COMPL2	completive 1, completive 2
CONC	concessive
COND	conditional
CONF	confirmation particle
CONJ	conjunction
CONN	connective
CONT	continuative, continuous, ongoing action
CONTR	contrastive
COP	copula, equational copula
CPD	compound, component derived by tone deletion
CSEC	consecutive
CTPL	contemplated aspect
CVB	converb
DAT	dative
DECL	declarative
DEF	definite
DEFRCLT	deferential clitic
DEG	degree (particle, word)
DEIC	deictic
DELIM	delimitative
DEM	demonstrative
DEP	dependent (pronoun)
DEPV	dependent verb
DESID	desiderative
DET	determiner
DETRANS	detransitivizing
DIM	diminutive
DIR	direction, directional
DISASS	disassociative
DISC	discourse marker
DISC.PCL	discourse particle
DIST	distal

Abbreviations

DISTR	distributive		INDF	indefinite
DO	direct object		INDP	independent
DS	different subject		INF	infinitive
DU	dual		INFL	inflectional marker
DUB	dubitative, uncertain knowledge		INGR	ingressive
DUMMY	dummy pronoun		INS	instrumental
DUR	durative		INSIST	insistence
EMPH	emphatic, emphasis		INT	intentional, intentionalis
ENCL	enclitic		INTENS	intensifier, intensitive, intensive, intensity
EPIST	epistemic		INTERJ	interjection
EQ.COP	equational copula		INTERM	intermediate (between distal and proximal)
ERG	ergative		INTFR	intensifier
EVID	evidential		INTIM	intimate
EXCL	exclusive		INTR	intransitive
excl	exclusive (in value boxes, §7 of Introduction)		INV	inverse marker
EXCLAM	exclamation		IO	indirect object
EXIST	existential		IPFV	imperfective
EXPL	expletive		IRR	irrealis
F	feminine, female		ITER	iterative
FAM	familiar		JUDG	judgment
FILL	filler (item)		LINK	link vowel, link consonant
FIN	finite		LK	linker
FOC	focus (marker)		LOC	locative
FPST	far past		LOCV	locative verb
FUT	future		LOG	logophoric personal pronoun
FV	final vowel		M	masculine
GEN	genitive		MIR	mirative
GENER	generic		MKD	marked
GER	gerund		MOD	modal (auxiliary, verb, particle), modality
H	high toneme		MOD.AUX	modal auxiliary
HAB	habitual		MODIF	modifier
HABIL	habilitative		MOOD	mood particle
HAVE	possession predicate		N	neuter
HL	highlighter		N-	non-
HON	honorific		NACCOMPL	non-accomplished
HORT	hortative		NARR	narrative
HUM	human		NECESS	necessity
IDENTITY.COP	identity copula		NEG	negation, negative
IDEO	ideophone		NEG.FIN	negator preceding a finite verb
IGN	ignorative		NEG2	2nd negative marker
IMM.PST	immediate past		NFIN	non-finite
IMP	imperative		NFUT	non-future
IMPRS	impersonal pronoun		NHON	non-honorific
INAB	inability		NMLZ	nominalizer, nominalization, nominalizing suffix
INACC	inaccomplished		NOM	nominative
INAN	inanimate		NP	noun phrase
INC	inchoative		NPST	non-past
INCEP	inceptive (future)		NSBJ	non-subject
INCL	inclusive		NSG	non-singular
INCOMPL	incompletive		NUM	number, numeral
INCORP	incorporated (noun)		OBJ	object (marker)
IND	indicative		OBL	oblique

Abbreviations

OBLIG	obligative (mood marker), obligatory	REL	relative, relativizer
OBV	obviative	REL.PCL	relative particle
OPT	optative	REL.PRO	relative pronoun
ORD	ordinal	REM	remote
ORD.NUM	ordinal numeral	REP	repetition, repetitive
P	patient-like argument of canonical transitive verb	REPORT	reportative
		REQ	requestative
PASS	passive	RES	resultative
PAUC	paucal	S	single argument of canonical intransitive verb
PCL	particle		
PERM	permission, permissive	SBJ	subject
PERMANENT	permanent state	SBJV	subjunctive
PFV	perfective, narrative perfective (marker)	SENT.PCL	sentence particle
PL	plural	SEQ	sequence marker
PM	predicate marker	SG	singular
POL	polite	shrd	shared (in value boxes, §7 of Introduction)
POSS	possessive, possessor, adpositional, possessive marker		
		SI	subject index
POSTP	postposition	SIML	similative
POT	potential	SM	subject marker
PRED	predicative	SPECUL	speculative
PREP	preposition	SS	same subject
PRESV	presentational, presentative	STANDARD.MARKER	comparative standard
PRET	preterite	STAT	stative
PRF	perfect	SUBORD	subordinator
PRO	pronoun, resumptive pronoun	SUPERL	superlative
PROG	progressive	SUPPL	suppletive
PROG2	second progressive	SVC	serial verb construction
PROH	prohibitive	TA	transitive animate
PROX	proximal/proximate	TAM	tense aspect mood
PRS	present (tense)	TEMP	temporal
PSREFL	pseudo-reflexive pronoun	TMA	tense mood aspect
PST	past, past before past	TNS	tense particle
PTCP	participle	TOP	topic
PURP	purpose, purposive	TR	transitive
Q	interrogative, question (word, particle, marker)	V	verb
Q.TAG	question tag	V.PREF	verbal prefix
QUANT	quantifier, quantitative	VAL	validator
QUOT	quotative	VBLZ	verbalizer
RECP	reciprocal	VOC	vocative
RED	reduplication	VOL	volitive
REFL	reflexive	VPCL	verb particle

ACKNOWLEDGEMENTS

The editors would like to express their gratitude to a number of institutions and people without whose help and collaboration the *Atlas of Pidgin and Creole Language Structures* (and the three accompanying *Survey* volumes) would not have been possible.

First, we are grateful to the Deutsche Forschungsgemeinschaft (DFG) for providing crucial funding for Susanne Maria Michaelis and Melanie Revis and for several Giessen-based student assistants over a period of three and a half years (2008–2011) through Justus Liebig University Giessen. The efficient administration at the DFG and in Giessen allowed us to concentrate on our research.

Second, we thank the Max Planck Institute for Evolutionary Anthropology (Leipzig), and in particular the director of the Department of Linguistics, Bernard Comrie, for generously funding seven conferences and workshops between 2006 and 2010, as well as providing funds for Leipzig-based assistants and reliable technical support.

Among the people who helped the editors in putting together the four volumes of the *APiCS* project, our collaborators Melanie Revis and Bradley Taylor stand out. In particular the handling of the different reviewed and revised dataset versions which are the basis for the chapters in this *Atlas* was largely in Melanie's hands. Brad's full control of the database and his patience with the contributors' questions was equally central for the project. Hans-Jörg Bibiko created all the maps in this atlas, patiently providing many sets of improved versions, and giving us crucial advice on various map-related questions. Claudia Schmidt helped us organize all the workshops and conferences, from the website to the coffee breaks and travel claim forms. Thanks to you all for your super-efficient work!

We had the pleasure to work with several highly motivated and committed student assistants, both in Giessen and in Leipzig: Oleg Batt, Tyko Dirksmeyer, Lea Gleixner, Alexander Jahraus, Christina Klempel, Sven Langbein, Verena Pietzner, Sandy Schaber, Eva-Maria Schmortte, Ulrike Schneider, and Bianca Widlitzki. No matter how fascinating a project may be, there will always be tasks of the more monotonous kind (such as checking consistency in the abbreviations of thousands of glosses in the database). It was our student assistants who bore the brunt of these chores, but we hope that they got a sense of the excitement of a large-scale collaborative project on some of the world's most intriguing languages.

We also use this opportunity to extend our thanks to Hagen Jung and Robert Forkel for developing *APiCS Online*, OUP's typesetter Peter Kahrel, and John Davey of Oxford University Press.

Finally, we would like to thank our contributors (the Consortium members) for their patience and devotion to a project that certainly demanded more personal commitment than the average publication. It is their perseverance that made *APiCS* possible.

Susanne Maria Michaelis, Philippe Maurer,
Martin Haspelmath, and Magnus Huber
Leipzig, Zürich, and Giessen, March 2013

ABOUT THE AUTHORS

ENOCH O. ABOH is currently Professor of Linguistics at the University of Amsterdam. He received his Ph.D. at the University of Geneva. His principal research interests are in theoretical syntax, comparative syntax (with a particular focus on Kwa languages), as well as discourse-syntax interface, language creation, and language change. He is the author of *The Morphosyntax of Complement-Head Sequences: Clause Structure and Word Order Patterns in Kwa* (OUP, 2004) and co-editor of *Complex Processes in New Languages* (John Benjamins, 2009, with Norval Smith). Recently he has been organizing the African Linguistics School in Accra and Porto-Novo.

DENISE ANGELO is a linguist and Senior Project Officer for English as a Second Language at the Department of Education and Training, Queensland, Australia. While being employed as the Senior Linguist and manager of the Diwurruwurru-Jaru Aboriginal Language Centre in Katherine, Northern Territory, she conducted research on Kriol as well as preparing Kriol materials for literacy courses and interpreter training. She is currently involved with research on creole languages spoken in Queensland and on language acquisition in the multilingual setting of remote north-east Australia.

UMBERTO ANSALDO specializes in language contact, linguistic typology and languages of China, South and Southeast Asia. He is currently Associate Professor of Linguistics in The School of Humanities of The University of Hong Kong. There he teaches courses in sociolinguistics, diversity and endangerment, war, and self-defence. He is the author of *Contact Languages. Ecology and evolution in Asia* (CUP, 2009) and is preparing a second monograph on simplicity and complexity for OUP.

PHILIP BAKER has published articles and books on Mauritian and related creoles since 1969. He has also done research and published on Chinese Pidgin English, various Pidgin Englishes of Australia and Melanesia, and the Creole English of St Kitts. His linguistic research has always been combined with other careers as a film editor, newspaper editor, in distance teaching and, currently, in publishing. He retired as Professor of Contact Linguistics at the University of Westminster in 2008 and now divides his time between London and Sri Lanka.

PETER BAKKER teaches linguistics at the University of Aarhus. His research combines typology with anthropological and historical linguistics. He focuses on contact languages, especially new languages. He has worked, among others, on Basque, Romani, and Algonquian (Amerindian) languages, also in contact with one another. His book on Michif (1997) was the first in-depth study of the genesis of a mixed language. Recently he has been working on deep prehistoric connections between Salish and Algonquian languages, the typological distinctness of creole languages, and universals of pidgins and pidginization.

MARLYSE BAPTISTA is Professor of Linguistics at the University of Michigan. She is the author of *The Syntax of Cape Verdean Creole* (John Benjamins, 2002) and the co-editor with Jacqueline Guéron of *Noun Phrases in Creole Languages* (John Benjamins, 2007). She specializes in the morpho-syntax of creole languages, their genesis, and development. She is also interested in their representation in education. More recently, she has started to examine the cognitive processes involved in creole formation and is currently collaborating on the design of experiments testing some of these processes.

ANGELA BARTENS is currently Docent of Ibero-Romance Philology at the University of Helsinki and Acting Chair of Spanish at the University of Turku. Previously, she worked as Visiting Scholar at the Graduate Center of the City University of New York, Assistant Professor at the Colombian National University in San Andrés, and she was Acting Chair of Ibero-Romance Languages at the University of Helsinki. Besides creole languages, her research interests include general contact linguistics, sociolinguistics, critical discourse analysis, and Latin American Spanish and Portuguese. She has done fieldwork on San Andrés and Providence Creole English.

ALAN N. BAXTER has until recently taught Linguistics in the Department of Portuguese of the University of Macau (China). He is now based at the Federal University of Bahia (Salvador, Brazil). His published work includes *A Grammar of Kristang (Malacca Creole Portuguese)* (Pacific Linguistics, 1988), the co-authored works *A Dictionary of Kristang – English* (Pacific Linguistics, 2004) and *O Português Afro-Brasileiro* (Afro-Brazilian Portuguese, 2009), in addition to descriptive papers in scholarly books and journals. He is primarily interested in language variation and contact involving Portuguese, and the description and typology of Asian varieties of Creole Portuguese.

NOËL BERNARD BIAGUI is currently a Ph.D. student at LLACAN (Paris), where he is writing a dissertation devoted to the linguistic description of his mother tongue, Casamancese Creole. He also has experience in Niger-Congo linguistics, having studied the grammar (phonology and class-system) of the Nyun dialect of Djibonker (Casamance, Southern Senegal) for his Masters in Linguistics, defended at Cheikh Anta Diop University (Dakar, Senegal) in 2005.

THERESA BIBERAUER is a senior research associate at the University of Cambridge. She specializes in theoretical, comparative and historical syntax, with interface, acquisition and contact issues also being a focus of interest. Much of her research has centred on the clause structure of the Germanic languages, with the peculiar patterns of variation and change exhibited by Afrikaans forming the heart of her doctoral work. She is currently working with Ian Roberts on the project "Reconsidering Comparative Syntax".

ANNEGRET BOLLÉE is Professor emerita of the University of Bamberg, where she taught Romance linguistics (French, Italian, and Spanish) from 1978 to 2002. Her research activities focused on Indian Ocean Creoles. She has published a grammar of Seychelles Creole based on fieldwork in the islands (1977) and a book on the development of Reunion Creole, based on an edition of eighteenth-century religious texts (2007). After completing the *Dictionnaire étymologique des créoles français de l'Océan Indien* (4 vols, 1993–2007) she is now preparing a *Dictionnaire étymologique des créoles français d'Amérique* in collaboration with Dominique Fattier (Cergy-Pontoise) and Ingrid Neumann-Holzschuh (Regensburg).

ADRIENNE BRUYN is a historical linguist with a special interest in language contact phenomena. Her PhD dissertation concerned the development of determiners and relative clauses in Sranan. Since then, she has investigated historical developments in various creole languages, including those of Suriname, with a focus on the interplay between grammaticalization and transfer from the substrate languages. She is involved in the Suriname Creole Archive (SUCA), containing digitized 18th-century Sranan and Saramaccan materials.

HUGO C. CARDOSO has conducted research mostly on Portuguese-lexified contact languages, especially the Indo-Portuguese Creoles of India but also Suriname's Saramaccan. His main interests include language description and documentation, language contact theory, typology, and historical linguistics. He has also published on topics of a sociolinguistic and ethnological nature. He is the author of *The Indo-Portuguese Language of Diu* (LOT dissertation, 2009) and co-editor of *Gradual Creolization; Studies Celebrating Jacques Arends* (John Benjamins, 2009).

J. CLANCY CLEMENTS is Professor of Linguistics and Spanish & Portuguese at Indiana University (Bloomington). He researches and teaches in the areas of functional syntax and contact linguistics, especially pidgins and creoles, with a focus on Asian-Portuguese creoles. His main publications are: *The Genesis of a Language: The Formation and Development of Korlai Portuguese* (John Benjamins,

About the Authors

1996) and *The Linguistic Legacy of Spanish and Portuguese: Colonial Expansion and Language Change* (Cambridge University Press, 2009).

SERGE COLOT is Associate Professor at The Université des Antilles et de la Guyane. He was trained at the University of Poitiers and the Université des Antilles et de la Guyane. He mainly works on lexical and grammatical aspects of his native language, Guadeloupean Creole, and the closely related Martinican Creole. Among his publications is *Guide de lexicologie créole* (Presses Universitaires Créoles, 2001).

HANS DEN BESTEN was associate professor at the University of Amsterdam and professor extraordinary in general linguistics at Stellenbosch University, South Africa. He passed away in July 2010. He was one of the major investigators of Afrikaans, but also published on Germanic languages in general and Khoekhoe. His research interests lay mainly in the field of syntax, but he has also published on the history of Afrikaans and Cape Dutch Pidgin. He is co-editor of *Afrikaans: een drieluik* (Stichting Neerlandistiek VU, 2009, co-edited by Frans Hinskens and Jerzy Koch) and *Afrikaans en variëteiten van het Nederlands* (Taal en Tongval, 1996, co-edited by Jan Goossens, Frits Ponelis, and Pieter van Reenen). In 2012, a selection of unpublished work was posthumously published as *Roots of Afrikaans* (John Benjamins, edited by Ton van der Wouden).

HUBERT DEVONISH is Professor of Linguistics at the University of the West Indies, Mona, Jamaica. He has published extensively on the suprasegmental systems of creole languages, as in his books, *Talking in Tones: A Study of Tone in Afro-European Creole Languages* (Karia Press, 1989) and *Talking Rhythm, Stressing Tone: The Role of Prominence in Anglo-West African Creole Languages* (Arawak Publications, 2002). With Dahlia Thompson, he has published a *Concise Grammar of Guyanese Creole* (Lincom Europa, 2010). In addition, he has researched and published widely in the areas of sociolinguistics, language variation, language planning, and language policy, with his best-known work in this area being *Language and Liberation: Creole Language Politics in the Caribbean* (2nd edn., Arawak Publications, 2007).

SABINE EHRHART is Associate Professor for ethnolinguistics at the University of Luxembourg and is mainly teaching in the teacher education programmes of the University of Luxembourg. She is an expert on language contact and educational policy in plurilingual settings; her research approach is focused on an ecological approach to plurilingualism. She received her Ph.D. for her thesis on contact languages in New Caledonia (especially Tayo) from Augsburg University and in 2006 she gained her habilitation on "Language Contact in Natural and Institutional Settings" from Sorbonne University, Paris. In 2006 she created the LACETS group with the objective of creating a link between theory, research, and school practices in the multicultural environment of Luxembourg.

GENEVIÈVE ESCURE is Professor of Linguistics in the English Department at the University of Minnesota-Minneapolis (USA). Her major interests include the morphosyntax and pragmatics of English-based creole languages (especially Central American varieties in Belize and Honduras), African American English (USA), and endangered languages (Garifuna), as well as other mixed varieties such as Chinese Pidgin English. She also investigates sociolinguistic aspects of identity and gender in postcolonial societies. Her books include Creole and Dialect Continua: Standard Acquisition Processes in Belize and China (1997) and Creoles, Contact and Language Change: Linguistic and Social Implications (co-edited with Armin Schwegler, 2004).

NICHOLAS FARACLAS is Professor of Linguistics at the University of Puerto Rico, Rio Piedras. Having received his Ph.D. from the University of California at Berkeley, a National Science Foundation Fellowship, and two Fulbright Fellowships, he has developed and taught courses and published a significant number of books and articles in the areas of theoretical, descriptive, socio-, and applied linguistics. Over the past three decades, he has been conducting research on colonial-era creole languages as well as promoting community-based literacy activities in Africa, the South Pacific, and the Caribbean.

About the Authors

JOSEPH T. FARQUHARSON is Lecturer in Linguistics at the University of the West Indies, St. Augustine (Trinidad and Tobago). He is founder and coordinator of the Jamaican Lexicography Project (Jamlex), which is preparing the web-based *Jamaican National Dictionary*. Farquharson has published on language contact, morphology, pragmatics, historical lexicography, and literature. His latest book-length publication is *Variation in the Caribbean: From Creole Continua to Individual Agency* (John Benjamins, 2011), co-edited with Lars Hinrichs (Texas).

DOMINIQUE FATTIER teaches linguistics at the University of Cergy-Pontoise (France). She is the author of *L'Atlas linguistique d'Haïti: cartes et commentaires* (1998). She is currently working on various topics: language evolution, genealogical aspects within creole studies (origins of creole vernaculars), lexicology, dialectology, grammatical description of Haitian Creole, teaching materials for closely related languages (Creoles – French), and regional French of Haiti.

MALCOLM AWADAJIN FINNEY is a Professor at California State University Long Beach. His research is two-fold. He investigates mental and social factors that influence the speed and efficiency of adult second language acquisition and processing. He further investigates the origins and properties of the Sierra Leone Krio (and other Atlantic creoles) to determine parallels between such properties and the developing grammatical systems of first and adult second language learners. In addition, he explores the extent to which the linguistic system of Krio may have been influenced by the grammatical properties of West African Kwa substrate languages.

WILLIAM A. FOLEY is University Professor of Linguistics at the University of Sydney. He is the co-author of *Functional Syntax and Universal Grammar* and author of *The Papuan Languages of New Guinea*, *The Yimas Language of New Guinea*, and *Anthropological Linguistics: An Introduction*, among many book chapters and journal articles. His research interests include the description of the Papuan languages of New Guinea, especially those of the Sepik region, grammatical theory and typology, and linguistic relativity. He has carried out extensive fieldwork in the Sepik region over many years and to a lesser extent in other areas of island Southeast Asia and the Pacific.

ANTHONY P. GRANT is Professor of Historical Linguistics and Language Contact at Edge Hill University, Ormskirk, UK. A specialist in the study of intimate language contact, typology and diachrony, and issues in lexical documentation of endangered languages, he has worked on Romani, English, and numerous Austronesian, Native North American and pidgin, creole and mixed languages. His work includes *Chamic and Beyond* (edited with Paul Sidwell, 2005) and forthcoming works include a cross-linguistic study of the boundaries and limitations of lexical and morphemic borrowing, and a collection of Trinidad Creole French texts (with Jo-Anne S. Ferreira).

LISA GREEN is Professor in Linguistics and the director of the Center for the Study of African American Language at the University of Massachusetts Amherst. Her research interests include syntax, syntactic variation, and acquisition of African American English. She is the author of *African American English: A Linguistic Introduction* and *Language and the African American Child* (both Cambridge University Press).

STEPHANIE HACKERT holds a Ph.D. from the University of Heidelberg and has taught at the universities of Heidelberg, Karlsruhe, Regensburg, and Augsburg. She is now Full Professor and Chair of English Linguistics at Ludwig-Maximilians-Universität in Munich. Her research interests centre around pidgins and creoles, variationist sociolinguistics, and historical discourse analysis; her publications include various articles in peer-reviewed journals as well as a monograph on urban Bahamian Creole English (John Benjamins, 2004). A monograph on the emergence of the concept of the native speaker in English is in preparation.

TJERK HAGEMEIJER is a researcher at the Centre of Linguistics of the University of Lisbon (CLUL). He is primarily interested in diachronic and synchronic aspects of the Gulf of Guinea creoles, particularly Santome, both from a theoretical and a descriptive point of view. His current research interests concern language and gene co-evolution in the formation and development of the

About the Authors

Gulf of Guinea creoles, standardization of these languages, and the syntax of L1 and L2 varieties of Portuguese spoken in Africa.

MARTIN HASPELMATH is senior scientist at the Max Planck Institute for Evolutionary Anthropology and Honorary Professor at the University of Leipzig. His research interests are primarily in the area of broadly comparative and diachronic morphosyntax (*Indefinite Pronouns*, 1997; *From Space to Time*, 1997; *Understanding Morphology*, 2002) and in language contact (*Loanwords in the World's Languages*, co-edited with Uri Tadmor, 2009). He is one of the editors of Oxford University Press's *World Atlas of Language Structures* (2005).

JOHN HOLM holds the chair of English Linguistics at the University of Coimbra in Portugal. He completed his doctoral dissertation at the University of London on the Creole English of Nicaragua's Miskito Coast in 1978 and then taught at the College of the Bahamas (1978–1980) and the City University of New York (1980–1998) before coming to Coimbra. His books include *Pidgins and Creoles* (1988–1989), *An Introduction to Pidgins and Creoles* (2000), *Languages in Contact: The Partial Restructuring of Vernaculars* (2004), and *Comparative Creole Syntax*, edited with Peter Patrick (2007). He was a founding member of SPCL and ACBLPE.

MAGNUS HUBER is Professor of English at the University of Gießen and has taught close to 100 courses in a wide variety of subjects in English linguistics. He is an expert on English-based pidgins and creoles and is particularly interested in these languages' historical evolution and present structure. He is the author of *Ghanaian Pidgin English in its West African Context* (1999) and edited *Spreading the Word: The Issue of Diffusion Among the Atlantic Creoles* (1999) and *Synchronic and Diachronic Perspectives on Contact Languages* (2007). His other research interests include World Englishes, (historical) sociolinguistics, dialectology, corpus linguistics, and historical linguistics particularly on the levels of phonetics/phonology, morphology, and syntax.

INCANHA INTUMBO was born in Guinea-Bissau and is a native speaker of Kriyol, its Portuguese-based creole. He is writing his doctoral dissertation on an ethnic variety of this language with John Holm at the University of Coimbra in Portugal. He is a member of Coimbra's linguistic research institute CELGA (Centro de Estudos de Linguística Geral e Aplicada). He has been working on substrate and superstrate influences on Guinea-Bissau Kriyol and publishing in this area since 2004. He is the author of the book *Estudo Comparativo da morfo-sintaxe do crioulo guineense, do balanta e do português* (Lincom Europa, 2008).

LILIANA INVERNO teaches linguistics and Portuguese as a Foreign Language at both undergraduate and postgraduate levels at the University of the Algarve in Portugal. She is a member of the University of Coimbra's linguistic research institute CELGA (Centro de Estudos de Linguística Geral e Aplicada). Her main area of research is the contact-induced restructuring of Portuguese morphosyntax in Angola, an area in which she has been publishing since 2003. Her doctoral dissertation, *Contact-induced Restructuring of Portuguese Morphosyntax in Interior Angola: Evidence from Dundo (Lunda Norte)*, supervised by John Holm, is the first in-depth description of this variety.

KHIN KHIN AYE is a lecturer at Swinburne University of Technology (Sarawak Campus, Kuching, Malaysia). She has worked on Bazaar Malay used in Singapore and the impact of Hokkien Chinese on this contact variety. Her research interests include descriptive linguistics, linguistic typology, contact linguistics, and learners' interlanguage. She is a co-author of the article "Bazaar Malay Topic" published in the special issue of *Journal of Pidgin and Creole Languages* (Vol. 25 no. 1) in 2010.

THOMAS B. KLEIN (Ph.D., University of Delaware) is Associate Professor in the Department of Writing & Linguistics at Georgia Southern University. His research interests are in theoretical and descriptive phonology and morphophonology as well as phonological typology, in particular with regard to creole languages. He focuses on Gullah/Geechee and other Atlantic varieties, but he has worked on Austronesian languages, too, especially Chamorro.

About the Authors

THOMAS A. KLINGLER is Associate Professor of French and Linguistics at Tulane University in New Orleans. His research focuses on French and Creole in Louisiana. He is the author of *'If I Could Turn My Tongue Like That': The Creole Speech of Pointe Coupee Parish, Louisiana* and co-editor of the *Dictionary of Louisiana Creole* and of the *Dictionary of Louisiana French as Spoken in Cajun, Creole, and American Indian Communities*.

SILVIA KOUWENBERG teaches linguistics at the Mona Campus of the University of the West Indies (Jamaica). Her research has focused on creole genesis scenarios, in particular pertaining to the role of the substrate in the emergence of Berbice Dutch, on creole grammar (Berbice Dutch; Papiamentu prosody; reduplicative processes with Darlene LaCharite), and on the sociohistorical context of creole emergence in Jamaica. She is co-editor, with John Victor Singler, of the *Handbook of Pidgin and Creole Studies* (Wiley-Blackwell, 2008).

SIBYLLE KRIEGEL is Professor of Linguistics at Aix-Marseille Université and group leader at the Laboratoire Parole et Langage (CNRS, UMR 7309) in Aix-en-Provence. She has published on the grammar of French creoles in the Indian Ocean and has developed a special interest in comparative linguistics and language contact. She is co-editor of the first online journal in creole studies, *Creolica* (http://www.creolica.net).

JÜRGEN LANG has held a chair for Romance Linguistics at the University of Erlangen-Nürnberg (Germany) for twenty years. After a Ph.D. thesis on the theoretical bases of dialectology he published work on grammar (French and Spanish), historical linguistics (mainly concerning Spanish), and pragmatics (mainly concerning French), finally becoming a creolist. He is the coordinator of a Creole-German-Portuguese dictionary of the creole of Santiago Island (Cape Verde) published in 2002, and the author of the book *Les langues des autres dans la créolisation: Théorie et exemplification par le créole d'empreinte wolof à l'île Santiago du Cap Vert* (2009).

MICHELLE LI obtained her Ph.D. from the University of Hong Kong. She worked on the grammar of Chinese Pidgin English and its historical connections with Hawai'i Creole English and Melanesian Pidgin for her Ph.D. dissertation. Her research interests lie in the area of contact languages, especially pidgins and creoles in Asia, language change, and the grammar of Cantonese. Her current research focuses on Portuguese elements in Chinese Pidgin English and the role Portuguese pidgin played in Canton trade.

LISA LIM's expertise lies in New Englishes, especially excolonial Asian varieties in multilingual ecologies, such as Singapore English/Singlish and Peranakan English, with particular focus on contact dynamics, involving both sociohistorical and linguistic investigation, and with particular interest in particles and suprasegmental features, including tone. She also works on issues of language choice, shift, endangerment, and identity in minority/diasporic Malay-speaking communities, such as the Cocos (Keeling) Island Malays, the Sri Lankan Malays, and the Peranakans. A more recent interest comprises the impact that globalization has on contact and change. She is currently completing a book (with Umberto Ansaldo) on *Languages in Contact* for CUP, and is setting up a website on linguistic minorities in Hong Kong. An Assistant Professor in the School of English at the University of Hong Kong, she directs and teaches in the Language and Communication programme, and in English Studies.

RALPH LUDWIG is Professor of Romance Linguistics at the University of Halle (Germany). His main research areas are orality studies, francophone and Latin American language variation, contact linguistics and creole studies, as well as francophone literature. He has, for example, co-edited the *Dictionnaire du créole guadeloupéen* (2nd edn., 2002) and the *Corpus créole. Textes oraux dominicais, guadeloupéens, guyanais, haïtiens, mauriciens et seychellois* (2001).

XAVIER LUFFIN teaches Arabic Language at the *Université Libre de Bruxelles* (Brussels, Belgium). He has published a grammar of Kenyan Kinubi (*Un créole arabe: le kinubi de Mombasa, Kenya*, Munich, Lincom Europa, 2005) and a bilingual collection of Kinubi texts from Kenya and Uganda

About the Authors

(*Kinubi Texts*, Munich, Lincom Europa, 2004). He has also compiled a survey of another Arabic pidgin/creole, Bongor Arabic (in Chad).

STEFANO MANFREDI is a postdoctoral researcher at the University of Turin. His main research interests are Arabic dialectology, creolistics, and contact linguistics in Sudan. He is primarily interested in the study of Juba Arabic and other Arabic-based pidgins and creoles. He also analysed different Arabic varieties spoken in western Sudan. His works include articles and chapters on the subjects of Arabic descriptive and comparative dialectology, Arabic-based secret languages, and language contact in the Nuba Mountains area.

STEPHEN MATTHEWS is Associate Professor in Linguistics at the University of Hong Kong. He gained a BA in Modern and Medieval Languages from Cambridge University and a Ph.D. in Linguistics from the University of Southern California. His interests include language typology, language contact, and bilingualism. He has published on Cantonese, the grammar of Chinese dialects, and contact languages such as Chinese Pidgin English. His work with Virginia Yip on bilingual development includes the monograph *The Bilingual Child: Early Development and Language Contact*, which received the Linguistic Society of America's Leonard Bloomfield Book Award.

PHILIPPE MAURER is a creolist working on Ibero-Romance-based creoles, mainly on Papiamentu (*Les modifications temporelles et modales du verbe dans le papiamento de Curaçao*, 1988) and on the Gulf of Guinea creoles (*L'angolar: un créole afro-portugais parlé à São Tomé*, 1995, and *Principense: Grammar, Texts, and Vocabulary*, 2009). A book on the extinct Portuguese-based Creole of Batavia and Tugu (Indonesia) appeared in 2011.

FELICITY MEAKINS is a postdoctoral research fellow at the University of Queensland. Her main research interests include Australian Aboriginal languages and language contact, in particular post-colonial language contact. Most of her work is on Gurindji Kriol, a mixed language spoken in northern Australia, and she is the author of *Case-marking in Contact: The Development and Function of Case Morphology in Gurindji Kriol* (2011). In addition, Meakins has done extensive documentation work on Gurindji and Bilinarra.

MICHAEL MEEUWIS is Professor of Lingala and African linguistics at the University of Ghent, Belgium. He has published widely on the political and missionary history of Lingala and its grammatical structures. His recent publications include *A Grammatical Overview of Lingala* (Munich, 2010), which includes a detailed account of the origins and early developments of the language.

RAJEND MESTHRIE is Professor of Linguistics at the University of Cape Town, where he holds a National Research Foundation (SARCHI) research chair on Migration, Language and Social Change. He is a past President of the Linguistics Society of Southern Africa (2001–2009). He has published in the fields of Sociolinguistics, with special reference to language contact and variation in South Africa. Amongst his publications are *World Englishes* (with Rakesh Bhatt, Cambridge University Press, 2008) and *A Dictionary of South African Indian English* (University of Cape Town Press, 2010). He is co-editor of the CUP journal *English Today*.

MIRIAM MEYERHOFF is currently Professor of Linguistics at The University of Auckland. Previously she held the position of Professor in Sociolinguistics at the University of Edinburgh. Sociolinguistics being her principal field of research, she has worked in particular on language variation and change in situations of language contact, gender and language, and pidgins and creoles (especially Bislama and other Pacific creoles), among other topics. Her publications include the textbook *Introducing Sociolinguistics* (2nd edn., Routledge, 2011). With Umberto Ansaldo, she is co-editor of the Creole Language Library series (John Benjamins).

SUSANNE MARIA MICHAELIS is currently a creolist at the Max Planck Institute for Evolutionary Anthropology in Leipzig. Between 2008 and 2011, she held a research position in the *APiCS* project at the University of Gießen. Her early work, at the University of Freiburg and at the

About the Authors

University of Bamberg, focused on French-based Indian Ocean creoles, in particular Seychelles Creole (*Temps et aspect en créole seychellois*, 1993; *Komplexe Syntax im Seychellen-Kreol*, 1994). More recently, she has adopted a comparative approach with a focus on substrate explanations (e.g. Ditransitive constructions: creole languages in a cross-linguistic perspective, *Creolica* 2003). She is also editor of *Roots of Creole Structures* (John Benjamins, 2008) and co-editor of the anthology *Contact Languages: Critical concepts in linguistics* (Routledge, 2008).

BETTINA MIGGE is Senior Lecturer in Linguistics at University College Dublin, Ireland. Her main research and teaching interests are contact linguistics, sociolinguistics, language and gender, language and migration, language and education, and descriptive linguistics. She has published on creole genesis, language variation and change in Suriname and French Guiana, and migration to Ireland. Her work focuses on the creoles of Suriname, varieties of Gbe and English.

MAARTEN MOUS is Professor of African linguistics at Leiden University. He has written descriptive and analytic studies on Cushitic and Bantu languages and he is the author of *The Making of a Mixed Language: The Case of Ma'a/Mbugu* (John Benjamins, 2003). His main areas of interest are language contact (mixed languages), language and identity (youth languages), and morphology, especially verb valency, and nominal gender.

SALIKOKO S. MUFWENE is the Frank J. McLoraine Distinguished Service Professor of Linguistics and the College at the University of Chicago and the editor of the *Cambridge Approaches to Language Contact* book series. His books include *The Ecology of Language Evolution* (2001), *Créoles, écologie sociale, évolution linguistique* (2005), *Language Evolution: Contact, Competition and Change* (2008). His current research bridges scholarship on emergence of creoles, on second language acquisition, and on language evolution (including language birth and death), all approached from an ecological perspective. He is a native speaker of Kikongo-Kituba and has also published on Gullah and Jamaican Creole.

SUSANNE MÜHLEISEN teaches English Linguistics at the University of Bayreuth, Germany. She is the author of *Creole Discourse: Exploring Prestige Formation and Change across Caribbean English-lexicon Creoles* (John Benjamins, 2002) and *Heterogeneity in Word-formation Patterns* (John Benjamins, 2010). She has edited *Creole Languages in Creole Literatures* (*JPCL* special issue, 2005) and co-edited *Politeness and Face in Caribbean Creoles* (with Bettina Migge, 2005) as well as *Linguistic Explorations of Gender and Sexuality* (with Don E. Walicek, *Sargasso* special issue, 2009). Her research interests include contact linguistics, intercultural pragmatics, word-formation, and translation studies.

PETER MÜHLHÄUSLER has carried out fieldwork and research on numerous pidgin and creole languages of Australia and the Pacific since 1972. He has visited Norfolk Island 18 times. He obtained his Ph.D. from the Australian National University and has lectured at the Technical University of Berlin and the University of Oxford before becoming the Foundation Professor of Linguistics at the University of Adelaide in 1992. He is a Supernumerary Fellow of Linacre College, Oxford and a Fellow of the Academy of Social Sciences in Australia.

PIETER MUYSKEN is Academy Professor of Linguistics at Radboud University Nijmegen (Netherlands), having previously taught at Amsterdam and Leiden. He has carried out research and fieldwork in the Andes, Curaçao, and the Netherlands. Recent books include *Bilingual Speech: A Typology of Code-mixing* (Cambridge University Press, 2000), *Functional Categories* (Cambridge University Press, 2008), and *Las lenguas de Bolivia I–IV* (with Mily Crevels, 2009–2011). Currently he is studying the effect of language contact at four time scales in Radboud University's Languages in Contact group (www.ru.nl/linc). He collaborates with Marianne Gullberg on the interaction of linguistic and processing models for code-switching.

INGRID NEUMANN-HOLZSCHUH is Professor of Romance Linguistics (French and Spanish) at the University of Regensburg (Germany). Her main academic interests are creole studies, the varieties

About the Authors

of French in North America, Spanish diachronic linguistics (especially syntax), as well as language change and language contact. She has published the first comprehensive grammar of Louisiana Creole (*Le créole de Breaux Bridge, Louisiane. Étude morphosyntaxique – textes – vocabulaire*, 1985) and is the author of a monograph on Spanish syntax (*Die Satzgliedanordnung im Spanischen: Eine diachrone Analyse*, 1997). She is currently working on a comparative grammar of Acadian and Louisiana French as well as on the *Dictionnaire étymologique des creoles des Antilles* (together with Annegret Bollée).

SCOTT PAAUW is an Assistant Professor of Linguistics at the University of Rochester (USA). His interests include typology, language contact, morphosyntax, and historical linguistics. He has worked on varieties of Malay resulting from language contact, including varieties found in eastern Indonesia and Sri Lanka. He is currently working on methods for detecting language contact occurring in prehistoric times and language contact situations in Africa.

ELENA PEREKHVALSKAYA is Leading Researcher in the Institute for Linguistic Studies (St Petersburg) of the Russian Academy of Sciences. Her main interest is the study of the languages of the Manchu-Tungusic group, in particular, Udihe; she has also studied Russian pidgins, language contacts, and language shift in the Russian Far East. Her habilitation dissertation on Russian pidgins was published in Russian. Currently she is carrying out fieldwork on South Mande languages in West Africa.

SARA PETROLLINO is a postgraduate student in African Linguistics at Leiden University. Her main research interests are language contact and descriptive linguistics. She has worked on Arabic-based pidgins and creoles spoken in Africa, on language attrition in Tanzania, and on codeswitching between Swahili and the Cushitic language Iraqw. She is also interested in Afroasiatic, Cushitic, and Omotic studies and at present she is working on the grammatical description of Hamar, a language of Ethiopia.

STEFAN PFÄNDER is Professor of Romance Linguistics at the University of Freiburg and also Director of the Hermann Paul School of Language Sciences. Previously he was Assistant Professor at the University of Halle-Wittenberg. His research interests focus on corpus-based linguistic description of modern Spanish and French grammar as well as regional variation, contact languages, and emergent language change, especially concerning the varieties spoken in South America, the Caribbean, and western Africa.

INGO PLAG is Professor of English Linguistics at the University of Düsseldorf, Germany. His monographs include *Sentential Complementation in Sranan* (1993, Niemeyer) and *Word-Formation in English* (Cambridge University Press, 2003). He is editor-in-chief of *Morphology*, and has published on the phonology, morphology, and syntax of English and creole languages in journals such as *English Language and Linguistics*, *Journal of Pidgin and Creole Languages*, and *Language*.

MARIKE POST studied General Linguistics at the University of Amsterdam. She wrote her MA thesis on Portuguese-based creoles of West Africa and is currently working on a description of the grammar of Fa d'Ambô. She has written a number of articles on the subject.

PAULA PRESCOD (Ph.D., Université Sorbonne-Nouvelle) is an associate member of LESCLaP (Université Jules Verne in Amiens, France) and LLACAN (Paris). Her research interests include syntax, morphology, phonology, and sociolinguistics. Her 2004 dissertation, entitled *Une description grammaticale du syntagme nominal dans le créole anglophone de Saint-Vincent-et-les-Grenadines* was published in 2006. The English version, *A Grammatical Description of the Noun Phrase in the English-based Creole of St Vincent and the Grenadines*, was published in 2010. She is also an external trainer of French and English as foreign languages to business and engineering students at the Grandes Écoles in Amiens.

NICOLAS QUINT is Directeur de Recherche in Linguistics at the CNRS and is currently a member of LLACAN (Paris), a research unit specialized in African languages. Since 1995, he has been regularly working on Afro-Iberian creoles, in particular Cape Verdean, Casamancese Creole, and Papiamentu, and has published several dozens of articles and books on these languages (including a Cape Verdean Grammar, comparative studies and dictionaries). His field of expertise includes Kordofanian (Koalib and other Heiban languages), Romance (Occitan, Spanish, and Portuguese), and descriptive linguistics.

MELANIE REVIS is currently pursuing her doctoral degree at Victoria University of Wellington about language maintenance among Colombians and Ethiopians in New Zealand. She was previously an assistant in the *APiCS* team at Justus Liebig University in Giessen, Germany. Her research interests include language contact, language maintenance, and structural aspects of pidgins and creoles.

SARAH J. ROBERTS is Lecturer of Linguistics at Stanford University. She is primarily interested in sociolinguistic theory and pidgin and creole languages, focusing her research on reconstructing the social context of language contact in colonial Hawai'i. She is working on a corpus of nineteenth century Hawaiian texts preserved in court records.

MARCEL ROSALIE is the current Director General for Culture of the Republic of Seychelles. He previously worked at the National Heritage Research Section and recorded and transcribed many spoken texts in Seychelles Creole. He is co-editor of *Parol ek Memwar* (1994, together with Annegret Bollée) and a close collaborator of Susanne Maria Michaelis, with whom he has worked on the grammar and lexicon of Seychelles Creole. His present work, as a member of the Seychelles Creole Language Committee, is focusing on the production of a Creole monolingual dictionary.

WILLIAM SAMARIN is Emeritus Professor of Linguistic Anthropology of the University of Toronto, Canada, retired since 1991. He lived for almost ten years in the Central African Republic, beginning in 1952, and continued linguistic and sociolinguistic research on Sango and Gbaya in 1962, 1966, 1979, 1988, and the 1990s. He has published on these languages and on African ideophones. Language and colonization in West Central Africa has been one of his preoccupations with a focus on Sango, Bangala-Lingala, and Kituba. Outside of African studies he has written about language in religion, especially on glossolalia.

ANNE SCHRÖDER is Professor of English Linguistics at Bielefeld University (Germany). She studied English and French at the universities of Caen (France), Bristol (UK), and Freiburg i. Br. (Germany), where she received her Ph.D. in English Linguistics. She previously worked at Martin Luther University Halle and at Chemnitz University of Technology (Germany). Her publications include *Status, Functions, and Prospects of Pidgin English: An Empirical Approach to Language Dynamics in Cameroon* (2003), the edition of *Crossing Borders: Interdisciplinary Approaches to Africa* (2004), and various articles on similar topics. She has also researched and published on morphological productivity.

EVA SCHULTZE-BERNDT completed her undergraduate degree at the University of Cologne and her Ph.D. at the Max Planck Institute for Psycholinguistics and the University of Nijmegen. She is now Professor of Linguistics at the University of Manchester. She has been conducting fieldwork in the Victoria River District in Northern Australia since 1993, resulting in publications on aspects of Jaminjung grammar such as spatial expressions, complex predicates, overt verb classification, and discontinuous noun phrases, as well as on language contact phenomena. Her typological research interests include secondary predication, complex predication, parts of speech and information structure.

ARMIN SCHWEGLER is Professor of Spanish linguistics at the University of California, Irvine. For several years, he has been co-editor of the *Journal of Pidgin and Creole Languages* and the *Revista Internacional de Lingüística Iberoamericana* (RILI). The author of over fifty scholarly articles and several books, his research emphasizes the study of Spanish, Palenquero (Colombia), and Palo Monte ritual speech (Cuba) from a linguistic perspective, while also exploring language in its

About the Authors

social, cultural, and historical contexts. He has lived in Palenque on many occasions, and speaks the creole fluently.

JEFF SIEGEL is Adjunct Professor in Linguistics at the University of New England in Australia. His main areas of research concern the processes involved in the development of contact languages, and the use of such languages in formal education. He has worked specifically on Melanesian Pidgin, Hawai'i Creole, Pidgin Fijian, and Pidgin Hindustani. His most recent books are *The Emergence of Pidgin and Creole Languages* (Oxford University Press, 2008) and *Second Dialect Acquisition* (Cambridge University Press, 2010).

EEVA SIPPOLA is the author of *Una gramática descriptiva de chabacano de Ternate (A descriptive grammar of Ternate Chabacano,* University of Helsinki, 2011). She has worked on the Chabacano varieties of Manila Bay, where she has done extensive fieldwork. Her current research interests are concentrated on descriptive and comparative linguistics of the Ibero-Asian creoles, the sociolinguistics of minority languages and pedagogical methodologies.

PETER SLOMANSON received his Ph.D. in 2005 from the City University of New York. He conducted postdoctoral fieldwork in Sri Lanka, funded by the American Institute for Sri Lankan Studies, and subsequently taught at the College of Staten Island. He is currently at Radboud University in Nijmegen and the University of Aarhus, in Denmark. Dr Slomanson is also affiliated with the Information Structuring and Typology research group of the French *Centre National de Recherche Scientifique* (CNRS). His research involves modelling non-canonical contact language development, and the roles of discourse-pragmatic accommodation and reanalysis in the development of contact language and second language grammars.

GEOFF P. SMITH is now retired after a career teaching in the UK, Ghana, Papua New Guinea, and Hong Kong. His main interest in the area of creolistics is in Tok Pisin and Chinese Pidgin English. He is the author of *Growing up with Tok Pisin* (2002), based on a corpus of spoken Tok Pisin collected between 1980 and 1992. He is also co-editor of a special edition of the *Hong Kong Journal of Applied Linguistics* entitled *Chinese Pidgin English: Text and contexts* (2005), based on an analysis of a corpus of Chinese language texts found in nineteenth-century Chinese documents.

IAN R. SMITH holds a doctorate in Linguistics from Cornell University. He has taught at Monash University, the National University of Singapore, the University of Sydney, and at York University, where he is Associate Professor of Linguistics. His primary research field is language contact. He has published works on South Asian languages, English, and Kugu Nganhcara. He has a long-standing interest in Sri Lanka Portuguese, and is the author of *Sri Lanka Creole Portuguese Phonology* as well as articles on its grammatical structure and historical development. He is working on a second book on the language.

NORVAL S. H. SMITH is Associate Professor in the Linguistics department of the University of Amsterdam, where he has worked since 1970; he retired in September 2011. He has done significant fieldwork on Strathearn Scots. He has worked principally on phonology and the creole languages of Suriname. In phonology, his special interests are vowel harmony and the phonologies of Scottish languages, Frisian languages, and Yokuts languages (California). In creole studies he is involved in the long-running debate on creolization. In Yokuts studies he is also interested in the wider contexts of ethnohistory and ethnogeography.

PATRICK O. STEINKRÜGER is a specialist in Romance languages, especially Catalan and Spanish-based creoles of South Asia. Currently he is a Visiting Professor at the Institute of Romance Linguistics and Literature at Frankfurt University, Germany. He has until recently taught at the ZAS (Centre for General Linguistics) in Berlin. He co-edited *On Inflection* (Mouton de Gruyter, 2009) with Manfred Krifka and published numerous articles on Zamboanga Chabacano.

DOMINIKA SWOLKIEN is an assistant lecturer at the University of Mindelo, Cape Verde. She is currently finishing her Ph.D. dissertation on the variety of Cape Verdean Creole spoken on the island of São Vicente with John Holm at the University of Coimbra, Portugal. Her research focuses on the role that socio-historical factors have played in shaping the modern morphosyntactic structure of this variety. She is involved in the Master's Program in Creolistics and Cape Verdean language run by the University of Cape Verde, being deeply concerned about the standardization of the language and dissemination of scientific knowledge about creoles within the creole-speaking community.

DAHLIA THOMPSON is a graduate student in the Department of Computing at the University of the West Indies, Jamaica. Her research focus is on the documentation, implementation, and evaluation of a speech synthesizer for the Jamaican (Creole) language. She recently co-authored *A Concise Grammar of Guyanese Creole* with Hubert Devonish (Lincom Europa, 2010). She has a multi-disciplinary background in languages, linguistics, and information technology. Her areas of interest include computational linguistics, creole languages and technology, the grammars of creole languages, the grammar of the Japanese language, techniques in the teaching of English to Speakers of Other Languages (ESOL), language acquisition, translation studies, and the virtual classroom.

MARGOT C. VAN DEN BERG is an NWO Veni postdoctoral researcher at the Radboud University of Nijmegen, coordinator of the Suriname Creole Archive (SUCA) and board member of *OSO*. In her current research project, titled "Creoles at birth? The role of nativization in language formation", she combines historical and experimental linguistics to explore the social and linguistic factors involved in language formation. Her work includes *A Grammar of Early Sranan* (2007) among other scholarly contributions on morphosyntactic topics in Sranan and Negerhollands and codeswitching in Ghana and Togo with Evershed Amuzu (University of Ghana) and Komlan Essizewa (Université de Lomé).

HEIN VAN DER VOORT is Visiting Researcher at the Museu Paraense Emílio Goeldi (Brazil). His interests include morphology, language description and documentation, language contact, areal and historical relationships, and anthropological linguistics. He has worked on creole languages, Arctic languages, and Amazonian languages, and is the author of *A Grammar of Kwaza* (Mouton de Gruyter, 2004).

ROBBERT VAN SLUIJS works at Radboud University of Nijmegen (Netherlands) on a Ph.D. project entitled "The rise and fall of Negerhollands", in which he studies the origin, development, and decline of the extinct creole language Negerhollands, with special focus on the TMA system. In addition, he is involved in the construction of the NEgerHOLands database (NEHOL), a CLARIN-NL project that aims to make the Negerhollands texts publicly available via the Max Planck Institute Nijmegen.

TONJES VEENSTRA is Research Fellow at the Centre for General Linguistics in Berlin. He has published on the morphosyntax and the development of English-, Dutch-, Portuguese-, and French-related creoles. His main research interests focus on modelling language variation, contact, and change, in particular the relation between models of language acquisition and language contact and creation.

VIVEKA VELUPILLAI is a research fellow at the Justus-Liebig-University of Gießen. She is the author of *Hawai'i Creole English: A Typological Analysis of the Tense-Mood-Aspect System* (Palgrave, Macmillan, 2003) and *An Introduction to Linguistic Typology* (John Benjamins, 2012) and the co-editor of *Synchronic and Diachronic Perspectives on Contact Languages* (John Benjamins, 2007). Her main interests are linguistic typology, pidgin and creole languages, contact linguistics, and historical linguistics, in particular how these linguistic domains complement and benefit each other.

DONALD WINFORD is Professor of Linguistics at the Ohio State University. His teaching and research interests are in creole linguistics, variationist sociolinguistics, contact linguistics, and African-American English, and he has published widely in those areas. His other main interest is the integration of linguistic and psycholinguistic approaches to contact phenomena, using

About the Authors

Van Coetsem's model of language contact as a basic theoretical framework. He is the author of *Predication in Caribbean English Creoles* (1993) and *An Introduction to Contact Linguistics*. He has been editor of the *Journal of Pidgin and Creole Languages* since August 2001.

KOFI YAKPO is Assistant Professor at the University of Hong Kong. Until recently, he worked at the Centre for Language Studies of Radboud University Nijmegen, where he was looking at language contact and multilingualism. Previous occupations include heading the Africa Desk of the human rights organization FIAN and serving as a Policy Advisor to the German Federal Parliament in Berlin. He holds a Magister Artium in Linguistics, Social Anthropology and Political Science from the University of Cologne and an MBA from the University of Geneva. He was awarded a Ph.D. in Linguistics by the Radboud University Nijmegen for his grammar of Pichi, the English-lexicon creole of Equatorial Guinea.

INTRODUCTION

1. The nature of this atlas

The *Atlas of Pidgin and Creole Language Structures* (*APiCS*) brings together the expertise of 88 language experts to provide a systematic comparison of key structural features of 76 creoles, pidgins, and mixed languages in the areas of syntax, semantics, morphology, lexicon, and phonology. It is accompanied by the three-volume *Survey of Pidgin and Creole Languages*, written by the same team of authors and editors.

To be able to address general questions about the nature and origin of contact languages, a broad comparative perspective is crucial. The languages need to be compared with their source languages (lexifiers, substrates, as well as other languages that have played a role in their history), but they also need to be compared with each other.

Since 2005, comparative linguists have had an important resource for the world-wide comparison of language structures, the *World Atlas of Language Structures* (*WALS*, Haspelmath et al. 2005, online since 2008 at wals.info). At about the time when *WALS* appeared, just after the "Conference on creole language structure between substrates and superstrates" (June 2005 in Leipzig), some creolists suggested that there should be a similar work dealing specifically with creole and pidgin languages. We took on this task in 2006, but we chose a different approach for gathering the data: while the maps on structural features in *WALS* were put together by comparative linguists who gathered the relevant information from grammatical descriptions of the languages, we adopted a consortium approach for *APiCS*. We invited experts on 76 languages and varieties to collaborate with us, supplying data on a detailed questionnaire of 130 features that we drew up, to serve as a basis for an atlas similar to *WALS*. In addition, we asked every author to write a chapter for the accompanying *Survey of Pidgin and Creole Languages*.[1]

The language experts have thus made two contributions to the overall project: they provided a "structure dataset" in response to our questionnaire, with detailed exemplification and comments, and they wrote a chapter for the *Survey*. The datasets are published together online at http://apics-online.info by the Max Planck Institute for Evolutionary Anthropology. Although there is no printed version of the datasets, they should be considered full-fledged scholarly publications, and cited as follows:

Mufwene, Salikoko. 2013. Kikongo-Kituba structure dataset. In: Michaelis, Susanne Maria & Maurer, Philippe & Haspelmath, Martin & Huber, Magnus (eds.), *Atlas of Pidgin and Creole Language Structures Online*. Leipzig: Max Planck Institute for Evolutionary Anthropology. (Available online at http:/apics-online.info/contributions/58)

2. The *APiCS* Consortium

The *Atlas* contains 130 world maps of structural linguistic features showing 76 languages. The database underlying the maps is joint work of the four editors and the authors or author teams for the 76 languages (88 authors in total). Each map is accompanied by a chapter written by one (or sometimes two) of the editors that explains and illustrates the feature and draws some conclusions. The input of the *APiCS* contributors was so crucial that we decided that they should be considered as co-authors of these chapters. In practical terms, listing all 88 authors with each chapter is impossible, so we adopted a convention from the natural sciences, where a team of scientists from different institutions who are working towards a common goal is called a "consortium". These consortia

---

[1] The four-volume work resulting from our six-year project also has the general title *Atlas and Survey of Pidgin and Creole Languages*, but this should not be used in bibliographical contexts. We have generally called our six-year project the '*APiCS* project' because it started with the one-volume *Atlas*, and the idea of editing the three-volume *Survey*, too, came later.

Introduction

can then be authors of research papers (e.g. Chimpanzee Sequencing and Analysis Consortium 2005). Thus, we call our 88 contributors the "*APiCS* Consortium" (listed in Table 1). This allows us to abbreviate the author designation for each chapter: "Philippe Maurer and the *APiCS* Consortium" means that there are actually 88 authors: Philippe Maurer (the editor who wrote the chapter) and the 87 other colleagues who contributed the database in response to our questionnaire. For this reason, the four editors appear as "editors" and not as "authors" of the *Atlas*, even though we wrote all the texts and put together all the maps in this book.

The 88 Consortium members who contributed to the *APiCS* database are listed in Table 1. Some people worked on several languages (or varieties), and the databases for some languages were contributed by several authors working together.

Table 1. **The *APiCS* Consortium members**

Aboh, Enoch O.	Saramaccan (with Tonjes Veenstra and Norval S. H. Smith)
Angelo, Denise	Kriol (with Eva Schultze-Berndt)
Ansaldo, Umberto	Singlish (with Lisa Lim)
Baker, Philip	Mauritian Creole (with Sibylle Kriegel)
Bakker, Peter	Michif
Baptista, Marlyse	Cape Verdean Creole of Brava
Bartens, Angela	(2) Nicaraguan Creole English, San Andres Creole English
Baxter, Alan N.	Papiá Kristang
Biagui, Noël Bernard	Casamancese Creole (with Nicolas Quint)
Biberauer, Theresa	Afrikaans (with Hans den Besten)
Bollée, Annegret	Reunion Creole
Bruyn, Adrienne	Early Sranan (with Margot C. van den Berg)
Cardoso, Hugo C.	Diu Indo-Portuguese
Clements, J. Clancy	Korlai
Colot, Serge	(2) Guadeloupean Creole, Martinican Creole (with Ralph Ludwig)
den Besten, Hans[a]	Afrikaans (with Theresa Biberauer)
Devonish, Hubert	Creolese (with Dahlia Thompson)
Ehrhart, Sabine	Tayo (with Melanie Revis)
Escure, Geneviève	Belizean Creole
Faraclas, Nicholas	Nigerian Pidgin
Farquharson, Joseph T.	Jamaican
Fattier, Dominique	Haitian Creole
Finney, Malcolm Awadajin	Krio
Foley, William A.	Yimas-Arafundi Pidgin
Grant, Anthony P.	Chinuk Wawa
Green, Lisa	African American English
Hackert, Stephanie	Bahamian Creole
Hagemeijer, Tjerk	Santome
Holm, John	Guinea-Bissau Kriyol (with Incanha Intumbo & Liliana Inverno)
Huber, Magnus	(editor) Ghanaian Pidgin English
Intumbo, Incanha	Guinea-Bissau Kriyol (with John Holm & Liliana Inverno)
Inverno, Liliana	Guinea-Bissau Kriyol (with John Holm & Incanha Intumbo)
Khin Khin Aye	Singapore Bazaar Malay
Klein, Thomas B.	Gullah
Klingler, Thomas A.	Louisiana Creole (with Ingrid Neumann-Holzschuh)
Kouwenberg, Silvia	(2) Berbice Dutch, Papiamentu
Kriegel, Sibylle	Mauritian Creole (with Philip Baker)
Lang, Jürgen	Cape Verdean Creole of Santiago
Li, Michelle	Chinese Pidgin English (with Stephen Matthews)
Lim, Lisa	Singlish (with Umberto Ansaldo)
Ludwig, Ralph	(2) Guadeloupean Creole, Martinican Creole (with Serge Colot)
Luffin, Xavier	Kinubi
Manfredi, Stefano	Juba Arabic (with Sara Petrollino)
Matthews, Stephen	Chinese Pidgin English (with Michelle Li)
Maurer, Philippe	(editor) (3) Angolar, Batavia Creole, Principense
Meakins, Felicity	Gurindji Kriol
Meeuwis, Michael	Lingala

Introduction

Mesthrie, Rajend	Fanakalo
Meyerhoff, Miriam	Bislama
Michaelis, Susanne Maria	(editor) Seychelles Creole (with Marcel Rosalie)
Migge, Bettina	Nengee
Mous, Maarten	Mixed Ma'a/Mbugu
Mufwene, Salikoko S.	Kikongo-Kituba
Mühleisen, Susanne	Trinidad English Creole
Mühlhäusler, Peter	Norf'k
Muysken, Pieter	Media Lengua
Neumann-Holzschuh, Ingrid	Louisiana Creole (with Thomas A. Klingler)
Paauw, Scott	Ambon Malay
Perekhvalskaya, Elena	Chinese Pidgin Russian
Petrollino, Sara	Juba Arabic (with Stefano Manfredi)
Pfänder, Stefan	Guyanais
Plag, Ingo	Sranan (with Donald Winford)
Post, Marike	Fa d'Ambô
Prescod, Paula	Vincentian Creole
Quint, Nicolas	Casamancese Creole (with Noël Bernard Biagui)
Revis, Melanie	Tayo (with Sabine Ehrhart)
Roberts, Sarah J.	Pidgin Hawaiian
Rosalie, Marcel	Seychelles Creole (with Susanne Maria Michaelis)
Samarin, William J.	Sango
Schröder, Anne	Cameroon Pidgin English
Schultze-Berndt, Eva	Kriol (with Denise Angelo)
Schwegler, Armin	Palenquero
Siegel, Jeff	(2) Pidgin Hindustani, Tok Pisin (with Geoff P. Smith)
Sippola, Eeva	(2) Ternate Chabacano, Cavite Chabacano
Slomanson, Peter	Sri Lankan Malay
Smith, Geoff P.	Tok Pisin (with Jeff Siegel)
Smith, Ian R.	Sri Lanka Portuguese
Smith, Norval S. H.	Saramaccan (with Enoch O. Aboh & Tonjes Veenstra)
Steinkrüger, Patrick O.	Zamboanga Chabacano
Swolkien, Dominika	Cape Verdean Creole of São Vicente
Thompson, Dahlia	Creolese (with Hubert Devonish)
van den Berg, Margot C.	Early Sranan (with Adrienne Bruyn)
van der Voort, Hein	Eskimo Pidgin
van Sluijs, Robbert	Negerhollands
Veenstra, Tonjes	Saramaccan (with Enoch O. Aboh & Norval S. H. Smith)
Velupillai, Viveka	Hawai'i Creole
Winford, Donald	Sranan (with Ingo Plag)
Yakpo, Kofi	Pichi

[a] Hans den Besten passed away on 19 July 2010.

3. The languages of *APiCS*

The *Atlas of Pidgin and Creole Language Structures* contains information about 76 languages, listed in Table 2. This is a large subset of the existing contact languages (Smith 1994 lists over 500 pidgins, creoles, and mixed languages), but including more languages was not possible with our resources. Besides pidgins and creoles we included a few mixed languages. All these languages are also covered in the three-volume *Survey of Pidgin and Creole Languages* (though there are a few mismatches between the *APiCS* Consortium and the *Survey* authors, set out in notes to Table 2).

Inevitably, the choice of languages for such an enterprise will be partially opportunistic and potentially controversial. For some little-studied languages that we would have liked to include, we did not find any authors that could have contributed a chapter. In choosing the languages, we were confronted with the problem that while there is a vibrant field of pidgin and creole language studies, there are no commonly agreed criteria by which the category of creoles and pidgins can be readily delimited. All experts in this field agree that pidgins and creoles are new languages that are distinct from the languages from which they took the bulk of their lexicon or their grammar, and not just

Introduction

Table 2. *APiCS* languages and Consortium members

Language (variety)	Lexifier	Consortium member
African American English	English	Lisa Green
Afrikaans[a]	Dutch	Hans den Besten & Theresa Biberauer
Ambon Malay	Malay	Scott Paauw
Angolar	Portuguese	Philippe Maurer
Bahamian Creole	English	Stephanie Hackert
Batavia Creole	Portuguese	Philippe Maurer
Belizean Creole	English	Geneviève Escure
Berbice Dutch	Dutch	Silvia Kouwenberg
Bislama	English	Miriam Meyerhoff
Cameroon Pidgin English	English	Anne Schröder
Cape Verdean Creole of Brava	Portuguese	Marlyse Baptista
Cape Verdean Creole of Santiago	Portuguese	Jürgen Lang
Cape Verdean Creole of São Vicente	Portuguese	Dominika Swolkien
Casamancese Creole	Portuguese	Noël Bernard Biagui & Nicolas Quint
Cavite Chabacano	Spanish	Eeva Sippola
Chinese Pidgin English	English	Michelle Li & Stephen Matthews
Chinese Pidgin Russian	Russian	Elena Perekhvalskaya
Chinuk Wawa	Coastal Chinook	Anthony P. Grant
Creolese	English	Hubert Devonish & Dahlia Thompson
Diu Indo-Portuguese	Portuguese	Hugo C. Cardoso
Early Sranan[b]	English	Margot C. van den Berg & Adrienne Bruyn
Eskimo Pidgin	Eskimo	Hein van der Voort
Fa d'Ambô	Portuguese	Marike Post
Fanakalo[c]	Zulu	Rajend Mesthrie (& Clarissa Surek-Clark)
Ghanaian Pidgin English	English	Magnus Huber
Guadeloupean Creole[d]	French	Serge Colot & Ralph Ludwig
Guinea-Bissau Kriyol	Portuguese	Incanha Intumbo, Liliana Inverno, & John Holm
Gullah	English	Thomas B. Klein
Gurindji Kriol	Gurindji/Kriol	Felicity Meakins
Guyanais	French	Stefan Pfänder
Haitian Creole	French	Dominique Fattier
Hawai'i Creole	English	Viveka Velupillai
Jamaican	English	Joseph T. Farquharson
Juba Arabic	Arabic	Stefano Manfredi & Sara Petrollino
Kikongo-Kituba	Kikongo-Kimanyanga	Salikoko S. Mufwene
Kinubi	Arabic	Xavier Luffin
Korlai	Portuguese	J. Clancy Clements
Krio	English	Malcolm Awadajin Finney
Kriol[e]	English	Eva Schultze-Berndt & Denise Angelo
Lingala	Bobangi	Michael Meeuwis
Louisiana Creole	French	Thomas A. Klingler & Ingrid Neumann-Holzschuh
Martinican Creole	French	Serge Colot & Ralph Ludwig
Mauritian Creole	French	Philip Baker & Sibylle Kriegel
Media Lengua	Spanish	Pieter Muysken
Michif	French/Cree	Peter Bakker
Mixed Ma'a/Mbugu	Cushitic/Maasai	Maarten Mous
Negerhollands	Dutch	Robbert van Sluijs
Nengee	English	Bettina Migge
Nicaraguan Creole English	English	Angela Bartens
Nigerian Pidgin	English	Nicholas Faraclas
Norf'k	English	Peter Mühlhäusler
Palenquero	Spanish	Armin Schwegler
Papiá Kristang	Portuguese	Alan N. Baxter
Papiamentu[f]	Spanish	Silvia Kouwenberg
Pichi	English	Kofi Yakpo
Pidgin Hawaiian	Hawaiian	Sarah J. Roberts

Introduction

Pidgin Hindustani	Hindustani	Jeff Siegel
Principense	Portuguese	Philippe Maurer
Reunion Creole	French	Annegret Bollée
San Andres Creole English	English	Angela Bartens
Sango	Ngbandi	William J. Samarin
Santome	Portuguese	Tjerk Hagemeijer
Saramaccan	English	Enoch O. Aboh, Tonjes Veenstra, & Norval S. H. Smith
Seychelles Creole	French	Susanne Maria Michaelis & Marcel Rosalie
Singapore Bazaar Malay	Malay	Khin Khin Aye
Singlish[g]	English	Lisa Lim & Umberto Ansaldo
Sranan	English	Donald Winford & Ingo Plag
Sri Lanka Portuguese	Portuguese	Ian R. Smith
Sri Lankan Malay	Malay	Peter Slomanson
Tayo	French	Sabine Ehrhart & Melanie Revis
Ternate Chabacano	Spanish	Eeva Sippola
Tok Pisin	English	Geoff P. Smith & Jeff Siegel
Trinidad English Creole	English	Susanne Mühleisen
Vincentian Creole	English	Paula Prescod
Yimas-Arafundi Pidgin	Yimas	William A. Foley
Zamboanga Chabacano	Spanish	Patrick O. Steinkrüger

[a] The chapter on Afrikaans for the *Survey* was written by Robbert van Sluijs.
[b] The chapter on Early Sranan for the *Survey* was written by Margot C. van den Berg & Norval S. H. Smith.
[c] Clarissa Surek-Clark is a co-author of the *Survey* chapter, but not of the *Atlas* dataset.
[d] The *Survey* has just a single combined chapter on Guadeloupean and Martinican Creole.
[e] The chapter on Kriol for the *Survey* was co-authored in addition by Felicity Meakins.
[f] The chapter on Papiamentu for the *Survey* was written by Philippe Maurer.
[g] The *Survey* lacks a chapter on Singlish.

"corrupted" or "broken" versions of their lexifiers (lexicon-providing languages). We know that all of them arose as a result of an unusually high degree of language contact influence in special social circumstances such as long-distance trade and forced or indentured labour. Sometimes these languages have therefore simply been called "contact languages" in recent years (cf. Holm & Michaelis (eds.) 2008). But the term "contact language" has also been used in a much broader sense, and since our focus was on the languages that are traditionally discussed under the heading of "pidgin" and "creole", this term was not suitable as a title for our project.

Our choice of the term "pidgin and creole languages" thus simply follows traditional ordinary usage in the field, and should not be taken to imply a particular definition of "pidgin" or "creole". Our main goal with this work (the *Atlas* and the *Survey*) has been to provide a new systematic and solid factual basis on which future work can build, not to engage in theoretical or ideological debates.

Languages which underwent an unusually high degree of contact are not only those languages widely known as pidgins and creoles, but also include languages which are more often discussed under the rubric of "mixed languages" (cf. Matras & Bakker 2003), of which there are various types (e.g. "bilingual mixed languages", "intertwined languages"). The debate on the nature and origin of all these varieties is ongoing, so we decided to include a number of these languages in both the *Atlas* and the *Survey*. Typical cases of languages which are regarded as mixed languages that are not pidgins or creoles are Michif, Media Lengua, Gurindji Kriol, and Mixed Ma'a/Mbugu. Moreover, we included languages with a history of high contact that are sometimes called "semi-creoles" (Holm 2004) and languages that are in other ways similar or related to pidgins or creoles, such as African American English, Afrikaans, and Sri Lankan Malay. Thus, our general approach was to be inclusive rather than exclusive. If a language is not included here that meets all the above criteria (and no doubt there are many such languages), this is for practical reasons, not for any principled reasons. We are aware that we were not able to fulfil everybody's wishes, but we are confident that our selection of languages can be seen as representative of the kinds of languages that contact linguists have focused their research on over the last few decades. Readers who wish to classify our languages according to their criteria into groups are invited to do so on the

Introduction

basis of the sociohistorical and structural information provided in the individual survey chapters.

Where we want to contrast the languages dealt with in *APiCS* with the world's languages, we rarely use the full description "creole languages, pidgin languages, and mixed languages", as it would be cumbersome. Instead, we simply talk about "the *APiCS* languages" (or sometimes we use the term "contact languages" to encompass all three kinds of languages). Note that all the varieties included in *APiCS* are full-fledged languages with fairly fixed conventions. We have not included any jargons, that is, speech forms that are used where no common full-fledged language is available and that do not have fixed conventions.

A factor that played no role in our choice of languages is the numerical or social significance of the language. Only a few of the languages can be regarded as having the status of "national language" of some sort, but most of these are languages of small countries, and where they are spoken throughout larger countries (like Haitian Creole and Nigerian Pidgin), they generally have low (or even very low) prestige. Since our interest is primarily in the language structures, this was irrelevant: we included languages regardless of their status and the number of their speakers. Some *APiCS* languages have very few speakers and never had many (e.g. Norf'k with 800 speakers, Tayo with about 3,000 speakers, Fa d'Ambô with about 5,000 speakers). Others were more vigorous in the past, but it is foreseeable that they will become extinct in the not so distant future (e.g. Papiá Kristang, Principense, Cavite Chabacano). Still others no longer have any speakers (e.g. Berbice Dutch, Batavia Creole, Eskimo Pidgin, Chinese Pidgin Russian). In one case, we included both an earlier and a modern variety of the same language: Early Sranan (based on the extensive documentation from the eighteenth century) and modern Sranan.

Sometimes the languages or varieties that the *APiCS* language experts described were not internally homogeneous, but different subvarieties (or lects) had different value choices for some feature. For example, in ordinary Guinea-Bissau Kriyol, "adjectives sometimes agree in gender with the head noun when the noun refers to a human" (Intumbo et al. 2013). But in the variety of the older generation, such gender agreement is entirely absent. In such cases, we allowed the authors to enter this information as well, but it is not reflected on the maps of this atlas, which only show the default lect. The information on such **non-default lects** is given only in *APiCS Online*. So the default lect that was primarily described by the contributors need not be representative for the entire language.

4. Classification by lexifier

To help the reader's orientation, we have classified our languages into English-based, Dutch-based, Portuguese-based, and so on (see the second column in Table 2). The 76 *APiCS* languages are shown in Map 0, with different colours for different lexifiers. Again, this classification is not entirely uncontroversial. On the one hand, contact languages are characterized by strong influence from multiple languages, so saying, for instance, that Haitian Creole is French-based is problematic, as it glosses over the very important contribution of the African languages, especially to the grammar of the language. For this reason, many authors have used expressions like "French-lexified", "Dutch-lexified", etc. for such languages, which only refer to the role of the European languages as primary lexicon-providers.[2] We agree that such terms are more precise, but they are also more cumbersome, so we have mostly used the older (and still much more widespread) manner of talking about groups of creoles and pidgins. We think that it is sufficiently well known that "English-based" (etc.) is not meant to imply anything other than that the bulk of the language's lexicon is derived from English.

On the other hand, the notion of being based on a language is problematic in the case of languages with several lexifiers, especially Gurindji Kriol and Michif. These are shown as having two lexifiers on Map 0 (see overleaf). There are a few other cases where it is not fully clear what the primary lexifier is. Saramaccan's vocabulary has a very large Portuguese component, but for simplicity we

---

[2] Still other authors have used expressions like "English-related" and "French-related", which make the role of the lexifier languages appear less central.

classify it as English-based here. Papiamentu is often thought to be originally (Afro-)Portuguese-based, but as it has long been influenced much more by Spanish, we classify it as Spanish-based.

We made no attempt to use a uniform system for the language names, so we used names such as "Bahamian Creole", "Nicaraguan Creole English", and "Trinidad English Creole" side by side. We used the names which the authors preferred, and which they think are most widely used, by scholars and/or by the speakers themselves. Since there is no agreement on what exactly a pidgin and a creole is, it was impossible to try to use these terms systematically in the language names. Moreover, quite a few of the languages have well-established names that do not contain the elements "pidgin" or "creole" at all (Bislama, Sranan, Tayo, Papiamentu, etc.). Note that when we refer to creole or pidgin languages in general, we never capitalize these terms. They are capitalized only as part of language names, and sometimes when "Pidgin" or "Creole" are used as abbreviations of a longer language name (as when "Creole" is used to refer to Seychelles Creole, in a context where it is clear that the creole of the Seychelles is referred to).

Of our 76 languages and varieties, 27 are English-based, 14 are Portuguese-based, 9 are French-based, and 6 are Spanish-based. Our sample of languages is thus not genealogically balanced at all. Most specialists of pidgins and creoles do not classify their languages by families, but the reasons why typologists usually work with genealogically balanced samples (e.g. D. Bakker 2011) also apply to pidgins and creoles: if the languages in the sample are not independent cases, it is easy to be misled, especially if one applies quantitative measures. Our sample of 76 languages does include a fair number of languages with non-European lexifiers, but most have European lexifiers, and almost half of those with European lexifiers are English-based. And these languages not only share a lexifier, but many of them (e.g. those in the Caribbean) share a significant part of their more recent history. Some of our languages are so similar to each other that they are mutually intelligible (e.g. Mauritian Creole and Seychelles Creole). Thus, when looking at the figures, one cannot translate "most *APiCS* languages have X" into "pidgin and creole languages generally have X". The reader is urged to interpret all quantitative statements that we make with great caution.

5. The structural features

Like the choice of languages, the choice of features involved some difficult decisions. Languages can be compared with respect to an indefinite number of diverse dimensions, and while we would ideally like to have a representative set of features covering all domains of language structure, it is not even clear what representativeness might mean here. So we had to proceed on the basis of our intuitions, choosing features that we regarded as interesting and that we hoped the users of this atlas would find interesting as well. We tried to include the classical features discussed in the literature on creoles (e.g. those discussed in the wake of Bickerton 1981). In deciding on the choice of features, we made ample use of inspiration from two sources: the *World Atlas of Language Structures* (*WALS*), and *Comparative Creole Syntax* (Holm & Patrick 2007). To a significant extent, the present work stands on the shoulders of these predecessors.

As in *WALS*, the features of *APiCS* are *synchronic structural features*, with a small set of (between two and nine) *fixed values*. In contrast to *WALS*, we decided to allow *multiple choice*, that is, a language can have two or more values on a given feature (see §7).

The features are **structural features** in the sense that they concern abstract structures of the languages, rather than concrete form-meaning combinations (morphs). In dialect atlases, one commonly finds maps displaying the distribution of specific morphs. For example, in Kortmann & Lunkenheimer (2011), Feature 1 is "*She/her* used for inanimate referents". This makes reference to the specific morphs *she* and *her*. Such features are not possible when one compares languages that are not closely related. In order to capture similarities and differences between languages that do not descend from a common ancestor, one needs to define abstract structural features that make reference to structural properties that can be identified in any language. These can be general concepts of language form such as "precedes/follows", "overt/zero", "identical/differ-

Introduction

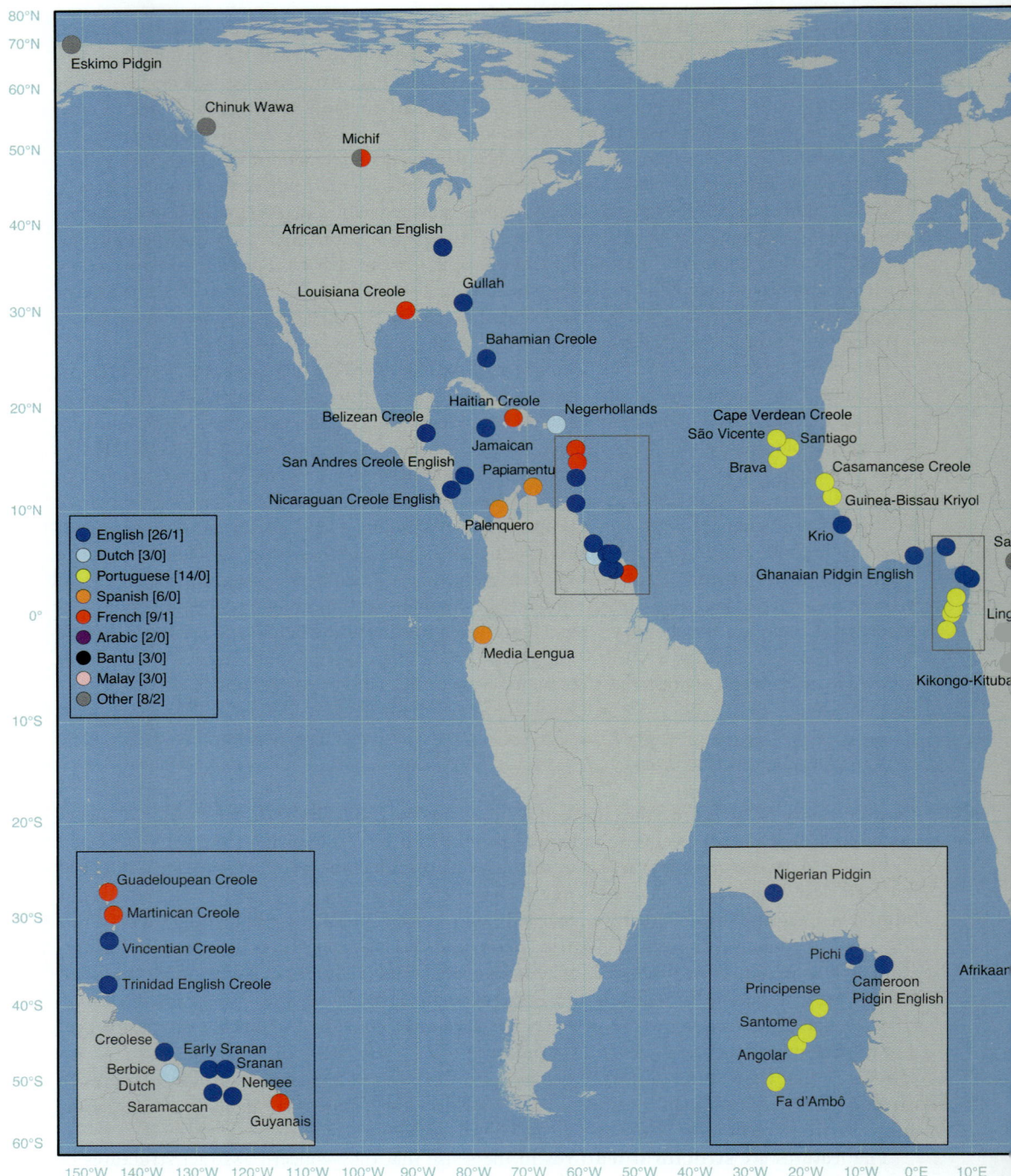

Map 0. The *APiCS* languages and their lexifiers

ent", or semantic-pragmatic concepts like "negation", "question", "focus", or more complex comparative concepts defined on the basis of such elementary formal concepts and semantic-pragmatic concepts (e.g. "subject", "pronoun").

The features are **synchronic features** in that they make no reference to the history of the relevant forms. Of course, in creole studies it is often diachronic changes that are of interest, and

Introduction

creolists often ask what the origin of particular forms is, for example, whether the plural marker originates from a third-person-plural pronoun (e.g. Papiamentu *kas-nan* 'houses', *nan* 'they'). But our perspective is synchronic, even though the *APiCS* authors often provide interesting information about diachronic sources of grammatical markers. However, we can ask only questions that can in principle be answered for any language, even if nothing is known about its history. Thus, we refrained from including diachronic features in the *Atlas of Pidgin and Creole Language Structures*.

Introduction

But in the comments to the value assignments in the database, the *APiCS* contributors have often included information about diachronic aspects, and we often included diachronic considerations in the chapter texts.

However, we made exceptions in two lexical features, Chapter 109 ("Pequenino") and Chapter 110 ("Savvy"). The Portuguese words *pequenino* 'little' and *saber* 'know' came to be widely used also in English-based pidgins and creoles (with forms such as *pickaninny* and *savvy*), so we thought that including them in *APiCS* would be interesting, even though these are specific forms, not abstract structures, and thus should not strictly speaking be part of a comparison of language structures.

The structural features have between two and nine different **fixed values**. Like the choice of features, the choice of values had to be based on our intuitions of what kinds of distinctions would give the most interesting results. For example, in Chapter 40 ("Gender agreement of adnominal adjectives"), we distinguish the four values in Table 3.

Table 3. **The value box of Chapter 40**

○	1. No adjective agrees with the noun	59
◯	2. Only few adjectives agree with the noun	12
◉	3. Many adjectives agree with the noun	2
●	4. All adjectives agree with the noun	1

Instead of four values, we could have distinguished only two (gender agreemeent exists/does not exist), or we could have made even more distinctions along any number of dimensions: optional/obligatory agreement, agreement depending on adjective position, agreement depending on semantic class of adjective, on animacy of head noun, and so on. Thus, there is nothing "natural" or "true" about the value choices that we made: These are our choices that we feel best capture the diversity and similarity among our languages, but alternative choices would always have been possible.

It is important to be aware that the concepts that we use to compare the languages in structural terms are a special set of comparative concepts (Haspelmath 2010) and need not be identical to the descriptive categories that one would use to describe these languages. Descriptive categories are defined in language-particular terms and thus not suitable for cross-linguistic comparison. For example, "adjective" may be defined in a variety of ways in different languages (Dixon 2004), making reference to the lack of marking in adnominal contexts, presence of a copula in predicative contexts, presence of comparative marking, use of special degree words, and so on. But for cross-linguistic comparison, we must limit ourselves to criteria that can be applied to all languages, that is, semantic criteria. In Chapter 3 ("Order of adjective and noun") we therefore define "adjectives" as words with property meanings such as 'hot', 'old', and 'blue', regardless of how they are treated grammatically in each language. Thus, in languages which do not make a grammatical adjective–verb distinction, it is still possible to answer the question about the order of the adjective and the noun. Likewise, in the chapters dealing with definite articles (Chapters 9, 28, 31), we provide a semantic definition of definite articles, and we classify some elements as definite articles that are normally regarded as demonstratives in the languages in question.

Some grammatical concepts are generally treated as if they had a cross-linguistically valid definition, though this is not in fact the case. The most striking example of this is the concept 'word' (as well as its counterparts, 'affix' and 'phrase'). Linguists often compare languages with respect to the contrast between morphological expression (by affixes) and syntactic expression (by words and phrases), and we do this occasionally in *APiCS* as well (e.g. in Chapters 37, 45–6, 62, 100), but one needs to be aware that it is very difficult to define 'affix' as a comparative concept (Haspelmath 2011b). Thus, a more precisely defined notion of "tightness of combination" (as in Chapters 45–6) is likely to give more information than the information about affixhood (which tends to primarily reflect writing traditions).

Introduction

6. Relationship between *APiCS* features and features in Holm & Patrick (2007) and in *WALS*

Table 4 shows those 48 *APiCS* features that are also represented in Holm & Patrick (2007) in one way or another, and those 48 features that are also represented in *WALS* (Haspelmath, Dryer, Gil, & Comrie 2005).

Table 4. *APiCS* features with counterparts in *Comparative Creole Syntax* and *WALS*

	APiCS chapter/feature title	Holm & Patrick number	*WALS* number
1	Order of subject, object, and verb		81
2	Order of possessor and possessum	16.1-2	86
3	Order of adjective and noun	15.9-10	87
4	Order of adposition and noun phrase		85
5	Order of demonstrative and noun	15.6-7	88
6	Order of cardinal numeral and noun		89
7	Order of relative clause and noun		90
8	Order of degree word and adjective		91
12	Position of interrogative phrases in content questions		93
13	Gender distinctions in personal pronouns	15.11	44
15	Inclusive/exclusive distinction in independent personal pronouns		39
18	Politeness distinctions in second-person pronouns		45
19	Interrogative pronouns	17.8	
21	Indefinite pronouns		46
22	Occurrence of nominal plural markers		34
23	Expression of nominal plural meaning		33
24	The associative plural	15.5	
25	Nominal plural marker and third-person-plural pronoun	15.4	
28	Definite articles	15.3	37
29	Indefinite articles	15.2	38
30	Generic noun phrases in subject function	(16.1)	
31	Co-occurrence of demonstrative and definite article	15.6-7	
32	Pronominal and adnominal demonstratives	15.6-7	42
33	Distance contrasts in demonstratives	15.6-7	41
34	Adnominal distributive numerals		54
35	Ordinal numerals		53
36	Sortal numeral classifiers		55
37	Marking of pronominal possessors	16.4	
38	Marking of possessor noun phrases	16.1-3	24
39	Independent pronominal possessors	16.5-6	
40	Gender agreement of adnominal adjectives	15.11	
41	Comparative adjective marking	12.7	
42	Comparative standard marking	(15.6–7, 14.5)	121
44	Internal order of tense, aspect, and mood markers	(7.2)	
45	Tightness of the link between the past marker and the verb	2.	
46	Tightness of the link between the progressive marker and the verb	3.	
47	Uses of the progressive marker	3.	
48	Uses of the habitual marker	4.	
51	Present reference of stative verbs and past perfective reference of dynamic verbs	1.2-4	
52	Aspect markers and inchoative meaning	3.4	
54	Suppletion according to tense and aspect		79
56	The prohibitive		71
58	Alignment of case marking of full noun phrases		98
59	Alignment of case marking of personal pronouns	17.1–17.6	99
60	Ditransitive constructions with 'give'		105
62	Expression of pronominal subjects		101
70	Comitatives and instrumentals		52
71	Noun phrase conjunction and comitative		63
72	Nominal and verbal conjunction		64

(*cont.*)

Introduction

Table 4. (*cont.*)

	APiCS chapter/feature title	Holm & Patrick number	*WALS* number
73	Predicative noun phrases	13.1	120
74	Predicative adjectives	13.3	
75	Predicative locative phrases	13.2	
76	Predicative noun phrases and predicative locative phrases		119
77	Predicative possession		117
78	Existential verb and transitive possession verb	13.6	
81	Motion-to and motion-from	(19.2)	
84	Directional serial verb constructions with 'come' and 'go'	14.1-2	
86	'Give' serial verb constructions	14.3	
88	Intensifiers and reflexive pronouns	17.7	47
89	Reciprocal constructions		106
90	Passive constructions	11.1-2	
91	Applicative constructions		109
92	Subject relative clauses	9.3 (15.8, 17.9)	122
93	Object relative clauses	9.4, 9.6 (17.9)	
94	Instrument relative clauses	(9.5, 17.9)	
95	Complementizer with verbs of speaking	8.5–8.7, 14.4	
96	Complementizer with verbs of knowing	8.5–8.7	
97	'Want' complement subjects		124
100	Negative morpheme types	10.1-2	112
101	Position of standard negation	10.1-2	
102	Negation and indefinite pronouns	10.3	115
103	Polar questions	(20.1)	116
104	Focusing of the noun phrase	13.5	
105	Verb doubling and focus	12.5	
107	Vocative markers	(20.2)	
108	Paralinguistic usages of clicks		142
112	'Hand' and 'arm'		129
120	Tone		13
122	Nasal vowels		10

In addition to these matching features, there are about 25 chapters that have a topic that is related to the topic of a *WALS* chapter, but the definition of the feature and/or the choice of feature values is so different that a direct comparison is not possible.

And even for those 48 features where there is a close match between the *WALS* features and the *APiCS* features (usually because the *APiCS* feature was explicitly modelled on the *WALS* feature), we had to change the *APiCS* values occasionally. Sometimes this was necessary because we wanted to include more information and avoid uninformative values such as "other" and "mixed" (see also §7, below, on multiple-choice features). In a number of cases we felt that more distinctions should be made than in *WALS*, and sometimes we ignored minor values that occur only in highly special circumstances and that would have been difficult to explain to our contributors. Another common situation is that certain values that occur in *WALS* do not occur in *APiCS* because they are rare and are not found in our relatively small sample of 76 languages.

While the Holm & Patrick (2007) features were specifically chosen in order to highlight properties that are characteristic of creoles, the features that were adopted from *WALS* are more neutral.

7. Multiple-choice features

In contrast to *WALS*, we decided to allow **multiple-choice features**, that is, features in which a language allows several possibilities. Thus, in Chapter 2 ("Order of possessor and possessum"), we have two values (see Table 5), but there are three types of language: those with possessor–possessum

Introduction

order (20 languages, exclusively value 1), those with possessum–possessor order (29 languages, exclusively value 2), and those with both orders (27 languages, sharing values 1 and 2).

Table 5. **The value box of a multiple-choice feature (Chapter 2)**

		excl	shrd	all
●	1. Possessor–possessum	20	27	47
●	2. Possessum–possessor	29	27	56

Languages which show multiple values for a given feature are shown by a **pie chart** in different colours on the map.

In *WALS*, by contrast, there are three values, and for each language a **single choice** must be made. Table 6 shows the three values of *WALS*'s Chapter 86 (Order of genitive and noun, Dryer 2005f; note that Dryer uses "genitive" in the same sense as *APiCS* uses "possessor"). If a language allows both orders and neither of the two orders is dominant (as in English, where one can say both *my friend's house* and *the house of my friend*), the language is assigned to the third type ("both").

Table 6. **Value distribution in Dryer's (2005f) *WALS* chapter**

1. Genitive–noun (GenN)	685
2. Noun–genitive (NGen)	467
3. Both orders occur with neither order dominant	96

If both orders are possible but one of the orders is marginal (e.g. genitive–noun order in Russian, which is possible under highly restricted conditions), then a language is classified in the *WALS* chapter according to the majority pattern, and the minority option is ignored.

In *APiCS*, we did not want to ignore minority patterns, and we wanted to distinguish between different situations of value combinations. Thus, we decided to add a weighting to the different values in a multiple-choice situation. Whenever more than two values were chosen for a feature, the contributors were asked to indicate the **relative importance** of each value, either numerically or by verbal description. There are five different degrees of relative importance as described verbally, which we translated into numerical values:

pervasive	90%	●
majority	70%	◐
about half	50%	◐
minority	30%	◑
marginal	10%	◔

So if there are two values, and one of them is described as "majority" and the other as "minority" by the contributor, the pie chart on the map shows 70 per cent of its area in the colour of the first value, and 30 per cent in the colour of the second value. It has to be kept in mind that relative importance can refer to different concepts. For example, in the feature "Order of subject, object, and verb" (Chapter 1) relative importance refers to text (or token) frequency. That is, it indicates how often a particular word order occurs in spoken or written language in comparison to the other word orders. On the other hand, token frequency is irrelevant for the feature "Female and male animals" (Chapter 117), where relative frequency expresses the paradigm frequency, that is, it indicates how many different animal names a particular sex-denoting word-formation process applies to, irrespective of whether the names are often or rarely used.

But the pies are not limited to 10% vs. 90%, 30% vs. 70%, and 50% vs. 50%. There are two ways in which other divisions of the values can come about. On the one hand, the contributors could also indicate the relative importance numerically, by entering exact percentages. Of course, just like the verbal importance indications, these numbers are usually based on impressionistic

Introduction

estimates rather than on text counts, but we felt that the impressionistic knowledge of language experts was a valuable resource that we wanted to include in the database when it was available. On the other hand, numerical distributions other than the ones implied by the five degrees listed above can come about when three (or more) different values are chosen. In such cases, the contributors often chose verbal relative-importance indications that add up to more than 100 per cent by the above correspondences. For example, if three values are chosen, and one of them is said to be "pervasive", while the other two values are "marginal", the figures add up to 110%. To turn such value choices into a pie chart, we had to normalize the figures: the pervasive pattern now gets 82% (= 90/110) instead of 90%, while the two other values get 9% each (= 10/110) instead of 10%. Occasionally, this kind of normalization was also necessary when only two values were chosen. For example, if one value is said to be "pervasive" (90%) and the other value "minority" (30%), we assign the resulting importance values 75% (= 90/120) and 25% (= 30/120).

Of the 130 structural features, 43 are multiple-choice features and 87 are single-choice features.

8. The chapter texts

Each chapter consists of a text that explains and exemplifies the different structural types (or values) of the feature, as well as of a world map showing the *APiCS* languages. In most cases, both the chapter text and the world map occupy two pages. However, for several features that show relatively little variation in our languages, we decided to make the map smaller (occupying just half a page rather than two pages), and to fit the text into one and a half pages. This concerns features 10, 15, 27, 36, 58, 91, and 99. Moreover, some of the phonological features, where we had less to say in the chapter texts, are treated differently: the texts for Chapters 118–19 occupy just a single page each, and those for Chapters 121–30 occupy just half a page each and are accompanied by smaller maps.

The chapter texts were written by the editors, but since the texts are based on the value assignments and the examples provided by the members of the *APiCS* Consortium, we decided to make the *APiCS* Consortium a co-author of each chapter (as mentioned earlier in §2). This may look a bit unusual, especially in the context of a work of linguistics where named author groups are not (yet) common. But it accurately reflects the enormous contribution made by the Consortium members. We would not have felt comfortable if the individual chapters of the *Atlas* were referred to as "Michaelis 2013" or "Maurer 2013", as if these were papers based entirely on our research. It must be emphasized that the co-authorship of the Consortium does not imply any responsibility for the interpretation of the results. An alternative would have been not to assign individual authorship to the chapters at all, but if we had chosen that option, the individual contributions of the editors would have been left unclear. As a rule, the first chapter author was responsible not only for writing the chapter, but also for reviewing and checking the corresponding feature dataset in the database (§10), as well as for formulating the feature values and the annotation in the first project phase. All this preparatory work was much more time-consuming than the actual writing of the chapter on the basis of the final database. When a chapter has two editors as co-authors, usually one of them did most of the preparatory work while the other one wrote most of the text.

The chapter texts explain the feature in question, define the (between two and nine) feature values, provide examples, discuss the geographical or historical distribution of the values, and situate it in a wider context, often relating it to debates in pidgin and creole studies or to the worldwide distribution of languages as reported in *WALS*. Because of the brevity of the *APiCS* chapters and the huge amount of relevant literature especially in creole studies, we were able to cite only a small part of it. Our chapters can thus be used as an introduction to the grammatical patterns of pidgins and creoles, but not as an overview of what has been written about them (see Holm 1988 for such an overview).

Each chapter contains a value box, which is largely identical to the value legend on the corresponding map (the value names are sometimes abbreviated on the maps). The value boxes of the single-choice features just give the number of languages in each value, while for the multiple-choice features, three numbers are given for each value: the number of languages that have this value exclu-

Introduction

sively, those that have this value among others ("shared"), and those that have this value at all (see Table 5, above).

Many of the chapters contain quite a few **examples** (usually example sentences) of the various phenomena from different languages of *APiCS*. These examples were almost all taken from the structure datasets supplied by the *APiCS* contributors, and in order to highlight these contributions, each example is accompanied by a reference to the structure dataset from which we took it. It should be noted that the examples often come from earlier published sources, which are mentioned in the structure dataset as published in *APiCS Online*.

The examples are usually accompanied by interlinear word-by-word glosses. For languages with more complex word-internal structure, we have often broken up the words into morphemes and provided morpheme-by-morpheme glosses. The interlinear glosses follow the conventions of the Leipzig Glossing Rules.

9. The maps

The maps show the world with country boundaries for orientation, and dot symbols (or pie charts) in different colours for each of the 76 languages. Each feature can have between two and nine different values. The colour of the dot tells the user for each language which value(s) it has for the given feature. The political boundaries are shown only for rough orientiation, and they should by no means be taken to endorse a particular political view. Online versions of the maps are also available in *APiCS Online* (at http://apics-online.info), but the chapter texts are available only in the printed form of the atlas.

The world map uses the Gall-Peters projection, which looks a bit unusual, because the shapes of the continents are different from what we are used to from the more frequently used projections. However, some of the commonly used projections have the disadvantage of enlarging the circumpolar regions, especially the well-known Mercator projection. Since the majority of *APiCS* languages are spoken in the circum-equatorial regions, the Gall-Peters projection with its specialized cylindrical equal-area representation of the world seemed best to us. Even so, two inset maps were necessary because of the high number of languages in these regions: One for the eastern Caribbean and one for the Gulf of Guinea. When information is lacking for a language (as happens in about 3% of the cases), the language is simply not shown on the map.

The different feature values are shown by dots with different colours. We tried to choose the colours in such a way that they facilitate the interpretation of the differences between the languages. The principles that have guided us are quite similar to those used in *WALS*:

– we avoid green dots because some readers cannot easily distinguish green and red;
– we use similar colours for similar values across different features;
– we use white dots for values expressing absence of a certain property;
– we normally use red and blue for the two main types (apart from absence of a property);
– we try to use light red and light blue for values that are similar to the two main types;
– we use yellow for identical coding of a function, red for different coding, orange for overlap, and black for identity and differentiation;
– for constituent order features such as the order of adposition and noun phrase (Chapter 4), we use red for the order where the head (or grammatical element) precedes, and blue for the order where it follows;
– for word-order features where there is no general correlation with the order of object and verb, we use yellow for the order where a modifier precedes the noun and purple for the order where it follows the noun;
– we use maximally distinct colours for rare types that need to be salient.

In addition to the main world maps showing the *APiCS* languages, we have included small inset maps cited from *WALS* for those 48 features that match *WALS* features. However, the maps cite

Introduction

only the data of *WALS*, not the actual map layout. In *WALS*, a different map projection and orientation is chosen, so we adjusted the *WALS* maps to the *APiCS* maps in this regard. The *WALS* maps sometimes had to be modified, as described in the map caption (e.g. "with minor values omitted"). There is no separate legend for the *WALS* insets—the dot colours have (at least largely) the same meaning as in the *APiCS* map. These inset maps allow the users to get a good sense of the worldwide distribution of the feature, thus allowing them to assess the likelihood that the feature is due to universal trends or substrate effects.

10. The *APiCS* project 2006–2012

The *Atlas of Pidgin and Creole Language Structures* is the result of intensive large-scale collaboration over several years. In this section we describe the process in its broad outlines.

The idea was originally proposed in the context of the *Groupe Européen de Recherche en Langues Créoles* in 2005 by Philippe Maurer. This proposal was taken up by Susanne Maria Michaelis, and Magnus Huber and Martin Haspelmath joined them as co-editors. Thus, the editorial team consisted of a specialist of Ibero-Romance-based creoles (Maurer), a specialist of French-based creoles (Michaelis), a specialist of English-based pidgins and creoles (Huber), and a general comparative linguist with an interest in language contact (Haspelmath).

Funding came from the Max Planck Institute for Evolutionary Anthropology (and its director Bernard Comrie), as well as (between 2008 and 2011) from the *Deutsche Forschungsgemeinschaft* through a grant to the University of Giessen (Susanne Maria Michaelis and Magnus Huber). This allowed Susanne Maria Michaelis to work primarily on this project for most of the project time, and covered the costs for a substantial number of student assistants, as well as our main assistant Melanie Revis and our database manager Bradley Taylor. We also had funding for regular meetings of the editors (mostly in Leipzig, but once in Aubonne near Lake Geneva). In addition, we were given the generous opportunity to organize seven workshops and conferences in Leipzig between 2006 and 2010 (February 2006, October 2006, March 2007, October 2007, June 2008, November 2009, November 2010). All *APiCS* Consortium members were invited to attend at least one of these events, and almost all of them came to Leipzig at least once. Finally, the *APiCS* project was presented by one or more of the editors at various conferences on (pidgin and) creole languages during this time, so that many members of the field had the chance to hear about it early on (January 2007 at the SPCL meeting in Anaheim, June 2007 at the SPCL meeting in Amsterdam, July 2008 at the SCL/SPCL meeting in Cayenne, January 2009 at the SPCL meeting in San Francisco, April 2009 at the Giessen Creolistics Workshop, August 2009 at the SPCL meeting in Cologne).

Most of the key design features of the *APiCS* database, of the resulting *Atlas*, and of the *Survey* volumes were intensively discussed during the meetings in the early phase of the project, and later meetings discussed first results from the database.

The most important aspect of the work of the editors in the first phase was to put together a set of features and feature values for the *APiCS* questionnaire. It would hardly have been possible to formulate the definitive questionnaire without a pilot phase, because the definition of the phenomena and the subdivision of the types depends on what is actually there. For this reason, we formulated a test questionnaire of 153 features in 2006 (inspired by Holm & Patrick 2007 and by *WALS*, see §6) that we asked a number of colleagues to fill in. After getting these preliminary datasets, we thoroughly revised the questionnaire and reduced it to 120 primary features. To this we added 28 sociolinguistic features (available only online) and over 100 segment features (for the phonological segments, we asked the contributors to give the complete inventory), which were much easier to fill in than the 120 primary features. The 130 maps of this atlas show the 120 primary features plus 10 particularly interesting segment features.

The feedback from the test questionnaires and discussions with the contributors during the meetings in 2006 and 2007 helped the editors to formulate the *APiCS* questionnaire in the best possible way. In many cases, we realized that some of the concepts that we had used were not suf-

Introduction

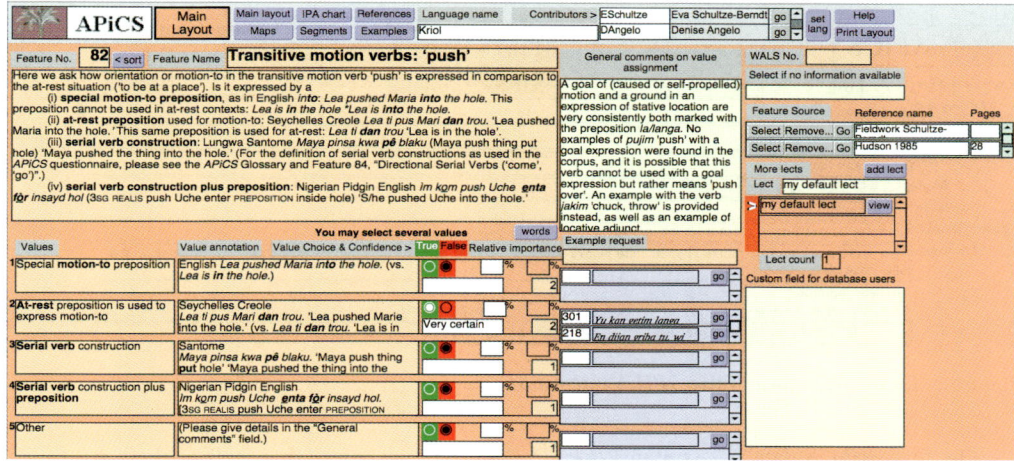

Figure 1. **Main layout of the *APiCS* questionnaire (application FileMaker Pro)**

ficiently clear and the definitions needed to be clarified (e.g. "definite article", "adjective", "serial verb"). Some of the contributors asked us what to do in case different subvarieties of their language show different types, so we allowed for the possibility of adding further lects, in addition to the default lect, to the database (note that the maps in this volume only show the distribution of values in the default lect). The question how to deal with multiple-choice features and how to indicate relative importance (by words or by estimated percentages, as mentioned in §7) was also discussed intensively.

The final questionnaire was sent out to the contributors in the spring of 2008, and we received most of the filled questionnaires by the end of the year. A screenshot of the database questionnaire (main layout) is show in Figure 1. The contributors' tasks were to carefully read the feature description in the upper left corner of the layout, to look at the feature values and their annotations, and to select the correct value (or several, in the case of multiple-choice features). They were asked to provide a bibliographical reference (in case the phenomenon was discussed in the literature on their language) and one or more examples, and they were given the opportunity to enter a prose comment into a comment field.

The resulting datasets were thoroughly reviewed by the editors. Each editor looked at the value choices, the comments, and the examples for the features that he or she was responsible for, and then provided comments to the contributors. In the majority of cases, the comment was limited to "OK", but in many other cases we had to ask a question or point out an omission. It turned out that some definitions of features and values were not fully clear and demanded revision, and there were cases where we later realized that even in the revised version of the questionnaire, some unclarities of definitions remained. This review by the editors was rather time-consuming, but it was very important to ensure the consistency of the datasets.

At the next stage, the contributors got their datasets back with our comments and were asked to revise them in accordance with our requests. Thus, the datasets were revised much more thoroughly than an average journal paper, and our contributors had to be very patient with us. For this reason, we kept stressing their crucial role in this enterprise, which is reflected in the fact that the *APiCS* Consortium is a co-author of every chapter of this *Atlas* (see §2).

In addition to the value assignment in the main layout, the contributors were asked to provide examples in a separate layout. This layout has fields for the primary text, an analysed text (with hyphenation for morpheme breakup), an interlinear gloss, and an idiomatic translation into English. We also asked the contributors to give an example reference and to specify the example type (spoken, written, constructed, etc.). Further optional fields can contain translations into other languages and general comments (see Figure 2 for a screenshot).

Introduction

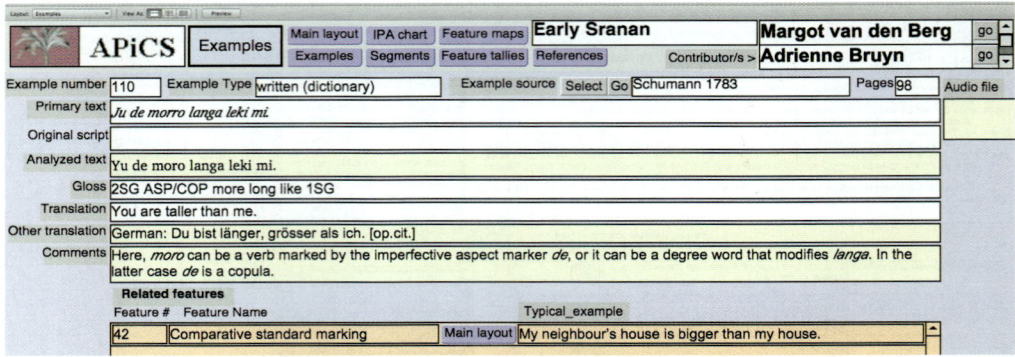

Figure 2. **Example layout of the *APiCS* questionnaire**

The final *APiCS* database contains over 15,000 examples, more than half of them naturalistic spoken examples. Over 1,000 of the examples were constructed by native-speaker linguists (at least ten of the contributors are native speakers of the languages they have described). The glossing style of the examples was made consistent across the entire database thanks to the hard work of our student assistants, who spent a lot of time tracking down the meanings of unusual abbreviations and homogenizing capitalization and punctuation conventions. A major role was played by our main assistant Melanie Revis, who coordinated the students and provided invaluable help in making other aspects of the database consistent (as well as editing the *Survey*). All examples are accessible via *APiCS Online* (apics-online.info). The chapter texts in this *Atlas* contain just a small selection of the examples that we collected. The *APiCS* example collection must be one of the largest sets of interlinear glossed text from multiple languages.

After the editors received the revised datasets from the contributors, we looked at each record of the database again, repeating the first reviewing step, to make sure that no inconsistency was left. Occasionally this involved further consultation with the contributors.

Throughout the project duration (between 2006 and 2013), we had the privilege to be assisted by our database manager Bradley Taylor, who programmed the database template in FileMaker Pro, provided software support to the contributors, aggregated all the contributor databases, and helped us to make the database usable and consistent by adding a wide variety of additional features.

Finally, the editors wrote the 130 chapter texts, defining each feature and its values as in the original feature annotation, selecting examples from the database, and drawing some conclusions about possible geographical or historical patterns. This was a daunting task that took us longer than we had expected. Basically, it would require excellent knowledge of pidgin and creole languages and earlier research in the field, excellent knowledge of the patterns that are possible in the world's languages (though often *WALS* helped here), and excellent knowledge of the domain of grammar in question. We may not have been able to fulfil all these demands simultaneously, but we enjoyed working on these tasks and we trust that the resulting *Atlas of Pidgin and Creole Language Structures* will be a valuable tool for our colleagues and future generations of linguists with an interest in contact languages.

WORD ORDER

Chapter 1
Order of subject, object, and verb

MAGNUS HUBER AND THE *APiCS* CONSORTIUM

1. Feature description

This feature is inspired by *WALS* feature 81 (Dryer 2011c) and concerns the ordering of subject, object, and verb in non-contrastive, non-focused transitive clauses without special topicalization; more specifically, declarative clauses with both the subject and object realized as full noun phrases (not as pronouns). We use subject and object in a semantic sense, to refer to the agent-like and patient-like constituents in a monotransitive clause, as in French, for example:

(1) $_S$[*Les souris*] $_V$[*mangent*] $_O$[*le fromage*]
ART mouse.PL   eat.PL   ART cheese
'The mice eat the cheese.'

As can be seen from this example, French has SVO order (subject-verb-object), because the subject *les souris* 'the mice' precedes the verb, and the object *le fromage* 'the cheese' follows it. Since we consider only non-contrastive, non-focused, non-topicalized clauses, cases like English *It is the cheese that the mice eat* (=OSV) are disregarded here.

Languages can have several word orders (e.g. German is SVO and VSO in main clauses and SOV in subordinate clauses), so several values can be true for this feature.

2. The values

There are six possible orders of subject, object, and verb, as shown in the value box, all of which are attested in the *APiCS* sample:

		excl	shrd	all
●	1. Subject–verb–object (SVO)	61	10	71
●	2. Subject–object–verb (SOV)	1	11	12
●	3. Verb–subject–object (VSO)	0	7	7
●	4. Verb–object–subject (VOS)	0	3	3
●	5. Object–subject–verb (OSV)	0	3	3
●	6. Object–verb–subject (OVS)	0	2	2

Value 1. **SVO** order is found in e.g. Fanakalo. This order is by far the most common order in the *APiCS* languages:

(2) *Lo kati buk-a lo inja.*
ART cat see-PRS ART dog
'The cat is looking at the dog.' (Mesthrie 2013)

Value 2. **SOV** order is illustrated by an example from Eskimo Pidgin:

(3) *wai'hinni artegi annahanna pûgmûmmi*
woman   coat   sew   now
'The woman is sewing a coat now.' (van der Voort 2013)

Value 3. Example (4), from Cavite Chabacano, has **VSO** order:

(4) *Ya coge el mga pulis con el ladron.*
PFV catch the PL police OBJ the thief
'The policemen caught the thief.' (Sippola 2013a)

Value 4. **VOS** is attested in Ternate Chabacano if the object is indefinite (otherwise the order is VSO):

(5) *Ya kumpra plor el baguntáw.*
PFV buy   flower the young.man
'The young man bought a flower.' (Sippola 2013b)

Value 5. The majority of sentences in Yimas-Arafundi Pidgin are **OSV**:

(6) *nuŋgum paymban awkura-mbi* [...].
man   eagle   take-DEP
'The eagle took the man and [...].' (Foley 2013)

Value 6. **OVS** order is marginally attested in Chinese Pidgin Russian:

(7) *Knifka xotfi d'elaj eta liudi.*
book   want make this person
'These people wish to compose a book.'
(Perekhvalskaya 2013)

Feature 1 is a multiple-choice feature and one language in our sample, the mixed language Michif, actually shows all six orders:

(8) SVO: *Trwaa lii   zom kii-tahkwamamw-ak*
    three ART.PL man PST-carry.INAN-3PL
    trwa lii   suutkees shaak.
    three ART.PL suitcase each
    'Three men carried three suitcases each.'

SOV: *La   shyenn lii   ptsi   shyaen*
DEF.ART.F.SG bitch ART.PL small dog
meekwaat ayaaw-eew.
PROG   have.ANIM-3.SBJ.3.OBJ
'The bitch is having pups.'

VSO: *Kii-wanist-aw   li   zhwal*
PST-lose.INAN-3 DEF.ART.M.SG horse
soo   likoo.
3.POSS.M halter
'The horse lost its halter.'

VOS: *Kii-uchi-pit-am   sa   tet*
PST-from-pull-3.OBJ.INAN POSS.3.F head
la   torcheu.
DEF.ART.F.SG turtle
'The turtle retracted its head.'

OSV: *Aen   beebii la   praenses*
INDF.M.SG baby DEF.ART.F.SG princess
kii-ayaw-eew.
PST-have.ANIM-3.SBJ.3.OBJ
'The princess had a baby.'

OVS: *Lii   zaray pwaencheu ayaa-wak*
ART.PL ear   pointed   have-3PL
li   loo pi li   minush.
DEF.ART.M.SG wolf and DEF.ART.M.SG cat
'Cats and wolves have pointed ears.'
(Bakker 2013)

APiCS documents all possible neutral word orders in a language regardless of their frequency, but the corresponding *WALS* feature 81 (Dryer 2011c) considers only the dominant one and disregards the rest, except when a language lacks a dominant word order (value 7, e.g. German). There is thus no exact match between *WALS* and *APiCS* for the order of subject, object, and verb.

3. Distribution

Numerical. SOV is the most frequent dominant order among the world's languages (565 out of 1,377 languages = 41% in Dryer 2011c), followed by SVO (488/1377 = 35%). By contrast, 71 of 76 languages in the *APiCS* sample (93%) have SVO, with 63 languages (83%) relying on this word order as the exclusive or dominant pattern. Only twelve *APiCS* languages (16%) show SOV. Of these, Sri Lanka Portuguese is exclusively SOV and another five languages predominantly rely on this word order. Nine of these SOV languages also have SVO, which clearly establishes SVO as the dominant *APiCS* pattern. Note, however, that the *APiCS* sample with its heavy bias towards European lexifier contact languages is not typologically balanced and that the above figures may therefore not necessarily be representative of pidgins and creoles in general. The four other word orders (VSO, VOS, OSV, OVS) are marginal in that there is no *APiCS* language that exclusively relies on any of these orders alone. However, the three Chabacano varieties exhibit VSO as a dominant pattern (probably as a result of the influence of Philippine languages) and Yimas-Arafundi Pidgin is dominantly OSV.

By lexifier/substrate. As with a number of other word-order features, word order in the *APiCS* languages seems to have been determined in most cases by that of the lexifier. For example, the 27 languages whose sole or predominant lexifier is English are all exclusively SVO. This is unsurprising in most cases since the substrates also have SVO; for example, substratal input to many Atlantic English-lexicon contact varieties of the African Diaspora came from slaves who spoke SVO languages (mainly Bantu, Kwa, Atlantic). However, some important substrate languages from the Senegambia region and Sierra Leone are SOV; examples are the Western Mande languages Mandinka, Susu, Mende, and Vai. Nevertheless, this order did not find its way into, for instance, Gullah or other creoles where these substrates are known to have provided a strong input. A similar case could be made for the French- and Portuguese-lexicon Atlantic varieties, which again are all exclusively SVO.

Turning to the Pacific, languages on the Papua New Guinea mainland are predominantly SOV, yet Tok Pisin is exclusively SVO. This probably results from the word order of the lexifier English and the fact that plantation workers were imported from the Bismarck Archipelago, where the languages are SVO (cf. e.g. Tolai). In the Indian Ocean, the French-lexicon creoles of Mauritius, Reunion, and the Seychelles (the latter indirectly through slaves from Mauritius and Reunion) received an early substratal input of VOS through slaves from Madagascar and of SOV from West Africa (Mandinka) and India. Yet, none of these orders were retained in the three creoles, all exclusively following French SVO.

However, there are also a few cases where substratal word order became the dominant pattern in the creole: for example, while 13 Portuguese-lexified creoles in *APiCS* show SVO only, Sri Lanka Portuguese and Korlai in the Indian Ocean adopted the SOV order of the Indian adstrates (a recent development, see Bakker 2008: 140). Another exceptional case is Pidgin Hawaiian, which retained the Hawaiian lexifier VSO pattern only as a minority choice but relies heavily on the SVO order of the substrates English, Cantonese, Hakka, and Portuguese. In the New World, Chinuk Wawa is exclusively SVO in spite of its major lexifier Chinook being VOS and the languages of the Pacific Northwest being mainly VSO. Again, the word order may well have been adopted from English and French, minor lexifiers of Chinuk Wawa.

1 Order of subject, object, and verb

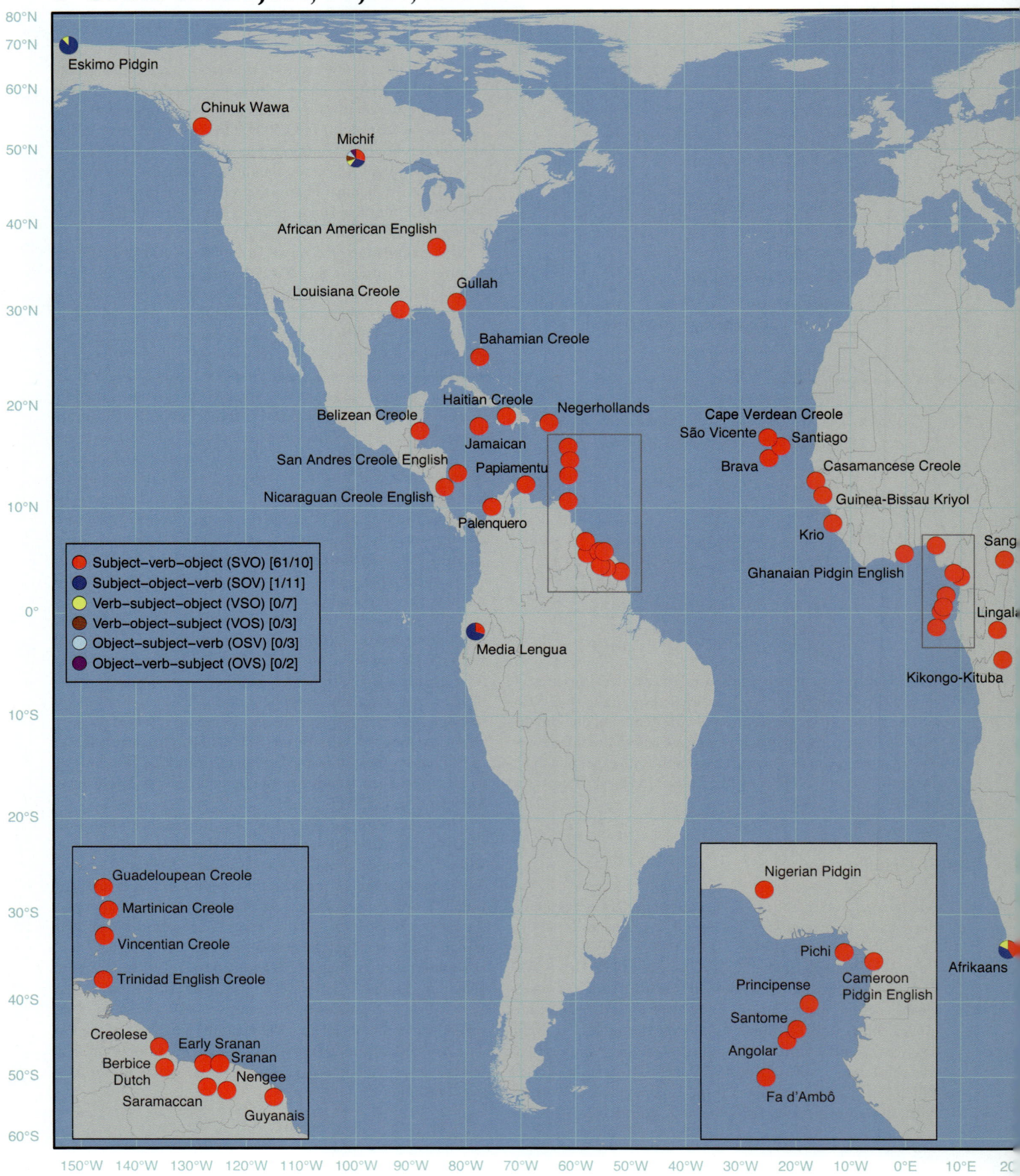

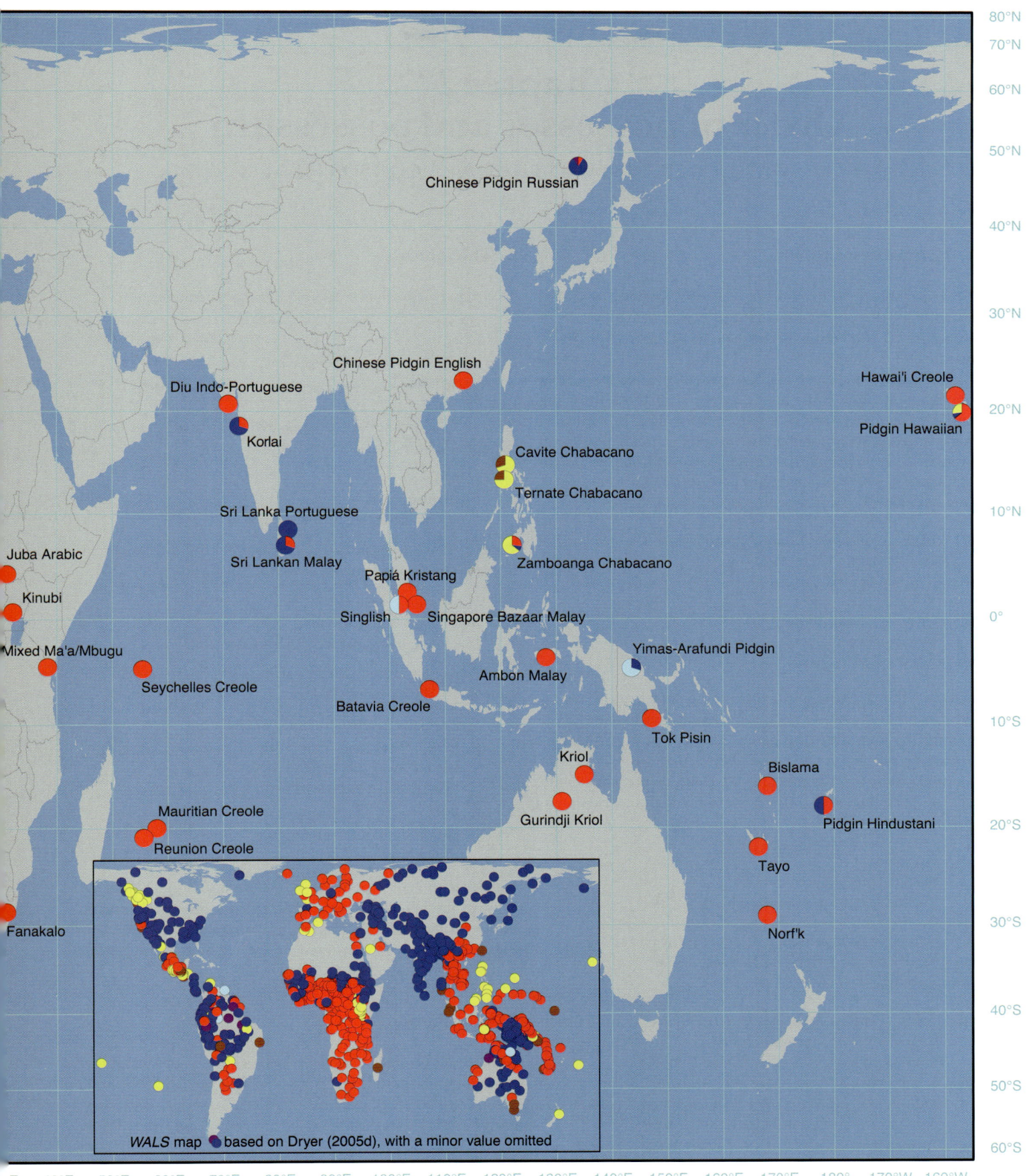

Chapter 2
Order of possessor and possessum
MAGNUS HUBER AND THE *APiCS* CONSORTIUM

1. Feature description

This map shows the word order in attributive possessive constructions—that is, the order of the possessor noun phrase with respect to the head noun (or possessum). It is based on *WALS* feature 86A (Dryer 2011d).

We restrict ourselves to the position of possessive noun phrases containing (full) nouns, rather than those involving only a pronominal word or a proper noun. This is because in some languages pronominal and/or proper noun possessors occur in different positions than nominal ones. Compare Pidgin Hindustani, where pronominal possessors follow the possessum but nominal possessors precede it (Siegel 2013):

(1) *Wau kii   kela papale wau.* (pronominal possessor)
    1SG fetch DET hat   1SG.POSS
    'I fetched my hat.'

(2) *Daya ke   kuta* (nominal possessor)
    Daya POSS dog
    'Daya's dog'

Whether the construction involves other words or affixes on the head or the possessor noun is irrelevant for this feature. For example, in a number of pidgins and creoles a third-person-possessive determiner is placed between the possessor and the possessum (cf. Chapter 38 "Marking of possessor noun phrases"), as illustrated by the possessor-initial construction of Berbice Dutch:

(3) *di potɛ man ʃi   toro*
    the old man 3SG.POSS eye
    'the old man's eye' (Kouwenberg 2013a)

The term possession is used in this context in a broad sense, including, of course, ownership, as in *the old lady's dog*, but also the following:

(a) kinship relations and body-part relations, as in German *Maria-s Mutter* [Mary-GEN mother] 'Mary's mother' and *Maria-s Fuß* [Mary-GEN foot] 'Mary's foot',
(b) the subjective and objective genitive, where the possessor would be the subject or object in a sentential paraphrase, e.g. *the teacher's efforts* or *the pupil's detention*.

2. The values

There are two possible orders of possessor and possessum:

	excl	shrd	all
1. Possessor–possessum	20	27	47
2. Possessum–possessor	29	27	56

Value 1. The **possessor–possessum** order is attested in, for example, African American English:

(4) *Sue house*
    Sue house
    'Sue's house' (Green 2013)

Value 2. The **possessum–possessor** order is illustrated by an example from Cape Verdean Creole of São Vicente:

(5) *káza d'un   senhor*
    house of=DET gentleman
    'the house of a gentleman' (Swolkien 2013)

Feature 2 is a multiple-choice feature, and 27 languages in our sample actually have both orders:

(6) Vincentian Creole (Prescod 2013)
    a. *misa Jesi god fren suhn*
       Mister Jessie good friend son
       'Mr Jessie's good friend's son'
    b. *di pikni fo di woman*
       ART child for ART woman
       'the woman's child(ren)'

Note that the corresponding *WALS* feature 86A, "Order of genitive and noun" (Dryer 2011d), records only the dominant value and disregards the less frequent alternative (except when a language lacks a dominant order = value 3, as in Norwegian).

3. Distribution

Numerical. Overall, possessor-final is the somewhat more common order in the *APiCS* sample. This tendency is a little stronger when one considers only those languages that show just one order ("excl" in the value box above) and also holds—

albeit to a lesser extent—when the *APiCS* values are reduced to match *WALS*: predominantly possessor-initial 33, predominantly possessor-final 36, no dominant order 8. This is somewhat against the trend among the world's languages: predominantly possessor-initial 685, predominantly possessor-final 467, no dominant order 96 (Dryer 2011d), but it has to be kept in mind that the *APiCS* sample is not typologically balanced.

By lexifier/substrate. Most African slaves in the Atlantic region originated from areas where Niger-Congo languages were spoken. These languages show a rather well-defined distribution regarding the order of possessor and possessum (see Dryer 2011d): in the extreme west, the Atlantic subfamily is mostly possessor-final. Further east, and stretching to the western border of Nigeria, other Niger-Congo subfamilies are possessor-initial, while Nigerian languages and the large Bantu genus again show a possessor-final order. Substratal input in the Atlantic contact languages thus often provided a mix of both orders.

While English also has both orders, it is interesting that of the 19 English-lexicon contact languages in the Atlantic, nine are exclusively possessor-initial but none is exclusively possessor-final. Also, in those languages that exhibit both orders, possessor-final is never the dominant one, with the sole exception of Early Sranan.

On the other hand, in nine of the ten Portuguese-lexified Atlantic creoles the possessor categorically follows the possessum. The explanation is probably that both Portuguese and the dominant substrates of the Gulf of Guinea and the Cape Verdean Creoles, Bantu, and Atlantic languages, too, are of this type. Papiamentu is the only Atlantic Ibero-Romance-lexified creole that has both orders. Slaves from the Togo-Benin area (see Maurer 2013d) or indeed the Dutch construction (e.g. *Jan zijn huis* [Jan his house] 'Jan's house') may have contributed the minority possessor-initial order.

The French creoles of the Caribbean and the Americas are exclusively possessor-final, following the lexifier French, although there must have been possessor-initial substratal input.

The Dutch-lexified languages Afrikaans and Negerhollands show both orders, but Berbice Dutch is an exclusive possessor-initial language, which may be due to the strong substratal influence of Ijo, a southern Nigerian possessor-initial language (see Smith 1999: 254ff.).

In all the African- and Arabic-lexified contact varieties in central and southern Africa the possessor can only follow the possessum, maybe because this is the dominant order in the main lexifiers and African substrates. On the other hand, Afrikaans allows both orders, just like its lexifier Dutch.

The picture is different when we turn to the Indian Ocean and South Asia: except for Reunion Creole, all French and Portuguese creoles allow the possessor-initial order to varying degrees. In the South Asian varieties Diu Indo-Portuguese, Korlai, and Sri Lanka Portuguese, the possessor-initial order can be explained by the fact that Indian languages overwhelmingly prefer this order. This may also be the reason why Sri Lankan Malay does not follow Standard Malay's possessor-final order (Prentice 1990: 928). The island creoles of Mauritius, Reunion, and the Seychelles received an early and strong substratal possessor-final input through slaves from Madagascar and later from the Kenya region. This agreed with the lexifier order and seems to have been the reason why there is a strong preference in these varieties for possessor-final, even though the other order was also imported to Mauritius and Reunion, from West Africa (Mandinka) and India. Where possessor-initial also occurs (Mauritian Creole, Seychelles Creole) it is in the minority and a more recent development, as in Mauritian Creole, where it "is not attested until about 1880" (Baker & Kriegel 2013a).

In the Pacific, Tok Pisin and the closely related Bislama are strictly possessor-final. For Tok Pisin this could be seen as surprising, since mainland New Guinea is predominantly possessor-initial (Dryer 2011d; and Yimas-Arafundi Pidgin too has this order) and Tok Pisin's lexifier English has both orders. As with Features 1 "Order of subject, object, and verb" and 3 "Order of adjective and noun", the answer is probably found in Tok Pisin's strong substratal input from the Bismarck Archipelago, where the majority of languages, including the important substrate Tolai, have a dominant possessor-final order (Dryer 2011d). The languages of Vanuatu, too, are overwhelmingly possessor-final and Bislama unsurprisingly follows this. Note also that Tok Pisin's and Bislama's possessive constructions of the *house belong father* type may have been consolidated by the phrasal correspondence in English (*the house belongs to father* or *the house that belongs to father*). The possessor-initial order of Chinese Pidgin English is easier to explain, Cantonese preferring that order. Kriol and Gurindji Kriol in Australia allow both orders, maybe because the Aboriginal languages in the Northern Territories are rather heterogeneous, too, in this respect. In Hawai'i Creole, there is a strong preference for possessor-initial, in spite of the fact that the substrates provided a mix of orders: Chinese and Japanese: possessor-initial; Hawaiian and Portuguese: possessor-final. The possessor can both precede and follow the possessum in Norf'k, probably because both English and the contributing language Tahitian (see Mühlhäusler 2013a) allow both orders.

2 Order of possessor and possessum

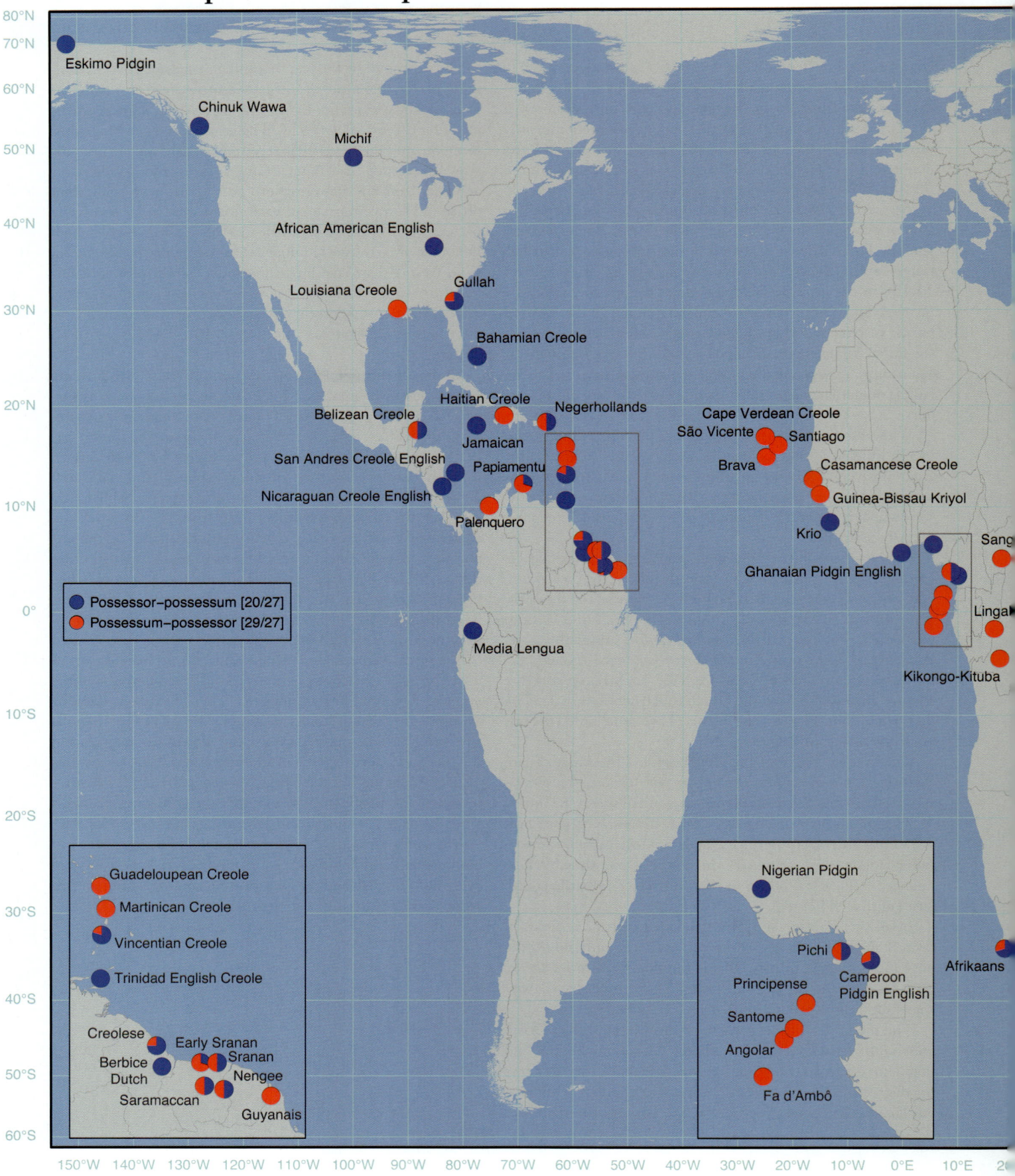

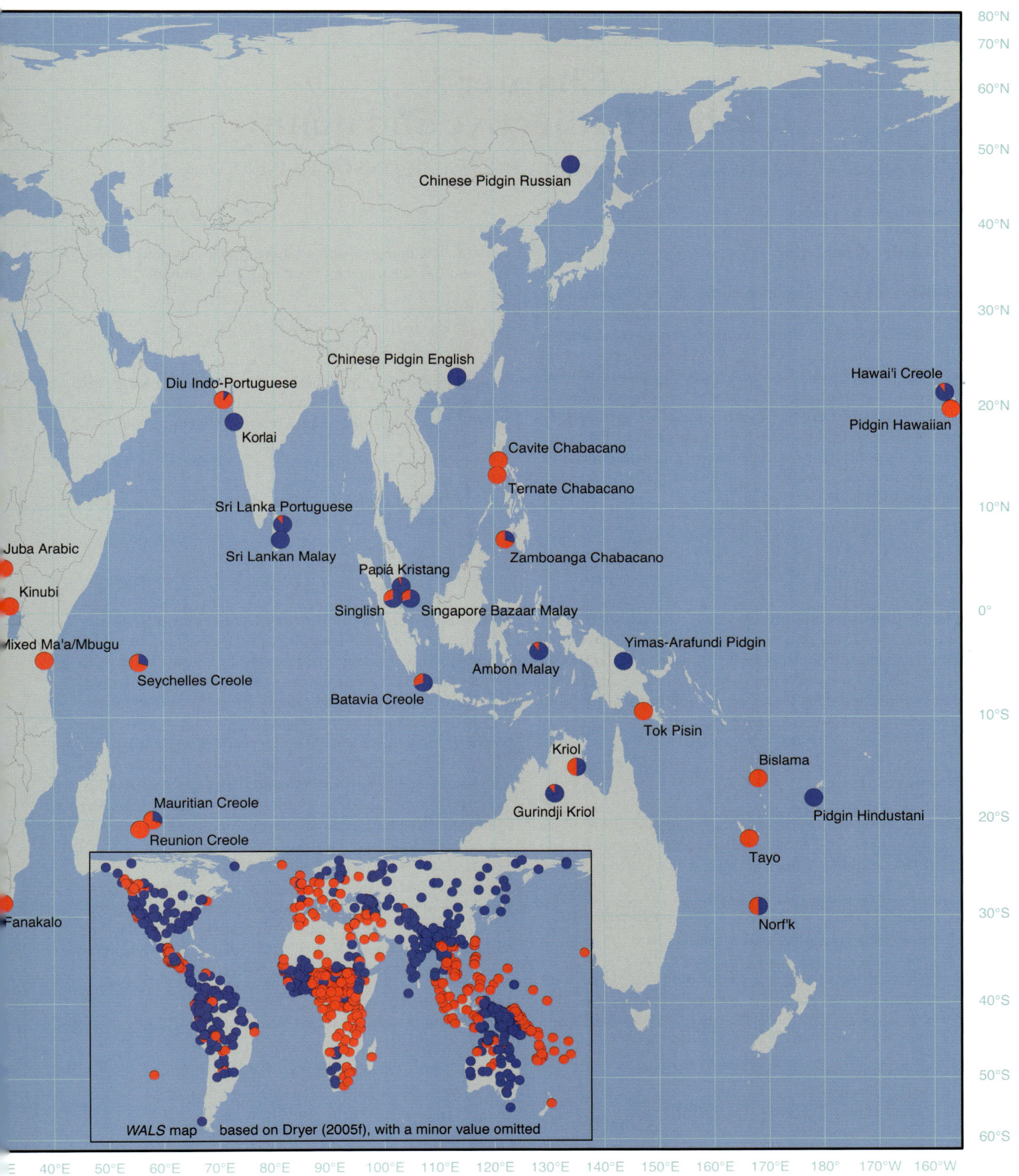

Chapter 3
Order of adjective and noun

MAGNUS HUBER AND THE *APiCS* CONSORTIUM

1. Feature description

Chapter 3 is about the position of the adjective relative to the noun it modifies. Here and in other *APiCS* features, the term *adjective* is defined purely in a semantic sense—as a word with a lexical meaning such as 'hot', 'old', or 'blue'. For this reason, we disregard demonstratives, numerals, and words meaning 'other'. In languages such as English and French, adjectives belong to a distinct class of words, but in other languages they are nouns or verbs. However, for the purposes of the present feature, a word is treated as an adjective as long as it denotes a property or quality, irrespective of its word class, thus including cases such as (1).

(1) Kikongo-Kituba (Mufwene 2013)
    muntu ya nda/ ngolo
    person of tallness/strength
    'tall/strong person'

The conception of the present feature follows *WALS* Feature 87 (Dryer 2011a) and thus considers only adjectives modifying a noun (i.e. attributive adjectives), as in English *the wicked man*. Chapter 3 is not concerned with predicative adjectives in clauses where the noun is the subject and the adjective is the predicate, as in English *The man is wicked*.

2. The values

There are two possible orders of the modifying adjective relative to the noun: either the adjective precedes the noun (value 1) or it follows the noun (value 2):

		excl	shrd	all
●	1. Modifying adjective precedes noun	34	35	69
●	2. Modifying adjective follows noun	7	35	42

Value 1. The adjective–noun order (modifying adjective precedes noun) is found in e.g. Chinese Pidgin Russian:

(2) malen'ki kurema
    small   jacket
    'small jacket' (Perekhvalskaya 2013)

Value 2. The noun–adjective pattern (modifying adjective follows noun) is illustrated by an example from Ambon Malay:

(3) ana~ana   kacil
    child~child small
    'small children' (Paauw 2013)

This feature is a multiple-choice feature in that a language can have both preceding and following adjectives. Thus, in Cape Verdean Creole of Santiago, adjectives can either precede or follow nouns:

(4) a. un   póbri bédju
       ART.INDF poor old
       'a poor old man' (Lang 2013)
    b. un   bédju póbri
       ART.INDF old   poor
       'a poor old man' (Lang 2013)

There is no perfect match with *WALS* Feature 87 (Dryer 2011a), which, in addition to the two *APiCS* values, has a third value "Both orders of noun and modifying adjective occur, with neither dominant" and a fourth value "Adjectives do not modify nouns, occurring as predicates in internally headed relative clauses". *WALS* value 3 represents only a subset of the cases where *APiCS* records both preceding and following adjectives: *WALS*'s "no dominant order" indicates that both alternatives are about equally common (Romance languages therefore appearing as noun–adjective), while *APiCS* records all occurring orders and in addition gives information on relative importance. *APiCS* does not have a value corresponding to *WALS*'s fourth value "Adjectives do not modify nouns, occurring as predicates in internally headed relative clauses", but two contributors note that, in addition to attributive adjectives, modification through relative clauses is regularly attested in their variety. This is found in Tayo (Ehrhart & Revis 2013) and in the mixed language Michif:

(5) Gii-miy-ikaw-in   aen   morsoo
    1.PST-give-PASS-1   INDF.ART.M   piece
    [kaa-mishaa-k]   la   vyaand.
    REL-be.big.INAN-3   DEF.ART.F.SG meat
    'He was given a piece of meat that was big.' or
    'He was given a big piece of meat.' (Bakker 2013)

3. Distribution

Numerical. Although noun–adjective is the prevalent order among the world's languages (768 of 1,005 languages in Dryer 2011a), a preceding adjective is clearly the dominant pattern among the (admittedly skewed sample of) languages represented in *APiCS* (69/76), with 34 varieties using this pattern exclusively and another 35 having preceding adjectives along with following adjectives. The noun–adjective pattern is found in 42 *APiCS* languages, of which only 7 are exclusively noun–adjective. These are Ambon Malay, Juba Arabic, Kikongo-Kituba, Kinubi, Lingala, Mixed Ma'a/Mbugu and Papiá Kristang.

Geographic/areal. While Dryer's *WALS* map shows rather well-defined areas of noun–adjective and adjective–noun languages, the two patterns appear to be more or less evenly spread around the world as far as *APiCS* languages are concerned. This may well be due to the fact that the contact languages documented in *APiCS* often involved large-scale migrations and that the concept of areality in the traditional sense is therefore problematic in this case.

By lexifier/substrate. For most *APiCS* languages, Feature 3 appears to be a rather clear case of lexifier influence: with only two exceptions (Media Lengua, Papiá Kristang) the 27 Romance language-lexified contact languages allow both the adjective–noun and the noun–adjective pattern, just as in French, Portuguese, and Spanish. A number of *APiCS* contributors note that similarities with the lexifier even extend to which adjectives may precede or follow nouns or to the meaning difference of the same adjective in pre- or postnominal position. Of the two exceptions mentioned above, the mixed language Media Lengua is exclusively adjective–noun, closely following the Quechua model, while Papiá Kristang's exclusive noun–adjective order seems to have been the result of a strong sub- or adstratal influence of Malay. As to the Germanic lexifier languages, 25 out of 28 varieties in our sample have only preceding adjectives, just as in English and Dutch. Among the non-European lexified contact languages, we find the same trend of copying the lexifier order. For example, Kikongo-Kituba, Lingala, and Mixed Ma'a/Mbugu (Bantu), Juba Arabic and Kinubi (Arabic), and Ambon Malay (Malay) copy the noun–adjective order of their lexifiers.

In some cases the lexifier and substrates have the same order of the adjective relative to the noun—as in Juba Arabic and Kinubi, whose Sudanese substrates are also noun–adjective—but Central African Sango copies the adjective–noun model of its lexifier Ngbandi in spite of the fact that the pidginizers spoke either languages that were predominantly noun–adjective (speakers from East and West Africa and from the equatorial regions of the Congo River) or had both patterns (French-speaking Europeans; see Samarin 2013a). Fanakalo's adjective–noun is a surprising exception, its main lexifiers Zulu and Xhosa as well as the Bantu substrates being noun–adjective languages. Here, the adjective–noun sequence is possibly modelled on the structure of the socially dominant English and Afrikaans-speaking pidginizers of Zulu and Xhosa.

The fact that Bislama, Kriol, and Tok Pisin (all spoken in the Australia-Pacific region) have both orders may also be due to substratal influence. Kriol in northern Australia is spoken in a region with a mix of languages allowing pre-, post-, and both pre and post modifying adjectives. Tok Pisin and Bislama are spoken in areas where the overwhelming majority of languages are premodifying, but there is historical evidence that both languages received a strong input from a pidgin spoken on plantations in Queensland (eastern Australia), an area where both orders are found. In addition, Tok Pisin was influenced by Tolai, one of the few languages in Papua New Guinea that has no dominant order according to *WALS*.

The rule for Bislama and Tok Pisin is that adjectives modified by *-fala/-pela* precede the noun while the other adjectives follow it:

(6) Bislama (Meyerhoff 2013)
long-fala maot
long mouth
'long beak'

(7) Tok Pisin (Smith & Siegel 2013)
man nogut
man bad
'bad man'

The case of the mixed language Michif (French nouns, Cree verbs) is interesting: Michif adjectives are of French origin and, as in French, they either precede or follow the noun (Cree does not have adjectives but expresses noun modification through relative clauses or by noun-prefixation (Bakker 1997: 106); compare example 5).

The three Malay-lexified varieties in *APiCS* show a wide variation with only Ambon Malay following the Malay lexifier noun–adjective order. Ambon Malay is spoken in an area of noun–adjective languages, just like Singapore Bazaar Malay, which however shows both orders. This is probably because Indian and Chinese languages (predominantly adjective–noun) were involved in the genesis of Bazaar Malay (see Khin Khin Aye 2013a). Sri Lanka Malay seems to have adopted Tamil's adjective–noun order (for the close contact between Malays and Sri Lanka Muslim Tamils (see Slomanson 2013a).

3 Order of adjective and noun

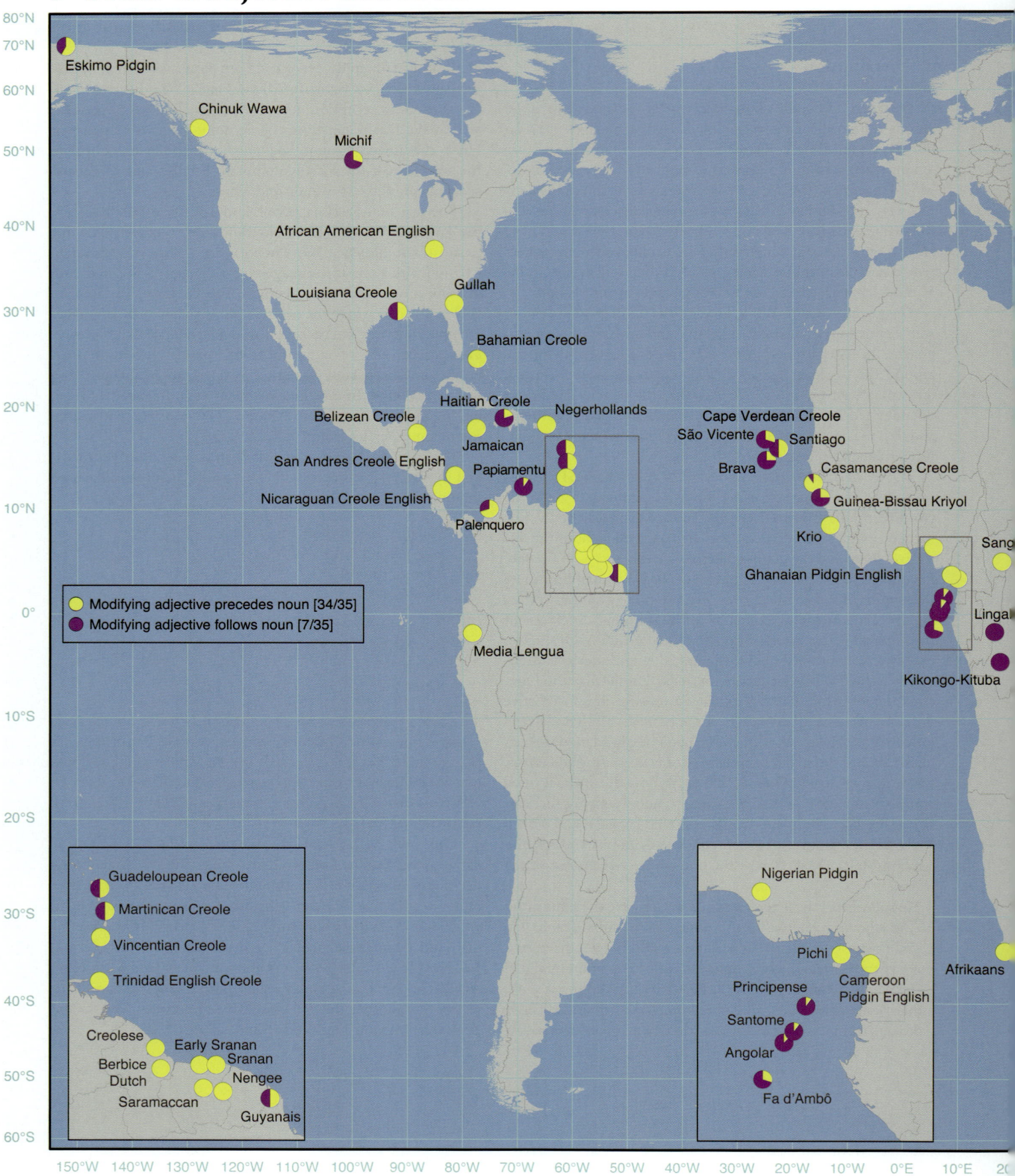

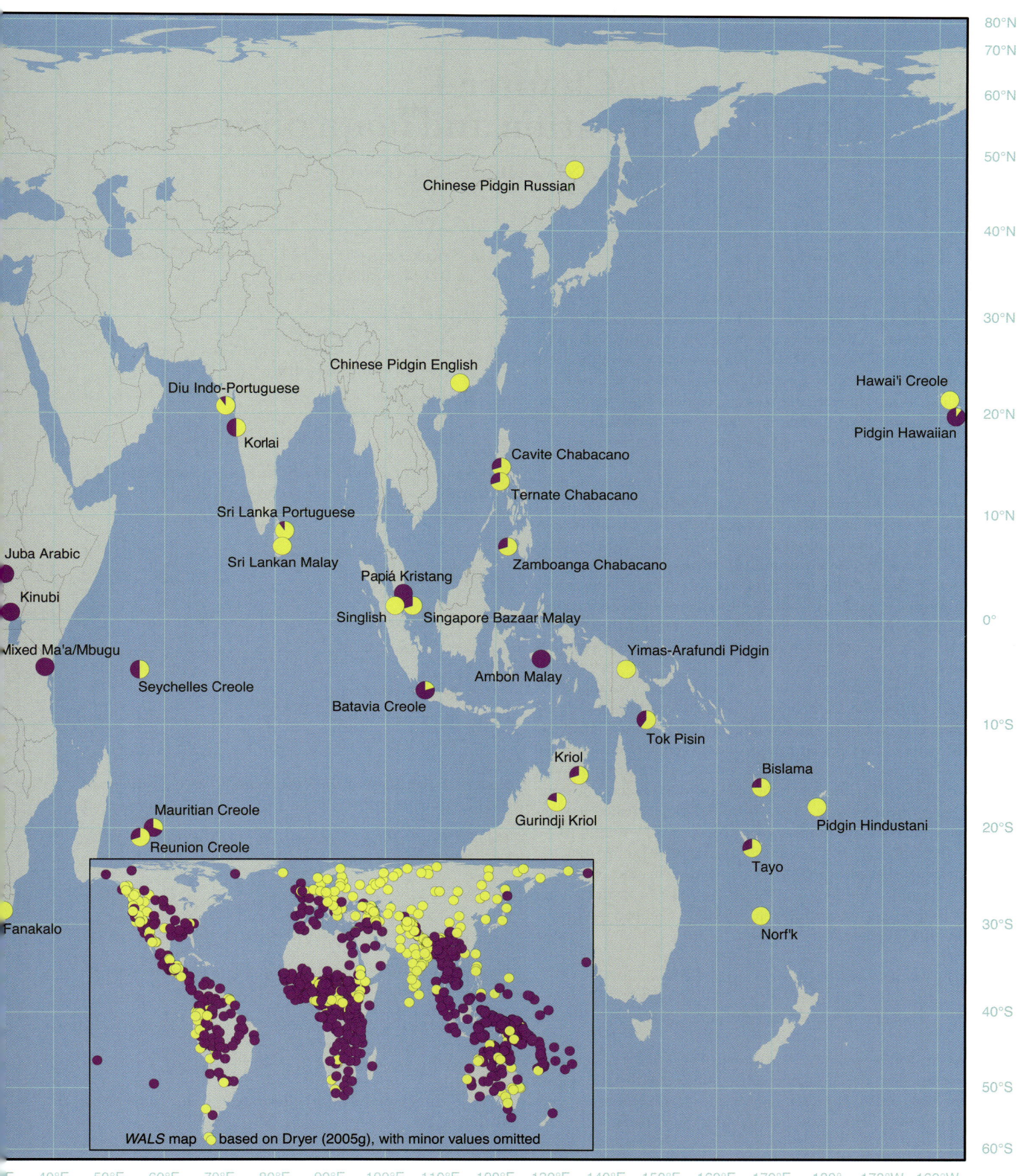

Chapter 4
Order of adposition and noun phrase

MAGNUS HUBER AND THE *APiCS* CONSORTIUM

1. Feature description

For this feature, which is based on Dryer (2011e), an adposition is defined as a separate free word that stands before, inside, or after a noun phrase and establishes a grammatical or semantic relationship between the noun phrase and a verb in the same clause. There are four types of adposition: prepositions stand before, postpositions after, circumpositions both before and after a noun phrase, while inpositions are situated inside the noun phrase. The latter type does not occur in our sample.

Since our criterion is that an adposition indicates some kind of relationship between a noun phrase and a verb, as in *speak of the devil*, attributive possessive constructions like *the tail of the dog* are disregarded here because *of* establishes a relationship between the nouns *tail* and *dog*, not between either of them and a verb. We also disregard case affixes on nouns, which in some languages have functions that are similar to adpositions in European languages. On the other hand, cliticized relation markers, which are phonologically integrated into the noun but whose position depends on the syntax, do count as adpositions for the purposes of this feature.

The type or token frequency of adpositions in a language is irrelevant for this feature. As long as there is at least one adposition, even if it has a low text frequency, its position relative to the noun phrase is what matters. For example, Gurindji Kriol has only two adpositions, *langa* and *bo*, which are quite rare (Meakins 2013), but since they always stand before the noun phrase whenever they occur, Gurindji Kriol is treated as a language that has only prepositions.

A number of *APiCS* languages use serialized verbs to encode meanings that are expressed by prepositions in other languages, for example, *come* for 'to', *go* for 'away', *take* for 'with', *pass* for 'through', etc. (see also Chapters 84–86). Compare *ba* 'give' = 'for' in Guyanais:

(1) Mo achté liv ba to.
     I buy book give you
     'I bought a book for you.' (Pfänder 2013)

As the degree of grammaticalization of such verbs is often hard to determine, they pose a potential problem for this feature and are disregarded. However, none of the *APiCS* languages relies on serialized verbs alone. For example, the instrumental meaning in Nengee can be expressed both through serialized *tek* 'take' and the preposition *anga* 'with':

(2) Nengee (Migge 2013)
     a. *A teke a   akisi piiti ala den   udu.*
        he take the axe   split all DET.PL wood
        'He split all the logs with the axe.'
     b. *A ondoo en goon anga how.*
        she cut   her field with machete
        'She cut the weeds in her field with a machete.'

The exclusion of serialized verbs from the present feature did therefore not result in a language being classified as having no adpositions.

2. The values

Three different values are distinguished for this feature:

		excl	shrd	all
●	1. Prepositions	62	9	71
●	2. Postpositions	5	9	14
●	3. Circumpositions	0	3	3

None of the languages in the *APiCS* sample has inpositions and there is no language that does not make use of adpositions at all.

Value 1. Most *APiCS* languages have only prepositions. Mixed Ma'a/Mbugu is an example:

(3) Ni-daha-íye na ndate.
     1SG-walk-PRF with stick
     'I walked with a stick.' (Mous 2013)

Value 2. A handful of languages have only postpositions, for example, Yimas-Arafundi Pidgin:

(4) Waɲəŋ kandək apanda-n anak.
     arrow with   shoot-FUT AUX
     '(We'll) shoot him with an arrow.' (Foley 2013)

Value 3. Circumpositions are illustrated by an example from Michif:

(5) *dans le   fridzh uhchi*
    LOC DEF.ART.M fridge from
    'out of the fridge' (Bakker 2013)

The *APiCS* languages Nengee, Early Sranan, Sranan, and the student lect of Ghanaian Pidgin English have constructions that look like potential circumpositions. Compare *na ... tapu* in the following example:

(6) Early Sranan (van den Berg & Bruyn 2013)
    Da   fowru de   sidon na eksi tapu.
    DET.SG chicken PROG sit LOC egg top
    'The chicken is sitting on the eggs.'

Such "circumpositions" consist of a general preposition (here, *na*) and a postposed locative or temporal nominal (*tapu*), whose degree of grammaticalization into a postposition is hard to determine (see Plag 1998). Since in all cases it is possible to interpret such constructions as a prepositional phrase containing a preposition and a possessive noun phrase ($_{PrepP}[_{Prep}na\ _{NP}[eksi\ tapu]]$ lit. 'on the egg's top'), these cases were not counted as circumpositions.

Feature 4 is a multiple-choice feature and nine languages in our sample allow adpositions to occur before (value 1) and after the noun (value 2). Compare, for instance, Berbice Dutch, where prepositions (7a) and postpositions (7b) occur with about the same frequency:

(7) Berbice Dutch (Kouwenberg 2013a)
    a. *Ju kan sɛtɛ sondro bita?*
       2SG can stay without clothes
       'Can you live without clothes?'
    b. *O   wa grui di lanfi ben   ka.*
       3SG PST grow the language inside NEG
       'He did not grow up in this language.'

All *APiCS* languages that have circumpositions also have both prepositions and postpositions. Compare the examples from Diu Indo-Portuguese (a. *pə* = preposition, b. *jũt* = postposition, c. *də ... jũt* = circumposition):

(8) Diu Indo-Portuguese (Cardoso 2013)
    a. *Lion vey   i   rasp-o   pə gat.*
       lion come.PST and scratch-PST ACC cat
       'The lion came and scratched the cat.'
    b. *Mĩ   jũt   nã te   muyt diɲer*
       1SG.OBL together NEG EXIST.NPST much money
       nã te.
       NEG EXIST.NPST
       'I don't have much money.'
       (lit. 'With me/next to me there isn't much money.')
    c. *Yo fik   d-εl   jũt.*
       1SG dwell.NPST of-3SG.F together
       'I live with her.' or 'I live next to her.'

Note that the corresponding *WALS* feature 85A, "Order of adposition and noun phrase" (Dryer 2011e), records only the dominant value and disregards the less frequent alternatives. By contrast, *APiCS* maps all possible orders in a language, regardless of their frequency.

3. Distribution

Numerical. Prepositions are by far the most common adpositions in the *APiCS* sample, with 62 languages relying exclusively on them and another nine having prepositions along with other adpositions. None of the three languages that make use of circumpositions—Afrikaans, Diu Indo-Portuguese and Michif—relies exclusively on them, and only in Afrikaans are they not marginal.

When the *APiCS* values are modified to match *WALS*, the following picture emerges: prepositions predominant 65, postpositions predominant 7, no dominant order 4. This is a stark contrast to the trend among the world's languages: postpositions 577, prepositions 512, no dominant order 58 (of a total of 1,158 languages). *APiCS* languages thus show a much stronger reliance on prepositions, but it has to be kept in mind that the *APiCS* sample is not typologically balanced.

By lexifier/substrate. For reasons of space, the following discussion will be restricted to postpositions, which are significantly less frequent in the *APiCS* sample than in the languages of the world. Dutch has pre-, circum-, and postpositions (Koopman 2000: 206), and postpositions are also found in Afrikaans and Berbice Dutch. Interestingly, postpositions are marginal in Afrikaans, even though the contributing language Khoekhoe has postpositions. In Berbice Dutch, on the other hand, prepositions and postpositions occur with about the same frequency. The reason is possibly that the strong Ijo substrate (Smith 1999: 254f.) has postpositions (Tepowa 1904: 122). Against this background it is surprising that the third Dutch-based language in our sample, Negerhollands, does not have postpositions at all, even though there was a strong postpositional input: Ewe (predominantly postpositions) and Akan (no dominant order; Dryer 2011e) were the major African substrates during the formative years of Negerhollands (van Sluijs 2013a). None of the five *APiCS* languages that rely exclusively on postpositions had a consistent postpositional input: either the lexifiers (predominantly) had prepositions and the substrates (predominantly) postpositions—as in Chinese Pidgin Russian, Sri Lanka Portuguese, and Sri Lankan Malay—or the other way around—as in Pidgin Hindustani and Yimas-Arafundi Pidgin.

4 Order of adposition and noun phrase

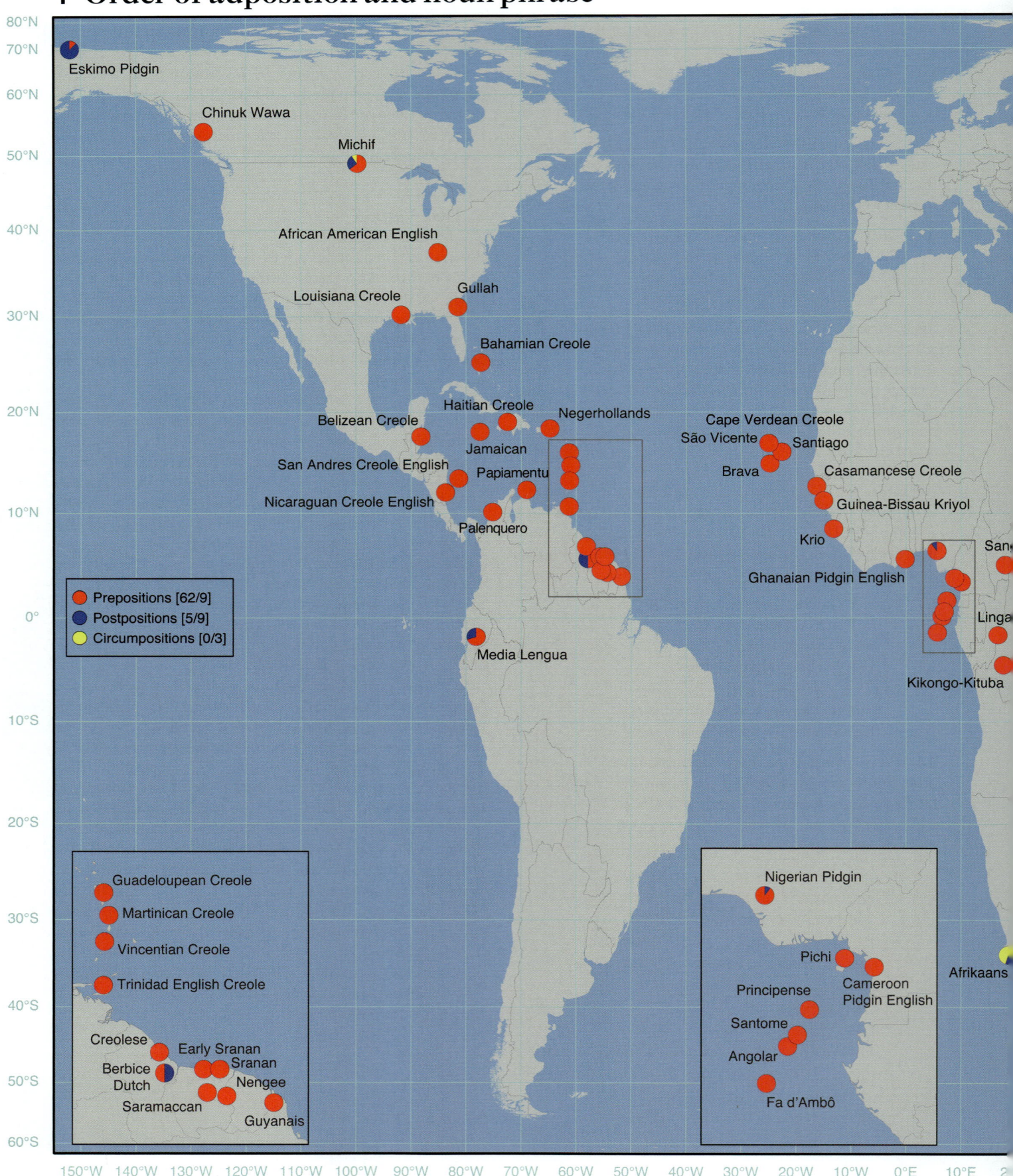

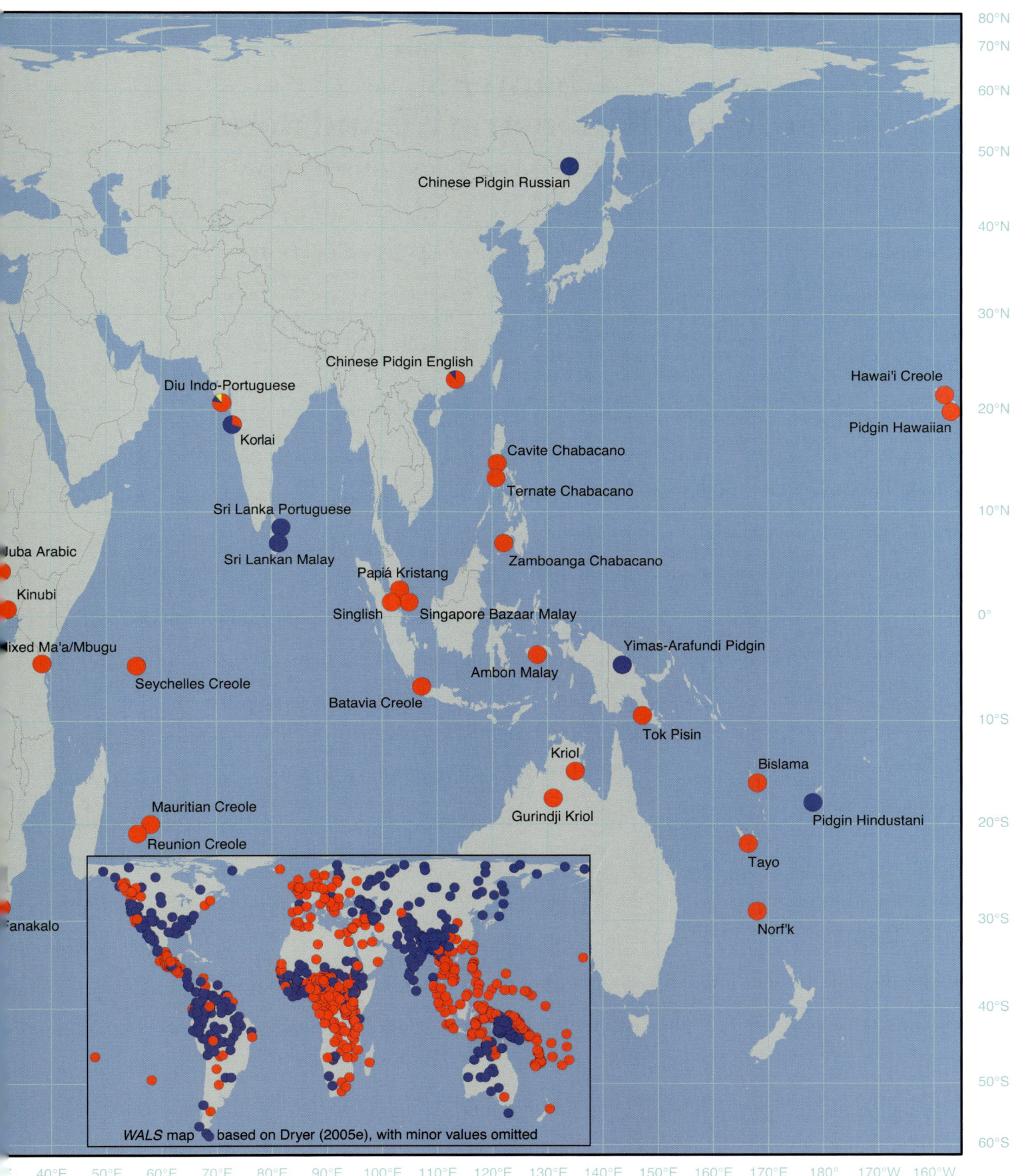

Chapter 5
Order of demonstrative and noun

PHILIPPE MAURER AND THE *APiCS* CONSORTIUM

1. Introduction

Demonstratives are deictic expressions such as English 'this' and 'that' which indicate the relative distance of a referent in the speech situation in relation to the speaker's location. This chapter considers the order of adnominal demonstrative and noun.

Demonstratives are often homonymous with, or derive from, deictic locational adverbs such as 'here' and 'there', and are sometimes difficult to distinguish from them. Among the criteria for the demonstrative status of such elements are the following:

(i) The demonstrative differs in shape from the spatial adverbs (French *cette femme-ci* 'this woman' vs. *ici* 'here').
(ii) The spatial adverbs are the only available demonstratives in the language, as in Papiamentu, where 'this house' can only be rendered by *e kas aki*, lit. 'the house here'; *e kas* without *aki* means 'the house' and not 'this house'.
(iii) The combination of the demonstrative and the adverb is obligatory, i.e. if in a given language only *this house here* may be used, but not **this house*.

This chapter is based on Dryer (2005h); see also Chapter 33 in this volume on distance contrasts in demonstratives.

2. The values

We distinguish the following three values:

		excl	shrd	all
🟡	1. Demonstrative word precedes noun	36	20	56
🟣	2. Demonstrative word follows noun	19	15	34
🔵	3. Demonstrative simultaneously before and after noun	0	7	7

Value 1 (**demonstrative word precedes noun**) is the most widespread value among the *APiCS* languages. It occurs in all areas and in all language types.

(1) Diu Indo-Portuguese (Cardoso 2013)
Ikəl kamiz ku verd i amrɛl flor ɛ də mĩ.
DEM shirt with green and yellow flower COP of 1SG.OBL
'This shirt with the green and yellow flowers is mine.'

(2) Jamaican (Farquharson 2013)
Dis uman waahn wahn kyaar fi bai.
DEM woman want ART car to buy
'This woman wants a car to buy.'

(3) Ghanaian Pidgin English (Huber 2013)
Dis mã ì bì tifmã.
DEM man 3SG COP thief
'This man is a thief.'

(4) Seychelles Creole (Michaelis & Rosalie 2013)
Tou sa bann landrwa mon 'n ale.
all DEM PL place 1SG PRF go
'It's to all these places that I have been.'

(5) Gurindji Kriol (Meakins 2013)
Nyawa yapakayi gel imin turrp im nidul-jawung.
DEM small girl 3SG.PST poke 3SG.OBJ needle-INS
'This small woman (nurse) jabbed her with a needle.'

(6) Chinese Pidgin English (Li & Matthews 2013)
Killum thisee piecee capon.
kill DEM CLF capon
'Kill this capon.'

(7) Pidgin Hindustani (Siegel 2013)
U larika baito maket kelage.
DEM boy COP market near
'That boy was near the market.'

Value 2 (**demonstrative word follows noun**), like value 1, occurs in all areas and in all language types, but is less frequent than value 1, although still fairly common.

(8) Angolar (Maurer 2013a)
Turu kwa e ma alê thêka fa [...].
all thing DEM REL king PROG say
'All these things the king was telling [...].'

(9) Papiamentu (Kouwenberg 2013b)
E minister ei ta biaha hopi.
ART minister DEM HAB travel much
'That minister travels a lot.'

(10) Early Sranan (van den Berg & Bruyn 2013)
Tee mie werie foe da Pliesierie datie [...].
when 1SG weary for ART pleasure DEM
'When I get tired of that pleasure [...].'

(11) Haitian Creole (Fattier 2013)
M renmen moun sa yo.
1SG love person DEM PL
'I love these people.'

(12) Lingala (Meeuwis 2013)
Búku óyo ya náni?
book DEM of who
'Whose book is this?'

(13) Juba Arabic (Manfredi & Petrollino 2013)
Ákil de kwes kális.
food DEM good very
'This food is very good.'

(14) Gurindji Kriol (Meakins 2013)
Dei karan-karra karu-walija-ngku-ma ngakparn-ku
3PL scratch-CONT child-PAUC-ERG-DISC frog-DAT

nyawa-rra-ma.
DEM-PL-TOP
'This group of kids are digging for frogs.'

(15) Singapore Bazaar Malay (Khin Khin Aye 2013)
Malam ini tentu hujan hebat.
night DEM sure rain tense
'Tonight, it will rain heavily.'

(16) Chinese Pidgin Russian (Perekhvalskaya 2013)
Iwo kuritfa jajtfy eta lamaj.
3SG chicken egg DEM break
'He broke those chicken eggs.'

Value 3 (**demonstrative simultaneously before and after noun**) only occurs as a shared value in seven languages. There are two subtypes: (i) the same element precedes and follows the noun, and (ii) the demonstrative precedes and a locative adverb follows the noun.

The first subtype only occurs in two Philippine creoles (Ternate and Zamboanga Chabacano).

(17) Ternate Chabacano (Sippola 2013b)
Si kabá ya rin éle éste ányo éste [...].
if finish already also 3SG DEM year DEM
'If she finishes also this present year [...].'

(18) Zamboanga Chabacano (Steinkrüger 2013)
Ése ómbre 'se ya-andá na tyángge.
DEM man DEM PFV-go LOC market
'This (very) man went to the market.'

The second subtype occurs in two English-based creoles (Creolese and Krio), in two French-based creoles (Martinican Creole and Reunion Creole), and in one Portuguese-based creole (Casamancese Creole). In Creolese, we find *dem tings o* [DEM.PL.DIST things DEM.DIST] 'those things' (Devonish & Thompson 2013), in Reunion Creole *se fanm-la* 'this/that woman' [DEM.SG woman DEM] (Bollée 2013), and in Casamancese Creole *e kacor-li* [DEM dog-here] 'this dog' (Biagui & Quint 2013). The other examples are:

(19) Krio (Finney 2013)
Da man de dɔn dai.
DEM man there PFV die
'That particular man is dead.'

(20) Mauritian Creole (Baker & Kriegel 2013)
Mo sipoze sa bann zanfan la sorti
1SG suppose DEM PL child DEM come.from

Kaznwayal.
Case-Noyale
'I imagine that these children come from Case-Noyale.'

Almost all authors claim that the constructions of both subtypes are topic constructions or otherwise emphatic.

Note that in the case of the second subtype of value 3, it is not fully clear whether criterion (iii) of §1 applies, so one might say that these circumposed elements are not demonstratives, but combinations of demonstratives and spatial adverbs (remember that all languages share this value with one of the other values which only imply one demonstrative element). It is only in Casamancese Creole that the situation is more complicated. The simple prenominal demonstrative *e* has only a deictic (proximal) function, whereas the simple prenominal demonstrative *kel* has exclusively anaphoric functions; in order to fulfil a deictic function, *kel* must obligatorily combine with a postnominal locative adverb.

3. Distribution and comparison with *WALS*

There is no specific areal distributional pattern for value 1 (noun–demonstrative) and value 2 (demonstrative–noun), and also no specific distributional pattern according to language type or lexifier(s).

The languages in *WALS* show a clearer picture: value 2 is predominant in Africa and Southeast Asia, whereas value 1 predominates in Europe, in the rest of Asia, and in the Americas. Numerically, there is almost no difference between value 1 and value 2 in *WALS*. The predominance of value 1 (against value 2) in the *APiCS* languages is related to the influence of the European lexifiers in the formation of these languages. Inversely, where *APiCS* languages have value 2, substrate influence may be invoked, except in cases where the lexifier itself has postnominal demonstratives, as is the case with Lingala or Juba Arabic.

5 Order of demonstrative and noun

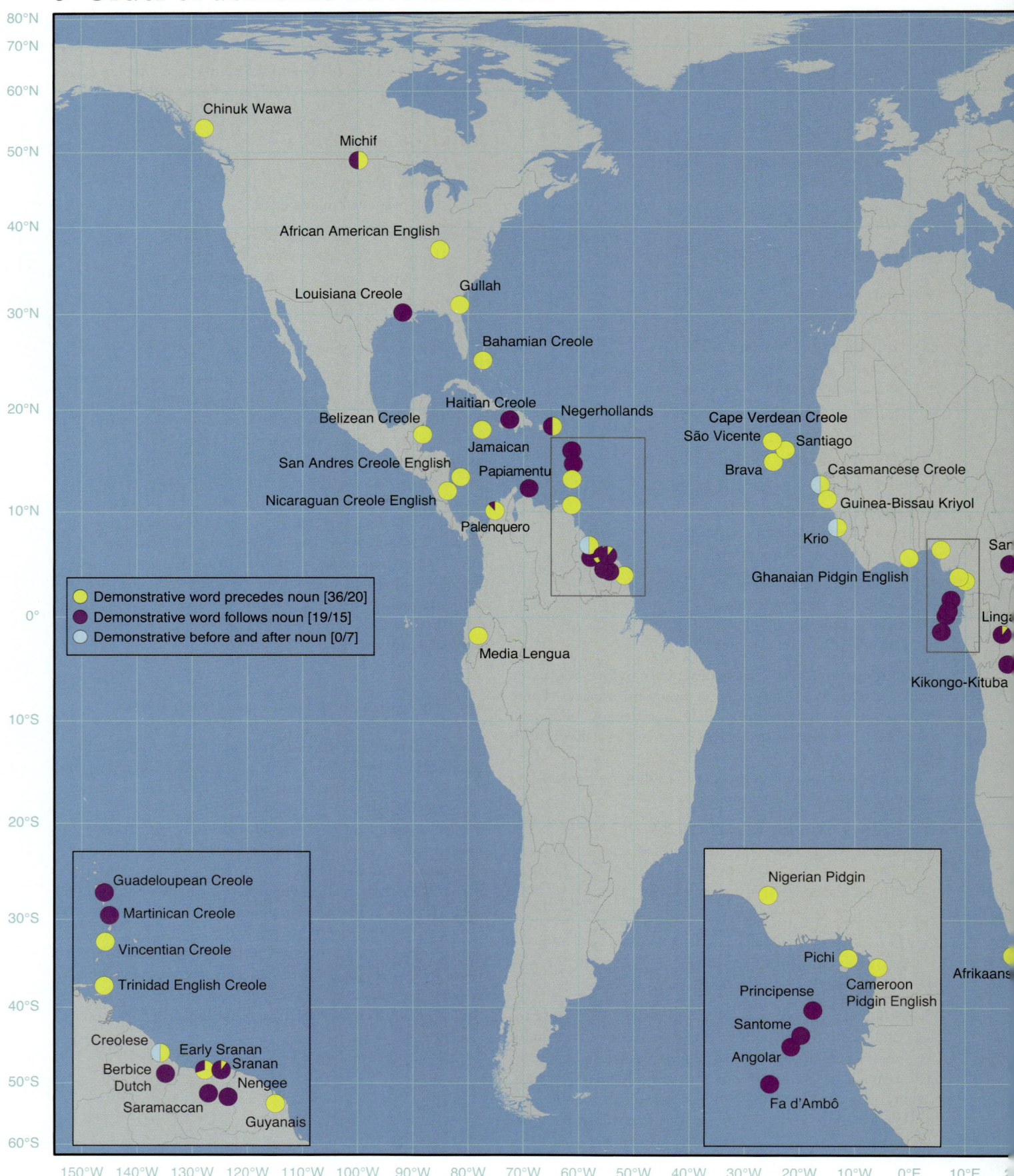

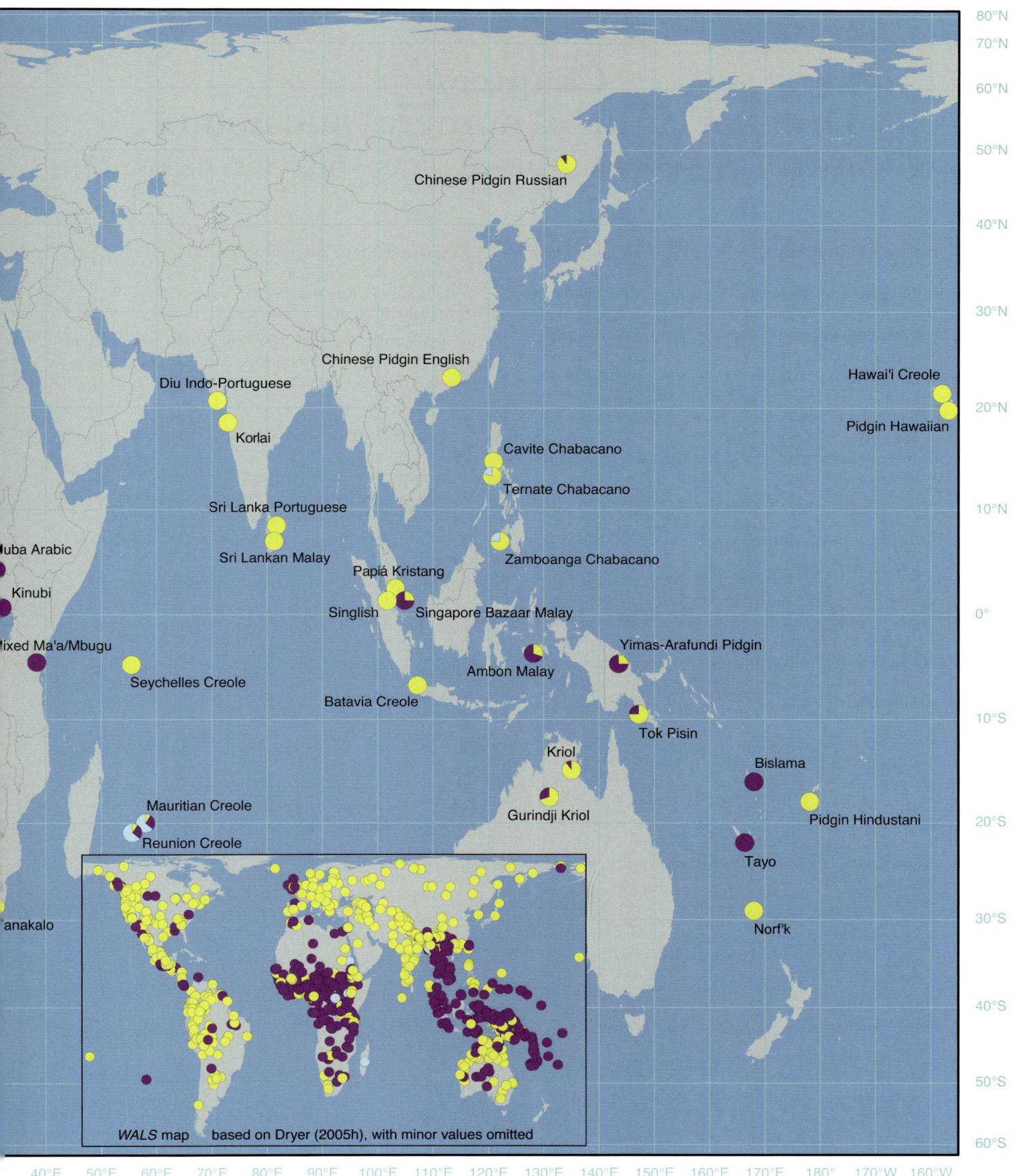

Chapter 6
Order of cardinal numeral and noun

MARTIN HASPELMATH, SUSANNE M. MICHAELIS, AND THE *APiCS* CONSORTIUM

1. Cardinal numerals

Cardinal numerals are numerals that denote the number of things in the set referred to by the noun phrase, as in *seven houses*. This chapter closely parallels Dryer's (2005i) *WALS* chapter.

Note that elsewhere, *APiCS* deals with distributive numerals (e.g. *two balls each*, Chapter 34), ordinal numerals (*the fifth street*, Chapter 35), and with numeral classifiers (Chapter 36). The complexity of numeral systems in pidgins and creoles is discussed by Hammarström (2008).

In the great majority of *APiCS* languages, the numeral precedes the noun:

		excl	shrd	all
🟡	1. Numeral precedes noun	61	8	69
⚫	2. Numeral follows noun	7	8	15

The world's languages are much more balanced, with most African and Southeast Asian languages as well as many languages in New Guinea and Australia showing postposed numerals (Dryer 2005i). In view of the generally strong African influence on Atlantic pidgins and creoles, one might have expected more postposed numerals.

2. Languages with preposed numerals only

In the great majority (61) of *APiCS* languages, numerals can only precede the noun. This is the case in almost all languages of the Americas, West Africa, and Asia. Evidently, the numeral–noun order follows the order of the European lexifier in most of these languages.

(1) Singlish (Lim & Ansaldo 2013)
*So your grandfather had **three** wives something like that ah?*
'So your grandfather had three wives or something like that?'

(2) Bahamian Creole (Hackert 2013)
*You get **five** card, and you play.*

(3) Diu Indo-Portuguese (Cardoso 2013)
*Dəpəy də **trey** di use vẽy volta-d.*
after of three day you come.NPST return-PTCP
'You will come back in three days.'

(4) Pidgin Hindustani (Siegel 2013)
*Ham lekeao **dui** katon stabi.*
1SG bring two carton stubby
'I brought two cartons of stubbies.'

Not accidentally, the indefinite article also precedes the noun in all these languages (see Chapter 10)—it almost always derives from the numeral 'one'.

3. Languages with postposed numerals only

Seven languages have only postposed numerals. They are all spoken in areas where the indigenous languages overwhelmingly show postposed numerals as well. The order numeral–noun in the central African languages follows the order in the Bantu and Ubangian lexifiers:

(5) Lingala (Meeuwis 2013)
*mibáli **míbalé***
men two
'two men'

(6) Kikongo-Kituba (Mufwene 2013)
*mu-ntu **mosi**; ba-ntu **zole***
SG-person one PL-person two
'one person; two persons'

(7) Sango (Samarin 2013)
*melenge ti lo **oko** a-mu koli*
child of 3SG one PM-take man
'His one child got married.'

Mixed Ma'a/Mbugu is similar, but the Bantu-based pidgin Fanakalo has preposed numerals: *mabili fan* [two boy] 'two boys'.

In Kinubi, all numerals follow the noun, even though in its Arabic lexifier, only a few lower numerals follow the noun. Thus, here the influence of the South Sudanese substrate languages seems to have imposed itself.

(8) Kinubi (Luffin 2013)
*yal-á **tísa***
child-PL nine
'nine children'

Another language where the African substrate overrides the order of the lexifier is the Portuguese-based Gulf of Guinea creole Fa d'Ambô:

22

(9) Fa d'Ambô (Post 2013)
*batel **tisy***
canoe three
'three canoes'

A language of New Guinea too has only postposed numerals:

(10) Yimas-Arafundi Pidgin (Foley 2013)
*aykum **kundamwin***
woman two
'two women'

This order is the same in Yimas (Foley 1991: 101) and in many other indigenous languages of New Guinea.

4. Languages with both orders of numerals

Eight languages have both orders, numeral–noun and noun–numeral. Often the same numeral can occur preposed or postposed to the noun, as in (11) and (12). Two of these languages are Gulf of Guinea creoles, where African influence was strong (as in Fa d'Ambô in (9)).

(11) Principense (Maurer 2013c)
  a. *kaxi **ũa***
     house one
     'one house'
  b. ***dexi** kaxi*
     ten house
     'ten houses'

(12) Santome (Hagemeijer 2013)
  a. *inen sun se **dôsu***
     PL.DEF man DEM two
     'these two men'
  b. ***dôsu** inen mina mosu se mu*
     two PL.DEF child boy DEM 1SG.POSS
     'those two boys of mine'

In both languages, the order with postposed numerals is much less common. In Principense, it now occurs only with the numeral *ũa* 'one', though in former times all numerals could follow the noun. In Santome, postposed numerals are rare and are most acceptable with low numerals. This suggests that postposed position (as in Fa d'Ambô) was once the norm in Principense and Santome, and that the preposed position is due to influence from Portuguese (with lower numbers resisting the change because of their higher frequency).

In Ambon Malay, too, postposed numerals occur particularly with the lower numerals (especially 1–10), and "the occurrence of numerals preceding the head noun may be due to recent influence from Indonesian" (Paauw 2013). Since postposed numerals are the norm in the indigenous languages throughout eastern Indonesia (Dryer 2005i), and the varieties of Malay that are spoken in its western homeland regions have preposed numerals, it is likely that the noun–numeral order is due to substrate influence.

(13) Ambon Malay (Paauw 2013)
  a. *parangpuang **tuju***   b. ***tuju** orang bidadari*
     woman seven   seven CLF nymph
     'seven women'   'seven nymphs'

Kriol and the mixed language Gurindji Kriol freely allow both orders, in line with the general freedom of word order in Australian languages:

(14) Kriol (Schultze-Berndt & Angelo 2013)
  a. *Tubala bin goawei na, kenggaru **tu-bala**.*
     3DU PST go_away now kangaroo two-NUM
     'The two went away then, the two kangaroos.'
  b. *Fes yu garra put-im det-lat **faib** ting la yu finga.*
     first you must put-TR DEM-PL five thing LOC you finger
     'First you have to put those five things in your hand.'

(15) Gurindji Kriol (Meakins 2013)
  a. *Im-in grab-im im leg **wan-bala**, nyila-ngku*
     3SG-PST grab-TR 3SG leg one-NUM that-ERG
     pujikat-tu.
     cat-ERG
     'That cat grabbed one of his legs.'
  b. *Nyawa **jirri-bala** malyju dei bin luk-aran bo*
     this three-NUM boy 3PL.SBJ PST look-around DAT
     kirrawa.
     goanna
     'These three boys are searching for goannas.'

In both these languages, numerals may carry the suffix *-bala*, which corresponds to *-pela* in Melanesian Pidgin (e.g. Tok Pisin *tri-pela haus* 'three houses'), ultimately deriving from English *fellow*.

The origin of postposed and preposed numerals in Eskimo Pidgin is unclear. It seems that Iñupiaq has preposed numerals (Lanz 2010: §5.1.2), but postposed numerals occur in the related West Greenlandic (Fortescue 1984: 110), so perhaps they were also present in some of the Eskimo varieties that contributed to the making of Eskimo Pidgin.

(16) Eskimo Pidgin (van der Voort 2013)
  a. *awoñ'a ca'vik ai'tcū, ila awoñ'a ekal'luk **ta'llimat** a'itcū*
     I knife give he I fish five give
     'I gave him a knife (for which) he gave me five fish.'
  b. ***malo** okio aipani*
     two winter long.ago
     'two winters ago'

6 Order of cardinal numeral and noun

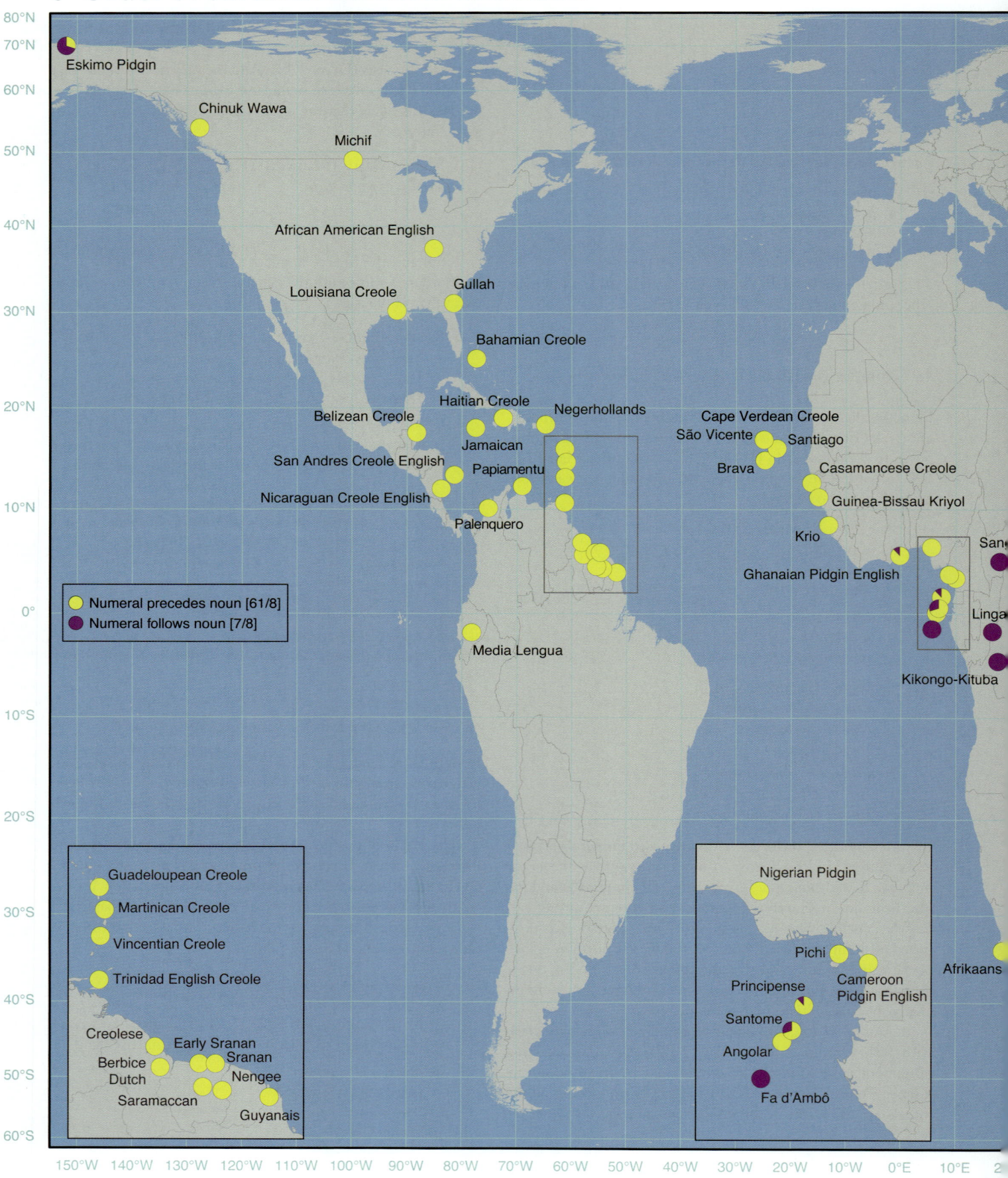

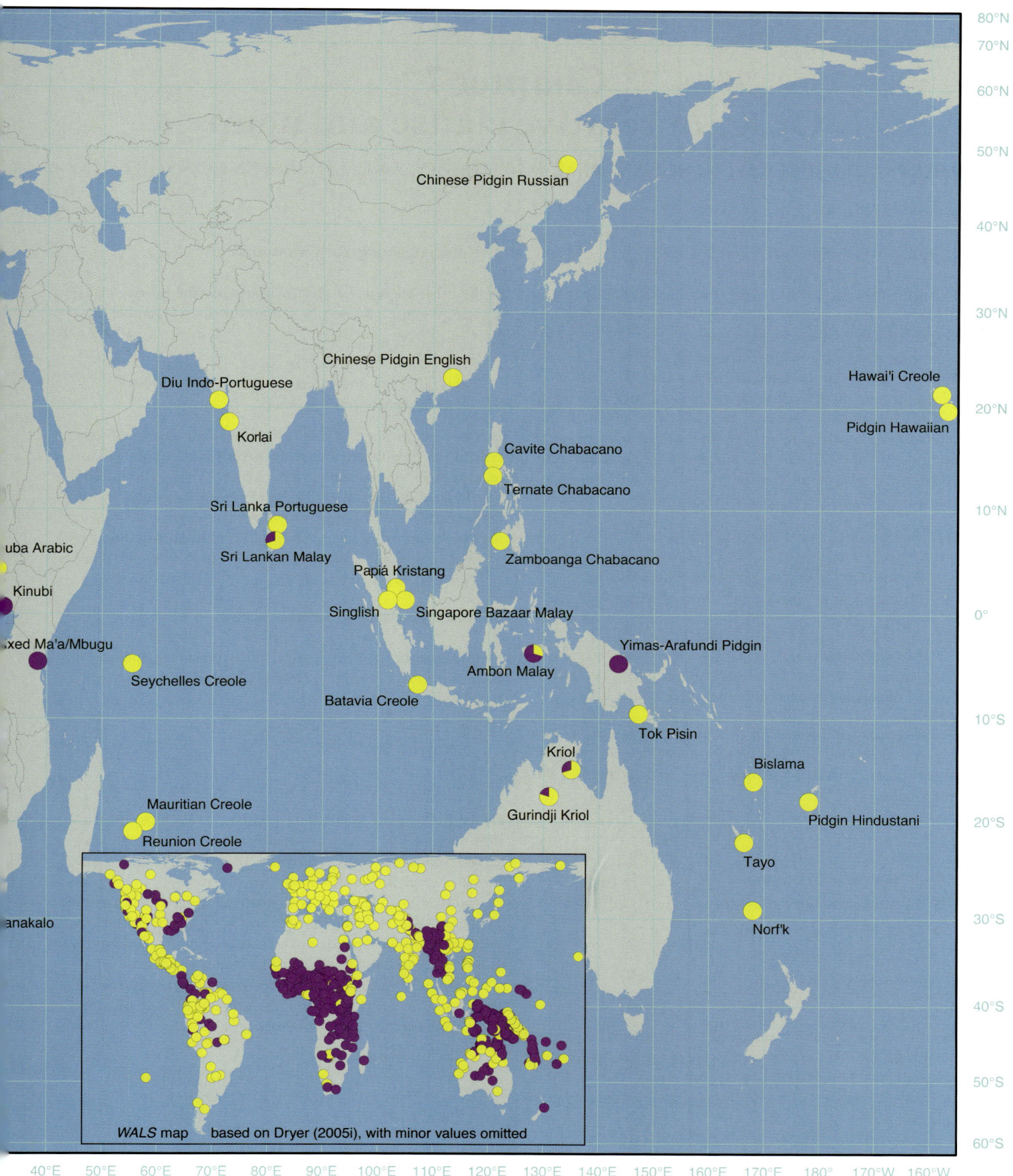

WALS map based on Dryer (2005i), with minor values omitted

Chapter 7
Order of relative clause and noun

MARTIN HASPELMATH, SUSANNE M. MICHAELIS, AND THE *APiCS* CONSORTIUM

1. Relative clauses

Following Dryer's (2005j) *WALS* chapter, this chapter looks at the order of relative clause and noun, as well as at some special, less widely known relative-clause types.

For this chapter, a relative clause is defined as a clause that helps narrow down the reference of a noun (the head) and in which the referent of the head noun has a semantic role. (Headless relative clauses are left aside here.) Relative clauses are most often clauses which occur adjacent to the head noun, as seen in examples (1) and (2). (In these and the other examples in this chapter, the head noun is given in boldface, and the relative clause is enclosed in brackets in the gloss line.)

(1) Seychelles Creole (Michaelis & Rosalie 2013)
I annan en koray ki apel koray Sidwes?
PM have a coral [REL call coral Sud.ouest]
'Is there a coral whose name is Sud-ouest coral?'

(2) Singapore Bazaar Malay (Khin Khin Aye 2013)
Di sini tinggal punya orang pun boleh jauh pergi beli.
[in here live REL] people even can far go buy
'Even people who live here can go far to buy [it].'

Only seven languages in *APiCS* have relative clauses of other types, as described in §4–6. We distinguish the following five types (a very rare sixth type that Dryer 2005j recognizes does not occur in *APiCS*).

		excl	shrd	all
●	1. Relative clause follows noun	64	8	72
●	2. Relative clause precedes noun	2	3	5
○	3. Internally headed relative clause	0	1	1
○	4. Correlative relative clause	1	2	3
○	5. Adjoined relative clause	0	3	3

Relative-clause constructions are further described in Chapters 92–4 from the point of view of the role of the head noun in the relative clause (subject relative clauses, object relative clauses, instrument relative clauses). This aspect is not considered in this chapter.

2. Relative clause follows noun

In the great majority of *APiCS* languages, the relative clause is adjacent to the head noun and follows it, as in (1) and in (3).

(3) Pichi (Yakpo 2013)
*Mi nà wan **human** we à siryɔs.*
1SG.EMPH COP one woman [REL 1SG.SBJ be.serious]
'I am a woman who is serious.'

It is not surprising that this is the overwhelmingly dominant type in our languages, because it is overwhelmingly the dominant type in the indigenous languages of Africa, Europe, and Southeast Asia, as well as in Austronesian languages (Dryer 2005j). In *APiCS*, there are only three languages which do not have postnominal relative clauses (all spoken in Asia: Sri Lankan Malay, Sri Lanka Portuguese, and Chinese Pidgin Russian).

3. Relative clause precedes noun

Five languages have prenominal relative clauses, and two of them, Sri Lanka Portuguese and Sri Lankan Malay, have only this option:

(4) Sri Lankan Malay (Slomanson 2013)
*poḍiyen si-billi **teegi***
[boy PST-buy] gift
'the gift that the boy just bought'

As the lexifiers lack prenominal relative clauses, this construction must be due to the Tamil substrate/adstrate in both languages (note that the *WALS* map for Sri Lanka shows only Sinhala, which has postnominal relative clauses).

Another Asian language with dominant prenominal order is Singapore Bazaar Malay, as seen in (2). In this language, the prenominal order must be due to substrate influence from the Chinese languages of the Bazaar Malay speakers.

Prenominal relative clauses are also found in two mixed languages in the Americas, Media Lengua and Michif, following the patterns of the indigenous languages:

(5) Michif (Bakker 2013)
*lii groo pale kaa-ayaa-chik **wishtawaw***
ART.PL [big palace REL-have-CONJ.3PL] they.also
'those who have big palaces'

4. Internally headed relative clause

Internally headed relative clauses have not been widely known until fairly recently. They are clauses which are not adjacent to the notional head, but contain it inside them. They occur especially in the languages of North America, but also sporadically elsewhere throughout the world. In *APiCS*, this type occurs only marginally in one language, Ternate Chabacano. Postposed relative clauses are much more common in this language, but (6) shows an internally headed relative clause.

(6) Ternate Chabacano (Sippola 2013b)
*Kel a-konosé bo **ómbri** agóra mi ermáno.*
[that PFV-know you man today] my brother
'The man you met today is my brother.' (lit. 'The—you met the man today—is my brother.')

5. Correlative relative clause

Three *APiCS* languages have correlative relative clauses, where the head occurs inside the relative clause together with a relative marker, and which are taken up by a resumptive demonstrative-like element in the main clause. Thus (7) from Pidgin Hindustani is literally 'Which camp they stayed at, that (was) dirty.'

(7) Pidgin Hindustani (Siegel 2013)
*Jon **kempa** u-lon baito, u maila.*
[REL camp 3-PL COP] 3SG dirty
'The camp that they stayed at was dirty.'

(8) Chinese Pidgin Russian (Perekhvalskaya 2013)
Это который люди колодица лазил, такой
*Eta katory **liudi** kaloditʃa lazil, **takoj***
this [which person well get.into-PFV] that
скажи.
skaʒi.
tell
'Tell about a person who got into the well.'

(9) Korlai (Clements 2013)
*Akə ɔm ɔ̃t ki yawe, Janna **pel** ulyo.*
[that man yesterday REL came] Janna OBJ.3SG see.PST
'Janna saw the man who came yesterday.'

Correlative relative clauses are particularly well known from Indo-Aryan languages (Dryer 2005j), so in *APiCS* we find them in Hindustani-lexified Pidgin Hindustani and in Portuguese-based Korlai (spoken in India, showing strong Indo-Aryan adstrate influence). The presence of the construction in Chinese Pidgin Russian may seem a bit more surprising, but similar constructions are actually found in colloquial Russian.

6. Adjoined relative clause

Three languages have adjoined relative clauses, that is, relative clauses which do not occur adjacent to the head noun and are not specially marked as relative clauses. That they help narrow down the reference of the head noun must be inferred from the context. Adjoined relative clauses are particularly well known from Australian languages, so we find them in Kriol, but also in Early Sranan and Michif.

(10) Kriol (Schultze-Berndt & Angelo 2013)
***Tubala** kam-in hiya we im=in hab-im tubala*
two come-PROG here [SUBORD 3SG=PST have-TR two
marrug.
hidden]
'The two are coming here, the ones that he (a white man) had kept hidden away.' (lit. 'The two are coming here, while he had hidden the two away.')

(11) Early Sranan (van den Berg & Bruyn 2013)
*Wan **uman** ben de dapeh, dissi habi wan jeje vo siki*
one woman PST COP there [DEM have one spirit of illness
sinsi tin na aiti jari.
since ten at eight year]
'There was a woman there who had a spirit of infirmity for eighteen years.'

(12) Michif (Bakker 2013)
*enn pitael pur **anikik** kaaya kwayesh kaa-ayaa-chik*
a hospital for DEM.PL [NEG right SUBORD-be-3PL
daa leu tet
LOC 3PL.POSS head]
'a hospital for those who are not right in the head (i.e. an asylum)'

We must admit here that the classifications in §§4–6 are not particularly certain. Internally headed relative clauses are often difficult to recognize, and correlative relative clauses could be confused with simple cases of left dislocation of the head noun together with the relative clause, as in (13).

(13) Bislama (Meyerhoff 2013)
***woman** we hem i aot finis, hem i pem buk ia*
woman [REL 3SG AGR out COMPL] 3SG AGR buy book DEF
'The woman who left already, she bought that book.'

Adjoined relative clauses are the least well defined. The case of Early Sranan could simply be regarded as a case of relative-clause extraposition, for example. The clearest case of an adjoined relative clause is the Kriol example in (10), where the subordinator *we* is not specific to relative clauses.

7 Order of relative clause and noun

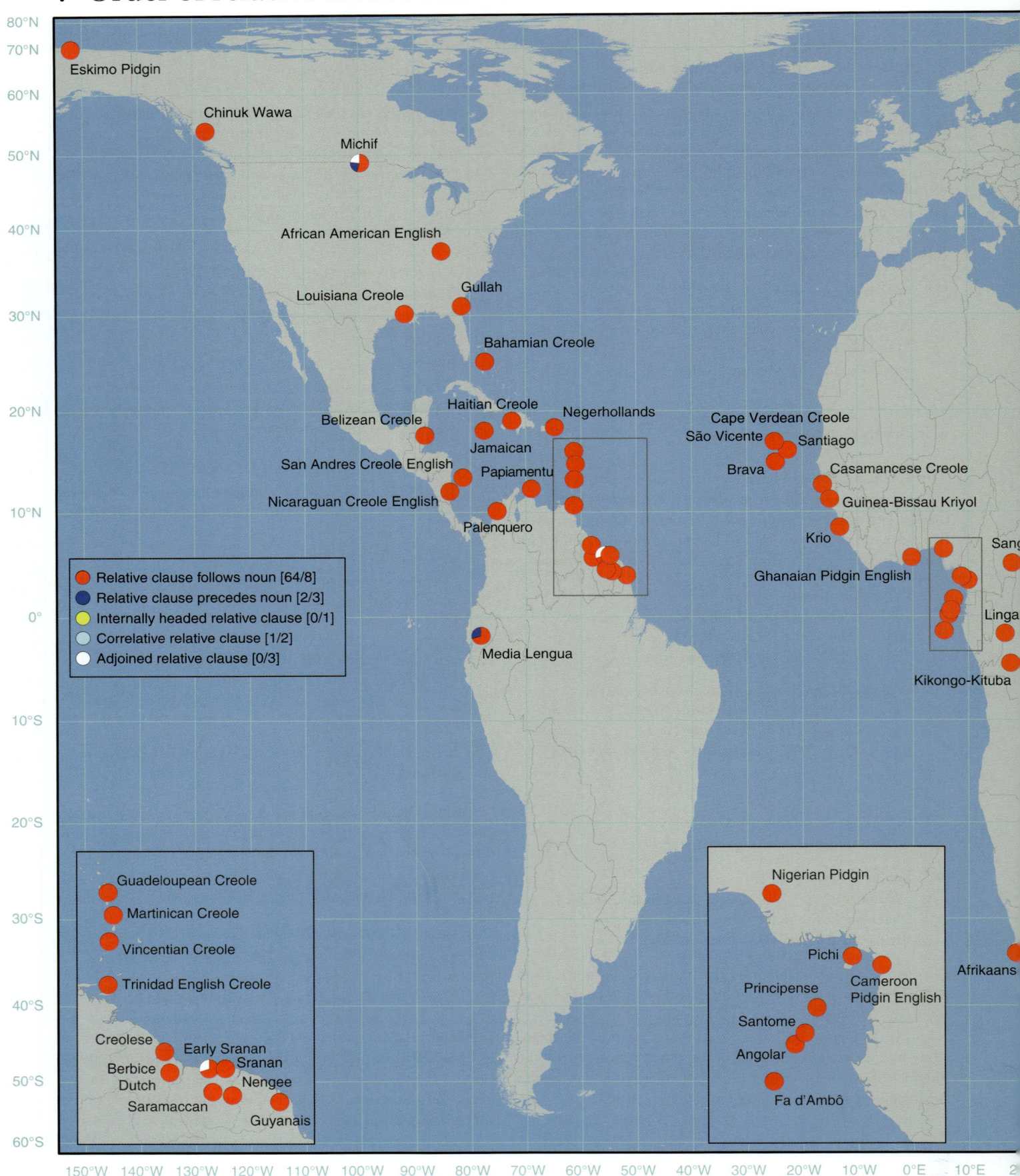

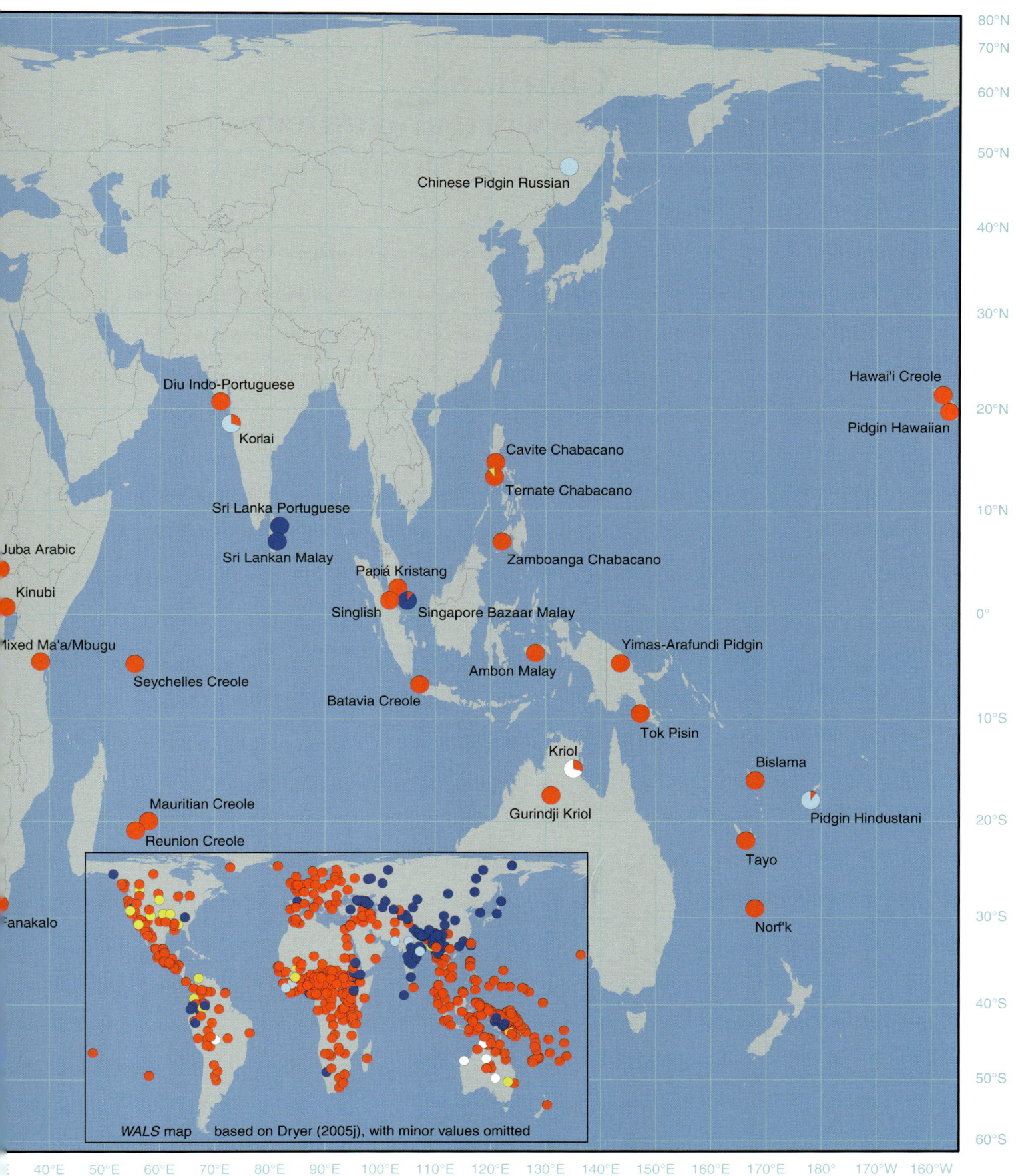

Chapter 8
Order of degree word and adjective

MARTIN HASPELMATH AND THE *APiCS* CONSORTIUM

1. Degree words

The order of degree word and adjective is more variable than orders of most other kinds of words. Only frequency adverbs (Chapter 11) show a similar variability across languages. **Degree words** (often called "degree adverbs") are words like 'very', 'a little', 'too', and 'more' in adjective phrases. This chapter closely parallels Dryer's (2005k) *WALS* chapter.

Some initial examples of degree words are given in (1) and (2).

(1) Guadeloupean Creole (Colot & Ludwig 2013a)
    a. *I   tibwen cho.*
       3SG [a.little hot]
       'It is a little hot.'
    b. *I   gran toubolman.*
       3SG [tall very]
       'He is very tall.'

(2) Cameroon Pidgin English (Schröder 2013)
    a. *I   tu dye.*
       3SG.SBJ [too dear]
       'It is too expensive.'
    b. *Di   pikin drai bad.*
       ART.DEF child [thin bad]
       'The child is very thin.'

There is a general preference for preposed degree words, but many languages have both preposed and postposed degree words.

		excl	shrd	all
●	1. Degree word precedes adjective	32	35	67
●	2. Degree word follows adjective	8	35	43
●	3. Degree word precedes and follows adjective	0	1	1

Only one language has a degree construction with both a preceding and a following word (value 3):

(3) Ambon Malay (Paauw 2013)
    paleng manganta lawang
    very painful very
    'very very painful'

2. Languages with preposed degree words only

About half of the *APiCS* languages have only preposed degree words. This includes quite a few English-, French-, and Ibero-Romance-based languages, and the position of the degree word in these languages is identical to the order in the lexifier. In many of these languages, the degree words are straightforwardly inherited from the lexifier.

(4) Batavia Creole (Maurer 2013b)
    Akel teng mutu karu.
    that COP [very expensive]
    'That one is too expensive.' (cf. Portuguese *muito*)

(5) Seychelles Creole (Michaelis & Rosalie 2013)
    I   en pti pe so.
    PM [a little bit hot]
    'It is a bit hot.' (cf. French *un petit peu*)

(6) Singlish (Lim & Ansaldo 2013)
    Singapore flat very expensive a21?
    'Are Singapore's apartments very expensive?'

(7) Pidgin Hindustani (Siegel 2013)
    Baut barawala ciz   nai baito jaise sako kato.
    [very big]   thing NEG COP like can cut
    'There aren't very big things [in the bush] of the kind that can bite you.' (cf. Hindi *bahut* 'very')

3. Languages with postposed degree words only

Eight languages have only postposed degree words. Seven of them are spoken in Africa; examples are in (8)–(10):

(8) Kinubi (Luffin 2013)
    ána g-ásma   kwes zaídi
    1SG ASP-understand [good very]
    'I understand very well.'

(9) Fanakalo (Mesthrie 2013)
    Yena pikinin stelek.
    it [small strong]
    'It is very little.'

(10) Sango (Samarin 2013)
 *karako ni a-le nzoni **mingi***
 peanuts DET PM-bear [good much]
 'The peanuts have borne very well.'

This areal concentration of obligatorily postposed degree words in Africa matches the worldwide trend (Dryer 2015k): Western and Central Africa has the strongest concentration of languages with postposed degree words. It is also interesting to note that the order of numeral and noun shows a similar areal picture, with a concentration of languages with postposed numerals in Africa (Chapter 6). Since degree words and numerals are both quantity modifiers, this word-order similarity is semantically sensible.

The only non-African language with exclusively postposed degree words is Tok Pisin, which is again not surprising as the indigenous languages of New Guinea overwhelmingly show postposed degree words.

(11) Tok Pisin (Smith & Siegel 2013)
 *Haus i bik-pela **tru**.*
 house PM [big-MOD very]
 'The house is very big.'

4. Languages with both orders of degree words

Thirty-five languages have both preposed and postposed degree words, among them 15 English-based languages and 9 Portuguese-based languages. In almost all cases, this variation in order is due to several different degree words occurring in different positions, not to the order of an individual degree word being free. Thus, degree words form the least coherent word-class from a word-order perspective.

In the English-based languages, inherited degree words like *very*, *too*, and *more* usually precede the adjective, while it is the degree words that do not derive from standard English that tend to follow the adjective (e.g. *bad*, *too much*, *true*, cf. also (2b) and (11)).

(12) Creolese (Devonish & Thompson 2013)
 a. *afta mi groo an mi get **lil mo** big*
  after I grow and I get [little more big]
  'after I grew up and got a little bigger'
 b. *di baai dootish **baad***
  DET boy [foolish very]
  'The boy is very foolish.'

(13) Ghanaian Pidgin English (Huber 2013)
 a. *pɔpjuleʃɛn **tu** gret*
  population [too great]
  'The population is too large.'
 b. *nima dɛti **tu** matʃ*
  Nima [dirty too much]
  'Nima is too/very dirty.'

(14) Jamaican (Farquharson 2013)
 a. *Di lili pikni **tuu** bad.*
  DET little child [too bad]
  'The little child is too rude.'
 b. *Di fuud hat **bad**.*
  DET food [hot very]
  'The food is very hot.'

In Haitian Creole, too, the inherited degree word *pi* (from French *plus*) precedes, while the new word *anpil* (French *en pile* 'in a pile') follows the adjective:

(15) Haitian Creole (Fattier 2013)
 a. *Wòb sa a **pi** bèl.*
  dress DEM SG [more beautiful]
  'This dress is more beautiful.'
 b. *Li cho **anpil**.*
  3SG [hot very]
  'He/She is very hot.'

Thus, we may speculate that in the Atlantic creoles and pidgins, the inherited degree words simply preserved the position they had in the lexifier, while the new degree words derive their position from the African substrates.

In a few languages, such as Early Sranan and Nengee, the order of the degree word depends on the function of the adjective: if the adjective is attributive and precedes a noun, the degree word precedes it, but if it is predicative, the degree word follows it:

(16) Early Sranan (van den Berg & Bruyn 2013)
 a. *wan **toemoesie Biegie** Soema*
  INDF.SG [very big] person
  'a very big person'
 b. *Lampo de fulu **tumussi**, a de go passa abra.*
  lamp IPFV [full too.much] 3SG.SBJ IPFV go pass over
  'The lamp is (getting) overfull, it is going to overflow.'

Berbice Dutch is somewhat similar. And in Jamaican, only predicative adjectives can be modified by a degree word. In Tok Pisin, prenominal adjectives can be modified by a degree word, but this cannot occur inside the adjective phrase and must be postposed:

(17) Tok Pisin (Smith & Siegel 2013)
 *Em i bik-pela haus **tru**.*
 3SG PM big-MOD house very
 'That's a very big house.'

8 Order of degree word and adjective

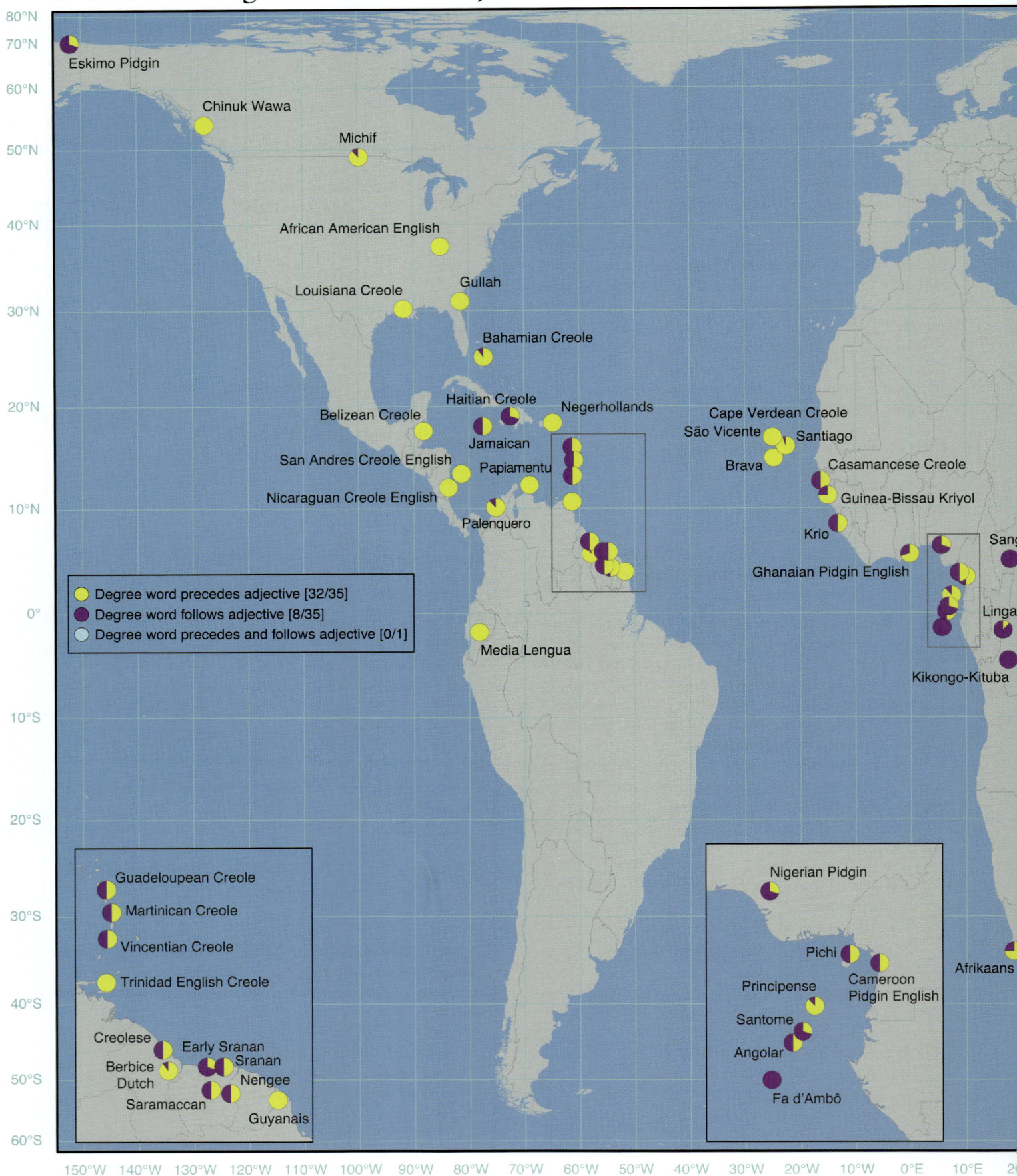

32

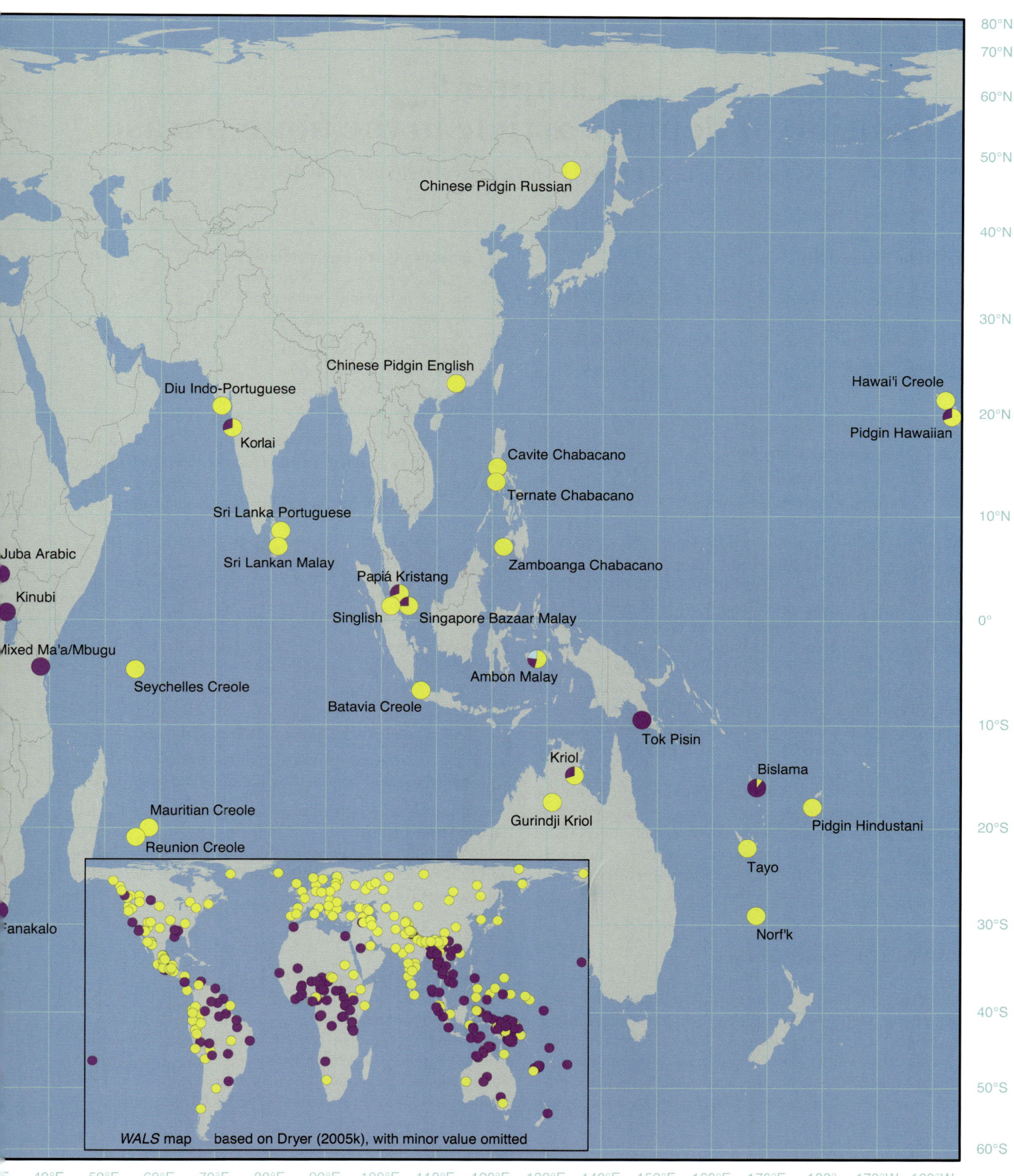

Chapter 9
Position of definite article in the noun phrase
MARTIN HASPELMATH AND THE *APiCS* CONSORTIUM

1. Definite articles

This chapter deals with the position of the definite article with respect to the noun in noun phrases. Three quarters of the *APiCS* languages have a definite article, which is either preposed, postposed, or circumposed:

		excl	shrd	all
○	1. Definite article is preposed	44	5	49
●	2. Definite article is postposed	7	2	9
○	3. Definite article is circumposed	0	3	3
○	4. The language has no definite article	19	0	19

As in Chapters 28 and 31, which treat definite articles from different perspectives, we define a definite article as a morpheme which accompanies nouns and which codes definiteness, like *the* in English. Definite articles need not be obligatory. Definite NPs are NPs whose referent can be uniquely identified by the hearer, as in anaphoric situations, to refer back to something mentioned in the preceding discourse (e.g. *I bought a new bicycle… My husband likes the bicycle*), or in associative contexts, to refer to something that is not mentioned in the preceding discourse but that is identifiable because of an associative relationship (e.g. *I bought a new bicycle. The saddle is very comfortable*; see also ex. (4), below).

In pidgin and creole languages, definite articles either go back to the definite article of the lexifier (as in many English-based languages), or they derive from adnominal demonstratives ('that', 'this') or locative demonstratives ('there') (see Chapter 28). In quite a few languages, they are still synchronically identical with demonstratives (see Chapter 31).

2. Preposed definite articles

Definite articles are (or can be) **preposed** (value 1) in the great majority of *APiCS* languages. This includes all English-based languages (except for Tok Pisin and Bislama, which lack definite articles), as well as those Ibero-Romance-based creoles that have definite articles. In all these languages, the preposed definite articles derive from preposed articles or adnominal demonstratives in the lexifiers.

(1) Ghanaian Pidgin English (Huber 2013)
 ì gò kam ritʃ **dɛ** ɔda ɛnt
 3SG IRR come reach DEF other end
 'It would reach the other side.'

(2) Papiá Kristang (Baxter 2013)
 nus sibrí **aké** pesi kanikaninu
 1PL use DEF fish small.small
 'We use the very small fish.'

Preposed definite articles are also found in Dutch-based languages and in two French-based creoles of the Indian Ocean, Reunion Creole and Seychelles Creole. These definite articles, too, derive from Dutch and French articles/demonstratives, respectively.

(3) Negerhollands (van Sluijs 2013)
 Di noli a sē […]
 DET donkey PST say
 'The donkey said: […]'

(4) Seychelles Creole (Michaelis & Rosalie 2013)
 Ou a bezwen sal li ek son lekay tou.
 2SG FUT need salt it with POSS.3SG scale all

 E ou tir **sa** gro zaret milye, ou tir latet.
 and 2SG pull DEF thick bone middle 2SG pull head
 'You had to salt them [the fish] with their scales. And you pulled the large bone in the middle, you pulled the heads.'

The mixed language Michif also has preposed definite articles, adopted from French.

In addition, we find preposed definite articles in Fanakalo and Pidgin Hawaiian, where the definite article is identical to the (preposed) demonstrative.

3. Postposed definite articles

Postposed definite articles (value 2) are found only in French-based languages and in two African languages, Sango and Kinubi. Among the French-based languages, they occur as the usual order in the Caribbean languages Guyanais, Guadeloupean and Martinican Creole, in Haitian Creole, and in older varieties of Louisiana Creole.

(5) Mauritian Creole (Baker & Kriegel 2013)
ban zanfan la   fer   tapaz
PL child   DEF make noise
'The children are making noise.'

(6) Kinubi (Luffin 2013)
azól de já   ma galamóyo
man DEF come with goat
'The man came with a goat.'

In all these languages they derive from postposed demonstratives. As Dryer (2005h) shows, demonstratives are overwhelmingly postposed in African languages, as well as in some languages on the western fringe of Europe (Basque and Celtic). French has preposed demonstratives, but these typically co-occur with postposed locative demonstratives, as in *cette maison-là* 'that house' (lit. 'this house there').

Lefebvre (1998: 81) argues that the syntactic and semantic properties of the postposed definite article in Haitian Creole derive from the substrate languages (for instance, Fongbe has a postposed definite article *ɔ́*, as in *vǐ ɔ́* [child the] 'the child'). But note that most of the properties of postposed *la* (or its phonological variants *a*, *an*, *nan*, *lan* in Haitian Creole) in Caribbean French creoles can be derived directly from the postposed French demonstrative *-là*, not only its shape and position, but also the fact that it cannot be used generically:

(7) Haitian Creole (Lefebvre 1998: 80)
Pen (*an) bon pou lasante.
bread (DEF) good for health
'Bread is good for one's health.'

There is thus no need to invoke substrate influence here, because definite articles that were recently grammaticalized from demonstratives are not expected to have the generic use (in fact, even English *the* does not have it (yet)). Moreover, if the postposed Haitian Creole article were primarily due to the substrate, we would expect to find postposed definite articles in English-based languages, too.

However, in Haitian Creole, the definite article is postposed not only to the noun, but also to a modifier following the noun such as an adjective, a possessor, or even a relative clause:

(8) Haitian Creole (Fattier 2013)
a. *machin wouj Mari   a*
   car   red Marie DEF
   'Marie's red car'
b. *M wè ti nèg ki frekan   an.*
   1SG see little man [REL insolent] DEF
   'I saw the little boy who is impertinent.'

This NP-final position is also found in Fongbe (Lefebvre 1998: 82), so this can be taken as an additional argument for the substrate effect. But we find this order of postposed *la* also in the Indian Ocean:

(9) Mauritian Creole (Baker & Kriegel 2013)
tifi ki pe   tini en   pupet la
girl [who PROG hold INDF doll] DEF
'the girl who is holding a doll'

Whether the substrate explanation also extends to Mauritian (whose substrate languages are generally East African and Malagasy rather than West African) remains to be seen.

4. Circumposed definite articles

In a few languages, the definite article is **circumposed** (value 3), that is, it consists of two parts, one preposed and the other postposed. This option is not so uncommon with demonstratives (see Chapter 5 on the position of demonstratives in the noun phrase). With definite articles, it occurs only in two Chabacano varieties, in one variety of Louisiana Creole (though only with marginal frequency), and apparently in Belizean Creole (where *di nɛt dɛ* [the net there] is said to represent an article use by Escure 2013).

(10) Zamboanga Chabacano (Steinkrüger 2013)
El ómbre el ya-bené.
DEF man   DEF PRF-come
'The (same) man has come.'

(11) Louisiana Creole (Neumann-Holzschuh & Klingler 2013)
tou le   jenn jan-ye
all DEF.PL young person-DEF.PL
'all the young people' (Pointe Coupée variety)

In Louisiana Creole, this has apparently arisen from the retention of the postposed third-person definite plural marker *-ye* ('they', cf. Chapter 25) in this conservative variety and the introduction of the preposed definite article from French (*les*). The origin of the "doubled" *el* (or *kel*) in Chabacano is more puzzling.

5. Languages lacking definite articles

Nineteen languages **lack definite articles** (value 4). There is a concentration of such languages in the Pacific region, in central Africa, among the Portuguese-based languages of West Africa (as well as Korlai in India), among the Malay-based languages, and among the northern pidgins (Eskimo Pidgin, Chinuk Wawa, and Chinese Pidgin Russian). Malay varieties, Bantu languages, and the substrates of the northern pidgins lack definite articles, so we do not expect the *APiCS* languages to have them, but the absence of definite articles is somewhat more surprising in the Portuguese-based West African languages, in Palenquero, and in Juba Arabic.

9 Position of definite article in the noun phrase

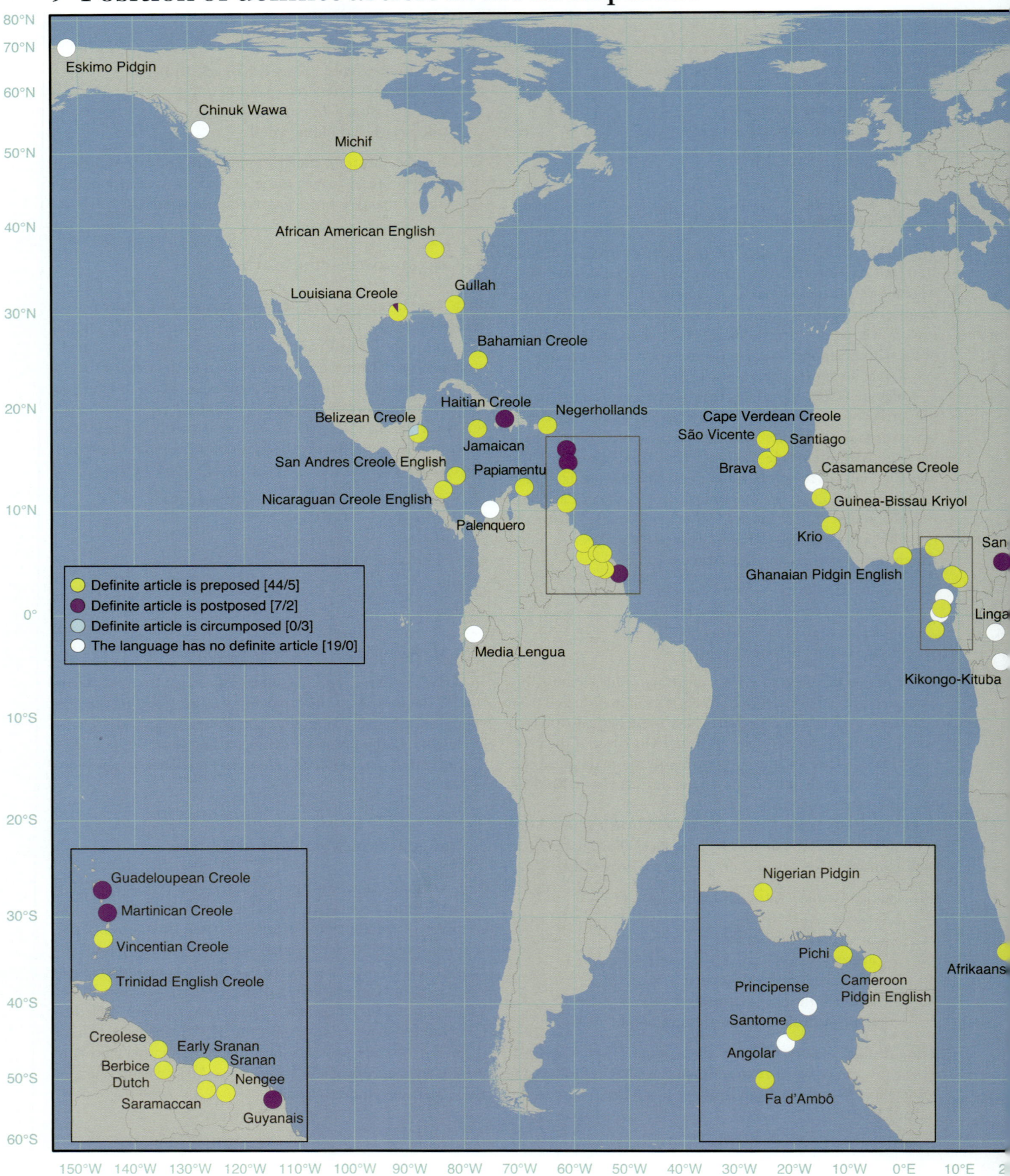

Chapter 10
Position of indefinite article in the noun phrase

MARTIN HASPELMATH AND THE *APiCS* CONSORTIUM

1. Indefinite articles

This chapter deals with the position of the indefinite article with respect to the noun in noun phrases. While there are more *APiCS* languages that have an indefinite article than a definite article (cf. Chapter 9), there is less variation: almost all indefinite articles precede the noun:

		excl	shrd	all
🟡	1. Indefinite article is preposed	63	1	64
🟣	2. Indefinite article is postposed	2	1	3
⚪	3. The language has no indefinite article	10	0	10

As in Chapter 29, we define an indefinite article as a morpheme that frequently occurs in noun phrases and signals that the referent is not uniquely identifiable by the hearer, as in *We have a cat*. In almost all languages where we have information about their origin, indefinite articles go back to the numeral 'one', and as a result, they are normally not used with plural noun phrases. As we show in Chapter 29, in many languages they are still synchronically identical to the numeral 'one'.

2. Preposed indefinite articles

Indefinite articles are **preposed** (value 1) in the great majority of *APiCS* languages. Some examples are given in (1)–(4).

(1) Jamaican (Farquharson 2013)
   Wahn dopi lik **wahn** man.
   [INDF ghost] hit [INDF man]
   'A ghost hit a man.'

(2) Tayo (Ehrhart & Revis 2013)
   nu ekri a ᵑgra let
   1PL write [INDF long letter]
   'We are writing a long letter.'

(3) Fa d'Ambô (Post 2013)
   Mala xoze **wa** bluz ku guya.
   Mary sews [INDF shirt] with needle
   'Mary sews a shirt with a needle.'

(4) Cavite Chabacano (Sippola 2013a)
   Ta escribi ele **un** carta.
   IPFV write 3SG [INDF letter]
   'He writes a letter.'

3. Postposed indefinite articles

Postposed indefinite articles (value 2) are found in only two *APiCS* languages in Africa, Kinubi and Principense, and in Sri Lankan Malay.

Since word order tends to be very strongly influenced by the lexifier (see e.g. Chapters 1–3), it is not surprising to find a postposed indefinite article in Arabic-lexified Kinubi, because in Arabic, the numeral 'one' is always postposed, like adjectives (e.g. *ṭiflun waahidun* 'one child'). Kinubi *wáy* derives from Arabic *waahid* 'one'.

(5) Kinubi (Luffin 2013)
   fi nyerekú **wáy** kamán rúo ma bába t-o
   EXIST [child INDF] too go with father GEN-his
   'There was also a child who went with his father.'

The other language where the indefinite article always follows the noun is Principense:

(6) Principense (Maurer 2013c)
   Kêdê mêzê Maa ka xikevê mi kata **ũa**.
   every month Maa HAB write 1SG [letter INDF]
   'Every month Maa writes me a letter.'

Principense and Kinubi are two of those few *APiCS* languages where the numeral may (or must) follow the noun (see Chapter 6). Since the indefinite article derives from the numeral 'one', it is precisely in these languages that we expect postposed indefinite articles. (Most of the other languages with postposed numerals lack indefinite articles.)

As we saw in Chapter 6, the postposed order of numerals in the African *APiCS* languages goes back to the indigenous African languages, which almost always have postposed numerals. In fact, even the postposed ordering of the numeral 'one' and the indefinite article in Kinubi may have to do with the indigenous languages of South Sudan and Uganda (rather than with the Arabic lexifier, as suggested earlier), because Kinubi has all numerals following the noun (e.g. *yal-á tísa* [child-PL nine]

Position of indefinite article in the noun phrase

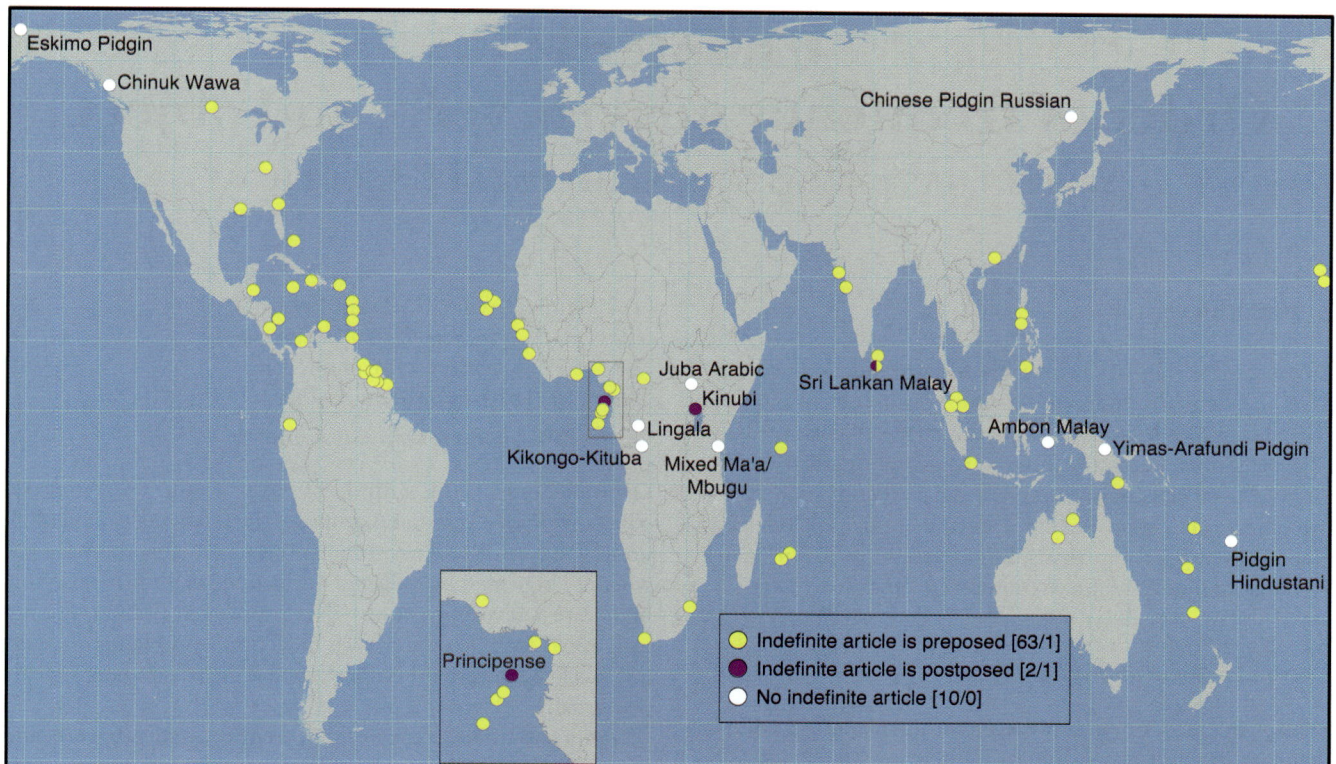

'nine children'), not just the numerals for 'one' and 'two', as in Arabic.

The third language that has a postposed indefinite article is Sri Lankan Malay, but here both orders of the indefinite article *attu* (from Malay *satu*) are allowed and about equally common:

(7) Sri Lankan Malay (Slomanson 2013)
    a. *Go panjang **attu** buk si-baca.*
       1SG [long   INDF book] PST-read
       'I read a long book.'
    b. *Go ayer mera kumbang **attu** yang e-klaatan.*
       1SG [water red   flower   INDF ACC] ASP-see
       'I saw a pink flower.'

In Sri Lankan Malay, the order of the indefinite article is actually quite free, as described in detail by Nordhoff (2009: 440–4). We see in (7a) that the indefinite article follows the adjective, for instance, but the reverse order would also be possible. As argued by Nordhoff (2012: 28–31), the widespread (and sometimes obligatory) use of the indefinite article is due to Sinhala influence. Nordhoff cites the Sri Lankan Malay example in (8) and the parallel Sinhala example in (9). So it seems clear that the postposed ordering is also due to Sinhala influence.

(8) Sri Lankan Malay
    ***hathu**=oorang=pe muuluth=dering **hathu**=criitha*
    INDF=man=POSS mouth=ABL   INDF=story

    kal-dhaathang
    when-come
    'when a story comes out of a man's mouth'

(9) Sinhala
    *minih-**ek**-gee   kaṭ-ing   kataav-**ak***
    man-INDF.ANIM-POSS mouth-ABL story-INDF.INAN
    ena   koṭa
    come when
    'when a story comes out of a man's mouth'

4. Languages lacking indefinite articles

Ten languages **lack in definite articles** (value 3). These are mostly the languages that have lexifiers which are not Germanic or Romance: Eskimo Pidgin, Chinuk Wawa, and Chinese Pidgin Russian in the north, Bantu-based Lingala, Kikongo-Kituba, and Mixed Ma'a/Mbugu (as well as Juba Arabic) in Africa, and Ambon Malay, Yimas-Arafundi Pidgin, and Pidgin Hindustani in the Pacific region. Since indefinite articles are actually not all that easy to distinguish from the numeral 'one' (see Chapter 29), it could be that the difference is primarily due to the descriptive tradition: Germanic and Romance languages are usually described as having indefinite articles, while in other languages indefinite articles are much less expected.

Chapter 11
Order of frequency adverb, verb, and object
MARTIN HASPELMATH AND THE *APiCS* CONSORTIUM

1. Introduction

Linguists generally pay relatively little attention to the order of adverbial elements in the clause. One reason for this is that adverbial elements occur less frequently than subjects, verbs, and objects; another reason is that their position tends to be more variable: even languages with fairly rigid order of subject, verb, and object often show flexible ordering of adverbial elements, especially temporal adverbials. English seems to be typical in allowing both initial and final temporal adverbs:

(1) a. *Yesterday I sold my house.*
     b. *I sold my house yesterday.*

Perhaps the most important reason for the neglect of adverbial elements in word-order studies is their heterogeneity. While noun phrase arguments and verbs are homogeneous classes that are quite readily comparable across languages, adverbial adjuncts are a class with great internal diversity, perhaps even best defined in negative terms ("an adverbial is everything that is not an argument or a verb").

To get a reasonably homogeneous class of items for this chapter, we decided to focus on the position of frequency adverbs such as 'always' and 'often' or their phrasal equivalents. In many creoles, expressions like 'all the time' are used, replacing the English word *often* and the French word *souvent*. Moreover, 'often' and 'always' are often not distinguished.

That such adverbial elements vary interestingly in their position across languages is well known from Pollock (1989), who noted that French allows postverbal pre-object order of such adverbs, while English does not, and instead allows preverbal post-subject order, which French disallows:

(2) French
     a. *Jean embrasse **souvent** Marie.*
     b. **Jean souvent embrasse Marie.*

(3) English
     a. **John kisses **often** Mary.*
     b. *John **often** kisses Mary.*

DeGraff (1994, 1997, 2005) notes that Haitian Creole shows the English ordering pattern, not the French one, even though it derives most of its word shapes from French:

(4) Haitian Creole (DeGraff 1997: 68)
     a. *Mwen **toujou** ekri manman mwen.*
        I   always write mother my
        'I always write to my mother.'
     b. **Mwen ekri **toujou** manman mwen.*

DeGraff connects this with the absence of inflectional morphology on Haitian verbs, and proposes the following explanation: underlying word order is uniformly subject–adverb–verb, but when a language has inflected verbs, the verb must raise to a higher, pre-adverb, position. This happens in French, but not in English with its poorer verb inflection, and Haitian Creole, too, has lost the verb movement, so that the adverb now appears preverbally.

Let us now look at the order of frequency adverb, verb, and object in the *APiCS* languages. There are six logically possible orders, all of which occur in at least one language:

		excl	shrd	all
●	1. Verb–adverb–object	1	16	17
●	2. Adverb–verb–object	12	36	48
●	3. Verb–object–adverb	12	39	51
●	4. Object–adverb–verb	0	7	7
●	5. Adverb–object–verb	0	7	7
●	6. Object–verb–adverb	0	1	1

We see that two-thirds of our languages have multiple ordering possibilities.

2. Verb–adverb–object

Adverbial position between the verb and the object (value 1), as seen in (2a) for French, is not very common in SVO languages, but most of the West African Portuguese-based creoles allow this order:

(5) Cape Verdean Creole of Santiago (Lang 2013)
     *Nhu   ta ten **txeu bes** surpréza.*
     2SG.POL.M IPFV have many time surprise
     'You often have a surprise.'

If one wanted to preserve DeGraff's generalization, one could try to argue that the West African Portuguese-based creoles have more verbal inflection than Haitian Creole. This might be argued for Cape Verdean and the varieties on the adjacent mainland, but it is certainly not true for the Gulf of Guinea creoles.

In addition, the verb-initial Chabacano languages allow pre-object adverbials, which follow not only the verb, but also the subject:

(6) Zamboanga Chabacano (Steinkrüger 2013)
 *Ta-besá si Patrick **pirmi** kun January.*
 IPFV-kiss AG Patrick often OBJ January
 'Patrick often kisses January.'

3. Adverb–verb–object

The preverbal order of adverbials is found in the majority of languages with verb–object order (value 2), in accordance with the expectation that initial and final order should generally be possible for temporal adverbs.

As in the case of verb–adverb–object order, the position of the subject is not considered here, so this value subsumes both subject–adverb–verb order (as in 7) and adverb–subject–verb order (as in 8).

(7) Diu Indo-Portuguese (Cardoso 2013)
 *Yo **sẽp** tə brĩka saykəl.*
 1SG always IPFV.NPST play.INF bicycle
 'I often/always play with my bicycle.'

(8) Nigerian Pidgin (Faraclas 2013)
 ***Planti taym** Mẹri dè kis Jọn.*
 plenty time Mary INCOMPL kiss John
 'Mary often kisses John.'

4. Verb–object–adverb

Post-object order of frequency adverbs (value 3) is even more common in our languages. Again, most of the languages with this order also allow other orders.

(9) a. Hawaiʻi Creole (Velupillai 2013)
  *a stɛ go kat gɹæs **al a taɪm**.*
  1SG IPFV ACT cut grass all ART time
  'I kept cutting grass all the time.'
 b. Pichi (Yakpo 2013)
  *À kìn si dan bɔy **bɔ́kú** nà tɔn.*
  1SG.SBJ HAB see that boy much LOC town
  'I often see that boy in town.'

5. Object–verb orders

When the object precedes the verb, so does the adverb in most cases. This reflects a more general pattern across languages: OV languages are much more often verb-final than VO languages are verb-initial (Dryer 1991). Object–adverb–verb order (value 4), as in (10), is about as common as adverb–object–verb order (value 5), as in (11). Most languages that use one of them also allow the other.

(10) Sri Lankan Malay (Slomanson 2013)
 *Farida nasi **mana-waktu-le** a-makan.*
 Farida rice which-time-COM PRS-eat
 'Farida often eats rice.'

(11) Chinese Pidgin Russian (Perekhvalskaya 2013)
 *Tiper maja **sigəda** iwo biristoj pali.*
 now 1SG always 3SG birch.bark burn
 'Now I always set them (wasp nests) on fire with the help of burning birch bark.'

Object–verb–adverb order (value 6) is attested only in the mixed language Michif, which has very flexible order, and actually allows all six orderings.

(12) Michif (Bakker 2013)
 *Aen susis ni-miyeeht-aen **aashkaw**.*
 INDF.M.SG sausage 1-like.TR.INAN-3.OBJ sometimes
 'I like a frankfurter sometimes.'

6. Further conditions on word order

So far we have been pretending that word order among frequency adverbs is homogeneous. But even though we limited ourselves to a small subclass of adverbials, we do of course find languages where different adverbs condition different orders. In Berbice Dutch, for instance, the native adverbial *idri titi* 'every time, always' precedes the subject, while the adverb *alwes*, borrowed from Creolese, occurs between the subject and the verb.

(13) Berbice Durch (Kouwenberg 2013a)
 a. ***idri tit'** o wa haf mu f' ɛkɛ*
  every time 3SG PST have.to go for 1SG
  'Every time he had to fetch me.'
 b. *af' u pruf di gu' di, ju ma **alwe'** suk' o*
  if 2SG taste the thing DEM 2SG IRR always want 3SG
  'If you taste this stuff, you will always want it.'

In Diu Indo-Portuguese, the adverb *sẽp* 'always, often' always occurs preverbally (see ex. 7), while the order of longer expressions such as *bastãt vez* 'many times' or *tud di* (or *tudi*) 'every-day' is much more flexible.

11 Order of frequency adverb, verb, and object

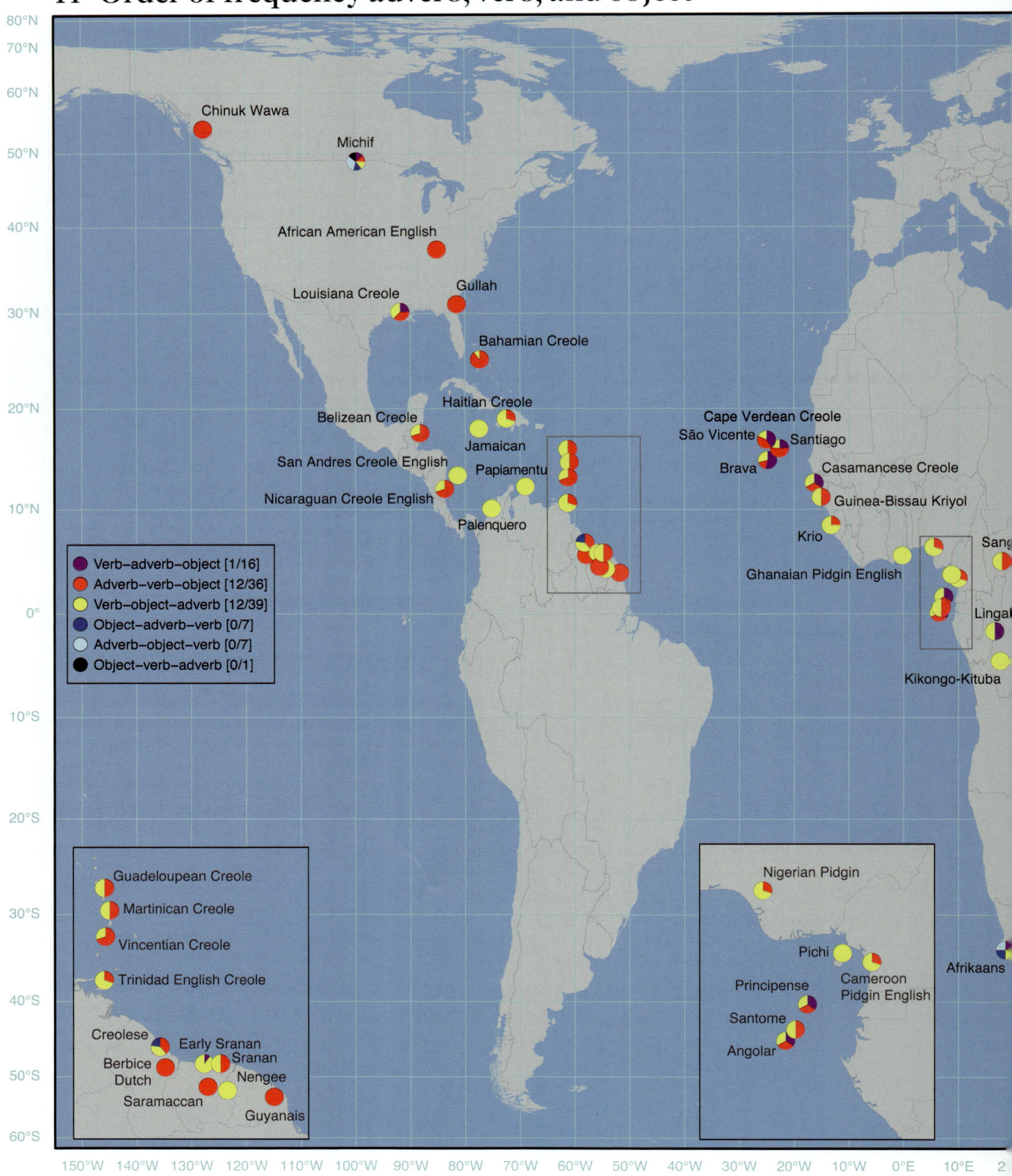

Chapter 12
Position of interrogative phrases in content questions

MARTIN HASPELMATH AND THE *APiCS* CONSORTIUM

1. Interrogative phrases

In many languages, in particular in languages with verb–object order, the interrogative phrase (or "wh-phrase") in content questions is normally or obligatorily fronted, that is, it occurs in a special initial position in the clause that is different from the position that the corresponding non-interrogative expression would occupy. An example is English:

(1) a. (non-interrogative)
   *The children are playing **in the garden**.*
  b. (interrogative)
   ***Where** are the children playing?*

In other languages, they can occur in the position in which they would occur in the corresponding declaratives ("**in situ**"), or in another special position (e.g. a preverbal focus position). An example comes from Bislama, where the object interrogative phrase occurs in the ordinary object position:

(2) Bislama (Meyerhoff 2013)
   *yu wantem karem **wanem**?*
   2SG want take what
   'What do you want to buy?'

2. The two types

Here we only distinguish two non-exclusive possibilities: **initial** (i.e. fronted) and **non-initial** (i.e. in situ, or in some other non-initial position), largely following Dryer (2005l). About half of the languages allow both possibilities.

		excl	shrd	all
🔴	1. Interrogative phrase initial	31	35	66
🔵	2. Interrogative phrase not initial	10	35	45

Two examples of initial position are given in (3a–b):

(3) a. San Andres Creole English (Bartens 2013b)
   ***Wa** yu waahn du wid ih?*
   what 2SG FUT do INS 3SG.N
   'What are you going to do with it?'

  b. Zamboanga Chabacano (Steinkrüger 2013)
   ***Kósa** tu ta-asé?*
   what you IPFV-do
   'What are you doing?'

Three examples of non-initial position are given in (4a–c):

(4) a. Sri Lanka Portuguese (Smith 2013)
   *poḍiyaas-ntu taam **kii** poy faya?*
   child-LOC also what HABIL do
   'What can the children do also?'

  b. Kikongo-Kituba (Mufwene 2013)
   *Nge me mona **nki**?*
   you PRF see what
   'What have you seen?'

  c. Tayo (Ehrhart & Revis 2013)
   *ta tape **ki**?*
   you hit whom
   'Whom did you hit?'

There may be further word-order peculiarities in content questions, as in English, where the subject inverts with some verbs (as in 1b), but these hardly occur in our languages and are not taken into account here.

Note that "initial position" does not necessarily mean absolute initial position. Initial interrogative phrases may be preceded by highlighting particles or copulas in cleft constructions, as in example (5).

(5) Jamaican (Farquharson 2013)
   *A **wa** Jan bai wid di moni?*
   FOC what John buy with DET money
   'What did John buy with the money?'

For this feature, we consider only interrogative phrases that do not normally occur initially in the clause, because with initially occurring elements (such as subjects), one cannot tell whether they are fronted. In example (6a), the interrogative phrase could be in situ or fronted, and it is only by analogy with (6b), where it is clearly fronted, that we may want to choose an analysis according to which (6a) is fronted as well.

(5) Guinea-Bissau Kriyol (Intumbo et al. 2013)
   a. ***Kin ki*** *ciga aonti?*
      who REL.SUBJ arrive.PST yesterday
      'Who arrived yesterday?'
   b. ***Kin ku*** *bu odja?*
      who REL.OBJ 2SG see.PST
      'Who did you see?'

It should be noted that in some languages that normally require fronting of interrogative phrases, occurrence of interrogative phrases in situ is possible in special echo questions (questions that copy part of an immediately preceding declarative sentence), as in Afrikaans and English:

(7) Afrikaans (den Besten & Biberauer 2013)
   *Jy het **WAT** ge-sê?*
   you PST what PTCP-said
   'You said WHAT?!' (Reaction to an utterance like 'I said that I'll marry him.')

Because of their highly specialized usage, echo questions have been excluded for this feature, so Afrikaans is classified as allowing only fronted interrogative phrases.

3. Languages with both orders

Many languages allow both fronting and in situ occurrence of interrogative phrases. Such languages are Guadeloupean Creole, Lingala, and Nigerian Pidgin:

(8) Guadeloupean Creole (Colot & Ludwig 2013a)
   a. ***Ki*** *koté ou té yé?*
      which place 2SG PST be
      'Where were you?'
   b. *Ou té **ki** koté?*
      2SG PST which place
      'Where were you?'

(9) Lingala (Meeuwis 2013)
   a. ***wápi*** *a-kend-ákí?*
      where 3SG-go-PST
      'Where did he go?'
   b. *a-kend-ákí **wápi**?*
      3SG-go-PST where
      'Where did he go?'

(10) Nigerian Pidgin (Faraclas 2013)
   a. ***Haw mọch mòni*** *dẹ̀m get?*
      how much money 3PL.SBJ have
      'How much money do they have?'
   b. *Dẹ̀m get **haw mọch mòni**?*
      3PL.SBJ have how much money
      'How much money do they have?'

There is often some semantic or pragmatic difference between the two construction types, but apart from echo questions (see above), such differences have been disregarded in our classification. For Bislama, Meyerhoff (2013) reports that in situ position (as in (2) above) is normal, while a question with fronted interrogative phrase is perceived as rude or aggressive. In Cape Verdean Creole of Santiago, in-situ position is especially used when the main verb is 'be':

(11) Cape Verdean Creole of Santiago (Lang 2013)
   *Kel (kumida) la **ê di kenha**?*
   that (food) there is of whom
   'Whose is that (food)?'

In Creolese, in situ position often occurs with a suggested answer, or when the answer is considered to be obvious:

(12) Creolese (Devonish & Thompson 2013)
   *yu jraa om **wid wo** - charkool?*
   you draw it with what charcoal
   'What did you draw it with? Charcoal?'

In some languages, different interrogative words behave differently. For instance, in Juba Arabic, *wen* 'where?' is always non-initial, whereas other interrogative pronouns may also be fronted (Manfredi & Petrollino 2013). Similarly, Santome *bô* 'where?' obligatorily occurs in final position, whereas for other interrogative phrases, initial position is more common (Hagemeijer 2013). (This particular case can be explained etymologically: *bô* was borrowed from Edo and is originally an interrogative copula.)

4. Geographical distribution of the types

In general, Atlantic pidgins and creoles show fronting of interrogative phrases, following the European model. In African languages, non-initial position is far more common (cf. Dryer 2005l), and the African pidgins and creoles also tend to show non-initial position (with the obvious exception of Afrikaans). In Asia, too, non-initial position is generally dominant in the indigenous languages, with the exception of Philippine languages, and this is reflected on the *APiCS* map, too. Thus, the position of interrogative phrases does seem to be susceptible to substrate influence in some areas, while in the Atlantic region the superstrate influence appears to be dominant. This is a puzzling pattern that requires further research.

12 Position of interrogative phrases in content questions

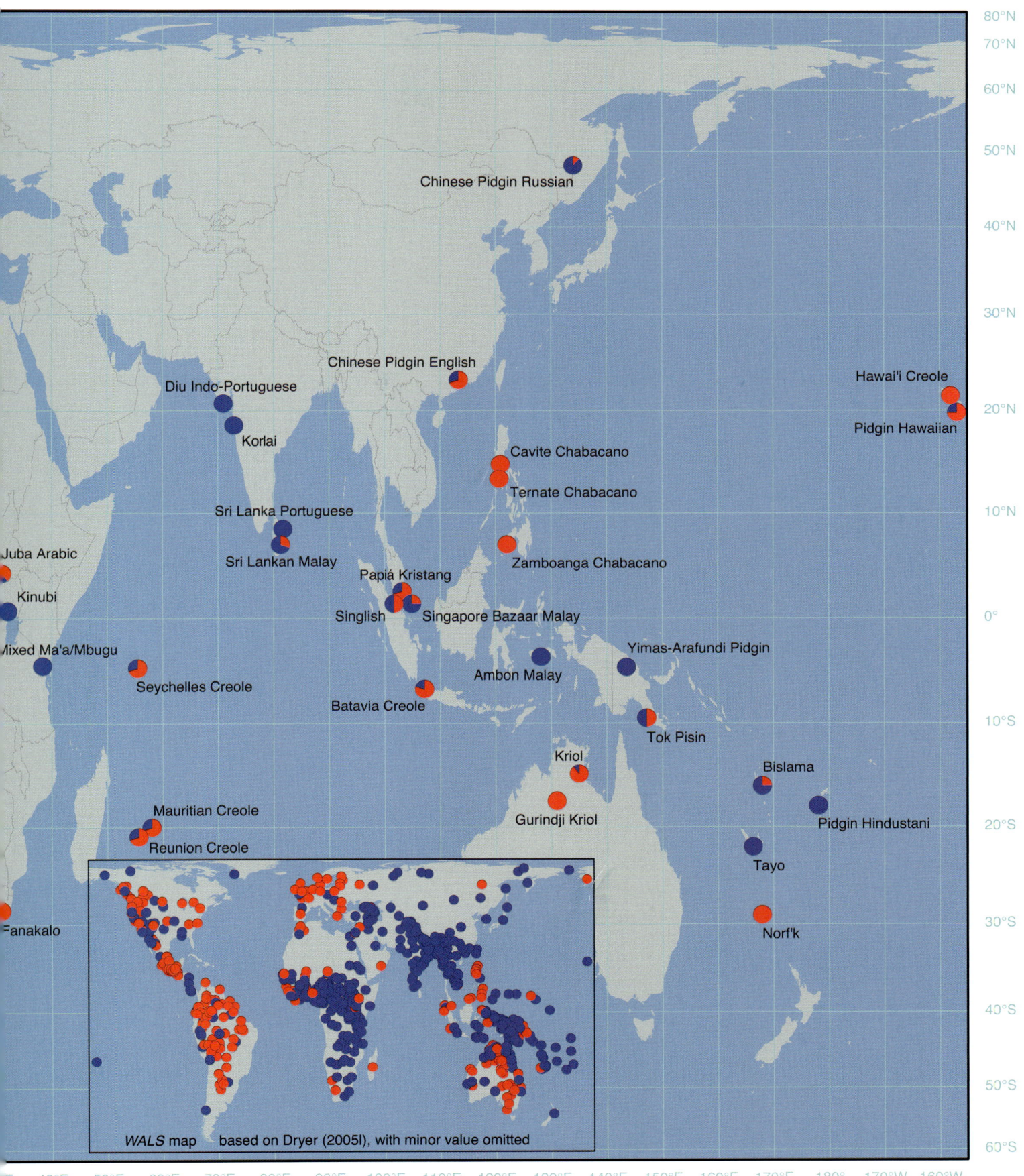

NOMINAL CATEGORIES

Chapter 13
Gender distinctions in personal pronouns

PHILIPPE MAURER AND THE *APiCS* CONSORTIUM

1. Introduction

Gender is not restricted here to oppositions such as male vs. female or masculine vs. feminine vs. neuter as in most European languages; gender also subsumes oppositions such as animate vs. non-animate or the Bantu noun-class systems.

Although most European languages (and others) display gender distinctions in personal pronouns, many *APiCS* languages lexically based on these languages do not, be they dependent (i.e. bound to the verb, as in Papiamentu *Mi ta traha* 'I am working') or independent (i.e. standing alone as, for instance, in elliptical answers; cf. Papiamentu *Ken ta traha? Ami.* 'Who is working?' 'Me.').

If in the *APiCS* languages gender distinctions do exist, they almost exclusively distinguish male and female referents. The only exceptions are Kikongo-Kituba, Lingala, and Michif, where the distinction is between animates and inanimates (see example 9).

This feature parallels *WALS* feature 44 (Siewierska 2005a).

2. The values

We distinguish the following values:

○	1. No gender distinctions	58
●	2. In 3rd person singular only	12
●	3. In 3rd person singular and plural only	4
●	4. In 2nd person but not 3rd person	2

As the value box shows, most *APiCS* languages (about 75%) make no gender distinctions in personal pronouns.

Value 1 (**no gender distinctions in pronouns**) occurs in pidgin languages (examples 1 and 2) and in creole languages of various lexical bases (examples 3–7).

(1) Chinese Pidgin Russian (Perekhvalskaya 2013)
 a. *Iwo ʃi-la iwo.*
   3SG sew-PFV 3SG
   'She sewed it.'

 b. *Iwo sioravno liudi, toko rubaʃəka dərugoj.*
   3SG all.the.same person only shirt different
   'It [a wild pig] is also a human in another appearance.'

(2) Singapore Bazaar Malay (Khin Khin Aye 2013)
 a. *Saya punya dia tak mahu, dia buang.*
   3SG POSS 3SG NEG want 3SG throw.away
   'She would throw away mine, which she does not want.'

 b. *Dia selalu di tenga jalan tipu-tipu sama olang.*
   3SG always in middle road cheat-cheat with person
   'He is always on the road cheating people.'

(3) Korlai (Clements 2013) (Portuguese-based)
 a. *Mhanje el ti andad lava kɔrp.*
   that.is 3SG PST go.PTCP wash body
   'That's to say, she went to take a bath.'

 b. *El tə hala ku muler [...].*
   3SG PROG say OBJ woman
   'He says to the woman [...].'

(4) Berbice Dutch (Kouwenberg 2013a) (Dutch-based)
 a. *ori mjato ʃi selfu*
   3SG make.PFV 3SG 3SG.POSS self
   'He made it himself.'

 b. *ori, o no-ko redi noko ka*
   3SG 3SG not-RES ready yet NEG
   'As for her, she wasn't ready yet.'

(5) Gullah (Klein 2013) (English-based)
 a. *E gone an marry Mary.*
   3SG go.PST and marry Mary
   'He went and married Mary.'

 b. *E gwine be wid chile.*
   3SG going be with child
   'She will be pregnant.'

(6) Reunion Creole (Bollée 2013) (French-based)
 a. *[...] li voi banann par isi.*
   3SG see banana over here
   '[...] she sees some bananas over there.'

 b. *[...] alor li na trode zanfan [...].*
   well.then 3SG have too.many child
   '[...] well, he had too many children [...].'

(7) Kinubi (Luffin 2013) (Arabic-based)
   a. *úwo gu-rúo ma baláma de*
      3SG PRS-go with balama DEM
      'She wears the balama (a kind of cloth).'

   b. *úwo captain*
      3SG captain
      'He is a captain.'

Of the twelve languages exhibiting value 2 (**gender distinction in third person singular only**; about 17 per cent of the *APiCS* languages), nine are English-based, two are Portuguese-based, and one is Dutch-based. In these languages, the gender distinction of the lexifier was retained.

(8) Trinidad English Creole (Mühleisen 2013)
   a. *Who say dat? Shi.*
      who say DEM.SG 3SG.F
      'Who said that?' 'She.'

   b. *Hi well laik shi.*
      3SG.M ADV like 3SG.F
      'He likes her all right (mostly).'

Value 3 (**gender distinctions in third person singular and plural only**) occurs in Kikongo-Kituba, Lingala, Michif, and Sri Lanka Portuguese. In Sri Lanka Portuguese, the distinction is between masculine and feminine referents (as in the Portuguese lexifier), whereas in Kikongo-Kituba, Lingala, and Michif it is between animates and inanimates. In Michif, the gender distinction has been retained from Cree and is restricted to dependent pronouns. In the case of Kikongo-Kituba and Lingala, the gender distinction represents a drastic reduction of the Bantu noun class system.

(9) Lingala (Meeuwis 2013)
   a. *na-món-ákí yé té*
      1SG-see-PST 3SG.ANIM NEG
      'I didn't see her/him.'

   b. *na-món-ákí yangó té*
      1SG-see-PST 3SG.INAN NEG
      'I didn't see it.'

In Lingala (as well as in Kikongo-Kituba), a number distinction exists only for human referents (*yé* vs. *bangó*); *yangó* may have singular or plural referents.

Value 4 (**gender distinctions in the second person, but not in the third person**) is restricted to Cape Verdean Creole of Brava and Cape Verdean Creole of Santiago; note, however, that it is only realized in polite pronouns: *nho* (< Portuguese *senhor* 'Sir') vs. *nha* 'you (f.)' (< Portuguese *senhora* 'Madam'); in the informal pronoun of the second person, *bo*, there is no gender distinction. In the third Cape Verdean variety contained in the *APiCS*, the São Vicente variety, there is no gender distinction in the polite pronoun, which is *bosé* 'you' (as opposed to the informal *bo*).

3. Distribution

Value 1 (no gender distinction) is found all over the world. Value 2 (gender distinctions in the third person singular only) occurs predominantly in English-based languages, but only in roughly one third of these languages. Half of the languages displaying value 2—six languages—are found in North America and the Caribbean; two languages are found in Africa, one in South Asia, two in Southeast Asia, and two in the Pacific.

4. Comparison with *WALS*

Our *APiCS* feature is not directly comparable with *WALS* feature 44 (Siewierska 2005a), because the *WALS* feature is concerned exclusively with independent personal pronouns, whereas in the *APiCS* feature, no distinction is made between independent and dependent personal pronouns.

Two *WALS* values are not represented in the *APiCS*: (1) gender distinctions in third person and in first and/or second person, (2) gender distinctions in third person non-singular only.

The *APiCS* languages display gender distinctions only in third persons, except for the two Cape Verdean varieties mentioned above, where a gender distinction is made in polite second-person pronouns. There is, however, a parallel between the *WALS* and the *APiCS* data: 67 per cent of the *WALS* languages do not display gender distinctions in independent pronouns, which parallels the 76 per cent of the *APiCS* languages whose pronouns, independent or not, do not show gender distinctions; 16 per cent of the *WALS* languages show gender distinctions in third-person singular only, which parallels the 17 per cent of those *APiCS* languages which have this same value.

The absence of gender distinctions in 75 per cent of the *APiCS* languages can certainly be attributed to the general process of morphological reduction in (extreme) contact situations; this process may have been reinforced by the fact that most West African and Southeast Asian substrate languages lack gender distinctions.

13 Gender distinctions in personal pronouns

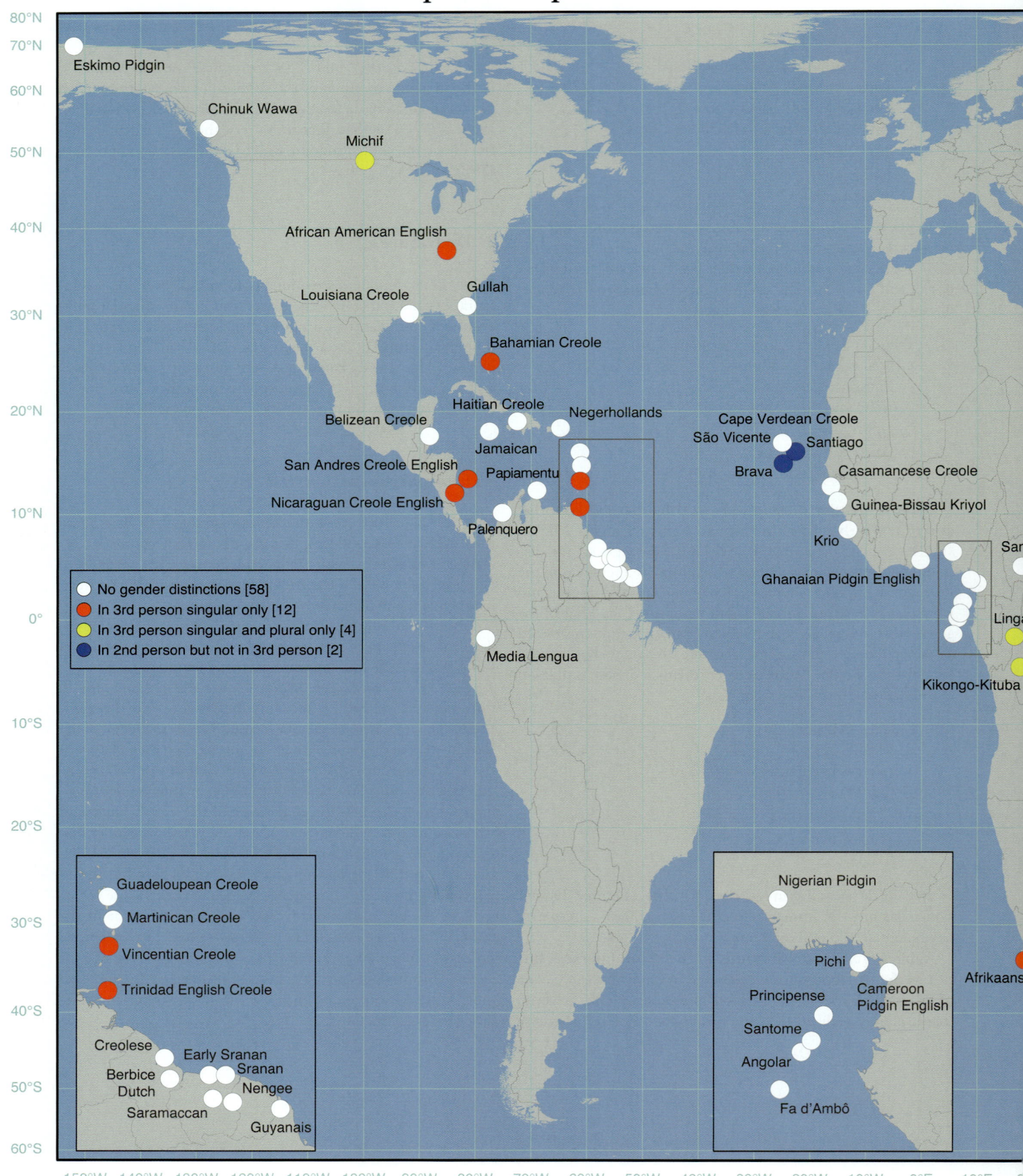

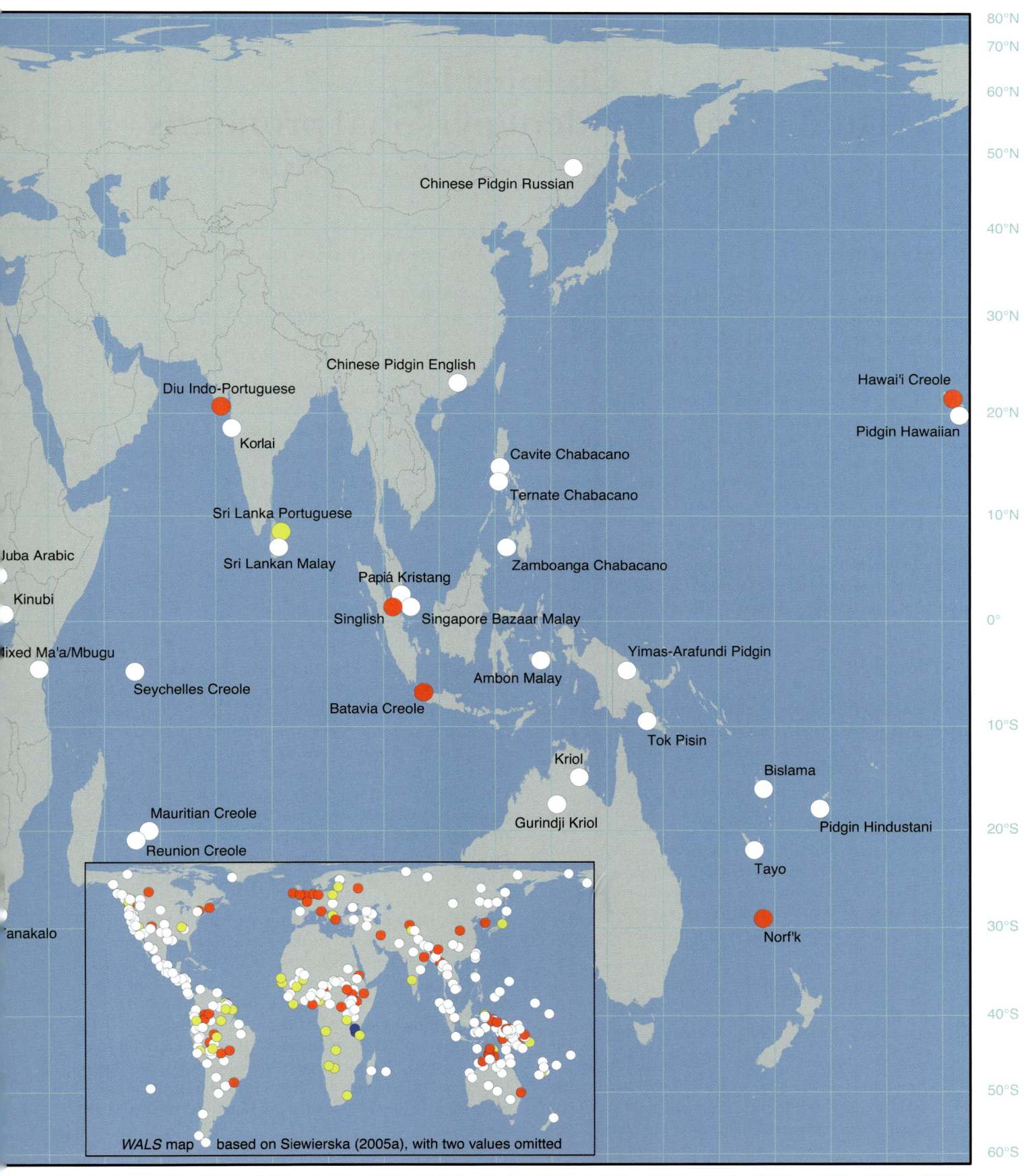

Chapter 14
Dual in independent personal pronouns

MARTIN HASPELMATH AND THE *APiCS* CONSORTIUM

1. Dual number

In the great majority of languages, personal pronouns make a number distinction, at least in some of the persons: for instance, a contrast between singular *I* and plural *we* in English, between singular *toi* and plural *vous* in French, and between singular *siya* 'she, he' and plural *sila* 'they' in Tagalog. This also applies to the great majority of pidgin and creole languages. But far fewer languages make a further distinction between dual number ('two') and plural number ('more than two'). An example is Classical Arabic, which has singular *huwa* 'he', dual *humaa* 'they (two)', and plural *hum* 'they (more than two)'. Such a distinction is made in some pidgin and creole languages, too. In this chapter, we look only at independent personal pronouns—that is, personal pronouns that can occur independently, in an utterance of their own, for example, in an elliptical answer (see also Chapters 13, 17). For dual marking in general, see Corbett (2000), and for duals of person forms, see Cysouw (2003: ch. 7).

2. The values

We distinguish three different values for this feature. The great majority of our languages lack a dual, so they have value 1.

○ 1. No special dual form	66
● 2. Dual form in all three persons	8
● 3. Dual form only in first person	1

In languages with dual forms of personal pronouns, we distinguish further between languages with a dual form in all three persons (value 2), and languages with a dual form only in the first person (value 3). A well-known example of a language with dual forms in all three persons is Tok Pisin (Smith & Siegel 2013a):

(1) | | 1st p. excl | 1st p. incl. | 2nd p. | 3rd p. |
|---|---|---|---|---|
| SG | *mi* | | *yu* | *em* |
| DU | *mitupela* | *yumitupela* | *yutupela* | *tupela* |
| PL | *mipela* | *yumi(pela)* | *yupela* | *ol* |

The one example of a language with a more restricted range of dual forms is Yimas-Arafundi Pidgin, which has *kapa* 'we two', but no dual–plural distinction in the second and third person.

A few examples of the use of duals are given in (2).

(2) a. Bislama (Meyerhoff 2013)
   hem i se "e, yutufala i stanap gud."
   3SG AGR say hey 2DU AGR stand.up good
   'She said "Hey, you guys, stand up straight".'

   b. Kriol (Schultze-Berndt & Angelo 2013)
   Wot kain yunmi gona toktok?
   what kind 1DU.INCL FUT RED.talk
   'What (i.e. which language) are we going to speak?'

   c. Pidgin Hawaiian (Roberts 2013)
   Maua hapai kela pohaku.
   1DU bring DET rock
   'The two of us brought the rock.'

3. Lexifier effects

None of the European lexifier languages has dual personal pronouns, so these cannot be the source of duals in pidgins and creoles with European lexifiers. In Old English, there was a distinction in the first person (*wit* 'we two' vs. *we* 'we (more than two)') and in the second person (*git* 'you two' vs. *ge* 'you (more than two)'), but this distinction disappeared by the end of the Old English period and the dual forms were lost. In Classical Arabic (and Modern Standard Arabic), there is a special dual form (as we saw in the first section above), but this form has been lost in most of the modern vernacular varieties of Arabic. Thus, it is not surprising that no dual is found in the Arabic-based languages.

Thus, the duals in our languages generally do not go back to the lexifiers, but there are three exceptions in the Pacific region. Dual forms are widely found in the Oceanic languages of the Austronesian family and in other languages of the region, particularly in New Guinea and in Australia. The dual form in Yimas-Arafundi Pidgin goes back to Yimas (Foley 1991: 111); one of the dual forms in the mixed language Gurindji Kriol, *ngali* 'we two', goes back to the Australian language Gurindji (Meakins 2013); and the dual forms in Pidgin Hawaiian go back to the duals in the Oceanic language Hawaiian (Polynesian sub-family):

(3) Pidgin Hawaiian (Roberts 2013)
   maua 'we two'
   olua 'you two'
   laua 'they two'

4. Substrate effects

It has long been known that in the English-based languages of Oceania and Australia, the existence of dual forms is due to substrate influence from the Oceanic and Australian languages. In (4), we see the dual forms of Bislama and Kriol; the very similar dual forms of Tok Pisin were given above in (1). (In Gurindji Kriol, *ngali* is used for the first person, but in the second and third persons, forms derived from Kriol are used.)

(4)
	Bislama	Kriol
1DU.EXCL	*mitufala*	*mindubala*
1DU.INCL	*yumitu*	*yunmi, minyu*
2DU	*yutufala*	*yundubala*
3DU	*tufala*	*tubala*

Similarly, in the French-based creole Tayo, the dual forms in (5) are used:

(5) Tayo (Ehrhart & Revis 2013)
   1DU.EXCL *nude*
   2DU *ude*
   3DU *lede*

These patterns are clearly due to the existence of a prominent dual–plural distinction in the Oceanic and Australian languages of the region.

In many of the Oceanic languages, the dual forms of personal pronouns are based on the numeral 'two' combined with the plural pronoun, and it is not surprising that the same method was chosen for creating personal pronoun duals in the pidgins and creoles. In the English-based languages, the dual marker is *tu* (from *two*), while in Tayo, it is *de* (from French *deux*).

This interpretation is corroborated by the fact that some languages are even reported to have trial forms, especially Tok Pisin (*mitripela*, *yutripela*, etc.). These forms also have corresponding trial forms in the Oceanic languages.

5. New duals elsewhere

Dual forms of personal pronouns have been posited for Norf'k, too (Mühlhäusler 2013):

(6) *hamii/himii; mii and hem* 'we (dual)'
   yutuu 'you (dual)'
   demtuu 'they (dual)'

And Yakpo (2009: 184) identifies duals in the West African language Pichi:

(7) Pichi (Yakpo 2013)
   Ùna-ɔ̀l-tú gò go de?
   2PL-all-two POT go there
   'Will the two of you go there?'

Yakpo notes that the use of these dual forms is not obligatory, but very frequent. This raises the question of how to delimit dual forms from phrases consisting of plural pronoun plus numeral.

One sufficient criterion would certainly be obligatoriness. If a form must be used when two referents are intended, then one would regard it as a grammaticalized dual number form, because numerals are never obligatory. But obligatoriness is not a necessary criterion. There are many languages with grammatical plural and dual forms that are not obligatory in semantically plural and dual contexts (see e.g. Chapter 22 for plurals).

Thus, we will say that a pronoun + numeral combination counts as a dual form if the numeral is used much more often than would be expected if the 'two' form were a numeral rather than a dual marker. For example, in Pichi, the use of the dual forms is very frequent, more frequent than the use of the numeral 'two' in other languages, so this was taken as a sufficient criterion for a dual number analysis. In Palenquero, the combinations *suto ndo* 'we two' and *utere ndo* 'you two' are also "fairly common in daily speech", but the author does not regard these combinations as dual forms (Schwegler 2013). They do not differ in their structure and use from combinations like *utere tre* 'the three of you'. For Ternate Chabacano, Steinkrüger (2007: 368) claims that the combination *mordós* (< *motro dós* 'we two') is a dual form, but the *APiCS* contributor on Ternate Chabacano, Eeva Sippola, does not regard this as a fully grammaticalized form. Thus, the distinction between phrases with numerals and dual forms is subtle and not easy to make in a cross-linguistically comparable way. This should be kept in mind when interpreting the data of this chapter.

14 Dual in independent personal pronouns

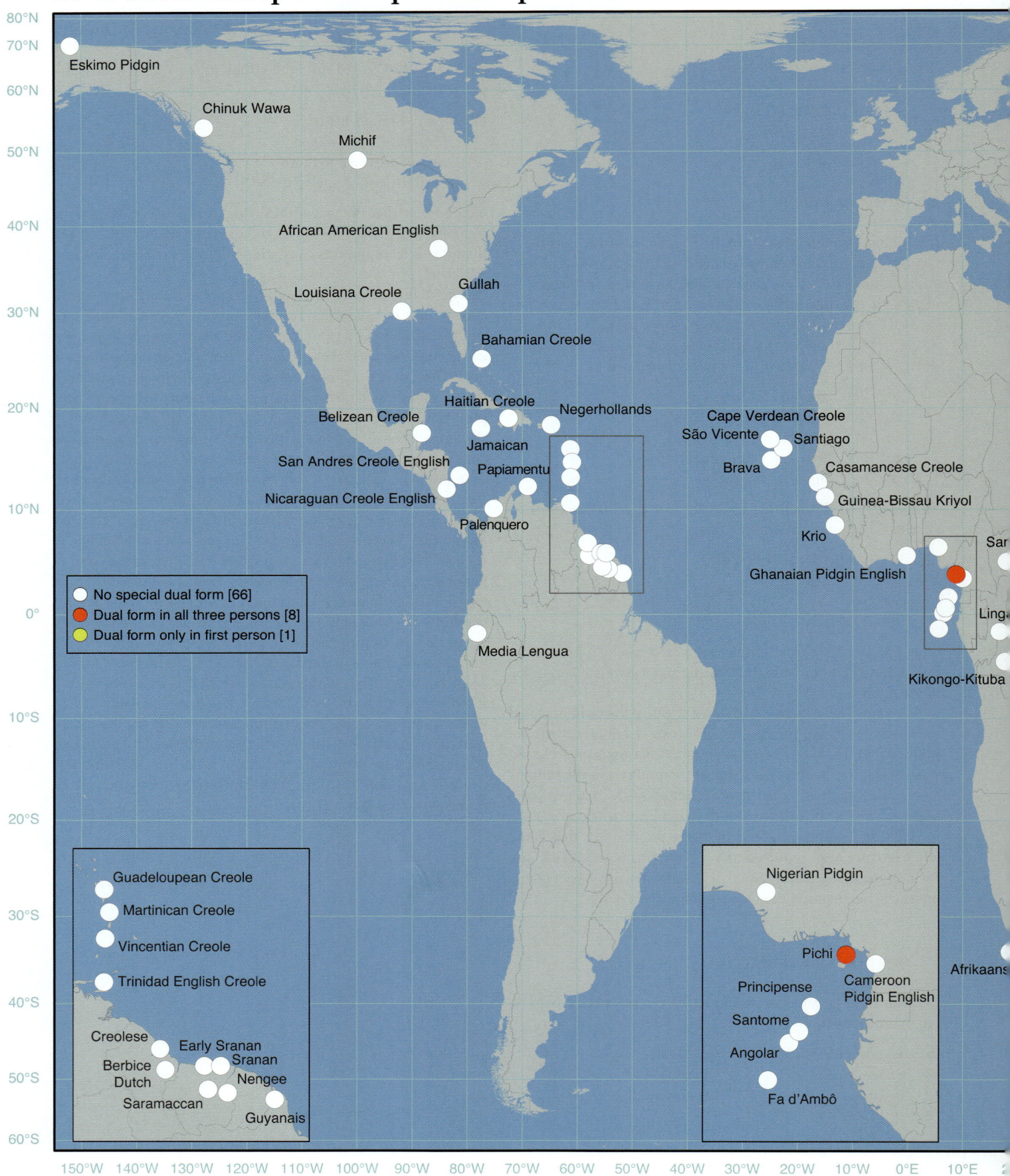

Chapter 15
Inclusive/exclusive distinction in independent personal pronouns

MARTIN HASPELMATH, SUSANNE M. MICHAELIS, AND THE *APiCS* CONSORTIUM

1. Introduction

Quite a few languages throughout the world have a distinction between inclusive and exclusive person forms, rather than a single non-singular person form 'we'. The inclusive form means 'you (singular or plural) and I', that is, it includes the hearer, while the exclusive form means 'he/she/they and I', excluding the hearer. Sometimes both inclusive and exclusive forms are called first-person forms, but the inclusive is perhaps better described as "1+2 person", while the exclusive form is "1+3 person".

As the corresponding *WALS* chapter (Cysouw 2005) shows, inclusive/exclusive distinctions occur only sporadically in Africa and Eurasia, but are common in Austronesian languages and northern Australian languages, as well as in the Americas. Some examples of the distinction in these languages are given in Table 1.

Table 1. Examples of inclusive and exclusive forms

		Inclusive	Exclusive
Austronesian lgs	Indonesian	*kita*	*kami*
	Tagalog	*tayo*	*kami*
	Hawaiian	*kakou*	*makou*
	Tolai	*dat*	*avet*
Australian lgs	Ungarinjin	*ŋarun*	*njarun*
	Bininj Gun-wok	*ngad*	*ngaye*
	Jaminjung	*yurri*	*yirri*

For the worldwide typology of the inclusive/exclusive distinction (also called clusivity), see also Filimonova (ed.) (2005).

2. The two values

We distinguish just two values, absence and presence of the distinction.

3. Inclusive/exclusive differentiation due to substrate

In four of our languages, the presence of the distinction is evidently due to Austronesian influence (see Table 2).

Table 2. Inclusive and exclusive forms

Language	Inclusive form	Exclusive form
Tok Pisin	*yumi*	*mipela*
Bislama	*yumi*	*mifala*
Kriol	*yunmi, minyu*	*minbala, mindubala*
Zamboanga Chabacano	*kita*	*kame*

The great majority of *APiCS* languages make no distinction between inclusive and exclusive forms, which is not surprising in view of the fact that this distinction is not found at all in European languages, and is hardly found in West African, Bantu, and Semitic languages. Thus, in *APiCS* we primarily find it in the Pacific region, where the Austronesian and Australian languages are spoken. We might have expected the distinction also in Sri Lankan Malay or Sri Lanka Portuguese, because Tamil has the distinction, but neither language adopted it from Tamil.

The case of English-based Melanesian pidgins and creoles is quite well known (see e.g. Keesing 1988, Siegel 2008), perhaps because it is so transparent to speakers of English: the exclusive form is *yumi*, which evidently comes from English *you (and) me*. The exclusive form *mipela* (and similar forms in Bislama and Kriol), by contrast, comes from the singular form *mi* 'I' plus the plural-indicating element *pela* (from *fellow*). Since Melanesian pidgins/creoles also have dual and trial forms like *(yu)mitupela* and *(yu)mitripela*, like the Oceanic (Austronesian) languages that were their main substrates, it has long been clear that the pattern must have been created on the basis of the substrates.

In Zamboanga Chabacano, the forms *kita* and *kame* were apparently borrowed from the Philippinic language Hiligaynon. The two other Chabacano varieties do not make the distinction.

Inclusive/exclusive distinction in independent personal pronouns

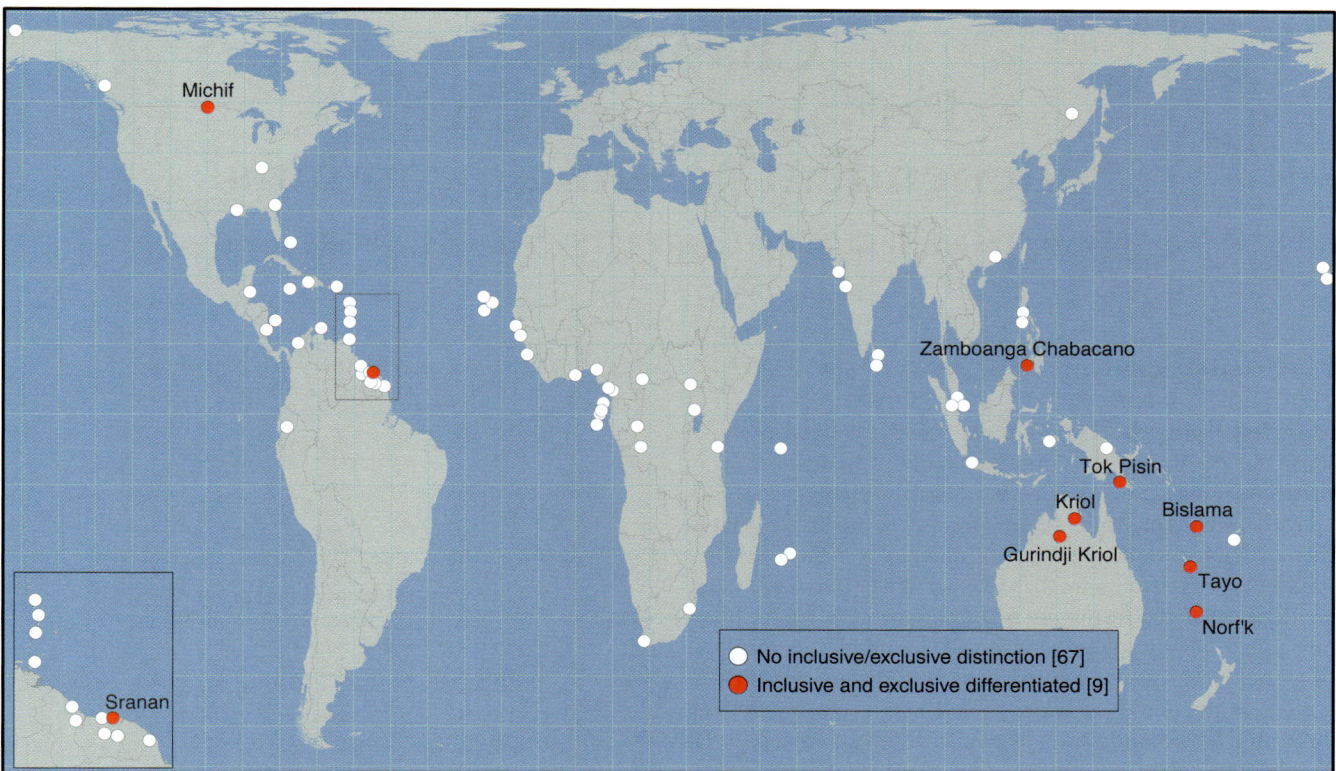

Interestingly, the inclusive/exclusive distinction was lost in the three Malay-based varieties in *APiCS*. While standard Malay has *kita* vs. *kami*, Ambon Malay only has *katong* 'we', Singapore Bazaar Malay only has *kita*(*-orang*) 'we' (with the plural-indicating *-orang*), and Sri Lankan Malay has *kitang* or *kitam-pəðə* 'we' (with the plural-indicating *-pəðə*). The distinction was also given up in Pidgin Hawaiian, where *kakou* and *makou* (Table 1) still exist but are not distinguished, and in Pidgin Fijian (Siegel 2008: 14).

In the two mixed languages Michif and Gurindji Kriol, the distinction is retained from the non-European contributing languages Cree and Gurindji, respectively (see Table 3).

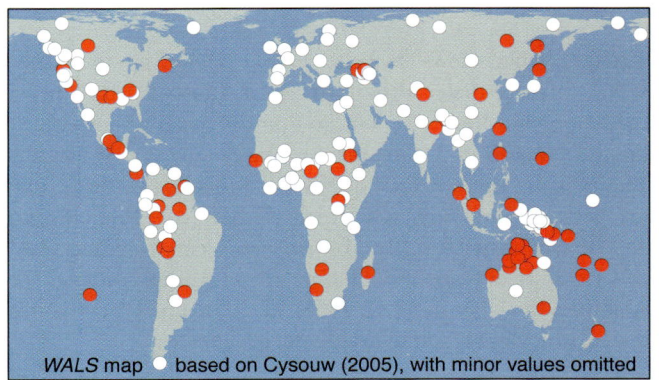

Table 3. **Inclusive and exclusive forms**

Language	Inclusive form	Exclusive form
Michif	*kiyanaan*	*niiyanaan*
Gurindji Kriol	*ngaliwa*	*ngantipa*

In Michif, the distinction is sometimes even made with affixal person forms, following Cree.

4. Newly introduced distinctions

In three *APiCS* languages, there is an inclusive/exclusive distinction that is not (or not clearly) derived from a substrate language or a lexifier. Sranan has the general form *wi* (which can mean 'we including you' or 'we excluding you'), but also the form *unu*, which can mean 'we excluding you', but also 'you (plural)' (see also Chapter 16). For Norf'k, Mühlhäusler (2013) reports a distinction between *himii* and *hamii* (dual inclusive, corresponding to the Melanesian form *yumi*) and the forms *miienhem*, *miienher* (dual exclusive, evidently from *me and him*, *me and her*). And Tayo has the forms *nuⁿde ave twa* [we.two with you] 'we (dual) inclusive' and *nuⁿde sa twa* [we.two without you] 'we (dual) exclusive' (Ehrhart & Revis 2013). Neither the Norf'k nor the Tayo cases may have sufficiently grammaticalized to be regarded as exhibiting this distinction.

Chapter 16
Person syncretism in independent personal pronouns
MARTIN HASPELMATH AND THE *APiCS* CONSORTIUM

1. Person syncretism

Most languages have distinct independent personal-pronoun forms for the three persons in both singular and plural, as in French (singular) *moi, toi, lui/elle*, (plural) *nous, vous, eux/elles*.

But in some languages, there is **person syncretism**, that is, there is a form in the paradigm of independent personal pronouns that serves for more than one person. (Alternatively, one could say that the forms for two different persons are homonymous.) This is cross-linguistically unusual and therefore of particular interest. An example of first–second-person syncretism in the plural is Haitian Creole *nou* 'we, you (PL)', and an example of second–third-person syncretism in the plural is Seychelles Creole *zot* 'you (PL), they'. In *APiCS*, person syncretism occurs only in the plural, in line with the well-known generalization that the singular tends to make more grammatical distinctions than the plural (Greenberg 1966: 27, Croft 2003: 95–6).

Some languages have other forms of syncretism as well, such as number syncretism (lack of singular–plural distinction, as in Standard English *you*) or gender syncretism (lack of masculine–feminine–neuter distinction, as in English *they*, contrasting with the distinction between *he*, *she*, and *it* in the singular). In this chapter, only person syncretism is considered.

This chapter distinguishes three types of language (with only a single choice being possible): no person syncretism, syncretism between first and second person, and syncretism between second and third person.

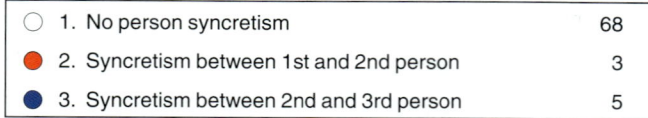

○	1. No person syncretism	68
●	2. Syncretism between 1st and 2nd person	3
●	3. Syncretism between 2nd and 3rd person	5

2. No person syncretism

The great majority of the *APiCS* languages have no person syncretism (value 1). Some examples of typical paradigms of personal pronouns are given in Tables 1–2.

Table 1. Independent personal pronouns in Afrikaans (van Sluijs 2013)

	SINGULAR	PLURAL
1	*ek*	*ons*
2	*jy*	*julle*
3	*hy, sy, dit*	*hulle*

Table 2. Independent personal pronouns in Cavite Chabacano (Sippola 2013a)

	SINGULAR	PLURAL
1	*yo*	*nisos*
2	*vo, tu, uste*	*vusos, ustedes*
3	*ele*	*ilos*

3. First- and second-person-plural syncretism

Three languages in the Caribbean region have syncretism between first and second person (value 2). Their personal pronoun paradigms are given in Tables 3–5.

Table 3. Independent personal pronouns in Haitian Creole (Fattier 2013)

	SINGULAR	PLURAL
1	*mwen*	*nou*
2	*ou*	*nou*
3	*li*	*yo*

Haitian Creole shows some variation: according to Fattier (1996), in some dialects the form *zot* is attested, which has a second-person-plural use, but no first-person use (however, it can also be used in a third-person sense, so that it shows another type of syncretism, as discussed in the next section). The first-person-plural form *nou* clearly derives from French *nous*, but the second-person-plural form *nou* seems to come from an African form (Igbo *únù*, Temne *nu*, or Adioukrou *uno*; see Goodman 1964: 41, Boretzky 1983: 35, 109). The syncretism is thus historically a result of accidental homonymy.

The form *unu/un/u* for the second person plural is found in many English-based creoles, too, but in two languages, Sranan and Nengee (both spoken in Suriname), it can also be used in a first-person-plural sense:

Table 4. Independent personal pronouns in Sranan (Plag & Winford 2013)

	SINGULAR	PLURAL
1	*mi*	*unu, wi*
2	*ju, i*	*unu*
3	*a, en*	*den*

Table 5. Independent personal pronouns in Nengee (Migge 2013)

	SINGULAR	PLURAL
1	*mi, m*	*u, wi*
2	*yu, i*	*u*
3	*a, en*	*de(n)*

We see that Sranan and Nengee have the alternative (and older) form *wi* for the first person plural. In fact, in Early Sranan, *unu* is not attested with first-person-plural use, so the use of *u(nu)* for the first-person plural seems to be secondary. The extension of *u(nu)* to the first person may be related to the fact that some West African languages have similar or identical forms for first and second person plural (e.g. Fongbe *mí* 1PL, *mì* 2PL, Goodman 1964: 41). Lefebvre (1998: 142), too, attributes the syncretism between first and second person plural in Haitian Creole to the influence from the Fongbe pattern; if this were correct, we would not need to assume Igbo influence in Haitian, and the similarity between Haitian *nou* (2PL) and Sranan *unu* (2PL) would be accidental.

4. Second- and third-person-plural syncretism

The three French-based creoles of the Indian Ocean, the African contact language Sango, and Ambon Malay have syncretism between second and third person (value 3). Table 6 shows the paradigm of Sango.

In Sango, originally *e* was the first-person-plural form, and *i* was the second-person-plural form (Diki-Kidiri 1977: 64–5). These tended to be confused for phonological reasons, and *ala* was extended from the third-person-plural form to express the second person plural as well. In Ambon Malay, the form is *dorang* (or the shortened version *dong*), derived from *dia* '(s)he' plus *orang* 'person', that is, the third-person-plural use is primary.

In the French-based creoles of the Indian Ocean, the extension seems to have gone in the other direction. Table 7 shows the paradigm of Mauritian Creole. The form *zot* derives from regional French *vous autres* 'you (PL)' (cf. Spanish *vosotros*).

Table 6. Independent personal pronouns in Sango (Samarin 2013)

	SINGULAR	PLURAL
1	*mbi*	*e, i*
2	*mo*	*ala*
3	*lo*	*ala*

Table 7. Independent personal pronouns in Mauritian Creole (Baker & Kriegel 2013)

	SINGULAR	PLURAL
1	*mwa*	*nu*
2	*twa, u*	*zot*
3	*li*	*zot*

In Seychelles Creole, the plural paradigm is the same (*nou*, *zot*, *zot*). Reunion Creole has an alternative form *bannla* (made up of *bann* 'group, PL' and *la* 'definite') for the third-person-plural pronoun, perhaps introduced in order to differentiate the third from the second person.

It is possible that the third-person-plural form *zot* derives from a third-person form in French (*eux autres*, or *les autres*), but such forms are not common in French in a pronominal sense, unlike *vous autres*. Moreover, French creoles of the Caribbean tend to have *zot* for the second person plural (cf. the Guadeloupean plural paradigm: *nou*, *zòt*, *yo*), and the extension to the third person is a development that is typical of the Indian Ocean varieties. For some reason, the original third-person-plural form *eux* (cf. Haitian and Guadeloupean *yo*) is not found in the French-based creoles of the Indian Ocean.

5. Macrofunctionality or homonymy

There are two ways of describing cases like Haitian Creole *nou* 'we; you (PL)' synchronically: as a single (macrofunctional) form with two renderings into English, or as two (homonymous) forms that happen to have the same shape. The term *syncretism* is used here, in preference to *homonymy*, because it makes no assumption about the correct description. It is quite possible that the syncretism is synchronically accidental (e.g. because Haitian Creole borrowed an African form and ended up with a second-person-plural form *nou* that happened to be identical to the descendant of French *nous*). But it is also possible, and in fact likely, that the syncretism is not accidental even synchronically. As Cysouw (2003: 123–34) notes, both first–second-person syncretism and second–third-person syncretism occur elsewhere in the world's languages. Such cases are not frequent, but not extremely rare either. It may well be best to characterize forms like *nou* as "non-third-person forms", and forms like *zot* as "non-first-person forms".

16 Person syncretism in independent personal pronouns

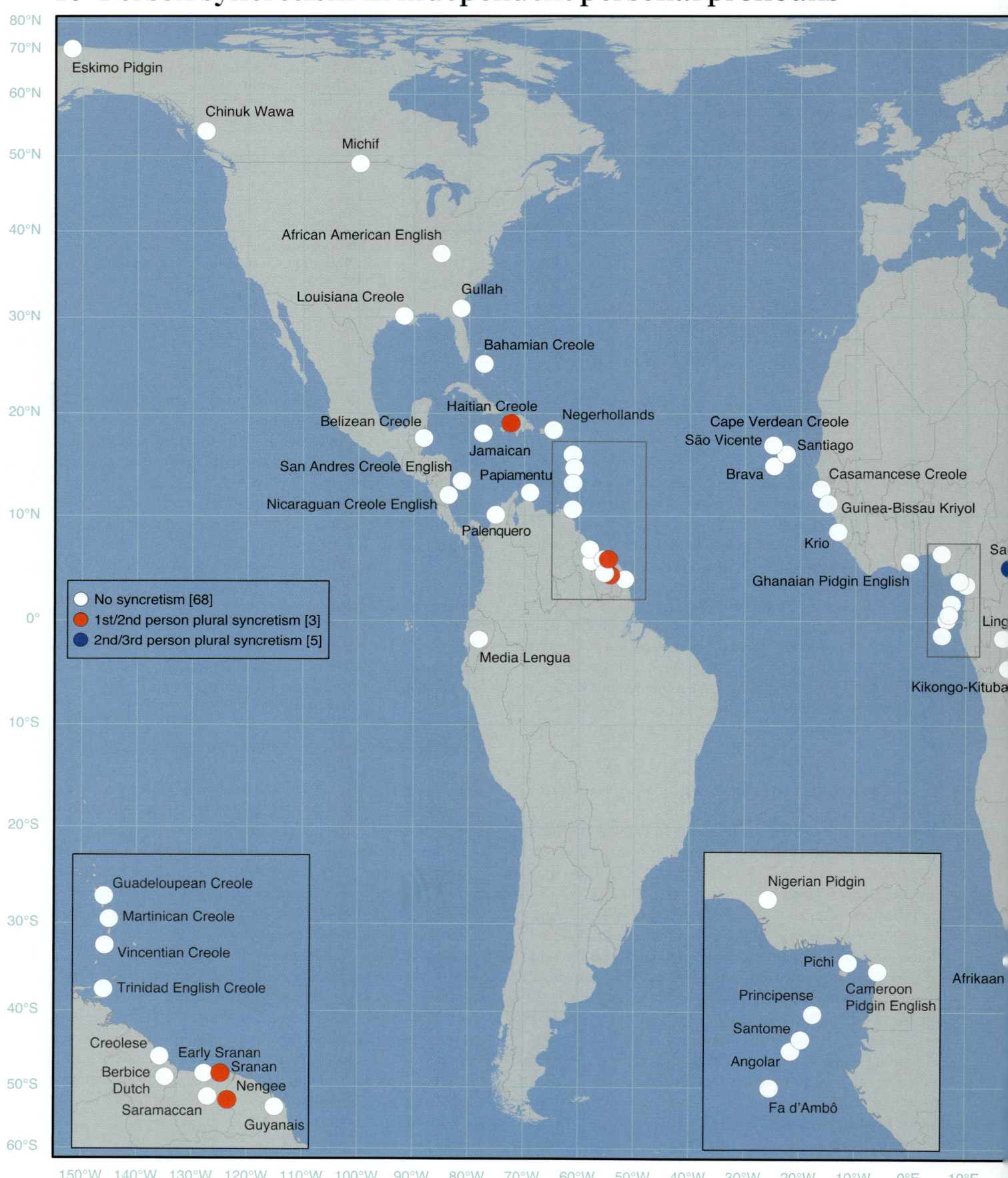

Chapter 17
Special dependent person forms for subject and object

MARTIN HASPELMATH AND THE *APiCS* CONSORTIUM

1. Independent personal pronouns and dependent person forms

All (or virtually all) languages have **independent personal pronouns,** that is, personal pronouns ('I', 'you', 'he/she', 'we', 'you (PL)', 'they', etc.) that can occur on their own, or at least not combined intimately with a verb. Some typical contexts where such independent personal pronouns occur are given in (1)–(4).

(1) elliptical answers
*Did you call me? No, **him**.*

(2) coordination
***you** and your sister*

(3) contrastive focusing
*It's **me** that they invited./They invited **me**.*

(4) additive focusing
***They**, too, will soon understand.*

In all these contexts, the personal pronouns are singled out in some way. We find separate words that are independent pronouns (or "free pronouns", "strong pronouns") in this sense in all the *APiCS* languages.

In addition, some languages also have **dependent person forms,** which always occur together with a verb (or sometimes another host). They cannot occur on their own as in (1), in coordination, as in (2), or in focusing constructions, as in (3) and (4). Their position with respect to their host is quite rigid, and they are often described as bound elements (clitics or affixes). Thus, the person markers in a language like Portuguese (*cant-o* 'I sing', *canta-s* 'you sing', *canta-mos* 'we sing', etc.) are also dependent person forms in this sense. Whether they can co-occur with a coreferential full NP or an independent pronoun is irrelevant here, though in most of the *APiCS* languages, this is not possible (in this regard, they differ from Portuguese). Dependent person forms on verbs are also called **verbal person markers** (Siewierska 2005c), or as **argument indexes** (Lazard 1998, Haspelmath 2013a+). In this chapter, we are concerned both with dependent subject forms (as in 5a, b) and dependent object forms (6a, b).

(5) a. Guadeloupean Creole (Colot & Ludwig 2013a)
An ka pati. (independent: *mwen*)
1SG prog leave
'I am leaving.'

b. Lingala (Meeuwis 2013)
a-táng-ákí (independent: *yé*)
3SG-study-PST
'he studied'

(6) a. Bahamian Creole (Hackert 2013)
*If I don't do **um**, he gwine kill me.* (indep.: *it*)
if I NEG do 3SG.N.OBJ he FUT kill me
'If I don't do it, he'll kill me.'

b. Santome (Hagemeijer 2013)
*men mu ka manda **mu** lekadu* (indep.: *ami*)
mother 1SG.POSS IPFV send me message
'My mother sends me a message.'

This chapter distinguishes four feature values, with just a single choice being possible.

○	1. No dependent person forms	29
●	2. Only dependent subject forms	19
●	3. Only dependent object forms	1
●	4. Dependent subject and object forms	26

2. Languages lacking dependent person forms

Many *APiCS* languages lack dependent person forms and use the same (independent) pronouns in contexts such as (1) to (4) and in contexts like (5) and (6). Some examples are given in (7) and (8), where the first example shows the "independent use" of the pronoun, while the second example shows its "dependent use".

(7) Tok Pisin (Smith & Siegel 2013)
a. *Husat i stap? **Mi**.*
who PM stay 1SG
'Who's there? Me.'

b. *Planti taim **mi** bin stap long ples.*
many time 1SG PST stay at village
'I often stayed in the village.'

(8) Diu Indo-Portuguese (Cardoso 2013)
   a. Kẽ sab   istɔr? Yo.
      who know.NPST story   1SG
      'Who knows a story? Me.'
   b. Yo   kɛr   fal-a.
      1SG want.NPST   speak-INF
      'I want to speak.'

This lack of special dependent person forms is particularly characteristic of pidgins (Chinese Pidgin English, Chinese Pidgin Russian, Eskimo Pidgin, Fanakalo, Pidgin Hawaiian, Pidgin Hindustani, Yimas-Arafundi Pidgin), which never preserve the dependent person forms of the lexifier language. But there are also quite a few creoles which lack special dependent person forms. Typically, both in pidginization and in creolization, the dependent person forms (such as the Portuguese endings -o, -s, -mos, etc., or the French clitics *je*, *tu*, *il*, *le*, *les*, etc.) are not preserved from the lexifier language, resulting in languages of the first type.

3. Languages with only dependent subject forms

If a language has any dependent person forms, it is very likely that these are subject forms. This is a very general trend (Siewierska 2005c: 414), and it is also true of the *APiCS* set, where 16 languages have dependent subject forms but no special dependent object forms. However, normally there is not a full set of dependent subject forms. Most of the languages have special forms only for part of the paradigm, especially for the third-person forms, and/or for the first and second person singular. Two exemplary paradigms are shown in Tables 1 and 2.

Table 1. **Jamaican (Farquharson 2013)**

	Dependent (subject)	Independent/object
1SG	*mi*	*mi*
2SG	*yu*	*yu*
3SG	*ihn* [ĩ]	*im*
1PL	*wi*	*wi*
2PL	*unu*	*unu*
3PL	*dehn* [dẽ]	*dem*

Table 2. **Palenquero (Schwegler 2013)**

	Dependent (subject)	Independent/object
1SG	*i*	*yo*
2SG	*(b)o*	*bo*
3SG	*e*	*ele*
1PL	*(s)uto*	*(s)uto*
2PL	*utere*	*utere*
3PL	*ané*	*ané*

Usually, the dependent forms are originally reduced forms of the independent forms, which explains why they are especially frequent for subject forms and for singular forms (these are the most frequent contexts, and reduction is conditioned by frequency).

Lingala, which has preserved the Bantu person subject prefixes, is exceptional in that it has a full paradigm (dependent subject forms *na-*, *o-*, *a*/*e-*; *to-*, *bo-*, *ba*/*e-*; contrasting with independent/object pronouns *ngáí*, *yó*, *yé*/*yangó*; *bísó*, *bínó*, *bangó*/*yangó*).

4. Languages with only dependent object forms

There is only one language which has special dependent object forms, but no special dependent subject forms, Bahamian Creole (see Table 3, where the three special dependent object forms are in boldface).

Table 3. **Bahamian Creole (Hackert 2013)**

	Dependent object	Independent/subject
1SG	*me*, **ma**	*I*, *me*
2SG	*you*	*you*
3SG	*'e*, **um**, *him*, *her*, *it*	*'e*, *he*, *she*, *it*
1PL	*we*, *us*	*we*
2PL	*you*, *yinna*, *you-all*	*you*, *yinna*, *you-all*
3PL	*they*, *them*, **um**	*they*, *them*

5. Languages with both dependent subject forms and dependent object forms

Quite a few languages have both dependent subject forms and dependent object forms. An example is Guinea-Bissau Kriyol (Table 4). Here it is clear that the independent pronouns were recreated with an initial element *a-* that is absent in the independent pronouns of its lexifier Portuguese.

Table 4. **Guinea-Bissau Kriyol (Intumbo et al. 2013)**

	Independent	Dependent subject	Dependent object
1SG	*ami*	*ŋ*	*ŋ*
2SG	*abo*	*bu*	*u*
3SG	*el*	*i*	*l*
1PL	*anos*	*no*	*nu*
2PL	*abos*	*bo*	*bos*
3PL	*elis*	*e*	*elis*

In other languages, the difference is less drastic. For example, in Pichi, the dependent forms (subject forms *à*, *yù*, *è*; *wì*, *ùna*/*ùnu*, *dɛ̀n*) differ mostly by their low tone from the independent pronouns (*mi*, *yu*, *in*; *wi*, *ùna*/*ùnu*, *dɛn*). The latter are also used as object forms, except that for the third person singular there is an alternative low-tone form *àn*. In Haitian Creole, the independent forms always have a full syllable (*mwen*, *wou*, *li*; *nou*, *nou*, *yo*), while the dependent forms are reduced to a single consonant when they are adjacent to a vowel (*m*, *w*, *l*; *n*, *n*, *y*).

17 Special dependent person forms for subject and object

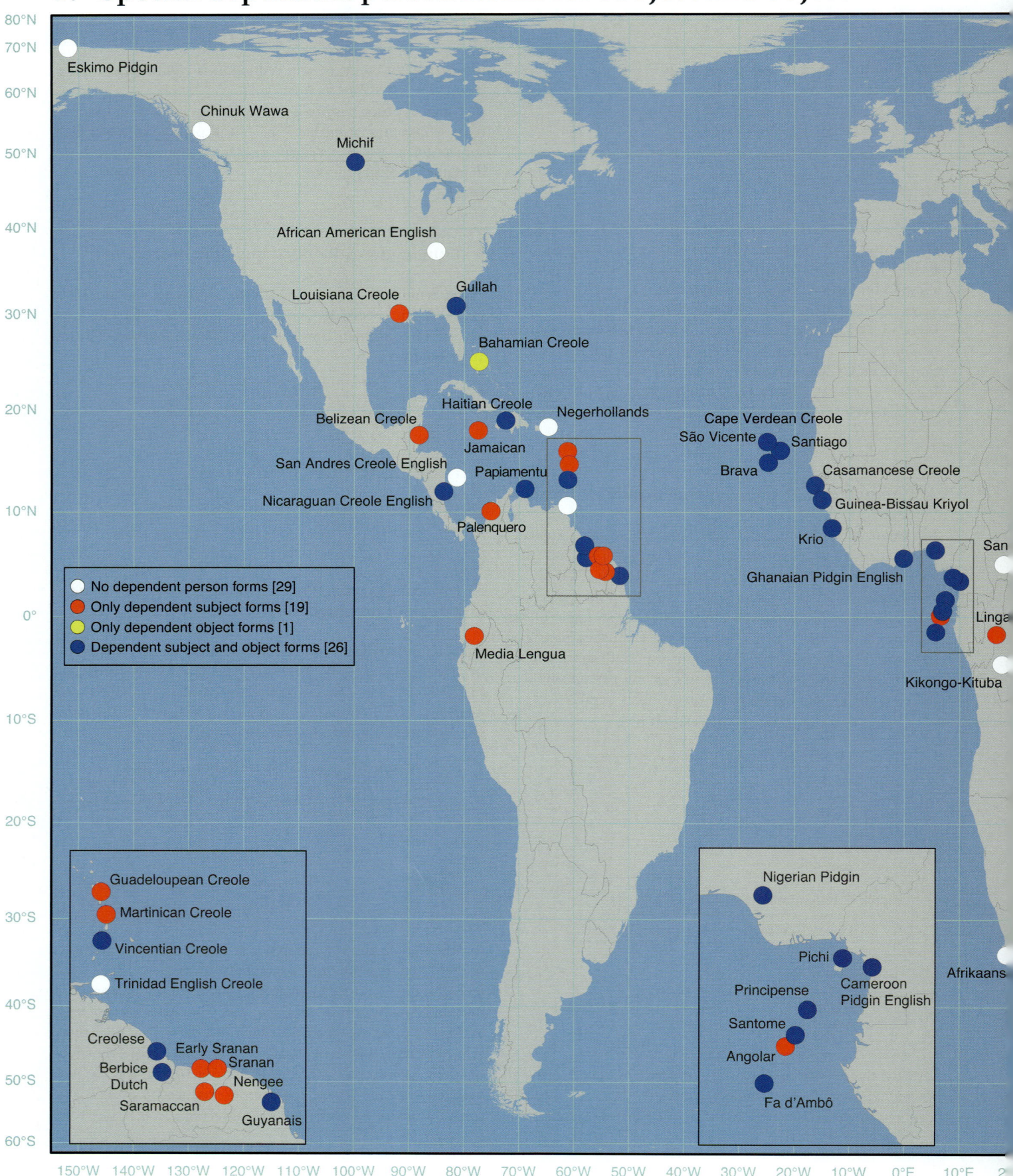

Chapter 18
Politeness distinctions in second-person pronouns

MARTIN HASPELMATH AND THE *APiCS* CONSORTIUM

1. Politeness in pronouns

In many languages, politeness is expressed not only in title nouns (*sir*, *master*, etc.), but also in second-person pronouns. In the best-known system, exemplified by French *tu* vs. *vous*, Spanish *tu* vs. *usted*, German *du* vs. *Sie*, and Russian *ty* vs. *vy*, one form is used for addressing children and intimates (family and friends), while the other form is used for polite address of other adults. But politeness forms can be used for other distinctions as well (special forms for royalty, or special forms for impolite address), and various terms have been used for distinctions of this kind (familiar–polite, informal–formal, plain–honorific, etc.). In this chapter, which is modelled on Helmbrecht's (2005) chapter in *WALS*, we ask whether a language has a politeness distinction in pronouns, and if so, whether it is a binary politeness distinction or whether more than two types are distinguished. The exact type of politeness is not important, and it is often poorly investigated for our languages. In addition, we single out languages where title nouns ('sir', 'uncle') or names can be used as second-person forms.

○	1. No pronominal politeness distinction	46
●	2. Binary pronominal politeness distinction	17
●	3. Multiple pronominal politeness distinction	3
●	4. Titles used as second-person forms	8

2. No pronominal politeness distinction

The majority of the *APiCS* languages make no politeness distinction in second-person pronouns. The English-based pidgins and creoles generally use the counterpart of *you* regardless of politeness, like Standard English. Similarly, pidgins do not normally make a politeness distinction (though Chinese Pidgin Russian and Singapore Bazaar Malay inherited their politeness distinctions from Russian and Malay, respectively). This is also the pattern of most of the languages based on non-European lexifiers, as pronominal politeness distinctions are not so common outside Eurasia.

In creoles based on French, Portuguese, and Spanish, the *tu* forms have typically disappeared, and the older *vous/vos* forms of the second person plural are used for second-person-singular reference, often regardless of politeness (the latter development is also found in some non-creole varieties). Examples are Guadeloupean Creole (*ou* < *vous*), Reunion Creole (*ou*), Tayo (*u*), Casamancese Creole (*bu* < *vós*), Papiá Kristang (*bos*), and Palenquero (*bo*).

3. Binary pronominal politeness distinction

Seventeen languages make a binary politeness distinction. In some of the French-based creoles, the French *tu*–*vous* distinction has been preserved in some form: Mauritian Creole (*to*–*ou*), Louisiana Creole (*twa*–*vou*), and Guyanais (*to*–*ou*). However, in Guyanais this distinction is disappearing in the younger generation.

In several of the Spanish-based and Portuguese-based languages, the politeness distinction is between a form that goes back to *vos/vós* and a form based on the polite pronoun *usted/você*. Examples are Ternate Chabacano (*bo*–*tédi*), Korlai (*wɔ–use*), Cape Verdean Creole of São Vicente (*bo*–*bosê*), and the Imbabura variety of Media Lengua (*bos*–*usti*; note that the map reflects the variety of Salcedo in Central Ecuador).

English-based languages often have new second-person-plural forms distinct from the second-person-singular form that derives from *you*. In some languages, such an innovated plural pronoun is used for polite second-person-singular reference:

(1) Nengee (Migge 2013; the 2SG form *i* is not possible here)
Gaanman, u mu yeepi den sama ya.
chief   2PL must help DET.PL person DEM
'Chief, you should help these people.' (*u* not from *you*)

(2) Bislama (Meyerhoff 2013)
be i gud yufala i talem olsem
but AGR good 2PL   AGR tell like
'But it's good you (SG) tell (me) this.'

In Bahamian Creole, there is a politeness distinction as well, but it is of a quite different nature. While in Nengee and Bislama a polite form was innovated (on the basis of the plural form), in Bahamian the innovated second-person-plural forms *yinna* and *you-all* (the latter illustrated in (3)) can NOT be used for polite address and are restricted to familiar contexts (probably because of their very basilectal nature). The form *you* can be used both in polite and in familiar contexts (cf. the first word of (3), where *you* is used in the same way as *you-all*). Note that Bahamian Creole is the only language where the politeness distinction is only made in the plural.

(3) Bahamian Creole (Hackert 2013)
You see what I tell you-all, I tell you-all something was go happen through here.
'You see what I told you! I told you something was going to happen here.'

A new politeness distinction in pronouns has also been created in the Portuguese-based creoles of the Cape Verdean Islands and the adjacent mainland. In these languages, the familiar form is *bo* or *bu* (from *vós*), and the polite form is *nhu* (masculine) and *nha* (feminine), deriving from *senhor/senhora*.

(4) Cape Verdean Creole of Santiago (Lang 2013)
Abo   bu ta fika, anho   nhu   pode bai.
2SG.INDP 2SG IPFV stay 2SG.POL.INDP 2SG.POL can go
'YOU (SG familiar) stay, (but) YOU (SG polite) can go.'

This is found in Cape Verdean Creole of Brava, too, and in Guinea-Bissau Kriyol, but apparently not in Casamancese Creole and in Cape Verdean Creole of São Vicente. A similar development has happened in the Gulf of Guinea creoles Santome and Principense, where the forms *sun* and *san* are used as polite pronouns, but these forms have not lost their non-pronominal uses yet and are therefore treated as titles (see §5).

In one Portuguese-based creole, Sri Lanka Portuguese, the second-person-plural form *botus* (< *vós outros* [you.PL others]) is used as a polite pronoun. But this language uses titles as pronouns as well, so it is assigned to type 4.

Sango is the only language with a non-European and non-Malay lexifier that has a politeness distinction: the familiar second-person-singular *mo* contrasts with the polite form *ala*, originally the second person plural. This form can be used for the third person plural as well, and in polite reference to a third person singular.

4. Multiple politeness distinction

Four languages have a ternary politeness distinction. In Cavite Chabacano and Zamboanga Chabacano, the Spanish form *tu* has survived, and there is a distinction between (*e*)*bo*(*s*) (intimate), *tu* (neutral, familiar), and *usted* (formal, polite).

In Korlai, there is a three-way distinction between *wɔ* (< *vós*, informal), *use* (< *você*, formal), and *udzo* (originally second-person plural, very formal).

Finally, Ambon Malay has a ternary politeness distinction between the neutral form *se*, the impolite form *os*(*e*), and the intimate form *al*(*e*). This language uses titles for polite address, and thus is assigned to type 4, but in addition it makes politeness distinctions in pronouns as well.

5. Use of titles as second-person forms

In some languages, polite second-person reference does not happen through pronouns, but through titles which are used as second-person forms, as in 'I admire Her Majesty'. The distinction between pronouns and titles is not always immediately apparent, because titles can become pronouns (as in the well-known example of Spanish *usted*, which derived from the title *Vuestra Merced* 'Your Grace'). We define a second-person pronoun as a form that cannot be used with third-person reference. Thus, the form *Sun* 'sir, you' in Principense is regarded as a title, even though it is used in a pronoun-like way, as in example (5).

(5) Principense (Maurer 2013c)
*Kasô **Sun** mêê **Sun** maxi dêkê mosa **Sun**.*
dog sir love sir more than girl sir
'Your dog loves you more than your wife does.'
(lit. 'Sir's dog loves sir more than sir's wife.')

The pronoun-like trait of *Sun* in (5) is that it recurs three times, instead of being replaced by a third-person pronoun in the second and third occurrence. But *Sun* can also be used as an ordinary noun with the meaning 'sir'.

One might be tempted to regard this recurrence of a title as a sufficient criterion for pronounhood, but there are languages where an open class of items can be used in this way. In Principense, for example, other nouns such as *arê* 'king', as well as proper names (e.g. *Pedu* 'Peter'), can be used in this way. Other examples come from Papiamentu and Afrikaans:

(6) Papiamentu (Kouwenberg 2013b)
Roberto tin Roberto su   buki?
Roberto have Roberto POSS book
'Do you have your book?' (lit. 'Does Roberto have Roberto's book?')

(7) Afrikaans (den Besten & Biberauer 2013)
Oom moet Oom gedra.
uncle must uncle behave
'You must behave yourself, uncle.'

As these examples show, kinship terms and proper names may behave like titles. If a language allows this use of titles, it is included in the fourth type, regardless of the distinctions among pronouns that it makes.

18 Politeness distinctions in second-person pronouns

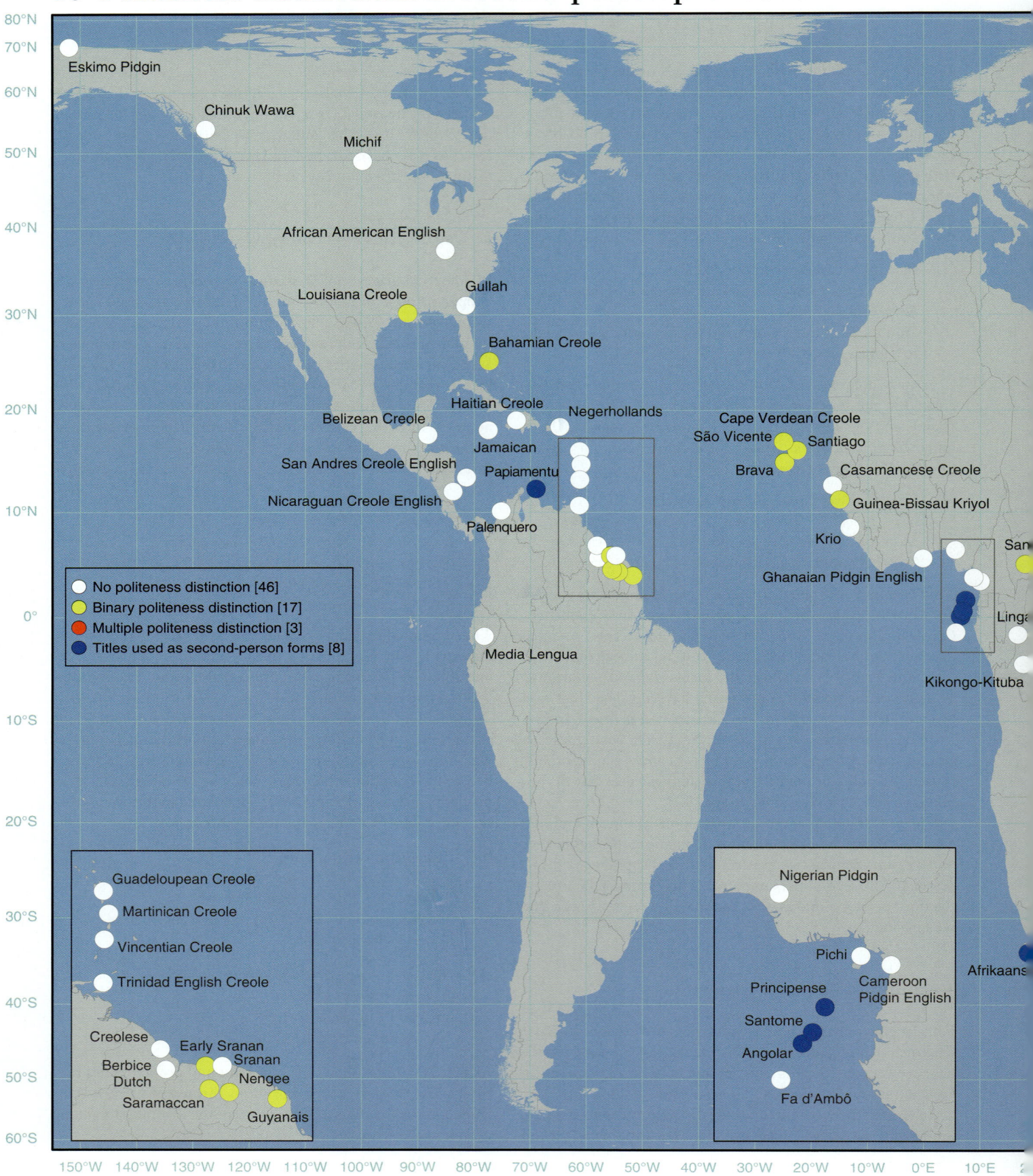

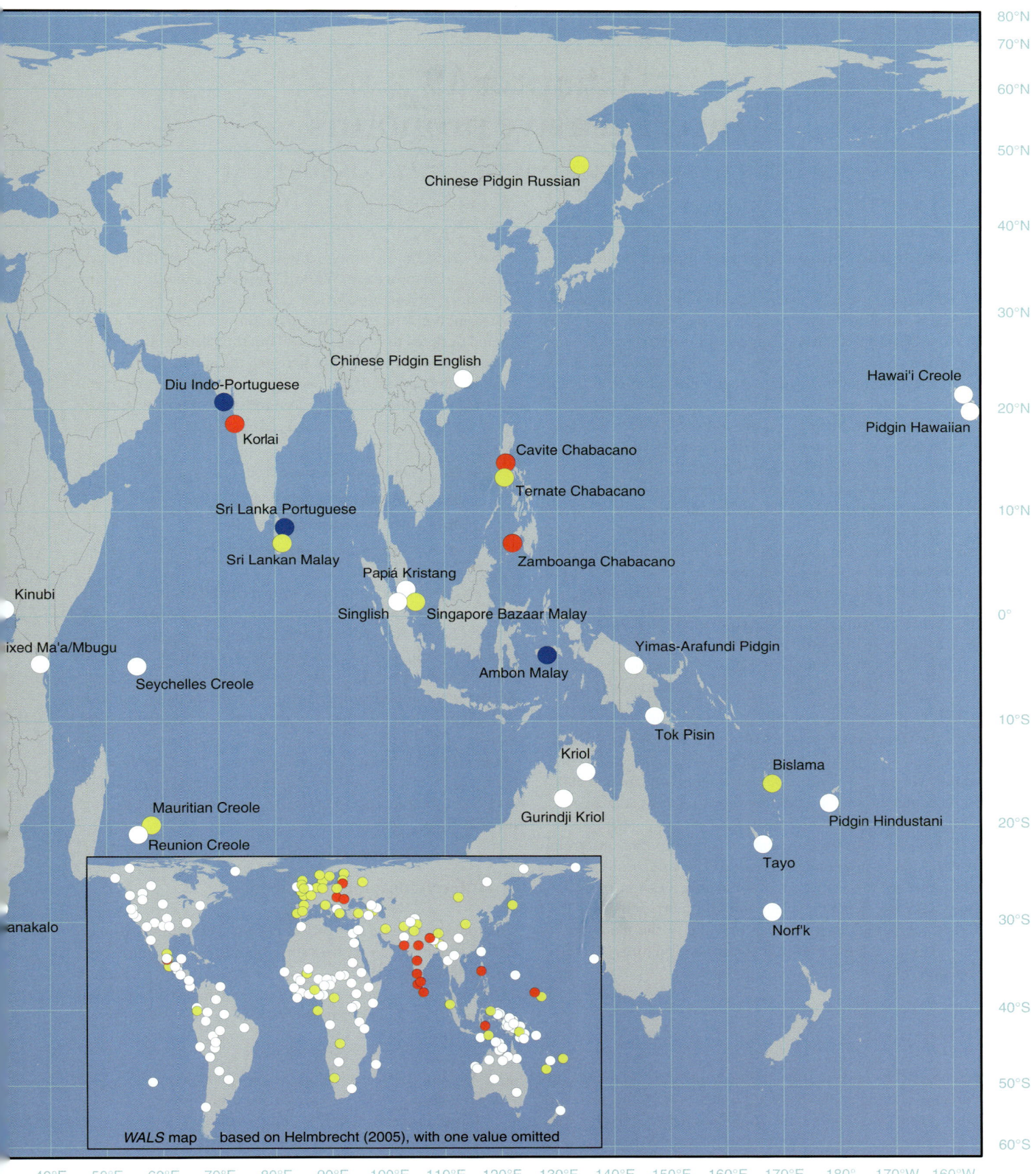

Chapter 19
Interrogative pronouns

MARTIN HASPELMATH AND THE *APiCS* CONSORTIUM

1. Simple and compound interrogative pronouns

All languages have interrogative pronouns for asking content questions, such as 'who', 'what', 'where', 'when', and 'how' (Idiatov 2007). In addition, languages normally have adnominal interrogative words such as 'which', which allow speakers to form complex interrogative noun phrases such as 'which house' or 'which girl'.

In this chapter, we focus on the contrast between two kinds of interrogative pronouns: **simple interrogative pronouns** (monomorphemic words such as English *who*, *how* and Spanish *quién*, *dónde*) and **compound interrogative pronouns**, which are composed of an adnominal interrogative word and a **generic noun** for one of the ontological categories (person, thing, place, time, manner). Such compound interrogatives are found, for example, in Guadeloupean Creole (Colot & Ludwig 2013a), which contrasts strikingly with its French lexifier:

(1)   *ki moun*   [which person]   'who'   (cf. *qui*)
     ki koté   [which side]   'where'   (cf. *où*)
     ki tan   [which time]   'when'   (cf. *quand*)
     ki jan   [which kind]   'how'   (cf. *comment*)

It is well known that pidgin and creole languages often replace the simple interrogatives of the lexifiers with such compounds consisting of adnominal interrogatives and generic nouns (Muysken & Smith 1990, Clements & Mahboob 2000). This chapter shows the extent to which different languages use simple and compound interrogatives.

It has sometimes been claimed that compound interrogatives in Atlantic pidgins and creoles are due to African substrate languages, but this explanation works only for some of the languages. A more general explanation (but more difficult to test) is that compound interrogatives are due to the tendency for pidgins and creoles to exhibit transparent structures (Seuren & Wekker 1986).

2. The values

We concentrate our attention on the counterparts of the four interrogatives 'who', 'where', 'when', and 'how'. Others, such as 'what', 'why' and 'how much', could have been added but were not taken into account here because they show less variation, 'what' being almost always simple, and 'why' and 'how much' compound in most cases. While the lexifiers generally have simple interrogatives, most of the *APiCS* languages have at least one compound interrogative pronoun among these four. (It should be noted that what is said about the relationship between pidgins/creoles and lexifiers here relates mostly to the European lexifiers; some of the non-European lexifiers may themselves have compound expressions for some of the categories.)

○	1. All simple words	22
●	2. One compound expression	18
●	3. Two compound expressions	17
●	4. Three compound expressions	10
●	5. Four compound expressions	7

Not suprisingly, languages with relatively little distance to the lexifier tend to have four simple words (e.g. Afrikaans, Reunion Creole, Singlish, African American English, Hawai'i Creole, Gullah), as do the mixed languages Michif and Mixed Ma'a/Mbugu. Also, the Arabic-based languages and Kikongo-Kituba lack compound interrogatives. The languages that most strongly favour compound interrogatives are the Atlantic English-based and French-based creoles. Spanish-based and Portuguese-based languages generally preserve the simple forms better. In the English-based languages, influence from English is often leading to a replacement of compound forms by English-like simple forms.

3. Different ontological categories

The four ontological categories (person, place, time, manner) differ in their propensity to occur as simple or compound interrogatives. The category that most strongly favours compound expression is time: more than two dozen languages have 'what time' or 'which hour' instead of 'when' in the lexifier, for example,

(2)   Ambon Malay   *apa tempo*   [which time]
     Angolar   *ora kutxi*   [hour which]
     Cape Verdean Creole   *ki tenpu*   [which time]
     Principense   *ki ora*   [which time]

Bahamian Creole	*what time*	[what time]
Bislama	*wanem taem*	[what time]
Pichi	*us tɛn*	[which time]
Lingala	*tángo níni*	[moment which]
Fanakalo	*(y)ini skati*	[which time]

The category that is the most resistant to replacement by an adnominal form plus generic noun is 'what', followed by 'who'. But Atlantic English-based languages not uncommonly have forms such as *witʃpɛsin/witʃman* (Ghanaian Pidgin English), *husman* (Cameroon Pidgin English), *wich badi/huu badi* (Creolese), and French-based languages have forms like *ki moun* (from French *monde* 'world, people, person').

The interrogatives 'where' and 'how' are intermediate. 'Where' is commonly replaced by 'what place' or similar forms:

(3) Vincentian Creole *wich paa(t)* [which part]
    Cameroon Pidgin English *hu-say* [which-side]
    Papiá Kristang *ki banda* [what side]
    Guinea-Bissau Kriyol *na kal ladu* [in which side]

'How' is commonly replaced by 'what manner' or similar forms:

(4) Seychelles Creole *ki mannyer* [what manner]
    Tok Pisin *olsem wanem* [like what]
    Batavia Creole *ki-lay* [what-sort]

4. Degrees of compoundness

Whether a form is regarded as compound is decided by its shape, not by evidence for analysability by the speaker. Maurer (2013b) notes that Batavia Creole *kilay* 'how' is always written as one word and also occurs with the shape *klay*. This suggests that synchronically this form is unanalysable. But as long as the generic noun *lay* still exists in the language and has a similar form as the relevant part of the interrogative pronoun, we regard them as compound.

If compoundness were defined purely in terms of morphological complexity, then even English *when*, *where*, etc. could be analyzed as *wh-en* [INTERROG-TEMP], *wh-ere* [INTERROG-LOC], etc. But we require identity of the generic noun with a noun with similar meaning in the language. Thus, Berbice Dutch *wanga*, which historically derives from *wa-anga* [what-place], is regarded as simple, because *anga* 'place' no longer occurs in the language (Kouwenberg 2013a). Similarly, Korlai *kɔr* 'when' (< Portuguese *que hora*) and *kilɛ* 'how' (< *que laia* 'what kind')

are no longer compound. But such cases of secondary opacity of interrogatives are not common. The adnominal interrogative word more often becomes opaque (e.g. in Pichi *us-*, e.g. *us-say* 'where', *us-tɛn* 'when', *us-pɔsin* 'who', deriving from *which* via a form *utʃ*), but forms with an opaque adnominal element are still regarded as complex.

Sometimes the adnominal element disappears completely, so that only the original generic noun is left, as in Martinican Creole *koté* 'where' (originally *ki koté* [which place], which is still possible; Colot & Ludwig 2013b). Such cases are considered to be simple interrogatives, but there are few cases of such "secondarily simple" forms that no longer occur side by side with the original complex form (e.g. Sranan *suma* 'who' < *hu-soma* [which-person], Angolar *ngê* 'who' < [person(+which)]).

Note also that morphological elements that are neither (similar to) generic nouns nor (similar to) adnominal interrogatives are disregarded, as in Gullah *whodat* 'who' (presumably < *who + that*), Reunion Creole *ki sa* 'who' (presumably < *qui + ça*), Papiamentu *na unda* [in where] 'where'. All these forms are not counted as compound interrogatives.

5. Co-occurrence of simple and compound forms

Many languages have simple and compound forms side by side. For example, Santome has the following forms (Hagemeijer 2013):

(5) 'who'   *kên*   *kê ngê*   [what person]
    'where' *an(dji)*   *kê xitu* [what place]
    'when'   *kê ola*   [what hour]
    'how'   *kuma*   *kê modu* [what manner]

In San Andres Creole English, besides the simple forms *huu*, *we*, *wen*, *hou*, there are compound forms such as *wa-paat* [what-part] 'where' and *wen-time* [when-time] 'when'.

Since we are primarily interested in the compound forms here, cases where both forms occur are classified in the same way as cases where only compound forms occur. It is only when the compound forms are very uncommon that they are disregarded. Thus, according to Hagemeijer (2013), "the frequency of compound expressions for 'where' and 'how' is very low", so Santome is counted as a language with two compound expressions (*kê ngê* and *kê ola*). Similarly, in present-day San Andres Creole English, the compound forms are not common, so this language is classified as having all simple words.

19 Interrogative pronouns

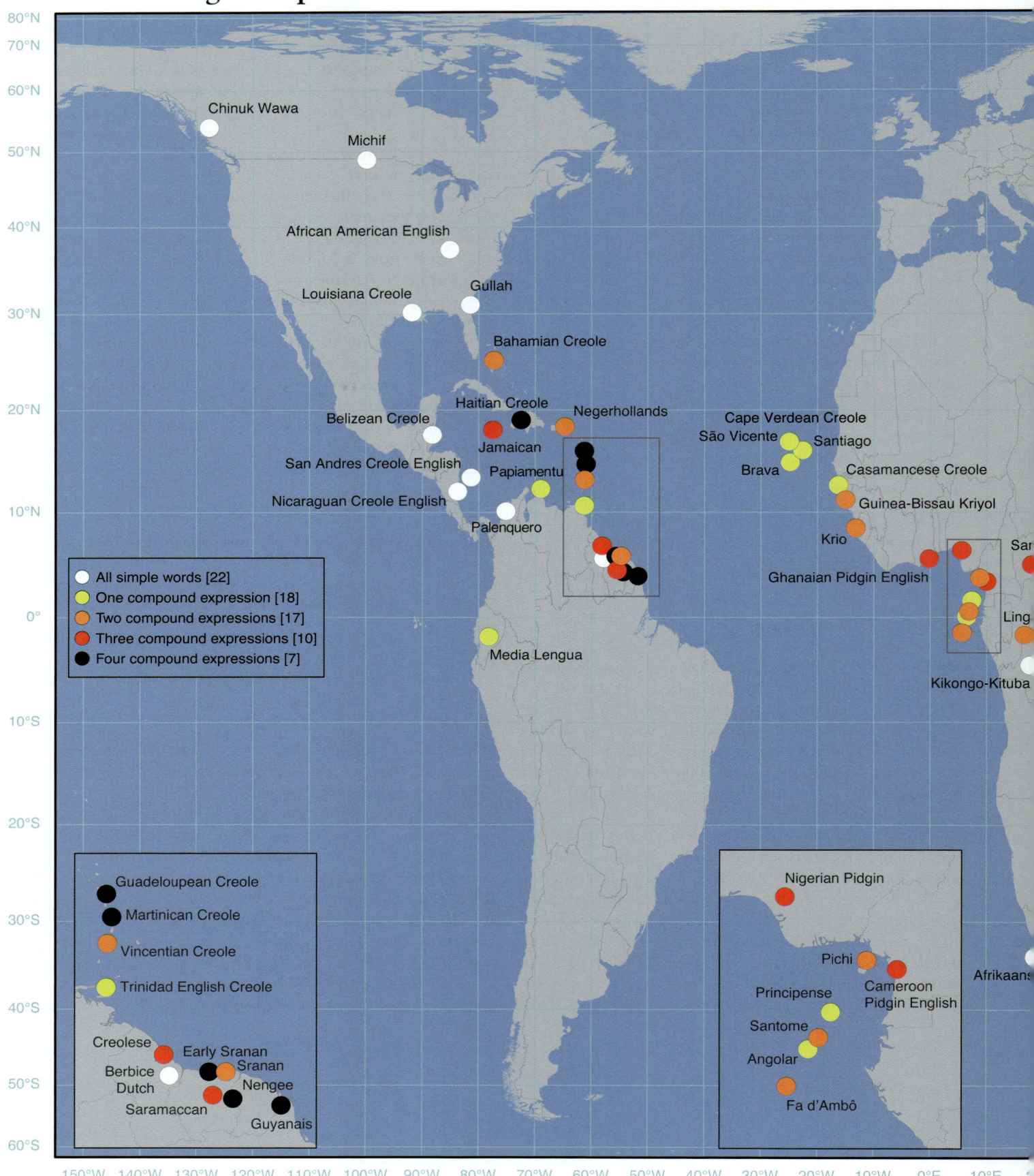

Chapter 20
Pronoun conjunction

MARTIN HASPELMATH AND THE *APiCS* CONSORTIUM

1. Expressing conjunction ('and')

The notion of conjunction ('A and B') is most straightforwardly expressed in languages by simple **juxtaposition** (*A B*), or by a construction with an overt **coordinator** (*A and B*) that links both **conjuncts**. In other chapters of this work, we ask whether the coordinator is also used to mark comitative participants (Chapter 71), or whether the same marking is used for coordinating nominal and verbal expressions (Chapter 72).

In this chapter, we focus on the expression of conjunction in cases when one of the conjuncts is a **personal pronoun**, because in such cases, some languages use a special **inclusory construction** (Lichtenberk 2000), as illustrated in (1a–c) from different non-*APiCS* languages.

(1) a. Tagalog (Schachter & Otanes 1972: 116)
    sila ni Juan
    they GEN Juan
    'he and Juan' (lit. 'they of Juan')

  b. Russian
    my s otcom
    we with father.INS
    'my father and I' (lit. 'we with father')

  c. Guugu Yimidhirr (Australian; Haviland 1979: 105)
    Ngaliinh *Dyaagi-ngun gambarr balga-y.*
    1EXCL.DU.NOM Jack-ERG pitch[ABS] make-PST
    'Jack and I made the pitch.' (lit. 'We Jack made the pitch.')

Inclusory constructions express conjunction and are rendered as 'A and B' in English, but they do this by means of a strategy that does not involve addition, but inclusion: one element of the construction (the **inclusory pronoun**) expresses the **total set** of participants, while the other element (the **subset NP**) expresses a **proper subset** of the participants. The resulting meaning is clearest in example (1c), where the inclusory pronoun means 'we (exclusive) two', and Jack is one subset. The other, complementary subset must therefore be 'I' ('Jack and I', i.e. we two). In (1a) and (1b), it is not so clear what the other subset is, because the pronouns are plural pronouns and the languages do not have duals. Thus, (1b) could mean 'father and I' or 'father and we'. But what is crucial is that one possible meaning is 'father and I', showing clearly that we are dealing with an inclusory construction, not a regular coordination construction. The inclusory pronoun is thus always a non-singular pronoun, and it can be first, second, or third person.

Among the *APiCS* languages, thirteen languages make use of a kind of inclusory construction. We distinguish five values overall, among them three different kinds of inclusory construction.

		excl	shrd	all
●	1. Singular pronoun overtly conjoined with other conjunct	55	12	67
●	2. Inclusory pronoun juxtaposed with subset NP	1	2	3
●	3. Inclusory pronoun plus marker plus subset NP	1	7	8
●	4. Inclusory pronoun plus numeral plus subset NP	0	2	2
○	5. Singular pronoun juxtaposed with other conjunct	0	1	1

The contributors were asked to concentrate on constructions with a first-person pronoun, and with a subset noun phrase expressed by a personal name.

2. Conjunction with overt coordinator

In most of the *APiCS* languages, just as in most of the European lexifiers, the only possibility is to coordinate pronouns and noun phrases by means of an overt coordinator between the two conjuncts (value 1), in other words, in the same way as two full noun phrases. Some examples are given in (2).

(2) a. Guadeloupean Creole (Colot & Ludwig 2013a)
    Mwen épi Jòj alé jwé boul.
    1SG and Georges go play ball
    'Georges and I went to play football.'

  b. Papiá Kristang (Baxter 2013)
    Yo ku yo sa mulé ja bai Muar.
    1SG COM 1SG GEN wife PFV go Muar
    'I and my wife went to Muar.'

(Interestingly, in the majority of examples the first-person pronoun precedes the other conjunct, unlike in English, where it follows it.)

3. Inclusory pronoun juxtaposed with subset noun phrase

In the first type of inclusory construction (value 2), the inclusory pronoun is juxtaposed with the subset noun phrase. This is found in Kriol and Gurindji Kriol, and is evidently influenced by the indigenous Australian languages, where this type is common (see 1c and Singer 2001).

(3) a. Kriol (Schultze-Berndt & Angelo 2013)
Mindubala Namij kol-im dardaga.
IDU.EXCL   Namij call-TR plant.species
'[In our language, Ngarinyman,] Namij and I call it *dardaga* [an edible plant].'

b. Gurindji Kriol (Meakins 2013)
*Mijij **ngali** wulaj nyangka!*
Mijij IDU.INCL hide look
'Mijij and I are hiding, look!'

As we see, the inclusory pronoun may precede or follow the subset NP. The only other *APiCS* language with a juxtapositional inclusory construction is Tok Pisin:

(4) Tok Pisin (Smith & Siegel 2013)
*Nau **mitupla** Beiko les.*
now IDU.EXCL Beiko tired
'Now me and Beiko were tired.'

However, in Tok Pisin this is a minority pattern; the overtly conjoined construction (*mi na Tomas* [I and Thomas]) is more common. As in the Australian *APiCS* languages, it is clear that this pattern is due to substrate influence: in many Oceanic languages of the area, a construction of this type is attested, as in (5):

(5) Toqabaqita (Lichtenberk 2000: 2)
kamareqa doqora-ku
IDU.EXCL brother-1SG.POSS
'my brother and I'

4. Inclusory pronoun plus marker plus subset NP

A more common type of inclusory construction (value 3) involves a marker between the inclusory pronoun and the subset NP, as in the examples in (6).

(6) a. Angolar (Maurer 2013)
Ane ki mengai rê kota fintxin pê.
3PL with wife POSS.3SG cut quarrel put
'He and his wife started to quarrel.'

b. Bislama (Meyerhoff 2013)
Mitufala wetem Charlie i wok.
IDU with Charlie AGR work
'Charlie and I were at work.'

c. Lingala (Meeuwis 2013)
Bisó na Marie to-kend-ákí na ndáko.
1PL with Mary 1PL-go-PST to house
'Mary and I went home.'

In all these cases, the inclusory pronoun precedes the marker and the subset NP, and the marker is identical to the 'with' preposition in the language. This is a very widespread pattern found in European languages too (e.g. in Russian, as we saw in 1b). It is particularly common in African languages, and Lingala shows the typical Bantu pattern. The Angolar construction is clearly due to its West African substrate. In view of the frequency of this construction in African languages, one could have expected to find it in more of the Atlantic creoles, but for some reason it does not seem to have been carried over very often.

5. Inclusory pronoun plus numeral plus subset NP

Two languages have an inclusory construction with a numeral 'two' between the two elements of the inclusory construction (value 4). This construction is common in Seychelles Creole (7a), but marginal in Reunion Creole (7b).

(7) a. Seychelles Creole (Michaelis & Rosalie 2013)
Nou de fre Zako nou a fer bon travay.
1PL two brother Zako 1PL FUT make good work
'Brother Zako and I will do a good job.'

b. Reunion Creole (Bollée 2013)
Alor, zot dé Maryann, i rantr dan le pti panyé.
then 3PL two Marianne FIN enter in DEF little basket
'So then he and Marianne stepped into the little basket.'

While this construction is similar to the inclusory constructions in Australian, Oceanic, and African languages, its origin clearly lies in dialectal French: in many varieties of French (especially in the north of France), this construction is possible as well (e.g. *nous deux mon chien* 'my dog and I'; this is not acceptable in Standard French, see Tesnière 1951).

6. Singular pronoun juxtaposed with other conjunct

One language allows a simple juxtaposition construction without overt marker (value 5). In Pidgin Hindustani, one can say *ham Biju* [I Biju] for 'Biju and I', though an overt marker is possible as well (*ham aur Vesu* [I and Vesu] 'Vesu and I').

20 Pronoun conjunction

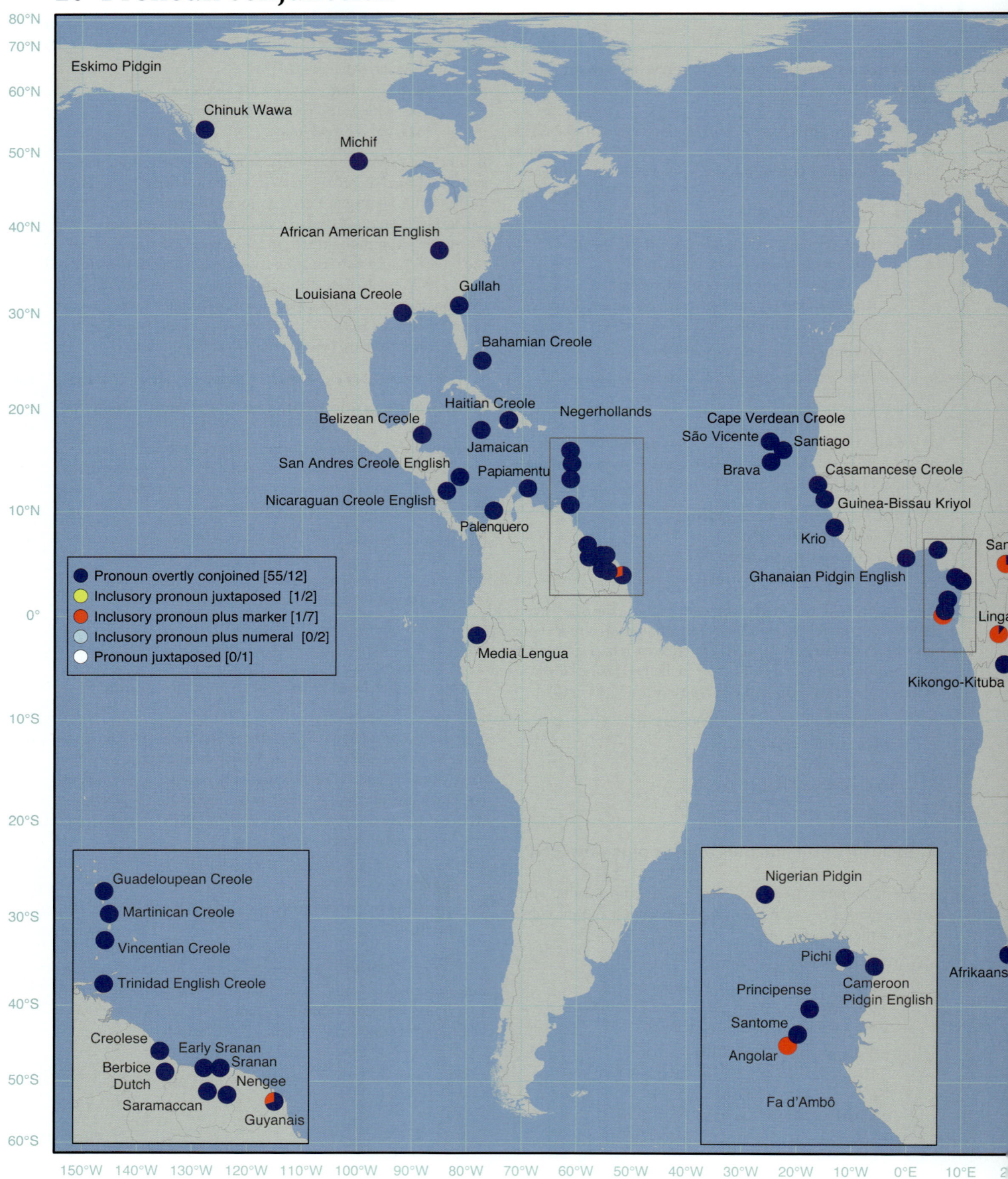

Chapter 21
Indefinite pronouns

MARTIN HASPELMATH AND THE *APiCS* CONSORTIUM

1. Indefinite pronouns

As in Haspelmath (2005b), in this chapter we ask how indefinite pronouns are formed, that is, the translational equivalents of 'somebody' and 'something'. In many languages, there are special expressions for these concepts which are undeniably pronouns (e.g. Spanish *algo* 'something'). In other languages, one simply says 'a person' or 'a thing', using a generic noun, as in (1) and (2).

(1) Sango (Samarin 2013)
 mo wara mbeni yi na ya ni?
 2SG find some thing PREP belly DET
 'Did you find something inside?'

(2) Haitian Creole (Fattier 2013)
 M ta bwè yon bagay.
 1SG COND drink INDF thing
 'I'd like to drink something.'

Nevertheless, the expressions corresponding to 'something' and 'somebody' here are considered as "indefinite pronouns" for the purposes of this chapter, because it is very difficult to draw a line between fully compositional noun phrases with generic nouns and special pronouns. In English, there is a stress contrast, and also a semantic difference, between the noun phrase *sòme thíng* and the pronoun *sómething*, and syntactically they behave differently, too (cf. *some nice things* vs. *something nice*). But these differences are very subtle and we cannot base our major classifications on them.

The question here is thus how 'something' and 'somebody' are expressed. The three main types are: (i) based on interrogative pronouns ('what', 'who'), (ii) based on generic nouns ('thing', 'person'), and (iii) special forms that are not synchronically based on anything. In addition, there is an intermediate type between (ii) and (iii), and languages may use existential constructions instead of indefinite pronouns.

When the 'somebody' expression in a language belongs to a different type than the 'something' expression, or when there are several different ways of expressing both indefinites, a language is shown as having multiple types.

Indefinite pronouns may also express ontological categories other than thing and person: place ('somewhere'), time ('sometime'), manner ('somehow'), and others. These typically behave

		excl	shrd	all
●	1. Interrogative-based indefinites	3	4	7
●	2. Generic-noun-based indefinites	37	9	46
●	3. Old generic-noun-based indefinites continuing *somebody*/*something*	17	4	21
●	4. Special indefinites	4	6	10
○	5. Existential construction	1	2	3

in the same way (see Haspelmath 1997), but in this chapter, we consider only the most frequent categories, thing and person.

Languages often have several different series of indefinite pronouns expressing different referential and modal types of indefiniteness, as in *something* vs. *anything* in English, or special negative indefinites such as *nothing* in English. In this chapter, we consider only indefinites that correspond to English *something* and *somebody* (but see Ch. 102 for negative indefinites).

2. Interrogative-based indefinites

Throughout North America, Australia, and Eurasia (with the exception of Western Europe), most languages have interrogative-based indefinites (e.g. Polish *kto* 'who', *kto-ś* 'someone', Japanese *nani* 'what', *nani-ka* 'something', see Haspelmath 1997). However, in the *APiCS* languages this type is not widespread and is found only in a few languages of North America and southern and eastern Asia. An example is (3).

(3) Sri Lankan Malay (Slomanson 2013)
 Go sapa-bɛkɛ-yang si-liiyat.
 1SG who-INDF-ACC PST-see
 'I saw somebody.'

In the Malay-based languages and in Michif and Chinuk Wawa, the pattern comes from the lexifier, but in Chinese Pidgin Russian, Ternate Chabacano, and Sri Lanka Portuguese, it must be due to the substrate.

3. Generic-noun-based indefinites

Generic-noun-based indefinites are found throughout Africa (with the exception of an area in northeastern Africa; Haspelmath 2005b), so it is not surprising that this is the dominant type in the Atlantic creoles. Moreover, English and the Romance languages, too, have many generic-noun-based indefinites. In English, *some-thing* is a clear case (based on *thing*), and *some-body* is a somewhat less clear case (but *body* must have meant 'person' originally here). In French, *quelque chose* [some thing] is clearly generic-noun-based, as is Portuguese *alguma coisa* [some thing]. But Spanish has special forms (*alguien* 'someone', *algo* 'something'), which are only diachronically analysable (from Latin *ali-quem*, *ali-quod*).

In the creoles based on English, French, and Portuguese, generic-noun forms may thus simply be inherited from the lexifiers, for example, Batavia Creole *alung kudja* 'something' < Portuguese *alguma coisa*, Louisiana Creole *kekchoz* < French *quelque chose*. In the English-based languages, forms directly derived from *somebody* and *something* are extremely common, but it is usually not clear whether these are still synchronically based on *thing* and *body*, so they are given special treatment (see §4).

In the Romance-based creoles, it is more common for generic-noun-based forms to be newly created. For example, in the Gulf of Guinea creoles, the generic noun *kwa* 'thing' (< Portuguese *coisa*) is used with the indefinite article rather than with *alguma* (Principense *kwa ũa* 'something'). In Cape Verdean Creole of Brava, 'somebody' is *algun djenti* [some person], not a form derived from Portuguese *alguem*. In French-based creoles, 'somebody' often comes from *monde* 'people' rather than from French *quelqu'un*, as in Reunion Creole *en moun*, Martinican Creole *an moun*. And in (2) above we saw *yon bagay* 'something' in Haitian Creole, which is unrelated to French *chose* 'thing'.

Some English-based creoles, too, have forms that are clearly innovated and do not continue *somebody/something*. Thus, Pichi has *sɔn pɔsin* 'somebody', and some of the Surinamese creoles have forms based on *sama* 'person' and *sani* 'thing', often with the indefinite article or numeral 'one':

(4) Nengee (Migge 2013)
   a. *I mu gi mi wan sani.*
      you must give me INDF thing
      'You have to give me something.'

   b. **Wan sama** *fufuu mi wagi.*
      INDF person steal my car
      'Someone stole my car.'

The form *sani* is said to derive from *something*, and *sama* from *somebody*, but they have become ordinary nouns.

Generic-noun-based indefinites are also found in African-based languages such as Sango (see example 1) and the Bantu-based Lingala, Kikongo-Kituba, and Mixed Ma'a/Mbugu, as well as in Eskimo Pidgin:

(5) Eskimo Pidgin (van der Voort 2013)
   ababa **innuk** *kaili*
   say man come
   'Tell someone (or some man, or the man) to come here.'

4. English-based indefinites continuing *somebody/something*

As we saw, many English-based languages have forms that go back directly to *somebody* (or sometimes *someone*) and *something* and that are still more or less transparently segmentable. These are assigned to an intermediate type here, because it is neither completely clear that they are analysable nor that they are unanalysable. Some examples are given in (6).

(6)
	from *somebody*	from *something*
Cameroon Pidgin Engl.	*sombodi*	*somtin(g)*
Hawai'i Creole	*sambari*	*samtin*
Kriol	*sambadi*	*jamjing*
Belizean Creole	*sambodi*	*samtn̩*
Vincentian Creole	*suhmbadi*	*suhmting*

5. Special forms

A few languages have special forms for 'somebody' and 'something' that are neither derived from interrogatives nor from generic nouns. Sometimes they are inherited from special forms of the lexifier (e.g. Afrikaans *iets* 'something', Pidgin Hindustani *koi* 'something, somebody', Michif *awiyak* 'someone', Papiamentu *algo* 'something', Diu Indo-Portuguese *aɲe* 'somebody' < Portuguese *alguem*).

In other cases, the special forms have arisen from transparent forms of the lexifier which have become completely unanalysable. English *somebody* and *something* have thus turned into special forms in Jamaican (*smadi/sitn*) and Saramaccan (*sɛmbɛ/sɔndi*).

6. Existential constructions

Occasionally, languages do not use pronominal expressions to render 'someone' and 'something', but existential constructions with free relative clauses (lit. 'There exists who came', i.e. 'Someone came'). This is found especially in some Austronesian languages, and in the *APiCS* languages where it occurs it is clearly due to the Austronesian influence.

(7) Cavite Chabacano (Sippola 2013a)
   Tiene que ya llega.
   EXIST who PFV come
   'Someone came.'

21 Indefinite pronouns

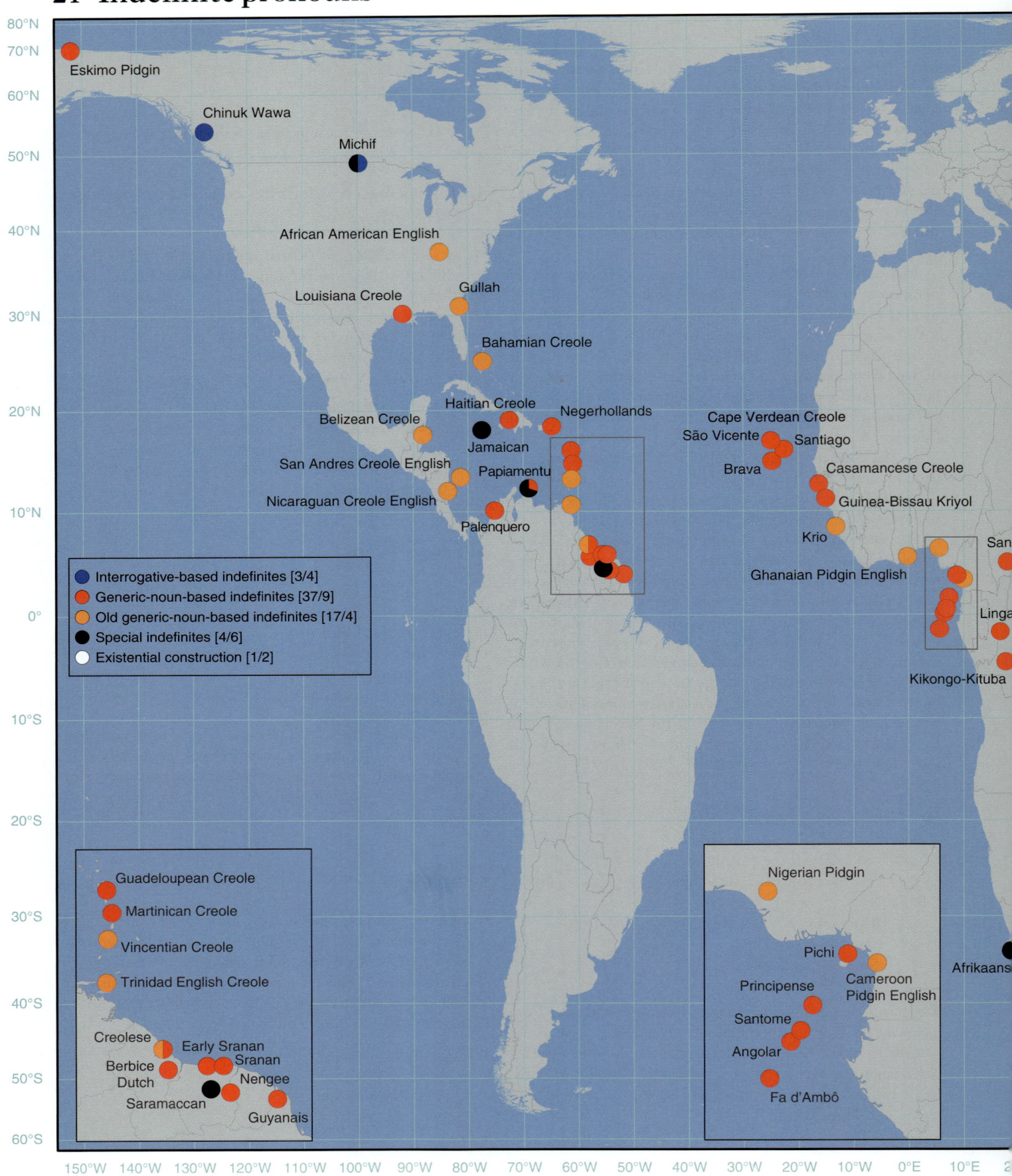

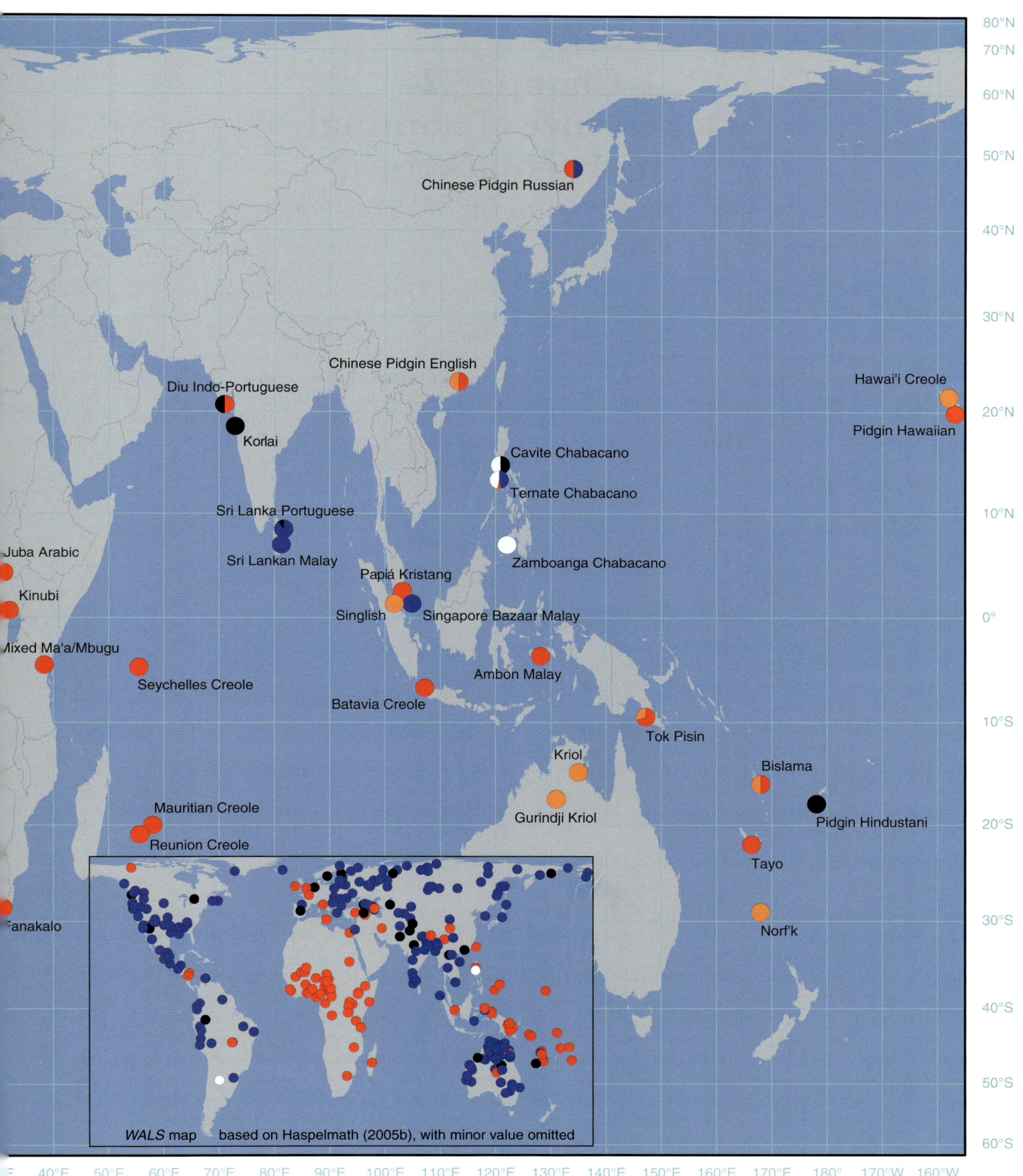

Chapter 22
Occurrence of nominal plural markers

MARTIN HASPELMATH AND THE *APiCS* CONSORTIUM

1. Variable extent of plural marking

In many languages, nouns with plural meaning are plural-marked, and in some languages, this plural marking is so thoroughgoing that it is difficult to find contexts where no overt plural marking occurs. In European languages such as English and Spanish, for example, plural marking occurs even when the noun is combined with a numeral and plural marking is thus completely redundant (1c). Plural marking may also occur both on the noun itself and on a modifier or determiner (1d).

(1)   English   Spanish
     a. *tree*   *árbol*
     b. *tree-s*   *árbol-es*
     c. *three tree-s*   *tres árbol-es*
     d. *these tree-s*   *est-os árbol-es*

Plural marking may be lacking only in compounding constructions in English (e.g. *tree plantation*), or with certain "collective" nouns that inherently denote a group of things or people (e.g. English *furniture*, Spanish *gente* 'people') and can never be used to refer to a single item.

But English and Spanish are fairly extreme. Many other languages have grammatical plural marking but do not require it when the meaning is plural, or restrict its use to certain kinds of words. In fact, there is an implicational scale that governs the ways in which plural marking can be limited (Smith-Stark 1974, Corbett 2000: 56):

(2)   speaker > hearer > 3rd person > kin > human > animate > inanimate

If a language allows or requires plural marking anywhere on the scale, then it also allows or requires plural marking for all higher positions on the scale. Moreover, when plural marking is optional, then the words higher on the hierarchy are more likely to bear a plural marker than the words lower on the hierarchy.

The pidgin, creole, and mixed languages of *APiCS* conform to this scale and sometimes use plural marking only with (personal pronouns and) human or animate nouns, not with inanimates. In addition to animacy, definiteness also often plays a role in plural marking, and again we find evidence for this in our languages: definite nouns are more likely to show plural marking, and in fact quite a few of the *APiCS* languages allow plural marking only for definite nouns.

Plural marking can take various forms, as we will see in Chapter 23. Note that it need not be marking on the noun itself, but can be marking of the entire noun phrase. Cases where plural marking is found only on the article (as with most nouns in French, where the written plural suffix *-s* is not pronounced) are also regarded as plural marking. For more on plural marking in various creoles, see also Mühlhäusler (1981), Janson (1984), Manessy (1985), Lang (1990), Déprez (2007).

2. The values

The distribution of the four different values is shown in the value box:

○	1. No plural marking	5
●	2. Variable plural marking of human nouns	4
●	3. Variable plural marking of human or inanimate nouns	51
●	4. Invariant plural marking	16

Whereas all European languages as well as Arabic (i.e. the main lexifiers of the *APiCS* languages) show invariant plural marking like English and Spanish, the great majority of pidgin and creole languages show variable plural marking.

2.1. Value 1: No plural marking

In some languages, there is so little nominal plural marking that they are classified here as having no plural marking. This concerns especially some of the pidgins, but there is also one creole in this category (Portuguese-based Korlai). A few exceptions are recorded, however: in Eskimo Pidgin, there is a single attested singular–plural pair, *innuk–innuit* 'man–men', and Korlai, too, has just a single exception, *mulɛr–mulǝris* 'woman–women'. Not accidentally, these exceptions are nouns denoting humans. Note that all that is claimed here is that these languages do not use plural marking with nouns. Personal pronouns are much more rarely neutral with respect to number (see the scale in 2), and in general these languages do make a number distinction in pronouns (e.g. Chinuk Wawa *náyka* 'I' vs. *ntsáyka* 'we', *máyka* 'you (SG)' vs. *mtsáyka* 'you (PL)').

2.2. Value 2: Variable plural marking of human nouns

In a few other languages, it is reported that plural marking is variable (i.e. does not occur under all circumstances) and is restricted to human nouns. Again, three of these are pidgins. Examples of plural use are Chinese Pidgin Russian *ibəŋka isio zenʃinə* [Japanese PL woman] 'Japanese women', Diu Indo-Portuguese (older generation lect) *moyrmoyr* 'Muslims' (singular *moyr*). The restriction to humans is not entirely certain for these languages; the three pidgins are extinct (or nearly extinct) and the data are somewhat limited. If plural marking was possible but uncommon for inanimate nouns, it may simply be unattested in the available materials. For Kriol, Schultze-Berndt & Angelo (2013) report that "plural marking with inanimates is rare and absence of plural marking with humans is rare, but variation is found in all categories." If Kriol were not as well attested, it might have been classified as belonging to this category, too.

2.3. Value 3: Variable plural marking of human or inanimate nouns

In the great majority of the *APiCS* languages, plural marking is variable but possible for all kinds of nouns. This concerns especially those plural markers that were newly created in the creoles, such as words deriving from 'all' (e.g. Tok Pisin *ol*, Diu Indo-Portuguese *tud*) or words deriving from a noun meaning 'group' (e.g. Seychelles and Mauritian Creole *bann*, < French *bande*; see Bollée 2000).

But the majority of languages with innovated plural markers have plural words deriving from third-person-plural pronouns (see Chapter 25):

(3) a. Papiamentu (Kouwenberg 2013b)
    baka-nan   'the cows'
    cow-(3)PL

 b. Bahamian Creole (Hackert 2013)
    de boy-dem   'the boys'
    DEF boy-(3)PL

Understandably, it is especially with plural markers of this latter type that a restriction to definite noun phrases is often reported. Personal pronouns are definite, so when a combination such as "they, children" becomes a single noun phrase, it is expected that it should retain the definiteness of the personal pronoun. In some of these languages, the plural marker is in fact described as a plural definite article. For instance, Sranan has the contrast *a oso* [DEF.SG house] vs. *den oso* [DEF.PL house]. This description is fully compatible with the view that *den* is a plural marker: it simply has a dual function, marking both definiteness and plurality.

In the Portuguese-based creoles Principense, Santome, and Angolar, the plural marker is restricted to definite noun phrases, but it does not suffice as a definite article, at least for inanimate nouns. The latter need to be marked as definite by a demonstrative:

(4) Angolar (Maurer 2013a)
    a. *ene n'na*   'the children'
       PL child
    b. *ane fuuta e* 'the breadfruits'
       PL fruit DEM

(5) Santome (Hagemeijer 2013)
    a. *inen mina*   'the children'
       PL child
    b. *inen fya se* 'these leaves'
       PL leaf DEM

In Palenquero, by contrast, the plural marker *ma* is compatible not just with an indefinite interpretation, but even with an indefinite article:

(6) Palenquero (Schwegler 2007, 2013)
    un   ma kusa
    INDF.ART PL thing
    'some things' (Spanish *unas cosas*)

As *ma* derives from the Kikongo (Bantu) gender–number prefix *ma-* rather than a definite element, this is not surprising.

2.4. Value 4: Invariant plural marking

Finally, invariant plural marking is reported for a number of languages. The Bantu-based languages Lingala, Kikongo-Kituba, and Mixed Ma'a/Mbugu have preserved Bantu singular and plural prefixes (e.g. Lingala *mo-báli* 'man', *mi-báli* 'men'), even though gender–number agreement has been lost in Lingala and Kikongo-Kituba. Invariant plural marking is also found in the mixed languages Michif (which uses the plural marker *lii*, from French *les*) and Sri Lankan Malay, as well as in African American English and Afrikaans. In some of the Portuguese-based West African creoles that have preserved (or reborrowed) the Portuguese plural suffix *-s*, this is also said to be invariant. Finally, plural marking is reportedly invariant in several French-based creoles in the Caribbean (Guadeloupean and Martinican Creole, Guyanais, Louisiana Creole) as well as in Tayo.

22 Occurrence of nominal plural markers

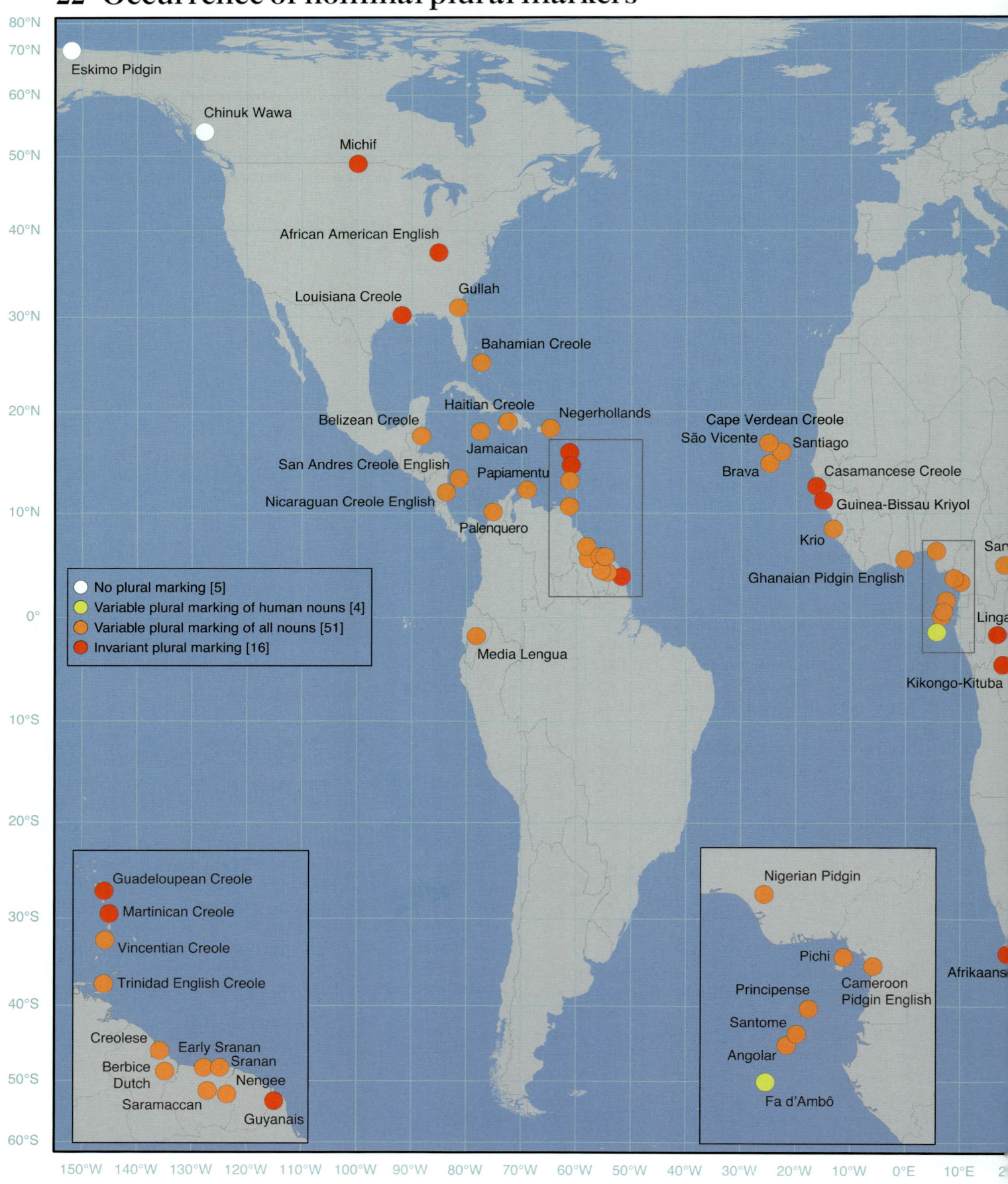

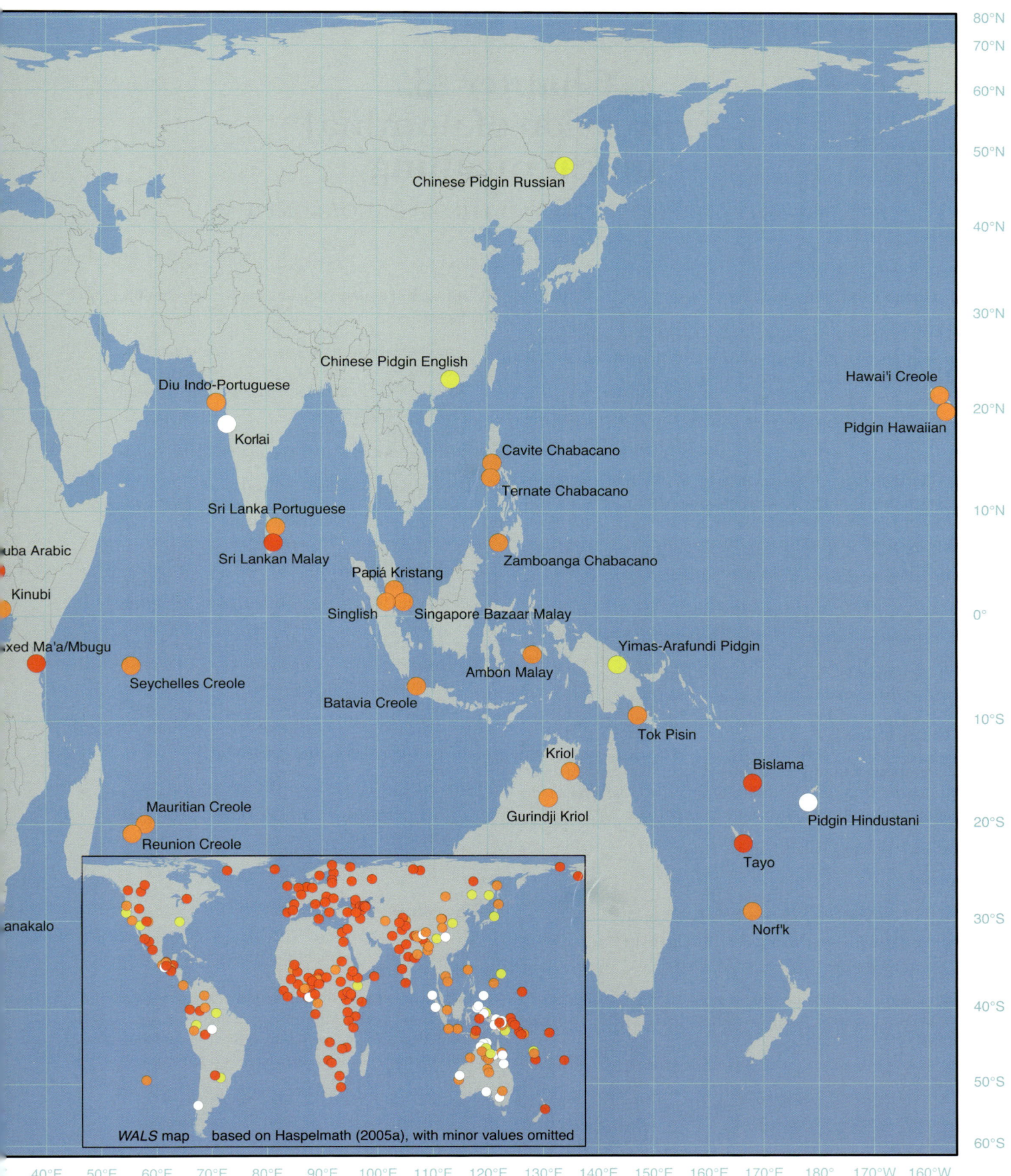
WALS map based on Haspelmath (2005a), with minor values omitted

Chapter 23
Expression of nominal plural meaning

MARTIN HASPELMATH AND THE *APiCS* CONSORTIUM

1. Types of plural marking

In this chapter, we look at the **formal type of plural expression** of nouns if plural is marked overtly. In some of our languages, nominal plural is not expressed overtly, and in many of them, plural expression is optional (see Chapter 22), and often uncommon in usage. Here, we look only at the form of plural markers, regardless of how they are used. The values are based on Dryer (2005a).

Plural marking on nouns can be by an affix (prefix or suffix), by stem change or tone change, by reduplication, or by a plural word that occurs in the noun phrase, normally next to the noun. A plural **prefix** and a plural **suffix** are illustrated in (1) and (2).

(1) Lingala (Meeuwis 2013)
 mo-báli   mi-báli
 SG-man   PL-man
 'man'   'men'

(2) Casamancese Creole (Biagui & Quint 2013)
 padidi   padidi-s
 wall   wall-PL
 'wall'   'walls'

Plural **stem change** is illustrated by (3a–c). This can be a slight change consisting only in a different vowel (as in 3a, b), or a radical change involving a new suppletive stem (as in 3c).

(3) a. Ghanaian Pidgin English (Huber 2013)
      uman 'woman'   *umɛn* 'women'
    b. Haitian Creole (Fattier 2013)
      madanm 'woman'   *medanm* 'women'
    c. Juba Arabic (Manfredi & Petrollino 2013)
      mára 'woman'   *nuswán* 'women'

Plural **tone or stress change** is attested only in a single language, Kinubi, where the stress shifts to the last syllable in some words:

(4) Kinubi (Luffin 2013)
 bágara 'cow'   *bagará* 'cows'
 sámaga 'fish'   *samagá* 'fish (PL)'

Reduplication is quite common, but is rarely the only type of plural form:

(5) Ambon Malay   *gunung gunung*   'mountains'
    Creolese   *buk buk*   'books (all over)'
    Kriol   *olgamanolgaman*   '(older) women'
    Papiá Kristang   *kaza kaza*   'houses'
    Papiamentu   *repirepi*   'strips'
    Zamboanga Ch.   *pyédra-pyédra*   '(all the) stones'

Finally, many languages have a **plural word**:

(6) a. Plural word preceding the noun
       Angolar   *ane alê*   'kings'
       Belizean Creole   *dem bway*   'boys'
       Saramaccan   *dɛɛ wɔmi*   'the men'
       Cavite Ch.   *manga estudiante*   'students'
       Juba Arabic   *nas zaráf*   'giraffes'
       Mauritian Creole *ban liv*   'books'
       Michif   *lii maenzon*   'houses'
       Palenquero   *ma nimá*   'animals'
       Tayo   *te kas*   'houses'
       Tok Pisin   *ol liklik dok*   'little dogs'
    b. Plural word following the noun
       Creolese   *di kou dem*   'the cows'
       Haitian Creole   *liv yo*   'the books'
       Negerhollands   *di mēnshi sinu*   'the girls'
       Nigerian Pidgin   *got dèm*   'goats'

2. The values

The distribution of the eight different values is shown in the value box.

Plural **prefixes** are primarily found in languages that inherited their plural marking from Niger-Congo languages, such as Bantu languages (Kikongo-Kituba, Mixed Ma'a/Mbugu, Lingala) and Ubangian-based Sango (see also ex. 1).

(7) a. Kikongo-Kituba   *mw-ana*   *b-ana*
                       'child'   'children'

b. Mixed Ma'a/Mbugu *ki-hlatú* *vi-hlatú*
'finger' 'fingers'
c. Sango *yi* *a-yi*
'thing' 'things'

		excl	shrd	all
○	1. Plural is not expressed overtly	7	0	7
●	2. Plural prefix	4	1	5
●	3. Plural suffix	8	24	32
●	4. Plural stem change	0	12	12
●	5. Plural tone or stress change	0	1	1
●	6. Plural reduplication	4	14	18
○	7. Plural word preceding the noun	16	11	27
○	8. Plural word following the noun	4	17	21

The plural marking in Louisiana Creole is based on the French plural article *les* (*lez ekol* '(the) schools') and is regarded as a prefix, too. None of the other French-based languages has this kind of plural-marking.

Plural **suffixes** are the norm in several of the Portuguese-based creoles (see Lang 1990, 1991), where the Portuguese plural suffix *-s* has been preserved (Cape Verdean Creole, Guinea-Bissau Kriyol, Sri Lanka Portuguese; see also ex. 2). The English plural suffix *-s* has also been preserved in many English-based creoles and pidgins, but is not as regularly used, and is often a more acrolectal form alongside a basilectal form with an innovated plural word. Kinubi and Juba Arabic have preserved some of the Arabic plural suffixation. New plural suffixes, which do not go back to plural markers of the lexifier, are found in Berbice Dutch (*-apu*) and Sri Lankan Malay (*-pədə*).

Plural **stem change** occurs quite marginally in the *APiCS* languages, and never as the only possibility of plural expression. Most of the cases are English-based languages that have preserved a few stem-changing plurals in high-frequency words (e.g. Bahamian Creole *women*, Gullah *tʃaːl* 'child' vs. *tʃɪlṇ* 'children', Hawai'i Creole *fit* 'feet', Singlish *mice*). The Ghanaian Pidgin English example in (3a), where the stem change has been extended analogically from *man/mɛn*, is unusual. Among the French-based languages, examples of preserved stem-changing plurals like (3b) from Haitian Creole are very unusual too, though Michif also has a few (e.g. *animal/zanimoo* 'animal(s)').

Plural **tone or stress change** only occurs in Kinubi, as seen in (4). The stress change is the only trace of the Arabic plural suffix *-aat*: In Standard Arabic, the corresponding forms are *báqara* 'cow', *baqar-áat* 'cows'. The long *aa* in the final closed syllable attracted the stress, and when the final *t* and the vowel length disappeared in Kunubi, only the final stress remained.

Plural **reduplication** occurs in many languages, but it is the only option for only a few Asian languages. Most of these are Malay-based (e.g. Ambon Malay, as in ex. 5) or under the strong influence of Malay (Batavia Creole, e.g. *albër albër* 'trees', Papiá Kristang *kren-krensa* 'children'). Only Diu Indo-Portuguese restricts its plural expression to reduplication (e.g. *muyɛmuyɛr* 'women') but was not influenced by Malay.

Perhaps the most prominent feature of creoles is the **plural word**, a category quite unknown in European languages, though typologically not uncommon (Dryer 1989). Plural words may be **preposed** or **postposed** (the latter almost exclusively in Caribbean creoles). Plural words commonly derive from third-person-plural pronouns, as is also the case in a number of African languages (Manessy 1985). Examples are Angolar *ane*, all the English-based languages that use a form of *them/dem* for plural expression, Negerhollands *sinu*, Papiamentu *nan*, and Caribbean French creoles which use a form derived from *eux* (Haitian *yo* and others). These forms are often restricted to marking definite plurals, and they are sometimes regarded as definite articles (see Janson 1984 for discussion). However, as they also mark plural, they are considered to be plural words here, too. See Chapter 25 for more discussion of the formal identity between third-person-plural pronouns and plural markers. Almost all postposed plural words derive from third-person-plural pronouns.

Another source of plural words is universal quantifiers meaning 'all'. The plural marker *ol* is found in English-based languages in the Pacific (Tok Pisin, Bislama, Kriol, see Mühlhäusler 1981), and Tayo *tule/tle/te* has the same origin (French *tous les* 'all the').

Plural words may also come from substrate or adstrate languages (Chabacano *manga*, Palenquero *ma*, see Schwegler 2007), and from nouns meaning '(group of) people' (Juba Arabic *nas*) or 'group' (Indian Ocean French creoles *ban*, from French *bande* 'group', see Bollée 2000).

Plural words are phrasal markers, and they need not be immediately adjacent to the noun. Thus, *ol* in *ol liklik dok* 'the little dogs' (see 6a) precedes the adjective. In Papiamentu, different orders of the postposed plural word are possible, with somewhat different interpretative possibilities:

(8) Papiamentu (Kouwenberg 2013b)
a. *e   buki-nan di skol*
   DEF book-PL of school
   'the books of the school, the schoolbooks'

b. *e   buki di skol-nan*
   DEF [book of school]-PL
   'the schoolbooks'

23 Expression of nominal plural meaning

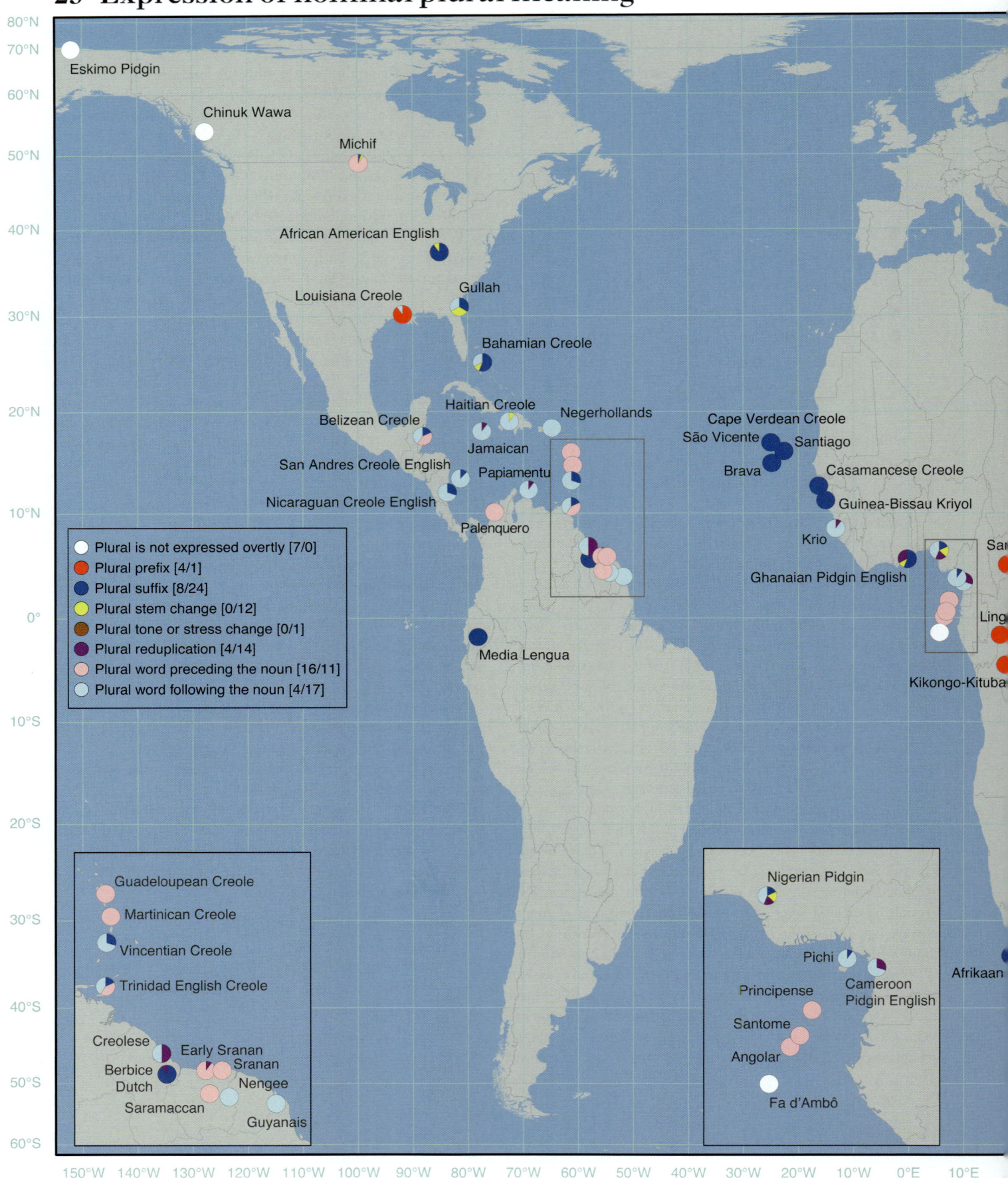

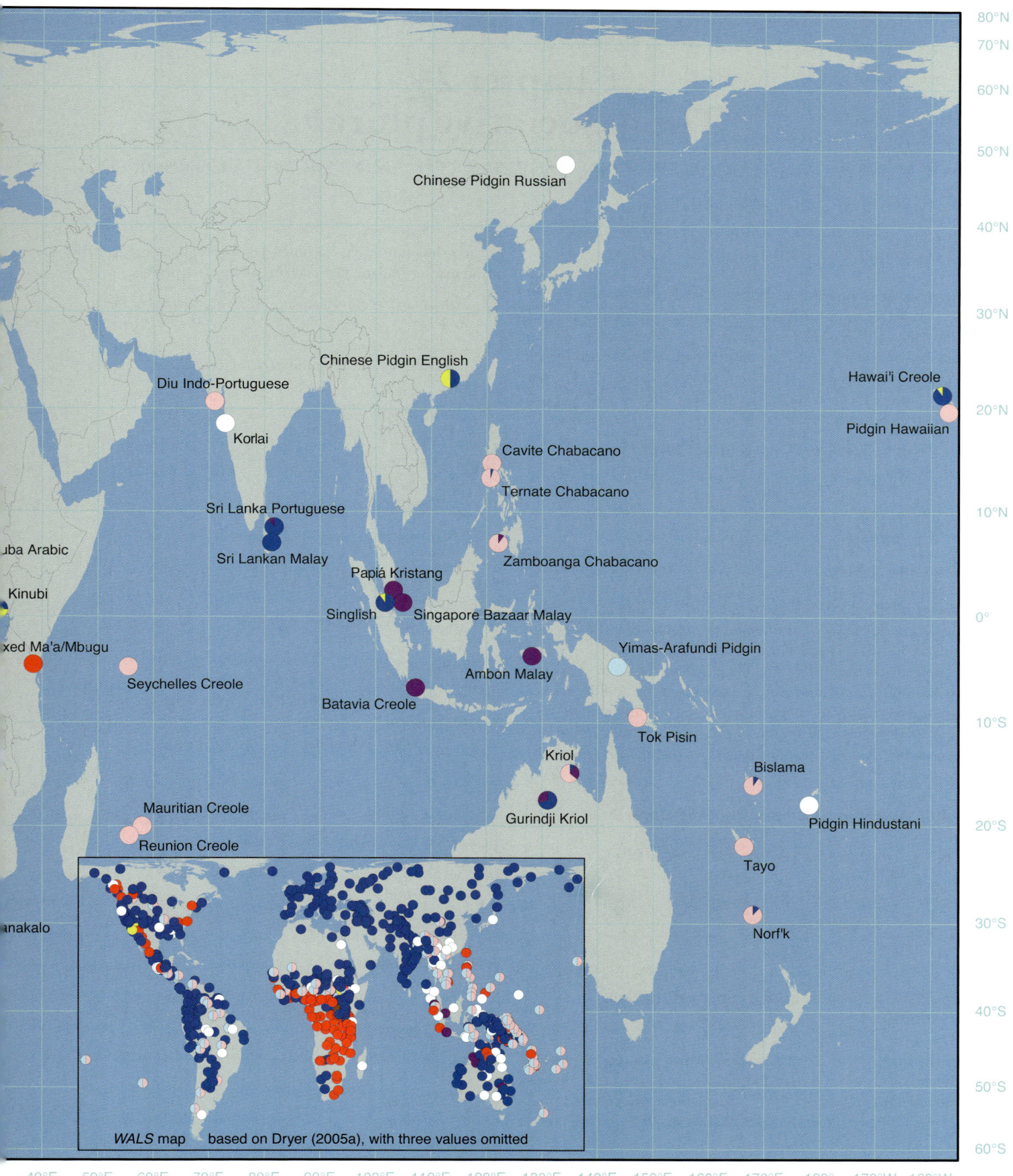

Chapter 24
The associative plural

SUSANNE M. MICHAELIS, MARTIN HASPELMATH, AND THE *APiCS* CONSORTIUM

1. Associative vs. additive plurals

An associative plural construction consists of a noun X and an associative plural marker and means 'X and associates'. It contrasts with an ordinary additive plural construction, which consists of a noun Y and an additive plural marker and means 'several instances of Y'. The contrast is illustrated in (1) from Kriol, where *-mob* is an associative plural marker and *ole* is an ordinary additive plural marker.

(1) Kriol (Schultze-Berndt & Angelo 2013)
    a. *Helen-mob*
        'Helen and her people'
    b. *ole boi*
        'the boys'

Associative plurals are not well known from European languages, but they occur very widely in the world's languages, as shown in Daniel & Moravcsik's (2005) *WALS* chapter, on which this chapter is based. For more on associative plurals, see Corbett (2000: 101–11) and Moravcsik (2003).

In general, the focal referent (e.g. 'Helen' in 1a) in an associative plural is a person name or a kinship term, and the associates refer to family members or friends of the person.

We distinguish four values. The majority of *APiCS* languages have associative plurals, and we distinguish three subtypes.

●	1. Associative plural marker identical to additive plural marker	29
●	2. Special associative plural marker identical to 3rd-plural pronoun	8
●	3. Other special associative plural marker	9
○	4. No associative plural marker	25

2. Associative and additive plural marker identical

In the majority of *APiCS* languages with associative plurals, **the same marker** is used for additive and associative plurals (value 1). In this regard, *APiCS* languages are no different from the world's languages (Daniel & Moravcsik 2005). These plural markers thus simply have a somewhat broader meaning than the plural markers in languages lacking associative plurals.

(2) Bahamian Creole (Hackert 2013): plural marker *them/dem*
    a. *B'Booky them*
        'B'Booky and his family/friends/associates'
    b. *de boy-dem*
        ART boy-PL
        'the boys'

(3) Nigerian Pidgin (Faraclas 2013): plural marker *dẹm*
    a. *Chidi dẹm*
        'Chidi and his people'
    b. *man dẹm*
        'men'

(4) Angolar (Maurer 2013a): plural marker *ane*
    a. *ane Peru*
        'Peru (Peter) and his friends'
    b. *ane fuuta*
        'breadfruits'

(5) Tok Pisin (Smith & Siegel 2013): plural marker *ol*
    a. *Sandy ol*
        'Sandy and the others'
    b. *ol dok*
        'dogs'

(Note that in Tok Pisin, the order of the marker is different in the associative use. This is disregarded here.)

(6) Seychelles Creole (Michaelis & Rosalie 2013): plural *bann*
    a. *bann Pyer*
        'Pyer and company'
    b. *bann danm*
        'women'

(7) Kikongo-Kituba (Mufwene 2013): plural marker *ba-*
    a. *ba-Petelo*
        'Petelo and his associates/family/the other members of his group'
    b. *ba-nkento*
        'women'

This type is particularly common among Atlantic and Indian Ocean languages in *APiCS*, which is very likely related to the fact that the type is very widespread also in the languages of West Africa and in Bantu languages.

Quite a few of the plural markers in this group are identical to the third-person-plural pronoun (see examples 2–5), especially among the Atlantic English-based languages. This identity of (ordinary and associative) nominal plural marker and third-person-plural pronoun will be discussed in the next chapter (Chapter 25).

3. Special associative plural marker identical to third-person-plural pronoun

In a number of languages, there is a special associative plural marker different from the additive plural marker, but is **identical to the third-person-plural pronoun** (value 2), as seen in (8)–(10).

(8) Afrikaans (den Besten & Biberauer 2013)
 Pa-hulle
 'Dad and one or more others' (*hulle* 'they')

(9) Bislama (Meyerhoff 2013)
 Sale olgeta
 'Sale and his family' (*olgeta* 'they')

(10) Sri Lankan Malay (Slomanson 2013)
 Miflal-derang
 'Miflal and his friends' (*derang* 'they')

4. Other special associative plural marker

There are also a few languages with a special associative plural marker which is **different from both the ordinary plural marker and the third-person-plural pronoun** (value 3). We already saw an example of this in (1). More examples are given in (11)–(13).

(11) Guinea-Bissau Kriyol (Intumbo et al. 2013)
 ba Djon
 ASS John
 'John and his associates'

(12) Gurindji Kriol (Meakins 2013)
 ngakparn-nyarrara
 frog-ASS
 'frogs and other animals'

(13) Pidgin Hawaiian (Roberts 2013)
 mama ma
 mother ASS
 'my mother and her friends'

Most of these forms seem to have been retained from non-European contributing languages. Thus, Pidgin Hawaiian *ma* is from Hawaiian *ma*, and Gurindji Kriol *-nyarrara* is from Gurindji.

5. Further considerations

Associative plurals are very similar to similative plurals (as also noted by Daniel & Moravcsik 2005), that is, constructions that refer to a plurality of entities which are similar to (rather than associated with) the focal referent. Thus, in Diu Indo-Portuguese, the construction in (14a) is a similative plural construction. Interestingly, the plural marker *tud* follows the noun here, whereas it precedes it when it has additive meaning (14b), much as in Tok Pisin.

(14) Diu Indo-Portuguese (Cardoso 2013)
 a. *mĩ nitiŋ tud*
  my grandchild SIML
  'my grandchildren and similar people'
 b. *ikəl tud koyz*
  DEM PL thing
  'those things'

Even though this is not strictly speaking an associative plural construction, we decided to count it as such for this chapter and subsumed Diu Indo-Portuguese under value 1. Likewise, the Korlai construction with duplifixation, exemplified by *korp bi-p* 'body and so forth' (where the beginning of the second reduplicant is replaced by *bi-*; see Chapter 26), has been considered an associative plural here, though this is an unconventional classification. Another language that seems to have similative plurals rather than associative plurals is the mixed language Gurindji Kriol. We already saw example (12), which is unlike the other examples in that the focal noun is an ordinary common noun rather than a proper name or a kinship term with unique reference. Maybe this should be translated as 'frogs and similar animals'. Gurindji Kriol has another marker, specialized for inanimate referents, which is translated as a kind of similative plural:

(15) Gurindji Kriol (Meakins 2013)
 ngapulu-purrupurru
 milk-ASS
 'milk and the like (other things that go with tea)'

The examples considered in this last section show that the diversity in associative plural marking is potentially quite rich, but most *APiCS* languages are simpler and have just a single separate marker that combines only with names or kinship terms, as in (1)–(10).

24 The associative plural

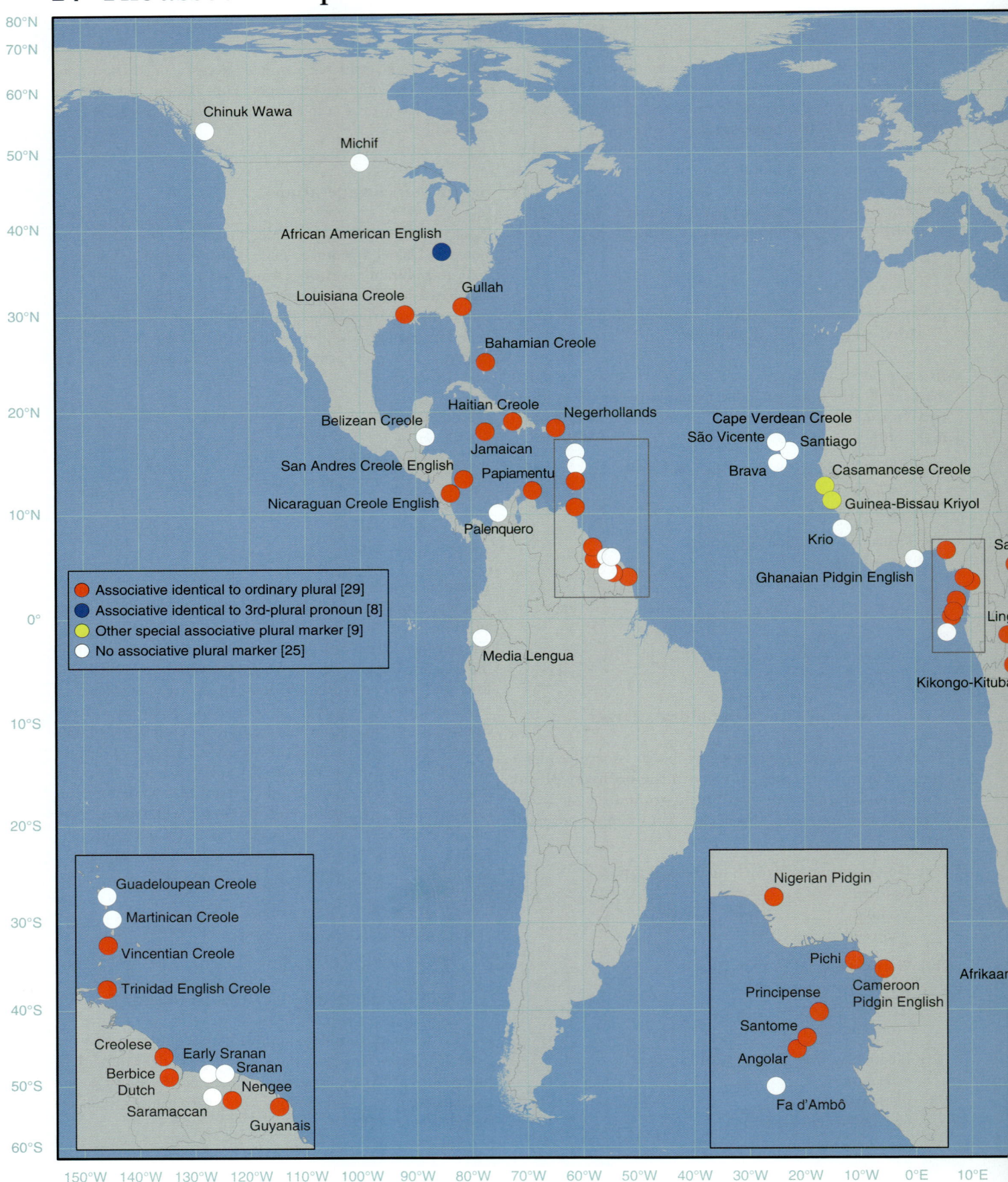

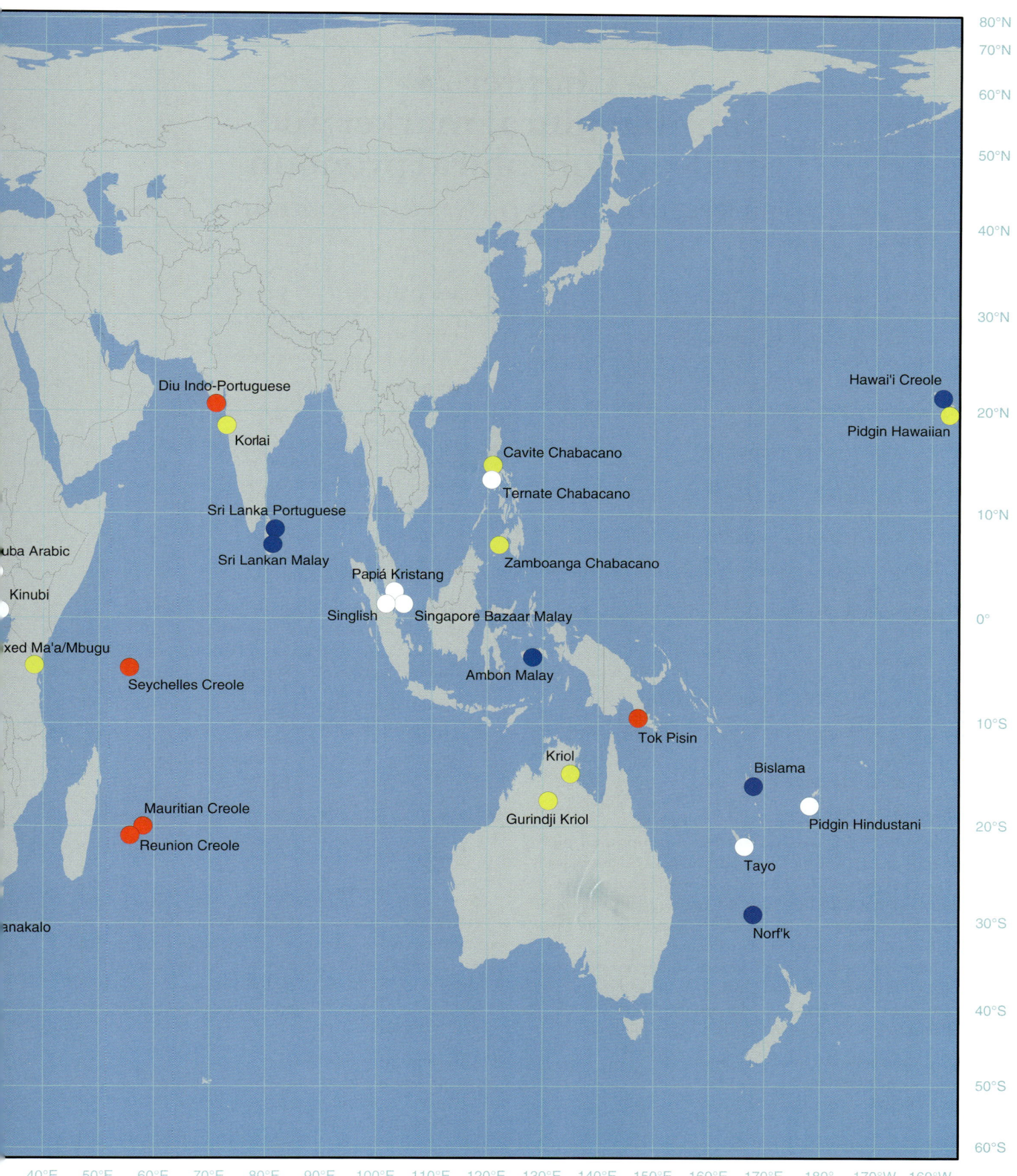

Chapter 25
Nominal plural marker and third-person-plural pronoun

PHILIPPE MAURER AND THE *APiCS* CONSORTIUM

1. Feature description

In quite a few languages, the nominal plural marker is formally identical to the—mostly independent—third-person-plural pronoun, as for instance in Cameroon Pidgin English:

(1) Cameroon Pidgin English (Schröder 2013)
  a. *Wich taym **dem** de go?*
   which time 3PL PROG go
   'When are they going?'
  b. ***Pikin dem** di pley futbol fo stad.*
   child PL PROG play football LOC stadium
   'The children are playing football at the stadium.'

This chapter is closely related to Chapter 22 on the occurrence of nominal plural markers and to Chapter 23 on the expression of nominal plural meaning.

2. The values

In this feature, four values are distinguished:

○	1. No nominal plural word	29
●	2. Identity	16
●	3. Differentiation	22
●	4. Overlap	9

Many *APiCS* languages **do not posses a nominal plural word** (value 1). The plural marking in these languages is discussed in Chapter 23. The most widespread strategies are the use of a plural suffix (e.g. *-s/-is* in Cape Verdean Creole of São Vicente), reduplication of the stem (as in Singapore Bazaar Malay), or stem change (Nigerian Pidgin).

Identity (value 2) means that there is only one word that is used both as a third-person-plural pronoun and as a nominal plural marker, as shown by (1). In example (1b), as well as in the following examples, the plural marker follows the noun:

(2) Negerhollands (van Sluijs 2013)
  *di mēnshi **sinu***
  ART girl PL
  'the girls'

(3) Pichi (Yakpo 2013)
  *Dì man para insay **pipul dεn**.*
  DEF man stand inside people PL
  'The man is standing amidst people.'

But the plural marker may also precede the noun:

(4) Belizean Creole (Escure 2013)
  *Sam a **dem bway** wuda gu awt.*
  some of PL boy would go out
  'Some of the boys want to go out.'

(5) Santome (Hagemeijer 2013)
  *Tudu **inen ngê** se ka môlê.*
  all PL people DEM FUT die
  'All people in question will die.'

(6) Tok Pisin (Smith & Siegel 2013)
  *Mi lukim **ol dok** i ranim pik bilong mi.*
  1SG see.TR PL dog PM run.TR pig POSS 1SG
  'I saw the dogs that chased my pig.'

Differentiation (value 3) means that there are two different words for the two functions, as in (7).

(7) Martinican Creole (Colot & Ludwig 2013b)
  a. ***Sé** zwéwo-a chapé.*
   PL bird-DEF escape
   'The birds flew away.'
  b. ***Yo** chapé.*
   3PL escape
   'They flew away.'

Overlap (value 4) means that there are two words and that one functions only as a pronoun and the other as a pronoun as well as a nominal plural marker, or the other way around. In the following examples (8a–c), taken from Bislama, *olgeta* functions as a personal pronoun as well as a nominal plural marker, but *ol* is only a nominal plural marker:

(8) Bislama (Meyerhoff 2013)
  a. ***Olgeta** oli drong.*
   3PL AGR drunk
   'They were drunk.'

b. *Olgeta UMP oli no laekem hem.*
   3PL UMP AGR NEG like 3SG
   'The UMP (people) didn't like him.'

c. *Ol haos oli fas~fas tumas.*
   PL house AGR RED~fast very
   'The houses are crowded together.'

Thirty-eight per cent of the *APiCS* languages do not have a nominal plural word; 29 per cent differentiate between the third-person pronoun and the plural marker; 21 per cent use the third-person-plural pronoun for nominal plural marking, and 12 per cent show overlap.

Out of the forty-seven languages with a nominal plural marker (values 2–4), twenty-two differentiate between the two functions, sixteen show identity, and nine overlap. In other words, 52 per cent of the languages to which the feature applies possess the feature, either exclusively or together with another marker.

3. A special case

A special case is found in Trinidad English Creole and Vincentian Creole. In these two languages, the plural marker may be a combination of the conjunction 'and' and the pronoun of the third-person plural. In Trinidad English Creole, this is the only possibility (value 3, differentiation):

(9) Trinidad English Creole (Mühleisen 2013)
Santa, yu see yu an dem chupid Reindeer an dem [...].
Santa 2SG see 2SG and DEM stupid Reindeer and them
'Santa, you see you and these stupid Reindeer [...].'

In Vincentian Creole, the conjunction 'and' is optional (value 4, overlap):

(10) Vincentian Creole (Prescod 2013)
a. *di maango an dem*
   ART mango and them
   'the mangoes'

b. *di maango dem*
   ART mango them
   'the mangoes'

4. Geographical distribution

The identity between the third-person-plural pronoun and the nominal plural marker, be it as value 2 (identity) or 4 (overlap), is almost exclusively an Atlantic feature, occurring on both sides of the ocean (seven languages in West Africa, 15 in the Caribbean). It is not restricted to a specific primary lexifier since it occurs, for example, in Santome (Portuguese-based), Krio (English-based), Haitian (French-based), or Negerhollands (Dutch-based).

In the Pacific area, this feature also occurs in three historically related English-based creoles, as identity in Tok Pisin and as overlap in Bislama and Norf'k.

5. Theoretical observations

According to some creolists, the third-person-plural pronoun used as a nominal plural marker in a given language is not a mere plural marker but a marker of (plural) definiteness or a plural article. We would like to show that, at least in Principense, this marker (realized as *ine*) is not a marker of definiteness or a plural article but a plural marker that is used only in definite contexts.

Like many creole languages, Principense does not overtly mark generic or indefinite plural noun phrases, and it does not mark plural noun phrases which are modified by a plural quantifier unless these are syntactically marked for definiteness, for example, with a demonstrative determiner or a relative clause:

(11) Principense (Maurer own field work)
kwatu omi [vs.] *ine kwatu omi sê*
four man   PL four man DEM
'four men'   'these four men'

In such cases, it is not *ine* that triggers a definite reading of the noun phrase but the occurrence of the (definite) demonstrative *sê* that triggers the use of *ine*. This means that for language-internal reasons many indefinite contexts exclude the use of a nominal plural marker.

If the noun is inanimate, it may only be modified by *ine* if the noun phrase is overtly definite, for example, because of the co-occurrence of the demonstrative *sê*:

(12) Principense (Maurer own field work)
*Ê tan ine laanza. [vs.] *Ê tan ine laanza sê.*
3SG take PL orange   3SG take PL orange DEM
'She took the oranges.' 'She took the/these oranges.'

Vocative noun phrases are intrinsically definite because of the extralinguistic context in which they are used. In sentences like (13) the plural marker does not add definiteness to the noun phrase—it only adds plurality.

(13) Principense (Maurer own field work)
Ningê ê! [vs.] *Ine ningê ê!*
person VOC   PL person VOC
'Sir!/Madam!'   'Ladies!/Gentlemen!'

The rules of Principense may of course not be applied to other languages, and each language must be examined separately. The important fact here is that in many creole languages, the third-person-plural pronoun can be used to express nominal plurality in one way or another.

25 Nominal plural marker and third-person-plural pronoun

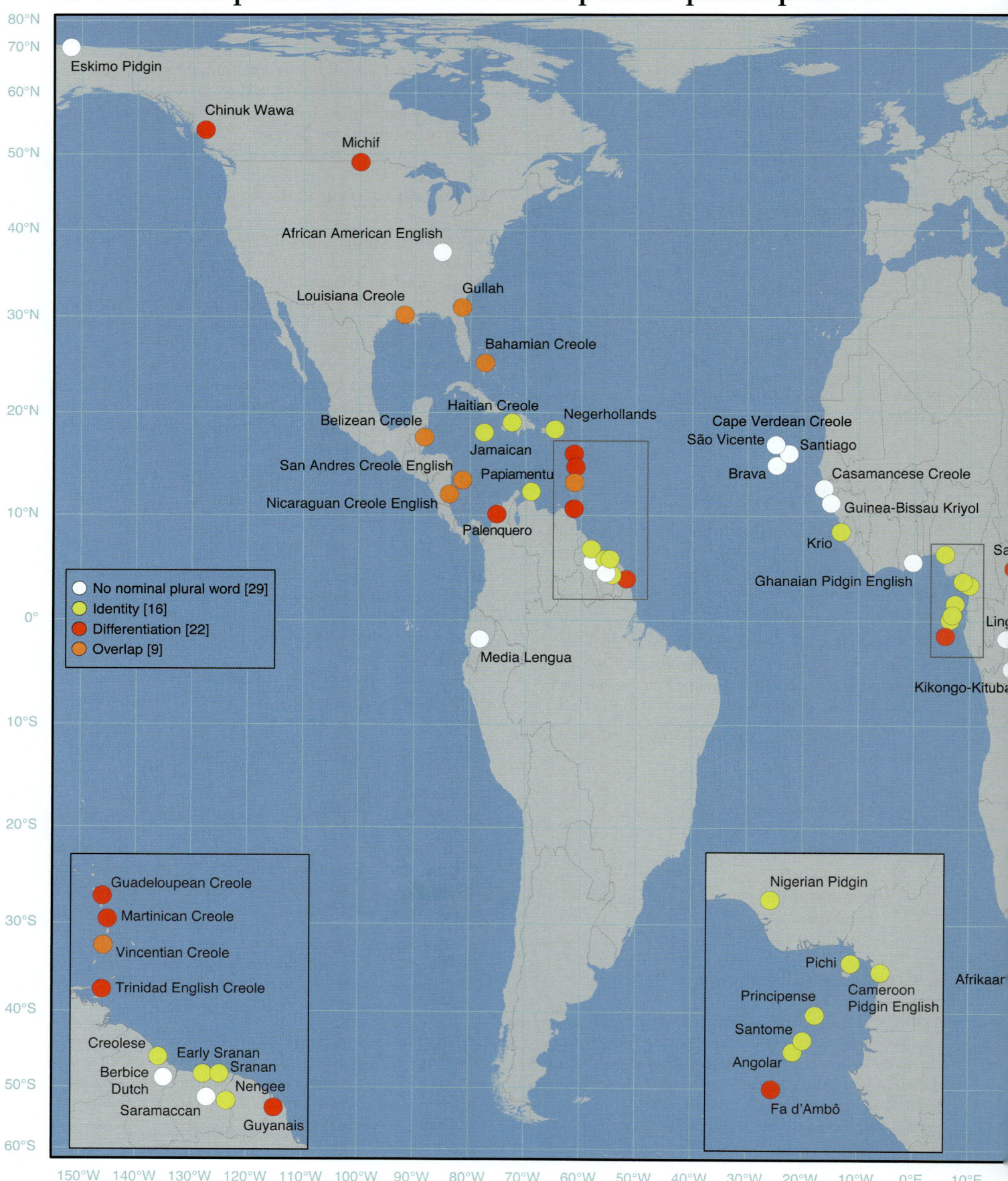

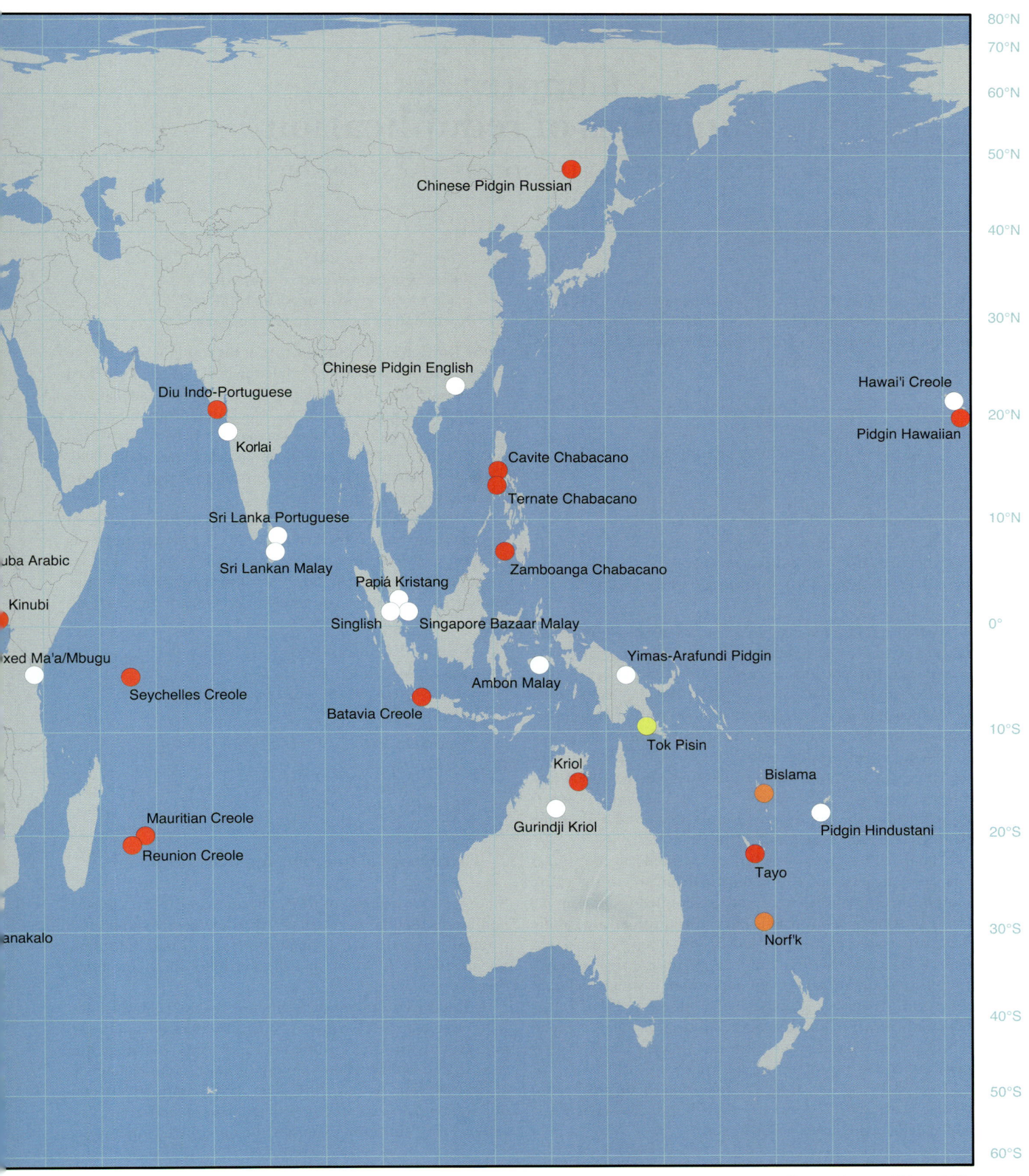

Chapter 26
Functions of reduplication

MARTIN HASPELMATH AND THE *APiCS* CONSORTIUM

1. Introduction

Reduplication is a pattern in which a linguistic form is (fully or partially) repeated directly before or after the base form in order to express a modification of its meaning. Most frequently, reduplication expresses intensity and iteration, as in (1) and (2).

(1) Media Lengua (Muysken 2013)
 yo-ga **bin-bin** *tixi-y-da pudi-ni*
 1SG-TOP well-well weave-INF-ACC can-1SG
 'I can weave very well.'

(2) Berbice Dutch (Kouwenberg 2013a)
 ʃi kɛn-apʰ masi **kor-kori**-*tɛ wɛrɛ*
 her person-PL must work-work-PFV again
 'Her people must have worked and worked again.'

Reduplication is notable in the context of pidgin and creole languages, as these have been found to exhibit a great variety of reduplicative phenomena, which are used frequently (e.g. Kouwenberg (ed.) 2003, Bartens 2004). What is not so clear is whether pidgins and creoles show an unusual amount of reduplication when seen in the context of the world's languages in general, rather than in comparison with the European lexifier languages. Reduplication is widely found in the world's languages (Moravcsik 1978, Hurch (ed.) 2005ff.), but it is poorly represented in the languages of Europe (Rubino 2005), which linguists often take as an intuitive baseline.

Almost all instances of reduplication found in the *APiCS* languages are cases of **full reduplication**, where the entire morpheme or even the entire word is repeated (as in example (1)). Much rarer in our data is **partial reduplication**, where only part of a morpheme is repeated, most often a syllable (e.g. Papiá Kristang *kren-krensa* 'children', Angolar *fo-foga* 'asthma', from *foga* 'suffocate'). Partial reduplication is widely found in the world's languages (Rubino 2005), but not in *APiCS*. It is not clear whether this is because the substrate languages tended to lack partial reduplication or because partial reduplication is more difficult to transfer from a substrate.

A special case of partial reduplication is **duplifixation** (Haspelmath 2002: 24), where a fixed segment sequence is added to the reduplicant, as illustrated by (3).

(3) Korlai (Clements 2013)
 kume bi-me; buni bi-ni; korp bi-p
 eat BI-eat; good BI-good; body BI-body
 'eat and so forth; good and all; body etc.'

In the Korlai pattern, only the part of the word that follows the first syllable is reduplicated, while the first syllable is replaced by the fixed element *bi-*. Sri Lanka Portuguese has a similar pattern, with the fixed element *ki-*. Such duplifixation patterns are widespread in South Asian languages, where they are often called "echo words" or "echo compounds" (see Stolz 2008). The creole patterns have clearly been adopted from the South Asian substrates or adstrates.

Full reduplication is sometimes difficult to distinguish from (re-)iteration (Stolz 2006, Aboh et al. 2012), where entire words or even short phrases are repeated. Such examples are also found in our data (see 4 and 5), but the great majority of our examples are repetitions of simple roots. Only the latter are regarded as reduplication here.

(4) Kinubi (Luffin 2013)
 yal-á al dugag-ín dugag-ín
 child-PL REL small-PL small-PL
 'the young children'

(5) Vincentian Creole (Prescod 2013)
 Shi baal shi baal.
 she bawl she bawl
 'She cried a lot.'

2. Three kinds of function and five values

Since the great majority of *APiCS* languages exhibit reduplication, we focused on the question what functions reduplicative patterns may have. We distinguish between iconic functions, the attenuating function, and the word-class-changing function.

Iconic functions subsume all those functions in which the reduplicated pattern expresses intensity, iteration, plurality, or distributivity. Almost all the examples seen so far are of this type, and we found that this is by far the most common function of reduplication. In fact, there is no *APiCS* language with reduplication that lacks the iconic function of reduplication. The **attenuating function** expresses the opposite of intensity: it refers to a low degree of intensity, as in Singlish *cough-cough* 'cough a little'. Reduplication may also have the purely grammatical function of transposition (**word-class-changing**), as in Cameroon Pidgin English *kwik-kwik* 'quickly' (adverb) from *kwik* (adjective).

Since all languages with reduplication have the iconic function, there are five different types of language:

○	1. No reduplication	10
●	2. Only iconic functions	43
●	3. Attenuating function	7
●	4. Word-class-changing function	9
●	5. Attenuating and word-class-changing function	7

3. Iconic functions

As mentioned earlier, the subfunctions of the iconic function are intensity, iteration, plurality, and distributivity. It is very common for gradable words (adjectives such as 'small', 'good', and 'dark', and adverbs) to have the intensity sense (see 6) when reduplicated, while action words have the iteration or continuation sense (7). Example (6b) shows that "triplication" is possible as well.

(6) a. Bahamian (Hackert 2013)
*when it get **dark-dark** night* [...]
'when the night turns really dark [...]'

b. Juba Arabic (Manfredi & Petrollino 2013)
*maál **tamán tamán tamán***
place good good good
'a very good place'

(7) a. Cameroon Pidgin English (Schröder 2013)
*Ren di **fol fol**.*
rain IPFV fall fall
'It's raining all the time.'

b. Afrikaans (den Besten & Biberauer 2013)
*Hulle **soek-soek** so tussen die bossies.*
3PL search-search so among the bushes
'They are searching among the bushes.'

Nouns have a plural sense in a few languages, for example, Ambon Malay *rusa rusa* 'deer (PL)', Diu Indo-Portuguese *muyɛ-muyɛr* 'women', Kriol *olgaman-olgaman* 'old women'. In Kriol, it is also possible for attributive adjectives to be reduplicated to show plurality of the noun phrase: *lilwan-lilwan kokiroj* [little-little cockroach] 'little cockroaches'.

The distributive sense occurs commonly with numerals (see Chapter 34), as in Tok Pisin *Ol i kam **tupela tupela*** [they PM come two two] 'They came two by two' (Smith & Siegel 2013). But it is also found in other kinds of situations, for example, with temporal nouns referring to regular occurrence (*día día* [day day] 'every day' in Ternate Chabacano), with adjectives (*teya teya* 'torn in many places, ragged' in Norf'k, *teya* < *tear*), or with verbs, to indicate that the action distributes over the participants:

(8) Santome (Hagemeijer 2013)
*Yô ngê **dêsê-dêsê**.*
many people descend-descend
'Many people went down (different people at different moments).'

4. Attenuating functions

The attenuating function is mostly found with adjectives:

(9) Nengee *fatu-fatu* 'fattish'
Saramaccan *wɛti-wɛti* 'whitish'
Jamaican *yala-yala* 'yellowish'
Seychelles Creole *vilenn-vilenn* 'a little ugly'

But verbal actions can also be attenuated (cf. also the Singlish example *cough-cough* mentioned earlier):

(10) Sranan (Winford & Plag 2013)
*Norfu e **férfi férfi**.*
Norfu ASP paint paint
'Norval is painting a bit.'

And Haitian Creole makes use of reduplication for diminutives, especially in child-directed speech:

(11) Haitian Creole (Fattier 2013)
*Ann al fè on ti **benbeny**!*
IMP.1PL go do INDF little bath
'Let's take a little bath!' (cf. *beny* 'bath')

5. Word-class-changing functions

The word-class-changing function of reduplication occurs much less systematically, and often seems to be restricted to a small group of lexical items. It never involves a change to a verb, creating only nouns and adjectives in our data. Here are a few examples (in addition to Cameroon Pidgin English *kwik-kwik* 'quickly' mentioned earlier):

(12) Verb to noun
Creolese *blow blow* [blow blow] 'a whistle'
Papiamentu *pega-pega* [stick-stick] 'gecko'

(13) Adjective to noun
Ghanaian P. E. *pɔ pɔ* [poor poor] 'poverty'
Jamaican *swiit swiit* [sweet sweet] 'perfume'

(14) Noun to adjective
Juba Arabic *móyo móyo* [water water] 'liquid'

26 Functions of reduplication

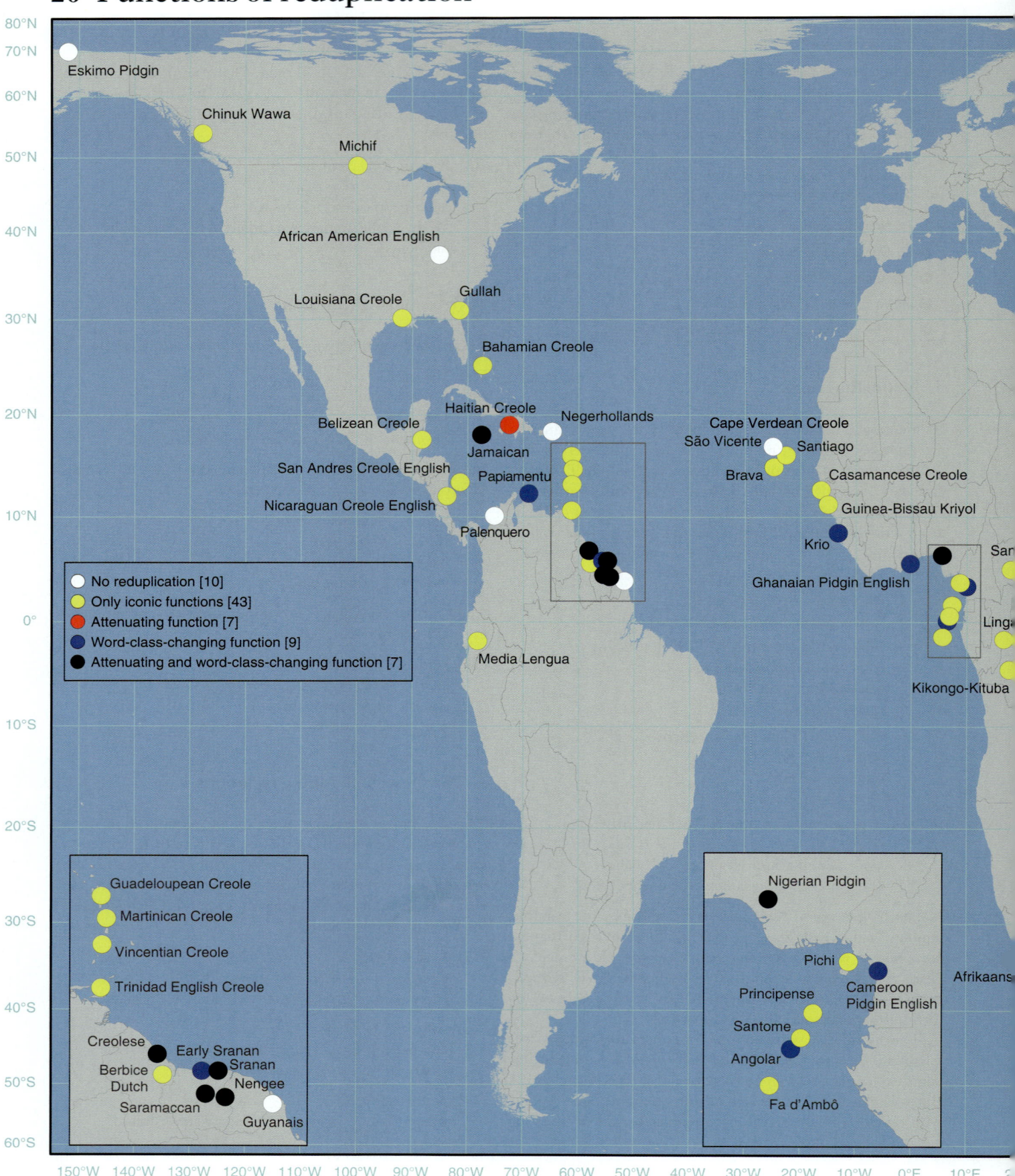

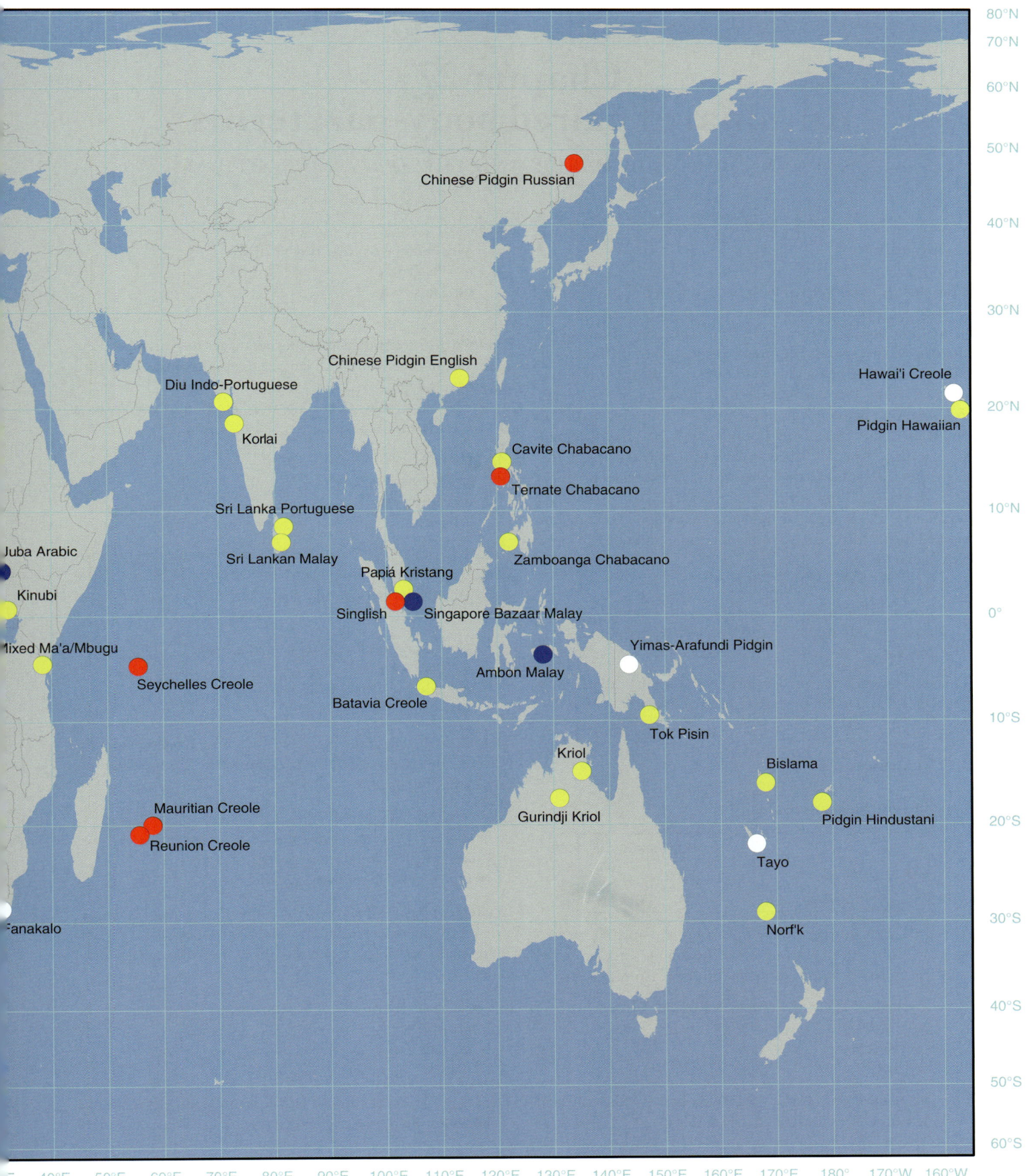

Chapter 27
Antidual of paired body-part terms

SUSANNE MARIA MICHAELIS AND THE *APiCS* CONSORTIUM

1. Introduction

This chapter is concerned with the expression of the notional singular of paired body-part terms (e.g. 'one eye', 'one ear', 'one hand', 'one arm', 'one foot'). In some languages, the notional singular of such words requires or often occurs with an overt singular-marking element, as in Hungarian *fél szem* 'one eye', lit. 'half eyes'. The normal way to express the concept 'eyes' in Hungarian is to use the non-marked form *szem*, that is, no plural marking is used (see Rounds 2001: 90). Such a singular-marking element is called an **antidual marker** here. Other languages with antidual marking use words like 'side' or 'grain' in the same way. Thus, an antidual marker is a special case of a singulative, which marks a singular form in opposition to a non-marked plural form. An example of antidual marking in a creole is given in (1):

(1) Reunion Creole (Bollée 2013)
   mon **kote** d zorey vs. mon de zorey
   POSS.1SG side of ear   POSS.1SG two ear
   'my ear'   'my ears'

This phenomenon seems to be rare cross-linguistically, and has not been studied in a comparative perspective.

2. The values

Two different values are distinguished:

		excl	shrd	all
●	1. Antidual	0	6	6
○	2. No antidual	68	6	74

As can be seen from the value box, there are only six *APiCS* languages in which an antidual construction for singular paired body-part terms is found (value 1). Another example is (2):

(2) Seychelles Creole (Michaelis & Rosalie 2013)
   en **kote** lipye
   a/one side leg
   'one leg'

The vast majority of *APiCS* languages do not show antidual marking (value 2), as illustrated in example (3):

(3) Vincentian Creole (Prescod 2013)
   a nooz hool
   INDF nose hole
   'a nostril'

None of the six antidual-marking languages has this option exclusively; in other words, all languages also have the unmarked option (value 2).

In Haitian Creole, we find the word *grenn* 'unit, seed' which is used as the antidual marker:

(4) Haitian Creole (Fattier 2013)
   gwo **grenn** zye
   big unit   eye
   'a big eye'

Baker & Kriegel (2013) state for Mauritian Creole that the antidual structure, as in Seychelles Creole expressed by *kote*, is attested in nineteenth-century texts, but that it is rarely used today:

(5) Mauritian Creole (Baker & Kriegel 2013)
   en **kote** lizye fer mal
   one side eye make bad
   'One eye is hurting.'

Migge (2013) suggests the same historical development for Nengee. She suspects that the antidual marking is the older option in this language:

(6) Nengee (Migge 2013)
   Wan se fufu langa moo a taa wan.
   one side foot long more DET.SG other one
   'One foot is longer than the other one.'

In Creolese the antidual construction with *said* 'side' is not restricted to specific lexical items (body-parts), but is very much contextually restricted in that it is rather used to emphasize one item in a pair.

(7) Creolese (Devonish & Thompson 2013)
   wan said eez
   one side ears
   'one ear'

The case of Trinidad English Creole is interesting. It is not one of the six antidual-marking languages because it does not mark

Antidual of paired body-part terms

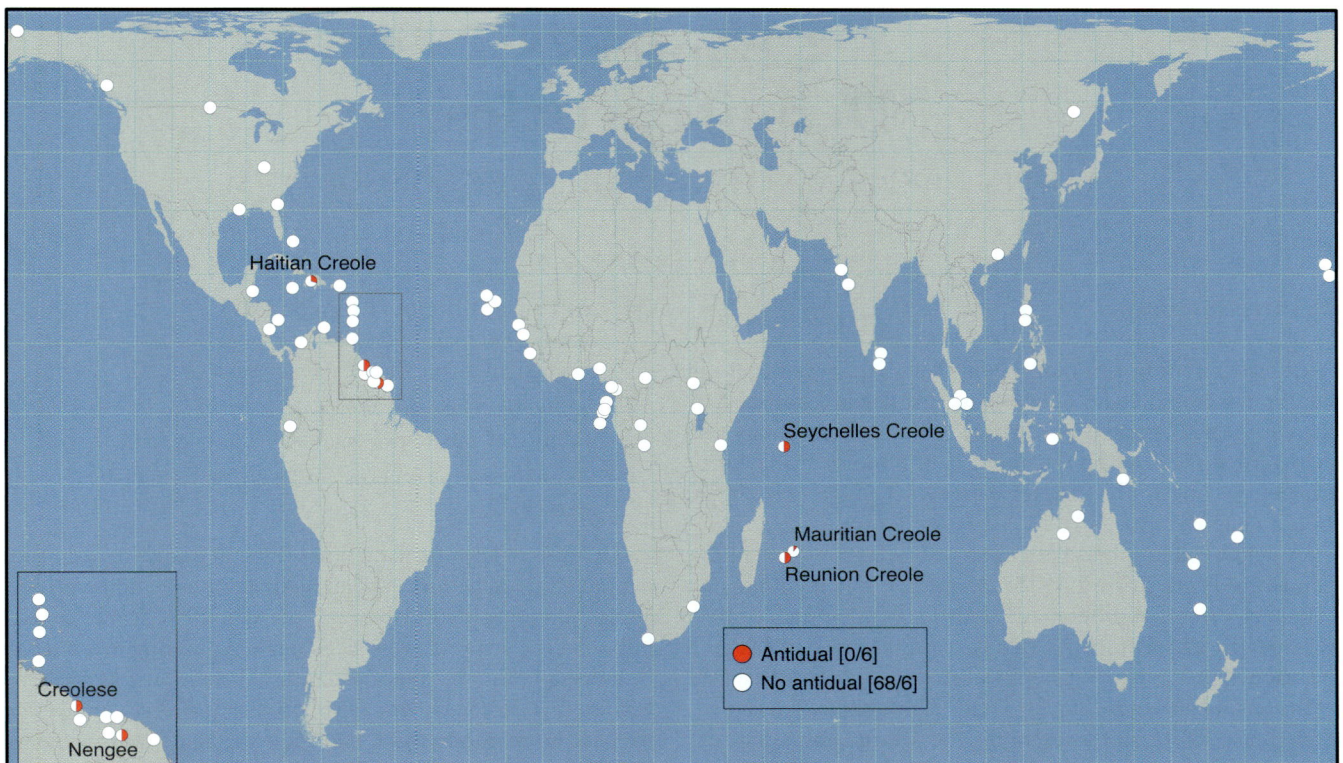

the singular in paired body-parts. But according to Mühleisen (2013), the use of 'side' referring to one entity of paired things is very common, as in *a side of shoe/earring/slipper* 'one shoe/earring/slipper'. Bollée (2013) also cites a similar example in Reunion Creole (*en kote soulye* [a side shoe] 'one shoe'). These uses are very similar because the paired objects are pieces of clothing or adornment that are closely associated with paired body-parts.

3. Geographic distribution

As can be seen from the figures and the map, this feature shows very little variation within the *APiCS* languages. But interestingly enough, all three French-based Indian Ocean creoles show this construction. As far as we know, there is no French dialectal model to this construction (see Chaudenson 1974; Philip Baker, p.c.). And neither of the major substratal sources for this group of creoles, Malagasy and Eastern Bantu languages, displays this construction (Maria Polinsky, p.c.; Maarten Mous, p.c.).

The other three antidual-marking languages are Haitian Creole, Creolese, and Nengee, one French- and two English-based creoles of the Caribbean. The origin of this pattern in the creole languages is thus an intriguing open question.

4. Lexicalization of plural body-parts in *APiCS* languages

From an etymological point of view, it is interesting to mention that in many creoles and pidgins it is the plural forms of the body-part terms in the base language which were reanalysed as the creole/pidgin lexeme unspecified for number, e.g. *lizye* 'eye(s)' (< French *les yeux* (pl.)), *zorey* 'ear(s)' (< French *les oreilles* (pl.)) in French-based creoles, *iez* 'ear(s)' in Jamaican (< English *ears*), *glaza* 'eye(s)' (< Russian *glaza* (pl.)) in Chinese Pidgin Russian. In Jamaican (Farquharson 2013) and Pichi (Yakpo 2013), the former English plural body-parts tend to get only the singular interpretation. If one wants to refer explicitly to the two members of a pair, one needs to use the postposed plural word, as in Jamaican *mi iez-dem* 'my ears', and Pichi *fut dɛn* 'legs'.

Chapter 28
Definite articles

MARTIN HASPELMATH AND THE *APiCS* CONSORTIUM

1. Introduction

A **definite article** is a morpheme that frequently occurs in noun phrases and codes definiteness, like *the* in English. Articles are usually treated as separate words, but they may also be regarded as affixes on the noun, as in Swedish (*kung* 'king', *kungen* 'the king'). This chapter is modelled on Dryer's (2005b) *WALS* chapter.

A definite noun phrase is a noun phrase whose referent can be **uniquely identified** by the hearer. Unique identifiability occurs in a range of different circumstances. One such context is in **anaphoric situations**, that is, when the referent has been mentioned previously. This is illustrated in (1), where 'the fish' in the second clause is uniquely identifiable because it was mentioned just before. In this example, the definite noun phrase is coded by the demonstrative *eta* 'that', but this could equally be translated by a definite article.

(1) Chinese Pidgin Russian (Perekhvalskaya 2013)
 Xetʃʒu liba kupi-la, eta liba pomilaj netu.
 Xeczu fish buy-PFV this fish die NEG
 'Xeczu bought a fish, that/the fish was alive.'

Unique identifiability also holds in **associative contexts**, where a referent has not been mentioned directly in the preceding context but is identifiable because of an association with a previously mentioned referent.

(2) Cape Verdean Creole of Brava (Baptista 2013)
 N kunpra un kaza ki kobra poku dinheru
 I bought INDF house that cost little money
 *y **kel** aldeia fika pertu di trabadju.*
 and DEF neighbourhood is close of work
 'I bought a house that cost little money and the neighbourhood is close to work.'

Here *aldeia* 'neighbourhood' has not been mentioned previously, but the noun *kaza* evokes various concepts such as 'roof', 'door', 'owner', 'neighbourhood' that can be uniquely identified when a house is mentioned.

Finally, a noun phrase may be uniquely identifiable because it is used **generically**, referring to the entire kind rather than to a particular instance, as in (3) (where 'fevers' is understood generically).

(3) Sri Lanka Portuguese (Smith 2013)
 *ingrees miziɲa dika **isti** fɛɛvri-s-pa*
 English medicine than the fever-PL-DAT
 malvaar-su miziɲa mee boom
 Tamil-GEN medicine FOC good
 'Tamil medicine is better for fevers than English medicine.'

Definite articles are sometimes difficult to distinguish from demonstratives, because a noun modified by a demonstrative is always uniquely identifiable, and the specific semantic contribution of the demonstrative need not be a pointing use, but can be an anaphoric use. Thus, example (1) could just as easily be rendered as 'Xeczu bought a fish, this fish was alive', and in fact we have no reason to think that the morpheme *eta* in Chinese Pidgin Russian is anything but a demonstrative. However, demonstratives are not used when the noun phrase is used associatively (see 2), or is used generically (see 3). If a morpheme can be used in one of these contexts for unique reference, it is considered a definite article.

Note that definite articles need not be obligatory. They are normally frequent when the referent is uniquely identifiable, but they are also often absent, for example, when a possessor is present (and especially when a demonstrative is present; cf. Chapter 31).

2. The values

Four different values are distinguished:

●	1. Definite article distinct from demonstratives	38
●	2. Definite article identical to a demonstrative	19
●	3. No definite article, but indefinite article	10
○	4. Neither definite nor indefinite article	9

Many pidgins and creoles are like English, Dutch, French, Spanish, and Portuguese in that they have **a special definite article that is distinct from a demonstrative**. Almost all English-based languages are of this type, and in almost all of them, the English distinction between *the* and *this/that* has survived. Examples are given in (4).

(4) a. Cameroon Pidgin English (Schröder 2013)
   di pikin   dat man
   the child   that man

 b. Nicaraguan Creole English (Bartens 2013a)
    di tiicha   dis ting
    the teacher this thing

 c. Sranan (Winford & Plag 2013)
    a son   a sani dati
    the sun   the thing that

The distinction has also survived in some of the Philippine Spanish-based creoles (cf. Spanish *el/la* vs. *este/esta*):

(5) Zamboanga Chabacano (Steinkrüger 2013)
   el ómbre   *éste ómbre*
   the man   this man

In some languages, demonstratives are expressed by postnominal spatial deictic elements:

(6) a. Papiamentu (Kouwenberg 2013b)
   e buki   *e buki aki*
   the book   the book here = 'this book'

 b. Nengee (Migge 2013)
    a osu   *a osu de*
    the house   the house there = 'that house'

And in some languages, the distinction is a purely prosodic one, with more stress or a higher pitch on the demonstrative:

(7) a. Pichi (Yakpo 2013)
   dì nem   *dí man*
   the name   this man

 b. Afrikaans (den Besten & Biberauer 2013)
    die motor *díé motor*
    the car   that car

In a few languages, the definite article occurs only in the plural and is simultaneously a plural marker (e.g. Santome *inen mosu* [3PL.DEF boy] 'the boys'). Such plural markers derive from the third-person-plural personal pronoun and are quite unrelated to demonstratives (see Chapter 25).

There are also many languages whose **definite article is not distinct from a demonstrative**. In all the cases where we know more about the history of the forms, the demonstrative use is the original use, and the word has been extended to a definite-article use, for instance:

(8) Chinese Pidgin English   *that*
    Diu Indo-Portuguese   *ikəl*
    Papiá Kristang   *aké*
    Seychelles Creole   *sa*
    Singapore Bazaar Malay   *itu*

Such definite articles are usually not obligatory, so to establish that they are really definite articles as well, it must be clear that they can be used associatively or generically. Examples (2) and (3) show definite articles that could also be used as demonstratives. Another example is (9), which has an occurrence of *kela* 'that, the' in a demonstrative use and another occurrence in an associative use ('priest' is evoked by 'church').

(9) Pidgin Hawaiian (Roberts 2013)
   kela *wahine Auroria hoi   mai ma ka halepule* [...]
   that woman Auroria return DIR LOC the church

   Wau olelo iaia noho malie, mahope huhu **kela** *kahunapule.*
   1SG speak 3SG stay quiet later angry the priest
   'That woman, Auroria, returned to the church with the girls [...] I told her to be quiet, or else the priest would get angry.'

The languages of the remaining two types have no definite articles. Value 3 comprises languages that at least have an **indefinite article** (see also Chapter 29). Example (10) shows two noun phrases, a definite and an indefinite one, and only the latter has an article.

(10) Sri Lankan Malay (Slomanson 2013)
    *Dia daging-yang piso-**attu**-ring e-potong.*
    3SG meat-ACC knife-INDF-INS PST-cut
    'She cut the meat with a knife.'

Finally, the languages of the last type do **not have any article**. In (11), again we see an indefinite and a definite noun phrase, and neither has an article.

(11) Eskimo Pidgin (van der Voort 2013)
    wai'hinni artegi annahanna pûgmûmmi
    woman coat sew now
    'The woman is sewing a coat now.'

Another such language is Chinese Pidgin Russian, illustrated in (1).

28 Definite articles

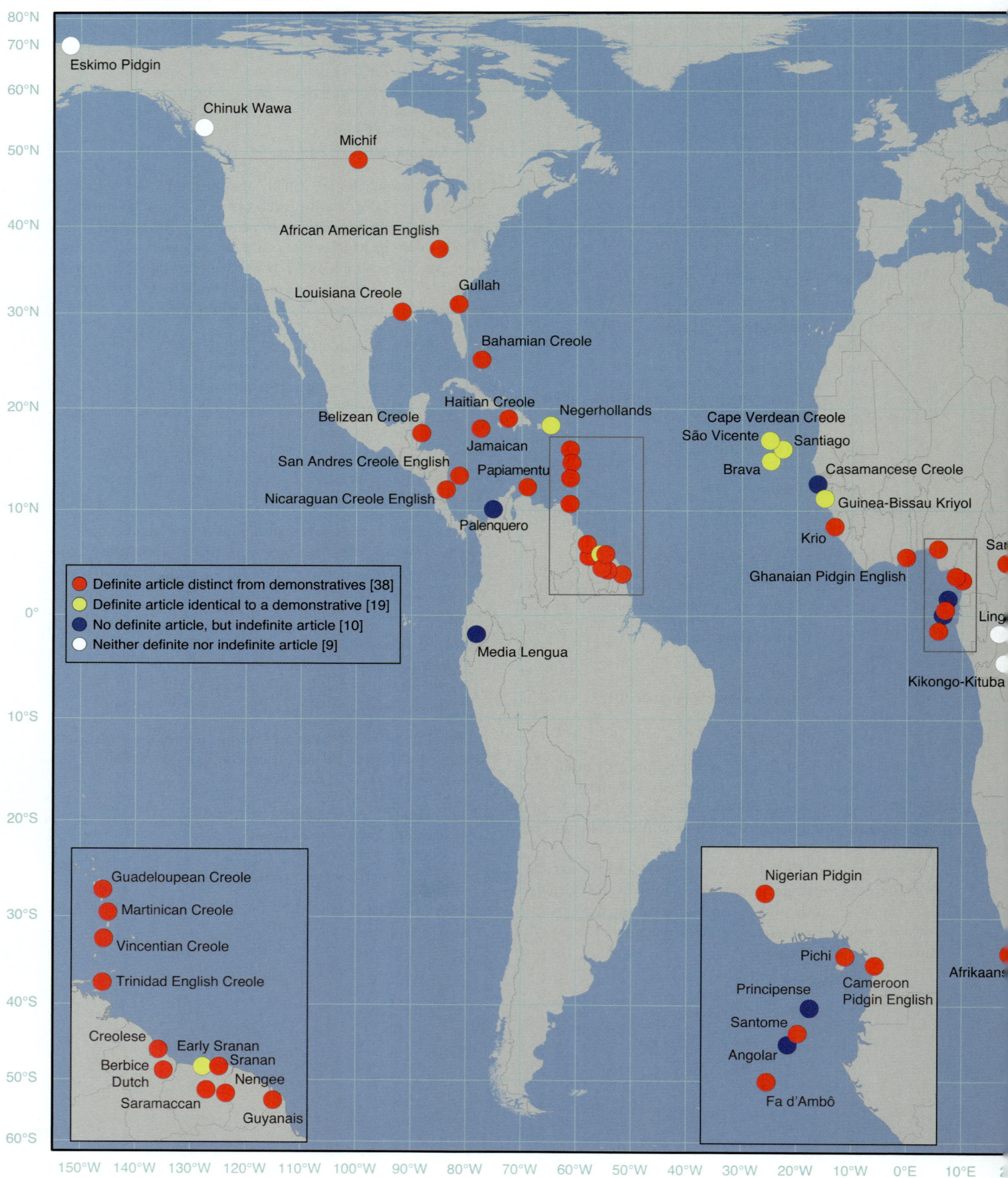

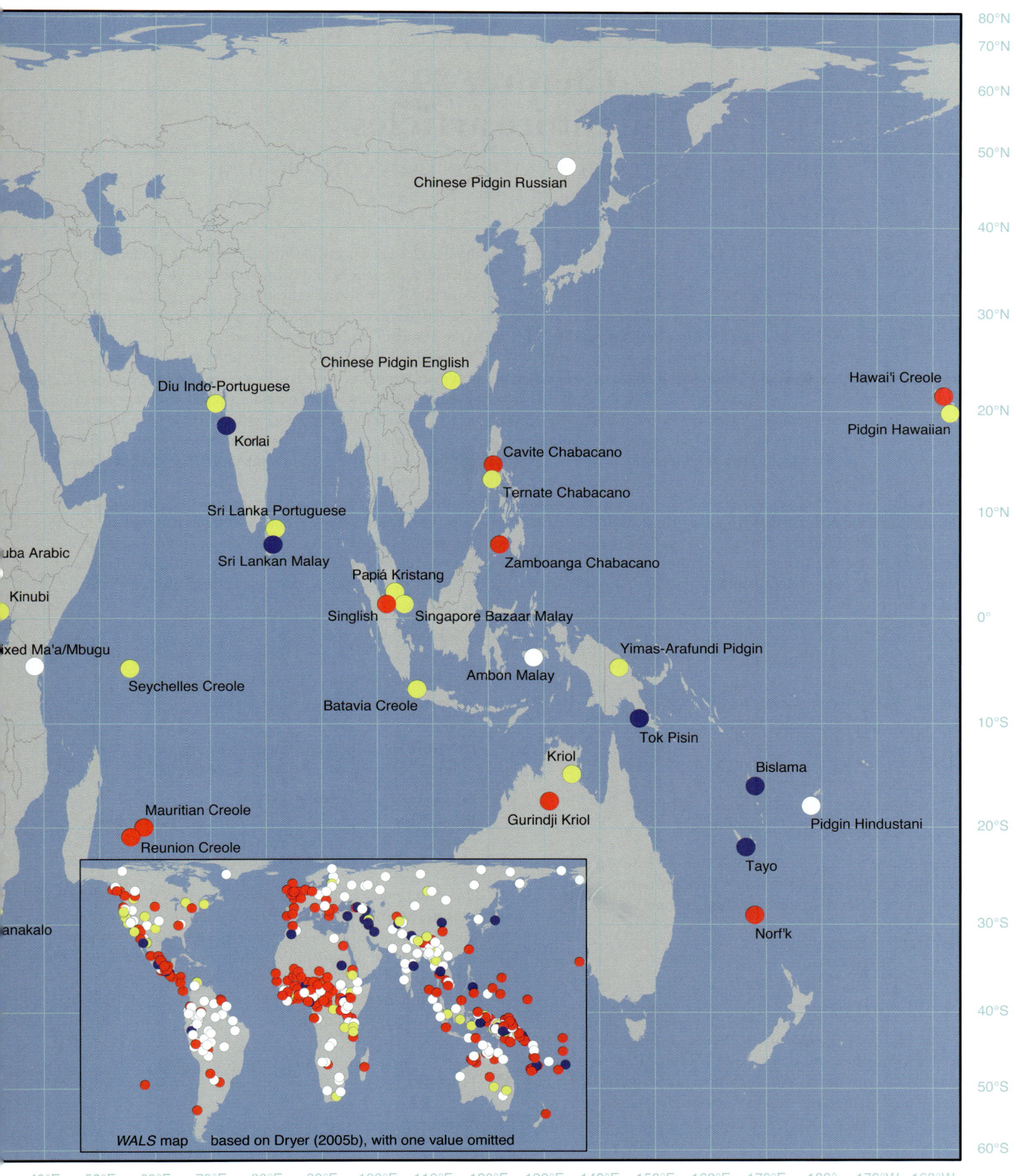

Chapter 29
Indefinite articles

MARTIN HASPELMATH AND THE *APiCS* CONSORTIUM

1. Introduction

An **indefinite article** is a morpheme that frequently occurs in noun phrases and signals that the referent is not uniquely identifiable by the hearer, as in *We have a dog*. The great majority of *APiCS* languages have not only a definite, but also an indefinite article. This chapter is modelled on the *WALS* chapter by Dryer (2005c).

Indefinite articles typically originate in the numeral 'one', and in the *APiCS* languages this is almost universally the case: in the Romance-based languages, the indefinite article is derived from the Romance indefinite article *un/um* (ultimately from Latin *unum* 'one'), and in the English-based languages, the indefinite article is derived from English *a* or *one* (both ultimately from Old English *ān* 'one'). As a result of their origin in a numeral, indefinite articles are most often restricted to count nouns (cf. **We have a money*) and to singular nouns (cf. **We have a dogs*).

Two examples of indefinite articles are given in (1) and (2).

(1) Santome (Hagemeijer 2013)
 Ũa migu mu bi ai.
 a friend 1SG.POSS come here
 'A friend of mine came here.'

(2) Early Sranan (van den Berg & Bruyn 2013)
 Kaba a si **wan** figaboom varreweh.
 and 3SG.SBJ see INDF.SG fig.tree far.away
 'And he saw a fig tree further down.'

There is just one clear example of an indefinite article in our data that does not appear to derive from the numeral 'one', the form *mbeni* in Sango (the Sango numeral 'one' is *oko*):

(3) Sango (Samarin 2013)
 I faa **mbeni** kota yaka.
 1PL cut a large garden
 'We made a large garden.'

Just as definite articles often originate in demonstratives and are therefore often still synchronically identical to them, indefinite articles are often still synchronically identical to the numeral 'one'. This is the case in Romance languages, in French for example, where *un ami* can mean 'a friend' or 'one friend'.

In Dryer's (2005c) worldwide study, 204 out of 473 languages have an indefinite article, and of these, 91 have an indefinite article word that is distinct from the numeral 'one' (like English *a*), while 90 languages have an indefinite article word that is identical to the numeral 'one' (like French *un*).

Distinguishing article use from numeral use in semantic-pragmatic terms is not easy. In the three examples above, a translation with 'one' would yield a slightly different meaning, but not unacceptable sentences ('One friend of mine came here.', 'He saw one fig tree.', 'We made one large garden.'). The basic difference is that the numeral underlines the cardinality, in implicit contrast with other cardinalities ('one fig tree', i.e. not two or three fig trees), while the indefinite article backgrounds the cardinality (even though it entails it as well). Thus, when a word that is also used as the numeral 'one' is used in a context where emphasizing the cardinality would be pointless, as in (4) and (5), we can be certain that we are dealing with an indefinite article.

(4) Bislama (Meyerhoff 2013)
 from hem i **wan** pikinini we hem i no save
 because 3SG AGR INDF.ART child REL 3SG AGR NEG HAB
 hangri
 hungry
 'because he's a child who doesn't feel hungry [but then gets headaches if he hasn't eaten]'

(5) Sranan (Winford & Plag 2013)
 Nanga den sma disi wi o abi **wan** taki-makandra.
 with the.PL person DEM we FUT have ART talk-about
 'We will have a conversation with these people.'

This criterion is fairly vague, so in practice, the criterion that was normally employed by the contributors was whether the word is often used accompanying an indefinite noun where English would use its indefinite article, not its numeral *one*. Note that in many *APiCS* languages, the indefinite article is not obligatory, and the precise conditions under which it is used or omitted are usually unknown.

2. The values

Four different values are distinguished:

Indefinite articles

🔴	1. Indefinite article distinct from numeral 'one'	20
🟡	2. Indefinite article identical to numeral 'one'	46
🔵	3. No indefinite article, but definite article	1
⚪	4. Neither indefinite nor definite article	9

Many pidgins and creoles are like English in that they have **a special indefinite article that is distinct from the numeral 'one'** (value 1). This is the case in quite a few English-based and Dutch-based languages where the English (and similarly Dutch) distinction between *a* and *one* has survived. Examples are given in (6).

(6) a. Gullah (Klein 2013)
    a bag   *one cent*
    a bag   one cent

    b. Afrikaans (den Besten & Biberauer 2013)
    'n kat   *een kat*
    a cat   one cat

But the indefinite article *a* has disappeared from many English-based languages, and has been replaced by the numeral *one* (mostly written *wan* in the pidgins and creoles), leading to identity (value 2, see below). In Jamaican and in Creolese, the indefinite-article use and the numeral use are said to be pronounced differently.

(7) a. Jamaican *wahn* [wã] 'a'   *wan* 'one'
    b. Creolese *wan* 'a'   *waan* 'one'

In some of the French-based languages, the indefinite article is occasionally differentiated from the numeral 'one' (*un* in French).

(8) a. Louisiana Creole *ẽ* 'a'   *enn* 'one'
    b. Michif *aen, enn* 'a'   *henn* 'one'

Another example of this type is Sango (see ex. 3), where the indefinite article does not derive from the numeral 'one'. But note that a mere stress difference is not sufficient: in many languages, the numeral 'one' can be distinguished from the indefinite article by stress (e.g. Mauritian Creole *en sát* 'a cat' vs. *én sát* 'one cat'). These cases are subsumed under the next value.

In the majority of our languages the **indefinite article is identical to the numeral 'one'** (value 2). This is the case in many Romance-based languages, where the nondistinctness of indefinite article and numeral was inherited from French/Spanish *un* and Portuguese *um*.

(9) Angolar (Maurer 2013a)
    a. *No ka konta ũa thoya* [...].
       1PL FUT tell   ART story
       'I am going to tell a story [...].'

    b. *M mêthê ũa litu vi.*
       1SG want one litre wine
       'I want one litre of palm wine.'

(10) Seychelles Creole (Michaelis & Rosalie 2013)
    Mon annan en sat.
    1SG have one cat
    'I have a/one cat.'

Nondistinctness is also found in many English-based languages, where *wan* (from *one*) is used in both ways (*wanpela* in Tok Pisin comes from *one fellow*):

(11) Tok Pisin (Smith & Siegel 2013)
    a. *Long dispela ples i gat **wanpela** lapun meri.*
       PREP this village PM have one   old woman
       'In this village there was an old woman.'

    b. *Long dispela tais saksak i gat **wanpela** traipela rot tasol.*
       PREP DEM swamp sago PM got one big road only
       'In this sago swamp there was only one big road.'

(12) Chinese Pidgin English (Li & Matthews 2013)
    a. 米其勞士温卑時雞品
       *Makee roastee **one** piecee capon.*
       make roast ART.INDF CLF capon
       'Roast a capon.'

    b. 米刻吠温三布
       My give you one sample.
       1SG give 2SG ART.INDF sample
       'I will give you one sample.'

When a language has two different indefinite articles, one of which is identical to the numeral and one of which is distinct, it is classified as value 1 (e.g. Nicaraguan Creole English, which has both *a* and *wan*).

The languages of the remaining two types have no indefinite articles. Value 3 comprises the one language that at least has a **definite article** (see Chapter 28), Yimas-Arafundi Pidgin. Finally, the languages of the last type (value 4) **do not have any article**; these are the same languages that have value 4 in Chapter 28. In (13), we see an indefinite and a definite noun phrase, and neither has an article.

(13) Juba Arabic (Manfredi & Petrollino 2013)
    kamán nesib-át bi=jáhizu háfla kebír
    also sister.in.law-PL IRR=prepare party big
    'The sisters-in-law also prepare a big party.'

29 Indefinite articles

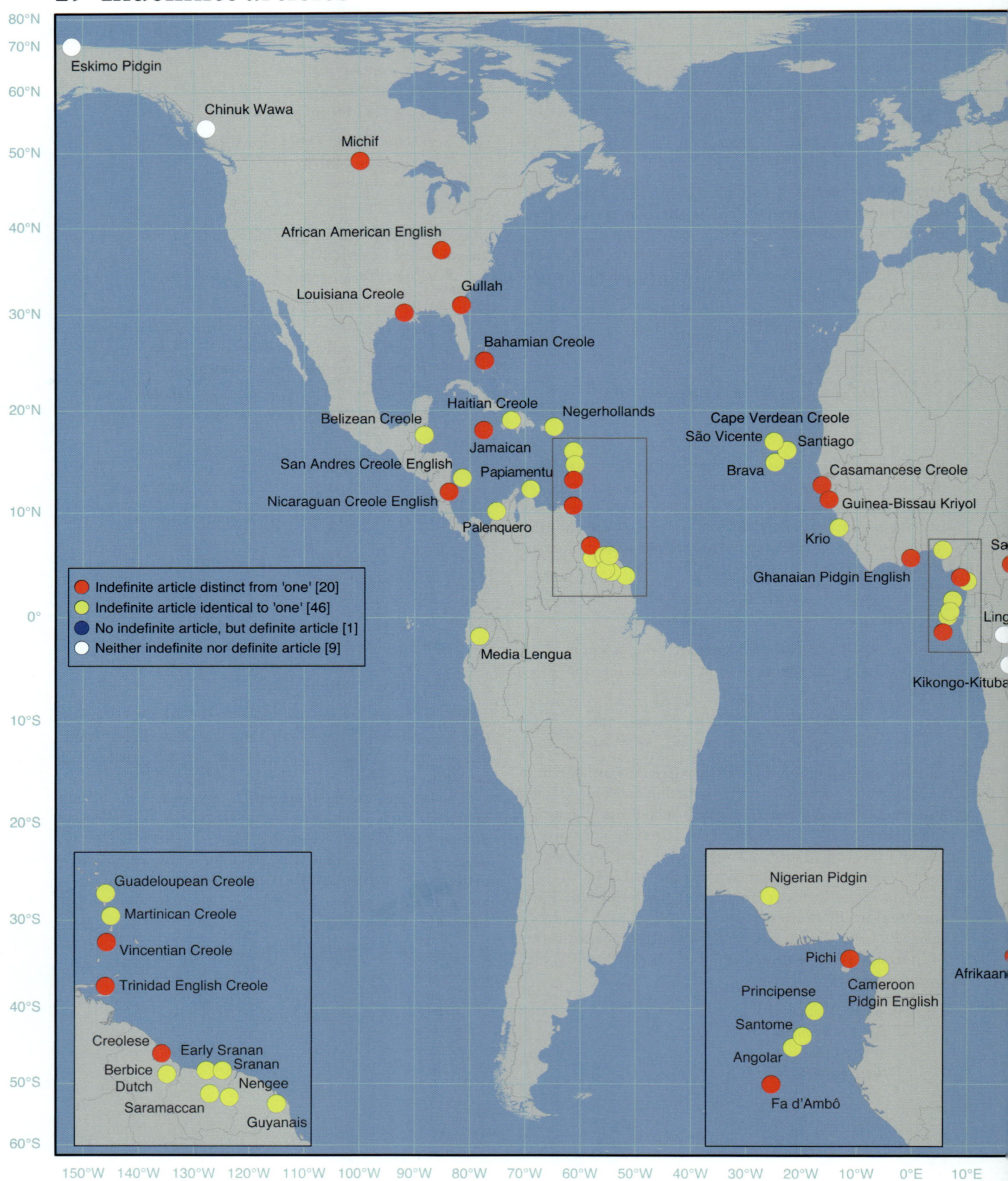

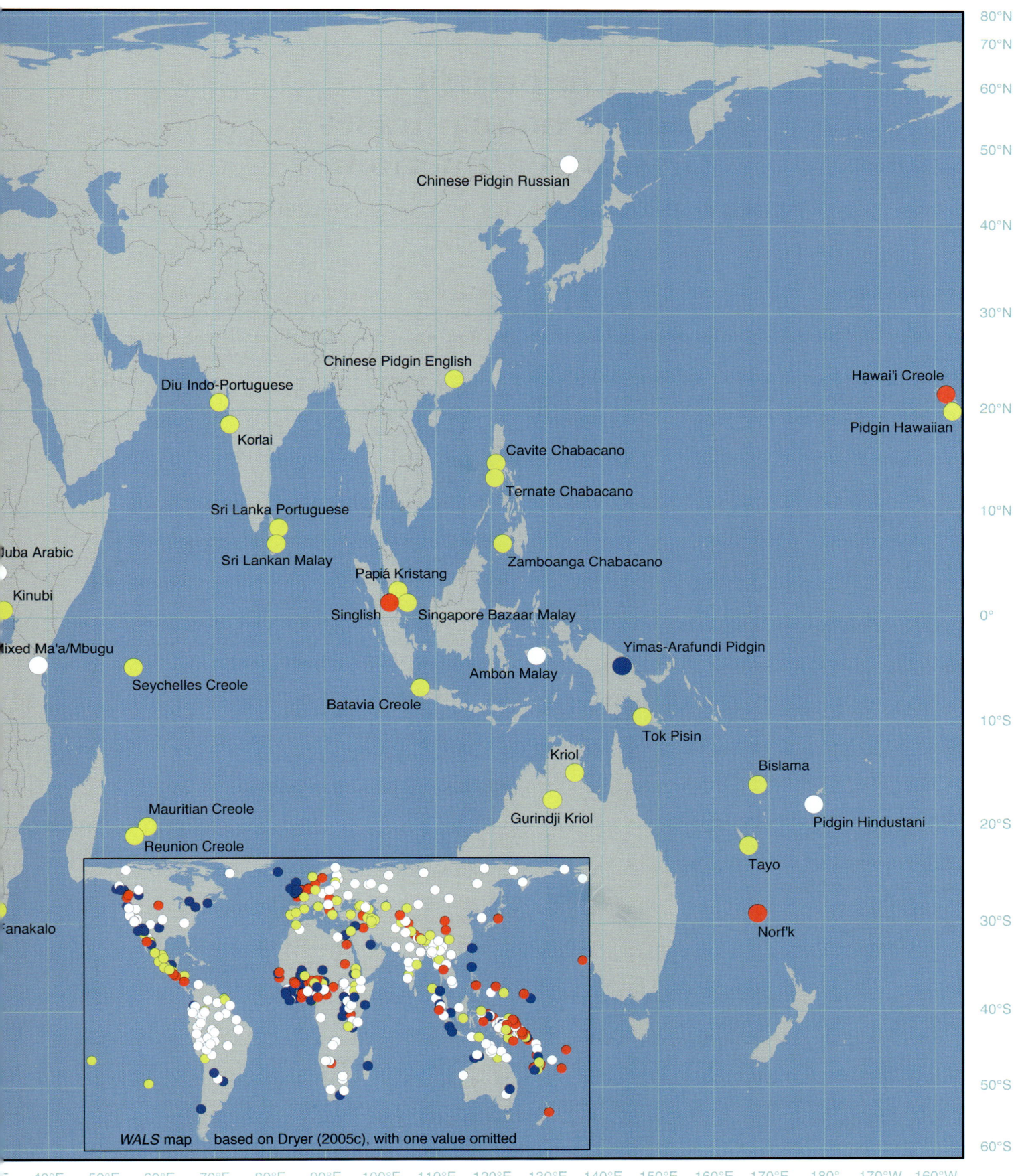

Chapter 30
Generic noun phrases in subject function

PHILIPPE MAURER AND THE *APiCS* CONSORTIUM

1. Introduction

A generic noun or noun phrase refers to a whole class and is thus non-specific.

For this feature, we consider only sentences where both the subject and the situation which the verb refers to are generic; we do not consider sentences where the subject, but not the verb phrase, is generic, as in 'The stamp was invented in the nineteenth century.'

2. The values

We distinguish the following values:

		excl	shrd	all
○	1. Languages without definite and indefinite article	9	0	9
●	2. Bare singular noun phrase in languages with definite article	28	14	42
●	3. Bare singular noun phrase in languages without definite article	6	0	6
●	4. Singular noun phrase with definite article	3	15	18
●	5. Bare plural noun phrase in languages with definite article	3	9	12
●	6. Bare plural noun phrase in languages without definite article	2	0	2
●	7. Plural noun phrase with definite article	2	10	12
●	8. Singular noun phrase with indefinite article	1	6	7
●	9. Singular noun phrase with adnominal possessive	0	1	1

Note that for the purposes of *APiCS*, a form is considered a definite article only if it also has the associative function (see Chapter 28 on definite articles). Furthermore, 'singular' means that there is no overt plural marking on the noun, and 'bare' means that there is no determiner in the noun phrase.

Value 1 (**languages without definite and indefinite article**) occurs in five pidgin languages (Chinese Pidgin Russian, Chinuk Wawa, Eskimo Pidgin, Pidgin Hindustani, Yimas-Arafundi Pidgin), in three Bantu-based languages (Kikongo-Kituba, Lingala, Mixed Ma'a/Mbugu), in Ambon Malay, and in Juba Arabic. In these languages, generic noun phrases are bare.

(1) Juba Arabic (Manfredi & Petrollino 2013)
 Nas fi júba úmon nas mutalimín wa
 people LOC Juba 3PL people educated.PL and
 muhtaramín.
 respectful.PL
 'Juba people are educated and respectful.'

Value 2 (**bare noun phrase in languages with definite article**) occurs in 55 per cent of the *APiCS* languages and is the most widespread value. It is present in twenty English-based languages, in ten Ibero-Romance-based languages, in six French-based languages, in Berbice Dutch, Sango, Kinubi, Singapore Bazaar Malay, Pidgin Hawaiian, and in the bilingual mixed language Gurindji Kriol.

(2) Diu Indo-Portuguese (Cardoso 2013)
 Ɛlifãt ɛ may fɔrt ki də nɔs.
 elephant COP.NPST more strong COMPAR of 1PL
 'Elephants are stronger than us.'

(3) Bahamian Creole (Hackert 2013)
 When cockroach give dance, he don't ask fowl.
 when cockroach give dance 3SG.M NEG ask fowl
 'When cockroaches have a dance, they don't ask the fowl [to attend].'

(4) Haitian Creole (Fattier 2013)
 Piti piti zwazo fè nich li.
 little little bird make nest POSS.3SG
 'Little by little, the bird builds its nest.'

Note that in languages without a singular definite article, some *APiCS* authors consider the nominal plural marker a plural definite article, hence value 2. But if these nominal plural markers are not considered definite articles, then value 3 would be correct for these languages (see comments in Chapter 25).

Value 3 (**bare singular noun phrase in languages without definite article**) occurs in the Portuguese-based creole languages Casamancese Creole, Angolar, Principense, and Korlai, as well as in Sri Lankan Malay and Media Lengua.

(5) Casamancese Creole (Biagui & Quint 2013)
Liyoŋ ta montiyá kasela.
lion HAB hunt gazelle
'Lions hunt gazelles.'

Value 4 (**singular noun phrase with definite article**) occurs in five Ibero-Romance-based languages, in six English-based languages, in three Dutch-based languages, in Fanakalo, Pidgin Hawaiian, and in Michif.

(6) Ternate Chabacano (Sippola 2013b)
Ta ladrá ba el gátu?
IPFV bark Q ART cat
'Do cats bark?'

(7) Kriol (Schultze-Berndt & Angelo 2013)
Im lib la keib, det larrpburniny.
3SG live LOC cave DEM wallaby
'It lives in caves, the wallaby.'

(8) Berbice Dutch (Kouwenberg 2013a)
Di jɛrma doko gaugau.
ART woman paddle quick-quick
'Women paddle with short, quick strokes.'

(9) Fanakalo (Mesthrie 2013)
Lo pikanin yena hayi thanda lo pelepele.
ART child 3SG NEG like ART pepper
'Children don't like pepper.'

Value 5 (**bare plural noun phrase in languages with definite article**) occurs in eight English-based languages, in two Ibero-Romance-based languages, and in two Dutch-based languages.

(10) Bislama (Meyerhoff 2013)
Ol boe tu oli kat sem raet.
PL boy too AGR have same right
'Boys, too, have the same rights.'

Value 6 (**bare plural noun phrase in languages without definite article**) occurs in Tayo and Tok Pisin.

(11) Tayo (Ehrhart & Revis 2013)
Tule fja le aᵐboje.
PL dog SI bark
'Dogs bark.'

Value 7 (**plural noun phrase with definite article**) occurs in three Ibero-Romance-based languages, in five English-based languages, in two French-based languages, in Berbice Dutch, in Fanakalo, and in Michif.

(12) Cavite Chabacano (Sippola 2013a)
Ta haci habol el mga perro con el mga gato.
IPFV make catch DEF PL dog OBJ DEF PL cat
'Dogs chase cats.'

(13) Hawai'i Creole (Velupillai 2013)
Da mɛnehuni-s kam aʊt naɪtaɪm.
ART menehune-PL come out at.night
'Menehunes ('little people') come out at night.'

(14) Louisiana Creole (Neumann-Holzschuh & Klingler 2013)
Jordi le mun nwar lib.
today DEF.ART.PL people black free
'Today black people are free.'

Value 8 (**singular noun phrase with indefinite article**) occurs in two Ibero-Romance-based languages (Cape Verdean Creole of São Vicente, Batavia Creole), in two French-based languages (Haitian Creole, Louisiana Creole), in Early Sranan, in Afrikaans, and in Michif.

(15) Cape Verdean Creole of São Vicente (Swolkien 2013)
Un om ka ta txorá.
INDF.ART man NEG PRS cry
'Men don't cry.'

(16) Early Sranan (van den Berg & Bruyn 2013)
Wan hessi hessi lobbi no bun [...].
INDF.SG quick quick love NEG be.good
'Fast love is no good [...].'

Value 9 (**singular noun phrase with adnominal possessive**) is only reported for Afrikaans:

(17) Afrikaans (den Besten & Biberauer 2013)
Jou Volkswagen is 'n goeie kar.
2SG.POSS Volkswagen is a good.INFL car
'Volkswagen is a good car.' or 'Volkswagens are good cars.'

Bare generic noun phrases, whether singular or plural (values 2, 3, 5, and 6), constitute the most widespread pattern; it occurs in 80 per cent of the *APiCS* languages. There is no particular areal distribution of these values.

Bare *singular* noun phrases (values 2 and 3) occur in 60 per cent of the *APiCS* languages. In the case of European-based *APiCS* languages exhibiting these values (55 per cent of the sample), this constitutes the most striking difference between them and their lexifiers, since in Portuguese, Spanish, French, English, and Dutch, generic noun phrases are either determined by an article or realized as a bare plural noun phrase.

Non-bare generic noun phrases (values 4, 7, 8, and 9) occur in 50 per cent of the *APiCS* languages.

30 Generic noun phrases in subject function

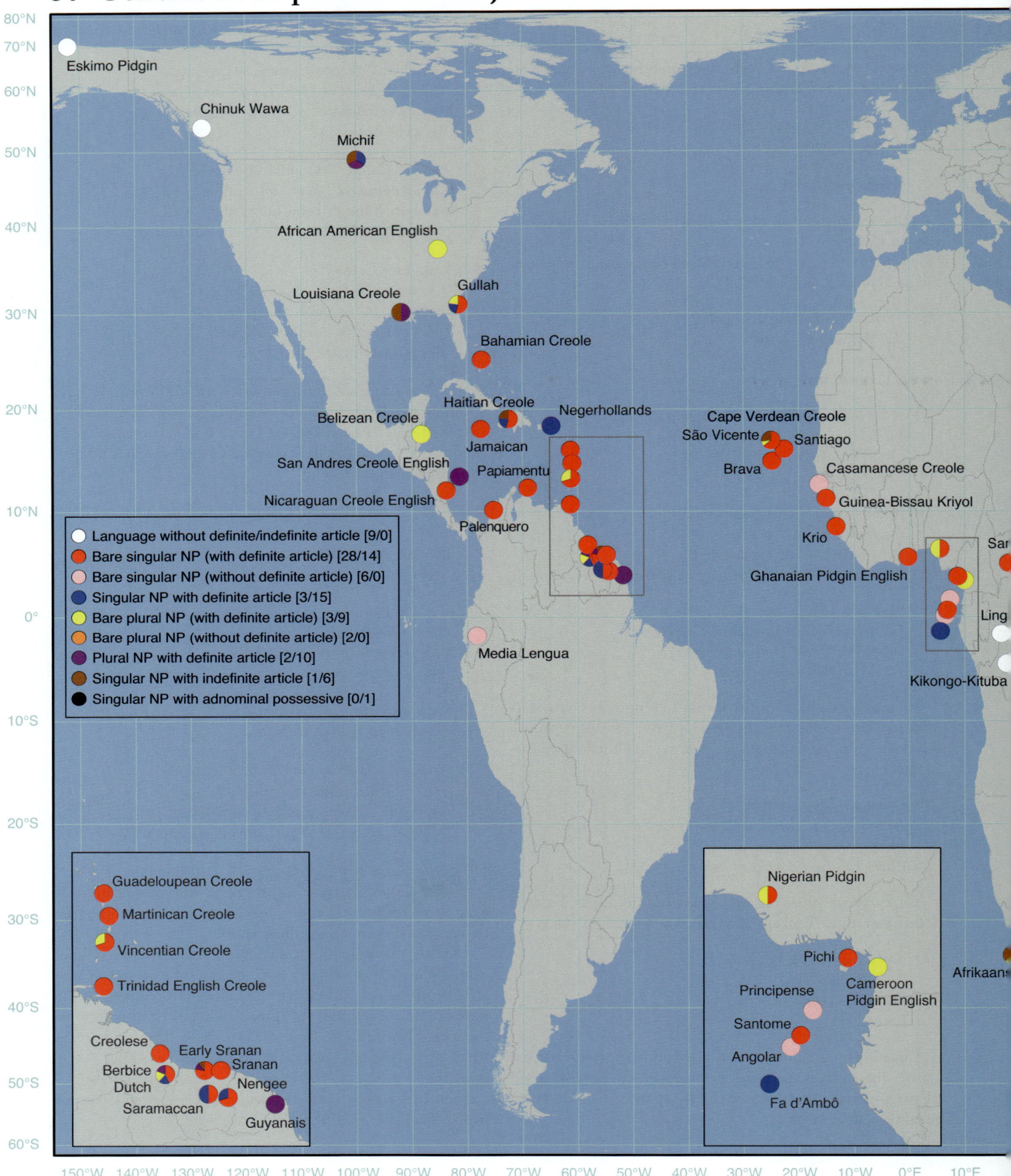

Chapter 31
Co-occurrence of demonstrative and definite article

MARTIN HASPELMATH AND THE *APiCS* CONSORTIUM

1. The four values

This chapter addresses the question whether a definite article can co-occur with an adnominal demonstrative in the same noun phrase. This is not possible in English (**this the book*) or French (**le ce livre-là*), but in many other languages, it is possible, as in (1) and (2).

(1) Spanish
 el hombre ese
 the man that 'that man'

(2) Egyptian Arabic
 il-haaga di
 the-thing this 'this thing'

In such constructions, the definite article does not add any information; thus, in Spanish the alternative construction *ese hombre* (with prenominal demonstrative and without the definite article) has the same meaning. But as noun phrases modified by a demonstrative are usually regarded as definite, the option of including a definite article is not surprising. On the other hand, since they cannot be indefinite, it is also not surprising that many languages are like English and French and dispense with the definite article in the presence of a demonstrative.

The basic contrast is thus between constructions like (1) and (2) with co-occurrence (value 1) and constructions like those of English with no co-occurrence of demonstrative and definite article (value 2). Both are well represented in our data. But in addition, there are cases where the definite article is identical to a demonstrative (see Chapter 28 on definite articles) so that the issue of co-occurrence does not arise (value 3). Finally, in some languages there is no definite article at all, and these, too, are irrelevant here (value 4). Note that all languages have demonstratives (Diessel 1999: 1).

	excl	shrd	all
● 1. Co-occurrence	13	7	20
● 2. No co-occurrence	19	7	26
○ 3. Demonstrative identical to definite article	18	1	19
○ 4. No definite article exists	19	0	19

2. Co-occurrence of demonstrative and article

Thirteen languages have only constructions with co-occurrence of demonstrative and definite article, and another seven languages have this as one possibility (value 1). Among the European-based languages, this option is found mostly in those that have a new definite article that is not derived from the lexifier. For example, in several French-based languages there is a new postposed definite article (*l*)*a*, which may combine with a demonstrative:

(3) a. Haitian Creole (Fattier 2013)
 chat sa a
 cat DEM ART
 'that cat'

 b. Guadeloupean Creole (Colot & Ludwig 2013a)
 kaz-la-sa
 house-ART-DEM
 'this house'

 b. Guyanais (Pfänder 2013)
 sa kaz-a
 DEM house-ART
 'that house'

However, in one Spanish-based language, both the Spanish demonstrative and the article have survived (though the construction shows a different order than that in (1)):

(4) Zamboanga Chabacano (Steinkrüger 2013)
 el éste póno
 ART DEM tree
 'this tree'

And in English-based Sranan, the article *a* (< *the*) and the demonstrative *dati* (< *that*) can co-occur (Winford & Plag 2013):

(5) *a man dati*
 ART man DEM
 'that man'

In the other Surinamese creoles, the postposed demonstrative is derived from a spatial adverb 'there'; the same pattern is found in Papiamentu:

(6) a. Saramaccan (Aboh et al. 2013)
 di wɔmi dɛ
 ART man there
 'that man'

 b. Nengee (Migge 2013)
 a pikin ya
 ART child here
 'this child'

 c. Papiamentu (Kouwenberg 2013b)
 e buki aki   *e buki ei*
 ART book here   ART book there
 'this book'   'that book'

3. No co-occurrence

Of the 19 languages in which non-co-occurrence (i.e. complementary distribution) of demonstrative and definite article is the only option, 15 are English-based languages which are relatively close to English, almost all of them from the Atlantic region. In these languages the non-co-occurrence pattern was inherited from English, alongside the demonstratives and definite article:

(7) a. Trinidad English Creole (Mühleisen 2013)
 dis book, dat book   *de book*
 'this book, that book'   'the book'

 b. Cameroon Pidgin English (Schröder 2013)
 dis rod, dat man   *di haus*
 'this road, that man'   'the house'

Non-co-occurrence occurs sporadically elsewhere, for example, in the mixed language Gurindji Kriol, which has the English/Kriol-derived definite article *thet* and Gurindji-derived demonstratives; the two do not co-occur (e.g. *nyawa ngumpit* [this man], *dat warlaku* [the dog]).

4. Demonstrative identical to definite article

As we saw in Chapter 28 on definite articles, 19 languages have a definite article that is identical to a demonstrative. All these languages have value 3 in this feature. Some examples are given in (8), with some possible translations.

(8) Batavia Creole   *akel ondra*   'the honour'
                  akel sepultura   'that grave'
 Ternate Chabacano   *kel ómbre*   'that man'
                  kel muhér   'the woman'

Some of the examples given for these languages include a postposed spatial adverbial, so that the construction becomes similar to that of (6a–c). However, in the examples in (6) the spatial adverbial is required for a demonstrative sense, whereas here it could be omitted and the meaning could still be demonstrative.

(9) a. Cape Verdean Creole of Santiago (Lang 2013)
 kes=pinton la
 DEM/ART.PL=chicken there
 'those chickens'

 b. Kriol (Schultze-Berndt & Angelo 2013)
 thet pab hiya
 DEM/ART pub here
 'this pub here'

5. No definite article exists

Nineteen languages have no definite article. These are irrelevant here, as they are for Feature 9 (on definite article order) and Feature 28 (on the presence and nature of definite articles).

6. Multiple possibilities

A number of languages allow several different options, because they have several different constructions of demonstratives, like Spanish, which allows both co-occurrence (in ex. 1) and non-co-occurrence (in the construction *ese hombre* 'that man').

In Belizean Creole, the demonstratives *dis/dat* precede the noun and cannot co-occur with the definite article, but the plural demonstrative *dem* follows the noun and co-occurs:

(10) Belizean Creole (Escure 2013)
 a. *dat ki*   [that caye]   'that caye'
 b. *di ki dem*   [the cayes those]   'those cayes'

Similarly, in Early Sranan the postnominal, but not the prenominal, demonstratives co-occur with the definite article:

(11) Early Sranan (van den Berg & Bruyn 2013)
 a. *disi pranasi*   [this plantation]   'this plantation'
 b. *dem pikin dissi*   [the children these]   'these children'

In Louisiana Creole, the (postnominal) demonstrative *sala* co-occurs with a prenominal definite article under certain conditions (e.g. obligatorily when the noun is plural and animate):

(12) Louisiana Creole
 (Neumann-Holzschuh & Klingler 2013)
 a. *dons sala*   [dance that]   'that dance'
 b. *le moun sala*   [the.PL people that]   'those people'

In Sango, Nigerian Pidgin, and Michif, the definite article seems to be optional when it occurs with a demonstrative.

In Early Sranan, the definite article (*da, dem/den*) that can co-occur with a postnominal demonstrative can also be used as a demonstrative by itself (e.g. *den dirkture* 'those managers'), so this language has value 3 in addition to 1 and 2.

31 Co-occurrence of demonstrative and definite article

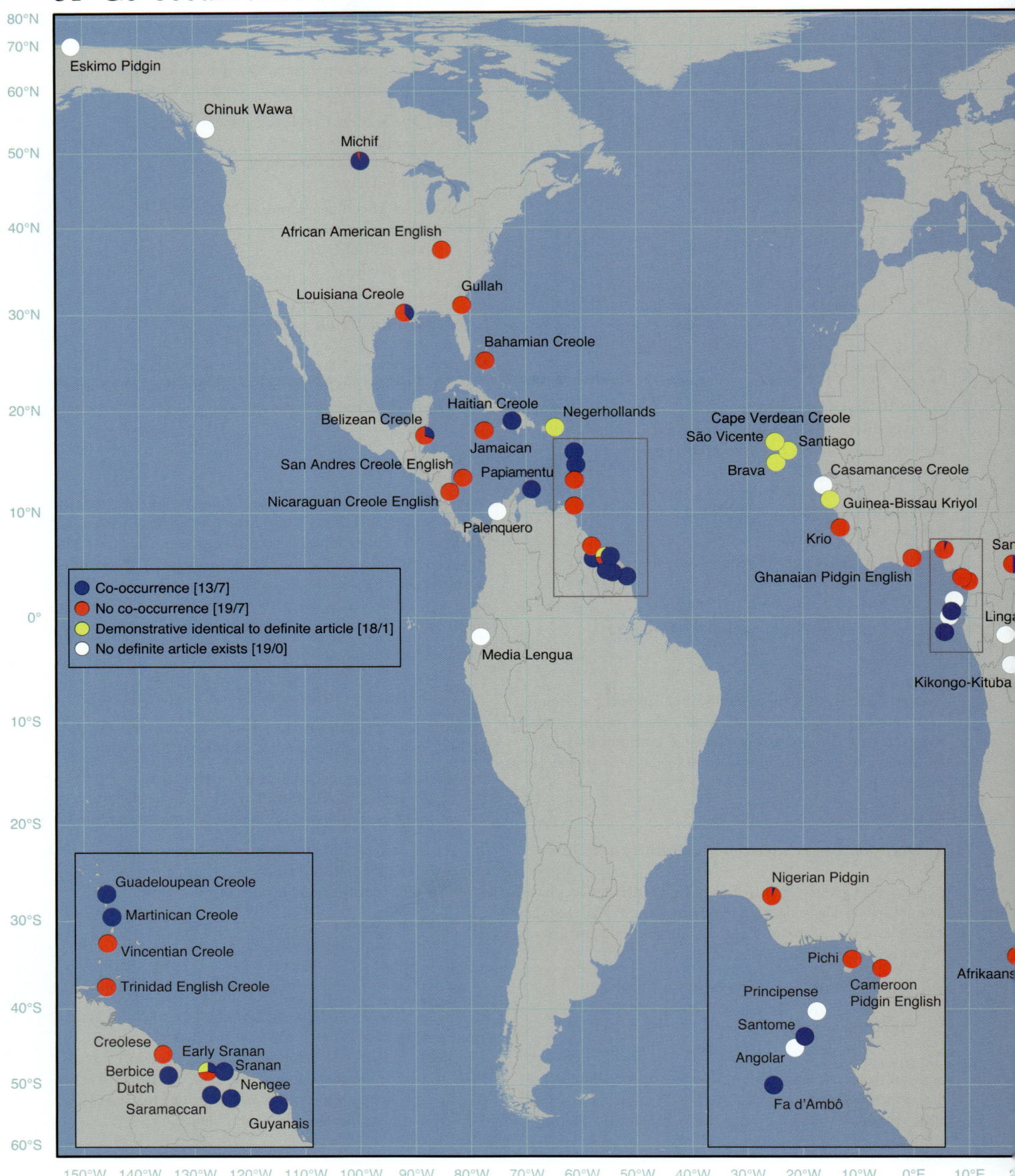

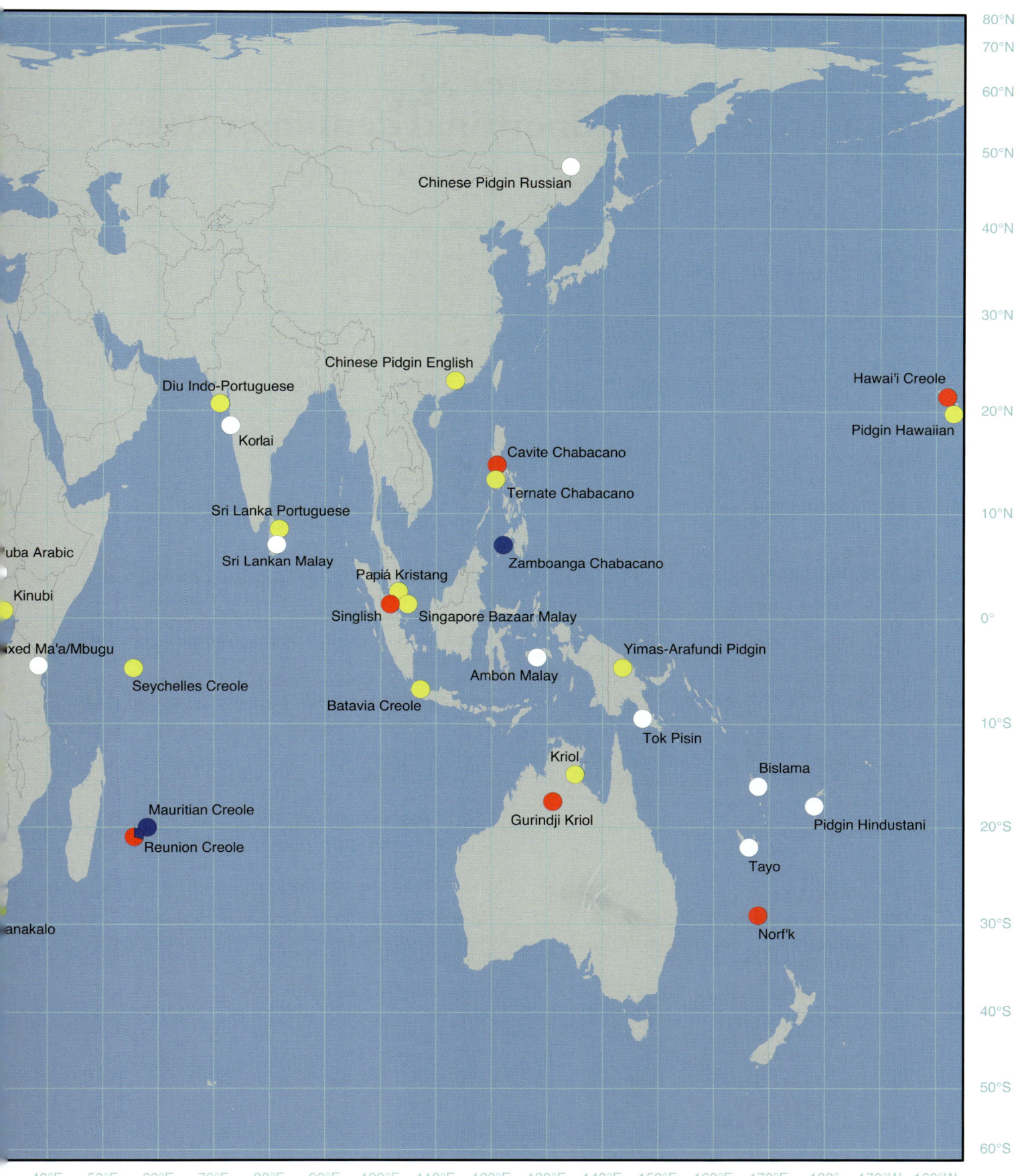

Chapter 32
Pronominal and adnominal demonstratives

PHILIPPE MAURER AND THE *APiCS* CONSORTIUM

1. Introduction

Demonstratives are commonly divided into pronominal demonstratives, which replace a noun or noun phrase (as in French *Je préfère celui-ci* 'I prefer this one'), and adnominal demonstratives, which determine a noun (as in French *Je préfère ce livre* 'I prefer this book'). This feature corresponds to *WALS* Feature 42 (Diessel 2005b).

2. The values

We distinguish the following three values:

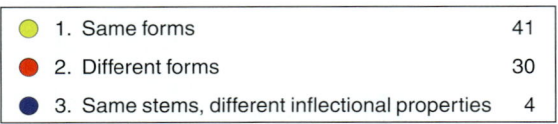

Value 1 (pronominal and adnominal demonstratives have the **same form**) is found in eleven Ibero-Romance-based languages, in twelve English-based languages, in three French-based languages, in three Malay-based languages, in two Arabic-based languages, in Negerhollands and Sango, in the mixed languages Media Lengua, Michif, and Mixed Ma'a/Mbugu, as well as in the pidgin languages Chinuk Wawa, Fanakalo, Pidgin Hawaiian, Pidgin Hindustani, and Yimas-Arafundi Pidgin.

(1) Batavia Creole (Maurer 2013a)
 a. *Eo apusta ki akel teng mintrodju.*
 1SG bet COMP DEM COP lie
 'I bet that that is a lie.'

 b. *Pertu di akel sepultura teng ung albër bringin.*
 near of DEM tomb EXIST ART tree fig
 'Near that tomb there was a fig tree.'

(2) Creolese (Devonish & Thompson 2013)
 a. *Da kyaahn wok.*
 DEM cannot work
 'That is not suitable.'

 b. *Da stoorii kyaahn wok.*
 DEM story cannot work
 'That story is not believable.'

(3) Sango (Samarin 2013)
 a. *Mbi ye so pepe.*
 1SG like this NEG
 'I don't like this.'

 b. *Mbi sara yi so ngbangati so mbi ke zo voko.*
 1SG do thing this because this 1SG COP person black
 'I do this (lit. this thing) because I'm an African.'

(4) Yimas-Arafundi Pidgin (Foley 2013)
 a. *Mən naŋga?*
 DEM where
 'Where is that?'

 b. *Yəm mən murimbi tanan kakan.*
 water DEM run.DEPV PROG.NFUT NEG
 'That water hasn't drained yet.'

Value 2 (pronominal and adnominal demonstratives are **formally distinguished**) occurs in fourteen English-based languages, in seven Ibero-Romance-based languages, in six French-based languages, in Afrikaans, Kikongo-Kituba, and in Chinese Pidgin Russian.

In Nengee, for instance, pronominal and adnominal demonstratives have different stems: *disi* is used pronominally and *a* NOUN *ya* is used adnominally:

(5) Nengee (Migge 2013)
 a. *Disi nyan mi meti.*
 this eat POSS.1SG meat
 'This one ate my meat.'

 b. *A dagu ya nyan mi meti.*
 DEF.SG dog DEM/here eat POSS.1SG meat
 'This dog ate my meat.'

In Santome (as well as in the other Portuguese-based Gulf of Guinea creoles), the adnominal demonstrative gets the prefix *i-* to form the pronoun:

(6) Santome (Hagemeijer 2013)
 a. *vin se*
 wine DEM
 'this wine'

 b. *Ise sa doxi.*
 DEM.PRO COP sweet
 'This one is sweet.'

Still other languages use one form for only one function, and another form for both functions; in other words, they show overlap. An example is Haitian *sa* 'this' (only pronominal) and *sa a* 'this' (pronominal and adnominal). These cases are subsumed under value 2.

(7) Haitian Creole (Fattier 2013)
    a. *M wè sa.*
        I see DEM
        'I see this.'
    b. *pitit sa a*
        child DEM SG
        'this child'
    c. *M wè sa a, m pa wè lòt la.*
        I see DEM SG I NEG see other DEF
        'I see this, I don't see the other.'

Value 3 (pronominal and adnominal demonstratives have **the same stems but different inflectional properties**) occurs in Sri Lanka Portuguese, in Berbice Dutch, in Lingala, and in the mixed language Gurindji Kriol.

In Sri Lanka Portuguese, the pronominal demonstrative is inflected for plural, whereas the adnominal demonstrative is not:

(8) Sri Lanka Portuguese (Smith 2013)
    a. *Muytu moosam=ley, isti luvaara-s!*
        very bad=like this place-PL
        'Very bad, these places!'
    b. *Isti-s ɛkavn-ntu ta-tiraa, naa!*
        this-PL account-LOC PRS-take TAG
        'These [guys] are buying on account, eh!'

In the mixed language Gurindji Kriol, the pronominal demonstrative is case-marked (9b), in contrast to the adnominal demonstrative (9a), which is not:

(9) Gurindji Kriol (Meakins 2013)
    a. *Nyila warlaku im gon kankula karnti-ngka*
        that dog 3SG go up tree-LOC
       nyila bi-walija-yu.
        that bee-PAUC-DAT
        'That dog goes up the tree after the bees.'
    b. *Im ged-im im na nyila-ngku.*
        3SG get-TR 3SG FOC that-ERG
        'That one gets it.'

3. Areal distribution

Value 1 (same form) is found in all regions, in contrast to value 2 (different forms), which is present on both sides of the Atlantic and in the Pacific but is absent from South and Southeast Asia.

Value 3 is represented by only four languages in different parts of the world: Berbice Dutch in the Caribbean, Lingala in Central Africa, Sri Lanka Portuguese in South Asia, and Gurindji Kriol in Australia.

4. Comparison with *WALS*

The comparison with *WALS* shows that the percentage of the values differs considerably: the percentage of *APiCS* languages having value 2 (different forms) is twice as big as the percentage of *WALS* languages having the same value:

		APiCS		*WALS*	
1	Same forms	41	54.6%	143	71.1%
2	Different forms	30	40.0%	37	18.4%
3	Different inflection	4	5.3%	21	10.4%

According to Diessel (2005b), value 2 is especially frequent in Northern and Central Africa; these, however, are areas where no *APiCS* languages are spoken (except for Sango, which displays value 1, see example 3). But in the *WALS* languages, value 2 is absent from South and Southeast Asia, as is the case in the *APiCS* languages.

What stands out with regard to the *APiCS* languages is the high concentration of value 2 in West Africa. Out of the fourteen West African languages, eleven show value 2, and only three show value 1, namely the three Cape Verdean varieties. Out of those languages which exhibit value 2, five are English-based (Cameroon Pidgin English, Ghanaian Pidgin English, Krio, Pichi, and Nigerian Pidgin English), and six are Portuguese-based (Angolar, Fa d'Ambô, Principense, Santome, Guinea-Bissau Kriyol, and Casamancese).

In the case of the English-based creoles, value 2 can be explained by English superstrate (or adstrate) influence. These languages are of the type *dat* (adnominal) vs. *datwon* (pronominal), as in Nigerian Pidgin English.

In the case of the Portuguese-based creoles, the situation is different since Portuguese exhibits value 1 (same form for both pronominal and adnominal demonstratives).

In the Gulf of Guinea creoles, the prefix *i-* is attached to the adnominal demonstratives to form the corresponding pronouns, as in the Santome example (6) above. Since this construction is not directly derived from Portuguese, it must be either an independent development or a case of African substrate influence. In Edo, an Edoid language spoken in Nigeria, the proximal adnominal demonstrative has the form *na/nà* and the pronominal *ɔna* (sg) and *ɛna* (pl) (Melzian 1937: 128, 167). Edo has value 3 (different inflections, since in contrast to the adnominal forms, the pronominal forms inflect for number); but in a contact situation, value 3 could have easily been reinterpreted as value 2, different forms.

32 Pronominal and adnominal demonstratives

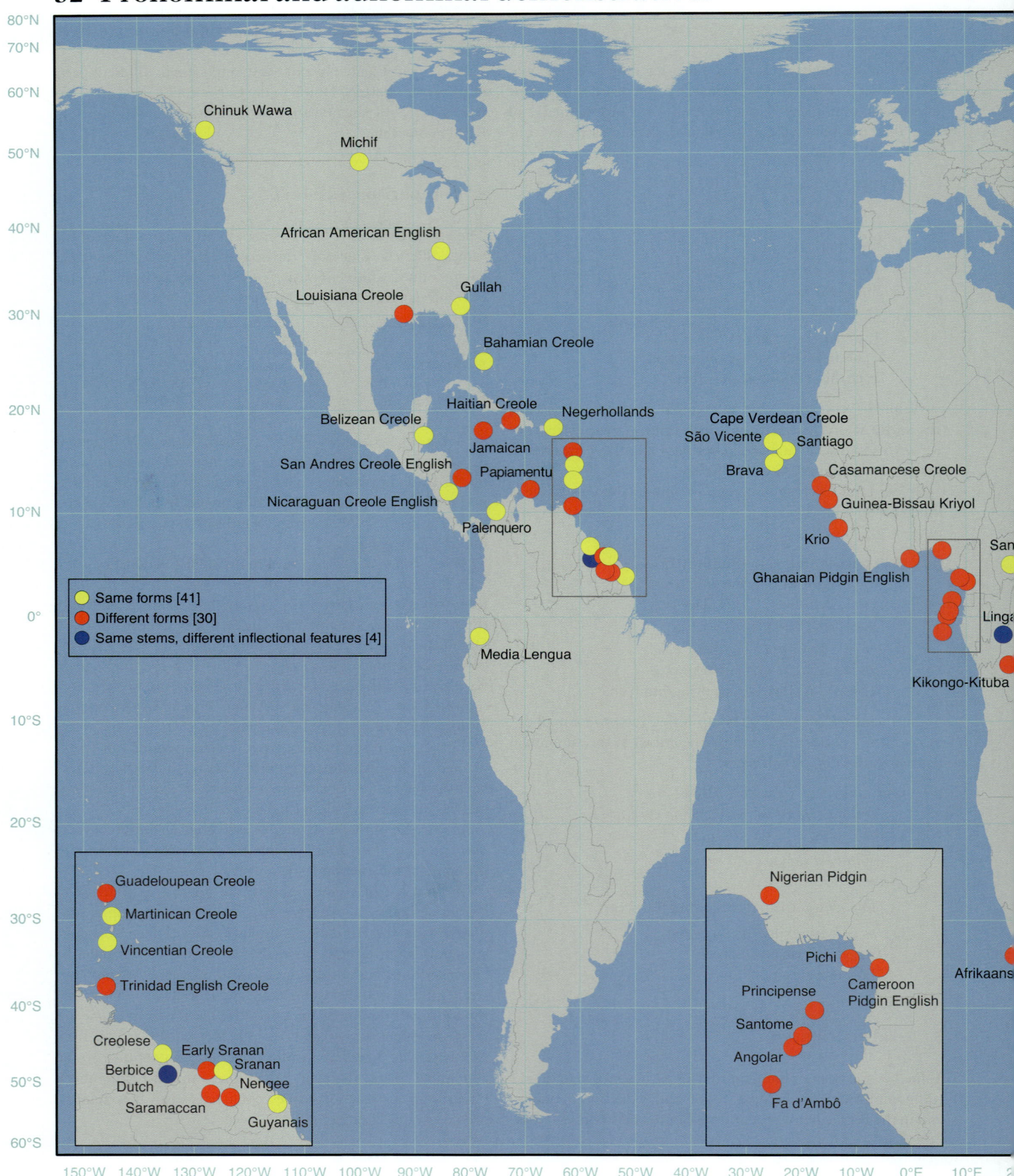

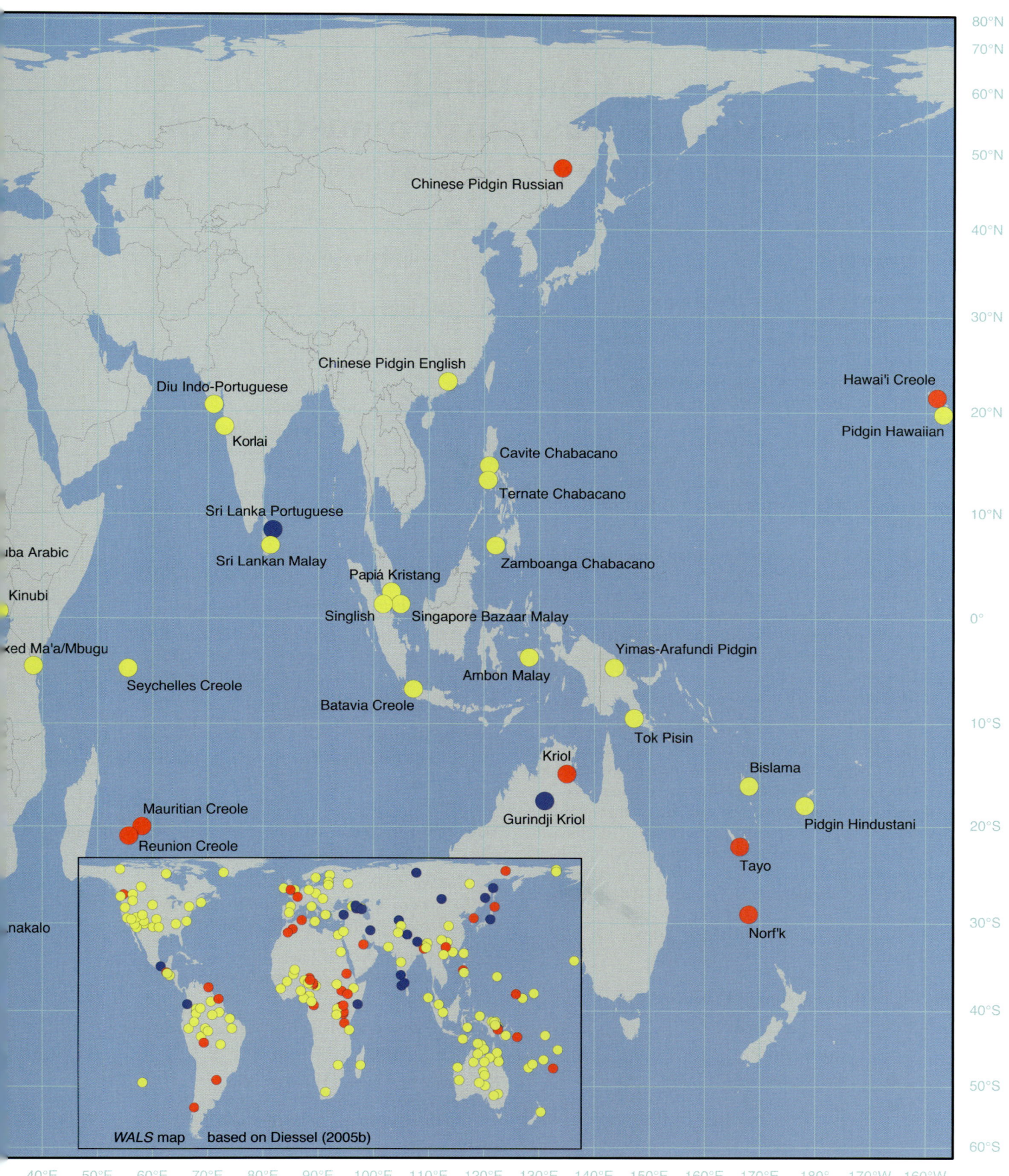

Chapter 33
Distance contrasts in demonstratives

PHILIPPE MAURER AND THE *APiCS* CONSORTIUM

1. Introduction

Demonstratives are deictic expressions such as English 'this' and 'that' which indicate the relative distance of a referent in the speech situation in relation to the speaker's location. When *this* and *that* are used contrastively, *this* denotes a referent in relative proximity to the speaker and *that* denotes a referent at a greater distance, as in **This is my pen and that one is yours** (see Diessel 2005a: 170).

Demonstratives often are homonymous with, or derive from, deictic locational adverbs such as 'here' and 'there', and are sometimes difficult to distinguish from them. Among the criteria for the demonstrative status of such elements are the following:

(i) The demonstrative differs in shape from the spatial adverbs (French *cette femme-ci* 'this woman' vs. *ici* 'here').
(ii) The spatial adverbs are the only available demonstratives in the language, as in Papiamentu, where 'this house' can only be rendered by *e kas aki*, lit. 'the house here'; *e kas* without *aki* means 'the house' and not 'this house'.
(iii) The combination of the demonstrative and the adverb is obligatory, that is, if in a given language *this house here* may be used, but not **this house*.

If pronominal and adnominal demonstratives behave differently (see Chapter 32 on pronominal and adnominal demonstratives), only adnominal demonstratives are considered.

This feature is only concerned with the number of distance contrasts and not with other categories encoded by demonstratives, e.g. visible vs. out of sight, uphill vs. downhill, or higher vs. lower elevation.

This feature is based on *WALS* feature 41 (Diessel 2005a).

2. The values

We distinguish the following four values:

○	1. No distance contrast	14
●	2. Two-way contrast	50
●	3. Three-way contrast	10
●	4. Four-way contrast	1

Value 1 (**no distance contrast**) is found in eight French-based languages:

(1) Guadeloupean Creole Noun + *lasa* (Colot & Ludwig 2013a)
    Martinican Creole Noun + *tala* (Colot & Ludwig 2013b)
    Haitian Creole Noun + *sa* (Fattier 2013)
    Louisiana Creole Noun + *sala* (Neumann-Holzschuh & Klingler 2013)
    Mauritian Creole *sa* + Noun (Baker & Kriegel 2013)
    Seychelles Creole *sa* + Noun (Michaelis & Rosalie 2013)
    Reunion Creole *se* + Noun (Bollée 2013)
    Tayo Noun + *la* (Ehrhart & Revis 2013)

It also occurs in three English-based languages:

(2) Belizean Creole *dis/dat* + Noun (Escure 2013)
    Bislama Noun + *ia* (Meyerhoff 2013)
    Tok Pisin *dispela* + Noun (Smith & Siegel 2013)

The other languages displaying this feature are:

(3) Chinuk Wawa *úkuk* + Noun (Grant 2013)
    Chinese Pidgin Russian *eta* + Noun (Perekhvalskaya 2013)
    Sango Noun + *so* (Samarin 2013)

Value 2 (**two-way contrast**) is the most widespread value and occurs in all types of *APiCS* languages.

(4) Sranan (Winford & Plag 2013)
    a man disi 'this man' (lit. 'the man this') vs.
    a man dati 'that man' (lit. 'the man that')

(5) Negerhollands (van Sluijs 2013)
    di shi 'this side' vs. *di dungku da* 'that night' (lit. 'the night there')

(6) Cape Verdean Creole of São Vicente (Swolkien 2013)
    es mes 'this month' vs. *kel altura* 'that time'

(7) Kikongo-Kituba (Mufwene 2013)
    muntu yayi 'this book' (lit. 'book this') vs.
    mukanda yina 'that book' (lit. 'book that')

(8) Sri Lankan Malay (Slomanson 2013)
ini kendera 'this chair' vs. *ittu kendera* 'that chair'

(9) Batavia Creole (Maurer 2013b)
isti belu 'this old man' vs. *ake sepultura* 'that tomb'

(10) Yimas-Arafundi Pidgin (Foley 2013)
andi nak 'this land' (lit. 'land this') vs.
kumbut mən 'that village' (lit. 'village that')

(11) Pidgin Hindustani (Siegel 2013)
i admi 'this man' vs. *u larika* 'that boy'

Fanakalo makes a tonal difference between the proximal and the distal demonstrative:

(12) Fanakalo (Mesthrie 2013)
Lò umfan ai enzile lo into, ló umfan yena enzıle.
PROX boy NEG do.PST ART thing DIST boy 3SG do.PST
'This boy didn't do the thing; that boy did.'

Value 3 (**three-way contrast**) occurs in six Ibero-Romance-based languages (Guinea-Bissau Kriyol, Angolar, Papiamentu, Cavite Chabacano, Ternate Chabacano, Zamboanga Chabacano), in two English-based languages (Nengee, Vincentian Creole), in Michif, and in Mixed Ma'a/Mbugu.

(13) Papiamentu (Kouwenberg 2013b)
e buki aki, e buki ei, e buki aya
DEF book here DEF book there DEF book over.there
'this book, that book, that book yonder'

(14) Nengee (Migge 2013)
a pikin ya, a pikin de, a pikin anda
DEF child here DEF child there DEF child over.there
'this child, that child, the child over there'

(15) Ternate Chabacano (Sippola 2013b)
ésti máno, ési manga mutʃátʃa, akél palabra
DEM hand DEM PL girl DEM word
'this hand, those girls, those words'

(16) Mixed Ma'a/Mbugu (Mous 2013)
lukándo ká, va'inyí yá, mbuvá hú
wall this children this field that
'this wall, these children, that field'

The Ibero-Romance languages, too, have three demonstratives, which, in a deictic situation, do not only express a difference of distance, but which are also bound to the speech act participants. In Spanish, *este* points to a referent near the speaker, *ese* near the hearer, and *aquel* is distant from both speaker and hearer (see (15) from Ternate Chabacano). In Papiamentu, for example, this difference was not retained; the three demonstratives refer to a relative distance to the location of the speech act, but they are not bound to the speech act participants. In other *APiCS* languages exhibiting this value, the situation is not clear. However, for Mixed Ma'a/Mbugu, Mous (2013) clearly states:

"The three degrees of distance refer roughly to (1) near speaker (*ká*), (2) near addressee or referential (*yá*), and (3) distant (*hú*)."

In Michif, the demonstratives encode not only distance constrasts, but also animacy contrasts. The following examples illustrate the demonstratives used for inanimates.

(17) Michif (Bakker 2013)
a. *uma li liiv*
DEM.INAN DEF.ART.M.SG book
'this book'

b. *li liiv anima*
DEF.ART.M.SG book DEM.INAN.INTERM.SG
'that book'

c. *li liiv anima neetee*
DEF.ART.M.SG book DEM.INAN.INTERM.SG over.there
'that book over there'

Value 4 (**four-way contrast**) only occurs in Saramaccan:

(18) Saramaccan (Aboh et al. 2013)
a. *di wɔmi aki* 'this man'
DEF.SG man here

b. *di wɔmi dɛ* 'that man'
DEF.SG man there

c. *di wɔmi na-a-dɛ* 'the man over there'
DEF.SG man LOC-3SG-there

d. *di wɔmi ala* 'the man over yonder'
DEF.SG man yonder

3. Distribution and comparison with *WALS*

Value 1 (no distance contrast) is present in the Americas, in the Caribbean, in the Indian Ocean, and in the Pacific, but is absent from insular and coastal West Africa, from South Asia, and from Southeast Asia. In *WALS*, this value is only present in Europe (French, German) and in North Africa. According to *WALS*, the French adnominal demonstrative *ce/cette/ces* is distance-neutral. This may explain why the great majority of the French-based creoles exhibit value 1, and also why this value is much more common in *APiCS* (19%) than in *WALS* (2%).

Value 2 (two-way contrast) is found in all regions in both *APiCS* and *WALS*; it is also the most widespread value in both atlases since it occurs in more than half of the languages: in 67 per cent of the languages in *APiCS* and in 54 per cent of the languages in *WALS*.

Value 3 (three-way contrast) is present in North America, in the Caribbean, in West Africa, as well as in the Philippines. In comparison with *WALS* (38%), this value is less widely found in *APiCS* (13%).

In *APiCS*, value 3 is well represented among the Ibero-Romance-based languages, and value 4 (four-way contrast) is restricted to Saramaccan (Caribbean).

33 Distance contrasts in demonstratives

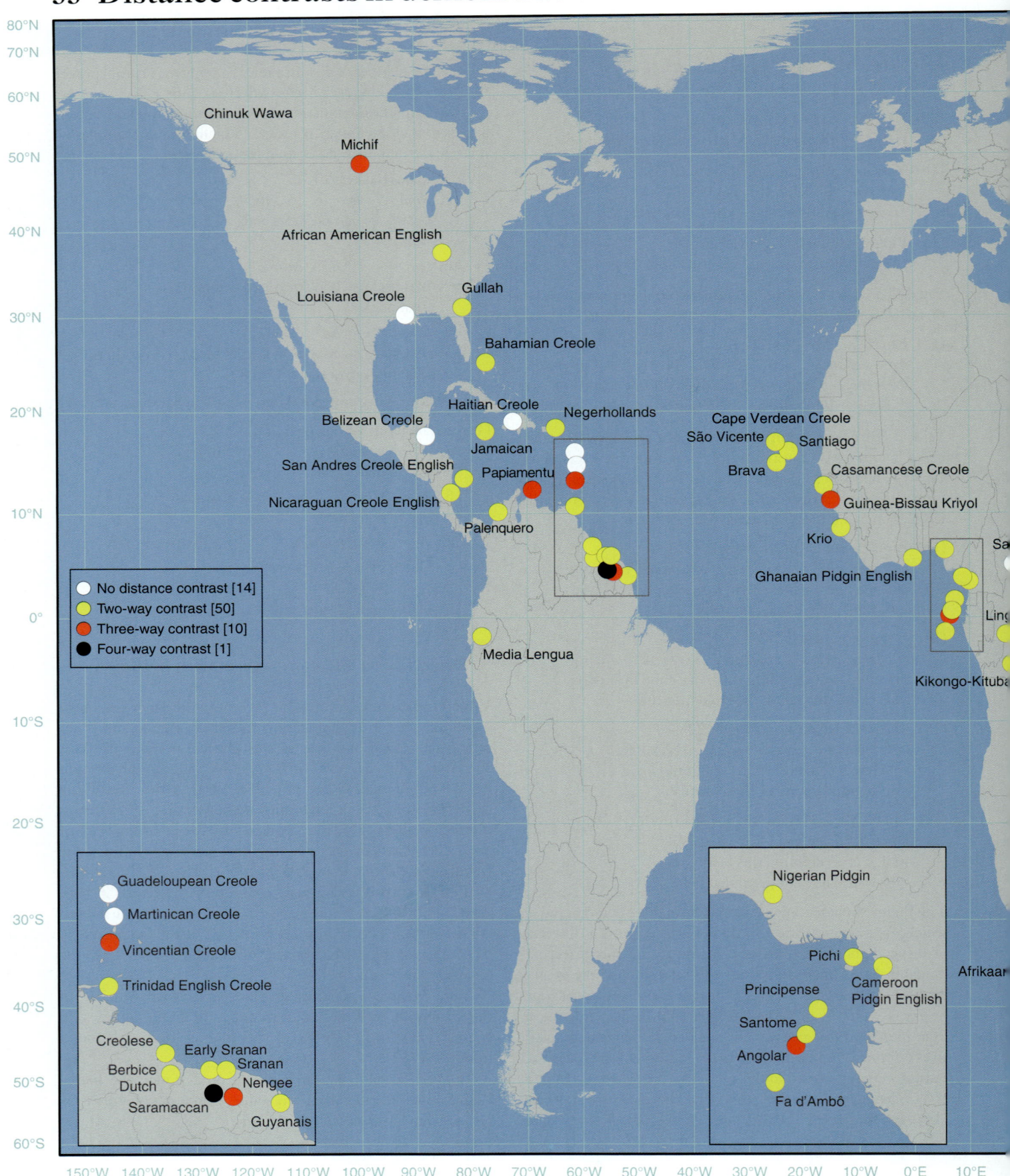

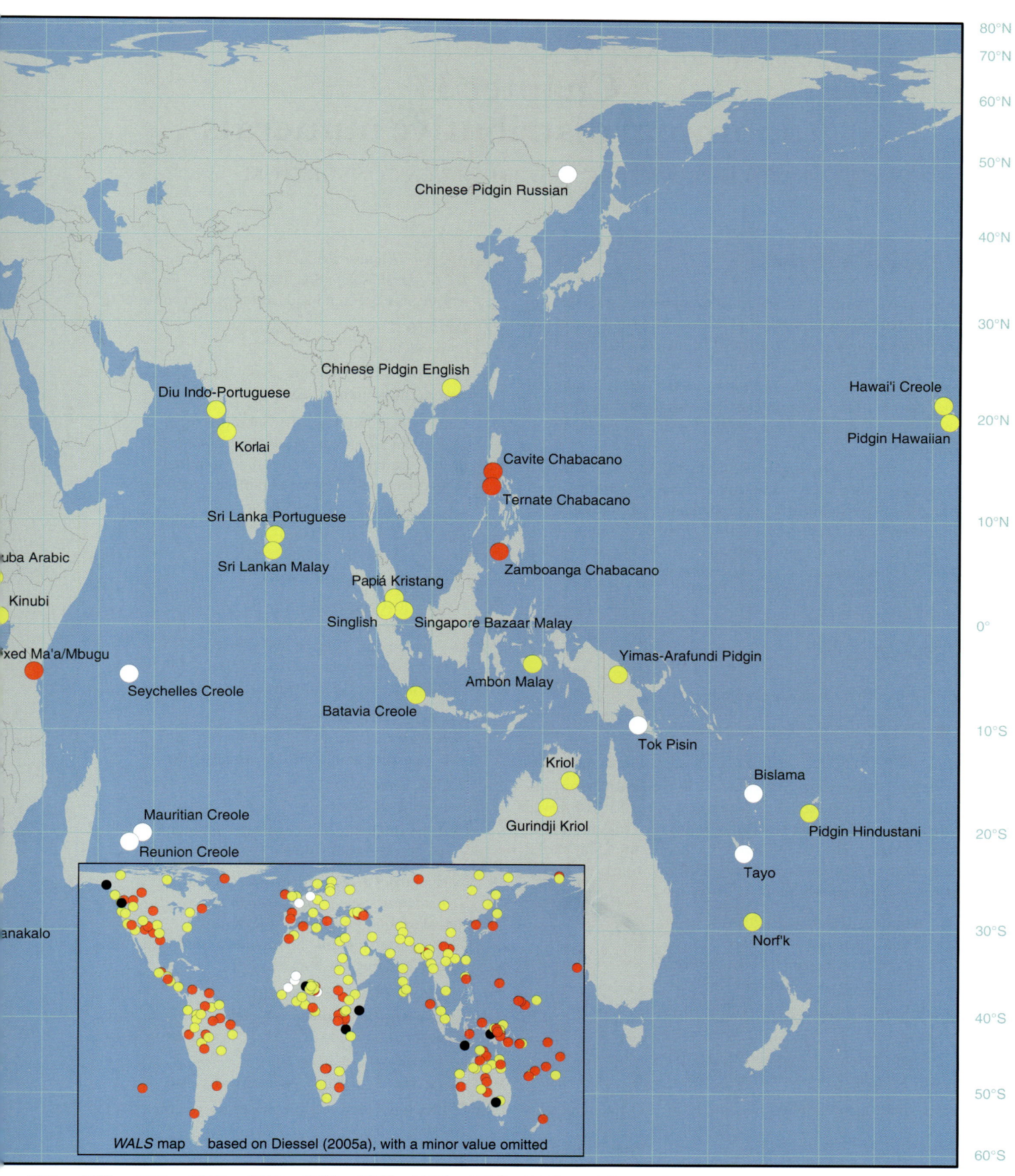

Chapter 34
Adnominal distributive numerals

PHILIPPE MAURER AND THE *APiCS* CONSORTIUM

1. Feature description

Distributive numerals are special adnominal numerals that express distributive relations, as in German *je drei* in the sentence *Die Männer trugen je drei Koffer.* 'The men carried three suitcases each.' English lacks distributive numerals, because in a sentence such as *They carried three suitcases each*, the numeral *three* does not form a continuous expression with the distributive word *each*, in other words, *three . . . each* does not qualify as a numeral.

Since the dividing line between distributive numerals and quantifiers is not always clear-cut, especially regarding 'one', examples with reduplicated adnominal numerals meaning 'one by one' or 'every' are also taken into account (see example 8).

This feature corresponds partially to *WALS* feature 54 (Gil 2005a). For reduplication in pidgins, creoles, and other contact languages, see also Kouwenberg (2003).

2. The values

We distinguish the following two values:

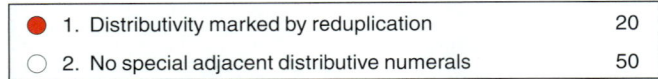

●	1. Distributivity marked by reduplication	20
○	2. No special adjacent distributive numerals	50

Value 1 (**distributivity marked by reduplication**) occurs in six Portuguese-based languages, in ten English-based languages, in Mauritian Creole, in Sango, in Fanakalo, and in Ambon Malay. The reduplication is generally total, but partial reduplication is found occasionally. The following examples illustrate partial reduplication:

(1) Santome (Hagemeijer 2013)
 Ê da dôsu ngê tlê-tlêxi fluta.
 3SG give two person three-three breadfruit
 'He gave two people three breadfruits each.'

(2) Diu Indo-Portuguese (Cardoso 2013)
 Tud di vay da trĩ-trĩt rupi.
 every day go.NPST give.INF thirty-thirty rupee
 'Every day I give them thirty rupees each.'

In the following examples, the reduplication of the numeral is total:

(3) Angolar (Maurer 2013a)
 Ka pê taya kôôndja lêtu fia e ki ũa ũa
 PST put slice coconut inside leaf DEM with one one
 taminha e.
 bowl DEM
 'They put slices of coconut in the [banana] leaves, [which were at the bottom of] every bowl.'

(4) Cameroon Pidgin English (Schröder 2013)
 Draiva bin tek dehm foh wan wan hohndred.
 driver PST take 3PL for one one hundred
 'The driver took them for a hundred francs each.'

(5) Nigerian Pidgin (Faraclas 2013)
 Dèm get tre tre pìkín.
 3PL have three three child
 'They have three children each.'

(6) Nengee (Migge 2013)
 Tu tu kabiten de a wan kondee.
 two two kaptain COP LOC one village
 'There are two captains in each village.' (lit. 'In one village there are two captains each.')

(7) Creolese (Devonish & Thompson 2013)
 Wan wan dotii doz bil dam, tuu tuu dotii
 one one dirt HAB build dam two two dirt
 doz bil am faasa.
 HAB build 3SG faster
 'A dam is built one bit of earth at a time, but two bits of earth at a time would build it faster.'

(8) Nicaraguan Creole English (Bartens 2013a)
 Deh staart tu bil wan wan hous.
 3PL start COMP build one one house
 'They started building houses one by one.' (lit. 'They started building one house each.')

(9) Tok Pisin (Smith & Siegel 2013)
 Tripela taim long wanpela wanpela yia yupela mas
 three time in one one year 2PL must
 makim bikpela de bilong lotu bilong mi.
 mark big day for worship POSS 1SG
 'Three times each year you must reserve a feast day for worship.'

(10) Bislama (Meyerhoff 2013)
[...] *be wan wan aelan blong Bankis hemi*
    but one one island POSS Banks 3SG.AGR
gat difren nem blong ol samting ia [...].
have different name POSS PL something DEF
'[...] but every island in the Banks has different names for these things [...].'

(11) Mauritian Creole (Baker & Kriegel 2013)
*Li don en brok dilo **kat kat** dimun.*
3SG give ART jug water four four person
'She gives a jug of water to each group of four people.'

(12) Sango (Samarin 2013)
*na ya ti abar **oko oko***
LOC belly of PL.bar one one
'in each one of the bars (site for drinking)'

(13) Fanakalo (Mesthrie 2013)
*Yena nigile lo gane **mabili mabili** switi.*
3SG give.PST ART child two two sweet
'She gave the children two sweets each.'

Value 2 (**no special adjacent distributive numeral**) is the most widespread value. Several constructions are possible in order to express distributivity. In the Cape Verdean Creole of Brava, the numeral is reduplicated, but it is not adjacent to the noun:

(14) Cape Verdean Creole of Brava (Baptista 2013)
*N kré karnéru ki ta pari **dós-dós**.*
1SG want sheep REL HAB deliver two-two
'I want sheep that deliver lambs by pairs/two by two.'

In other languages, expressions like 'everyone' or 'every man' are used:

(15) Cape Verdean Creole of Santiago (Lang 2013)
*Es leba **kada un** tres maléta.*
3PL carry every one three suitcase
'They carried three suitcases each.'

(16) Vincentian Creole (Prescod 2013)
***Evri man** tek a suutkeiz (iich/fo iself).*
every man take a suitcase each/for himself
'Each man took one suitcase.'

(17) Chinuk Wawa (Grant 2013)
***Kánawi man** tk'up makwst stik.*
all man cut two tree
'The men cut two trees each.'

(18) Kikongo-Kituba (Mufwene 2013)
***Konso bakala** nat-aka valise zole.*
each man carry-PST suitcase two
'Each man carried two suitcases.'

3. Distribution

Reduplication of the numeral for distributive functions (value 1) is totally absent from Spanish-based languages, Dutch-based languages, bilingual mixed languages, and also from most French-based languages (the only exception being Mauritian Creole); regarding the English-based languages, it is absent in 17 out of 27 languages.

Distributivity expressed by reduplication occurs in somewhat less than a third of our languages. It is present in the Atlantic as well as in Asia, from the Indian Ocean to the Pacific.

4. Comparison with *WALS*

Comparing this feature with the corresponding *WALS* feature (Gil 2005a), we can observe the following:

1. The *WALS* languages show many more different types (affixation, preceding word, following word, other strategies) than the *APiCS* languages.
2. Reduplication is the most widespread value in the *WALS* languages (84 out of 250 languages, i.e. roughly one third), whereas absence of adnominal distributive numerals is found in roughly a quarter of the languages. In the *APiCS* languages, reduplication is the only strategy found, with more or less the same percentage as in *WALS*; absence of adnominal distributive numerals is found in more than two-thirds of the languages.
3. In the *WALS* languages, reduplication is the predominant strategy in sub-Saharan Africa, in South Asia, and, to a lesser extent, in insular Southeast Asia and the Pacific, as well as in other areas. These areas correspond more or less to the sub- or adstrate languages of those *APiCS* languages which exhibit reduplication for this feature.

On the one hand, we can reasonably assume that the reduplication strategy in European-based *APiCS* languages is due to their substrate or adstrate languages. On the other hand, the high percentage of absence of adnominal distributive numerals seems to derive from the fact that the European superstrate languages Portuguese, Spanish, English, and French lack such numerals.

34 Adnominal distributive numerals

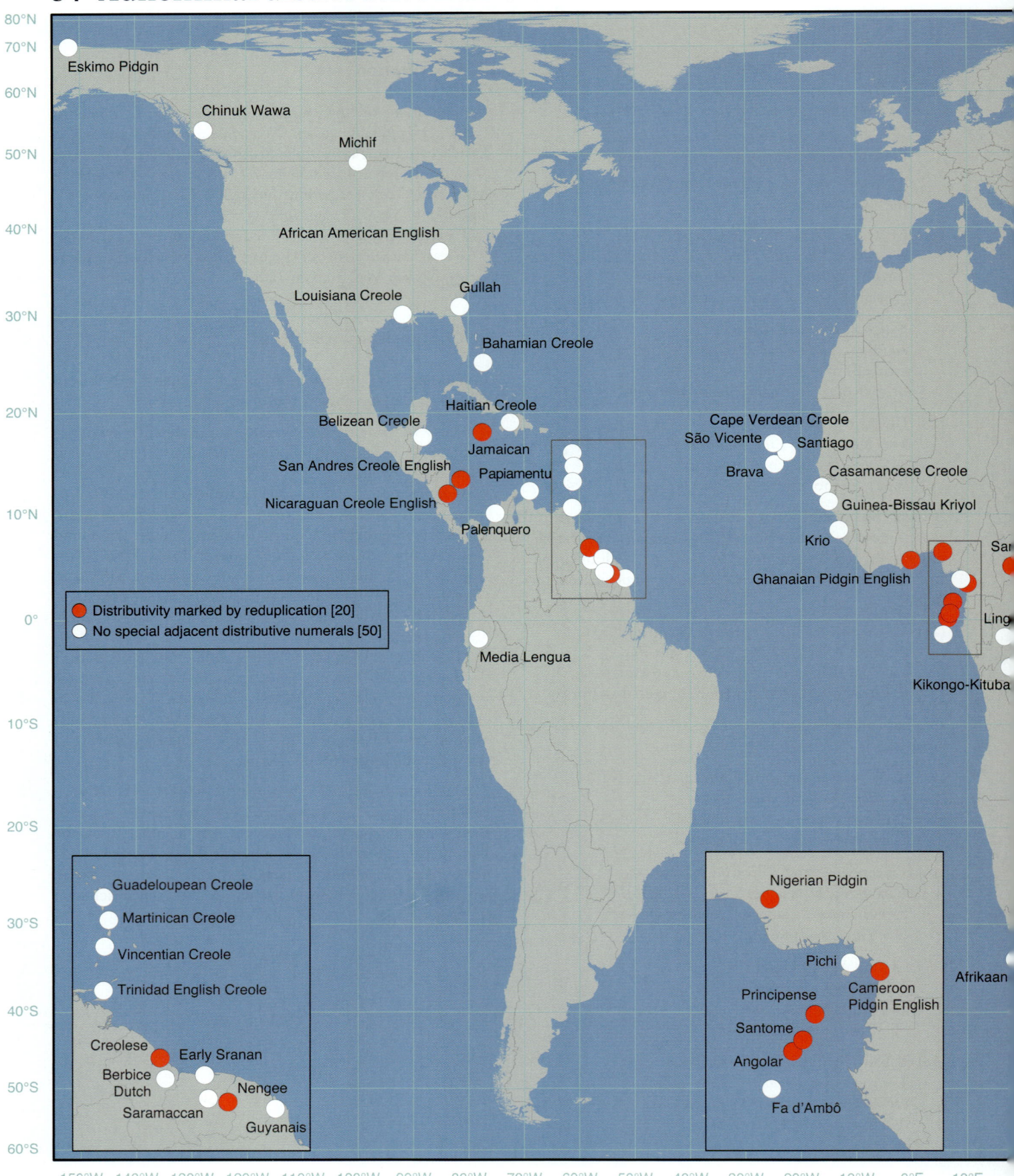

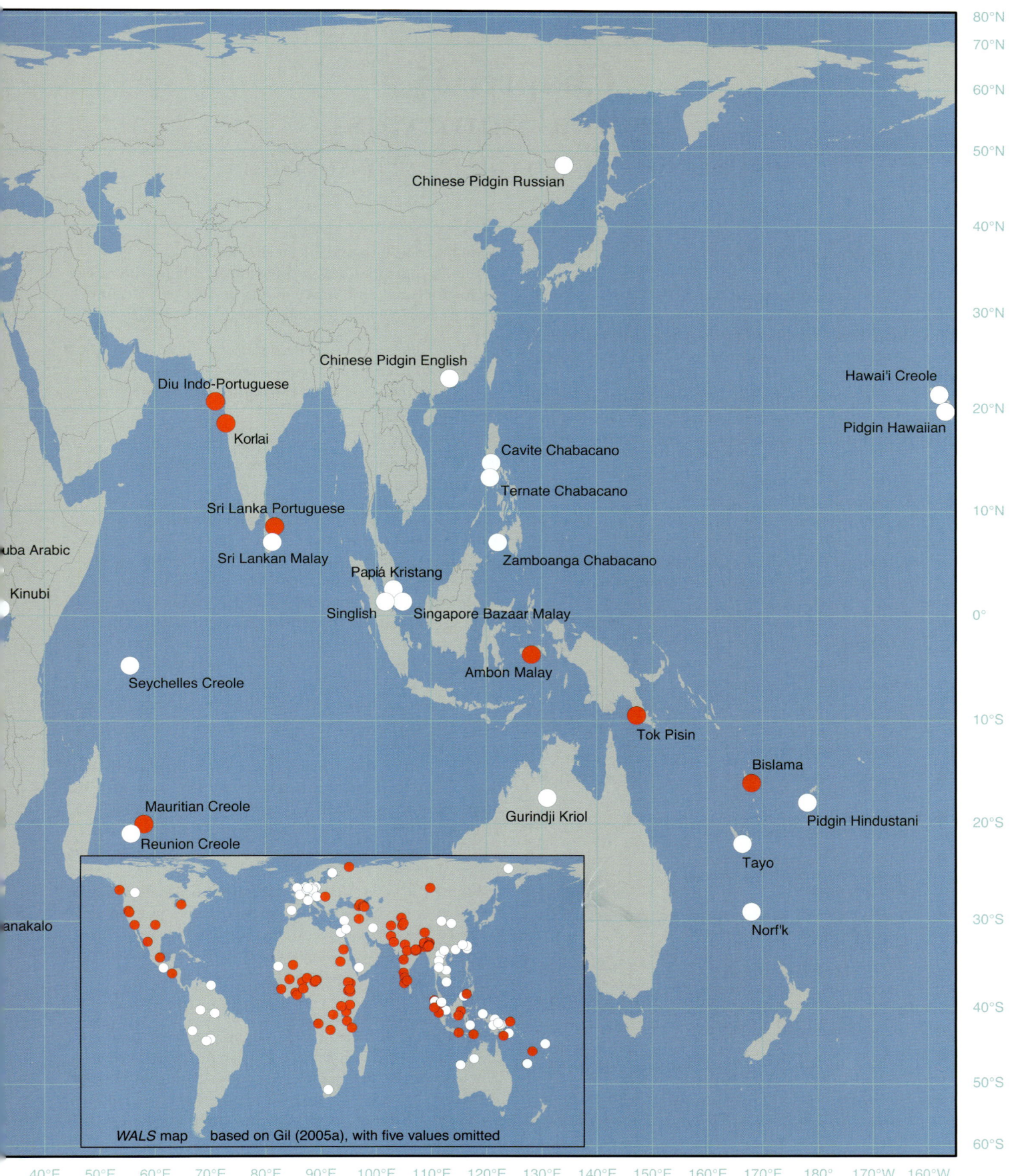

Chapter 35
Ordinal numerals

PHILIPPE MAURER AND THE *APiCS* CONSORTIUM

1. Feature description

This feature compares ordinal numerals ('first', 'second', 'third', etc.) with adnominal cardinal numerals ('one', 'two', 'three', etc.). There are different ways in which ordinal numerals are formed, especially with regard to 'first' and 'second', which are often irregular.

Since we are considering only synchrony, words like English *third* and *fifth* are not considered derived from *three* and *five*, although from a diachronic perspective they are of course derived.

This feature corresponds partially to *WALS* feature 53 (Stolz & Veselinova 2005).

Three derivational strategies occur in the *APiCS* languages: (a) **affix** (e.g. Cavite Chabacano *ika-dos* 'second'), (b) **"number" + numeral** (Tok Pisin *nambafaiv* 'fifth'), and (c) **genitive particle** (Kinubi *ta itnášer* 'twelfth', lit. 'of twelve').

2. The values

We distinguish the following eight values:

		excl	shrd	all
○	1. Ordinal numerals do not exist	4	0	4
●	2. Cardinal and ordinal numerals are identical except for 'one' and 'first'	5	1	6
●	3. All ordinal numerals are synchronically derived from cardinal numerals	4	4	8
●	4. All ordinal numerals are synchronically derived from cardinals, but 'first' may also be suppletive	3	0	3
●	5. 'First' is suppletive, all other ordinals are synchronically derived from cardinal numerals	20	3	23
●	6. 'First', 'second', or more are suppletive, the others are synchronically derived from cardinal numerals	12	7	19
●	7. All ordinal numerals are suppletive	6	1	7
●	8. Other solutions	5	2	7

Value 1 (**ordinal numerals do not exist**) pertains to only four languages: Berbice Dutch, the bilingual mixed language Gurindji Kriol, Tayo, and Pidgin Hindustani.

Value 2 (**cardinal and ordinal numerals are identical except for 'one' and 'first'**) occurs in Angolar, Fa d'Ambô, Ternate Chabacano, Early Sranan, Sango, and Lingala.

(1) Early Sranan (van den Berg & Bruyn 2013)
 na fossi kakka-kreh; na tu kakka-kreh; na dri
 at first rooster-cry at two rooster-cry at three
 kakka-kreh
 rooster-cry
 'at the first rooster crow, at the second rooster crow, at the third rooster crow'

Value 3 (**all ordinal numerals are synchronically derived from cardinal numerals**) occurs in five English-based languages, in two Malay-based languages, and in Papiá Kristang.

Two strategies are used: "number" + cardinal numeral and derivational affix. "Number" + cardinal numeral occurs in Papiá Kristang (*namba dos* 'second'), Cameroon Pidgin English (*namba wan* 'first', *namba tu* 'second'), Ghanaian Pidgin English (*nɔmba wan* 'first', *nɔmba tu* 'second'), Nigerian Pidgin (*nọmba wọn, nọmba tu*), Creolese (*maan nomba faiv* 'the fifth man'), Tok Pisin (*nambawan* 'first', *nambafaiv* 'fifth'), and Singapore Bazaar Malay (*namar satu* 'first'). A derivational affix is used in Sri Lankan Malay (*kə-sattu* 'first', *kə-ðua* 'second').

Value 4 (**all ordinal numerals are synchronically derived from cardinal numerals, but 'first' may also be suppletive**) occurs in Bislama (*nambawan* vs. *fes* 'first', *namba-tri* 'third'), Chinese Pidgin English (*number one* vs. *first*, *number five* 'fifth'), and Kinubi (*ta wáy* 'of one', *ta awalán* 'of first', *ta itnášer* 'of twelve').

Value 5 (**'first' is suppletive, all other ordinals are synchronically derived from cardinals**) occurs in five Ibero-Romance-based languages, in four English-based languages, in eight French-based languages, in three Bantu-based languages, as well as in Negerhollands, Ambon Malay, Mixed Ma'a/Mbugu, and Michif.

In European-based languages exhibiting value 5, the word for 'first' is derived from the European base language (Portuguese *primeiro*, Spanish *primero*, English *first*, French *premier*, Dutch *eerste*), as, for example, Sri Lanka Portuguese *primeer* or *prumeer*, Nengee *fosi*, Guyanais *premyè*, and Negerhollands *estə*. Cavite Chabacano exhibits an unusual strategy: it uses the

Spanish masculine form *uno* for 'one' and the feminine form *una* for 'first'. In Lingala, we find *ya libosó* 'of front'.

Regarding the derived forms for 'two' upwards, four different strategies occur in the *APiCS* languages.

One derivational strategy is to use lexifier-based or adstrate-based affixes:

(2) Sri Lanka Portuguese   *doz-er*   'second'
     Guadeloupean Creole and others *dé-zyèm*   'second'
     Negerhollands   *twee-də*   'second'
     Ambon Malay   *ka-dua*   'second'
     Cavite and Zamboanga Chabacano *ika-dos*   'second'

Note that in Portuguese, the suffix *-eiro* exists only in *prim-eiro* 'first' and *terc-eiro* 'third'; in Sri Lanka Portuguese, this suffix has been extended to the other numerals.

Another strategy is to use the genitive particle to form ordinals from cardinals: *di* in Casamancese Creole and Papiamentu (*di tres* 'third'), *fu* in Nengee and Sranan (*fu tu* 'second'), or the (originally gender-agreeing) genitive particle *-a/ya* in Bantu-based languages (Kikongo-Kituba, Lingala, Mixed Ma'a/Mbugu) (e.g. Kikongo-Kituba *ya zole* 'second'). This strategy is found also in Guinea-Bissau Kriyol and Early Sranan, but only for pronominal, not adnominal, ordinals: *di unzi* 'the eleventh', *di fu dri* 'the third'.

Still another strategy is "number" + cardinal numeral, which is found in Pichi and Fanakalo.

Finally, Saramaccan uses 'for make': *di fu mbei tu* 'the second', literally 'the for make two'. This strategy is found in Early Sranan, too, but only for pronominal ordinals: *disi fu meki tri* 'the third' (see also Santome in example 3 for a similar strategy involving the verb 'do, make').

Value 6 (**'first', 'second', or more are suppletive, the others are regular**) occurs in three Ibero-Romance-based languages, in sixteen English-based languages, in Mauritian Creole, and in Juba Arabic. Some examples are:

(3) Santome: *plumê* 'first', *sêgundu* 'second', *tlusêlu* 'third', *ku ka fe dôzê* [REL HAB make twelve] 'twelfth'
     Cameroon Pidgin English: *fes, sekend, nomba tri*
     Gullah: *firs, secon, thuteen-t*
     Juba Arabic: *áwal* 'first', *táni* 'second', *ta sitta* 'sixth'

Value 7 (**all ordinal numerals are suppletive**) occurs almost exclusively in Ibero-Romance-based languages, though not in all: in the three Cape Verdean varieties (Brava, Santiago, São Vicente), in Guinea-Bissau Kriyol, in Ternate Chabacano, and in Palenquero. The only non-Ibero-Romance-based language having this value is Krio.

(4) Cape Verdean Creole of Brava: *primeru* 'first', *segundu* 'second', *terseru* 'third', *kuartu* 'fourth'
     Palenquero: *primero* 'first', *segundo* 'second', *tersero* 'third', *kuarto* 'fourth'

Value 8 (**other solutions**) is attested in seven languages. Afrikaans has suppletive forms for 1 and 3, and the others derived (*een/eerste* 'one/first', *drie/derde* 'three/third', vs. *twee/tweede* 'two/second', *vier/vierde* 'four/fourth', *vyf/vyfde* 'five/fifth').

In Nicaraguan Creole English and San Andres Creole English, the forms for 1 to 5 are suppletive, and the others are identical to the cardinal numerals. A similar situation is found in Creolese: 'first' and 'third' are suppletive, the others are identical to the cardinal numerals.

Korlai uses ordinals borrowed from the adstrate language Marathi, and in Diu Indo-Portuguese, Portuguese-derived ordinals from 1 to 6 are suppletive (*pimer* 'first' vs. *ũ* 'one'). Some speakers use the suffix *-m* to derive ordinals from cardinals above six: *ɔyt-m* 'eigth' vs. *ɔyt* 'eight'; there is, however, a tendency to use English ordinals in everyday speech.

Pidgin Hawaiian differentiates cardinals from ordinals syntactically. Cardinals usually have the order numeral + noun, while ordinals have the order noun + numeral: *alima manawa* 'five times', *kani akolu* 'third sound', literally 'sound three'.

3. Distribution

There is no particular areal distribution of the values of this feature, and the comparison with *WALS* does not show any similarity, except for the fact that the *APiCS* values 5 and 6 are also the most widespread values in *WALS* (34% and 19%, respectively).

With respect to the lexifier, the English-based languages have a strong tendency to exhibit value 6 ('first', 'second', or more are suppletive, the others are regular), namely 16 out of 27 languages. Value 7 occurs almost exclusively in Portuguese- and Spanish-based languages.

Regarding the derivational strategies, the most common strategy is the use of a lexifier-based or adstrate-based affix (23 languages). It occurs in four Ibero-Romance-based languages, in seven English-based languages, in nine French-based languages, in Negerhollands, in Sri Lankan Malay, and in Ambon Malay.

The strategy 'number + cardinal numeral' occurs in eight English-based languages, in Fanakalo, in Singapore Bazaar Malay, and in Papiá Kristang. It occurs in three true pidgins (Chinese Pidgin English, Fanakalo, Singapore Bazaar Malay), but is absent from French-based and Ibero-Romance-based languages (with the exception of Papiá Kristang), and, generally speaking, is absent from the Caribbean (including most of the English-based languages).

The strategy involving the genitive adposition or affix is used in two Ibero-Romance-based languages (Casamancese Creole, Papiamentu), two English-based languages (Nengee, Sranan), three Bantu-based languages (Kikongo-Kituba, Lingala, Mixed Ma'a/Mbugu), and two Arabic-based languages (Juba Arabic and Kinubi). It is also present in Guinea-Bissau Kriyol and Early Sranan but only with pronominal ordinals.

35 Ordinal numerals

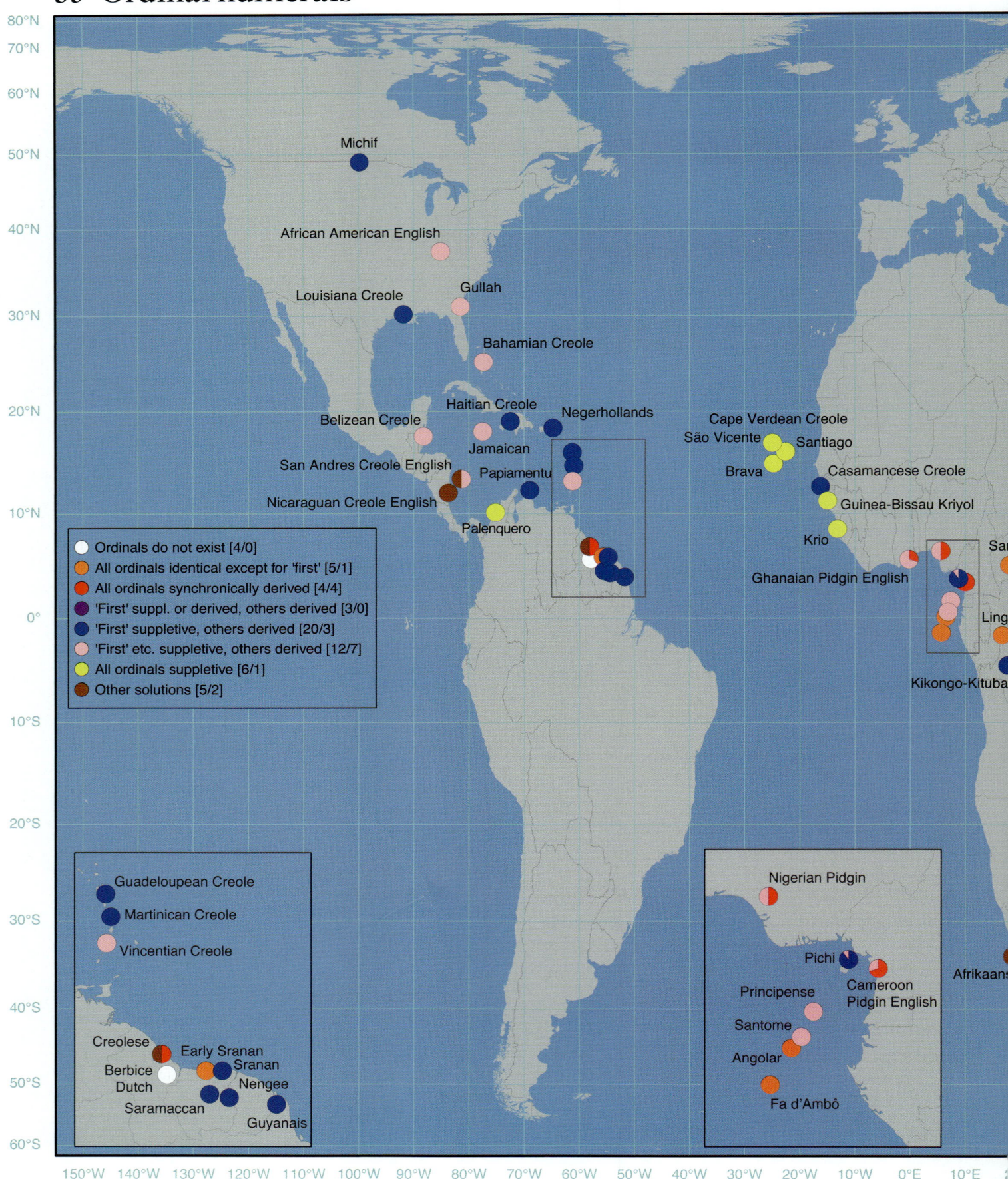

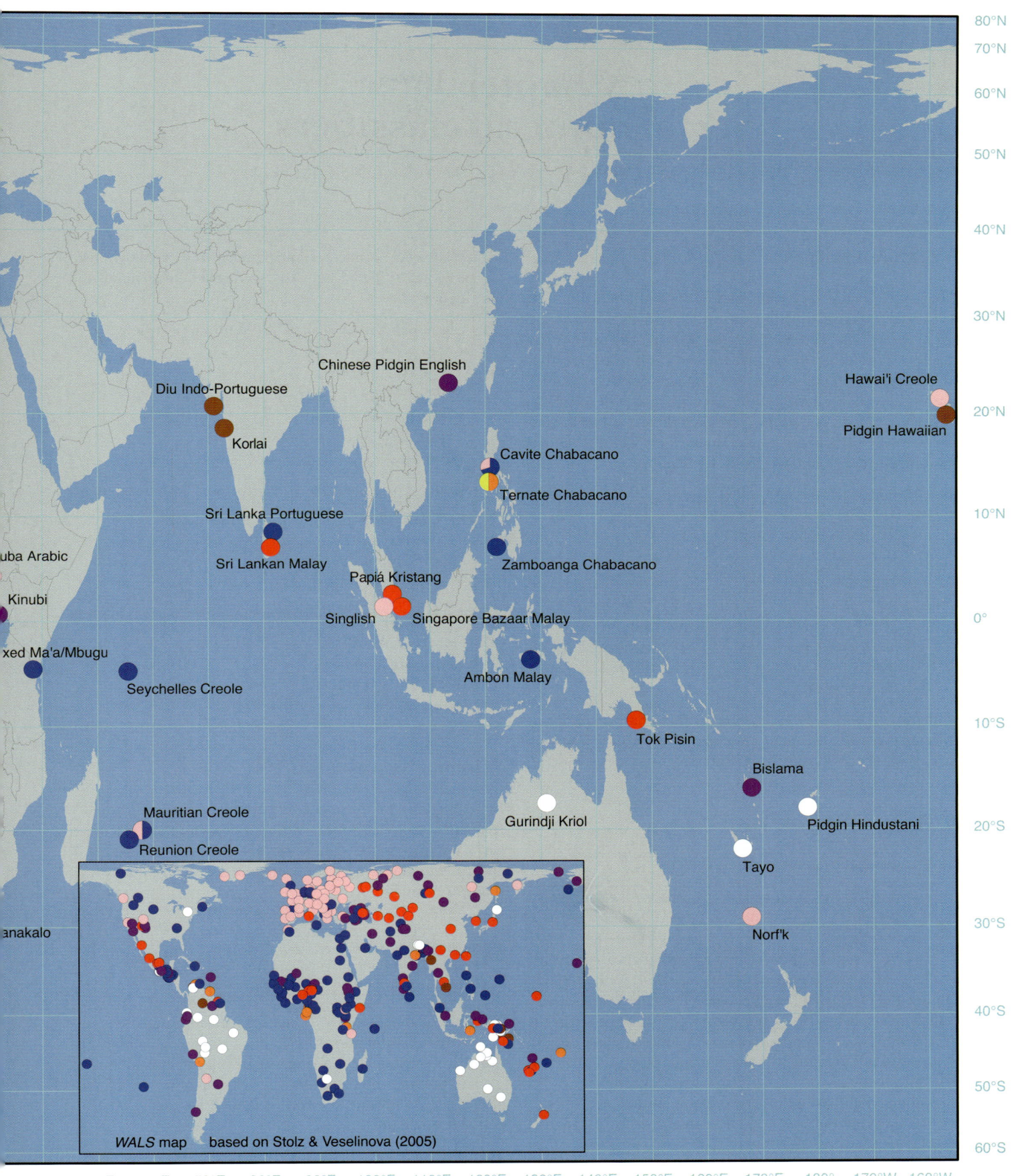

Chapter 36
Sortal numeral classifiers

PHILIPPE MAURER AND THE *APiCS* CONSORTIUM

1. Feature description

Two types of numeral classifier may be distinguished. One type is referred to as **mensural numeral classifiers**, like *pound* in *two pounds of gold*. The second type—which is the topic of this chapter—is referred to as **sortal numeral classifiers**; they "divide the inventory of count nouns into semantic classes, each of which is associated with a different classifier" (Gil 2005b).

Ambon Malay, for example, possesses three main sortal classifiers: *orang* 'person' for human nouns, *ekor* 'tail' for nonhuman animate nouns, and *bua* 'fruit' for inanimates:

(1) Ambon Malay (Paauw 2013)
    a. *laki~laki dlapang orang*
       RED~male eight   CLF
       'eight men'
    b. *ikang sapol ekor*
       fish ten CLF
       'ten fish'
    c. *mangga lima bua*
       mango five CLF
       'five mangoes'

In Ambon Malay, these classifiers are optional, but optionality is not taken into account for the *APiCS* feature. This feature is based on *WALS* Feature 55 (Gil 2005b).

2. The values

We distinguish the following values:

○	1. The language has no numeral classifiers	72
●	2. The language has numeral classifiers	4

In the *APiCS* languages, sortal numeral classifiers occur in only four languages, and they are optional in all four: Ambon Malay, Chinese Pidgin English, and Sri Lanka Portuguese in Asia, and Gullah in North America. Note that the confidence given by the *APiCS* authors for Ambon Malay and Chinese Pidgin English is 'very certain', but for Sri Lanka Portuguese and Gullah it is only 'intermediate'.

Ambon Malay has at least three common numeral classifiers, as shown in example (1). In the other three languages, the numeral classifiers are very limited, mostly restricted to human nouns. Chinese Pidgin English uses *piecee* for human nouns and *chop* for others:

(2) Chinese Pidgin English (Li & Matthews 2013)
    a. *two piecee coolie*
       two CLF coolie
       'two coolies'
    b. *thisee chop tea*
       this CLF tea
       'this tea'

Sri Lanka Portuguese uses *pesaan* 'person' for human nouns:

(3) Sri Lanka Portuguese (Smith 2013)
    nosa   jeentis doos pesaan
    POSS.1PL people two CLF
    'two of our people'

Gullah uses *head of* for human nouns, especially for children:

(4) Gullah (Klein 2013)
    seven head of children
    seven CLF   child.PL
    'seven children'

3. Comparison with *WALS*

In the languages of the world, sortal numeral classifiers are very frequent in Southeast Asia, Mesoamerica, and the Amazonian basin, but in many parts of the world they are almost absent (Gil 2005b). The following table compares the *WALS* values with the *APiCS* values:

	WALS	*APiCS*
1. The language has no numeral classifiers	260	72
2. The language has optional numeral classifiers	62	4
3. The language has obligatory numeral classifiers	78	0

This table shows that in a substantial part of those *WALS* languages that allow for numeral classifiers, these classifiers are optional, like the four *APiCS* languages displaying this value.

The presence of sortal numeral classifiers in *APiCS* languages is certainly due to substrate influence—except for Gullah, which is an unclear case.

Sortal numeral classifiers

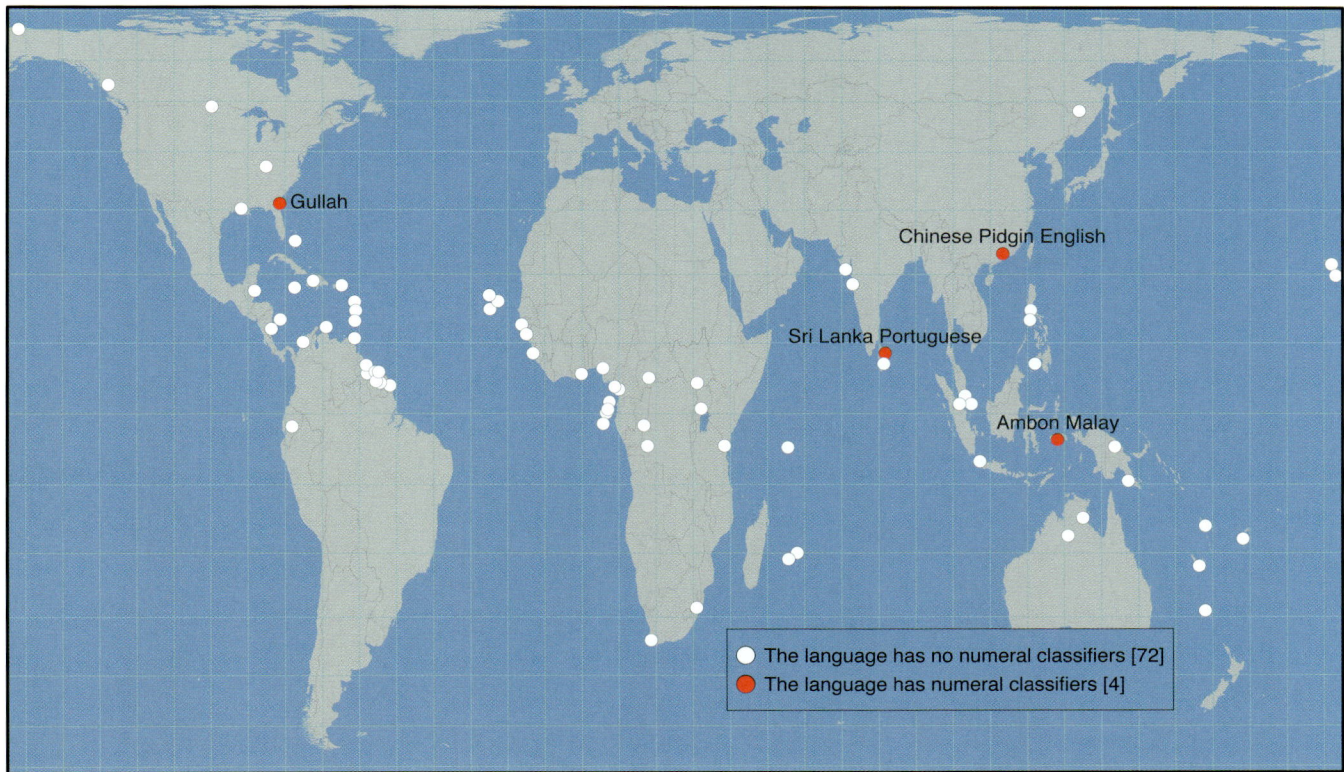

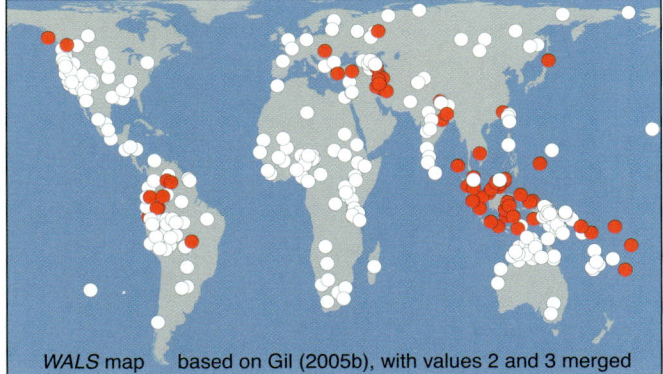

According to Smith (2013), the optional use of *pesaan* 'person' as a classifier for humans in Sri Lanka Portuguese is modelled on Tamil and Sinhala (but note that according to *WALS*, there are no numeral classifiers in Sinhala).

In Ambon Malay, the use of numeral classifiers is clearly of Indonesian origin. Interestingly, for the other *APiCS* languages based on Malay, or where Malay is an important sub- or adstrate language, no numeral classifiers are reported. This pertains to Sri Lankan Malay, Singapore Bazaar Malay, Papiá Kristang, and Batavia Creole.

Regarding Chinese Pidgin English, its contact language, Cantonese, has a rich variety of obligatory classifiers, which means that the two optional classifiers in Chinese Pidgin English represent a drastic reduction of the classifier system of the Sinitic contact language.

NOMINAL SYNTAX

Chapter 37
Marking of pronominal possessors

MARTIN HASPELMATH AND THE *APiCS* CONSORTIUM

1. Adnominal personal-pronoun possessors

The topic of this chapter is the expresssion of personal-pronoun possessors modifying a possessed noun, as in *my mother* and *her house*. In Chapter 2, the order of possessor and possessum was dealt with, and in this and the following two chapters, the grammatical coding of possessors is at the centre of our attention. Since pronominal possessors and full NP possessors are often treated differently in languages, there are two different chapters for the marking of these two possessor types. The marking of full NP possessors is the topic of the next chapter (Chapter 38). In addition to the coding types, this chapter also takes into account the order of pronominal possessor and possessum, as Chapter 2 is restricted to full NP possessors.

As in the other chapters on adnominal possessive constructions, possession is defined as comprising ownership, body-part, and kinship relations. Of course, other relationships are often coded in the same way as these (e.g. *our school*, *your chair*), but these other relationships are more difficult to characterize, and we leave them aside. We do not consider contrasts between ownership on the one hand and kinship and body-part relations on the other. Such grammatical contrasts (known as alienable–inalienable contrasts) seem to play (almost) no role in pidgin and creole languages (see McWhorter 2001: 126, 153) and are therefore not taken into account here.

In this chapter, only non-contrastive, non-focused adnominal possessors with an overt possessed noun are taken into account. Focused adnominal possessors (e.g. YOUR *house*) and independently used possessors (e.g. *yours*) are often coded differently (see Chapter 39 for independent pronominal possessors).

Predicative possession (as in *He has a big house*) is treated in Chapter 77.

2. The values

Three coding types (possessive word, adpositional phrase, affix) and two ordering types (preceding, following) are distinguished, which yields six feature values.

When the pronominal possessor is a single word, it is often called **possessive pronoun**. These **precede the possessum** (value 1) in most Atlantic and Indian Ocean pidgins and creoles with European lexifiers, as illustrated in (1)–(3).

		excl	shrd	all
●	1. Preceding word	24	31	55
●	2. Following word	3	11	14
●	3. Adpositional phrase preceding the possessum	3	15	18
●	4. Adpositional phrase following the possessum	9	23	32
●	5. Prefix	0	1	1
●	6. Suffix	0	2	2

(1) Guyanais (Pfänder 2013)
 to kaz
 2SG house
 'your house'

(2) Guinea-Bissau Kriyol (Intumbo et al. 2013)
 nha fidju (*nha* < Portuguese *minha*)
 1SG.POSS child
 'my child'

(3) Nicaraguan Creole English (Bartens 2013a)
 Mai mama se dat haar grani
 1SG.POSS mother say COMP 3SG.POSS.F granny
 mama woz fram Jamieka.
 mother COP.PST from Jamaica
 'My mother told me that her grandmother was from Jamaica.'

Similar constructions are also found in English- and Dutch-based languages elsewhere (e.g. Singlish, Chinese Pidgin English, Hawai'i Creole, Afrikaans), as well as in Asian Spanish- and Portuguese-based creoles. In all these cases, the forms are fairly close to the corresponding forms of the lexifier. In most languages, the actual forms of the possessive pronouns are different from the subject or object pronouns, but in some they are always identical (e.g. in Chinese Pidgin English, where the possessive pronouns are identical to object pronouns, e.g. *you pidgin* 'your business', or in Singapore Bazaar Malay).

Possessive pronouns **follow the possessum** (value 2) in far fewer languages. The most striking group is the Atlantic French-based creoles and the Portuguese-based creoles of the Gulf of Guinea, and another example is Palenquero:

(4) Martinican Creole (Colot & Ludwig 2013b)
   yich mwen (orthographic: *yich-mwen*)
   child my
   'my children'

(5) Angolar (Maurer 2013a)
   kai no
   house our
   'our house'

(6) Palenquero (Schwegler 2013)
   ¡Moná mi, miní aká!
   son   my come here
   'My son, come here!'

It seems that this ordering is substrate-influenced, though this is not easy to demonstrate (but see Schwegler 2002 for Palenquero, Lefebvre 1998: 143–7 for Haitian Creole). Other languages with a following possessive word are Juba Arabic, Pidgin Hawaiian and Mixed Ma'a/Mbugu.

When the pronominal possessor is marked by an adposition (normally a preposition), this adpositional phrase more typically follows the possessum. But **adpositional phrases preceding the possessor** (value 3) are found, for example, in several Caribbean English-based creoles (ex. 7). However, in Jamaican (and maybe also in others) this pattern seems to have a special contrastive sense.

(7) Creolese (Devonish & Thompson 2013)
   fo   awii buk
   POSS 1PL book
   'our book'

In addition, it is found in a number of Asian languages and in Kriol. The use of prepositional phrases as preposed possessors is unexpected, because "in languages with prepositions, the genitive almost always follows the governing noun" (Greenberg 1963, Universal 2).

(8) Diu Indo-Portuguese (Cardoso 2013)
   D-use kurəsãw ɔn   te?
   of-2 heart   where be.NPST
   'Where is your heart?'

(9) Ternate Chabacano (Sippola 2013b)
   kel di mótru pamílya
   that of 1PL   family
   'our family'

(10) Kriol (Schultze-Berndt & Angelo 2013)
   bla   mibala   bos
   POSS   1PL.EXCL boss
   'our boss'

Other languages with preposed adpositional phrases have postpositions, as is more expected from the point of view of word-order typology. Interestingly, both Batavia Creole and Ambon Malay (as well as Singapore Bazaar Malay) have postpositions (rather than prepositions) as possessive markers, suggesting that Batavia Creole is influenced by Malay. However, etymologically the postposition *sua* comes from a possessive pronoun (in indexing function, as described in Chapter 38).

(11) Ambon Malay (Paauw 2013)
   antua   pung rambu
   3SG.FORMAL POSS hair
   'her hair'

(12) Batavia Creole (Maurer 2013b)
   Eo teng vose sua sirbidor.
   1SG COP 2SG POSS servant
   'I am your servant.'

In Sri Lankan Malay and in Yimas-Arafundi Pidgin, the postpositions are written jointly with the possessor noun, so they might be case suffixes.

(13) Yimas-Arafundi Pidgin (Foley 2013)
   ama-nakən tam
   1SG-POSS   dog
   'my dog'

Adpositional phrases following the possessor (value 4) are the second-most widespread type. Since this is by far the most widespread type when the possessor is a full NP, it is not surprising that quite a few languages use the same pattern with personal pronouns, as in (14).

(14) Tayo (Ehrhart & Revis 2013)
   kas   pu mwa
   house of me
   'my house'

However, occasionally a different preposition is used for pronoun and full NP possessors, as in Kikongo-Kituba (and similarly in Lingala):

(15) Kikongo-Kituba (Mufwene 2013)
   a. *mwana na mono*
      child of me
      'my child'
   b. *mwana ya Petelo*
      child of Petelo
      'Peter's child'

Finally, **prefixes** (value 5) and **suffixes** (value 6) are quite marginal in *APiCS*. Prefixes occur in Michif, but only in those (relatively few) nouns that derive from Cree (e.g. *ki-tawakay-a* [2SG-ear-PL.INAN] 'your ears'). Suffixes occur in Sango (marginally) and in Kinubi, again marginally, following the Arabic pattern (e.g. *abú-i* 'my father'). And it should be kept in mind that the preceding and following words of values 1 and 2 are also often affix-like.

37 Marking of pronominal possessors

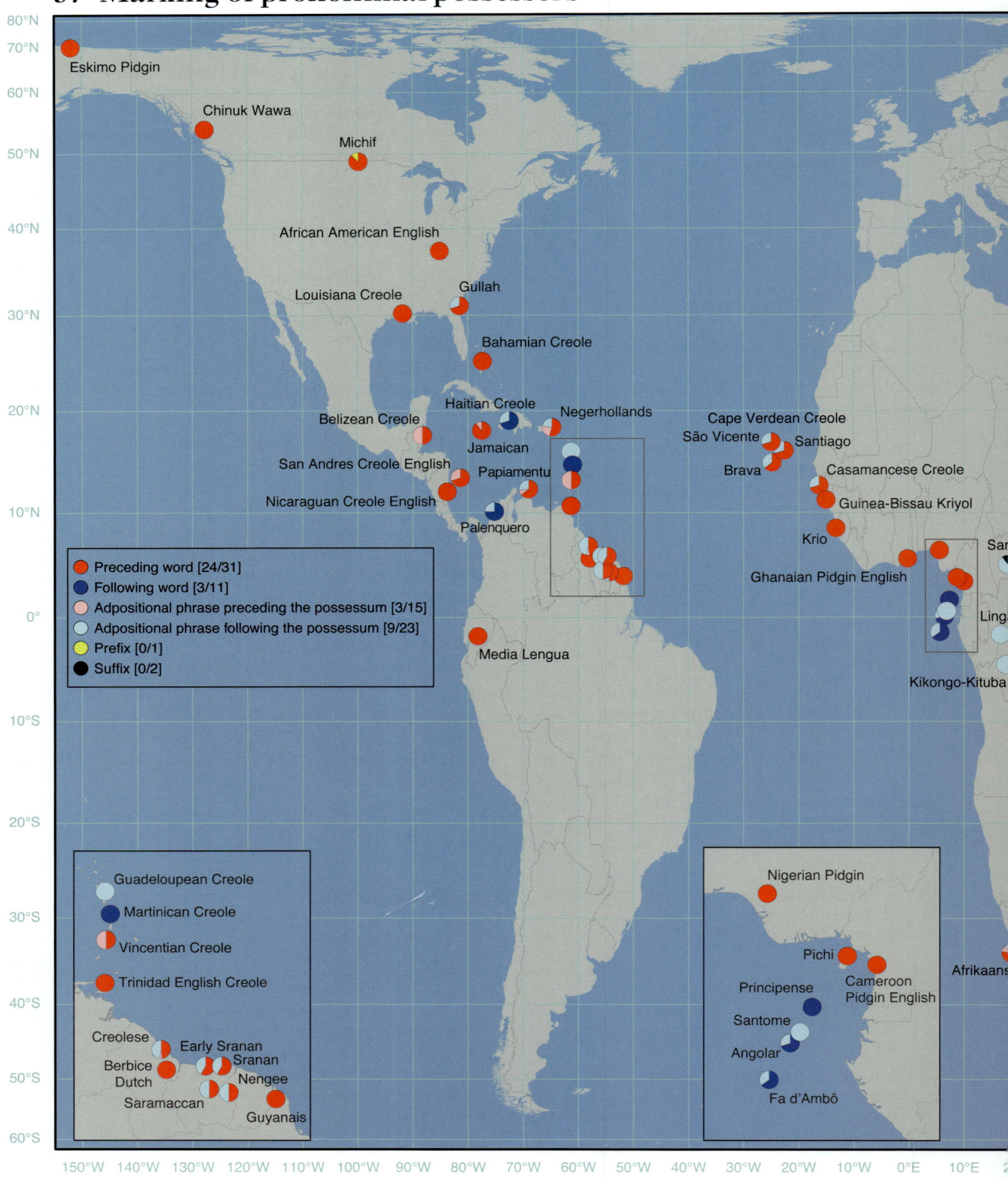

Chapter 38
Marking of possessor noun phrases

MARTIN HASPELMATH AND THE *APiCS* CONSORTIUM

1. Possessor noun phrases

In this feature, we look at the coding of possessor noun phrases, that is, full noun phrases (not personal pronouns) that express the possessor in an ownership, body-part, or kinship relationship, as in *the girl's bed*, *Pedro's foot*, and *mother's uncle*. Personal-pronoun possessors are treated in the preceding chapter. In this chapter, only coding by adposition or case, by person-indexing, or by juxtaposition is considered. Word order is the topic of Chapter 2 and is not taken into account here. The corresponding *WALS* chapter is Nichols & Bickel (2005).

There are just three possibilities that are distinguished here:

		excl	shrd	all
●	1. Adpositional or case marking of possessor	30	26	56
○	2. No marking	12	30	42
●	3. Person-indexing on possessum	2	11	13

2. Adpositional or case marking of the possessor

In the most frequent case, the possessor is marked by an adposition or a case affix on the possessor (value 1), as in English (preposition: *the house of my brother*, case suffix: *my brother's house*) or the Romance languages (Spanish, preposition: *la casa de mi hermano*).

In many languages, there is a preposition that is derived from the 'of' preposition of the lexifier, e.g. Afrikaans *van*, Cape Verdean Creole *di*, Guinea-Bissau Kriyol *di*, Zamboanga Chabacano *di/de*, and Mixed Ma'a/Mbugu *-a*. Two further examples are given in (1) and (2):

(1) Santome (Hagemeijer 2013)
 pe di mosu
 father of boy
 'the boy's father'

(2) Gullah (Klein 2013)
 de foot ob de tree
 'the foot of the tree'

Pidgin Hindustani uses the postposition *ke*, from its lexifier Fiji Hindi:

(3) Pidgin Hindustani (Siegel 2013)
 Daya ke kuta
 Daya POSS dog
 'Daya's dog'

Mixed Ma'a/Mbugu has the gender-agreeing preposition *-a*, while Fanakalo and Lingala (other Bantu-based languages that have lost gender) have the fossilized prepositions *ga* and *ya* (deriving from *-a*), respectively.

(4) Lingala (Meeuwis 2013)
 ndáko ya mobáli
 house of man
 'the house of the man'

In a few English-based languages, the genitive case marker (*'s*) survives, for example, in Singlish and Hawai'i Creole:

(5) Hawai'i Creole (Velupillai 2013)
 diz gaɪ-z nɛk
 this guy-GEN neck
 'this guy's neck'

But there are also quite a few *APiCS* languages which have a newly developed possessive preposition. The Pacific English-based languages have a preposition deriving from *belong* (Kriol *blanga*, Tok Pisin *bilong*), while quite a few other languages have a preposition deriving from 'for' (Sranan *fu*, Saramaccan *u* from English *for*, Tayo *pu* from French *pour*).

(6) Kriol (Schultze-Berndt & Angelo 2013)
 blanga men kantri
 POSS man country
 'the man's country'

(7) Sranan (Winford & Plag 2013)
 a plan fu a Masra
 DET plan of DET Master
 'the Lord's plan'

Similarly, the Juba Arabic preposition *ta* comes from a noun meaning 'possession' (used as a possessive preposition in many Arabic vernaculars), and Guadeloupean and Haitian Creole *a* apparently comes from the French preposition *à* 'to'. In other languages, the origin of the possessive adposition is unknown (e.g. Sango *ti*, Ambon Malay postposition *pung*, Sri Lankan Malay genitive suffix *-pe*).

Less expectedly, a possessive postposition may derive from a personal pronoun, in an indexing construction like the one described in §4. This occurs in Korlai (*su*), Sri Lanka Portuguese (*-su*), and Papiá Kristang (*sa*), as well as in Afrikaans (*se*).

(8) Korlai (Clements 2013)
pay su kadz
father POSS house
'father's house'

This Korlai pattern clearly derives from an original construction of the type 'father, his house'. That *su* is now a postposition in Korlai is clear from the fact that the possessive postpositional phrase can alternatively be postposed (*kadz pay su*). Another language where this occurs is Papiamentu (see 9a, b). That *su* is now a postposition in Papiamentu rather than a possessive pronoun is clear from the fact that it occurs not only with third-person possessors, but also with second-person possessors (see 9b).

(9) Papiamentu (Kouwenberg 2013b)
a. *Hose su kas*
José POSS house
'José's house'

b. *boso tur su trabou*
2PL all POSS work
'the work of all of you'

3. No marking

The possessor and the possessum may simply be juxtaposed, with no segmental marking (value 2). This occurs widely in the English-based and Romance-based creoles of the Atlantic, but also elsewhere. However, most of the languages that allow juxtaposition also have an alternative construction with overt marking, sometimes with a subtle meaning difference.

It seems that these constructions derive from prepositional or case-marked constructions in the lexifier from which the overt marker (*'s*, *de*) has simply been dropped: this is apparent from the word order, which is identical to the word order of the lexifier: preposed possessor in English-based languages, postposed possessor in French-based languages. (Interestingly, English-based languages never have possessum–possessor order in constructions without marking, so simple dropping of *of* does not seem to have occurred, for whatever reason.)

(10) Early Sranan (van den Berg & Bruyn 2013)
da man nem
that man name
'that man's name'

(11) Gullah (Klein 2013)
God work
'God's work'

(12) Berbice Dutch (Kouwenberg 2013a)
di jɛrma papa
the woman father
'the woman's father'

(13) Seychelles Creole (Michaelis & Rosalie 2013)
lakaz Marcel
house Marcel
'Marcel's house'

(14) Angolar (Maurer 2013a)
mulu kai
wall house
'the wall of the house'

A construction with no marking is also found in a number of pidgins:

(15) Chinese Pidgin Russian (Perekhvalskaya 2013)
eta bərata synə
that brother son
'the brother's son, the nephew'

4. Indexing of the possessor on the possessum

In our third type, the marking is by a person form associated with the possessum, as in 'the father, his house' (value 3). This construction is sometimes called head marking (Nichols 1986), but here it is called person-indexing (Haspelmath 2013a+).

(16) Krio (Finney 2013)
di man ĩ os
DET man 3.POSS house
'the man's house' (lit. 'the man, his house')

(17) Negerhollands (van Sluijs 2013)
di mēnshi shi hā
DET girl 3.POSS hair
'the girl's hair' (lit. 'the girl, her hair')

(18) Chinuk Wawa (Grant 2013)
man yáka kánim
man 3SG canoe
'the man's canoe' (lit. 'the man, his canoe')

Krio and Chinuk Wawa are the only languages where this is reported to be the only existing construction. This construction is particularly common in the West African English-based languages. As in the Korlai and Papiamentu constructions discussed in §2, the indexing person forms in these constructions may be on their way toward reanalysis as postpositions, but here we have no evidence that they are not simple person-indexing constructions.

38 Marking of possessor noun phrases

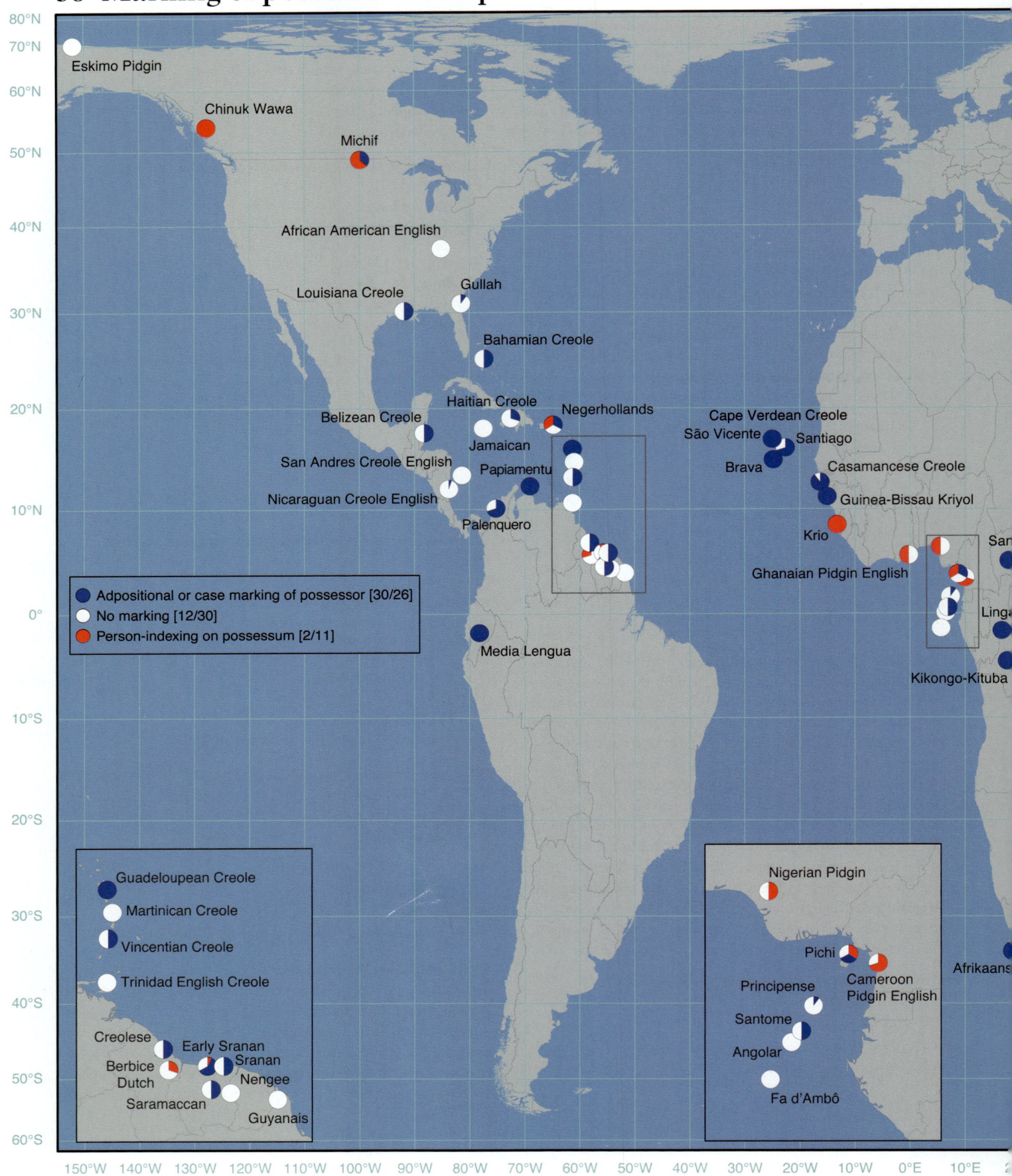

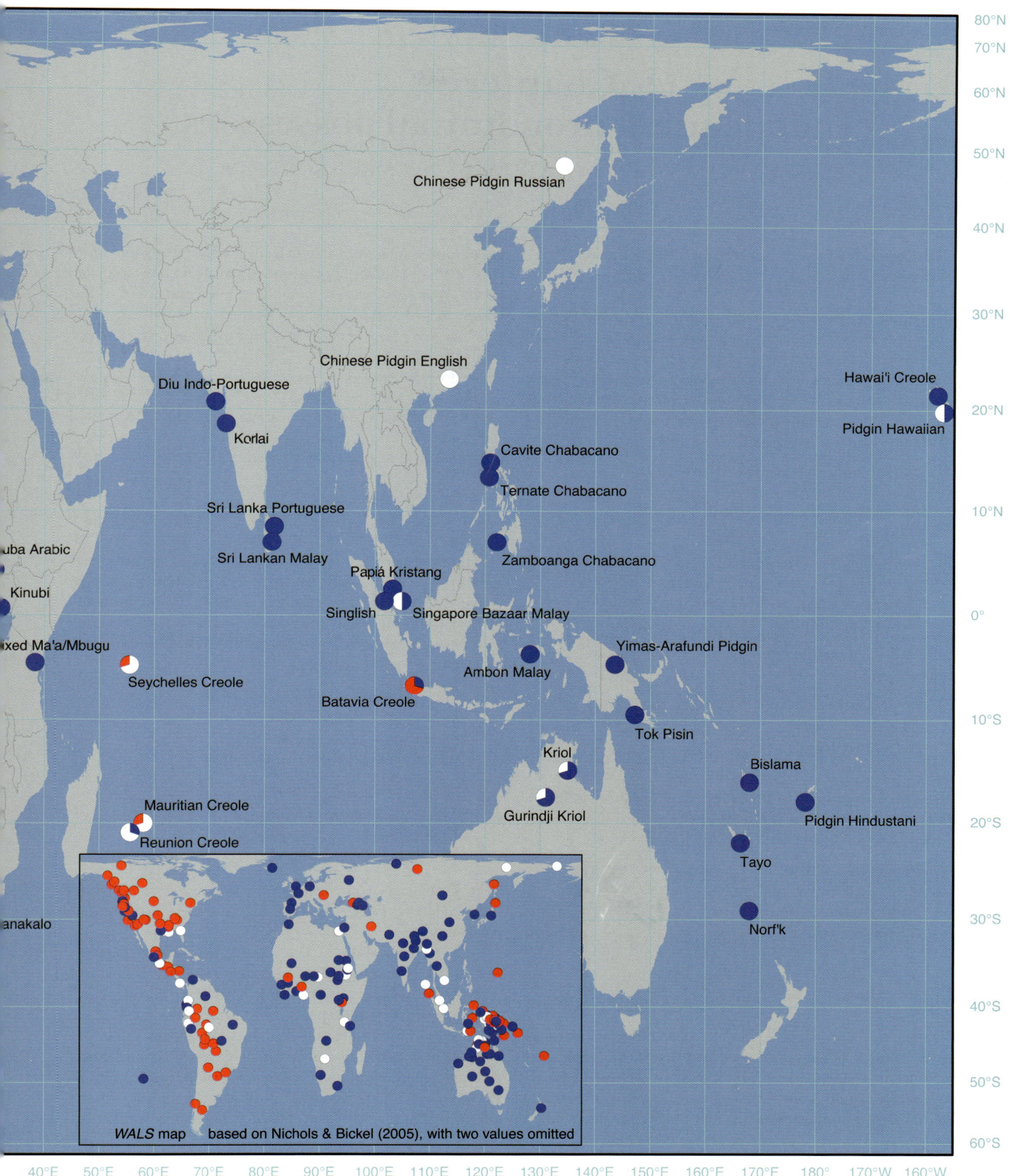

Chapter 39
Independent pronominal possessors

MARTIN HASPELMATH AND THE *APiCS* CONSORTIUM

1. Independent vs. dependent pronominal possessors

In Chapter 37, we looked at dependent pronominal possessors that occur with an overt possessed noun, as in *my house*. Here we will look at independent pronominal possessors, such as *mine*. Independent pronominal possessors are used when the possessed noun is not overt but must be inferred from the context, for example in comparative constructions (1) or in elliptical answers (2).

(1) San Andres Creole English (Bartens 2013b)
Mi nieba hous biga an fi mi.
my neighbour house bigger than for me
'My neighbour's house is bigger than mine.'

(2) Gurindji Kriol (Meakins 2013)
An wijan-tu warlaku nyawa? Ngayiny!
and who-DAT dog this 1SG.DAT
'And whose dog is this?' 'Mine!'

Independent pronominal possessors are also common in predicative position, as in (3).

(3) Cavite Chabacano (Sippola 2013a)
Di ele ese camisa.
of 3SG that dress
'That dress is hers.'

When they occur in an ordinary argument position, as in (4), there must be an antecedent in the earlier context (e.g. 'Didn't you say that your brother and you both lost your keys?').

(4) Pichi (Yakpo 2013)
À dɔn si yù yon.
1SG.SBJ PRF see 2SG own
'I have seen yours.'

2. The values

What we study primarily is the form of the independent personal pronoun possessor in comparison with the dependent personal pronoun possessor. The two can be **formally identical** (as in Gurindji Kriol: *ngayiny walaku* 'my dog' vs. *ngayiny* 'mine'), or a **special preposition** may be used for independent possessors (as in Guinea-Bissau Kriyol: *nha fidju* 'my son' vs. *di mi* 'mine'), or another **special word** may be used (as in Pichi: *yù hia* 'your hair', *yù yon* 'yours'), or a **special form** of the possessive personal pronoun may be used (as in Afrikaans: *haar seun* 'her son', *hare* 'hers'). Thus, four different feature values are distinguished:

		excl	shrd	all
○	1. Identical to dependent pronominal possessor	28	6	34
○	2. Special preposition plus pronoun	9	4	13
●	3. Special word plus dependent pronominal possessor	13	6	19
●	4. Special pronoun form	10	8	18

The most common type of language has the **same form for both the dependent and the independent possessor** (value 1). This occurs especially in languages whose pronominal possessors include an overt possessive marker, e.g. Sri Lankan Malay (*go-pe bapa* [I-GEN father] 'my father') and Bislama (*woman blong yu* 'your wife'):

(5) Sri Lankan Malay (Slomanson 2013)
Ini sapa-pe buk-pədə? Go-pe.
DEM who-POSS book-PL 1SG-POSS
'Whose books are these? Mine.'

(6) Bislama (Meyerhoff 2013)
ol loli ia blong mi o blong yu?
PL lolly DEF POSS 1SG or POSS 2SG
'Are those sweets mine or yours?'

APiCS languages with formally simple possessive pronouns (like English *my mother*) never seem to use these also for independent possessors.

Value 1 is chosen also if a language has two different dependent constructions, and the independent possessor is identical with just one of them. For example, in Belizean Creole, independent possessors are expressed by the preposition *fu* (e.g. *Da aysbaks fu i* 'This icebox is his'). This is also one option for dependent possessors (*fu dem mone* 'their money'), which exists alongside another option (*i hɛd* 'his head'). It appears that in all these cases, the independent possessor is identical with the longer (overtly marked) form of the dependent pronominal possessor. Another example comes from Ternate Chabacano, where the independent possessor is marked by *di*, as in (7a), like the longer form of the dependent possessor (as in 7b), and unlike the shorter form (as in 7c). Singapore Bazaar Malay is similar.

(7) Ternate Chabacano (Sippola 2013b)
 a. *Di kyen ésti líbru?* ***Di mi****, di mi késti líbru.*
  of who DEM book of 1SG.POSS of 1SG.POSS this book
  'Whose book is this?' 'Mine. This book is mine.'
 b. *el bida **di** mi*
  DEF life of 1SG.POSS
  'my life'
 c. *mi gargánta*
  1SG.POSS throat
  'my throat'

In some languages, there is a **special possessive preposition** (value 2) that is used for independent possessors, but not for dependent possessors. Some examples are given in (8). This occurs particularly in Caribbean English-based creoles, in Indian Ocean French-based creoles, and in some Portuguese-based creoles of the Gulf of Guinea. A sentence example is (9).

(8)
	Dependent possessor	Independent possessor
a. Jamaican	*mi*	*fi mi*
b. Seychelles Creole	*mon*	*pour mwan*
c. Guinea-Bissau Kriyol	*nha*	*di mi*
d. Angolar	*m*	*ri m*
	'my'	'mine'

(9) Palenquero (Schwegler 2013)
 ¿Libro ese, ri kiene fue? É ri bo.
 book this of who be be of 2SG
 'Whose book is it?' 'It is yours.'

(Note that the preposition *ri* is not excluded in adnominal position. Palenquero allows expressions such as *moná ri ele* [daughter of he] 'his daughter', but prefers possessives without preposition such as *moná mi* 'my son'. For this reason, the use of *ri* in (9) is regarded as a "special preposition".)

In languages of the third type, there is a **special word** that takes the place of the possessum and that is **combined with the ordinary dependent possessives** (value 3). This occurs especially in the English-based and the French-based languages, and is found almost exclusively in the Atlantic region. In the former group, the English words *one* and *own* have given rise to such special words (e.g. Singlish *his one* 'his'; Gullah *hənə own* [2PL own] 'yours', Cameroon Pidgin English *ma on* 'mine', Vincentian Creole *foyu oon* 'yours'). In the French-based languages, the special word is *pa* (Haitian Creole *pa m* 'mine'), or *ta* (Martinican Creole *ta mwen* 'mine'), or *kenn/tchenn* (Louisiana Creole *mo-kenn* 'mine', *so-kenn* 'hers'). Of these, *pa* seems to be derived from French *part* 'part'. Special words also occur in two of the Portuguese-based Gulf of Guinea creoles: Fa d'Ambô has *xa* (e.g. *xa-bo* [thing-2SG] 'yours'), and Principense, illustrated in (10), has *ki*, which behaves like a noun and may go back to *coisa* 'thing'.

(10) Principense (Maurer 2013c)
 *Kaxi sê **ki** tê.*
 house DEM thing POSS.2SG
 'This house is yours.'

One may ask whether there is such a clear difference between such a special word and a special preposition (value 2). In fact, for Guadeloupean and Martinican Creole, the word *ta* (as in *ta mwen* 'mine') is called a preposition by Colot & Ludwig (2013a, b), and is even glossed 'of'. However, in contrast to the prepositions in value 2, this element does not occur anywhere else in the language. (So by "special preposition" we really mean a word that occurs elsewhere in the language as a preposition, but not in possessive constructions with dependent pronoun.)

In the fourth type, there is a **special pronoun form** of the independent possessive pronoun, as in English (*mine, yours, hers, ours,* etc.). This mostly occurs in English-based languages, which sometimes preserve the kind of distinction that exists in English, especially when they are influenced by English (e.g. African American English *mine* or *mines*, Gullah *mine*, Hawai'i Creole *maɪn*, Nicaraguan Creole English *owɑrz*). Similarly, in Cavite Chabacano the Spanish distinction between *mi* 'my' and *mío* 'mine' has been preserved. The form in (11) is another possibility, alongside the form with *di* illustrated above in (3).

(11) Cavite Chabacano (Sippola 2013a)
 Mio *esi bicicleta na enfrente de niso casa.*
 mine that bicycle LOC front of 1PL.POSS house
 'The bicycle in front of our house is mine.'

In Spanish, the dependent forms *mi, tu, su* are simply shortened forms of the independent forms *mío, tuyo, suyo*. This also occurs in some *APiCS* languages. For example, in Cape Verdean Creole of São Vicente, the form *nha* 'my' (as in *nha káza* 'my house') appears to be just a shortening of *minha* 'mine' (from Portuguese *minha* 'my, mine'). Similarly, in Juba Arabic, *tai* 'my' (*ida tai* 'my hand') is a shortened form of *bitai* 'mine' (*de bitai* 'this is mine'). The origin is a noun *bita-* 'possession', which takes pronominal suffixes (*bita-i* 'mine' < 'my possession', *bita-ki* 'yours' < 'your possession', etc.). In Afrikaans, too, the independent form *hare* is a non-reduced variant of the dependent form *haar*.

In Michif, the independent pronominal possessor derives from Cree, whereas the dependent pronominal possessor derives from French (*ma liivr* 'my book').

(12) Michif (Bakker 2013)
 Awaana soo liiv ooma? ***Niya****.*
 who 3.POSS.M book this.INAN 1SG
 'Whose book is this?' 'Mine.'

39 Independent pronominal possessors

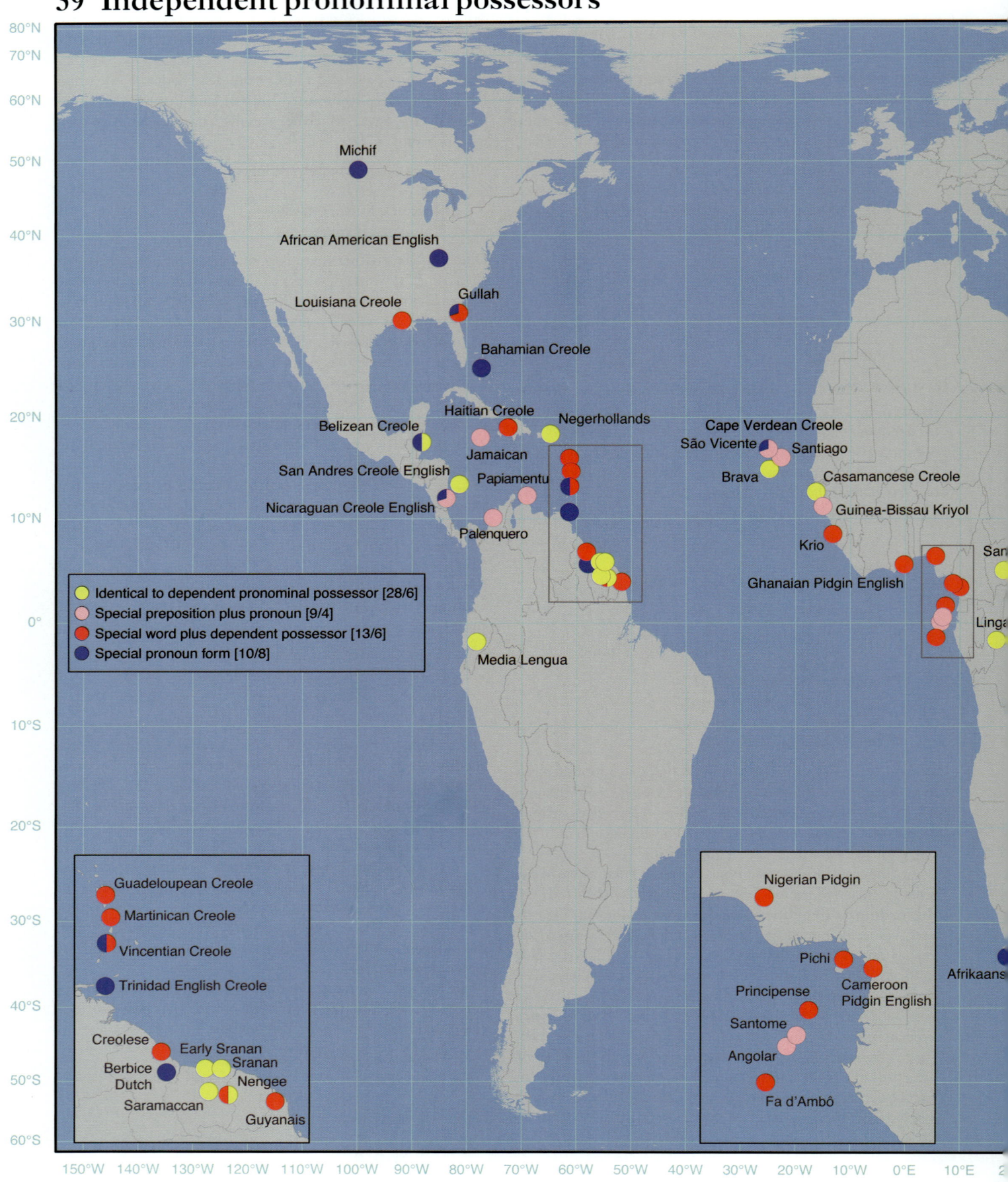

Chapter 40
Gender agreement of adnominal adjectives

PHILIPPE MAURER AND THE *APiCS* CONSORTIUM

1. Introduction

In linguistics, gender may be subdivided into two types: sex-based and grammatical-based gender (see e.g. Corbett 2005a, b, c). Sex-based distinctions are probably found in all languages of the world; in Papiamentu (Caribbean, Ibero-Romance-based), for example, there is a contrast between *mama* 'mother' and *tata* 'father'. This contrast, however, is a matter of lexical semantics. On the other hand, grammatical gender requires syntactic evidence, called agreement. Agreement may be exhibited, for example, by verbs, adjectives, determiners, and numerals. An example of a language displaying agreement is French, as in *un grand clocher* 'a (m.) big (m.) church steeple' vs. *une grande table* 'a (f.) big (f.) table'. In these examples, both the indefinite article and the adjective agree with their noun in gender.

Note that in many languages, not only adnominal adjectives but also predicative adjectives agree in gender with the subject noun phrase, but here we deal mainly with adnominal adjectives.

In pidgin and creole languages, which tend to be isolating languages, agreement is a very rare phenomenon; nevertheless, it exists in some rare cases of adnominal adjectives which agree in gender with their nouns.

For this feature, it is not relevant whether agreement is obligatory or optional; what matters is whether agreement exists at all. In the *APiCS* languages, cases of gender were inherited from the lexifier languages, though often in reduced form.

2. The values

The following four values are distinguished:

○	1. No adjective agrees with the noun	60
●	2. Only few adjectives agree with the noun	12
●	3. Many adjectives agree with the noun	2
●	4. All adjectives agree with the noun	1

As mentioned before, pidgins and creoles tend to be of the isolating type; therefore it is not surprising that the great majority of the *APiCS* languages (60 out of 74 languages, or 81 per cent) have **no gender agreement with adnominal adjectives** (value 1). Note that for the *WALS* languages, Corbett (2005a) states that in his sample of 254 languages, 57 per cent lack a gender-agreement system.

(1) Diu Indo-Portuguese (Cardoso 2013)
   bunit   rapas, bunit   muyɛr
   beautiful boy   beautiful woman
   'handsome boy, beautiful woman'

(2) Cameroon Pidgin English (Schröder 2013)
   ol man, ol wuman
   'old man, old woman'

(3) Negerhollands (van Sluijs 2013)
   ēn klēn mēⁿshi, ēn klēn jung
   ART small girl   ART small boy
   'a small girl, a small boy'

(4) Kinubi (Luffin 2013)
   mária núbi, rági núbi
   woman Nubi man Nubi
   'a Nubi woman, a Nubi man'

For English- and Malay-based *APiCS* languages, it is not surprising that they lack cases of gender agreement since neither English nor Malay have gender agreement; but French-based languages (seven out of nine) show that the whole French agreement system has been lost, as in Seychelles Creole.

(5) Seychelles Creole (Michaelis & Rosalie 2013)
   en vye tonton, en vye tantin
   ART old man   ART old woman
   'an old man, an old woman'

The twelve languages which display value 2 (**only few adjectives** agree with their noun) all belong to the Ibero-Romance-based creoles: the three Cape Verdean varieties, Guinea-Bissau Kriyol, Casamancese Creole, and Principense in West Africa; Papiá Kristang, Cavite Chabacano, Ternate Chabacano, and Zamboanga Chabacano in Southeast Asia; and finally Papiamentu and Palenquero in the Caribbean. In all these twelve languages gender agreement is restricted to adjectives that modify human nouns; with the exception of Zamboanga Chabacano, agreement of the adjective is optional.

The following examples illustrate West African creoles. In Cape Verdean Creole of Brava, we find *branku* (m.) vs. *branka* (f.) 'white (of persons)', *altu* vs. *alta* 'tall', *kabuverdianu* vs. *kabuverdiana* 'Cape Verdean'. In Guinea-Bissau Kriyol, agreement is restricted to the acrolect, and in Casamancese Creole, only two adjectives may agree with their noun: *dudu* vs. *duda* 'crazy', and *beju* vs. *beja* 'old'. In Principense, there is only one adjective agreeing with its noun: *finu* vs. *fina* 'nice', as in *ũa mye fina* (but also *ũa mye finu*) 'a nice woman'.

In Southeast Asia, Ternate Chabacano has *boníta muhér* 'beautiful woman' vs. *boníto ómbri* 'handsome man', and Zamboanga Chabacano, as already mentioned, is the only language displaying value 2 where gender agreement is obligatory, although only with a dozen adjectives:

(6) Zamboanga Chabacano (Steinkrüger 2013)
    a. *Éste muhér byen lóka.*
       this woman quite crazy.F
       'This woman is quite crazy.'
    b. *Lóko ya si Jeffrey.*
       crazy.M already AG Jeffrey
       'Jeffrey is crazy, already.'

In the Caribbean, Palenquero has, for example, *guapo* 'handsome' vs. *guapa* 'beautiful', and Papiamentu has only optional gender agreement with adjectives referring to nationality, for example, *kolombiano* vs. *kolombiana* 'Colombian'.

Note that not all Ibero-Romance-based languages exhibit gender agreement in adnominal adjectives; Santome and Angolar in the Atlantic area, Diu Indo-Portuguese (see example 1), Korlai, and Sri Lanka Portuguese in South Asia, as well as Batavia Creole in Southeast Asia do not.

Value 3 is represented by the French-based Louisiana Creole as well as by the bilingual mixed language Michif. The following example illustrates Louisiana Creole:

(7) Louisiana Creole (Neumann-Holzschuh & Klingler 2013)
    en gro nèg, en gros fom
    ART big.M black.man ART big.F woman
    'a big black man, a big woman'

Gender agreement of adnominal adjectives

Note, however, that agreement is not obligatory in Louisiana Creole either, as shown by *en vyè fam* 'an old woman' vs. *en vyè hòm* 'an old man'.

In Michif, the elements of the noun phrase (nouns, adjectives, determiners) are French-based, so Michif inherited gender agreement from French.

In Michif, agreement of adnominal adjectives depends on word order: adjectives preceding the noun show agreement, whereas postnominal adjectives do not. The following example illustrates a prenominal adjective:

(8) Michif (Bakker 2013)
    a. *la pchit fiy*
       the little.F girl
       'the little girl'
    b. *aen pchi bwa aan noor*
       a little.M wood of gold
       'a little wooden stick'

The only language representing value 4 is the bilingual mixed language Mixed Ma'a/Mbugu. In this language, **all adjectives agree with their nouns**:

(9) Mixed Ma'a/Mbugu (Mous 2013)
    Lu-hige lu-kuhlo ní yá.
    11-door 11-nice is this
    'The good door is this.'

This example shows that Mixed Ma'a/Mbugu has retained the Bantu gender system, which is not the case with the other Bantu-based languages of our sample, namely Lingala, Kikongo-Kituba, and Fanakalo.

40 Gender agreement of adnominal adjectives

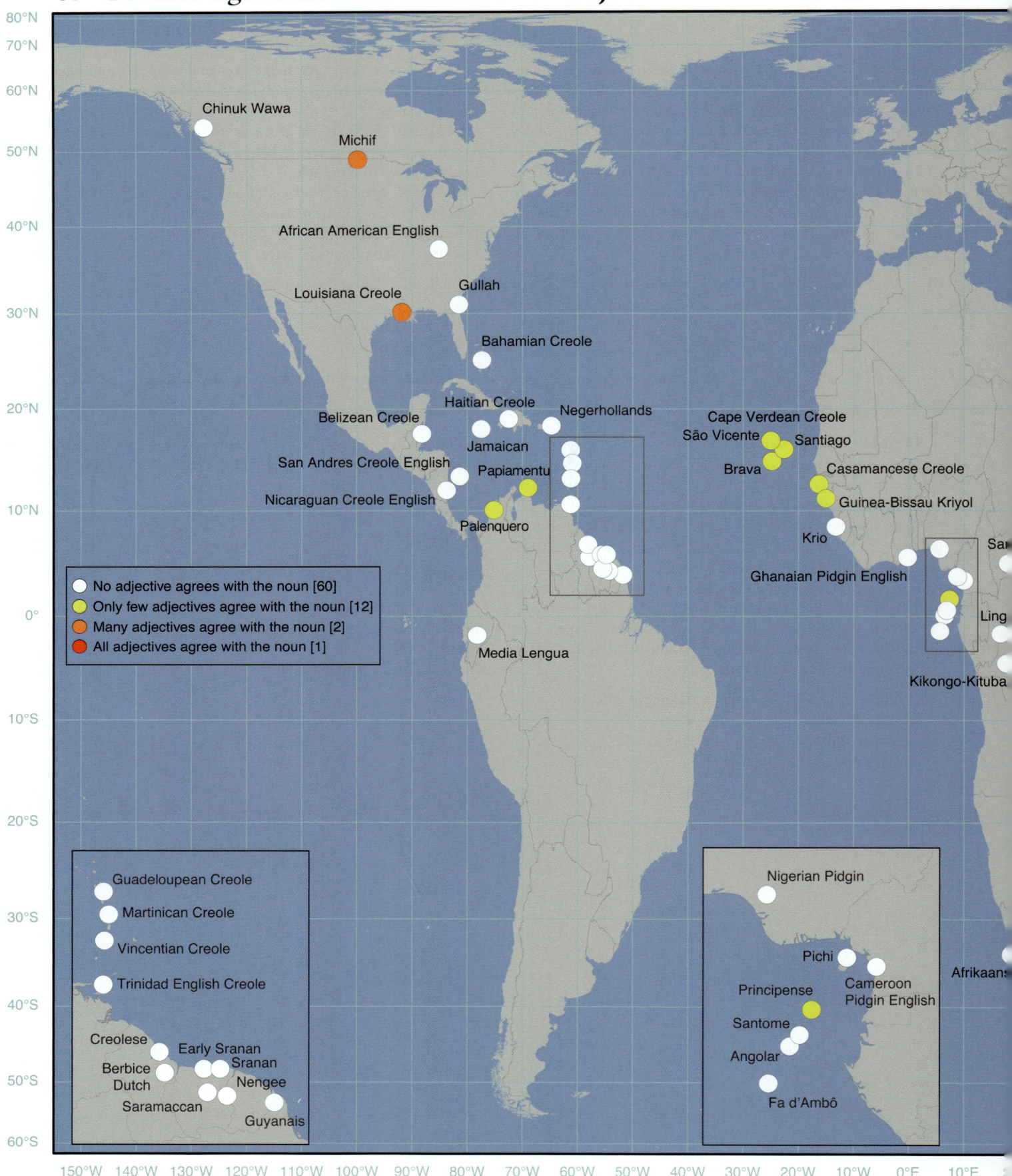

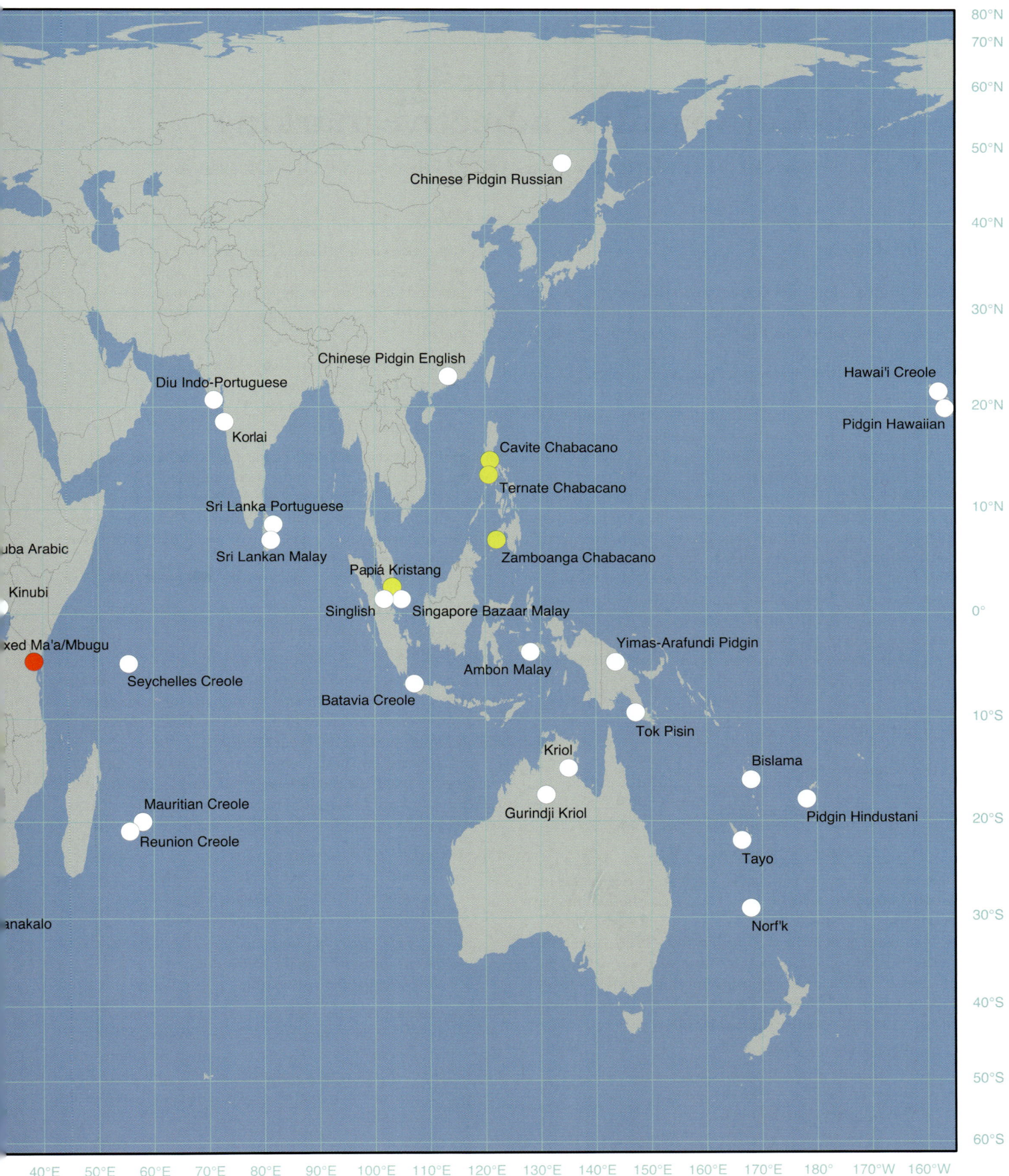

Chapter 41
Comparative adjective marking

SUSANNE MARIA MICHAELIS AND THE *APiCS* CONSORTIUM

1. Introduction

In this chapter, we ask how degree is marked on adjectives when they occur in comparative constructions of inequality such as English *Mary is taller than Peter*, where a comparee NP (*Mary*) is compared with a standard NP (*Peter*) with respect to a parameter (*tallness*). In such constructions, many (especially European) languages mark the comparative degree on the adjective either by a suffix, for example, English *-er* in *tall-er*, or by a degree word, as in French *plus* 'more' in *plus grand* 'bigger'.

We use *adjective* here in a semantic sense to refer to gradable property concepts, for example, 'big', 'small', 'short', 'long' (cf. also Chapter 3 on order of adjective and noun). Morphosyntactically these property concepts can be encoded as verbs, nouns, or as a separate word class (adjectives). In comparative constructions, the standard can be marked in various ways (see Chapter 42 on comparative standard marking). For the present chapter, we only consider constructions in which the standard is present (e.g. *Peter* in *Mary is taller than Peter*), not constructions in which the standard is contextually omitted (*Mary is taller*), because some languages use a different construction when the standard is not expressed.

2. The values

In this feature, we distinguish two values:

		excl	shrd	all
●	1. Adjective is marked	36	23	59
○	2. Adjective is not marked	15	23	38

If comparative degree marking is optional, we regard this here as two different constructions, and in this case both values have been chosen.

The most prominent type within the *APiCS* languages is represented by value 1, where the **adjective is marked**, most often by a particle or degree word meaning 'more' (e.g. *masi* in Angolar, *pli* in Mauritian Creole, *lebih* in Singapore Bazaar Malay, *moa* in Bislama, *mɛr* in Berbice Dutch):

(1) Angolar (Maurer 2013a)
 Ũa tha masi dhangaru patha ôtô.
 one be more high surpass other
 'One is higher than the other.'

(2) Mauritian Creole (Baker & Kriegel 2013)
 mo tur lavi lontan inpé pli bon ki astér
 1SG find life before bit more good than today
 'I find that life in former times was a bit better than today.'

(3) Singapore Bazaar Malay (Khin Khin Aye 2013)
 John lebih tinggi dari Jimmy.
 John more high from Jimmy
 'John is taller than Jimmy.'

In some English-based *APiCS* languages, the adjective suffix *-er* and the degree word *more* can be used simultaneously to mark the adjective, as in Trinidad English Creole, African American English, Bahamian Creole, and others (cf. also the feature "Double comparatives and superlatives" in *eWAVE*, Kortmann & Lunkenheimer 2011, feature 78):

(4) Trinidad English Creole (Mühleisen 2013)
 Hi more bigger dan mi.
 3SG more big.COMP than 1SG
 'He is bigger than me.'

In French-based *APiCS* languages, we find a similar double marking with *pli* (< French *plus* 'more') and some suppletive comparatives inherited from French, for example in Seychelles Creole *pli meyer* 'better' (< French *meilleur*).

As for the position of the comparative marker with regard to the property word, there is some variation across and within the *APiCS* languages. In Berbice Dutch, the comparative marker *mɛr(ɛ)* can either precede (5a) or follow the adjective (5b).

(5) Berbice Dutch (Kouwenberg 2013a)
 a. *dida mɛr stifu an mɛr tarki dɛn katun*
  that more stiff and more strong than cotton
  'That is stiffer and stronger than cotton.'
 b. *o tarki mɛr af di tibiʃiri*
  3SG strong more than the palmstraw
  'It is stronger than palmstraw.'

Some languages allow for great variability in comparative adjective marking. For example, in Vincentian Creole, the adjective suffix *-a* can occur on its own (6a), or it can combine with two different degree words, preposed *mo* (6b) and postposed *moo* (6c). Finally, the two degree words can occur circumposed to the adjective (6d):

(6) Vincentian Creole (Prescod 2013)
   a. *hi taal-a dan shi*
      3SG tall-er than 3SG
      'He is taller than her.'
   b. *hi mo taal-a dan shi*
      3SG more tall-er than 3SG
      'He is taller than her.'
   c. *hi taal-a moo dan shi*
      3SG tall-er more than 3SG
      'He is taller than her.'
   d. *hi mo taal moo dan shi*
      3SG more tall more than 3SG
      'He is taller than her.'

In some languages, the comparative marking of the adjective is discontinuous, that is, the comparative marker and the adjective are not adjacent, as can be seen in example (7) from Korlai. Here the comparative marker *mayz* is separated from the adjective *piken* 'small' by the noun phrase representing the standard (*ki Pedru* 'than Pedru').

(7) Korlai (Clements 2013)
    Lwiz mayz ki Pedru piken tɛ
    Lwiz more than Pedru small COP
    'Lwiz is smaller than Pedru.'

Sometimes it seems difficult to distinguish comparative markers (which belong to the adjective) from standard markers (which belong to the standard), especially when no standard marker is used. The following example from Casamancese Creole is such a case:

(8) Casamancese Creole (Biagui & Quint 2013)
    Jon ma(s) Pidru riku.
    John more Peter rich
    'John is richer than Peter.'

In example (8), *ma(s)* could be interpreted as an ambiguous comparative adjective/standard marker. But when the standard is absent, as in example (9), it becomes obvious that *ma(s)* is the comparative adjective marker, and that the standard *Pidru* is inserted between this comparative adjective marker and the adjective *riku*:

(9) Casamancese Creole (Biagui & Quint 2013)
    Jon ma(s) riku.
    John more rich
    'John is richer.'

This means that the Casamancese Creole example in (8) is parallel to the Korlai example in (7): both show insertion of the standard with the difference that the standard is not marked in (8) (see Chapter 42 on standard marking).

Languages displaying value 2 do **not mark the adjective** in comparative constructions. Here we can distinguish two subtypes. In languages like Fanakalo (10) and Gullah (11), the adjective is not marked, but from the presence of a standard (with its standard marker) the hearer can infer that the two entities are being compared.

(10) Fanakalo (Mesthrie 2013)
     Lo Themba yena makhulu ga lo sistela ga yena.
     DEF.ART Themba he big than DEF.ART sister POSS he
     'Themba is bigger than his sister.' (lit. 'Themba is big from his sister.')

(11) Gullah (Klein 2013)
     E tall pas me.
     3SG tall pass me
     'He is taller than me.'

Another subtype of value 2 consists in juxtaposing two separately asserted predications. The comparison again has to be inferred from the context. One example comes from Pidgin Hawaiian:

(12) Pidgin Hawaiian (Roberts 2013)
     Lanai maikai, Lahaina aole maikai
     Lanai good Lahaina NEG good
     'Lanai is better than Lahaina (as a place to dock).'
     (lit. 'Lanai is good, Lahaina is not good.')

Twenty-three *APiCS* languages show both values 1 and 2. Pichi is typical in this respect. The two constructions are parallel: they are serial verb constructions with a secondary 'pass' verb (see also Chapter 42 on comparative standard marking), the only difference being that in example (13a), representing value 1, the adjective is marked by the degree word *mɔ*, whereas in example (13b), illustrating value 2, the adjective *big* is not marked.

(13) Pichi (Yakpo 2013)
   a. *[...] ya mɔ dia pas de.*
      here more be.expensive pass there
      '[...] here is more expensive than there.'
   b. *[...] wan say we è big pas di wan.*
      one side SUBORD 3SG.SBJ be.big pass this one
      '[...] a place that is bigger than this one.'

Other languages with values 1 and 2 show a European comparative construction type, where the adjective is marked by a degree word like in Guadeloupean Creole: *I pli gran ki mwen.* [3SG more tall than 1SG] 'He/she is taller than me'. Additionally, these languages have a secondary 'pass' construction where the adjective is not marked as in (13b) from Pichi.

41 Comparative adjective marking

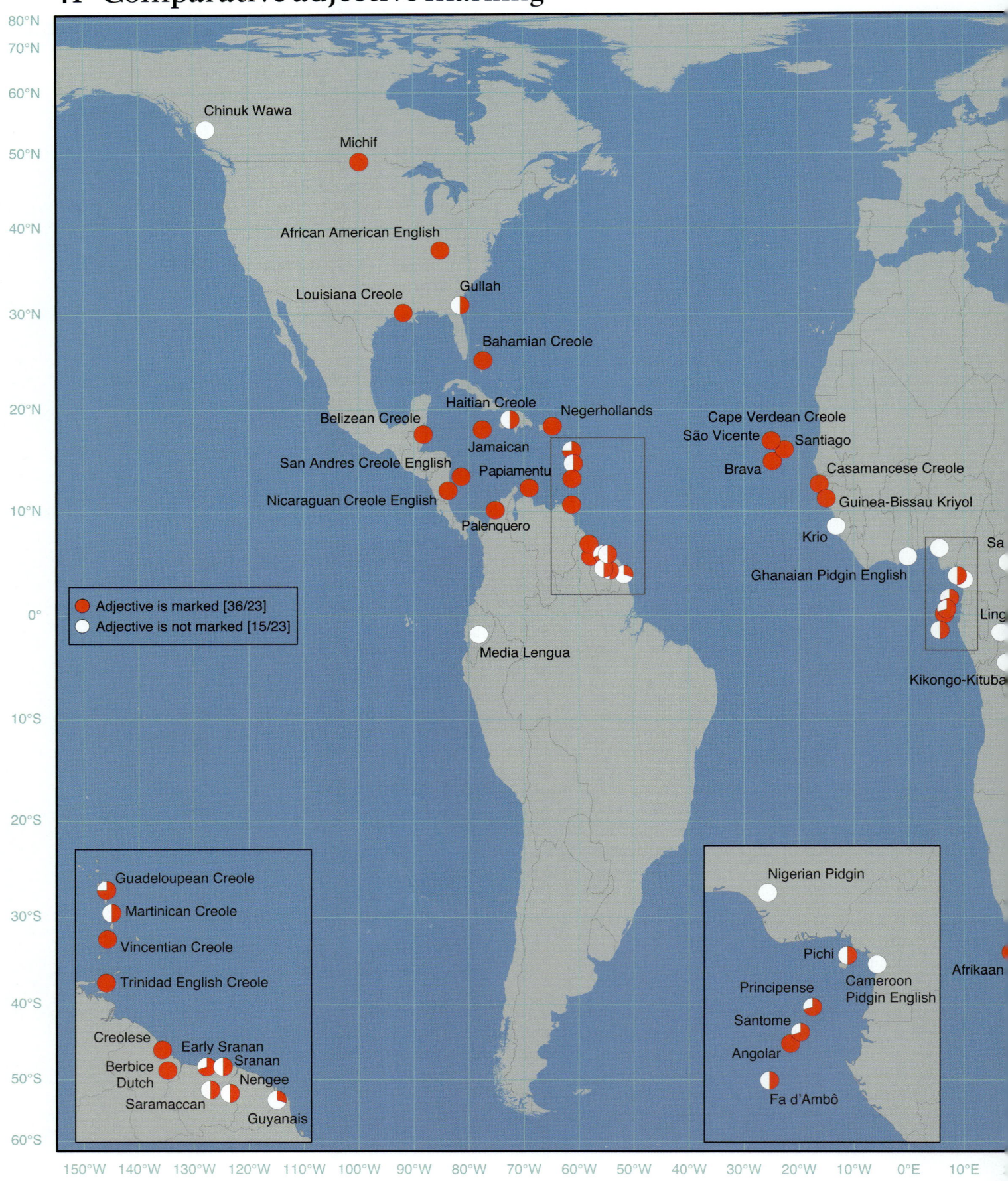

Chapter 42
Comparative standard marking

SUSANNE MARIA MICHAELIS AND THE *APiCS* CONSORTIUM

1. Introduction

Like the previous Chapter 41 on comparative adjective marking, this chapter, too, deals with comparative constructions of inequality. In this feature, following Stassen (2005e), we are interested in the marking of the standard. In a comparative construction, for example

(1) *Mary is taller than Peter*

the standard of comparison is the entity Y (*Peter*) to which the comparee X (*Mary*) is compared. In example (1) the standard *Peter* is marked by the particle *than*. The parameter of comparison is an adjective, taken in a semantic sense (as a gradable property word), as in Chapters 3 and 41.

The standard markers are here classified by the salient other meanings that they have in addition to that of marking the standard. Thus, **surpass markers** also occur as (or are closely related to) verbs meaning 'surpass' or 'exceed'. **Locational markers** have a locational sense (ablative, allative, essive), or a dative sense. **Particle markers** are elements, which are specialized for standard marking, or at least have no 'surpass' or locational meaning (e.g. English *than* and French *que*).

2. The values

In this multiple-choice feature, we distinguish seven values:

		excl	shrd	all
●	1. Primary surpass marking	0	5	5
●	2. Secondary surpass marking	7	20	27
●	3. Locational marking	6	7	13
●	4. Particle marking	22	21	43
●	5. Locational plus particle marking	2	4	6
○	6. Standard is not overtly marked	1	5	6
●	7. Conjoined marking	2	5	7

In the first two types, the standard of comparison is encoded by a 'surpass' verb. We call the first construction type **primary surpass marking** (value 1). In examples representing this value, a 'surpass' verb is the only verb of the construction, and the standard is encoded as its direct object. The parameter of comparison is expressed as a prepositional phrase (*na molaí* 'in tallness' in the following example).

(2) Lingala (Meeuwis 2013)
   Pierre a-lek-í   Jean na molaí
   Pierre 3SG-surpass-PRS.PRF Jean in tallness
   'Pierre is taller than Jean.' (lit. 'Pierre surpasses Jean in tallness.')

A much more widespread construction type within the *APiCS* languages is **secondary surpass marking** (value 2). Here a 'surpass' verb behaves like the second verb of a serial verb construction. The standard is the object of this serial 'surpass' verb (see e.g. Winford 1993: 248ff. for an extensive discussion of this construction in Caribbean English-based creoles).

(3) Ghanaian Pidgin English (Huber 2013)
   wì plɛnti   pas dɛ̀m
   1PL be.plentiful pass 3PL
   'We are more numerous than they are.'

(4) Martinican Creole (Colot & Ludwig 2013b)
   I gran pasé mwen.
   3SG tall pass 1SG
   'He is taller than me.'

The basic verb meaning in this type can also be 'win' (*winim* in Tok Pisin and *gana* in Media Lengua).

(5) Media Lengua (Muysken 2013)
   Takunga-mi   riko ga-n Salsedo-da gana-n
   Latacunga-AFF rich be-3SG Salcedo-ACC win-3SG
   'Latacunga is richer than Salcedo.'

The third value is **locational marking**, that is, the standard marker is also used to mark a locational relation, for example, allative ('to'), ablative ('from'), or essive ('at'). An example for ablative marking (*se* 'from') comes from Pidgin Hindustani:

(6) Pidgin Hindustani (Siegel 2013)
   Ham u   larika se   bara.
   1SG DEM boy   from big
   'I am bigger than that boy.'

In Zamboanga Chabacano the locational notion 'against' (*kóntra*) is used to mark the standard:

(7) Zamboanga Chabacano (Steinkrüger 2013)
    *Mas gránde dimíyo ermáno **kóntra** kon éle.*
    more big my brother against OBJ s/he
    'My brother is bigger than him/her.'

The most prominent standard marking type within the *APiCS* languages is **particle marking** (value 4), which is the type of marking displayed in all European lexifiers (e.g. English *than*, Romance *que*, see Stassen 2005e). This heterogeneous category comprises various markers which are neither 'surpass' nor locational markers.

(8) Early Sranan (van den Berg & Bruyn 2013)
    *Ju de morro langa **leki** mi.*
    2SG ASP/COP more long like 1SG
    'You are taller than me.'

(9) Norf'k (Mühlhäusler 2013)
    *Shi morgara **dan** mii.*
    she slim.COMPAR than me
    'She is thinner than I.'

In French-based creoles, we find reflexes of the French standard marker *que*, which is typically identical to the relative pronoun and the complementizer. The standard markers in the creoles are *ke* and *ki*:

(10) Louisiana Creole (Neumann-Holzschuh & Klingler 2013)
     *Li pa plu rich **ke** John.*
     3SG NEG more rich than John
     'He's not richer than John.'

A small group of Portuguese-based creoles also belong to this value. Here, the marker diachronically reflects two units: one derives from a possessive marker, the other from a relative marker. But in a synchronic perspective the two components do not express the two functions anymore and have been lexicalized into a single marker.

(11) Principense (Maurer 2013c)
     *Txi maxi gôdô **dêkê/dôkê** mi.*
     2SG more fat than 1SG
     'You are fatter than I am.'

In Sri Lanka Portuguese, the lexicalized marker *dika* is postposed to the standard.

The next value consists of a combination of **locational and particle marking** (regardless of the order of the marker). It is found only in Portuguese-based creoles. The marker is composed of reflexes of Portuguese *do* and *que* which are still synchronically transparent (possessive/ablative marker; relative marker). This transparency criterion puts these languages apart from their related sister languages Principense and Sri Lanka Portuguese (just mentioned earlier for value 4, particle marking). Examples for this value come from Casamancese Creole (ex. 12), where the locational part precedes the particle, and from Diu Indo-Portuguese (13), where the locational part follows the particle:

(12) Casamancese Creole (Biagui & Quint 2013)
     *Jon ∅ ma(s) **di ki** Pidru riku.*
     John PFV more of COMPAR Peter rich
     'John is richer than Peter.'

(13) Diu Indo-Portuguese (Cardoso 2013)
     *ɛlifãt ɛ may fɔrt **ki dǝ** nɔs.*
     elephant COP.NPST more strong COMPAR of 1PL
     'Elephants are stronger than us.'

See Cardoso (2012) for an in-depth study of comparative constructions in Portuguese-based creoles in Asia.

Value 6 comprises languages where the **standard is not overtly marked**. Only few *APiCS* languages show this pattern. Chinese Pidgin English is the only language where this strategy is the only one available in the language.

(14) Chinese Pidgin English (Li & Matthews 2013)
     You no got more better thisee?
     2SG NEG got more better this
     'Have you not got any better than this?'

Value 7 is represented by languages which do not use a specific comparison construction, but where comparison is expressed by two separately asserted predications. The comparison has then to be inferred by the hearer. This technique is called **conjoined marking**.

(15) Kriol (Schultze-Berndt & Angelo 2013)
     Dijan lilbit bigwan, dijan lilwan lilbit.
     PROX.ADJ somewhat big.ADJ PROX.ADJ small.ADJ somewhat
     'This is somewhat big, this is somewhat small.'

3. Geographical distribution

The geographical distribution of the different standard-marking strategies is not random. We see clear areal effects: Central African contact languages with either African or European lexifier languages tend to show 'surpass' marking. 'Surpass' marking also extends to the Caribbean (even though not as the only possible strategy). This type of serial verb construction in Atlantic creoles has long been traced back to African substrate languages; see e.g. Boretzky (1983: 104ff., 172, 184), Holm (1988: 189f.), Parkvall (2000: 73f.). Particle marking prevails in North America, the Caribbean and the Indian Ocean. East Africa and areas east of it prefer locational marking, whereas Australian contact languages have conjoined marking. Comparison with the worldwide picture shows very clear substrate effects (compare the corresponding *WALS* map by Stassen 2005e).

42 Comparative standard marking

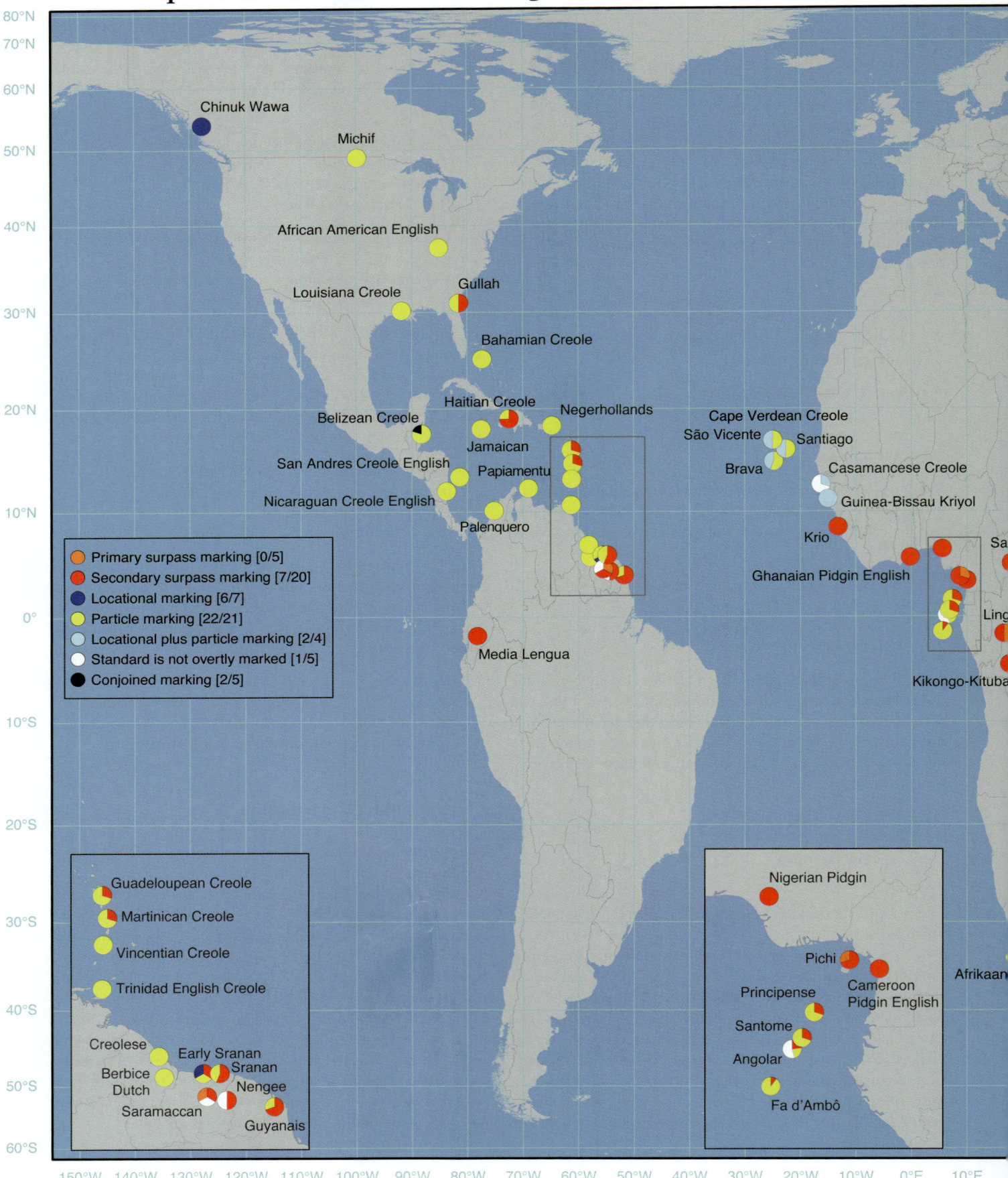

VERBAL CATEGORIES

Chapter 43
Position of tense, aspect, and mood markers in relation to the verb

PHILIPPE MAURER AND THE *APiCS* CONSORTIUM

1. Feature description

This chapter considers the position of tense, aspect, and mood markers in relation to the verb.

The term *aspect* is used in a restricted way (imperfective vs. perfective, see the definitions given in Chapter 49), which means that we do not look at other aspectual categories such as completive, resultative, or iterative.

2. The values

In many languages, TAM markers may occur in different positions. This is why this feature is a multiple-choice feature.

We distinguish the following five values:

		excl	shrd	all
●	1. Immediately preceding the verb	22	38	60
●	2. Immediately following the verb	4	17	21
●	3. In a leftward position	4	31	35
●	4. In a rightward position	1	5	6
○	5. No TAM markers	3	0	3

Value 1 (**TAM markers immediately precede the verb**), which occurs in almost 80 per cent of the *APiCS* languages, means that the marker is immediately adjacent to the verb, without any other intervening elements, except for other tense, aspect, and mood markers.

Value 1 is present in all types of languages: European-, Arabic-, Bantu-, and Malay-based pidgins and creoles, as well as bilingual mixed languages.

(1) Krio (Finney 2013)
 Yestade, a bin de wok.
 yesterday 1SG PST PROG work
 'Yesterday I was working.'

(2) Kinubi (Luffin 2013)
 Íta gu rúo búkra.
 2SG FUT go tomorrow
 'You will leave tomorrow.'

(3) Lingala (Meeuwis 2013)
 A-ko-tánga.
 3SG-FUT-study
 'He will study.'

(4) Singapore Bazaar Malay (Khin Khin Aye 2013)
 Sekarang suda tukar.
 now PFV change
 'Now it's already changed.'

Value 2 (**TAM markers immediately follow the verb**) is found in six Ibero-Romance-based languages, in four English-based languages, in two Dutch-based languages, in three Bantu-based languages, as well as in Michif, Media Lengua, Mixed Ma'a/Mbugu, Gurindji Kriol, Yimas-Arafundi Pidgin, and Chinese Pidgin Russian.

(5) Yimas-Arafundi Pidgin (Foley 2013)
 Ama andə-nan.
 1SG hear-NFUT
 'I heard.'

(6) Media Lengua (Muysken 2013)
 Kuri-xu-ngi.
 run-PROG-2SG
 'You are running.'

Value 3 (**TAM markers in a leftward position**) covers situations where object pronouns, negators, or lexical items occur between the TAM marker(s) and the verb. This value corresponds partially to values 3 and 4 of Chapters 45 and 46, which deal with the tightness of the link between the past and the progressive marker and the verb. For examples regarding the position of the past marker and the progressive marker, see Chapter 45, examples (14)–(17), and Chapter 46, examples (16)–(19).

Value 3 occurs in six Ibero-Romance-based languages, in twelve English-based languages, in nine French-based languages, in two Dutch-based languages, as well as in Fanakalo, Juba Arabic, Ambon Malay, Pidgin Hawaiian, and the bilingual mixed languages Gurindji Kriol and Michif.

In Louisiana Creole, Tayo, Fanakalo, Juba Arabic, and Ambon Malay, it is the negator that intervenes between a TAM marker and the verb:

Position of tense, aspect, and mood markers in relation to the verb

(7) Louisiana Creole (Neumann-Holzschuh & Klingler 2013)
Si mo te konnen li te la, mo se pa vini.
if 1SG PST know 3SG PST there 1SG COND NEG come
'If I'd known he was there, I wouldn't have come.'

(8) Juba Arabic (Manfredi & Petrollino 2013)
Wókit ána kan ma geisténna íta íta wósulu.
time 1SG PST NEG PROG.wait 2SG 2SG arrive
'When I was no longer waiting for you, you arrived.'

(9) Fanakalo (Mesthrie 2013)
Yena zo ai hamba khaya.
3SG FUT NEG go home
'He will not go home.'

In 25 languages, some adverbs (especially time adverbs) may occur between a TAM marker and the verb:

(10) Principense (Maurer 2013c)
Mene xintxi ya jingantxi sa kwaji xiga.
Mene feel COMP ogre PROG almost arrive
'Mene felt that the ogre was almost arriving.'

In Papiamentu, Bislama, and Tok Pisin, the future marker is located before the subject pronoun.

(11) Papiamentu (Kouwenberg 2013b)
Ma bobo ku e ta, el a konta su
but stupid COMP 3SG COP 3SG PFV tell POSS.3SG
kompader ku lo e gaña morto.
friend COMP FUT 3SG pretend dead
'But stupid that he is, he told his friend that he intends to play dead.'

(12) Bislama (Meyerhoff 2013)
Bae mi soemoat long yu.
FUT 1SG show PREP 2SG
'I'll show [them] to you.'

In Michif, an object noun phrase may intervene between the progressive marker *mekwaat* and the verb:

(13) Michif (Bakker 2013)
Li shyaen mekwaat aen zoo maamaakwaht-em.
ART dog PROG ART bone chew-3SG > 3SG
'The dog is chewing on a bone.'

In Afrikaans, open-class items may intervene between the auxiliary verb and the past participle in compound tenses, and Kriol allows the quantifier *ol* 'all' to occur between the past marker and the verb.

The future markers of Papiamentu, Tok Pisin, and Bislama behave differently from the other languages exhibiting value 3 because these future markers are located outside the clausal core. Their position is due to their adverbial etymology: Portuguese *logo* 'right away, soon' for Papiamentu and English *by and by* for Tok Pisin and Bislama.

As with value 3, some examples of value 4 (**TAM markers in a rightward position**) can be found in Chapter 45 (example 18) and in Chapter 46 (example 20).

This value is found in three Ibero-Romance-based languages (Guinea-Bissau Kriyol, Casamancese Creole, Palenquero), in Tok Pisin, in Chinese Pidgin Russian, and in Pidgin Hawaiian. It is only in Pidgin Hawaiian that this value is found exclusively, but this follows from the fact that Pidgin Hawaiian has only one TAM marker (example 17).

In Guinea-Bissau Kriyol, the past marker may be separated from the verb by the causative marker and an object pronoun:

(14) Guinea-Bissau Kriyol (Intumbo et al. 2013)
Jon tciga-nta-l-ba ja.
John arrive-CAUS-3SG-PST already
'John had already put it aside.'

In Palenquero, an object pronoun may intervene between the past progressive marker and the verb:

(15) Palenquero (Schwegler 2013)
¿Utere asé-ba kandá-lo-ba por
2PL HAB-PST.PROG sing-3SG-PST.PROG for
kuanto ría?
how.many day
'You were usually singing to (lamenting) him for how many days?'

In Chinese Pidgin Russian, the negator may separate the future marker from the verb:

(16) Chinese Pidgin Russian (Perekhvalskaya 2013)
Siwodəni maja səpi ni budu.
today 1SG sleep NEG FUT
'I will not sleep today.'

In Pidgin Hawaiian, a lexical item, *hou* 'again', may intervene between the imperfective marker and the verb:

(17) Pidgin Hawaiian (Roberts 2013)
Olelo hou ana.
speak again IPFV
'He was speaking again.'

In Casamancese Creole, an object pronoun or an object noun may intervene between the verb and the past marker *baŋ*, and in Tok Pisin an object noun may intervene between the verb and the progressive marker *istap*.

Value 5 (**no TAM markers**) only concerns Chinuk Wawa, Eskimo Pidgin, and Pidgin Hindustani.

The distribution of the different values of this feature does not show any particular areal pattern.

43 Position of tense, aspect, and mood markers in relation to the verb

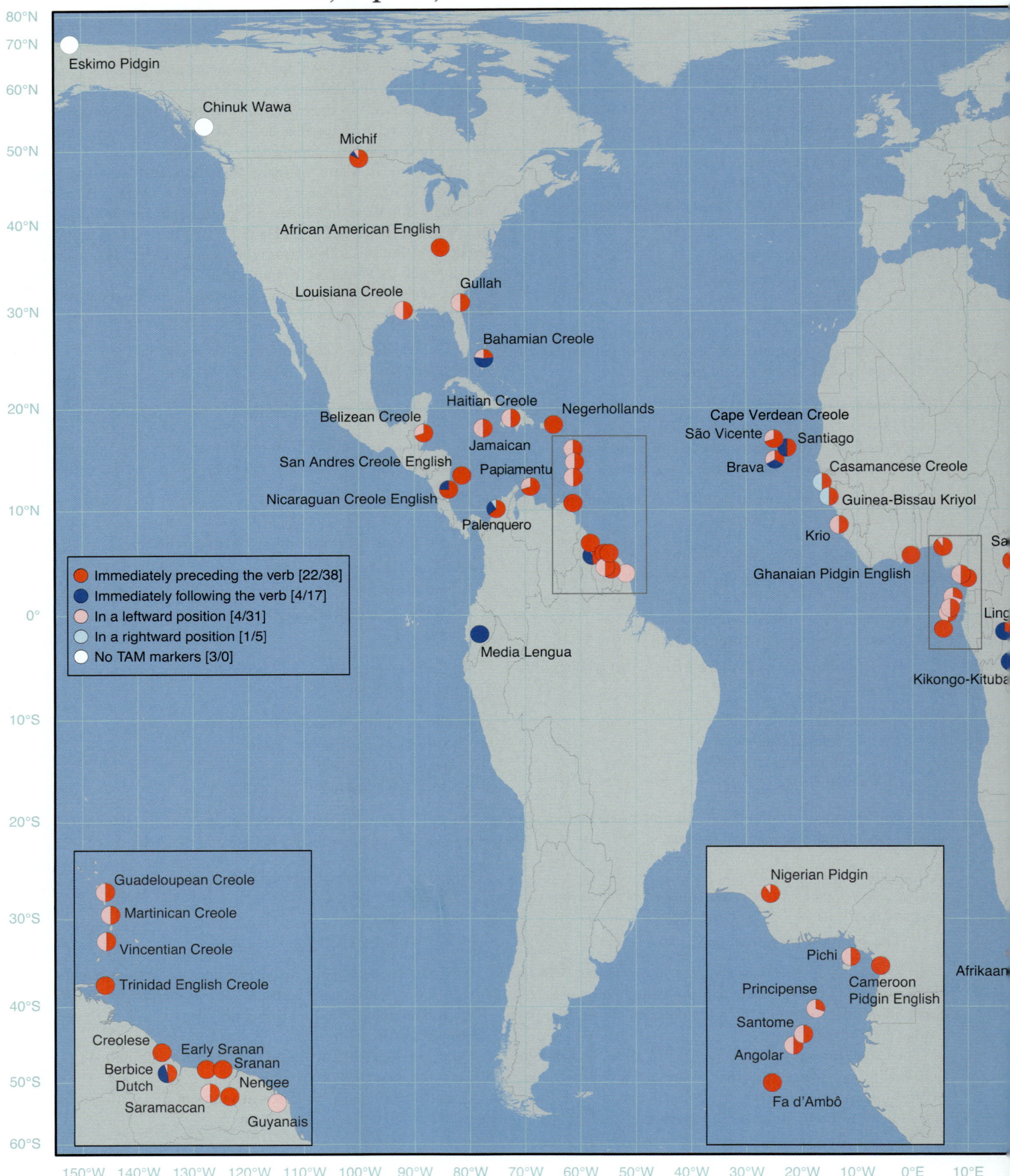

Chapter 44
Internal order of tense, aspect, and mood markers

PHILIPPE MAURER AND THE *APiCS* CONSORTIUM

1. Introduction

In this feature we ask about the order of tense, aspect, and mood markers (TAM markers) with respect to each other. To qualify for this feature, it is important that the three markers be adjacent to each other. A context which favours the combination of the TAM markers is counterfactual clauses, where the tense marker usually corresponds to a past marker, the aspect marker to an imperfective marker, and the mood marker to a future marker (used modally). An example is Creolese, where the order of the three markers is tense-aspect-mood (TAM):

(1) Creolese (Devonish & Thompson 2013)
*Dem **bin a go** raab mi.*
3PL TNS ASP MOOD rob 1SG
'They would have robbed me.'

Note that we consider markers to be adjacent even if lexical items such as adverbs may intervene between them (see Chapter 45 and Chapter 46 on the tightness of the link between the past and the progressive marker with the verb); what matters is that the markers are located on the same side of the verbal complex.

There are many *APiCS* languages to which this feature does not apply, either because they do not possess three markers, or, if they have three markers, they do not allow them to combine or to be adjacent to each other.

As in other chapters, we use "aspect" in a restricted sense, applying it only to the opposition between perfective and imperfective aspect.

This feature has played an important role in creole studies since it was one of the features of Bickerton's language bioprogram hypothesis. According to Bickerton, creole languages display the order TMA when the three markers combine (see below our value 1), where the category mood is defined as 'irrealis', referring to markers which express future, counterfactual, conditional, and similar functions (Bickerton 1980: 6). Note, however, that Bickerton was not the first linguist to make this claim. To our knowledge the first linguist was Voorhoeve (1957: 384).

2. The values

We distinguish the following four values:

		excl	shrd	all
●	1. Tense–Mood–Aspect	11	1	12
●	2. Tense–Aspect–Mood	2	0	2
●	3. Mood–Tense–Aspect	3	1	4
○	4. The feature does not apply	56	0	56

This box shows that the possibility of using tense, aspect, and mood markers adjacent to each other is restricted to a relatively small subset of *APiCS* languages (about 25%); furthermore, the box also shows that the logically possible combinations MAT, ATM, and AMT are not attested in our languages.

Value 1 (**Tense–Mood–Aspect**) occurs in six English-based and in six French-based languages.

(2) Krio (Finney 2013)
*If ren nɔ **bin de kam**, wi **bin fɔ de ple** bɔl.*
if rain NEG PST PROG come 1PL PST MOOD PROG play ball
'If it hadn't been raining, we would have been playing soccer.'

(3) Mauritian Creole (Baker & Kriegel 2013)
*Li **ti ava pe** aprann si li ti anvi pas so lexame.*
3SG PST MOOD ASP learn if 3SG PST want pass POSS.3SG exam
'She would have been studying if she had wanted to pass her exams.'

Value 2 (**Tense–Aspect–Mood**) is found in Creolese (see example 1) and in Kinubi:

(4) Kinubi (Luffin 2013)
*kan **bi gi** ruwa*
PST FUT PROG go
'would have been going'

Value 3 (**Mood–Tense–Aspect**) is found in Santome, in Principense, and in Reunion Creole; note, however, that in Reunion Creole the confidence value is given as 'uncertain'.

(5) Santome (Hagemeijer 2013)
Xi ê ká ta ka kume, ami tudaxi ka kume.
if 3SG MOOD PST IPFV eat 1SG also IPFV eat
'If he had been eating, I also would have been eating.'

(6) Principense (Maurer 2013c)
Xi non ka tava sa xivi wosê, non ka tava tê
if 1PL MOOD PST PROG work now 1PL MOOD PST have
dyô.
money
'If we were working now, we would have money.'

In some languages, for example Guyanais, Kinubi, and Principense, the mood marker occurring in combination with the tense and the aspect marker also functions as a future marker, but in other languages like Nengee or Krio this is not the case. In Nengee, for instance, the future marker is *o* and the counterfactual marker is *sa*, and in Krio the markers are *go* and *fɔ*. However, it looks as if there has been some diachronic change from future AND counterfactual marker to only counterfactual marker, at least in Sranan (which is closely related to Nengee). In Early Sranan, *sa* is the only marker attested as a future marker, and it also occurs in counterfactual and similar contexts. The following example illustrates value 1 (TMA):

(7) Early Sranan (van den Berg & Bruyn 2013)
Joe ben sa dee leesie?
2SG PST FUT ASP be.lazy
'Would you be lazy?'

In modern Sranan, *sa* only occurs in counterfactual and similar contexts, and the future marker is *go*. This suggests that the grammaticalization of the verb *go* as a future marker and the specialization of *sa* as a (non-future) mood marker is a later development.

Modern Sranan is the only *APiCS* language that allows different orders. Example (8) illustrates value 1 (TMA) and example (9), value 3 (MTA):

(8) Sranan (Winford & Plag 2013)
Efu John ben de dya, a ben sa e sribi now.
if John PST COP here 3SG PST MOOD PROG sleep now
'If John were here, he would be sleeping now.'

(9) Sranan (Winford & Plag 2013)
Nownow de Tanti M. sa ben e ferteri stori efu
now there Aunt M. MOOD PST IPFV tell story if
a ben de na libi ete.
3SG PST COP LOC life yet
'Aunt M. would have been telling stories right now if she were still alive.'

Note that according to Winford & Plag (2013), example (9) was accepted by one older informant only.

Internal order of tense, aspect, and mood markers

As noted above, value 4 (**the feature does not apply**) concerns (i) languages which do not have all three markers, (ii) languages which do not allow them to combine, or (iii) languages which do not allow them to be adjacent to each other. Among this last group we find for example Papiamentu, where the future marker *lo* has partly retained the pre-subject position of its Portuguese adverbial etymon (*logo* 'right away') and where the past marker *taba* has fused with the originally progressive marker *ta* (note that *taba* is not used without *ta* except for the verbs *ta* 'be' and *tin* 'have', as in the following example):

(10) Papiamentu (Maurer own knowledge)
Lo e tabata traha si e tabatin tempu.
FUT 3SG PST.PROG work if 3SG PST.have time
'He would be working if he had time.'

In several languages, some markers are preverbal and others postverbal (see also the examples in Chapter 43 on the position of TAM markers in relation to the verb):

(11) Guinea-Bissau Kriyol (Intumbo et al. 2013)
N' na ta bay ba skola ma N' sta ba dwenti.
1SG PROG FUT go PST school but 1SG COP PST sick
'I would have gone to school, but I was sick.'

(12) Kriol (Schultze-Berndt & Angelo 2013)
Im-in oldei nes-im-bat tu jet faiya.
3SG-PST always nurse-TR-PROG too DEM fire
'It used to look after the fire too.'

(13) Fanakalo (Mesthrie 2013)
Yena zo gate hamb-ile.
3SG FUT ANT go-PST
'He will have gone.'

3. Distribution

Among the *APiCS* languages, the possibility of combining tense, aspect, and mood markers adjacent to each other occurs only in creole languages. This possibility is also restricted areally: it occurs in the Atlantic, the Indian Ocean, and in East Africa. In the Atlantic, it occurs in Portuguese-based, in English-based, and in French-based creoles; in the Indian Ocean, it occurs in the three French-based creoles. Note that the Portuguese-based creoles exhibiting this feature are restricted to the Gulf of Guinea; in East Africa, this feature occurs in Kinubi, which is Arabic-based.

The results of this chapter cast some doubts on Bickerton's claim that the TMA pattern is universal. First, the possibility of combining the tense, the aspect, and the mood marker only occurs in seventeen languages; second, these seventeen languages are areally restricted, and third, six of the seventeen languages which do allow the combination of the three markers do not have TMA, but TAM or MTA.

44 Internal order of tense, aspect, and mood markers

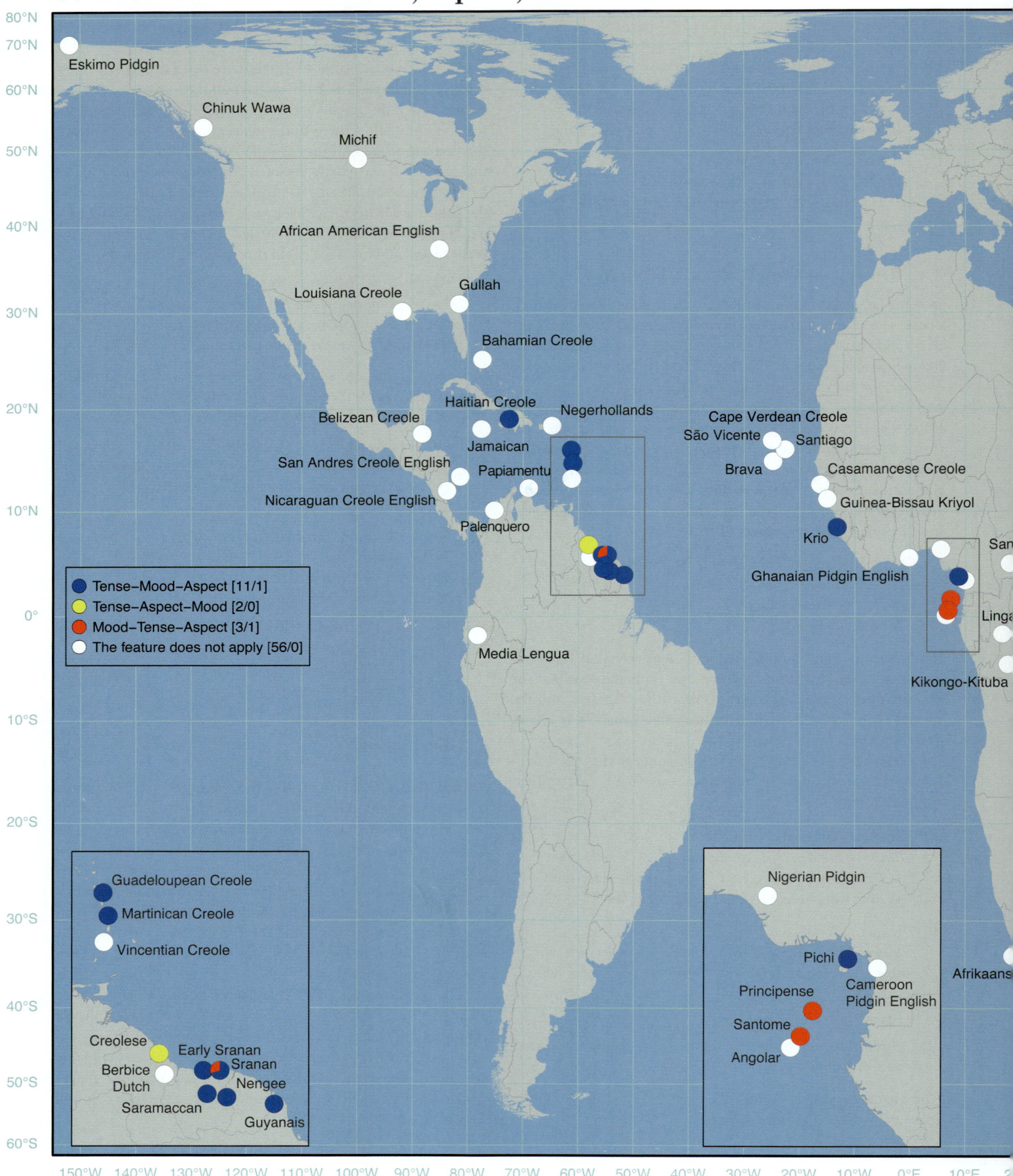

Chapter 45
Tightness of the link between the past marker and the verb

PHILIPPE MAURER AND THE *APiCS* CONSORTIUM

1. Introduction

This feature asks how tightly combined the overt past marker and the verb form are, especially which elements (if any) may intervene between the past marker and the verb.

If a language has an overt perfective past marker as well as an overt imperfective past marker, we take into account only the past marker which is used in imperfective contexts (typically with stative predicates to denote past and with nonstative predicates to denote past progressive or past habitual).

This chapter parallels Chapter 46 on the tightness of the link between the progressive marker and the verb.

2. The values

For this feature, we distinguish seven values:

●	1. Affix	13
●	2. Particle, nothing can intervene	4
●	3. Particle, only grammatical markers can intervene	17
●	4. Particle, a few lexical items may intervene	22
●	5. Particle, open-class items may intervene	2
●	6. Particle, clause-second position	1
○	7. No overt past marker exists	16

Value 1 (the past marker is an **affix**) occurs in four Portuguese-based languages (Cape Verdean Creole of Brava, Cape Verdean Creole of Santiago, Korlai, Sri Lanka Portuguese), in two English-based languages (African American English, Singlish), in three Bantu-based languages (Fanakalo, Kikongo-Kituba, Lingala), as well as in Media Lengua, Michif, Sri Lankan Malay, and Mixed Ma'a/Mbugu.

(1) African American English (Green 2013)
He crossed the street yesterday.

(2) Sri Lanka Portuguese (Smith 2013)
Poḓiyaas sudu aka-ntu mee ya-nasa, aka kaaza-ntu.
children all that-LOC FOC PST-be.born that house-LOC
'The children were all born there, in that house.'

(3) Fanakalo (Mesthrie 2013)
Mina buk-ile yena: yena gate khona lapha.
1SG see-PST 3SG 3SG ANT COP there
'I saw him: he was there.'

(4) Media Lengua (Muysken 2013)
Ki-da azi-ndo chaiku-mu-rka-ngi?
what-ACC do-SUBORD tire-CIS-PST-2SG
'What did you do to get so tired?'

(5) Sri Lankan Malay (Slomanson 2013)
Anak nasi si-makan.
child rice PST-eat
'The child ate rice.'

Value 2 (the past marker is a **particle**, and **nothing can intervene**) only occurs in four languages (Diu Indo-Portuguese, Nicaraguan Creole English, Trinidad Creole, and Reunion Creole). Note that in Chapter 46 (on the tightness between the progressive marker and the verb), the same value 2 is the most widespread value (31 languages), and this would corroborate Bybee's (1985: 33–5) hypothesis that aspect is located more closely to the verb than tense.

(6) Diu Indo-Portuguese (Cardoso 2013)
Ali nɔs uki tiŋ brĩka?
there 1PL what PST.IPFV play
'What were we playing there?'

(7) Nicaraguan Creole English (Bartens 2013a)
Joan harikien did bos opm di biich.
Joan hurricane PST bust open DEF.ART beach
'Hurricane Joan destroyed the entire beach.'

The dividing line between an affix and a particle which does not allow for an element to intervene between it and the verb is not always clear-cut. This means that, for some of the languages with value 2, value 1 might be more adequate.

Value 3 (the past marker is a **particle, only grammatical markers may intervene**) occurs in nine English-based, in three Ibero-Romance-based, in one French-based, in two Dutch-based, and in two Arabic-based languages. In these languages, other TAM markers and negators are reported to intervene between the past marker and the verb.

(8) Early Sranan (van den Berg & Bruyn 2013)
Effi a ben jeri, a ben sa komm.
if 3SG PST hear 3SG PST FUT come
'If he had heard, he would have come.'

(9) Fa d'Ambô (Post 2013)
Dyiabeza poxodul bi ska laba apotose.
day.already people PST PROG wash water.lake.DEM
'Formerly, people used to wash in this lake.'

(10) Haitian Creole (Fattier 2013)
M t ap boukannen manyòk.
1SG PST PROG cook.over.wood.fire manioc
'I was cooking manioc over a wood fire.'

(11) Negerhollands (van Sluijs 2013)
En-andə nashi a kā kō fo figití mi sinə.
a-other nation PST COMPL come for fight with 3PL
'Another people had come to fight with them.'

(12) Berbice Dutch (Kouwenberg 2013a)
ɛk wa sa kutɛ en ar twe fan eni an tem eni
1SG PST IRR catch-PFV one or two from 3PL and tame 3PL
'I would have caught one or two of them and tamed them.'

(13) Juba Arabic (Manfredi & Petrollino 2013)
Úwo kan g-wónusi morú.
3SG PST PROG-speak Moru
'He was speaking Moru.'

Value 4 (the past marker is a **particle**, and **a few lexical items may intervene**) occurs in ten English-based languages, in five Ibero-Romance-based languages, in six French-based languages, and in the bilingual mixed language Gurindji Kriol. In these languages, adverbs (especially time adverbs) and object pronouns are reported to occur between the past marker and the verb. Note that object pronouns occur only in Guinea-Bissau Kriyol, whose past marker follows the verb (in contrast to the other languages exhibiting this feature, whose past markers precede the verb).

(14) Cape Verdean Creole of São Vicente (Swolkien 2013)
Na Olánda, Ailton táva só trubaiá.
in Holland Ailton PST.IPFV only work
'While in Holland, Ailton only worked.'

(15) Nigerian Pidgin (Faraclas 2013)
À bin jọst dè go.
1SG PST just PROG go
'I had just been going.'

(16) Mauritian Creole (Baker & Kriegel 2013)
Ganes ti pe aṅkor travay.
Ganesh PST PROG still work
'Ganesh was still working.'

(17) Gurindji Kriol (Meakins 2013)
I bin til faind-im nyanuny Mummy na
3SG PST still find-TR 3SG mother FOC
dat yapakayi-ngku.
the small-ERG
'It still found its mother, the little one did.'

Value 5 (the past marker is a **particle**, and **open-class items may intervene**) only occurs in Casamancese Creole and in Gullah:

(18) Casamancese Creole (Biagui & Quint 2013)
Antu k-i na febursé, i ta korenté karu baŋ.
before REL-3SG FUT fall.ill 3SG HAB drive car PST
'Before he fell ill, he used to drive cars.'

Value 6 (**particle, clause-second position**) pertains only to Afrikaans. Afrikaans has a past auxiliary, *het*, which is strictly adjacent if it occurs in non-finite contexts; if it occurs in finite sentences, it occupies a clause-second position, and therefore many items may intervene between *het* and the verb, as in the following example:

(19) Afrikaans (den Besten & Biberauer 2013)
Hy het dit gister vir sy broer ge-wys.
3SG PST it yesterday OBJ POSS.3SG brother PTCP-show
'He showed it to his brother yesterday.'

Value 7 (**no overt past marker**) occurs in five Ibero-Romance-based languages (Batavia Creole, Cavite Chabacano, Papiá Kristang, Ternate Chabacano, Zamboanga Chabacano), in two English-based languages (Bislama, Ghanaian Pidgin English), in two Malay-based languages (Ambon Malay, Singapore Bazaar Malay), as well as in Tayo, in Chinese Pidgin Russian, in Chinuk Wawa, in Sango, in Pidgin Hawaiian, in Pidgin Hindustani, and in Yimas-Arafundi Pidgin.

Out of these 16 languages, 10 are purely aspectual languages (see Chapter 49 on tense–aspect systems, value 1). Value 7 of this chapter and value 1 of Chapter 49 are related, since purely aspectual systems lack a past tense marker. Note that perfective aspect markers do not count as past markers in this context.

45 Tightness of the link between the past marker and the verb

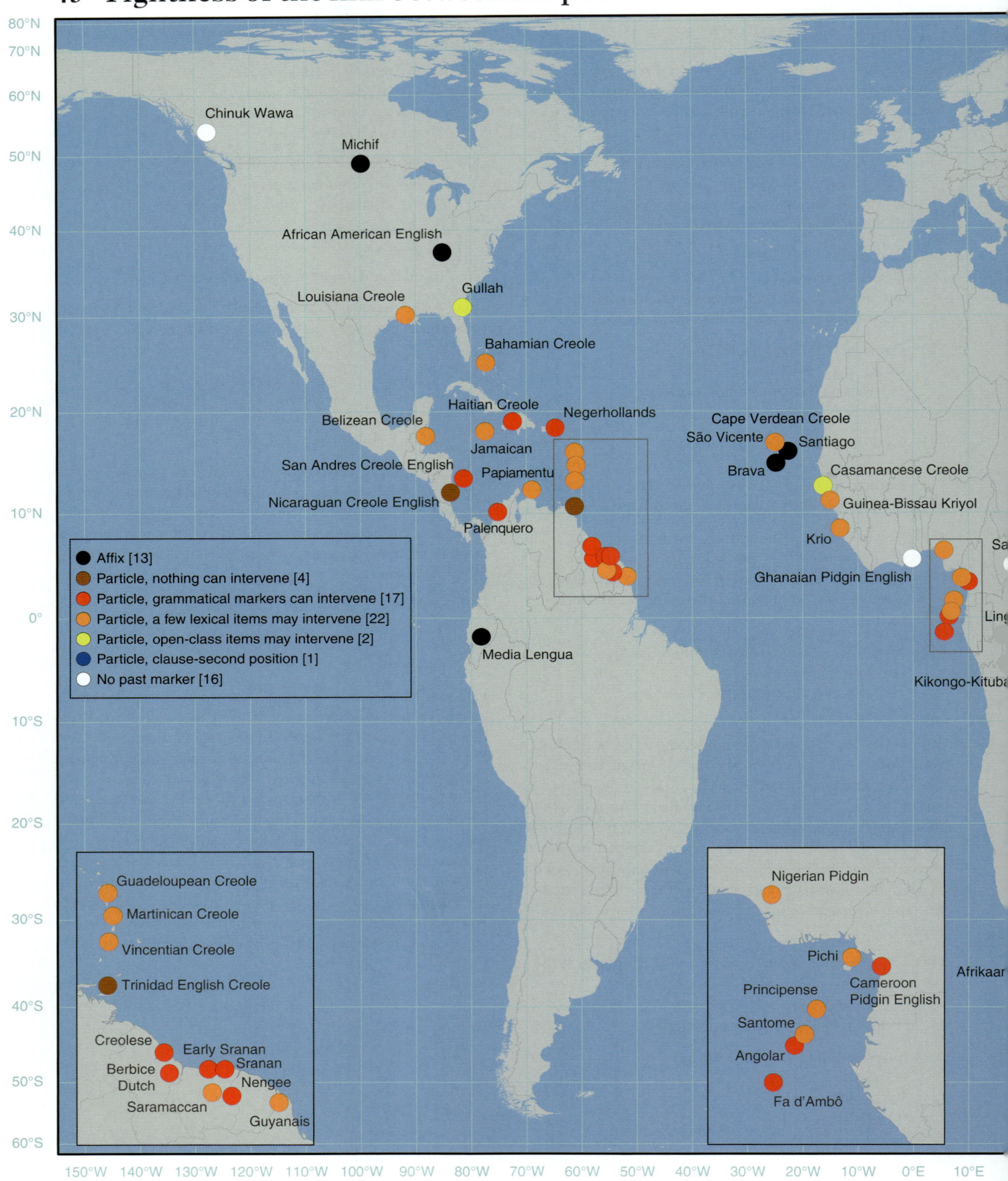

Chapter 46
Tightness of the link between the progressive marker and the verb

PHILIPPE MAURER AND THE *APiCS* CONSORTIUM

1. Introduction

This feature asks how tightly linked the (overt) progressive marker and the verb are, and especially enquires which elements (if any) may intervene between the progressive marker and the verb.

A progressive construction refers to ongoing activities, as in English *she is working*. It does not matter whether this marker has other functions as long as the construction has a progressive interpretation; in this sense, the French present tense *elle travaille* 'she is working, she works' is a progressive construction, although it also fulfils other functions (e.g. present habitual). However, the French construction does not display an overt progressive marker and therefore would not be relevant for this feature.

We distinguish between progressive affixes and progressive particles, that is, separate words. If the progressive marker is an auxiliary (e.g. Tok Pisin *istap*), this also counts as a particle. And if there are two or more different progressive markers in the language, only the more grammaticalized one is taken into account.

2. The values

The following six values are distinguished:

●	1. Affix	14
●	2. Particle, nothing can intervene	31
●	3. Particle, only grammatical markers can intervene	6
●	4. Particle, a few lexical items may intervene	15
○	5. Particle, open-class items may intervene	3
○	6. No overt progressive marker	5

Value 1 (the **progressive marker is an affix**) occurs in seven English-based languages (African American English, Bahamian Creole, Hawai'i Creole, Kriol, Nicaraguan Creole, Norf'k, Singlish), in three Ibero-Romance-based Creoles (Korlai, Sri Lanka Portuguese, Zamboanga Chabacano), in Berbice Dutch, in Media Lengua, in Mixed Ma'a/Mbugu, and in the mixed language Gurindji Kriol.

(1) Media Lengua (Muysken 2013)
I-xu-ni kaza-mu.
go-PROG-1SG house-ALL
'I am going home.'

In all English-based languages displaying value 1, the progressive affix goes back to the English gerundial construction with *-ing* (*sing-ing*), as in Singlish:

(2) Singlish (Lim & Ansaldo 2013)
*Hey, I think the driver try**ing** to be funny, you know.*

In the Portuguese-based creole Korlai, the progressive affix goes back to the Portuguese gerundial construction with *-ndo* (*canta-ndo* 'singing'):

(3) Korlai (Clements 2013)
*Teru sirwis hedze-**n**.*
Teru work do-PROG
'Teru is working.'

The only European-based languages whose progressive marker does not go back to a European gerund construction are Berbice Dutch, Sri Lanka Portuguese, and Zamboanga Chabacano.

(4) Berbice Dutch (Kouwenberg 2013a)
O wa riſa.
3SG PST swell.PROG
'He was swelling.'

(5) Zamboanga Chabacano (Steinkrüger 2013)
Ta-kantá kamó.
PROG-sing 2PL
'You are singing.'

Value 2 (the progressive marker is a **particle**, and **nothing can intervene**) is the most widespread type. Note that the dividing line between an affix (value 1) and a particle which does not allow for an element intervening between it and the verb is not always clear-cut. This means that, for some of the languages exhibiting value 2, value 1 might be more adequate.

(6) Casamancese Creole (Biagui & Quint 2013)
*Gósiŋ i ka podé kudí-bu parbiya i **na** tarbajá.*
now 3SG NEG can answer-2SG because 3SG PROG work
'He/She cannot answer you because he/she is working.'

(7) Nigerian Pidgin (Faraclas 2013)
*À bin d<u>o</u>n k<u>o</u>m **dè** go.*
1SG PST COMPL REALIS PROG go
'I had actually been going.'

(8) Early Sranan (van den Berg & Bruyn 2013)
*Hangri **de** killi mi.*
hunger PROG kill 1SG
'I am hungry.' (lit. Hunger is killing me.)

(9) Negerhollands (van Sluijs 2013)
*Sinu a **lo** wandu.*
3PL PST PROG walk
'They were walking.'

(10) Chinuk Wawa (Grant 2013)
*Man **hai-tl'kup** lup.*
man PROG-cut rope
'The man is cutting the rope.'

(11) Kinubi (Luffin 2013)
*Generation ta ásede **gi-**ábidu ágara.*
generation GEN today PROG-start study
'This generation starts to study.'

(12) Tayo (Ehrhart & Revis 2013)
*Ta atraⁿ **de** fe kwa se mata?*
2SG PROG PROG do what DEM morning
'What are you doing this morning?'

Value 3 (the progressive marker is a **particle**, but **only grammatical markers** like other TAM markers **may intervene**) occurs in Ambon Malay, Cape Verdean Creole of Santiago, Ghanaian Pidgin English, Guinea-Bissau Kriyol, Palenquero, and Yimas-Arafundi Pidgin. In these languages, only other TAM markers are reported to intervene between the progressive marker and the verb.

(13) Ambon Malay (Paauw 2013)
*Iyo, beta **ada** mo pi.*
yes 1SG PROG FUT go
'Yes, I'm about to go.'

(14) Ghanaian Pidgin English (Huber 2013)
*Nau dɛ tin **dè** kam sprɛd.*
now DEF thing PROG SEQ spread
'[And] now the thing was starting to spread.'

(15) Yimas-Arafundi Pidgin (Foley 2013)
*Ama tɛpa-**mbi** ta-nan.*
1SG bathe-DEPV PROG-NFUT
'I'm washing.'

Value 4 (the progressive marker is a **particle**, and **a few lexical elements may intervene**) occurs in four Ibero-Romance-based languages (Angolar, Cape Verdean Creole of Brava, Principense, Papiamentu), in seven French-based languages (Guyanais, Haitian Creole, Mauritian Creole, Reunion Creole, Seychelles Creole, Guadeloupean Creole, Martinican Creole), in two English-based languages (Pichi, Vincentian Creole), in Lingala, and in Pidgin Hawaiian. In these languages, only adverbs, especially time adverbs, are reported to occur between the progressive marker and the verb (besides other TAM markers as in value 3).

(16) Cape Verdean Creole of Brava (Baptista 2013)
*Maria **sta** senpri **ta** pensa na se mininu.*
Maria PROG always ASP think of POSS child
'Maria is always thinking of her child.'

(17) Guyanais (Pfänder 2013)
*Mo **ka** jis krè zombi-a ka egzisté.*
1SG PROG just believe zombie-DEF IPFV exist
'I'm about to believe that the zombie exists.'

(18) Vincentian Creole (Prescod 2013)
*Hi **a** juhs sel sprat.*
3SG PROG just sell sprat
'He is only selling sprat.'

Value 5 (the progressive marker is a **particle**, and **open-class items may intervene**) only occurs in Afrikaans, in Michif, and in Tok Pisin:

(19) Michif (Bakker 2013)
*Li shyaen **mekwaat** aen zoo*
DEF.M.SG dog PROG INDF.M.SG bone
maamaakwaht-em.
chew.INAN-3 > 3
'The dog is chewing on a bone.'

(20) Tok Pisin (Smith & Siegel 2013)
*Ol lapun meri i mumu-im kaikai **istap**.*
PL old woman PM earth.oven-TR food PROG
'The old women are cooking food in an earth oven.'

Value 6 (**no overt progressive marker**) occurs in Chinese Pidgin English, Chinese Pidgin Russian, Eskimo Pidgin, Pidgin Hindustani, and Fanakalo.

There is no particular geographical distribution for the different values, except for the fact that value 4 (the progressive marker is a particle, some lexical items may intervene) is absent from South and Southeast Asia.

46 Tightness of the link between the progressive marker and the verb

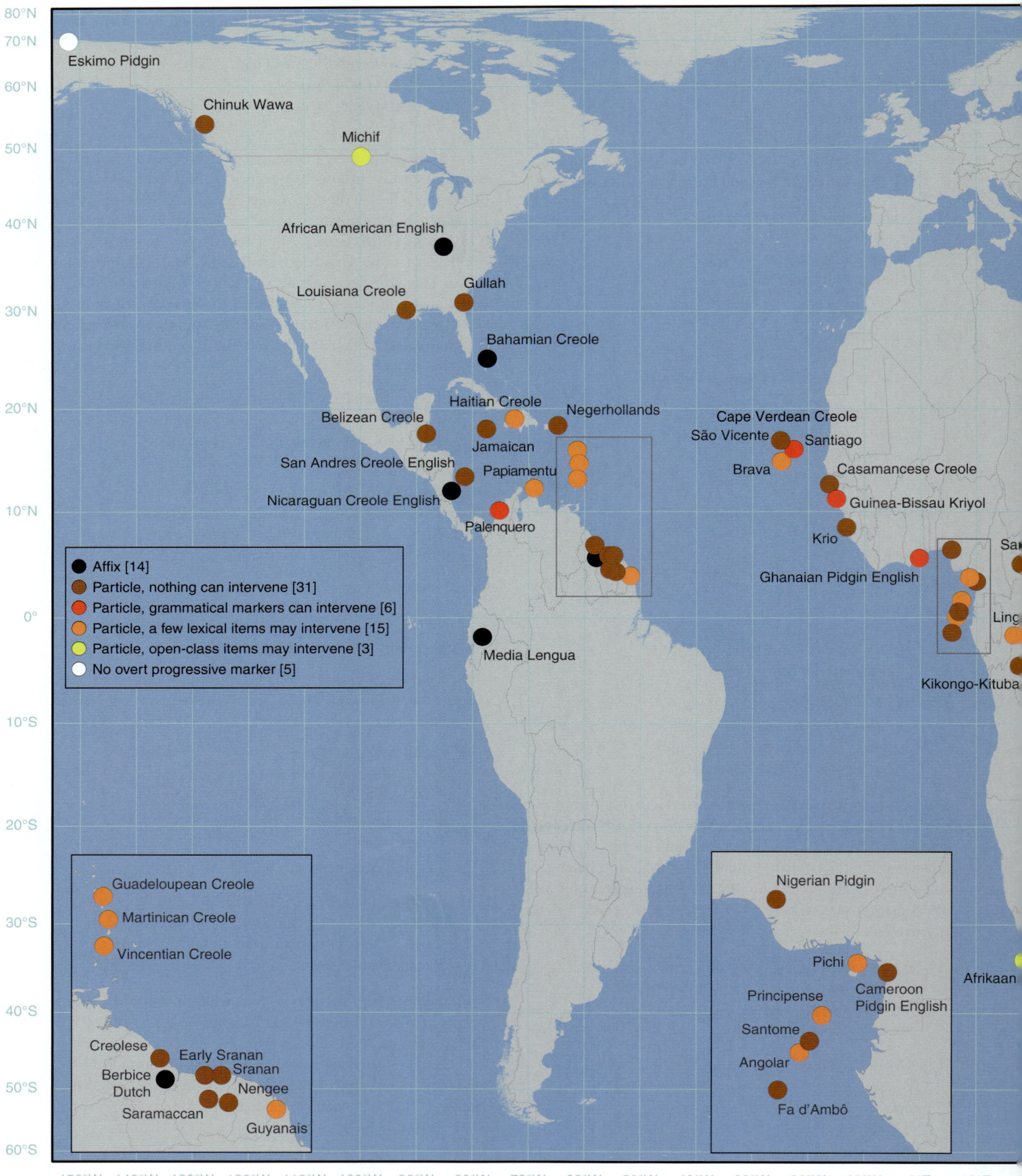

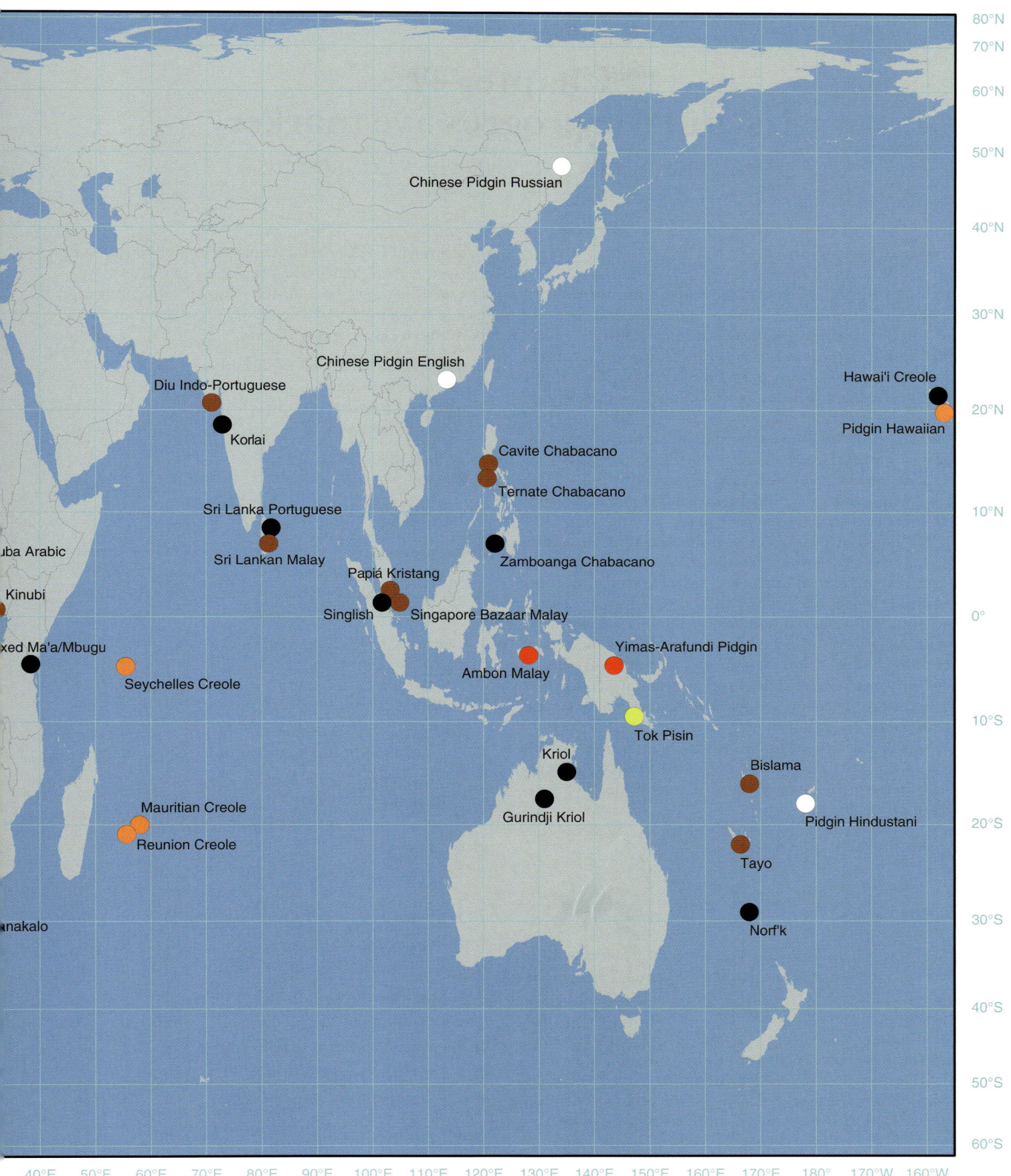

Chapter 47
Uses of the progressive marker

PHILIPPE MAURER AND THE *APiCS* CONSORTIUM

1. Feature description

An aspect marker which expresses progressive aspect—that is, which refers to ongoing activities at the time of speech or at some other temporal reference point—often fulfils other functions as well. A progressive marker may also express habitual situations, current states, and future situations. This feature asks about these three other potential functions that an overt progressive marker may have.

If a language has both a present progressive and a past progressive marker, the past progressive marker is disregarded.

With "current state", we refer to permanent states like 'love', 'hate', 'have', and 'know', which are true at the time of speech or at some other temporal reference point.

The progressive marker of languages that allow this marker to modify current states does not necessarily mark all verbs which refer to current states. For instance, Papiamentu uses the marker *ta* obligatorily with some stative verbs (e.g. with *kere* 'believe'), but the modal verbs *sa* 'know', *por* 'can', and *mester* 'must' (as well as other verbs) are zero-marked for present reference. The point at issue is whether the progressive marker can mark some verbs referring to permanent states (values 4, 6, 8), or whether it cannot mark any verb referring to permanent states (values 2, 3, 5, 7).

Note that we look only at overt markers. If the progressive is expressed by the bare verb without any overt marker (as for example in German), we treat the language as lacking a progressive marker (value 1).

This chapter is closely related to Chapter 48, which deals with the uses of the habitual marker.

2. The values

We distinguish the eight values set out in the table. Value 1 (**no overt progressive marker**) is found exclusively in pidgin languages: Chinese Pidgin English, Chinese Pidgin Russian, Chinuk Wawa, Eskimo Pidgin, Pidgin Hindustani, and Fanakalo. Note, however, that Singapore Bazaar Malay, Pidgin Hawaiian, and Yimas-Arafundi Pidgin have an overt progressive marker.

Value 2 (**only progressive function**) is the most widespread feature, occurring in about 40 per cent of the *APiCS* languages. It is present in nine Ibero-Romance-based languages, in eight English-based languages, in five French-based languages, in three Malay-based languages, as well as in Afrikaans, in Kikongo-Kituba, in the bilingual mixed language Gurindji Kriol, in Hawai'i Creole, in Pidgin Hawaiian, in Yimas-Arafundi Pidgin, and in Michif.

(1) Papiamentu (Kouwenberg 2013b)
 Mi ta drech-ando un auto.
 1SG COP repair-GER ART car
 'I am repairing a car.'

(2) Krio (Finney 2013)
 A de sing.
 3SG PROG sing
 'I am singing.'

Value 3 (**progressive and habitual**) occurs in four English-based languages (Belizean Creole, Cameroon Pidgin English, Nigerian Pidgin, Singlish), in Fa d'Ambô, Lingala, Juba Arabic, and in Mixed Ma'a/Mbugu.

(3) Belizean Creole (Escure 2013)
 a. *Hi de se di preya.*
  3SG PROG say ART prayer
  'She is saying the prayer.'
 b. *Wen a de wok lang di ki ya*
  when 1SG HAB work along ART caye 2SG
  hia wan li 'kilin-kilin'.
  hear ART little kilin-kilin
  'When I work along the caye, you hear a noise like "kilin-kilin".'

		excl	shrd	all
○	1. No overt progressive marker	5	0	5
●	2. Only progressive function	32	1	33
●	3. Progressive and habitual	8	0	8
●	4. Progressive and current state	1	0	1
●	5. Progressive and future	3	0	3
●	6. Progressive, habitual, and current state	12	0	12
●	7. Progressive, habitual, and future	6	0	6
●	8. Progressive, habitual, current state, and future	8	1	9

Value 4 (**progressive and current state**) occurs only in Cape Verdean Creole of Santiago.

Value 5 (**progressive and future**) occurs in Guinea-Bissau Kriyol, Casamancese Creole, and in Haitian Creole.

(4) Casamancese Creole (Biagui & Quint 2013)
   a. *Gósiŋ i ka podé kudí-bu parbiya i*
      now 3SG NEG can answer-2SG because 3SG
     na tarbajá.
     PROG work
     'She cannot answer you now because she is working.'
   b. *I ka na beŋ amañaŋ.*
     3SG NEG FUT come tomorrow
     'He will not come tomorrow.'

Value 6 (**progressive, habitual, and current state**) occurs in six Ibero-Romance-based languages (Batavia Creole, Cape Verdean Creole of São Vicente, Diu Indo-Portuguese, Cavite Chabacano, Ternate Chabacano, Zamboanga Chabacano), in four English-based languages (Early Sranan, Sranan, Ghanaian Pidgin English, Bislama), in Berbice Dutch, and in Media Lengua.

(5) Early Sranan (van den Berg & Bruyn 2013)
   a. *Da vool de slibi na eksi tappo.*
     ART chicken PROG sleep LOC egg top
     'The chicken is sitting on the eggs.'
   b. *Mi hatti de lobbi ju.*
     POSS.1SG heart IPFV love 2SG
     'I love you.'
   c. *Da somma de prodo, da wan prodoman,*
     ART person HAB boast COP one boaster
    a lobbi prodo.
    3SG like boast
    'That person boasts, he is a real boaster, he likes to boast.'

Value 7 (**progressive, habitual, and future**) is present in Creolese, Jamaican, Vincentian Creole, Louisiana Creole, Negerhollands, and Sango.

(6) Negerhollands (van Sluijs 2013)
   a. *Mi lō lō a mi grani.*
     1SG PROG go LOC POSS.1SG grandma
     'I am going to my grandma.'
   b. [...] *sinu lō mā di flut sinu.*
        3PL HAB make ART flute PL
     '[...] where they make those flutes.'
   c. *Morək mi lō lō.*
     tomorrow 1SG FUT go
     'Tomorrow I will go.'

Value 8 (**progressive, habitual, current state, and future**) occurs in Papiamentu, in Bahamian Creole, in Gullah, in Nengee, in Saramaccan, in Pichi, in Guadeloupean Creole, in Martinican Creole, and in Kinubi.

(7) Martinican Creole (Colot & Ludwig 2013b)
   a. *I ka dòmi.*
     3SG PROG sleep
     'He is sleeping.'
   b. *Man ka sipozé i la.*
     1SG IPFV suppose 3SG there
     'I suppose he is here.'
   c. *I ka jwé foutbol.*
     3SG HAB play football
     'He is a football player.'
   d. *I ka vini dimen.*
     3SG FUT come tomorrow.
     'He is coming tomorrow.'

3. Diachronic observations

Except for value 7, which occurs only in the Caribbean and in Africa, the different values of this feature do not show a particular areal distribution.

From a diachronic perspective, we can observe that the English-based languages which possess the marker *de* show the different stages in the grammaticalization path that a progressive marker may take. According to Bybee et al. (1994: 148), a progressive marker turns into a general imperfective marker by adopting the functions of habitual and current state. In the case of the English-based *APiCS* languages, Krio illustrates the initial stage where *de* only has the progressive function (example 2); in Belizean Creole, *de* marks progressive and habitual events (example 3), and in Early Sranan (as well as in Modern Sranan) *de* fulfils all three functions (progressive, habitual, current state; example 5), having thus reached the status of a general imperfective marker. Note that this development in Sranan is not recent; the Early Sranan examples date from 1781.

Papiamentu, which among the *APiCS* languages is the only language displaying two progressive markers—a gerund construction (example 1) and the marker *ta*—illustrates what may happen when an etymologically progressive marker (Papiamentu *ta* < Portuguese/Spanish *estar* + infinitive or gerund) reaches the stage of a general imperfective marker (or even a present tense marker; see Maurer 2003): a new progressive construction that puts particular emphasis on the progressive meaning is developed or borrowed.

47 Uses of the progressive marker

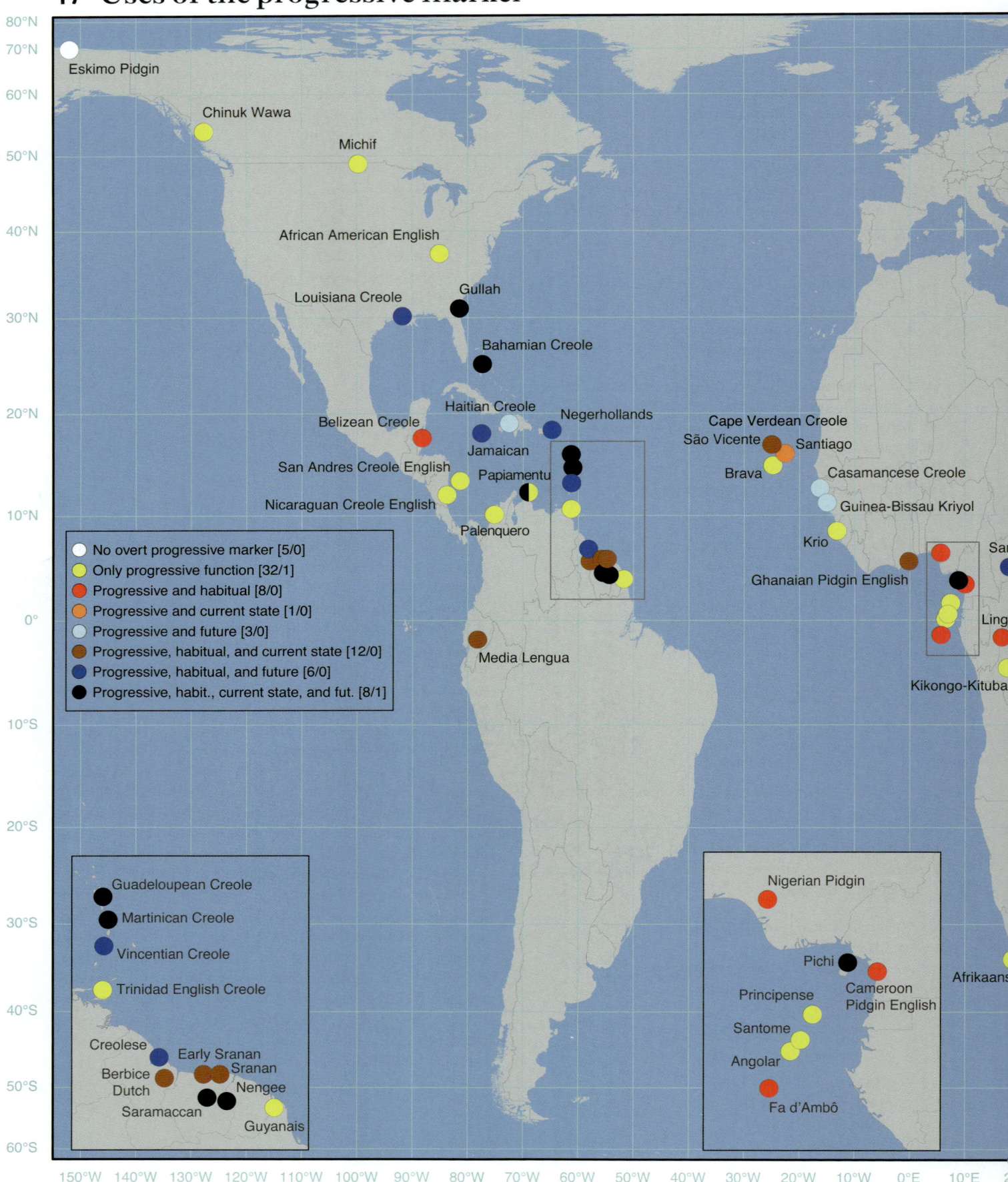

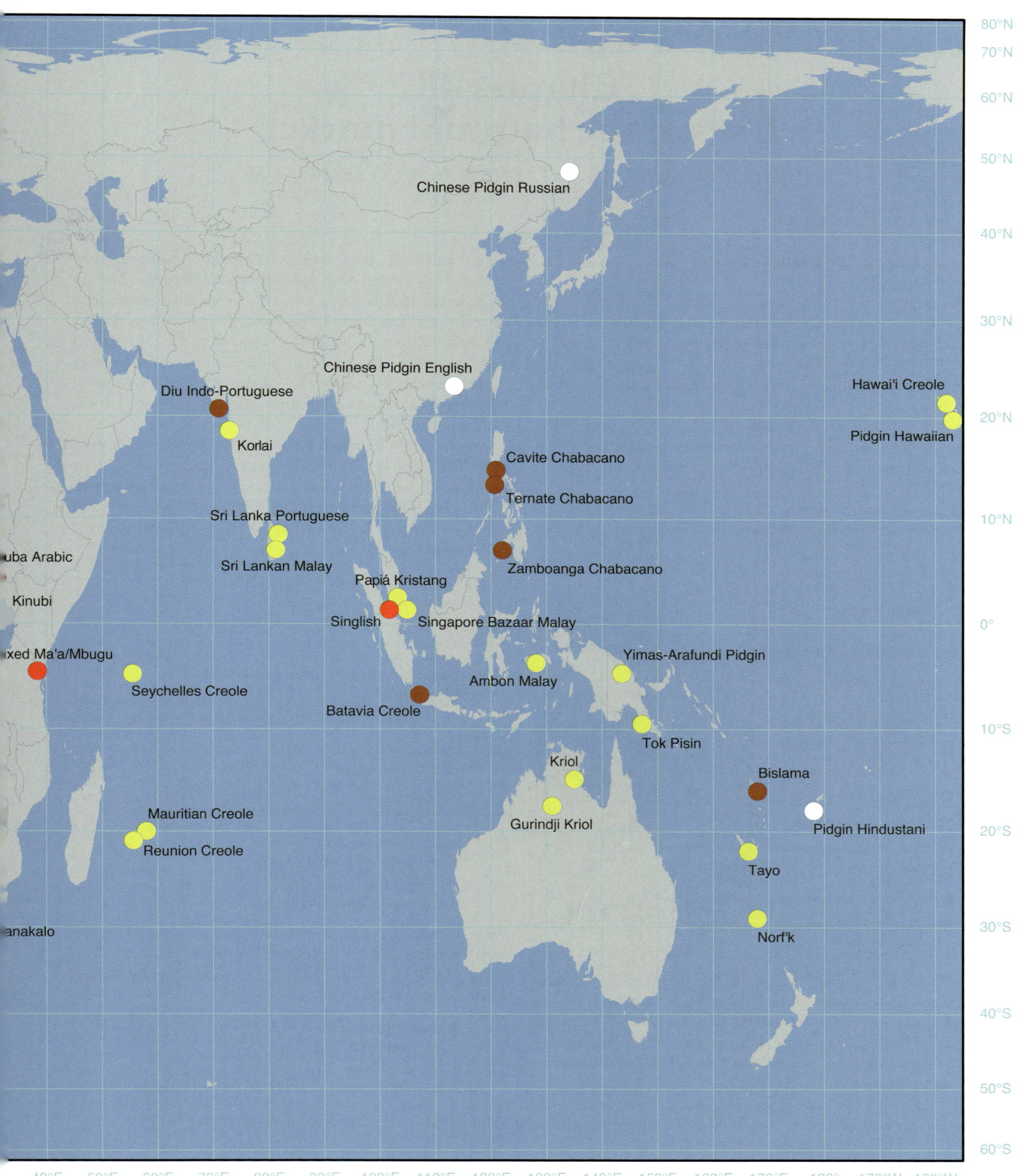

Chapter 48
Uses of the habitual marker

PHILIPPE MAURER AND THE *APiCS* CONSORTIUM

1. Feature description

An overt marker which expresses habitual aspect often fulfils other functions as well. This feature asks about the additional functions that an overt habitual marker may have.

From our comparative perspective, it is not important whether the habitual function of the marker is the basic function.

We only look at overt markers. If habituality is expressed by the bare verb without any overt marker (as for example in English), we treat the language as lacking a habitual marker (value 1).

This chapter is closely related to Chapter 47, which deals with the uses of the progressive marker (see that chapter for some definitions).

2. The values

We distinguish the following nine values:

		excl	shrd	all
○	1. No overt habitual marker	17	0	17
○	2. Only habitual function	17	13	30
●	3. Habitual and progressive	5	2	7
●	4. Habitual and current state	1	0	1
●	5. Habitual and future	2	0	2
●	6. Habitual, progressive, and current state	9	2	11
●	7. Habitual, current state, and future	5	1	6
●	8. Habitual, progressive, and future	1	5	6
●	9. Habitual, progressive, current state, and future	5	5	10

Note that most values of this feature are very similar to values of feature 47 on the uses of the progressive marker since in many languages the progressive and the habitual function can be expressed by the same marker. The differences are due to the fact that some languages use a specific habitual marker or a specific progressive marker.

Value 1 (no overt habitual marker) occurs in all nine *APiCS* pidgin languages, in five French-based languages (Guyanais, Mauritian Creole, Reunion Creole, Seychelles Creole, Tayo), in two Malay-based languages (Ambon Malay, Sri Lankan Malay), and in Afrikaans. Note that in some languages with several overt tense and aspect markers, such as Guyanais or Seychelles Creole, the habitual is rendered by the zero-marked verb, which then has a functional load. This contrasts with (mostly pidgin) languages which have no, or only one, overt tense and aspect marker and where the zero-marked verb has no functional load.

Value 2 (only habitual function) is the most widespread value. It is found in six Ibero-Romance-based languages, in fifteen English-based languages, in two French-based languages, in two Dutch-based languages, in Kikongo-Kituba, Sango, in Hawai'i Creole, and in the bilingual mixed languages Michif and Gurindji Kriol.

(1) Casamancese Creole (Biagui & Quint 2013)
 Tudu diya, N ta kumé na fugoŋ.
 every day 1SG HAB eat LOC kitchen
 'I eat in the kitchen every day.'

(2) African American English (Green 2013)
 She be telling people she eight.
 'She is always telling people she is eight.'

(3) Haitian Creole (Fattier 2013)
 Kòlbè konn vann liv bò isi a.
 Colbert HAB sell book around here DEF
 'Colbert usually sells books around here.'

(4) Sango (Samarin 2013)
 Baa ala nyon-'ka samba pepe.
 see 2PL drink-HAB beer NEG
 'Look, I don't drink beer.'

Value 3 (habitual and progressive) occurs in four English-based languages (Belizean Creole, Cameroon Pidgin English, Nigerian Pidgin, Singlish), in Kikongo-Kituba, in Juba Arabic, and in Mixed Ma'a/Mbugu.

(5) Nigerian Pidgin (Faraclas 2013)
 À dè wosh plet.
 1SG IPFV wash plate
 'I wash dishes (every day).'/'I am washing dishes.'

Value 4 (habitual and current state) is only found in Lingala.

(6) Lingala (Meeuwis 2013)
   a. *Na-sál-aka na Kinshása.*
      1SG-work-HAB LOC Kinshasa
      'I work in Kinshasa (habitually).'
   b. *Na-báng-aka Nzámbe.*
      1SG-fear-IPFV God
      'I fear God.'

Value 5 (**habitual and future**) occurs in Guinea-Bissau Kriyol and Papiá Kristang.

(7) Papiá Kristang (Baxter 2013)
   a. *Sédu sédu eli lo bai mar.*
      early early 3SG FUT go sea
      'He will go fishing very early.'
   b. *Stanley niora niora lo bebé sura.*
      Stanley due.course due.course HAB drink toddy
      'Stanley often drinks toddy.'

Value 6 (**habitual, progressive, and current state**) occurs in five Ibero-Romance-based languages (Diu Indo-Portuguese, Batavia Creole, Cavite Chabacano, Ternate Chabacano, Zamboanga Chabacano), in four English-based languages (Early Sranan, Sranan, Ghanaian Pidgin English, Bislama), as well as in Berbice Dutch and in Media Lengua.

(8) Ternate Chabacano (Sippola 2013b)
   a. *Ta trabahá éle na Las Pínyas.*
      IPFV work 3SG LOC Las Pínyas
      'He works in Las Pínyas.'
   b. *Ta esperá yo kon bo ayer.*
      IPFV wait 1SG OBJ 2SG yesterday
      'I was waiting for you yesterday.'
   c. *Ta kré lótru na kel milágru sánto nínyo.*
      IPFV believe 2SG in DEF miracle holy child
      'They believe in the miracles of the holy child.'

Value 7 (**habitual, current state, and future**) is present in five Portuguese-based languages (Cape Verdean Creole of Brava and of Santiago, Santome, Angolar, Principense), and in Juba Arabic.

(9) Cape Verdean Creole of Brava (Baptista 2013)
   a. *Nu ta fika ku bontadi di panha otu, ma ka ten.*
      1SG HAB stay with longing of take other but NEG have
      'We would long for more but there was not any more.'
   b. *N ta lenbra kuma nu tinha, tinha falta.*
      1SG IPFV remember COMP 1PL had had need
      'I remember that we were in need.'
   c. *N fra-z, kuazi N ta bai Praia.*
      1SG tell-3PL maybe 1SG FUT go Praia
      'I told them that maybe I'll go to Praia.'

Value 8 (**habitual, progressive, and future**) occurs in three English-based languages (Creolese, Jamaican, Vincentian Creole), as well as in Louisiana Creole, in Negerhollands, and in Sango.

(10) Sango (Samarin 2013)
   a. *Nyen' aso mo si mo eke toto tongaso?*
      what SM.hurt 2SG then 2SG COP/PROG cry thus
      'What ails you that you are crying like this?'
   b. *Mo yeke te nyama ti nyen'?*
      2SG COP/HAB eat meat of what
      'What kind of meat do you (habitually) eat?'
   c. *Mbi ke leke tere ti mbi ti kiri.*
      1SG COP/FUT fix body of 2SG to return
      'I'll prepare myself to return.'

Value 9 (**habitual, progressive, current state, and future**) occurs in two Ibero-Romance-based languages (Cape Verdean Creole of São Vicente, Papiamentu), in five English-based languages (Bahamian Creole, Gullah, Nengee, Saramaccan, Pichi), in two French-based languages (Guadeloupean Creole, Martinican Creole), and in Kinubi.

(11) Kinubi (Luffin 2013)
   a. *Úmun gi-ákul ákil ta Núbi*
      3PL HAB-eat food GEN Nubi
      'They eat the Nubian food.'
   b. *Nyerekú de bi-gi-rúa fi bé.*
      child DEM FUT-PROG-go LOC house
      'The child will be going home.'
   c. *Ána gi-kumbúka wázi.*
      1SG IPFV-remember well
      'I remember well.'
   d. *Íta gu-rúo búkra.*
      2SG FUT-go tomorrow
      'You will leave tomorrow.'

The values of this feature do not display any particular areal distribution, except for value 7, which occurs in five out of nine West African Portuguese-based creoles (as well as in Juba Arabic), and value 9, which only occurs in the Atlantic area (as well as in Kinubi).

In some languages, the habitual marker is derived from a full verb that does not function as a marker of habituality in the lexifier languages. Examples are the verb 'can' (*kan* in Negerhollands, *kin* in Krio, *kin* in Pichi), 'know' (*konn* in Haitian Creole, *kone* in Louisiana Creole, *sa* in Papiamentu, *sa ~ save* in Tok Pisin, *save* in Bislama), and 'love' (Saramaccan *lo*).

48 Uses of the habitual marker

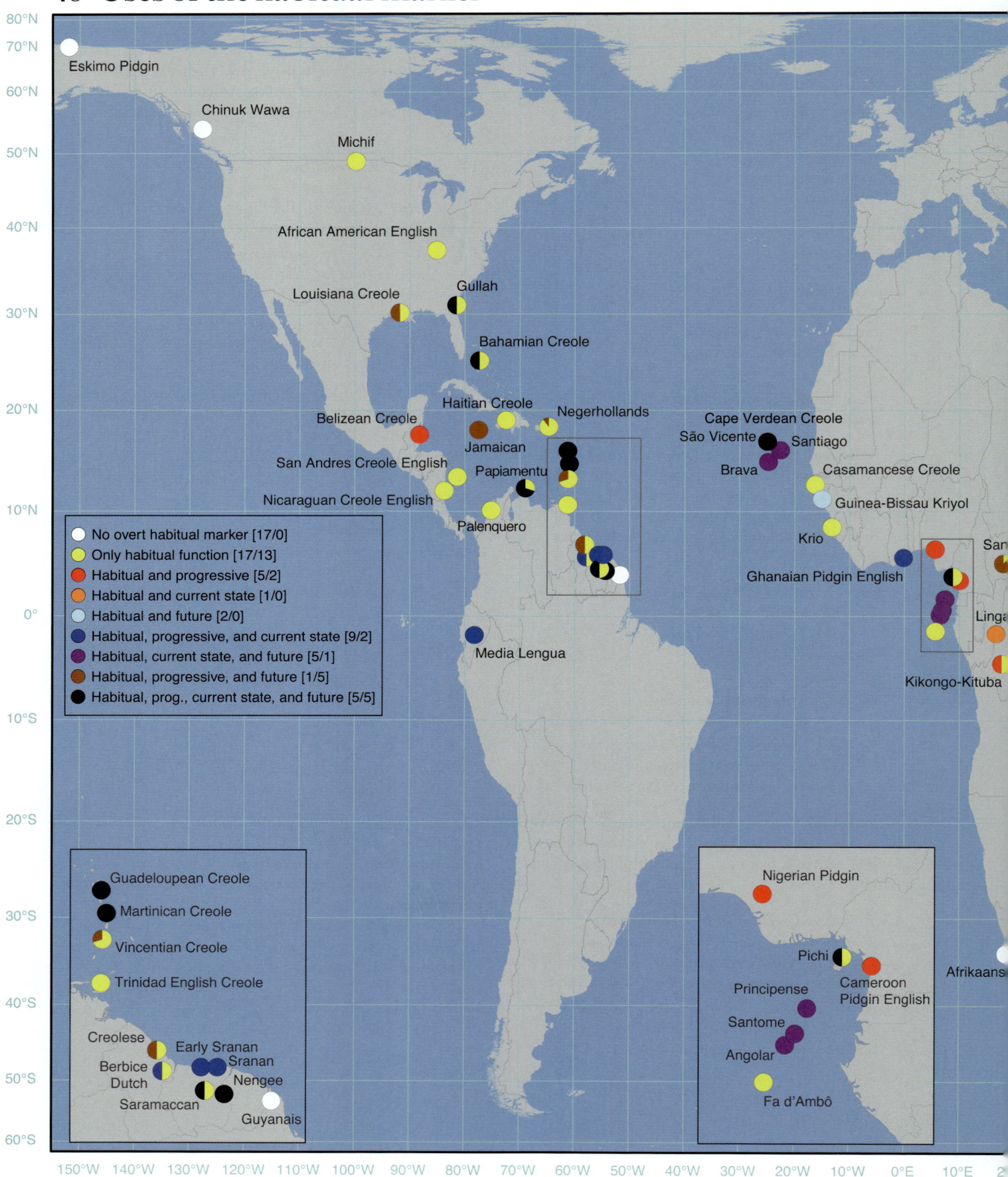

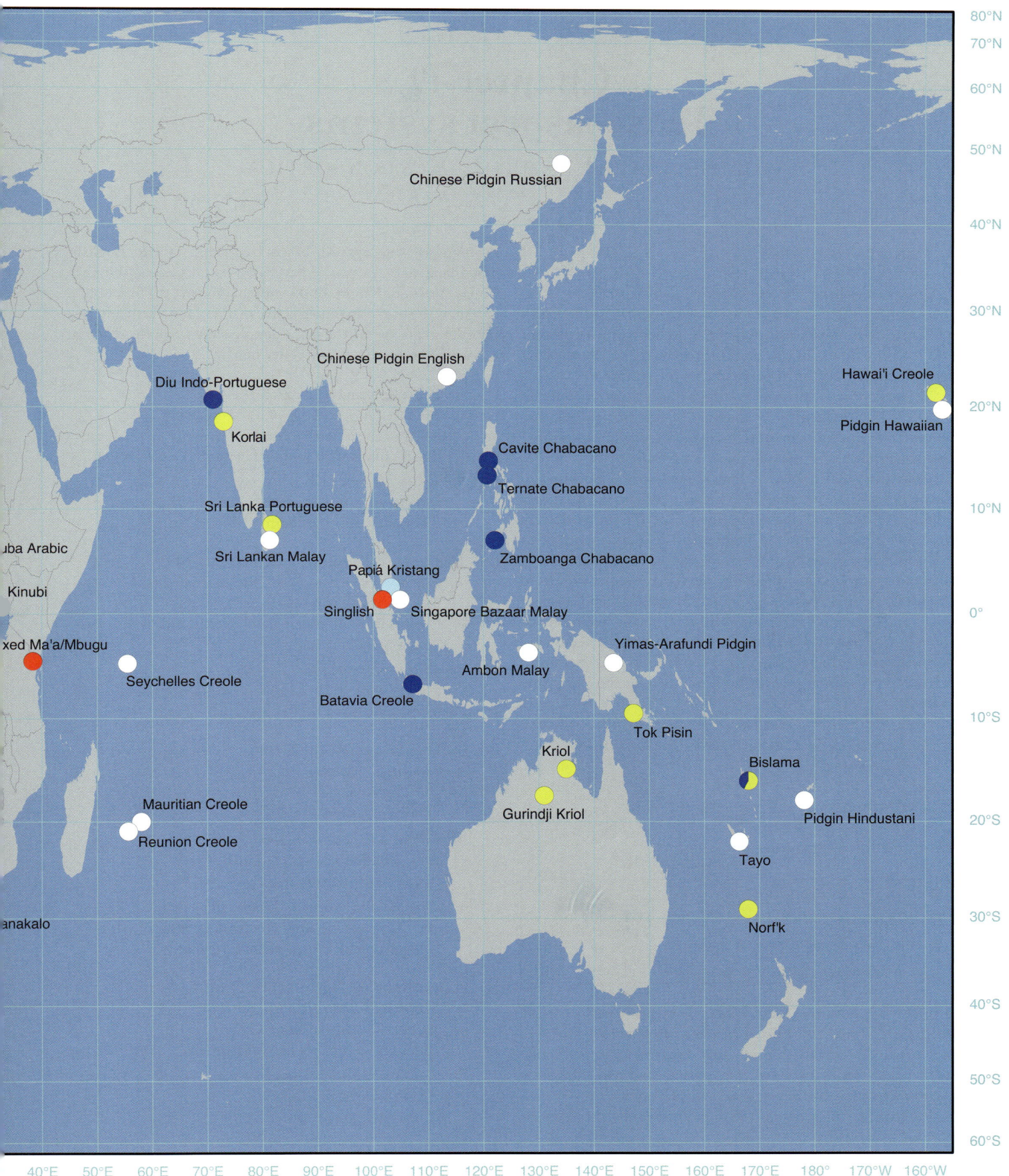

Chapter 49
Tense–aspect systems

PHILIPPE MAURER AND THE *APiCS* CONSORTIUM

1. Feature description

Languages may have different kinds of tense–aspect systems. In this feature, we do not look at the whole range of possible aspect and tense categories. Regarding tense, we look only at present and past situations; in the aspectual domain, we restrict ourselves to the opposition of perfective vs. imperfective.

Tense concerns the order relations that a situation denoted by a verb may have with the moment of utterance or another temporal-deictic moment of reference. Three relations are distinguished: anteriority, simultaneity, and posteriority.

Grammatical aspect is understood here as referring to the marking of the internal temporal structure of an event (beginning, middle, and end). The **imperfective aspect** refers to a point of time within the boundaries (beginning, end) of an event. In narrative texts, imperfective markers are often used to refer to backgrounded events. The **perfective aspect** refers to the whole situation, with beginning, middle, and end. Perfectively marked stative verbs may also refer to the beginning of the state (inchoative function). In narrative texts, perfective aspect markers—which in pidgin and creole languages are mostly zero-markers—often refer to foregrounded events (story line events).

Note that there are other aspectual categories like resultative or completive, but these are disregarded for this feature.

2. The values

We distinguish the following four values:

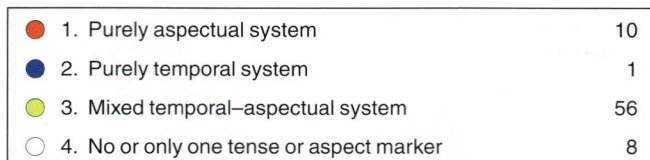

A **purely aspectual system** (value 1) only has a perfective aspect marker (possibly realized as a zero morpheme) that normally refers to perfective past situations, and an imperfective marker that can be used for both present and past situations (ongoing process, current state, or habitual event).

Purely aspectual systems are found in five Southeast Asian Portuguese- and Spanish-based languages, in two English-based languages, in two Malay-based languages, as well as in Yimas-Arafundi Pidgin. In the examples below, the first or first two show the use of an imperfective marker for present and past time reference, while the last example shows a perfective past situation expressed by a perfective marker.

(1) a. Papiá Kristang (Baxter 2013)
 Eli ta papiá ku John.
 3SG IPFV speak with John
 'He is talking with John.'/'He was talking with John.'

 b. *Eli ja bai mar onti anoti.*
 3SG PFV go sea yesterday night
 'He went fishing last night.'

(2) Zamboanga Chabacano (Steinkrüger 2013)
 a. *Éste el ómbre kon kyen tu ta-konversá.*
 DEM ART man with whom 2SG IPFV-talk
 'This is the man you are talking to.'/'This is the man you were talking to.'

 b. *Éle ya-matá pwérko gat alyá gránde.*
 3SG PFV-kill pig really there big
 'S/he killed a really big pig there.'

(3) Ambon Malay (Paauw 2013)
 a. *Dong ada makang.*
 3PL PROG eat
 'They are eating.'

 b. *Katong ada dudu tado-tado [...].*
 1PL PROG sit quiet~quiet
 'We were sitting very quietly [...].'

 c. *Dong su makang deng balong galap lai.*
 3PL PFV eat and not.yet dark also
 'They have eaten, and it is not dark yet.'

(4) Yimas-Arafundi Pidgin (Foley 2013)
 a. *Mən manba ambi ta-nan.*
 3SG PL eat.DEP PROG-NFUT
 'They are eating.'/'They were eating.'

 b. *Mən manba ambi məndəkə-nan.*
 3SG PL eat.DEP finish-NFUT
 'They have already eaten.'

(5) Ghanaian Pidgin English (Huber 2013)
   a. *Witʃples dɛ faia dè   bɛn?*
      where ART fire PROG burn
      'Where is the fire burning?'
   b. *Wî dè   dig àm wit pikaks* [. . .].
      1PL PROG dig 3SG with pickaxe
      'We were digging it out with pickaxes [. . .].'
   c. *Dè ∅ go fɔ Dagɔmba tʃif   haus.*
      3PL PFV go to Dagomba chief house
      'They went to the Dagomba chief's house.'

Note that in most languages with a purely aspectual system, the perfective marker is an overt marker; the exception to this is Ghanaian Pidgin English.

Languages with **a purely temporal system** (value 2) only mark present, past, and future situations, regardless of aspect. The only language exhibiting this feature is Afrikaans.

(6) Afrikaans (den Besten & Biberauer 2013)
   a. *Hy ∅   weier dit.*
      3SG.M PRS refuse 3SG.N
      'He refuses it.'
   b. *Hy   het dit ge-weier.*
      3SG.M PST 3SG.N PTCP-refuse
      'He refused it.'/'He has refused it.'
   c. *Hy   sal dit   weier.*
      3SG.M FUT 3SG.N refuse
      'He will refuse it.'

Languages with a **mixed temporal–aspectual system** (value 3) are the most widespread type. (For this value, it is not important whether tense marking is obligatory, optional, or bound to certain contexts.) In these languages, imperfective marking can be combined with a present–past distinction, as the (a) and (b) examples below show.

(7) Cameroon Pidgin English (Schröder 2013)
   a. *I di waka fo fores.*
      3SG PROG walk LOC forest
      'S/he is walking in the forest.'
   b. *I bi di waka fo fores.*
      3SG PST PROG walk LOC forest
      'S/he was walking in the forest.'
   c. *A ∅ si-am.*
      1SG PFV see-3SG
      'I saw him/her.'

(8) Kinubi (Luffin 2013)
   a. *Mátará gi-wága.*
      rain.PL PROG-fall
      'It is raining.'
   b. *Úwo kan g-wónusi   morú.*
      3SG PST PROG-speak Moru
      'He was speaking Moru.'
   c. *Núbi ∅ wósul Mombása bédir.*
      Nubi PFV arrive Mombasa early
      'The Nubi arrived early in Mombasa.'

(9) Media Lengua (Muysken 2013)
   a. *I-xu-ni   kaza-mu.*
      go-PROG-1SG house-ALL
      'I am going home.'
   b. *Kaza-mu i-xu-rka-ni.*
      house-ALL go-PROG-PST-1SG
      'I was going home.'
   c. *Yo-ga   bini-ngi zi-ka-ni.*
      1SG-TOP come-2SG say-PST-1SG
      'I said that you should come.'

The difference between a purely aspectual system and a mixed tense–aspect system lies in the domain of the imperfective: purely aspectual systems cannot mark the difference between present imperfective and past imperfective, whereas mixed tense–aspect systems do.

Value 4 (**no or only one tense and aspect marker**) refers to languages that use only time adverbs or have only one overt tense or aspect marker (future markers are not relevant for this feature). Value 4 occurs in Chinuk Wawa, Eskimo Pidgin, and Pidgin Hindustani (have no tense and aspect markers), in Chinese Pidgin English (has only a perfective aspect marker *hab*), in Chinese Pidgin Russian (has only a perfective suffix *-la*), in Pidgin Hawaiian (has only an imperfective marker *ana*), in Sango (has only a habitual marker *ka*), and in Tayo (has only a progressive marker *atraⁿde*).

3. Distribution

Whereas mixed temporal–aspectual systems prevail in nearly all regions, purely aspectual systems are found almost exclusively in Southeast Asia and the Pacific, with the exception of Ghanaian Pidgin English in the Atlantic area. The fact that the Southeast Asian languages exhibit purely aspectual systems is due to Malay and Philippine substrate or adstrate influence.

49 Tense–aspect systems

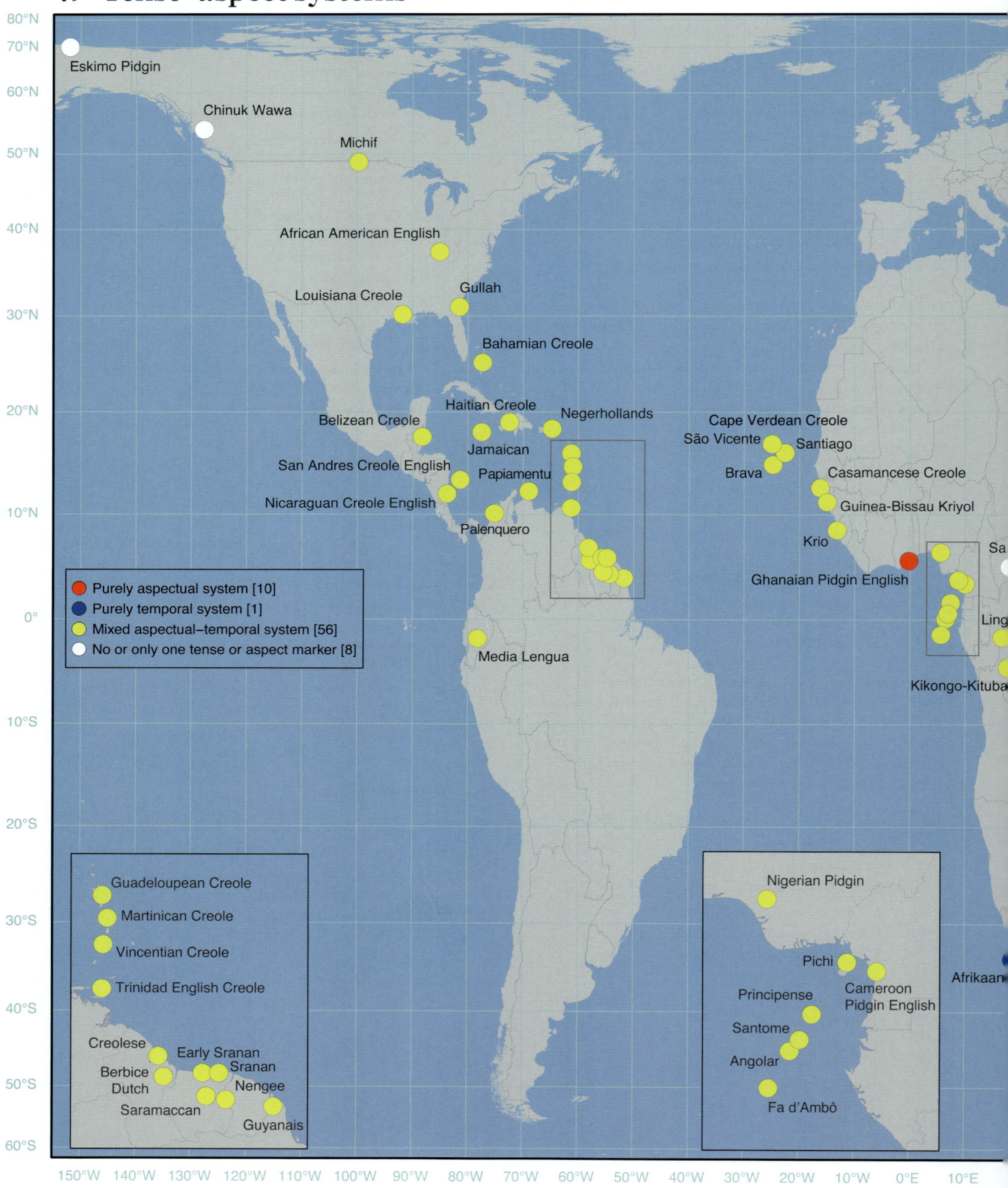

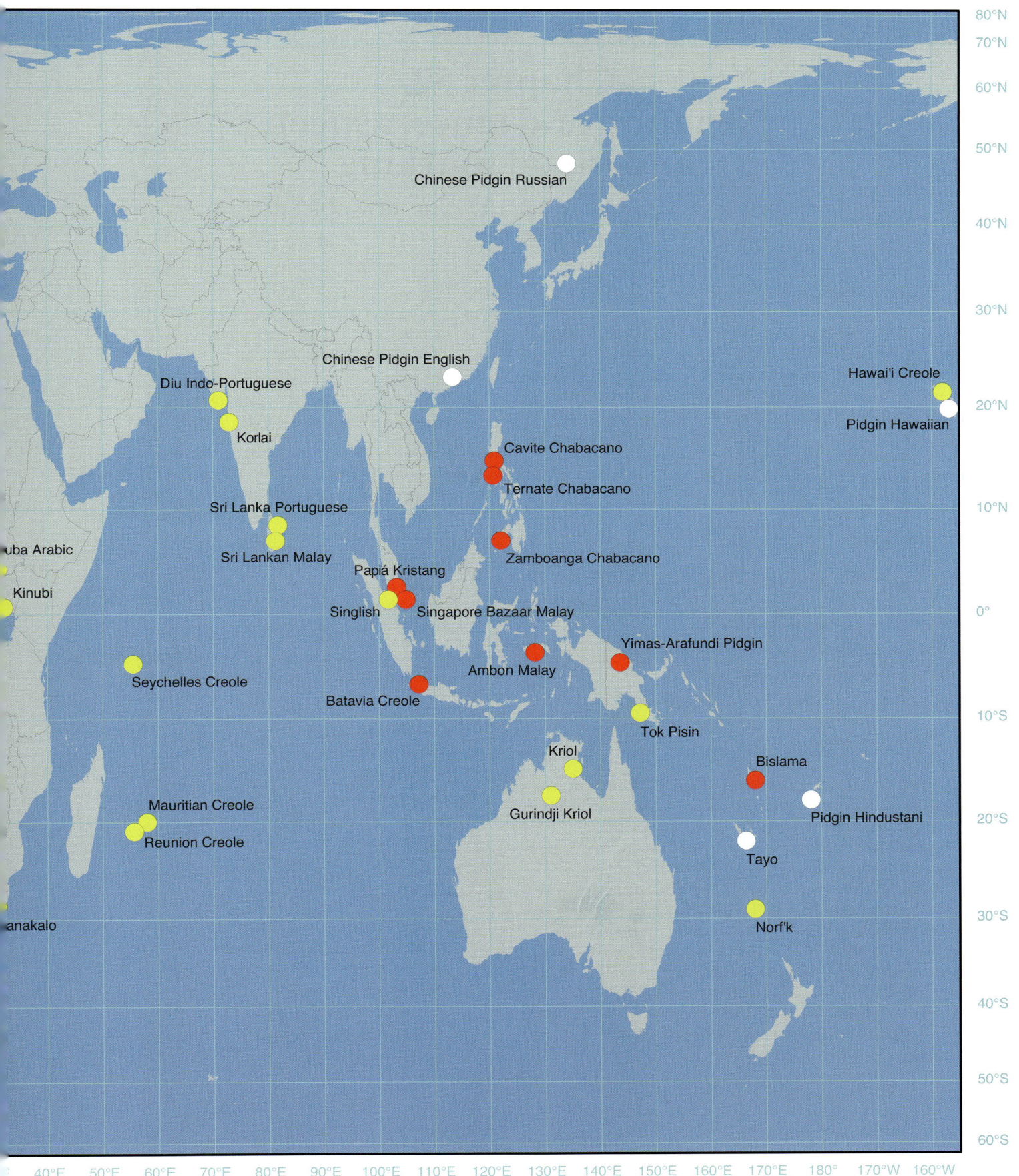

Chapter 50
Negation and tense, aspect, and mood marking

PHILIPPE MAURER AND THE *APiCS* CONSORTIUM

1. Feature description

Some *APiCS* languages do not allow the standard negator (the negator occurring in declarative main clauses; see Miestamo 2005) to co-occur with one or more tense, aspect, or mood markers. In some languages, the TAM marker is deleted, in other languages, it is replaced by another TAM marker, and in still other languages, the TAM marker is replaced by a special marker (or negator) which does not belong to the set of markers which occur in affirmative sentences.

2. The values

We distinguish the following five values:

●	1. Same TAM marking in negated clauses	47
●	2. Reduced TAM marking in negated clauses	10
●	3. Different TAM marking in negated clauses	9
●	4. Reduced and different TAM marking in negated clauses	2
○	5. No TAM marker	3

Value 1 (**same tense, aspect, and mood marking** in negated clauses as in affirmative clauses) is the most widespread value; it occurs in almost two thirds of the *APiCS* languages.

Value 2 (**reduced tense, aspect, and mood marking in negated clauses compared to affirmative clauses**) occurs in Principense (Portuguese-based), in Kriol, Bahamian Creole, and Chinese Pidgin English (English-based), in Reunion Creole and Mauritian Creole (French-based), in Berbice Dutch, in Ambon Malay, in Sri Lankan Malay, and in Chinese Pidgin Russian. Reduction can mean less differentiation (as in 1), less overt marking (2–4), or less variation (5 and 6).

In Principense negated sentences, the habitual/future marker *ka* may not be used; instead, the progressive marker *sa* replaces *ka*:

(1) Principense (Maurer 2013c)
 a. *Amanhan n ka kume ki Zwan.*
  tomorrow 1SG FUT eat with John
  'Tomorrow I will eat with John.'
 b. *Amanhan n sa kume ki Zwan fa.*
  tomorrow 1SG PROG eat with John NEG
  'Tomorrow I won't eat with John.'

In Berbice Dutch, the perfective marker *-tɛ* may not co-occur with the standard negator *ka*. The stative verb *nimi* 'know' is normally modified by the perfective marker *-tɛ* for present reference (as *nimi* in the object clause of the following example), but when negated, *nimi* occurs without *-tɛ*:

(2) Berbice Dutch (Kouwenberg 2013a)
 ɛkɛ nimi hoso eni nimi-tɛ dida ka
 1SG know [how 3PL know-PFV that] NEG
 'I don't know how they know that.'

In Ambon Malay, the progressive marker *ada* cannot co-occur with the standard negator:

(3) Ambon Malay (Paauw 2013)
 a. *De ada makang.*
  3SG PROG eat
  'He is eating.'
 b. *De seng makang.*
  3SG NEG eat
  'He isn't eating.'

In Sri Lankan Malay, negation precludes the use of any tense, aspect, or mood marker.

(4) Sri Lankan Malay (Slomanson 2013)
 a. *Inçian ruma dua si-kuttumun.*
  3SG.HON house two PST-see
  'She just saw two houses.'
 b. *Go attu=le ta-kelaatan.*
  1SG one=QUANT NEG.FIN-see
  'I didn't see anything.'

In Reunion Creole, the perfect can be marked with *la* or *la fin/fini*, but in negative sentences only *la* occurs.

(5) Reunion Creole (Bollée 2013)
    a. *Moin la fine ariv la kaz.*
       1SG PRF   arrive ART house
       'I have arrived at home.'
    b. *Li la pa rantré.*
       3SG PRF NEG come.back
       'He has not come back home.'

In Mauritian Creole, *va* marks the uncertain future and *pu* the definite future. *Va* cannot co-occur with the negator, whereas *pu* and all other preverbal markers can.

(6) Mauritian Creole (Baker & Kriegel 2013)
    a. *Mo pa pu kasyet sa.*
    b. *Mo pa *va kasyet sa.*
       1SG NEG FUT hide   3SG
       'I will not hide it.'

Value 3 (**different tense, aspect, and mood marking**) occurs in seven English-based languages (Belizean Creole, San Andres Creole English, Cameroon Pidgin English, Ghanaian Pidgin English, Nigerian Pidgin, Pichi, Hawai'i Creole) and in two Portuguese-based languages (Korlai, Batavia Creole).

In the English-based languages, it is invariably a negative past marker *neva* (< English *never*) which precludes the use of general past markers, perfective aspect markers, perfects, or completive aspect markers (depending on the language).

(7) San Andres Creole English (Bartens 2013b)
    a. *We yu wehn sii di ishili?*
       where 2SG PST   see ART lizard
       'Where did you see the lizard?'
    b. *Di gyal neva wiek Jack.*
       ART girl NEG.PST wake Jack
       'The girl didn't wake Jack up.'

(8) Hawai'i Creole (Velupillai 2013)
    a. *ʃi wɛn ɹaɪʔ wan buk*
       3SG.F PST.PFV write ART book
       'She wrote a book.'
    b. *aɪ dono waɪ dɛ neva pur ɔm in a mirol*
       1SG NEG.know why 3PL NEG.PST put 3SG in ART middle
       'I don't know why they didn't put it in the middle.'

In Korlai, most tense, aspect, and mood markers used in affirmative sentences are replaced by other markers or constructions in negative sentences; for example, the affirmative present progressive *katan* '(she) is singing' is replaced by *nu tɛ katan* '(she) is not singing'. In Batavia Creole, the affirmative future marker *lo* is replaced by the negative future marker *nada*.

Value 4 (**reduced and different tense, aspect, and mood marking**) only occurs in Papiá Kristang, and in Sri Lanka Portuguese.

In Papiá Kristang, negators do not co-occur with the progressive aspect marker *ta* or the perfective marker *ja* (hence reduced marking). Furthermore, the future marker *lo*(*gu*) is replaced by *nádi* in negated sentences (hence the different marking).

(9) Papiá Kristang (Baxter 2013)
    a. *Eli ta drumí na chang.*
       3SG PROG sleep LOC floor
       'He is sleeping on the floor.'
    b. *Taté ja olá ku bela Rozil.*
       Taté PFV see OBJ old Rozil
       'Taté saw old Rozil.'
    c. *Eli ńgka bai mar.*
       3SG NEG go sea
       'He isn't/wasn't going fishing./He doesn't go fishing./He didn't go fishing.'
    d. *Sédu sédu eli lo bai mar.*
       early early 3SG FUT go sea
       'He will go fishing very early.'
    e. *Taté nadi bai mar ozi anoti.*
       Taté NEG.FUT go sea today night
       'Taté won't go fishing tonight.'

As for Sri Lanka Portuguese, Smith (2013) notes that "there is not always a one-to-one correspondence between positive and negative forms. The negative markers signal aspect and modality rather than tense; they cannot be accompanied by tense markers."

Value 5, **no TAM markers**, refers to languages that use only time adverbs. This value occurs in three pidgin languages: Chinuk Wawa, Eskimo Pidgin, and Pidgin Hindustani.

3. Distribution

The *same* tense, aspect, and mood marking in affirmative and negated sentences (value 1) occurs in all areas, but *not the same* marking (values 2–4) is concentrated in West Africa and, generally speaking, in Asia, from the Indian Ocean to the Pacific area.

The only particular distribution according to the lexifiers is value 3 (different marking): out of nine languages exhibiting this feature, seven are English-based, the other two being Portuguese-based. Note, however, that the other twenty English-based *APiCS* languages do not display this value.

50 Negation and tense, aspect, and mood marking

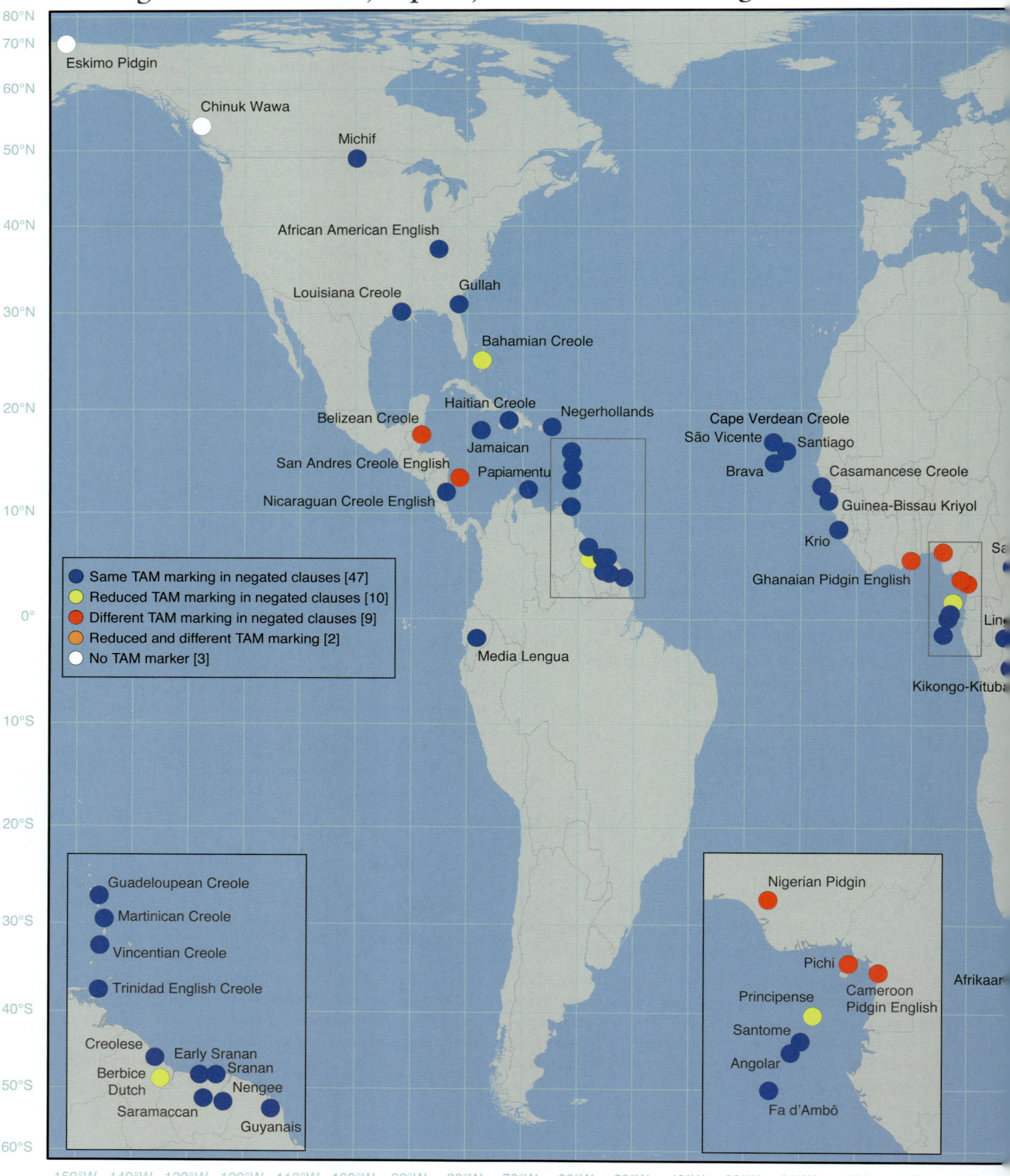

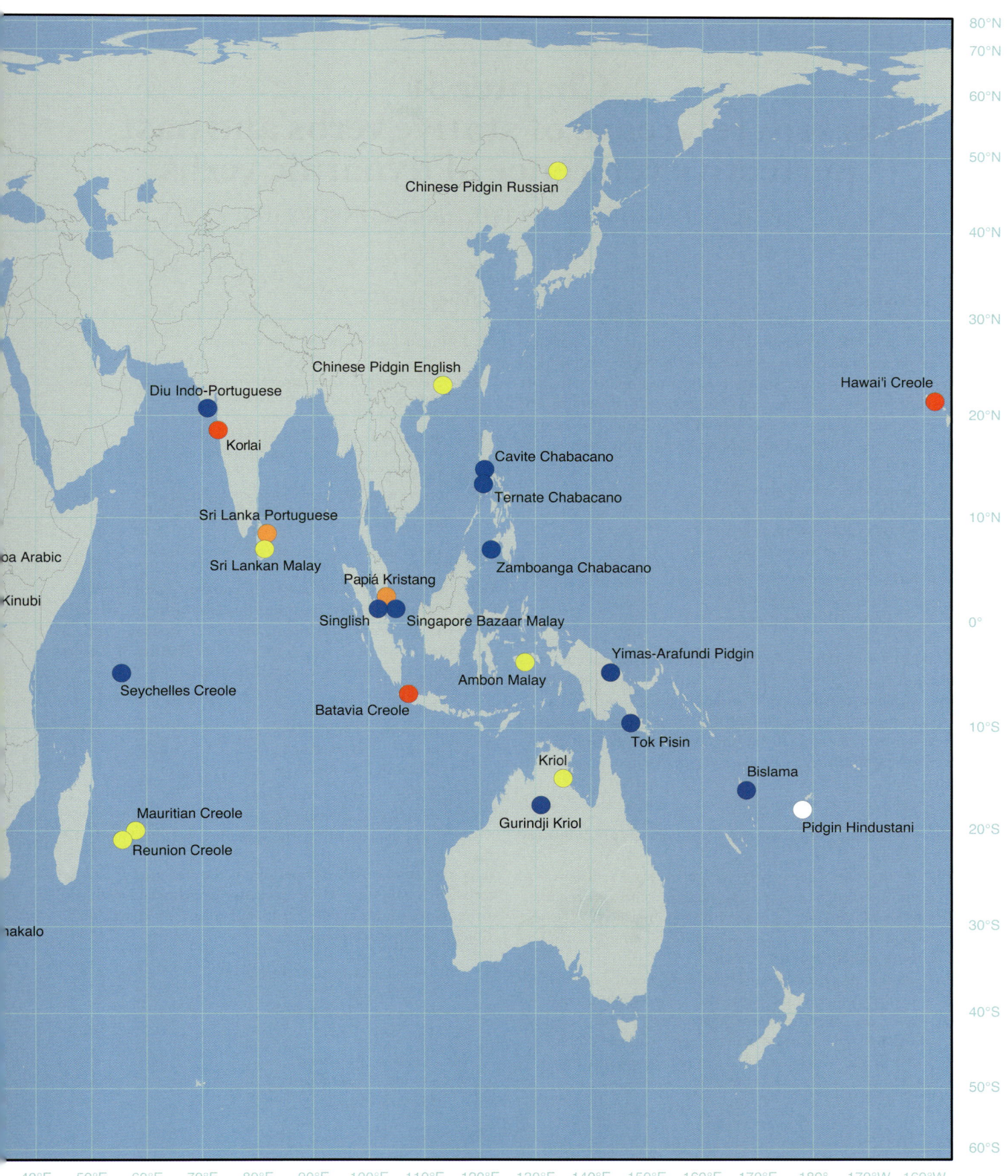

Chapter 51
Present reference of stative verbs and past perfective reference of dynamic verbs

PHILIPPE MAURER AND THE *APiCS* CONSORTIUM

1. Introduction

Bickerton (1981: 58) claimed that, according to his language bioprogram hypothesis, in creole languages the zero-marked verb refers to a present situation (the a-examples) with stative verbs and has a past perfective function with dynamic verbs (b-examples) (which corresponds to *APiCS* value 1, below). The following Belizean Creole examples illustrate this:

(1) Belizean Creole (Escure 2013)
    a. *Dey no ∅ wan du it.*
       3PL NEG PRS want do 3SG
       'They don't want to do it.'
    b. *A ∅ fayn di bɛs rowp.*
       1SG PFV find ART best rope
       'I found the best rope.'

This chapter examines how verbs referring to permanent states like 'can', 'know', 'love', or 'want' are marked for present reference and how dynamic verbs are marked for (past) perfective aspect (or past reference, if the language has no dedicated perfective aspect marker). If the language has no dedicated perfective aspect marker, a past tense or a perfect tense marker has been retained.

For this feature, it is not important

(i) whether the overt tense and aspect markers are obligatory or optional;
(ii) whether only some verbs referring to permanent states are zero-marked for present reference and others are modified by an overt marker (as in the Gulf of Guinea creoles, where some stative verbs are zero-marked and others marked by *ka* for present reference); and
(iii) whether the covert and overt markers retained for this feature have other functions besides referring to present tense in the case of stative verbs and to (past) perfective aspect with dynamic verbs (as with the zero-marked verb in Haitian Creole, which may also refer to habitual situations).

2. The values

We distinguish the following four values:

🔴	1. Stative verbs with present reference and dynamic verbs with past perfective reference are both unmarked	38
🟠	2. Stative verbs with present reference and dynamic verbs with past perfective reference are marked with the same overt marker	3
🔵	3. Stative verbs with present reference and dynamic verbs with past perfective reference are marked differently	26
⚪	4. The language has no or only one TAM marker	6

Value 1 (**stative verbs with present reference and dynamic verbs with past perfective reference are both unmarked**) is the most widespread value among the *APiCS* languages and, as mentioned above, corresponds to one of the features of Bickerton's (1981) language bioprogram hypothesis.

(2) Sango (Samarin 2013)
    a. *A-mbeni a-hinga ape.*
       PL-some PM-know NEG
       'Some don't know.'
    b. *Kol ni a-mu mama ni a-faa lo.*
       man DET PM-take mother DET PM-kill 3SG
       'The man took the (wife's) mother and killed her.'

Value 2 (**stative verbs with present reference and dynamic verbs with past perfective reference are marked with the same overt marker**) only occurs in Lingala, in Mixed Ma'a/Mbugu, and in Palenquero.

(3) Mixed Ma'a/Mbugu (Mous 2013)
    a. *Ni-áa-kwaha.*
       1SG-PFV-be.tired
       'I am tired.'
    b. *É-áa-bibi itoru.*
       3SG-PFV-throw spear
       'He threw a spear.'

(4) Palenquero (Schwegler 2013)
a. *Suto a polé ta arí-ndo no.*
    1PL PFV can PROG laugh-GER NEG
    'We can't be laughing.'
b. *Suto a miní ayé.*
    1PL PFV come yesterday
    'We arrived yesterday.'

In contrast to Lingala and Mixed Ma'a/Mbugu, the marker is optional in Palenquero for stative verbs with present reference as well as for dynamic verbs with past perfective reference.

The following Seychelles Creole and Ternate Chabacano examples illustrate value 3 (**stative verbs with present reference and dynamic verbs with past perfective reference are marked differently**). This value is the normal case in European languages.

(5) Seychelles Creole (Michaelis & Rosalie 2013)
a. *Mon ∅ konn gete.*
    1SG PRS can watch
    'I know how to watch.'
b. *Apre ou 'n al Sent Ann.*
    then 2SG PRF go Saint Anne
    'Then you went to Saint Anne.'

(6) Ternate Chabacano (Sippola 2013b)
a. *∅ Tyéni yo úna íha.*
    PRS have 1SG one daughter
    'I have a daughter.'
b. *Ya ganá yo na eleksyón.*
    PFV win 1SG LOC election
    'I won the elections.'

Those languages in which the overt marking of the perfective aspect is not obligatory are also subsumed under this value. An example is Gurindji Kriol:

(7) Gurindji Kriol (Meakins 2013)
a. *Im ∅ want to kurru yu nyawa-ngku nangari-ngku.*
    3SG PRS want to listen 2SG this-ERG Nangari-ERG
    'This Nangari wants to listen to you.'
b. *Hau i bin lungkarra na?*
    how 3SG PFV cry SEQ
    'How did he cry, then?'
c. *Kyle-tu-ma parl im ∅ put-im.*
    Kyle-ERG-TOP pile 3SG PFV put-TR
    'Kyle put them in a pile.'

Value 4 (**the language has no or only one TAM marker**) concerns five pidgin languages (Chinese Pidgin Russian, Chinuk Wawa, Eskimo Pidgin, Pidgin Hawaiian, Yimas-Arafundi Pidgin), and Tayo.

3. Distribution

There is a clear areal distribution of the primary contrast between value 1 (unmarked stative verbs have present reference, unmarked dynamic verbs have past perfective reference) and value 3 (dynamic and stative verbs are not marked the same way for the relevant functions): value 1 predominates on both sides of the Atlantic (including the Americas and continental Africa), whereas value 3 occurs mainly in the other areas, from the Indian Ocean to the Pacific – with some exceptions for both values.

Distribution according to the lexifier shows that value 1 occurs in languages with all lexical bases (19 English-based languages, nine Portuguese-based languages, five French-based languages, four African or Arabic-based languages, and Ambon Malay). Value 3 occurs somewhat more commonly in the Romance-based languages (11 out of 30) than in the Germanic-based languages (7 out of 30).

4. Other issues

From a semantic or functional point of view, values 1 and 2 are the same: present states and past perfective dynamic situations are marked the same way, covertly with value 1 and overtly with value 2.

Covert marking of both functions is widespread among non-Bantu West African languages (e.g. Yoruba); therefore it is probable that the Atlantic creole languages having value 1 were influenced by their West African substrate languages.

Overt marking of both functions is well represented among Bantu languages: in many of these languages, present states cannot be marked with a present tense marker; they must occur in the Perfect (which is aspectually perfective) or a similar tense. This means that in these languages, states can only be referred to inchoatively: the Perfect tense indicates that the beginning of the state has been achieved. Note that this feature is not restricted to the Bantu-based contact varieties Lingala and Mixed Ma'a/Mbugu, but that it also occurs in non-contact Bantu varieties like Kimbundu, spoken in Angola.

Overtly marked functions are easier to establish than covertly marked functions; therefore it is possible to infer from the languages with value 2 that the languages exhibiting value 1—or at least some of them—have the same pattern, in the sense that present states can only be referred to inchoatively. This means thus that the zero-marked stative verbs have the same function as the zero-marked dynamic verbs, namely perfective aspect.

The data presented here furthermore show that Bickerton's feature (which corresponds to *APiCS* value 1) is the most widespread value among the *APiCS* languages (about 52%), but that it does not apply to all creole languages: in the *APiCS* language sample, this feature is absent from 17 creole languages.

51 Present reference of stative verbs and past perfective reference of

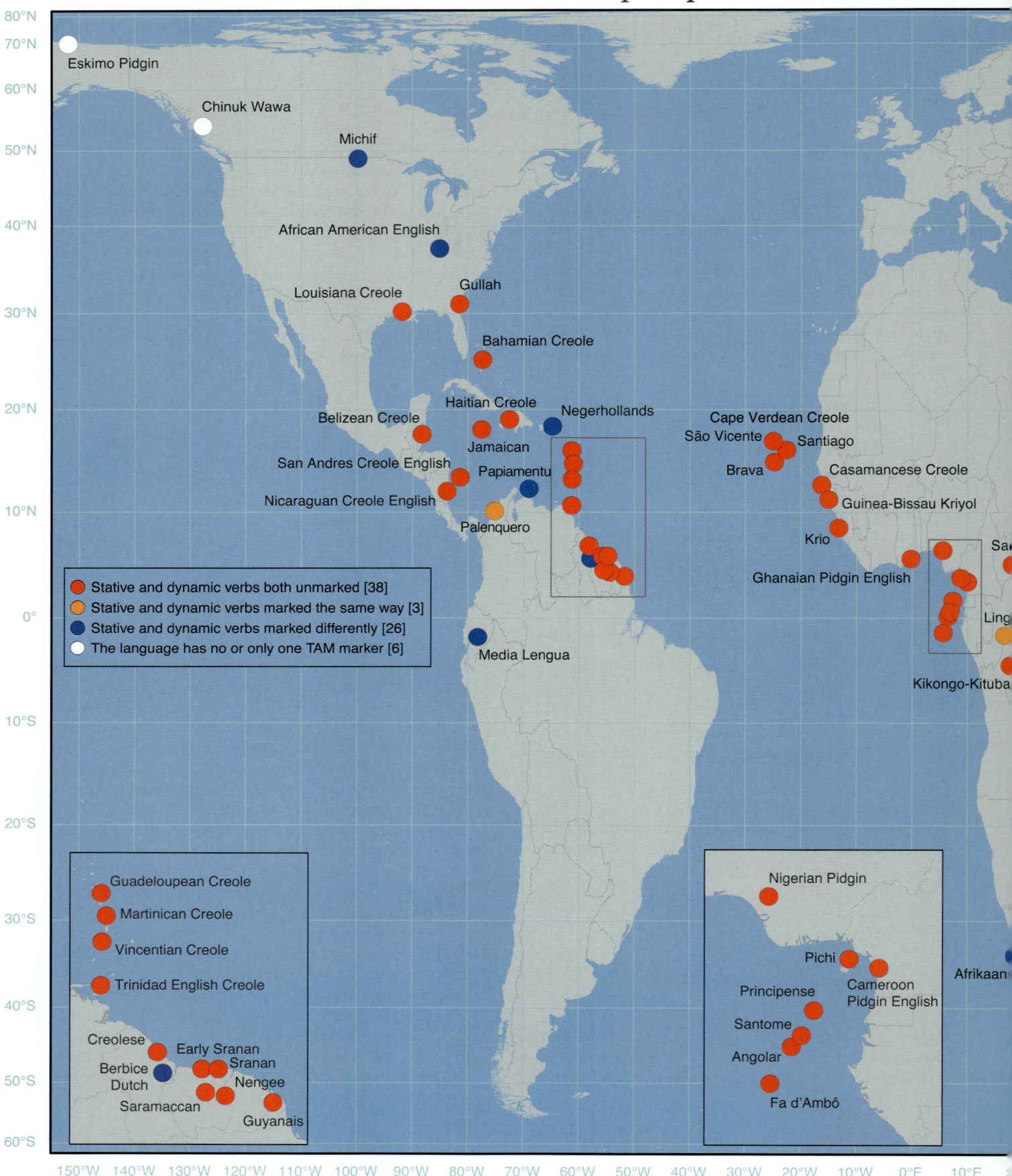

202

Chapter 52
Aspect markers and inchoative meaning

MARTIN HASPELMATH, SUSANNE M. MICHAELIS, AND THE *APiCS* CONSORTIUM

1. Introduction

A striking feature of many creole languages is that words denoting physical and psychological states such as 'ripe', 'sick', 'fat', 'red', and 'know', when combined with progressive or completive aspect markers, can take on an inchoative meaning, that is, a sense of becoming. This is illustrated in (1a) for a marker that otherwise expresses progressive aspect (cf. 1b), and in (2a) for a marker that otherwise expresses completive aspect (cf. 2b).

(1) Nengee (Migge 2013)
 a. *Den koosi e nati.*
  DET.PL clothes IPFV wet
  'The clothes are getting wet.'
 b. *Nownow mi e wasi beenki.*
  now.now I IPFV wash dishes
  'I'm washing dishes now.'

(2) Seychelles Creole (Michaelis & Rosalie 2013)
 a. *Tu pu mwa i 'n mir.*
  all for me PM PRF ripe
  'All my [bananas] have become ripe (and are now ripe).'
 b. *Eski Thomas in manze?*
  Q Thomas PRF eat
  'Has Thomas eaten?'

That this feature, which is absent from the European lexifiers, occurs in Atlantic, Indian Ocean, and Pacific creoles was noted by Bickerton (1981: 69). Note that it does not matter for this feature whether the state words are classified as "adjectives" or as "verbs".

2. The values

We distinguish five mutually exclusive types:

○	1. No inchoative meaning with aspect markers	33
○	2. Inchoative expressed by progressive marker	20
●	3. Inchoative expressed by completive marker	9
●	4. Inchoative expressed by progressive and completive markers	10
●	5. No aspect markers	1

Slightly less than half of the languages have aspect markers that lack the inchoative meaning (value 1), and one language lacks aspect markers entirely (value 5). A progressive marker has inchoative meaning far more frequently than a completive marker. About one third of the languages with this feature have both progressive and completive markers with inchoative meaning (value 4).

3. Aspect markers do not express inchoative meaning

Where aspect markers cannot express the inchoative meaning, this is generally expressed by 'become' verbs, as in (3)–(4).

(3) Kriol (Schultze-Berndt & Angelo 2013)
 Wel im=in git kwait na.
 well 3SG=PST get quiet now
 'Well, he became quiet then.'

(4) Palenquero (Schwegler 2013)
 Fluta ta ngobbé madulu.
 fruit PROG turn ripe
 'The fruit is becoming ripe.'

Overt progressive or imperfective markers are usually not used with state words in these languages, but occasionally they can be used (also alongside the copula) and then have habitual meaning, as in Cape Verdean Creole (and similarly in Guadeloupean and Martinican Creole):

(5) Cape Verdean Creole of Santiago (Lang 2013)
 Túnika di nhu pádri ta sta sénpri bránku álbu sima névi.
 robe of our priest IPFV be always white white as snow
 'The robe of our priest is always spotlessly white, as snow.'

4. Inchoative meaning expressed by progressive marker

Another example of value 2 is (6).

(6) Louisiana Creole
 (Neumann-Holzschuh & Klingler 2013)
 M ape fatige ek te zistwar.
 1SG PROG tired with 2SG.POSS.PL story
 'I'm getting tired of hearing your stories.'

Progressive markers that have inchoative meaning with state words occur widely in Atlantic creoles, and also sporadically elsewhere. It should be noted that the progressive marker need not express progressive meaning exclusively, but can also have other meanings (which may even be more prominent than the progressive meaning, see Chapter 47).

This pattern has been attributed to West African substrate influence, for example, by Migge (2003: 87), who cites the following Gbe example:

(7) Xwela Gbe
 Emɛ lɔ nɔ ga.
 person DET PROG big/fat
 'The person is getting fat.'

5. Inchoative meaning expressed by completive marker

Somewhat less commonly than progressive markers, completive markers may have inchoative meaning (value 3).

(8) Casamancese Creole (Biagui & Quint 2013)
 Mangu-s kabá burmeju.
 mango-PL COMPL red
 'The mangoes have become ripe.'

(9) Cameroon Pidgin English (Schröder 2013)
 Hoa yu bin 'don 'no 'yi?
 how 2SG.SBJ PST PFV know 3SG.OBL
 'How did you get to know him?'

In addition to typical completive markers (often based on *done* in English-based languages and on *acabar* 'finish' in Ibero-Romance-based languages), which put special emphasis on the completion of an event, perfect and perfective markers may be used in this way as well. Thus, Seychelles Creole (*i*)*n* (as in (2)) is generally a perfect marker, and in Korlai, the ordinary perfective past tense can be used with inchoative meaning:

(10) Korlai (Clements 2013)
 Teru sabew ki ʌnkɔl tɛ aki.
 Teru know.PFV.PST that uncle COP.PRS here
 'Teru found out that uncle is here.'

Korlai forms like *sabew* are inherited from the Portuguese lexifier, where the perfective past tense also has inchoative meaning with some state verbs. So conservative cases such as (10) are rather different from cases like (8)–(9), which represent innovations vis-à-vis the lexifier. However, since completive and perfective forms are difficult to distinguish in a general way, they have been lumped together here.

Languages with a completive marker with inchoative meaning are found in the Caribbean and West Africa, but also outside this region. At least in languages that have been in contact with Chinese, this pattern can be attributed to Chinese influence. For example, in Singlish, the completive marker *already* is used in much the same way as Hokkien *liau* (corresponding to Mandarin *le*), and this in turn corresponds to Singapore Bazaar Malay *sudah*.

(11) Singlish (Bao 2005: 239)
 *The tongue red **already**.*
 'The tongue {has turned/turned} red.'
 (not: 'The tongue was red.')

For the Atlantic creoles, the source of the completive marker with inchoative meaning is not equally clear. But it is striking that languages where both a progressive marker and a completive marker have inchoative meaning occur only in West Africa and the Caribbean.

6. The nature of the state words

For the classification of our languages, we simply asked whether the inchoative effect occurs at all, not whether it occurs with all state words. There seems to be considerable variability in this regard. For example, in Jamaican, *im de taiyad* (with the progressive marker *de*) means 'he is becoming tired', but *di bwai de bad* means 'the boy is being bad', not 'the boy is becoming bad' (Farquharson 2013). In Louisiana Creole (see 6), only a few state words such as *fatige* 'tired' and *choke* 'angry' allow this meaning of the marker *ape*.

For this feature, we have assumed that the variation between languages concerns the meaning of the progressive markers, but one might also look at it differently, from the point of view of the meaning of the "state words". It might be that at least in some languages, the meaning of words that translate as 'tired', 'ripe', 'big', 'wet', and so on is not a state meaning, but a dynamic meaning, that is, these words really mean 'become tired', 'ripen', 'become big', 'become wet', etc. The inchoative meaning with progressive and completive markers would thus not be surprising, because it is the basic meaning of the words. The state meaning ('is tired', 'is ripe', 'is wet', etc.) arises in a perfect(ive) context, and perfective is of course often expressed by zero: as we saw in the preceding chapter, unmarked dynamic verbs often have past (perfective) reference. A clear example of this is the word *wô* in Principense: *Bana sê sa wô* [plantain the PROG ripen] means 'The plantain is ripening', and the state 'The plantain is ripe' is expressed by the zero-marked perfective aspect: *Bana sê ∅ wô* [plantain the PFV ripen] 'The plantain (has) ripened (i.e. is ripe)' (Maurer 2013c). The word *wô* cannot be used attributively by itself, but needs the participial suffix *-du* (*bana wôdu* 'ripe banana'). According to Migge (2003: 87), a similar situation is found in Nengee and Gbe, and probably more widely in Atlantic creoles.

52 Aspect markers and inchoative meaning

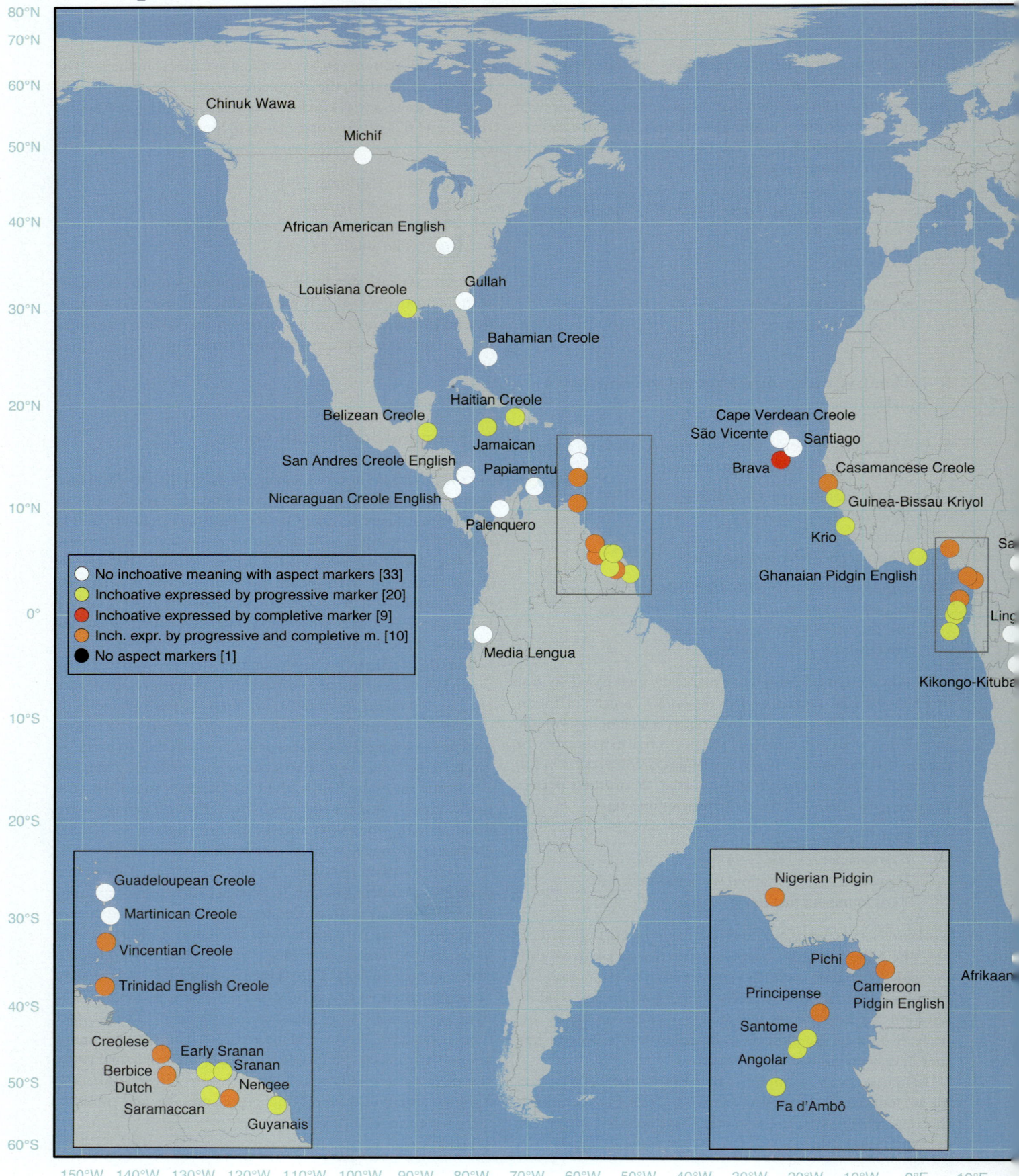

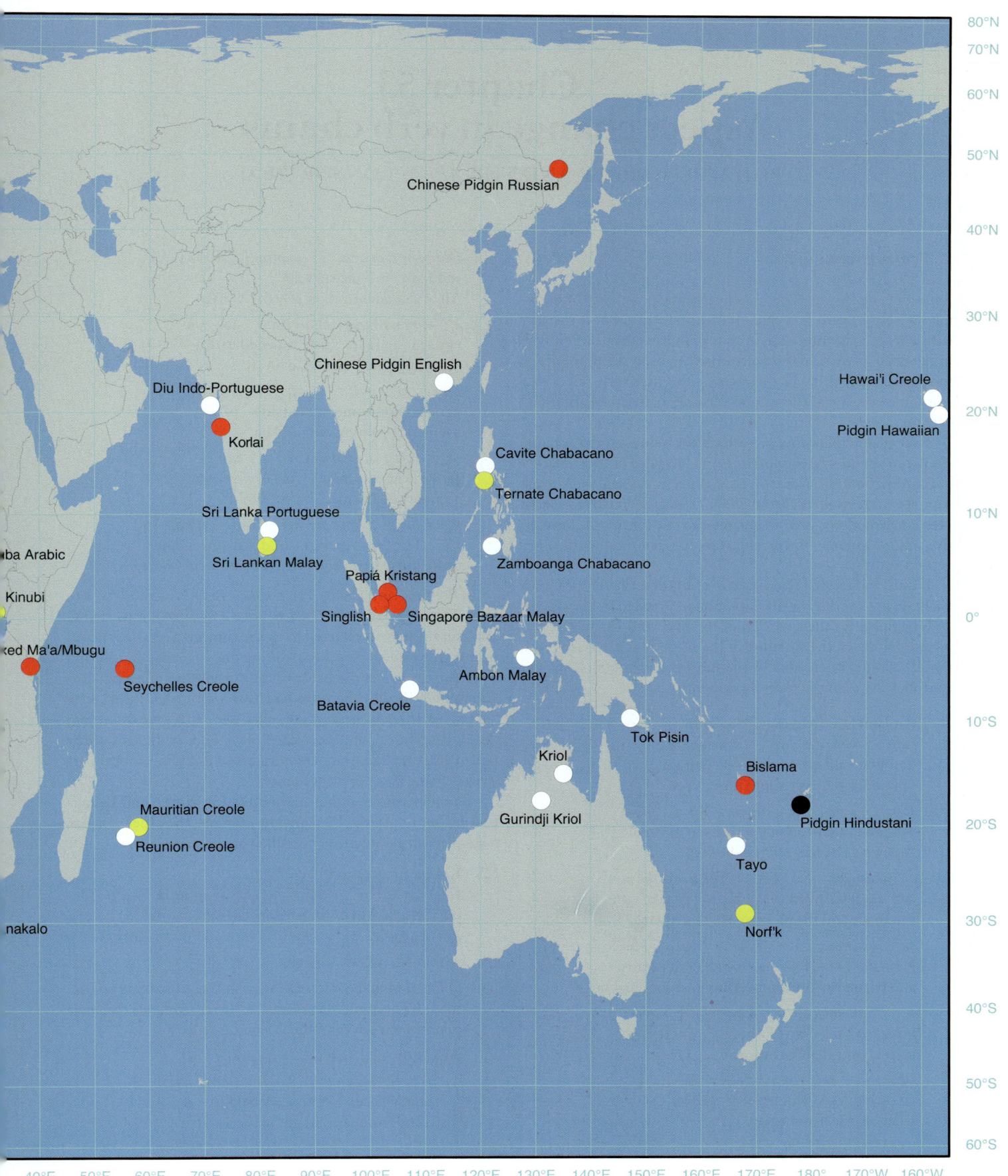

Chapter 53
Aspect change in verb chains
PHILIPPE MAURER AND THE *APiCS* CONSORTIUM

1. Feature description

Aspect change in verb chains concerns the possibility of marking the second verb in a chain for imperfective aspect (usually with a progressive function) in spite of the fact that the first verb in the chain is marked—or zero-marked, as in many creoles—for perfective aspect. In these cases, the first verb refers to a story line event, and the second verb refers to a backgrounded event.

Note that in this context, **verb chain** is understood as being similar to **serial verb constructions** (absence of overt marker of coordination, subordination, or syntactic dependency of any sort, see Aikhenvald & Dixon 2006: 1); but, in contrast to serial verb constructions, verb chains refer to two (or more) consecutive actions whereby the second verb does not modify the other verb in any way.

It must be stressed that the two events described by the verb chain do not overlap, i.e. the situation referred to by the second verb begins after the situation of the first verb has been completed. However, the situation of the second verb overlaps with the situation(s) referred to by the subsequent verb(s). Consider the following example from Papiamentu:

(1) Papiamentu (Maurer 1988: 260)
Yan a kana bai dirèkt den santana.
Yan PFV walk go directly LOC church
'Yan walked directly into the church.

Pareu ku Yan a yega, Yan a mira
as.soon.as that Yan PFV arrive Yan PFV see
As soon as he had arrived, he saw

e skòp ku e piki. Yan a kohe nan
ART spade with ART pickaxe Yan PFV take 3PL
the spade and the pickaxe. He took them

ta bai kas. Pero apénas Yan a bira
PROG go home but no.sooner Yan PFV turn
and began walking home. But no sooner had he

su lomba el a tende: [. . .]. Yan a
POSS.3SG back 3SG PFV hear Yan PFV
turned over than he heard: [. . .]. He

sigui ta bai, Yan a bolbe tende: [. . .].
go.on PROG go Yan PFV REP hear
went on. He heard again: [. . .].

Di ripiente un stèm a puntra: [. . .] Yan [. . .]
suddenly a voice PFV ask Yan
All of a sudden, a voice asked: [. . .] Yan

a mira un buraku mitar habrí, ku un
PFV see a hole half opened with a
saw a hole, half opened, with

hende ta sali afó. [. . .] el a
person PROG come.out outside 3SG PFV
somebody coming out [. . .] he

yega serka e hòmbër, el a bati'é
arrive near ART man 3SG PFV hit=3SG
approached the man, he hit him

mata, der'é na drechi i sali bai kas.
kill bury=3SG on right and leave go home
dead, buried him correctly, left and went home.'

In the first verb chain, *Yan a kohe nan ta bai kas*, *ta bai kas*, literally 'was going home', starts after *a kohe nan* 'took them'; but Yan, the person referred to by the subject, performs the action of going home (*ta bai kas*) during the whole paragraph, and so *ta bai kas* forms the background for all the following situations, described by the verbs *bira* 'turn over', *tende* 'hear', *sigui* 'go on', *bolbe tende* 'hear again', *mira* 'see', *bati'e mata* 'hit him dead', *dera* 'bury', and *sali* 'leave'. It is only at the end of the paragraph that Yan, the person referred to by the subject, arrives at home (*bai kas* 'went home').

A similar construction can be found in Korlai and Batavia Creole, but unlike the Papiamentu example, the aspect change takes place in paratactic or coordinated constructions:

(2) Korlai (do Couto 1996: 275)
Rhat ja tumo patɛk. El marcha-n
rat PFV take.PVF watermelon 3SG walk-PROG

ku kami. El ja kaso.
with road 3SG PFV tire.PFV

'The rat took the watermelon, then began walking on the road. It got tired.' (Portuguese: 'O rato tomou a melancia e continuou seu caminho. Ficou cansado.')

(3) Batavia Creole (Maurer 2011: 54f.)
[. . .] e ∅ acha por ola di londji ung
and PFV get PURP see from far ART
'[. . .] and from far they got to see a

liang [...]. *Di medu ilotër ste kore e*
lion   of fear 3PL IPFV run and
lion. [...]. Being afraid they began running away and

∅ *chega na sidadi.*
PFV arrive LOC city
arrived at the city.'

In other words, the aspect change illustrated in examples (2) and (3) does not take place in a verb chain and is therefore not regarded as an aspect change in a verb chain.

Notice that in European languages like Portuguese and English it is not possible, or at least not common, to have such an aspect change in two coordinated or two paratactic sentences:

(4) Portuguese
Eles viram   um leão. */?Eles estavam
3PL see.PST.PFV a lion 3PL   COP.3PL.PST

a   correr e chegaram   à cidade.
PREP run   and arrive.PST.PFV at city
'They saw a lion. They */? were running and arrived at the city.'

In both Portuguese and English, an inceptive-aspect verb is used: *continuou seu caminho* and **began walking**, or *começaram a correr* and **began running**. But the fact that the Portuguese and English translations use an inceptive-aspect verb does not mean that the creole progressive markers have an inceptive-aspect function. If they did, they could not form the background for subsequent situations since inceptive verbs refer to the beginning of a situation and not to its duration. In Portuguese, it is the noun phrase *seu caminho* and the infinitive *correr* that form the background, and in English the gerunds *walking* and *running*.

2. The values

For this feature, the following three values are distinguished:

●	1. Aspect change in verb chains is possible	17
●	2. Aspect change in verb chains is not possible	24
○	3. Verb chaining does not exist	25

Value 1 (**Aspect change in verb chains**) is an almost exclusively Atlantic feature occurring in West Africa (eight languages) as well as in the Caribbean (also eight languages), the exception being Mauritian Creole in the Indian Ocean.

This value is found in eight Ibero-Romance-based languages, in four English-based languages, in four French-based languages, and in Berbice Dutch. It occurs exclusively in creole languages. Examples (5) to (10) illustrate the phenomenon further.

(5) Cape Verdean Creole of São Vicente (Swolkien 2013)
No táva te   andá, un d'es   ∅   vrá te   xutá-nos.
1PL PST PROG walk one of.DEM PFV turn PROG kick-1PL
'We were walking, one of them turned [and began] to kick us.'

(6) Guinea-Bissau Kriyol (Intumbo et al. 2013)
N ∅ sai na   yanda ba na   strada,
1SG PFV leave PROG walk PST LOC road

katcur ladran   toki N   tciga kasa.
dog   bark.1SG until 1SG arrive home
'I left [and while I] was walking on the road, a dog barked at me till I got home.'

Note that in example (6), the second verb is not only marked for aspect (*na*), but also for tense (*ba*).

(7) Principense (Maurer 2013c)
N   xyê sa   ke   n'ifi-kumin, kasô kupa mi ten
1SG leave PROG IPFV.go LOC=road   dog bark 1SG till

txyô.
farm
'I left [and while I] was walking on the road, a dog barked at me till I got home.'

(8) Creolese (Devonish & Thompson 2013)
Mi ∅ lef mi   hous a   waak dong
1SG PFV leave POSS.1SG house IPFV walk down

di   rood an daag kom baak bihain mi.
DEF road and dog come bark behind 1SG
'I left my house and was walking down the road, when a dog came behind me barking.'

(9) Saramaccan (Aboh et al. 2013)
A   ∅   fáa   páu tá   túe.
3SG PFV chop tree PROG fall
'He is felling the tree (i.e. at this very moment the tree is falling).'

(10) Guadeloupean Creole (Colot & Ludwig 2013a)
An ∅   pati ka   maché tou byen, mwen enki
1SG PFV leave PROG walk all good 1SG suddenly

vwè on   chyen douvan mwen.
see INDF dog   in.front.of 1SG
'I left and as I was walking idly, I suddenly saw a dog in front of me.'

This almost exclusively Atlantic construction needs more investigation to establish its exact syntactic status.

53 Aspect change in verb chains

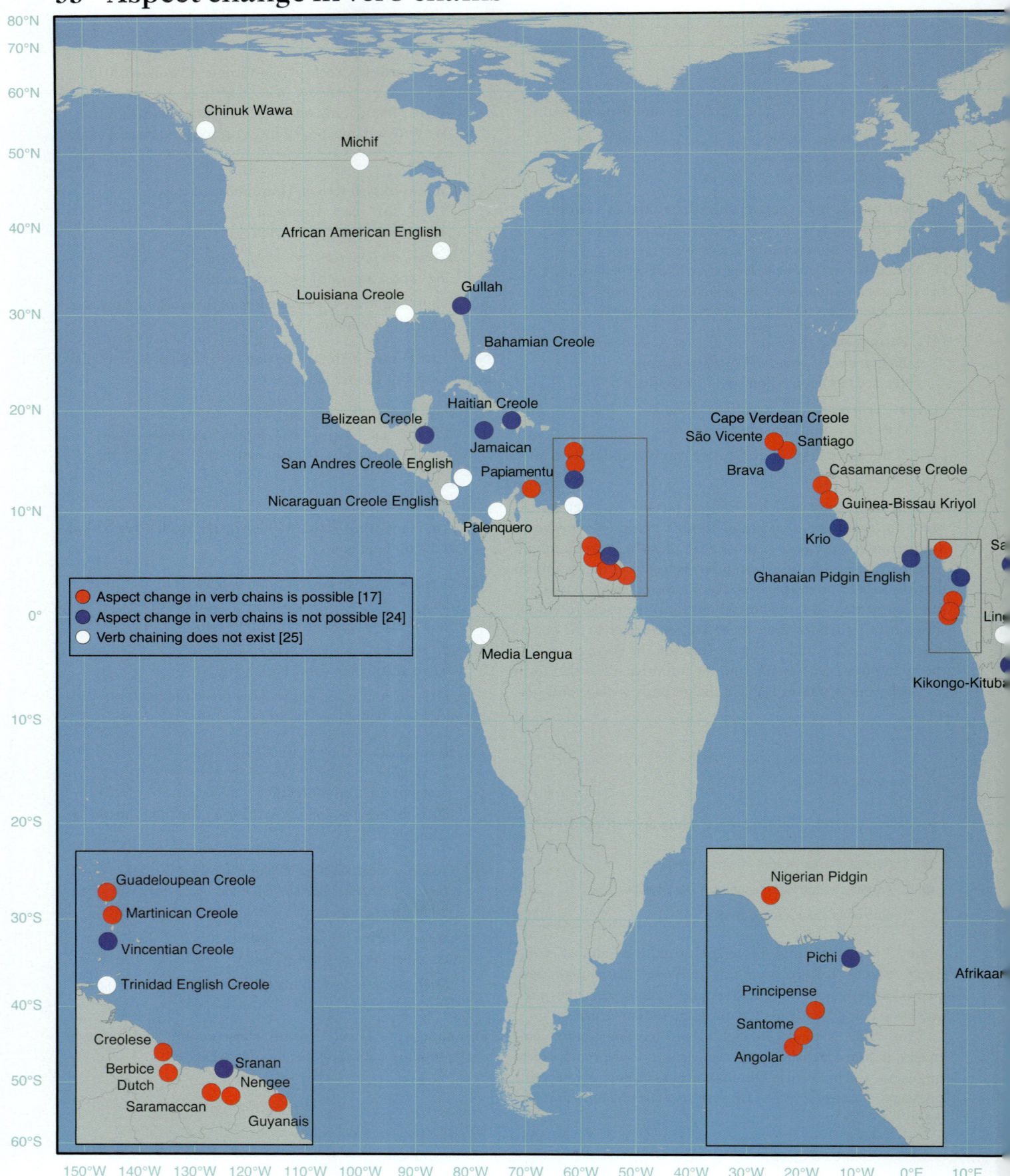

210

Chapter 54
Suppletion according to tense and aspect

PHILIPPE MAURER AND THE *APiCS* CONSORTIUM

1. Feature description

In this chapter, we ask whether verbs exhibit suppletion (different stems in different grammatical contexts) depending on different tense or aspect forms. We distinguish two degrees of suppletion. In **strong suppletion**, there are two different stems that share no phonological material at all (as English *go* vs. *went*), whereas in **weak suppletion**, the two irregularly related stems share some phonological material (as English *think* vs. *thought*).

It is irrelevant for this feature how many verbs in a given language exhibit strong or weak suppletion. It suffices that verbal suppletion exists in only one verb. Note that in most *APiCS* languages, suppletion occurs only in a few high-frequency verbs.

We consider only stem suppletion (as English *go* vs. *went*). Formal irregularity is determined by synchronic, not by diachronic, criteria; therefore, the historical origin of the suppletive forms and their etymologies are not taken into account here.

This feature is related to *WALS* feature 79 (Veselinova 2005).

2. The values

We distinguish the following six values:

○	1. Weak suppletion according to tense only	6
●	2. Strong suppletion according to tense only	17
○	3. Weak suppletion according to aspect only	2
●	4. Strong suppletion according to aspect only	1
●	5. Strong suppletion according to both tense and aspect	5
○	6. No suppletion according to tense or aspect	45

Less than half of our languages show any suppletion, and in most of them, suppletion is according to tense (generally present vs. past tense).

Value 1 (**weak suppletion according to tense only**) is found in four Ibero-Romance-based languages (Cape Verdean Creole of Brava, Palenquero, Papiamentu, Cavite Chabacano), as well as in Kinubi and Norf'k.

(1) Cape Verdean Creole of Brava (Baptista 2013)
   a. *N ten fidju ki ten seti fidju.*
      1SG have child REL have seven child
      'I have a child that has seven children.'
   b. *Es tinha ses kazinha ma es ben bende.*
      3PL have.PST POSS.3PL house but 3PL come sell
      'They had their house but they came to sell it.'

(2) Kinubi (Luffin 2013)
   a. *ána kun "well organized"*
      1SG COP.PRS well organized
      'I am well organized.'
   b. *Úmun kan ásker.*
      3PL COP.PST soldier
      'They were soldiers.'

Weak suppletion should be taken to mean 'at most weak suppletion'. If a language shows both weak and strong suppletion, it is classified as having strong suppletion.

Value 2 (**strong suppletion according to tense only**) occurs in six Ibero-Romance-based languages, in seven English-based languages, in two French-based languages, and in two Dutch-based languages.

(3) Negerhollands (van Sluijs 2013)
   a. *Jack, ju skun mi skon.*
      Jack 2SG shoe COP.PRES clean
      'Jack, your shoes are clean.'
   b. *[…] mushi fan sinu a wēs me am.*
      many of 3PL PST COP with 3SG
      '[…] many of them were with him.'

(4) Hawai'i Creole (Velupillai 2013)
   a. *Ai no is da seim wan […].*
      1SG know COP.PRS ART same one
      'I know it's the same one […].'
   b. *Sambaɾi waz ɹaɪd dɛa.*
      somebody COP.PST right there
      'Somebody was right there.'

(5) Reunion Creole (Bollée 2013)
   Mwen lé byen kontan./ Mwen lété byen
   1SG COP.PRS well pleased 1SG COP.PST well

kontan.| Mi sra byen kontan.
pleased 1SG COP.FUT well pleased
'I am very pleased./I was very pleased./I will be very pleased.'

In the Reunion Creole example, the opposition between *le* vs. *lete* is a case of weak suppletion according to tense, but the opposition between these two markers and *sra* is a case of strong suppletion according to tense.

(6) Nicaraguan Creole English (Bartens 2013a)
   a. *Wat dat iz?*
      what DEM COP.PRS
      'What is that?'
   b. *Ai liv-d tu sii hou wi woz obiidient.*
      1SG live-PST to see how we COP.PST obedient
      'I lived at the time and recall how obedient we were.'
   c. *Aligieta gou ap tu footiin fiit.*
      alligator go.PRS up to fourteen feet
      'Alligators measure up to fourteen feet.'
   d. *Hou yu gwain hevn an noh hav*
      how 2SG go.PRES.PROG heaven and not have
      wing fa flai?
      wing for fly
      'How are you going to heaven even though you don't have wings to fly?'
   e. *Wi gaan de twelv oklak.*
      1PL go.PST there twelve o'clock
      'We went there at twelve o'clock.'

In the Nicaraguan Creole English examples, the opposition between *iz* and *woz* shows strong suppletion according to tense, the opposition between *gou* and *gaan* illustrates weak suppletion according to tense, and *gwain* refers to weak aspect suppletion. Remember that in languages with strong suppletion, weak suppletion is not taken into account in order to assign the value.

Value 3 (**weak suppletion according to aspect only**) occurs in San Andres Creole English and in Saramaccan.

(7) Saramaccan (Aboh et al. 2013)
   a. *Mi go a di wosu.*
      1SG go LOC ART house
      'I went to the house.'
   b. *Me ta ko, mi nango.*
      1SG.NEG PROG come 1SG PROG.go
      'I am not coming, I am leaving.'

Value 4 (**strong suppletion according to aspect only**) occurs only in Chinese Pidgin Russian: *xodi* 'go (imperfective)' vs. *pafola* 'has gone (perfective)'.

Value 5, **strong suppletion according to both tense and aspect**, occurs in four Portuguese-based creoles (Cape Verdean Creole of São Vicente, Casamancese Creole, Principense, Korlai), as well as in Creolese.

(8) Cape Verdean Creole of São Vicente (Swolkien 2013)
   a. *N ka sabê.| N ka sabia.*
      1SG NEG know. 1SG NEG know.PST.IPFV
      N sub.
      1SG know.PST.PFV
      'I don't know./I didn't know./I got to know.'
   b. *Última foi| éra| e*
      last COP.PST.PFV COP.PST.IPFV COP.PRS
      nha tia.
      POSS.1SG aunt
      'The last one was/is my aunt.'

Example (8a) illustrates weak suppletion according to tense and aspect, and example (8b) illustrates strong suppletion according to tense and aspect.

(9) Korlai (Clements 2013)
   yo tanan| yo ti andan| yo ti anda
   1SG go.PROG.PRS 1SG PST go.PROG 1SG PST go.HAB
   yo yafoy
   1SG go.PST.PFV
   'I am going/I was going/I used to go/I went'

3. Distribution

Suppletion, strong or weak, occurs in 31 *APiCS* languages, or 41 per cent of the sample. It is present in all regions of the world, except in Southeast Asia and the Pacific, but almost exclusively in creole languages, the exceptions being African American English, Afrikaans, and Chinese Pidgin Russian.

In the *APiCS* languages, only few verbs show suppletion according to tense and aspect; in most cases, these verbs are statives ('be', 'have', 'know'); the most frequent dynamic verb showing suppletion is 'go'. All these verbs are very frequently used verbs, in the lexifier languages as well as in the *APiCS* languages themselves.

In the *WALS* languages (see Veselinova 2005), tense and aspect suppletion occurs mainly in Europe and Western Asia up to South Asia, whereas in the *APiCS* languages, it is very frequent in the Caribbean and West Africa. In most *APiCS* languages, tense and aspect suppletion is inherited from their European lexifiers.

54 Suppletion according to tense and aspect

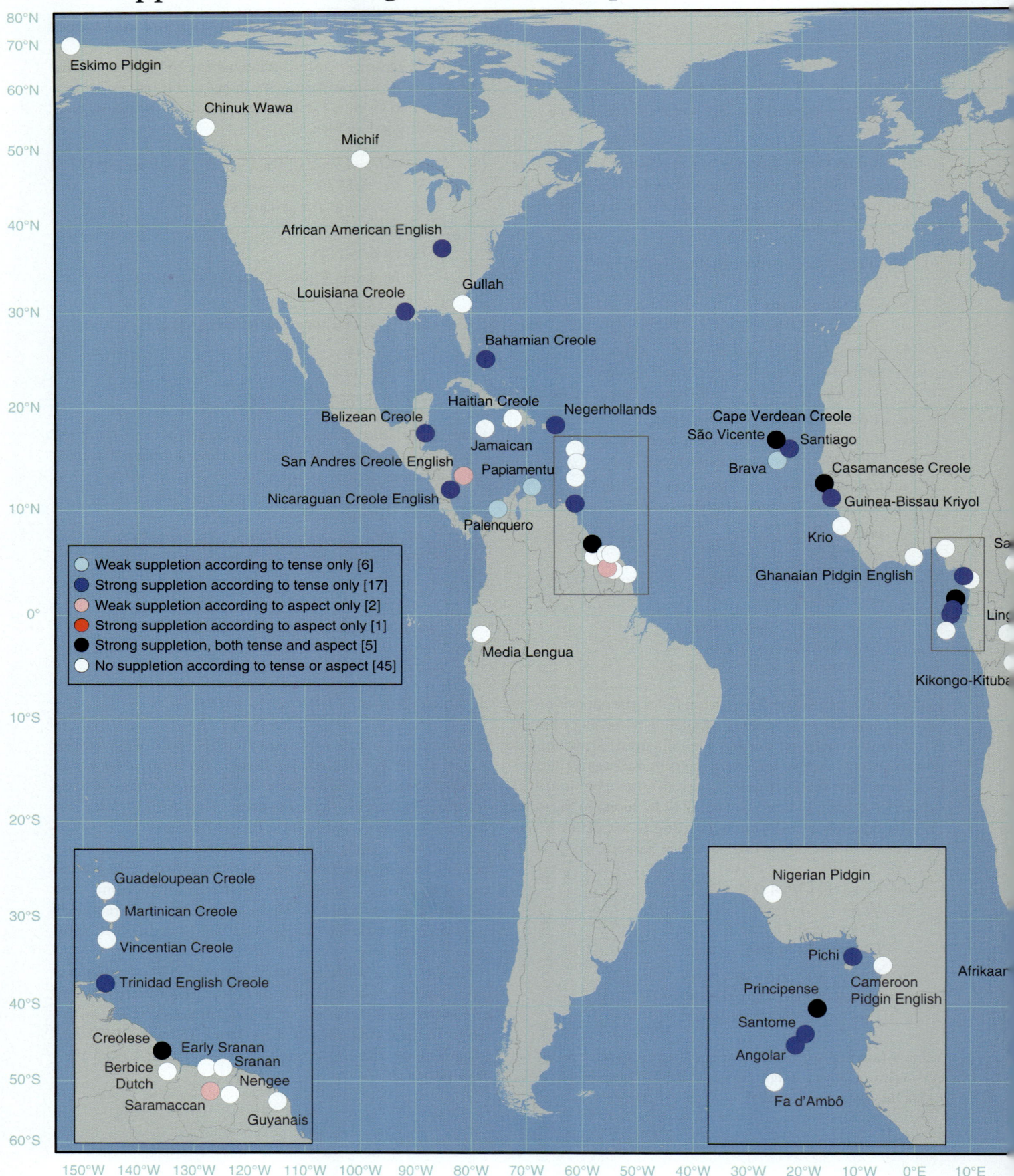

Chapter 55
Ability verb and epistemic possibility

PHILIPPE MAURER AND THE *APiCS* CONSORTIUM

1. Feature description

In quite a few languages, epistemic possibility may be expressed by the same verb as ability. For example, German *kann kommen* can mean 'is able to come' (ability) or 'may come' (epistemic possibility).

By **ability**, we refer broadly to various non-epistemic possibility types comprising **mental participant-internal ability** (French *savoir* 'know, can': *il sait nager* 'He can swim'), **physical participant-internal ability** ('He can lift 100 kilograms'), and **participant-external possibility** ('She can go to town by bus', e.g. because there is a bus connection).

Epistemic **possibility** concerns the speaker's judgement as to the truth value of the sentence, as exemplified by the English adverbs 'perhaps' or 'possibly'. See also *WALS* feature 76 ("Overlap between situational and epistemic modal marking", van der Auwera & Ammann 2005), which is concerned not only with possibility, but also with necessity.

2. The values

We distinguish the following three values:

🔴	1. Ability verb also expresses epistemic possibility	32
🔵	2. Ability verb cannot express epistemic possibility	41
⚪	3. No ability verb	2

Value 1 (the ability verb can also express epistemic possibility) occurs in 42 per cent of the *APiCS* languages. It is present in ten Ibero-Romance-based languages, in eight English-based languages, in seven French-based languages, in three Dutch-based languages, as well as in Lingala, Mixed Ma'a/Mbugu, Sango, and Sri Lankan Malay. In the examples below, (a) shows an ability verb, and (b) shows its use to express epistemic possibility.

(1) Papiamentu (Kouwenberg 2013b)
 a. *E ora nan lo mester por papia ingles*
  ART hour 3PL MOOD must can speak English
  ku e turistanan.
  with DEF tourist.PL
  'In that case they have to be able to speak English with the tourists.'

 b. *Lo e tabata por ta traha den kurá*
  MOOD 3SG PST can PROG work LOC yard
  ora b'a bèl.
  when 2SG=PFV call
  'He was possibly working in the yard when you called (on the phone).'

(2) Sri Lanka Portuguese (Smith 2013)
 a. *Tɔɔna aka midisaam inda uŋa-pa*
  afterwards DEM measurement yet one-DAT
  araa naa poy-ski.
  go.wrong NEG.FUT can-REPORT
  'Subsequently, it won't be possible for the measurement to be misinterpreted by someone else, apparently.'

 b. *Asii mee kii see pooy teem.*
  so FOC what COND can COP
  'It may be something like that.'

(3) Cavite Chabacano (Sippola 2013a)
 a. *Ya pudi cumpra yo aquel nuevo libro.*
  PFV can buy 2SG DEM new book
  'I was able to buy that new book.'

 b. *Puede llega el carta mañana.*
  can arrive ART letter tomorrow
  'The letter may arrive tomorrow.'

(4) Saramaccan (Aboh et al. 2013)
 a. *A taánga téee. A sa hópo wán hóndo kiló.*
  3SG strong IDEO 3SG can lift.up one hundred kilo
  'S/he is strong, s/he can lift a hundred kilos.'

 b. *A sa gó a húku.*
  3SG can go LOC hook
  'She might have gone fishing.'

(5) Seychelles Creole (Michaelis & Rosalie 2013)
 a. *Be en zwazo konmyen dizef i kapab ponn?*
  but ART bird how.many egg 3SG can lay
  'But a bird, how many eggs can it lay?'

 b. *Mon ti kapab annan 'pepre dan trez an par*
  1SG PST can have about in thirteen year through
  la.
  there
  'I was probably about thirteen years old.'

(6) Negerhollands (van Sluijs 2013)
a. *Ham na **kan** ris də stēn.*
   3SG NEG can lift ART stone
   'He cannot lift the stone.'

b. *Am ha sē, Adinja na **kan** sē am ēntēn lik:*
   3SG PST say Adinja NEG can say 3SG no lie
   di fo ha sómgut am maṅké am fo du.
   DET must have something 3SG want 3SG to do
   'He said, Adinja cannot have told him any lie: there must be something he wants him to do.'

(7) Mixed Ma'a/Mbugu (Mous 2013)
a. *Símúru ku'onhi na gomaé.*
   1SG.NEG.can 15.wash with clothes
   'I can't swim with clothes.'

b. *Hahali mikó ishirini i-lit-íye*
   16.other PL.year twenty 4-come-PRF
   ki-múru kulá.
   7-can 15.get.lost
   'Otherwise, in twenty years the language may get lost.'

(8) Sango (Samarin 2013)
a. *Gi Nzapa oko **alingbi** ti sara so.*
   only God one PM-be.able of do DEM
   'Only God can do that.'

b. *Ala **lingbi** ti si kekereke ape.*
   3PL can of arrive tomorrow NEG
   'They might not arrive tomorrow.'

(9) Sri Lankan Malay (Slomanson 2013)
Anakpədə na koolangyang məsubrang na
child.PL DAT lake.ACC INF.cross DAT
məbərənang na boolɛ.
INF-swim DAT can
'The children can swim across the lake.'/'The children might swim across the lake.'

Value 2 (**the ability verb cannot express epistemic possibility**) occurs in 55 per cent of the *APiCS* languages, and value 3, there is **no ability verb** in the language, concerns only Chinuk Wawa and Yimas-Arafundi Pidgin.

3. Geographical distribution

From the Atlantic to South Asia, the distribution of value 1 (ability verb can express epistemic modality) and value 2 (ability verb cannot express epistemic modality) is about equal, but value 1 is virtually absent from Southeast Asia and the Pacific, the only exception being Cavite Chabacano.

4. Etymological considerations

Interestingly, not all ability verbs in the English- and French-based languages are derived from the lexifiers' ability verbs (English *can*, French *pouvoir*). In English-based creoles and pidgins, we find *sa* (< Portuguese *saver*?) in Nengee and Saramaccan, *fit* (< English *be fit*) in Cameroon Pidgin English, Ghanaian Pidgin English, Nigerian Pidgin, and Pichi, *save* (< Portuguese *saber* 'know') in Bislama, *ebul* and *ell* (English < *be able*) in Krio and Norf'k, and *inap* (English < *enough*) in Tok Pisin.

French-based creoles often show verbs deriving from French *être capable de* 'be able to': *kapab/kab* in Haitian, *kapab* in Louisiana Creole, Reunion Creole, and Seychelles Creole, as well as *kapav* in Mauritian Creole (see also Kriegel et al. 2003). Tayo shows *mwaya* (French < *avoir les moyens* de 'have the means to'). These expressions all denote only ability in the lexifiers, so the extension to epistemic use must have occurred at a later stage.

5. Theoretical issues

In some *APiCS* languages, the complement of the modal verb may take tense and aspect markers when the 'can' verb has epistemic meaning, as in example (1b) or in the following example:

(10) Guadeloupean Creole (Colot & Ludwig 2013a)
I pé ka manjé.
3SG can PROG eat
'He may be eating.'

In Early Sranan, according to van den Berg & Bruyn (2013), "[t]he epistemic reading of *kan* seems possible only with progressives, and perhaps statives, including the copula *de*." In other languages, Papiamentu for example, the present (imperfective) marker *ta*, the past imperfective marker *tabata*, and the perfective marker *a* may modify the complement of the modal verb; only the future marker *lo* is precluded (see Maurer 1988: 277–90).

This raises the question of the syntactic status of 'can' (and other modal verbs): is it a verb or should it rather be considered as belonging to the set of tense, aspect, and mood markers? Of course, there can be only language-specific answers to this question. In Papiamentu, for example, there are two arguments that point to the verbal status of *por* 'can': it may stand alone, and it may itself be modified by the future marker *lo* or the past imperfective marker *tabata* (see 1b).

The syntactic status of modals and the possibility of modifying the complement of modal verbs with tense and aspect markers merits a thorough cross-linguistic investigation.

55 Ability verb and epistemic possibility

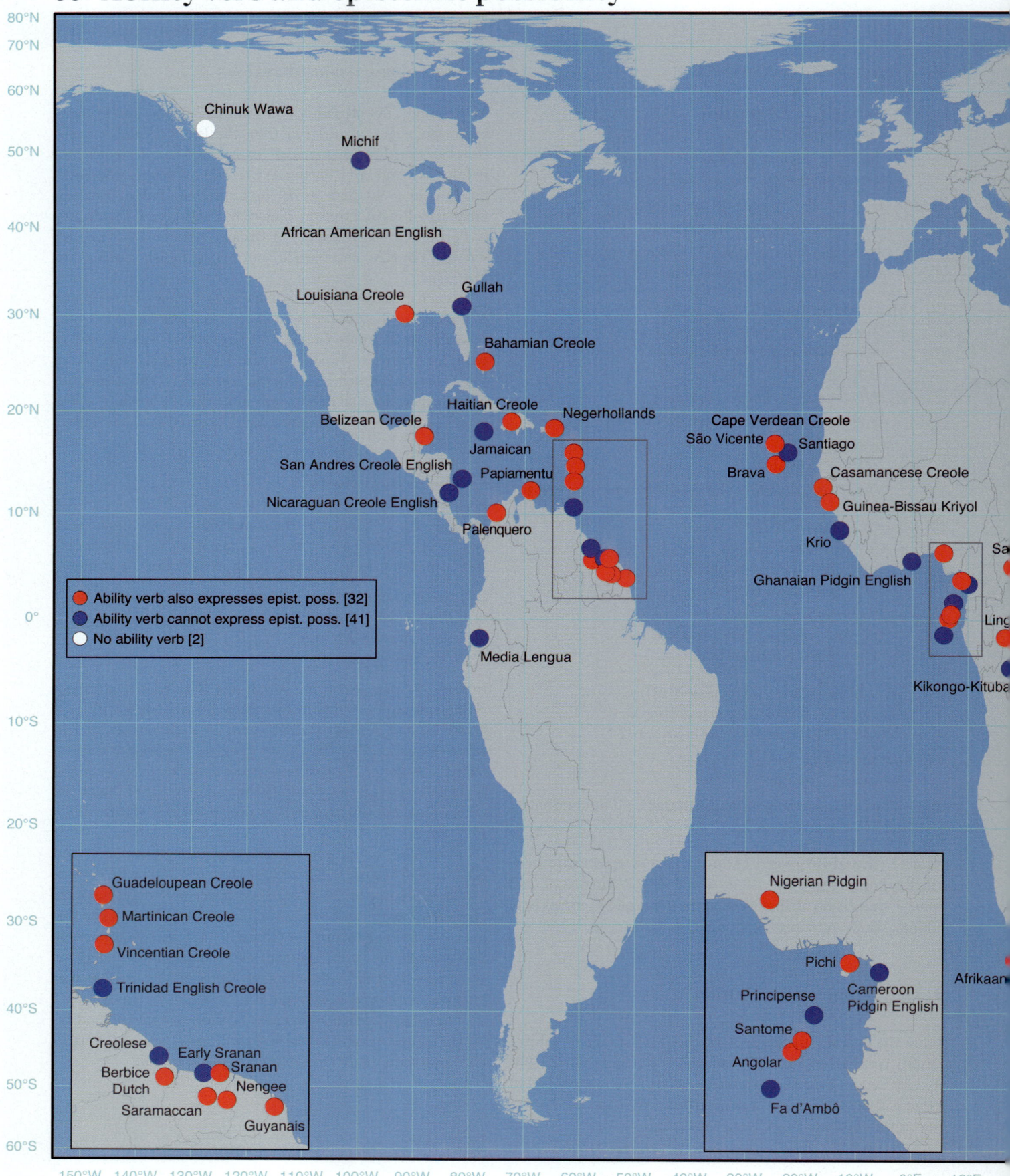

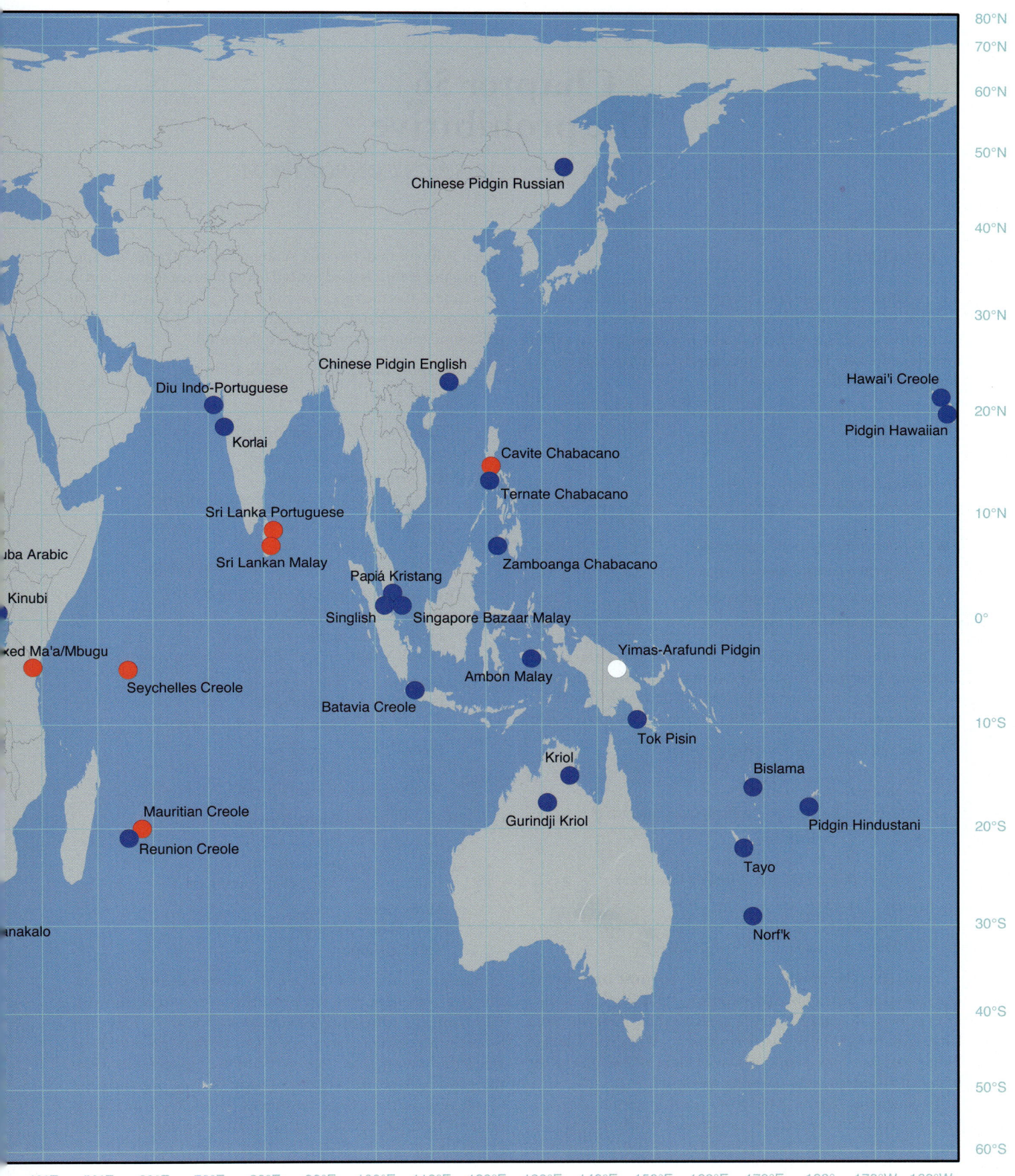

Chapter 56
The prohibitive

PHILIPPE MAURER AND THE *APiCS* CONSORTIUM

1. Introduction

The prohibitive is the negated counterpart of the affirmative imperative, as in Papiamentu *No bai!* 'Don't go!' Only the singular prohibitive is considered here, that is, prohibition addressed to a single addressee. The corresponding *WALS* chapter is van der Auwera et al. (2005).

2. The values

We distinguish the following values:

		excl	shrd	all
●	1. Normal imperative, normal negator	45	7	52
●	2. Normal imperative, special negator	13	4	17
●	3. Special imperative, normal negator	8	2	10
●	4. Special imperative, special negator	1	1	2

The prohibitive may have the same form as the affirmative imperative (**normal imperative construction**) and the same sentential negative construction found in declarative sentences (**normal negator**) (value 1). This is the most widespread value.

(1) Berbice Dutch (Kouwenberg 2013a)
 a. *lu ju-jɛ nau*
 look 2SG-NMLZ now
 'Now look at yours!' (affirmative imperative)
 b. *ɛkɛ-jɔ mja dida ka*
 1SG-NMLZ do that NEG
 'Mine doesn't do that.' (normal negator)
 c. *bu so-fɛlɛ ka*
 drink so-much NEG
 'Don't drink so much!' (prohibitive)

Sometimes the prohibitive uses the **normal imperative construction but a special negator** (value 2). This occurs in five Ibero-Romance-based languages, three English-based languages, three Malay-based languages, Afrikaans, Chinese Pidgin Russian, Juba Arabic, Michif, Pidgin Hawaiian, and the bilingual mixed language Gurindji Kriol.

In Singapore Bazaar Malay the special negator *jangan* is used in prohibitive sentences, as opposed to the negator *tak*, which is found in declarative sentences; in Afrikaans, the special negator *moenie* is used instead of the first negator *nie*, and in Juba Arabic, it is the special negator *máta* which is used instead of the normal negator *ma* (but see example 6, Kinubi, which looks similar but was interpreted differently).

(2) Singapore Bazaar Malay (Khin Khin Aye 2013)
 a. *Tengok!*
 look
 'Look!' (affirmative imperative)
 b. *Dia tak ada kerja sekarang.*
 3SG NEG PROG work now
 'He is not working now.' (normal negator)
 c. *Jangan lupa jumpa saya.*
 PROH forget meet 1SG
 'Don't forget to visit me.' (prohibitive)

(3) Afrikaans (den Besten & Biberauer 2013)
 a. *Praat Xhosa, asseblief!*
 speak Xhosa please
 'Speak Xhosa, please!' (affirmative imperative)
 b. *Ek praat nie Engels nie.*
 1SG speak NEG English NEG
 'I don't speak English.' (normal negator)
 c. *Moenie Duits praat nie!*
 PROH German speak NEG
 'Don't speak German!' (prohibitive)

(4) Juba Arabic (Manfredi & Petrollino 2013)
 a. *Ruwa!* b. *Bolís ma bi-ásalo.*
 go police NEG IRR-ask
 'Go!' 'The police doesn't ask.'
 c. *Máta bíga zalán.*
 PROH.SG become angry
 'Don't be angry!'

The prohibitive may also use the **same negator** as in declarative sentences, but the **prohibitive construction differs from the affirmative imperative** (value 3). This value is relatively rare (ten languages). There are three possibilities in which this value may be realized. In the five Upper Guinea Portuguese-based creoles (Guinea-Bissau Kriyol, Casamancese Creole, and the three Cape Verdean varieties), in Cavite Chabacano, in Belizean Creole, and in Kinubi, the negator is used both in declarative and prohibitive sentences, but, in contrast to the affirmative imperative, the subject pronoun is obligatory in the prohibitive.

(5) Casamancese Creole (Biagui & Quint 2013)
   a. *Kantá!*
      sing
      'Sing!' (affirmative imperative)
   b. *Bu ka kantá.*
      2SG NEG sing
      'You did not sing.' (normal negator)
   c. *Ka bu kantá.*
      NEG 2SG sing
      'Don't sing!' (prohibitive)

(6) Kinubi (Luffin 2013)
   a. *Rúa!*   b. *Íta ma gi-rúa.*
      go   2SG NEG TAM-go
      'Go!'   'You don't go.'
   c. *Ma ta rúa.*
      NEG 2SG go
      'Don't go!'

Another possibility illustrating value 3 is found exclusively in Lingala. In this language, the negator *té* is used both in declarative and prohibitive sentences; however, in this case, the prohibitive construction differs from the affirmative imperative in that it does not use the imperative suffix *-á* (with a high tone, as opposed to the final vowel *-a*, with a low tone).

(7) Lingala (Meeuwis 2013)
   a. *Sál-á!*
      work-IMP
      'Work!' (affirmative imperative)
   b. *O-sál-áki té.*
      2SG-work-PST NEG
      'You did not work.' (normal negator)
   c. *Ko-sál-a té!*
      INF-work-FV NEG
      'Don't work!' (prohibitive)

The last subtype of value 3 occurs only in Pichi. In this language, the prohibitive uses the same negator *no* as in declarative sentences, but additionally, the subjunctive particle *mek* may head a prohibitive sentence; in such cases, the subject pronoun is obligatory.

(8) Pichi (Yakpo 2013)
   a. *Laf!*
      laugh
      'Laugh!' (affirmative imperative)
   b. *Á no laf.*
      1SG.SBJ NEG laugh
      'I didn't laugh.' (normal negator)
   c. *Mek yù no laf!*
      SBJV 2SG NEG laugh
      'Don't laugh!' (prohibitive)

Value 4 (**special negator** and **a special prohibitive construction**) occurs only in Haitian Creole and in Mixed Ma'a/Mbugu. In Mixed Ma'a/Mbugu, the prohibitive uses a subject prefix, which is not the case in affirmative imperatives, and the negator used in the prohibitive sentence (*si*) differs from the one used in the declarative sentence (*te*).

(9) Mixed Ma'a/Mbugu (Mous 2013)
   a. *Líta íʔi!*
      come here
      'Come here!' (affirmative imperative)
   b. *Te-tú-ila-íye ité hé-lo vahe*
      NEG-1PL-know-PRF PURP 16-have people
      vé-di-ye iʔi.
      2-stay-OPT here
      'We didn't know that there were people staying here.' (normal negator)
   c. *U-si-hlati lunige!*
      2SG-NEG-close door
      'Don't close the door!' (prohibitive)

In Haitian Creole, the other language exhibiting this value, the special prohibitive negator *pinga* may be used (as opposed to *pa*, which is used in declarative sentences); in this case, the subject pronoun is obligatory, which is not the case in affirmative imperatives.

3. Areal distribution

Value 1 (normal imperative construction and normal negator, found in 52 languages) is present everywhere, although this value is dominant in the Atlantic (32 languages), especially in the Caribbean. Value 2 (normal imperative and special negator) is predominant in all parts of Asia (13 out of 17 languages) but is almost absent from Africa (exceptions: Afrikaans and Juba Arabic) and the Americas (exceptions: Palenquero and Michif). Value 3 (11 languages) is concentrated on the African side of the Atlantic as well as in Central Africa, and value 4 occurs only in Mixed Ma'a/Mbugu (East Africa) and in Haitian Creole (Caribbean).

Except for value 3, the distribution of the four values in the *WALS* languages differs considerably from the distribution in the *APiCS* languages (value 1: 23% vs. 68%; value 2: 37% vs. 22%; value 3: 11% vs. 14%; value 4: 29% vs. 2%).

56 The prohibitive

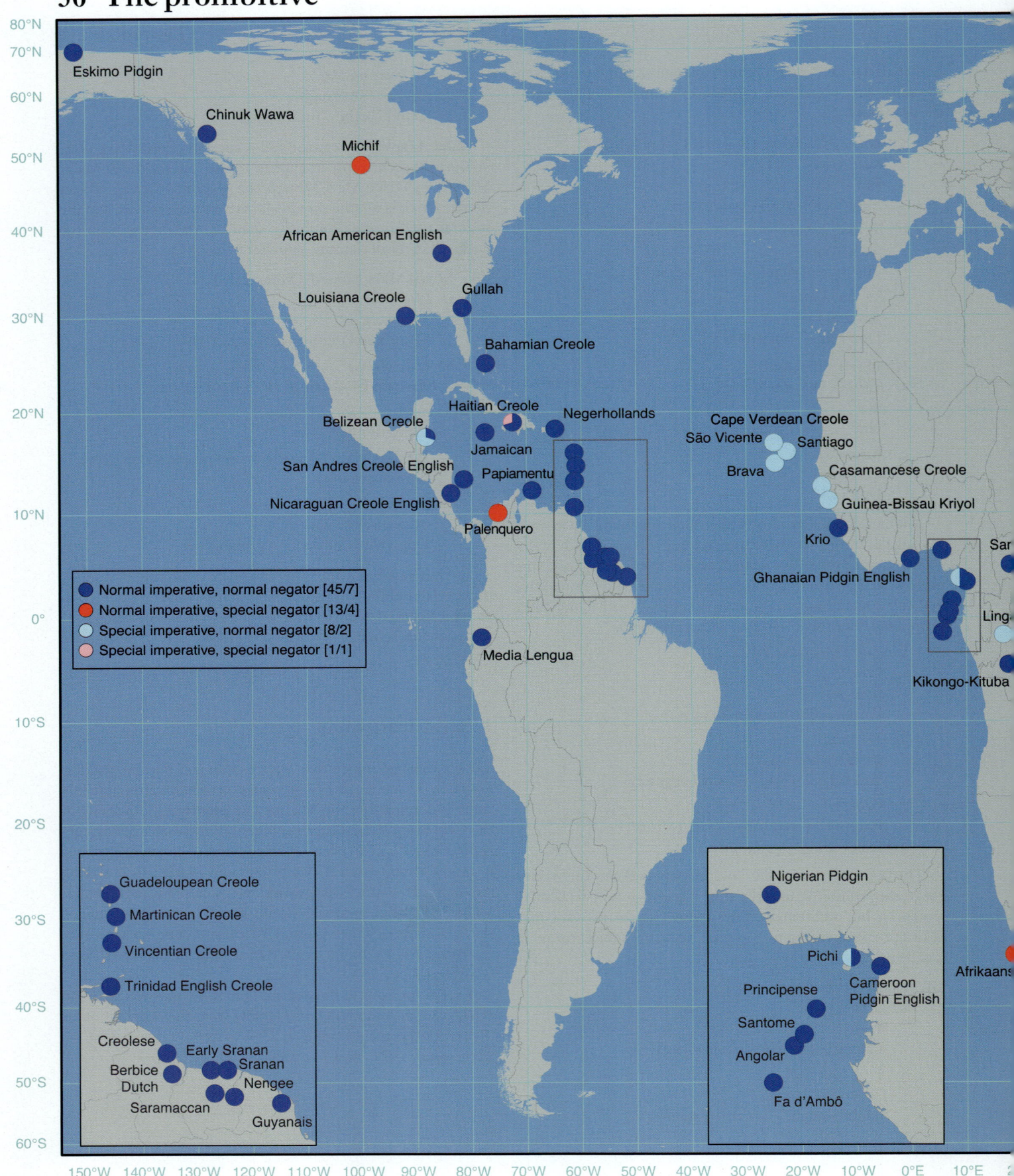

222

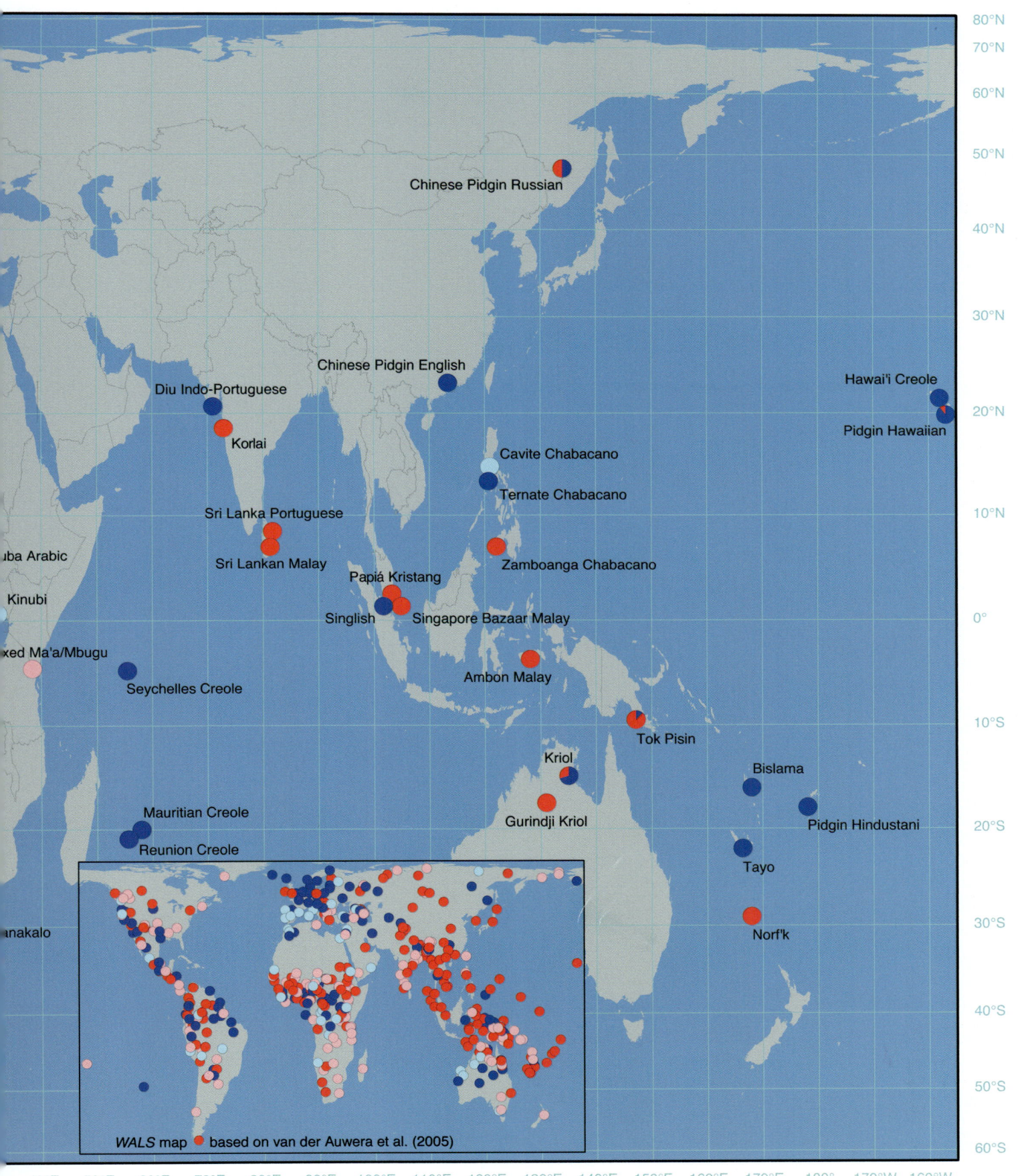

ARGUMENT MARKING

Chapter 57
Marking of patient noun phrases

MARTIN HASPELMATH AND THE *APiCS* CONSORTIUM

1. Patient marking of full noun phrases

In many languages, the patient argument of a typical transitive clause is coded in some overt way (i.e. not just by word order) to distinguish it from the agent. Such markers are well known from Latin and are typically called accusative markers (see 1).

(1) Latin
In principio creavit Deu-s caelu-m et
in beginning created God-NOM heaven-ACC and
terra-m.
earth-ACC
'In the beginning God created the heavens and the earth.'

Accusative markers can be case affixes, as in Latin, but they can also be prepositions, as in many of the examples below, for example, in (7a–c).

As will be seen in Chapter 58, some languages have overt coding of the transitive agent instead, but in this chapter we consider only coding of patients. Moreover, we do not consider patient coding by means of person–number indexing (or cross-referencing, or agreement) on the verb, as is found in Río de la Plata Spanish (2) and many Bantu languages such as Swahili (3). (Note that Spanish has both an object person marker on the verb and an accusative marker on the noun phrase.)

(2) Río de la Plata Spanish
Lo veo a Juan.
3SG.OBJ I.see ACC Juan
'I see Juan.'

(3) Swahili
Ni-li-mw-uliza Ali.
1SG.SBJ-PST-3SG.OBJ-ask Ali
'I asked Ali.'

Finally, we do not consider the coding of personal pronouns here. Many languages treat full noun phrases and personal pronouns differently (typically restricting accusative marking to pronouns, as in English), and pronouns will be dealt with in Chapter 59.

Thus, for this feature we ask only whether full noun phrases (i.e. non-pronominal noun phrases) have an overt accusative case affix or adposition. This marker need not be unique to patients (cf. Spanish *a* in (2), which also codes recipients in ditransitive constructions), but it must serve to distinguish patients from agents.

2. The feature values

Overt patient marking is not common in *APiCS* languages.

○	1. No marking of patient NPs	62
●	2. Only definite patient NPs are marked	2
●	3. Only animate patient NPs are marked	8
●	4. Only definite and animate patient NPs are marked	2
●	5. All patient NPs are marked	2

Most of our languages have the first feature value, **no marking of patient NPs**.

(4) a. Krio (Finney 2013)
di bɔbɔ kik di bɔl
ART boy kick ART ball
'The boy kicked the ball.'

b. Cape Verdean Creole of Brava (Baptista 2013)
Dotor kura omi duenti.
doctor cure man sick
'The doctor cured the sick man.'

This is expected for three reasons: (i) the languages also tend to have fixed SVO word order (cf. Chapter 1), so that the patient NP need not be overtly marked (see Sinnemäki 2010); (ii) the European lexifiers English, French, Portuguese, and Dutch do not have overt patient marking; and (iii) hardly any of the relevant African and Oceanic substrate languages have overt patient marking. Thus, overt patient marking is generally found only in Asian pidgins and creoles as well as in some mixed languages.

In the world's languages, accusative marking of patients is not uncommon, but most languages with accusative marking use this marking only on a subclass of prominent patients, especially animate and definite patients. This situation, known as **differential object marking** (Bossong 1998, Aissen 2003), is more common than consistent object marking, and this is reflected in our languages as well. Moreover, in many cases object marking is optional and its use depends on a complex set of factors. Thus, when we say that only patients of a certain type are marked, this does not imply that these patients must be marked, or that marking of other patients is categorically excluded.

In Sri Lankan Malay and Pidgin Hawaiian, **only definite patients are marked** (value 2). In both languages, there is variability, but examples (5) and (6) show that accusative marking of inanimate patients is at least possible when they are definite.

(5) Sri Lankan Malay (Slomanson 2013)
Go itu buk-pəðə-yang ati-baça.
1SG DEM book-PL-ACC FUT-read
'I will read those books.'

(6) Pidgin Hawaiian (Roberts 2013)
pehea oe aihue i ka dala
why 2SG steal OBJ DEF dollar
'Why did you steal the dollar?'

In Pidgin Hawaiian, object marking with *i* (inherited from its lexifier Hawaiian) is in fact uncommon, but when the object is indefinite, it does not occur at all. In Sri Lankan Malay, the accusative marker probably arose under the influence of Tamil. Classical Malay has no accusative marking, and the patient marker *sama* that is sometimes used in colloquial Malay is not likely to have played a role.

In a number of languages in South Asia and Southeast Asia, **only animate patients are marked** (value 3). A few examples are given in (7a–c).

(7) a. Batavia Creole (Maurer 2013b)
      Choma kung kusir.
      call OBJ coachman
      'Call the coachman.'
   b. Korlai (Clements 2013)
      Yo ulyo ku padgar.
      I see.PST OBJ priest
      'I saw the priest.'
   c. Cavite Chabacano (Sippola 2013a)
      Ya coge el mga pulis con el ladron.
      PFV catch the PL police OBJ the thief
      'The policemen caught the thief.'

In the Spanish- and Portuguese-based languages, the accusative marker typically derives from the preposition *con/com* 'with'. In Diu Indo-Portuguese and in Sri Lanka Portuguese, the accusative marker is *-pa/-pə*, from Portuguese *para* or *por*.

(8) Sri Lanka Portuguese (Smith 2013)
eev vosa kuɲaadu-pa kada ɔɔra
1SG 2SG.GEN brother.in.law-ACC every time
ki-lembraa
HAB-remember
'I often think of your brother-in-law.'

In the mixed language Michif, patient marking is restricted to animates, too, but the marker in question is traditionally called *obviative* rather than accusative, because strictly speaking, it marks non-topic status rather than patienthood. Under certain circumstances, it may be used on arguments other than patients. It is counted as a patient marker here because in practice it mostly occurs on patients.

(9) Michif (Bakker 2013)
Li shyaen kii-nawashwaat-eew li sha-wa.
ART dog PST-chase-3SBJ.3OBJ ART cat-OBV
'The dog chased the cat.'

In Afrikaans and Papiá Kristang, **only patients that are both definite and animate** get accusative marking (value 4).

(10) Afrikaans (den Besten & Biberauer 2013)
Ons het nie vir Piet ge-sien nie.
1SG PST NEG for Pete PTCP-seen NEG
'We didn't see Pete.'

(11) Papiá Kristang (Baxter 1988: 156)
yo ja olá ku Maria sa pai
1SG PFV see ACC Maria GEN father
'I saw Maria's father.'

Finally, in two languages **all patient noun phrases are** (or may be) marked with accusative case (value 5). In Zamboanga Chabacano, accusative marking is obligatory on patients that are definite and human, but optionally possible for all patients.

(12) Zamboanga Chabacano (Steinkrüger 2013)
Pírmi si Peter ta-besá kun Joan.
often AG Peter IPFV-kiss OBJ Joan
'Peter often kisses Joan.'

In the mixed language Media Lengua, accusative marking is as ubiquitous as in the grammatifier Quechua, even though it is not absolutely necessary in all cases.

(13) Media Lengua (Muysken 2013)
kura bindizia-xu-n nwibu iskwila-da
priest bless-PROG-3SG new school-ACC
'The priest blesses the new school.'

57 Marking of patient noun phrases

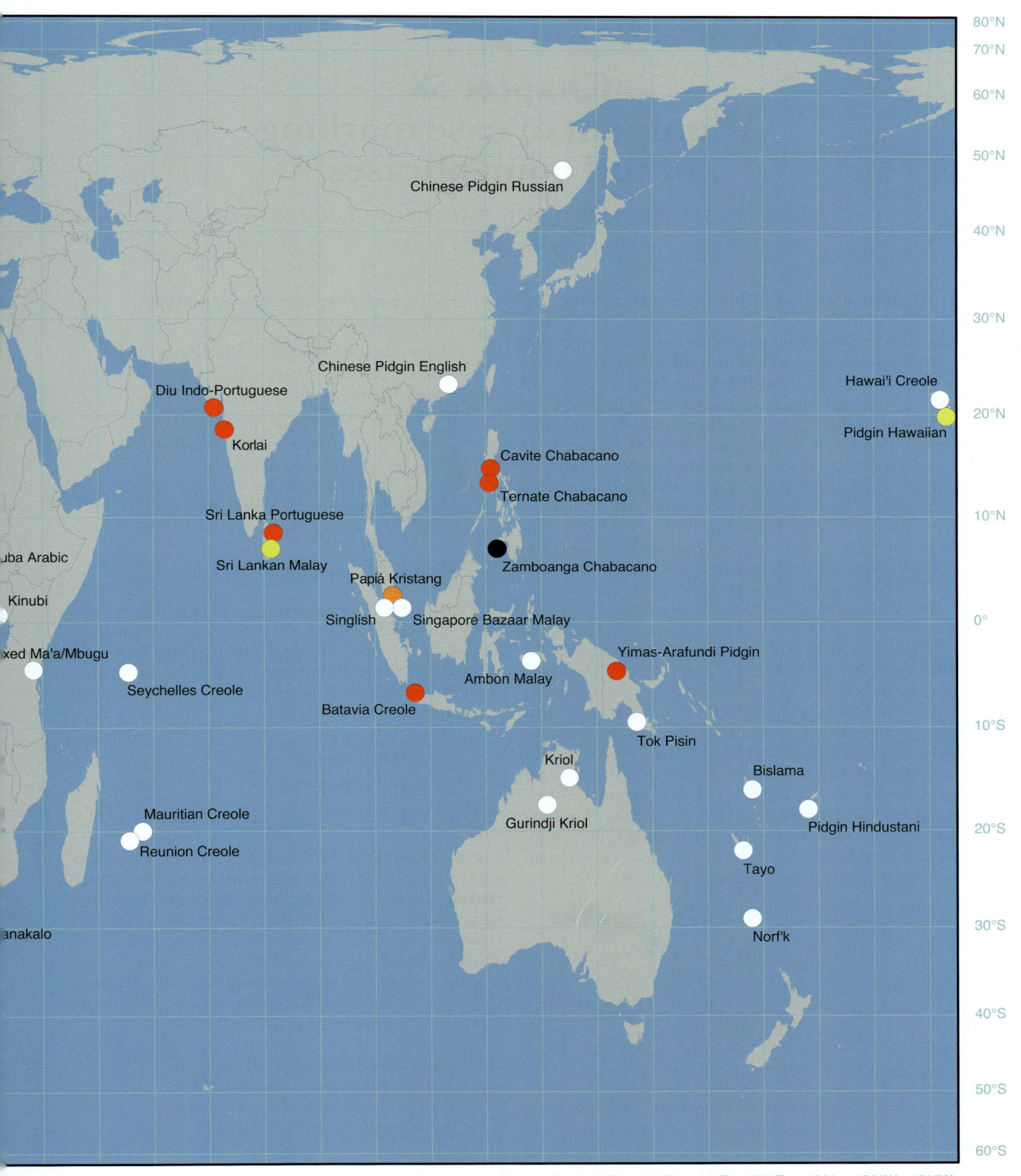

Chapter 58
Alignment of case marking of full noun phrases

MARTIN HASPELMATH AND THE *APiCS* CONSORTIUM

1. Alignment in monotransitive constructions

Like the preceding chapter, this chapter considers role-marking patterns (case marking and adpositional marking) in monotransitive clauses, that is, clauses with a typical physical-effect verb such as 'break' and 'kill'. In accordance with widespread typological practice (see Comrie 2005, Haspelmath 2011a), we compare the coding of the monotransitive agent (A) and patient (P) with the coding of the sole argument of a single-argument intransitive clause (S). This kind of comparison is usually called **alignment** (it can be carried out in a similar way with ditransitive clauses, see Chapter 60). In *APiCS* we limit ourselves to alignment of cases and adpositions, and in this chapter we consider only full noun-phrase arguments (for personal pronouns, which often behave differently, see Chapter 59).

When comparing the coding of the agent and patient with the intransitive sole argument, there are five logical alignment possibilities, of which only three are relevant in practice: the pattern with identical coding of sole argument and agent, and special coding of the patient (called accusative alignment), the pattern with identical coding of sole argument and patient, and special coding of the agent (called ergative alignment), and the pattern in which the agent and the patient are coded identically and in the same way as the sole argument (called neutral alignment, always with zero coding). The three patterns are illustrated in (1–3), from English, Quechua (a South American language), and Garrwa (an Australian language). The corresponding intransitive clause, not given here for lack of space, has an S argument with zero coding. See Figure 1.

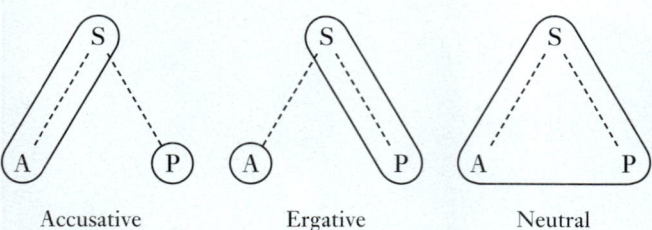

Figure 1. The three main monotransitive alignment patterns

(1) English: neutral alignment (no case marking)
The farmer-Ø killed the duckling-Ø.

(2) Quechua: accusative alignment (only P-marking)
Hwan-Ø Tumas-ta maqa-n.
Juan-NOM Tomás-ACC hit-3
'Juan hits Tomás.' (Huallaga Quechua, Weber 1989: 15)

(3) Garrwa: ergative alignment (only A-marking)
daba-yi miya-Ø nana-yi djukai-wanji
hit-PST snake-ABS that-ERG boy-ERG
'That boy hit the snake.' (Leeding 1976: 385)

2. The feature values

The three main alignment types are the three feature values shown on the map. Only the first two are at all common in our languages. (The other two logical patterns, with different coding of A, S, and P (tripartite pattern), or with identical coding of A and P contrasting with the coding of S (horizontal pattern), are not attested at all in *APiCS*.)

○	1. Neutral alignment	61
●	2. Accusative alignment	14
●	3. Ergative alignment	1

The map is quite similar to the map for patient marking (Chapter 57), as neutral alignment is identical to absence of patient marking in practice, while accusative alignment is identical to the possibility of patient marking (whether patient marking is variable and optional, as it is in most cases, or obligatory).

The only difference between Chapter 57 and this chapter is the presence of an ergative pattern in the mixed language Gurindji Kriol, which has inherited its ergative case from the Australian Aboriginal language Gurindji; see (4).

(4) Gurindji Kriol (Meakins 2013)
Karu-ngku im pangkily im marluka-Ø.
child-ERG 3SG hit.on.head 3SG old.man-ABS
'The kid hit the old man on the head.'

Alignment of case marking of full noun phrases

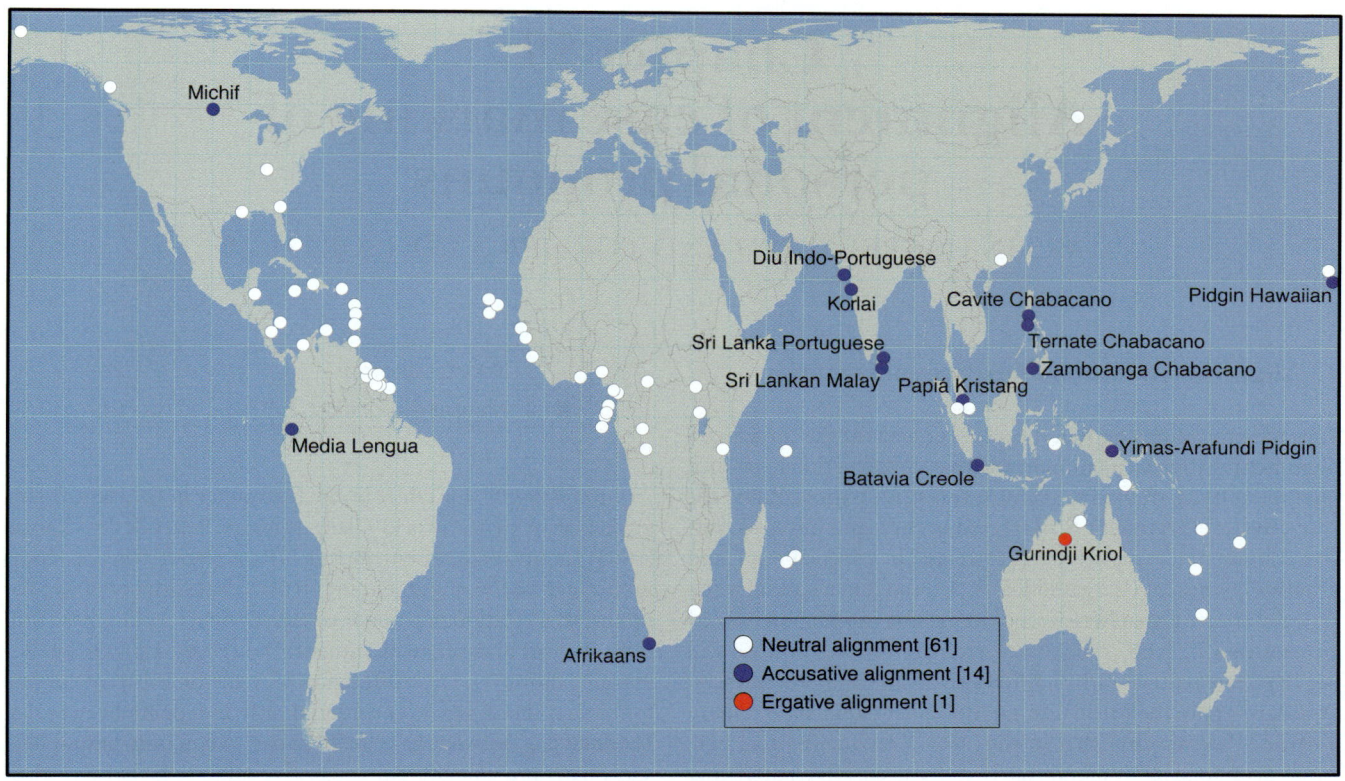

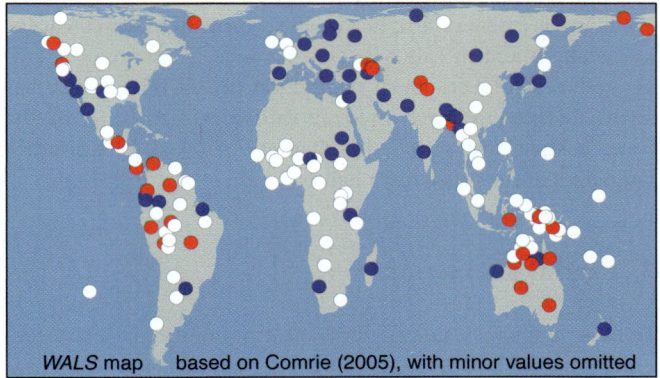

WALS map based on Comrie (2005), with minor values omitted

Like accusative marking in most *APiCS* languages with an accusative pattern, ergative marking is variable in Gurindji Kriol (Meakins 2011: 209–39).

The small map, adapted from *WALS* (Comrie 2005), shows the distribution of the three types in the world's languages. Tripartite and active–stative alignments, which do not occur in *APiCS*, have been omitted from this map. We see that ergative alignment is found widely in Australia, and accusative alignment is found in South Asia, which explains some of the patterns in *APiCS*.

Chapter 59
Alignment of case marking of personal pronouns

MARTIN HASPELMATH AND THE *APiCS* CONSORTIUM

1. Alignment in monotransitive constructions

Like the preceding chapter, this chapter looks at the three main alignment patterns in monotransitive constructions: neutral alignment (with transitive agent A, transitive patient P, and intransitive sole argument S all treated in the same way), accusative alignment (A treated like S, P treated in a special way), and ergative alignment (P treated like S, A treated in a special way). The difference is that here we look at the way in which **personal pronouns** ('I', 'you', 'she', 'we', etc.) are treated, and we will see that they pattern rather differently from full noun phrases. As elsewhere in the world's languages (Silverstein 1976, Dixon 1994: 83–94), we find that in the *APiCS* languages, too, personal pronouns show significantly more accusative patterning than full NPs, as well as less ergative marking.

In fact, there is no ergative alignment with personal pronouns attested in our languages at all: the only language with an ergative pattern of full NPs, Gurindji Kriol, shows accusative alignment with personal pronouns, for example, the contrast *dei* ('they', A and S) vs. *dem/jem* ('them', P):

(1) Gurindji Kriol (Meakins 2013)
   a. ***Dei***   *bin luk det ngakparn gat nyanuny femli.*
       3PL.SBJ PST see DET frog   with 3SG.DAT family
       'They saw the frog with his family.'
   b. *Lamawurt-ku wi*   *kan teik-im **jem**.*
       grub-DAT   1PL.SBJ can take-TR 3PL.OBJ
       'We will take them to get witchetty grubs.'

Note that when a language has a distinction between independent and dependent person forms (see Chapter 17), we consider only the dependent person forms here, because these are much more commonly used as subjects and objects.

2. The feature values

The two feature values are thus only (i) neutral alignment (no subject–object distinction in personal pronouns) and (ii) accusative alignment (a subject–object distinction). It turns out that more than half of the *APiCS* languages have accusative alignment, that is, a subject–object distinction in person forms.

○	1. Neutral alignment	22
●	2. Accusative alignment	54

Interestingly, this effect is much stronger in the *APiCS* languages than in the world's languages in general. In Comrie (2005), neutral alignment in full NPs is about twice as common as accusative alignment in full NPs, but with personal pronouns, this relationship is not reversed: neutral alignment still prevails over accusative alignment, though by a much smaller margin. However, this difference may to some extent be due to the fact that Comrie considered only independent personal pronouns; as Siewierska (2005b) shows, when only bound person forms are considered, accusative alignment is more than twice as common as neutral alignment in the world's languages, so the preference for accusativity is even stronger.

There is a general implicational relationship between accusative alignment in full NPs and personal pronouns: if a language has a subject–object distinction in full NPs, it also has such a distinction in person forms (Silverstein 1976). Thus, the 54 accusative languages in this chapter include all 14 accusative languages of the preceding chapter.

3. Partial distinctions

In most languages, not all personal pronouns make a subject–object distinction. A few paradigms of languages with accusative alignment are given below.

(2) Ambon Malay (Paauw 2013)

	Subject	Object
1SG	*beta; bet; be*	*beta*
2SG	*ose; os; se*	*ose; os; se*
2SG	*ale; al*	*ale*
3SG	*dia; di; de*	*dia*
3SG.FORMAL	*antua; ontua;* …	*antua; ontua;* …
3SG.N	*akang*	*akang; kang; ang*
1PL	*katong; tong*	*katong*
2PL	*dorang; dong*	*dorang; dong*
3PL	*dorang; dong*	*dorang; dong*

(3) Ghanaian Pidgin English (Huber 2013)

	Subject	Object
1SG	à	mì
2SG	jù	jù
3SG	ì	àm
1PL	wì	wì, ɔs
2PL	jù	jù
3PL	dè, dɛ̀m	dɛ̀m

(4) Guinea-Bissau Kriyol (Intumbo et al. 2013)

	Subject	Object
1SG	ŋ	ŋ
2SG	bu	u
3SG	i	l
1PL	no	nu
2PL	bo	bos
3PL	e	elis

These paradigms are quite typical, also in that they do not show a consistent pattern, that is, no specific accusative marker can be discerned. Case marking is thus suppletive, and for this reason, these forms are not normally treated as different (nominative vs. accusative) cases, but as different subject and object forms. (From our perspective, however, there is no difference between these two ways of talking about the contrasts.)

In some languages, the distinction is even more partial than in the three languages above. For example, in Atlantic English-based languages, typically only the first-person singular and/or the third-person singular makes a distinction:

(5)

	1SG	3SG
Creolese		ii/am
Gullah	I/me	ee/um
Kriol	ai/mi	
Nengee		a/en

Note that even these very partial paradigms have been counted as exhibiting accusative alignment. A limiting case is Papiamentu, where there is only a single distinction in some varieties of the language (second-person-singular accusative *bu*, contrasting with the neutral form *bo*, only in the Curaçao variety), so this language has been considered to show neutral alignment.

4. Origins of accusative marking on personal pronouns

The *APiCS* languages can be grouped into three diachronic types with respect to the origin of their accusative marking.

In the first type, the accusative forms derive from special accusative prepositions or postpositions/case suffixes. This is the case with those languages that have patient markers in full NPs, too, especially Portuguese- and Spanish-based creoles in South and Southeast Asia:

(6)

Korlai (Clements 2013)	pe-l 'him' (per < Portuguese para)
Diu Indo-Portuguese (Cardoso 2013)	a el 'him' (a < Portuguese a)
Sri Lanka Portuguese (Smith 2013)	elis-pa 'them' (-pa < Portuguese para)
Batavia Creole (Maurer 2013b)	kung eo 'me' (kung < Portuguese com)
Zamboanga Chabacano (Steinkrüger 2013)	kun-éle 'him' (kun- < Spanish con)

A French-based language in which the person forms have preposition-derived accusative forms is Reunion Creole (*a-mwen* 'me', *a-li* 'him', *a-nou* 'us', etc., from French *à*).

In the second type, the special nominative and accusative forms, were inherited from the lexifier. This is the case with many English-based languages, such as Ghanaian Pidgin English in (3), as well as the languages shown in (5). The English lexifier is different from the Romance lexifiers in that it has no clitic personal pronouns, so the case distinctions of the independent pronouns sometimes survived. In the Romance-based languages, the clitic personal pronouns were invariably lost, so no case distinctions generally survived from the lexifiers. (An exception is the distinction between *i* and *li* in Seychelles Creole, which seems to go back to the French *il–lui* contrast.) It should be noted, however, that in some of the more basilectal Caribbean English-based varieties, no case distinctions are made, and it is only due to contact with English that the distinctions are reemerging.

Accusative pronoun forms were also inherited from a source language in some of the mixed languages such as Media Lengua, Michif, and Mixed Ma'a/Mbugu.

In the third type, the nominative–accusative contrast has come about by sound changes, which often affect subject pronouns more than object pronouns, so that they tend to be shorter. This can be seen in some of the forms in (4) from Guinea-Bissau Kriyol, and also in the forms in (7).

(7)

			Subject	Object
Louisiana Creole		1SG	mo	mwa
		2SG	to	twa
Principense		1SG	(i)n, (u)n	mi, n
		3SG	ê	li, e
San Andres Creole English		3SG	ihn [ĩ]	im
		3PL	dehn [dẽ]	dem

More reduction in the subject forms than in the object forms is also generally found in Ambon Malay (see (2)), but the opposite may also be found (in the third-singular-neutral form *akang* vs. *ang*).

59 Alignment of case marking of personal pronouns

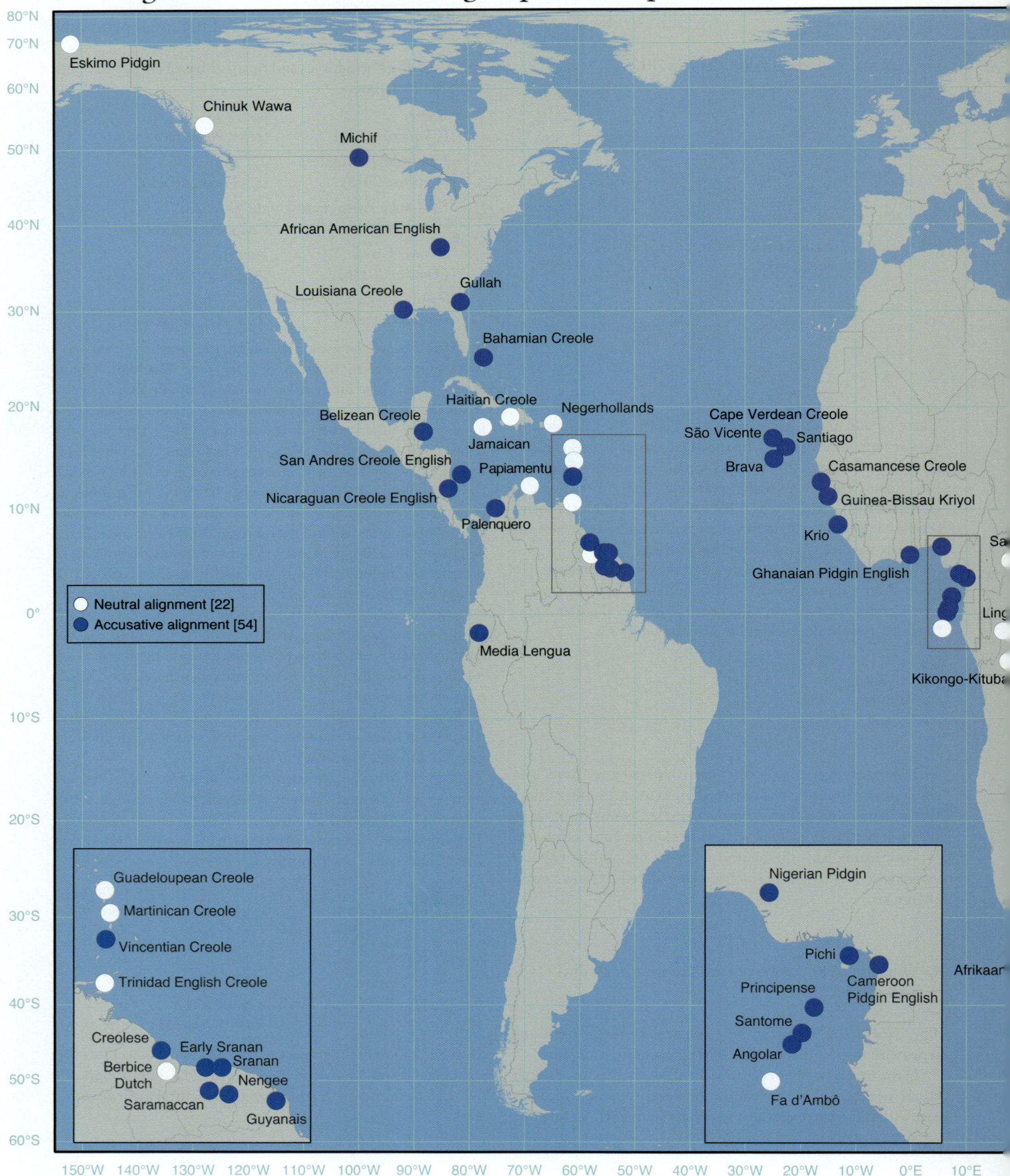

Chapter 60
Ditransitive constructions with 'give'

MARTIN HASPELMATH, SUSANNE MARIA MICHAELIS,
AND THE *APiCS* CONSORTIUM

1. Ditransitive constructions

A **ditransitive construction** is a monoclausal construction containing a verb of physical or mental transfer and three arguments: an agent, a theme (the thing that is transferred), and a recipient or addressee (see Malchukov et al. 2010). The most frequent physical transfer verb is 'give', so when different ditransitive verbs show a different pattern, this chapter focuses on the behaviour of 'give' (as in Haspelmath 2005d, the corresponding *WALS* chapter). In this chapter, we consider the coding of the theme (T) and the recipient (R), comparing it to the coding of the patient (P) in monotransitive (agent–patient) clauses. The marking of the agent is almost always identical in monotransitive and ditransitive clauses, so we leave it aside here. Word order in ditransitive clauses is dealt with in the next chapter.

When comparing the coding of the recipient and theme with the monotransitive patient, there are five logical alignment possibilities, of which only three are relevant in practice: the pattern with identical coding of patient and theme, and special coding of the recipient (called **indirect-object** or **indirective construction**), the pattern with identical coding of patient and recipient, and special coding of the theme (called **secondary-object** or **secundative construction**), and the pattern in which the theme and the recipient are coded identically and in the same way as the patient (called **double-object** or **neutral** construction) (see Fig. 1).

The three patterns are illustrated with English examples in (1a–c). As in most pidgins and creoles, the monotransitive patient is zero-coded here, so we find overt (prepositional) coding only in the indirect-object construction (on the recipient, *to*) and in the secondary-object construction (on the theme, *with*). The double-object construction in (1c) has no overt coding of the objects.

(1) a. *The mother gave money **to** her three children.*
b. *The government provides us **with** enough funding.*
c. *The boy gave his mother a new computer.*

In many languages, personal pronouns show different coding, so for the purposes of this chapter, we only consider the coding of full noun phrases.

2. The values

The three main constructions are the three values shown on the map. The secondary-object construction is almost inexistent, and many languages have both the indirect-object construction and the double-object construction.

	excl	shrd	all
1. Double-object construction	31	29	60
2. Indirect-object construction	16	28	44
3. Secondary-object construction	0	1	1

In the creoles of the Atlantic and Indian Ocean regions, the most widespread pattern is the **double-object construction** (or neutral alignment). This is the case independently of the lexifier. We find this pattern not only in English-based creoles (2a, b), but also in French-based (3) and Ibero-Romance-based creoles (4a, b), despite the fact that the Romance lexifier languages lack a double-object construction and use a preposition (*a*/*à*, *para*) to code the recipient.

(2) a. Krio (Finney 2013)
di uman gi di titi sɔm mɔni
the woman give the girl some money
'The woman gave the girl some money.'

b. Jamaican (Farquharson 2013)
Di uman gi di bwai di fuud.
the woman give the boy the food
'The woman gave the boy the food.'

(3) Seychelles Creole (Michaelis & Rosalie 2013)
Mon 'n donn Marcel en mang.
1SG PRF give Marcel a mango
'I gave Marcel a mango.'

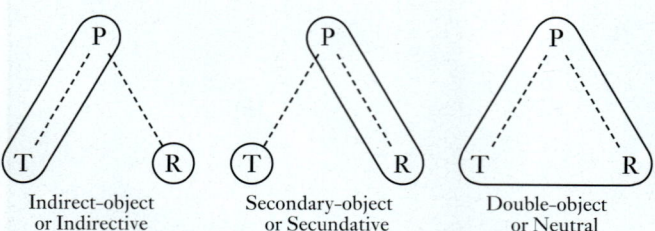

Figure 1. The three main ditransitive alignment patterns

(4) a. Papiamentu (Kouwenberg 2013b)
Duna mi ruman hòmber e yabi.
give 1SG sibling man DEF key
'Give my brother the key.'

b. Guinea-Bissau Kriyol (Intumbo et al. 2013)
No da Djon un prenda.
1PL give.PST John INDF gift
'We gave John a gift.'

The predominance of the double-object construction in these languages has been noted by Bruyn et al. (1999) and explained in universalist terms, but Michaelis & Haspelmath (2003) pointed out that a substratist explanation is more likely, given that the West African and Bantu substrate languages of Atlantic and Indian Ocean creoles tend to show the double-object construction (see also Michaelis 2008).

In Asian and Melanesian creoles, by contrast, the **indirect-object construction** is much more common, as illustrated by (5a–c).

(5) a. Papiá Kristang (Baxter 2013)
eli sa tiu ja bendé aké prau ku yo
3SG GEN uncle PFV sell that boat DAT 1SG
'His uncle sold the boat to me.'

b. Tayo (Ehrhart 1993: 224)
sola done fam pu lja
they gave wife for him
'They gave him a wife.'

c. Tok Pisin (Smith & Siegel 2013)
Givim mani long papa bilong yu.
give money PREP father POSS 2SG
'Give your father the money.'

Indirect-object constructions are also found in some Atlantic creoles, but usually in varieties that are closer to the lexifier. In Louisiana Creole, the traditional construction is a double-object construction similar to (3), and "the indirect object construction is the more recent construction" (Neumann-Holzschuh & Klingler 2013).

(6) Louisiana Creole (Neumann-Holzschuh 1985: 256)
Mo don ponye-la a ma moman.
1SG give basket-ART.DEF.SG to 1SG.POSS mother
'I give the basket to my mother.'

3. Some issues of classification

For some constructions, the classification as indirect-object or secondary-object requires further discussion. One case concerns languages which have variable coding of monotransitive patients and where the patient marker is also used as the recipient marker. This is illustrated by Ternate Chabacano, where inanimate patients are uncoded (7a), but human patients are coded with the preposition *kon* (7b) (see Chapter 57). Recipients are treated unlike themes and inanimate patients, but like human patients in that they are coded by the preposition *kon* (see 7c).

(7) Ternate Chabacano (Sippola 2013b)
a. *Ta kortá lótro kel mánga grándi pónu.*
IPFV cut 3PL DEF PL big tree
'They cut the big trees.'

b. *a mirá rin mánang Lóling kon kel ómbri*
PFV see also sister Loling OBJ DEF man
'Loling too saw that man.'

c. *Ya dáli Lóling sen kon Lólet.*
PFV give Loling money OBJ Lolet
'Loling gave money to Lolet.'

It was decided to compare the coding of the ditransitive construction to the coding of the monotransitive construction with inanimate patients, because patients are more typically inanimate. Thus, the Ternate Chabacano pattern is classified as an indirect-object construction.

Another pattern requiring discussion is a serial verb construction with the verb 'give'. This is not uncommon in Atlantic pidgins and creoles, under the influence of Niger-Congo languages (see 8) (see also Chapter 86).

(8) Ghanaian Pidgin English (Huber 2013)
à gò faind sɔm mɔni giv mà mɔoda
1SG FUT find INDF money give 1SG.POSS mother
'I will (find and) give some money to my mother.'

If the serial verb *giv* is regarded as a kind of recipient marker here, as seems reasonable, then this is an indirect-object construction. Occasionally, this construction is even used when the main verb is 'give' itself, so that there are two instances of 'give', and an indirect-object construction results:

(9) Fa d'Ambô (Post 2013)
Amu da wan kuzu da bo.
1SG give ART thing give 2SG
'I gave you something.'

But it is also possible that the 'give' verb in second position is the main verb, and the first verb is regarded as a theme marker. In (10), the 'take' verb does not translate as 'take', but only adds a nuance of deliberateness to the meaning (see Chapter 85).

(10) Creolese (Devonish & Thompson 2013)
mi tek di baal gi Jaan
1SG take the ball give John
'I gave the ball to John deliberately.'

Thus, this construction is classified as a **secondary-object construction** (value 3). It is the only construction of this kind in our data.

60 Ditransitive constructions with 'give'

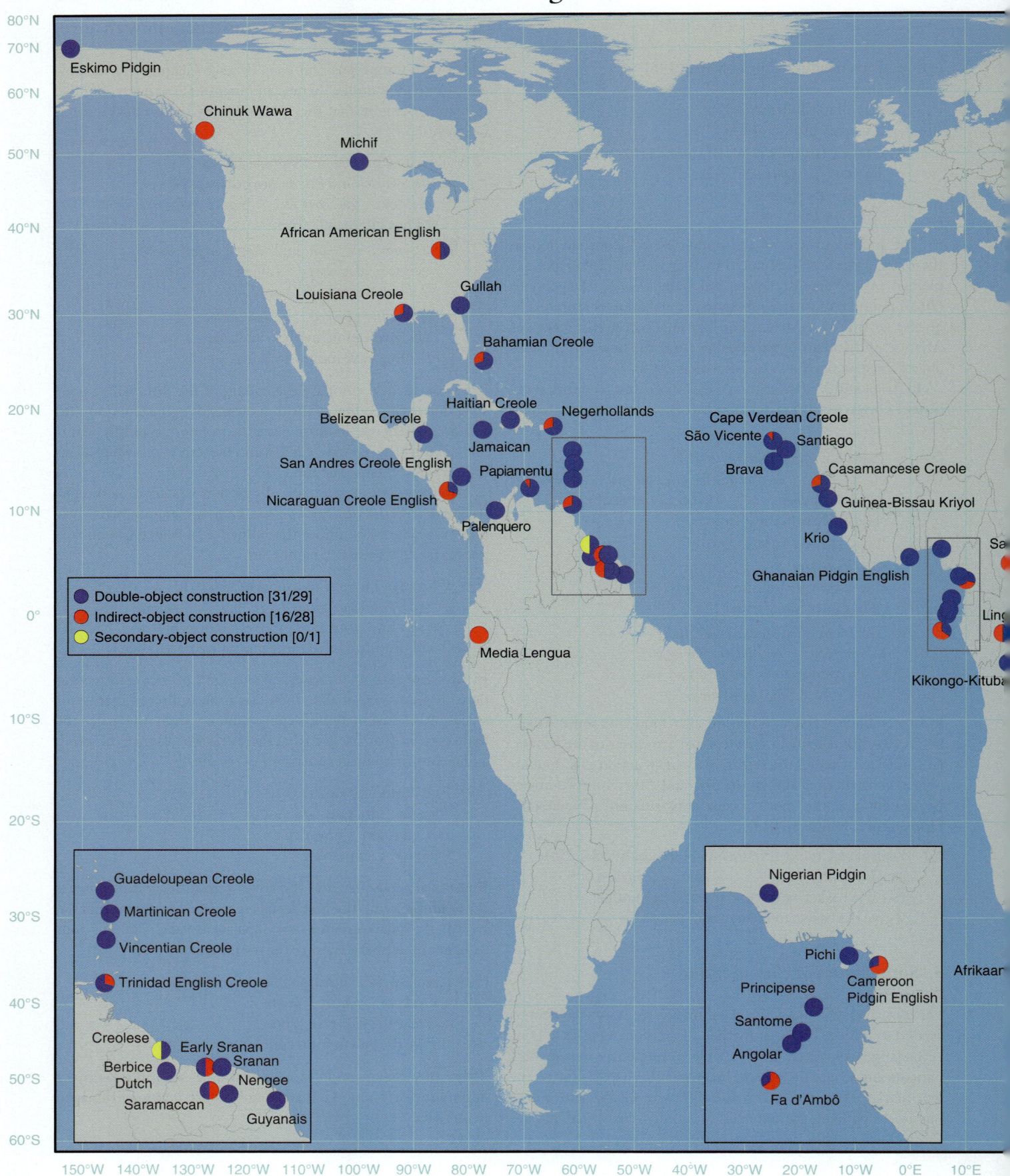

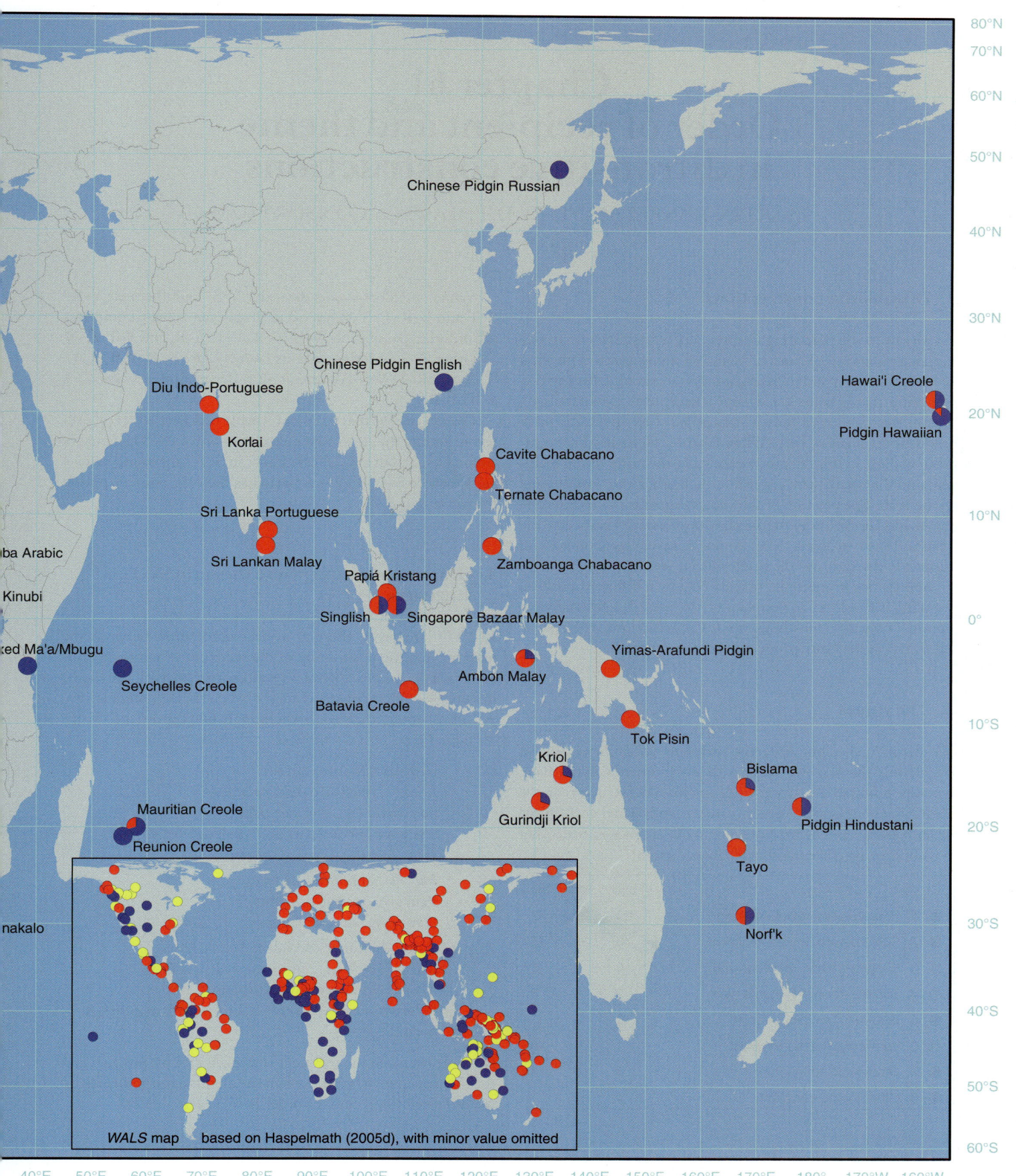

Chapter 61
Order of recipient and theme in ditransitive constructions

MARTIN HASPELMATH AND THE *APiCS* CONSORTIUM

1. Ditransitive constructions

As we saw in the preceding chapter, a **ditransitive construction** is a monoclausal construction containing a verb of physical or mental transfer and three arguments: an **agent**, a **theme** (i.e. the thing that is transferred) and a **recipient** (or addressee). Again, this chapter is mostly concerned with 'give', the most frequent ditransitive verb. While Chapter 60 focused on argument coding, in this chapter we consider the order of the recipient and the theme with respect to each other and with respect to the verb. The position of the subject/agent is not so interesting, as it is almost always in the same position with respect to the verb and the two objects as in monoclausal constructions (with respect to the verb and the single object, see Chapter 1).

Sometimes pronominal objects occupy a different position from full NP objects. In this chapter, the special position of pronominal objects is mostly ignored. Constructions with special information structure properties are also ignored.

2. The values

We distinguish eight different ordering possibilities, out of which only the first two occur with any frequency in our data, corresponding to the strong tendency for SVO structure in the *APiCS* languages. SOV order (values 3 and 4) and verb-initial order (values 5 and 6) are quite rare in our languages. Still other possibilities are quite marginal (values 7 and 8).

	excl	shrd	all
1. Subject–verb–recipient–theme	23	39	62
2. Subject–verb–theme–recipient	6	39	45
3. Subject–theme–recipient–verb	0	5	5
4. Subject–recipient–theme–verb	2	6	8
5. Verb-initial recipient–theme	0	3	3
6. Verb-initial theme–recipient	1	4	5
7. Other recipient–theme	0	3	3
8. Other theme–recipient	0	2	2

Value 5 in effect means the order V–S–R–T (because V–R–S–T and V–R–T–S do not occur at all), but value 6 comprises the ordering possibilities V–S–T–R, V–T–S–R, and V–T–R–S.

Other R–T ordering options (value 7) are S–R–V–T, R–V–T–S, and R–T–V–S. Another T–R ordering option (value 8) is S–T–V–R.

Overall, we see that recipient–theme ordering is clearly preferred among the *APiCS* languages, not only in SVO languages (value 1 vs. 2), but also, if less clearly, in SOV languages (value 4 vs. 3), where S–R–T–V is reported as the only possible option for two languages.

3. Ordering of recipient and theme in SVO languages

In SVO languages, there is a clear correlation between the marking and the positioning of the recipient: when the recipient is not coded in a special way and co-occurs with the theme in a double-object construction (i.e. when the alignment is neutral, cf. Chapter 60), we overwhelmingly find the order S–V–R–T (value 1):

(1) a. Angolar (Maurer 2013a)
É ra Têtêuga ũa kiba palaxu.
he give turtle one part palace
'He gave Turtle a part of his palace.'

b. Haitian Creole (Fattier 2013)
Pòl ba Anita yon mango.
Paul give Anita INDF mango
'Paul gave Anita a mango.'

c. Kriol (Schultze-Berndt & Angelo 2013)
Missis bin oldei giv-it mibala boks-is.
Missus PST always give-TR 1PL.EXCL box-PL
'The Missus used to give us boxes (with matches, to burn the grass).'

By contrast, when the recipient is marked by a preposition and the theme is unmarked (i.e. when the alignment is indirective), we overwhelmingly find the order S–V–T–R (value 2):

(2) a. Diu Indo-Portuguese (Cardoso 2013)
Yo a da kriãs pə tɛtɛ.
1SG IRR.NPST give.INF child DAT aunt
'I will give the children to (my) aunt.'

b. Chinuk Wawa (Grant 2013)
máyka pátlač kámuks kápa tánas
2SG give dog PREP small
'You're giving the child a dog.'

In quite a few *APiCS* languages, there is an alternation between a double-object construction (see 3a and 4a) and an indirective construction (see 3b and 4b), with the word order alternating as well, just as in the English Dative Alternation:

(3) Papiamentu (Kouwenberg 2013b)
a. *Bo por pasa mi e skalchi?*
2SG can pass 1SG DEF dish
'Can you pass me the dish?'

b. *Bo por pasa e skalchi pa mi?*
2SG can pass DEF dish for 1SG
'Can you pass the dish to me?'

(4) Singapore Bazaar Malay (Khin Khin Aye 2013)
a. *Dia kasi kita ini.*
3SG give 1PL DEM
'He gave us this.'

b. *Jangan kasi wang sama ini macam punya olang.*
don't give money with DEM like of person
'Don't give money to people like him.'

This kind of ordering alternation is found not only when the recipient is marked by a preposition, but also when it is marked by a serial verb, as in (5b):

(5) Saramaccan (Aboh et al. 2013)
a. *Di womi da di mujee wan buku.*
DEF.SG man give DEF.SG woman one book
'The man gave the woman one book.'

b. *Di womi da tu buku da di mujɛɛ.*
DEF.SG man give two book give DEF.SG woman
'The man gave two books to the woman.'

Moreover, it is found far beyond English-based languages, so English influence explains the pattern only for a few of the languages. And the preference for R–T ordering with double–object constructions and T–R ordering with indirective constructions seems to be general in the world's languages (Heine & König 2010).

4. Deviating orders

Deviations from the general pattern are quite uncommon. Recipient–theme order with prepositional recipients tends to be found only when the recipient is a pronoun and hence quite short, as in (6) and (7).

(6) Juba Arabic (Manfredi & Petrollino 2013)
úo wedí le ána gurúʃ
3SG give to 1SG money
'He gave me money.'

(7) Kriol (Schultze-Berndt & Angelo 2013)
giv-it bek langa im thet taka blanga im
give-TR back LOC 3SG DEM tucker DAT/POSS 3SG
'Give that food of hers back to her.'

The opposite pattern, T–R order in an SVO language with a double-object construction, is rare but is occasionally found in the Indian Ocean:

(8) Reunion Creole (Bollée 2013)
I fo ou donn pa manzé marmay la!
FIN must 2SG give NEG food child DEM
'You should not give these children food!'

5. Ordering of recipient and theme in SOV and verb-initial languages

When the usual order is subject–object–verb, there seems to be a general preference for recipient–theme order, but no clear correlation with the type of coding. In these languages, the coding may be by a postposition or case suffix:

(9) Sri Lanka Portuguese (Smith 2013)
trees poɖiyaas-pa tyuviʃan ta-daa
three child.PL-DAT tuition PRS-give
'[They] are giving tuition to three children.'

And among the languages that allow verb-final order, there are some (such as Afrikaans and Michif) that have many different orders, with complicated syntactic or pragmatic conditioning.

Verb-initial order is found especially in the Spanish-based languages of the Philippines, and since these have prepositional recipients, it is not surprising that they generally show V–T–R order (rather than V–R–T order), e.g.

(10) Ternate Chabacano (Sippola 2013b)
Ya dáli Lóling sen kon Lólet.
PFV give Loling money OBJ Lolet
'Loling gave money to Lolet.'

61 Order of recipient and theme in ditransitive constructions

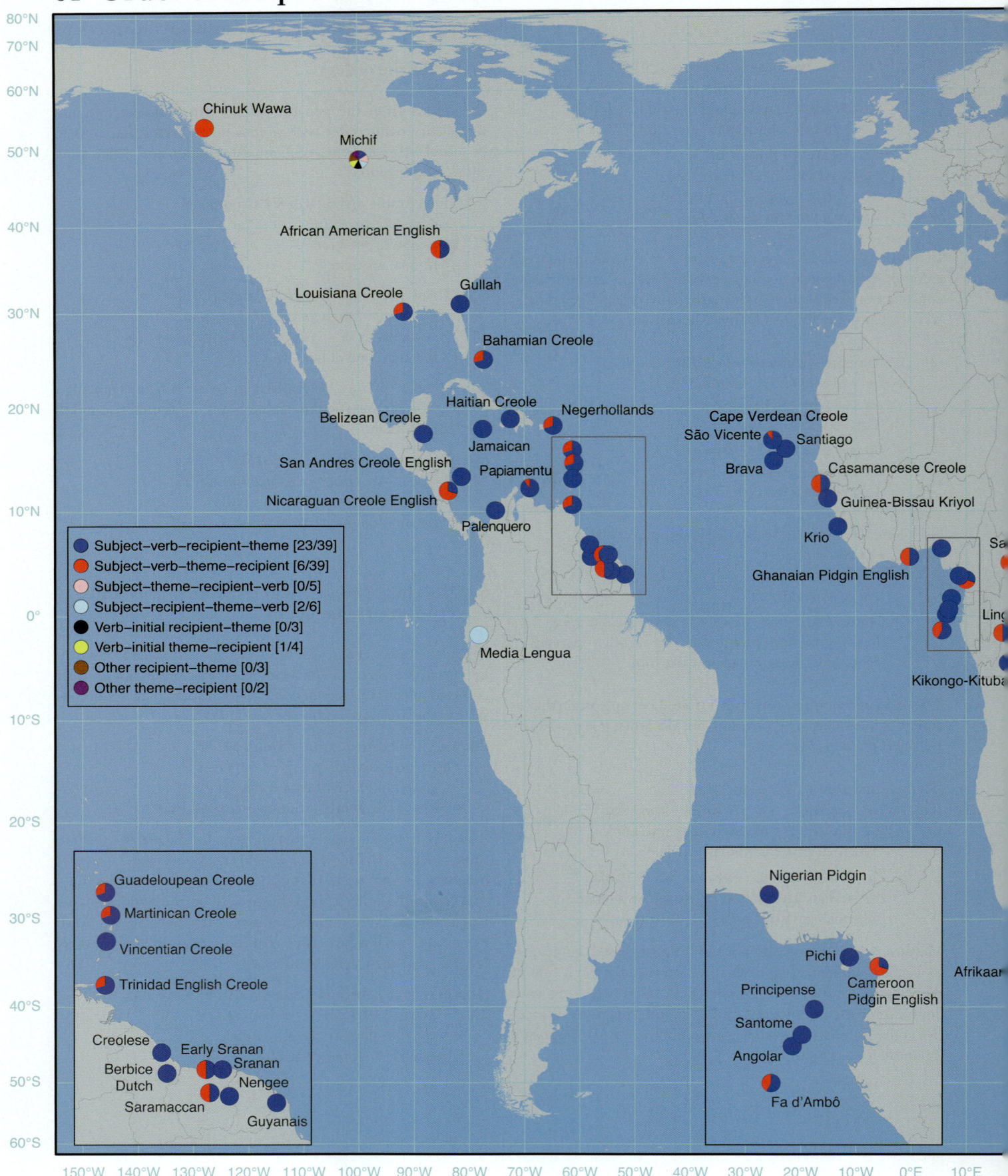

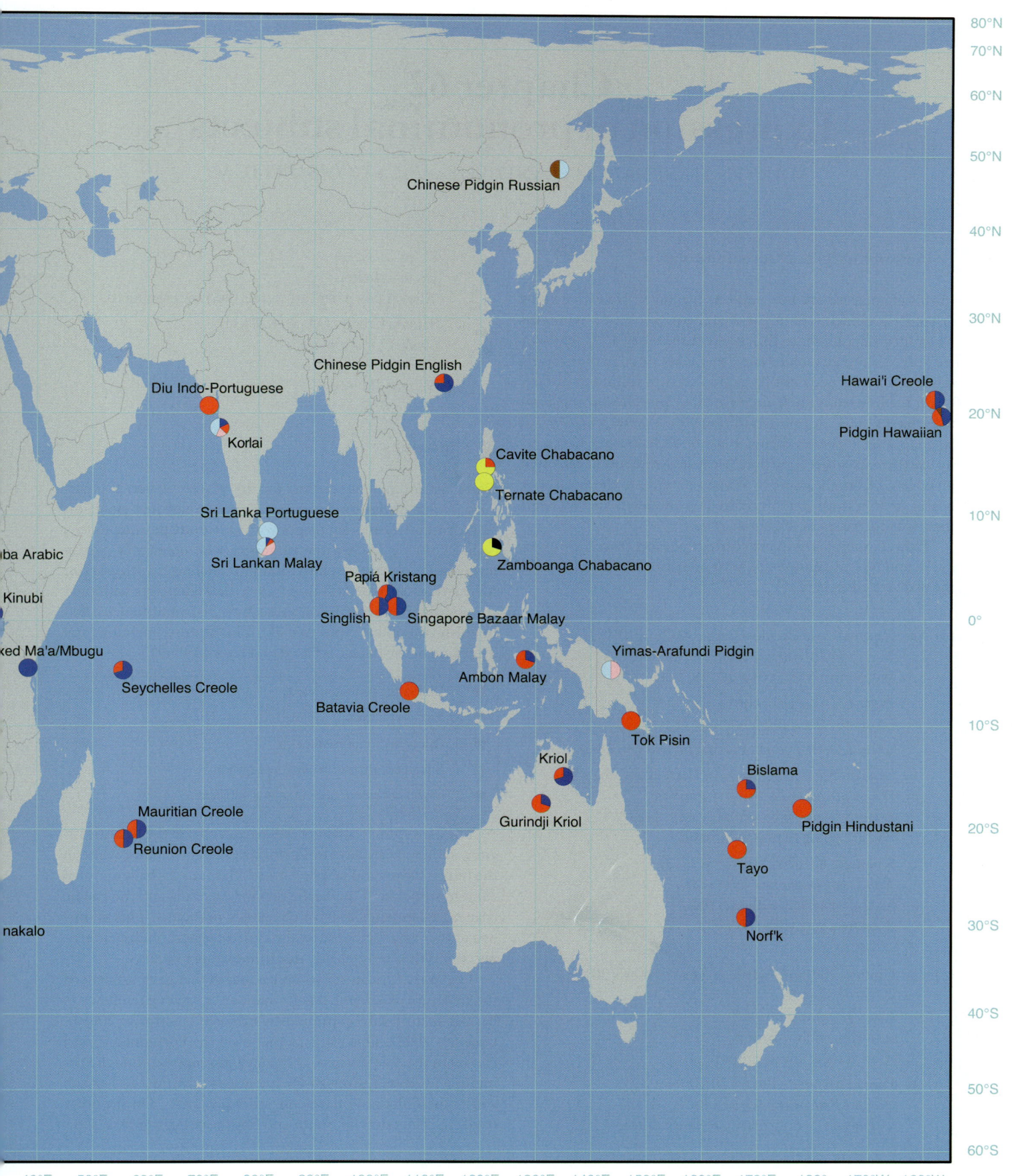

Chapter 62
Expression of pronominal subjects

MARTIN HASPELMATH AND THE *APiCS* CONSORTIUM

1. Person forms and zero anaphora

In this chapter we ask how subjects (agents of transitive verbs or single arguments of single-argument verbs) are expressed when they refer either to the speaker or hearer ('I', 'you', 'we', etc.) or to a third-person referent that is activated in the hearer's mind and hence need not be expressed by a full noun phrase. Overt forms used in such circumstances are called *person forms* (Siewierska 2004) or (more traditionally) *personal pronouns*. All languages have person forms, but not all languages necessarily use them in subject position, because their content can often be inferred from the context. When reference to the speaker or hearer or to a third-person referent is intended and no overt form is used, we speak of *zero anaphora*.

Typical examples of **overt subject person forms** are given in (1), and typical examples of **zero anaphora** (marked by ∅ in the text) are given in (2).

(1) a. Casamancese Creole (Biagui & Quint 2013)
   N   kudá bay kumá bu   sebé
   1SG.SBJ think PST COMP 2SG.SBJ know
   kumá i   bey kasa.
   COMP 3SG.SBJ come house
   'I thought that you knew that he had come home.'

   b. San Andres Creole English (Bartens 2013b)
   Wi gwain go pruuv di   kies!
   1PL FUT   go prove ART.DEF case
   'We are going to prove the case!'

   c. Kikongo-Kituba (Mufwene 2013)
   Yandi sonik-aka na   biki yayi.
   he/she write-PST with pen this
   'He/she wrote with this pen.'

(2) a. Chinese Pidgin English (Li & Matthews 2013)
   (口件)結治暑廉
   Can ∅   catchee shrimp?
   can you catch   shrimp
   'Can you get any shrimps?'

   b. Papiá Kristang (Baxter 2013)
   eli ja santá naké-úngua basu   di albi,
   3SG PFV sit   LOC-that   beneath of tree
   ∅ ja sombrá
   3SG PFV shelter
   'She sat down beneath a tree, (and she) sheltered.'

   c. Batavia Creole (Maurer 2013b)
   Undi ∅ dja anda?
   where he PFV go
   'Where did he go?'

2. The values

The most prominent contrast for this feature is between languages with **obligatory person forms in subject position** (values 1 and 2) and languages with **optional person forms** (value 3, ex. 2). Within the languages with obligatory person forms, we can make a subdivision into languages with **person forms that are words** (value 1, ex. 1) and languages with **person forms that are affixes** (value 2, ex. 3). In addition, we distinguish two minor types (see §4). This feature, including the definition of the values, is based on Dryer (2005m).

●	1. Obligatory pronoun words	49
●	2. Pronoun affixes	4
●	3. Optional pronoun words	18
○	4. Subject pronouns in different position	2
●	5. Mixed behaviour of pronominal subjects	3

The map shows a striking areal regularity: in the Atlantic region, all languages have obligatory subject pronouns, while in the Indian Ocean and in Asia, almost all languages have optional subject pronouns. The Pacific region (Australia and the Pacific islands) again tends to have obligatory pronouns. This is thus one of the features that show the clearest geographical patterning, and is thus most clearly due to substrate influence.

The West African substrate languages that have influenced the structure of Atlantic creoles show a very strong tendency to have obligatory subject pronoun words or affixes (Dryer 2005m, Creissels 2005). This explains that even the Portuguese-based creoles in the Atlantic have obligatory pronouns, although Portuguese (at least European Portuguese, in contrast to English and French) does not have obligatory pronouns. On the other hand, the languages of South and Southeast Asia tend to show optional pronouns, which is reflected in the Portuguese-based and Spanish-based creoles of the region as well as Chinese Pidgin English and Chinese Pidgin Russian, and the languages based on Malay. Why the French-based languages of the Indian Ocean pattern with the Asian languages is less clear. In the Pacific islands, the Austronesian languages tend to be like the African languages in requiring obligatory subject pronouns, so again the fact that Tok Pisin and Tayo have obligatory pronouns may be explainable by the substrate.

Affixal pronouns (value 2), which are always obligatory, are found only in those *APiCS* languages that are closely related to non-European languages with affixal pronouns, especially the mixed languages Michif, Media Lengua, and Mixed Ma'a/Mbugu, but also in the Bantu-based Lingala. An example is (3).

(3) Media Lengua (Muysken 2013)
     nu tini-ni warmi kunki-un no kaza-y pudi-ni
     NEG have-1SG woman who-INS not marry-INF can-1SG
     'I do not have a woman whom I can marry.'

(Affixal person forms are often called "agreement markers", but we do not use this terminology, for the reasons given in Haspelmath 2013a+.)

It should be noted, however, that the distinction between affixal pronouns and pronoun words of the sort seen in (1a) and (1b) is difficult to draw. For example, French weak subject pronouns are written separately, but they have all the properties of prefixes (Miller 1992). Creissels (2005) notes that the same is true of West African languages: weak subject pronouns are often written separately as in English or French, but really behave like prefixes. In general, making a distinction between affixes and clitics (dependent words that cannot occur on their own) is difficult (Haspelmath 2011b). And most of the languages with obligatory pronoun words in subject position (value 1) have special dependent person forms for the subject (values 2 and 4 of Chapter 17). Whether one describes these special dependent person forms as clitics or affixes is typically a matter of descriptive tradition, and not so much due to real differences.

Note also that our major distinction, between obligatory and optional pronouns, is rather different from another well-known distinction, between "pro-drop" (or "null-subject") and "non-pro-drop" languages. The latter correspond roughly to our types 1 and 4, and the former can be seen as corresponding to type 2 and 3 (cf. Meyerhoff 2000), but we prefer not to use this terminology and this way of grouping the phenomena (see also Haspelmath 2013a+).

3. Distinguishing optional and obligatory use

There are many intermediate cases between the two extremes of languages where person forms are always used and languages where they are never used in non-contrastive contexts. Almost all languages allow the omission of subject person forms in imperatives, and many allow their omission in coordinate structures.

The criterion for optionality (type 3) that we asked our contributors to adopt was whether person forms are omitted strikingly more often than in English. According to den Besten & Biberauer (2013), this is not the case in Afrikaans, for instance, even though this language allows the omission of the first-person-singular pronoun in the spoken language (*Verstaan nie* = *Ek verstaan nie* 'I don't understand'), but English is similar. For Berbice Dutch, Kouwenberg (2013a) argues that pronominal arguments cannot be considered optional, because they cannot be omitted in out-of-the-blue sentences, as would be the case in a pro-drop language, even though pronominal subjects are frequently omitted in discourse. This is probably the most extreme case where a different decision would have been possible.

4. The minor types

In one of the minor types, the subject person form is **in a different position than the full-NP subject** (value 4). One example comes from Papiamentu, where weak person forms usually follow the modal particle *lo* (see 4a), but full-NP subjects precede it (see 4b).

(4) Papiamentu (Kouwenberg 2013b)
   a. *Lo e por ta kome.*
      MOOD 3SG be.able TNS eat
      'He may be eating.'
   b. *E kambio di gobièrnu lo no trese*
      DEF change of government MOOD NEG bring
      kambio den esaki.
      change in one.DEM.PROX
      'The change of government will not bring any change in this regard.'

In Eskimo Pidgin, pronoun subjects follow the verb (e.g. *tuktu mûkki ila* [caribou kill he] 'He killed the caribou'), but full-NP subjects precede it (e.g. *wai'hinni artegi annahanna* [woman coat sew] 'The woman is sewing a coat').

In the final type, first- and second-person-subject forms behave differently from third-person-subject forms. For example, in Singapore Bazaar Malay, first- and second-person pronouns are optional, but third-person pronouns are obligatory:

(5) Singapore Bazaar Malay (Khin Khin Aye 2013)
   a. *Sekarang tua ah tak kerjar.*
      now old TOP NEG work
      'Now [that I am] old, [I do] not work.'
   b. ***Dia** mau pukul dia sendiri.*
      3SG want hit 3SG REFL
      'He wanted to hit himself.'

62 Expression of pronominal subjects

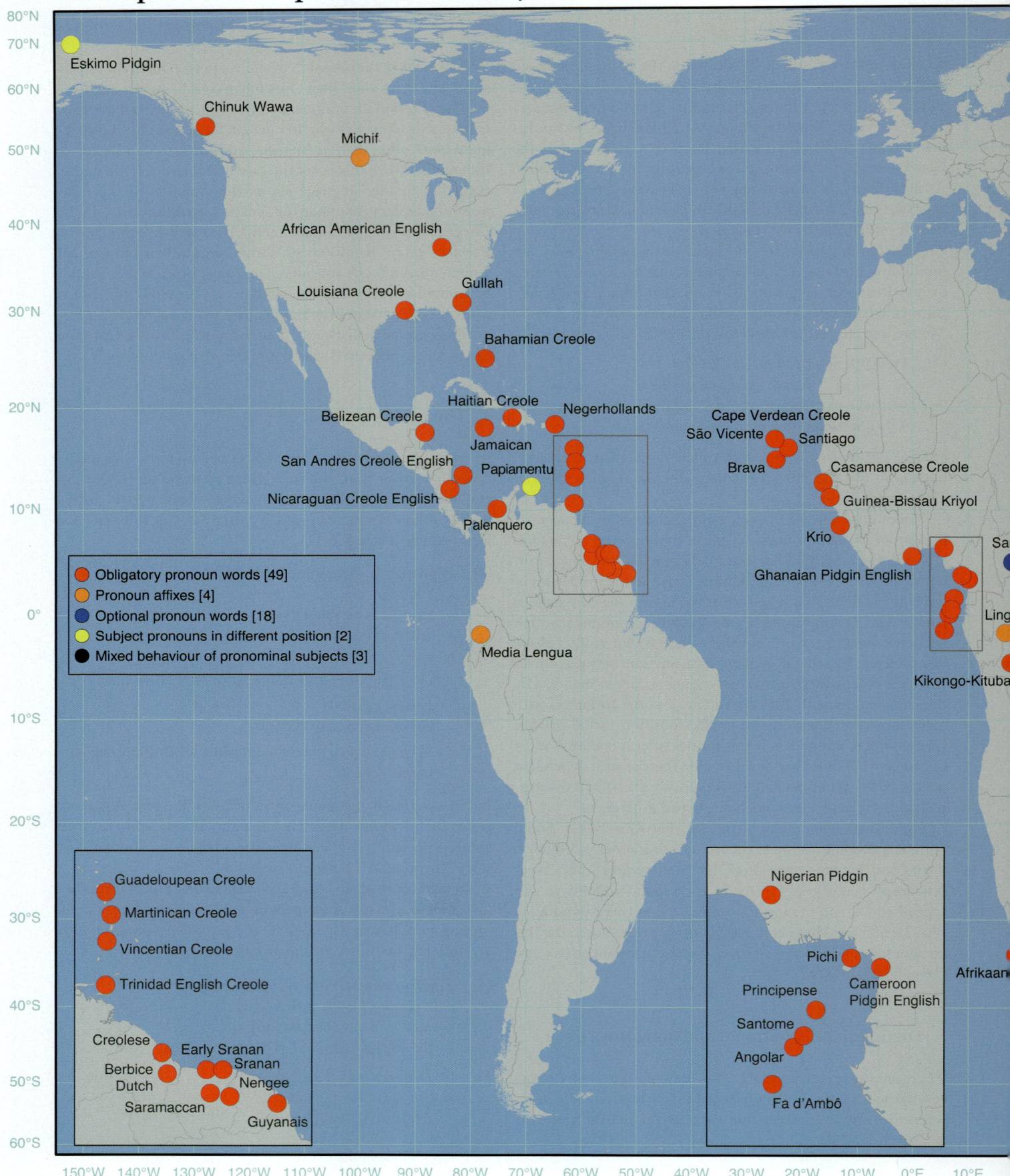

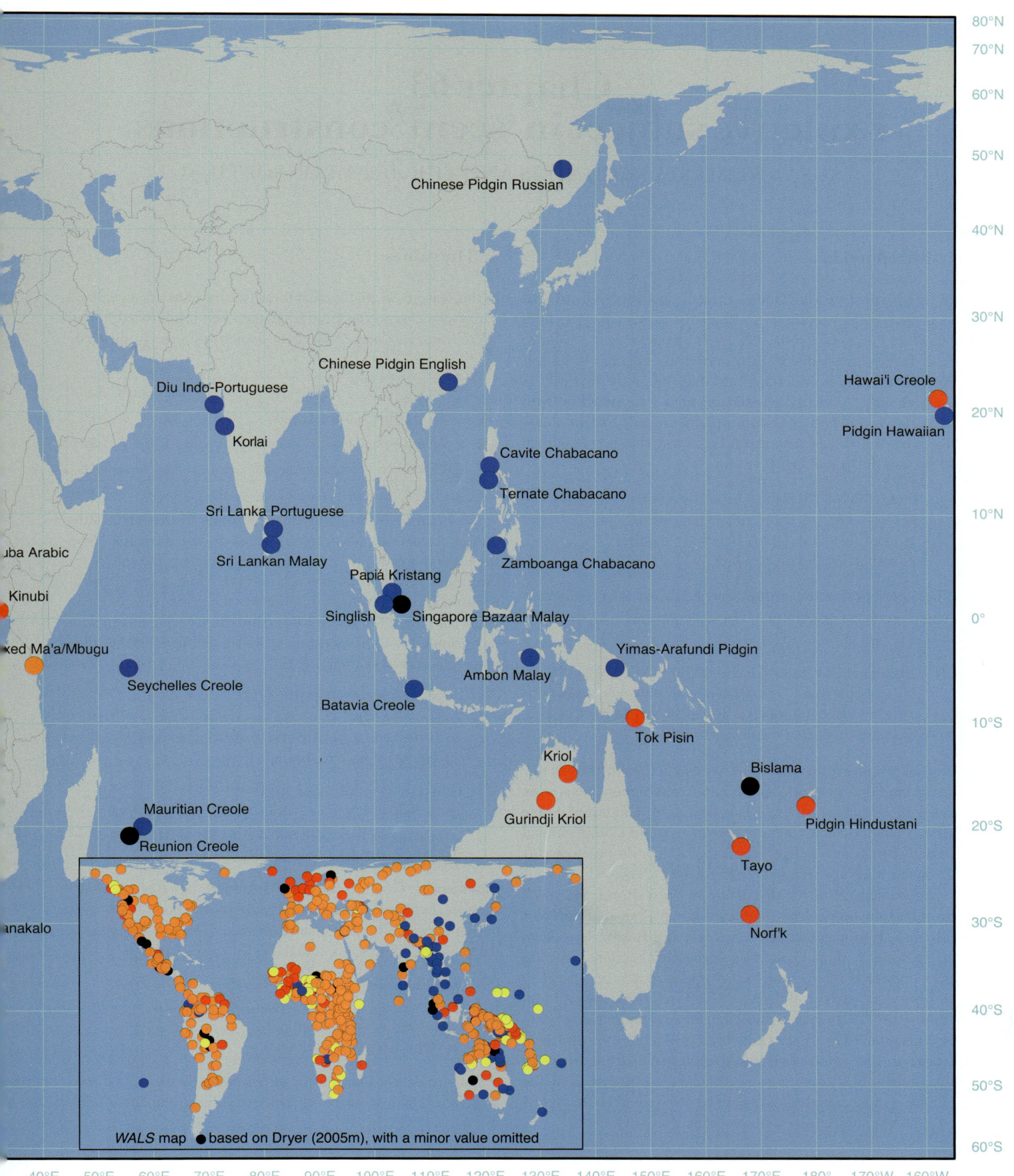

Chapter 63
Expletive subject in 'seem' constructions

SUSANNE MARIA MICHAELIS AND THE *APiCS* CONSORTIUM

1. Introduction

In this chapter we ask whether there is an **expletive subject** in a 'seem' construction, as in English *It seems (that) we have stayed long enough/ It looks like.../ It appears that it is going to rain*. An expletive subject is a pronoun-like element in subject position that has no reference and that functions primarily as a placeholder. A **'seem' construction** is a construction with a matrix verb denoting a propositional attitude ('seem', 'look like', 'resemble') and a complement clause that is its notional subject, as illustrated in (1):

(1) Pichi (Yakpo 2013)
 È fiba se Bòyé gɛt mɔ̀ní.
 3SG.EXPL resemble [QUOT Boye have money]
 'It seems that Boye has money.'

The experiencer of the attitude may be absent as in (1), or present as an object or oblique (*It seems to me that . . .*), as shown in (2):

(2) Casamancese Creole (Biagui & Quint 2013)
 I parsí-m kumá i na cobé awosi.
 3SG.EXPL seem-1SG.OBJ [COMP 3SG.SBJ FUT rain today]
 'It seems to me that it will rain today.'

Not all languages have a 'seem' construction in the narrow sense intended in this chapter, this construction apparently being more typical of European (standard) languages. Some *APiCS* languages only have experiencer-subject propositional attitude constructions like 'I think that . . .', or they may use adverbs meaning 'apparently, seemingly' (see §2, below).

In the context of the discussion of "pro-drop languages", the question of expletive subjects has played an important role: pro-drop languages (e.g. Spanish and Italian) have been claimed *not* to show expletive subject constructions, whereas the opposite holds for non-pro-drop languages (e.g. English and Swedish; see e.g. Roberts 1997). Under this assumption, as most *APiCS* languages show obligatory pronominal subjects (see Chapter 62) and are therefore considered non-pro-drop languages, one would expect these languages also to show expletive subjects in a 'seem' construction. But as the data show, the picture is more complex (as discussed in §3; see also Chapter 64 on expletive subjects in existential constructions).

2. The values

In this feature, we distinguish three feature values. Values 1 and 2 may co-occur in the same language when it has two different 'seem' constructions, or when the expletive subject is optional.

		excl	shrd	all
●	1. An expletive subject is used	20	8	28
●	2. An expletive subject is not used	15	8	23
○	3. There is no 'seem' construction	26	0	26

Value 1 languages, which exclusively show an **expletive subject** construction, are nearly all English-based creoles. Here, the English words *(be) like* or *look like* are often the source for the creole 'seem' verbs, as in (3) and (4). Most often the third-person-singular pronoun functions as the expletive subject. In Nigerian Pidgin (3), the third-person-singular dependent subject pronoun is always used in its shortened form *i* rather than in its full form *im* (Faraclas 2013).

(3) Nigerian Pidgin (Faraclas 2013)
 Ì bí làyk se wì dɔn taya.
 3SG.EXPL be like [COMP 1PL.SBJ COMPL be.tired]
 'It seems that we have become tired.'

(4) Jamaican (Farquharson 2013)
 It luk laka se im ago kil im wid lik.
 3SG.EXPL look like [COMP 3SG FUT kill 3SG with blow]
 'It appears that he is going to beat him to death.'

Casamancese Creole is the only Portuguese-based creole which shows an expletive subject in the 'seem' construction as its only option (see ex. 2), whereas in Papiá Kristang and Principense the expletive subject is optional (i.e. they also have value 2).

(5) Papiá Kristang (Baxter 2013)
 (yo) parsé lo kai chua
 (3SG.EXPL) seem [FUT fall rain]
 'It seems (to me) it will rain.'

Singapore Bazaar Malay is the only language with a non-European base which requires an expletive subject, the demonstrative *ini*.

(6) Singapore Bazaar Malay (Khin Khin Aye 2013)
Ini macam sula tau paham saya pinya celita.
DEM.EXPL seem [PFV know understand 1SG POSS story]
'It seems [as if you] have already known [and] understood my language.'

There are 23 value-2 languages, which do not use any expletive subject. For 15 of them this construction is the only option. These include the Ibero-Romance-based creoles Papiamentu, Palenquero, the Cape Verdean Creole varieties, Guinea-Bissau Kriyol, Korlai, and Cavite Chabacano.

(7) Cape Verdean Creole of São Vicente (Swolkien 2013)
Parsê-m éra kel dia.
seem-1SG COP.PST DEM day
'It seems to me that it was on that day.'

(8) Cavite Chabacano (Sippola 2013a)
Ta pareci que dela niso paga con ele el debe mañana.
IPFV seem that must 1PL pay OBJ 3SG DEF debt tomorrow
'It seems that we must pay him the debt tomorrow.'

There are also three English-based creoles which lack an expletive subject: Bislama, Tok Pisin, and Hawai'i Creole. Singlish and Vincentian Creole show both constructions with and without the expletive subject. The interesting cases are Tok Pisin, Hawai'i Creole, and Vincentian, which are clear non-pro-drop languages, but do not require an expletive subject here (see discussion in §3 and Chapter 62).

As for the French-based creoles, many of them show both construction types, too:

(9) Mauritian Creole (Baker & Kriegel 2013)
a. *li paret ki fin ena en kudeta*
3SG.EXPL seem that COMPL have INDF coup.d'état
'It seems that there has been a coup d'état.'
b. *paret ki lapli pu tombe dan en ti mama*
seem that rain FUT fall in INDF little moment
'It seems that it will start raining in a moment.'

Reunion Creole is the only French-based creole which never uses an expletive subject.

Roughly a third of the *APiCS* languages do not have a **'seem' construction** in the narrow sense of our definition (value 3). Some of these languages use experiencer-subject propositional attitude verbs such as 'I think that . . .', for example,

(10) Pidgin Hawaiian (Roberts 2013)
Wau manao akahi pihi nui iaia paani kela wai.
1SG think INDF fish big 3SG play DET water
'I thought that a huge fish was playing in the water.'

Lingala, Sango, Fanakalo, Ambon Malay, Chinese Russian Pidgin, and Tayo show the same construction type. Other languages with value 3 use adverbs meaning 'apparently, seemingly'. These adverbs may have lexicalized from verbal source constructions in the European base languages, for example, *pares* 'apparently' in Diu Indo-Portuguese goes back to Portuguese *parece* 'it seems', whereas *laik* in Creolese goes back to English (*it looks*) *like*. The fact that these lexical items are no longer combinable with negation or TAM markers is evidence that they are not verbal elements any more in the creole languages. Martinican Creole *asiparé* 'apparently' even goes back to a phrasal expression in French, *à ce qu'il paraît* 'as it seems' (lit. 'to that which it seems').

3. Discussion

Two aspects are of interest when looking at the map: (i) what is the relation between the 'seem' construction in the creole and its (European) base language? and (ii) does the pro-drop parameter make the right predictions for this feature?

For all English- and French-based creoles with value 2 (either exclusively or shared: e.g. Vincentian Creole, Tok Pisin, Hawai'i Creole, Haitian Creole, Louisiana Creole, Mauritian Creole), there is a mismatch between the expletive subject construction in the base languages English and French (*it seems that/il semble que*) and the non-use of an expletive subject in the corresponding creole languages. The same holds the other way round for Portuguese- and Spanish-based creoles. Here the base languages lack expletives (∅ *parece*), and one might expect the corresponding creoles to show the same value. But Principense, Papiá Kristang, and Casamancese Creole have expletive subjects (the latter exclusively).

Can the pro-drop parameter then make the right predictions here? As can be seen from Chapter 62, the majority of the *APiCS* languages have obligatory pronoun words in subject position, with a clear areal pattern: in the Atlantic all languages have obligatory subject pronoun words, in the Indian Ocean nearly all languages allow for optional pronouns, while in Australia and the Pacific again the obligatory pattern prevails. One would expect that languages with an obligatory subject pronoun word also have an obligatory expletive pronoun in the 'seem' construction, and vice versa. But the *APiCS* data clearly contradict this simplistic picture. Many languages with value 2 are non-pro-drop languages, in other words, have obligatory subject pronouns. The English-based creoles Tok Pisin, Hawai'i Creole, and Vincentian Creole were mentioned earlier. But here we also find the Portuguese-based creoles of the Cape Verde Islands, Guinea-Bissau Kriyol, Palenquero, Juba Arabic, and Kinubi. Conversely, five languages in the Indian Ocean and Southeast Asia (Mauritian and Seychelles Creole, Singlish, Singapore Bazaar Malay, Papiá Kristang) allow expletive subjects but can drop their subject pronouns (see Chapter 62).

63 Expletive subject in 'seem' constructions

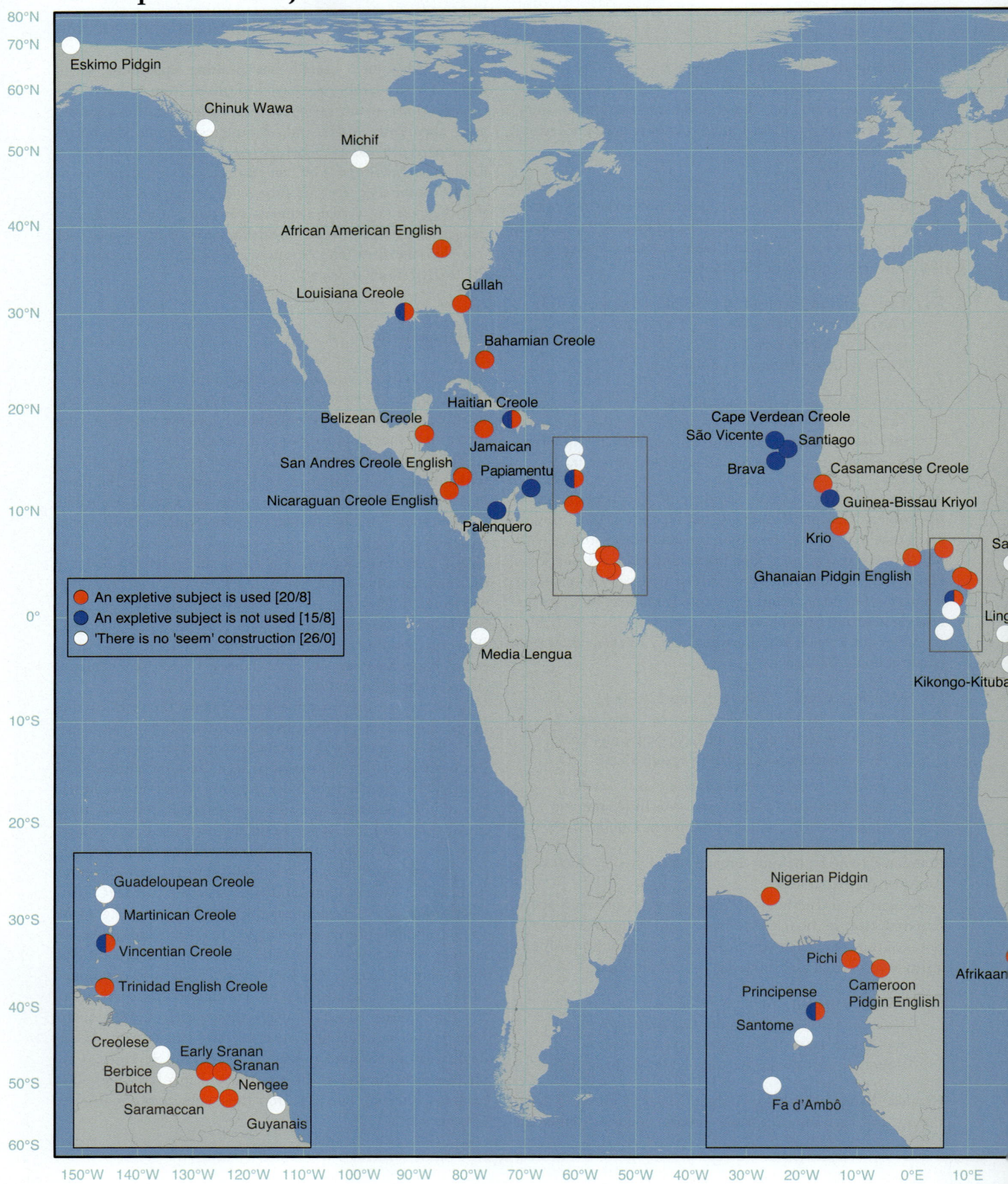

Chapter 64
Expletive subject of existential verb

MARTIN HASPELMATH AND THE *APiCS* CONSORTIUM

1. Existential verb and expletive subject

Most languages use an **existential verb** in existential constructions such as (1a–c). In addition, an existential construction contains an **existential argument** (e.g. 'a big well' in 1a) and an optional locational phrase ('in town' in 1c).

(1) a. Batavia Creole (Maurer 2013b)
   *Nu meo di matu **teng** ung pos grandi.*
   in middle of forest EXIST a well big
   'In the middle of the forest, there was a big well.'

   b. Jamaican (Farquharson 2013)
   *Yu **gat** som piipl we groj yu*
   2SG EXIST some people REL grudge 2SG

   fi evriting yu gat.
   for everything 2SG have

   'There are some people who covet everything you have.'

   c. Sranan (Winford & Plag 2013)
   *Merki no **de** srefisrefi a foto.*
   milk NEG EXIST at.all LOC city
   'There isn't any milk at all in town.'

The existential verb often has other uses as well; in particular, it may be used as a transitive possession verb 'have', like *teng* in (1a) and *gat* in (1b) (see Chapter 78 for more details), or it may be identical with the locational copula, as in Sranan (see 1c, cf. the use of *de* as a copula: *den pikin de na skoro* 'the children are at school'). But a language may also have an existential verb that is used only in this function, like Juba Arabic *fi*:

(2) Juba Arabic (Manfredi & Petrollino 2013)
   fi béled geríb ma júba
   EXIST village near with Juba
   'There is a village near Juba.'

In SVO languages, the existential argument is subject-like when it precedes the verb (as in 1c), and object-like if it follows the verb (as in 1a–b, 2). The latter case is more common, and in such existential constructions, there may be an **expletive subject**, that is, a pronoun-like element that occupies the preverbal subject position but does not have any specific meaning of its own. Two examples of existential constructions with expletive subjects are given in (3) (another one was given in 1b).

(3) a. Santome (Hagemeijer 2013)
   Ê tê dja ku n na ka kume fa.
   3SG.EXPL EXIST day REL 1SG NEG IPFV eat NEG
   'There are days on which I don't eat.'

   b. Trinidad English Creole (Mühleisen 2013)
   It have rum in de house.
   3SG.EXPL EXIST rum PREP DET house
   'There is rum in the house.'

The expletive may also be a locational demonstrative such as 'there', as in (4).

(4) Afrikaans (den Besten & Biberauer 2013)
   Daar is 'n probleem.
   LOC.EXPL EXIST INDF.ART problem
   'There is a problem.'

Only two types are distinguished in this chapter:

	excl	shrd	all
● 1. An expletive subject is used	10	17	27
● 2. An expletive subject is not used	48	17	65

2. Constructions with expletives

The majority of our languages do not have expletive subjects in existential constructions, but such expletives are not uncommon in the Atlantic creoles, especially English-based and French-based languages. This pattern can be explained in part by lexifier influence, because both English (*there is*) and French (*il y a*) use expletive subjects, while Portuguese (*há*) does not use an expletive subject.

However, the pidgins and creoles do not simply continue the lexifier pattern. In the English-based languages, a construction with *get/got* is common (see 5a–b, 1b), or the verb *have* may be used (3b):

(5) a. Krio (Finney 2013)
   dɛn gɛt bɔku pipul dɛm de
   3PL have a.lot.of people PL LOC
   'There were a lot of people there.'

b. Kriol (Schultze-Berndt & Angelo 2013)
I got-im big gata maitbi theya, thet-said.
3SG have-TR big gutter maybe there DEM-side
'Maybe there is a big gutter, on that side.'

Likewise, French-based languages tend to show a 'have' verb (*gen* in 6a, *ni* in 6b) that is distinct from the old 'have' verb of the lexifier (*avoir*).

(6) a. Louisiana Creole (Neumann-Holzschuh & Klingler 2013)
Ye te janmen gen pir blan dan la Louzyaen
3PL PST never have pure white in DEF Louisiana
ye tou mele.
3PL all mixed
'There have never been pure whites in Louisiana, they're all mixed.'

b. Guadeloupean Creole (Colot & Ludwig 2013a)
I ni onlo moun.
3SG have much people
'There are a lot of people.'

In Dutch-based creoles, too, there are existentials with 'have', and here, too, they are innovated with respect to the lexifier.

(7) Negerhollands (van Sluijs 2013)
Ēen tid di a ha ēn frou.
INDF time 3SG PST have INDF woman
'Once upon a time there was a woman.'

Thus, these Atlantic creoles have not simply inherited their constructions with expletives from their lexifiers (though it may of course be that the innovative verbs like *got* and *gen* were already present in the dialects of the lexifiers that were the input to creolization).

It seems that the expletive in the subject position has more to do with the fact that the languages have obligatory subject pronouns (cf. Chapter 62). Obligatory subject pronouns are also found in some Portuguese-based creoles, and some of them have existential expletives as well, such as Santome (in 3a) and Guinea-Bissau Kriyol:

(8) Guinea-Bissau Kriyol (Intumbo et al. 2013)
I ten un igreja na e prasa.
3SG have a church in this town
'There is a church in this town.'

Recall that Portuguese has no expletive subject in existential constructions (*há* 'there is'), and no obligatory subject pronouns.

The expletive subject is normally a third-person-singular personal pronoun, but other person–number forms are possible as well. In (1b) we saw a second-person-singular form, and in (5a) and (6a) a third-person-plural form. The first person plural also occurs:

(9) Ghanaian Pidgin English (Huber 2013)
wì gɛt difrɛn frɛnɛs we dè dè kam
1PL get different foreigners COMP 3PL HAB come
'There are different foreigners who come.'

There are only three languages where the expletive is a locational demonstrative, all very close to the lexifiers English and Dutch: Afrikaans (see 4), Singlish, and less basilectal Nicaraguan Creole English (*dier wil aalwiez bii* 'there will always be'). Bantu languages also have expletives, as illustrated by the expletive use of the gender 16 prefix *hé-* in Mixed Ma'a/Mbugu:

(10) Mixed Ma'a/Mbugu (Mous 2013)
hé-lo isonhka i-kumure
G16-have dust(G5) G5-many
'There is a lot of dust.'

3. Constructions without expletives

Existential constructions without expletives are the norm in languages with non-European lexifiers, and in SOV languages. They are also found in the Cape Verdean varieties and in the Spanish-based languages of the Philippines:

(11) Ternate Chabacano (Sippola 2013b)
Tiene nah rio ung grande bangka motor.
EXIST LOC river INDF big boat motor
'There is a big motor boat on the river.'

In several English-based languages, existential constructions have the existential argument in subject position. We already saw an example from Sranan in (1c), and (12a–b) show two further examples. (Note that (12a) is one of the few examples of an existential construction without an existential verb.)

(12) a. San Andres Creole English (Bartens 2013b)
Tu moch hous iina Nort End.
too much house in North End
'There are too many houses in North End.'

b. Krio (Finney 2013)
it de na di tebul
food EXIST LOC ART table
'There is food on the table.'

Some languages even allow the existential argument in subject position when there is no locational phrase (e.g. Saramaccan *Hía ló bi de* [many tribes TNS be] 'There were many tribes').

A special type of existential construction that is not found in European languages at all is a construction with a quantificational expression in predicate position:

(13) Lingala (Meeuwis 2013)
ba-to ba-zal-ákí ebelé
PL-person 3PL-be-PST many
'There were many people.' (lit. 'persons were many')

64 Expletive subject of existential verb

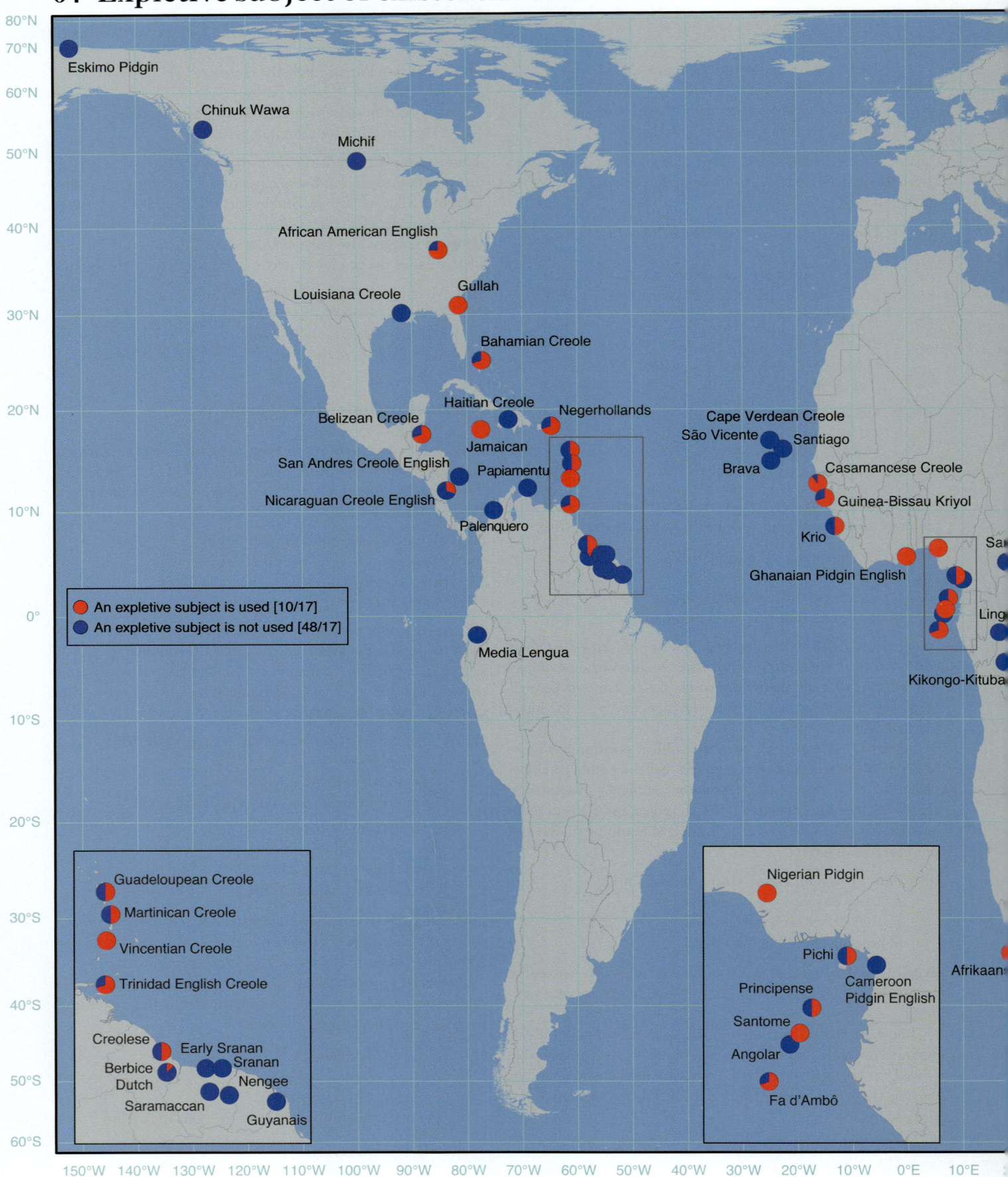

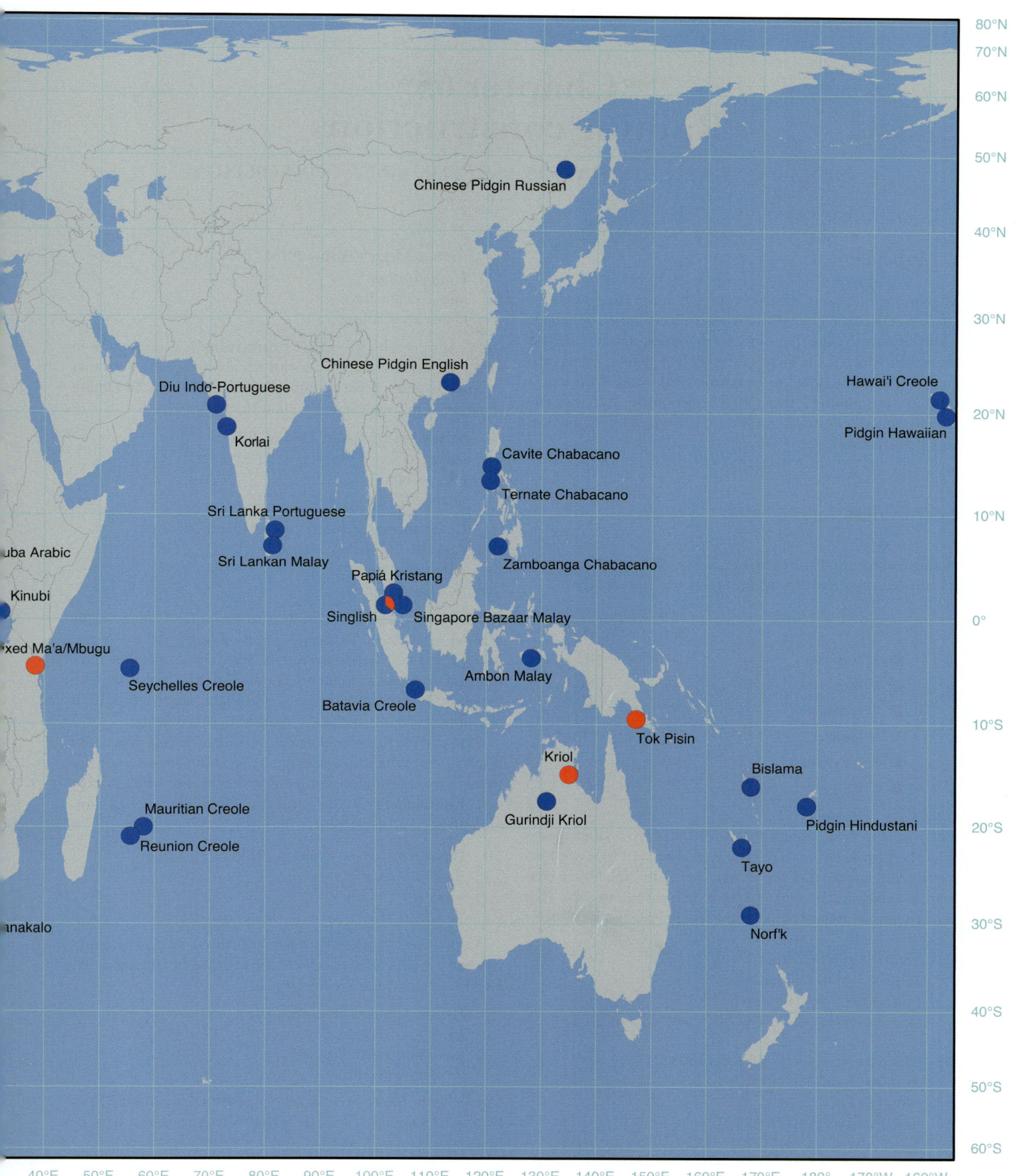

Chapter 65
Raining constructions

SUSANNE MARIA MICHAELIS AND THE *APiCS* CONSORTIUM

1. Introduction

Meteorological events are not expressed uniformly across languages (cf. Eriksen et al. 2010, 2012 for recent cross-linguistic work), and they also exhibit interesting variation in the *APiCS* languages, which is the focus of the present chapter. Since languages often code different meteorological events ('the sun is shining', 'it is raining', 'there is a thunderstorm', etc.) with different syntactic constructions, we consider exclusively the situation 'it is raining'.

2. The values

In this feature we distinguish six values. A language can have several raining constructions belonging to different types.

		excl	shrd	all
●	1. Rain falls	34	14	48
●	2. Rain rains	3	7	10
●	3. It rains	6	10	16
●	4. Raining	9	8	17
●	5. It gives rain	0	1	1
●	6. Rain exists	1	1	2

By far the most common type in the *APiCS* languages is value 1 ('**rain falls**'), where raining is expressed by a word referring to the natural element 'rain' or 'water' in subject position accompanied by a general verb such as 'fall' or 'hit'. This construction is not restricted to any specific geographical area.

(1) Haitian Creole (Fattier 2013)
 Lapli a pral tonbe talè.
 rain DEF FUT.go fall soon
 'It will rain very soon.' (lit. 'Rain will fall soon.')

(2) Mauritian Creole (Baker & Kriegel 2013)
 lapli pu tombe
 rain FUT fall
 'it will rain' (lit. 'Rain will fall.')

(3) Ambon Malay (Paauw 2013)
 Ujang turung.
 rain come.down
 'The rain is falling.'

In constructions of value 2 ('**rain rains**'), a 'rain' noun in subject position is combined with a 'rain' verb, i.e. a verb that exclusively (apart from metaphorical usages) refers to raining situations. Only ten languages show this construction.

(4) Mixed Ma'a/Mbugu (Mous 2013)
 mare í-si
 rain 9-rain
 'it rained'

(5) Casamancese Creole (Biagui & Quint 2013)
 Coba na cobé.
 rain PROG rain
 'It is raining.'

Here, the geographical restriction to Africa (and some nearby islands) is striking. Besides Kikongo-Kituba, Mixed Ma'a/Mbugu, and Guinea-Bissau Kriyol, which have only this 'raining' construction, it is found as one option in Cape Verdean Creole of Brava, Casamancese Creole, Pichi, and the three Gulf of Guinea creoles Principense, Santome, and Angolar.

Papiamentu is the only creole outside of Africa which also displays this value. In this language it is the lexical noun for 'water' *awa*, and not for 'rain', which is combined with a raining verb. Kouwenberg (2013b) notes that this construction is common in the Aruban dialect.

(6) Papiamentu (Kouwenberg 2013b)
 Awa tawata jobe.
 water PST rain
 'It was raining.'

Value 3 constructions ('**it rains**') consist of an expletive subject and a 'rain' verb, as is well documented in languages like English (*it rains*) and French (*il pleut*).

(7) Hawai'i Creole (Velupillai 2013)
 its gɔna ɹeɪn
 3SG.is FUT rain
 'It's going to rain.'

Interestingly, most of the 16 languages with this value are English-based languages, and out of the six languages that have no other construction, five are English-based languages (African American English, Bahamian Creole, Nicaraguan Creole English, San Andres Creole English, and Hawai'i Creole). The sixth language is Afrikaans, a Dutch-based language. This provides a striking parallel to Chapter 63 ('seem' constructions), where the expletive subject construction occurs almost exclusively in English-based creoles as well. But some Portuguese-based languages too (Santome, Guinea-Bissau Kriyol, Casamancese Creole) have the construction with an expletive subject:

(8) Santome (Hagemeijer 2013)
Ê ka sôbê muntu fan.
3SG IPFV rain a.lot PCL
'It rains a lot!'

The only French-based creole with an expletive subject is Haitian Creole:

(9) Haitian Creole (Fattier 2013)
Petèt i ka fè lapli.
maybe it can make rain
'It is possible that it will rain.'

The next type is value 4 ('**raining**'), where there is just a 'rain' verb without any subject (as in Spanish *llueve* and Portuguese *chove* 'it rains').

(10) Ambon Malay (Paauw 2013)
Mo ujang.
FUT rain
'It's going to rain.'

(11) Chinese Pidgin English (Li & Matthews 2013)
Long lain [...].
long rain
'It has been raining for a long time [...].'

Here, we again see some geographical patterning: the 17 languages with this value are spoken in Asia, the Pacific, North and South America, and on the Cape Verde Islands, but not in mainland Africa, the Gulf of Guinea, the Caribbean (except for Papiamentu and Palenquero), or Australia. Palenquero, the Cape Verdean Creoles, and Norf'k have obligatory pronoun words in subject position (cf. Chapter 62), but do not feature an expletive subject pronoun in their 'raining' constructions.

Among the English-based creoles, only the languages spoken in Asia and the Pacific (Chinese Pidgin English, Singlish, Bislama, Norf'k) show no expletive subject. This is in line with the lack of obligatory pronoun words in subject position discussed in Chapter 62 for all languages (except for Norf'k, which has obligatory pronoun words).

(12) Singlish (Lim & Ansaldo 2013)
***Rain** already.*
rain PRF
'It's raining.' OR: 'It has started raining.' OR: 'It has rained.'

(13) Norf'k (Mühlhäusler 2013)
***Rienen** haad.*
rain.CONT hard
'It is raining hard.'

There is just one language with value 5 ('**it gives rain**'), where 'rain' is object noun of a general verb:

(14) Cape Verdean Creole of São Vicente (Swolkien 2013)
Aont, dá txuva.
yesterday give rain
'It rained yesterday.'

Value 6 ('**rain exists**') reflects a construction type with an existential verb and a lexical argument referring to 'rain'. There are only two *APiCS* languages which feature this type, Sri Lankan Malay as its only option and Tayo (with the alternative widespread 'rain falls' construction, value 1):

(15) Sri Lankan Malay (Slomanson 2013)
Ujang ambɛ aɖa.
rain PROG EXIST
'It is raining.'

3. Origins of the different constructions

As already mentioned, the construction of value 1 ('rain falls') is by far the most frequent construction in the *APiCS* languages and is found in all areas of the world. Eriksen et al. (2010) observe that this construction is also widespread worldwide. Despite this fact, there is good evidence for substrate influence in this particular 'raining' construction. Koopman (1986) and Lefebvre (1998) have pointed out the parallel syntactic constructions in West African languages, in particular in Fongbe, which is one of the most important substrates for Haitian Creole (cf. 1):

(16) Fongbe (Lefebvre 1998: 252)
Jí jà.
rain fall
'It is raining.' (lit. 'Rain falls.')

Similar constructions are found in Bantu languages, giving rise to the same structures, for instance, in the French creoles of the Indian Ocean (see 2 from Mauritian Creole). Schultze-Berndt & Angelo (2013) also argue for substrate influence in Kriol in constructions of value 1 ('rain falls'). More detailed research will probably show that the substrate languages also imposed their structure on the raining constructions of other creole languages.

65 Raining constructions

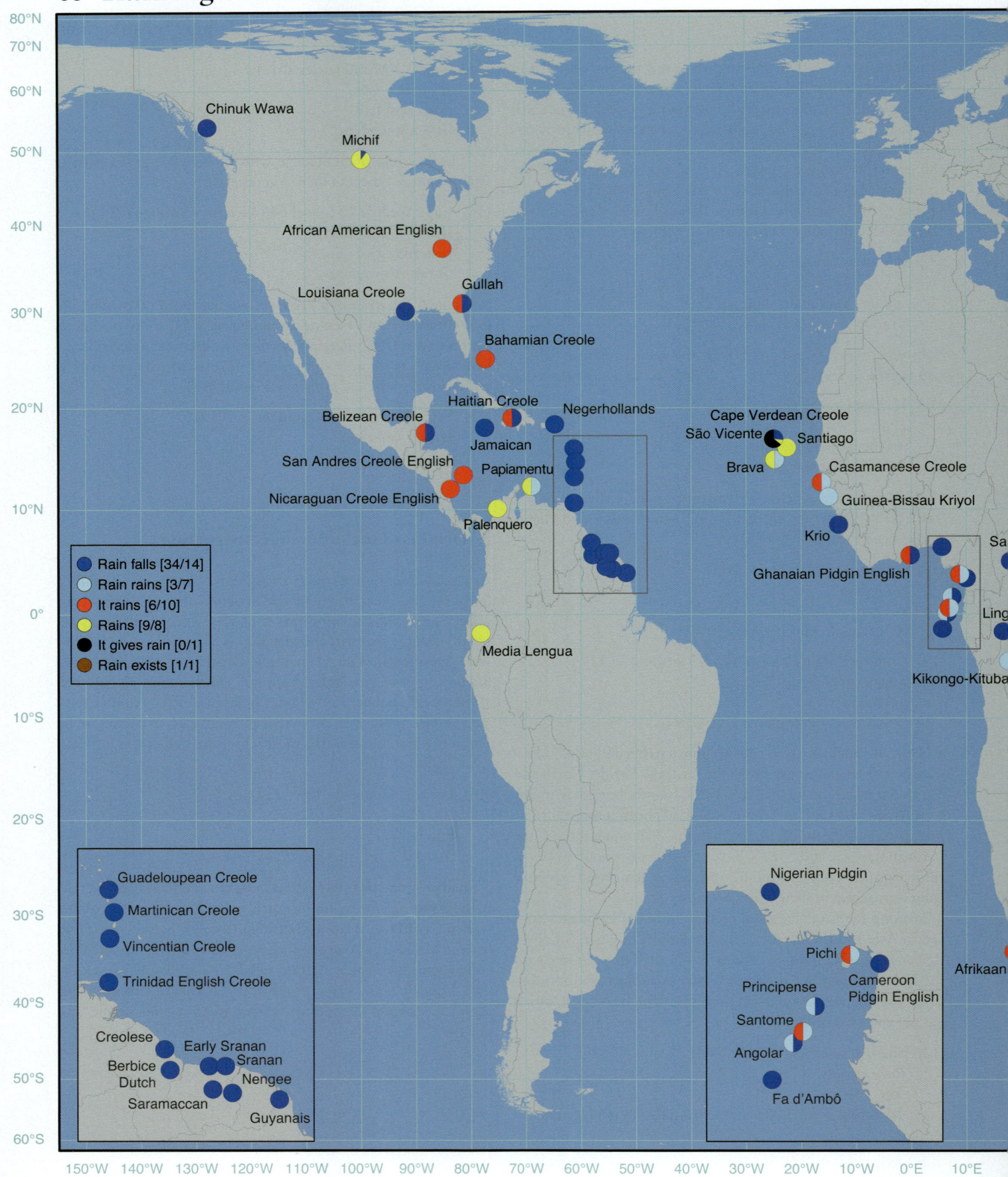

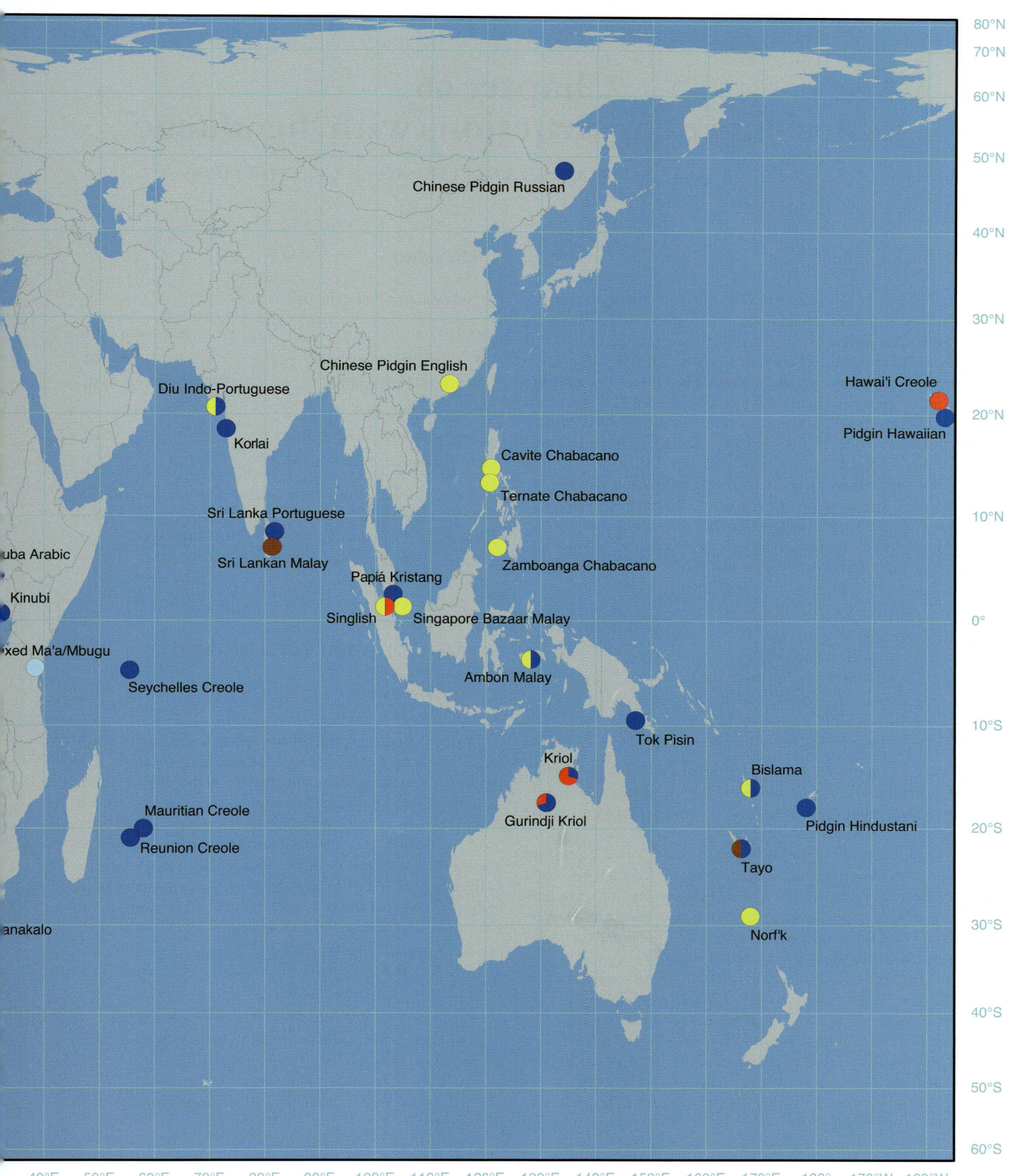

Chapter 66
Experiencer constructions with 'headache'

SUSANNE MARIA MICHAELIS AND THE *APiCS* CONSORTIUM

1. Introduction

In this and the following two chapters we will look at different kinds of **experiencer constructions**, expressing situations involving **'headache'** (Chapter 66), **'liking'** (Chapter 67), and **'fear'** (Chapter 68). There is little systematic typological literature on experiencer constructions. The few studies available focus on European languages (see Bossong 1998, Haspelmath 2001). A study that is of interest for creoles with West African substrates is Ameka (1990), where experiencer constructions in Ewe are analyzed.

Experiencer constructions vary significantly depending on the more specific type of experience; for example, languages may have a different construction for expressing sensations like pain, emotions like fear, and cognitive experiences like hearing. For example, in Korlai, having a headache is expressed differently from having a cold:

(1) Korlai (Clements 2013)
 a. *Kabes duwen mi.*
  head hurt.PROG me
  'I have a headache.' (lit. 'The head hurts me.')
 b. *pari difludz hikad*
  me.DAT cold be/become.PTCP
  'I have a cold.' (lit. 'To me has become cold.')

In the questionnaire, we asked for the expression of 'headache', but some contributors could not provide a 'headache' example from their language. In this case, examples expressing similar pain experiences were also accepted.

So here we ask about the types of construction expressing pain, and more specifically headache, as in English *She has a headache*. Such **headache constructions** involve three participants, an **experiencer**, who experiences the pain sensation ('she'), the **sensation** itself ('ache'), and potentially a **body-part** ('head') to which this sensation is related.

There is a lot of interesting variation in such constructions. However, in this feature, we focus on the question which of the three participants is coded in subject position. *Subject* is defined here as an argument that is coded like the typical agent in a monotransitive clause, or the single argument of an intransitive clause.

Many languages are reported to have several different 'headache' constructions.

2. The values

In this feature we distinguish five values.

		excl	shrd	all
●	1 Experiencer is subject	16	20	36
●	2 Body-part is subject	31	24	55
●	3 Pain is subject	0	4	4
●	4 Experiencer is dative	1	2	3
●	5 Incorporated body-part noun	0	1	1

The first value is shown by languages which code the **experiencer as subject**, as in 'She has a headache' (value 1). This type is fairly widespread among the *APiCS* languages.

(2) Ambon Malay (Paauw 2013)
 De saki kapala.
 3SG sick head
 'She has a headache.'

(3) Juba Arabic (Manfredi & Petrollino 2013)
 ána índu wója ras
 1SG have pain head
 'I have a headache.'

In the second type, the **body-part is coded as the subject** of the sentence, as in 'Her head is aching' (value 2). This type is the most prominent construction in the *APiCS* sample. Within the languages showing value 2, there are several subtypes. The experiencer can be retrievable via the object of the transitive verb 'hurt', as in example (4a) from Angolar and example (4b) from Cape Verdean Creole of São Vicente (see also 1a from Korlai), but it can also be expressed as a possessor of the body-part noun, as shown in examples (5a, b), again from Angolar and from Chinese Pidgin English.

(4) a. Angolar (Maurer 2013a)
  N'tê thêka rue m.
  head PROG hurt me
  'I have a headache.' (lit. 'The head is hurting me.')
 b. Cape Verdean Creole of São Vicente (Swolkien 2013)
  Kabésa ta doe-m senpr.
  head PRS hurt-1SG always
  'I always have a headache.' (lit. 'The head always hurts me.')

(5) a. Angolar (Maurer 2013a)
N'tê m tha ruê.
head 1SG.POSS PROG ache
'I have a headache.' (lit. 'My head is aching.')

b. Chinese Pidgin English (Li & Matthews 2013)
My foot hap got pain.
1SG.POSS foot has got pain
'I have a pain in my foot.' (lit. 'My foot has pain.')

Ghanaian Pidgin English shows a third subtype: the experiencer is expressed both through the possessive pronoun *ma* and the object pronoun *mi*.

(6) Ghanaian Pidgin English (Huber 2013)
mà hɛd dè pen/nak mi
1SG.POSS head PROG pain/knock 1SG.OBJ
'I have a headache.' (lit. 'My head is hurting/knocking me.')

In yet another construction type for value 2, the experiencer is not expressed at all and has to be inferred from the linguistic or extra-linguistic context. One example comes from Diu Indo-Portuguese.

(7) Diu Indo-Portuguese (Cardoso 2013)
kabes tə dw-e.
head IPFV.NPST hurt-INF
'(My) head is hurting.'

The third value is only marginally represented within the *APiCS* sample. Here the **'pain'** itself is coded as **subject**, as in 'Headache is affecting her'. An example comes from Sranan:

(8) Sranan (Winford & Plag 2013)
Ede-hati e kiri mi.
head-hurt IPFV kill me
(lit.) 'A headache is killing me.'

In the next construction type (value 4), the **experiencer is marked as dative**, that is, like the recipient of a typical ditransitive verb like 'give'. In the following examples, the preposition *a* in (9) and the case suffix *-ðang* in (10), which otherwise occur on recipients, mark the human experiencer (see also 1b from Korlai):

(9) Diu Indo-Portuguese (Cardoso 2013)
A mĩ tə sĩti dor də kabes.
DAT 1SG.OBL IPFV.NPST feel.INF pain of head
'I have a headache.' (lit. 'To me is feeling headache.')

(10) Sri Lankan Malay (Slomanson 2013)
Go-ðang kupala a-pinning a-peegang.
1SG-DAT head PRS-pain PRS-pound
'I have a splitting headache.' (lit. 'To me the head is aching, pounding.')

Alternatively, example (10) could have been classified as an instance of value 2 (body-part is subject). But here the dative marking of the experiencer is the more characteristic property of the construction, therefore we have subsumed this construction under value 4.

Finally, value 5 represents an **incorporation construction**, which is found only in the mixed language Michif. In this language, nouns are normally from French and verbs from Cree. But in this construction the nominal stem 'head' (the body-part) is a Cree lexical element incorporated into the verb 'hurt'.

(11) Michif (Bakker 2013)
Dee-ushtikwaan-aa-n.
1.hurt-head-INCORP-1
'I have a headache.'

3. Distribution of the values

As one can see on the map, values 1 and 2 (experiencer is subject and body-part is subject) are by far the most widespread options in the *APiCS* languages. There is no clear patterning either along the pidgin–creole distinction, lexifier, or geographical area. Nevertheless, it is interesting to note that many *APiCS* languages with English, Dutch, and French as their lexifiers *only* have body-part subjects (e.g. Nengee, Jamaican, Seychelles Creole, Tayo). This option is at best one possible construction in these European lexifiers, but it is certainly not the most prominent construction, as the most neutral way of referring to this experience is to express the experiencer in subject position, as in *I have a headache*, French *J'ai mal à la tête* [I.have pain at the head].[1] This leads us to suspect substrate influence, and indeed Ameka's (1990) description of Ewe—a Kwa language of West Africa—shows that the body-part subject in 'headache' situations is the only construction type available in this language. Thus, quite a few of the Atlantic creoles showing only value 2 are probably influenced by their substrates.

The construction type represented by value 4 (experiencer is dative) is geographically restricted. The three languages with this value are all located in South Asia: Diu Indo-Portuguese, Sri Lanka Portuguese, and Sri Lankan Malay. If one looks at the relevant substrate/adstrate languages, one finds that the corresponding pattern of dative-marked experiencers is widespread in South Asian languages. In the literature this construction is called **dative subject construction** (see also Chapter 67 on experiencer constructions with 'like'). The marking of experiencers in the South Asian *APiCS* languages by this kind of dative case or adposition can thus clearly be traced back to their substrates/adstrates.

---

[1] But Spanish and Portuguese show a dative-marked experiencer with postverbal body-part as subject, as in Portuguese *Doi-me a cabeça* [hurt-me the head].

66 Experiencer constructions with 'headache'

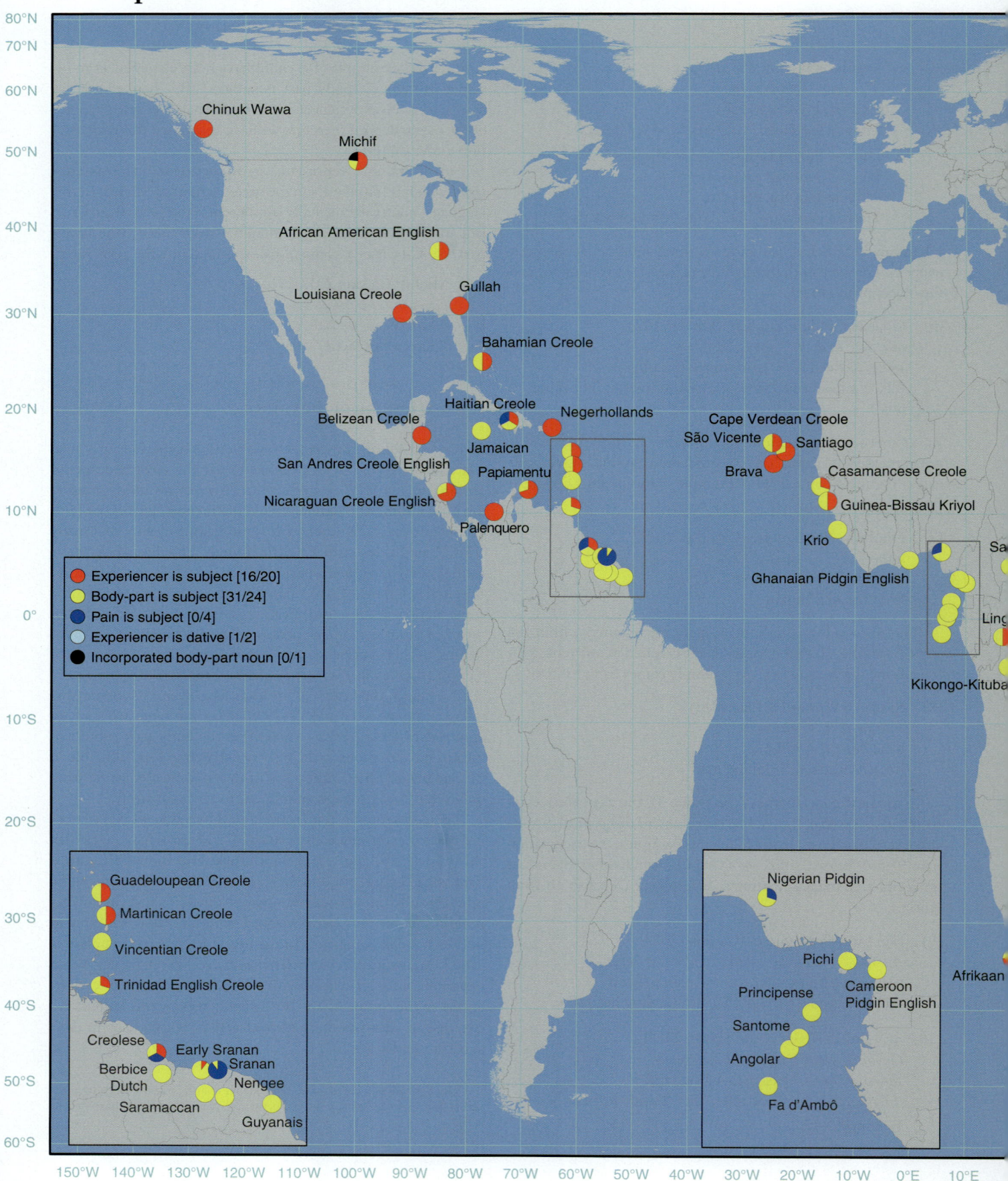

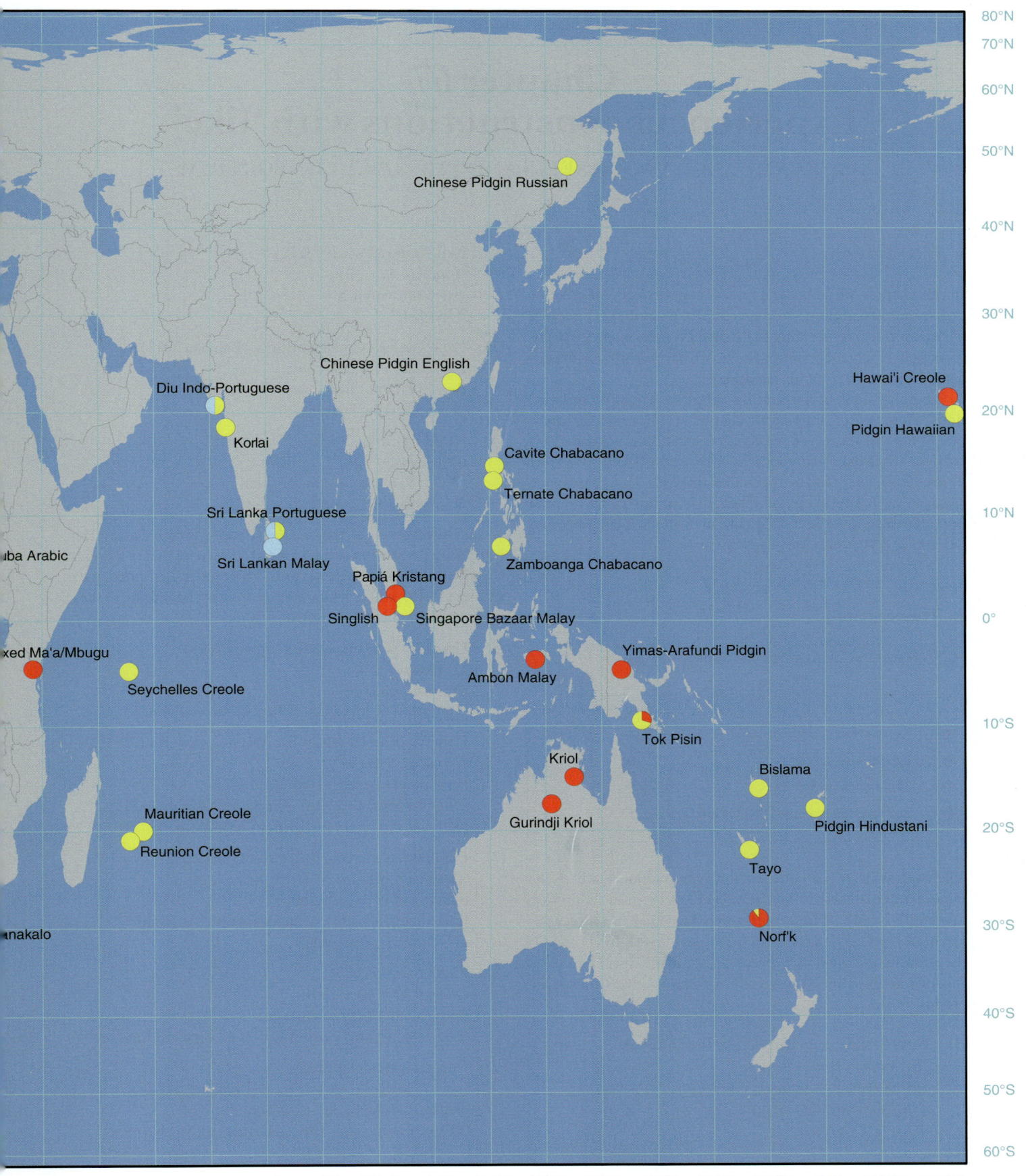

Chapter 67
Experiencer constructions with 'like'

SUSANNE MARIA MICHAELIS AND THE *APiCS* CONSORTIUM

1. Introduction

In this chapter, we consider a type of experiencer construction expressing an emotion. More specifically, we look at expressions of situations corresponding to English *Lea likes mangoes*. 'Like' (experiencer) constructions involve two participants, an experiencer (*Lea*) and a stimulus (*mangoes*).

There is a lot of interesting variation in such constructions. However, in the present chapter we focus on the question of how the **experiencer** is expressed. It may be treated as a **subject** ('Lea likes mangoes'), as a **(direct) object** ('Mangoes please Lea'), or it may be marked as **dative** ('To Lea mangoes are pleasing'). Another possibility is to treat **both experiencer and stimulus as objects** ('Me like mangoes'). A language may have several different 'like' constructions.

2. The values

In this feature we distinguish four values:

	excl	shrd	all
1. Experiencer is subject	54	15	69
2. Experiencer is object	0	11	11
3. Experiencer is dative	3	4	7
4. Both experiencer and stimulus are objects	1	0	1

The most widespread construction type is value 1, where the **experiencer is coded like the subject** of a typical action verb like 'pull' or 'talk'. The stimulus may be coded as a direct object or oblique, as illustrated in examples (1)–(4). In (1) and (4) the stimulus is coded as a direct object, while in (2) and (3) it is coded as an oblique phrase (i.e. a phrase coded by a special preposition).

(1) Early Sranan (van den Berg & Bruyn 2013)
No, mi no lobi bori-wan.
NEG 1SG NEG love boil(ed)-one
'No, I don't like boiled ones.'

(2) Fa d'Ambô (Post 2013)
Amu-ngo ku pisyi.
1SG-want with fish
'I like fish.'

(3) Cape Verdean Creole of Brava (Baptista 2013)
Es gostaba di rapazinhu.
they like.ANT of little.boy
'They liked the little boy.'

(4) Kinubi (Luffin 2013)
úwo gi-híbu béle t-ómun
3PL IPFV-like country GEN-their
'They like their country.'

In constructions of value 2, the stimulus is coded as subject, whereas the **experiencer is treated like an object** of a typical transitive verb like 'break' or 'kill'. This type is illustrated in examples (5)–(9), where literal translations are added. In all these cases, the stimulus is the subject.

(5) Creolese (Devonish & Thompson 2013)
di jook swiit mi
the joke sweet me
'I enjoyed the joke.' (lit. 'The joke sweeted me.')

(6) Cape Verdean Creole of São Vicente (Swolkien 2013)
Ketxupa ta keí-m ben.
ketxupa PRS please-1SG well
'I like *ketxupa* a lot.' (lit. '*Ketxupa* pleases me well.')
(*Ketxupa* is a regional dish.)

(7) Casamancese Creole (Biagui & Quint 2013)
Maŋgu ø sabi-mi.
mango PFV nice-1SG.INDP
'I like mangoes.' (lit. 'Mangoes are nice (to) me.' or 'Mangoes please me.')

(8) Pichi (Yakpo 2013)
Dan gal dè fayn mi.
that girl IPFV be.fine 1SG.EMPH
'I find that girl to be beautiful.' (lit. 'That girl fines me.')

(9) Lingala (Meeuwis 2013)
sósó e-sepel-is-aka ngáí
chicken 3SG-be.happy-CAUS-HAB 1SG
'I like chicken.' (lit. 'Chicken causes me to be happy.')

None of the *APiCS* languages which show value 2 has this type as the only option to express 'like'. As is apparent from the examples, the meaning of value 2 (experiencer is object) constructions may differ slightly from the meaning of value 1 (experiencer is subject) constructions since value 2 constructions present the emotion situation from the perspective of the stimulus. Nevertheless, our definition is wide enough to subsume these cases here.

In the next construction type (value 3), the **experiencer is marked as dative**, that is, like the recipient of a typical ditransitive verb like 'give', as in examples (10)–(14). The coding of the recipient is also discussed in Chapter 60 (on ditransitive constructions with 'give'). The dative marker may be a preposition as in Sango (10), a serial verb as in Nengee (11), or sometimes a case affix, as in the South Asian languages (12)–(14):

(10) Sango (Samarin 2013)
mango a-nzere **na mbi** *mingi*
mango PM-taste.good PREP 1SG much
'I like mangoes a lot.'

(11) Nengee (Migge 2013)
A nyanyan switi **gi mi** *tee.*
DET food please.give me very.much
'I like the food very much.'
or 'The food pleases me very much.'

(12) Korlai (Clements 2013)
Mari *ye buk tə awru.*
me.DAT this book PRS like
'I like this book.'

(13) Sri Lanka Portuguese (Smith 2013)
per-mi *teem dizeey isti siriviis*
DAT-1SG be please this work
'I like this work. / I am pleased with this work.'

(14) Sri Lankan Malay (Slomanson 2013)
Mangga-pəḍə ***go-ḍang*** *suuka.*
mango-PL 1SG-DAT like
'I like mangoes.'

So far we have not considered word order in this chapter. But looking at languages which show value 3, there is some variation in the position of the dative experiencer. It follows the verb in SVO languages, and it precedes the verb in SOV languages, that is, it behaves like the object in transitive constructions (see also Chapter 1 on order of subject, object, and verb). The first two examples, (10) and (11), from Sango and Nengee, are from languages with SVO order. Here the dative-marked experiencer follows the (main) verb. The South Asian languages in (12)–(14) mainly show SOV order. Here the experiencer is in preverbal position, but often it precedes the stimulus as seen most clearly in (12) and (13).

In yet another construction type, both **the stimulus and the experiencer are coded as objects** (value 4). Media Lengua is the only *APiCS* language which shows this pattern. Here accusative marking makes it clear that both arguments are objects.

(15) Media Lengua (Muysken 2013)
ami-da-ga *papa frita-da-mi kumi-naya-n*
1SG.OBJ-ACC-TOP potato fried-ACC-AFF eat-DESID-3
'I like eating fried potatoes.'

3. Distribution

As shown in the value box, constructions with a subject experiencer (value 1) are by far the most widespread among the *APiCS* languages. The construction type of value 2 (experiencer is object) is found in eleven *APiCS* languages, of which none has this type as the only option to express a 'like' situation. Value 3 (experiencer is dative) is represented by only seven languages, of which Sango, Sri Lankan Malay, and Tayo show this option as their only one.

As for the geographical distribution, the most widespread construction type (value 1, experiencer is subject) is found in all regions of the world, in creoles, pidgins, and mixed languages alike, and it is not restricted to a certain lexical base of the contact language.

Of the eleven languages showing value 2 (experiencer is object), nine are Atlantic creoles: eight are English-based languages of the Caribbean (Bahamian Creole, Creolese, Jamaican, Vincentian) and West Africa (Ghanaian Pidgin English, Cameroon Pidgin English, Pichi, Nigerian Pidgin). The three others are two Portuguese-based languages, Cape Verdean Creole of São Vicente and Casamancese Creole, and the Bantu-based language Lingala. As the "experiencer is object"-pattern is not very prominent in the relevant European lexifiers English and Portuguese (the English type *It pleases me* is marginal), one may suspect substrate influence (Ameka 1990 has some pertinent discussion regarding experiencer constructions in Ewe).

Value 3 (experiencer is dative) is exhibited by seven languages, three of which are spoken in India and Sri Lanka. If we look at the substrates/adstrates of the South Asian contact languages, we find clear parallel constructions called "dative subject constructions" in the literature (e.g. Verma & Mohanan 1991). In these South Asian languages too, the argument expressing the human experiencer is coded as a dative argument, which typically occurs in the topical initial position of the sentence (unlike the Sango and Nengee examples in (10) and (11), which show the dative experiencer in postverbal position).

The rare construction type (value 4) of Media Lengua, where both experiencer and stimulus are marked as objects, is modelled on the Quechua pattern.

67 Experiencer constructions with 'like'

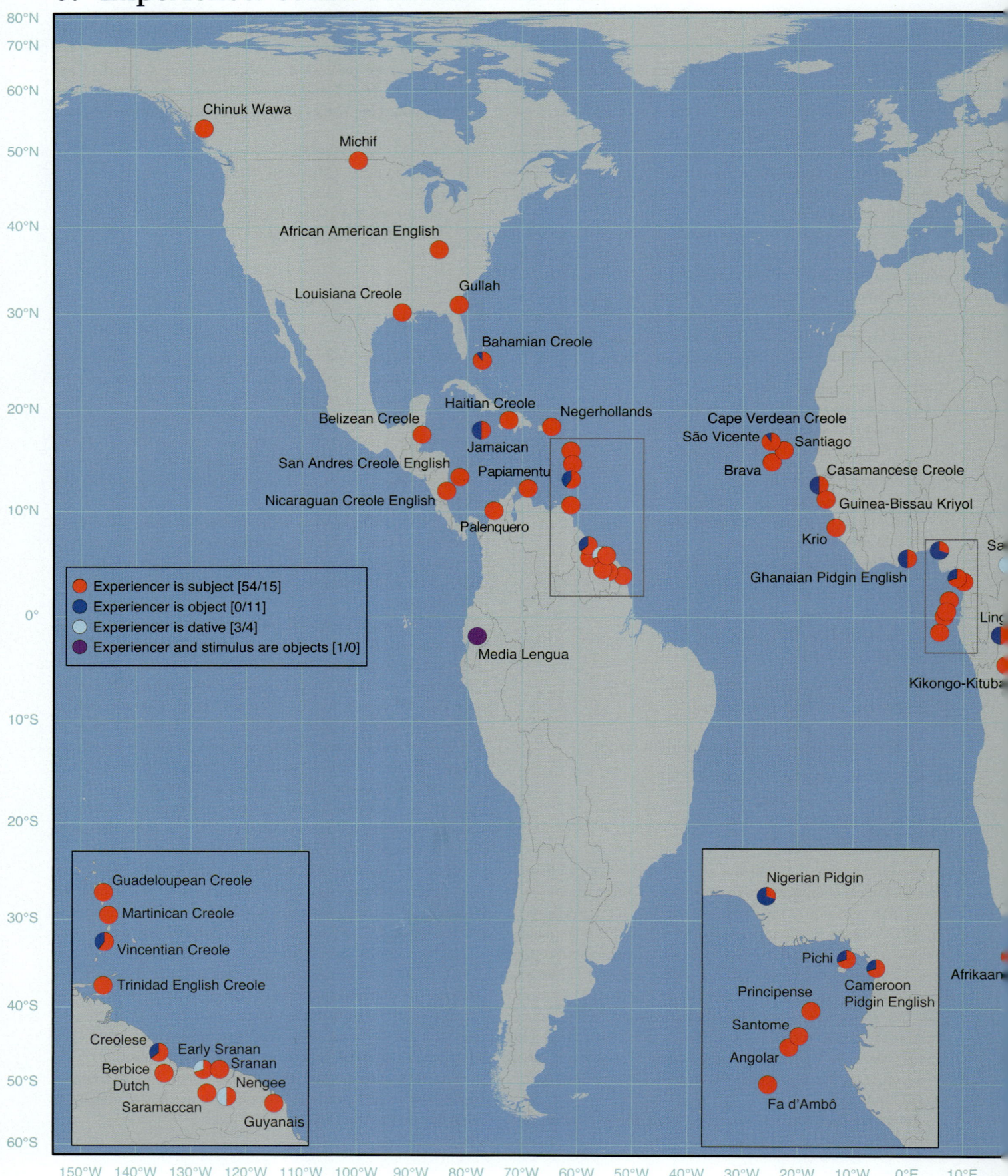

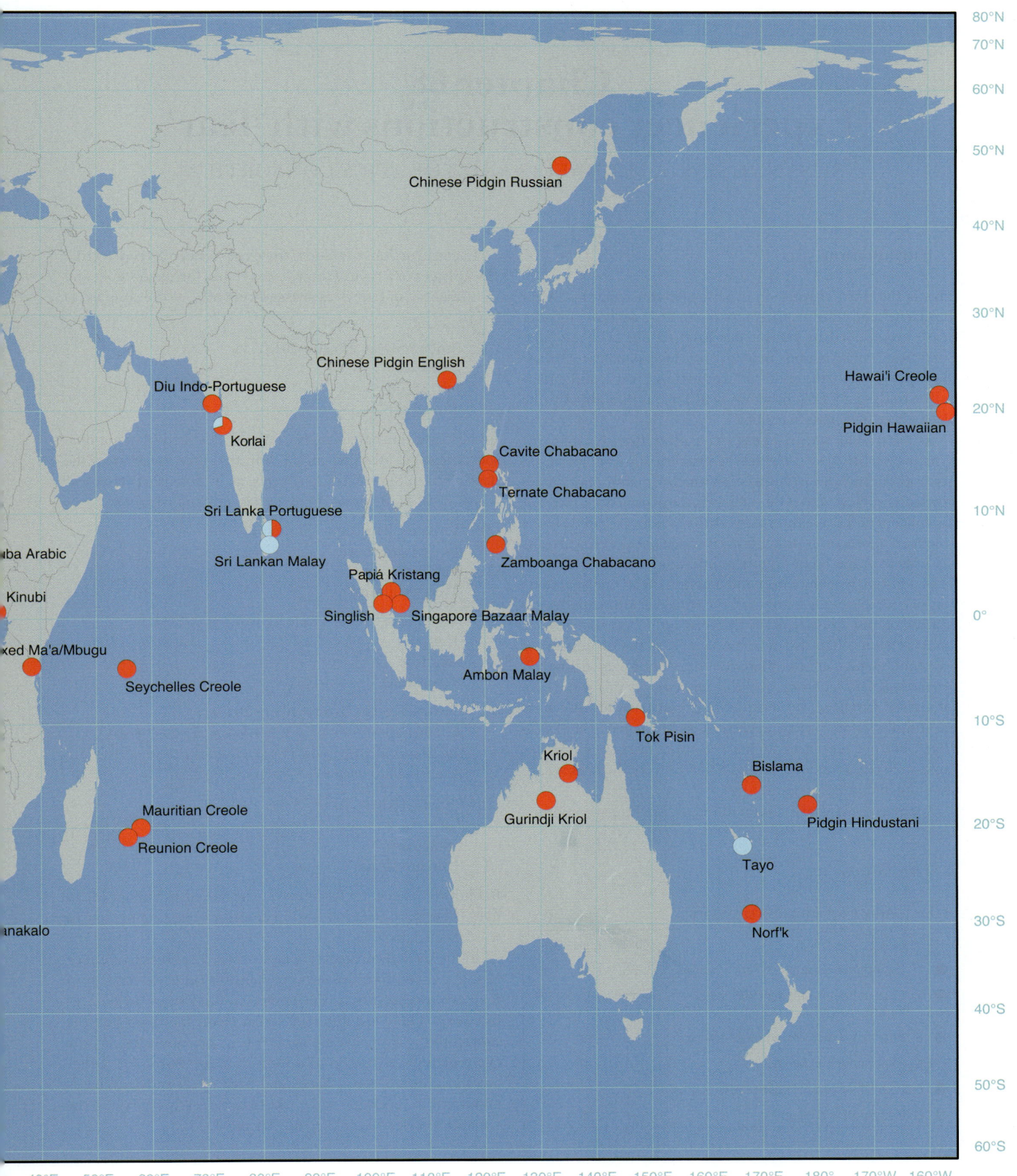

Chapter 68
Experiencer constructions with 'fear'

SUSANNE MARIA MICHAELIS AND THE *APiCS* CONSORTIUM

1. Introduction

This is the third chapter on experiencer constructions. After 'headache' and 'like' in Chapters 66 and 67, we now consider 'fear', exemplified by clauses like English *The child is afraid*. Such 'fear' constructions may involve three semantic entities: the **experiencer** ('the child'), the **emotion** ('fear'), and potentially a **body-part** ('my heart/my soul') that is thought of as the place where the emotion resides.

As was true for the previous two chapters, there is a lot of interesting variation in such 'fear' constructions, too. However, here we concentrate on the question which semantic entity is expressed as subject, and if the subject is the experiencer, whether the concept of fear is expressed verbally or non-verbally. *Subject* is defined here as an argument that is coded like the typical transitive agent or the single argument in a monotransitive clause.

In addition to experiencer and emotion, 'fear' constructions may of course include a stimulus, the entity that the experiencer is afraid of, but this is typically optional and we do not consider its expression. Note that in some languages the expression of the stimulus may entail different constructions, as in English *I am afraid (of the storm)* vs. *I fear the storm*. If this is the case for a given language, we consider only constructions in which the stimulus is not overtly expressed, as in English *The child is afraid*, but not sentences such as *The child fears the storm*, because such constructions may be different from the ones we are studying in this feature.

A language may have several different 'fear' constructions.

2. The values

In this feature we distinguish six values:

		excl	shrd	all
●	1. Experiencer is subject, 'fear' is verbal	35	20	55
●	2. Experiencer is subject, 'fear' is non-verbal	11	17	28
●	3. 'Fear' is subject, experiencer is object	0	10	10
●	4. Experiencer is dative	1	2	3
●	5. 'Fear' is subject, experiencer is oblique	0	1	1
●	6. Body-part is subject	0	6	6

In constructions of value 1, **the experiencer is treated like the subject** of a typical transitive verb like 'break' or 'kill', and the semantics of **fear is expressed verbally**, as in examples (1) to (5):

(1) Ambon Malay (Paauw 2013)
  Beta tako
  1SG afraid
  'I'm afraid.'

In the European-based creoles, reflexes of adjectival or nominal source lexemes meaning 'afraid, fear (n.)' often make up for the 'fear' verb in the *APiCS* languages, as in Spanish/Portuguese *miedo/medo*, French *peur*, Dutch *bang*, and English *afraid*.

(2) Ternate Chabacano (Sippola 2013b)
  Ta myédu mótro.
  IPFV fear 1PL
  'We were afraid.'

(3) Martinican Creole (Colot & Ludwig 2013b)
  Man pè.
  1SG fear
  'I am afraid.'

(4) Berbice Dutch (Kouwenberg 2013a)
  di boko-apu bin bangi di doto kenɛ
  the Amerindian.person-PL PST afraid the dead person
  'Amerindians used to be scared of the dead.'

(5) Gullah (Klein 2013)
  I don fraid.
  I NEG fear
  'I am not afraid.'

In Gullah, the negator *don* is used to negate verbs but not adjectives. Therefore *fraid* is verbal in contrast to its English source word (see Klein 2013).

In the second construction type (value 2), **the experiencer is** still **treated like the subject**, but this time the concept of **fear is expressed in a non-verbal noun-like or adjective-like way**. There are different verbal elements which link the subject to the noun-like element 'fear'. The copula 'be' is only one type here, as can be seen from examples (6) to (9). Other linking verbs are 'stay', 'have', and 'feel' (see 7 and 8). What is important in this value is the fact that the lexeme carrying the semantics of 'fear' is not verbally encoded:

(6) Afrikaans (den Besten & Biberauer 2013)
Ek is bang.
1SG.NOM am afraid
'I am afraid.'

(7) Cape Verdean Creole of Brava (Baptista 2013)
*Omi ka ta **ten medu** di omi, omi ta **ten medu** di dios.*
man NEG HAB have fear of man man HAB have fear of God
'Men do not fear men, men fear God.' (lit. 'have fear of')

(8) Louisiana Creole (Neumann-Holzschuh & Klingler 2013)
Le Kadjen te gen poer.
ART.DEF.PL Cajun PST have fear
'The Cajuns were afraid.' (lit. 'The Cajuns have fear.')

In the next construction type (value 3), **'fear' is treated as the subject, and the experiencer is coded like the object** of a transitive verb. The relationship between the emotion and the experiencer is expressed by a general affect verb ('do').

(9) Sango (Samarin 2013)
mbito a-sara ala
fear PM-do 3PL
'They're afraid.' (lit. 'Fear does them.')

Constructions of value 4 again treat **'fear' as subject**, but the **experiencer is coded as dative**, that is, like the recipient of a typical ditransitive construction. The three *APiCS* languages which show this value are Chinuk Wawa, Korlai, and Diu Indo-Portuguese:

(10) Chinuk Wawa (Grant 2013)
kwas kápa náyka
fear to 1SG
'I'm scared.' (lit. 'Fear is to me.')

(11) Diu Indo-Portuguese (Cardoso 2013)
A el te med.
DAT 3SG EXIST.NPST fear
'He is scared.' (lit. 'To him is fear.')

In example (10) the dative experiencer follows the 'fear' subject argument, but in the two cases from South Asian languages—Diu Indo-Portuguese and Korlai—the dative experiencers are in preverbal position and precede the 'fear' argument, which is sentence-final (see 11). We already saw this construction type in the two other chapters on experiencer constructions with 'headache' and 'like' (Chapters 66 and 67).

The fifth type (value 5) has the **experiencer treated as an oblique with a 'fear' subject**. The only *APiCS* language showing this value is Cape Verdean Creole of São Vicente:

(12) Cape Verdean Creole of São Vicente (Swolkien 2013)
Med dá na es.
fear give on 3PL
'They became overcome by fear.' (lit. 'Fear is giving on them.')

The last option to express fear is value 6: a **body-part ('heart') is treated as subject, and the experiencer is coded as a possessor**:

(13) Nengee (Migge 2013)
Mi ati saka.
my heart drop
'My heart dropped.' or 'I was afraid.'

For none of the six *APiCS* languages with this value is this the only way to express 'fear' in sharp contrast to Chapter 66 ('headache'), where 31 *APiCS* languages have the body-part construction as their only means to express 'to have a headache'.

3. Distribution

By far the most widespread construction type in the *APiCS* languages is the one with the experiencer treated as subject, and 'fear' is treated either verbally (value 1, 55 languages) or non-verbally (value 2, 28 languages). Many *APiCS* languages have one of the two values exclusively, that is, they show just one construction type. For all remaining values (3)–(6), which only cover few languages, no *APiCS* language has one of these values as its only option (except for Chinuk Wawa, which shows only value 4).

As for potential substrate/adstrate influence, we can confidently trace back the "dative subjects" in Diu Indo-Portuguese and Korlai to their South Asian substrates/adstrates (see also the relevant discussion in Chapters 66 and 67).

Looking at the bulk of the other European-based *APiCS* languages, it is noteworthy that they have verbal 'fear' constructions as their only option (e.g. Angolar, Guinea-Bissau Kriyol, Ghanaian Pidgin English, Tayo). It is true that the European base languages mostly also have the verbal construction type, but this is certainly not the most prominent option. Moreover, the creole 'fear' lexemes do not go back to these verbal constructions (see also §2). For example, the Seychelles Creole verb *pe* 'be.afraid' goes back to French non-verbal *j'ai peur* [I=have fear], not to verbal *je crains* [I fear], and the Bislama verb *frait* goes back to English non-verbal *I am afraid*, not to verbal *I fear*. In addition, Spanish and Portuguese show only non-verbal constructions with a nominal 'fear' lexeme (Portuguese *Tenho medo* [I.have fear]), thus not offering a model for the verbal constructions in the related creole languages. Therefore, it seems appealing to look for an explanation in the sub-/adstrate languages. But, unfortunately, there is too little data on experiencer constructions in West African languages, for example (Ameka 1990 on Ewe is the only work we know of).

68 Experiencer constructions with 'fear'

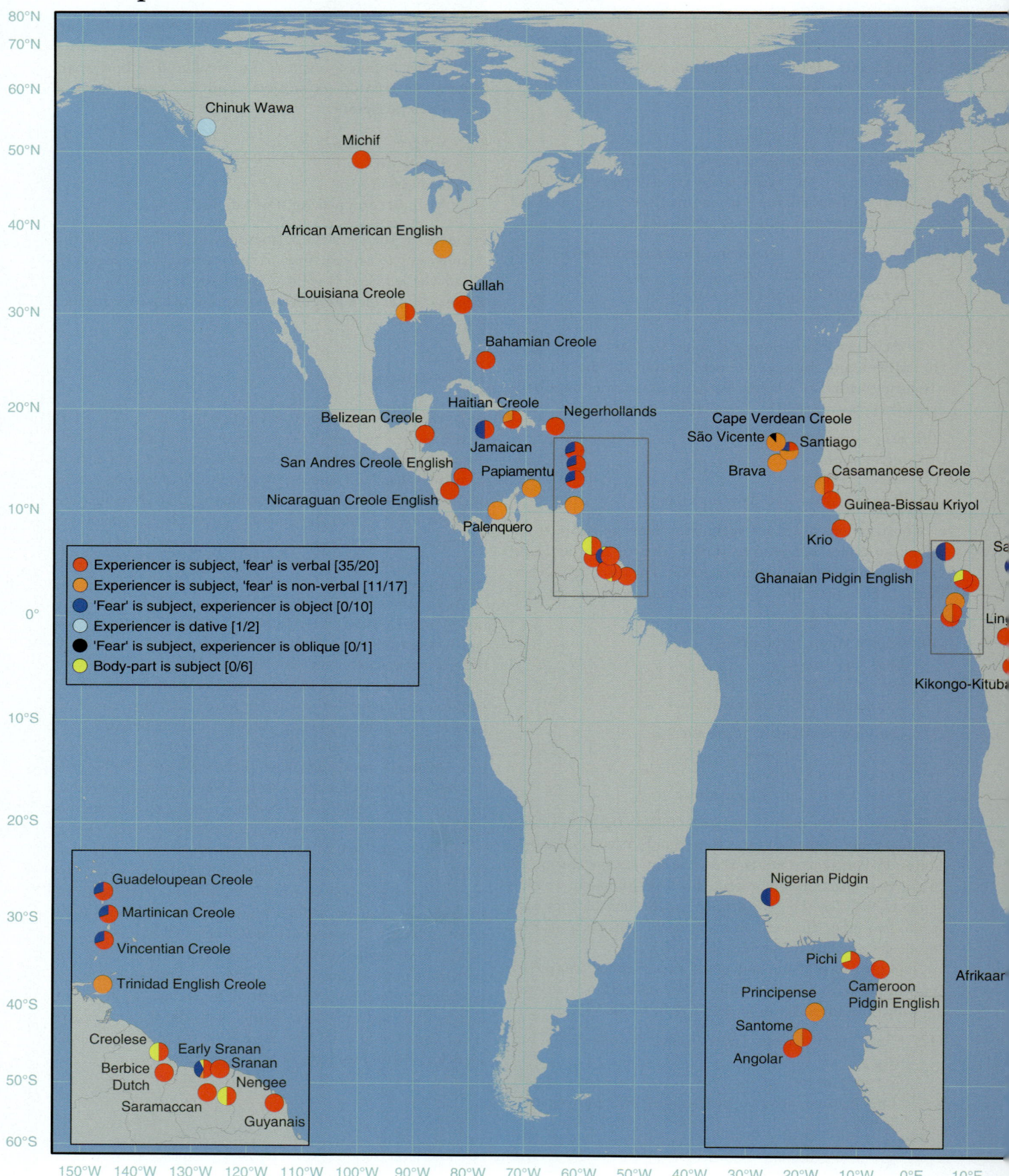

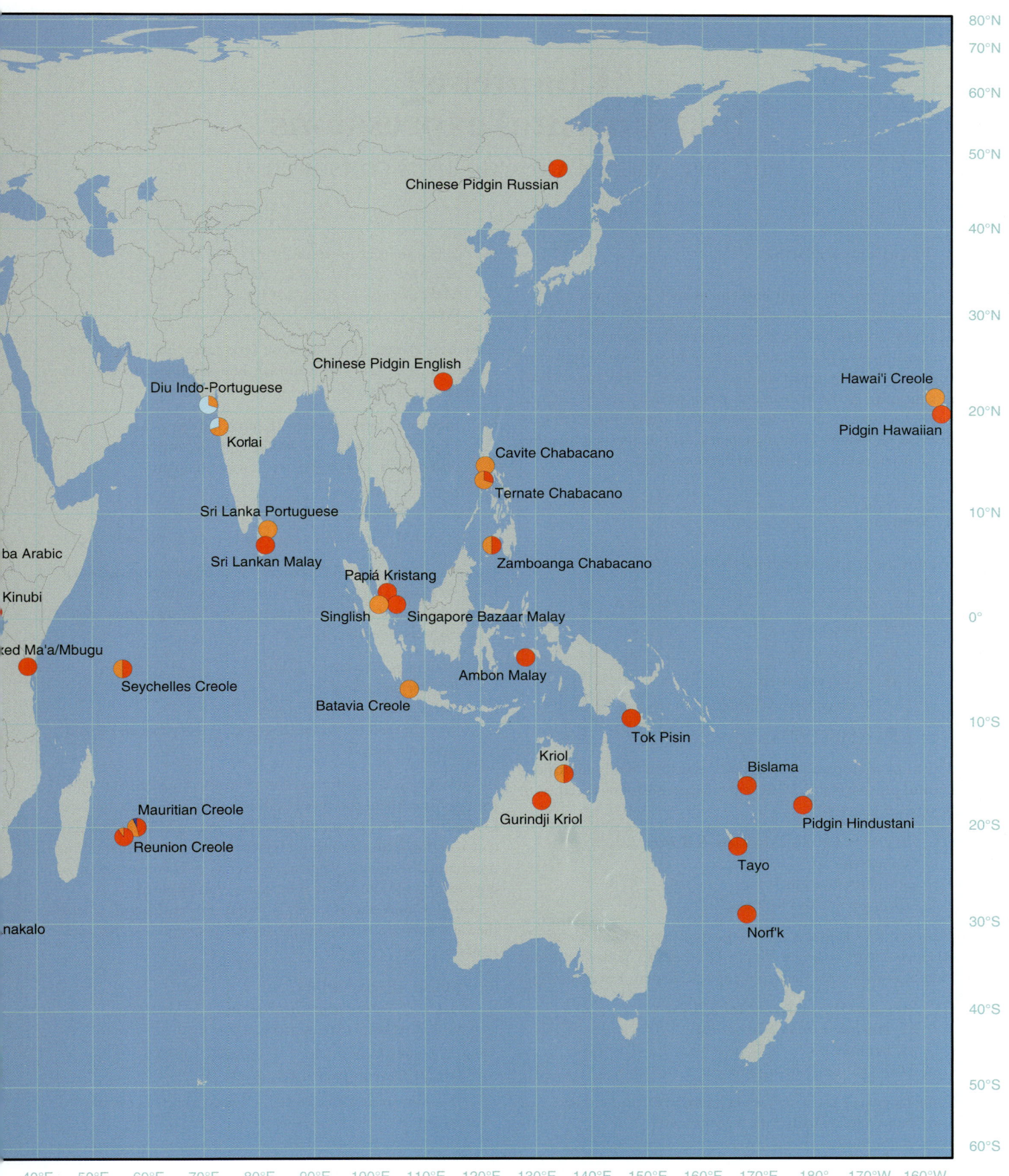

Chapter 69
Instrumental expressions
PHILIPPE MAURER AND THE *APiCS* CONSORTIUM

1. Feature description

An instrument can be an implement such as a knife, a body-part such as a finger, a means such as water, or a vehicle such as a boat. In this feature, we consider only instruments which are instrumental complements of a verb, or, in serial verb constructions, arguments of the first verb which function, at least semantically, as the instrument of the second verb. Therefore, *knife* in sentences like *He bought a knife* are not considered here because, although a knife is an instrument, it does not function as an instrumental complement of the verb *buy*.

2. Values

For this feature, we distinguish the following five values:

	excl	shrd	all
● 1. Adposition	43	27	70
● 2. Serial verb	1	23	24
○ 3. Non-serial verb	0	1	1
○ 4. Unmarked noun phrase	1	5	6
● 5. Case marker	2	2	4

The most widespread instrumental construction is an **adpositional phrase** (value 1). In general, a preposition is used, as in Seychelles Creole:

(1) Seychelles Creole (Michaelis & Rosalie 2013)
 Ou kas li ek ti laas.
 2SG chop 3SG INS little axe
 'You chop it with a little axe.'

However, four languages use a postposition, Michif alongside other constructions, and Pidgin Hindustani, Yimas-Arafundi Pidgin, as well as Sri Lanka Portuguese display it exclusively:

(2) Sri Lanka Portuguese (Smith 2013)
 Eli martel vɔɔnda prɛɛv ja-daay.
 3SG hammer INS nail PST-hit
 'He hit the nail with a hammer.'

Some languages use a **serial verb construction** (value 2; see also Chapter 86), usually with the verb TAKE:

(3) Jamaican (Farquharson 2013)
 Mieri tek di naif kot di bred.
 Mary take DEF knife cut DEF bread
 'Mary cut the bread with the knife.'

Singapore Bazaar Malay uses the verb *pakai* 'use', in combination with *pergi* 'go' (for a similar, non-serial construction in Michif, see example 6):

(4) Singapore Bazaar Malay (Khin Khin Aye 2013)
 Ini orang tua ah dia pakai ayer sabon pergi
 DEM people old TOP 3SG use water soap go
 cuci ini tangga.
 clean DEM staircase
 'This old man, he used soap water to clean the staircase.'

Except for Jamaican, all languages which allow an instrumental serial verb may also use an instrumental adposition.
 In many cases, a literal interpretation of the instrumental serial verb is also possible, as in (5):

(5) Principense (Maurer 2013c)
 E tan masadu va inha.
 3SG take axe cut firewood
 'She cut the firewood with an axe.' ~ 'She took an axe and cut the firewood.'

In most cases, the difference between the construction with the adposition and the serial verb is left unexplained, but see Devonish & Thompson (2013) on Creolese, who state that the construction with the adposition "is open to an accidental or unintended reading", whereas the serial verb construction is not (see also the alternative translation of example 6).

Value 3, **non-serial verb**, is found only in Michif, where the verb *apahchit* 'to use' introduces the instrument of the verb *kishkish* 'to cut':

(6) Michif (Bakker 2013)
 Aen kuto kii-apahchit-aaw
 INDF.M.SG knife PST-use.INAN-3OBJ
 chi-kishkish-ak la vyaand.
 FUT.COMPL-cut-1SG DEF.F.SG meat
 'I cut the meat with a knife.' ~ 'I used a knife to cut the meat.'

Note that in the case of Michif we cannot speak of a serial verb construction since the first verb is marked for past, and the second verb for future; according to the definition of serial verb constructions which we use in *APiCS*, different tense marking on the two verbs of a series is precluded (see e.g. Chapter 85).

Six languages (Chinese Pidgin Russian, Eskimo Pidgin, Korlai, Nigerian Pidgin, Pichi, and Pidgin Hawaiian) may use an **unmarked noun phrase** (value 4) to express the instrumental:

(7) Chinese Pidgin Russian (Perekhvalskaya 2013)
Nada liipaxoza   katera tʃo   vazila.
must logging.enterprise boat something carry.PFV
'I had to carry something to the logging enterprise by a cutter boat.'

(8) Eskimo Pidgin (van der Voort 2013)
Nuna sinani   kamotik elekta awoña.
land alongside sled   go   I
'I travelled by sled along the coast.'

(9) Korlai (Clements 2013)
Pɛ dal!
foot hit
'Kick it with your foot!'

(10) Nigerian Pidgin (Faraclas 2013)
Ìm   chuk mì   nayf.
3SG.SBJ pierce 1SG.OBJ knife
'S/he stabbed me with a knife.'

(11) Pichi (Yakpo 2013)
Dèn chuk-àn   nɛf.
3PL pierce-3OBJ knife
'They stabbed him with a knife.'

(12) Pidgin Hawaiian (Roberts 2013)
Aole laau wau hahau iaia.
NEG stick 1SG strike 3SG
'I didn't strike him with a stick.'

This construction also exists in Tugu Creole, a Malayo-Portuguese variety closely related to Batavia Creole:

(13) Tugu Creole (Maurer 2013b)
[…] *tapi aka korda bambu miste rusa djantong figu.*
     but DEM string bamboo must rub blossom banana
'[…] but the strings must be rubbed with banana blossoms.'

Note that Eskimo Pidgin is the only *APiCS* language for which only unmarked instrumental noun phrases are reported.

Value 5, **instrumental case marker**, occurs in four languages (Chinese Pidgin Russian, the mixed language Gurindji Kriol, Media Lengua, and Sri Lankan Malay):

(14) Chinese Pidgin Russian (Perekhvalskaya 2013)
Parka-m zakrywaj.
stick-INS close
'[I] close [it (= the door)] with a stick.'

(15) Gurindji Kriol (Meakins 2013)
Marluka-ma dei   bin kil-im
old.man-DISC 3PL.SBJ PST hit-TR
pangkily kurrupartu-yawung.
hit.head boomerang-INS
'The old man, they hit him on the head with a boomerang.'

(16) Media Lengua (Muysken 2013)
Inki kuchillu-n-di   korta-ka-ngi pan-da?
what knife-INS-EMPH cut-PST-2SG bread-ACC
'With what knife did you cut the bread?'

(17) Sri Lankan Malay (Slomanson 2013)
Dia daging-yang piso-attu-ring e-potong.
3SG meat-ACC   knife-INDF-INS PST-cut
'She cut the meat with a knife.'

3. Distribution

Except for six languages (Chinese Pidgin English, Chinese Pidgin Russian, Eskimo Pidgin, Jamaican, Media Lengua, and Sri Lankan Malay), all languages make use of an **adposition**, be it exclusively or alongside other constructions. **Serial verb constructions** are mainly used on both sides of the Atlantic, but this construction also occurs in Papiá Kristang (Portuguese-based, Southeast Asia) and Seychelles Creole (French-based, Indian Ocean). **Non-marked noun phrases** occur in one North American language (Eskimo Pidgin), in two languages of the Atlantic (Nigerian Pidgin and Pichi), in one South Asian language (Korlai), in one East Asian language (Chinese Pidgin Russian), and in one Pacific language (Pidgin Hawaiian). The use of a **case marker** occurs in bilingual mixed languages scattered over the world (Media Lengua in South America, Sri Lankan Malay in South Asia, and Gurindji Kriol in Australia), as well as in Chinese Pidgin Russian (East Asia).

69 Instrumental expressions

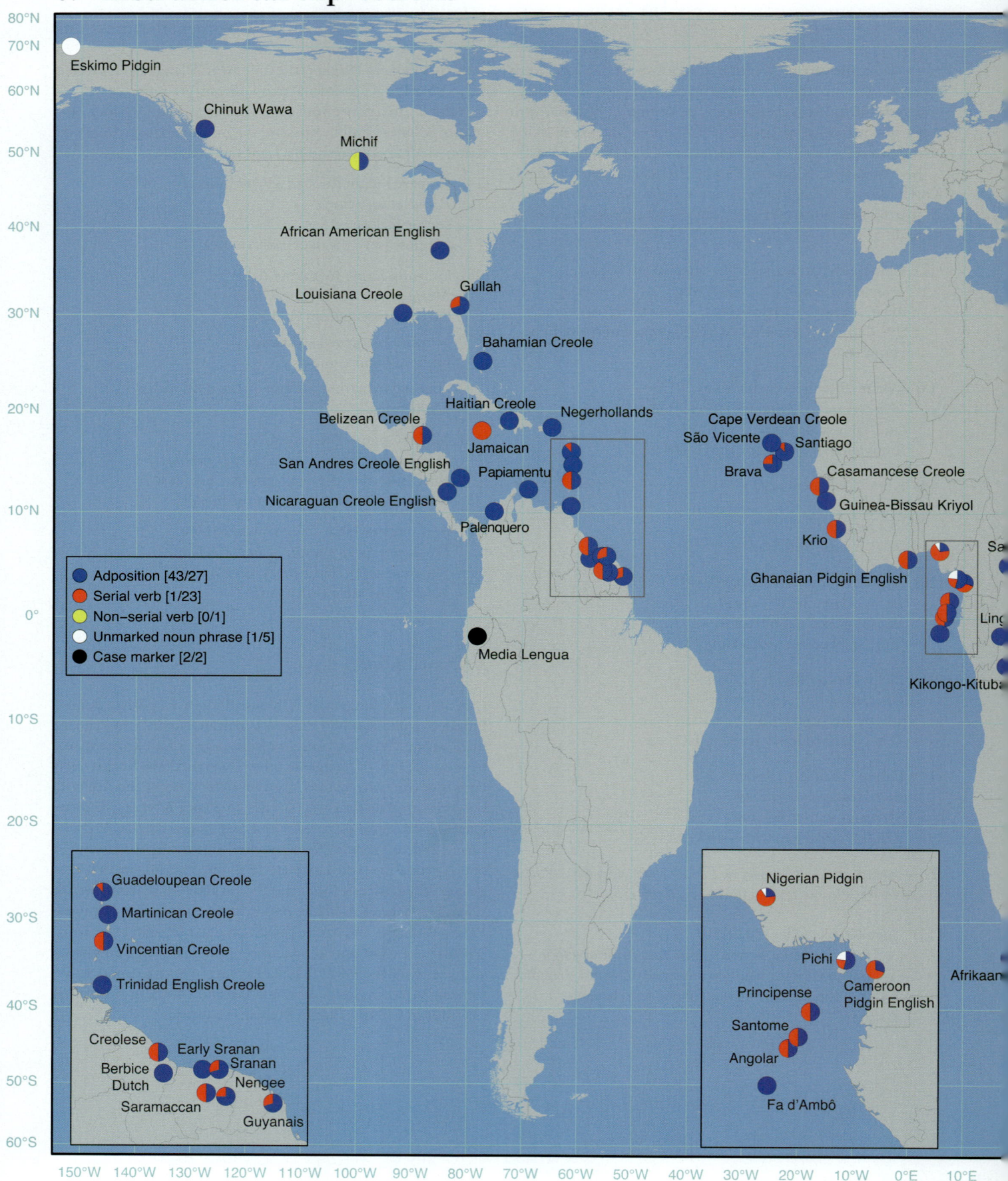

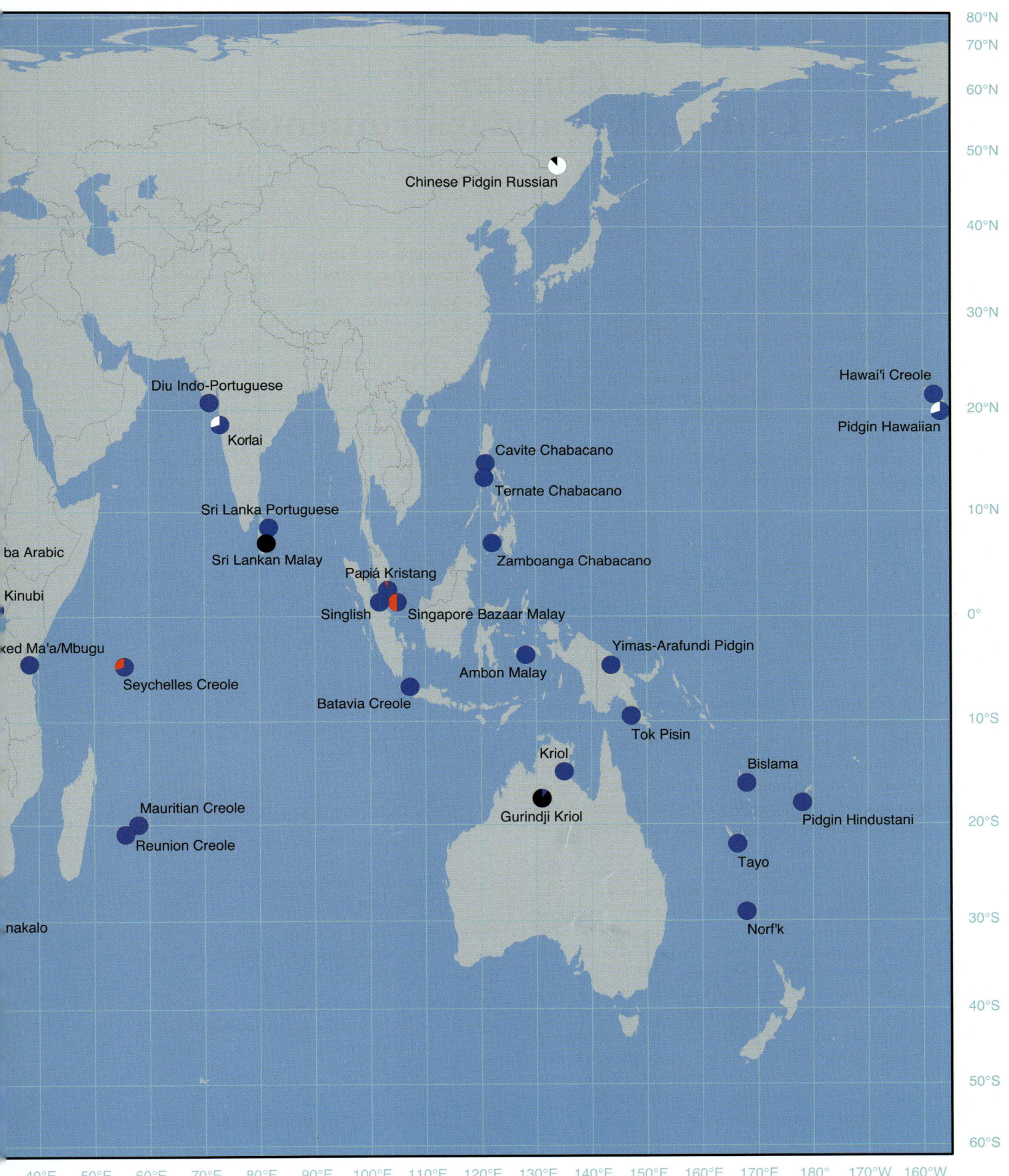

Chapter 70
Comitatives and instrumentals

PHILIPPE MAURER AND THE *APiCS* CONSORTIUM

1. Feature description

The concept 'with, together with' (comitative) can be expressed in the same way as the concept 'with' (instrumental); it may also be expressed differently (see *WALS* Chapter 52, Stolz et al. 2005). Instrumentals and comitatives may be rendered by different constructions in different languages; in this feature, serial verb constructions expressing comitatives and instrumentals are not taken into account unless they are the only way to express these concepts.

This chapter is closely related to Chapter 69 on instrumental expressions and Chapter 85 on TAKE serials.

2. Feature values

The following values occur:

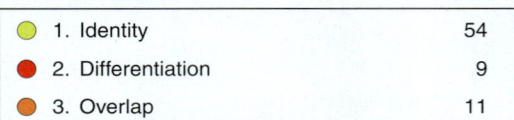

Identity means that there is only one marker for both functions (as in French *avec*). **Differentiation** indicates that there are two different markers for the two functions (as in Eskimo Pidgin *kápa* 'instrumental' vs. *kánamakwst* 'comitative'). **Overlap** refers to the existence of two markers, one of which fulfils only one of the functions, while the other one can be used for both functions (as in Casamancese, where *ku* fulfils both the function of instrumental and comitative, whereas *juntu ku* only refers to the comitative).

The most widespread value for this feature is value 1, **identity** between instrumental and comitative markers (72%). Differentiation (value 2) represents 12 per cent, and overlap (value 3) 16 per cent. This result strongly contrasts with the *WALS* languages (Feature 52 of the *WALS*), where 76 languages out of 322 (24%) show value 1, 213 languages (66%) value 2, and 33 languages (10%) value 3 (which is called "mixed" in the *WALS*). The overrepresentation of value 1 in the *APiCS* languages might be due to the fact that the European languages, which are the major lexifiers of creoles and pidgins represented in the *APiCS*, almost exclusively show value 1 on the corresponding *WALS* map. This holds equally for Dutch and Spanish, which are not represented on the *WALS* map.

An example of **identity** comes from Media Lengua, where instrumental and comitative are expressed by the suffix *-n*:

(1) Media Lengua (Muysken 2013)
 a. *Inki kuchillu-n-di korta-ka-ngi pan-da?*
 what knife-INS-EMPH cut-PST-2SG bread-ACC
 'With what knife did you cut the bread?'
 b. *Fernando tayta-n-lla parisi-xu-n.*
 Fernando father-INS-DELIM resemble-IPFV-3
 'Fernando looks like his father.'

Another example of identity can be found in the bilingual mixed language Gurindji Kriol, which possesses two different markers, a preposition and a suffix, which can be used for both functions:

(2) Gurindji Kriol (Meakins 2013)
 a. *I bin hiya na nyanuny Mami-yawung.*
 3SG.SBJ PST here FOC 3SG.DAT mother-COM
 'She was here with her mother.' (comitative)
 b. *An kengkaru i bin kilim kurrupartu-*
 and kangaroo 3SG PST hit boomerang-
 yawung dat karu-ngku.
 INS DET child-ERG
 'And the child hit the kangaroo with a boomerang.' (instrumental)
 c. *Dei bin luk det ngakparn gat nyanuny femli.*
 3PL PST see DET frog with 3SG.DAT family
 'They saw the frog with his family.' (comitative)
 d. *Deim kilim wan marluka gat kurrupartu.*
 3PL hit one old.man with boomerang
 'They hit one old man with a boomerang.' (instrumental)

Differentiation can be exemplified by Sri Lankan Malay, where the comitative is realized by the postposition *samma*, and the instrumental by the suffix *-ring*:

(3) Sri Lankan Malay (Slomanson 2013)
 a. *Go pe tummanpədə go samma Kirinde-na*
 1SG POSS friend.PL 1SG COM Kirinda-DAT
 e-datang (aða).
 ASP-come (AUX)
 'My friends have come to Kirinda with me.' (comitative)

b. *Go go pe nama penna-**ring** e-tuulis (aða).*
   1SG 1SG POSS name pen-INS ASP-write (AUX)
   'I have written my name with a pen.' (instrumental)

Another case of differentiation is represented by Chinese Pidgin Russian, where the instrumental is unmarked and the comitative rendered by postposed *kampani* 'company':

(4) Chinese Pidgin Russian (Perekhvalskaya 2013)
   a. *Nada kuʃaj **malen'li riumka**, nimnoʃka nalej.*
      must eat small glass a.little pour
      'One should take it with a small glass of wine, just a little bit.'
   b. *Sorok diviata iwo **kampani** tam ʒiwi.*
      forty ninth 3SG company there live
      'I lived with her since 1949.'

Languages showing **overlap** may have one marker which refers both to comitative and instrumental, and one which is only comitative and monomorphemic (Cape Verdean Creole of São Vicente, Reunion Creole):

(5) Reunion Creole (Bollée 2013)
   a. *Li travay **ek** son tonton.*
      3SG work with POSS.3SG uncle
      'He works with his uncle.' (comitative)
   b. *Lontan té i fé **èk** sak trésé an vakoi.*
      in.the.past PST FIN do with bag woven of vacoa
      'In the past it was done with a bag made of vacoa.' (instrumental)
   c. *Alon partir la butik **ansanm** li.*
      IMP.1PL leave DEF shop with 3SG
      'Let's go to the shop with him.' (comitative)

Another possibility for languages with overlap is to have one marker which refers to comitative and instrumental, and one which is exclusively comitative and bimorphemic, that is, 'together with' (Casamancese Creole, Cavite Chabacano, Diu Indo-Portuguese, Haitian Creole, Guinea-Bissau Kriyol, Ternate Chabacano):

(6) Casamancese Creole (Biagui & Quint 2013)
   a. *N bay Sicor **ku** ña yermoŋ.*
      1SG go Ziguinchor with POSS.1SG sibling
      'I went to Ziguinchor with my brother/sister.' (comitative)
   b. *N kortá karna **ku** faka.*
      1SG cut meat with knife
      'I cut the meat with a knife.' (instrumental)
   c. *N bay Sicor **juntu ku** ña yermoŋ.*
      1SG go Ziguinchor together with POSS.1SG sibling
      'I went to Ziguinchor with my brother/sister.' (comitative)

A third possibility, which exists only in Bislama, is to have one marker, *wetem*, which refers to instrumental as well as to comitative, and one marker, *long*, which is exclusively instrumental:

(7) Bislama (Meyerhoff 2013)
   a. *I had blong yu spoelem **wetem** finga blong yu.*
      AGR hard PURP 2SG spoil with finger POSS 2SG
      'It's hard to ruin it with your fingers [alone].' (instrumental)
   b. *Mifala i stap **wetem** olfala olgeta.*
      1PL.INCL AGR stay with old.one 3PL
      'We were standing with all the old guys.' (comitative)
   c. *[. . .] yu karem **long** wan smol samting [. . .].*
      2SG bring INS INDF small something
      '[. . .] you bring it (= pollen) [to the flower] with something small [. . .].' (comitative)

3. Areal distribution

The areal distribution of the three values of this feature shows that identity (value 1) and overlap (value 3) are represented in all regions, whereas differentiation (value 2) is almost absent from the Americas, where only Chinuk Wawa displays this feature, and from Africa, where it only occurs in Fanakalo.

70 Comitatives and instrumentals

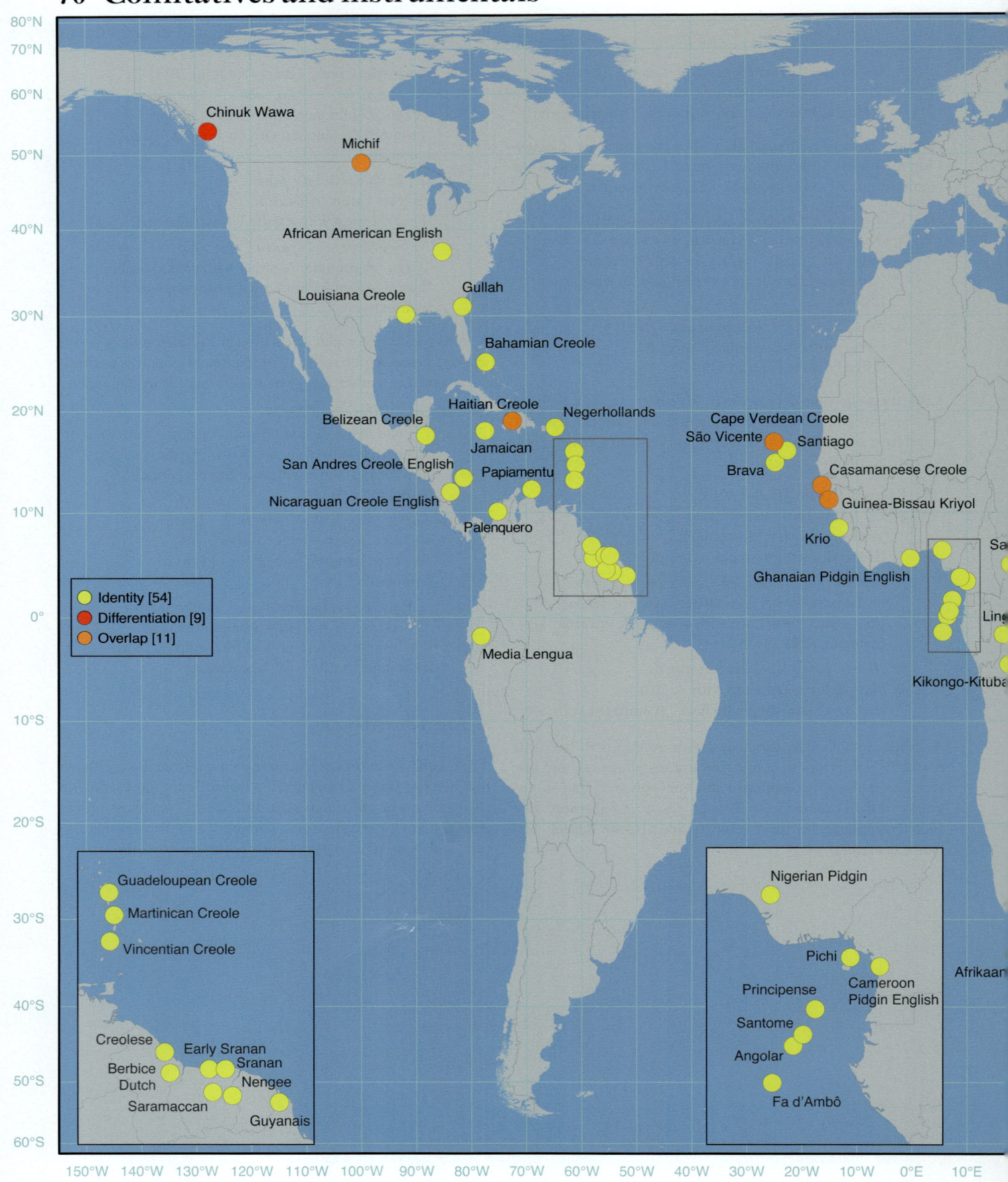

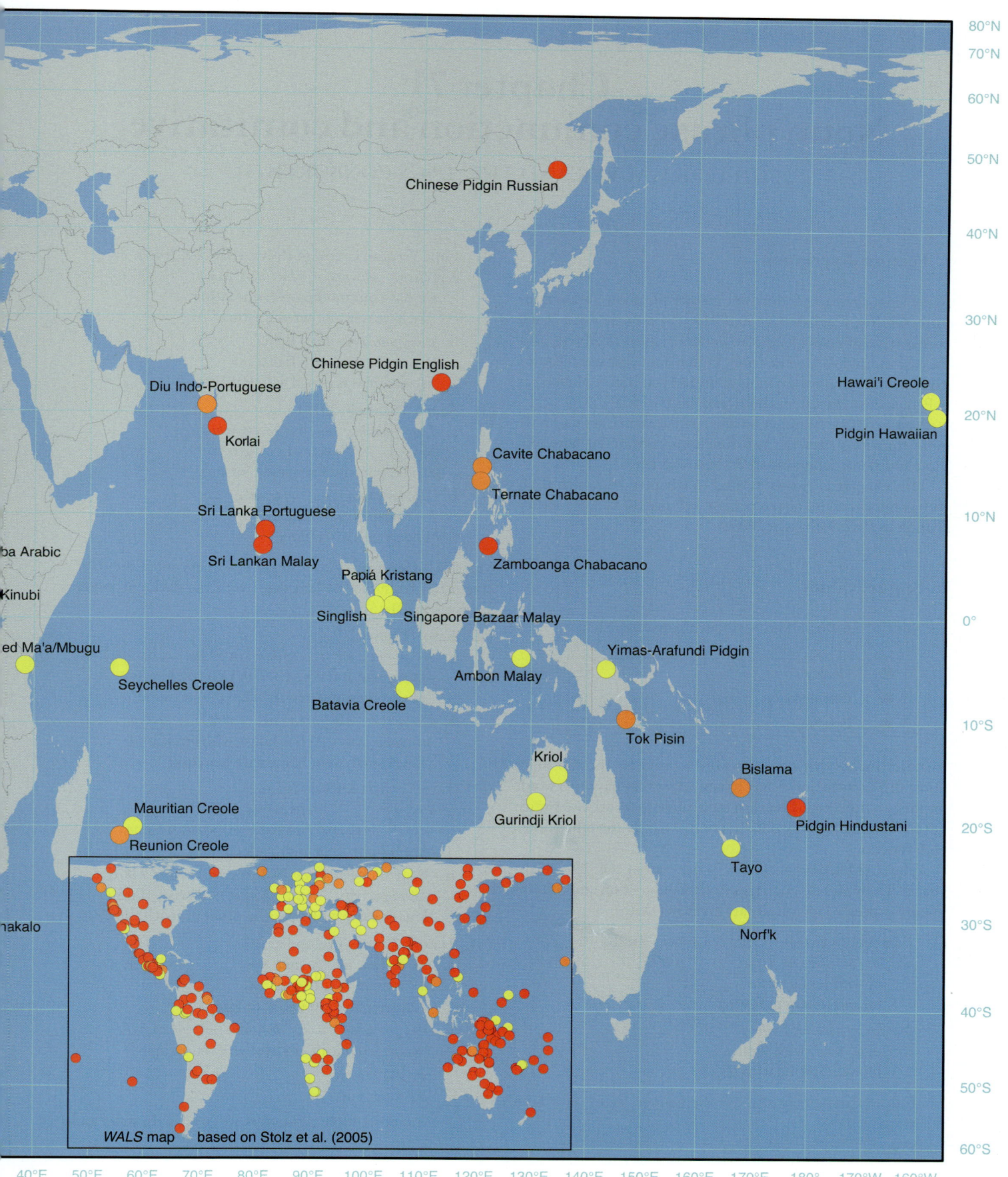

Chapter 71
Noun phrase conjunction and comitative

PHILIPPE MAURER AND THE *APiCS* CONSORTIUM

1. Feature description

Some languages have a different marker for noun phrase **conjunction** (e.g. English *John and Mary went to the movies*) and **comitative** phrases (*John went to the movies with Mary*), as is the case in English (*and* vs. *with*). Other languages use the same marker for noun phrase conjunction and comitative phrases, as in Principense (*ki* renders both 'and' and 'with').

A noun phrase conjunction or a comitative marker may have more functions than the two functions considered here, but these additional functions are disregarded here.

This chapter is closely related to Chapter 70, which deals with comitatives and instrumentals; see also the corresponding chapter in *WALS* (Stassen 2005a).

2. Feature values

For this feature, the following values are distinguished:

🟢	1. Identity	25
🔴	2. Differentiation	30
🟠	3. Overlap	18

Identity means that only one word is used for the two functions; **differentiation** refers to languages that have two words for the two functions. **Overlap** means that there are two words, but that one fulfils only one function, whereas the other fulfils both functions.

Value 1 (**identity**) occurs in 34 per cent of the *APiCS* languages. Examples of languages where conjunction and comitative are expressed identically are given in (1)–(3).

(1) Martinican Creole (Colot & Ludwig 2013b)
   a. *Joj épi Jéra ay péché.*
      Joj with Jéra go fish
      'Joj and Jéra went fishing.'
   b. *Joj ay péché épi Jéra.*
      Joj go fish with Jéra
      'Joj went fishing with Jéra.'

Martinican Creole may also use the markers *ek* or *é* for both functions.

(2) Cape Verdean Creole of Brava (Baptista 2013)
   a. *Nu ten nos mai ku nos pai.*
      we have our mother with our father
      'We have our mother and father.'
   b. *Benjamin kria ku Bahia.*
      Benjamin raise with Bahia
      'Benjamin was raised with Bahia.'

(3) Sango (Samarin 2013)
   a. *Laso mbi na mo, i ke gwe biani.*
      today I with you we COP go truly
      'Today you and I are going for sure.'
   b. *Mbi lango na ita ti mbi.*
      I sleep with sibling of I
      'I lived with my sibling.'

Value 2 (**differentiation**) is found in 41 per cent of the *APiCS* languages. Examples of languages with the different markers are given in (4)–(6).

(4) Krio (Finney 2013)
   a. *Di uman ɛn ĩ pikin dɔn go na os.*
      ART woman and POSS child PFV go LOC house
      'The woman and her child have gone home.'
   b. *Di uman dɔn go na os wit ĩ pikin.*
      ART woman PFV go LOC house with POSS child
      'The woman went home with her child.'

(5) Tayo (Erhart & Revis 2013)
   a. *Frer-ta epi ser-ta le vja?*
      brother-POSS.2SG and sister-POSS.2SG SI come
      'Are your brother and sister coming?'
   b. *Ma fe vwajaf ave(k) Marie pu visite Tahiti.*
      1SG make trip with Marie PURP visit Tahiti
      'I made a trip with Marie in order to visit Tahiti.'

(6) Hawai'i Creole (Velupillai 2013)
   a. *Da wahine no go wid him.*
      ART woman NEG go with 3SG
      'The woman didn't go with him.'
   b. *Mi kapo o ra bɹaraz wi go ap baɪ*
      1SG.OBL couple of ART brothers 1PL go up by
      ra waɾə tæŋ.
      ART water tank
      'Me and a couple of the guys, we go up to the water tank.'

In example (6b), there is no overt noun phrase conjunction, but a conjunction may occur, as for example in *mi æn papa* 'me and Papa'.

The bilingual mixed language Michif displays three comitative constructions: *avik/avek*, *wiichi*, and the verb *peeshaw* 'bring', as well as three noun phrase conjunctions: *pi*, *miina*, and *eekwa*.

Value 3 (**overlap**) is less widespread than value 1 and value 2, but it still occurs in 25 per cent of the *APiCS* languages. In most cases, it is the marker of noun phrase conjunction ('and') which fulfils only one function:

(7) Negerhollands (van Sluijs 2013)
    a. *Ananshi **mi** Tekoma sinu a lo it.*
       Ananshi with Tekoma 3PL PST go out
       'Ananshi and Tekoma went outside.'
    b. *Am a wun **mi** ēn hou mulā.*
       3SG PST live with ART old miller
       'He lived with an old miller.'
    c. *Ananshi **en** Tekoma sinu a lo it.*
       Ananshi and Tekoma 3PL PST go out
       'Ananshi and Tekoma went outside.'

(8) Cape Verdean Creole of São Vicente (Swolkien 2013)
    a. *Mi **má** Adrianu trubaiá djunt n'un bárk.*
       1SG with Adrianu work together on=DET ship
       'Adrianu and I worked together on a ship.'
    b. *El bai pa Praia **má** se irmon.*
       3SG go to Praia with 3SG.POSS brother
       'He went to Praia with his brother.'
    c. *Relasãu entre mi **y** nha mãi*
       relationship between 1SG and POSS.1SG mother
      senpr foi mut bon.
      always COP.PST very good
       'The relationship between my mother and me was always very good.'

(9) Kinubi (Luffin 2013)
    a. *Núbi ta Kíbra **ma** Mombása ma 'endisi tofaúti.*
       Nubi GEN Kibera with Mombasa NEG have difference
       'The Nubi of Kibera and the ones of Mombasa are not different.'
    b. *Úmun já **ma** British.*
       3PL come with British
       'They came with the British.'
    c. *Kan bes anás ta Mijikénda **u** anás ta Rabái.*
       ANT only people GEN Mijikenda and people GEN Rabai
       'There were just the Mijikenda and the Rabai.'

In languages which use constructions similar to English 'together with', it is the comitative marker which expresses only one function. This is the case in Casamancese Creole and Haitian Creole. In Casamancese Creole, *ku* 'and, with' connects noun phrases and heads comitatives, while *juntu ku* 'together with' is restricted to comitatives. In Haitian Creole, *ak* 'and, with' and its variants connect noun phrases and head comitatives, and *ansanm avèk* 'together with' heads only comitatives.

A similar situation can be found in Nigerian Pidgin. In this language one marker is used for both functions, but two markers are restricted to one function each. *Wit* 'and, with' fulfils both functions; *and* 'and' is restricted to the conjoining of noun phrases, and the serial verb *folo* 'follow' is restricted to the comitative:

(10) Nigerian Pidgin (Faraclas 2013)
    *Ìm gò **folo** dɛ̀m dans.*
    3SG FUT follow 3PL dance
    'S/he will dance with them.'

Nigerian Pidgin is the only *APiCS* language with a serial verb expressing comitative.

3. Distribution

There is a certain concentration of value 1 (**identity**) in the Atlantic area (15 out of 25 languages). These 15 languages are all European-based, and since all the European base languages have differentiation, an African substrate influence is very likely in this domain. Identity is predominant in sub-Saharan Africa (see below).

Value 2 (**differentiation**) is more common in South and Southeast Asia, with some languages in the Atlantic. Almost half of the languages exhibiting value 2 are English-based. There are only four English-based creoles exhibiting value 1 (the three Suriname creoles and Bislama).

Value 3 (**overlap**) is represented more or less equally in all regions.

WALS (Stassen 2005a) has only two values for this feature: identity and differentiation. Identity is predominant in sub-Saharan Africa and in the Pacific, whereas differentiation is found predominantly in Europe and South Asia. The numbers are almost identical for the two *WALS* values (103 out of 234 languages exhibit identity, or 44%, and 131 differentiation, or 56%). This parallels the situation in the *APiCS* languages, where there are somewhat fewer languages that show identity than languages that show differentiation.

71 Noun phrase conjunction and comitative

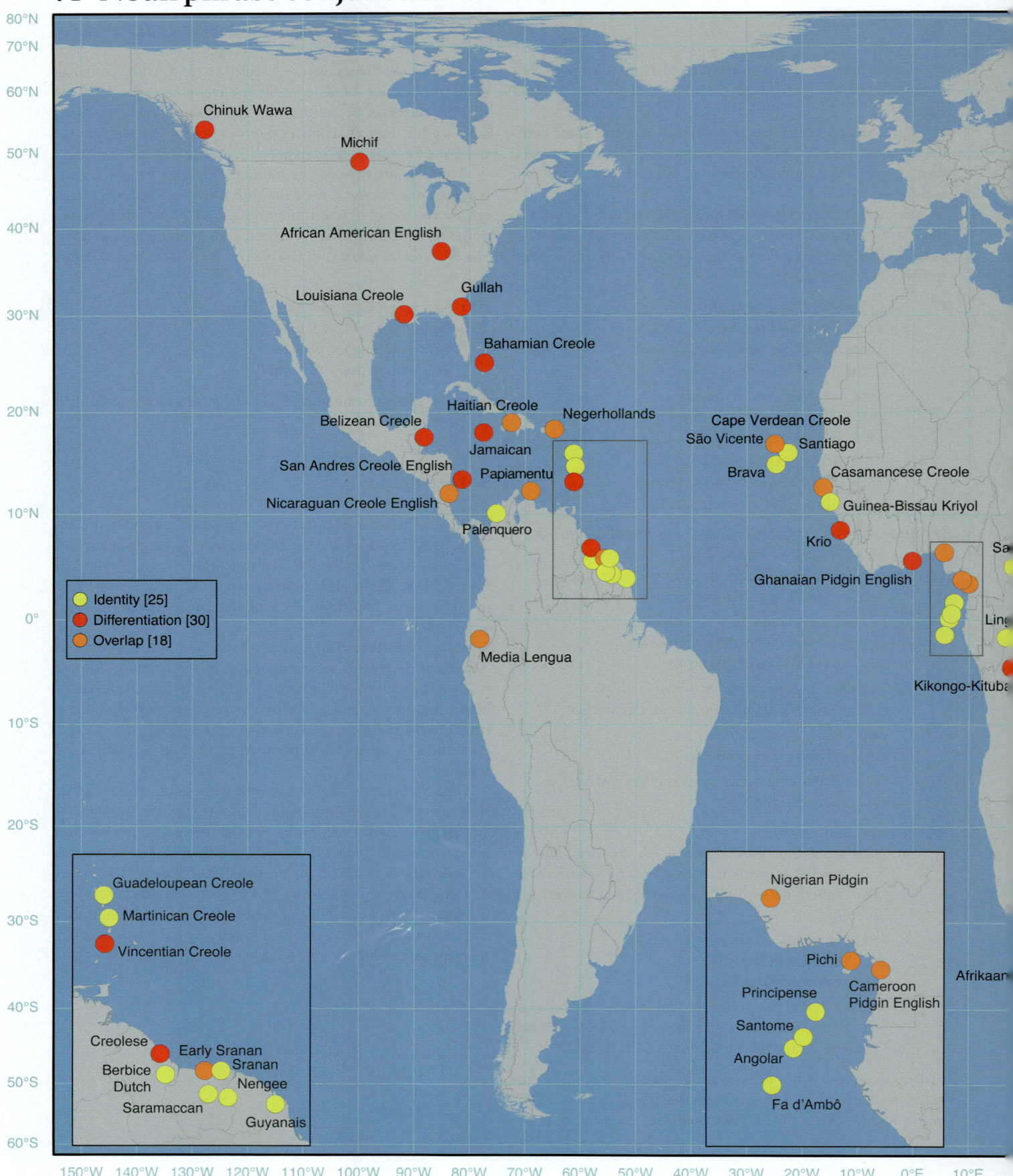

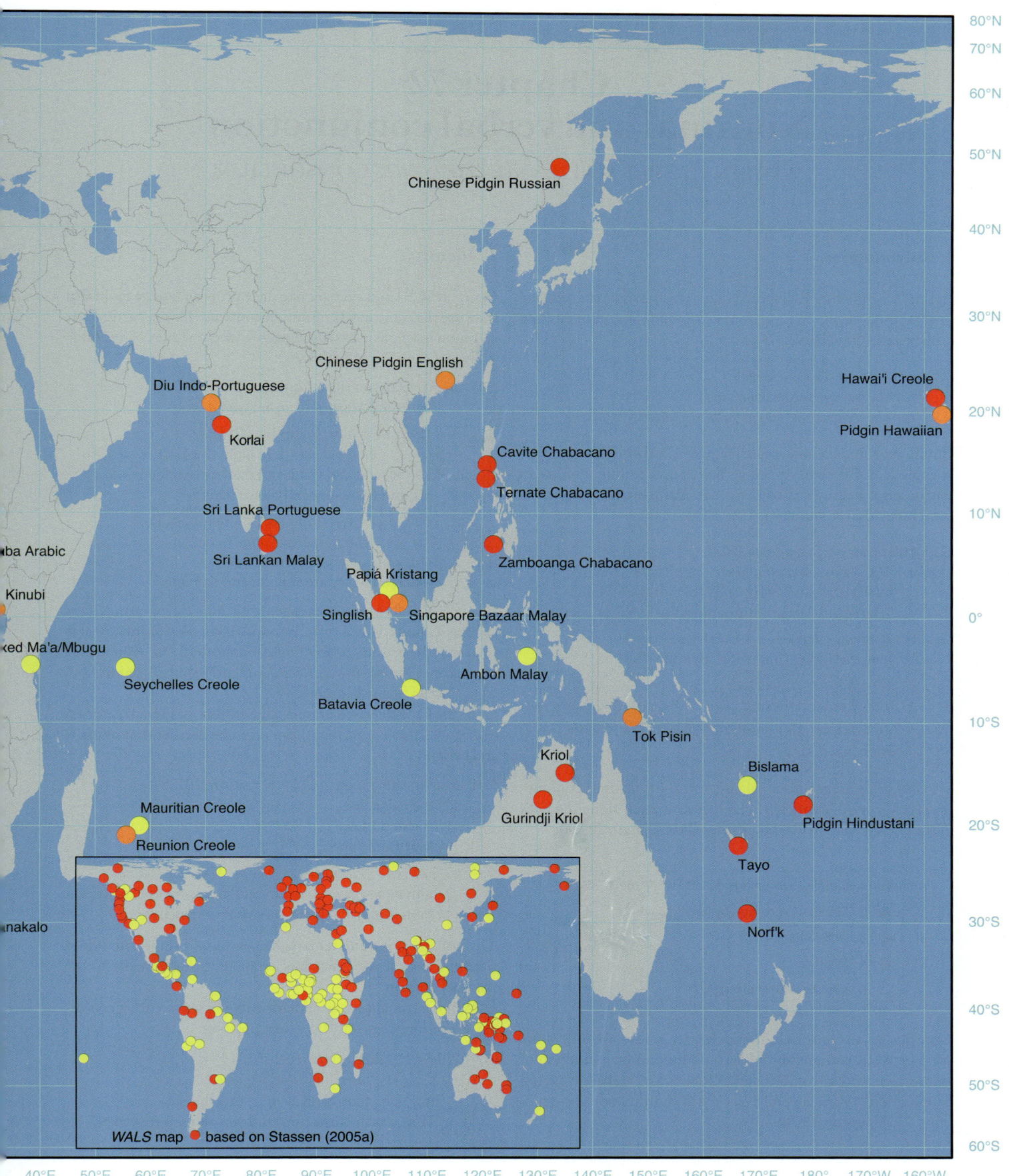

Chapter 72
Nominal and verbal conjunction

MARTIN HASPELMATH AND THE *APiCS* CONSORTIUM

1. Introduction

In English and other European languages, the same coordinator (*and*) is used for the conjunction of NPs and the conjunction of verb phrases and clauses:

(1) a. *the house **and** the garden*
b. *She was singing **and** dancing.*
c. *The children are playing **and** the adults are talking.*

But in many pidgin and creole languages, nominal conjunction is expressed differently from verbal/clausal conjunction, as in Palenquero, where *ku* is used for nominal conjunction and *i* is used for clausal conjunction:

(2) Palenquero (Schwegler 2013)
a. *Malia **ku** Ana ta etulé aí kasa Bitto.*
Maria with Ana PROG study there house Victor
'Maria and Ana are studying at the house of Victor.'
b. *Juan ta kumé **i** muhé si toabía ta*
Juan PROG eat and wife his still be
aí kusina trabahando.
there kitchen working
'Juan is (already) eating and his wife is still in the kitchen working.'

We thus ask whether nominal and verbal (or clausal) conjunction is expressed identically or is differentiated, along the lines of the corresponding *WALS* chapter (Haspelmath 2005c):

○ 1. Identity, overtly expressed		37
● 2. Identity, expressed by juxtaposition		1
● 3. Differentiation		26
● 4. Overlap		7
○ 5. Identity and differentiation		4

Note that for the purposes of this chapter, we are not differentiating between conjunction of verb phrases and conjunction of clauses, so "verbal conjunction" is short for 'verbal or clausal conjunction'. (For a general overview of coordination constructions, see Haspelmath 2007.)

2. Identity

Many *APiCS* languages are like the European languages in that they use the same marker for both contexts. This is particularly common in English-based languages, where a reflex of *and* often survives (as well as in Afrikaans):

(3) a. African American English (Green 2013)
*Bruce **and** his friend laughed **and** danced.*
b. Hawai'i Creole (Velupillai 2013)
mi æn papa siŋ æn dans (tugera)
1SG.OBL and Papa sing and dance (together)
'Me and Papa sing and dance together.'
c. Afrikaans (den Besten & Biberauer 2013)
*Jan **en** Marie sing **en** dans.*
John and Mary sing and dance
'John and Mary are singing and dancing.'

But it is also found in languages with non-European lexifiers such as Chinuk Wawa (*pi*), Ambon Malay (*deng*), Juba Arabic (*wa*, inherited from Arabic), and Sango (*na*). In Zamboanga Chabacano, the borrowed form *pati* 'and' can be used in both ways (just as Spanish-derived *i*).

In the French-based creoles, the words *e* (< French *et*) or *epi* (< French *et puis* 'and then') can often be used both nominally and verbally:

(4) Martinican Creole (Colot & Ludwig 2013b)
a. *Mari **épi** Jan*
Mary and John
'Mary and John'
b. *Jan ka kwenyen tanbou **épi** Mari ka dansé.*
John PROG play drum and Mary PROG dance
'John is playing drum and Mary is dancing.'

This use of *épi* is quite remarkable, because it shows the extension of a coordinator that was originally used verbally to the nominal domain.

While most languages with identity possess an overt coordinator, one language only uses juxtaposition:

(5) Pidgin Hindustani (Siegel 2013)
a. *Kaise ek taim Simi tum-log senge jao?*
how one time Simi 2-PL together go
'How was the time Simi and you all went together?'

b. *U-loŋ ekdam cup ekdam kape.*
   3-PL EMPH quiet EMPH fearful
   'They were really quiet and absolutely shaking (with fear).'

3. Differentiation

Quite a few of the *APiCS* languages show the differentiating pattern seen above in (2) for Palenquero, with two different coordinators. In the European-based languages, the nominal conjunction marker is typically different from the lexifier's nominal coordinator and derives from the preposition 'with' (cf. Palenquero *ku* < Spanish *con*), while the verbal conjunction marker was retained from the lexifier (cf. Palenquero *i* < Spanish *y*). This is found in most of the Portuguese-based creoles as well as in the more radical creoles of the Caribbean region, such as Berbice Dutch, Saramaccan and Nengee, and Guyanais and Haitian Creole (see also Chapter 71 on nominal conjunction and comitative function), as in (6), for example:

(6) Nengee (Migge 2013)
   a. *Baa Dagu **anga** Baa Koo be go piki manyan.*
      Mr Dog with Mr Turtle PST go pick mango
      'Mr Dog and Mr Turtle had gone mango picking.'
   b. *Baa B. be e sikiifi biifi **da** Baa D. be*
      Mr B. PST IPFV write letter and Mr D. PST
      e leisi buku.
      IPFV read book
      'Mr B. was writing letters and Mr D. was reading.'

The use of a conjunction marker that also (and originally) means 'with'—which is restricted to nominal conjunction—is a striking example of a substrate-influenced feature (see Michaelis & Rosalie 2000 and Chapter 71). The corresponding *WALS* data (Haspelmath 2005c) show that while differentiation is found throughout the world (except in western Eurasia), it is particularly common in Africa. Characteristically, differentiation is also found in the Bantu-based languages Lingala, Kikongo-Kituba, Fanakalo, and Mixed Ma'a/Mbugu. However, these languages tend to use juxtaposition rather than a distinct coordinator for verbal/clausal conjunction.

Note that also in many other languages, juxtaposition is an additional option, especially with verbal conjunction (as in English, where *and* can be omitted from 1c). For this chapter, juxtaposition was taken into account only where it was the only or the major option. For example, in Papiá Kristang, juxtaposition is explicitly said to be the major option for verbal conjunction:

(7) Papiá Kristang (Baxter 2013)
   a. *yo sa papa **ku** yo sa kanyong*
      1SG GEN father COM 1SG GEN elder.brother
      'my father and my brother'

b. *eli ta bebé sura, ta kumí seba*
   3SG PROG drink toddy PROG eat pig.ear
   'He is drinking palm wine and eating pig's ear.'

4. Overlap

Seven languages have two forms, one of which can be used in both ways (identity) and one of which is restricted (differentiation). Interestingly, in all cases, the form with broader distribution is the coordinator of the European (or Arabic) lexifier, while the form with narrower distribution derives from a comitative marker and is restricted to the nominal function:

(8)
	From lexifier (nominal/verbal)	From comitative (nominal only)
Cape Verdean (São V.)	*y*	*ma*
Diu Indo-Portuguese	*i*	*ku*
Chinese Pidgin English	*and*	*long*
Nigerian Pidgin	*ànd*	*wit, folo*
Reunion Creole	*é*	*ek*
Mauritian Creole	*e*	*avek*
Kinubi	*u*	*ma*

In Reunion Creole, for example, *é* comes from French *et* and can be used nominally (9a) and verbally (9b), while *ek* comes from *avec* 'with' and is only used nominally (9c):

(9) Reunion Creole (Bollée 2013)
   a. *Zan Pyer é Zan René*
      'Jean-Pierre and Jean-René'
   b. *Ma lanp la etin é la ralumé.*
      POSS.1SG lamp PRF go.out and PRF light.up
      'My lamp went out and lighted up again.'
   c. *Le papa ek le maman lé trakasé.*
      DEF father with DEF mother COP.PRS worried
      'The father and the mother are worried.'

5. Identity and differentiation

Finally, a few languages have three different forms, one of which can be used nominally and verbally, while the other two forms can be used only nominally and only verbally, respectively. For example, in Pichi, *àn* 'and' can be used nominally and verbally, *wìt* 'with, and' can be used only nominally, and *we* can be used only for clausal conjunction. The other three languages in this group are Bislama (*mo*, *wetem*, juxtaposition), Early Sranan (*en*, *nanga*, *kaba*), and Media Lengua (*-bish*, *-un*, *i*).

72 Nominal and verbal conjunction

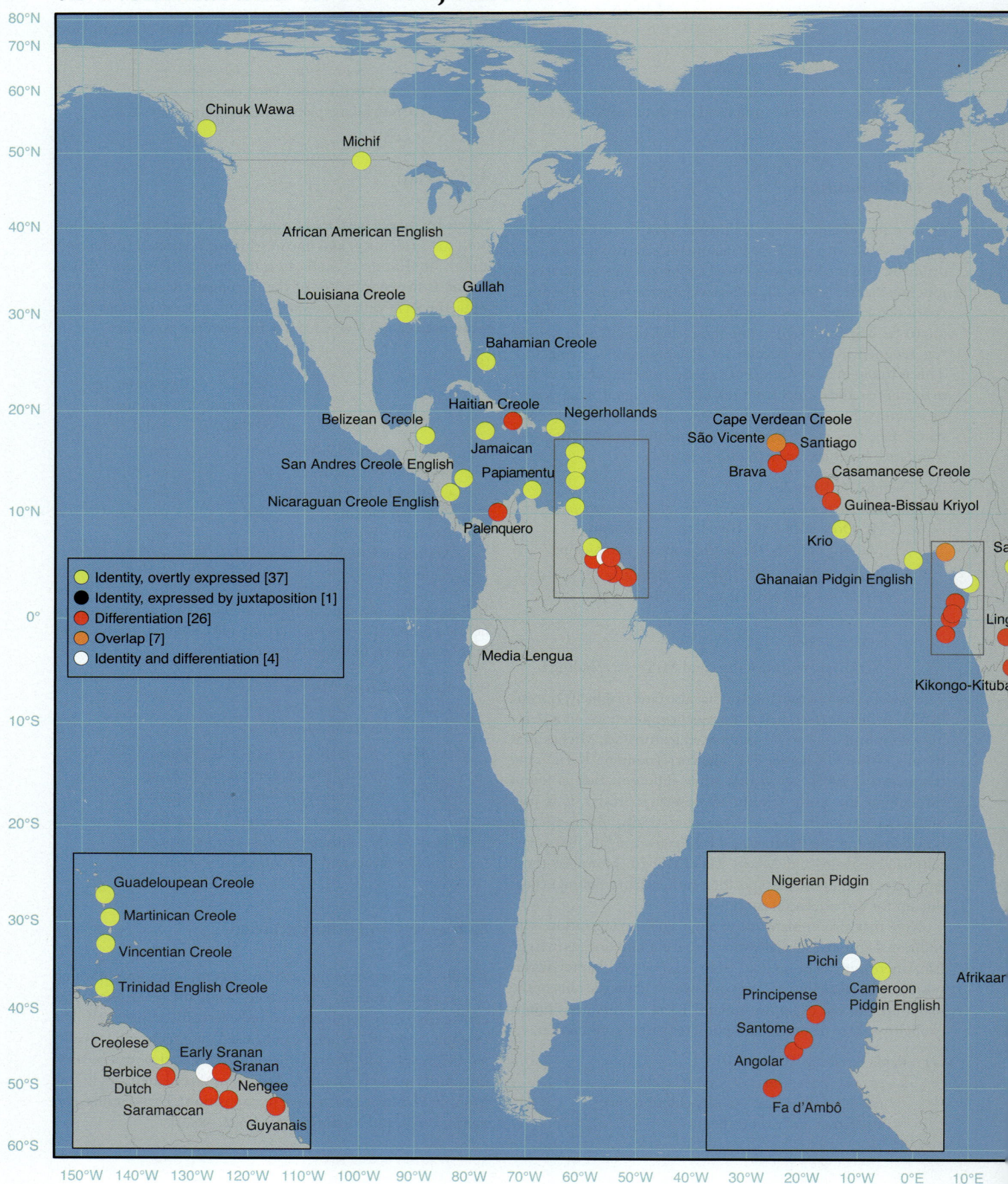

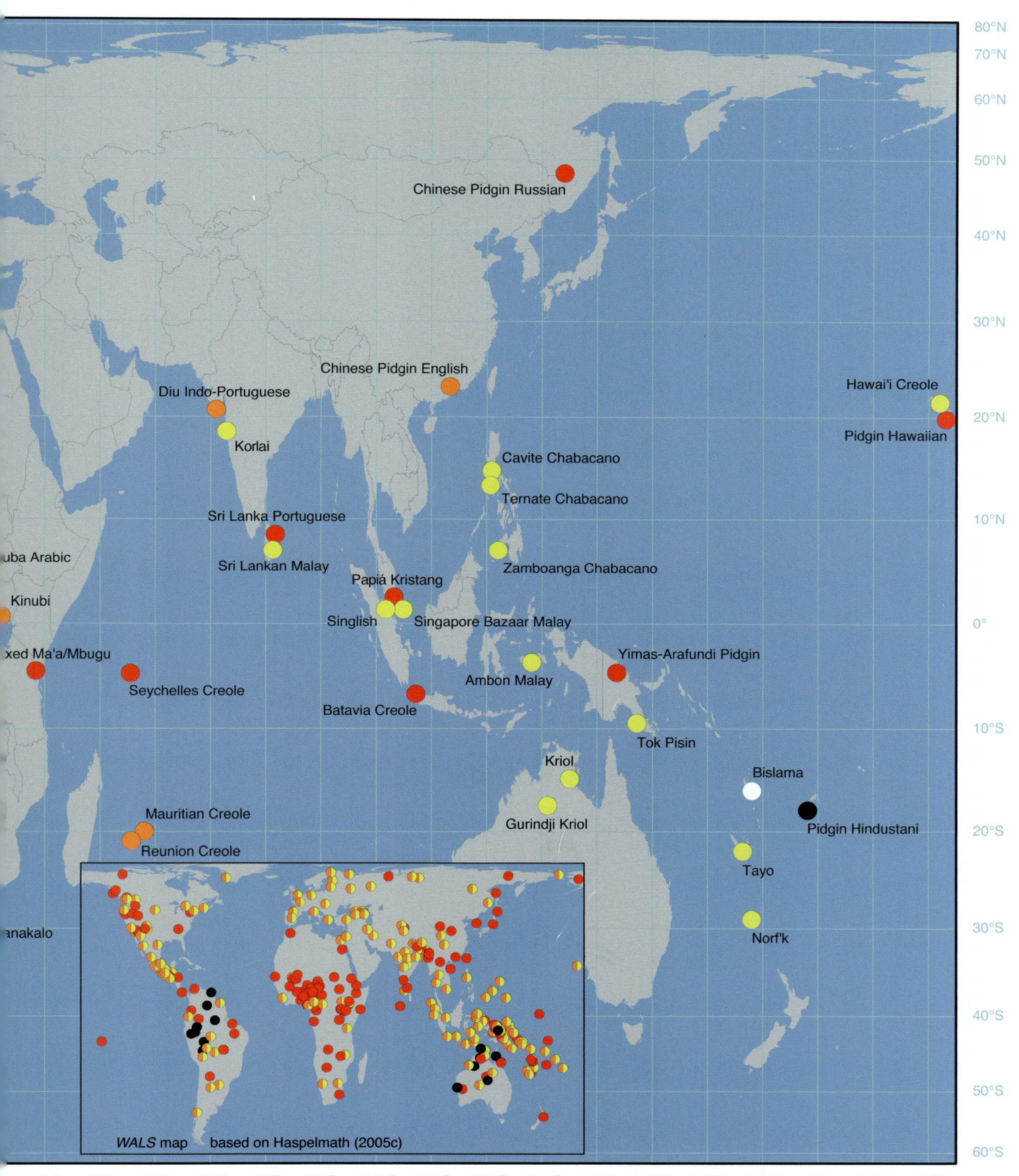

CLAUSAL SYNTAX

Chapter 73
Predicative noun phrases

SUSANNE MARIA MICHAELIS AND THE *APiCS* CONSORTIUM

1. Introduction

This chapter is about the presence or absence of a copula in clauses with predicative noun phrases with class-inclusion function (based on Stassen 2005d). Thus we study how a situation like 'Mary is a singer' is expressed in the *APiCS* languages. In class-inclusion constructions, the predicative noun phrase ('a singer') is indefinite and non-referential. We disregard predicative noun phrases with identification function as in 'My sister is the woman next to the singer', where the predicative noun phrase is definite and referential. Moreover, we restrict our comparison to stative situations, that is, we leave aside situations like 'Mary became a singer'.

A copula is defined as any overt element that occurs in such clauses apart from the subject and the predicative noun phrase and that does not normally occur in verbal clauses. The copula need not be a verb. Thus, resumptive pronouns, as in Hebrew *David hu student* [David he student] 'David is a student', are also considered as copulas. However, the Seychelles Creole predicate marker *i*, as in *David i letidyan* [David PM student] 'David is a student', is not a copula because it occurs in verbal clauses as well (*David i vini* 'David comes'). Discourse or focus markers, too, can function as copulas in the definition proposed here (see ex. 5 from Belizean Creole). In Belizean Creole, the particle *da*, which Escure (2013) analyzes as a focus particle, is still classified as a copula within the *APiCS* comparison. Thus our definition of copula as a cross-linguistic comparative concept does not have to coincide with language-particular definitions of copula (compare also our definition of *adjective* as a cross-linguistic comparative concept contrasting with language-specific definitions in Chapter 3, Order of adjective and noun).

For this chapter, only present-tense clauses are taken into account because where copula use is variable, it most often depends on tense: in the present tense, no copula is used, while in other tenses, a copula must be used (e.g. in Russian and Arabic).

2. The values

In this feature we distinguish three values. Thirty-three *APiCS* languages have an **invariant copula**, by which we mean that the copula obligatorily occurs under all circumstances (value 1).

●	1. Invariant copula	33
○	2. No copula	22
●	3. Variable copula	21

(1) Norf'k (Mühlhäusler 2013)
*Tarzan **es** bas draiwa.*
Tarzan COP bus driver
'Tarzan is a bus driver.'

(2) Pidgin Hindustani (Siegel 2013)
*U nas **baito**.*
3SG nurse COP
'She's a nurse.'

(3) Cape Verdean Creole of Brava (Baptista 2013)
*Jematu **e** piskador.*
Jematu COP fisherman
'Jematu is a fisherman.'

In Guyanais the copula *sa* is used if no TAM markers are present, which means that it is obligatory in the present tense:

(4) Guyanais (Pfänder 2013)
*i **sa** gran-grèk*
she COP professor/researcher
'She is a professor at university.' (*Gran-grèk* literally means 'old Greek'.)

In Belizean Creole, predicative noun phrases have to occur with the copula *da* (see 5a), which also functions as a focus particle or topicalizer (see 5b):

(5) Belizean Creole (Escure 2013)
a. *Dog pa fi dem pap **da** wan big dog.*
dog father for them pup COP a big dog
'These puppies' father is a big dog.'
b. ***Da** fɛl haya di bowt fra djimi.*
FOC Shell hire the boat from Jimmy
'It's Shell that rented Jimmy's boat.'

In 22 *APiCS* languages, a **copula is never used** (value 2). The following *APiCS* languages show this value, for example:

(6) Fanakalo (Mesthrie 2013)
    Yena lo ticha.
    he ART teacher
    'He is a teacher.'

(7) Guadeloupean Creole (Colot & Ludwig 2013a)
    Mari pa dòktè, Mari enfirmyèz.
    Mary NEG doctor Mary nurse
    'Mary is not a doctor, she is a nurse.'

Since we disregard tense forms other than the present tense, languages which show copulas in non-present tenses (like Russian and Arabic) also fall into this type. This is the case in Zamboanga Chabacano, where in present contexts there is no copula with predicative noun phrases (see ex. 8a), whereas in past contexts a copula (*estaba*, see ex. 8b) is required:

(8) Zamboanga Chabacano (Steinkrüger 2013)
    a. *Hendéq 'le amerikáno.*
       NEG s/he American
       'S/he is not an American.'
    b. *Un estudyánte estába si Teresa.*
       a student was AG Teresa
       'Teresa was once a student.'

Finally, in 21 *APiCS* languages the use of a **copula is variable**: it occurs under certain conditions (other than tense, as pointed out earlier), but not under others (value 3). Examples of languages which show optional copulas not conditioned by grammatical factors, in other word, in free variation, are Bahamian Creole and Singlish:

(9) Singlish (Lim & Ansaldo 2013)
    a. *My dad is a doctor.*
       1SG.POSS father COP ART doctor
       'My father is a doctor.'
    b. *He quite poor thing also lɔ33.*
       3SG quite poor thing also PCL
       'He is quite a poor thing as well [resignedly].'

Other languages with a variable copula have grammatical conditioning factors for the presence or absence of a copula with predicative noun phrases. One prominent condition is negation. For example, in Vincentian Creole, affirmative sentences (see 10a) show a copula, whereas negated sentences (10b) lack one (*a* being the copula and not the indefinite article).

(10) Vincentian Creole (Prescod 2013)
     a. *Hi a paasta.*
        3SG COP pastor
        'He is a pastor.'
     b. *Hi na (no) paasta.*
        3SG NEG (INDF) pastor
        'He is not a pastor.'

Another condition for the occurrence of a copula is main clause vs. (specific) subordinate clauses. In Principense the copula *sa* is excluded from most contexts, main clauses included (see 11a). But in certain subordinate clauses, for example, relative clauses and some complement clauses, the presence of the copula is obligatory (see 11b).

(11) Principense (Maurer 2013c)
     a. *Ê ladran mutu.*
        3SG thief very
        'He is a big thief.'
     b. *M mêsê pa txi sa dôtô.*
        1SG want COMP 2SG COP doctor
        'I want you to be a doctor.'

3. Distribution

All three values are quite evenly distributed over the *APiCS* languages. There seem to be some geographical patterns. Copula languages (languages showing value 1 or value 3) are concentrated in the Americas, the Atlantic region, in Africa, and in northern India. Languages in which a copula cannot occur are mainly found in the Indian Ocean, South Asia, Southeast Asia, Australia, and the Pacific. Interestingly, the two French-based languages, Martinican and Guadeloupean Creole (see ex. 7), are the only creoles in the Caribbean which have no copula.

If one compares the *APiCS* data with the corresponding *WALS* data, one finds first that the West African substrates of the Atlantic creoles have obligatory copulas, so that it is not surprising that the Atlantic creoles have them too. More interesting languages are those where the substrate languages diverge from the European lexifier, and where the contact languages follow the substrates in allowing zero-copulas, as is the case in Sri Lanka Portuguese, Tok Pisin, and Kriol.

One often cited claim in the literature is that pidgins—as very simplified languages—do not show any copula in such constructions (Ferguson 1971: 141ff.). And this is indeed the case for some of the *APiCS* languages: Eskimo Pidgin, Pidgin Chinese Russian, Fanakalo (see ex. 6), and Pidgin Hawaiian. But there are also pidgins with a copula: Yimas-Arafundi Pidgin, Pidgin Hindustani, and Chinese Pidgin English, the latter showing optional copulas (see also Baker 1995: 8 on the role of the copula in pidgins and creoles). As for Yimas-Arafundi Pidgin, at least Yimas, one of the contributing languages, also shows a copula construction.

73 Predicative noun phrases

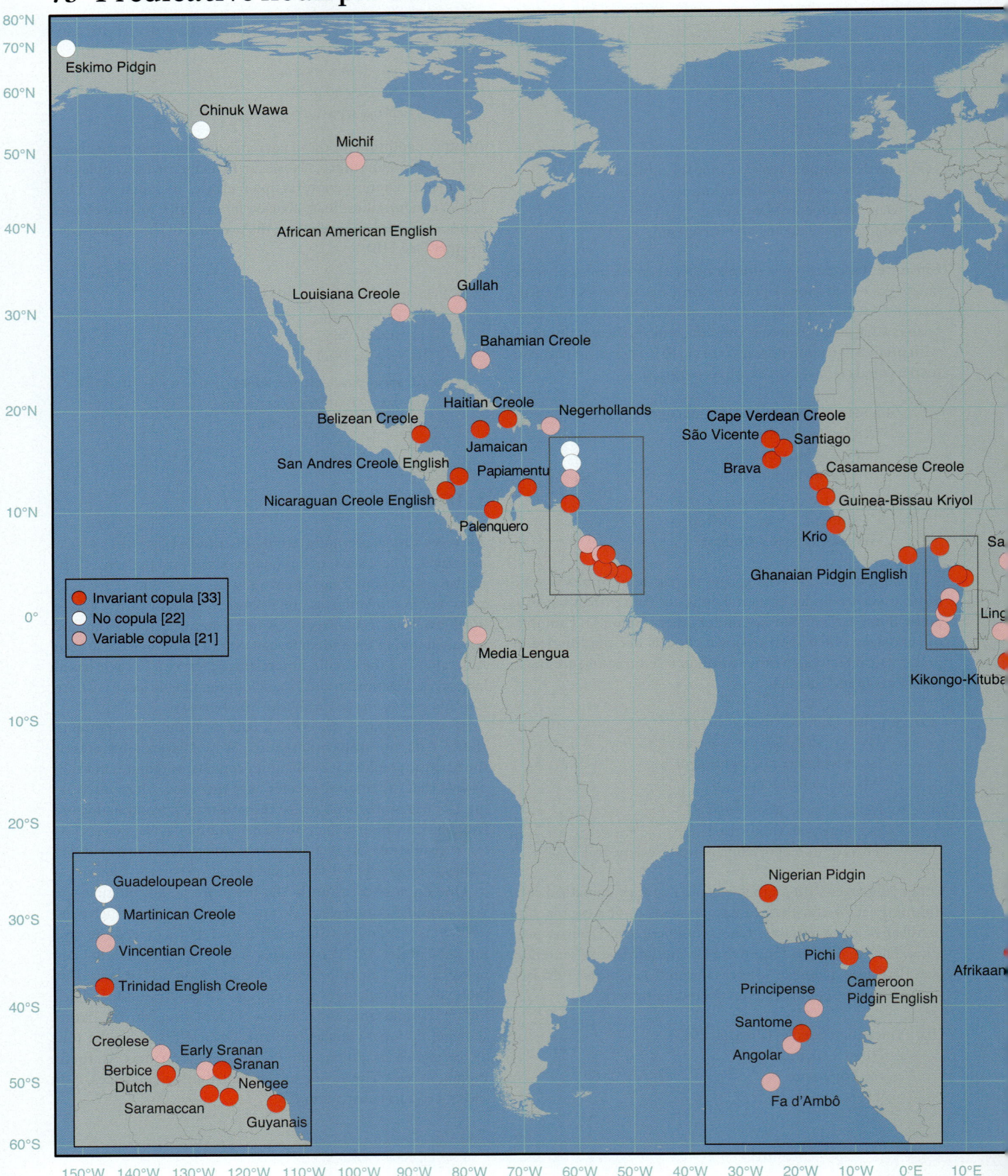

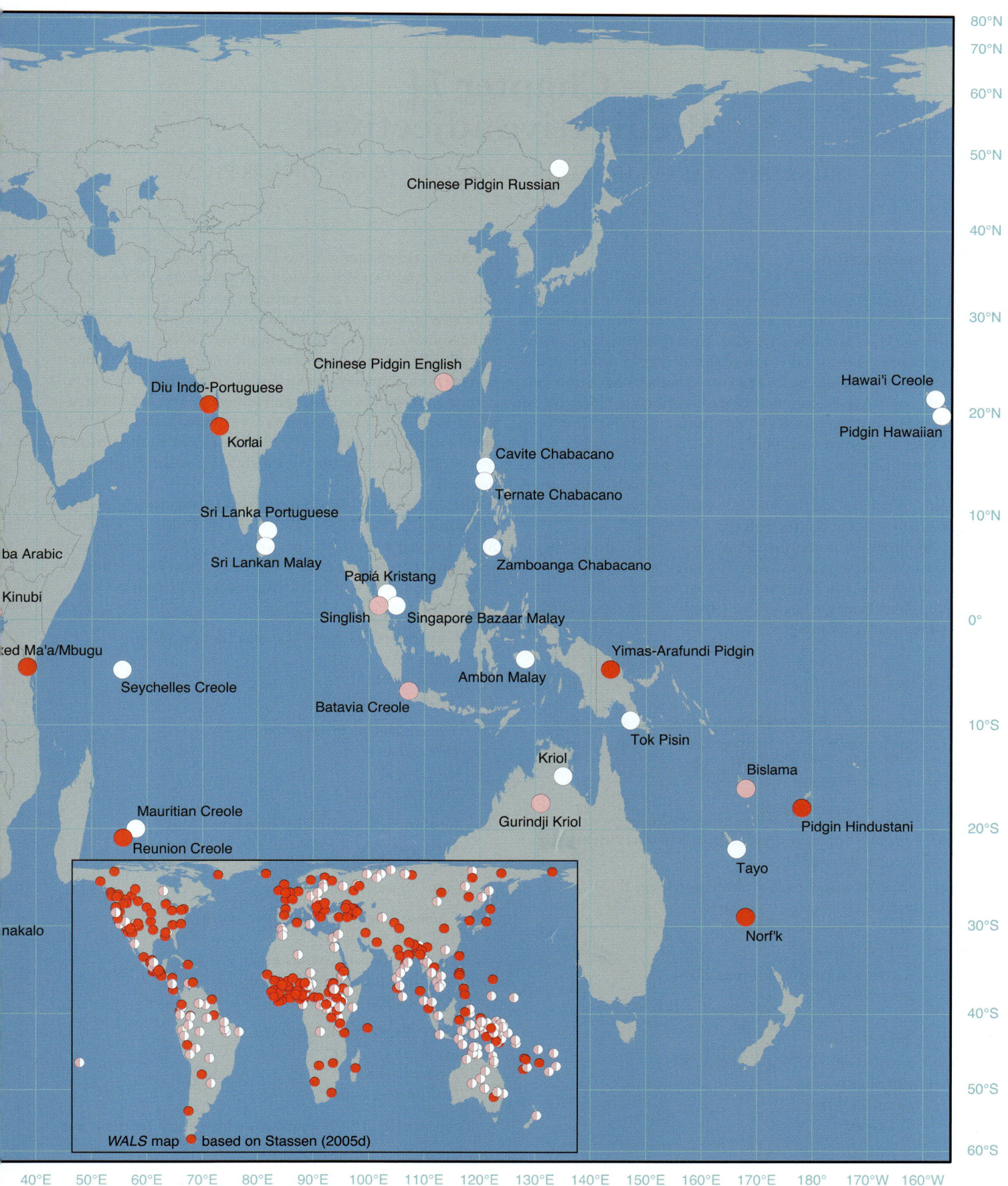

Chapter 74
Predicative adjectives

SUSANNE MARIA MICHAELIS AND THE *APiCS* CONSORTIUM

1. Introduction

This chapter is about the presence or absence of a copula in clauses with predicative adjectives. We ask how a situation such as 'Mary is old' is expressed. Note that "adjective" is defined purely semantically: a word that denotes a property such as 'red', 'big', 'old', 'bad'. The issue whether such words "are really verbs" or belong to a separate word class "adjective" is left aside for the purposes of this feature (see also Chapter 3, "Order of adjective and noun").

As in Chapter 73 ("Predicative noun phrases"), a copula is defined as any overt element that occurs in such clauses apart from the subject and the predicative adjective and that does not normally occur in clauses with action verbs.

Similarly, as in the preceding chapter, only present-tense clauses are taken into account. Moreover, we only look at stative predicative adjectives, so we do not consider inchoative situations like 'Peter got angry' (see Chapter 52 on aspect markers and inchoative meaning).

2. The values

In this feature we distinguish three values:

●	1. Invariant copula	14
○	2. No copula	34
●	3. Variable copula	28

In 14 *APiCS* languages, predicative adjectives **must occur with a copula** (value 1):

(1) Cape Verdean Creole of Santiago (Lang 2013)
 *Pamodi ki=bu=**sta** tristi?*
 why COMP=2SG=COP sad
 'Why are you sad?'

(2) Kikongo-Kituba (Mufwene 2013)
 *Yandi **kele** ngolo.*
 s/he COP strong
 'S/he is strong.'

(3) Yimas-Arafundi Pidgin (Foley 2013)
 *mən panmas **anak***
 3SG good COP
 'It's good.'

In some languages there are two different copulas. The choice for one or the other depends on whether the property assigned to the subject is conceived of as a permanent or a transitory state. This is the case in, for example, Diu Indo-Portuguese (Cardoso 2013) and in some varieties of Cape Verdean Creole (Baptista 2013 and Lang 2013). These creoles seem to continue the similar distinction between permanent and transitory states that is also found in their European base language Portuguese. But not all Portuguese-based *APiCS* languages have two copulas that make this kind of distinction. Other *APiCS* languages mark this distinction by different means (see e.g. Pichi and Ghanaian Pidgin English under value 3).

In the majority of *APiCS* languages (34 languages), the **copula cannot occur** in predicative adjective clauses (value 2). Such languages are often described as expressing property words by stative verbs rather than by adjectives. This is the case in most Caribbean languages, languages of the Indian Ocean, Asia, and in the Pacific.

(4) Guadeloupean Creole (Colot & Ludwig 2013a)
 Diana bèl.
 Diana beautiful
 'Diana is beautiful.'

(5) Vincentian Creole (Prescod 2013)
 Dem dotish.
 3PL stupid
 'They are stupid.'

(6) Juba Arabic (Manfredi & Petrollino 2013)
 kanísa de jedíd
 church DEM.PROX new
 'This church is new.'

(7) Chinese Pidgin English (Li & Matthews 2013)
 利士宅頓都宅治乞
 Thisee mutton too muchee hard.
 DEM mutton too much hard
 'This mutton is too hard.'

(8) Tayo (Ehrhart & Revis 2013)
 ta ʃa:ti pu mwa!
 2SG nice PREP 1SG
 'You are nice to me!'

There are 28 *APiCS* languages which **may or may not**

have a copula in predicative adjective phrases (value 3). For many languages, the contributors mention that the variation does not seem to be conditioned by grammatical factors. This is the case in, for instance, Gullah (ex. 9), Angolar, Nigerian Pidgin, Sango, Singlish, and the mixed language Gurindji Kriol. The variation may be governed stylistically or socially.

(9) Gullah (Klein 2013)
Man, the weather('s) bad.
man the weather(=COP) bad
'Man, the weather is bad.'

But in some languages there are grammatical, semantic, or lexical conditioning factors for the presence or absence of a copula. In Ghanaian Pidgin English, time-stable adjectives occur without a copula (ex. 10a), whereas transitory states like 'sick' require the locative copula *de* (ex. 10b).

(10) Ghanaian Pidgin English (Huber 2013)
 a. *dɛ hol siti ful*
  ART whole city full
  'The whole city is full.'
 b. *pɛsin we ì de sik*
  person REL 3SG COP sick
  'a person who is sick'

In Pichi (Yakpo 2013) and Nengee (Migge 2013), similar factors seem to condition the use of the copula.

In Sranan, the copula is used only with a small class of adjectives (see ex. 11b), most of which are loanwords from Dutch, such as *enthoesiast* 'enthusiastic', *bezig* 'busy', *ernstig* 'serious', *vrij* 'free', and *moi* 'nice' (Winford 1997: 283). All other adjectives occur without a copula (see ex. 11a).

(11) Sranan (Winford & Plag 2013)
 a. *A liba bradi.*
  DET river broad
  'The river is wide.'
 b. *A agu dati de moi kaba.*
  DET hog DEM COP nice already
  'That pig is already nice and fat.'

In Principense, in most syntactic contexts no copula occurs (ex. 12a). But in certain types of subordinate clause (complement clauses and desiderative clauses headed by *pa*, see ex. 12b), a copula is used with predicative adjectives (similar syntactic restrictions also hold for predicative noun phrases in Principense, see Chapter 73):

(12) Principense (Maurer 2013c)
 a. *Têtuuga, txi rwin mutu.*
  Turtle 2SG wicked very
  'Turtle, you are too wicked.'
 b. *Pa ine minu sê sa bôn.*
  COMP PL child DEM COP good
  '(I hope) that these children are good.'

In Santome the pattern with the copula is dominant (see 13a). The copula may be absent if the adjective shows a special intonation pattern (high pitch and vowel lengthening, not indicated in 13b):

(13) Santome (Hagemeijer 2013)
 a. *Mama sa ve za.*
  mama COP old already
  'Mama is already old.'
 b. *Kani makaku, ê doxi muntu.*
  meat monkey 3SG sweet very
  'Monkey meat, it's very tasty.'

3. Distribution

Interestingly, eight out of fourteen *APiCS* languages with invariant copula use (value 1) are Ibero-Romance-based languages: Palenquero, Papiamentu (both being the only invariant-copula languages of the Americas), the three Cape Verdean Creole varieties, Diu Indo-Portuguese, Korlai, and Batavia Creole. Only one French-based language, Reunion Creole, requires a copula, and there is no English-based *APiCS* language where the predicative adjective must occur with the copula.

The languages with value 2, where the copula cannot occur, are not restricted lexifier-wise or area-wise. The most striking picture is presented by the Caribbean, where the overwhelming majority of English- and French-based languages show no copula in predicative adjective constructions (with the exception of Palenquero and Papiamentu, as noted above). This is in sharp contrast to the geographical pattern in predicative noun phrase constructions (see the previous Chapter 73), where many of these Caribbean (and other Atlantic) creole languages have an obligatory copula.

Yimas-Arafundi Pidgin (see ex. 3) is the only pidgin in *APiCS* which shows a copula in predicative adjectives (as in Chapter 73 with predicative noun phrases). All other pidgins, even those which have a copula in predicative noun phrases (Pidgin Hindustani and Chinese Pidgin English), do not have a copula in this feature.

Variation in the treatment of property words is dealt with in Stassen's (2005f) *WALS* chapter too, but the three types he distinguishes are a bit different. He looks at verbal/non-verbal encoding (with mixed as a third option). Verbal encoding roughly corresponds to "no copula", non-verbal encoding to "invariant copula", and mixed to "variable copula" in our chapter. West African languages, which are the substrate languages for most Atlantic creoles, overwhelmingly show verbal encoding or mixed encoding. Many of the Atlantic creoles seem to mirror these substrate patterns (see also Boretzky 1983: 159ff.). The same holds for Indonesia, the Philippines, Melanesia, and Polynesia. Most *APiCS* languages with substrates and adstrates in these parts of the world also lack copulas in predicative adjectives.

74 Predicative adjectives

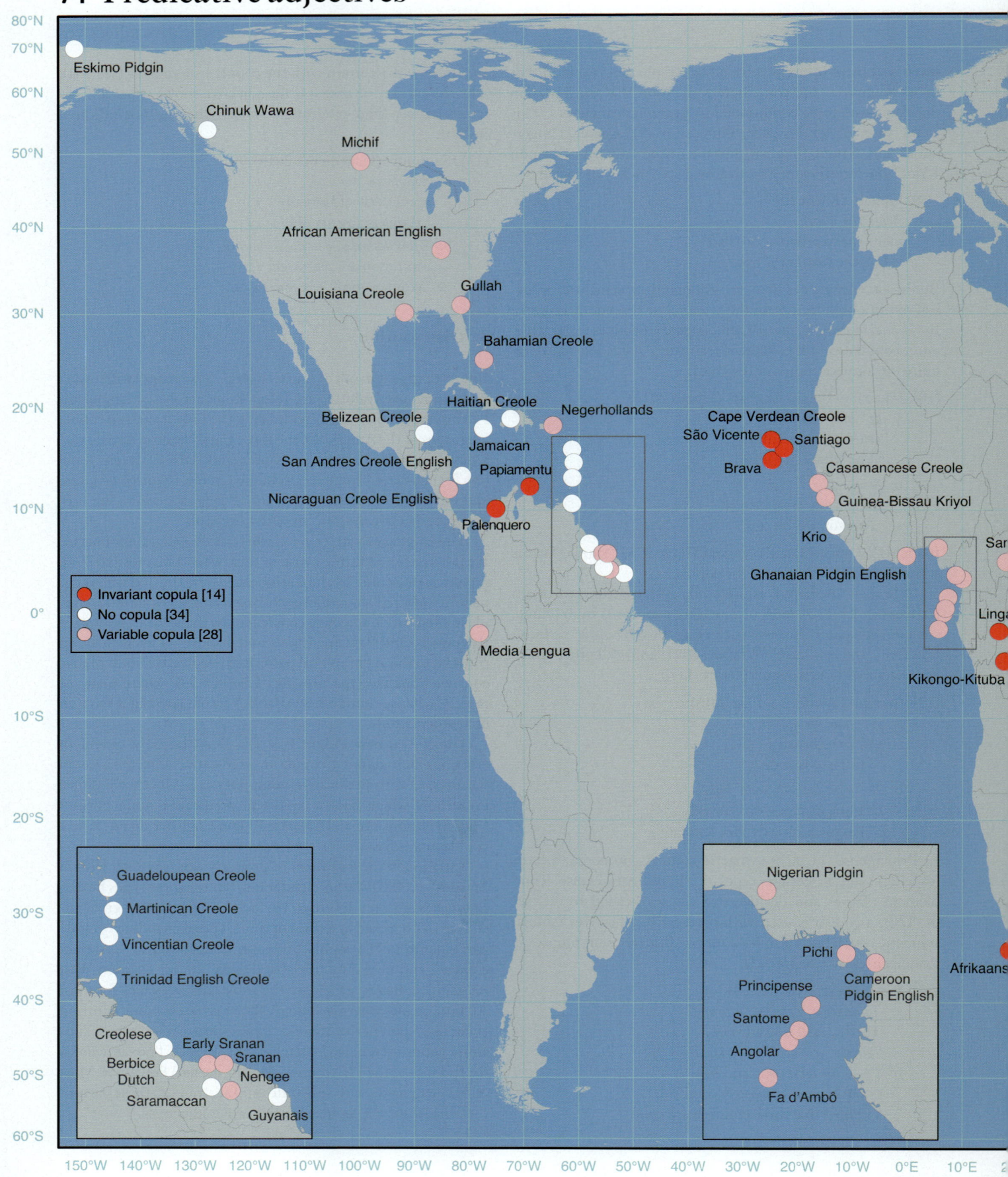

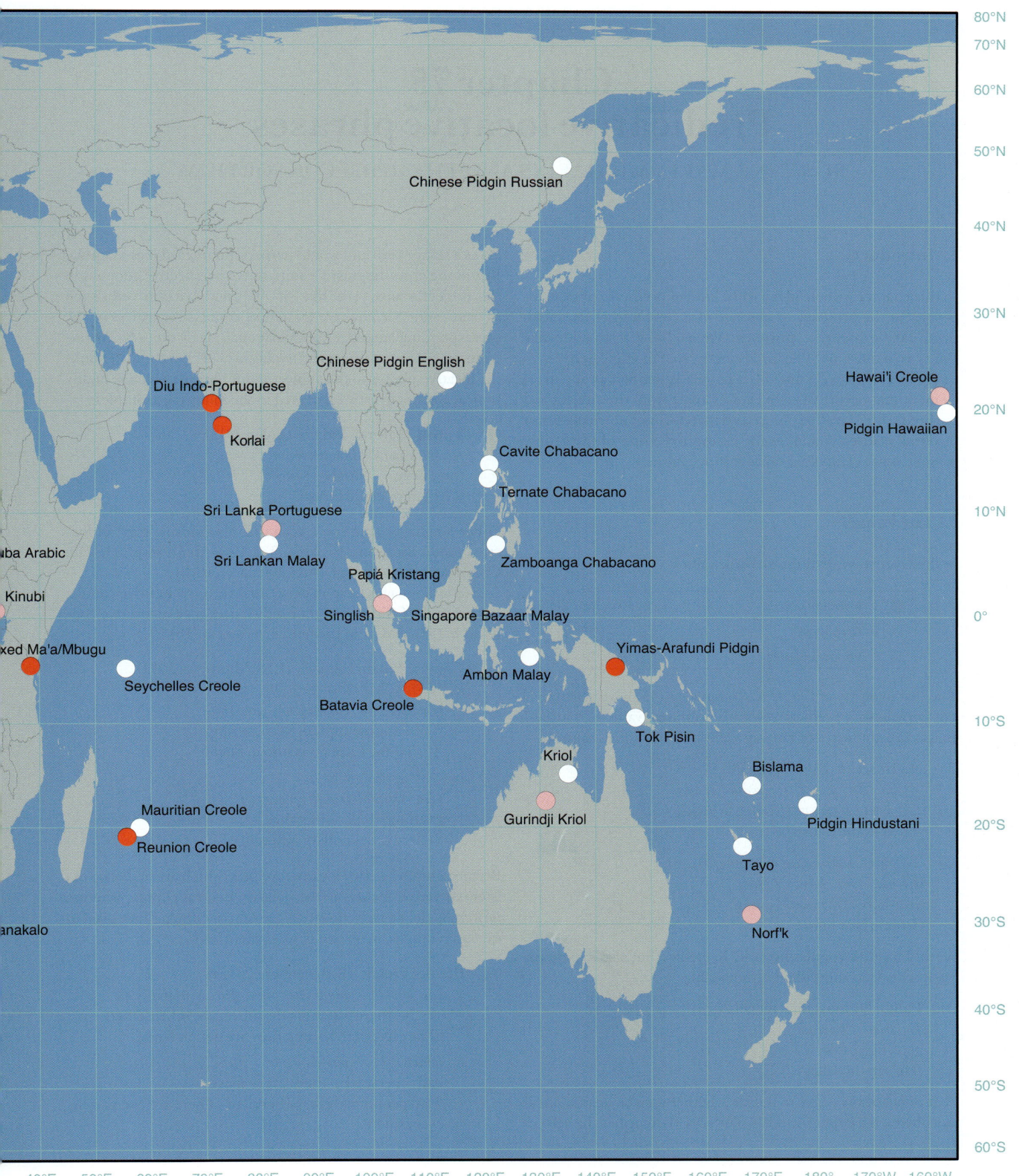

Chapter 75
Predicative locative phrases

SUSANNE MARIA MICHAELIS AND THE *APiCS* CONSORTIUM

1. Introduction

In this chapter we consider a third kind of predicate phrase, focusing on the presence or absence of a copula in clauses with **predicative locative phrases**. We ask how a situation like 'Mary is in town' or 'The bird is on the tree' is expressed.

As in Chapters 73 and 74, a copula is defined as any overt element that occurs in such clauses apart from the subject and the predicative locative phrase and that does not normally occur in verbal clauses. Again, as for predicative noun phrases, only present-tense clauses are taken into account.

2. The values

In this feature we distinguish three values:

●	1. Invariant copula	45
○	2. No copula	10
●	3. Variable copula	21

The vast majority of the *APiCS* languages (45) have an **invariant copula** with predicative locative phrases (value 1). The languages are not restricted to a specific area or lexifier language.

(1) Saramaccan (Aboh et al. 2013)
    *A ta **de** a di wósu dendu.*
    3SG ASP COP LOC DEF.SG house inside
    'He is in the house.'

(2) Ternate Chabacano (Sippola 2013b)
    Ta-akí na kása Loling.
    COP-here LOC house Loling
    'Loling is at home.'

We find locative copulas not only in creoles, but also in pidgins, e.g. in Fanakalo and Pidgin Hindustani.

(3) Pidgin Hindustani (Siegel 2013)
    *U koro **baito**.*
    3SG village COP
    'He's in the village.'

It is not always easy to decide whether a given grammatical morpheme is a copula or not. Foley (2013) describes the verb in (4) as a stance verb and would perhaps not regard it as a copula. But in the cross-linguistic comparative perspective adopted in this project, stance verbs like 'sit', 'lie', and dynamic verbs such as 'stay' and 'become' are treated as copulas regardless of the corresponding language-particular analysis by the *APiCS* contributor. We therefore regard *tandaukə* in (4) as a copula: it links the locative phrase to the subject noun phrase (which is highly topical and not overtly expressed in the following example).

(4) Yimas-Arafundi Pidgin (Foley 2013)
    pucəm kandək tandaukə-nan
    jungle OBL sit/stay-NONFUT
    '(We) were in the forest.'

Other languages showing a verb that also means 'stay' in locative predications are Bislama, Tok Pisin (both *stap*), Hawai'i Creole (*stɛ*), Tayo (*rester*), and Guyanais (*fika*).

Some languages have an existential verb as a locative copula. For example, Chinese Pidgin English uses *got* as a locative copula as in (5a), and as an existential verb as in (5b).

(5) Chinese Pidgin English (Li & Matthews 2013)
    a. 濕波素急頓糯吉涉
       [...] *supposo captain no **got** ship.*
       suppose captain NEG COP ship
       '[...] if the Captain is not on board.'
    b. 吉顛打鏷地化倫士
       ***Got** ten dollar differencee.*
       EXIST ten dollar difference
       'There is ten dollars difference.'

Berbice Dutch has two locative copulas, which are both also existential verbs. *Jen(da)* is the polarity neutral copula, whereas *furi(da)* is the negative locative/existential copula (both used in ex. 6a as copulas, in 6b and 6c as existentials).

(6) Berbice Dutch (Kouwenberg 2013a)
    a. *eni **jɛn-da** mingi ben eni **furi** alandi ka*
       3PL be-there water inside 3PL not.be on.land NEG
       'They live in the water, they are not on land.'
    b. *lombo kɛnɛ **jɛn-da** idri plɛkɛ*
       bad person be-there every place
       'Bad people are everywhere.' or 'There are bad people everywhere.'

c. *helpu furi-da ka*
help not.be-there NEG
'There was no help.'

In ten *APiCS* languages **there is never a copula** in locative predications (value 2). Strikingly, six (out of the nine) French-based *APiCS* creoles show this value: Haitian Creole, Martinican and Guadeloupean Creole, Seychelles Creole, Mauritian Creole, and Louisiana Creole (but only in the variety of the older generation, which is not displayed on the map).

(7) Guadeloupean Creole (Colot & Ludwig 2013a)
Boul-la anba tab-la.
ball-DEF under table-DEF
'The ball is under the table.'

(8) Louisiana Creole (older generation, Neumann-Holzschuh & Klingler 2013)
Djiabe dan cabanne.
devil in house
'The devil is in the hut.'

There are only two English-based creoles which never show a copula with locative phrases, namely Trinidad English Creole and Kriol (but there are other English-based creoles with variable copula, see below).

(9) Trinidad English Creole (Mühleisen 2013)
John in de yard.
John PREP DET yard
'John is in the yard.'

In Kriol there is no copula in present-tense clauses (see ex. 10), but the copula *be* must be used with future time reference.

(10) Kriol (Schultze-Berndt & Angelo 2013)
Thei langa yad.
3PL LOC yard
'They are in the yard.' (referring to chickens)

As we restrict our study of predicative locative phrases to present tense, Kriol ends up having value 2.

In 21 languages, **copula use is variable** (value 3), that is, a copula may or may not be used with predicative locative phrases. Out of these languages, 11 are English-based creoles of the Caribbean, where the locative copula is *de* (< English *there*). For many languages with value 3, there do not seem to be any grammatical factors determining when to use the copula.

(11) Vincentian Creole (Prescod 2013)
Shi (de) in di hous.
3SG (LOC.COP) in ART house
'She's in the house.'

(12) Singlish (Lim & Ansaldo 2013)
Mama (is) at (the) market.
grandmother (COP) at (DET) market
'Grandmother is at the market.'

Creolese shows a subtle semantic difference between copula and non-copula use.

(13) Creolese (Devonish & Thompson 2013)
Jaan (de) in de
John (is) in there
'John is/can be found in there.'

The copula is used when the speaker wants to give specific locational information, but when they want to give general information about the subject, the copula is omitted.

3. Comparison with predicative noun phrases and predicative adjectives (Chapters 73 and 74)

Of all three non-verbal predication types, it is the locative predication which requires an invariant copula most often (45 languages). Predicative noun phrases show an invariant copula in only 33 languages, and predicative adjective phrases show the lowest number of languages with invariant copula use (14 languages; for a comparison of predicative noun phrase and predicative locative phrase strategies, see Chapter 76). We already mentioned in Chapter 74 that in many *APiCS* languages property words are encoded as verbs and therefore do not take a copula.

The languages which cannot have a copula in locative predications (value 2) form an interesting set. As mentioned above, six French-based languages have this pattern, four of which are spoken in the Caribbean (including an older variety of Louisiana Creole). Some Caribbean English-based creoles allow variable copulas (value 3), but the Surinamese and West African English-based creoles nearly exclusively show invariant copulas in locative predication (value 1). Therefore, this picture is puzzling because the French-based Caribbean languages have the same or typologically very similar West African substrate languages as the English-based Caribbean languages. And these substrates have locative copulas (see Boretzky 1983: 160f., for Fongbe, Lefebvre & Brousseau 2002: 147ff., 300), and the French lexifier also has a copula in such contexts. The same holds for the two French-based creoles of the Indian Ocean. Mauritian and Seychelles Creole also have zero copulas in locative phrases even though the eastern Bantu substrate languages do require a copula in such constructions. If one interprets the zero copula as a simplification strategy in second-language use, one wonders why this strategy would have failed in so many English-based Atlantic creoles, radical and less radical ones (see Sharma & Rickford 2009, who argue against the imperfect-learning hypothesis).

75 Predicative locative phrases

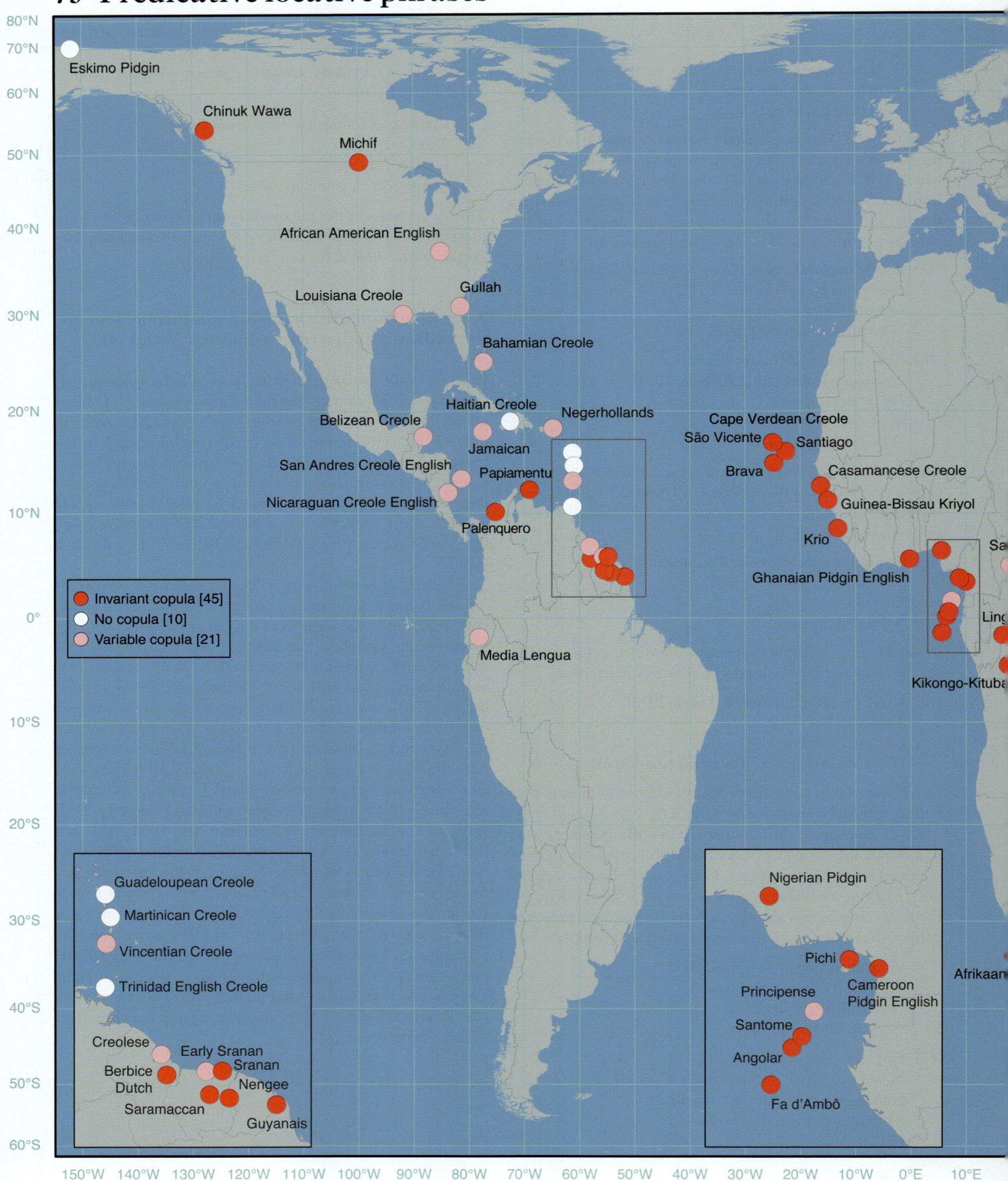

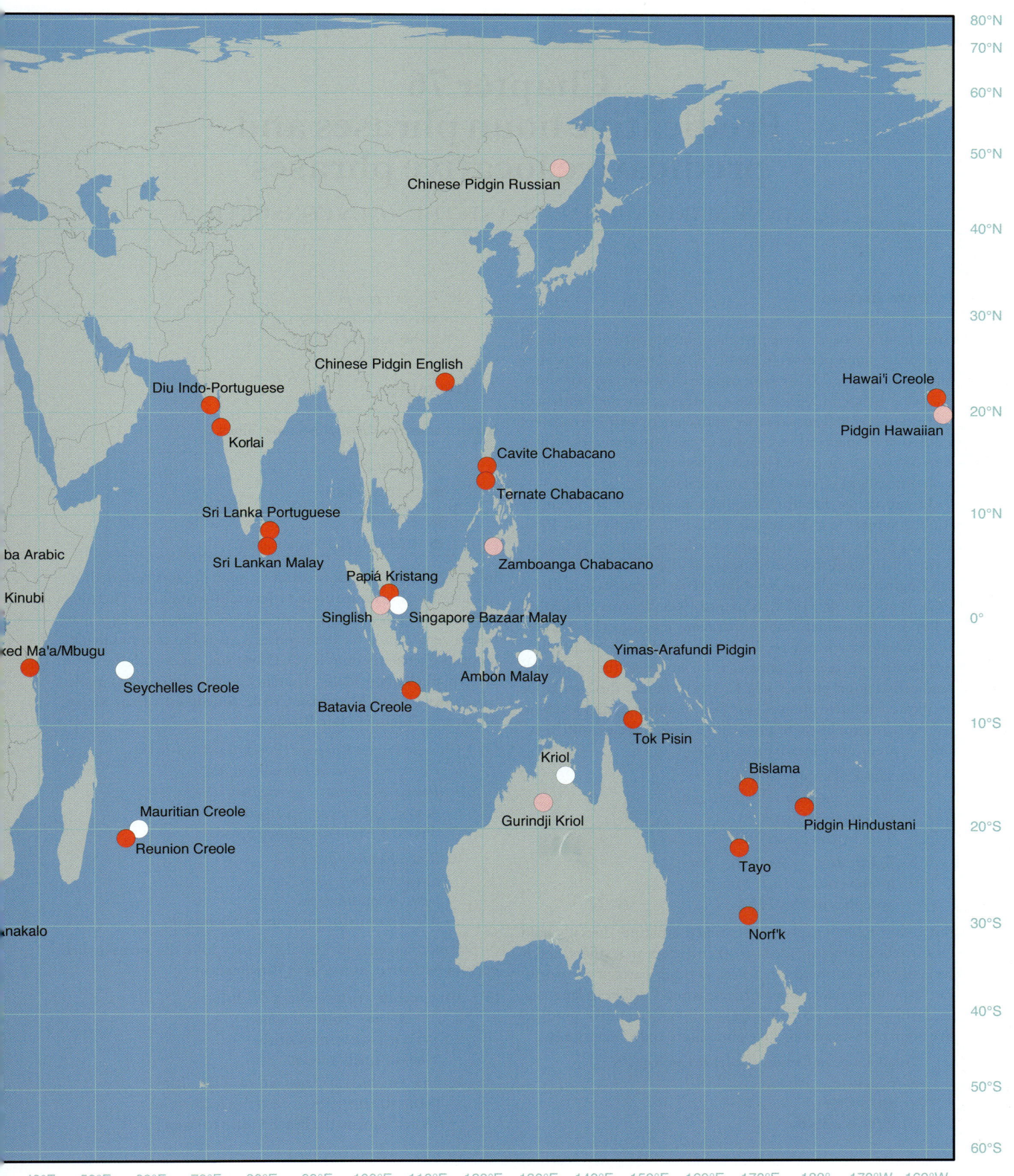

Chapter 76
Predicative noun phrases and predicative locative phrases

SUSANNE MARIA MICHAELIS AND THE *APiCS* CONSORTIUM

1. Introduction

After having looked at the presence and absence of copulas in predicative noun phrases (Chapter 73) and predicative locative phrases (Chapter 75), we here compare the two constructions, following Stassen (2005c). The question is whether sentences corresponding to 'I am a teacher' and 'I am in town' are coded in a different or identical way. If one or the two strategies involve zero coding (i.e. no copula is used), this zero-coding also counts as a strategy and is part of the comparison.

In the creole literature, copulas have been an intensely studied subject (e.g. Bickerton 1981: 67f., Arends et al. 1995: 323ff.). Substantial comparative work has mainly been concerned with English-based languages, that is, African American English and related Caribbean creole languages (e.g. Holm 1984, Winford 1993: 155ff., Rickford 1998, Sharma & Rickford 2009). It is thus widely known that many languages have different strategies to encode predicative noun phrases and predicative locative phrases. In Jamaican, for instance, the copula for predicative noun phrases is *a* (see 1a) whereas the copula for predicative locative phrases is *de* (see 1b; throughout this chapter, the (a) examples show predicative noun phrases, the (b) examples, predicative locative phrases).

(1) Jamaican (Farquharson 2013)
　a. *Mi a sia-man*.
　　1SG COP seer-man
　　'I am a (male) seer.'
　b. *Juoziv de (ina) Mie Pen*.
　　Joseph COP.LOC (in) May Pen
　　'Joseph is in May Pen.'

But in the present chapter, we see that this picture does not hold for Caribbean creoles based on other European lexifiers, and it certainly does not hold for creoles in other parts of the world. Corresponding data from a French-based Caribbean language in (2a, b) show that a copula is lacking in both contexts: predicative noun phrases and locative phrases are coded identically.

(2) Guadeloupean Creole (Colot & Ludwig 2013a)
　a. *I dòktè*.
　　3SG doctor
　　'S/he is a doctor.'
　b. *I anlè pon-la*.
　　3SG on bridge-DEF
　　'S/he is on the bridge.'

2. The values

In this feature we distinguish four values.

🟢	1. Identity	25
🔴	2. Differentiation	38
🟠	3. Overlap	12
⚫	4. Identity and differentiation	1

In 25 *APiCS* languages, predicative noun phrases and predicative locative phrases are **coded identically** (value 1). There are different ways in which this can happen. First, languages may have a zero copula for both contexts, as is the case in Guadeloupean Creole in example (2). Other languages with the same pattern are Ambon Malay, Haitian Creole, Martinican Creole, Seychelles Creole, Mauritian Creole, Singapore Bazaar Malay, Kriol, and Chinese Pidgin Russian.

(3) Chinese Pidgin Russian (Perekhvalskaya 2013)
　a. Поудза – китайса памэпушика.
　　Poudʒə - kitajsa pampuʃəkə.
　　pouze Chinese steamed.bread
　　'Pouze is Chinese steamed bread.'
　b. Щаса Шаньдун иво.
　　ʃasa ʃandun iwo.
　　now Shandong 3SG
　　'He is now in the province of Shandong.'

Second, languages with value 1 may have the **same overt copula** for both contexts, as in Papiamentu:

(4) Papiamentu (Kouwenberg 2013b)
　a. *E ta un muhé chikitu*.
　　3SG COP INDF woman small
　　'She is a small woman.'
　b. *Ora mi ta na lamá mi ta siña landa* [...].
　　hour 1SG COP LOC sea 1SG TNS learn swim
　　'When I am on the beach I learn to swim [...]'.

This is also the pattern of the European base languages English, Dutch, and French as well as of the following *APiCS* languages: Fa d'Ambô, Santome, Afrikaans, Kikongo-Kituba, Reunion Creole, Korlai, Batavia Creole, and Pidgin Hindustani.

There is yet a third possible identity pattern, which can be best described as "two-fold identity". Here, predicative noun phrases and locative phrases can each be coded by two different strategies, but each of the two strategies can occur in both contexts. In the Tugu variety of Batavia Creole, for example, predicative noun phrases can be expressed with the copula *teng/ting* and with no copula. Likewise predicative locative phrases can occur with and without a copula. Other *APiCS* languages which show this pattern are African American English, Media Lengua, and Singlish.

Thirty-eight *APiCS* languages code predicative noun phrases and predicative locative phrases **differently** (value 2). Here again we can observe different subtypes. The first pattern is illustrated in the examples from Jamaican above (ex. 1), where two different overt copulas are used: *a* for predicative noun phrases, *de* for predicative locative phrases. Most English-based Caribbean creoles and English-based West African pidgins and creoles show this pattern whereas their lexifier, English, does not show different copulas (Guyanais and Tayo being the only French-based creoles with value 2). But this type also exists in other languages, for example, Sri Lankan Malay and Mixed Ma'a/Mbugu:

(5) Mixed Ma'a/Mbugu (Mous 2013)
    a. *kilúgwi ni kinyongôlé*
       chameleon COP insect:Q
       'Is the chameleon an insect?'

    b. *é-re-áta i'í*
       1-BGND-COP here
       'He was here.'

Some of the Upper Guinea Portuguese-based creoles (e.g. the Cape Verdean Creole varieties and Guinea-Bissau Kriyol) too, have two different overt copulas, *e* and *sta* (with even more complex differentiation in the predicative NPs). They preserve the differentiation from the base language Portuguese, where the copula *é* is used with predicative noun phrases whereas *está* is used with predicative locative phrases.

The most frequent subtype (14 languages) in this value consists of a zero copula in predicative noun phrases and an overt copula in locative phrases. Examples come, for instance, from Vincentian Creole, Principense, Juba Arabic, Fanakalo, Papiá Kristang, and Chinuk Wawa.

(6) Chinuk Wawa (Grant 2013)
    a. *náyka dáktin*
       1SG doctor
       'I am a doctor.'

    b. *náyka **mitlayt** kápa tawn*
       1SG sit at town
       'I'm in town.' (lit. 'I sit in town.')

There are only two *APiCS* languages, Trinidadian English Creole and Haitian Creole, with a copula for predicative noun phrases but no copula for predicative locative phrases. This marking pattern seems to be very rare, at least in the *APiCS* languages.

Languages with value 3 show **overlap** in the coding of the two predicative contexts. In Angolar (Maurer 2013a), for instance, predicative noun phrases may or may not have the copula *tha*, whereas locative phrases always require this copula. Some languages with this value have one copula which is used in both noun-phrase predication and locative predication, and one copula which only occurs in noun-phrase predication. This is the case, for instance, in Negerhollands (*a* for NP, and *we:s* for NP and locative) and Saramaccan (*da* for NP, and *de* for NP and locative). Other languages do it the other way around: noun phrases show two copulas, whereas locative phrases show only one copula. This pattern exists in Casamancese Creole (*i* and *sa* NP, *sa* for locative).

Value 4 (**identity and differentiation**) is assigned to languages which show three different copulas, one copula for both contexts, another copula only for predicative noun phrases, and yet another copula only for predicative locative phrases. Only one *APiCS* language, Cameroon Pidgin English, shows this pattern. In this language the copula *bi* is used in both contexts, the copula *na* only in noun phrase predication, the copula *de* only in locative predication.

3. Distribution

When comparing the *APiCS* data with the corresponding *WALS* data in Stassen (2005c), we can detect clear substrate influences. West African languages *exclusively* show the different-copula pattern, which is retained in many Atlantic pidgins and creoles (see Boretzky 1983: 157ff., Sharma & Rickford 2009). In New Guinea and the Pacific islands, too, the indigenous languages overwhelmingly show different copulas, as do the *APiCS* languages spoken in these areas.

Zero–zero encoding as one possible pattern of identical marking (see ex. 2 from Guadeloupean Creole) seems to be rare cross-linguistically (Stassen 2005c), but present in nine *APiCS* languages, regardless of lexifier, area, or pidgin–creole distinction.

76 Predicative noun phrases and predicative locative phrases

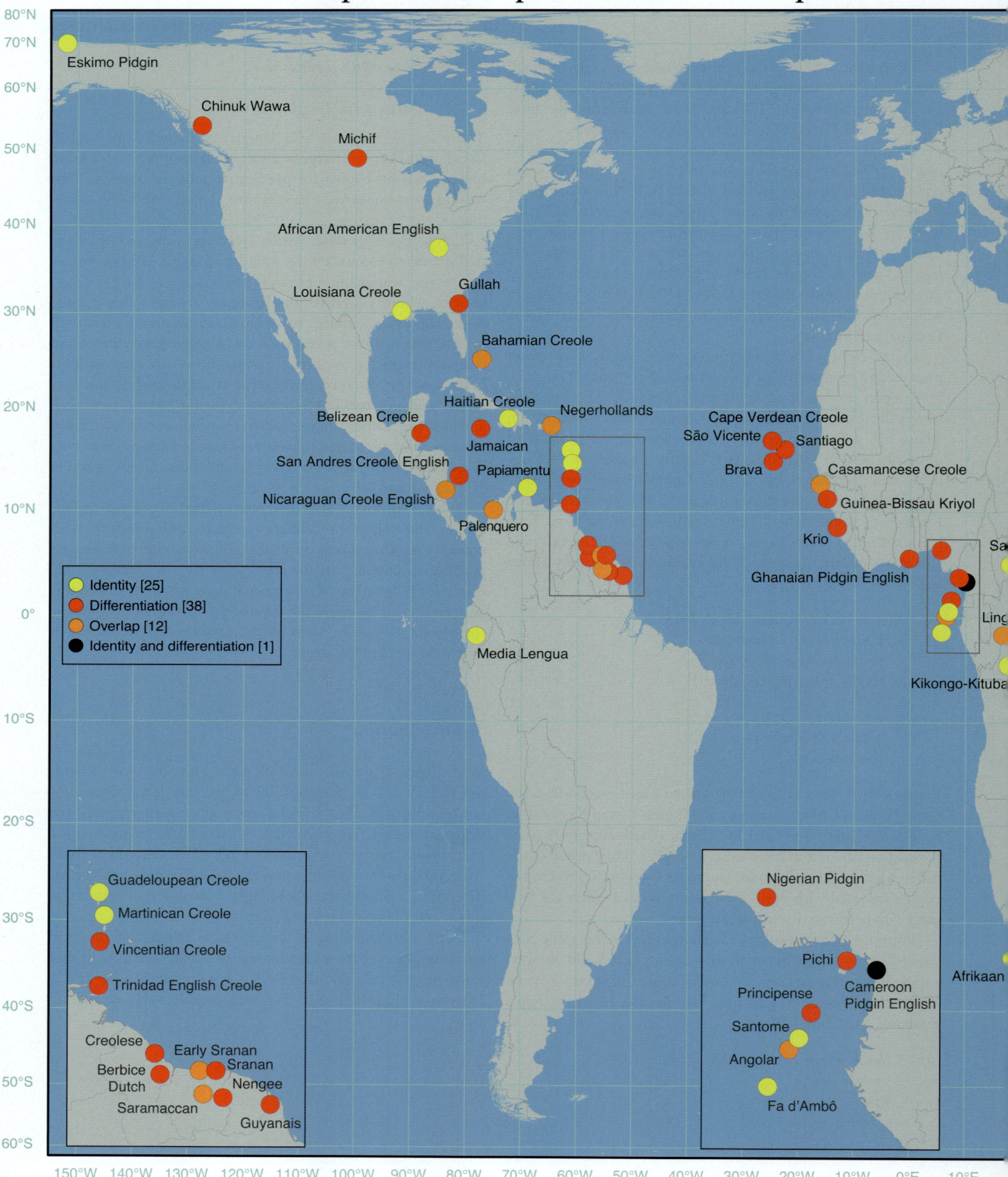

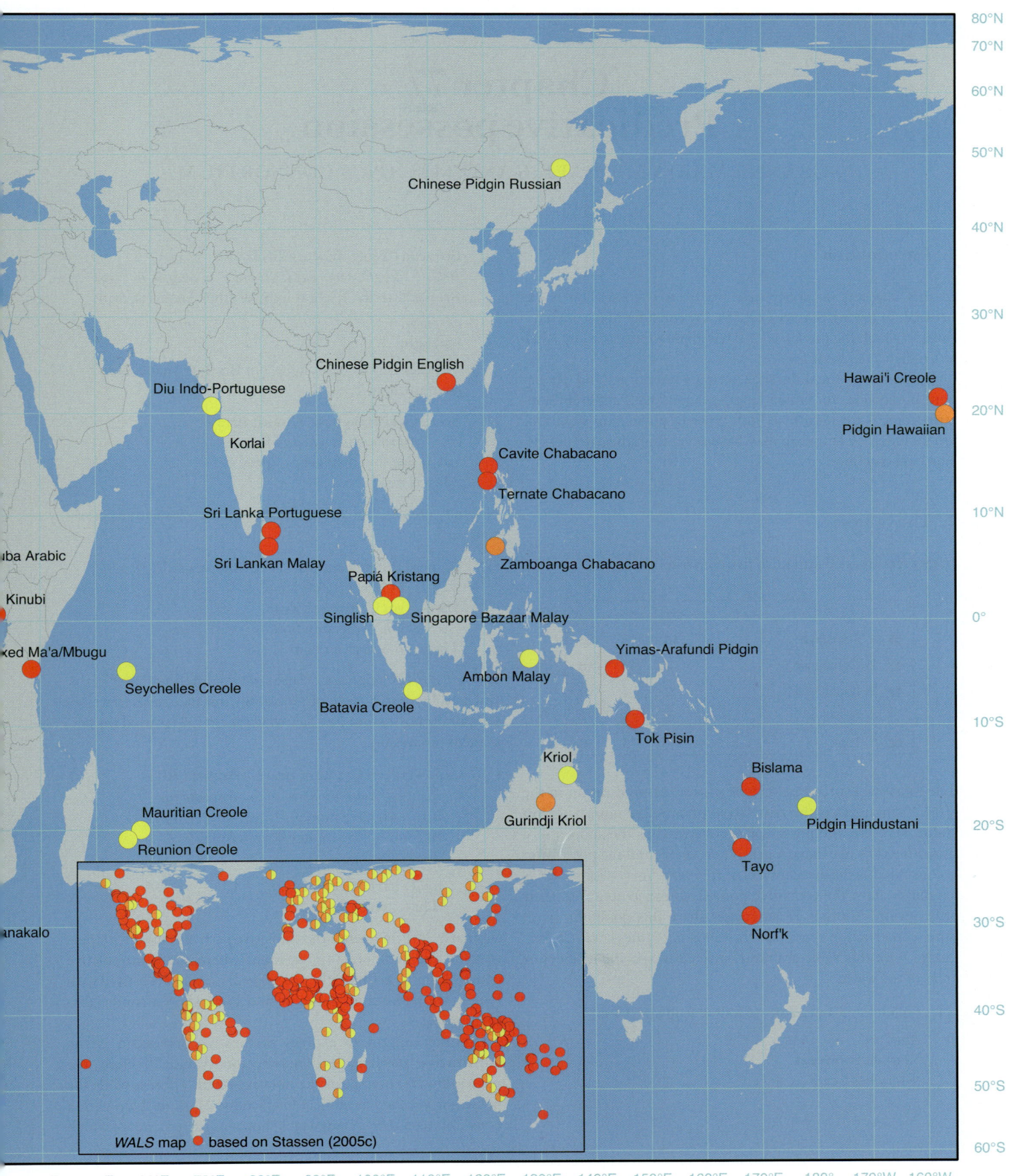

Chapter 77
Predicative possession

SUSANNE MARIA MICHAELIS AND THE *APiCS* CONSORTIUM

1. Introduction

In this chapter, we study how predicative possession is expressed, following Stassen (2005b). We consider only constructions in which the possessed NP has an indefinite reading, such as English *John has a horse*.

In this study, the difference between temporary and permanent possession, for which languages may have different constructions, is irrelevant, so both types of possession situations are included. A language may have several predicative possession constructions.

2. The values

In this feature we distinguish five construction types:

	excl	shrd	all
1. Transitive	48	18	66
2. Comitative	2	14	16
3. Locational	2	7	9
4. Genitive	2	5	7
5. Topic	1	5	6

The most widespread pattern of possessive predication in the *APiCS* languages is the **transitive possessive construction** (value 1). Here, the possessor is construed as the subject of a transitive verb like 'have', 'grasp', or 'keep', and the possessum is construed as the direct object of this verb. Forty-eight *APiCS* languages have the transitive possessive construction as their only option. Another 18 languages share this possibility with other construction types (see the following values). *APiCS* languages with this value are not restricted to specific lexifiers or areas of the world:

(1) Guadeloupean Creole (Colot & Ludwig 2013a)
Mari ni on chat.
Mary have one cat
'Mary has a cat.'

(2) Belizean Creole (Escure 2013)
Bra fayaflay im gat layt bra anansi no gat no layt.
Brother Firefly 3SG got light Brother Anansi NEG got NEG light
'Brother Firefly had a light, but Brother Anansi didn't have any light.'

(3) Sri Lanka Portuguese (Smith 2013)
eli askruuva jaa-gardaa teem
3SG.M rice PST-keep PRF
'He has rice.'

Not only creoles, but also pidgins can have a transitive possession verb:

(4) Chinese Pidgin English (Li & Matthews 2013)
米哪吉咩(竹+厘)(口件)乎簍也
My no got (A)merican flour.
1SG NEG got American flour
'I have no American flour.'

In some *APiCS* languages, there are two different 'have' verbs. In Cape Verdean Creole of Brava, for instance, *tene* expresses temporary possession (see 5a), whereas *ten* (5b) is used for permanent possession.

(5) Cape Verdean Creole of Brava (Baptista 2013)
a. *Si'N ka tene dinheru, N ta trabadja uji.*
if.I NEG have money I ASP work today
'If I don't have money, I work today.'
b. *Mi'N ten des fidju.*
me.I have ten child
'I have ten children.'

Similarly, in Principense the transitive verb *tê* is used with permanent and temporary possession, whereas the intransitive construction *sa ki* ('be with', see value 2) is exclusively used with temporary possession. Santome and Pichi show a similar distinction.

Another option to express predicative possession is the **comitative possessive construction** (value 2). Here, the possessum is expressed as a comitative ('with') phrase while the possessor is coded as subject (as in value 1), as in 'I am with a book'. Sixteen *APiCS* languages show this pattern, out of which

14 languages are spoken in Africa or on islands close to Africa. For Lingala and Kikongo-Kituba, this construction type is the only one available in the language.

(6) Lingala (Meeuwis 2013)
a-zal-ákí **na** *mwána*
3SG-be-PST with child
'He had a child.'

Another 14 languages (e.g. Fa d'Ambô and the mixed language Gurindji Kriol) have the comitative possession construction beside the transitive possession construction.

In Gurindji Kriol the comitative marker is a case suffix:

(7) Gurindji Kriol (Meakins 2013)
Nyawa-ma tu karu baisikul-jawung.
this-DISC two child bicycle-COM
'Here two kids have bicycles.'

The next value is the **locational possessive construction** (value 3), which may show an existential verb. The possessor is expressed as a locational or oblique phrase, whereas the possessum is the subject of the 'exist' or 'be' predicate, like 'At me there is a book' or 'A book is at me.' Nine *APiCS* languages show this value. In example (8), the oblique possessor is introduced by the general preposition *na* 'to, at, with':

(8) Sango (Samarin 2013)
ngombe a-ke **na** *mbi ape*
gun PM-COP PREP 1SG NEG
'I don't have a gun.' (lit. 'A gun is not at me.')

This construction type is also found in the four *APiCS* languages spoken in South Asia, of which Korlai and Sri Lankan Malay have it as their only option. However, in these languages it is not a locational marker but the dative marker ('to', 'for') which introduces the possessor NP, as can be seen in (9).

(9) Sri Lankan Malay (Slomanson 2013)
Go-ðang mera attu kumbang aða.
1SG-DAT red INDF flower EXIST
'I have a red flower.' (lit. 'To me there is a red flower.')

Even though this dative marker may not be used to express locative phrases, we still subsume it under locational possessive constructions following Stassen (2005b), in order to keep the *WALS* and *APiCS* data comparable.

Languages with value 4 show a **genitive possessive construction**: the possessor is coded as genitive modifier of the possessum. The possessum NP is linked to the subject of an 'exist' or 'be' predicate, as in 'My book exists'. Seven *APiCS* languages have this value, Tayo and Yimas-Arafundi Pidgin being the only two languages which have it as their only possessive construction.

(10) Tayo (Ehrhart & Revis 2013)
na a ŋgra lafamij **pu** *lja*
EXIST INDF.ART big family GEN 3SG
'He has a big family.' (lit. 'There exists a big family of his.')

The adnominal possessive construction in Tayo is constructed in exactly the same way: *kas pu mwa* [house GEN 1SG] 'my house'.

Example (11) from Kinubi shows that genitive possessors tend to be topicalized (*Morú*), so that this construction could be regarded as topic possession (see value 5).

(11) Kinubi (Luffin 2013)
Morú fí rután **t-ómun**
Moru EXIST language of-them
'The Moru have their own language.' (lit. 'The Moru, their language exist.')

The last value is **topic possession** (value 5). Here, the possessor is marked as a topic, and the possessum is the subject of an existential predicate (as was the case in value 4) '(As for Peter), there is a knife', meaning 'Peter has a knife'. There are six *APiCS* languages which show this construction.

(12) Sango (Samarin 2013)
ti lo, nginza a-ke oko ape
of 3SG money PM-COP one NEG
'As for him/her, he/she doesn't have any money at all.'

The other five languages have no overt topic marking other than the possessor being coded in the leftmost position in the sentence.

3. Substrate influence

There are three areas where substrate influence is clearly detectable. First, as mentioned above, the comitative construction is almost exclusively present in Africa and nearby islands. When we compare the situation with the *WALS* data (Stassen 2005b), we see that Africa and Australia are two areas of the world where there are many languages with comitative constructions. As the European lexifiers show this pattern only marginally (e.g. Portuguese *Estou com fome* 'I am hungry', lit. 'I am with hunger'), we can quite confidently invoke substrate influence here. Secondly, all four *APiCS* languages spoken in South Asia show only, or at least to some degree, locational marking (see 9 from Sri Lankan Malay). Again, when comparing these data with the *WALS* patterns, the parallels are striking: South Asia is entirely locational-marking. Thus, locational marking in the South Asian *APiCS* languages is due to their substrates. Thirdly, the French-based creole Tayo spoken in New Caledonia has the genitive possessive construction (see 10). Tinrin, one of its New Caledonian substrates, also has this cross-linguistically rare pattern (see Stassen 2005b).

77 Predicative possession

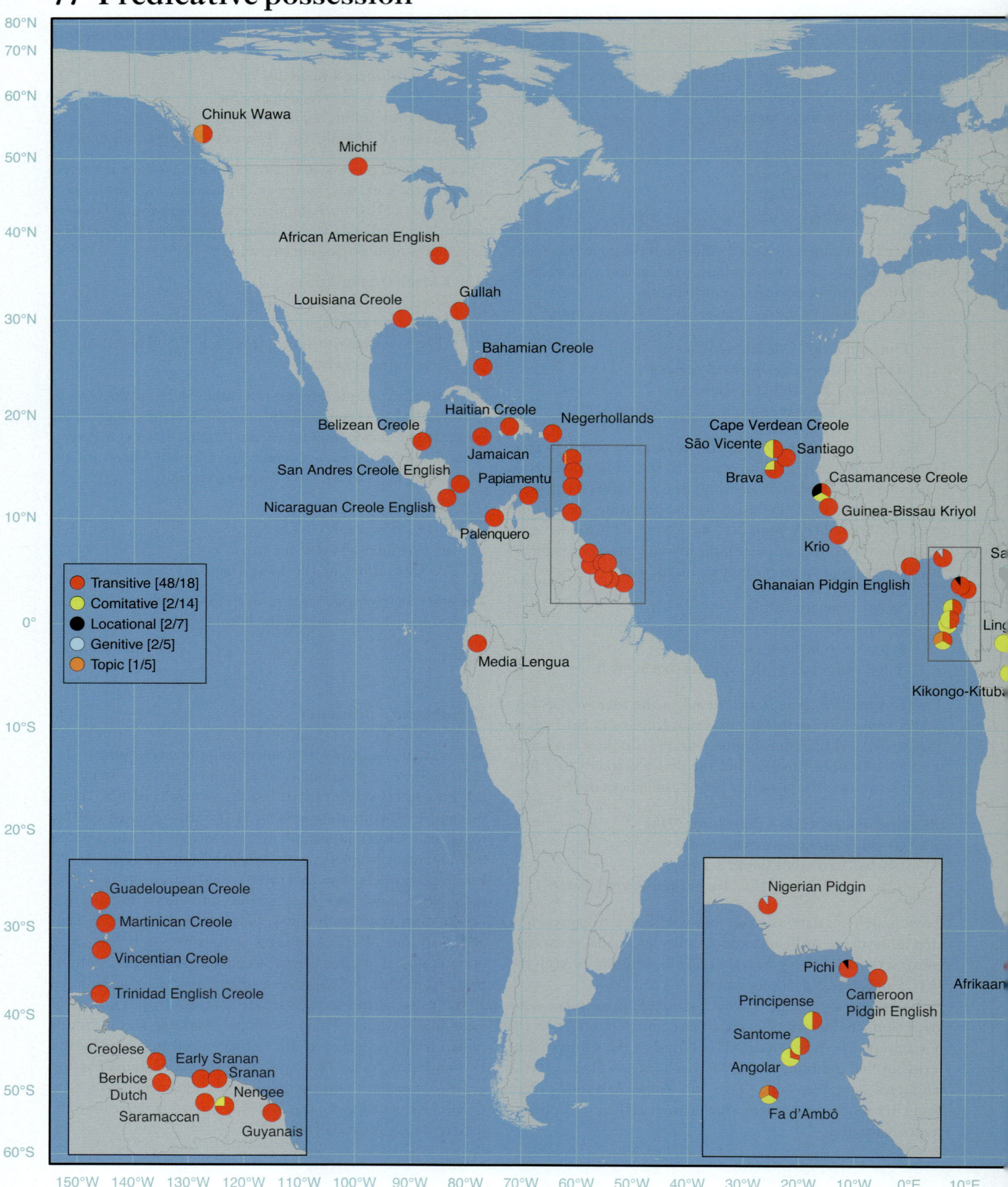

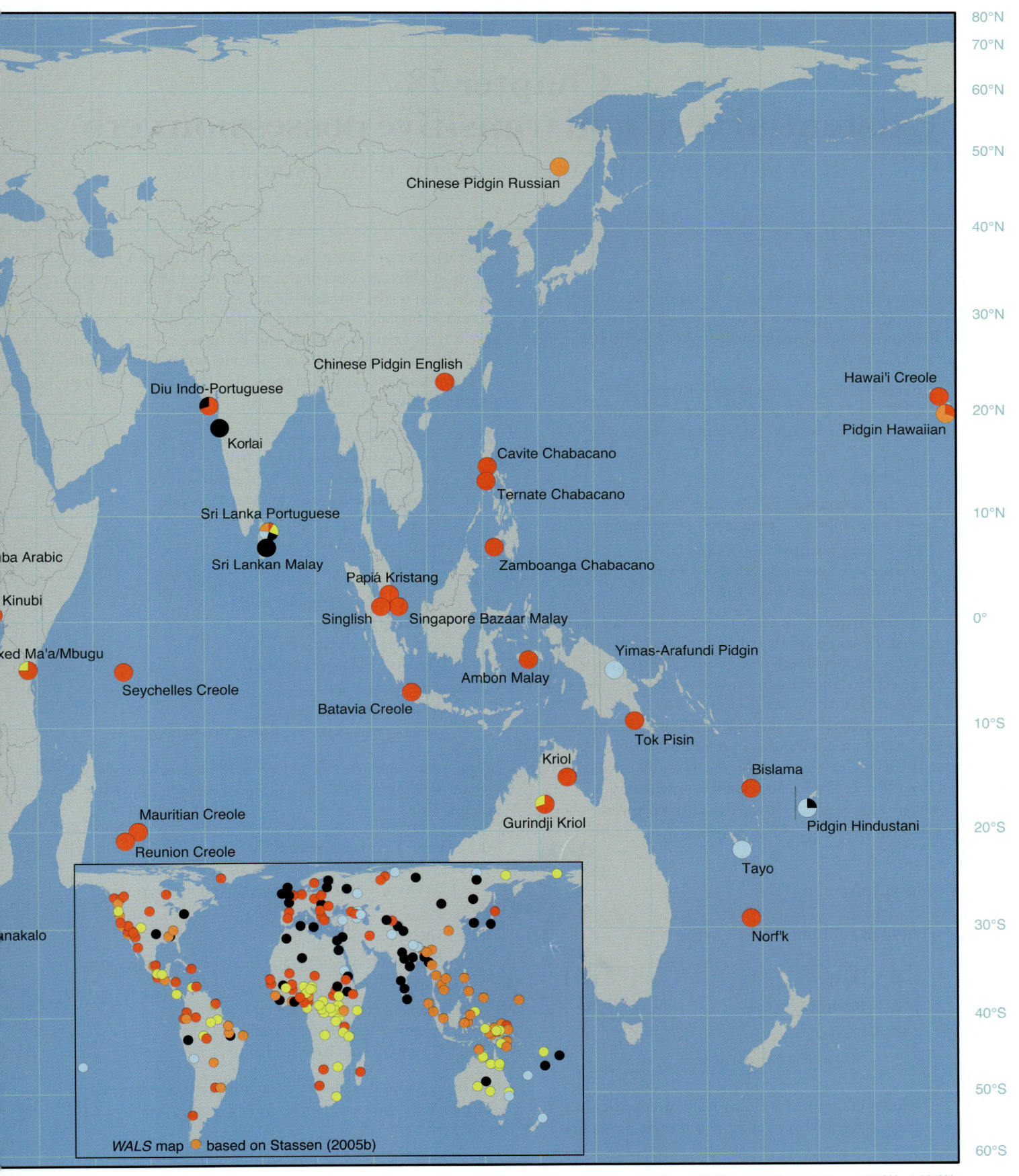

Chapter 78
Existential verb and transitive possession verb

SUSANNE MARIA MICHAELIS AND THE *APiCS* CONSORTIUM

1. Introduction

This feature investigates whether the existential verb ('there is') is identical to the transitive verb of possession 'have' (cf. value 1 in Chapter 77, and Chapter 64 on expletive subject of existential verb), as in (1a–b).

(1) Seychelles Creole (Michaelis & Rosalie 2013)
    a. *Be ler i annan koudvan zot pa reste lo sa* [...]
       but when PM EXIST hurrican 3PL NEG stay on DEM
      zil?
      island
      'But when there is a hurricane, they don't stay on the [...] island?' (lit. 'when it has a hurricane')
    b. *sa zoli lakaz ki ou annan la*
      DEM nice house REL 2SG have there
      'this nice house which you have'

By "existential verb" we refer to the element corresponding to English *there is* in existential clauses like *There is food on the table*. If the existential verb is not identical to the transitive possession verb, it is identical to a copula verb or includes an additional fixed element such as *there* in English.

Some languages have multiple predicative possession constructions, not just a transitive predicative verb like 'have'. In such languages, we only consider the transitive possession verb, not the other predicative possession constructions.

Other languages lack a transitive possession verb. They will be classified under value 4 (see below).

2. The values

In this feature we distinguish four values:

🟢 1. Identity		41
🔴 2. Differentiation		17
🟠 3. Overlap		8
⚪ 4. No transitive possession verb		9

The majority of the *APiCS* languages show **identical expression** of the existential verb and the transitive possession verb (value 1). As can be seen from the map, this pattern is represented in different areas of the world. It is found in pidgins, creoles, and mixed languages alike. Note that this type is also present in French (*il y a* 'there is'; *il a* 'he has'), whereas it is absent from English, Spanish, and Portuguese (but cf. Brazilian Portuguese existential *tem*). Throughout this chapter, the (a) examples show existential verbs, the (b) examples illustrate transitive possession verbs.

(2) Cavite Chabacano (Sippola 2013a)
    a. *Tiene mucho hielo na frigider.*
      EXIST plenty ice LOC refrigerator
      'There is plenty of ice in the refrigerator.'
    b. *Tieni yo casa.*
      have 1SG house
      'I have a house.'

(3) Hawai'i Creole (Velupillai 2013)
    a. *gɛʔ big kaɪn ʃak-s*
      EXIST big kind shark-PL
      'There are big sharks (here).'
    b. *luk laɪk ju gɛt indʒɛn*
      look like 2SG have Indian
      'It looks like you've got Indian (blood in you).'

In some languages, the 'have' verb combines with the second-person pronoun to yield the existential meaning, as shown in example (4a):

(4) Belizean Creole (Escure 2013)
    a. *Yu had di djadj yu had dis seym gavmɛn*
      2SG have the judge 2SG have this same government
      laya.
      lawyer
      'There was the judge, and there was that government lawyer.'
    b. *Anansi neva had no layt.*
      Anansi ANT.NEG have no light
      'Anansi did not have any light.'

In Mixed Ma'a/Mbugu the existential verb is expressed by using the locative noun class prefix *hé* as subject marker on the 'have' verb -*lo*.

(5) Mixed Ma'a/Mbugu (Mous 2013)
    a. *hé-lo isonhka i-kumure*
       16-have dust 5-many
       'There is a lot of dust.'
    b. *é-lo ina i-kuhlo*
       3SG-have face 5-nice
       'She has a nice face.'

As in other chapters (e.g. Chapter 76 on predicative noun phrases and predicative locative phrases), here too, the identity value can subsume a pattern which can be best described as "two-fold identity". Here, existential situations and possessive situations can each be coded by two different verbs, but each of the two verbs can occur in both contexts. An example comes from African American English, where *got* and *have* are used in existentials (5a and a′) and possessive contexts (5b/b′) alike:

(6) African American English (Green 2013)
    a. *Dey got a fly messing with me.*
       EXPL got.EXIST a fly messing with me
       'There is a fly bothering me.' (lit. 'There is a fly messing with me').
    b./b.′ *I have/got a table.*
       'I have a table.'
    a.′ *It had some breaded chicken sticks.*
       EXPL have.PST.EXIST some breaded chicken sticks
       'There were some breaded chicken sticks.'

Seventeen *APiCS* languages have **different existential and possessive verbs** (value 2). These are mostly creoles and mixed languages.

(7) Saramaccan (Aboh et al. 2013)
    a. *Buku dɛ.*
       book be
       'There is a book.'
    b. *Mi abi wan buku.*
       1SG have INDF book
       'I have a book.'

(8) Juba Arabic (Manfredi & Petrollino 2013)
    a. *fi nas bi=fékir ínu ma kwes kéda*
       EXIST people IRR=think COMP NEG good like.this
       'There are people who think that it is not good this way.'
    c. *tijára abáo le zol al ma éndu róksa*
       business forbid\PASS to individual REL NEG have permission
       'Business is forbidden to the one who doesn't have permission.'

Interestingly, pidgins do not show this value, except for Chinuk Wawa (whereas other pidgins show the identity pattern or do not have a transitive possession verb, see value 4).

(9) Chinuk Wawa (Grant 2013)
    a. *mákmak mitlayt kápa latáb*
       food sit PREP table
       'There is food on the table.'
    b. *náyka t'úwən kyútan*
       1SG have horse
       'I have a horse.'

Languages with the next value show an **overlap** pattern (value 3): there are two verbs, one of which means both 'there is' and 'have', whereas the other one has only one of these meanings. For example, in Creolese the verb *gat* is used in existential and in possessive constructions, whereas the verb *de* is used only in existential constructions (Devonish & Thompson 2013). Languages which show a similar coding pattern are Berbice Dutch, Bahamian Creole, Sranan, Angolar, and Fa d'Ambô. It turns out that all cases of overlap show one 'have' verb which can be used in both contexts and one verb which only occurs in existentials. So the range of possibilities to express existentials is wider than for possessive situations.

Nine *APiCS* languages, all outside the Americas, do not have a transitive possession verb and therefore cannot take part in the comparison here (compare with Chapter 77 on transitive possession verbs, where these languages have values other than value 1). These languages thus have value 4.

3. Distribution

As mentioned above, the identity pattern is widespread and can be found in all areas of the world. But there is also some areal clustering worth mentioning. One such area is the central Caribbean region where all languages, without exception, show identity, irrespective of the European base language. So we find English-, French-, and Spanish-based creoles all showing the same verb for existential and possessive situations. Interestingly, the mainland languages in the Guianas show either different marking or overlap (except for Guyanais, which features the identity pattern).

Worldwide cross-linguistic data show that in many languages existential and possessive constructions are expressed by the same verb (Stassen 2009). Diachronically, one can trace both ways of grammaticalization: (i) from an existential construction ('at me is a book') to a transitive possessive construction ('I have a book'; this is the case in Finnish, see Creissels 2011), and (ii) from a transitive possessive construction 'have', 'hold' or 'grasp' ('she has') to an existential construction ('it has, there is', see the French example above; see Creissels 2011, Heine 1997).

78 Existential verb and transitive possession verb

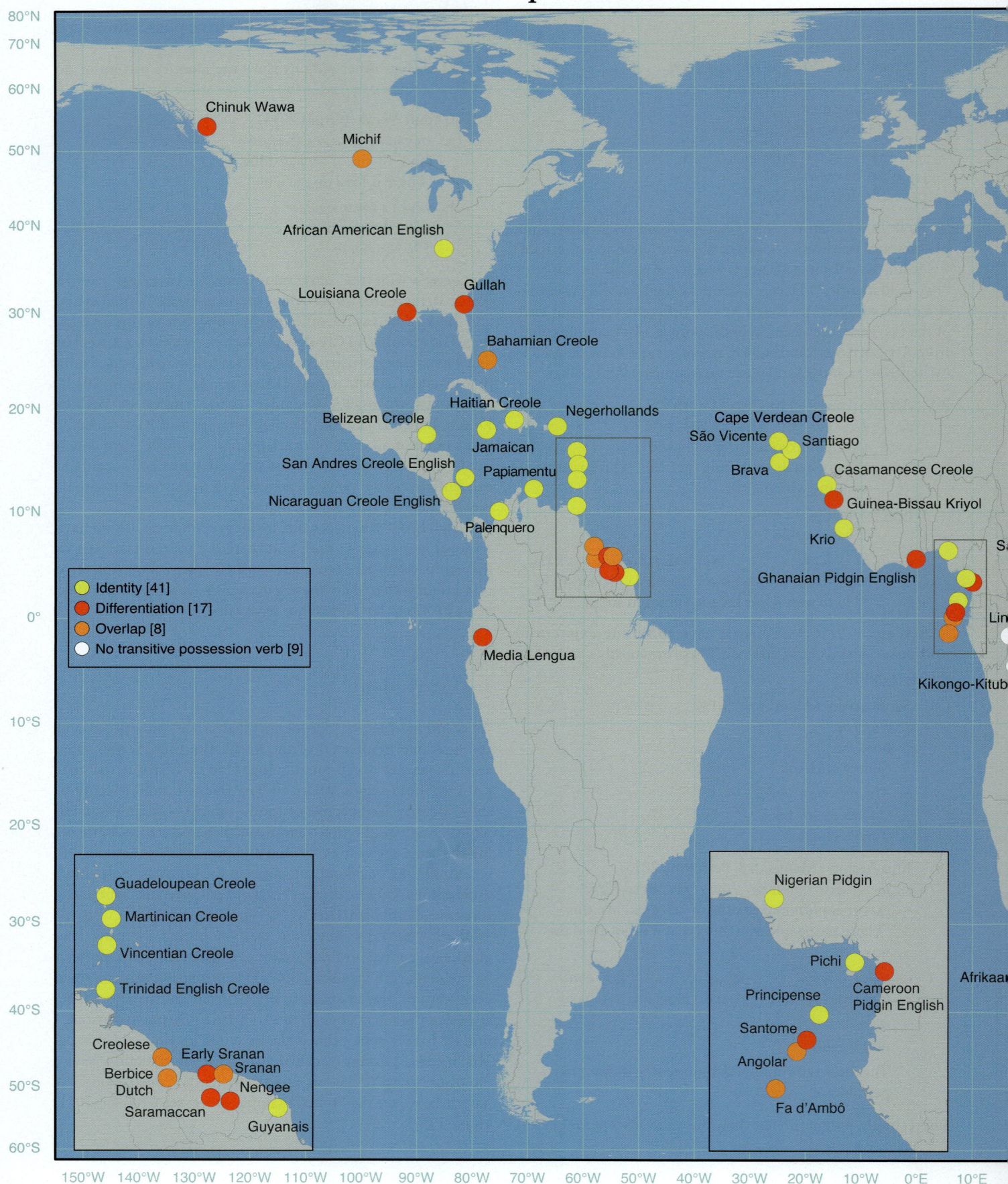

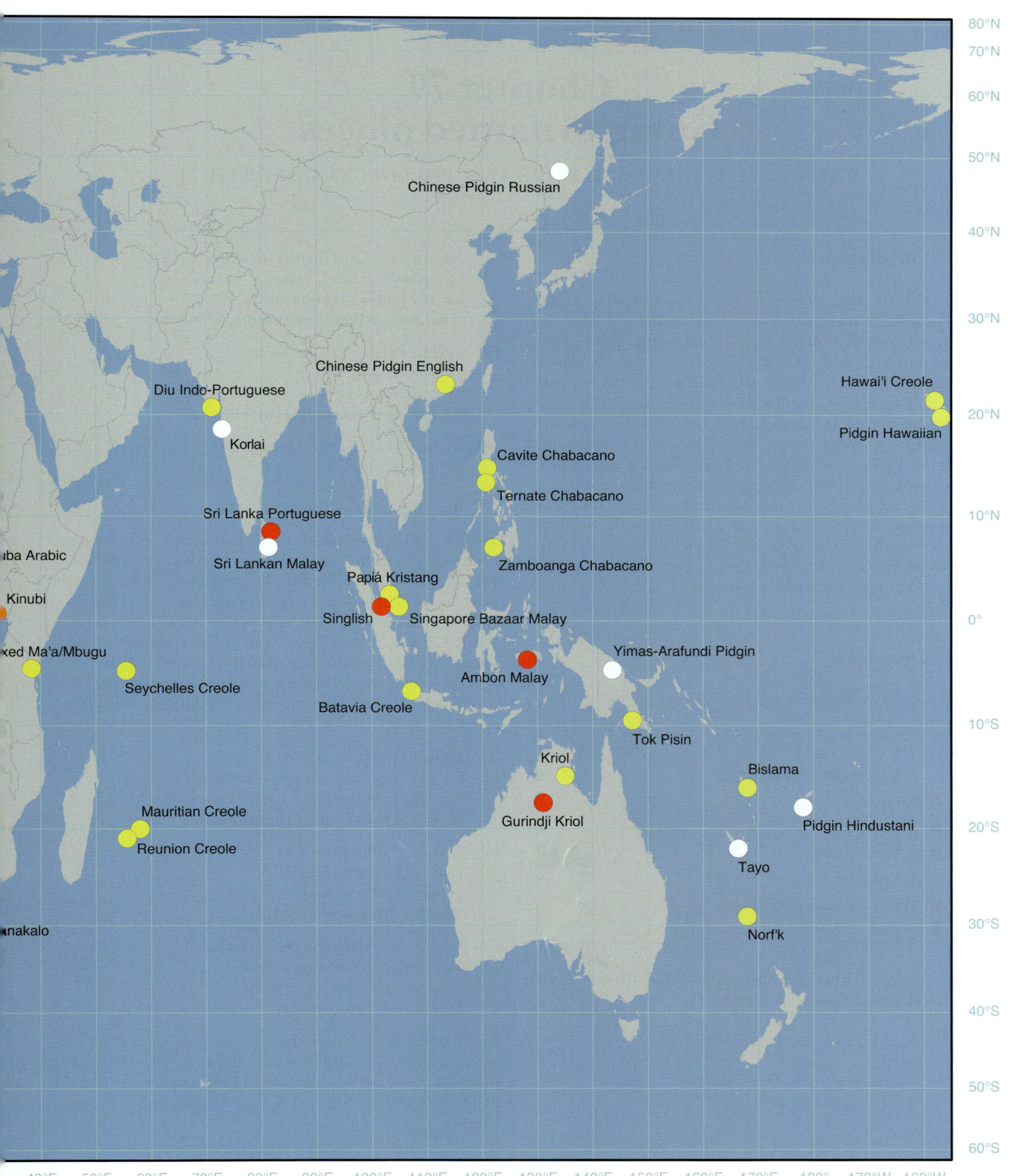

Chapter 79
Going to named places

SUSANNE MARIA MICHAELIS AND THE *APiCS* CONSORTIUM

1. Introduction

This is the first of several chapters investigating intransitive and transitive motion constructions. In the present chapter, we study the different means to express the action of going to named places, as in English *She went to Leipzig*. Here the named place, *Leipzig* (the goal), is preceded by the preposition *to* which expresses a particular orientation. We call this orientation 'motion-to' in the relevant *APiCS* chapters, as opposed to 'motion-from' and 'at-rest' orientations (following Comrie & Smith 1977). As we will see, different languages use different means to express orientation in directed motion events.

We restrict ourselves to goals which are named places, such as names of villages, cities, and countries (for the highly frequent goal/source 'market', see Chapter 81 on motion-to and motion-from) because in many languages different kinds of goals are expressed in different ways.

2. The values

In this feature we distinguish seven values:

		excl	shrd	all
○	1. No adpositional/case marking	22	31	53
●	2. Preposition	12	34	46
●	3. Postposition	2	2	4
●	4. Circumposition	0	1	1
●	5. Serial verb	0	8	8
●	6. Serial verb plus preposition	1	10	11
●	7. Case	1	1	2

In 53 *APiCS* languages, there is **no adpositional or case marking** of the named place (value 1).

(1) Mauritian Creole (Baker & Kriegel 2013)
    mo pe al Vakwa
    1SG ASP go Vacoas
    'I am going to Vacoas.'

(2) San Andres Creole English (Bartens 2013b)
    A gwain Pravidens tumara.
    1SG FUT Providence tomorrow
    'I am going to Providence tomorrow.'

(3) Eskimo Pidgin (van der Voort 2013)
    awoña iglupûk ĕlĕkta
    I barracks go
    'I am going (I went) to Fort McPherson.'

(4) Mixed Ma'a/Mbugu (Mous 2013)
    [. . .] *vé-so nhonga.*
          2-go Konga
    '[. . .] they went to Konga.'

Twenty-two languages show this pattern as their only option. Here we find nearly *all* French-based creoles (except for Louisiana Creole and Guyanais), three Caribbean English-based creoles, the Portuguese-based creoles of the Gulf of Guinea and Guinea-Bissau Kriyol, most pidgins (Eskimo Pidgin, Chinuk Wawa, Chinese English Pidgin, and Pidgin Hindustani), and some mixed languages (Michif and Mixed Ma'a/Mbugu).

The second most frequent motion-to construction (46 *APiCS* languages) uses a **preposition** to mark the named place (value 2).

(5) Gullah (Klein 2013)
    [. . .] *an fom dey we gone ta Patara.*
           and from there we go.PST to Patara
    '[. . .] and from there we went to Patara.'

(6) Kinubi (Luffin 2013)
    grup tán rúo fi Ankóle
    group other go in Ankole
    'Another group went to Ankole.'

(7) Cavite Chabacano (Sippola 2013a)
    Di anda el hombre na Manila.
    CTPL go DEF man LOC Manila
    'The man will go to Manila.'

For 12 languages this is the only marking type: some English-based creoles of the Caribbean and the Pacific, Negerhollands and Palenquero, the Spanish-based Chabacano varieties of the Philippines, and two African languages (Kinubi and Kikongo-Kituba).

The use of a preposition does not necessarily imply that this preposition is a specific motion-to preposition. As will be shown in Chapter 81, some of the preposition-marking languages with value 2 use the very same preposition also to mark motion-from. Thus, the preposition in such languages does not express the motion-to orientation towards the named place, but only some spatial feature of the goal, here the named place. Early Sranan is such a language: it has the preposition *na* in motion-to situations, though van den Berg & Bruyn (2013) stress that this preposition is neutral as to the motion-to/motion-from differentiation (for further discussion see Chapter 81):

(8) Early Sranan (van den Berg & Bruyn 2013)
*Mekie wie go **na** Combee.*
make 1PL go LOC Kombe
'Let us go to Kombe.'

This situation also holds for Saramaccan, Pichi, Krio, Lingala, Kikongo-Kituba, Ternate Chabacano, Tok Pisin, Bislama, and Pidgin Hawaiian.

Very few *APiCS* languages have a **postposition** (value 3) to mark motion to a named place. Sri Lankan Malay and Yimas-Arafundi Pidgin (see 9) show only this value, whereas Afrikaans and Sri Lanka Portuguese share this strategy with others.

(9) Yimas-Arafundi Pidgin (Foley 2013)
Pəpənəŋ kandək mənda wa-nan.
Pepeneng OBL then go-NFUT
'Then (they) went to Pepeneng (name of a lake).'

Here again, the postposition *kandək* does not exclusively mark motion-to, but is also used in motion-from contexts (see Chapters 80 and 81).

Afrikaans is the only language in which motion to a named place can be expressed by a **circumposition** (value 4). The postpositional part *toe* 'to' is optional:

(10) Afrikaans (den Besten & Biberauer 2013)
Hulle verhuis na Kaapstad (toe).
3SG.PL.NOM move to Cape.Town (to)
'They're moving to Cape Town.'

The next two values involve serial verb constructions with a **serial verb** 'reach, go (down)' (value 5; eight languages, see ex. 11) and with a **serial verb plus a preposition** (value 6; eleven languages, see ex. 12). Except for Papiá Kristang and Tok Pisin, all serializing languages are spoken in narrowly confined areas, namely in the Guianas (with Jamaican as an outlier) and in West Africa.

(11) Guyanais (Pfänder 2013)
nou vin désann Kayèn
we come go.down Cayenne
'We went to Cayenne.'

(12) Nengee (Migge 2013)
*Den lei **go a** Soolan.*
they drive go LOC St.Laurent
'They drove to St. Laurent.'

Nengee is the only *APiCS* language that marks motion-to exclusively by a serial verb construction (with an additional preposition).

In Cameroon Pidgin English (Schröder 2013), the serial verb construction (with or without a preposition) *rich* (*fo*) (see ex. 13) signals unintentional reaching of a goal, whereas this connotation is not implied in the other strategy available in this language, prepositional marking (value 2):

(13) Cameroon Pidgin English (Schröder 2013)
A go rich (fo) Bamenda.
1SG.SBJ go reach for Bamenda
'I went to Bamenda.'

Only two *APiCS* languages mark motion-to by a **case suffix** (value 7): the two mixed languages Gurindji Kriol and Media Lengua. In Media Lengua, the allative suffix *-mu* marks motion to a named place, here *Otavalo*:

(14) Media Lengua (Muysken 2013)
*Otabalo-**mu** i-gi-xu-ni*
Otavalo-ALL go-INC-PROG-1SG
'I am going to go to Otavalo.'

3. Distribution

In 53 *APiCS* languages, named place goals may lack any adpositional or case marking (value 1). For the languages with a European base (41 languages), these results are somewhat puzzling, especially for those languages which only have the zero pattern. Apparently the model of the base languages has not been taken over: in European languages, orientation towards a goal is always marked by a preposition; examples are English *I go to Paris*, French *Je vais à Paris* 'I go to Paris', and Spanish/Portuguese *Voy*/*Vou à*/*para Paris* (expressions like *I go home* being quite exceptional). One could argue that in *APiCS* languages with value 1, the lack of the preposition is due to the simplification forces of the pidginization/creolization process. In fact, many pidgins in *APiCS* show value 1. But this leaves us with the question why Saramaccan, for instance, known as a radical creole, does show overt prepositional marking (value 2), a pattern which is also very widespread in *APiCS* (46 languages).

After examining the coding of coming-from constructions in the next chapter, we will be in the position to evaluate the data in terms of different hypotheses in Chapter 81 on motion-to and motion-from. We will see that an interpretation in terms of retention of substrate patterns is very plausible.

79 Going to named places

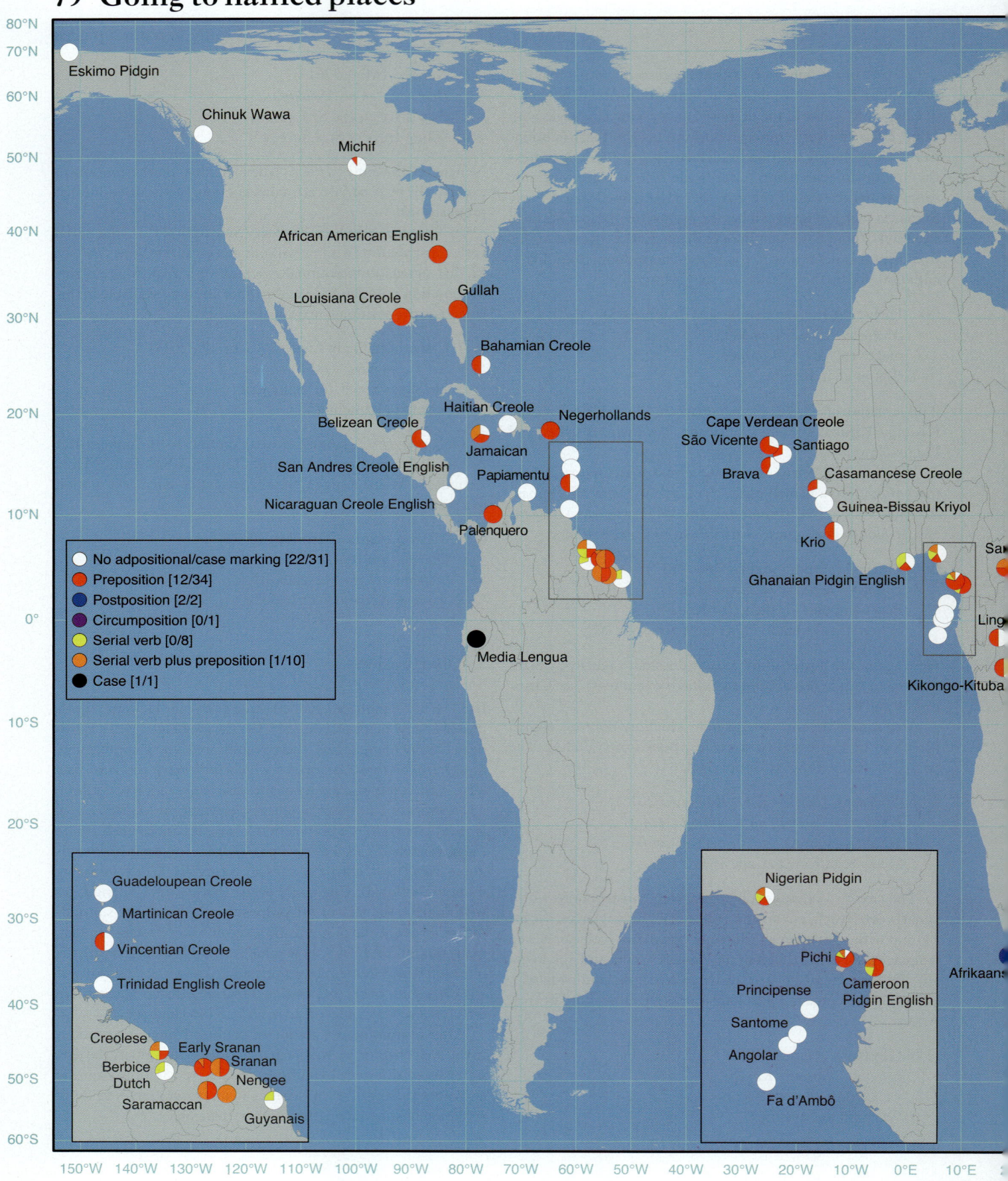

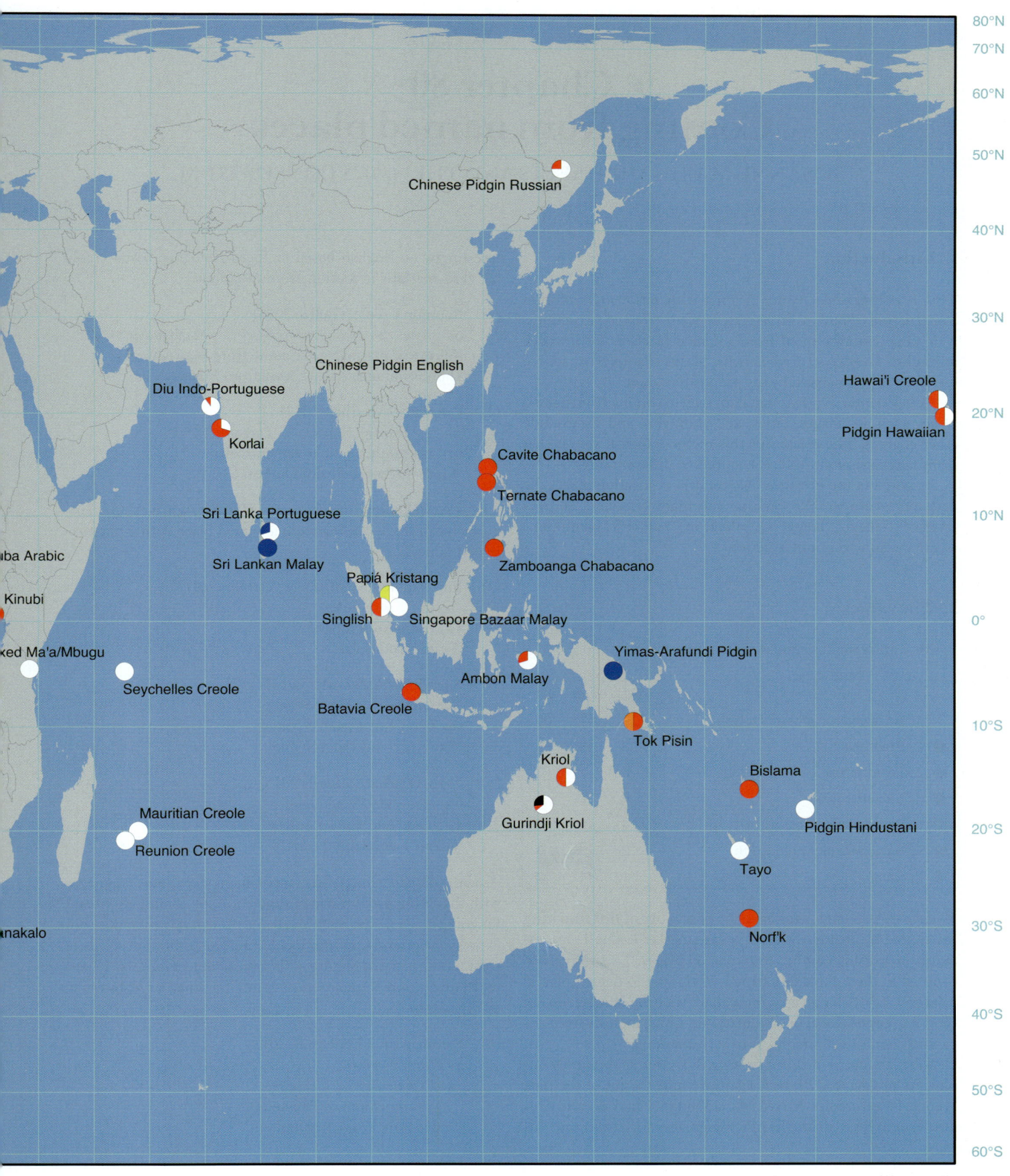

Chapter 80
Coming from named places

SUSANNE MARIA MICHAELIS AND THE *APiCS* CONSORTIUM

1. Introduction

This is the second chapter dealing with intransitive motion constructions. Here we investigate motion-from constructions, which express movement from a named place, as for instance in English *I came back from Leipzig*. In this example, the source term, *Leipzig*, is marked by the preposition *from*.

As in Chapter 79, we restrict our data to coming from named places such as villages, cities, and countries, and we exclude other sources. The reason for this methodological step is that many languages code different sources in different ways.

As noted in the previous chapter, this restriction makes the data more comparable. Data on the highly frequent sources 'market', 'village', 'home' is available in Chapter 81 on motion-to and motion-from constructions.

2. The values

In this feature we distinguish seven values:

		excl	shrd	all
○	1. No adpositional/case marking	9	11	20
●	2. Preposition	38	15	53
●	3. Postposition	6	1	7
●	4. Circumposition	0	2	2
●	5. Serial verb	4	1	5
●	6. Serial verb plus preposition	2	3	5
●	7. Case	1	1	2

Twenty *APiCS* languages have the possibility of **not marking** the source by an adposition or a case marker (value 1) in sentences expressing coming from named places. This is in sharp contrast to the figures in Chapter 79 (Going to named places) where 53 *APiCS* languages, more than twice the number, do not show any adpositional or case marking. Thus, motion-from apparently lends itself much less to zero-marking.

Nine languages of this type have this value as their only option. As in Chapter 79, here again we find six out of the nine French-based creoles. Mixed Ma'a/Mbugu, Fanakalo, and Chinese Pidgin Russian are the other languages with this value. Interestingly, no English-based or Ibero-Romance-based creole has zero-marking in motion-from situations.

(1) Reunion Creole (Bollée 2013)
 Sé pa le maï ki sort Madagascar.
 this.is NEG DEF maize REL come.from Madagascar
 'This is not maize that comes from Madagascar.'

(2) Fanakalo (Mesthrie 2013)
 Lo mama buy-ile Thegwin.
 DEF.ART mother return-PST Durban
 'Mother returned from Durban.'

The overwhelming majority of *APiCS* languages (53 languages) can mark coming from a named place with a **preposition** (value 2).

(3) Juba Arabic (Manfredi & Petrollino 2013)
 ána ja min júba
 1SG come from Juba
 'I came from Juba.'

(4) Norf'k (Mühlhäusler 2013)
 She kamen frum Sydney.
 she come.CONT from Sydney
 'She is arriving from Sydney.'

(5) Tayo (Ehrhart & Revis 2013)
 ma vja ⁿde Saint-Louis
 1SG come DIR Saint-Louis
 'I came from Saint-Louis.'

As with going to named places (see Chapter 79), some languages with this value use the same preposition for coming-from and for going-to contexts. Such an all-purpose preposition does not express the orientation (motion-to/motion-from), but seems to refer to some spatial feature of the placed object (see also Chapter 81 on motion-to and motion-from). Saramaccan shows such a preposition.

(6) Saramaccan (Aboh et al. 2013)
 a. Motion-from
 A kumutu a Damsko.
 3SG come.out LOC Amsterdam
 'He came from Amsterdam.'

Compare the example for going to a named place, showing the same preposition *a*:

(6) b. Motion-to
Mi go a Foto.
1SG go LOC Paramaribo
'I went to Paramaribo.'

The following languages have the same pattern: Early Sranan, Pichi, Krio, Lingala, Kikongo-Kituba, Ternate Chabacano, Tok Pisin, Bislama, and Pidgin Hawaiian.

Seven *APiCS* languages have **postpositions** to mark the source (value 3).

(7) Pidgin Hindustani (Siegel 2013)
Ham Suva se ao.
1SG Suva from come
'I came from Suva.'

The areal restriction is interesting here: five out of the six *exclusively* postpositional marking languages are spoken in South Asia and Melanesia (see also Chapter 4 on adposition order).

The next value is **circumpositional** marking (value 4), which is very rare in *APiCS*. Only Pidgin Hawaiian and Afrikaans show this value. In Afrikaans the second part *af* 'off' is optional:

(8) Afrikaans (den Besten & Biberauer 2013)
My ma het van Kaapstad (af) terug
1SG.POSS mother PST from Cape.Town (off) back
ge-kom.
PTCP-come
'My mother has returned from Cape Town.'

The next value involves a **serial verb** 'come from' (value 5). Here, we find five languages, of which four have this construction as their only option. All four languages are Portuguese-based creoles of the Gulf of Guinea: Principense, Santome, Angolar, and Fa d'Ambô.

(9) Angolar (Maurer 2013a)
Ê vutuka fõ Angene.
3SG return come.from Angene
'She returned from São João dos Angolares.'

There are five languages with value 6, **serial verb plus preposition**. One example comes from Nengee:

(10) Nengee (Migge 2013)
Den wagi e rei komoto na Albina (kon).
DET.PL car IPFV drive come.from LOC Albina (come)
'The cars are coming (back) from Albina.'

Here the construction with the serial verb *komoto* 'come from' and the preposition *na* 'at, in' can be combined with another op-

tional serial verb *kon* 'come', which is postposed to the source *Albina*.

When comparing the use of the serial verb strategy (with and without a preposition) with the situation in Chapter 79 (on going to named places), it is interesting to note that serial verbs are less frequently used to express motion-from (ten languages) than motion-to (19 languages).

Two mixed languages have ablative **case marking** on the source argument (value 7): in Gurindji Kriol, case marking is one option besides prepositional marking (value 2), while in Media Lengua case marking is the only option.

(11) Gurindji Kriol (Meakins 2013)
I bin kombek Katherine-nginyi.
3SG.SBJ PST come.back Katherine-ABL
'He came back from Katherine.' (Katherine is a town.)

It is far from clear on which grounds we decide what is a case marker and what is an adpositional marker. It seems that it has a lot to do with grammaticographic traditions which are linked to writing systems. These often suggest that something is an affix only because it is written in one word or at least hyphenated. It is beyond the scope of this project to come up with systematic tests for wordhood or affixhood. But the diversity of criteria in particular *APiCS* languages has made us aware of the difficulty of finding appropriate comparative concepts for deciding which morphemes should be regarded as free morphemes, and which morphemes should be classified as affixes (with clitics somewhere in between, see Haspelmath 2011b).

3. Discussion

Lack of prepositional or case marking is confined to 20 languages, of which nine (six French-based languages) stand out as having this option as their only one. Interestingly, in contrast to what one might expect, pidgins as simplified languages are not overrepresented in this value. Instead, they show adpositional marking, for example, in Pidgin Hawaiian, Pidgin Hindustani, Yimas-Arafundi Pidgin, Chinuk Wawa, Singapore Bazaar Malay, and Chinese Pidgin English. Only the last two pidgins also show zero-marking besides the prepositional marking.

For a more detailed interpretation of the data of this chapter in terms of substrate influence, see Chapter 81 on motion-to and motion-from.

80 Coming from named places

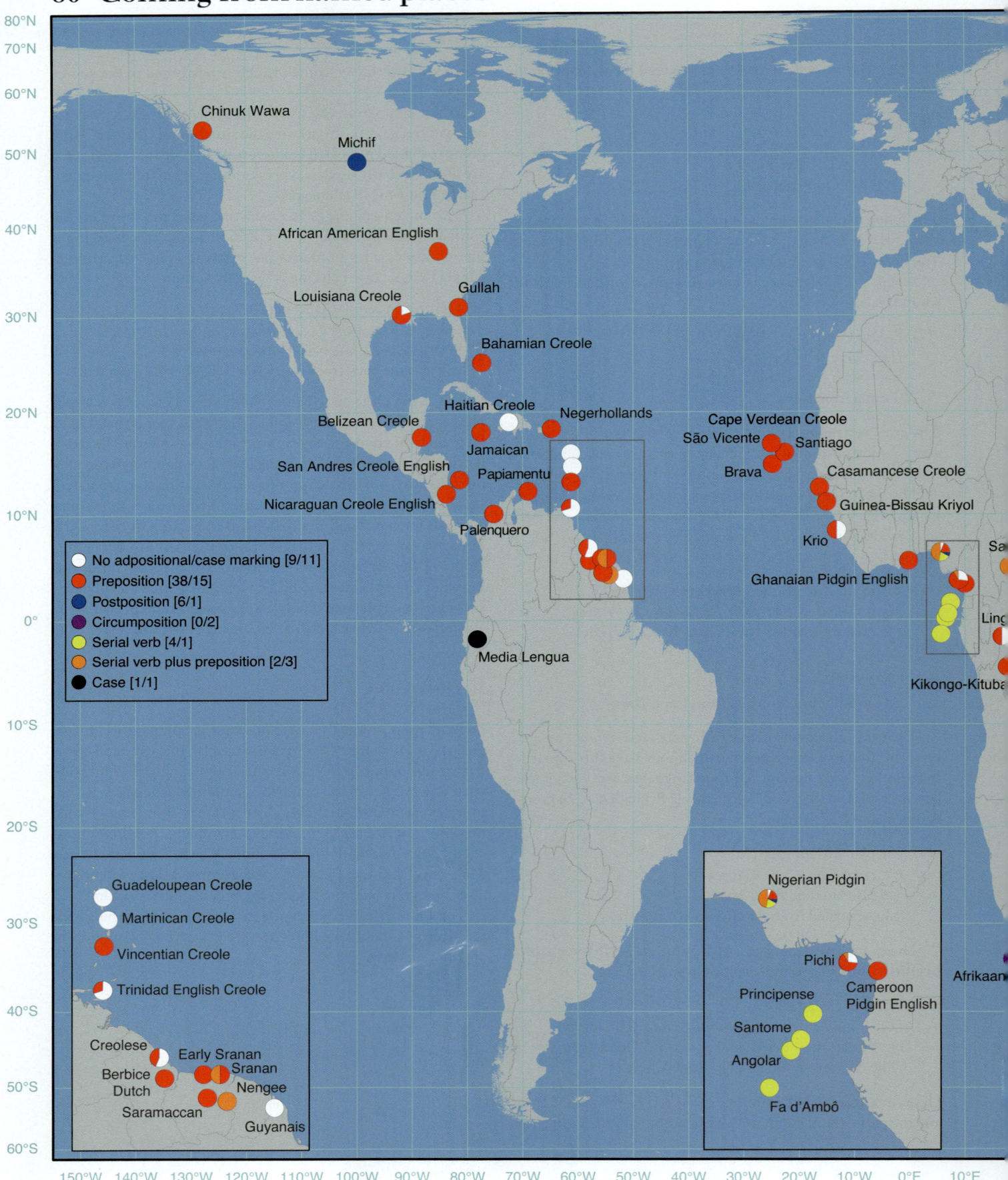

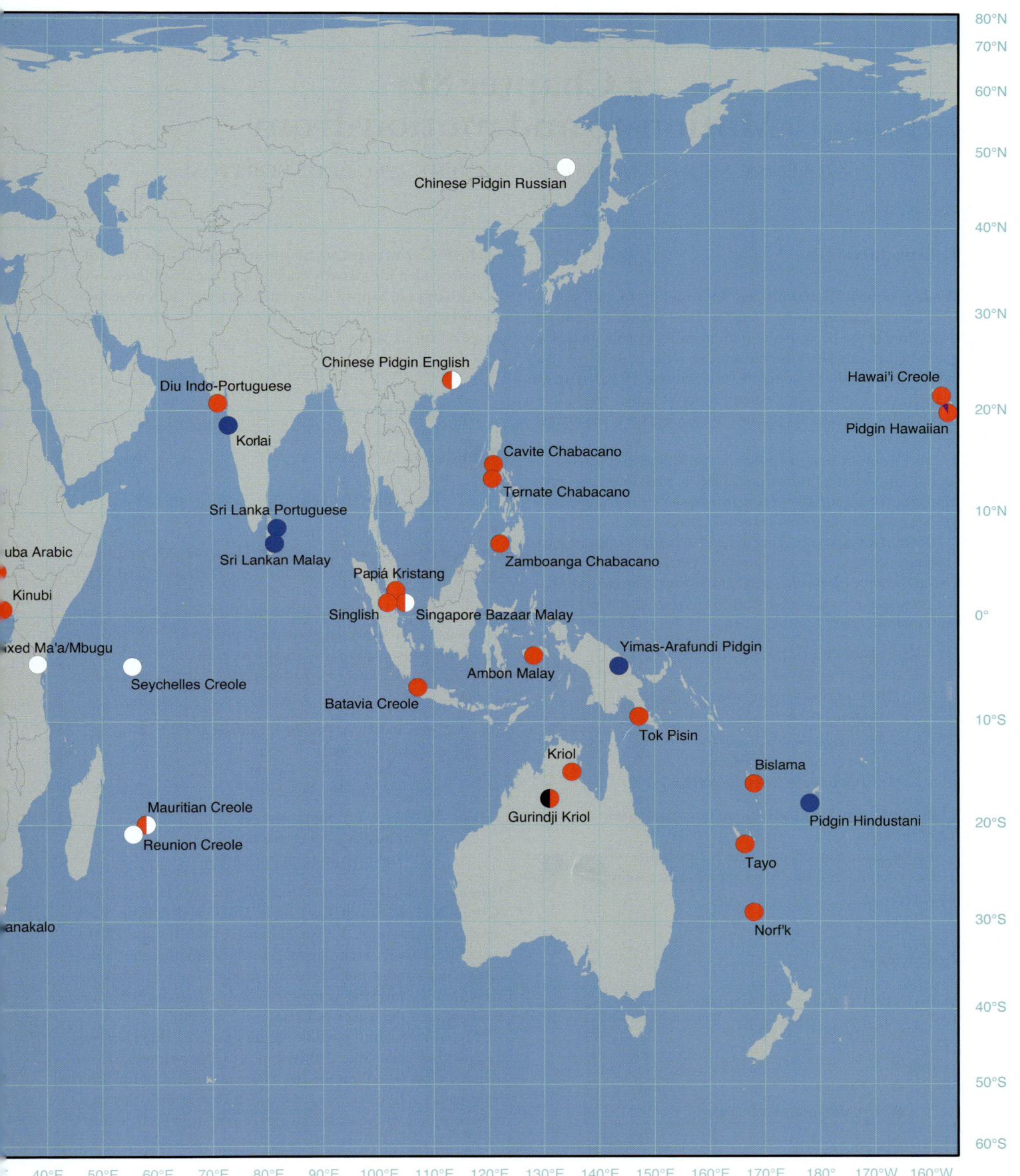

Chapter 81
Motion-to and motion-from

SUSANNE MARIA MICHAELIS AND THE *APiCS* CONSORTIUM

1. Introduction

While Chapters 79 and 80 deal with motion-to and motion-from constructions, respectively, in this chapter we compare the coding of the two types of motion construction: we investigate whether languages use the same strategy or different strategies to express the two opposite orientations. However, in this chapter, the goal/source element is not a named place, but a highly frequent place like 'home', 'town', 'village', 'the market', or 'the woods'.

All European base languages have different constructions for motion-to and motion-from a place in that different prepositions are used: English *to town*/*from town*, French *à la maison*/*de la maison*, Portuguese *ao mercado*/*do mercado*.

But in *APiCS*, it is striking to see that many European-based languages do not follow the European pattern and instead mark goal and source *identically*. In the following example from Krio the preposition *na* occurs in both contexts, motion-to (1a) and motion-from (1b):

(1) Krio (Finney 2013)
    a. *a di go **na** di makit*
        1SG PROG go LOC ART market
        'I am going to the market.'
    b. *a jɛs kɔmɔt **na** di makit*
        1SG just come LOC ART market
        'I just came back from the market.'

The hearer has to infer the relevant orientation from the meaning of the verb.

Throughout this chapter, the (a) examples show motion-to constructions and the (b) examples show motion-from constructions.

2. Values

In this feature we distinguish four values:

○	1. Identity	21
●	2. Differentiation	43
●	3. Overlap	9
●	4. Identity and differentiation	2

In 21 *APiCS* languages, motion-to and motion-from constructions are coded **identically** (value 1). There are different ways in which this can happen. First, languages may show **no adpositional or case marking** in both constructions. One such language is Chinuk Wawa:

(2) Chinuk Wawa (Grant 2013)
    a. *náyka tlátwa tawn*
        1SG go town
        'I'm going to town.'
    b. *náyka čáku tawn*
        1SG come town
        'I'm coming from town.'

Here, both orientations are identically coded: neither goal nor source *tawn* 'town' are marked. However, this type is rare in *APiCS* (another language with this pattern is Mixed Ma'a/Mbugu).

The much more widespread second subtype of value 1 consists in using the **same adposition**, both in motion-to and motion-from constructions, as shown in examples (1a, b) from Krio (*na* 'at, in') and (3a, b) from Martinican Creole (*anba* 'under'):

(3) Martinican Creole (Colot & Ludwig 2013b)
    a. *Man ka alé **anba** marché.*
        1SG PROG go under market
        'I am going to the market.'
    b. *Man sòti **anba** marché.*
        1SG come.back under market
        'I am coming back from the market.'

Languages which show the same pattern are Haitian Creole, Reunion Creole, Seychelles Creole, Bislama, Tok Pisin, Early Sranan, Saramaccan, Pidgin Hawaiian, and Ternate Chabacano. Interestingly, many languages which show identical preposition marking in motion-to and motion-from contexts also show identical marking in going-to/coming-from named places, this time zero-marking (see Chapters 79 and 80).

There is yet a third possible identity pattern, which has been described as "two-fold identity" in previous chapters with an identity value (e.g. Chapter 76). Here, motion-to and motion-from constructions can each be coded by two different strategies, but each of the two strategies can occur in both contexts.

Mauritian Creole belongs to this subtype. Here the goal/source *lafore* 'forest' can either be marked in both contexts by the preposition *dan* 'in', or it can be (left) unmarked.

(4) Mauritian Creole (Baker & Kriegel 2013)
 a. *mo ti al (dan) lafore*
  1SG PST go LOC forest
  'I went into the forest.'
 b. *mo ti sort (dan) lafore*
  1SG PST leave LOC forest
  'I came from the forest.'

Lingala and Kikongo-Kituba show the same pattern with the optional preposition *na* 'with, to, from, in, on'.

The vast majority of *APiCS* languages (43) code motion-to and motion-from **differently** (value 2). This can be achieved through three coding subtypes. First, a language has two different adpositions or cases to mark motion-to and motion-from. This is the case for instance in Bahamian Creole, Palenquero, and Batavia Creole, where different prepositions are used. Media Lengua shows two different cases, allative and ablative. Sri Lankan Malay has two different postpositions.

(5) Sri Lankan Malay (Slomanson 2013)
 a. *Rihan pasar na e-pi (aða).*
  Rihan market to ASP-go AUX
  'Rihan went to the market.'
 b. *Rihan pasar ring e-baalek (aða).*
  Rihan market from ASP-return AUX
  'Rihan returned from the market.'

The second subtype of value 2 consists of an optional adposition to express motion-to, but a different obligatory adposition to express motion-from. Here we find languages like Creolese, Papiamentu, two Cape Verdean Creole varieties, Kriol, Sri Lanka Portuguese, and Singlish. In Singlish (Lim & Ansaldo 2013), for instance, motion-to can be marked by the preposition *to* or zero, whereas motion-from must be marked by the preposition *from*.

In a third subtype of value 2, motion-to is never marked, whereas motion-from is always marked by an adposition or a serial verb. Jamaican, Casamancese Creole, Guinea-Bissau Kriyol, Papiá Kristang, and Tayo have prepositions (*frahn, di, de*) for expressing motion-from.

(6) Jamaican (Farquharson 2013)
 a. *Mieri go maakit yeside.*
  Mary go market yesterday
  'Mary went to [the] market yesterday.'
 b. *Mieri kom frahn maakit yeside.*
  Mary come from market yesterday
  'Mary came from the market yesterday.'

Pidgin Hindustani and Sri Lanka Portuguese show postpositions, and the Gulf of Guinea creoles (Angolar, Principense, Santome, and Fa d'Ambô) mark motion-from with the serial verb *fŏ/fo* 'come from'.

In nine languages there is **overlap** in the coding of motion-to and motion-from constructions (value 3). In Cameroon Pidgin English (Schröder 2013), for instance, the preposition *fo* 'in, at, on, to, from' can be used in both orientation contexts, whereas motion-to can additionally be expressed without any marker.

Two languages (Chinese Pidgin English and Louisiana Creole) show an **identity and differentiation** pattern (value 4). Here, there are at least three different coding patterns for motion-to and motion-from contexts. One pattern occurs in both orientations, whereas another pattern occurs only in motion-to and yet another only in motion-from contexts.

3. Distribution

First, when comparing the marking patterns of motion-to and motion-from in *APiCS*, one can formulate an implicational universal (Fanakalo and Zamboanga Chabacano being the only two out of 75 languages that show some contradicting data):

(7) Motion-from is coded in at least as complex a way as motion-to.

This asymmetry seems to hold universally across languages and probably has to do with the greater usage frequency of motion-to expressions (Haspelmath 2008b).

Second, we observe an interesting split between English- and French-based creoles: all French-based creoles (except for Tayo) show the identity pattern, whereas the English-based Atlantic creoles mostly show the differentiation pattern. It is only the Surinamese creoles (Early) Sranan and Saramaccan, Trinidad English Creole, and the West African English-based languages which show identical coding or overlap. Other Caribbean English-based creoles, such as Jamaican, Belizean Creole, and Gullah, follow the English differentiation pattern. And note that no Portuguese-based creole shows identical coding.

Third, we find substrate effects: In many West African and Bantu languages, which are substrates of the Atlantic and Indian Ocean contact languages, motion-to and motion-from are not overtly marked, but orientation is expressed through the semantics of the verb (see Michaelis 2008, Wälchli & Zúñiga 2006: 292ff.). If prepositions are used, they do not refer to orientation (motion-to/motion-from), but to the local region of the located object. Tayo, by contrast, has Oceanic substrates which differentiate motion-to and motion-from prepositions (Rivierre 1980: 220, 351, Osumi 1995: 80f., Bril 2002: 296, 309).

81 Motion-to and motion-from

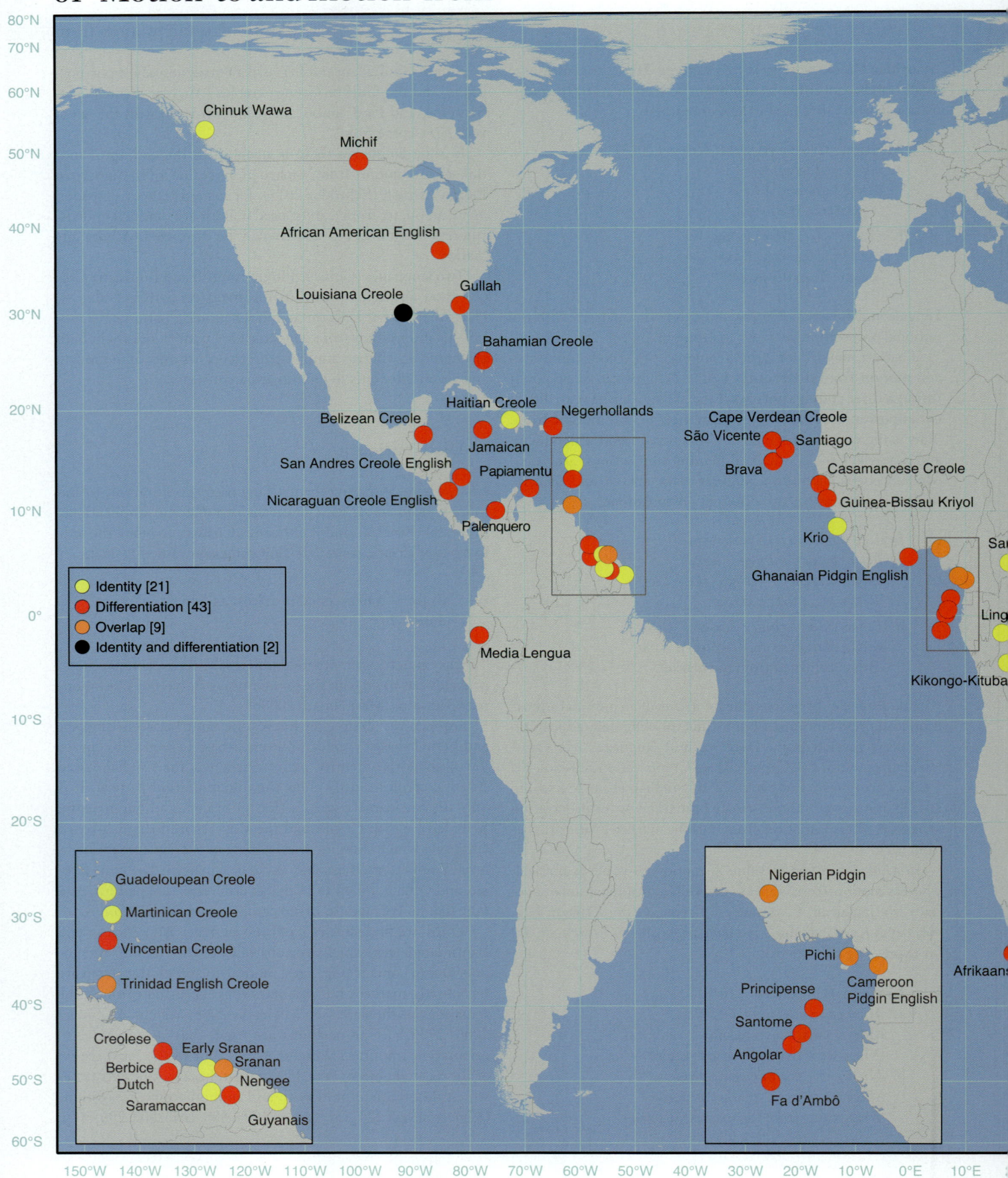

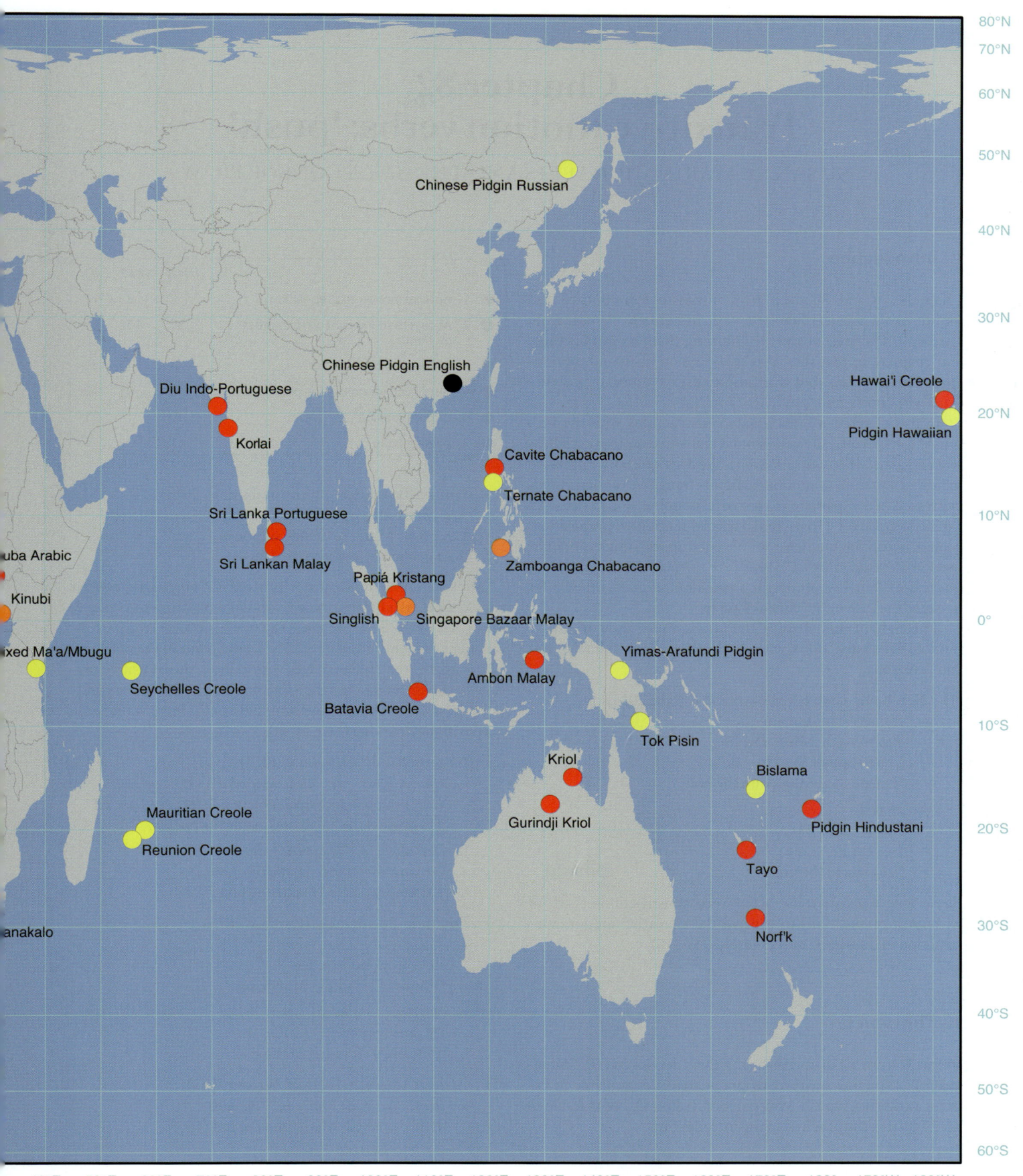

Chapter 82
Transitive motion verbs: 'push'

SUSANNE MARIA MICHAELIS AND THE *APiCS* CONSORTIUM

1. Introduction

Chapters 79 and 80 dealt with intransitive motion-to and motion-from constructions (e.g. 'I go to Leipzig', 'I come from Leipzig'). The present and the following chapters parallel these two chapters in that they also analyse motion-to and motion-from constructions, but this time transitive motion constructions with 'push' and 'pull'.

In this chapter, we investigate constructions with the verb 'push' (or semantically very similar transitive motion verbs), as in *Lea pushed Maria into the hole*. We are especially interested in how orientation or motion-to in this transitive motion verb is expressed in comparison to the corresponding at-rest situation ('to be at a place'). Do we find a special motion-to preposition, such as *into* in the English example cited above, which cannot be used in at-rest contexts (**Lea is into the hole*)? Or does the language use the at-rest preposition also for motion-to, which is for instance the case in Seychelles Creole?

Throughout this chapter, the (a) examples show transitive motion-to constructions, whereas the (b) examples show at-rest constructions.

(1) Seychelles Creole (Michaelis & Rosalie 2013)
    a. transitive motion-to
       *Lea ti pus Mari **dan** trou*
       Lea PST push Mari in hole
       'Lea pushed Maria into the hole.'
    b. at-rest
       *Lea ti **dan** trou.*
       Lea PST in hole
       'Lea was in the hole.'

Some languages may use serial verb constructions (with or without a preposition) to express the transitive motion construction in question, as in examples (8)–(10).

2. The values

In this feature we distinguish six values. In eleven *APiCS* languages, a **special motion-to preposition** is available to express a transitive 'push' construction (value 1), comparable to the English example cited in the introduction.

	excl	shrd	all
1. Special motion-to preposition	2	9	11
2. At-rest marking is used to express motion-to	32	18	50
3. Serial verb construction	4	4	8
4. Serial verb construction plus preposition	6	9	15
5. Circumposition	0	1	1
6. Allative case	1	0	1

(2) Guinea-Bissau Kriyol (Intumbo et al. 2013)
    *Lea pintca Maria **pa** dentru di kasa.*
    Lea push Maria to inside of house
    'Lea pushed Maria into the house.'

For the overwhelming majority of *APiCS* languages, **at-rest marking is used to express transitive motion-to** (value 2; see ex. 1). By "at-rest" we mean the two basic local regions containment ('in') and attachment ('at'), as in 'I am **in** the hole' and 'she is **at** the tree'. In languages with value 2, the transitive motion-to construction uses the same marking as the corresponding at-rest construction. In examples (3)–(5), there is the same prepositional marking (*bini*, *nə*, *in*):

(3) Negerhollands (van Sluijs 2013)
    a. *Ham a pus di klēn hon **bini** shi sak.*
       3SG PST push DET small dog inside 3SG.POSS pocket
       'He pushed the small dog inside his pocket.'
    b. *Dzhanwus a bli **bini** di gat.*
       Dzhanwus PST stay inside DET hole
       'Dzhanwus stayed inside the hole.'

(4) Diu Indo-Portuguese (Cardoso 2013)
    a. *Tud atər-a **nə** mar.*
       all throw-INF LOC sea
       'Throw everything into the sea.'
    b. *Nɔs t-iŋ nad-a **nə** mar.*
       1PL IPFV-PST swim-INF LOC sea
       'We were swimming in the sea.'

(5) African American English (Green 2013)
    a. *Bruce push(ed) Marie **in** the hole.*
       'Bruce pushed Marie into the hole.'

b. *He **in** the kitchen.*
  'He is in the kitchen.'

Other languages with this value have the same postposition or case marker to mark at-rest and transitive motion-to constructions. Two examples are Berbice Dutch and Sri Lankan Malay:

(6) Sri Lankan Malay (Slomanson 2013)
  a. *Pompang-kutti poðiyen-yang loobang-**ka** e-tolak-*
     female-girl boy-ACC.DEF hole-in ASP-push-
     lupa aða.
     leave AUX
     'The girl pushed the boy into the hole.'
  b. *Karang jo kutti sini-**ka** a-duuduk*
     now FOC girl there-in PRS-stay
     'Now she is (in) there.'

There is also the possibility that both situations are not overtly marked at all. This is the case in Chinese Pidgin Russian, where the goal *butyka* 'bottle' in (7a) and the locus *sopəka* 'mountain' in (7b) show no marking:

(7) Chinese Pidgin Russian (Perekhvalskaya 2013)
  a. Курица яйцы купила, бутыка апускайла.
     *Kuritʃa jajtsy kupi-la, **butyka** apuskaj-la.*
     chicken egg buy-PFV bottle put.into-PFV
     'He bought chicken eggs and put them into a bottle.'
  b. Моя постоянно сопка живи.
     *Moja pastajanna **sopəka** ʒivi.*
     1SG always mountain live
     'I permanently live in mountains.'

There are 23 languages which feature **serial verb constructions** either without (value 3; 8 lgs) or **with a preposition** (value 4; 15 lgs). The four languages that have only simple serial verb constructions at their disposal are the four Gulf of Guinea creoles Principense, Santome, Angolar, and Fa d'Ambô.

(8) Fa d'Ambô (Post 2013)
  *M' piza-l **ba** omal.*
  1SG push-3SG go sea
  'I pushed him into the sea.'

The languages which have serial verb constructions with a preposition show a certain concentration in the Caribbean, the Guianas, West Africa, Southeast Asia, and the Pacific.

(9) Saramaccan (Aboh et al. 2013)
  *A tuusi di tatai **go a** di aguja baaku.*
  3SG push DEF.SG thread go LOC DEF.SG needle hole
  'She pushed the thread through the needle's eye.'

(10) Tok Pisin (Smith & Siegel 2013)
  *Em pusim han i **go insait long** bilum.*
  3SG push hand PM go inside PREP string.bag
  'She pushed her hand into the bilum (a string bag).'

Only one language is attested as having **circumpositional** motion-to marking (value 5):

(11) Afrikaans (den Besten & Biberauer 2013)
  *Leah stoot Marie **by** die gat **in**.*
  Leah pushes Mary by the hole in
  'Leah pushes Mary into the hole.'

Den Besten & Biberauer (2013) note that this construction belongs to colloquial varieties of Afrikaans.

The last type of coding is represented only by the mixed language Gurindji Kriol, which exclusively uses the **allative case** *-ngkirri* (value 6) to express transitive motion-to:

(12) Gurindji Kriol (Meakins 2013)
  Dat jangkarni ngakparn-tu-ma i bin puj-im
  the big frog-ERG-TOP 3SG.SBJ PST push-TR
  *im na ngawa-**ngkirri**.*
  3SG.OBJ SEQ water-ALL
  'The big frog pushed him into the water then.'

For 11 languages there is no information about this feature.

3. Discussion

The overwhelming majority of *APiCS* languages use at-rest marking to express motion-to (value 2). This pattern is also widespread in the European base languages. French, for instance, uses *dans* in both contexts: *Je suis **dans** la cuisine* 'I am in the kitchen', *Je la pousse **dans** la cuisine* 'I push her into the kitchen.' In some varieties of English, too, causative motion verbs like *put* and *push* may show the preposition *in*, as in *She put her gloves **in** the pocket*, where the more standard variety would have the motion-to preposition *into* (*She put her gloves **into** the pocket*). Portuguese and Spanish do not seem to have these constructions. Therefore, this marking pattern in French- and English-based creoles may well be inherited from the European lexifier languages. But there are numerous Portuguese- and Spanish-based creoles which also show at-rest marking to express motion-to, as in Diu Indo-Portuguese in (4). Here, a different explanation must be sought. Maybe the relevant substrates show the same pattern.

The use of serial verb constructions in transitive motion verbs, however, has clear substrate sources. Lawal (1989: 10) cites parallel examples from Yoruba, where the serial verbs 'go', 'reach', 'come' are used in transitive motion-to constructions, as in (8) from Fa d'Ambô. Unfortunately, there is currently little cross-linguistic data on transitive motion constructions as outlined in this chapter.

82 Transitive motion verbs: 'push'

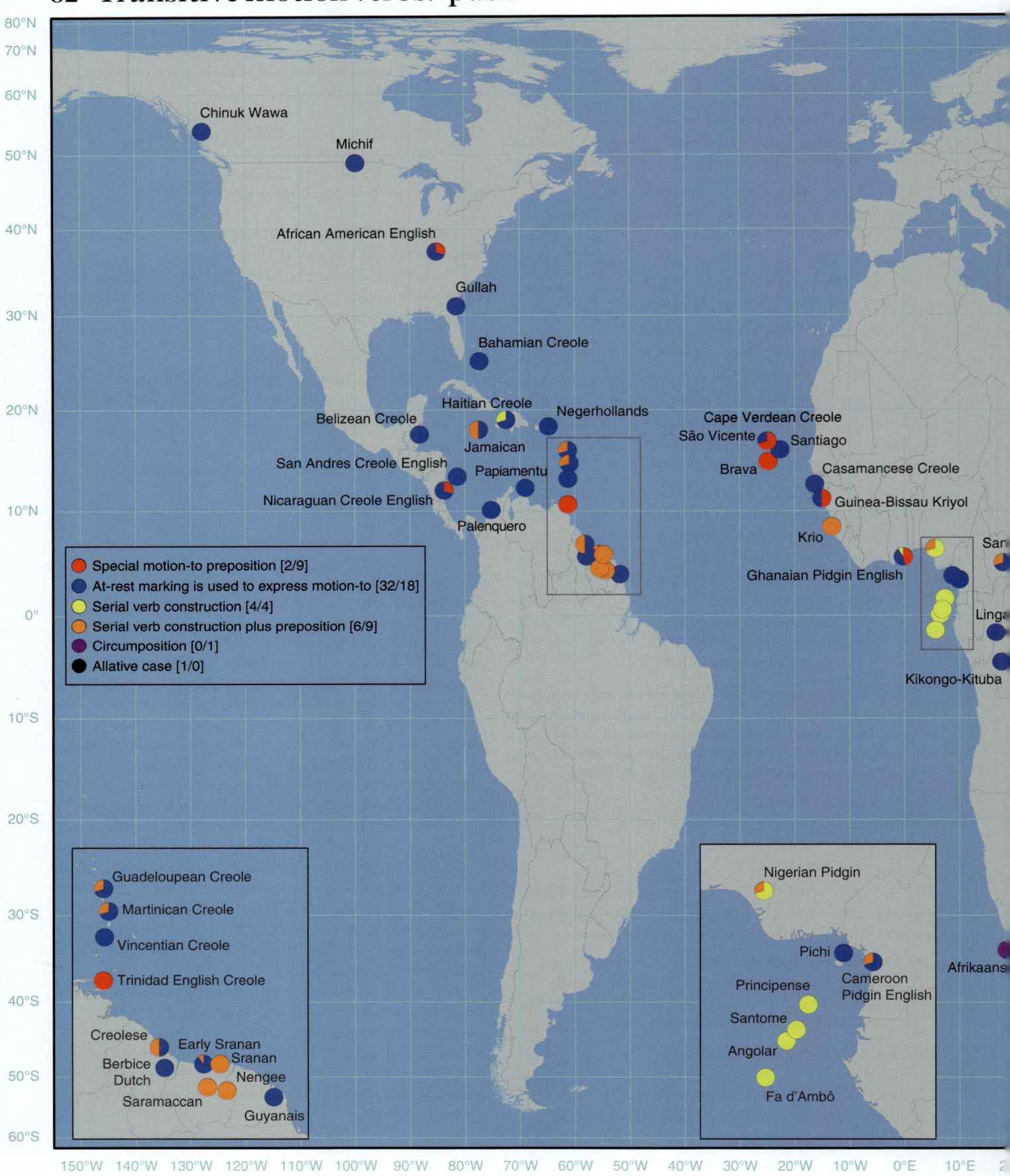

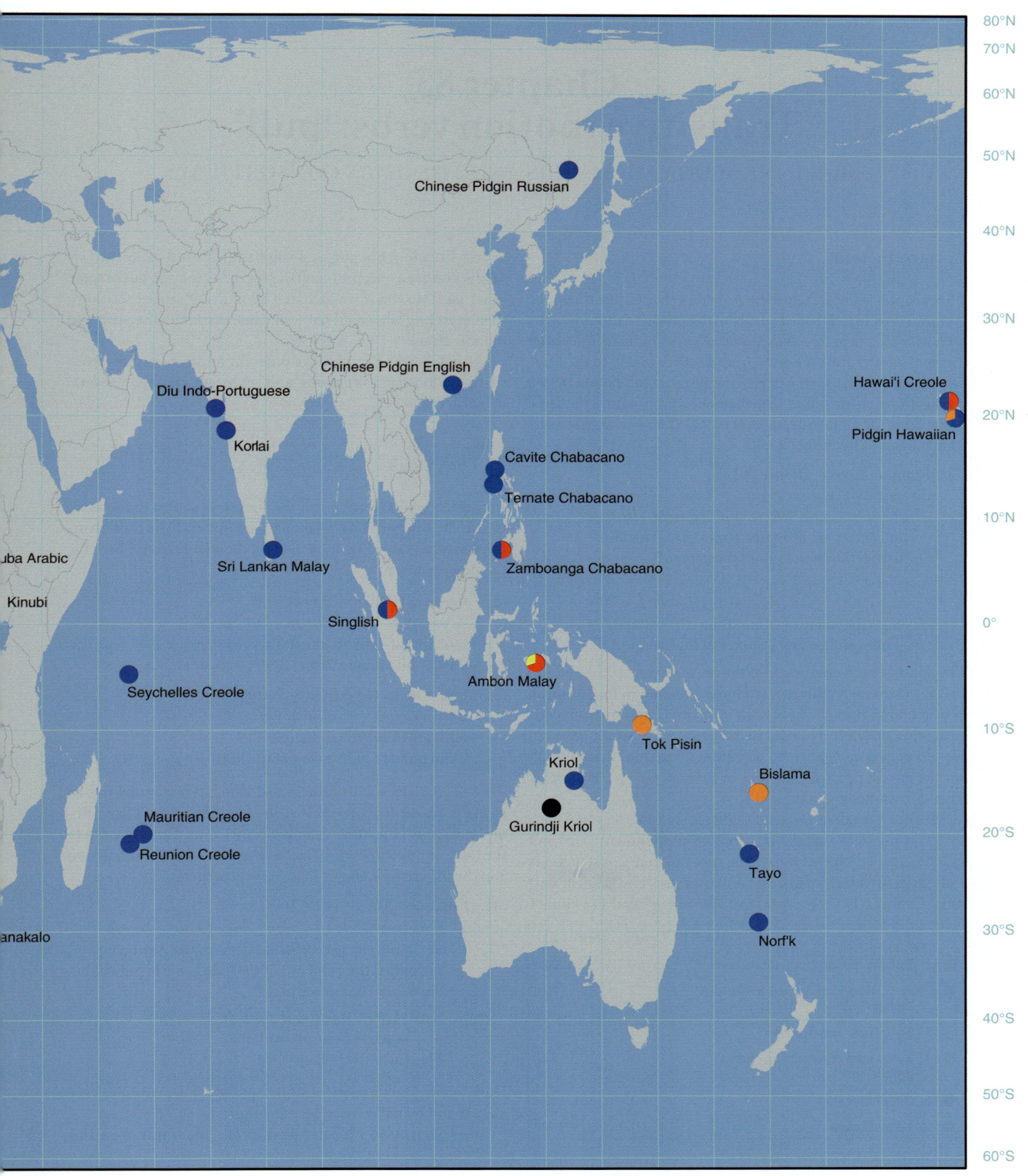

Chapter 83
Transitive motion verbs: 'pull'

SUSANNE MARIA MICHAELIS AND THE *APiCS* CONSORTIUM

1. Introduction

This chapter complements the previous chapter on transitive motion verbs like 'push'. It deals with transitive motion verbs such as 'pull', as in *Lea pulled Gabriel out of the hole*, where the theme (*Gabriel*) is moved away from a source (*hole*). In the English construction, the source is marked by a combination of two prepositions, *out of*. Other languages, however, feature the same preposition in motion-from contexts (1a) and in at-rest contexts (1b), as in Reunion Creole:

(1) Reunion Creole (Bollée 2013)
   a. transitive motion-from
     *tir le   gale /le ros **dan** la ter*
     pull DEF.PL stone DEF.PL stone LOC DEF soil
     'to pull the stones out of the ground'
   b. at-rest
     *Nana tro   d gale/ ros **dan** la ter.*
     EXIST too.many of stone stone LOC DEF soil
     'There are too many stones in the ground.'

This kind of polysemous use of the preposition *dan* in Reunion Creole is strikingly different from the situation in its European base language French. In French, transitive motion-from constructions obligatorily show the ablative preposition *de*, as in *tirer des pierres de la terre* 'to pull stones out/from the ground', not the at-rest prepositions *dans* or *sur* (*Les pierres sont dans la terre* 'The stones are in the soil').

When we speak of at-rest situations, we refer—as in Chapter 82—only to the spatial relations of containment ('in') and attachment ('at') and compare the motion-from constructions with these two kinds of at-rest constructions. The English sentence *Gabriel is out of the hole* may also be regarded as a kind of at-rest situation, but here it is implied that the location of *Gabriel* is a derived one, the result of precisely a motion out of some other location. So if we included all kinds of spatial relations, then even English would have the same marking for at-rest and motion-from.

As in Chapter 82, there are different means to express transitive motion-from situations, and languages may show several construction types.

2. The values

In this feature we distinguish the six values shown in the value box. In half of the *APiCS* languages, a **special motion-from adposition** (value 1) is used to mark the source from which the theme is removed.

(2) Belizean Creole (Escure 2013)
   *A   wan pul wan mame **fa**   tri fi yu.*
   1SG FUT pull one mame from tree for you
   'I will pull a mame (fruit) from the tree for you.'

(3) Juba Arabic (Manfredi & Petrollino 2013)
   *jon júru gódi   **min** hófra*
   John pull Godfrey from hole
   'John pulled Godfrey out of the hole.'

The 22 languages with value 2 use their **at-rest marking to express motion-from**, as was already shown in (1) from Reunion Creole. One other example comes from Fanakalo, where the (a) example shows the transitive motion-from construction and the (b) example shows an at-rest construction.

(4) Fanakalo (Mesthrie 2013)
   a. *Yena keep-ile lo   gane **duze** ga lo   godi.*
     he   pull-PST DEF.ART child near of DEF.ART hole
     'He pulled the child out of the hole.' or 'He pulled the child from out of the hole.'
   b. *Yena khona   **duze** ga lo   mgodi.*
     he   COP.LOC near of ART hole
     'He is near the hollow.'

Here, the spatial relation 'near' occurs, which we consider very close to the spatial relation of attachment.

Interestingly, *all* French-based creoles in *APiCS* show this

		excl	shrd	all
●	1. Special motion-from adposition	26	6	32
●	2. At-rest marking is used to express motion-from	12	10	22
●	3. Serial verb construction	4	3	7
●	4. Serial verb construction plus preposition	7	7	14
●	5. Circumposition	1	1	2
●	6. Ablative case	1	1	2

polysemous marking pattern, whereas there are only very few English-based languages with this value: Early Sranan, Krio, Ghanaian Pidgin English, Pichi, and marginally Tok Pisin.

Languages with the next two values express a transitive motion-from construction with **serial verbs** (value 3; 7 languages) or with **serial verbs followed by a preposition** (value 4; 14 languages). Within the languages with value 3, we find all four Portuguese-based creoles of the Gulf of Guinea.

(5) Angolar (Maurer 2013a)
Maya thaa Tonha fõ vuvu.
Maria pull Tonha come.from hole
'Maria pulled Tonha out of the hole.'

The behaviour of transitive motion-from constructions strikingly parallels the behaviour of transitive motion-to constructions (Chapter 82), where the Gulf of Guinea creoles, too, constitute a compact linguistic area of serial verb marking.

Languages with value 4 (serial verb constructions with a preposition) are mostly found in the Guianas, West Africa, and the Pacific.

(6) Sranan (Winford & Plag 2013)
Kofi hari a ston puru na ini a olo.
Kofi pull DET stone remove LOC in DET hole
'Kofi pulled the stone out of the hole.'

Here too, there is a clear parallel with transitive motion-to constructions (see Chapter 82). Sranan, Nengee, Tok Pisin, and Bislama mark both transitive motion-to and motion-from constructions with serial verb constructions plus a preposition.

Two languages show **circumpositional marking** (value 5), Michif and Afrikaans:

(7) Afrikaans (den Besten & Biberauer 2013)
Leah het Marie uit die gat uit getrek.
Leah PST Mary out DEF.ART hole out pulled
'Leah pulled Mary out of the hole.'

Two languages have **ablative case** to mark the source (value 6), the mixed languages Sri Lankan Malay and Gurindji Kriol:

(8) Gurindji Kriol (Meakins 2013)
I bin pulim hol-nginyi.
3SG.SBJ PST pull.TR hole-ABL
'He pulled it out of the hole.'

Afrikaans and Gurindji Kriol have circumpositional and case marking, respectively, in the transitive motion-to constructions as well, although with different morphemes (*in/by...in* and allative case).

3. Discussion

When comparing the value distribution in the two chapters on transitive motion verbs (82 and 83), it is noteworthy that the values of serial verb constructions with and without a preposition (values 3 and 4), circumposition (value 5), and case marking (value 6) are very similarly distributed.

The most striking differences in the distribution of the values concern the first two values "special motion-to/motion-from adposition" and "at-rest marking used to express motion-to/motion-from". Here we see very different proportions in both chapters. Compared to the 50 languages which treat 'push' verbs in the same way as the corresponding at-rest situation, only less than half of this number (22 languages) allow this option with 'pull' verbs. Accordingly, there are three times as many languages with special motion-from adpositions than languages with special motion-to adpositions.

Unfortunately, there are no worldwide cross-linguistic data on transitive motion constructions. But considering the data in *APiCS*, there seems to be a correlation between intransitive and transitive motion marking (see Chapters 79, 80, and 81 for intransitive motion verbs). There is a general tendency for languages which mark intransitive motion-to and motion-from identically (lit. 'I go **in** the forest', 'I leave **in** the forest') also to mark transitive motion-to and motion-from identically (lit. 'I push s.o. **in** the hole', 'I pull s.o. **in** the hole'). *APiCS* contains no chapter which compares transitive motion-to and motion-from constructions, analogous to Chapter 81 on intransitive motion constructions (see Chapter 81). But from the data we have, we can infer that languages which treat 'pull' constructions as at-rest constructions also mark 'push' constructions in the same way. Reunion Creole is an example of this. We already saw the transitive motion-from construction (1). The corresponding transitive motion-to construction (9a) is marked in the same way as are the intransitive counterparts (9b, c):

(9) Reunion Creole (Bollée 2013)
a. *I met trwa gren dan en trou.*
FIN put three grain in INDF hole
'You put three grains into a hole.'
b. *I rant dan en pti boukan* [...].
FIN enter in INDF small hut
'He goes into a little hut [...].'
c. *Li la sort dan la kaz si-l-tar.*
3SG PRF leave in DEF house late
'He left the house late.'

Boretzky (1983: 172ff.) already identifies West African substrate languages with the same marking pattern. And there is some evidence that eastern Bantu languages also show this polysemy marking in transitive motion-to/-from constructions (see Michaelis 2008). See also Chapter 81 on intransitive motion-to/motion-from constructions, which likewise identifies substrate influence as the key to explaining the creole data.

83 Transitive motion verbs: 'pull'

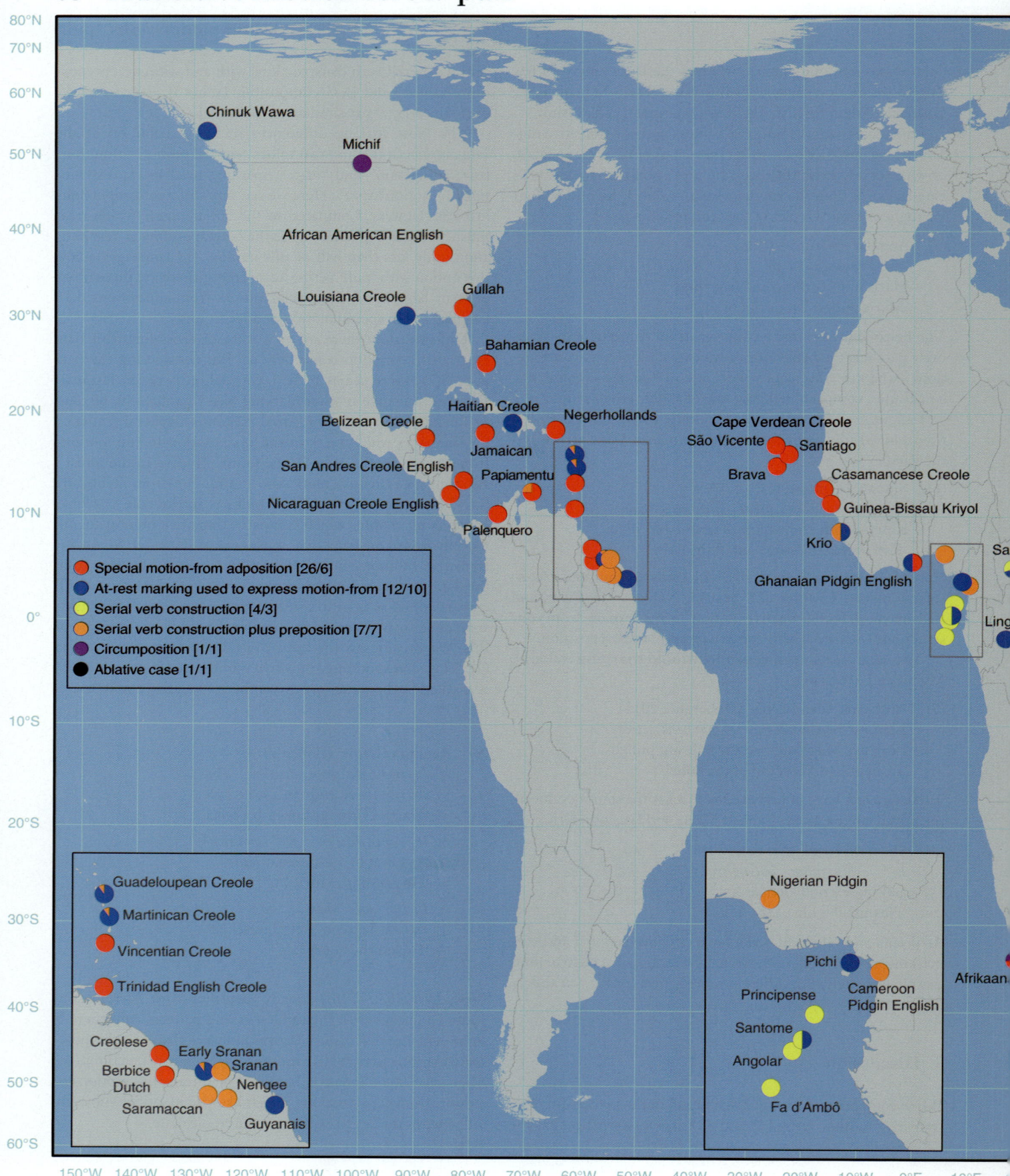

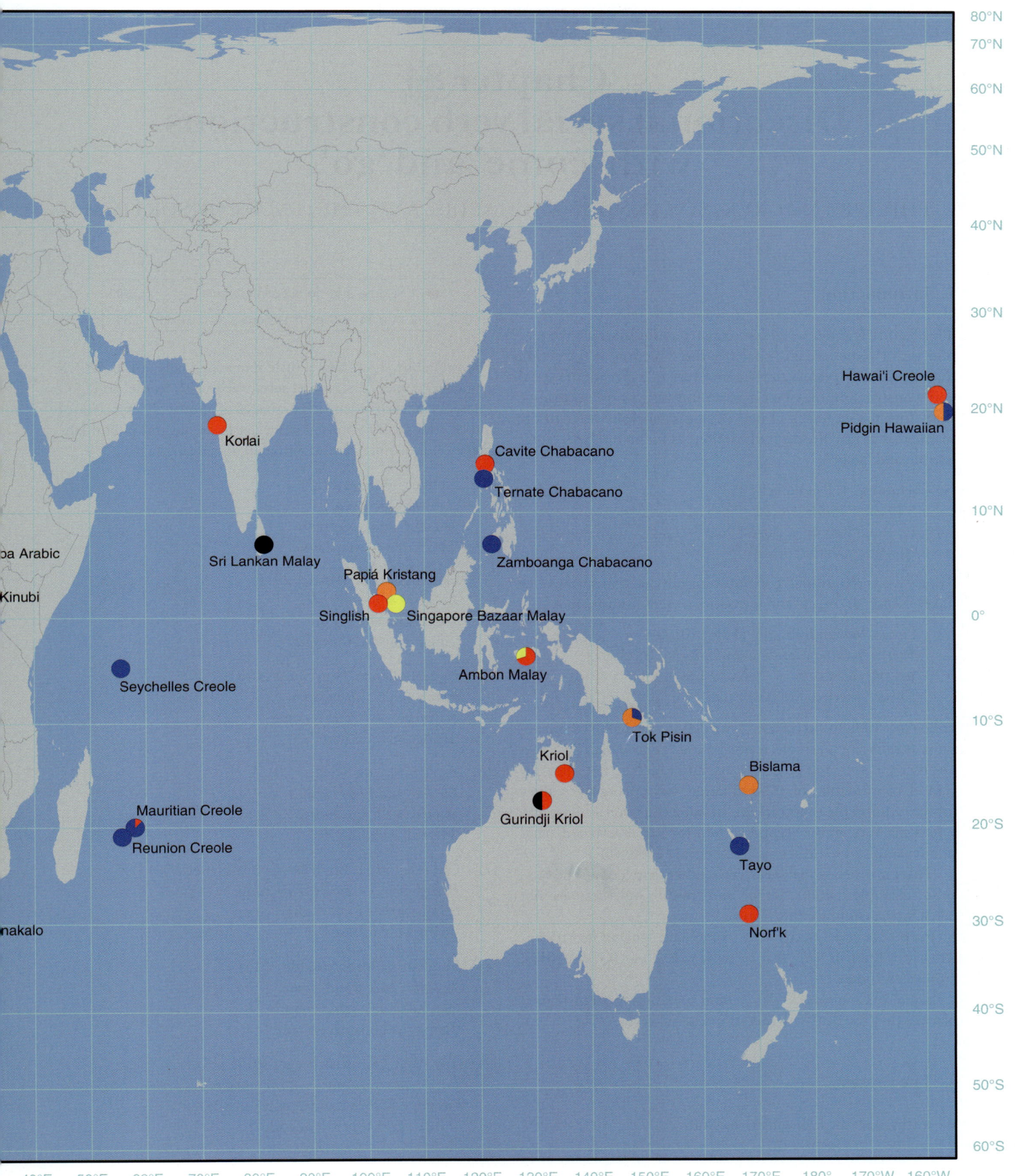

Chapter 84
Directional serial verb constructions with 'come' and 'go'

PHILIPPE MAURER, SUSANNE M. MICHAELIS, AND THE *APiCS* CONSORTIUM

1. Introduction

This feature is about serial verb constructions in which the second verb ('come' or 'go') specifies the direction of the action that the first verb refers to. The first verb of a directional serial verb construction may be either an intransitive or a transitive verb. Intransitive verbs in first position generally refer to the manner or to the direction of motion, as in 'go on foot', 'run', 'swim', and 'go up'.

(1) Santome (Hagemeijer 2013)
 Nansê ka **subli ba** *ôbô ê!*
 2PL IPFV go.up go forest PCL
 'You go up to the forest!'

Transitive verbs in first position typically have meanings like 'take', 'send', or 'carry' and introduce a theme argument:

(2) Yimas-Arafundi Pidgin (Foley 2013)
 Mən **pambaysambi wambi** *taŋgay kandək.*
 3SG.OBJ carry.DEP go.DEP beach OBL
 '[They] carried it to the beach.'

Following Aikhenvald (2006: 1), we define serial verb constructions as referring to single, monoclausal events which have just one tense, aspect, and polarity value and which do not show any sign of coordination or subordination. Some languages allow for (or require) the repetition of the subject as well as tense and aspect markers on the second verb of the serial verb construction (examples 14–18; see also Aikhenvald 2006: 40f.).

There are directional serial verbs other than 'come' and 'go', as for example 'enter', 'leave', and 'reach', but these are not taken into account for this feature.

Purposive serial verbs with 'come' and 'go', as in African-American English *After that we **went take** a nap* (Green 2013), are also excluded.

See also Chapters 79–80 (Going to/Coming from named places); they too deal with directional serial verbs.

2. The values

We distinguish the following two values:

●	1. 'Come' and 'go' directionals exist	39
○	2. 'Come' and 'go' directionals do not exist	36

The value box shows that a little more than half of the *APiCS* languages possess directional serial verbs with 'come' and 'go'. These serial verbs occur in languages of almost all lexical bases and of almost all regions. They exist in creole and pidgin languages, but do not occur in bilingual mixed languages.

(3) Nengee (Migge 2013)
 A **subi go** *anda.*
 3SG climb go over.there
 'He climbed over there.'

(4) Haitian Creole (Fattier 2013)
 Li **voye bòn** *nan* **ale**.
 3SG send maid ART go
 'She dismissed the maid.'

(5) Negerhollands (van Sluijs 2013)
 Bring *di difman* **ko**.
 bring DEF.ART thief come
 'Bring the thief here!'

(6) Papiá Kristang (Baxter 2013)
 Eli ja **andá bai** *kaza.*
 3SG PFV walk go house
 'He walked home.'

(7) Chinese Pidgin English (Li & Matthews 2013)
 Bring *one piecee chair* **come**.
 bring INDF.ART CLF chair come
 'Bring a chair here.'

(8) Singlish (Lim & Ansaldo 2013)
 Take the book **bring come**.
 take ART book bring come
 'Bring the book here/to me.'

(9) Tok Pisin (Smith & Siegel 2013)
 Baga ia **torome kam** *autsaid ia.*
 bugger FOC throw.away come outside FOC
 'The bugger threw it outside.'

(10) Singapore Bazaar Malay (Khin Khin Aye 2013)
Hari-hari jalan-jalan sini datang Geylang Bahru
day~day walk~walk here come Geylang Bahru
Kampong.
village
'Every day, I walk here to Geylang Bahru.'

In many examples in our database, the first verb refers to a past perfective situation (either zero-marked as in ex. 3 or marked by an overt perfective marker as in ex. 6), but the Negerhollands, Chinese Pidgin English, and Singlish sentences (exx. 5, 7, and 8) display an imperative in first position, and the Singapore Bazaar Malay sentence (10) has a zero-marked verb with a habitual reading. The following Guyanais example shows the first verb of the series marked by progressive *ka*:

(11) Guyanais (Pfänder 2013)
Manman ka voyé timoun alé lékol.
mother PROG send child go school
'Mom is sending her child to school.'

Directional serial verbs are not incompatible with (general) locative adpositions, as illustrated by Vincentian Creole and Pidgin Hawaiian:

(12) Vincentian Creole (Prescod 2013)
Shi sen i pikni go a shap.
3SG.F send POSS.3SG child go LOC shop
'She sent her child to the shop.'

(13) Pidgin Hawaiian (Roberts 2013)
Moaka lawe kela wahine ia Kipau hele ma Koloa.
Moaka take DET wife OBJ Kipau go LOC Koloa
'Moaka took Kipa's wife away to Koloa.'

As noted in the introduction, tense and aspect marking as well as the marking of the subject may occur on both verbs in the series. In Berbice Dutch, the past marker -*tɛ* co-occurs on both verbs:

(14) Berbice Dutch (Kouwenberg 2013a)
afti ifi skifu-tɛ kumu-tɛ difi-kandi
after 1PL move-PST come-PST this-side
'after we moved to this place'

San Andres Creole English, too, is a case of double tense and aspect marking; in the following example the first verb is zero-marked for (past) perfective aspect and the directional verb is marked for past.

(15) San Andres Creole English (Bartens 2013b)
Beda Taiga ∅ swim gaan shuo.
brother Tiger PFV swim go.PST shore
'Brother Tiger swam to the shore.'

In Casamancese Creole, Seychelles Creole, and Bislama, the subject is marked on both verbs. Note however that in the case of Casamancese Creole the marking on the second verb is not obligatory, and that in Bislama, it is the agreement marker which occurs on both verbs.

(16) Casamancese Creole (Biagui & Quint 2013)
Jon koré (i) bay Sicor.
John run 3SG go Zinguinchor
'John went at once to Ziguinchor.'

(17) Seychelles Creole (Michaelis & Rosalie 2013)
La nou kouri nou ale.
then 1PL run 1PL go
'Then we ran away.'

(18) Bislama (Meyerhoff 2013)
Hem i pusum i go.
3SG AGR push AGR go
'She pushed it forward.'

3. Distribution

Directional serial verbs are present in almost all regions: Caribbean (18 languages), West Africa (11 languages), Indian Ocean (2 languages), Southeast Asia (5 languages), and Pacific (3 languages). The only region where they are absent is South Asia.

As already mentioned, directionals are present in pidgins and creoles but absent from the bilingual mixed languages represented in *APiCS*.

Regarding the absence of directionals according to the lexifier, we can observe that they are absent from the Bantu-based languages, the Arabic-based languages, and from almost all Spanish-based creoles (with the exception of Papiamentu).

If we look at the distribution by lexifier and region, we can see that in the domain of the Ibero-Romance-based creoles (and only here), there are some subregions where directionals are absent: the Cape Verde islands (Upper Guinea), South Asia, and the Philippines. By contrast, directionals are present in the two Upper Guinea varieties spoken on the African mainland (Guinea-Bissau Kriyol, Casamancese Creole), in the four Gulf of Guinea creoles (Santome, Principense, Angolar, Fa d'Ambô), and in Southeast Asia. These differences can partly be explained by the substrates or adstrates of these languages. Philippine languages, some important substrate languages of the Cape Verdean varieties like Wolof, and South Asian languages lack directionals, whereas the substrate or adstrate languages of Guinea-Bissau Kriyol and Casamancese (e.g. Balanta), the Gulf of Guinea creoles (Yoruba), and the Southeast Asian languages (Hokkien Chinese) have them.

In the *APiCS* languages with lexical bases other than Portuguese or Spanish, the situation is similar.

84 Directional serial verb constructions with 'come' and 'go'

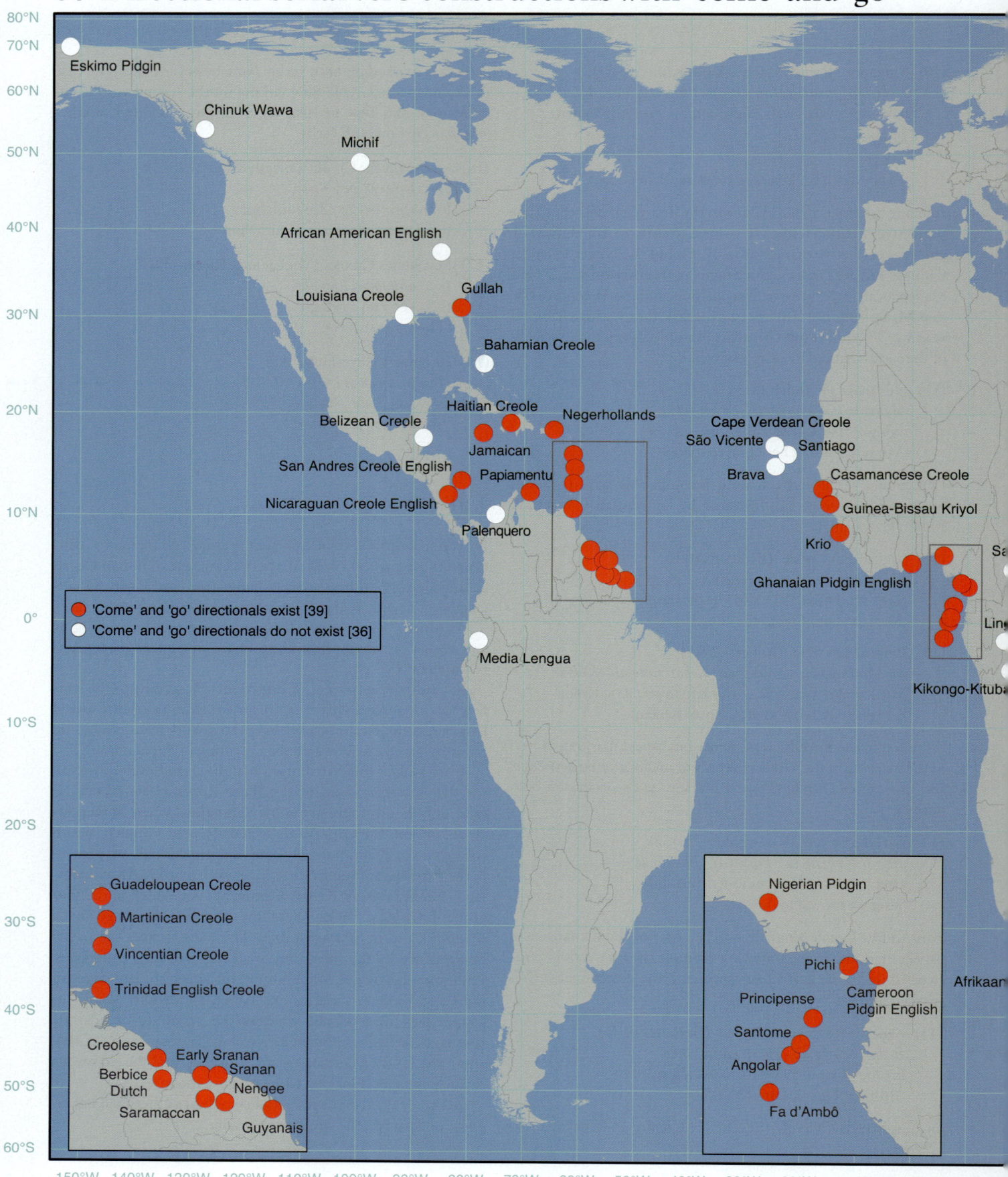

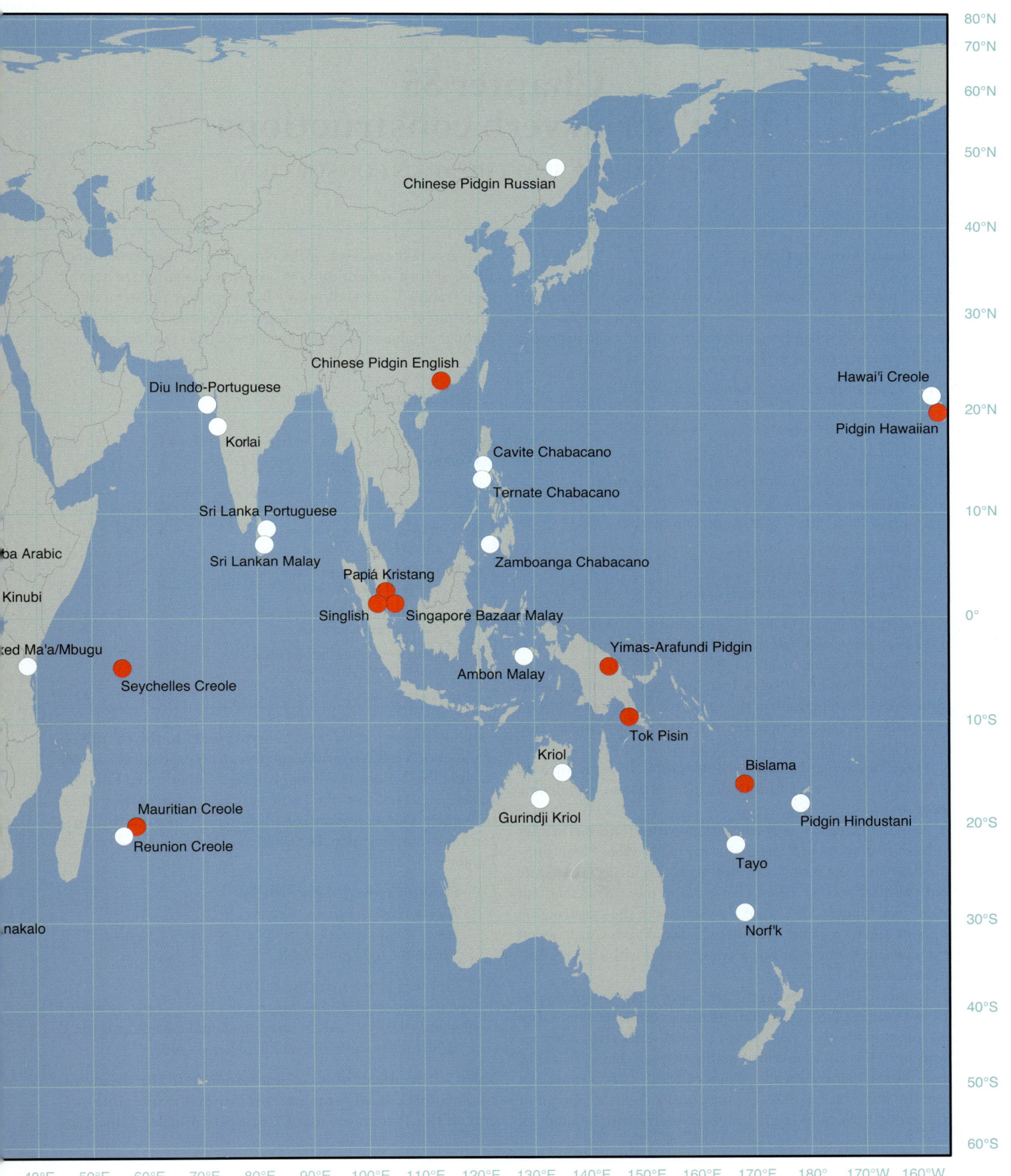

Chapter 85
'Take' serial verb constructions

PHILIPPE MAURER AND THE *APiCS* CONSORTIUM

1. Feature description

In this feature we consider serial verb constructions in which one of the two verbs (almost always the first one) means 'take' (or has a closely related meaning such as 'raise') and expresses an instrumental role as in (1), or a theme role as in (2).

(1) Guadeloupe Creole (Colot & Ludwig 2013a)
 I **pwan** hach a-y koupé bwa.
 3SG take axe POSS-3SG cut wood
 'He cut the wood with the axe.'

(2) Cape Verdean Creole of Santiago (Lang 2013)
 Katxor **toma** pónta di si rábo e **po**
 dog take tip of POSS.3SG tail 3SG put
 dibáxu di si bariga.
 under of POSS.3SG belly
 'The dog put the end of his tail under his belly.'

Following Aikhenvald (2006: 1), we define serial verb constructions as referring to single, monoclausal events which have just one tense, aspect, and polarity value and which do not show any sign of coordination or subordination. Some languages allow (or require) the repetition of the subject as well as tense and aspect markers on the second verb of the serial verb construction (examples 2, 5, and 8; see also Aikhenvald 2006: 40f.).

'Take' serials may have different functions; in our feature, we will focus on instrumental-introducing and theme-introducing 'take' serials.

Some languages allow constructions with an optional marker of coordination, as in Papiamentu *kue kuchú kòrta karni* (literally 'take knife cut meat') 'cut meat with a knife' or 'take a knife and cut meat' vs. *kue kuchú i kòrta karni* 'take a knife and cut meat' (see Maurer 1988: 256). In such cases, the construction without a marker is not considered a serial verb construction but a variant of the coordinate construction with the coordination marker.

In most *APiCS* languages 'take' serials can be given a biclausal reading (as in the Papiamentu examples). This raises the question whether 'take' serials are real serial verb constructions in all the cases described in this chapter, that is, that they describe a single event and are monoclausal. This is especially problematic if the 'take' serial introduces a theme argument of the second verb, allowing for a literal interpretation (value 1), and, generally speaking, if the object of the 'take' serial functions, at least semantically, as an instrumental of the second verb (values 3 and 4). It is only in cases where no literal interpretation of the construction is possible (value 2) that we know without any doubt that these are cases of true 'take' serials.

2. The values

We distinguish the following five values; values 1–4 refer to the role of the object of 'take':

		excl	shrd	all
●	1. Theme of the second verb, literal interpretation possible	9	22	31
●	2. Theme of the second verb, literal interpretation impossible	0	12	12
●	3. Instrument of the second verb, no resumptive pronoun	3	19	22
●	4. Instrument of the second verb, with resumptive pronoun	0	7	7
○	5. No 'take' serials	41	0	41

Value 1 (**the object of 'take' corresponds to the theme of the second verb, a literal interpretation is possible**) occurs in eight Ibero-Romance-based languages, in fourteen English-based languages, in three French-based languages, as well as in Berbice Dutch, in Sango, in Kikongo-Kituba, in Sri Lankan Malay, in Singapore Bazaar Malay, and in Yimas-Arafundi Pidgin.

(3) Batavia Creole (Maurer 2013b)
 Lanta komer *tridji* na medja.
 raise food bring LOC table
 'Bring the food to the table.'

(4) Gurindji Kriol (Meakins 2013)
 Kirringku im **teikim** lajap karu nyanuny.
 woman.ERG 3SG take.TR carry.on.shoulders child 3SG.DAT
 'The woman carries his child on her shoulders.'

Value 2 (**the object of 'take' corresponds to the theme of the second verb, a literal interpretation is impossible**) occurs in five Portuguese-based languages (Angolar, Cape Verdean Creole of Santiago, Fa d'Ambô, Principense, Santome), in six English-based languages (Creolese, Ghanaian Pidgin English, Nigerian Pidgin, Pichi, Sranan, Vincentian Creole), and in Berbice Dutch.

(5) Pichi (Yakpo 2013)
Mì man tek ìn yay è putàn
1SG.POSS man take 3SG.POSS eye 3SG put.3SG
bɔtɔn grɔn so.
bottom ground so
'My husband diverted his gaze to the ground.'

(6) Berbice Dutch (Kouwenberg 2013a)
Di wɛtɛ kɛnap justu dek di kurkur
ART white person.PL PST.HAB take ART black
kɛnap mɛ slev.
person.PL make slave
'The white people used to make slaves out of the black people.'

In example (7), a literal interpretation is not possible either; however, the object of 'take' does not correspond to the theme complement of the following verb but to its temporal complement:

(7) Nigerian Pidgin (Faraclas 2013)
À gò tek midnayt du-am.
1SG FUT take midnight do-3SG
'I'll do it at midnight.'

The following Sranan example illustrates aspect repetition on the second verb in the series:

(8) Sranan (Winford & Plag 2013)
[...] *den man e teki a sani e meki grap.*
ART.PL man IPFV take DET thing IPFV make joke
'Hey, they are making a joke of the matter.'

Value 3 (the object of 'take' corresponds to the instrument of the second verb, without resumptive pronoun) occurs in six Portuguese-based languages, in eleven English-based languages, in two French-based languages, as well as in Kikongo-Kituba, Singapore Bazaar Malay, and Chinuk Wawa.

(9) Chinuk Wawa (Grant 2013)
Náyka iskam máskit mámuk tlxwap.
1SG take gun make hole
'I make a hole with a gun.'

Value 4 (the object of 'take' corresponds to the instrument of the second verb, with resumptive pronoun) occurs in five Portuguese-based languages and in two English-based languages.

(10) Angolar (Maurer 2013a)
N tambu faka kota situ ku ê.
1SG take knife cut meat with 3SG
'I cut the meat with a knife.'

(11) Nigerian Pidgin (Faraclas 2013)
Ìm tek nayf chuk mì fɔr ay wìt am.
3SG take knife pierce 1SG LOC eye with 3SG
'S/he stabbed me in the eye with a knife.'

The possibility of resuming the object of 'take' as an argument of the second verb casts some doubt on the status of these constructions as serial verb constructions since the instrumental would be marked twice within the same clause. It is therefore not surprising that the authors of two Cape Verdean varieties and Casamancese Creole translate 'take' only literally in their examples (e.g. 'I took a knife and cut the meat').

Most *APiCS* languages with an instrumental serial verb also possess an instrumental adposition. The difference between the two constructions is left unexplained in most cases. An exception to this is Creolese.

(12) Creolese (Devonish & Thompson 2013)
Ii tek wan klaat waip di teebl.
3SG take ART cloth wipe ART table
'He wiped the table with a cloth.'

In Creolese, the serial verb construction implies that the action is deliberate and planned, which is not the case with the corresponding adpositional construction (*Ii waip di teebl wid wan klaat* 'He wiped the table with a cloth').

This means that more research is needed in order to establish the exact syntactic and semantic status, and possibly the pragmatic status of the different 'take' serial verb constructions discussed in this chapter.

Value 5 (**no 'take' serials**) occurs in 54 per cent of the *APiCS* languages—in creoles, in pidgins, and in bilingual mixed languages in all geographical areas.

3. Distribution

Although 'take' serials occur mainly in the Atlantic area (23 languages), they do occur in 12 languages outside this area: Chinuk Wawa in North America, Kikongo-Kituba and Sango in continental Africa, Seychelles Creole in the Indian Ocean, Sri Lankan Malay in South India, Papiá Kristang, Batavia Creole, Singapore Bazaar Malay, and Chinese Pidgin English in Southeast Asia, Gurindji Kriol in Australia, and Yimas-Arafundi Pidgin in the Pacific area.

85 'Take' serial verb constructions

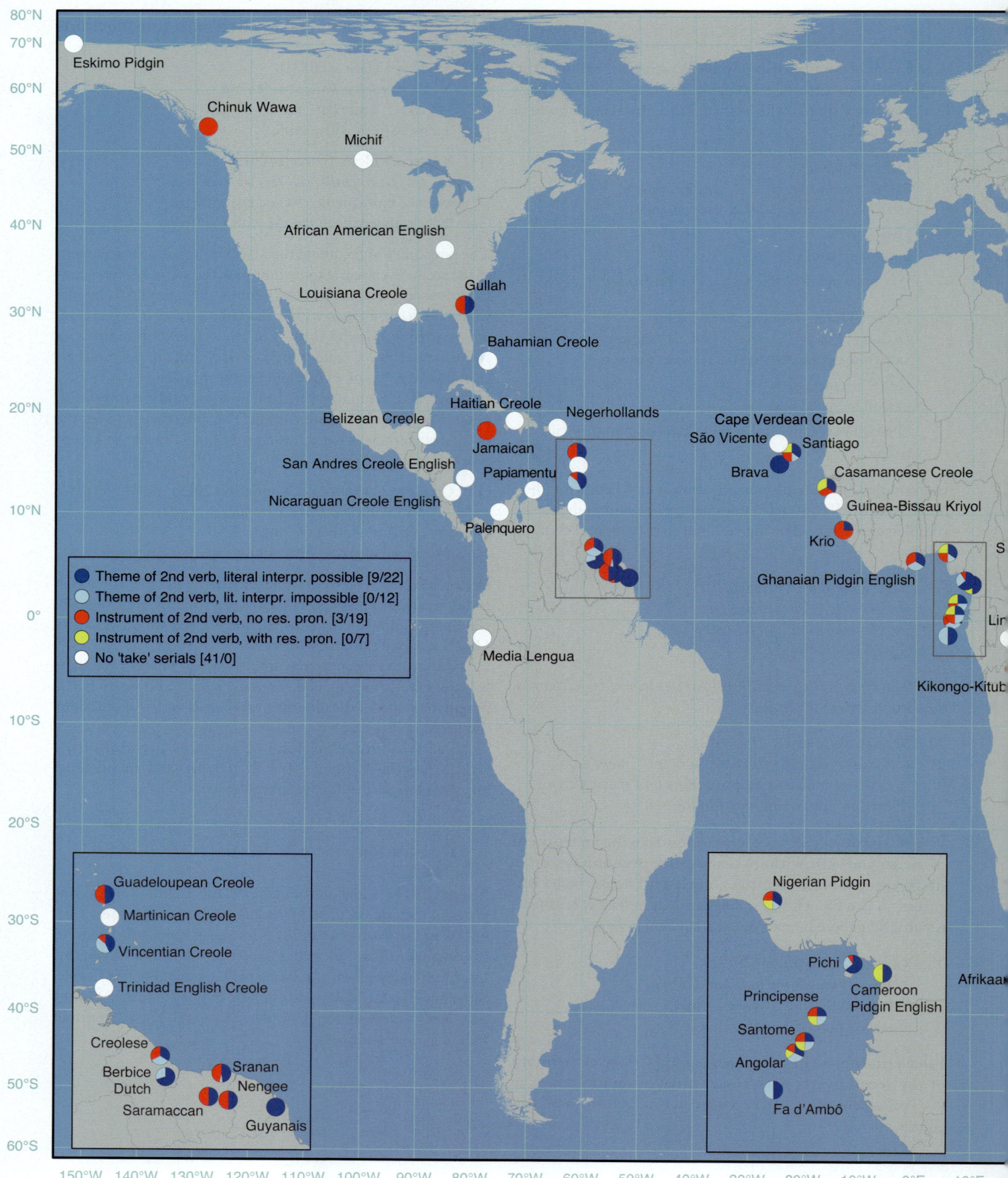

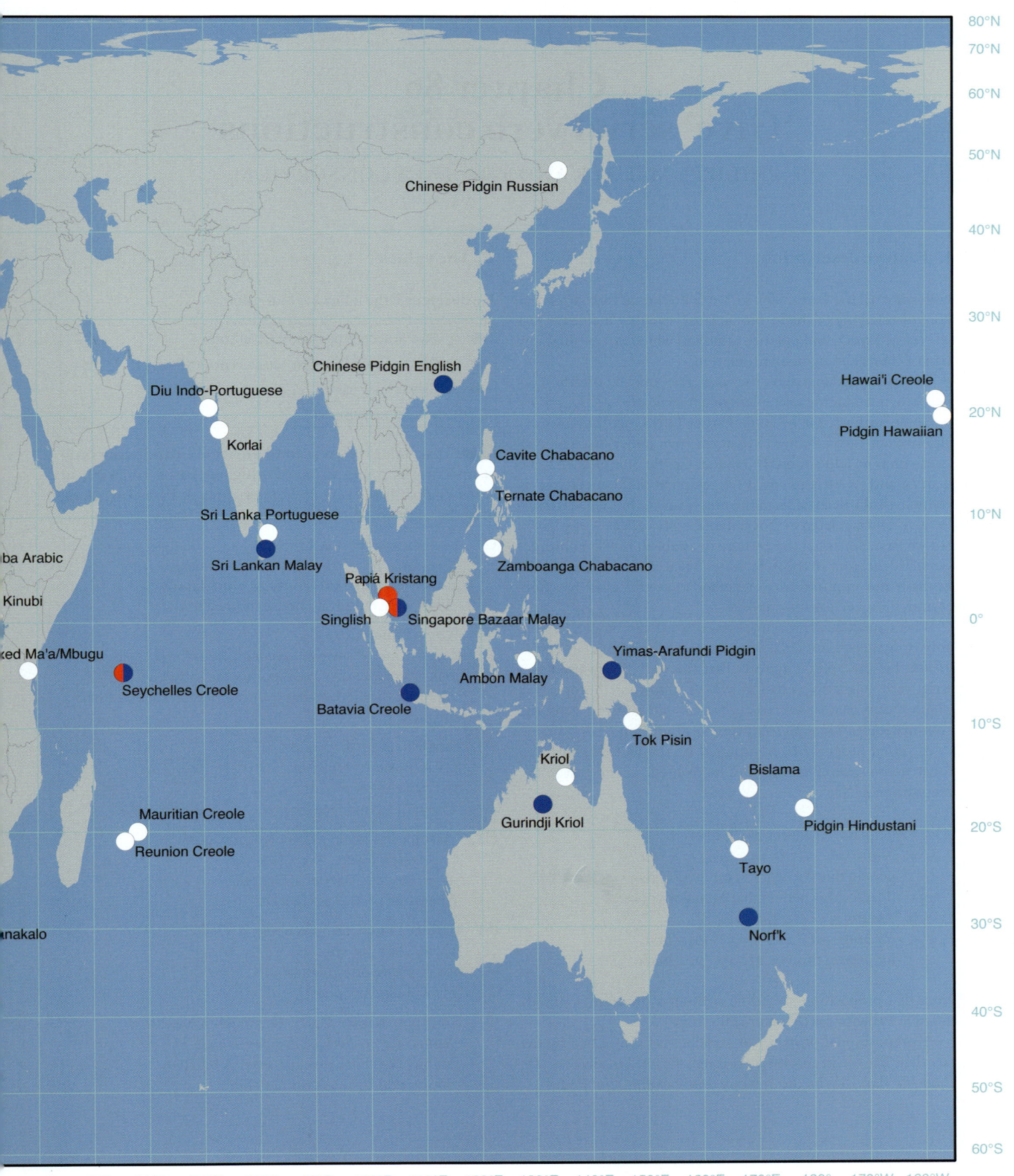

Chapter 86
'Give' serial verb constructions

PHILIPPE MAURER AND THE *APiCS* CONSORTIUM

1. Feature description

Following Aikhenvald (2006: 1), we define serial verb constructions as referring to single, monoclausal events which have just one tense, aspect, and polarity value and which do not show any sign of coordination or subordination.

In serializing languages, the verb 'give' may be used as a serial verb, introducing a recipient or a beneficiary.

Some authors, for instance Fattier (2013, on Haitian Creole), are not sure whether to treat the item under discussion as a verb or as an adposition. In Haitian Creole, it is clear that the item *ba* and its variants, used for recipient and benefactive, is etymologically derived from the now obsolete French verb *bailler* 'give' and is related to the Haitian Creole verb *ba ~ bay* 'give', but we have not asked the authors to establish the (synchronic) syntactic category of the item under discussion; in other words, we have not inquired as to whether the verb 'give' has fully grammaticalized into an adposition.

The syntactic category of a given word can be determined only by syntactic tests. Looking at the verb *da* 'give' in Principense, for example, it appears that this verb, when used as a serial verb, possesses verbal as well as adpositional properties, which means that this serial verb is located halfway along the grammaticalization path from verb to adposition.

A verbal property is exemplified by the fact that in focus constructions, serial *da* may not be fronted, in contrast to the preposition *pô* 'for':

(1) Principense (Maurer 2009: 110)
  a. ***Ningê sê** êli ki n kopa livu **da**.*
     person this FOC REL 1SG buy book give
     'It is for this person that I bought books.'
  b. *****Da** ningê sê ki n kopa livu.*
  c. ***Pô ningê sê** ki n kopa livu.*
     for person this FOC.REL 1SG buy book

Note that preposition stranding without a pronoun is not allowed in Principense (Maurer 2009: 107f.).

A prepositional property of serial *da* is exemplified by the fact that, like the preposition *pô*, it may be used in answers: *Da Pedu./Pô Pedu.* '(Who did you buy this book for?) For Pedu.'

2. The values

We distinguish the following four values:

●	1. 'Give' in second position, recipient only	12
●	2. 'Give' in second position, recipient or beneficiary	14
●	3. 'Give' in first position, recipient only	6
○	4. No 'give' serials exist	43

Value 1 (**serial 'give' in second position introducing only recipients**) is found in one Portuguese-based language, in seven English-based languages, in two French-based languages, in Berbice Dutch, and in Singapore Bazaar Malay.

(2) Fa d'Ambô (Post 2013)
   *A ska fe wan xadyi **da** na-namay.*
   3GEN PROG make ART house give ART-family
   'They were building a house for the family.'

(3) Krio (Finney 2013)
   *Luk di klos we yu mama dai lɛf **gi** yu*
   look ART clothes REL POSS mother die leave give you
   'Here are the clothes that your mother left for you when she died.'

(4) Singlish (Lim & Ansaldo 2013)
   *I buy chok **give** you.*
   1SG buy congee give 2PL
   'I bought rice congee for you.'

(5) Martinican Creole (Colot & Ludwig 2013b)
   *I matjé an let **ba** Joj.*
   3SG write ART letter give George
   'She wrote a letter to George.'

(6) Berbice Dutch (Kouwenberg 2013a)
   *O ma tiri en **pi** ɛkɛ.*
   3SG FUT send one give 1SG
   'He will send me one.'

(7) Singapore Bazaar Malay (Khin Khin Aye 2013)
   *Dia beli itu buku **kasi** dia punya anak ah.*
   3SG buy DEM book give 3SG POSS child PCL
   'She bought the book for her child.'

Value 2 (**serial 'give' in second position introducing recipient or beneficiary**) occurs in four Portuguese-based languages, in seven English-based languages, in two French-based languages, and in Negerhollands.

(8) Early Sranan (van den Berg & Bruyn 2013)
 a. *Kaba dem tu sissa senni muffe gi Jesus* [...].
  and PL two sister send word give Jesus
  'And the two sisters sent a message to Jesus [...].'
 b. *Dem sa hoppo dorro gi hem.*
  3PL FUT open door give 3SG
  'They will open the door for him.'

(9) Negerhollands (van Sluijs 2013)
 a. *Di difi sini am a kan goi mais mi ris gi sini.*
  DET dove 3PL 3SG PST HAB throw corn with rice give 3PL
  'To the doves, he used to throw corn and rice to them.'
 b. *Ju ha fo fin di gi mi.*
  2SG have for find DEM give 1SG
  'You have to find it for me.'

(10) Guyanais (Pfänder 2013)
 a. *Mo achté liv ba to.*
  1SG buy book give 2SG
  'I bought a book for you.'
 b. *Mo ké véyé timoun ba to.*
  1SG FUT look.after child give 2SG
  'I shall look after the child for you.'

Value 3 (**serial 'give' in first position introducing only recipients**) is found in Ambon Malay as well as in the two Southeast Asian Portuguese-based languages and in the three Spanish-based languages of the Philippines.

(11) Ambon Malay (Paauw 2013)
 Lalu antua kasi pulang kembali itu anak.
 then 3SG.FORMAL give go.home return DEM child
 'Then she returned the children to their homes.'

(12) Papiá Kristang (Baxter 2013)
 E ja da mpustá ku yo aké langgiáng.
 3SG PFV give borrow OBJ 1SG DEM push-net
 'He loaned me that push-net.'

(13) Batavia Creole (Maurer 2013b)
 Isti belu da sabe kung ile ki esta teng lugar [...].
 DEM old.man give know OBJ 3SG COMP DEM COP place
 'The old man told him that this was the place [...].'

(14) Cavite Chabacano (Sippola 2013a)
 Ya dale mira ele el retrato conmigo.
 PFV give look 3SG ART picture OBJ.1SG
 'She showed me the picture.'

Note that in the case of value 3, serial 'give' and the second verb form a syntactic unit; this can best be seen in example (14), where the subject *ele* follows *dale mira* 'give look', in other words, 'show'.

3. Distribution

Out of the 32 languages possessing serial 'give', the great majority (26 languages) show this verb in second position, as opposed to six languages which have serial 'give' in first position.

The geographical distribution of the values shows a very clear picture: value 1 and value 2 occur almost exclusively in the Atlantic area, whereas value 3 is restricted to Southeast Asia.

Diachronically, this feature is due to substrate (or adstrate) influence, although from different sources. The fact that values 1 and 2 (serial 'give' in second position) occur in the Atlantic area is without doubt due to West African influence, whereas the presence of the same two values in Southeast Asia (value 1 in Singlish and in Singapore Bazaar Malay, see examples 4 and 7) is most probably due to Sinitic influence.

As for value 3 (serial 'give' in first position), the origin of the construction is Malay and other related languages.

Value 4, no 'give' serials, is represented all over the world, in all the bilingual mixed languages but also in some Atlantic creoles with West African substrate influence such as Belizean Creole, Louisiana Creole, Papiamentu, and Pichi, as well as Sri Lankan Malay, which, although spoken in South India, is partially derived from Malay and might have been expected to exhibit value 3 as Ambon Malay does.

86 'Give' serial verb constructions

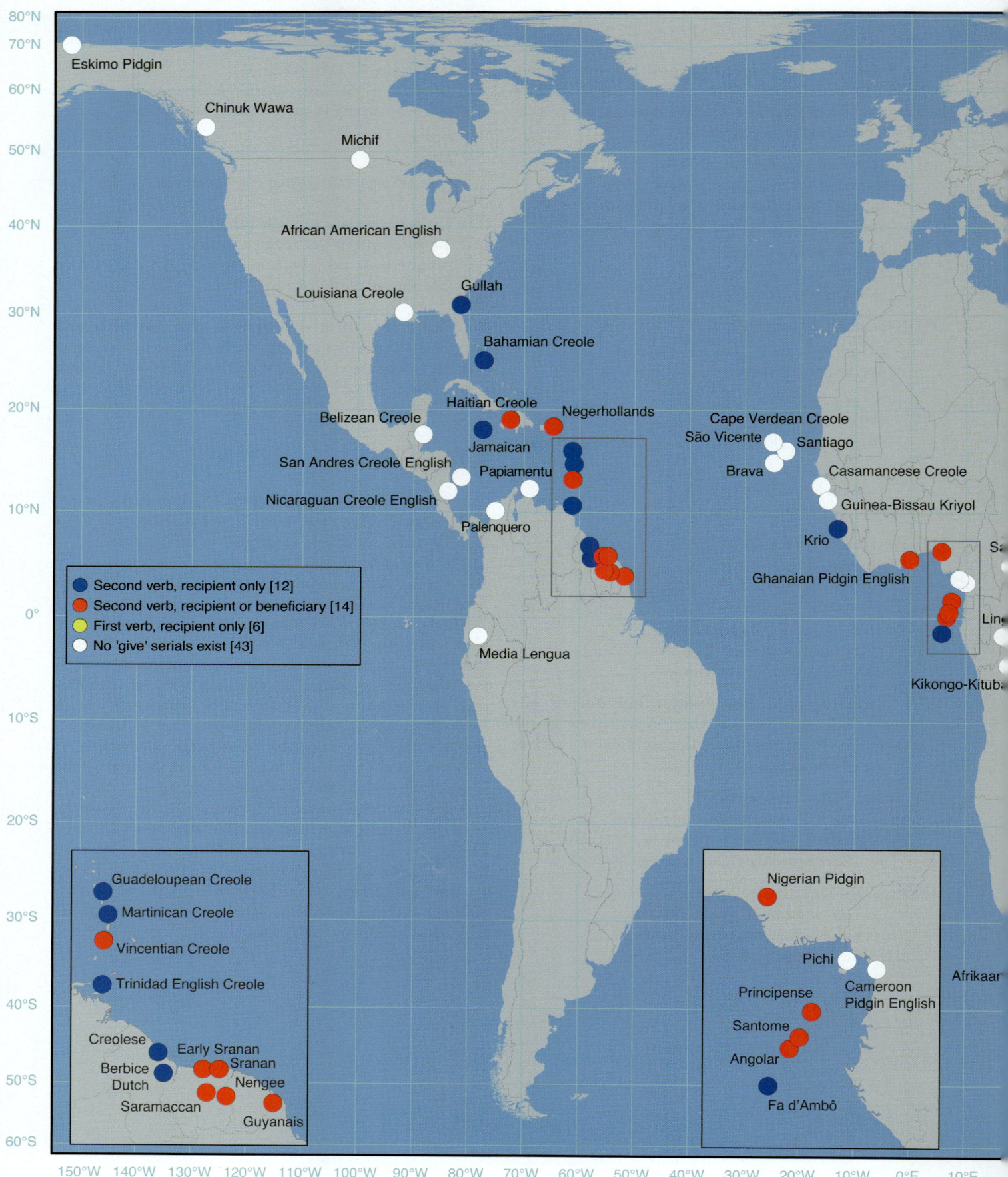

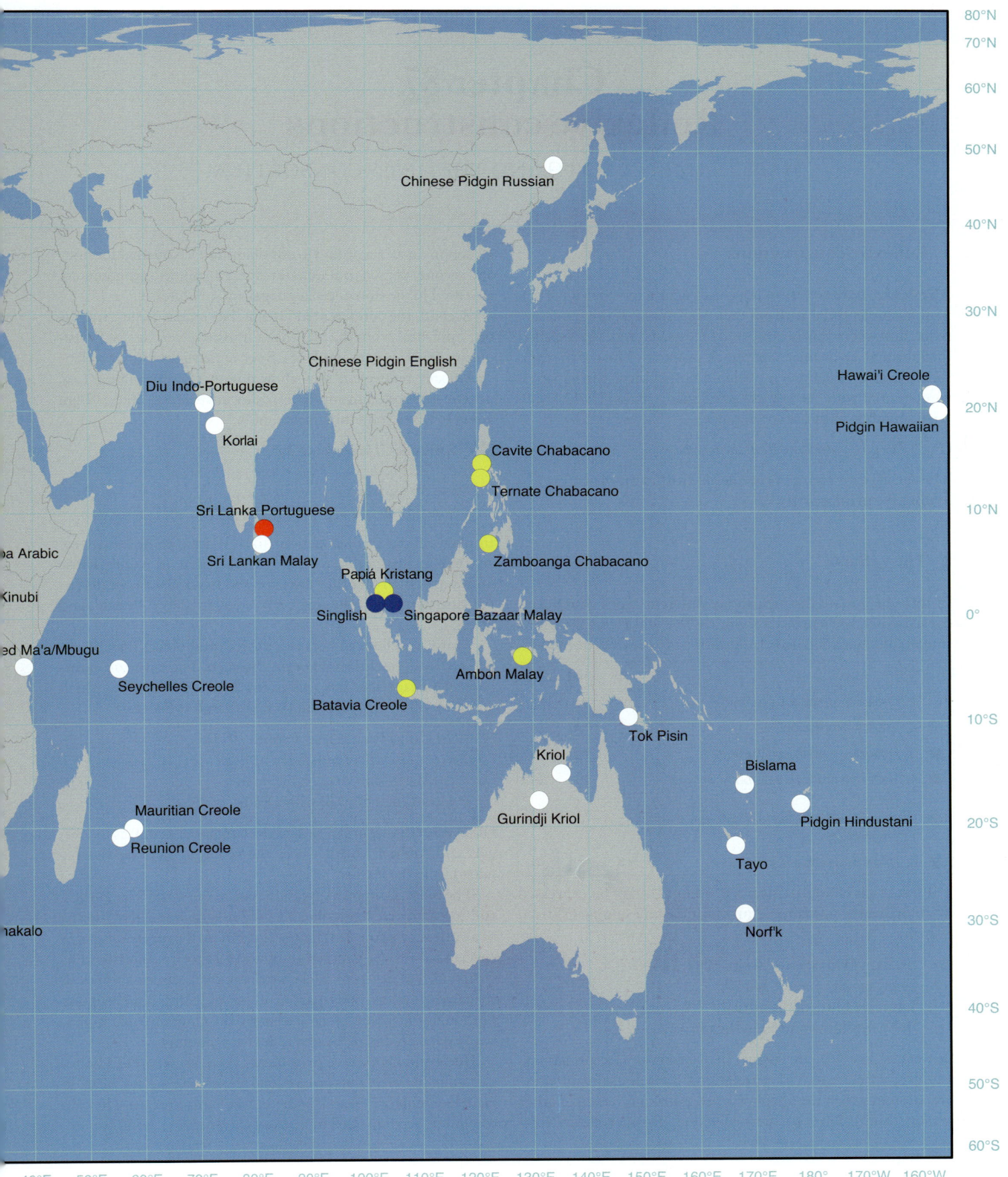

Chapter 87
Reflexive constructions

MARTIN HASPELMATH AND THE *APiCS* CONSORTIUM

1. Reflexive constructions

A **reflexive construction** is a construction in which a participant is coreferential with another participant of the same sentence, and where this is expressed in a special way, that is, other than through an ordinary anaphoric pronoun. Most of the time, this concerns situations in which a non-subject participant is coreferential with the subject participant, as in (1). The subscript numbers indicate coreference.

(1) [*The girl*]$_1$ *saw herself*$_1$ *in the mirror.*

The special expression of coreference within the clause in (1) is a **reflexive pronoun** (*herself*).

2. The values

In this chapter we distinguish six different types of reflexive construction (see Muysken & Smith 1994 and Heine 2005 for a similar, but more detailed classification of reflexives in creoles).

		excl	shrd	all
○	1. Ordinary anaphoric pronoun	4	14	18
○	2. Implicit expression	0	4	4
●	3. Reflexive marking on the verb	5	0	5
●	4. Reflexive pronoun with 'body' or body-part	8	27	35
○	5. Compound reflexive pronoun with emphasizer	17	26	43
●	6. Dedicated reflexive pronoun	4	2	6

First, a coreferential situation as in (1) may be expressed by an **ordinary anaphoric pronoun**, as in example (2) from Sranan.

(2) Sranan (Muysken & Smith 1994: 284)
John$_1$ *syi en*$_{2/1}$ *ini a spikri.*
John see him in the mirror
'John saw him/himself in the mirror.'

Sentences like (2) are vague between two interpretations: a subject-coreferential interpretation ('himself'), and an interpretation in which the anaphoric pronoun *en* refers to another person ('him'). Thus, such constructions are not reflexive constructions at all according to our definition. (Note that for first- and second-person pronouns, ordinary anaphoric pronouns are also used in the Romance languages and in Dutch.)

Second, the coreferential interpretation may be left **implicit**, inferrable from the fact that a transitive verb is used without an object, as in example (3). Such constructions may well be specifically reflexive if they allow no other interpretation (e.g. no non-reflexive interpretation with unspecified object 'I am going to warm something/someone').

(3) Santome (Hagemeijer 2013)
N ga ba kenta.
1SG IPFV go warm
'I am going to warm myself.'

Implicit reflexive constructions like (3) seem to be mostly restricted to "naturally reflexive" verbs, that is, verbs whose meaning is such that they are expected to occur in a coreferential situation (e.g. grooming verbs such as 'shave', 'wash', and 'dress').

Third, coreference between subject and object may be expressed by a **special marker on the verb**. The only European-based language that has this is Sri Lanka Portuguese, which seems to follow a Tamil model (cf. the Tamil suffix *-koḷ*).

(4) Sri Lanka Portuguese (Smith 2013)
eli ja-cucaa-taam faaka vɔɔnda
3SG.M PST-stab-REFL knife with
'He stabbed himself with a knife.'

Otherwise this occurs in two mixed languages as well as in Lingala and Ambon Malay, where the reflexive marking was retained from the lexifier.

The most common expression type in the world's languages, and in particular in creole and pidgin languages, is by means of a **reflexive pronoun**, that is, a referential expression that is specialized for the expression of coreference in reflexive constructions (values 4–6). Here we distinguish three subtypes of reflexive pronoun: body-part expressions, compound reflexive pronouns consisting of an anaphoric pronoun and an emphasizing particle, and dedicated reflexive pronouns.

Body-part reflexive pronouns (value 4) consist of a body-part noun (possibly plus pronominal possessor), such as 'head' in Haitian Creole (ex. 5) and 'body' in Fa d'Ambô (ex. 6). They are commonly accompanied by a possessive pronoun, as in Haitian.

(5) Haitian Creole (Fattier 2013)
*Li tiye **tèt li**.*
3SG kill head POSS.3SG
'He killed himself.' (lit. 'He killed his head.')

(6) Fa d'Ambô (Post 2013)
*Yabeza poxodul bi ska laba **ogé poto-se**.*
before people ANT PROG wash body lake-DEM
'Formerly people washed (themselves) in this lake.'

Such body-part reflexives are often ambiguous in that they can still be used in their original body-part sense. Thus, Haitian Creole *Li wè tèt li* [3SG see head 3SG.POSS] can mean either 'She saw herself' or 'She saw her head' (Déchaine & Manfredi 1994: 205).

Compound reflexive pronouns (personal pronoun plus emphasizer, value 5) are very common in the *APiCS* languages. The **emphasizer** is usually an element going back to an intensifier in the lexifier (see Chapter 88), such as *self* in English-based creoles and *mesmo* in Portuguese-based creoles.

(7) Jamaican (Farquharson 2013)
*A chuu bikaazn se unu hiet **unuself**.*
FOC through because COMP 2PL hate 2PL.REFL
'It's because you all hate yourselves.'

(8) Principense (Maurer 2013c)
*M mendu **ami mesu**.*
1SG fear 1SG self
'I am afraid of myself.'

Dedicated reflexive pronouns (value 6) are simple pronouns that do not have any other use apart from the reflexive use. Well-known examples are Spanish *se*, French *se*, and German *sich*. In the *APiCS* languages this type is rare, but an example is provided by Gurindji Kriol (reflexive pronoun *mijelp*):

(9) Gurindji Kriol (Meakins 2013)
*dat karu bin karan **mijelp***
the child PST scratch REFL
'The child scratched himself.'

Note that *mijelp* derives from Kriol (and ultimately from English *myself*), but it is synchronically not analysable.

3. Some issues of classification

One important issue in assigning the *APiCS* languages to the six types is that the expression of coreference may be different for different verbs.

Thus, in some languages the body-part reflexives are used primarily with concrete verbs where it is indeed the body or a body-part that is affected. For example, in Papiamentu verbs of physical action may use the body-part reflexive *kurpa* (cf. Spanish *cuerpo* 'body'), as in (10).

(10) Papiamentu (Muysken & Smith 1994: 286)
*El a hoga **su kurpa** na lama.*
he PST drown his body in sea
'He has drowned himself in the sea.'

Here the alternative compound reflexive (*su mes* [his self]) is also possible. But with mental verbs, *kurpa* is impossible, and only *su mes* is allowed (*M'a ekiboká mi mes* 'I confused myself, I made a mistake'). In a number of English-based creoles, a 'head' reflexive is used, but only with a restricted number of verbs, in a fairly idiomatic interpretation (e.g. Vincentian Creole *mi naa bada mi brein* 'I am not worrying', lit. 'I am not bothering my brain', Prescod 2013).

As noted above, the implicit construction is used primarily with grooming verbs. These often behave differently from other verbs with respect to the expression of coreference (Haiman 1983, Kemmer 1993), and the *APiCS* editors therefore tried to exclude them from consideration. This was not always successful, also because in spontaneous language use such verbs probably account for the majority of coreferential examples (Haspelmath 2008a). The ordinary anaphoric pronoun strategy (value 1), too, is restricted to particular verbs in a number of languages (see Corne 1988, 1989, Kriegel 1996, 2000 for Mauritian Creole, Muysken 1993 for Papiamentu).

4. Distribution of the types

The body-part reflexives and the compound reflexives are clearly the major types, and both are about equally common in our languages. There are also quite a few languages that use both of these types. Body-part reflexives are particularly common in Atlantic creoles, and there seems to be no question that their use is due to the influence from African substrate languages (e.g. Carden 1993, Muysken & Smith 1994: 279–82, Lefebvre 1998: 169–71, Parkvall 2000: §4.1; cf. Schladt 2000).

Compound reflexive pronouns of the type *himself*, *lui-même*, *ele mesmo* could be retentions from the lexifier languages. However, in the Romance languages these forms are not the ordinary reflexive pronouns, but rather intensifier forms which have become reflexive pronouns in the creoles (cf. Chapter 88). In English-based creoles, the compound reflexives cannot be simple retentions when the forms of the pronouns do not match (as in Sranan *wi-srefi* 'ourselves', *unu-srefi* 'yourselves'). Such cases must be novel creations or analogical remodellings.

The use of ordinary anaphoric pronouns has sometimes been thought to be an extremely idiosyncratic feature of some pidgin and creole languages (Carden & Stewart 1988). It is not found in European and African languages, but it is quite widespread in the Austronesian languages, and it apparently occurs in many other languages throughout the world.

87 Reflexive constructions

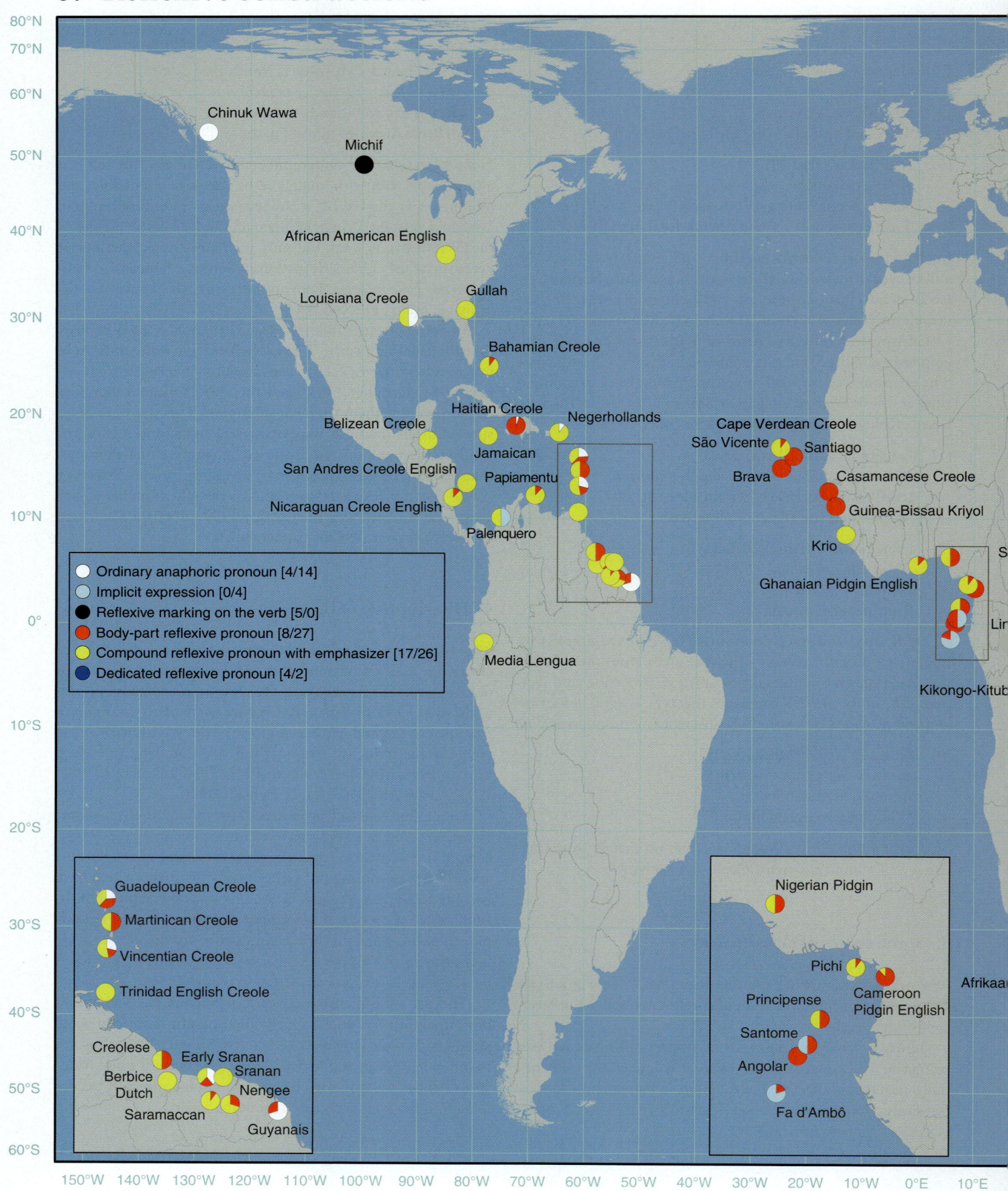

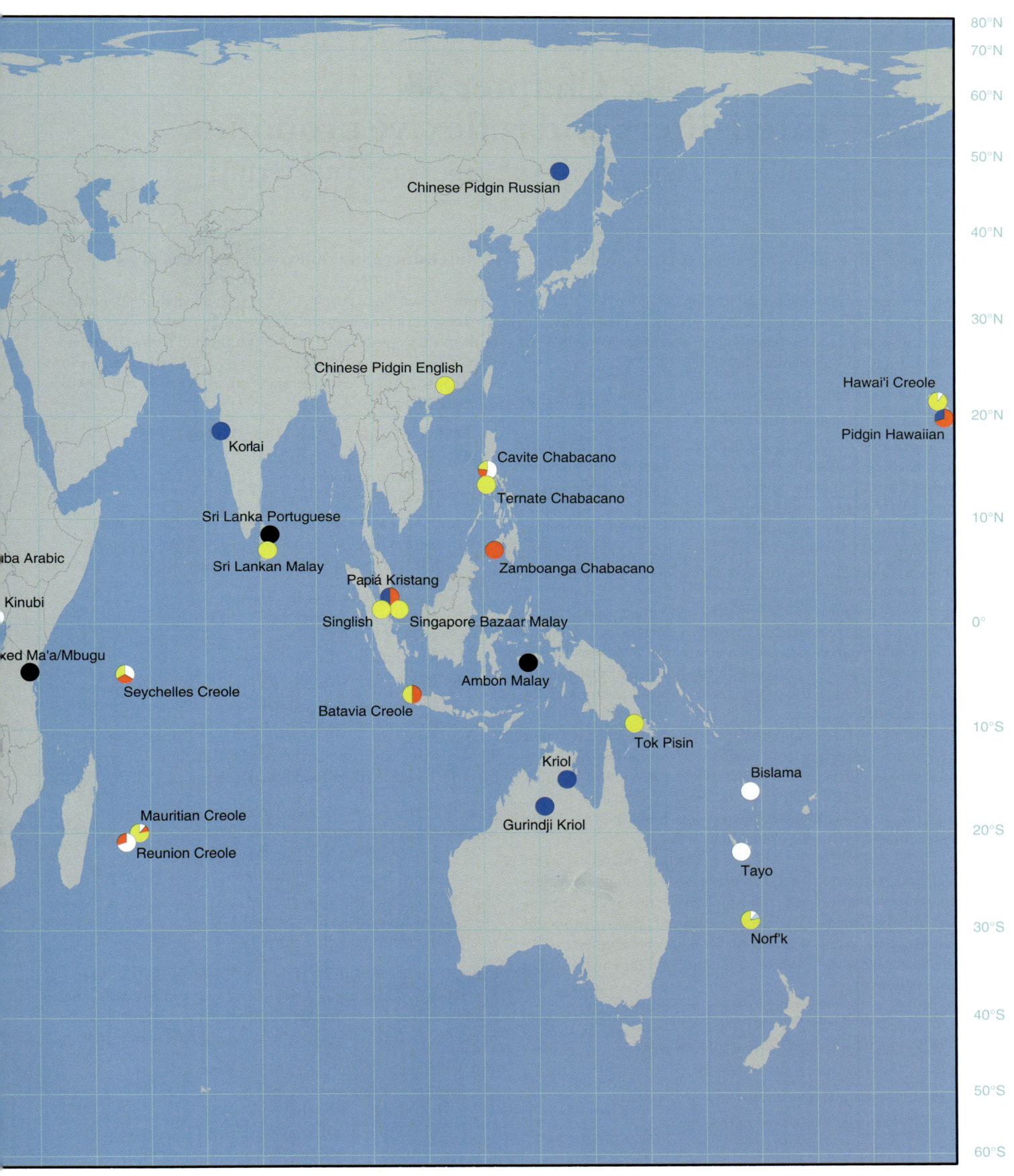

Chapter 88
Intensifiers and reflexive pronouns

MARTIN HASPELMATH AND THE *APiCS* CONSORTIUM

1. Intensifiers and how they give rise to reflexives

An **intensifier** is defined here as a focusing particle that singles out an entity as playing a central role or as being involved in an event without the participation of others (see König & Gast 2006). Typical English examples are (1) and (2).

(1) *The audience waited until the chairman **himself** spoke.*
(2) *I managed to solve the problem **myself**.*

These two uses of *-self* in English are different (e.g. in that the first is adnominal while the second is adverbal), but they are lumped together for the purposes of this chapter, which is based on the *WALS* chapter by König et al. (2005).

In quite a few languages around the world, intensifiers are expressed identically (or very similarly) to **reflexive pronouns**, and this seems to happen mostly by a change from (personal pronoun plus) intensifier to reflexive pronoun. A sentence such as *He saw himself*, where *himself* now simply signals coreference, derives from an earlier structure *He saw him self*, where it indicated focused status with a central role ('He saw the person himself', i.e. the person with the most central status, i.e. the same referent as the subject) (see König & Siemund 2000, Keenan 2003).

Within the European languages, intensifier–reflexive coexpression is characteristic of English, whereas other languages mostly have different (and older) reflexive pronouns. Such reflexive vs. intensifier contrasts are found, for instance, in German *sich* vs. *selbst*, Russian *sebja* vs. *sam*, Spanish *se* vs. *mismo*, Portuguese *se* vs. *mesmo*, French *se* vs. *même*.

In this chapter, we ask whether intensifiers and reflexives are identical or differentiated. If there is more than one intensifier and/or more than one reflexive pronoun, there may also be overlap. Finally, some languages have no special reflexive pronouns but use their ordinary anaphoric pronouns for coreference. In these languages, the question of identity or differentiation does not really arise.

○	1. Intensifiers and reflexives are identical	27
○	2. Intensifiers and reflexives are differentiated	24
○	3. Intensifiers and reflexives overlap	12
●	4. Identical and differentiated	1
○	5. No special reflexive pronouns exist	6

2. Intensifiers and reflexives are identical

Twenty-seven languages are like English in that they show identity between intensifiers and reflexives. Not surprisingly, most of them are English-based, and in almost all of them, the intensifier/reflexive is derived from English *self*. (In all examples in this chapter, the (a) sentences show intensifier uses, and the (b) sentences, reflexive uses.)

(3) Chinese Pidgin English (Li & Matthews 2013)
   a. *Myself wonshi looksee!*
      1SG.REFL want look.see
      'I want to see it for myself!'
   b. *He too much sorry inside, and have killum **he-self**.*
      3SG too much sorry inside and PFV kill 3SG-REFL
      'He felt very sad and killed himself.'

(4) Saramaccan (Aboh et al. 2013)
   a. *Hén seei bì dú hén.*
      3SG self TNS do 3SG
      'He himself did it.'
   b. *Hén a náki hén seéi tu.*
      and.then 3SG hit 3SG self also
      'And then he hit himself too.'

The only English-based language where the intensifier/reflexive is not based on *self* is Tok Pisin, which has *yet*:

(5) Tok Pisin (Smith & Siegel 2013)
   a. *Em **yet** em go hant.*
      3SG FOC 3SG go hunt
      'He himself went hunting.'
   b. *Em go na em kilim em **yet**.*
      3SG go and 3SG kill 3SG REFL
      'He went and killed himself.'

Reflexive–intensifier identity is also found in the Caribbean Spanish-based languages Palenquero and Papiamentu. The form is derived from Spanish *mismo*, which was originally only an intensifier, but has become the marker of reflexives as well:

(6) Palenquero (Schwegler 2013)
   a. *¡Ele **memo** ta-ba aí!*
      he/she self be-PROG there
      'He/she himself/herself was there.'

b. *Ele ta miná ele-memo.*
   he/she PROG look he-self
   'He/she is looking at himself/herself.'

In English, intensifiers and reflexives are literally identical, as the intensifiers include the personal pronouns (*my+self*, *him+self*, etc.). In some of our languages, the reflexive pronoun consists of pronoun + intensifier, but we counted this as identity, too. Some examples:

(7)   Intensifier   Reflexive pronoun
    Creolese   *self*   *ii-self*
    Nengee   *seefi*   *en seefi*
    Mauritian Creole *mem*   *li-mem*

3. Intensifiers and reflexives are differentiated

In twenty-four languages, intensifiers and reflexive pronouns are **formally differentiated**. Three examples of this type are given below.

(8) Guinea-Bissau Kriyol (Intumbo et al. 2013)
  a. *Djon propi korta pon.*
     John self cut bread
     'John himself cut the bread.'
  b. *I lanha si kabesa.*
     3SG cut 3SG head
     'He cut himself.'

(9) Haitian Creole (Fattier 2013)
  a. *Li kapab fè sa li menm.*
     3SG can do DEM he himself
     'He/she can do that him/herself.'
  b. *M ap gade kò mwen.*
     1SG PROG look body POSS.1SG
     'I look at myself.'

(10) Cameroon Pidgin English (Schröder 2013)
  a. *Darekto yi sef-sef tek we go pati.*
     director 3SG.SBJ self-self take 1PL.SBJ go party
     'The director himself took us to the party.'
  b. *Mary si im bodi fo lookin-glas.*
     Mary see 3SG.POSS body for mirror
     'Mary saw herself in the mirror.'

In these examples, the intensifiers are inherited from the lexifier, while the reflexive pronoun is a new creation on the basis of a body(-part) noun (see Chapter 87 on reflexive constructions). This seems to be typical: intensifiers tend to be older and more resistant to change than reflexive pronouns.

In other languages (e.g. Ambon Malay, Lingala, Michif, Mixed Ma'a/Mbugu), affixal markers are used as reflexive pronouns, and these are never identical to intensifiers. The old distinction between *se* and *même/mesmo/mismo* (see §1) has not survived in any of the Romance-based languages.

4. Intensifiers and reflexives overlap

In some languages, there are two different expressions, and one of them can be used in both ways, while the other is used only in one way. In Ghanaian Pidgin English, for example, *sɛf* ('self') can be used as intensifier or reflexive, while *bɔdi* ('body') is only a reflexive pronoun. Similarly, in Principense, *mesu* ('self') can be used as intensifier or reflexive, while *igbê* ('body') is only a reflexive pronoun. On the other hand, in Nicaraguan Creole English, *ihnself* (etc.) can be used as intensifier or reflexive, while *wan* ('one') can only be used as an intensifier (*mi wan* 'myself').

5. Identical and differentiated

In Cape Verdean Creole of São Vicente, we find both identity and differentiation. This language has four relevant forms: *prop* and *mesmu* ('self') are used only as intensifiers, while *kabésa* ('head') is used only as a reflexive pronoun, giving us differentiation. The fourth form, *mes*, is used both as intensifier and as reflexive, yielding identity.

(11) Cape Verdean Creole of São Vicente (Swolkien 2013)
  a. *Ma kulpód é nos mesmu.*
     but guilty COP.PST 1PL self
     'But we ourselves were guilty.'
  b. *El matá (se) kabésa.*
     3SG kill (POSS.3SG) head
     'He killed himself.'
  c. *El oiá el mes na spei. El mes brí pórta.*
     3SG see 3SG self in mirror 3SG self opened door
     'He saw himself in the mirror. He himself opened the door.'

6. No special reflexive pronouns exist

The six languages Bislama, Chinuk Wawa, Fanakalo, Juba Arabic, Kinubi, and Tayo lack special reflexive pronouns and generally express coreference by their ordinary anaphoric pronouns (see Chapter 87). In these languages, the issue of identity or differentiation thus does not arise (as intensifiers are presumably always distinct from the ordinary anaphoric pronouns).

88 Intensifiers and reflexive pronouns

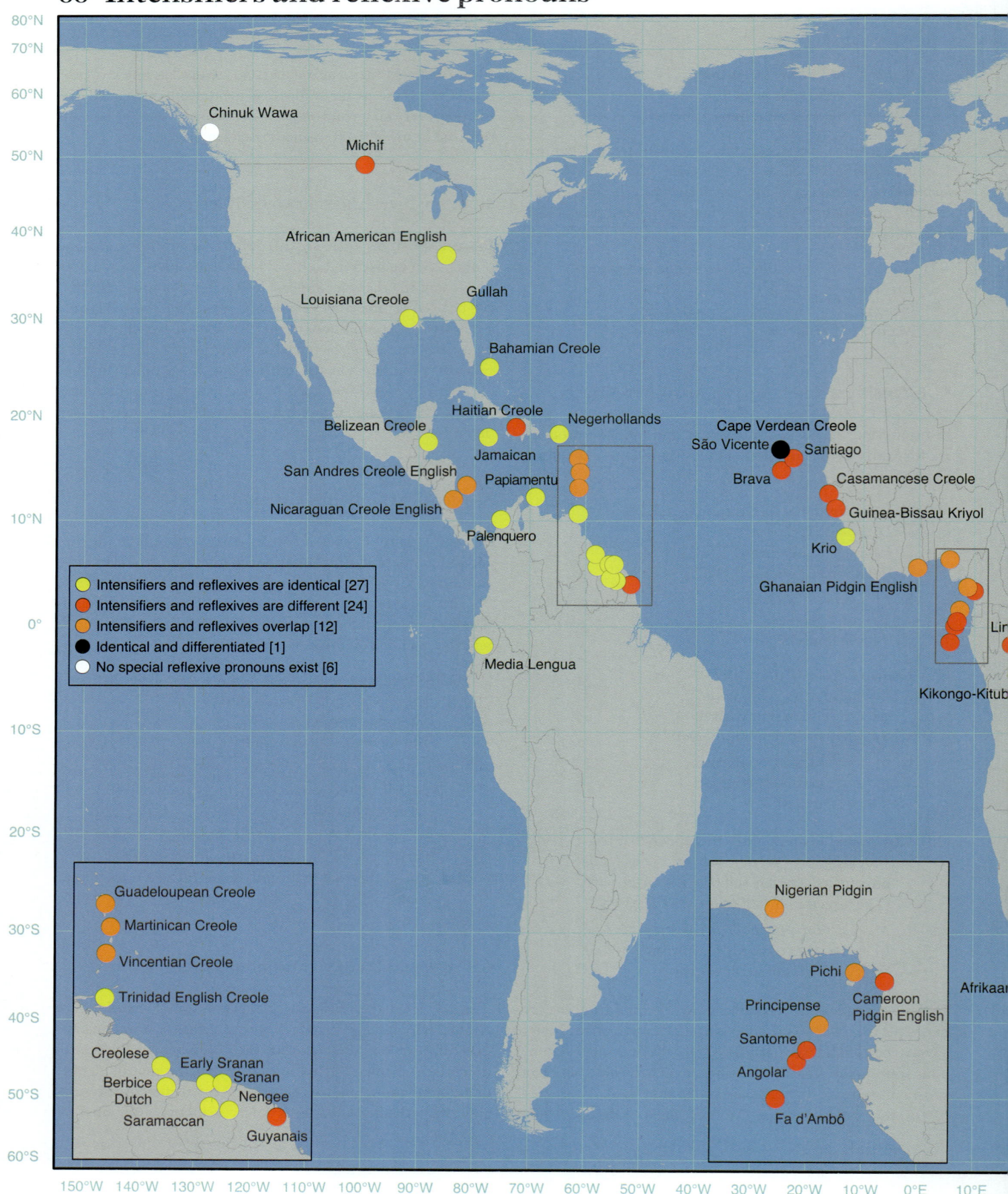

352

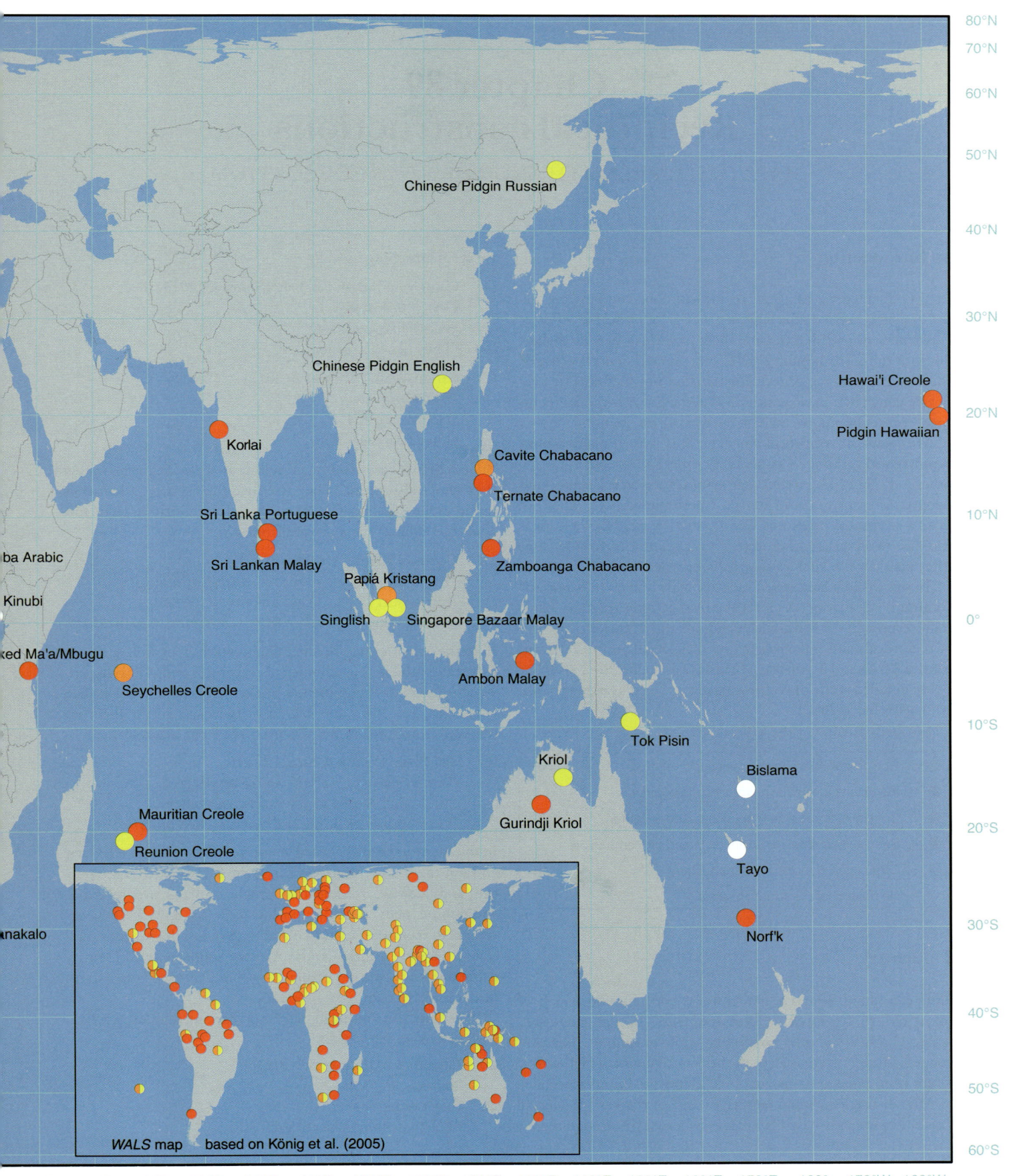

Chapter 89
Reciprocal constructions

MARTIN HASPELMATH AND THE *APiCS* CONSORTIUM

1. Introduction

In this chapter we ask how reciprocal constructions are expressed, and in particular whether they are identical to reflexive constructions or different from them (see Maslova & Nedjalkov 2005 for the corresponding *WALS* chapter). In most languages, there is a special reciprocal construction not identical to a reflexive construction, so within the languages with special reciprocal constructions, we make some further distinctions.

We focus on reciprocal constructions with transitive non-symmetrical verbs such as 'see' ('The girl and the boy saw each other'). It should be noted that symmetrical verbs sometimes behave differently, as in English, where the verb *kiss* does not need a reciprocal pronoun (*The boy and the girl kissed*). This is the case in some creoles too (e.g. Guadeloupean Creole *yo bo* 'they kissed'), but such cases are disregarded here.

In the world's languages, identity with reflexives is not uncommon, but distinct reciprocal constructions are more common, especially in Eurasia. Outside of the Americas, identity of reciprocals and reflexives is found especially in western and central Africa and in Australia (Maslova & Nedjalkov 2005). For a very detailed study of reciprocals in the world's languages, see Nedjalkov (ed.) (2007).

We distinguish six different values:

○	1. Reciprocal construction identical to reflexive	10
●	2. Identical and special reciprocal construction	9
○	3. Special reciprocal construction based on 'other'	25
○	4. Special reciprocal construction based on 'companion'	7
○	5. Other special reciprocal construction	15
○	6. No reciprocal construction exists	3

2. Identity

Nineteen languages have a reciprocal construction which is **identical to a reflexive construction**. In ten languages (value 1) this is the only possibility, while in nine further languages (value 2) there is also another construction which is different from reflexive constructions. Identity is found especially in African English-based languages and in the very basilectal Caribbean English-based languages, where *self* is used in reciprocal constructions as well:

(1) Cameroon Pidgin English (Schröder 2013)
Dem laik dem-sef.
3PL.SBJ like 3PL-REFL
'They like each other.'

(2) Saramaccan (Aboh et al. 2013)
De lobi de seei.
3PL love 3PL self
'They love each other.'

Such sentences are usually ambiguous in these languages in that they could also mean 'They like/love themselves'. Identity is found in the Australian languages Kriol and Gurindji Kriol too, again based on a form deriving from *self*:

(3) Gurindji Kriol (Meakins 2013)
"Watja watja" jei bin tok mijelp nganta.
hurry hurry 3PL.SBJ PST talk RECP DOUBT
'"Hurry hurry", I reckon they were saying to each other.'

Both the Atlantic and the Australian patterns may well be due to substrate influence, as identity of reciprocal and reflexive constructions occurs prominently in West African and Australian languages. Tok Pisin, too, has identity, based on the form *yet* (derived from English *yet*, also used as a focus marker):

(4) Tok Pisin (Smith & Siegel 2013)
Pikinini bik-pla na ol maret-im ol yet.
child big-MOD and 3PL marry-TR 3PL FOC
'The children grew big and married each other.'

In the Atlantic English-based languages, only the *self* reflexives, and not the 'body' reflexives can normally be used as reciprocals, and likewise, in Mauritian Creole, only the *mem* reflexive, and not the 'body' reflexive (with *so lekor* 'his body') can be extended to reciprocal use (see Chapter 87 on reflexive constructions). However, there is one African language with identity using the 'body' word: in Sango, *tere* 'body' is used both as a reflexive and as a reciprocal pronoun.

Palenquero is unique in that zero-marking has both a reflexive and a reciprocal sense:

(5) Palenquero (Schwegler 2013)
Ané ndo a besá.
they two PST kiss
'The two of them kissed each other.'

3. Special reciprocal constructions

Most of the *APiCS* languages have a special reciprocal construction. Frequently, this involves **a reciprocal pronoun deriving from or including the element 'other'** (value 3). The English-based varieties that are closer to English usually have a form deriving from *one another* (or occasionally *each other*), and the French-based varieties that are closer to French have a form deriving from French *l'un l'autre* [the.one the.other]. Some Portuguese-derived languages have a form such as Guinea-Bissau Kriyol *un utru* [one other], Casamancese Creole *ɲutur* (< *uɲ utru*).

But there are also 'other'-based forms that are less close to the lexifiers and that are clearly innovative with respect to them. In the Gulf of Guinea creoles, 'other' by itself may be used as in Santome, or 'other' is used both in subject position and in object position, as in Principense (similarly in Batavia Creole):

(6) Santome (Hagemeijer 2013)
 Ũa ska mat' ôtlô.
 one PROG kill other
 'They are killing each other.'

(7) Principense (Maurer 2013c)
 Ôtô sa mêê mata ôtô.
 other PROG want kill other
 'They wanted to kill each other.'

'Other' by itself, as in Santome, is also found in Caribbean French-based creoles (as well as in Papiamentu):

(8) Martinican Creole (Colot & Ludwig 2013b)
 Yonn ka gadé lot.
 one PROG look other
 'They are looking at each other.'

This category also includes Afrikaans *mekaar*, derived from Dutch *malk-ander* 'each other'.

Innovative reciprocal pronouns may also be **derived from a 'companion' word** (value 4), as in Cape Verdean Creole and in some French-based languages:

(9) Cape Verdean Creole of Brava (Baptista 2013)
 Nu ta sai, ta spia kunpanheru, pa kaminhu.
 we HAB go.out HAB look companion on way
 'We would go out, looking at each other on the way.'

(10) Guyanais (Pfänder 2013)
 yé konnèt yé kompannyen
 they know them friend
 'They know each other.'

(11) Seychelles Creole (Michaelis & Rosalie 2013)
 Nou pa zwenn kanmarad.
 1PL NEG meet comrade
 'We don't meet each other.'

In addition, the special form *matii* in Creolese (which was also borrowed into Berbice Dutch as *mati*) originally meant 'friend, companion':

(12) Creolese (Devonish & Thompson 2013)
 dem hog op matii
 3PL hug up friend
 'They hugged up each other.'

In addition, various **other special reciprocal markers** occur in our languages (value 5):

— reciprocal affixes derived from Bantu (in Lingala, Kikongo-Kituba and Mixed Ma'a/Mbugu), from Philippine languages (in some of the Chabacano varieties), from Malay (in Ambon Malay), from Quechua (in Media Lengua) and from Cree (in Michif);
— the reduplicated numeral 'two' in Papiá Kristang (*dos dos*), and the reduplicated numeral 'one' in Singapore Bazaar Malay (*satu satu*):

(13) Papiá Kristang (Baxter 2013)
 Pedru ku Maria dos dos busidu
 Pedru COM Maria two~two hate
 'Pedru and Maria hate each other.'

— the reciprocal marker *badum* in Juba Arabic and Kinubi (inherited from Arabic *baʕdu-hum* 'beside them, together');
— the auxiliary *hugá* 'play' in Ternate Chabacano:

(14) Ternate Chabacano (Sippola 2013b)
 Ta hugá keré lótro dos.
 IPFV play.RECP love 3PL two
 'The two of them love each other.' (lit. 'The two of them play loving.')

4. Non-existence

Some languages **simply lack a special reciprocal form or construction** (value 6) and use an "iconic" mode of rendering mutual situations: the two situations are expressed by two clauses with the participants expressed twice.

(15) Bislama (Meyerhoff 2013)
 yu yu save mi, mi mi save yu
 2SG 2SG know 1SG 1SG 1SG know 2SG
 'You know me and I know you.' (= 'We know each other.')

89 Reciprocal constructions

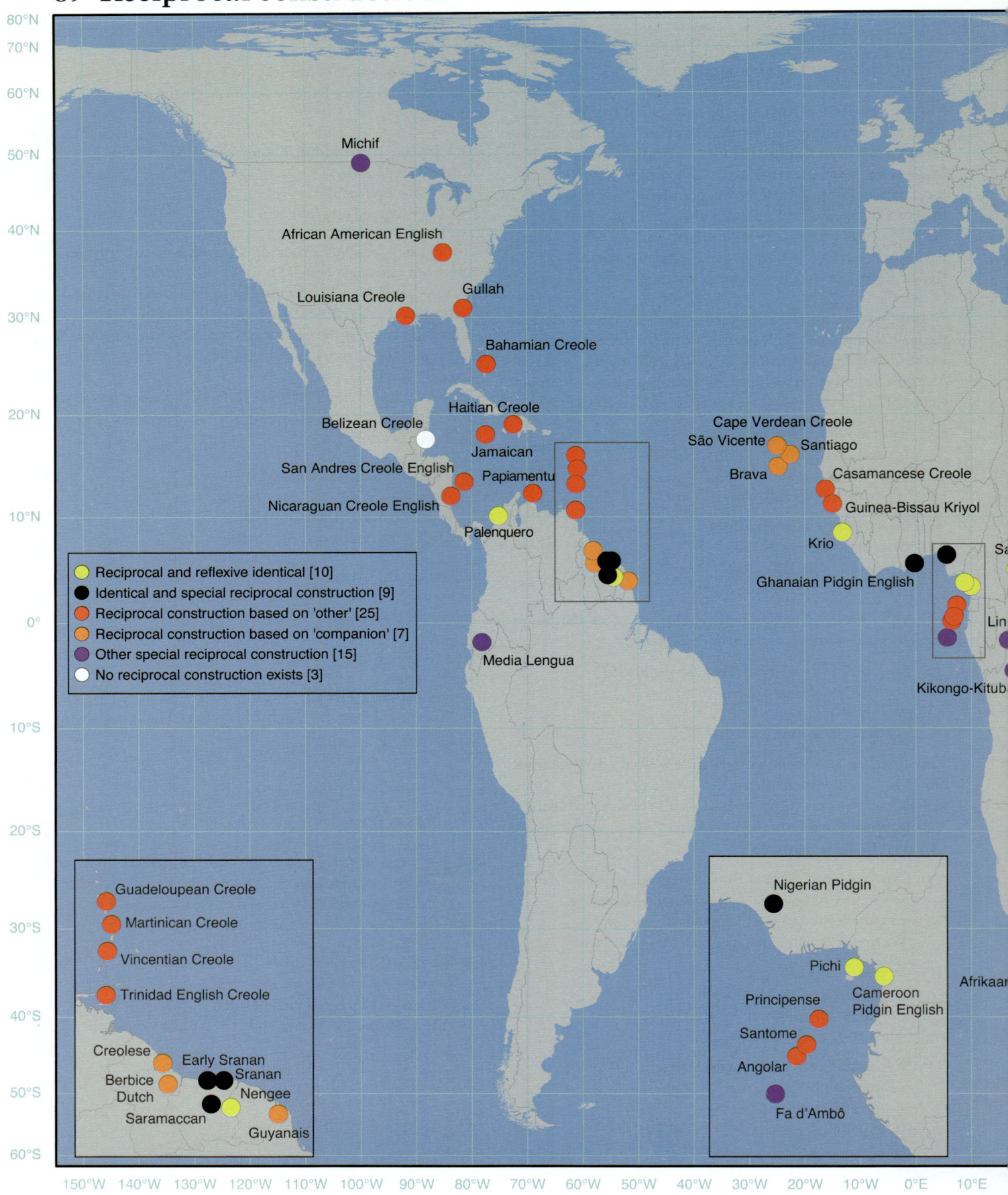

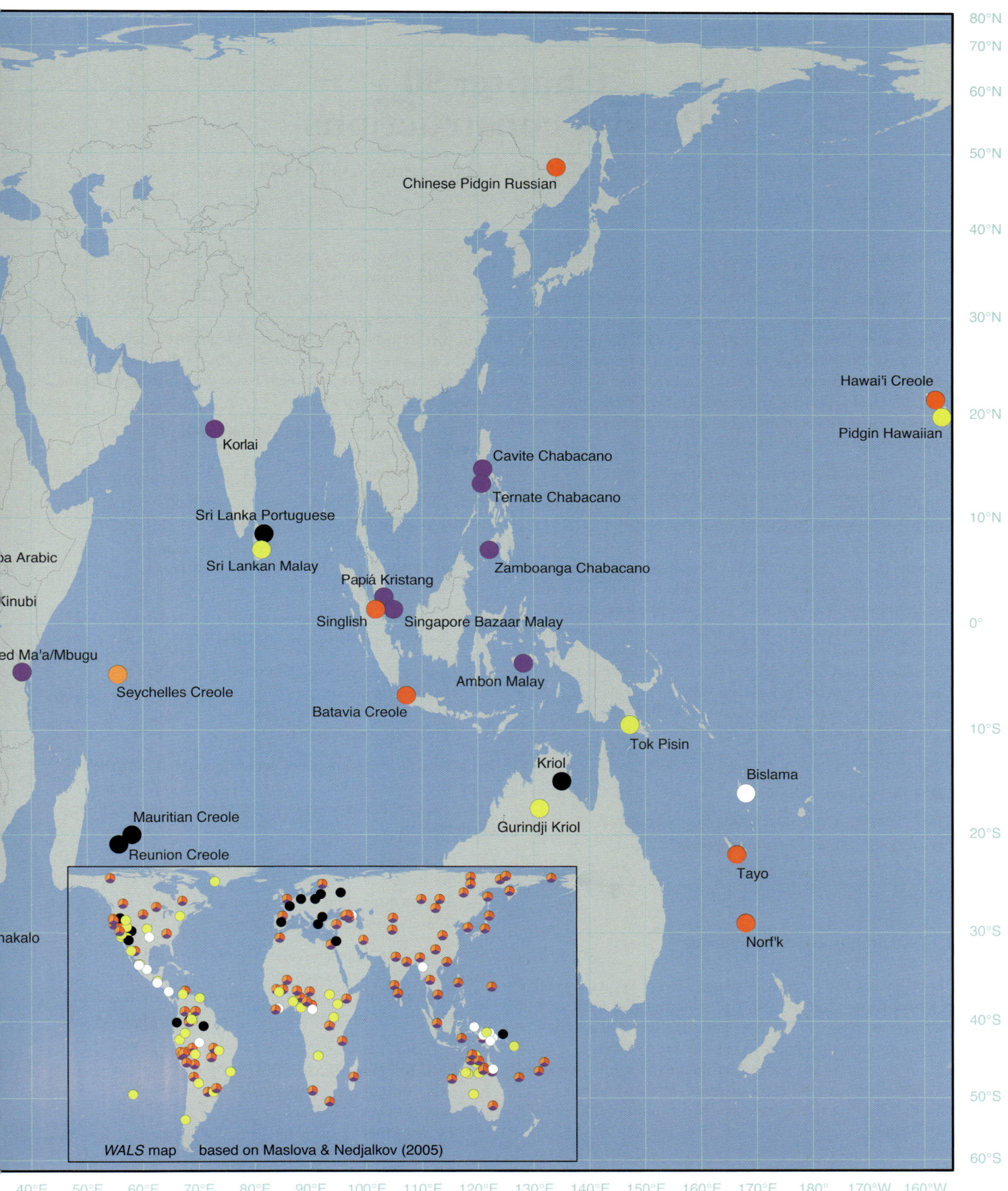

Chapter 90
Passive constructions

MARTIN HASPELMATH AND THE *APiCS* CONSORTIUM

1. Introduction

A passive construction is a special construction with a transitive verb (a verb that normally takes two arguments, an A and a P argument, as explained in Chapter 58) in which the argument that is normally the P is treated like the S in an intransitive clause, while the argument that is normally the A is either omitted or is treated like some oblique argument. An English example of an active (i.e. an ordinary, non-special construction) and a corresponding passive construction is given in (1).

(1) a. *Many people* (A) *have bought this book* (P).
    b. *This book* (S) *has been bought by many people.*

In the following, the P argument will be called "object", and the A and S arguments will be called "subject" for convenience.

In the *WALS* chapter on the passive construction (Siewierska 2005d), there is only a simple binary presence–absence distinction. Somewhat less than half of the world's languages have a passive construction, but in Europe, all languages have one. In the *APiCS* languages, presence of a passive is more common than absence, and to some extent this seems to be due to the influence of the European lexifiers. But the pidgins and creoles are very far from being simple copies of their lexifiers.

We distinguish four different types:

		excl	shrd	all
●	1. Typical passive construction	18	19	37
●	2. Passive without verbal coding	12	17	29
●	3. Other atypical passive construction	4	2	6
○	4. Absence of passive construction	23	0	23

2. Typical passive construction

About half of the *APiCS* languages have a **typical passive construction** (value 1) with the following five features that characterize passives cross-linguistically (Siewierska 2005d):
 (i) it contrasts with another construction, the active;
 (ii) the subject of the active corresponds to a non-obligatory oblique phrase of the passive or is not overtly expressed;
 (iii) the object of the active corresponds to the subject of the passive;
 (iv) the construction is pragmatically restricted in some way relative to the active;
 (v) the construction displays some special verbal (morphological or auxiliary verb) coding.

In the English-based languages, the passive marker is usually the auxiliary *get*; passives with a 'be' verb are rare in our languages; an example is Spanish-based Papiamentu, where the passive can be formed with *ser*.

(2) Trinidad English Creole (Mühleisen 2013)
    Hi get ketch.
    3SG get catch
    'He was caught.'

(3) Papiamentu (Kouwenberg 2013b)
    Nos a ser risibí dor di nos amigu-nan.
    1PL PFV PASS received by of 1PL friend-PL
    'We were received by our friends.'

In some of the Portuguese-based languages, the passive is formed with the passive-participle suffix *-du*:

(4) Guinea-Bissau Kriyol (Intumbo et al. 2013)
    E livru skribi-du pa Djon.
    DEM book write-PASS by Djon
    'This book was written by Djon.'

In the French-based languages, innovative verbs tend to be used as passive markers, such as *trouve* (< French *trouver* 'find') in Louisiana Creole and *ganny* (< French *gagner* 'win, get') in Seychelles Creole.

(5) Louisiana Creole (Neumann-Holzschuh & Klingler 2013)
    Piti-sa-la trouve taye par so popa.
    child-DET-DEM find beat by 3SG.POSS father
    'The child was beaten by his father.'

In the Southeast Asian languages, the passive is often restricted to adversity situations, where the patient is negatively affected by the action. This is also found with the overtly coded passive in Papiá Kristang, which uses the passive auxiliary *toka* ('touch'):

(6) Papiá Kristang (Baxter 2013)
    eli ja toka pegá di churikati
    3SG PFV PASS catch of goblin
    'He was caught by a goblin.'

Such a restriction of a new passive auxiliary is also reported for Mauritian Creole (Baker & Kriegel 2013), where *gany* (< French *gagner* 'win, get') is only used with a few verbs with meanings like 'beat' or 'punish'.

In one *APiCS* language, the Tugu variety of Batavia Creole, a passive marker was borrowed from a substrate or adstrate language (*di-* from Malay):

(7) Batavia Creole, Tugu variety (Maurer 2013b)
 bar   lama ki   dja fai   **di**-bira bar di garu
 earth mud   REL PFV make PASS-get   earth of harrow
 'the muddy ground which has been turned into soil by the harrow'

For several of the languages, it is noted by the contributors that the passive construction is acrolectal, or more typically used in the written language, and often it is noted that it is not frequently used, which probably means that it is less common than in English.

3. Passive without verbal coding

A surprisingly high number of creole languages show a construction that is like the typical passive construction in all respects except (v), that is, it has **no verbal coding** (auxiliary or affixal) (value 2). Such constructions are not common in the world's languages (Haspelmath 1990 even claimed that they do not exist), but they occur widely in *APiCS*, in English-, French-, and Portuguese-based languages, in the Atlantic and Indian Ocean (and often side by side with a typical passive construction):

(8) Saramaccan (Aboh et al. 2013)
 Dí dí gánia kíi, dí onkoóku kó kái.
 then the chicken kill the misfortune come fall
 'At the same time the chicken was killed, misfortune started to happen.'

(9) Guadeloupean Creole (Colot & Ludwig 2013a)
 Chanm-la ja   baléyé.
 room-DEF already sweep.up
 'The room has already been swept up.'

(10) Papiá Kristang (Baxter 2013)
 aké albi ja sunyá
 that tree PFV plant
 'The tree was planted.'

This construction is unusual, and authors have sometimes been reluctant to call it a passive construction, though syntactically it behaves just like other passives (see e.g. LaCharité & Wellington 1999 for Jamaican). It is similar to the phenomenon of ambitransitive verbs in English (e.g. *break*, which can mean 'cause to break' or 'break by itself'), but intransitive counterparts cannot normally be formed from agent-oriented verbs like 'plant' or 'sweep up' (Levin & Rappaport Hovav 1995). Thus, these cases are uncoded passives, not ambitransitives. The origin of these uncoded passives is not clear.

4. Other atypical passive construction

The third value subsumes a number of special constructions that are difficult to generalize over. We classify a construction as an atypical passive if it lacks one or two of the properties of typical passive constructions. For example, Singlish has a construction such as *John give his boss scold* 'John was scolded by his boss', which is clearly calqued on a similar Hokkien Chinese construction, where the active object becomes the subject, and the active subject becomes the object of the passive auxiliary, rather than an oblique-marked phrase. In Michif, there is a special inverse construction (for which Algonquian languages are famous) that must be used when the object is more topical than the subject, for example, when it is a pronoun and the subject is a full NP (as in *The police overtook him*).

5. Absence of passive construction

Many pidgins and creoles lack passives. This is true especially of the languages of the Pacific region, which fits with the worldwide picture in Siewierska (2005d), where the most striking passive-less region is the New Guinea area. Instead of passive constructions, languages often use constructions with a generic third-person-plural form:

(11) Cameroon Pidgin English (Schöder 2013)
 Dem   don kill king.
 3PL.SBJ PFV kill king
 'They killed the king./The king was killed.'

This construction type is well known from European languages, too. Another non-passive type that can be used in some languages is a construction where the subject is simply omitted but the object remains an object, as reported for two of the Chabacano varieties:

(12) Ternate Chabacano (Sippola 2013b)
 Kayá   lang a matá kon éle.
 therefore just PFV kill OBJ him
 'That's why he was killed.'

Since Chabacano has the object-marking preposition *kon*, it is particularly clear here that the object's status is not affected. The cross-linguistic distribution of this construction type (called *desubjective* in Haspelmath 1990) has not been studied yet.

90 Passive constructions

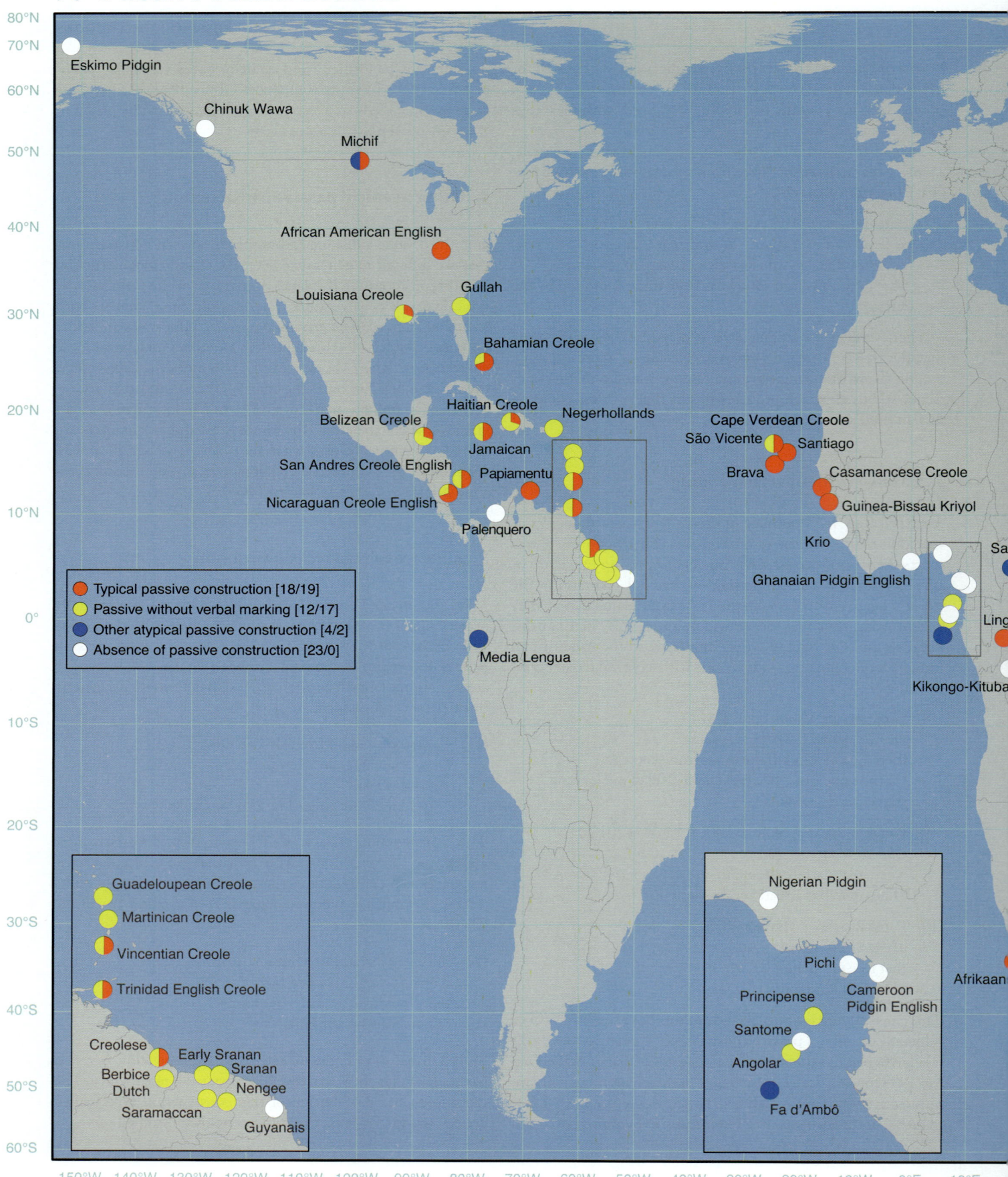

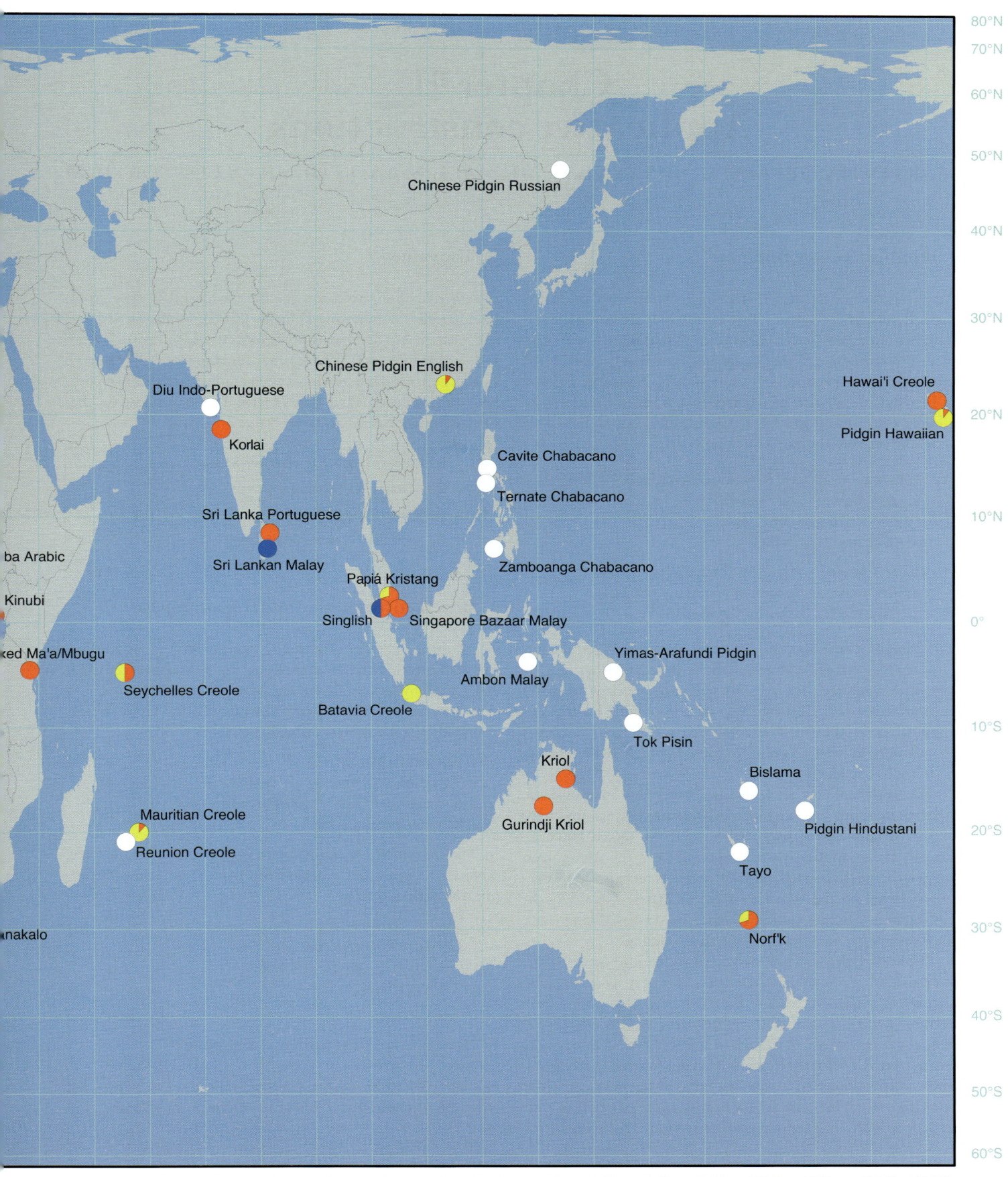

Chapter 91
Applicative constructions

MARTIN HASPELMATH, SUSANNE M. MICHAELIS, AND THE *APiCS* CONSORTIUM

1. Applicative constructions

An applicative construction is a construction with an overtly marked verb and a valency that is different from the corresponding unmarked verb (= base verb) in that there is a P argument ("direct object") that could not be a P argument in the unmarked construction. For example, in Shuswap (spoken in British Columbia), a beneficiary that is coded like the P argument (introduced just by the determiner) can be used only when the verb has the applicative suffix -*xt*:

(1) Shuswap (Salishan; Kiyosawa & Gerdts 2010: 150)
    a. *m-k'úln-s   y   mimx*
        PRF-make-3.SBJ DET basket
        'She made the basket.'

    b. *m-k'úl-xt-s   y   núx̌ʷənx̌ʷ tə   mimx*
        PRF-make-APPL-3.SBJ DET woman   OBL basket
        'She made a basket for the woman.'

The P argument in the derived construction is called the applied P. The erstwhile P argument is coded with an oblique preposition in (1b), but in many languages (including Bantu languages, see below), it can keep its non-oblique coding. For applicatives in the world's languages, see Peterson's (2007) monograph, as well as Polinsky (2005), which is the corresponding *WALS* chapter.

The great majority of *APiCS* languages lack an applicative construction, but four languages with Bantu background have preserved applicatives from Bantu, and the mixed language Michif has an applicative construction from the Algonquian language Cree. In two languages, P status is recognized by person indexing on the verb (pre-stem in Mixed Ma'a/Mbugu, post-stem in Michif), and in the four Bantu-based languages, the P occurs in immediately postverbal position.

Applicative markers are usually considered to be verbal affixes, that is, grammatical markers that are very closely associated with the basic verb stem. But affixal categories often have periphrastic (i.e. non-affixal) counterparts, so Creissels (2010) defines a category of "periphrastic applicatives". The applicative marker is a separate element deriving from the verb 'give'. Such constructions are treated as 'give' serial verb constructions here (see Chapter 86). Applicatives are restricted to constructions with a marker that is never separated from the verb.

2. The values

Benefactive applicatives are the most widespread type cross-linguistically, so following Polinsky (2005), we distinguish between languages that have only benefactive applicatives (values 1–2) and languages that have other functions as well (value 3). In addition, we distinguish between applicatives that can combine only with transitive bases (value 1) and applicatives that can combine with any base verb (value 2).

●	1. Benefactive function and transitive base	2
●	2. Benefactive function and any base	1
●	3. Benefactive and other functions	2
○	4. No applicative construction exists	70

3. Benefactive function and transitive base

The Zulu-based pidgin Fanakalo is reported to have an applicative with transitive bases only. According to Mesthrie (2013), it is not used by less proficient speakers of the pidgin, so it may often be used under the direct influence of Zulu. However, it is also used by some speakers who do not speak Zulu.

(2) Fanakalo (Mesthrie 2013)
    Theng-el-a   mina lo   sinkwa.
    buy-APPL-IMP 1SG DEF.ART bread
    'Buy the bread for me.'

In Michif, which has adopted its verb grammar from Cree, there is an applicative construction from Cree, using the applicative suffix -*amuw*:

(3) Michif (Bakker 2013)
    *George ushipeeh-**amuw**-eew.*
    George write-APPL-3.SBJ.3.OBJ
    'George writes for him.'

4. Benefactive function and any base

In Kikongo-Kituba, the benefactive applicative can be used not only with transitive bases, but also with intransitive bases, as in (4b):

Applicative constructions

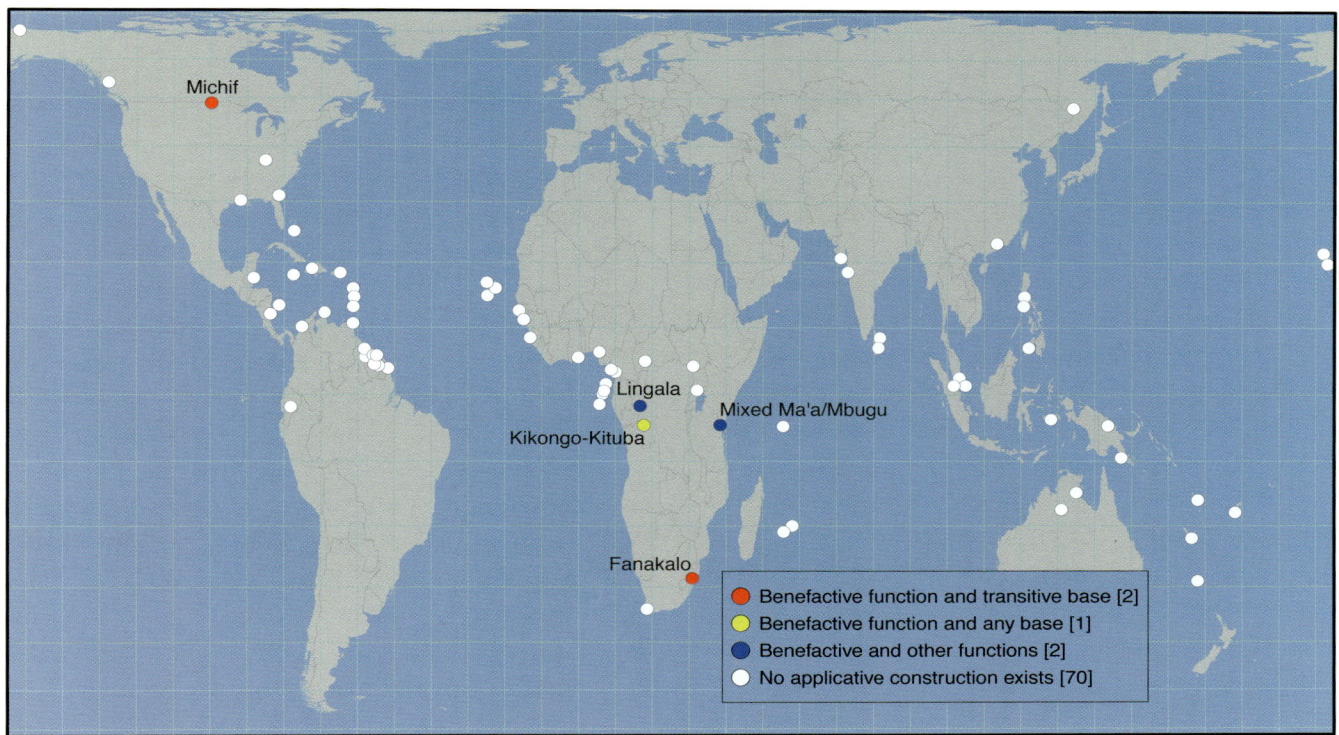

(4) Kikongo-Kituba (Mufwene 2013)
   a. *Sumb-il-a mono mukanda yayi!*
      buy-APPL-IMP me book this
      'Buy me this book!'
   b. *Muntu mene kuf-il-a mono.*
      person PRF die-APPL-INF 1SG
      'The person has died on me.'

However, in (4b) the meaning is malefactive rather than benefactive. This is not so surprising, because languages often use their benefactive construction more generally, allowing also malefactive meanings (so the construction can be said to be more generally "affactive"; see Zúñiga 2011).

5. Benefactive and other functions

In two of the Bantu-based languages, the applicative construction can have other semantic functions in addition to the benefactive function. In Lingala, the suffix *-él* can mark benefactive (5) and locative situations (6) (Meeuwis 2013):

(5) a. *a-pon-ákí elambá*
       3SG-choose-PST cloth
       'He chose a cloth.'
    b. *a-pon-él-ákí ngáí elambá*
       3SG-choose-APPL-PST 1SG cloth
       'He chose a cloth for me.'

(6) a. *a-fánd-ákí*
       3SG-sit-PST
       'He sat down.'
    b. *a-fánd-él-ákí kíti*
       3SG-sit-APPL-PST chair
       'He sat down on a chair.'

Likewise in Mixed Ma'a/Mbugu, the suffix *-ya* can mark benefactive (7) and locative situations (8) (Mous 2013):

(7) *ni-ne-ku-saga-ya mʔo ghó*
    1SG-FUT-OBJ.2SG-send-APPL voice my
    'I'll send you my news.'

(8) *vé-ne-gugulu-ya hé-hospitari*
    2-FUT-run-APPL 16-hospital
    'They'll run to the hospital.'

Mixed Ma'a/Mbugu has preserved the preverbal object indexes (*ku-* in 7) typical of Bantu languages, whereas Fanakalo (2), Kikongo-Kituba (4), and Lingala (5) use postverbal independent pronouns.

In Polinsky's (2005) worldwide sample, this is actually the most widespread type, and languages with only benefactives are less common. Almost all Bantu languages seem to have further applicatives in addition to benefactives, though Cree has only benefactive applicatives.

COMPLEX SENTENCES

Chapter 92
Subject relative clauses

SUSANNE M. MICHAELIS, MARTIN HASPELMATH, AND THE *APiCS* CONSORTIUM

1. Relative clauses

Following Comrie & Kuteva's (2005) *WALS* chapter, this and the following two chapters look at the marking of relative clauses and at the way in which the head's role is indicated inside the relative clause.

As in Chapter 7 (on the order of relative clause and noun), a relative clause is defined as a clause that helps narrow the reference of a noun (the head) and in which the referent of the noun head has a semantic role. (Headless relative clauses are again left aside.)

Relative clauses can be marked as such by a special morpheme that occurs at the beginning (or more rarely at the end) of a relative clause, which we call **relative particle** (as in (1), where the particle *ya* is glossed REL). Alternatively, overt marking may be lacking (**zero**) (as in (2)).

(1) Kikongo-Kituba (Mufwene 2013)
 muntu ya _ kwis-aka
 person [REL _ come-PST]
 'the person who came'

(2) Fanakalo (Mesthrie 2013)
 Mina bona lo muntu yena gula.
 I see DEF.ART man [he be.sick]
 'I see the man who is sick.'

The role of the head inside the relative clause can be indicated by a **gap** (no overt expression) (as in (3)), or by a **resumptive pronoun** (as in (4)). The gap is indicated by an underline (_) in this and the next two chapters.

(3) Guinea-Bissau Kriyol (Intumbo et al. 2013)
 Mindjer ki _ da-n e livru i nha kolega.
 woman [REL _ give-1SG ART book] COP my colleague
 'The woman who gave me the book is my colleague.'

(4) Cameroon Pidgin English (Schröder 2013)
 'man 'we i di 'pas fo 'rot
 man [REL 3SG.SBJ IPFV pass for road]
 'the man who is crossing the road' (lit. 'the man that he is crossing the road')

Most relative clause constructions can be classified by these two parameters: Whether they are marked by a particle or not, and whether the head's role is indicated by a resumptive pronoun or not. This yields four types of constructions (values 2–5).

In addition, there is the possibility of marking the relative clause and the head's role by the same element, a **relative pronoun**, as in (5).

(5) Angolar (Maurer 2013a)
 ome si ki ba tamba
 man DEM [REL.SBJ go fish]
 'the man who went fishing'

The relative pronoun *ki* marks the beginning of the relative clause (like a relative particle), and at the same time it indicates that the head is a subject inside the relative clause (it contrasts with the object form *ma*).

2. Seven types of subject relative clause

In this chapter, we study subject relative clauses, that is, relative clauses where the head has the subject role in the relative clause, as in (1)–(5). (The next two chapters look at object relative clauses and instrument relative clauses.) We distinguish seven subtypes:

		excl	shrd	all
○	1. Relative pronoun	5	7	12
●	2. Relative particle and gap	20	32	52
●	3. Relative particle and resumptive pronoun	3	9	12
●	4. Zero and gap	4	25	29
○	5. Zero and resumptive pronoun	2	9	11
○	6. Non-reduction	1	2	3
●	7. Verbal affix	1	2	3

The first type is **relative pronoun** (value 1). The best-known cases of relative pronouns, as found in Latin, inflect for case, like other pronouns and nouns. In the *APiCS* context, a relative clause marker is regarded as a relative pronoun if it has different subject and object forms (as is the case in Angolar, whose subject relative clause we saw in (5)), or if it can be combined with an adposition. For example, the marker *kyen* in Chabacano counts as a relative pronoun because it can be combined with the object marker *kun*, as seen in (6b).

(6) Zamboanga Chabacano (Steinkrüger 2013)
   a. *Akél el ómbre **kyen** ya-bené ayér.*
      that the man [who PRF-come yesterday]
      'That is the man who came yesterday.'
   b. *Akél el ómbre (**kun**) kyen ya-mirá yo ayér.*
      that the man [(OBJ) who PRF-see 1SG yesterday]
      'That is the man whom I saw yesterday.'

Example (6b) shows a **pied-piping** construction—a relative clause construction where the preposition is fronted along with the relative pronoun (this construction is more common in instrument relative clauses, Chapter 94).

Relative pronouns are uncommon worldwide (Comrie & Kuteva 2005), and they mostly occur in European languages. In *APiCS*, relative pronouns are found only in languages with European lexifiers, and one suspects that the pied-piping constructions are often due to later lexifier influence. The case of Angolar, which has a subject–object distinction independently of its lexifier, is quite unusual (another case is Casamancese Creole, see Chapter 93).

The most common way of forming subject (and object) relative clauses is by marking the relative clause with a **particle** and leaving the head's role implicit via a **gap** (value 2). We already saw examples of this type in (1) and (3), and another one is (7):

(7) Guadeloupean Creole (Colot & Ludwig 2013a)
   Mwen konnèt on ti boutik ki _ ka vann
   1SG know INDF little shop [REL _ PROG sell
   bèbèl kréyòl.
   fancy.jewels creole]
   'I know a little shop which sells creole fancy jewels.'

The difference between particles like *ya* (in 1), *ki* (in 3), *ki* (in 7) and *we* (in 8) and pronouns like *kyen* (in 6a) is that particles do not contribute to indicating the head's role. That the head is a subject inside the relative clause must be inferred from the gap in preverbal position. Some of the particles used in this construction were inherited from the European lexifiers (*ki/ku* in Portuguese-based creoles, from *que*; *dat* in Trinidad English Creole, from *that*). But others are new, or are at least not found in the standard variety of the lexifier, for example, *we* in West African English-based languages (apparently deriving from *where*) and *di* in English-based creoles in Suriname (apparently deriving from *this*). See Kortmann & Lunkenheimer (2011: features 189, 190) for non-standard relativizers in varieties of English.

In a few *APiCS* languages, especially in West Africa, subject relative clauses contain both a **relative particle and a resumptive pronoun** (value 3) (see also ex. 4).

(8) Pichi (Yakpo 2013)
   èf yù chɔp ɔl dis chɔp we è no dɔn, tumɔro
   if 2SG eat all this food [REL 3SG.SBJ NEG done] tomorrow
   yù gò sik.
   2SG POT be.sick
   'If you eat all this food that is not well-done, tomorrow you will be sick.'

Resumptive pronouns are not common in subject position (e.g. Hawkins 1999: 258), but they do occur in West African indigenous languages, so in some languages this construction seems to be due to substrate influence.

Zero-marked subject relative clauses with a simple **gap** in subject position (value 4) are also quite common, despite the fact that they introduce local ambiguity (i.e. the head noun could be mistaken for the subject of the relative clause verb).

(9) Reunion Creole (Bollée 2013)
   Sak létablisman na in klos _ i fé lèv azot.
   each sugar.estate has INDF bell [_ FIN make wake OBL.3PL]
   'Each sugar estate has a bell which wakes them up.'

(10) Pidgin Hawaiian (Roberts 2013)
   Mahope kela pake _ holo mai hemo kela puka.
   later DET Chinese [_ run DIR] open DET door
   'Then the Chinese who was running to me opened the door.'

In a few languages, the relative clause is **zero**-marked, but there is an overt subject pronoun, which functions as a **resumptive pronoun** (value 5, see also ex. 2).

(11) Juba Arabic (Manfredi & Petrollino 2013)
   sídi úo gáni bi=wedí gurúf
   owner [3SG rich] IRR=give money
   'The (shop) owner who is rich pays well.'

Three languages have internally headed or correlative relative clauses (see Chapter 7). These are subsumed under the category "non-reduction" here (value 6). And in three languages, subject relative clauses are marked by a verbal affix (value 7).

3. Discussion

Kuteva & Comrie (2012) argue that creole languages tend to have at most a single relative marker, whereas non-creoles often have multiple relative markers. While we did not specifically ask their question, our data seem to confirm their conclusion. Another question is whether there is any substrate influence on relative clauses, but this has to await future study (see also Kuteva & Comrie 2005) on relative clauses in African languages).

92 Subject relative clauses

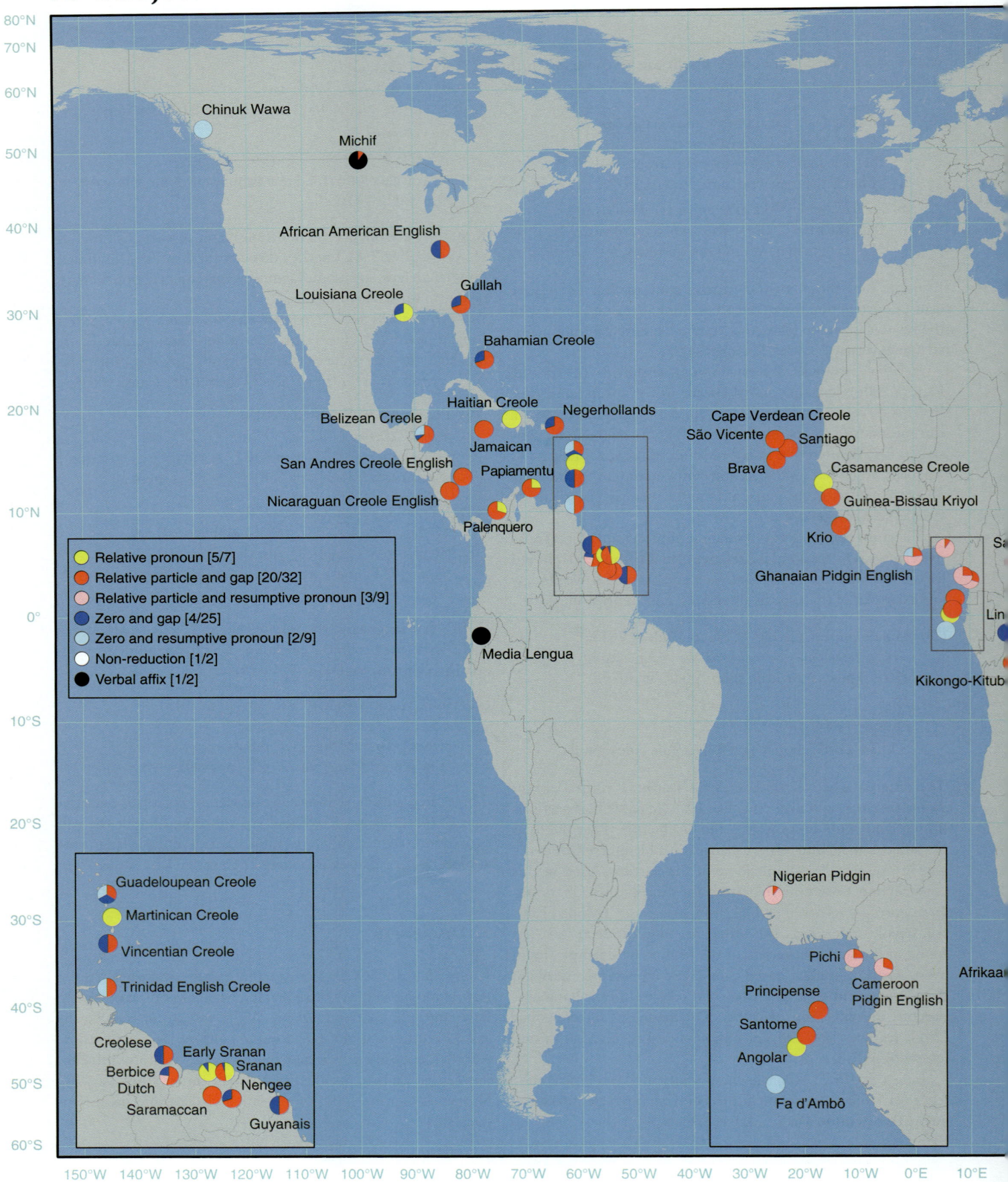

Chapter 93
Object relative clauses

SUSANNE M. MICHAELIS, MARTIN HASPELMATH, AND THE *APiCS* CONSORTIUM

1. Relative clauses

This chapter looks at the marking of object relative clauses and at the way the role of the head is indicated in them. A relative clause is defined as a clause that helps narrow the reference of a noun (the head) and in which the referent of the noun head has a semantic role.

As in Chapter 92 on subject relative clauses, (direct) object relative clauses can be marked as such by a special morpheme that occurs at the beginning or end of a relative clause, which we call relative particle (see 1, where the particle *wa* is glossed REL). Alternatively, overt marking may be lacking (zero) (see 2).

(1) Negerhollands (van Sluijs 2013)
Di man wa ju kā bring _.
DET man [REL 2SG COMPL bring _]
'the man that you have brought (with you)'

(2) Tok Pisin (Smith & Siegel 2013)
Dispela meri mi luk-im _ asde em i nais-pela tru.
this woman [1SG see-TR _ yesterday] 3SG PM nice-MOD really
'This woman I saw yesterday is really beautiful.'

The role of the head inside the relative clause can be indicated by a **gap** (no overt expression) (as in 1–2), or by a **resumptive pronoun** (3).

(3) Cameroon Pidgin English (Schröder 2013)
di wuman we wi bin luk-am
the woman [REL we PST look-3SG.OBL]
'the woman whom we saw'

Most relative-clause constructions can be classified by these two parameters: whether they are marked by a particle, and whether the head's role is indicated by a resumptive pronoun. This yields four types of constructions (values 2–5).

In addition, there is the possibility of marking the relative clause and the head's role by the same element, a **relative pronoun**, as in (4).

(4) Casamancese Creole (Biagui & Quint 2013)
Miñjer ku Pidru wojá bonitu.
woman [REL.OBJ Peter see] pretty
'The woman whom Peter has seen is pretty.'

The relative pronoun *ku* marks the beginning of the relative clause, and at the same time it indicates that the head is an object inside the relative clause (it contrasts with the subject form *ki*).

2. Seven types of object relative clause

Object relative clauses are clauses where the head has the direct object (or P) role in the relative clause (see Chapter 92 on subject relative clauses and Chapter 94 on instrument relative clauses). We distinguish the same seven subtypes that we saw for subject relative clauses, plus an eighth type, "impossible".

		excl	shrd	all
●	1. Relative pronoun	3	9	12
●	2. Relative particle and gap	16	37	53
●	3. Relative particle and resumptive pronoun	1	14	15
●	4. Zero and gap	5	34	39
●	5. Zero and resumptive pronoun	0	5	5
○	6. Non-reduction	2	1	3
●	7. Verbal affix	3	1	4
●	8. Impossible	1	0	1

The numerical distribution is quite similar for subject and object clauses. The main significant difference is that object relative clauses have the type "zero and gap" more often.

A relative-clause marker is regarded as a **relative pronoun** (value 1) if it has different subject and object forms (as is the case in Casamancese Creole, whose object relative clause we saw in (4)), or if its relative marker can be combined with an adposition. For example, the marker *kẽ* in Diu Indo-Portuguese counts as a relative pronoun because it can be combined with the preposition *a*, as seen in (5b).

(5) Diu Indo-Portuguese (Cardoso 2013)
a. *Ikəl raprig kẽ vẽde-w jərnal a mĩ ɛr bẽy piken.*
DEM girl [who sell-PST newspaper DAT 1SG.OBL] was very small
'The girl who sold me the newspaper was very small.'

b. *ikɔl ɔm   a   kẽ   use atər-o*
   DEM man [ACC who 2SG push-PST]
   'the man whom you pushed'

Example (5b) shows a **pied-piping** construction, that is, a relative-clause construction in which the preposition is fronted along with the relative pronoun.

The most common way of forming object (and subject) relative clauses is by marking the relative clause with a **particle** and leaving the head's role implicit via a **gap** (value 2). We already saw an example of this type in (1), and more are given below:

(6) Krio (Finney 2013)
   di man we wi si _ yɛstade   na mi padi
   ART man [REL 1PL see _ yesterday] COP POSS friend
   'The man that/whom we saw yesterday is my friend.'

(7) Tayo (Ehrhart & Revis 2013)
   si ta ko:ta ⁿde wajaʃ   sa nu fe   _ laᵐba Tene
   if 2SG happy of journey [REL 1PL make _ down Tene]
   'whether you are happy with the journey we made to Tene'

That the head is a direct object inside the relative clause must be inferred from the gap in postverbal position.

In a number of *APiCS* languages, there is a **relative particle** and the object is indicated by a **resumptive pronoun** (value 3), e.g.

(8) Cape Verdean Creole of Santiago (Lang 2013)
   Kárta ki N skebe-l   el   perde.
   letter [REL 1SG write-3SG 3SG.INDP] go.astray
   'The letter that I wrote to him got lost.' (lit. 'that I wrote it to him')

However, this is almost never the only option, and it is rarely the majority option. Object gaps can be recognized easily, so resumptive pronouns are not particularly important and hence not widely found worldwide (Hawkins 1999: 258). Two more examples:

(9) Gurindji Kriol (Meakins 2013)
   dat marluka wen warlaku bin katurl im leg-ta
   the old.man [REL dog   PST bite 3SG leg-LOC]
   'the old man whom the dog bit (lit. bit him) on the leg'

(10) Nigerian Pidgin (Faraclas 2013)
   Dì buk (we) à   rid(-am)   de dyar.
   the book (REL) 1SG.SBJ read(-3SG.OBJ) COP there
   'The book that I read (lit. read it) is there.'

Note that Nigerian Pidgin actually allows four different possibilities (values 2–5).

Zero-marking with a simple gap that indicates the role of the head (value 4) is more common in object relative clauses than in subject relative clauses. This must be because object relative clauses do not introduce local ambiguity (i.e. a danger of misparsing), unlike subject relative clauses. In English-based languages, as in (11), this pattern is not surprising because it exists in English (see also (2), above).

(11) Gullah (Klein 2013)
   The woman love the girl she boy marry _.
   the woman loves the girl [her boy marry _]
   'The woman loves the girl that her boy married.'

But it is also found in non-English-based languages, e.g.

(12) Martinican Creole (Colot & Ludwig 2013b)
   Mi an boutjé flè   manman-mwen ka vréyé _
   here a bunch.of flowers [mother-1SG PROG send _
   ba'w.
   for.2SG]
   'Here is a bunch of flowers which my mother sent to you.'

(13) Papiá Kristang (Baxter 2013)
   prau bo fai   _ ŋgua sumana ŋgka balé
   boat [2SG make _ one week] NEG value
   'A boat that you make in a week is useless.'

(14) Lingala (Meeuwis 2013)
   kíti (óyo) na-sómb-ákí e-zal-ákí   mabé
   chair [REL 1SG-buy-PST] 3SG.INAN-be-PST bad
   'The chair that I bought was bad.'

In a few languages, the relative clause is **zero**-marked, but there is an overt object pronoun, which functions as a **resumptive pronoun**.

(15) Ghanaian Pidgin English (Huber 2013)
   dɛ mã à dè draiv àm nau
   ART man [1SG PROG drive 3SG.OBJ now]
   'the man that I am driving now'

3. Other values

For the non-reduction type (value 6), see Chapter 7. The verbal-affix type (value 7) is represented by Media Lengua:

(16) Media Lengua (Muysken 2013)
   yo-ga no da-shka-ni-chu kopia azi-shka-da
   1SG-TOP not give-EVID-1SG-NEG copy [make-REL-ACC]
   'I did not give the copy that (I) made.'

Finally, in Chinuk Wawa, object relative clauses are not possible (value 8), and instead two separate independent clauses must be used (Grant 2013).

93 Object relative clauses

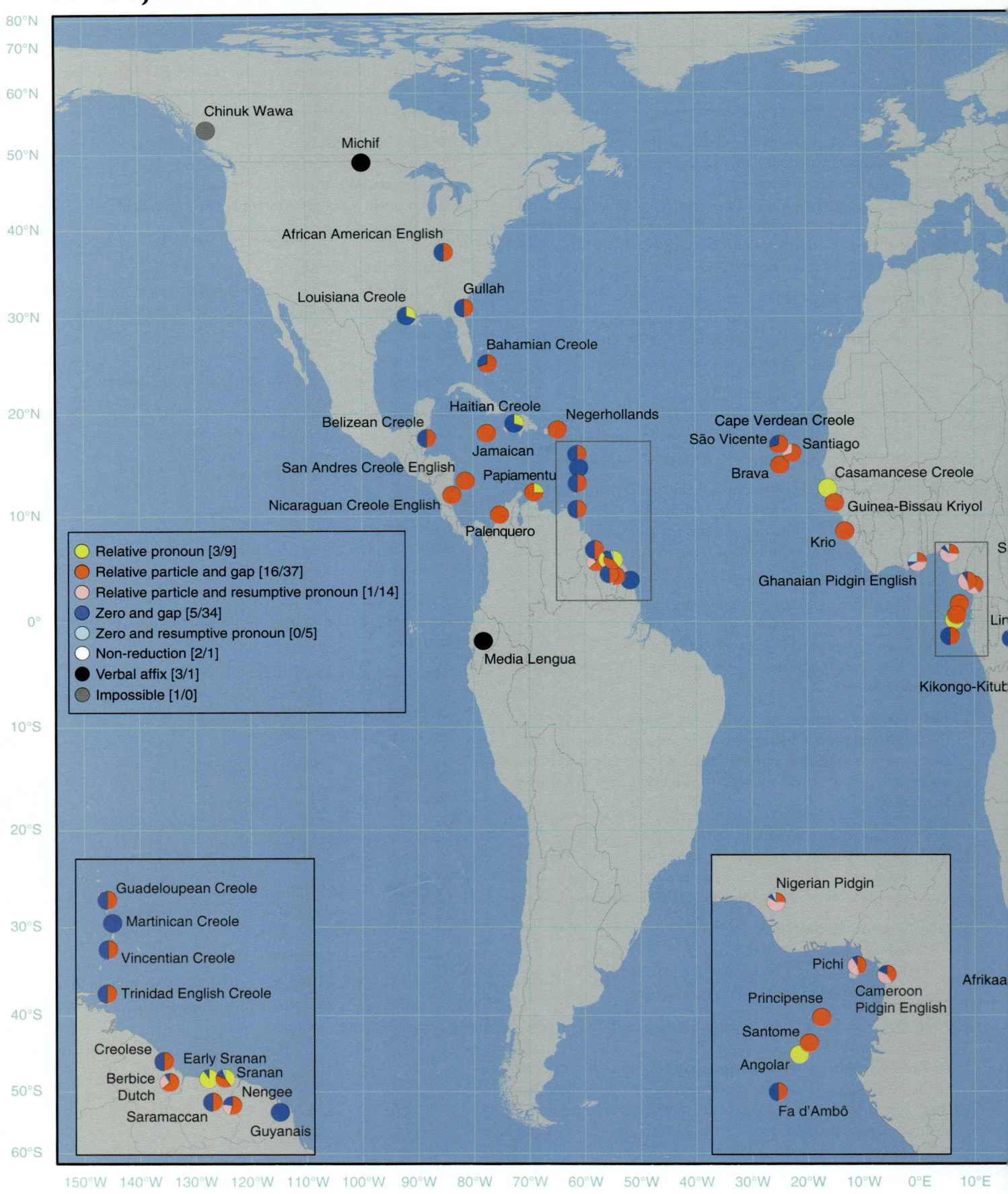

Chapter 94
Instrument relative clauses

MARTIN HASPELMATH, SUSANNE M. MICHAELIS, AND THE *APiCS* CONSORTIUM

1. Relative clauses

After Chapters 92 and 93 on subject and object relative clauses, here we consider instrument relative clauses, that is, relative clauses where the role of the head inside the relative clause is an instrument.

Such relative clauses can be marked by a special morpheme that occurs at the beginning or end of a relative clause, which we call relative particle (see 1, where the particle *wa* is glossed REL). Alternatively, overt marking may be lacking (zero) (see 2).

(1) Creolese (Devonish & Thompson 2013)
da a   di sizaz wa ii kot di peepa wid _
that EQ.COP the scissors [REL she cut the paper with _]
'Those are the scissors with which she cut the paper.'

(2) Reunion Creole (Bollée 2013)
Zafèr i koup kane   avèk _ la, koman i apèl?
thing [FIN cut sugar.cane with _ there] how FIN call
'The tool with which you cut sugar cane, what do you call it?'

The role of the head inside the relative clause can be indicated by a **gap** (no overt expression) (indicated by an underscore, as in (1)–(2)). A gap in relative-clause constructions is very common in the world's languages when the role of the head is subject or direct object, but it is much less common if it is an instrument or some other role that is typically expressed by an oblique phrase. Thus, the occurrence of the gap after the preposition in (1) and (2) goes by the special name **preposition stranding**.

Alternatively, the role of the head can be indicated by a **resumptive pronoun** (as in 3).

(3) Guyanais (Pfänder 2013)
sa kouto-a i ka koupé ké li
that knife-ART [he PROG cuts with it]
'the knife he cuts with'

Most relative clause constructions can be classified by these two parameters: whether they are marked by a particle, and whether the head's role is indicated by a resumptive pronoun. This yields four types of constructions.

In addition, there is the possibility of marking the relative clause and the head's role by the same element, a **relative pronoun**, as in (4).

(4) Palenquero (Schwegler 2013)
Ma tihera ku lo k'   i tan kottá papé ata
PL scissors [with REL REL which I FUT cut paper] be
aí.
there
'The scissors with which I am going to cut the paper are (over) there.'

The relative pronoun *lo ke* marks the beginning of the relative clause, and it is the complement of a preposition which indicates that the head is an instrument inside the relative clause. This kind of construction in which the relative pronoun is fronted but still has a preposition preceding it is called **pied-piping**.

2. Seven types of instrument relative clause

Instrument relative clauses are clauses in which the head has the instrument role in the relative clause. We distinguish eight subtypes, six of which are found in object relative clauses as well. Additionally there are two minor types, "relative pronoun with resumptive pronoun" (value 6), and "instrument meaning is left implicit" (value 7). Note that for twelve languages, we lack data on instrument relative clause formation, as this kind of relative clause is very rare in corpora. The type "non-reduction" does not occur in our data.

	excl	shrd	all
1. Relative pronoun with pied-piping	3	8	11
2. Relative particle and gap with preposition stranding	7	12	19
3. Relative particle and resumptive pronoun	9	11	20
4. Zero and gap with preposition stranding	1	8	9
5. Zero and resumptive pronoun	6	8	14
6. Relative pronoun with resumptive pronoun	1	1	2
7. Instrument meaning is left implicit	5	6	11
8. Impossible	7	0	7

Compared to subject and object relative clauses, instrument relative clauses are special in that resumptive pronouns are used in them much more often—in fact, resumptive pronouns are more common than preposition stranding. This is in line with Hawkins's (1999) observation that resumptive pronouns tend to be used primarily for such oblique roles. Moreover, the instrument meaning is often left implicit (value 7), and seven languages do not allow instrument relative clauses (value 8).

Value 1. A relative-clause marker is regarded as a relative pronoun if it has different subject and object forms, or if its relative marker can be combined with an adposition. Thus, all cases of pied-piping are cases of relative pronouns (see also ex. 4).

(5) Seychelles Creole (Michaelis & Rosalie 2013)
*Sa i kouto ek **ki** Zak ti koup pwason.*
this PM knife [with REL Jacques PST cut fish]
'This is the knife with which Jacques cut the fish.'

In two languages, Angolar and Casamancese Creole, there are relative pronouns (which have distinct subject and object forms), but these require a resumptive pronoun in instrument relative clauses (value 6).

(6) Angolar (Maurer 2013a)
*piongo **ma** n pega taba ku ê*
nail [REL.NSBJ 1SG nail plank with it]
'the nail with which I nailed the planks'

Value 2. Preposition stranding is most common in English-based languages, especially in the Atlantic. In 19 languages it occurs with a relative particle.

(7) Trinidad English Creole (Mühleisen 2013)
*de cotlass **dat** she kot it wid _*
DET cutlass [that 3SG.F cut 3SG with _]
'the cutlass that she cut it with'

Another example was seen in (1) above. Preposition stranding is also found in Sango, where the preposition occurs before the direct object:

(8) Sango (Samarin 2013)
*zeme **so** mbi doroko na _ nyami ni a-za*
knife [REL 1SG chop PREP _ meat DET] PM-be.sharp
nzoni ape
well NEG
'The knife with which I chop the meat is not very sharp.'

Value 3. As noted earlier, **resumptive pronoun**s are more common in instrument relative clauses than in subject and object relative clauses. In 20 languages they occur with a relative particle.

(9) Principense (Maurer 2013c)
*Kumin **ki** ine têêxi ufaka sê **ki** n txya ivin*
place REL PL three knife DEM [REL 1SG extract wine
kôli sa n' êli?
with.3SG be in 3SG]
'Where are the three knives I extracted palm wine with?'

Value 4. Zero-marked instrument relative clauses with a gap with preposition stranding are mostly found as an alternative in languages that also have preposition stranding with a relative particle (value 2). (Another example was seen in (2).)

(10) Vincentian Creole (Prescod 2013)
Sho mi di sezez yo kuht uhm wid _.
show 1SG ART scissors [2.SBJ cut 3.OBJ with _]
'Show me the scissors with which you cut it/him/her.'

Value 5. In a number of languages, the relative clause is zero-marked, and there is an overt pronoun following the preposition that functions as a resumptive pronoun. (Another example was seen above in (3).)

(11) Guadeloupean Creole (Colot & Ludwig 2013a)
*kouto-la ou ka sèvi épi'**y** la*
knife-DEF [2SG use cut with.3SG DET]
'the knife with which you cut'

Value 7. In quite a few languages, it is possible not only to have a gap for the instrument phrase, but even to leave the role of the instrument phrase in the relative clause implicit. Thus, (12) is literally 'The knife [I cut up the meat] is not sharp'.

(12) Haitian Creole (Fattier 2013)
Kouto m koupe vyann _ nan pa file.
knife [1SG cut meat _] DEF NEG sharpen
'The knife with which I cut up the meat is not sharp.'

In Nengee, including the preposition *anga* 'with' (and a resumptive pronoun) is not allowed.

(13) Nengee (Migge 2013)
*a pan **di** i e baka kasaba (*anga/*anga en)*
the pan [REL you IPFV bake cassava (with/with it)]
'the pan with which you roast cassava'

Value 8. In quite a few languages, instruments cannot be relativized at all, and they have to be turned into the direct objects of verbs like 'use' or 'take'. (This construction is somewhat similar to 'take' serials, see Chapter 85.)

(14) Korlai (Clements 2013)
*Fak **ki** tum-o _ kharm ki korta drɛt nu tɛ.*
knife [REL take-PST _ meat COMP cut] good NEG COP.PRS
'The knife she took to cut the meat is not good.'

94 Instrument relative clauses

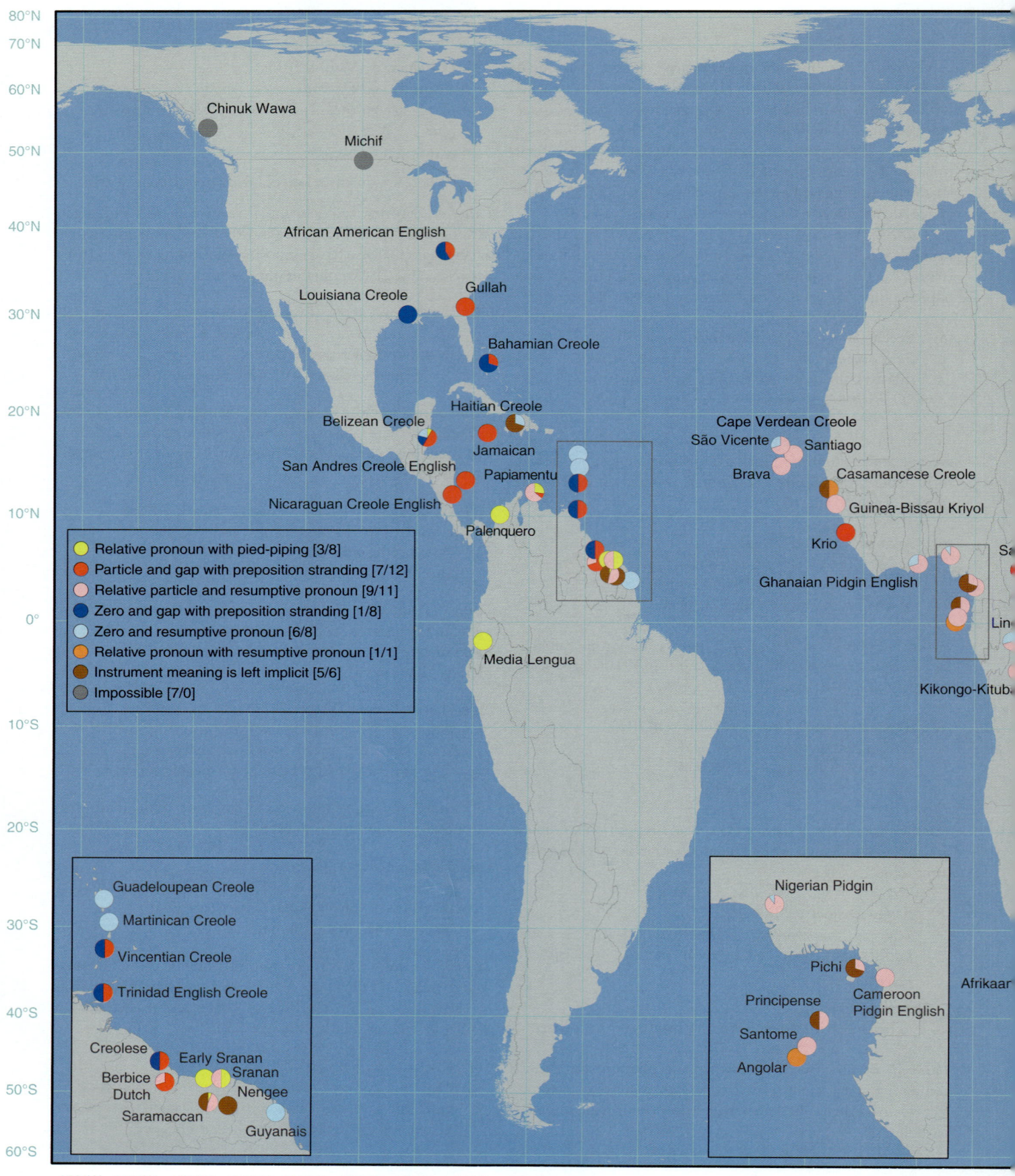

Chapter 95
Complementizer with verbs of speaking

SUSANNE MARIA MICHAELIS AND THE *APiCS* CONSORTIUM

1. Introduction

This chapter deals with complementizers (such as English *that*) used with verbs of speaking such as 'say', 'tell', 'ask', 'shout', 'whisper', in a reported-speech construction such as *She told me that she knew it*. In general, the constructions that interest us are indirect-speech constructions (with person shift), but when a language does not have a special indirect-speech construction, we also consider direct-speech constructions (see Güldemann 2008 and 2012 for an in-depth typological study of quotatives).

Complementizers are defined here as elements that link the reported speech to the verb of speaking, not belonging either to the verb of speaking or to the text of the reported speech. Examples are *say* in African American English (1), *te* in Lingala (2), and postposed *puris* in Korlai (3):

(1) African American English (Green 2013)
*She told me **say** she wasn't going to church.*
'She told me that she wasn't going to church.'

(2) Lingala (Meeuwis 2013)
a-lob-ákí **te** mbúla e-ko-bét-a
3SG-say-PST [COMP rain 3SG-FUT-hit-FV]
'She said that it was going to rain.'

(3) Korlai (Clements 2013)
El hal-o el lə vi **puris**.
3SG say-PST [3SG FUT come COMP]
'He said that he would come.'

In quite a few languages, a form of the verb 'say' is used as a complementizer with verbs of speaking. If the 'say' form is a bare stem, the pattern is often considered as a kind of serial verb construction. Such serial verb constructions have given rise to a large amount of literature in the field of creole studies which we cannot possibly refer to here, but see, for example, Winford (1993: 291ff.) for an in-depth discussion of 'say' complementizers in English-based Caribbean creoles.

In this feature we investigate asserted reported speech sentences such as 'She said that the boy did not feel well', not sentences with directive modality like 'She told the boy to stay in bed', because these latter constructions often yield different syntactic structures.

Languages often show several different complementizer constructions.

2. The values

In this feature we distinguish four values:

		excl	shrd	all
○	1. Complementizer identical to bare 'say'	5	24	29
●	2. Complementizer consists of 'say' plus some other marker	1	4	5
●	3. Complementizer not synchronically related to 'say'	5	38	43
○	4. No complementizer	14	47	61

There are 29 *APiCS* languages with a complementizer which is **identical to the bare verb 'say'** (value 1). It is not always easy to decide on the degree of grammaticalization of these verbs/complementizers (see Güldemann 2008, who criticizes the overgeneralization of the grammaticalization path 'say verb' > complementizer/quotative marker for many African languages, and who instead proposes a whole range of other sources for such elements, such as similarity markers 'be like, like this', deictics, presentationals). But this matter is not of interest here. We only ask whether a verb which means 'say', 'speak' is used to introduce the content of the reported speech.[1] One example was seen in (1), and more examples are in (4) to (8).

(4) Krio (Finney 2013)
di titi tɛl mi **se** i lɛk mi
ART girl tell me [COMP 3SG like me]
'The girl told me that she liked me.'

In the Surinamese creoles the complementizer is *taki* or *táa* (< *talk*):

(5) Sranan (Winford & Plag 2013)
A bonuman taigi a frow **taki** a musu weri
ART medicine.man tell ART woman [COMP 3SG must wear
wan bereketi [...]
ART belly.chain]
'The medicine man told the woman that she had to wear a chain around her waist [...].'

[1] It could be that some of the *se*-forms in the English-based Atlantic creoles were directly borrowed from Akan quotatives/complementizers *sɛ, se* ('to be like', 'to say') (see e.g. Lord 1993: 181f.). But since the Surinamese creoles have *taki* as their 'say' verb (see ex. 5), and non-English-based creoles (e.g. Guinea-Bissau Kriyol with *kuma*) have similar constructions, the Akan forms had at best a reinforcing influence on the English lexeme *say*, see §3 below.

In San Andres Creole English, the main verb *se* 'say' can be combined with the complementizer *se*.

(6) San Andres Creole English (Bartens 2013b)
Taiga se se him neva de kech no fish.
Tiger say [COMP 3SG NEG.PST PROG catch NEG fish]
'Tiger said he wasn't catching any fish.'

In other languages this is impossible, for instance in Jamaican, where the complementizer *se* does not co-occur with *se* 'say' and *piik* 'speak', but with all other verbs of speaking (Farquharson 2013), like *taak* 'talk' in (7):

(7) Jamaican (Farquharson 2013)
Dem taak se a mi a kyar nyuuz.
3PL talk [COMP FOC 1SG PROG carry news]
'They are saying that I am the one spreading gossip.'

Only five languages have a complementizer which consists of the verb **'say' in combination with some additional marker** (value 2): Berbice Dutch (*bifi dati* 'say COMP'), Seychelles Creoles (*poudir* 'for.say'), Sri Lanka Portuguese (*falaa-tu* 'say-PFV'), Yimas-Arafundi Pidgin (*maria-k* 'say-IRR'), and Angolar (*fala ma* 'say COMP').

(8) Angolar (Maurer 2013a)
Ê fa m fala ma karu e ka n'dja Potave.
3SG tell 1SG [say COMP car this HAB stop Ponte.Tavares]
'He told me that this car used to stop at Ponte Tavares.'

In addition to the verb *fala* 'say', Angolar uses the usual complementizer for object clauses *ma*. This construction (besides the construction with bare 'say') is used only when the recipient of the verb of speaking, here *m* 'to me', is expressed (Maurer 2013a).

Value 3 subsumes languages in which the **complementizer is not synchronically related to 'say'** even though there may be a diachronic link. Only five languages have this as their only complementizer strategy, whereas 38 languages share this option with another one. Here, we find complementizers going back to the various European lexifiers, for example, *ki*, *ke*, *que*, *dat*, complementizers/quotatives like *nde* in Kikongo-Kituba (see 10), but also new compound complementizers like Tok Pisin *olsem* (< *all the same*) as in (11):

(9) Tayo (Ehrhart & Revis 2013)
sa ⁿdi ke la ʃa:ti, fam-la
3PL say [COMP 3SG nice woman-DEM/DEF]
'They say that the woman is nice' (lit. 'They say that she is nice, that woman').

(10) Kikongo-Kituba (Mufwene 2013)
Yandi tuba nde: beto ata kutana mbasi.
3SG say [COMP 1PL FUT meet tomorrow]
'S/he said: We will meet tomorrow.'

(11) Tok Pisin (Smith & Siegel 2013)
Em tok olsem mi mas skul na kisim gut-pela save.
3SG talk [COMP 1SG must school and get good-MOD knowledge]
'He said I must go to school and acquire good knowledge.'

Smith & Siegel (2013) note that "in rapid speech the complementizer *olsem* may be reduced to a form which fortuitously is identical to *se*". But *se* is not the lexeme for 'say, talk' in Tok Pisin (which is *toktok*) and therefore should not be interpreted as a serial verb.

Sixty-one *APiCS* languages (14 of them exclusively) show **no complementizer** or linking element between the verb of speaking and the text of the reported speech (value 4). This strategy is not restricted to any area or lexifier, but, remarkably, 7 out of the 14 exclusively zero-marking languages are pidgins.

(12) Singapore Bazaar Malay (Khin Khin Aye 2013)
Ah dua olang dia cakap mao lawan siapa busat ah siapa busat.
PCL two person 3SG speak [want fight who big Q who big]
'These two, they said they wanted to fight (compete) [to find out] who was bigger.'

3. Discussion

Besides the specific value distribution in the *APiCS* languages, it is interesting to note that only 25 languages show just one value, but all other languages have two, three, or even all four values at their disposal. With an average of 1.82 value choices (close to two different options per language on average) this feature has the highest number of different values per language.

Bare 'say' constructions are almost exclusively concentrated in Africa and the Atlantic creoles. As has been extensively discussed (e.g. Lord 1993: 151ff., Boretzky 1983: 176ff., Holm 1988: 185ff., Parkvall 2000: 64ff.), these 'say' constructions have clear counterparts in the African substrate languages. But we also find some languages in India and Southeast Asia, with Bislama as an outlier. As (Southeast) Asian languages also show bare 'say' constructions in complementizer function (e.g. Lord 1993: 207ff., Bisang 1992: 398f.) we can invoke substrate/adstrate influence here, too.

A final puzzling point: in this feature we see a striking difference between English- and French-based creoles. No single French-based creole shows a bare 'say' serial. We have no explanation for this, but there are other features where French-based and English-based creoles differ in a surprising way (e.g. Chapter 71 on noun-phrase conjunction and comitative, and Chapter 112 on 'hand' and 'arm').

95 Complementizer with verbs of speaking

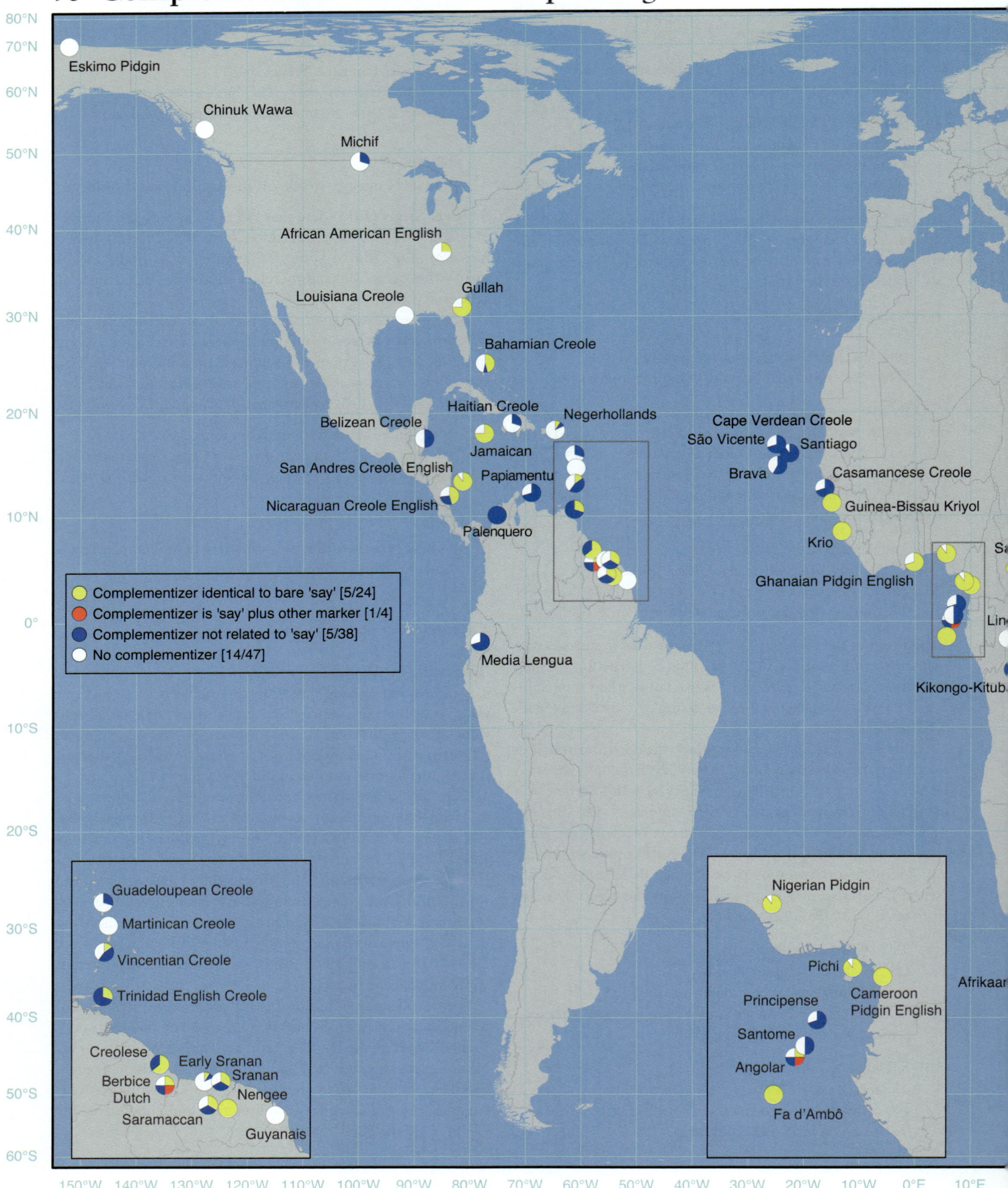

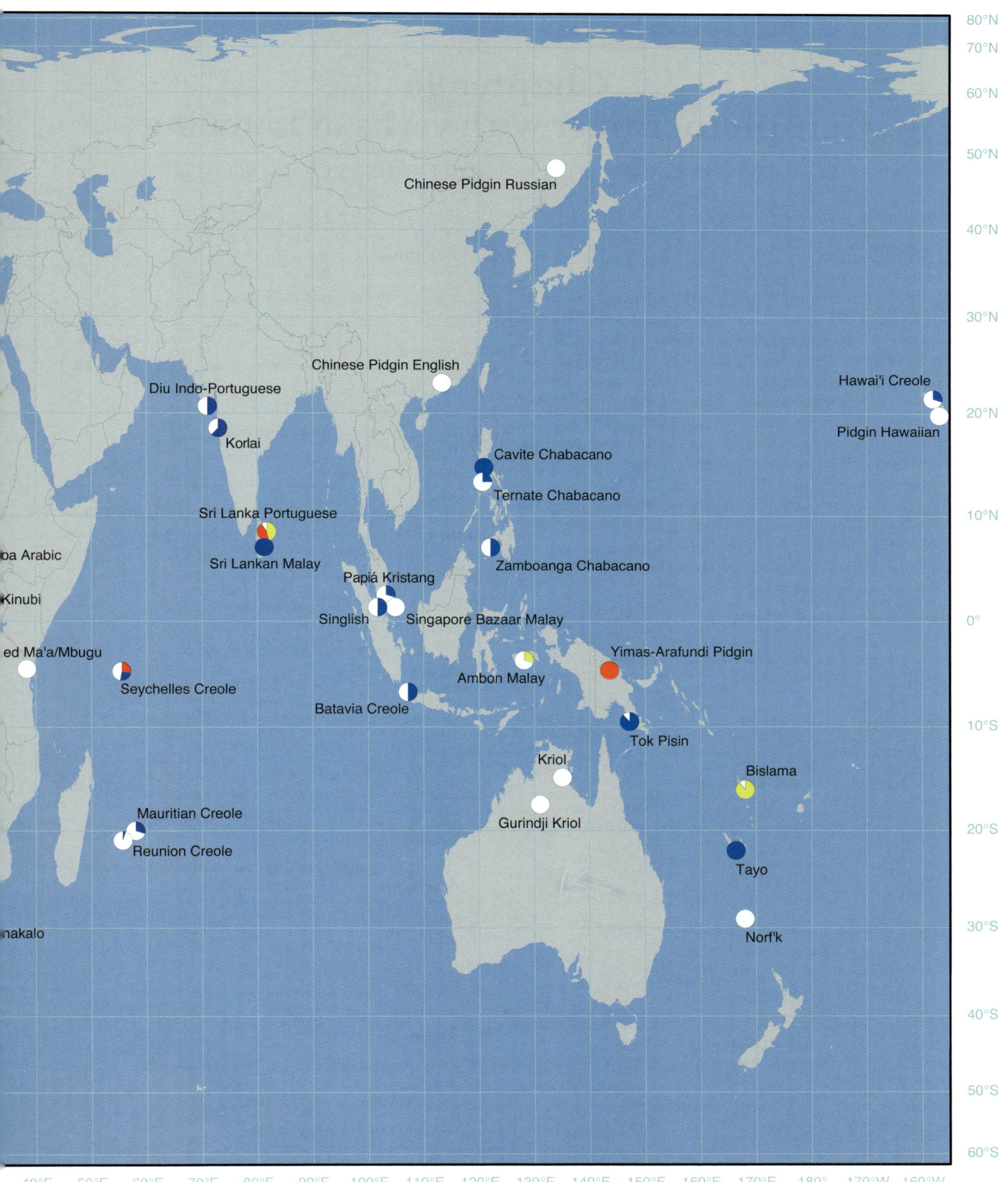

Chapter 96
Complementizer with verbs of knowing

SUSANNE MARIA MICHAELIS AND THE *APiCS* CONSORTIUM

1. Introduction

This is the second chapter which deals with complementizers (like English *that*). In this feature, we investigate a different verb class from Chapter 95, namely verbs of knowing, such as 'know', 'forget', and 'learn' in sentences like *We knew that they had come*. Verbs of knowing belong to the group of **factive verbs** where the content of the knowledge—expressed in the complement clause—is entailed. This fact puts factive verbs apart from non-factive verbs such as 'think', 'believe', and 'trust', where the complement clause can be questioned or denied. (For 'think' complements, see Chapter 98.)

Complementizers are defined here as elements that link the embedded clause to the verb of knowing, not belonging either to the verb of knowing or to the embedded clause. Examples are *fa* in Fa d'Ambô (1), *ité* in Mixed Ma'a/Mbugu (2), and *kay* in Zamboanga Chabacano (3):

(1) Fa d'Ambô (Post 2013)
*Fo desyi-se nge tudu sé **fa** bibi na sa patu*
since day-DEM person all know [say bibi NEG be bird
d'ogó-f.
of.jungle-NEG]
'Since then everybody knows that the *bibi* is not a jungle bird.'

(2) Mixed Ma'a/Mbugu (Mous 2013)
*te-tú-ila-íye **ité** hé-lo vahe vé-di-ye*
NEG-1PL-know-PRF [COMP 16-have people 2-stay-OPT
i?í
here]
'We didn't know that there were people staying here.'

(3) Zamboanga Chabacano (Steinkrüger 2013)
*Sábe silá **kay** ay-bené le légu.*
know they [COMP IRR-come 3SG later]
'They know that she will come later.'

Indirect questions like 'I don't know where . . .' or 'I don't know whether . . .' are ignored in this feature.

As in Chapter 95, quite a few languages use a form of the verb 'say' as a complementizer with verbs of knowing. As these serial verb constructions have been intensely discussed in the creole literature, we are interested in their distribution as well.

2. The values

In this feature we distinguish four values:

		excl	shrd	all
○	1. Complementizer identical to bare 'say'	7	18	25
●	2. Complementizer consists of 'say' plus some other marker	0	3	3
●	3. Complementizer not synchronically related to 'say'	11	31	42
○	4. No complementizer	16	38	54

In 25 *APiCS* languages we find a **complementizer which is identical to a 'say' verb** (value 1). Seven of these languages have this type as their only option (out of which San Andres Creole English is one):

(4) San Andres Creole English (Bartens 2013b)
*An di daata nuo **se** da neva ihn*
and ART.DEF daughter know [COMP FOC NEG.PST 3SG.POSS
muma.
mother]
'And the daughter knew that it wasn't her mother.'

(5) Gullah (Klein 2013)
*Den dey gwine know **say** wa dey been-a do*
then they going know [COMP what they PST-PROG do
ain right.
NEG.AUX right]
'Then they are going to know that what they have been doing is not right.'

In the Surinamese creoles, the complementizer is *taki/táa* 'say' (< English *talk*):

(6) Saramaccan (Aboh et al. 2013)
*Mi sábi **táa** á búnu.*
1SG know [say 3SG.NEG good]
'I know that it is not good.'

(7) Sango (Samarin 2013)
*lo hinga a-**tene** ni eke wali*
3SG know [PM-say 3SG.LOG COP woman]
'She knows that she's a woman.'

One could classify the predicate marker *a-* in Sango as illustrating value 2 ('say' plus some additional marker, see next value). But as the predicate marker expresses person information, we interpret it as being part of the verb complex and therefore classify it as value 1.

Only three languages show a 'say' verb with some additional marker (value 2): Berbice Dutch (*bi dato* 'say that'), Sri Lanka Portuguese (*falaa-tu* 'say-PFV'), and Seychelles Creole (*pourdir* 'for.say'):

(8) Seychelles Creole (Michaelis & Rosalie 2013)
*Pa konnen **pourdir** i pe mor, i 'n mor.*
NEG know [COMP 3SG PROG dead/die] 3SG PRF dead/die
'One didn't know whether he was going to die, (but) he died.'

The next two values are by far the most frequent values in this feature. Forty-two languages show a complementizer which is not synchronically related to 'say'.

(9) Cape Verdean Creole of Brava (Baptista 2013)
*Es sabe **ma** na kel tenpu, es tinha ses kazinha.*
they know [COMP in that time they had their home]
'They know that during that time, they had their house.'

(10) Mauritian Creole (Baker & Kriegel 2013)
*mo kóne **ki** li en kúyoṅ*
1SG know [COMP 3SG INDF fool]
'I know that he is a fool.'

Complementizers can be complex, as for instance in Vincentian Creole *da hou* (where both parts, *da* and *hou*, can be used on their own as complementizers).

(11) Vincentian Creole (Prescod 2013)
*Hi no **da hou** shi sik.*
3SG know [that how 3SG sick]
'He knows that she is ill.'

In Korlai we find a circumpositional complementizer composed of the general complementizer *ki* and the element *puris*:

(12) Korlai (Clements 2013)
*Yo sab **ki** vɔ parmi lə mustra **puris**.*
1SG know [COMP 2SG.INFORMAL 1SG.OBJ FUT show COMP]
'I know that you will show me.'

In Michif and Media Lengua, complementizers are affixes on the subordinate verb, *ee-* (13) and *-shka-* in (14):

(13) Michif (Bakker 2013)
*Robert kishkeeht-am Mari **ee**-aahkoshi-yi-t.*
Robert know.it-3.SBJ.3.OBJ [Mary COMP-be.ill-OBV-3]
'Robert knows that Mary is ill.'

(14) Media Lengua (Muysken 2013)
*no sabi-ni-chu Xwan bini-**shka**-da*
NEG know-1SG-NEG [Juan come-NMLZ-ACC]
'I don't know that John has come.'

Fifty-four *APiCS* languages allow for **no complementizer** after verbs of knowing (value 4), 16 of which have this as their only option:

(15) Negerhollands (van Sluijs 2013)
[. . .] fodima ju wēt, mi ha fo jet oka.
because 2SG know [1SG have for eat too]
'[. . .] because you know that I have to eat too.'

(16) Kriol (Schultze-Berndt & Angelo 2013)
Ai nomo bin jabi yu bin go, Nangari.
1SG NEG PST know [2SG PST go Nangari]
'I didn't know that you went away, Nangari.'

Interestingly, all pidgins in *APiCS* show exclusively this value.

(17) Eskimo Pidgin (van der Voort 2013)
innuk ababa tusara awoña
[man say] understand I
'I know that a man is talking.'

3. Discussion

An interesting question is whether languages which have the bare 'say' construction in Chapter 95 (with verbs of speaking) also have a bare 'say' construction in this feature. And indeed, it is striking that the values for the *APiCS* languages in Chapters 95 and 96 are nearly identically distributed, not only regarding the bare 'say' constructions. But there are some languages which show differences between complements of saying and knowing—Angolar, Ambon Malay, and Vincentian Creole—where the bare 'say' construction is not possible with verbs of knowing whereas it is possible with verbs of saying. In Papiá Kristang and in Hawai'i Creole, verbs of saying show both strategies (with the complementizer *ki/dæt* and no complementizer) whereas verbs of knowing only show no complementizers. In Diu Indo-Portuguese and Batavia Creole the option of a zero complementizer is only found with verbs of saying, and not with verbs of knowing.

APiCS languages show far fewer possible construction types with verbs of knowing than with verbs of saying (1.63 vs. 1.82 average value choices per language).

For a substratal explanation of the bare 'say' constructions, see § 3 in Chapter 95.

96 Complementizer with verbs of knowing

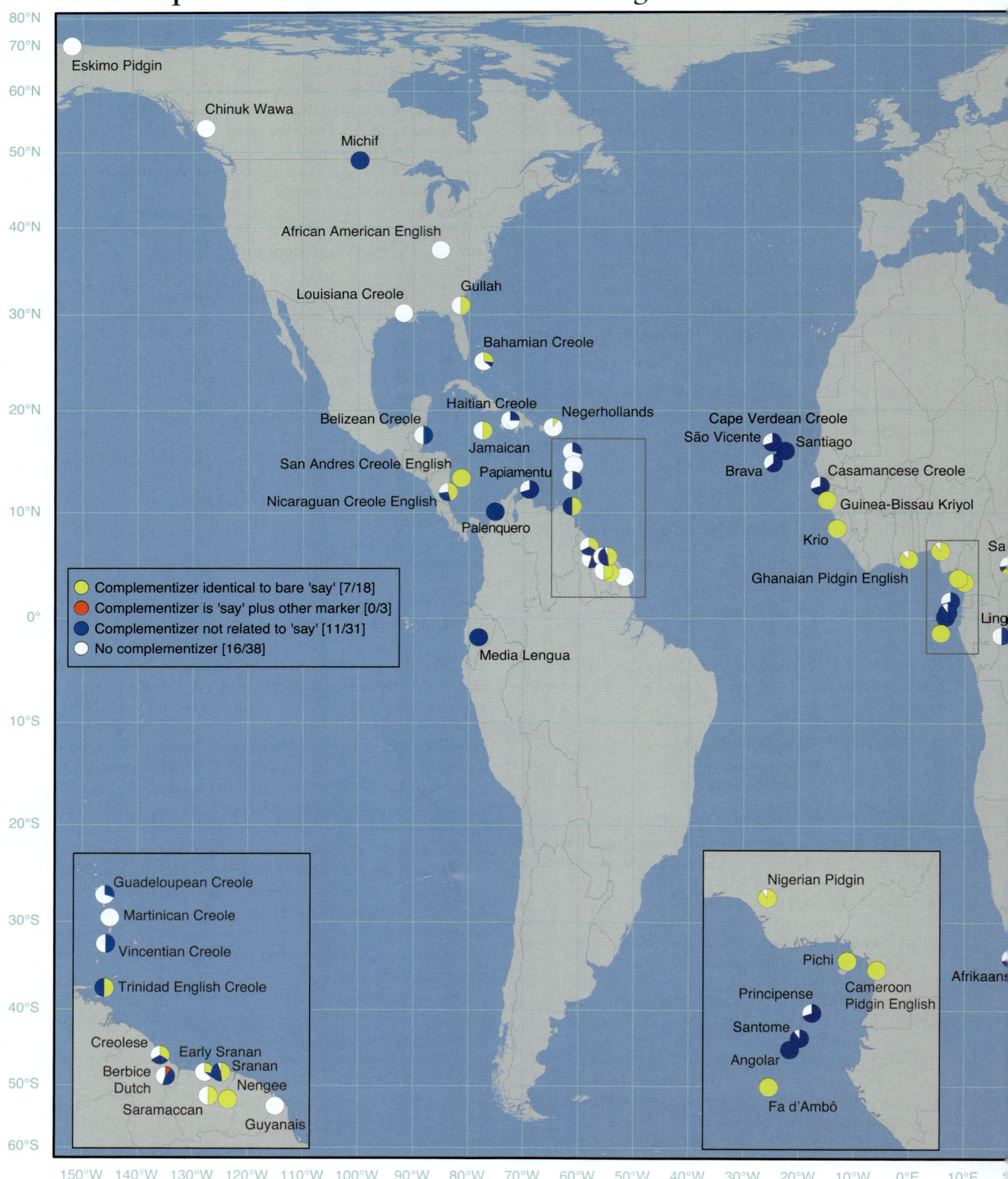

Chapter 97
'Want' complement subjects

SUSANNE M. MICHAELIS, MARTIN HASPELMATH, AND THE *APiCS* CONSORTIUM

1. 'Want' complements

In a complement clause, the subject can be either referentially different from or referentially identical to the superordinate subject. For 'want' complement clauses, these two possibilities are illustrated in (1a, b).

(1) a. *He₁ wants [∅₁ to come home].* (same subject)
    b. *He₁ wants [her₂ to come home].* (different subject)

In English and the other well-known European languages, same-subject complement clauses have an **implicit subject** (indicated by ∅ in example 1a). This is economical, because with 'want', subject identity is far more common than subject distinctness (Haspelmath 2013b+).

But in some languages, the subject of the 'want' complement clause is **expressed overtly** even when it is identical to the superordinate subject:

(2) Angolar (Maurer 2013a)
    Ê₁ mêthê p' ê₁ m'me ũa kwa rosi.
    3SG want that 3SG eat one thing sweet
    'He wants to eat something sweet.' (lit. 'He wants that he eat something sweet.')

This chapter follows Haspelmath's (2005f) *WALS* chapter. It considers only same-subject 'want' constructions (for different-subject 'want' constructions, see Chapter 98). We primarily ask whether the complement clause has an implicit subject or whether it is expressed overtly. The distribution of the four values distinguished here is shown in the value box. As can be seen, the great majority of *APiCS* languages follow the implicit-subject pattern in (1a).

2. Implicit-subject 'want' constructions

Implicit-subject 'want' constructions (value 1) are found in the great majority of *APiCS* languages, illustrated below. (In all examples in this chapter, the complement clause is enclosed in brackets in the gloss line.)

(3) Louisiana Creole (Neumann-Holzschuh & Klingler 2013)
    Si to olé vini padna no va fouyé ein pi.
    if 2SG want [become friend] 1PL FUT dig a well
    'If you want to be my friend, we will dig a well.'

	excl	shrd	all
● 1. The complement subject is left implicit	58	13	71
● 2. The complement subject is expressed overtly	0	13	13
● 3. Desiderative verbal affix	1	1	2
● 4. Desiderative particle	1	0	1

(4) Bahamian Creole (Hackert 2013)
    they don't want work
    'they don't want to work'

(5) Papiamentu (Kouwenberg 2013b)
    Hulanda no ke paga sierto debe nan di gobièrnu.
    Holland NEG want [pay certain debt PL of government]
    'Holland does not want to pay certain government debts.'

In many Indo-European languages, the verb 'want' combines with a special "infinitive" form of the verb, but in most pidgin and creole languages, the form of the verb is the simple verb stem, without any marking. The stem typically derives from the infinitive of the lexifier, but occasionally it may derive from another form. In the English-based languages, the infinitival *to* is preserved only in varieties that are quite close to the lexifier. For example, it is missing in Bahamian Creole in (4).

In some English- and Dutch-based languages of the Caribbean region, a special "infinitival" (or subjunctive) form based on a preposition deriving from *for* may be used in 'want' complements:

(6) Jamaican (Farquharson 2013)
    Jan waahn fi ga-a skuul.
    John want [INF go-to school]
    'John wants to go to school.'

(7) Negerhollands (van Sluijs 2013)
    Am mangkē fo gi am twaləfhondərt patakón[...]
    3SG want [INF give 3SG twelvehundred patacons]
    'He wants to give him twelve hundred patacons (currency name)[...]'

3. 'Want' constructions with overtly expressed subject

In 13 *APiCS* languages the subject may be overtly expressed (value 2, already seen in (2)). However, in none of the languages is this the only possibility, or even the majority option, and in some it is marginal. Most of these languages are spoken in central and western Africa. In the European-based languages, there is usually a complementizer present, such as *pa* in Angolar (2) and Santome (8), *pou* in Haitian Creole (9), *fu/fa* in Saramaccan (10), and *se* in Nigerian Pidgin (11). These complementizers are used in different-subject 'want' constructions too (see Chapter 98).

(8) Santome (Hagemeijer 2013)
 Sun na mêsê pa sun be ku mosu se f=ô?
 2SG.M NEG want [COMP 2SG.M go with boy DEM NEG]=PCL
 'Don't you want to go with the boy?'

(9) Haitian Creole (Fattier 2013)
 Mwen vle pou m marye ak ou.
 1SG want [COMP 1SG marry with 2SG]
 'I want to get married to you.'

(10) Saramaccan (Aboh et al. 2013)
 A ké faa go.
 3SG want [COMP.3SG go]
 'He wants to go.'

(11) Nigerian Pidgin (Faraclas 2013)
 À want se mek à go tawn.
 1SG.SBJ want [COMP SBJV 1SG.SBJ go town]
 'I want to go to town.'

Since all these languages also have the simple implicit-subject constructions of the type seen earlier, the existence of the more complex overt-subject constructions is particularly surprising. Examples (12) and (13) show the corresponding implicit-subject patterns for Angolar and Haitian Creole.

(12) Angolar (Maurer 2013a)
 Ê mêthê m'me ũa kwa rosi.
 3SG want [eat one thing sweet]
 'He wants to eat something sweet.'

(13) Haitian Creole (Fattier 2013)
 M vle tounen lakay.
 1SG want [come.back house]
 'I want to go back home.'

It seems that the only conceivable explanation is that the patterns in (2) and (8)–(11) are due to West African substrate influence. And indeed, Haspelmath (2005f) found that overt-subject constructions with 'want' are particularly common in West Africa:

(14) Fongbe (Lefebvre & Brousseau 2002: 280)
 É jló nú é ní yì.
 he want [COMP he SBJV leave]
 'He wants to leave.'

(15) Obolo (Faraclas 1984: 112)
 Ḿ-wèèk ǹ-gê íkpá
 1SG-want [1SG-write letter]
 'I want to write a letter.'

One of the *APiCS* languages with an African lexifier also has this pattern as an option:

(16) Lingala (Meeuwis 2013)
 a-ling-í á-kenda
 3SG-want-PRS.PRF [3SG.SBJV-go]
 'He wants to go.'

A very special overt-subject construction is found in Media Lengua:

(17) Media Lengua (Muysken 2013)
 profesora-ga no bini-sha zi-n-chu
 teacher-TOP NEG [come-1SG.FUT] say-3-NEG
 'The teacher does not want to come.'

Here the complement-clause subject is first person, and (17) is literally 'The teacher does not say I will come'.

4. Desiderative verbal affix

Two languages (Michif and Media Lengua) have a verbal affix that expresses 'want' (value 3). Here the subject is expressed only once, as in value 1, but not necessarily in close association with 'want'.

(18) Michif (Bakker 2013)
 Ki-maato-n ee-wii-ituhtee-yin la dans.
 2-cry-2 [COMP-want-go-2 ART.F.SG dance]
 'You are crying because you want to go to the dance.'

5. Desiderative particle

One language has an uninflected particle that expresses the notion 'want':

(19) Sri Lanka Portuguese (Smith 2013)
 etus-pa kapstaay=ley noos kera mustraa
 [3PL.HON-DAT cleverness=like 1PL want/VOL show
 kam-falaa, noos mes-prenda
 COND-say] 1PL OBLIG-study
 'If we want to/are going to demonstrate cleverness to them (i.e. the government), we must study.'

97 'Want' complement subjects

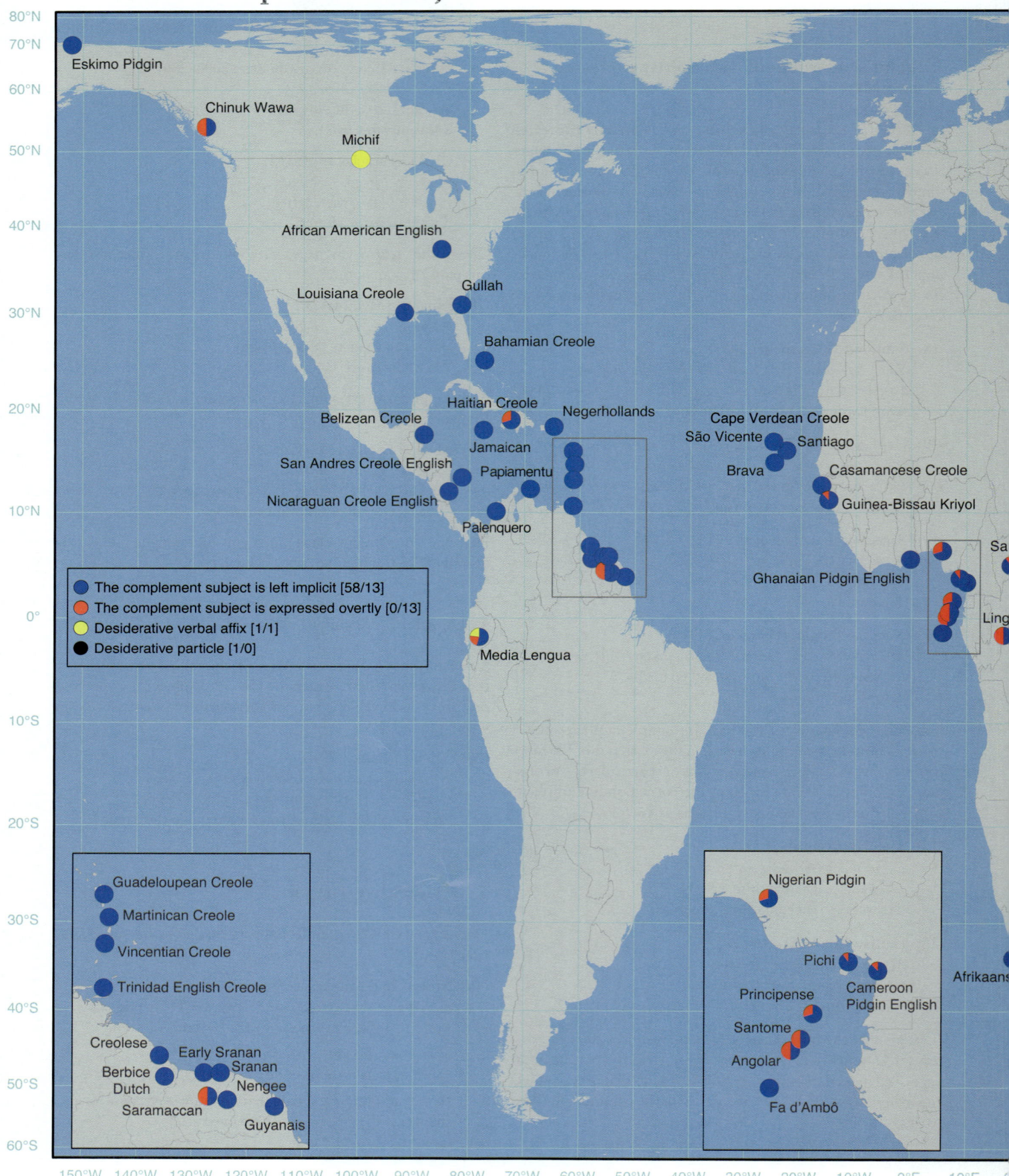

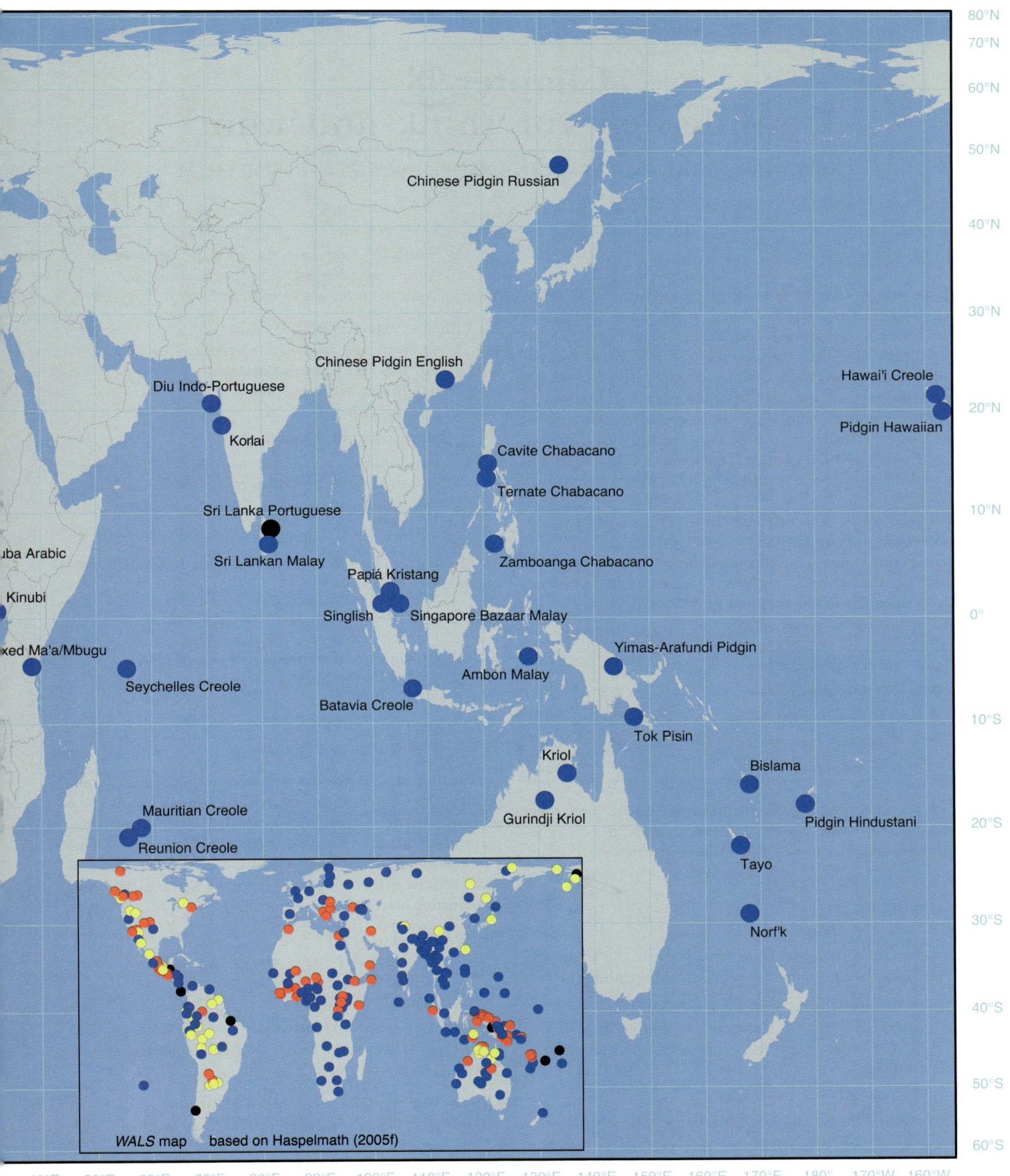

Chapter 98
Complements of 'think' and 'want'

SUSANNE MARIA MICHAELIS AND THE *APiCS* CONSORTIUM

1. Introduction

In the present chapter we consider the similarities and differences between two types of complement clause. On the one hand, we consider complement clauses which depend on the verb 'think' and where the subject of the main clause is different from the subject in the complement clause (e.g. English *She thinks that her son is at home*). On the other hand, we look at complement clauses of 'want' where the subject of the matrix clause is again different from the subject in the complement clause (e.g. English *She wants her son to come home*). For same-subject complements of 'want', see Chapter 97 ("'Want' complement subjects").

In comparing these two complement clause types, two separate parameters are relevant:
(i) whether there is an overt complementizer, and
(ii) if so, whether both complement types show the same complementizer or different complementizers.

We distinguish five feature values:

○ 1	Identical complementizer	15
● 2	Different complementizer	14
● 3	Only 'think' complement has a complementizer	19
○ 4	Only 'want' complement has a complementizer	1
○ 5	No complementizer	24

If several different 'think' complement constructions or several different 'want' constructions are possible, the contributors were asked to choose the dominant construction.

2. The values

Fifteen *APiCS* languages show value 1, where the 'think' and 'want' complement clauses show the **same complementizer**.

(1) Afrikaans (den Besten & Biberauer 2013)
  a. *Sy glo **dat** haar seun by die*
     3SG.F.NOM thinks [that 3SG.F.POSS son by DEF.ART
   huis is.
   house is]
   'She thinks that her son is at home.'

  b. *Anna wil **dat** haar seun huis toe gaan.*
    Anna wants [that 3SG.F.POSS son house to go]
   'Anne wants her son to go home.'

(2) Bislama (Meyerhoff 2013)
  a. *mi ting **se** bae mi lukaotem*
    1SG think [COMP IRR 1SG look.out]
   'I think that I'll go find [one].'

  b. *plante taem hem i wantem*
    plenty time 3SG AGR want
   ***se** man i mas folem ting~ting blong hem*
   [COMP man AGR must follow think~think POSS 3SG]
   'There are lots of times when she wants everyone to do what she thinks.'

The fourteen languages displaying value 2 show **different complementizers**.

(3) Guinea-Bissau Kriyol (Intumbo et al. 2013)
  a. *I pensa **kuma** si fidju sta na kasa.*
    3SG think [COMP POSS son COP at home]
   'She thinks that her son is at home.'

  b. *I misti **pa** si fidju bay kasa.*
    3SG want [COMP POSS son go home]
   'She wants her son to go home.'

The third value comprises languages in which the two complement types differ in that **only 'think' complements have a complementizer** (perhaps optionally), while 'want' complements lack one. This type is fairly widespread, too. One example comes from Pichi (see 4a–b), where we find the complementizer *se* in the 'think' construction, whereas in the 'want' construction there is no complementizer.

(4) Pichi (Yakpo 2013)
  a. *À bìn chɛk **se** ren gò fɔl.*
    1SG.SBJ PST think [COMP rain POT rain]
   'I thought it might rain.'

  b. *À want mek yù du mi sɔ̀n febɔ.*
    1SG.SBJ want [SBJV 2SG do 1SG.EMPH some favour]
   'I want you to do me a favour.'

Likewise, the examples from Ambon Malay in (5a–b) show an optional complementizer (*kata*) introducing the 'think' complement clause, whereas the 'want'-complement clause does not allow any complementizer.

(5) Ambon Malay (Paauw 2013)
   a. *De piker (**kata**) mo ka Natsepa par peknek kalo seng*
      3SG think [COMP FUT to Natsepa for picnic if   NEG
      ujang.
      rain]
      'He thought he would go to Natsepa for a picnic if it didn't rain.'
   b. *De mau de pung ana pulang.*
      3SG want [3SG POSS child go.home]
      'She wants her son to go home.'

In Berbice Dutch, the verb *glofu* 'believe' can introduce complement clauses marked by the complementizer *dati* 'that', by the serial complementizer *bi(fi)* 'say', or by a zero complementizer. However, in complement clauses depending on the verb *suku* 'want', no complementizer position is available.

The fourth value is the mirror image of value 3: **'want' complements have a complementizer**, while 'think' complements lack one. But this type is found only in Louisiana Creole, where the verb *ole* 'want' optionally has the complementizer *ke*, whereas *krwar* 'believe' generally shows no complementizer.

In 24 *APiCS* languages both complement clause types have **no overt complementizer** (value 5). Examples come from Papiá Kristang and Kinubi.

(6) Papiá Kristang (Baxter 2013)
   a. *eli lembrá bos já bai kaza*
      3SG think [2SG PFV go home]
      'He thinks you have gone home.'
   b. *eli kere bos bai kaza*
      3SG want [2SG go home]
      'He wants you to go home.'

(7) Kinubi (Luffin 2013)
   a. *ána féker lúga de bi-já   wóduru*
      I   think [language DET TAM-come disappear]
      'I think that this language will disappear.'
   b. *ána ázu íta rúo*
      I   want [you go]
      'I want you to go.'

3. Other differences between the two complement types

'Think' complements and 'want' complements often differ in ways that are unrelated to the presence, absence, or form of the complementizer. In particular, the 'want' complements often carry a "subjunctive" or "infinitive" marker of some sort, which is lacking in 'think' complements. In this way, there can be a fairly striking difference between the two clause types even when the language has value 1 (same complementizer) or 5 (no complementizer in both cases).

Thus, in Nigerian Pidgin, different-subject 'think' and 'want' complement clauses are introduced by the same complementizer *se*, but the 'want' complement clause (8b) shows the subjunctive marker *mek* (from English *make*; see Ihemere 2006 for the use of *mek* in Nigerian Pidgin, and Yakpo 2009 for a similar situation in Pichi; see also (4)).

(8) Nigerian Pidgin (Faraclas 2013)
   a. *À   tink se dèm   go tawn.*
      1SG.SBJ think [COMP 3PL.SBJ go town]
      'I think that they went to town.'
   b. *À   want se mek dèm   go tawn.*
      1SG.SBJ want [COMP SBJV 3PL.SBJ go town]
      'I want them to go to town.'

And in quite a few Atlantic English-based languages, the 'want' complement clause has a marker such as *fi*, *fo*, or *fu* (deriving from *for*), corresponding to the infinitival marker *to* in English:

(9) San Andres Creole English (Bartens 2013b)
   Ihn waahn evribady fi get hapi.
   3SG want [everybody to get happy]
   'He wants everybody to become happy.'

See also examples (6)–(7) in Chapter 97. Such markers have often been called "infinitival" markers (cf. Mufwene & Dijkhoff 1989) or even "complementizers", but we do not consider them complementizers here, as they do not occur in a clause-peripheral position. Their immediately preverbal position makes them more similar to modality markers. We did not single them out as a special type because one cannot readily distinguish such markers from other modality markers such as *gò* in (10).

(10) Ghanaian Pidgin English (Huber 2013)
   à wɔn se dè gò kam fiks àm
   1SG want [COMP 3PL FUT come fix 3SG.OBJ]
   'I want them to come and fix it.'

Another way in which 'want' complements may be distinct from 'think' complements is that they may lack person marking, as in Seychelles Creole in (11), where the third-person marker *i* is missing (see also Michaelis 1994: 82–91).

(11) Seychelles Creole (Michaelis & Rosalie 2013)
   Mari ti a oule son   garson al kot lakour.
   Mari PST FUT want [POSS.3SG son   go at house]
   'Mari would like her son to go home.'

Since most of the *APiCS* languages lack such agreement markers, this criterion cannot be used generally to classify the languages either.

98 Complements of 'think' and 'want'

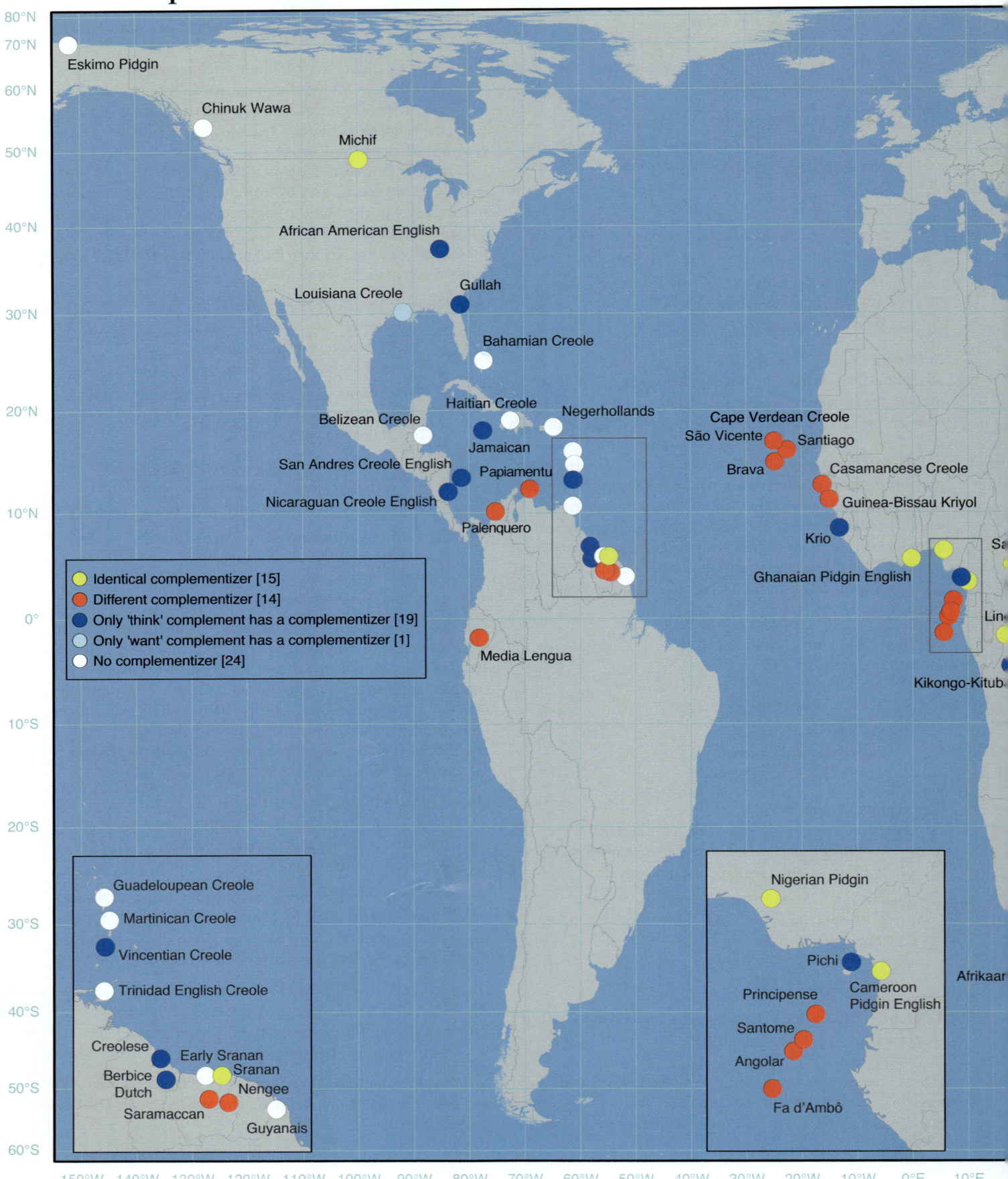

Chapter 99
Verb doubling in temporal clauses

SUSANNE M. MICHAELIS, MARTIN HASPELMATH, AND THE *APiCS* CONSORTIUM

1. Verb doubling

In a number of creole languages, temporal clauses can be expressed by constructions in which the verb is copied or reduplicated, as in (1) and (2).

(1) Haitian Creole (Fattier 2013)
 Parèt pwofesè ki mabyal la **parèt**, tout elèv
 [appear prof REL strict DEF appear] all student
 pè.
 be.afraid
 'As soon as the strict professor appears, all students are afraid.'

(2) Sri Lankan Malay (Slomanson 2013)
 Omong-omong Musba ruma na a-pi.
 [talk-talk] Musba house POSTP PRS-go
 'While talking, Musba goes (i.e. drives) home.'

Verb-doubling constructions occur widely in Atlantic creoles and pidgins to express focus (see Chapter 105), but they are rare in the function of marking temporal clauses. In our sample, they are found only in seven languages (plus an obsolete variety of an eighth language; see below):

- ● 1. Verb doubling is possible in temporal clauses 7
- ○ 2. Verb doubling is not possible in temporal clauses 67

2. More examples

Verb doubling in temporal clauses is found in five Atlantic languages, as well as in Sango and Sri Lankan Malay (see 2). In addition to Haitian Creole, we find it in Guadeloupean and Martinican Creole:

(3) Martinican/Guadeloupean Creole (Colot & Ludwig 2013a, b)
 Fini i *fini*, i *chapé*.
 [finish 3SG finish] 3SG escape
 'As soon as he finished, he left.'

Verb doubling is found in Berbice Dutch:

(4) Berbice Dutch (Kouwenberg 2013a)
 di **drai** wat ju **drai**-tɛ, o ku-tɛ ju
 [the turn REL 2SG turn-PFV] 3SG catch-PFV 2SG
 'As soon as you turn around, it catches you.'

In Nicaraguan Creole, it is not found in the modern language studied by Bartens (2013a), but it was attested at an earlier stage:

(5) Nicaraguan Creole English (Holm 1978: 235)
 di **kom** yu **kom**
 PST come 2SG come
 'as soon as you come'

Finally, we find it described for a variety of Cape Verdean Creole:

(6) Cape Verdean Creole of Santiago (Lang 2013)
 Na **kume** k' es ta **kume**, e nguli spinhu,
 [in eat COMP 3PL IPFV eat] 3SG swallow fishbone
 e ka xinti.
 3SG NEG feel
 'While they were having lunch, he swallowed a fishbone and didn't even notice.'

According to Lefebvre (2011: 21–2), such constructions are also found in Saramaccan and Papiamentu, but our contributors on these languages did not confirm this.

3. Structural properties

The verb-doubling constructions illustrated by (1)–(6) are fairly heterogeneous. In particular, the Sri Lankan Malay pattern in (2) is divergent, as it shows adjacent doubling, that is, a pattern that is best described as reduplication. (Note that in Chapter 105 on verb doubling and focus, we also find reduplication as a special rare type.)

The other five constructions share the order "verb$_1$–subject–verb$_2$", but the simplest pattern is found only in the French-based creoles of Haiti, Guadeloupe, and Martinique. In the Nicaraguan example (5), we see tense marking in the first instance of the verb, which is impossible in Haitian (Lefebvre & Ritter 1993: 68).

In Berbice Dutch, the first instance of the verb seems to be a kind of nominal form, as it is preceded by the definite article *di* and followed by the relative marker *wat*, so (4) is literally

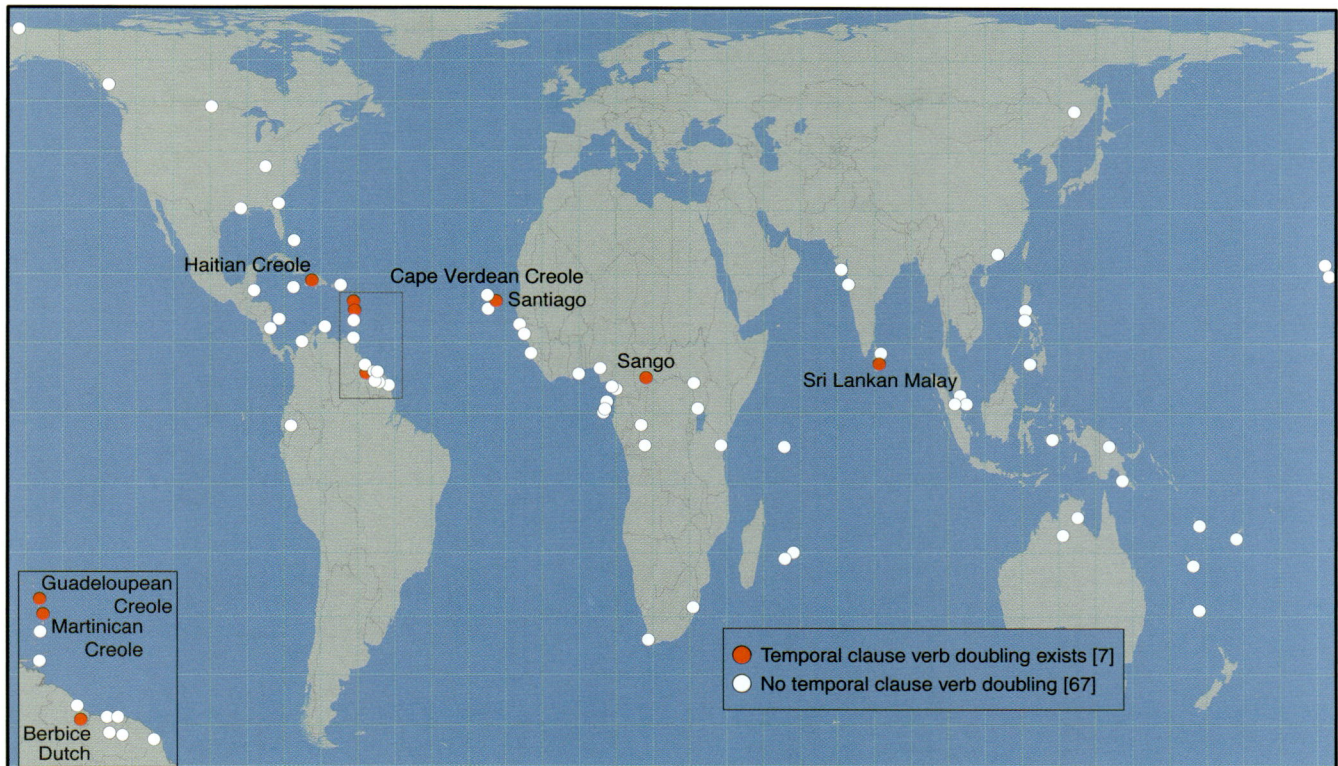

'the turning that you turned', which looks like a kind of cognate nominalized object. However, the relative-clause marker is not obligatory (Kouwenberg 2013a):

(7) di pak' ɛkɛ **paka** fan di rum ben,
[the emerge 1SG emerge from the room inside]
ɛkɛ kiki di kɛn-a latop-ar' o bringi
1SG see the person-PL lift-IPFV 3SG bring
'As I came out of the room, I saw them carrying him here.'

In Haitian Creole, too, the first instance of the verb can take a definite article (postposed *la/a*) (see 8a), so Lefebvre (1998: 369) regards it as a kind of nominalized form. However, the situation in Haitian is complex, and the definite article may also follow the second instance of the verb (8b).

(8) Haitian Creole
 a. ***Rive*** *a Jan **rive** (epi) Mari pati.*
    arrive DEF Jean arrive (and) Marie leave
    'As soon as John arrived, Marie left.'
    (Lefebvre 1998: 369)
 b. ***Rive*** *Jan **rive** a, Mari pati.*
    arrive Jean arrive DEF Marie leave
    'As soon as John arrived, Marie left.'
    (Lefebvre & Ritter 1993: 65)

A nominalization interpretation is readily available also for the Cape Verdean Creole example in (6), which can be translated literally as 'in the eating that they ate'. However, it must be kept in mind that this nominal occurs only in this construction (otherwise 'eating' is *kumida*).

It should be noted that, at least in Haitian Creole, such verb-doubling constructions can also have a causal sense ('because Jean arrived') and a factive sense ('the fact that Jean arrived') (see Lefebvre 1998: §12.6).

4. Substrate origin

According to Lefebvre (1998: §12.6), very similar patterns are found in Gbe languages, as shown by (9) from Fongbe (a Kwa language spoken in Benin) (see also Lefebvre & Brousseau 2002: ch. 16):

(9) Fongbe (Lefebvre 1998: 363)
 Wá *Jan **wá*** (trɔ́lɔ́) bɔ̀ Màrí yì.*
 [arrive Jean arrive (as.soon.as)] and Marie leave
 'As soon as Jean arrived, Marie left.'

We know of no comparative research on this kind of doubling construction in West African languages, and it remains to be seen whether the substrate explanation extends to the other Atlantic creoles. For Sri Lankan Malay, Nordhoff (2009: §7.5.4) notes that this pattern has been attributed to Sinhala influence, so here we have a non-lexifier source as well.

NEGATION, QUESTIONS, AND FOCUSING

Chapter 100
Negative morpheme types

MARTIN HASPELMATH, SUSANNE M. MICHAELIS, AND THE *APiCS* CONSORTIUM

1. Three types of negative morpheme

Negation is always signalled by an overt morpheme, and in this chapter we consider three different types of such morpheme: affix (see 1), particle (2), and auxiliary verb (3). Languages which mark negation by two morphemes in different positions (see 4) are the fourth type that is distinguished here.

(1) Sri Lankan Malay (Slomanson 2013)
Skul-ser pintu-yang tərə-tutup.
school-sir door-ACC NEG-close
'The teacher did not close the door.'

(2) Hawai'i Creole (Velupillai 2013)
ðat **no** saʊn ɹaɪt tu mi
DEM NEG sound right to 1SG.OBL
'That doesn't sound right to me.'

(3) Kriol (Schultze-Berndt & Angelo 2013)
Jad sineik **din** rili laik-im jad lilboi.
DEM snake NEG.PST really like-TR DEM little.boy
'The snake didn't really like the little boy.'

(4) Fa d'Ambô (Post 2013)
Eli ne ske da bo-f.
3SG NEG IRR give 2SG-NEG
'He will not give it to you.'

Languages can have several different negative morpheme types:

	excl	shrd	all
○ 1. Negative affix	2	6	8
● 2. Negative particle	53	15	68
○ 3. Negative auxiliary verb	1	10	11
○ 4. Bipartite negative marker	4	2	6

Note that we consider only standard negation (Miestamo 2005) here, as in the next chapter on the position of standard negation. This chapter loosely follows Dryer (2005n).

In addition to segmentable negative markers, some languages also have some verbs with suppletive negation marking, for example, *kaa* 'cannot' in Norf'k (Mühlhäusler 2013), which is in a suppletive relation to *ell* 'can' (< *able*). Such cases are not taken into account in this chapter.

For the six languages with a bipartite negative marker, see the next chapter on the position of standard negation.

2. Negative affix

A few languages have a negative affix. This is the only option in two languages, Sri Lankan Malay (see (1) above) and Mixed Ma'a/Mbugu:

(5) Mixed Ma'a/Mbugu (Mous 2013)
tú-si-tú mahóra
1PL.SBJ-NEG-dig pits
'Let us not dig pits.'

We also regard the Chinese Pidgin Russian form *ne* (e.g. *ne magu* 'I cannot'), the Zamboanga Chabacano form *no-* (*nosábe yo* 'I don't know'), and the Sri Lanka Portuguese form *nuku-* (*nuku-sava* 'doesn't know') as prefixes. Vincentian Creole (e.g. *wod-n* 'wouldn't') and Afrikaans (*kan-nie* 'cannot') are said to have a negative suffix that occurs with some modal verbs. However, these value assignments must be regarded as rather uncertain: distinguishing between affixes and non-affixed function words is generally very difficult or impossible (Haspelmath 2011b), and the criteria used here are probably not consistent across languages. Many of the negative particles of value 2 are probably equally tightly bound to the verb as the affixes of value 1.

In Sri Lanka Portuguese, there is reason to treat *nuku-* differently from the other negator *naa* (e.g. *naa vii* 'won't come'), because *naa* has a long vowel, unlike all other prefixes. In Zamboanga Chabacano, *no-* is different from the other negator *nuáy*, which is followed by the subject rather than directly by the verb:

(6) Zamboanga Chabacano (Steinkrüger 2013)
Nuay 'le ya-komprá este líbro.
NEG he PFV-buy this book
'He didn't buy this book.'

But these are language-particular criteria that do not generalize to other languages.

3. Negative particle

The great majority of *APiCS* languages have at least one negative morpheme that is classified as a negative particle. This particle typically occurs next to the verb (see the next chapter).

(7) Bislama (Meyerhoff 2013)
yu **no** save shopping blong ol man wetem blong yu
2SG NEG can shopping POSS PL man with POSS 2SG
'You can't do everyone else's shopping and yours.'

(8) Pichi (Yakpo 2013)
Dèn **no** gò flay nà Bàta mɔ.
3PL NEG POT fly LOC Bata more
'They're not going to fly to Bata any more.'

(9) Guinea-Bissau Kriyol (Intumbo et al. 2013)
Ze **ka** riba aonti.
Zé NEG return yesterday
'Zé did not return yesterday.'

It is often unclear whether such a negative morpheme should be regarded as a particle or a verbal affix. One suspects that writing habits influence our view of the grammatical nature of these elements. Particle status is clear when an argument phrase can come between the verb and the negative morpheme, as in (6) from Chabacano, and in the seven languages where the particle follows the object (value 3 in Chapter 101; but note that even in such a case, the negative morpheme can be written as an affix, as in (4) above).

4. Negative auxiliary verb

A negative auxiliary verb is a negative morpheme that has verbal properties such as tense marking or person marking. The best-known example comes from English, where negation is marked by the negative auxiliary *don't/doesn't* and *didn't* with most verbs (as well as *ain't* in non-standard varieties).

Interestingly, many English-based pidgins and creoles use a different strategy, the particle *no* preceding the verb (see (2), (7), and (8)). However, quite a few English-based languages have negative auxiliaries, retained from English (or perhaps reborrowed from English in decreolization):

(10) African American English (Green 2013)
They **ain't** leaving tomorrow.
they NEG.AUX leaving tomorrow
'They are not leaving tomorrow.'

(11) Trinidad English Creole (Mühleisen 2013)
Leah **eh** eat de food.
Leah NEG.AUX eat DET food
'Leah didn't eat the food.' (*eh* < *ain't*)

(12) Gullah (Klein 2013)
I **ain** gine worry a soul.
1SG.SBJ NEG.AUX going worry a soul
'I am not going to worry a soul.'

These elements might alternatively be considered negative particles, but we treat them as auxiliaries because they show a tense contrast. Thus, Trinidad English Creole has *doh* (< *don't*) as a present-tense counterpart of *eh*: *Leah doh eat de food* 'Leah doesn't eat the food'. And Kriol has *don* as a present-tense counterpart of *din* (cf. (3) above):

(13) Kriol (Schultze-Berndt & Angelo 2013)
Hi **don** want-im olabat hab-em.
3SG NEG.AUX want-TR 3PL have-TR
'He doesn't want them [i.e. the children] to have them.'

In Gullah, the auxiliary-verb status of *ain(t)* (seen earlier in 12) is shown by its ability to occur before the subject pronoun in questions:

(14) **Aint** you know say comin back rebel time?
NEG.AUX you know COMP coming back slavery time
'Don't you know that slavery is coming back?'
(Klein 2013)

In a number of Atlantic English-based languages, the preverbal negative morpheme *never* (or *neva*, *neba*, etc.) is classified as a negative auxiliary because it does not mean 'never', but is the simple negation of a past (or anterior) situation, that is, it is inherently tense-marked and occurs in an auxiliary slot.

(15) Belizean Creole (Escure 2013)
Yu **neva** ivn̩ memba dat if a **neva** kum
2SG ANT.NEG even remember that if 1SG ANT.NEG come
ya kum tɛl yu.
here come tell 2SG
'You would not even have remembered if I had not come to tell you.'

(16) Nigerian Pidgin (Faraclas 2013)
À **nẹva** bay nyam.
1SG.SBJ NEG.COMPL buy yam
'I didn't buy/haven't bought yams.'

5. Discussion

Since we cannot distinguish easily between affixes and particles, it is unclear whether it is significant that negative particles are found in almost all *APiCS* languages and negative affixes are rare in our languages, whereas negative affixes are very common in the world's languages (Dryer 2005n). However, we observe that short negative morphemes such as English *-n't*, French *ne*, and Portuguese *não* tend to get lost and be replaced (by *no* as in (7), *ka* as in (9), from Portuguese *nunca* 'never'). And where the old forms are preserved, they are often found only in a few high-frequency verbs (as with *no-* in Zamboanga Chabacano *no-sábe* 'don't know', and *-n* in Vincentian Creole *wod-n* 'wouldn't').

100 Negative morpheme types

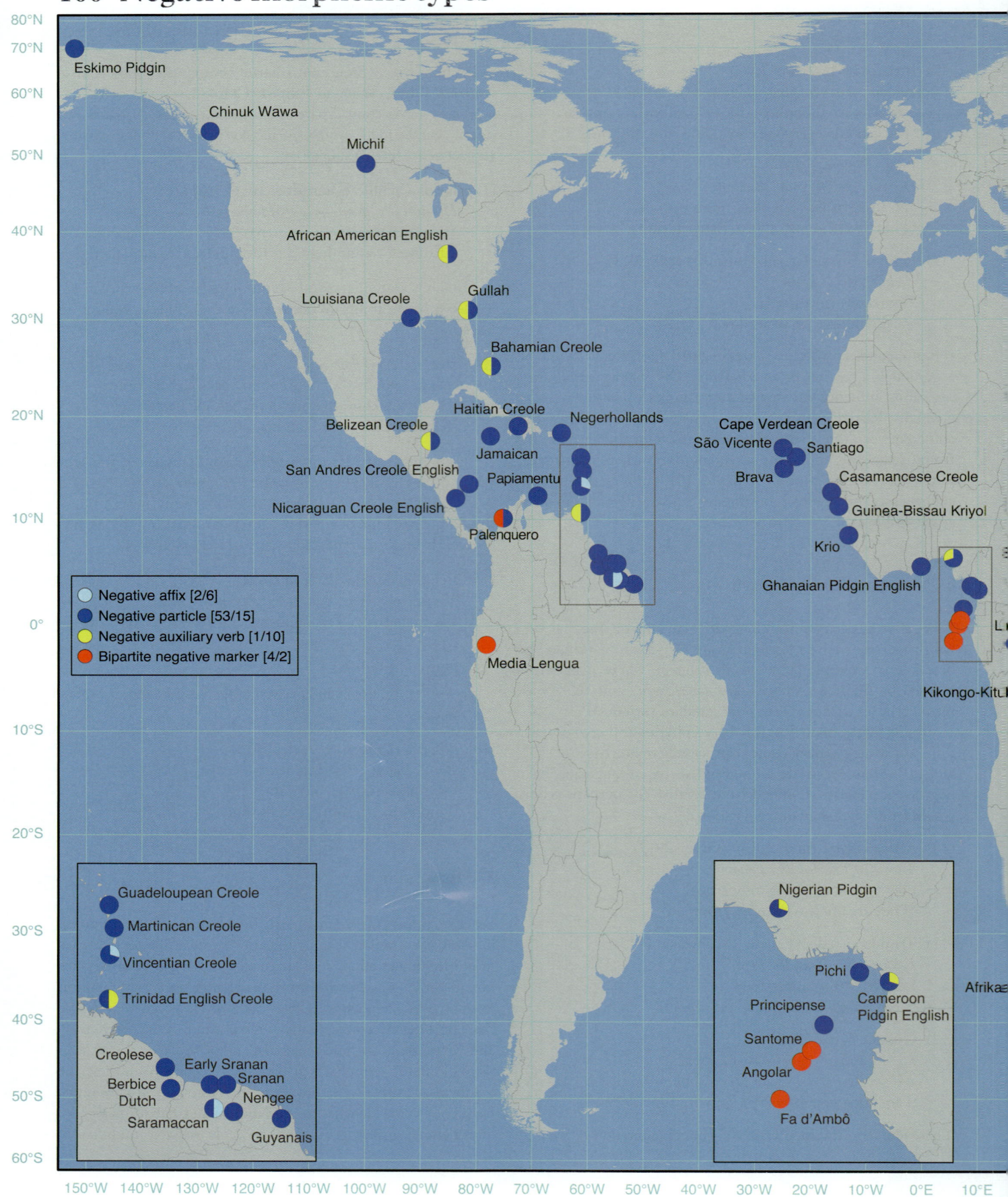

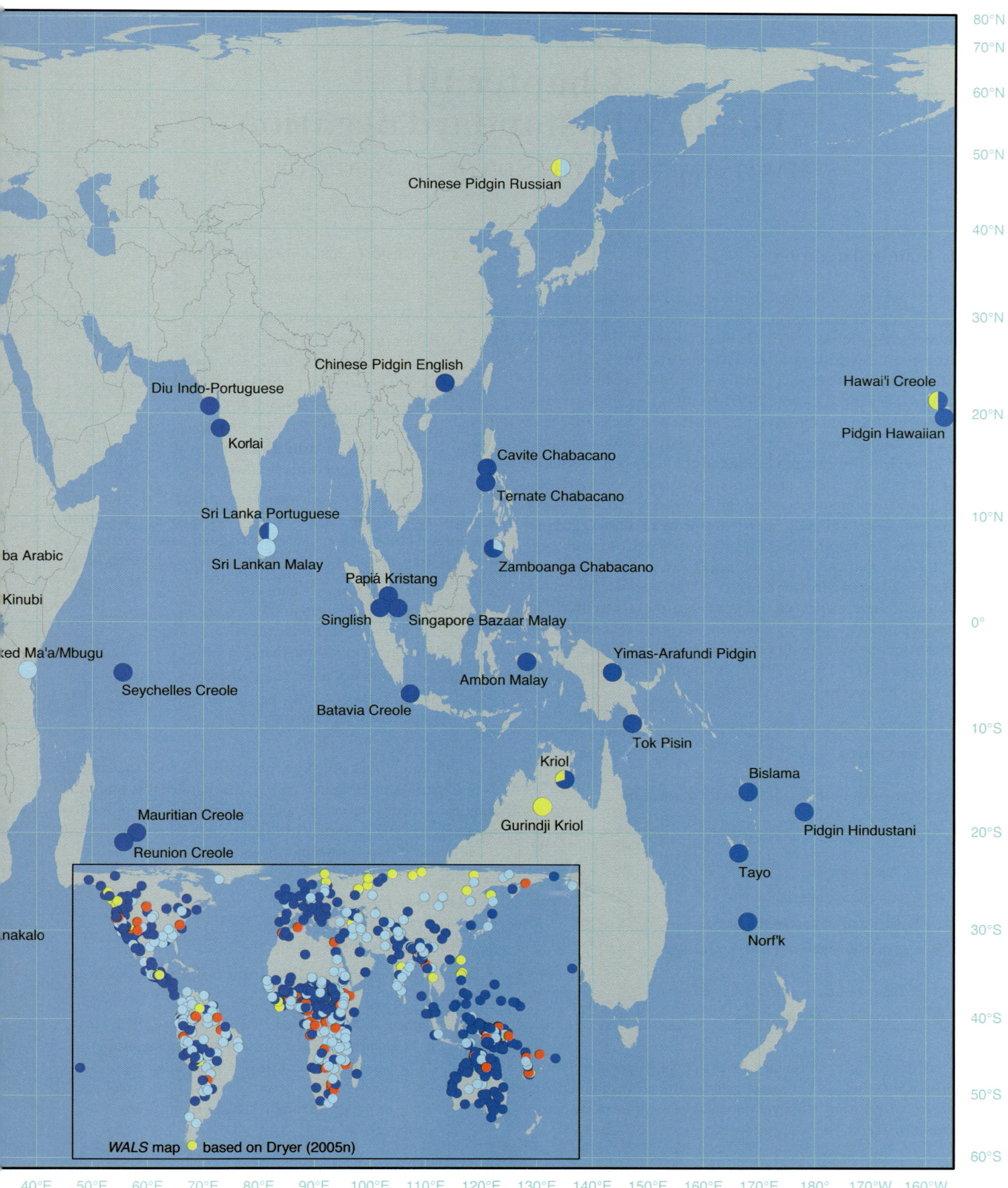

Chapter 101
Position of standard negation

MARTIN HASPELMATH AND THE *APiCS* CONSORTIUM

1. Standard negation

In this feature, we ask what the position of the negative marker is with respect to the main verb. In most of our languages, it immediately precedes the verb, but a number of languages deviate from this pattern in interesting ways. We focus on one particular type of negative construction, called **standard negation** (following Miestamo 2005). By this we mean the negative marker that is used for sentential negation in declarative main clauses, as in *She did not come*. Non-standard negation constructions such as constituent negation (e.g. *Not she came*), negation in subordinate clauses, in questions (e.g. *Didn't she come?*), and in imperatives are disregarded for this feature. See Chapter 56 for some information on negative imperatives (also called prohibitives). In considering the position of negative markers here, it does not matter whether the negative marker is a free word (=particle) or an affix (see Chapter 100 on negative morpheme types). If there are several different negative markers with different positions, or the negative marker may occur in different constructions, several values have been selected for a single language. In *WALS*, Dryer (2011b) examines the position of negative morphemes with respect to the verb.

2. The values

We distinguish six different values for this feature:

		excl	shrd	all
🔴	1. Before the verb	57	8	65
🔵	2. Immediately after the verb	2	5	7
🔵	3. After verb plus postverbal object	5	2	7
🟣	4. Bipartite, before verb and immediately after	0	1	1
🟡	5. Bipartite, before verb and after object	3	1	4
⚫	6. Bipartite, other possibilities	1	0	1

By far the most common type in our languages is **preverbal position** (value 1). This practically always means immediately preverbal position (though typically preceding other tense–aspect markers). Some examples are given in (1a–c).

(1) a. Seychelles Creole (Michaelis 1994: 185)
   Nou pa zwenn kanmarad.
   1PL NEG meet each.other
   'We don't meet each other.'

   b. Bahamian Creole (Hackert 2013)
   I ain't exactly know what kind of work he used to do.
   'I don't exactly know what kind of work he used to do.'

   c. Pidgin Hindustani (Siegel 2013)
   Ham-log nai kao pio tin roj kalas.
   I-PL NEG eat drink three day finish
   'We didn't eat or drink for three days.'

The preverbal negation element may preserve the lexifier's negative marker, or it may contain a new negative marker, such as *no* (or sometimes *never*, *nomore*) in English-based creoles (2a), (*nun*)*ka* (from *nunca* 'never') in Portuguese-based creoles (2b).

(2) a. Belizean Creole (Escure 2013)
   Yu no waak da ridj de.
   2SG NEG walk that ridge there
   'You don't walk along that ridge.'

   b. Casamancese Creole (Biagui & Quint 2013)
   Jon ka kumé biyanda.
   John NEG PFV.eat cooked.rice
   'John did not eat rice.'

It is only rarely that preverbal negation precedes the subject as well. In Pidgin Hawaiian (see 3), this pattern was inherited from the lexifier (Hawaiian), and it alternates with a more distinctively pidgin pattern with subject–negation–verb order. (Chabacano also has pre-subject negation.)

(3) Pidgin Hawaiian (Roberts 2013)
   Aole wau pepehi kela kepani.
   NEG 1SG beat DET Japanese
   'I didn't beat up that Japanese.'

Immediately **postverbal position** (value 2) is much less common:

(4) a. Chinese Pidgin Russian (Perekhvalskaya 2013)
   За женушека месяза посиди нету, адали чужой.
   Za ʒenuʃeka mesiaza pasidi netu, adali tʃuʒoj.
   TOP wife place sit NEG like stranger
   'They never sit near their wives as if they were strangers.'

b. Eskimo Pidgin (van der Voort 2013)
*ababa tusa'ra **pī'tcûk***
say hear not
'I heard no talking.'

This is of course the pattern of standard French (with main verbs), so some French-based creoles have this as one possibility (see 5). However, since the French negator *pas* follows auxiliaries which precede the main verb, these languages generally also allow preverbal negation in some patterns (see 6), or require it (see 1a).

(5) Reunion Creole (Bollée 2013)
*Mi touch **pa** aou.*
1SG.PRS touch NEG OBL.2SG
'I do not touch you.'

(6) Louisiana Creole (Neumann-Holzschuh & Klingler 2013)
*Ye **pa** kone parle kreol.*
3PL NEG know.how speak Creole
'They don't know how to speak Creole.'

A pattern that is almost as common as immediately postverbal negation is **negation that follows** not only a verb, but **also a postverbal object** (value 3). This is found especially in a number of languages in Africa (Lingala, Sango, Principense, but also Berbice Dutch).

(7) Principense (Maurer 2013c)
*Amanhan n sa kume pêxi **fa**.*
tomorrow 1SG FUT eat fish NEG
'Tomorrow I won't eat fish.'

The negator usually follows not only an object, but other postverbal elements as well, even subordinate clauses. In such cases, it may have scope over the main clause only, over the subordinate clause only, or even (as in 8) over both.

(8) Berbice Dutch (Kouwenberg 2013a)
*ɛkɛ suku mu titi ori jɛn-da **ka***
1SG want go time 3SG be-there NEG
'I don't want to go when he is not there.' or 'I want to go when he is not there.' or 'I don't want to go when he is there.'

A few contact languages also show **bipartite negation**, such as French *ne . . . pas*, though no French-based language has preserved this. Note that bipartite negation is particularly common in central and western Africa (Dryer 2011b), so here the *APiCS* languages clearly show African influence. The two markers can precede and **immediately follow the verb** (as in Standard French) (value 4). In *APiCS* this is found only in Media Lengua (9), with preverbal *no* from Spanish and postverbal *-chu* from Quechua.

(9) Media Lengua (Muysken 2013)
*llubi-xu-kpi mañana **no** i-sha-**chu***
rain-PROG-SUBORD tomorrow NEG go-1SG.FUT-NEG
'If it rains tomorrow I won't go.'

But the second marker can **also follow an object** (value 5), or even a subordinate clause, as in (10). This occurs mainly in the Portuguese-based Gulf of Guinea creoles.

(10) Santome (Hagemeijer 2013)
*Maji n **na** sêbê xi n ga nganha ala **fa**.*
but 1SG NEG know if 1SG IPFV arrive there NEG
'But I don't know if I will get there.'

A Caribbean creole that has this is Palenquero, where both elements are *nu* (see example 11; but note that single *nu* is also possible, either preverbally or following the object).

(11) Palenquero (Schwegler 2013)
*I **nu** sabé eso **nu**.*
I NEG know this NEG
'I don't know this.'

The most complex kind of bipartite negation is found in Afrikaans (value 6), where both negation morphemes are *nie*. The first *nie* follows the main verb in VO order (see 12a) and precedes it in OV order (see 12b). The second *nie* follows at the end.

(12) Afrikaans (den Besten & Biberauer 2013)
a. *Hy gaan **nie**$_1$ huistoe **nie**$_2$.*
he go NEG home NEG
'He does not go home.'
b. *omdat hy **nie**$_1$ huistoe gaan **nie**$_2$*
because he NEG home go NEG
'because he does not go home'

If the two negation morphemes were to occur next to each other, only one occurs (*hy gaan nie* 'he does not go').

3. Comparison to *WALS*

In the world's languages, negative markers tend to precede the verb, but the tendency is somewhat less strong than in the *APiCS* languages. In Dryer's (2011b) sample of 1,326 languages, about half of the languages have a preverbal negative morpheme, while less than a third have a postverbal negative morpheme. (Among postverbal negative morphemes, affixes are more common than negative words; only one-quarter of negative words is postverbal.) About one-sixth of the world's languages have bipartite negation.

101 Position of standard negation

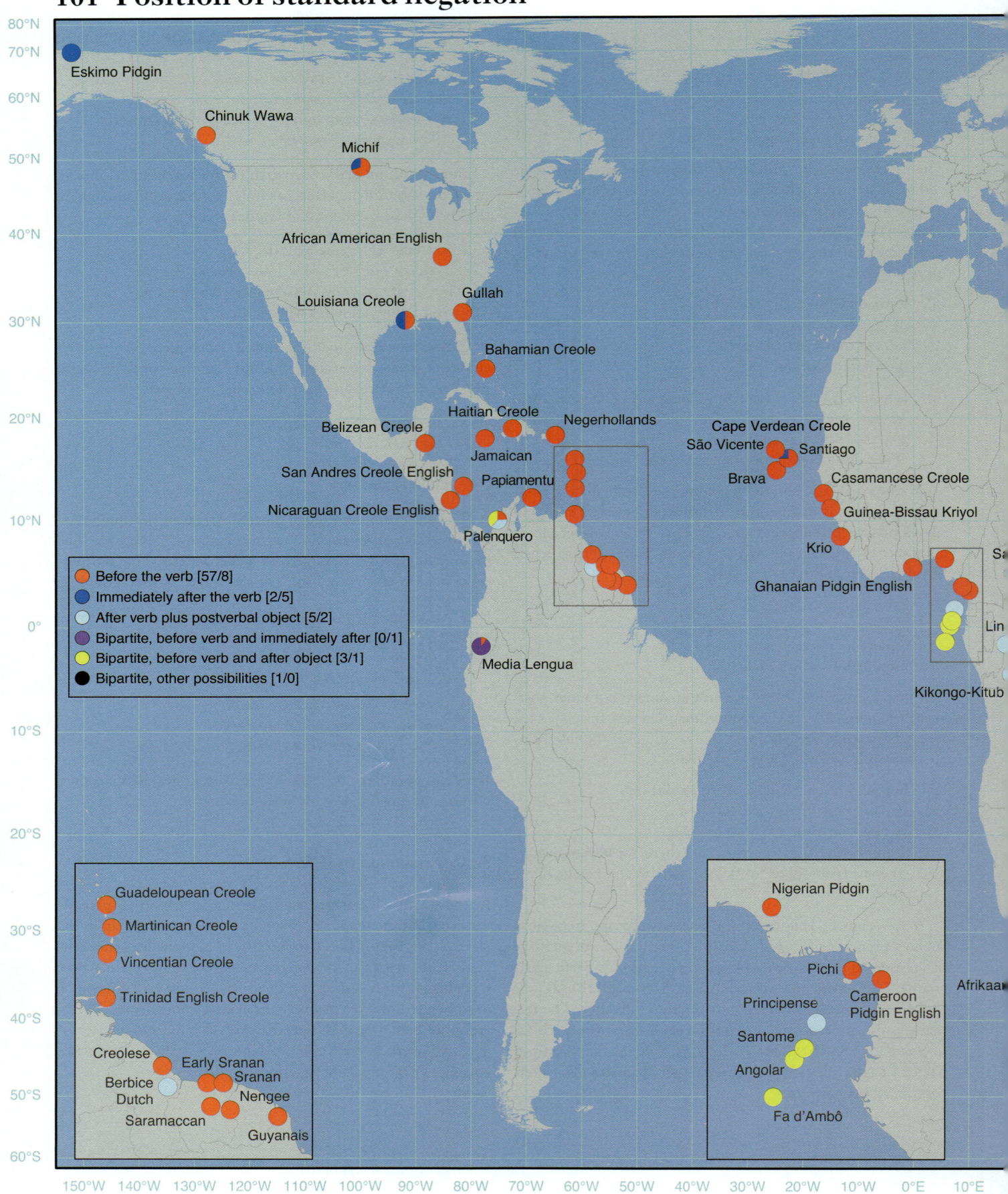

Chapter 102
Negation and indefinite pronouns

MARTIN HASPELMATH AND THE *APiCS* CONSORTIUM

1. Introduction

This chapter deals with indefinite pronouns that are semantically in the scope of negation, as in (1).

(1) a. *Nobody saw me.*
    b. *I saw nobody.*
    c. (*Anybody did not see me.*)
    d. *I did not see anybody.*

The main question that we ask here is whether a language requires the use of ordinary **predicate negation** with such negatively used indefinite pronouns, as in (1d), or whether it allows predicate negation to be absent, as in (1a, b), so that the negative sense is rendered only by the indefinite pronoun. We mostly focus on 'nobody' and 'nothing', but 'never' is also regarded as an indefinite pronoun.

In the world's languages, co-occurrence of indefinite pronouns with predicate negation is by far the most common type (see Haspelmath's 2005e *WALS* chapter and Haspelmath 1997: ch. 8), but in some European languages, most notably Latin and German (as well as Dutch), negatively used indefinites always **preclude** predicate negation (i.e are incompatible with it), at least on the intended sense:

(2) Latin
    Timeo nihil. (*non timeo nihil*)
    'I fear nothing.'

(3) Dutch
    Niemand heeft opgebeld. (*niemand heeft niet opgebeld*)
    'Nobody has called.'

Some languages show variability of the use of predicate negation. In Spanish (and likewise in Portuguese), for example, the occurrence of predicate negation depends on the **position** of the indefinite: If it precedes the verb, predicate negation is precluded, but if it follows the verb, it is required:

(4) Spanish
    a. *Nadie vino.* (*nadie no vino*)
       'Nobody came.'
    b. *No vi nada.* (*vi nada*)
       NEG I.saw nothing
       'I saw nothing.'

English shows variability in the use of predicate negation as well, and here, too, word order is one relevant factor (cf. 1c with 1d). But the primary factor is the **type of indefinite pronoun**: *nobody/nothing* precludes predicate negation, while *anybody/anything* may co-occur with predicate negation.

Some authors make a distinction between "inherently negative indefinites" and other negatively used indefinites, but no such distinction is made here. Determining which indefinites are "inherently negative" is not possible, as we are only looking at ordinary negative contexts as in (1)–(4), where indefinites are negative by definition. Even expressions with generic nouns as in (5) count as indefinite pronouns for current purposes (this is in line with Chapter 21 on indefinite pronouns).

(5) Kikongo-Kituba (Mufwene 2013)
    Muntu mosi ve kwis-aka.
    person one not come-PST
    'Nobody came.'

2. Co-occurrence with predicate negation

As the value box shows, the great majority of languages show the co-occurrence type (value 1), represented by (1d) and (4b) (*I did not see any body*, *No vi nada*). Preclusion of predicate negation by negative indefinites is not common.

● 1. Co-occurrence with predicate negation		59
● 2. Preclusion possible with preverbal indefinites		6
● 3. Preclusion possible under other conditions		4
● 4. Negative existential construction		4

The *APiCS* languages thus pattern with the majority of the world's languages in showing a massive preference for "double negation" or "multiple negation" (as the co-occurrence pattern is sometimes called). But they contrast strikingly with the major lexifier languages, all of which prohibit co-occurrence at least with preverbal indefinites. Thus, we find the following sentences with subject indefinites, whose direct counterparts in the lexifiers are ungrammatical:

(6) San Andres Creole English (Bartens 2013b)
    Nonbady no waahn daans wid Taiga.
    nobody NEG want dance COM Tiger
    'Nobody wanted to dance with Tiger.'

(7) Papiamentu (Kouwenberg 2013b)
Ningun di nan **no** a laga **nada** lòs tokante nan plan.
no.one of 3PL NEG PFV let nothing loose about 3PL plan
'Not one of them has revealed anything about their plan.'

(8) Cape Verdean Creole of Santiago (Lang 2013)
Náda ka ta leba-m dexa nha-s fidju.
nothing NEG IPFV carry-1SG abandon my-PL child
'Nothing will make me abandon my children.'

(9) Seychelles Creole (Michaelis & Rosalie 2013)
Personn pa ti vini.
nobody NEG PST come
'Nobody came.'

In Standard French, negative indefinites show partial co-occurrence with the bipartite negator *ne . . . pas*, in that the negative indefinite co-occurs with *ne*, but not *pas* (*personne n'est venu* 'nobody has come'). In the French-based creoles, *ne* plays no role, and *pa* (< *pas*) always co-occurs with negative indefinites. Note in this connection that those Gulf of Guinea creoles that have a bipartite negator (see Chapter 101) are different from Standard French in that they exhibit full co-occurrence, that is, both elements of the bipartite negator co-occur with the indefinite:

(10) Angolar (Maurer 2013a)
n **na** tô tê **kwa** fa me **va**
I NEG REP have thing say self NEG
'I didn't have anything to say any more.'

Co-occurrence with predicate negation is also widely found in languages not based on western European languages, but here it is unsurprising, because the vast majority of languages outside western Europe have co-occurrence.

(11) Chinuk Wawa (Grant 2013)
wik náyka mákmak **ikta**
NEG 1SG eat thing
'I didn't eat anything.'

(12) Chinese Pidgin Russian (Perekhvalskaya 2013)
Ничего не делай его, только работай конторе.
Nitʃiwo ni delaj iwo, tol'ko rabotaj kantore.
nothing NEG do 3SG only work office
'She does not do anything, she only works in the office.'

3. Preclusion of predicate negation

There is not one single *APiCS* language that is like Latin, German, and Dutch in that it never allows the co-occurrence of indefinites with predicate negation. But in a number of English-based languages, preclusion of predicate negation by the negative indefinite is found under conditions similar to those in English. Thus, Cameroon Pidgin English has co-occurrence with postverbal indefinites (*A no get nating* 'I have nothing'), but not with preverbal ones (*No peson bin kom* 'Nobody came'; Schröder 2013). A number of West African and Caribbean English-based languages are similar. It should be noted, however, that it is not always clear under what exact conditions predicate negation can be omitted. Sometimes it appears that the type of indefinite is decisive, rather than the position. This is the case in Standard English, which allows (1b) (*I saw nobody*), that is, preclusion with a postverbal indefinite. If we have no evidence that postverbal indefinites can co-occur with negation, such a language is classified as showing value 2.

A few languages are classified as value 3 (preclusion possible under other conditions), for example, Singlish, which allows preclusion with postverbal indefinites as in *I understand nothing*, and Norf'k, which has *Ai sii noebohdi* 'I saw nobody'. What exactly allows or requires preclusion in these languages is not clear. The mixed language Michif is particularly complicated and puzzling. With French-based indefinites, there is no predicate negation (in striking contrast to the French-based creoles):

(13) Michif (Bakker 2013)
Zhamaen ni-muw-aaw la bish.
never 1-eat-3.SBJ.3.OBJ ART.F.SG elk
'I never ate elk.' (*zhamaen* < French *jamais* 'never')

With Cree-based indefinites, the negator *noo* precedes the indefinite rather than the verb, and it is not quite clear whether the NEG+indefinite complex should be regarded as a unit (analogous to English *no-where*, etc.) or whether an example like (14) should be seen as showing ordinary predicate negation.

(14) **Noo naandaw** ni-mishkaw-aaw la shayeer.
NEG somewhere 1-find.ANIM-3.OBJ ART.F.SG pail
'I can't find the pail anywhere.'

4. Negative existential constructions

In a few languages, a negative existential construction is used to express the notion of 'nobody' and 'nothing' (value 4). This occurs especially in the languages of the Philippines, and is thus found in the Chabacano varieties:

(15) Zamboanga Chabacano (Steinkrüger 2013)
Nuáy kyen ya-andá na dimiyo kása.
NEG.EXIST who PRF-go LOC my house
'Nobody came to my house.'
(lit. 'Doesn't exist who came to my house.')

This is not the only possible construction, and Cavite Chabacano, for example, also allows *no sabi nada* '(s/he) knows nothing'. But the existential construction is so salient that it is singled out here as a separate type in these languages (as well as in Juba Arabic).

102 Negation and indefinite pronouns

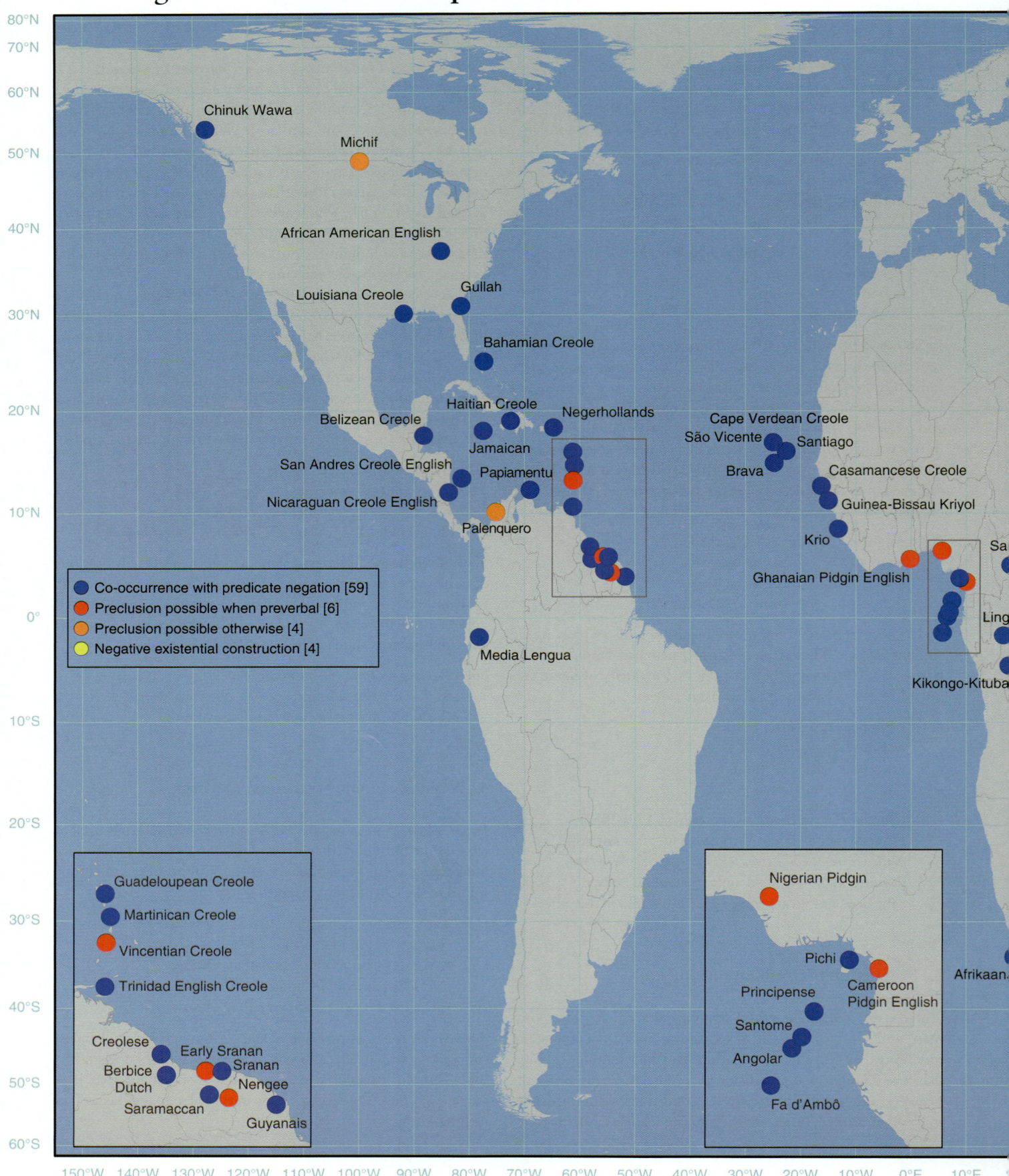

Chapter 103
Polar questions

MARTIN HASPELMATH AND THE *APiCS* CONSORTIUM

1. Polar questions

A **polar question** is a question that asks about the truth of a proposition rather than requesting additional information concerning a particular aspect of a proposition. Polar questions thus expect an answer like 'yes' or 'no', and are also known as *yes–no questions*. All languages have polar questions, and they are quite easy to identify and delimit from content questions (see Chapter 12 on the position of interrogative phrases in content questions). In this chapter, as in the corresponding *WALS* feature (Dryer 2005o), we ask how polar questions are marked as such, that is, how the addressee knows that the speaker intends a question rather than a statement. Such marking is more important in polar questions than in content questions, because the latter can typically be recognized by the presence of a specific interrogative phrase.

2. The values

Seven different values are distinguished, but only three of them occur with any frequency, the other four being rare.

		excl	shrd	all
○	1. Only interrogative intonation	35	36	71
●	2. Interrogative word order	1	3	4
○	3. Initial question particle	1	13	14
●	4. Final question particle	2	20	22
○	5. Question particle in other position	0	7	7
●	6. Interrogative verb morphology	1	0	1
○	7. A-not-A question	0	2	2

By far the most common type is represented by constructions where there is no special formal marking apart from **interrogative intonation** (value 1). This is the only option in about half of the languages, and it is one possibility in almost all the others (only Afrikaans, Sri Lankan Malay, Media Lengua, Kikongo-Kituba, and Saramaccan do not have this possibility). Some examples are given in (1).

The exact nature of the intonational marking is rarely specified, reflecting the fact that intonation is not well understood by linguists and rarely described well. Most commonly, it seems

(1) a. Chinese Pidgin English (Li & Matthews 2013)
   You likee makee boilum?
   2SG like make boil
   'Do you want it cooked?'

b. Gurindji Kriol (Meakins 2013)
   Yu garram kengkaruyu minti?
   2SG have kangaroo-DAT bottom
   'Do you have the kangaroo's bottom?'

c. Nigerian Pidgin (Faraclas 2013)
   Yù go makét?
   2SG.SBJ go market
   'Did you go to the market?' (Final rising intonation)

that polar questions are distinguished by a rising intonation at the end. For Chinese Pidgin English, Hall's (1944: 97) description is unusually explicit: "When no specifically interrogative word or phrase is present, pitch rises to the highest point on the stressed syllable of the last word in the sentence" (cited by Li & Matthews 2013). Concerning (1b), Meakins (2013) says: "The only thing that indicates that this is a question is rising intonation".

In a number of European languages, but only very few languages elsewhere, a special verb-initial **interrogative word order** (value 2) signals polar questions (cf. Dryer's 2005o *WALS* chapter). In *APiCS*, this is found in only a few English-based languages (e.g. 2a), as well as in Afrikaans, in other words, in languages that are fairly close to their Germanic lexifiers:

(2) a. Gullah (Klein 2013)
   Aint you know say comin back rebel time?
   NEG.AUX you know that coming back slavery time
   'Don't you know that slavery is coming back?'

b. Afrikaans (den Besten & Biberauer 2013)
   Het jy dit ge-sien?
   PST 2SG.NOM 3SG.N PART-seen?
   'Did you see it?'

A cross-linguistically very common method of signalling polar questions is by means of question particles, and this also occurs in *APiCS*. In quite a few languages, we find an **initial question particle** (value 3), as in (3a, b). In French-based creoles, this particle generally derives from the French expression *est-ce que*.

(3) a. Martinican Creole (Colot & Ludwig 2013b)
    Es i pati?
    Q 3SG leave
    'Did he leave?'
  b. Kikongo-Kituba (Mufwene 2013)
    Nki yandi me kwisa?
    Q s/he PERF come
    'Did s/he come?'

Even more common in *APiCS* are languages with a **final question particle** (value 4), as illustrated in (4). Note that questions marked by question particles may also show special interrogative intonation, but if there is segmental marking, intonation is not taken into account here.

(4) a. Ambon Malay (Paauw 2013)
    Pap mara katong ka?
    father angry 1PL Q
    'Would father be angry with us?'
  b. Santome (Hagemeijer 2013)
    Bô ka lembla non an?
    2SG IPFV remember 1PL Q
    'Do you remember us?'

Typical question particles are not separated intonationally from the question clause, whereas question tags are separated in this way. But since intonation is difficult to take into account systematically, we have not excluded question tags. Quite a few of the cases of final question particles could be question tags, and these elements often have other meanings such as 'not'. Two examples are shown in (5a, b) (other languages with such 'no' question tags are Gullah, Norf'k, Saramaccan, and Mauritian Creole).

(5) a. Sranan (Winford & Plag 2013)
    A film ben span, no?
    DET movie PST exciting no
    'The movie was exciting, wasn't it?'
  b. Kinubi (Luffin 2005: 383)
    Sébi de árab, meš?
    Sebi COP Arabic NEG
    'Sebi is an Arabic name, isn't it?'

Question particles are most often in a peripheral position, but they may also occur **in some other position** inside the clause (value 5). For Singapore Bazaar Malay, it is reported that the particle may occur immediately after the questioned constituent (cf. 6a), while in Chabacano and Michif, the particle may occur in second position (see 6b–c).

(6) a. Singapore Bazaar Malay (Khin Khin Aye 2013)
    Bagus, tak paham ka bagus?
    good NEG understand Q good
    '*Bagus*? Don't (you) understand *bagus* ('good')?'
  b. Ternate Chabacano (Sippola 2013b)
    Tédi ba ta kré?
    2PL Q IPFV believe
    'Do you believe?'
  c. Michif (Bakker 2013)
    Kit-ayaa-naan chii lii zavis di bwaa?
    2-have-1PL Q ART.PL screw of wood
    'Do we (inclusive) have any lag screws?'

We also subsume Guinea-Bissau Kriyol under this value, but the language is unusual in that it allows both an initial and a final question particle in polar questions (cf. 7). Both particles are optional, so Kriyol has four options (both initial and final particle, only initial, only final, no particle).

(7) Guinea-Bissau Kriyol (Intumbo et al. 2013)
    (*Ke*) *friu ten* (*me*)?
    Q cold exist Q
    'It's cold, right?'

A single *APiCS* language was classified as having special **interrogative verb morphology** (value 6). However, the element *-chu* might well be a clitic.

(8) Media Lengua (Muysken 2013)
    ayuda-sha-chu?
    help-1.FUT-Q
    'Shall I help you?'

Finally, two languages have **A-not-A questions** (value 7), that is, questions marked by repetition of the questioned element, with a 'not' word in between. This pattern is found in Chinese languages, as well as in two pidgins influenced by Chinese, as in (9) (an example from Chinese Pidgin English is *Can no can?* 'Can you do so?').

(9) Chinese Pidgin Russian (Perekhvalskaya 2008: 226)
    Ju den'gi mej ju?
    exist money NEG exist
    'Do you have money?' (lit. 'Have money not have?')

3. Comparison to *WALS*

In the world's languages, polar questions are most often marked by interrogative particles or interrogative verb morphology. Intonation as the sole means of marking questions is of course also found, but in Dryer's (2005o) sample, in not more than one-sixth of the languages. Thus, pidgins and creoles are far more likely to use nothing but intonation to mark polar questions than other languages. It should also be noted that *APiCS* languages that use question particles can usually also form polar questions without a particle. This, too, shows the general dominance of the intonation-only strategy.

103 Polar questions

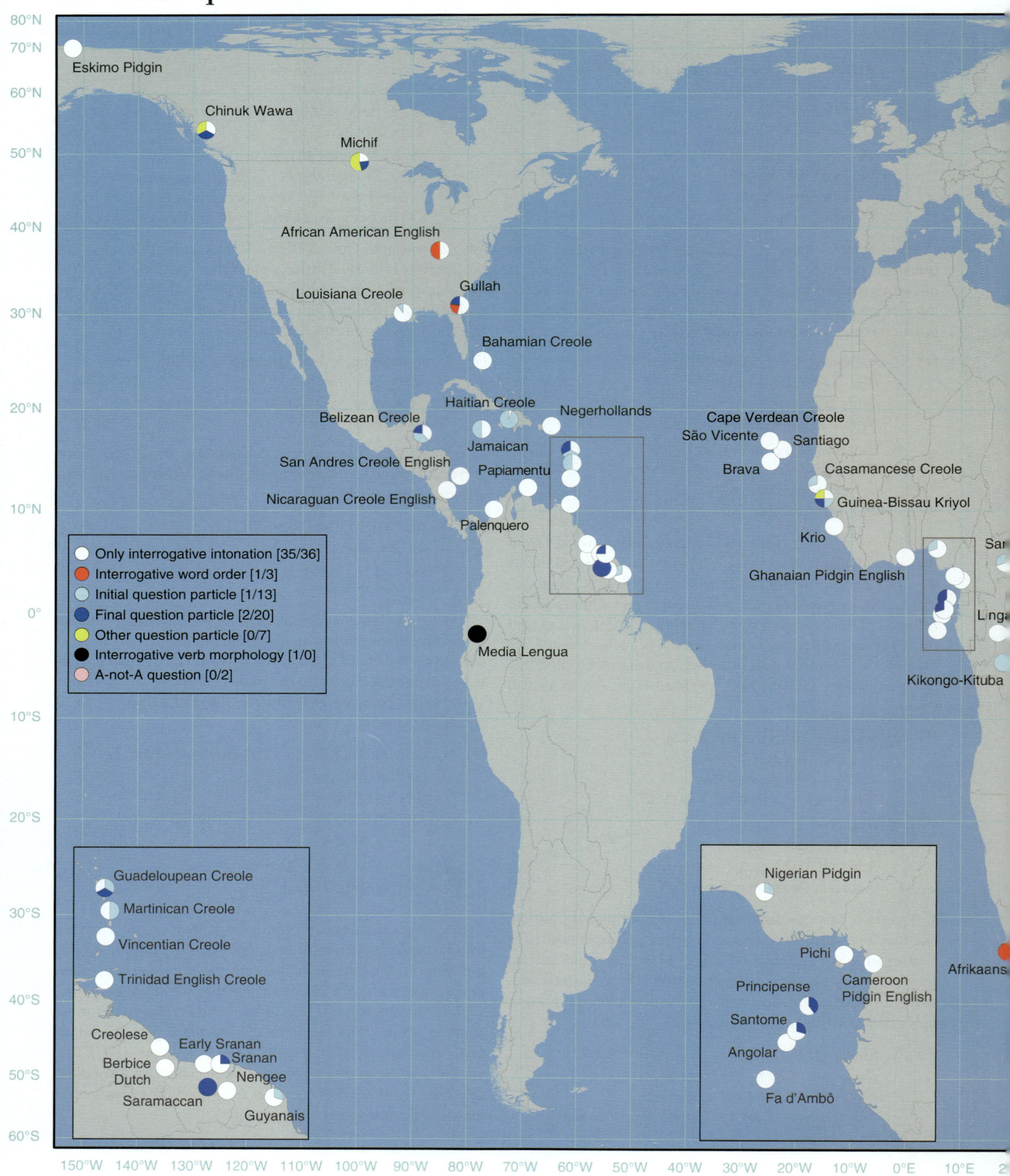

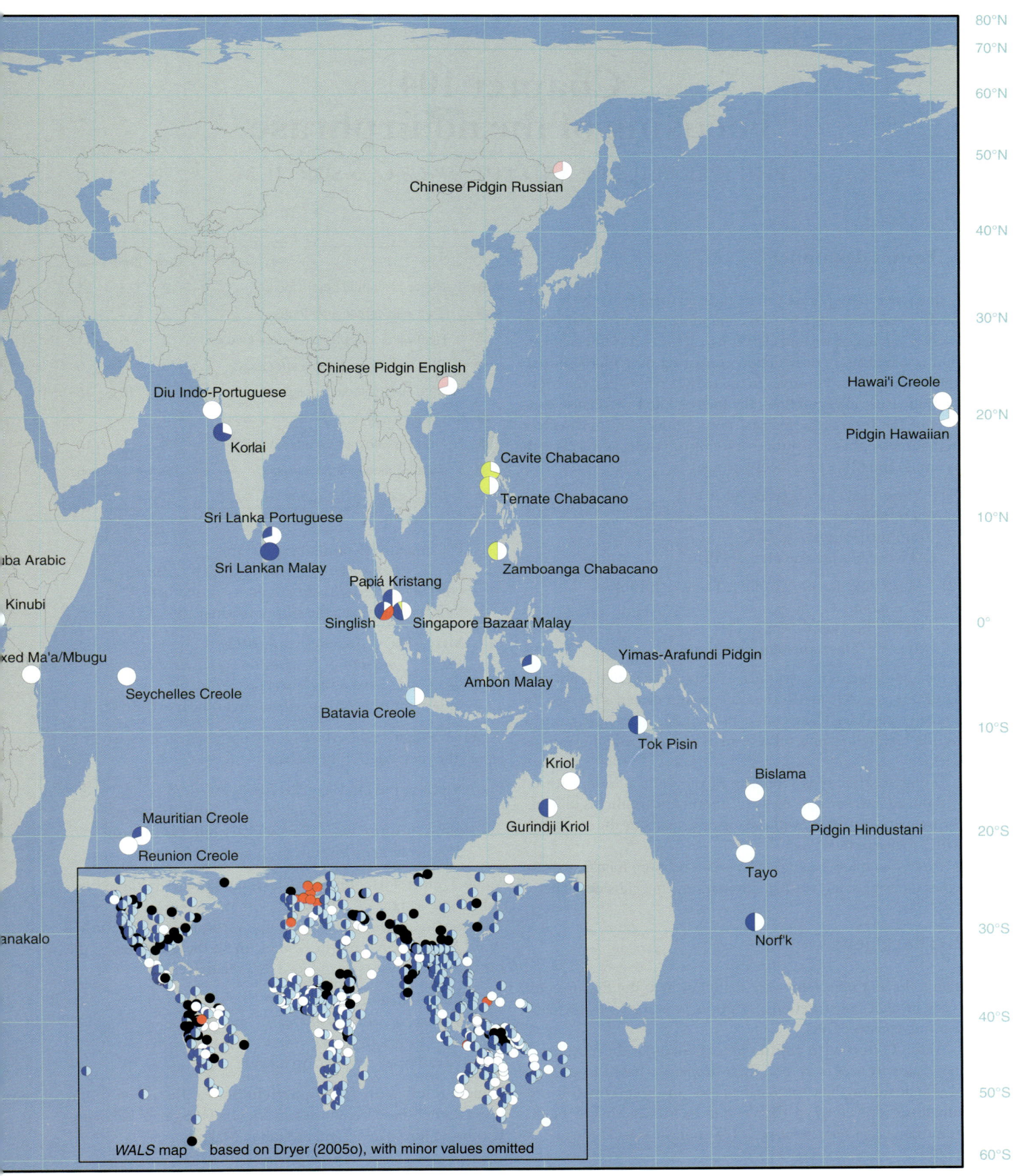

Chapter 104
Focusing of the noun phrase

PHILIPPE MAURER AND THE *APiCS* CONSORTIUM

1. Feature description

A noun or a noun phrase can be focused (contrastively) by different means. Among the most commonly used strategies in the *APiCS* languages, we find cleft constructions. A cleft construction is a biclausal construction consisting of a **focus clause** and a **background clause** (in the *APiCS* languages, the background clause always follows the focus). The focus clause consists of the **focus** (the focused noun phrase) and normally a highlighter, either a **copula** or a **focus particle**, as in (1) (with a copula) and (2) (with a focus particle).

(1) Vincentian Creole (Prescod 2013)
 Di man iz hu se so.
 [ART man] COP REL say so
 'The man is the one who said that.'

(2) Martinican Creole (Colot & Ludwig 2013b)
 Sé papa ki fè kay-la.
 FOC [father] REL do house-DEF
 'It is my father who built this house.'

If the highlighter is not a copula, a focus construction is not recognizable as a cleft unless the background clause is marked by a relative particle. Thus, cleft constructions must have either a copula highlighter or a relative-marked background clause or both.

Another strategy is **fronting** of the noun phrase, with or without a focus particle. And still another possibility is to focus the noun in situ, that is, without moving it outside the clause but with a focus particle.

Note that many languages have two or more focusing strategies; focusing solely through intonation is not considered here.

2. The values

The following nine values are distinguished; the first five are types of cleft constructions, values 6 to 8 are types of focus fronting constructions.

Value 1 (**cleft with copula before focus**) is the most common value. It occurs in nine Ibero-Romance-based languages, in seventeen English-based languages, in three Dutch-based languages, in Mauritian Creole, and in Mixed Ma'a/Mbugu. Some languages use a relativizer (2), some do not (1) and (3).

		excl	shrd	all
●	1. Cleft with copula before focus	19	12	31
●	2. Cleft with copula after focus	2	4	6
●	3. Cleft with focus particle before focus	3	8	11
○	4. Cleft with focus particle after focus	0	6	6
○	5. Bare cleft (without highlighter)	5	10	15
●	6. Fronting with particle before focus	3	5	8
●	7. Fronting with particle after focus	7	6	13
●	8. Bare fronting (without particle)	2	3	5
●	9. In situ focusing (with particle)	3	3	6

(3) Papiamentu (Kouwenberg 2013b)
 Ta e kakalaka e vruminganan a kome.
 COP [ART cockroach] ART ant.PL PFV eat
 'It is the cockroach the ants have eaten.'

(4) Mixed Ma'a/Mbugu (Mous 2013)
 Si mzemó akutí'i haráza.
 NEG.COP [I.herd.NMLZ] 3SG.COND.carry in.river
 'It is not the herdsman who brought them to the river.'

Nigerian Pidgin and Berbice Dutch optionally use a particle to signal the right edge of the focus.

(5) Nigerian Pidgin (Faraclas 2013)
 Ì bì mà fada shà wę byud dì haws.
 EXPL COP [POSS.1SG father PCL] REL build ART house
 'It is my father who built the house.'

Value 2 (**cleft with copula after focus**) occurs in three English-based languages (Belizean Creole, Vincentian Creole, Nicaraguan Creole English), in Cape Verdean Creole of São Vicente, in Afrikaans, and in Kinubi. In all these languages, the background clause is introduced by a relativizer.

(6) Kinubi (Luffin 2013)
 Ána ya al ásuru kurá tái dé.
 1SG COP REL tie.up leg POSS.1SG DEF
 'I am the one who tied up my leg.'

Value 3 (**cleft with focus particle before focus**) occurs in seven French-based languages, in Nigerian Pidgin, in Kikongo-Kituba, in Juba Arabic, and in Ambon Malay.

(7) Kikongo-Kituba (Mufwene 2013)
Si mukanda ya yi ya yandi sumbaka.
FOC book DEM REL 3SG buy.PST
'It is this book he bought.'

Value 4 (**cleft with focus particle after focus**) occurs in two Portuguese-based creoles (Angolar, Principense), in two French-based languages (Seychelles Creole, Mauritian Creole), in Nigerian Pidgin, and in Sango.

(8) Angolar (Maurer 2013a)
Balele thô ki tê vungu si
kind.of.dance FOC REL.SBJ have melody DEM
ma a ka kata [...].
REL.NSBJ GENER HAB sing
'It is the *balele* that has this melody that they would sing [...].'

Value 5 (**bare cleft, without highlighter**) occurs in seven Ibero-Romance-based languages, in two English-based languages, in five French-based languages, and in Michif.

(9) Batavia Creole (Maurer 2013b)
Sertu ile teng sorti. Nos ki teng mofinedja.
sure 3SG have luck 1PL REL have bad.luck
'He certainly is lucky. It is we who are unlucky.'

(10) Seychelles Creole (Michaelis & Rosalie 2013)
Bann zonm ki danse sa tinge.
PL man REL dance DEM tinge
'It was only the men who danced the *tinge*.'

(11) Michif (Bakker 2013)
Mu nipaenglet awa kaa-wanih-ak.
1.POSS clasp DEM REL-lose.him-1SBJ.3OBJ
'It is this clasp of mine that I lost.'

Value 6 (**fronting with particle before focus**) occurs in three English-based languages (San Andres Creole English, Nigerian Pidgin, Gullah), in three French-based languages (Louisiana Creole, Reunion Creole, Tayo), in Singapore Bazaar Malay, and in the bilingual mixed language Gurindji Kriol.

(12) Gullah (Klein 2013)
Duh Sara we duh talk about.
FOC Sarah 1PL PROG talk about
'It's Sara we are talking about.'

(13) Singapore Bazaar Malay (Khin Khin Aye 2013)
Itu selalu tinggal sini punya orang pakai ini
FOC always live here POSS person use DEM
pasar ah.
market EMPH
'It is the people living here who use this market.'

Value 7 (**fronting with particle after focus**) occurs in five Portuguese-based languages, in four English-based languages, in Sango, in Lingala, in Juba Arabic, and in Pidgin Hawaiian.

(14) Bislama (Meyerhoff 2013)
Ol papa blong mi nomo oli bildim haos ia.
PL father POSS 1SG FOC AGR build house DEF
'It was my father and uncles who built the house.'

(15) Juba Arabic (Manfredi & Petrollino 2013)
Anína yáwu birówa géru haját del.
1PL FOC FUT.go change thing.PL DEM.PL
'It's us that will change these things.'

(16) Pidgin Hawaiian (Roberts 2013)
Oe ka mea pepehi kela wahine oe.
2SG FOC thing beat DET wife POSS.2SG
'You're the one who beats your wife.'

Value 8 (**bare fronting, without particle**) occurs in Casamancese Creole, in Papiamentu, in Chinese Pidgin English, in Hawai'i Creole, and in Berbice Dutch.

(17) Papiamentu (Kouwenberg 2013b)
Bo buki mi a lesa.
2SG book 1SG PFV read
'It is your book I read.'

Value 9 (**in situ focusing with particle**) is found in Sri Lanka Portuguese, in Sri Lankan Malay, in Tok Pisin, and in Media Lengua.

(18) Sri Lankan Malay (Slomanson 2013)
Go aayər jo miinung.
1SG water FOC drink
'It's water that I am drinking.'

In Cape Verdean Creole of São Vicente, there is a construction COP NP COP REL background, and in Korlai, the focus construction is NP REL COP background.

3. Distribution

Most *APiCS* languages (92%) use one of the possible cleft constructions (values 1 to 5), and 35 per cent use fronting of the focused noun or noun phrase (values 6 to 8). As mentioned above, value 1 (copula + focus + background clause) is the most widespread value; it occurs mainly in the Atlantic area (23 out of 31 languages).

104 Focusing of the noun phrase

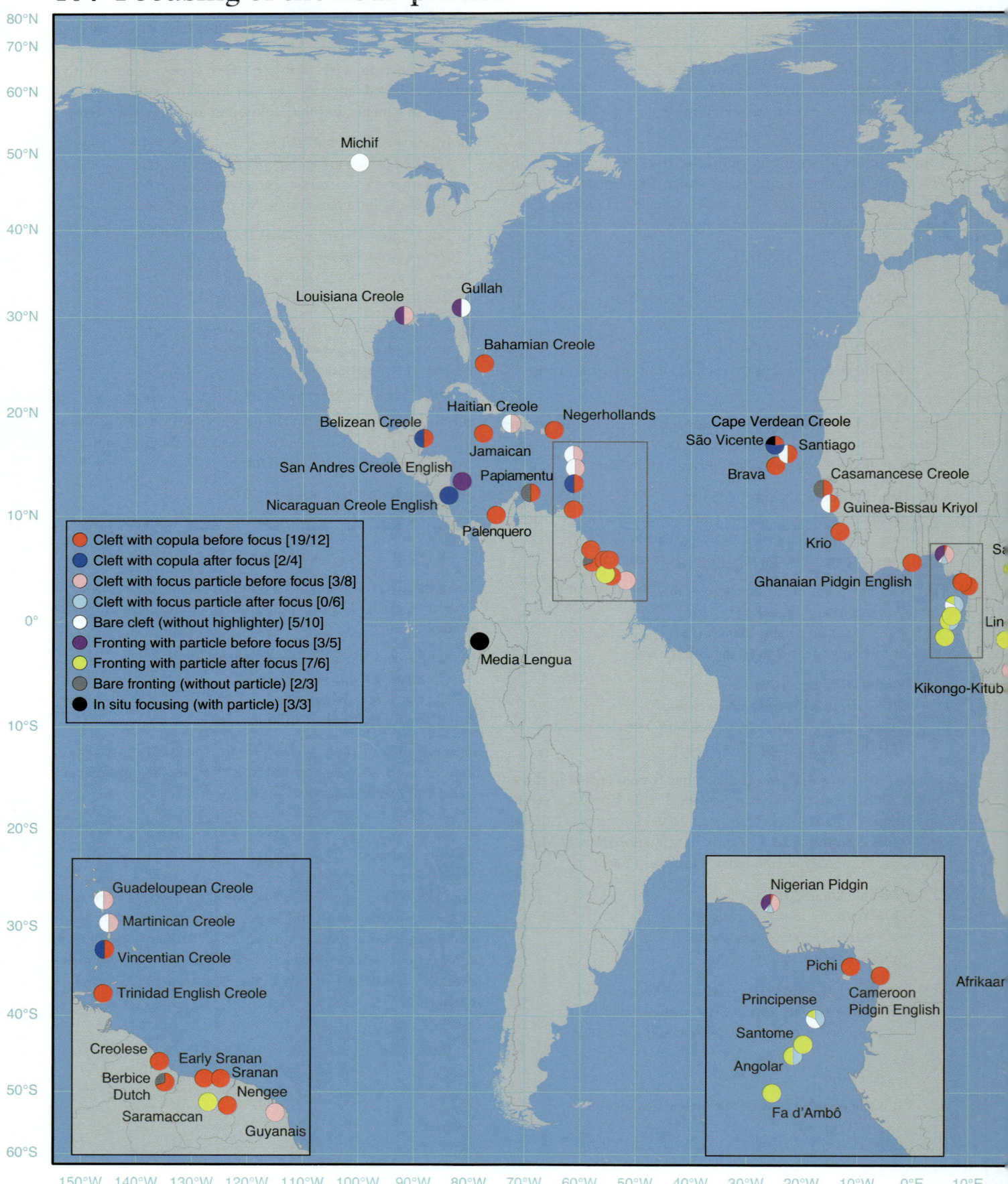

Chapter 105
Verb doubling and focus

PHILIPPE MAURER AND THE *APiCS* CONSORTIUM

1. Feature description

This feature is about the possibility of doubling the verb in order to focus on the situation referred to by the verb.

There are two main kinds of verb doubling construction: the fronting of the verb with a copy of the verb left in the background clause (ex. 1), and the reduplication of the verb within the matrix clause (ex. 2).

(1) Early Sranan (van den Berg & Bruyn 2013)
Da koksi ju koksi mi.
COP mock 2SG mock 1SG
'You are really mocking me.' (lit. 'It is mocking you are mocking me.')

(2) Sango (Samarin 2013)
Mbi vo vo-ngo pepe.
1SG buy buy-NOM NEG
'I didn't buy it (because someone gave it to me).'

The fact that in example (2) the second verb is nominalized is not important here; in verb-doubling constructions involving a copula, it is the copula that nominalizes the verb.

2. The values

The following three values are distinguished:

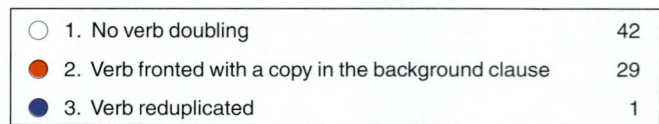

○ 1. No verb doubling		42
● 2. Verb fronted with a copy in the background clause		29
● 3. Verb reduplicated		1

Value 1 (**no verb doubling**) is found in more than half of the *APiCS* languages. The following examples show constructions in which the verb is focused, but without doubling:

(3) Cape Verdean Creole of São Vicente (Swolkien 2013)
Tánia so andá, el ka korrê.
Tánia only walk 3SG NEG run
'Tania only walked, she didn't run.'

(4) Hawai'i Creole (Velupillai 2013)
dei plɛin ɔ faitin? dei plɛin
3PL play.PROG or fight.PROG 3PL play.PROG
'Are they playing or fighting? They are playing.'

Value 2 (**verb fronting with a copy in the background clause**) is found in creoles and pidgins of different lexical bases. The constructions are sometimes cleft-like, and they may vary according to the following parameters: presence or absence of a highlighter, copular or non-copular highlighter, presence or absence of a relativizer (or relative pronoun) heading the background clause, and a combination of these three parameters.

Verb clefting implies the use of a relativizer (exx. 8 and 11–13); the difference between the clefting of verbs and the clefting of nouns (see Chapter 104) is that in nominal clefting (and fronting), no copy is left in the background clause, as in *It's mother that I saw ∅*.

In Early Sranan (ex. 1), there is a copular highlighter and no relativizer; this construction occurs in other creole languages as well:

(5) Negerhollands (van Sluijs 2013)
[...] *a lak am lo lak!*
COP laugh 3SG PROG laugh
'[...] he was laughing!'

(6) Trinidad English Creole (Mühleisen 2013)
Iz walk he walkin.
COP walk 3SG walk.PROG
'He really is walking (and not taking the bus).'

Berbice Dutch has the same construction, but it may add the focus marker *so* to the verb:

(7) Berbice Dutch (Kouwenberg 2013a)
Da mu so o wa mutɛ.
COP go FOC 3SG PST go.PFV
'He had really gone.'

Example (8) contains a copular highlighter and a relativizer:

(8) Cameroon Pidgin English (Schröder 2013)
Na waka we a waka, a no bin run.
COP walk REL 1SG walk 1SG NEG PST run
'It was walking that I did, not running.'

The following examples illustrate the construction with a non-copular highlighter without a relativizer:

(9) Santome (Hagemeijer 2013)
Bô ska bêbê!—Inô, kume so n ska kume.
2SG PROG drink NEG eat HL 1SG PROG eat
'You are drinking!—No, I am eating.'

(10) Haitian Creole (Fattier 2013)
Se chire Siltana te chire rad la.
HL tear Sultana ANT tear clothes DEF
'Sultana had torn the clothes.'

In the following examples, there is a non-copular highlighter as well as a relativizer:

(11) Nigerian Pidgin (Faraclas 2013)
Nà wàka wẹ à wàka.
HL walk REL 1SG walk
'It is walking that I did.'

(12) Principense (Maurer 2013c)
Txi sa kume a?—Ade ô, bêbê êli ki
2SG PROG eat Q no VAL drink FOC REL
n sa bêbê.
1SG PROG drink
'Are you eating?—No, I am drinking.'

Guinea-Bissau Kriyol uses no highlighter, but a relativizer:

(13) Guinea-Bissau Kriyol (Intumbo et al. 2013)
Kuri ku i na kuri, i ka na bua.
run REL 3SG PROG run 3SG NEG PROG fly
'He is running, he is not flying.'

Martinican Creole and Saramaccan use a construction without a highlighter and without a relativizer:

(14) Martinican Creole (Colot & Ludwig 2013b)
Achté man achté-y.
buy 1SG buy-3SG
'I did buy it.'

(15) Saramaccan (Aboh et al. 2013)
Síki dí wómi síki.
be.sick DEF man be.sick
'The man is really sick.'

Value 3 (**reduplication of the verb**) exists only in Sango (see ex. 2). As shown by (16), the main verb and the nominalized verb are not obligatorily adjacent; in this particular case, the two verbs are separated by *gi* 'only'.

(16) Sango (Samarin 2013)
A-zo a-vo gi vo-ngo.
PL-person PM-buy only buy-NMLZ
'People just buy it (without subscribing to the newspaper).'

3. Distribution

Value 1 (no verb doubling) is found in 9 Caribbean, South American, and North American languages, as well as in 33 African and Asian languages (i.e. 48% of all languages), whereas value 2 (verb fronting leaving a copy in the background clause), which is present in 40 per cent of the *APiCS* languages, is an essentially Atlantic feature (17 in the Caribbean and 9 in West Africa). The only three non-Atlantic languages displaying value 2 are Lingala and Kikongo-Kituba in Africa, as well as Korlai in South Asia. In Kikongo-Kituba, the fronted verb is nominalized with the infinitive prefix *ku-*:

(17) Kikongo-Kituba (Mufwene 2013)
Ku-dia yayi ya yandi ke dia.
INF-eat DEM REL 3SG COP eat
'It is the particular way he is eating.'

In Lingala, the fronted verb is inflected for person and tense:

(18) Lingala (Meeuwis 2013)
A-défis-ákí yó yangó ko-défis-a,
3SG-lend-PST 2SG 3SG.INAN INF-lend-FV
a-kabél-ákí yó té.
3SG-offer-PST 2SG NEG
'She *lent* it to you, she didn't *give* it.'

In Korlai, the fronted verb is modified by the same tense and aspect suffix that modifies the verb in the background clause:

(19) Korlai (Clements 2013)
Khure-n el nu ti khure-n, el ti martʃa-n.
run-PROG 3SG NEG PST run-PROG 3SG PST walk-PROG
'S/he wasn't running, she was walking.'

Verb doubling used as a means of focusing on the situation referred to by the verb is a feature that does not exist (or that exists only marginally) in European languages; in contrast, it is widespread in West African languages. Since this feature occurs almost exclusively in Atlantic creoles, a West African substrate influence on these creoles is highly probable.

105 Verb doubling and focus

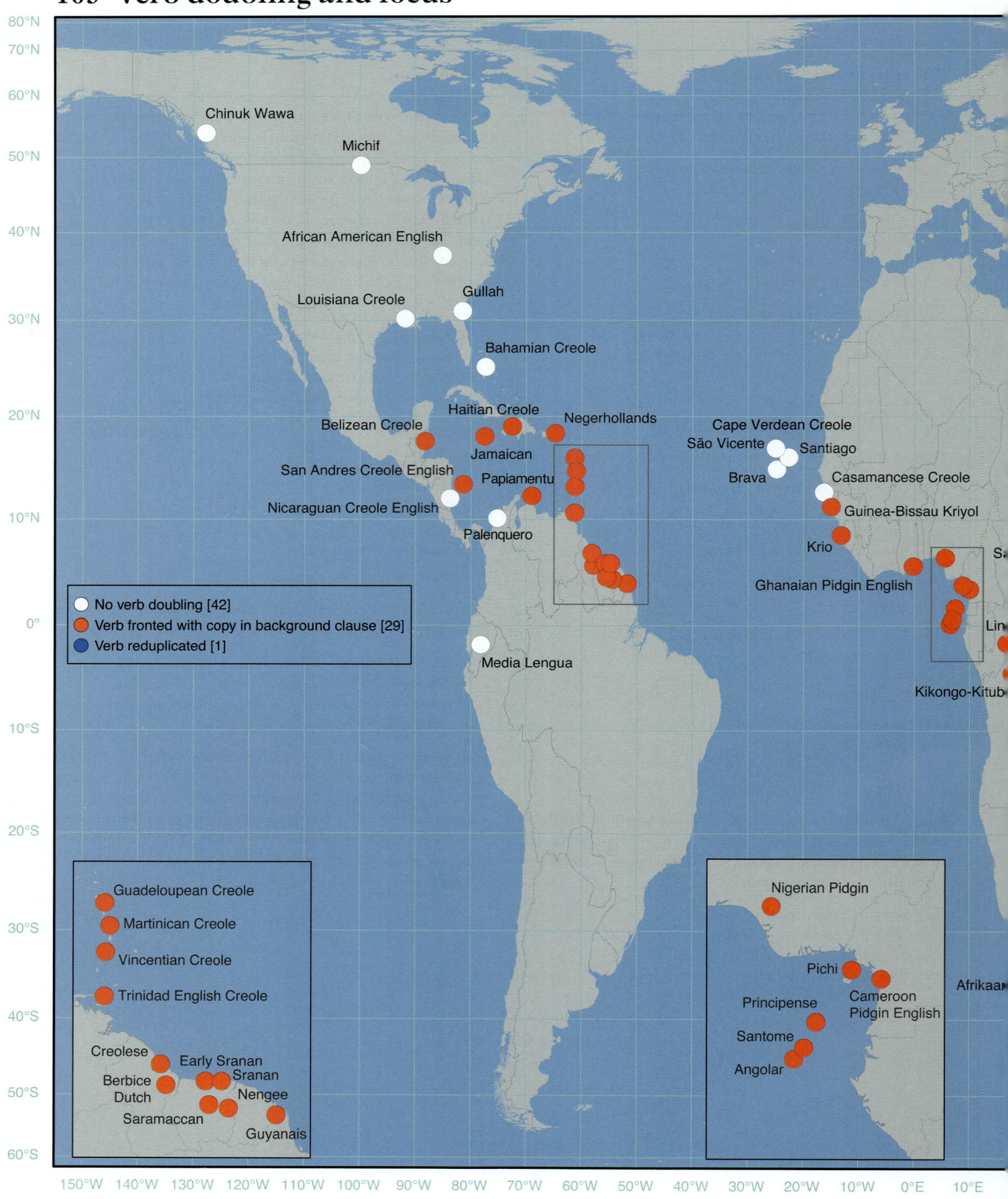

Chapter 106
Focus particle 'also'

MARTIN HASPELMATH, SUSANNE M. MICHAELIS, AND THE *APiCS* CONSORTIUM

1. Introduction

Additive focus particles that translate as 'too' or 'also' have the function of indicating that a proposition applies to an element in addition to other, contextually given, elements. Examples are given in (1).

(1) a. *My mother liked my cake, and* MY BROTHER, *too, liked it.*
    b. *Kim already knew it. Finally I also told* PAT.
    c. *First they danced and then they also* KISSED.

There is always an implicit or explicit contrast between the additional element and the other element(s), so additive constructions like (1) are a type of focus construction. The additive marker (in boldface in 1a–c) is typically adjacent to the element that is in focus (in small caps in 1a–c), but it may also be non-adjacent, as in (1b). The focused element is typically a noun phrase, but it can be any other focusable expression, including a verb, as in (1c). But almost all of our examples involve focused noun phrases.

All European languages have special words that function in this way, so the term *focus particle* has become widely used for such words (König 1991). But the same function can be fulfilled by affixal markers, so *focus operator* would be a more precise term (see Gast & van der Auwera 2011). We retain the term focus particle here, as additive affixes are quite marginal in the present context (though the suffix *-sh* occurs in the mixed language Media Lengua, following Quechua, e.g. *otro muchacho-guna-sh* [other boy-PL-ADD] 'other boys, too').

In a few of the *APiCS* languages it is not clear that there are special additive particles, because the element that is used to render 'also' is also used in the meaning 'again' or 'himself'. European languages distinguish strictly between 'Jane herself' and 'Jane, too', and between 'they also kissed' and 'they kissed again'. The latter distinction is not made in Yimas-Arafundi Pidgin, for example, and quite a few English-based languages use the *self* word also to render 'also', so it may well be that it is a general contrast marker that is vague between intensifier usage (see Chapter 88) and additive focus operator usage. Be that as it may, we regard all these overt elements which occur as translation equivalents of English 'also' as focus particles for the purposes of this chapter.

2. The four values

The question we ask about focus particles is whether they occur adjacent to the focused element (values 1 and 2) or not (values 3 and 4), and whether they precede or follow it. This yields four different positional options, which are not exclusive. In fact, multiple options are quite common: twenty-six languages allow two orders, and four languages allow three orders. Most commonly, the same focus particle occurs in different positions, but a language may have two different particles with different positional properties (like English *too* and *also*).

We see that adjacent position is more common than non-adjacent position, and particle-after-focus is much more common than particle-before-focus.

Unfortunately, it is difficult to assess these results with respect to the issue of universal trends vs. substrate influence, because very little comparative research has been done on the position of focus particles in the world's languages. Impressionistically one can say that the English-based and Romance-based languages tend to be similar to their lexifiers. However, there are a number of clearly innovative focus particles, such as *again* or *self* (meaning 'also') in English-based languages.

3. Before the focused element and adjacent

Only one language, Chinuk Wawa, has adjacent particle-before-focus position as the only option:

(2) Chinuk Wawa (Grant 2013)
    pi Sáli yáka cáku
    also Sally 3SG come
    'Sally, too, came.'

Adjacent preceding position is found especially in a few African languages, including Arabic-based and Bantu-based languages,

		excl	shrd	all
●	1. Before the focused element	1	9	10
●	2. After the focused element	39	29	68
●	3. Non-adjacent preceding	0	5	5
●	4. Non-adjacent following	4	21	25

as in Lingala *aliákí pé lípa* [he.ate also bread], which occurs alongside *aliákí lípa pé* [he.ate bread also]. In English-based languages, it is very marginal, but it occurs in Afrikaans (*ook Jan* 'Jan, too') and in Cape Verdean Creole:

(3) Cape Verdean Creole of Santiago (Lang 2013)
 Tánbi na Káuberdi ta kumedu txeu midju.
 also in Cape.Verde IPFV eat.PASS much maize
 'In Cape Verde, too, they eat a lot of maize.'

4. After the focused element and adjacent

In most languages, the focus particle immediately follows the focused element. In thirty-nine languages this is the only option, as in the following:

(4) Fa d'Ambô (Post 2013)
 M' ten sxa-bay.
 I too TMA-go.there
 'I, too, go there.'

(5) Palenquero (Schwegler 2013)
 Ana tambié a miní ku suto.
 Ana also PST come with us
 'Ana, too, came along (with us).'

(6) Mauritian Creole (Baker & Kriegel 2013)
 Zaṅ osi ti vini
 John also PST come
 'John also came.'

(7) Tok Pisin (Smith & Siegel 2013)
 Em tu i kam.
 3SG also PM come
 'He also came.'

(8) Pidgin Hindustani (Siegel 2013)
 Tum bi bia pio?
 2SG also beer drink
 'Do you, too, drink beer?' (*bi* from Hindi/Urdu *bhii*)

In the Portuguese- and Spanish-based languages, the word *também/también* has usually survived in some form, and in the French-based languages, *aussi/osi* is widely used. Some French-based languages have preserved the older or dialectal form *tou*, which also follows its focus:

(9) Haitian Creole (Fattier 2013)
 Yo arete l tou.
 3PL arrest 3SG also
 'They have stopped her, too.'

In the English-based languages, *too* is more widely found than *also*; the latter is only found in acrolectal Nicaraguan Creole English (see (12) below), Singlish, and Hawai'i Creole. Kriol has both *too* and *again*, both of which follow their focus:

(10) Kriol (Schultze-Berndt & Angelo 2013)
 a. *Teik-im Nawurla tu.*
 take-TR Nawurla too
 'Take Nawurla, too.'
 b. *Ya gumilan igen mibala kol-im.*
 yes gumilan too 1PL call-TR
 'Yes, we also call it [a palm species] *gumilan* [in addition to a name from a neighbouring language].'

5. Non-adjacent

In quite a few languages, the 'also' word may be non-adjacent. Non-adjacent occurrence **before the focus** (value 3) is uncommon and is never the only option. In Chabacano, it involves the particle *rin* from a Philippinic language, and in English-based languages, it occasionally occurs as in Standard English (see 12).

(11) Cavite Chabacano (Sippola 2013a)
 Luego ya anda rin alla Domingo.
 later PFV go also there Domingo
 'Later on, Domingo, too, came there.'

(12) Nicaraguan Creole English (Bartens 2013a)
 Yu kan aalso mek yuor rondon wid miit.
 2SG can also make 2SG.POSS rundown INS meat
 'You can make your rundown with meat, too.'

Non-adjacent occurrence **after the focus** (value 4) is quite common, especially with words deriving from English *too*, but also with words from French *aussi* and from Portuguese *também*:

(13) Norf'k (Mühlhäusler 2013)
 Yorlye comen tuu.
 2PL come.CONT also
 'You, too, are coming.'

(14) Guyanais (Pfänder 2013)
 Marie ké vin osi
 Mary FUT come also
 'Mary will come, too.'

(15) Guinea-Bissau Kriyol (Intumbo et al. 2013)
 N tene fidju. Maria tene tambi.
 1SG have.PRS child Maria have.PRS also
 'I have children. Maria has children, too.'

One problem with the value assignment is that non-adjacent position is not always easily distinguishable from adjacent position. Thus, in (10a), *tu* 'too' occurs immediately after the focus, but is simultaneously clause-final. It may well be that not all value assignments reflect the most general statement of the ordering rules in the language. The position of the focus particle is an under-researched domain both in pidgin and creole studies and in general comparative linguistics.

106 Focus particle 'also'

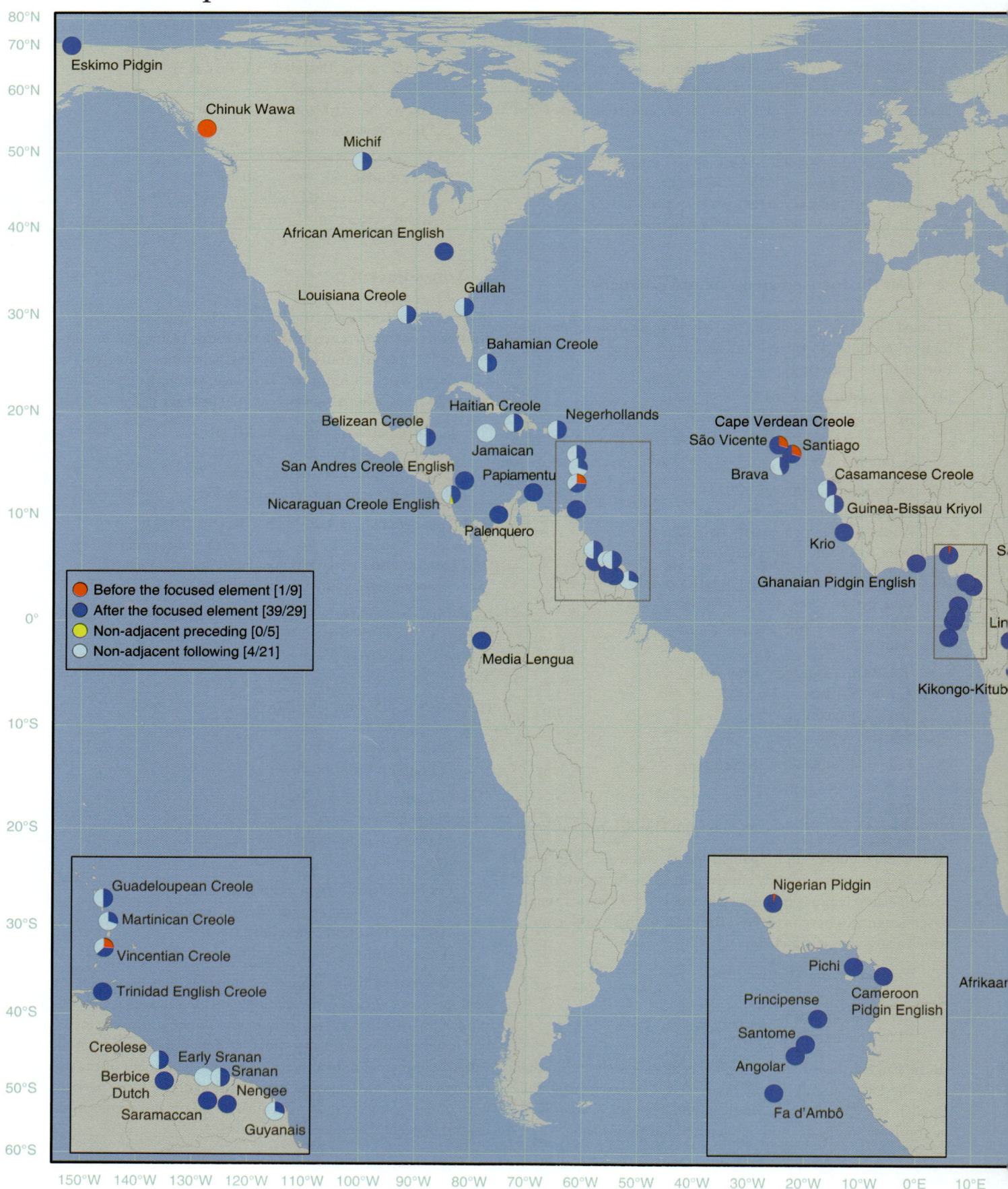

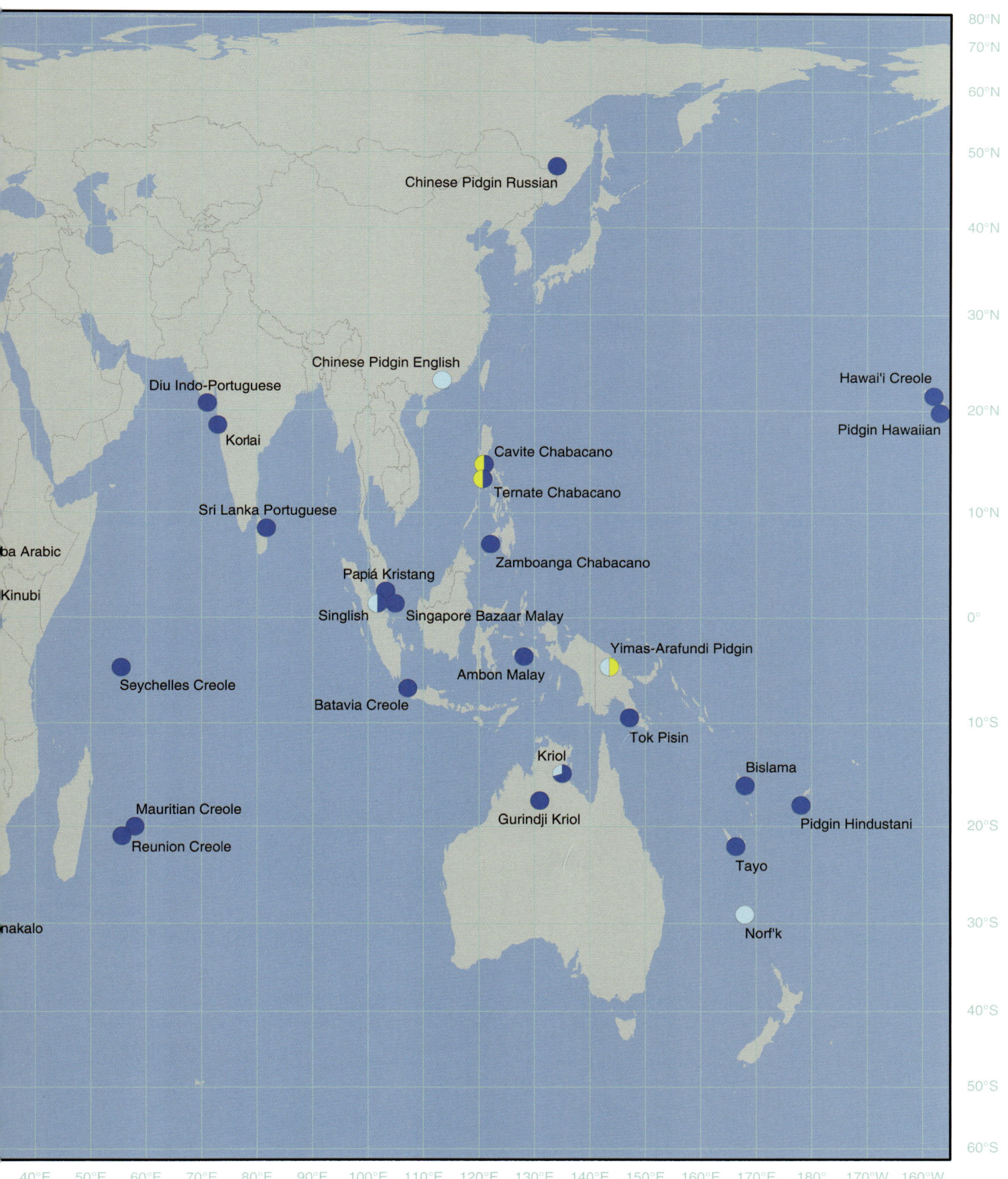

LEXICON

Chapter 107
Vocative markers

SUSANNE M. MICHAELIS, MARTIN HASPELMATH, AND THE *APiCS* CONSORTIUM

1. Vocative phrases and vocative markers

Vocative phrases are nominal expressions referring to the hearer, and are used to attract the hearer's attention (as in 1) or to signal and maintain the social link in a conversation (as in 2). The noun is a personal name or another address form, such as a kinship term, a title, or some other person-denoting noun (or rarely, a personal pronoun of the second person).

(1) Seychelles Creole (Michaelis & Rosalie 2013)
Marcel-o, donn mwan sa bolpenn.
Marcel-VOC give me DEM ballpen
'Marcel, give me this ballpen.'

(2) Chinese Pidgin Russian (Perekhvalskaya 2013)
Стреляй не надо! Моя люди! Спасибо, капитан!
Stərəlaj ninada! Maja liudi! Səpasiba, kapitan!
shoot NEG.IMP 1SG person thank.you captain
'Do not shoot! I am human! Thank you, captain!'

A vocative phrase may contain a **vocative marker**, that is, an element that does not occur when the nominal expression is used in the ordinary way, to refer to a third person. We see the vocative marker –*o* in (1), and a vocative phrase lacking a vocative marker in (2). In this chapter, we ask whether a language has a vocative marker and if it does, whether the vocative marker precedes or follows the nominal expression. (Vocative markers are sometimes treated as cases, as in Daniel & Spencer 2009, but our languages do not have case paradigms, so there is no reason to call vocative markers cases here.)

There is not much earlier research on vocative phrases that we were able to rely on, so we defined *vocative marker* in a very general way, as an element that accompanies the address term and appears to mark it as vocative. One could argue that elements such as *hey* in English and similar forms in related languages (e.g. in 3) are not vocative markers because all they do is attract the hearer's attention: they can also be used without address terms, and they have no particularly close association with nominal expressions.

(3) Belizean Creole (Escure 2013)
Ey Jeni yu now wen i mos hapn da ina Len.
VOC Jeni you know when it most happen TOP in Lent
'Hey Jenny, you know, it usually happens around Lent.'

But many languages have particles that are clearly specialized for marking address terms, and since we had no good way of telling them apart from more general particles like *hey*, we included them. (However, attention-drawing interjections were excluded from consideration when we had no evidence that they can occur adjacent to address terms.)

We distinguish the following five values:

● 1.	Optional vocative marker preceding noun	27
● 2.	Optional vocative marker following noun	19
● 3.	Optional vocative markers in both positions	4
● 4.	Obligatory vocative marker preceding noun	1
○ 5.	No vocative marker	19

The value names mention the position with respect to the "noun", because in most cases the nominal is a single noun, but it may also be a complex phrase with modifiers, as in (4).

(4) Sango (Samarin 2013)
mama ti mbi o, ala kwi ngbangati nyen'?
mother of 1SG VOC 2PL die for what
'Mom, why did you die?'

In the following, we discuss and illustrate the first four types. (The absence of a vocative marker is illustrated by (2).)

2. Optional vocative marker preceding noun

The most frequent type is the optional vocative marker **preceding the noun** (value 1). This is also the position where vocative markers occur in the European lexifiers, and the two most frequent particles (*h*)*e*(*y*) and *o* are clearly derived from European sources.

(5) a. Louisiana Creole (Neumann-Holzschuh & Klingler 2013)
Hè M., en bon file!
VOC M. ART.INDF good shot
'Hey M., (give me) a good shot (of whiskey)!'

b. Kriol (Schultze-Berndt & Angelo 2013)
Ei imiyu, yu gad-im eni mejik?
VOC Emu 2SG have-TR any magic
'Hey Emu, do you have any magic?'

(6) a. Cape Verdean Creole of São Vicente (Swolkien 2013)
    O Miriam, ben li!
    VOC Miriam come here
    'Hey Miriam, come here!'
  b. Early Sranan (van den Berg & Bruyn 2013)
    O Gado, sari mi.
    oh God have.pity 1SG
    'Oh God, take pity on me!'

We have no systematic data about the conditions under which optional vocative markers occur, but it seems that they are especially common when the vocative phrase is used to attract attention (rather than to maintain the social link).

3. Optional vocative marker following noun

Vocative markers that **follow the noun** (value 2) are also quite common in pidgins and creoles, but these do not derive from European languages. But interestingly, their shapes are again most commonly *e* (see 7) and *o* (see 8):

(7) a. Angolar (Maurer 2013a)
    Têtêuga ê, [...] bô tha n' e a!
    turtle VOC you be in it EMPH
    'Turtle, [...] you were here, weren't you!'
  b. Ambon Malay (Paauw 2013)
    Ana dua tu manangis: "Mama e!"
    child two DEM cry mother VOC
    'The two children cried: "Hey, Mama!"'

Other languages with *e* following the noun are Principense and Santome (two other Gulf of Guinea creoles). The following are examples with *o* following the noun:

(8) a. Pichi (Yakpo 2013)
    Paquita o, Maura o, ùna dè si=àn?
    Paquita VOC Maura VOC 2PL IPFV see=3SG.OBJ
    'Paquita, Maura, do you see it?'
  b. Haitian Creole (Fattier 2013)
    Marilèn o, kote ou ye?
    Marylene VOC where 2SG PRO
    'Hey Marylene, where are you?'
  c. Lingala (Meeuwis 2013)
    Cathy o!
    'Hey Cathy!'

Further languages with postposed *o* are English-based Nigerian and Cameroon Pidgin English, Creolese (10a) and Nengee, and French-based Guyanais, Guadeloupean and Martinican Creole, and Mauritian and Seychelles Creole (see 1).

In addition to postposed *o*, we also sometimes find postposed *oi* in English-based Caribbean creoles (also in Jamaican and Vincentian Creole):

(9) San Andres Creole English (Bartens 2013b)
    Alma-oi!
    'Hey Alma!'

There seems to be no doubt that the postposed vocative marker *o* is due to African substrate influence. For example, Yoruba has a particle *o* that follows a greeting and that is used to attract the addressee's attention (Rowlands 1969: 50). Bartens (2011: 219) mentions the postposed vocative marker *-e* in Twi and the postposed marker *o* in Fante, and concludes that "postposed vocative markers are a substratal feature in [San Andres Creole English]". We know of no systematic research on African languages, but it appears from our examples of Sango (see 4) and Lingala (see 8c) that the postposed *o* may well be more common in the area and not even restricted to West Africa.

4. Optional vocative markers in both positions

Four languages have **two different markers** (value 3), one following the nominal (always *o*) and one preceding the nominal (*e* or *we*). There are no vocative markers that show flexible order.

(10) Creolese (Devonish & Thompson 2013)
  a. *Nenen Jeenii oo?*
    Nenen Jeenii VOC
    'Nenen Jeenii (where are you)?'
  b. *eey baai*
    'You, boy!'

Devonish & Thompson (2013) call the preposed marker *eey* a "proximal vocative" because "it tends to be used for people who are within sight of the caller", while the postposed marker *oo* is a "distal vocative", used "to call to people who are out of sight, as, for example, inside a house". They also note that the distal vocative is regarded as old-fashioned, which of course fits well with its proposed African origin. (The obsolescence of the postposed vocative marker is noted for Guyanais and San Andres Creole English as well.)

Portuguese-based Casamancese Creole is very similar, with preposed *(h)ey* and postposed *o*, as are Guadeloupean and Martinican Creole, except that they have the preposed marker *wé* (*wé Diana* 'hey Diana!')

5. Obligatory vocative marker

One language, Juba Arabic, has an obligatory vocative marker *ya*, which occurs before the nominal (the same form occurs in Kinubi, and both are retained from Arabic):

(11) Juba Arabic (Manfredi & Petrollino 2013)
    yesúa kélim le úo gále ya Zakéo
    Jesus speak to 3SG say VOC Zacchaeus
    'Jesus said to him, oh Zacchaeus!'

107 Vocative markers

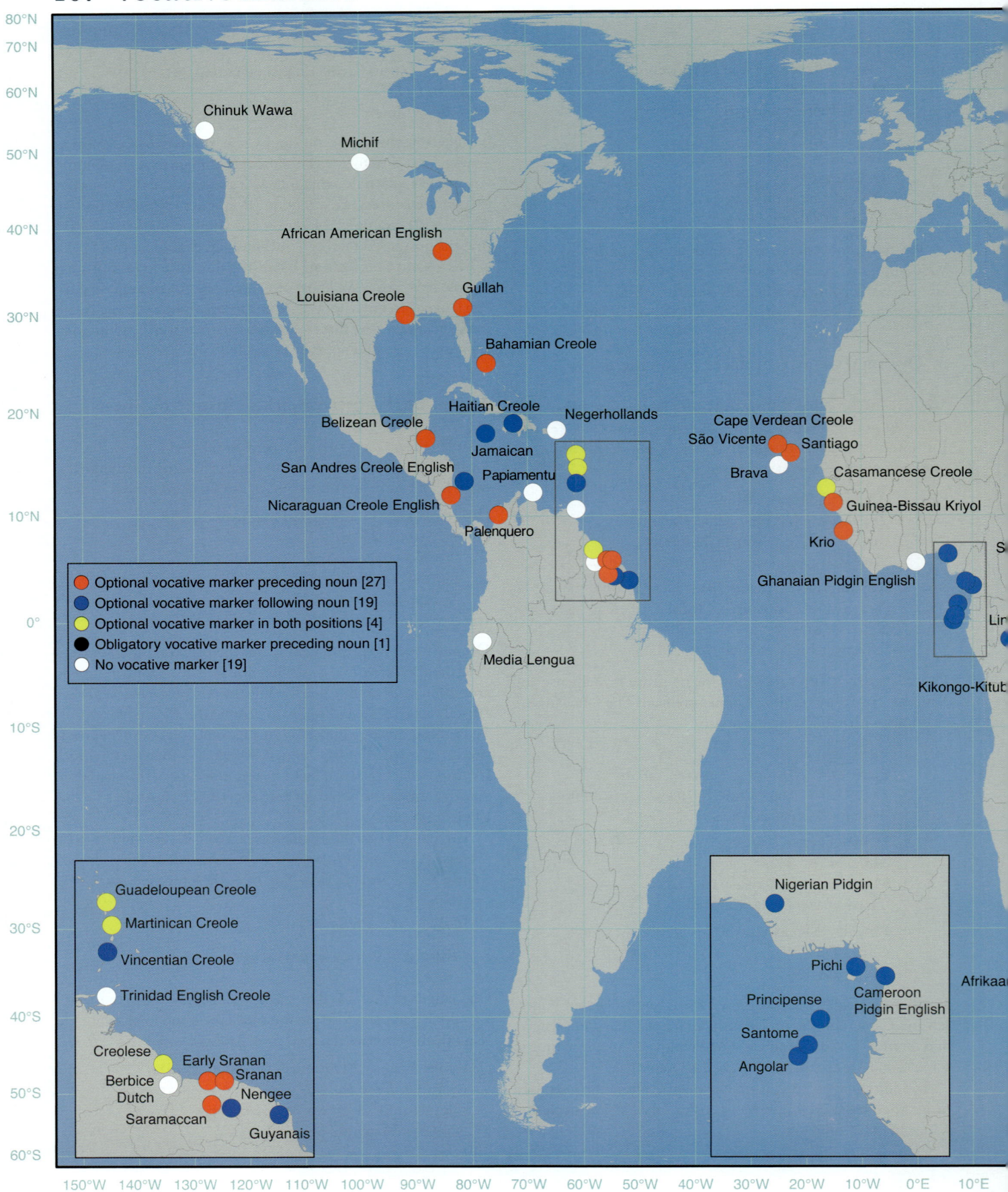

Chapter 108
Para-linguistic usages of clicks

MARTIN HASPELMATH AND THE *APiCS* CONSORTIUM

1. Introduction

This chapter looks at a phenomenon that does not belong to the standard canon of linguistic topics: the use of click sounds in languages that do not make use of clicks as regular phonemes. As Gil (2005c) has shown in his *WALS* chapter, this phenomenon is widespread in the world's languages, at least in Africa and western and southern Eurasia. Gil calls such click usages **para-linguistic** because they make use of sounds that do not occur elsewhere in the language, express a very restricted range of meanings, and are like interjections in that they are not integrated into the grammatical structure of the language. As a result, they are sometimes perceived as being non-linguistic gestures, but it is important to recognize that their form and meaning differ across languages, that is, they are learned together with other linguistic features.

Such click sounds are not normally written, but in the depiction of lively dialogue, authors may write the English dental click as *tsk tsk*, or as *tut tut*. In phonetic transcription, this would be [|], using the single pipe character, a technical symbol for dental clicks used by specialists of the Khoisan languages (which have phonemic clicks). In the following, however, we will use makeshift transcriptions of the *tsk tsk* type because the precise phonetic characteristics of the click sounds of the various languages have not been investigated yet.

2. The four values

According to Gil (2005c), the two most prominent para-linguistic usages of clicks are **logical uses**, to express affirmation or negation, and **affective uses**, to express negative affects (such as indignation, anger, annoyance) or positive affects (approval or appreciation). The value box shows the distribution of the *APiCS* languages over the four types.

We see that only 18 of our languages are reported as lacking para-linguistic clicks. It should be noted, however, that the existence of such clicks requires a very intimate knowledge of the language in its colloquial form. Thus, for 12 languages in the *APiCS* set, information on this feature is lacking, and it may be that further study will reveal the existence of clicks also in some of the languages of type 1.

Gil (2005c) also mentions other uses of click sounds, such as in addressing babies or for interacting with animals, but these seem to be much less widespread than affective and logical uses and are left aside for the classification. However, Michaelis & Rosalie (2013) mention that in Seychelles Creole, clicks can be used to court a woman or for the meaning 'I got it'. And Meyerhoff (2013) notes that "also very widespread in Vanuatu is the use of tightly pursed-lipped ingressives and dental fricatives as a means of summonsing people".

3. Affective meanings

In the clear majority of languages where the meanings of para-linguistic clicks have been described, they express negative affects, such as "anger, annoyance or exasperation" (African American English, Green 2013), "disapproval, skepticism or frustration" (Ambon Malay, Paauw 2013), "doubt, dismissal, challenge" (Belizean Creole, Escure 2013), "disagreement, reproach, exasperation, or annoyance" (Bahamian Creole, Hackert 2013). This is thus similar to the use of *tsk tsk* in English and other European languages. However, in many Caribbean languages, the click sound to express negative affect is quite different from English, and it has in fact frequently been remarked upon in the literature as having a distinct character and as being prominent in the languages. While English has no specific word for the *tsk tsk* gesture, in many English-based Caribbean languages, the expression "suck teeth" (or sometimes "kiss teeth") is used for a click sound expressing negative affect. Rickford & Rickford (1976) describe the use of this gesture in Creolese in some detail and claim that it is very similar in other Caribbean varieties. For example, the use of the gesture by children in the presence of adults is generally considered rude. They also note that the African Americans they interviewed were mostly familiar with the gesture, while White Americans were not.

Specific words for the "suck-teeth" gesture have been reported for several languages: *stchoops* or *chups* in Creolese (Rickford & Rickford 1976), *steups* or *cheups* in Trinidad Eng-

○ 1. No para-linguistic clicks		18
● 2. Clicks can express only affective meanings		34
● 3. Clicks can express only logical meanings		2
○ 4. Both logical and affective meanings		10

lish Creole (Mühleisen 2013), *tyuri* in Sranan (Winford & Plag 2013), *tuipe/kuipe/tchipe/tchwipe* in Haitian Creole (Fattier 2013), *kiyá/ciyá* in Casamancese Creole (Biagui & Quint 2013), and *chocho* in Santome (Hagemeijer 2013). In English-based Caribbean varieties, it may be written *cho* or *choo*. Some examples in context follow.

(1) a. Creolese (Devonish & Thompson 2013)
Speaker 1: Gyal mi laik di wee yu waak.—
'Speaker 1: Girl, I like the way you walk.—
Speaker 2: Schuups!
Speaker 2: Go away!'

b. San Andres Creole English (Bartens 2013b)
An wen ihn kom, ihn sei: "Cho! Unu nuo se ai gat trobl shitin an ai kyaan gou paati."
'And when he came, he said: "Cho! You know I have such a hard time shitting that I can't go to the party."'

c. Sranan (Winford & Plag 2013)
A   kon, a   langa   en mofo, a   man
3SG come 3SG lengthen 2SG mouth DET man
meki wan tyuri, dan a   gwe.
make ART smack then 3SG go.away
'He came, he pouted, the guy made a "suck teeth" and went away.'

In two languages of the Pacific region, a positive-affect meaning of the click has been reported. "The *tsk tsk* used for disapproval in English is widely used in Tok Pisin, but to show appreciation for something impressive" (Smith & Siegel 2013). Similarly, in the mixed language Gurindji Kriol, dental clicks are used to express agreement or approval (Meakins 2013).

(2) Tok Pisin (Smith & Siegel 2013)
Gut-pela tru! Tst   tst!
good-ADJ very click click
'Very good!'

4. Logical meanings

In twelve *APiCS* languages, a click can be used to express logical meanings, that is, negative answers, or rarely positive answers, to polar questions. There are two languages where **only logical meanings** (value 3) can be expressed by clicks, Diu Indo-Portuguese and Palenquero. Concerning Palenquero, Schwegler (2013) observes that negation-expressing clicks are found in different varieties of its lexifier Spanish, but since affect-expressing clicks are also found elsewhere in Hispanic varieties, the situation in Palenquero is surprising after all.

In the other ten languages, **clicks can have both logical and affective meanings** (value 4). This does not necessarily mean that a single click is ambiguous or polysemous. In Juba Arabic, for example, there are two different clicks for the two meanings: "The logical meaning 'yes' is realized as a palatal click, while the affective value is realized as a alveo-palatal click" (Manfredi & Petrollino 2013). In Nigerian Pidgin, "alveolar and palatal clicks are used with logical meaning ('no'/ negation) and lateral clicks are used with affective meaning (suck teeth/disgust)" (Faraclas 2013). Two further examples are given in (3).

(3) a. Tayo (Ehrhart & Revis 2013)
ta vja^n dema?—[click]
2SG come tomorrow—[click]
'Are you coming tomorrow?—No.'

b. Casamancese Creole (Biagui & Quint 2013)
Bu   wojá-l?   —[apical-click]/[labial-click]
2SG.SBJ see-3SG.OBJ — yes/no
'Did you see him/her? — Yes/No.'

Casamancese Creole is one of the few *APiCS* languages where a click can be used for positive answers, but note that there are two different clicks for positive and negative answers.

In some languages, the descriptions are not totally clear and the sound may not be strictly speaking a click. For Sango, Samarin (2013) describes "a labio-dental ingressive fricative that expresses disgust, disapproval, etc.", and writes it as "ff". Similarly, Devonish & Thompson (2013) describe the Creolese sound as "an ingressive fricative passing through either the front teeth, or more often laterally along the side of the mouth and then through the teeth". Mufwene (2013) says that "Clicks are not significant in Kikongo-Kituba, although there is a practice of sucking teeth for displeasure. However, it is not clear whether sucking teeth falls in the category of clicks." Clicks are ingressive, but they always involve two closures and a release of one closure. Thus, a study that would take the precise articulation of these special sounds into account is needed and would reveal more diversity.

5. Geographical distribution and substrates

Gil's (2005c) *WALS* chapter seems to presuppose that having logical usages of clicks implies having affective usages, but we have found two languages in which only logical usages are reported to be possible. The geographical pattern of the *WALS* map is of course not replicated here, because the areas with no or little usage of clicks (northeastern Eurasia, the Americas) have not been important for our languages. We do not find clear substrate or lexifier effects either, as African and European languages do not behave very differently with respect to the simple existence of clicks. However, Rickford & Rickford (1976) make a strong case for an African origin of the specific Caribbean "suck teeth" pattern. The *WALS* and *APiCS* distinctions are not fine-grained enough to detect this correlation.

108 Para-linguistic usages of clicks

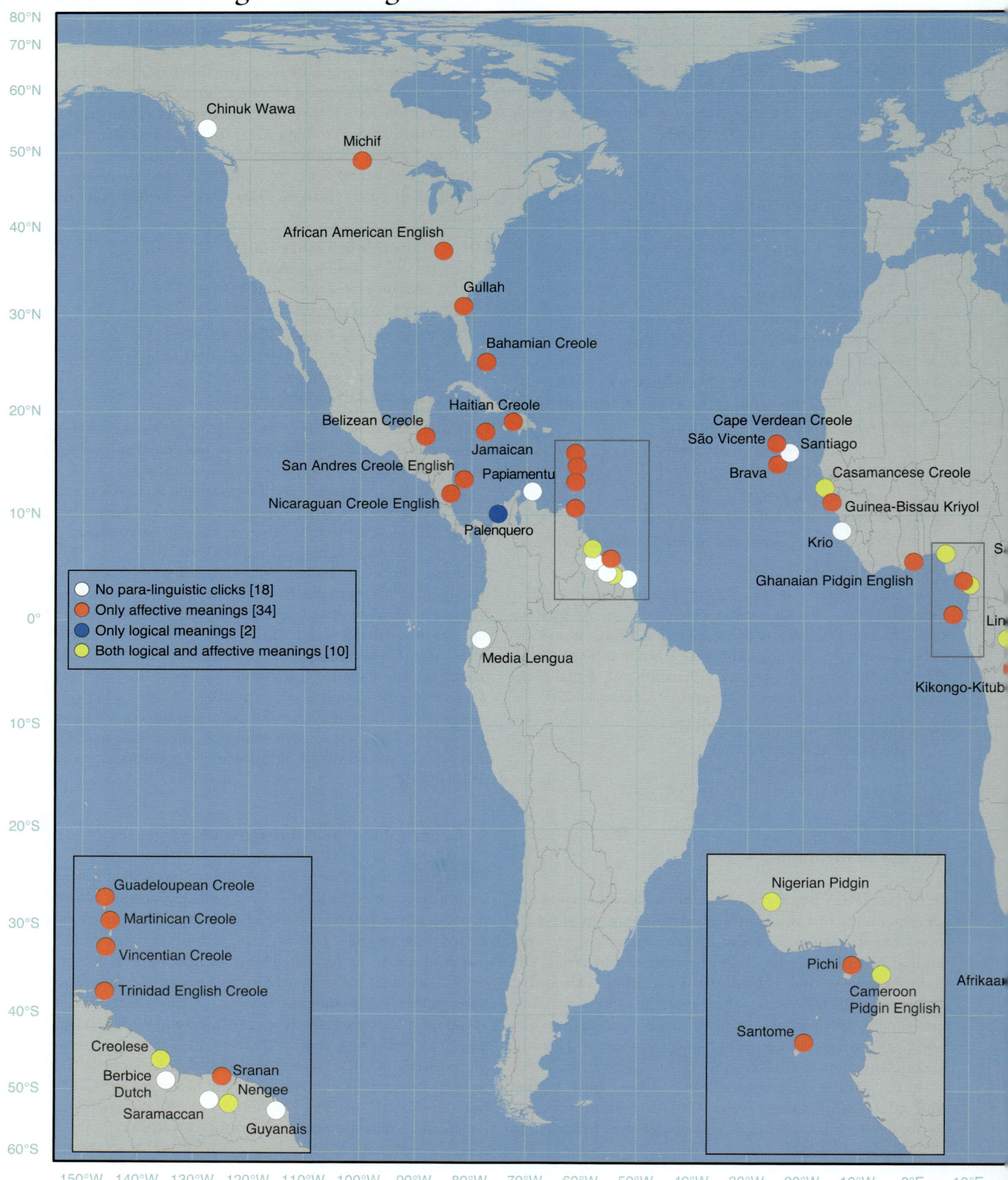

Chapter 109
Pequenino

MAGNUS HUBER AND THE *APiCS* CONSORTIUM

1. Feature description

Many pidgins and creoles around the world have a word such as *piccaninny*, *pikin*, or *pickney* for 'child, offspring; small, little' or similar meanings. It is commonly supposed that these words go back to Portuguese *pequeno/-a*, *pequenino/-a*, or even *pequenininho/-a* (with double diminutive marking), all meaning '(very) small'.

Pequenino is among a small number of Portuguese words with a worldwide distribution in pidgins and creoles, others being *grande* 'big' or *save* 'know' (see Chapter 110). Portuguese overseas exploration and contact with non-Europeans started in the second half of the fifteenth century and *piccaninny*, *grande*, and *save* are attested quite early both in Portuguese-lexicon and non-Portuguese-lexicon contact languages.

2. The values

Since a word can only be present or absent, two values are possible for this feature:

●	1. A word derived from *pequenino* exists	39
○	2. A word derived from *pequenino* does not exist	37

Value 1. *Pequenino* is attested in a great variety of forms, from disyllabic to tetrasyllabic and with various phonological changes, as illustrated in the following examples:

(1) disyllabic
   piknin (Creolese; Devonish & Thompson 2013)
   pikni (Belizean Creole; Escure 2013)
   pikín (Ghanaian Pidgin English; Huber 2013)
   piki (Saramaccan; Aboh et al. 2013)
   ninny (Bahamian Creole; Hackert 2013)

(2) trisyllabic
   pikanin(i) (Fanakalo; Mesthrie 2013)
   piknini (Nicaraguan Creole English; Bartens 2013a)
   pinini (Angolar; Maurer 2013a)
   pikina (Santome; Hagemeijer 2013)
   kəninu (Papiá Kristang; Baxter 2013)

(3) tetrasyllabic
   pikanini (Kriol; Schultze-Berndt & Angelo 2013)
   pinkinine (Early Sranan; van den Berg & Bruyn 2013)
   mikaninnee (Eskimo Pidgin; van der Voort 2013)
   pikinóti (Cape Verdean Creole of Santiago; Lang 2013)
   bikanene (Pidgin Hawaiian; Roberts 2013)

It is comparatively easy to trace the Portuguese-lexicon creole forms back to their respective Portuguese etyma. For example, Cardoso (2013) derives the Diu Indo-Portuguese forms as follows: "the word *pikənin* [from Portuguese *pequenino*] co-exists with *piken* [from Portuguese *pequeno/pequena*]". By contrast, the etymological history of *pequenino* in the non-Portuguese-lexicon contact languages is very complex and beyond the scope of this article.

Value 2. Those languages which do not have a word derived from *pequenino* use lexifier (4) or substrate words (5) to refer to 'child' or 'small':

(4) Papiamentu (Kouwenberg 2013b)
   juw, *mucha*; *chiki(tu)*; *pokito* (< Portuguese/Spanish)
   'child; small; little'

(5) Gurindji Kriol (Meakins 2013)
   karu (< Gurindji)
   'child'

3. Distribution and function

Numerical. A little over half of the *APiCS* languages (39) have a word derived from *pequenino* but, as will be shown below, *pequenino* is only found in two main groups of contact languages.

By lexifier. *Pequenino* is attested in 12 of the 14 Portuguese-lexified creoles in *APiCS* and it is an adjective ('small, little') in these languages (cf. e.g. Batavia Creole *pikninu*; Maurer 2013b). Note that the Portuguese words for 'child' are unrelated to *pequenino/pequeno*. They are *criança* 'child', *menino/-a* 'boy, girl' and *filho/-a* 'son, daughter'. Unsurprisingly, Portuguese-lexicon contact languages derive their words for 'child' from these etyma rather than from *pequenino*. Compare for example Fa d'Ambô *(na)min(a)* (Post, p.c.) or Principense *minu* (Maurer, p.c.), both from *menino*. The one Portuguese-lexified creole where a reflex of *pequenino* can also be used as a noun is basilectal Cape Verdean Creole of Santiago, where *pikinóti* is an adjective but can also refer to a child ('little one'; Lang 2013).

While most Portuguese-lexified creoles thus derive their words for 'small' from Portuguese *pequeno* etc. and their words for 'child' from *menino* etc., the Gulf of Guinea Portuguese-lexicon creoles present an exception in that *pequenino* is either marginal or completely absent: Angolar has an ideophone *pinini* which always co-occurs with *txo* 'small' (Maurer 2013a) and possibly derives from *pequenino* or *pequenininho*, and in Principense, the words for the adjective 'small' are *kêtê* (from Bantu or Edo) and *kitxi* (unclear etymology; Maurer, p.c.). The same is true for Fa d'Ambô, where 'small' is *kitsyi* (Post, p.c.).

There is an indication in Cape Verdean Creole of Santiago that the more basilectal varieties use forms derived from etyma with diminutives while more acrolectal varieties prefer the simplex form: "*Pikénu* 'small' exists only in the acrolect. In basilectal creole 'small' is *pikininu* or, more often, *pikinóti*" (Lang 2013, general comments).

It is striking that of the 27 non-Portuguese-lexified contact languages in *APiCS* that have a word derived from *pequenino*, a full 23 are pidgin or creole Englishes. The other four—Afrikaans, Eskimo Pidgin, Fanakalo, and Pidgin Hawaiian—have had some contact with or input from (pidgin) English in their history (van Sluijs 2013b; van der Voort 2013a; Mesthrie & Surek-Clark 2013a; Roberts 2013a). The only English contact languages where *pequenino* is not attested are African American English, modern Hawai'i Creole (but *pequenino* existed at earlier stages, the first attestation being from 1791; Baker & Huber 2001: 202), and Singlish, which is a rather young contact language and has a separate development.

There is no evidence whatsoever in *APiCS* of *pequenino* in any of the French, Spanish, and—except for the languages mentioned in the previous paragraph—African or other creoles, even if they are spoken in close proximity to the English creoles, as for instance in the Caribbean. This suggests that *pequenino* is a characteristic feature of English-lexicon contact languages and that the early form *piccaninny* (together with some other Portuguese words) formed part of a

repertoire of techniques and lexical items which was built up gradually and informally as anglophones exploited the trading routes pioneered earlier by the Portuguese … [W]henever an anglophone ship was a first such vessel to call at a particular settlement on the coast of Africa, Asia, America, or at a Pacific island there would be people on board with prior experience of communicating with non-anglophones who would draw on that experience. In this way words and other linguistic features could be spread far and wide without the existence of a stable nautical pidgin. (Baker & Huber 2001: 192–3)

It is interesting that all 23 English-lexified contact languages with a reflex of *pequenino* converted the Portuguese adjective into a noun, rather than adopting the Portuguese word meaning 'child' (the phonological similarity between *menino* 'child' and *pequenino* 'small' may have played a role in this process). Adjectival uses exist, but they are only found in Chinese Pidgin English, Early Sranan, Nengee, Saramaccan, and Sranan, that is, in early English-lexicon contact languages and in the "deep" creoles of Suriname. This suggests that adjectives derived from *pequenino* may have been more widespread in earlier stages of pidgin and creole Englishes.

4. History

In Baker & Huber's (2001: 197–204) list of earliest attestations in English-lexicon contact languages, *piccaninny* or similar variants with four syllables are the only forms attested in Pacific pidgin and creole Englishes (found from *c*.1800 on). The examples in the *APiCS* database show that this is still the case today; an example is Norf'k *pikinini* (Norf'k *nini* seems to be a secondary development, through clipping of *piki-*). The tetrasyllabic variants are also the earliest forms in the Atlantic English creoles. They appear from the mid-seventeenth century on, for example, *pinkinine* or *pekinini* in Early Sranan. Already at that time, however, they varied with disyllabic *pikien*, *pikin*, *pekin*. According to *APiCS*, tetrasyllabic or derived trisyllabic variants are today found in only six of the 17 modern Atlantic English creoles, in three of which they are in competition with disyllabic forms: Bahamian Creole *pickaninny*, Gullah *pickaninny* ~ *pickney*, Jamaican *pikini* ~ *pikni*, Nicaraguan Creole English *piknini*, San Andres Creole English *pikniny*, and Vincentian Creole *pikinani* ~ *pikni*.

The earliest attestations gathered by Baker & Huber (2001: 200) suggest that in Atlantic English creoles disyllabic *pikin*, *pikni*, and their variants started to replace tetrasyllabic *piccaninny* from the second half of the eighteenth century onwards. It is possible that the disyllabic form developed in one anglophone creole location and then spread through population replacement. However, since disyllabic forms may well have come into being independently in several locations through normal language change, more research is necessary here.

109 *Pequenino*

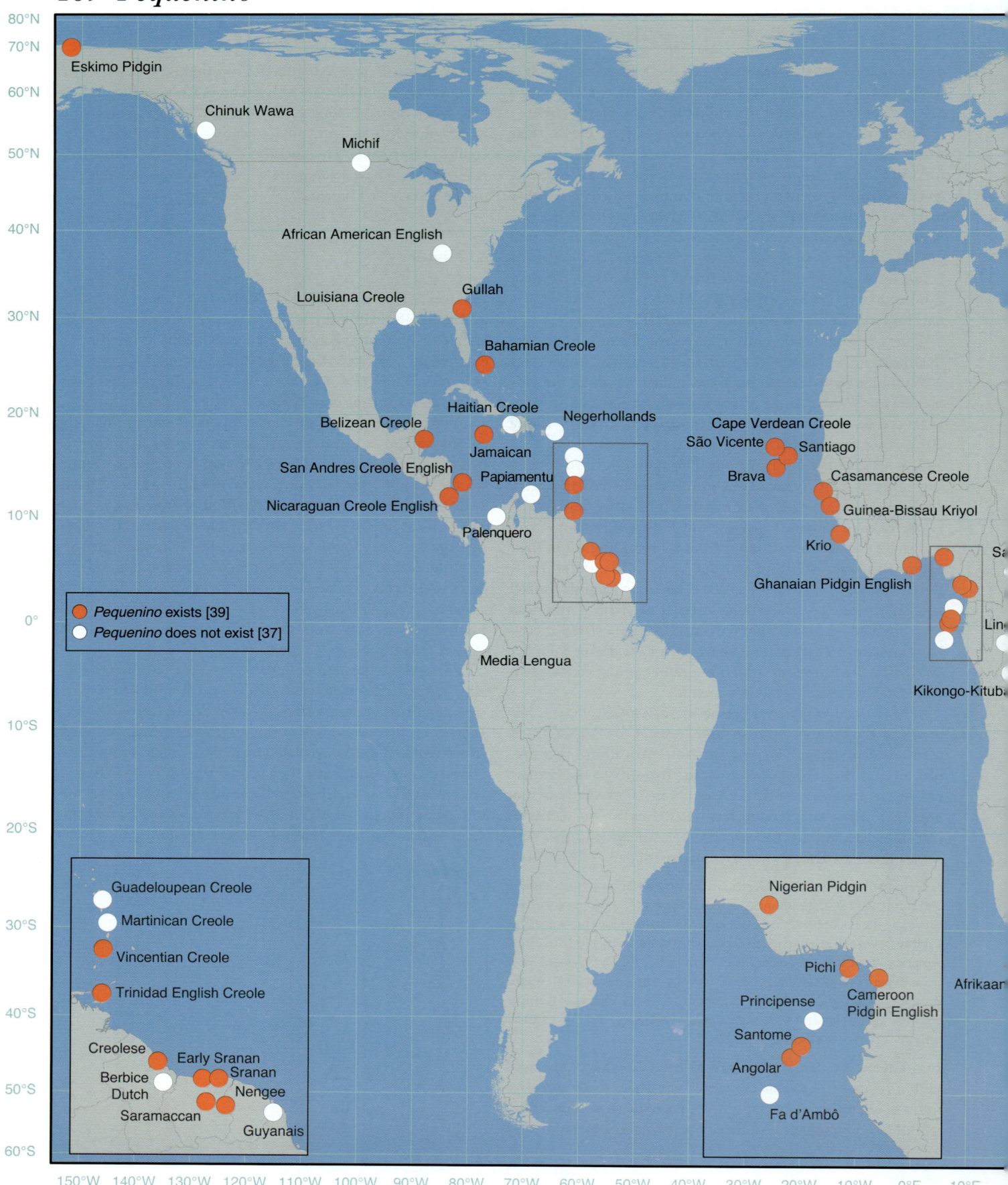

Chapter 110
Savvy

MAGNUS HUBER AND THE *APiCS* CONSORTIUM

1. Feature description

Many contact languages have words like *savvy*, *save*, or *sabi* with the meaning 'know' (or similar), deriving ultimately from Portuguese *saber* or from the etymologically closely related words *saber* and *savoir* in Spanish and French. *Savvy* can have grammaticalized modal, copular, or other meanings, but this feature only concerns the lexical meaning 'know' (although the former will also be commented on below).

Savvy is among a small number of Romance words with a worldwide distribution in pidgins and creoles, others being *grande* 'big' and *pequenino* 'small' (see Chapter 109). Portuguese overseas exploration and contact with non-Europeans started in the second half of the fifteenth century and Spain followed suit soon after. Interestingly, *savvy*, *grande*, and *pequenino* are attested quite early in non-Romance contact languages as well.

2. The values

This feature has two values, presence (value 1) and absence (value 2) of a *savvy* word:

- 1. A *savvy* word exists — 40
- 2. A *savvy* word does not exist — 36

Value 1. Unsurprisingly, the form used in the majority of the Portuguese-lexicon creoles in *APiCS* is *sabe*, which directly derives from the Portuguese etymon *saber*. But there are other forms as well, as illustrated in the following examples:

(1) sabe (Cape Verdean Creole of Santiago; Lang 2013)
 saba ~ sava (Sri Lanka Portuguese; Smith 2013)
 sab (Korlai; Clements 2013)
 sa (Papiamentu; Kouwenberg 2013b)
 sebé (Casamancese Creole; Biagui & Quint 2013)
 se (Fa d'Ambô; Post 2013)

It is remarkable that Portuguese-derived *savvy* words are also common in English-lexicon contact languages, where the forms are:

(2) sabe (Gullah; Klein 2013)
 sabi (Krio; Finney 2013)
 save (Bislama; Meyerhoff 2013)
 jabi (Kriol; Schultze-Berndt & Angelo 2013)

Spanish- and French-lexified creoles most probably derived their words for 'know' from the respective etyma in their lexifier, not from Portuguese. The different forms are listed in (3) for Spanish- and in (4) for French-lexified creoles:

(3) sabé (Ternate Chabacano; Sippola 2013b)
 sabi (Media Lengua; Muysken 2013)

(4) savé (Guyanais; Pfänder 2013)
 sav (Martinican Creole; Colot & Ludwig 2013b)

Value 2. Languages that do not have a word derived from *savvy* use lexifier or substrate words for 'know', for example,

(5) kámtaks (Chinuk Wawa, < Niuuchahnulth; Grant 2013)
 tahu (Singapore Bazaar Malay, < Malay; Khin Khin Aye 2013)
 kone (Reunion Creole, < French; Bollée 2013)
 nuo ~ nou (Nicaraguan Creole English, < English; Bartens 2013a)

3. Distribution and form

Numerical distribution. Over half of the *APiCS* languages (40) have a *savvy* word but, as will be shown below, *savvy* is found only in European lexifier contact languages.

Distribution by lexifier. Since the words for 'know' are phonologically very similar in Portuguese (*saber* /sɐber/), Spanish (*saber* /saβer/) and partly also in French (particularly the infinitive /savwar/ and plural forms *savons* /savɔ̃/, *savez* /save/, *savent* /sav/), it is at times impossible to unambiguously identify the etymon of a *savvy* word in a Romance-lexified creole. This is particularly difficult in the Spanish creoles which had some measure of Portuguese input and a little easier for the French creoles, which had less contact with Portuguese in their history. Common sense suggests that the likelihood is that *savvy* words in Spanish- and French-lexicon contact languages are derived from the Spanish and French etyma and not from Portuguese, and vice versa. However, this is only a rule of thumb and identifying the etymon remains difficult for a number of contact languages. For example, Papiamentu has had both Spanish and Portuguese influence (Maurer 2013d), which means that *sa* could have been derived from either or both. In-depth studies of the etymology of *savvy* are needed for individual contact languages, but these are beyond the scope of this chapter.

Since Portuguese, Spanish, and French were the lexifiers of Romance creoles, it is relatively unspectacular that we should find *savvy* words in these languages. What is more interesting, and will be discussed further below, is (1) that *savvy* is absent from a number of Romance creoles and (2) that it is present in some non-Romance lexifier contact languages.

Savvy is found in 19 of the 20 Portuguese and Spanish lexicon creoles included in *APiCS*, the one exception being the Gulf of Guinea creole Angolar, which uses (*e*)*ta* (etymology unknown; Maurer 2013a).

Savvy words meaning 'know' are also reported for three of the nine French creoles—Guadeloupean Creole *sav*(*é*) (Colot & Ludwig 2013a), Guyanais *savé* (Pfänder 2013), and Martinican Creole *sav* (Colot & Ludwig 2012b), the /v/ pointing towards a French (or, less probably, Spanish) origin. Incidentally, Neumann-Holzschuh & Klingler (2013) report that *se* (< *sais*, *sait*) is attested in the Pointe Coupee variety of Louisiana Creole. They also found one dubious instance of *sabai* in the earliest Louisiana Creole text, representing the language around 1720. The majority (6) of the French-lexified creoles in *APiCS*, however, derive their words for 'know' from French *connaître* rather than *savoir*, for example Reunion Creole *kon*(*e*)(*tr*) (Bollée 2013) or Haitian Creole *konn*(*en*) (Fattier 2013). The latter is interesting because although Haitian Creole has a *connaître*-derived verb to express 'know', modal (epistemic and deontic) meanings can be encoded by a *savoir*-derived word. Compare

(6) *Eske ou **konn** on moun ki bezwen al Chicago?*
    Q   2SG know INDF person REL need.to go Chicago
    'Do you know somebody who needs to go to Chicago?'

(7) *Mwen vini pou m **sa** palé avè w.*
    1SG come PREP 1SG MOD talk PREP 2SG
    'I have come in order to talk to you.' (Fattier 2013)

Nevertheless, since this chapter is concerned only with the lexical meaning 'know', Haitian Creole is counted as a language without a *savvy* word.

Savvy was also grammaticalized into a habitual marker in Palenquero and Tok Pisin:

(8) Palenquero (Schwegler 2013)
    *Ané **sabé**-ba asé eso nu.*
    they HAB-PST.HAB do this NEG
    'They did not use to do this.'

(9) Tok Pisin (Smith & Siegel 2013)
    *Papa na mama **save** go long gaden.*
    father and mother HAB go PREP garden
    'The parents would go to the garden.'

While a strong presence of *savvy* in the Romance creoles is not surprising, an interesting finding is that of all the non-Romance-lexified *APiCS* languages, *savvy* is attested only in pidgin and creole ENGLISHES. Within this group it is rather common: *savvy* is attested in 18 of the 27 English-lexicon contact languages, that is, in two-thirds. The proportion of *savvy* languages in this group would probably be even higher if earlier language stages were taken into account. The *APiCS* contributors for Creolese (Devonish & Thompson 2013), Hawai'i Creole (Velupillai 2013), Jamaican (Farquharson 2013), and Trinidad Creole English (Mühleisen 2013) report that the word is archaic in their language, which could be taken as an indication that it may already have been lost in others.

Phonological form. With one exception (Sri Lanka Portuguese, which has a /b/ ~ /v/ alternation), the second consonant in *savvy* words is realized as a bilabial plosive /b/ in Portuguese and Spanish creoles and as a labiodental fricative /v/ in the French creoles. The picture in the English-lexified contact languages is a little more varied. While the Pacific varieties tend to have /v/—Bislama *save* (Meyerhoff 2013), Chinese Pidgin English *savvy* (Li & Matthews 2013), Tok Pisin *save* (Smith & Siegel 2013)—the other 15 pidgin or creole Englishes have /b/. Nevertheless, spellings indicating a /v/ are clearly preferred in early sources referring to Pacific pidgin Englishes, but there is the occasional ⟨b⟩ and sometimes one and the same source even varies between ⟨v⟩ and ⟨b⟩—Wendeland (1939: 76, 97), for example, referring to the Tok Pisin of 1894–1915.

In the Atlantic, today's pidgin and creole Englishes are exclusively /b/ but there is considerable ⟨b⟩ ~ ⟨v⟩ variation in older texts. For example, in my collection of early West African Pidgin English, ⟨v⟩ is attested until circa 1930 (in competition with ⟨b⟩). It may be objected that ⟨v⟩ was only a conventionalized spelling for what actually was a /b/, influenced by English *savvy* (itself possibly derived from a creole form). However, both *b*- and *v*-spellings are found in non-English sources as well and Thomas (1860: 111), referring to West Africa around 1855, explicitly mentions both forms: "*saby* or *sava* is used on the whole coast as synonymous with understand". If *savvy* in English-lexified pidgins and creoles does indeed go back to a Portuguese etymon, the presence of /v/ is a puzzle: Portuguese *saber* derives from Vulgar Latin *sapere* 'to taste', whose intervocalic /p/ changed to /b/ in Portuguese (Cardoso, p.c.). There is thus no evidence of an earlier /v/ that could have found its way into the English-lexifier contact languages. More research is certainly needed here, but it seems that early contact Englishes around the world had two *savvy* forms, /savi/ and /sabi/, while today the Pacific varieties prefer /v/ forms and the Atlantic varieties exclusively rely on /b/ forms.

110 Savvy

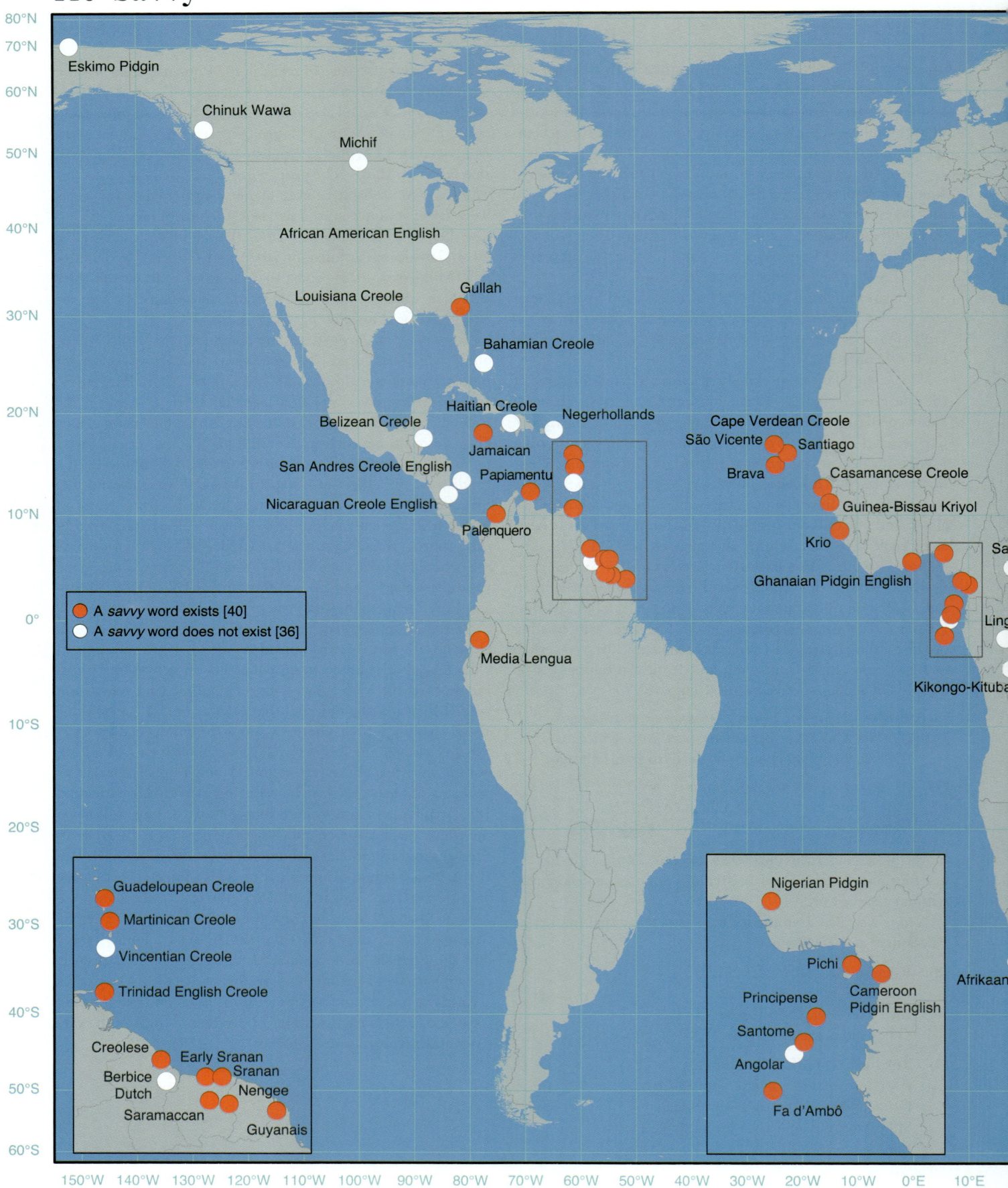

Chapter 111
'Tears'

MAGNUS HUBER AND THE *APiCS* CONSORTIUM

1. Feature description

Several contact languages around the world have a bimorphemic word for 'tear(s)', literally meaning 'eye-water' or something similar. In others, there is no separate word for tears and reference to the phenomenon is made via phrasal expressions like 'water in eye' or circumlocutions such as 'water is in eye'. Map 111 looks at the distribution of lexical or phrasal choices that *APiCS* languages make to refer to tears.

2. The values

There are three values for this features and languages can have more than one value:

		excl	shrd	all
●	1. Monomorphemic	28	10	38
●	2. Bimorphemic	19	8	27
●	3. Phrase/circumlocution	6	9	15

Value 1. The majority of *APiCS* languages (38) have a **monomorphemic word** for tears. In all cases, this word derives from (one of) the lexifier(s):

(1) tears   Norf'k (Mühlhäusler 2013)
         (< English *tears*)
     lag   Diu Indo-Portuguese (Cardoso 2013)
         (< Portuguese *lágrima*)
     larm   Tayo (Ehrhart & Revis 2013)
         (< French *larme*)
     lagrimas   Cavite Chabacano (Sippola 2013a)
         (< Spanish *lágrimas*)
     nsanga   Kikongo-Kituba (Mufwene 2013)
         (< Kimanyanga *nsanga*)
     traan   Afrikaans (den Besten & Biberauer 2013)
         (< Dutch *traan*)
     mikara   Gurindji Kriol (Meakins 2013)
         (< Gurindji *mikara*)
     maʔililma   Mixed Ma'a/Mbugu (Mous 2013)
         (< Dahalo *ʔilíma*)

Only in Zamboanga Chabacano does the Spanish-derived *lágrimas* vary with a substrate word, Visayan *lúhaq* (Steinkrüger 2013). In French-lexifier Guadeloupean Creole, Louisiana Creole, Martinican Creole, and Seychelles Creole, the word for 'tears' is identical with that for 'water' but there sometimes is another word that only means 'tears'. Compare, for example:

(2) Seychelles Creole (Michaelis & Rosalie 2013)
     delo/dilo 'water, tear' (< French *de l'eau* 'water')
     larm 'tear' (< French *larme*)

The situation is similar in Portuguese-lexified Cape Verdean Creole of São Vicente, where both *ága* 'water, tear' and *lágrima* 'tear' are attested (Swolkien 2013). *Lágua* 'water, tear' in the Santiago variety of Cape Verdean Creole also goes back to Portuguese *água* 'water', with a possible influence of Portuguese *lágrima* 'tear' (Lang 2013). Sri Lanka Portuguese *cooru* 'tears' (Smith 2013) is an exceptional case among the value 1 languages in that it is derived from Portuguese *choro* 'lament, weeping, crying'.

Value 2. **Bimorphemic combinations** for 'tears' are found in a total of 27 *APiCS* languages. Apart from true 'eye-water' compounds, this value also subsumes possessive constructions of the NP1 NP2 type, in other words, the simple juxtaposition of possessor and possessum. In the 42 *APiCS* languages that have such a zero marking of possessive constructions (see Chapter 38) the expression for 'tear' could either be a compound ('eye-water') or a possessive noun phrase ('water of eye'). The latter would in fact be a candidate for value 3, but since we lack data to differentiate between such noun phrases and compounds, all bimorphemic combinations without overt marking are treated as instances of value 2.

Bimorphemic combinations are directly taken from the lexifier (3), an adstrate (4), or a substrate (5):

(3) Singapore Bazaar Malay (Khin Khin Aye 2013)
     air mata (< Malay *air mata*, lit. 'water' + 'eye')

(4) Sri Lankan Malay (Slomanson 2013)
     kannir (< Tamil *kaṇṇīr*, lit. 'eye' + 'water')

(5) Berbice Dutch (Kouwenberg 2013a)
     toro-mingi (< Eastern Ijo *toro-mingi*, lit. 'eye' + 'water')

Another possibility is that the compound has been calqued on a substrate form, using the lexifier words for 'eye' and 'water', as in (6).

(6) *ai-waata*   Creolese (Devonish & Thompson 2013)
                  (< English *eye* + *water*)
    dlo-wey   Guyanais (Pfänder 2013)
                  (< French *de l'eau* 'water' + *œil* 'eye')
    móya éna   Juba Arabic (Manfredi & Petrollino 2013)
                  (< Sudanese Arabic *móya* 'water' + *éna* 'eye')
    awa wê   Santome (Hagemeijer 2013)
                  (< Portuguese *água* 'water' + *olho* 'eye')
    wátá-wóyo   Saramaccan (Aboh et al. 2013)
                  (< English *water* + Portuguese *olho* 'eye')

Value 3. This value includes the 15 cases where the concept of 'tears' is referred to by **phrasal expressions** with overt marking like 'water of eye' or **circumlocutions** like 'water is in my eye'. Among the *APiCS* languages we find constructions involving prepositional phrases (7) and possessive phrases (8):

(7) Cameroon Pidgin English (Schröder 2013)
    wata fo   ay
    water PREP eye
    'tear' (lit. 'water in eye')

(8) Chinuk Wawa (Grant 2013)
    síxwst yáka čak
    eye   3SG water
    'tear' (lit. 'eye his water')

The Batavia Creole possessive phrase *olu su lagër* [eye POSS tear] (Maurer 2013b) is interesting since it contains a monomorphemic word meaning 'tear' (*lagër* < Portuguese *lágrima*), but apparently this only occurs in the possessive phrase 'the tear of the eye'.

Two languages, Nigerian Pidgin and Krio, can refer to 'tears' only by circumlocution:

(9) Nigerian Pidgin (Faraclas 2013)
    Wòta de mì   fɔr ay.
    water COP 1SG.SBJ LOC eye
    'Water is in my eyes.'

(10) Krio (Finney 2013)
    wata di   kɔmɔt na ĩ   yai.
    water PROG come LOC POSS eye
    'He/she is crying.' (lit. 'Water is coming out of his eyes.')

Combination of values. Fifty-three *APiCS* languages (80% of the languages for which information is available for this feature) rely on one value only. Vincentian Creole is the only *APiCS* language that has all three values:

(11) Vincentian Creole (Prescod 2013)
    a. *Waip yo   tei-z.* (Monomorphemic)
       wipe 2.POSS tear-PL
       'Wipe your tears.'
    b. *Aal mi ai waata duhn.* (Bimorphemic)
       all 1SG eye water done
       'I have no more tears left.'
    c. *Shi krai lang waata out shi ai.* (Circumlocution)
       3SG cry long water out 3SG eye
       'She cried long tears.'

However, four languages—Bahamian Creole, Belizean Creole, Gullah, and Trinidad English Creole—have both a monomorphemic and a bimorphemic word for 'tears'; five languages—Cape Verdean Creole of Santiago, Cape Verdean Creole of São Vicente, Fanakalo, Lingala, and Papiamentu—combine value 1 (monomorphemic) and value 3 (phrase/circumlocution); and three languages—Early Sranan, Pichi, and Sango—have value 2 (bimorphemic) and value 3 (phrase/circumlocution).

3. Discussion

'Eye-water' compounds or phrases like 'water of/in eye' are not uncommon in the world's languages (Urban 2012: 875–6). However, they are not found in the major lexifiers in *APiCS*, English, French, Portuguese, and Spanish, which all have monomorphemic words for 'tears' (value 1). Nevertheless, not all contact languages adopted these from their European lexifier and there is a marked difference regarding the lexical choices made by the English-lexified *APiCS* languages on the one hand and by the Romance language-lexified ones on the other: 13 (52%) English-lexified *APiCS* languages actually do not have a monomorphemic word for 'tears' at all, and as many as 15 (60%) have a bimorphemic 'eye-water' word. On the other hand, only 7 (25%) Romance language-lexified contact languages lack a monomorphemic word, and a mere 5 (18%) have a bimorphemic one.

These non-European strategies are obviously a result of African substratal input. With the exception of Tok Pisin, all of the 20 English- and Romance language-lexified contact languages that do not have a monomorphemic word for tears and all 20 languages that have a bimorphemic word are located in the Atlantic region. Virtually all of these developed in plantation colonies characterized by the importation of African slaves. Curiously enough, four of the five African language-lexified contact languages are value 1 (monomorphemic) languages and do NOT have bimorphemic forms: Fanakalo, Kikongo-Kituba, Lingala, and Mixed Ma'a/Mbugu. Sango is the exception in that it does not have a monomorphemic but a bimorphemic form.

The above figures also show that there is a much stronger tendency among the English-lexified *APiCS* languages than in the Portuguese/French/Spanish-lexified ones to avoid the monomorphemic lexifier word and to calque a bimorphemic one. The reasons for this are not quite clear, but further research will possibly reveal a stronger African substratal influence in the English-lexified contact languages in this particular aspect.

111 'Tears'

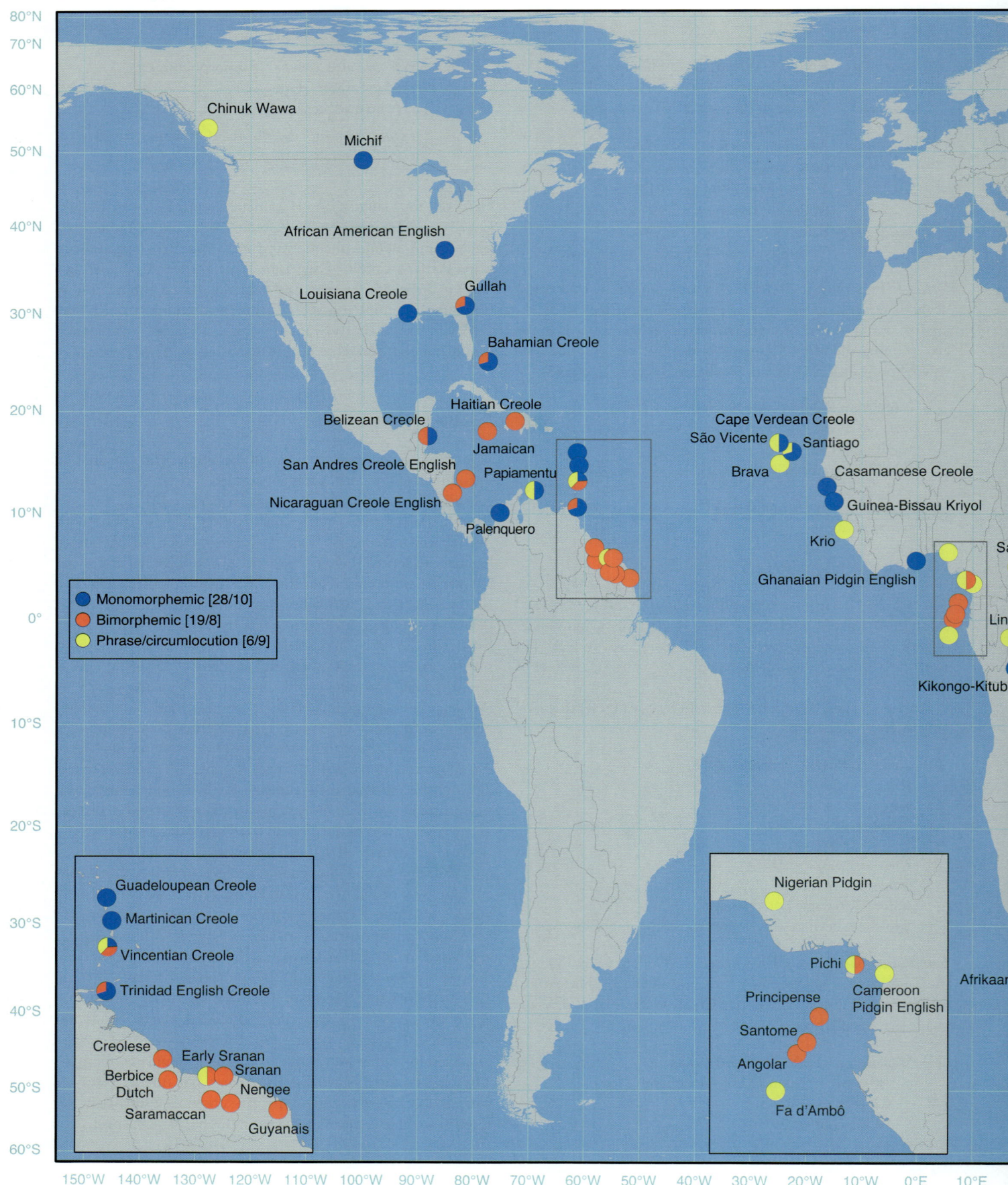

Chapter 112
'Hand' and 'arm'

MAGNUS HUBER AND THE *APiCS* CONSORTIUM

1. Feature description

This feature is inspired by *WALS* feature 129 (Brown 2005) and concerns the semantic identity or differentiation between the words meaning 'hand' and 'arm'. There are languages that have different words for forearm and upper arm (like Gurindji, one of Gurindji Kriol's lexifiers, which has *wartan* 'hand and forearm' and *murlku* 'upper arm'; Meakins 2013), but for the purposes of this feature, we consider only the forearm, from the elbow downwards. Of the several logical possibilities to partition the semantic space of the upper limb, Brown (2005) maps two: (a) identity, where one word means both 'hand' and 'arm' and (b) differentiation, where there are two words, one denoting 'hand' and another 'arm'. Brown's identity subsumes cases where there are two different (possibly related) words, but one of them denotes 'hand and arm' and the other only 'hand' or only 'arm', but we assign this constellation to a different value, overlap. A fourth constellation, identity and differentiation, where there are at least three words—one denotes 'hand', one denotes 'arm', and the third denotes 'hand and arm'—is not attested among the *APiCS* languages.

2. The values

Three strategies to refer to hand and/or arm are found among the contact languages in *APiCS*:

Value 1. 'Hand/arm' **identity** is the most frequent value in our sample, 43 languages (57%) showing this strategy. All *APiCS* languages with non-European lexifiers show 'hand and arm' identity, for example:

(1) Pidgin Hawaiian (Roberts 2013)
    a. *Iaia* [...] *nanao*   *no*   *kela* **lima** [...].
        3SG   thrust.into.opening INTENS DET hand/arm
        'He thrust his hand inside.'

    b. *Mahope wau moe malalo* [...] *onioni kela* **lima** [...]
        later   1SG rest below   stretch DET hand/arm
        'Then I reclined down, having my arms outstretched.'

(2) Sango (Samarin 2013)
    a. *lo mu zembe na* **maboko** *ti lo*
        3SG take knife PREP hand/arm of 3SG
        'He took a knife (with his hand).'

    b. *yoro*   **maboko** *ti ala na*   *nduzu*
        stretch.out hand/arm of 2PL PREP upward
        'Raise your arms.'

There are also some contact languages with a European lexifier that have 'hand and arm' identity:

(3) Casamancese Creole (Biagui & Quint 2013)
    a. *Ña*   **moŋ**   ∅ *teŋ siŋku dedu.*
        POSS.1SG hand/arm PFV have five   finger
        'My hand has five fingers.'

    b. *Lutador* ∅ *kebrá* **moŋ**.
        wrestler PFV break hand/arm
        'The wrestler broke his arm.'

(4) Nengee (Migge 2013)
    a. *Den naki* **ana**   *gi*   *mi gwlapgwlapgwlap.*
        they hit   hand/arm give me IDEO
        'They clapped for me.'

    b. *ala en ondoo* **ana**   *fuu tjafutjafu kwakwakwaa*
        all his under hand/arm full IDEO   IDEO
        'All of his lower arm is full with boils.'

Value 2. **Differentiation**, that is, two different words for 'hand' and 'arm', is found in 27 *APiCS* languages (36%), all of them having a European lexifier. Compare:

(5) Haitian Creole (Fattier 2013)
    a. *Se de* **men** *m* *genyen.*
        TOP two hand 1SG have
        'I only have two hands.'

    b. *M tonbe sou* **bra** *m.*
        1SG fall   on arm 1SG.POSS
        'I fell on my arm.'

(6) Cavite Chabacano (Sippola 2013a)
   a. *Debe laba tu el **mano** bago come.*
      should wash 2SG DEF hand before eat
      'You should wash your hands before eating.'
   b. *Tiene eli tattoo na su **brazo**.*
      have 3SG tattoo LOC 3SG.POSS arm
      'He has a tattoo on his arm.'

Value 3. Only five of the languages sampled in *APiCS* (7%) show semantic **overlap**, that is, two different (possibly related) words, of which one denotes 'hand AND arm' and the other 'hand OR arm'. Again, all these languages have a European lexifier: Bahamian Creole, Cape Verdean Creole of São Vicente, Chinese Pidgin English, Ghanaian Pidgin English, and Sri Lanka Portuguese. In all cases, it is the lexifier word designating the hand which means 'hand and arm' in the contact language, while the lexifier word designating the arm means 'arm' only. Compare Cape Verdean Creole of São Vicente, where *mon* (< Portuguese *mão* 'hand') refers to the hand and the arm, while *bros* (< Portuguese *braço* 'arm') refers to the arm only:

(7) Cape Verdean Creole of São Vincente (Swolkien 2013)
   a. *N kebrá **bros** skerd y **mon** dreita.*
      1SG break arm left and hand/arm right
      'I have broken my left arm and right hand.'
   b. *El po mnin na **mon**.*
      3SG put child in hand/arm
      'She took the child into her arms.'

3. Discussion

Differentiation is the most frequent value in Brown (2005), with 389 of 617 languages (63%) following this pattern. By contrast, 48 of 75 *APiCS* languages (64%) show 'hand and arm' identity (in value 1 and value 3). This is all the more remarkable in view of the facts that (i) 61 of 76 *APiCS* languages have a primary European lexifier and (ii) all European lexifiers in *APiCS* except Russian differentiate between 'hand' and 'arm'. The explanation may lie in Brown's (2005: 522) observation that there are more identity languages closer to the equator: most substrates of *APiCS* languages derive from these latitudes and the overall substrate pull would have been towards 'hand and arm' identity.

With only one exception (Berbice Dutch, where *bara* comes from the substrate Ijo *bárá* 'hand and arm'), *APiCS* languages derive the words designating parts of the upper limb from their lexifier languages. Thus, value 1 languages either inherited the 'hand and (fore)arm' identity from the lexifier or generalized one word from a 'hand' vs. 'arm' differentiating lexifier to cover both 'hand and (fore)arm'. Identity appears to be inherited from the lexifier in, among several others, Ambon Malay, Singapore Bazaar Malay, and Sri Lankan Malay, which derive their words from Malay *tangan* 'hand, forearm', and Chinese Pidgin Russian, whose *ruka* 'hand, arm' mirrors the semantics of the Russian etymon *ruka*. Interestingly, if the lexifier differentiates between 'hand' and 'arm' but the contact language shows 'hand and arm' identity, it was the lexifier word for 'hand'—and not that for 'arm'—that was generalized to mean 'hand and arm'. Presumably this is because the hand is the most salient part of the upper limb. This happened both in languages with a European lexifier (e.g. Bislama *han* 'hand, arm' < English *hand*, Diu Indo-Portuguese *mãw* 'hand, arm' < Portuguese *mão* 'hand', and Media Lengua *manu* 'hand, arm' < Spanish *mano* 'hand') as well as in those with non-European lexifiers (e.g. Fanakalo *sandla* 'hand, arm' < Zulu *isandla* 'hand' and Gurindji Kriol *wartan* < Gurindji *wartan* 'hand and forearm' as opposed to Gurindji *murlku* 'upper arm'). Yimas-Arafundi Pidgin, which may have generalized Yimas *maŋkaŋ* 'arm' rather than *nuŋkara* 'hand', possibly constitutes the only exception to this rule, but Foley (2013) is "uncertain" about the value 1 status of this language.

Similarly, with regard to value 3 (overlap) it is the lexifier word for 'hand' that is widened to mean 'hand and arm' in the contact language, while the word for 'arm' does not undergo any semantic change. Compare example (7), above, or Sri Lanka Portuguese:

(8) Sri Lanka Portuguese (Smith 2013)
   a. *isti pee **maam** tudu pa-duva*
      this foot hand/arm all INF-hurt
      'My legs and arms ache.'
   b. *maam pee lo-kosaa*
      hand/arm leg FUT-itch
      '(Your) arms and legs will itch.'
   c. *maam-braasu*
      hand/arm-arm
      'arm (above the hand)'

The semantic widening of lexifier 'hand' to contact language 'hand and arm' (as covered by value 1 "identity" and value 3 "overlap") is found to varying degrees in English-lexifier (21 of 27 English-lexifier *APiCS* languages), Portuguese-lexifier (10/14), and Spanish-lexifier (1/5) *APiCS* languages. However, not a single one of the ten French-lexifier contact languages in *APiCS* abandoned the *main* 'hand' vs. *bras* 'arm' differentiation of French, even though there must have been a considerable substrate pressure at least in the Caribbean and on New Caledonia (most West and Central African languages as well as most Melanesian languages showing 'hand and arm' identity; Brown 2005: 524–5).

112 'Hand' and 'arm'

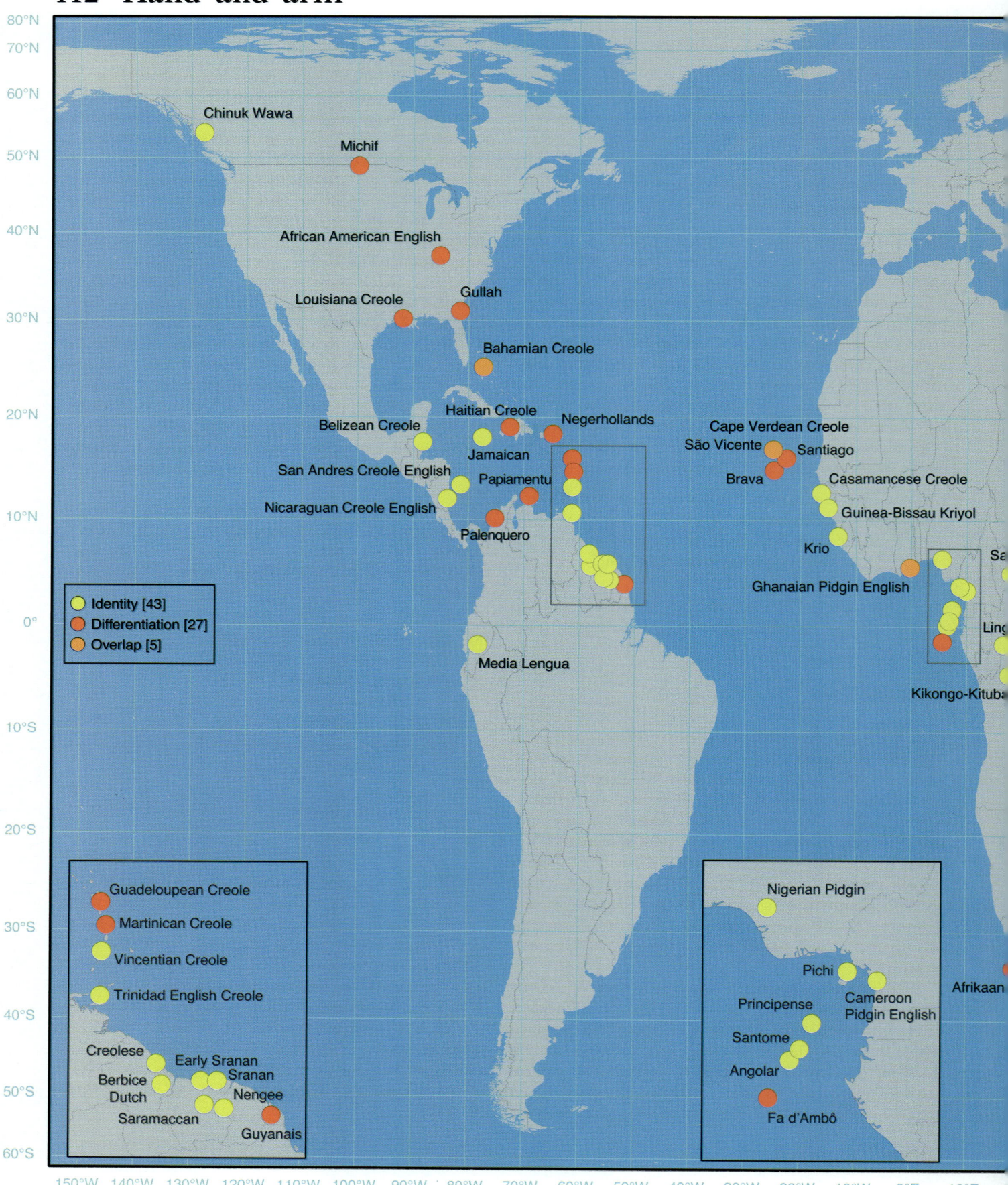

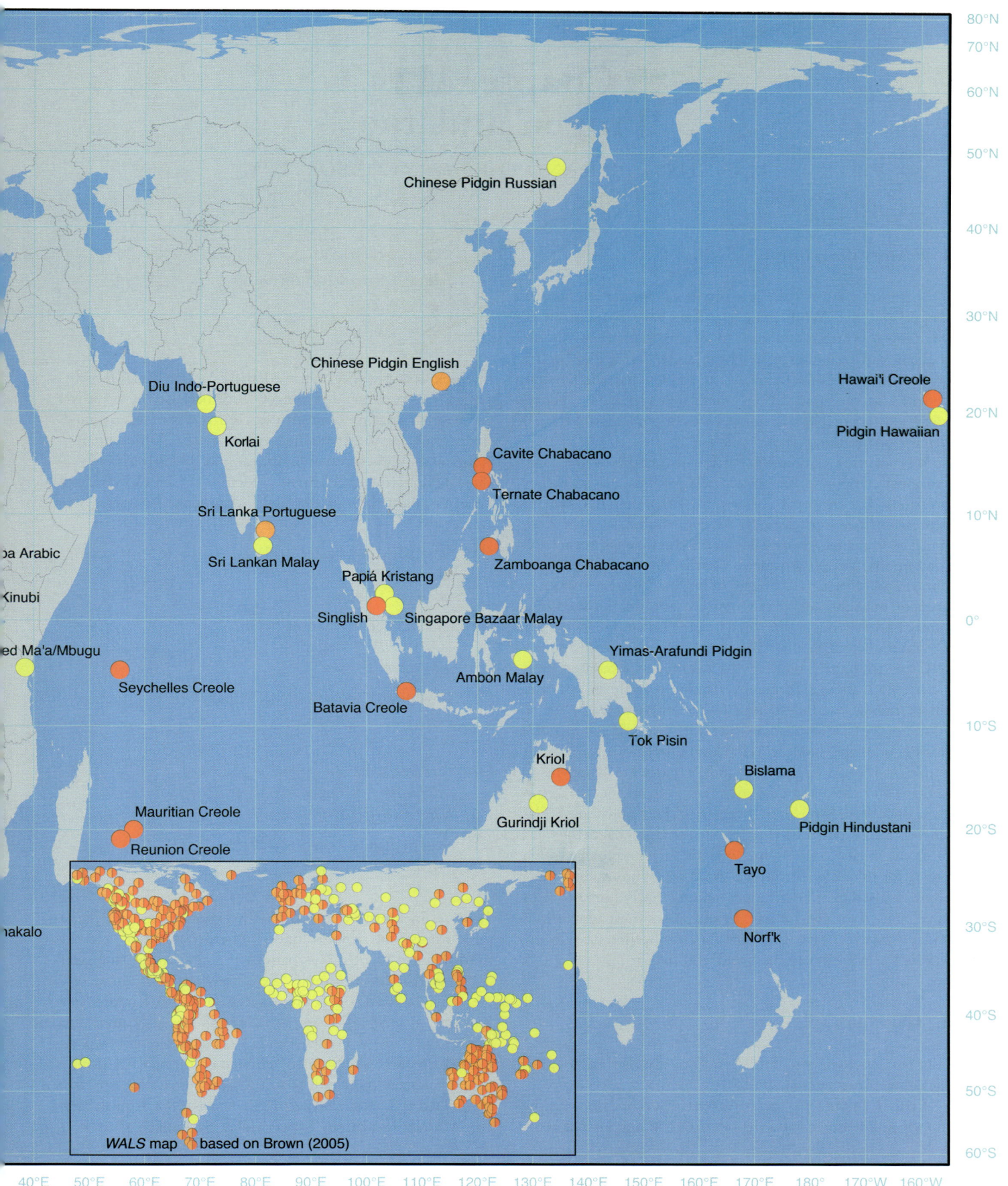

Chapter 113
'Finger' and 'toe'

MAGNUS HUBER AND THE *APiCS* CONSORTIUM

1. Feature description

This feature concerns the identity or differentiation between 'finger' and 'toe'. While some languages have two separate expressions for 'finger' and 'toe', there are others where one and the same expression refers to 'finger' and to 'toe' ('digit' or 'finger/toe' identity in the following) and in which disambiguation depends on the context. Yet other languages have a general 'digit' expression but additional words or phrases with the particularized meanings 'finger' and 'toe'.

It is not always straightforward to distinguish between conventional compound (or phrasal) expressions and ad hoc expressions. For practical reasons, we simply assume that the expressions that were given by the contributors are all conventional expressions. Also, we do not differentiate between words, compounds, and phrases here. That is, the Cavite Chabacano phrase *dedo de su pies* (lit. 'finger of his foot') is treated as an expression meaning 'toe' in the same way as is the Berbice Dutch compound *bwa fingri* (lit. 'foot finger') or the Guadeloupean Creole monomorphemic *zòtèy* 'toe'. Further, words/phrases referring to 'finger' and 'toe' are counted as separate expressions even if there is formal overlap between them, as, for instance, in Nigerian Pidgin *finga* 'finger' and *finga fòr leg* 'toe'. In addition, the fact that a language may have several synonyms referring to 'finger' and 'toe' is irrelevant for this feature. For example, in Haitian Creole *dwèt* and *dwèt men* are synonyms for 'finger', and *zòtèy* and *dwèt pye* are synonyms for 'toe'. However, since there is no 'digit' expression, Haitian Creole is classified as a differentiating language. In some languages the words meaning 'finger' and/or 'toe' include larger segments of the limbs, for example, Gurindji Kriol *martan* 'upper limb below elbow' is used to refer to 'finger' and *fut* 'lower limb below the knee' is used to refer to 'toe'. In such cases these semantically wider words were taken as a basis for classification (see Chapter 112 for the overlap between 'hand' and 'arm').

2. The values

Four patterns to refer to 'finger' and 'toe' are discernible among the contact languages in *APiCS*:

Value 1. In 'finger'–'toe' **differentiation** one word denotes 'finger' and another word denotes 'toe'. As mentioned above,

● 1. Differentiation		39
● 2. Identity and differentiation		14
● 3. Overlap		11
● 4. Identity		3

this includes cases of formal overlap like Ambon Malay *jari* 'finger' vs. *jari kaki* 'toe' (lit. 'finger foot') because the latter is a compound and as such constitutes a separate word even though it is partially identical with the word for 'finger'. Differentiation is the most frequent value in our sample, 39 languages (58%) showing this strategy. With the exception of Chinuk Wawa and Fanakalo, all of these are lexified by European languages. Examples are:

(1) Norf'k (Mühlhäusler 2013)
finger
toe

(2) Batavia Creole (Maurer 2013b)
dedu 'finger'
dedu di peo 'toe'

(3) Martinican Creole (Colot & Ludwig 2013b)
dwet 'finger'
zòtey 'toe'

(4) Ternate Chabacano (Sippola 2013b)
dédo, dedíto 'finger'
dedíto del pyés 'toe'

(5) Negerhollands (van Sluijs 2013)
finggu 'finger'
tesi 'toe'

Value 2. In **identity and differentiation** there are at least three words; one denotes 'finger', one denotes 'toe', and the third denotes 'digit'. This pattern is found in 14 languages (21%) of the *APiCS* sample. Six of these are Portuguese creoles (Angolar, Fa d'Ambô, Guinea-Bissau Kriyol, Korlai, Papiá Kristang, Principense), one is a Spanish creole (Zamboanga Chabacano), one a French creole (Reunion Creole), one an English creole (Early Sranan), and one is an English/Gurindji mixed language (Gurindji Kriol). Of the remaining four, two are lexified by Bantu languages (Kikongo-Kituba, Lingala) and two by Malay (Singapore Bazaar Malay, Sri Lankan Malay):

(6) Fa d'Ambô (Post 2013)
    dedu   'digit'
    dedu omá   'finger'
    dedu opé   'toe'

(7) Gurindji Kriol (Meakins 2013)
    nantananta   'digit'
    wartan   'finger'
    fut   'toe'

(8) Kikongo-Kituba (Mufwene 2013)
    musapi   'digit'
    musapi ya diboko   'finger'
    musapi ya dikulu   'toe'

(9) Sri Lankan Malay (Slomanson 2013)
    jirji   'digit'
    tangan jirji   'finger'
    kaki jirji   'toe'

Value 3 covers cases of semantic **overlap**, where there are two different words, one of which denotes 'digit' and the other one denotes only 'finger' or only 'toe'. All 11 languages in *APiCS* showing overlap (16%) have Romance lexifiers: the three Cape Verdean Creoles, Casamancese Creole, Cavite Chabacano, Mauritian Creole, Palenquero, Papiamentu, Santome, Sri Lanka Portuguese, and Tayo.

(10) Cape Verdean Creole of Brava (Baptista 2013)
     dedu   'digit'
     dedu di pe   'toe'

(11) Palenquero (Schwegler 2013)
     lelo   'digit'
     lelo ri pie   'toe'

(12) Tayo (Ehrhart & Revis 2013)
     ⁿdwa   'digit'
     ⁿdwa ⁿde pje   'toe'

Value 4. In the **identity** constellation, there is 'digit' but there is no word that denotes only 'finger' or only 'toe'. Only three languages (4%) show 'finger/toe' identity without separate words for 'finger' or 'toe' – Juba Arabic (*asbá*), Mixed Ma'a/Mbugu (*kihlatú*), and Nengee (*finga*).

3. Discussion

Of the 62 *APiCS* languages with a European lexifier, only Nengee is an identity language (value 4). These languages have almost consistently incorporated the European 'finger'–'toe' differentiation in their system. Portuguese-lexified creoles tend to have either overlap (7 of 14 Portuguese-lexified languages) or identity and differentiation (6/14), French-lexified creoles tend to be differentiating (7/10), but there is no clear pattern in the Spanish-lexified creoles. On the other hand, there is a very strong tendency for English- and Dutch-lexified contact languages to be differentiating (26/29). As to languages with a non-European lexifier, there is no language that shows overlap, but there is roughly equal distribution over the other three values.

Comments by the *APiCS* contributors suggest that in contact languages that have a 'digit' word (found in values 2–4), the default interpretation tends to be 'finger' and that contextual disambiguation is necessary for a 'toe' reading. This is probably because fingers are the more salient members, which may also be the reason why the expressions for 'toe' are often compounds or phrases involving the word for 'finger', formed on the basis of the proportional metaphor "the toes are the fingers of the foot" (Miller 1993: 383) as, for example, in Lingala *mosapi ya lokolo* 'toe' (lit. 'finger of foot').

That the majority of the Romance-lexified *APiCS* languages (24/28) have such a polymorphemic 'finger (of) foot' word/phrase is hardly surprising since the lexifiers Portuguese, Spanish, and French provide similar phrasal models (apart from the mixed language Michif, only the French-lexified creoles of Guadeloupe, Martinique, Louisiana, and Haiti derive their words for 'toe' from French *orteil* 'toe', Haitian Creole in addition to a 'finger of foot' phrase). Quite a number of the Romance-lexified contact languages also have 'finger (of) hand' expressions, mirroring the *dedo da mão*, *doigt de main*, and *dedo del mano* phrases of their lexifiers: these are Angolar, Fa d'Ambô, Guinea-Bissau Kriyol, Haitian Creole, Korlai, Papiá Kristang, Principense, Reunion Creole, Zamboanga Chabacano, and possibly Sri Lanka Portuguese and Ternate Chabacano.

By comparison, 'finger (of) hand/foot' expressions are much less frequent in the 29 English- and Dutch-lexified *APiCS* languages: 'finger (of) foot' is found only in Berbice Dutch, Nigerian Pidgin, Saramaccan, Sranan, and Tok Pisin, while 'finger of hand' occurs only in Early Sranan.

Polymorphemic expressions for 'toe' (7/11) and 'finger' (5/11) are found in about half of the non-European lexifier *APiCS* languages.

The implicational hierarchies in (13) and (14) are true for the *APiCS* sample:

(13) 'finger (of) hand' < 'finger (of) foot' < 'digit'/'finger'

That is, there is no *APiCS* language that has 'finger (of) hand' without also having 'finger (of) foot' as well as a monomorphemic word for either 'digit' or 'finger', and there is no language that has 'finger (of) foot' without also having a monomorphemic word for either 'digit' or 'finger', but not the other way round.

(14) 'toe' < 'finger'

That is, there is no *APiCS* language that has a monomorphemic word for 'toe' that does not also have a monomorphemic word for 'finger'. Monomorphemic 'toe' is found only in value 1 (differentiation) languages.

113 'Finger' and 'toe'

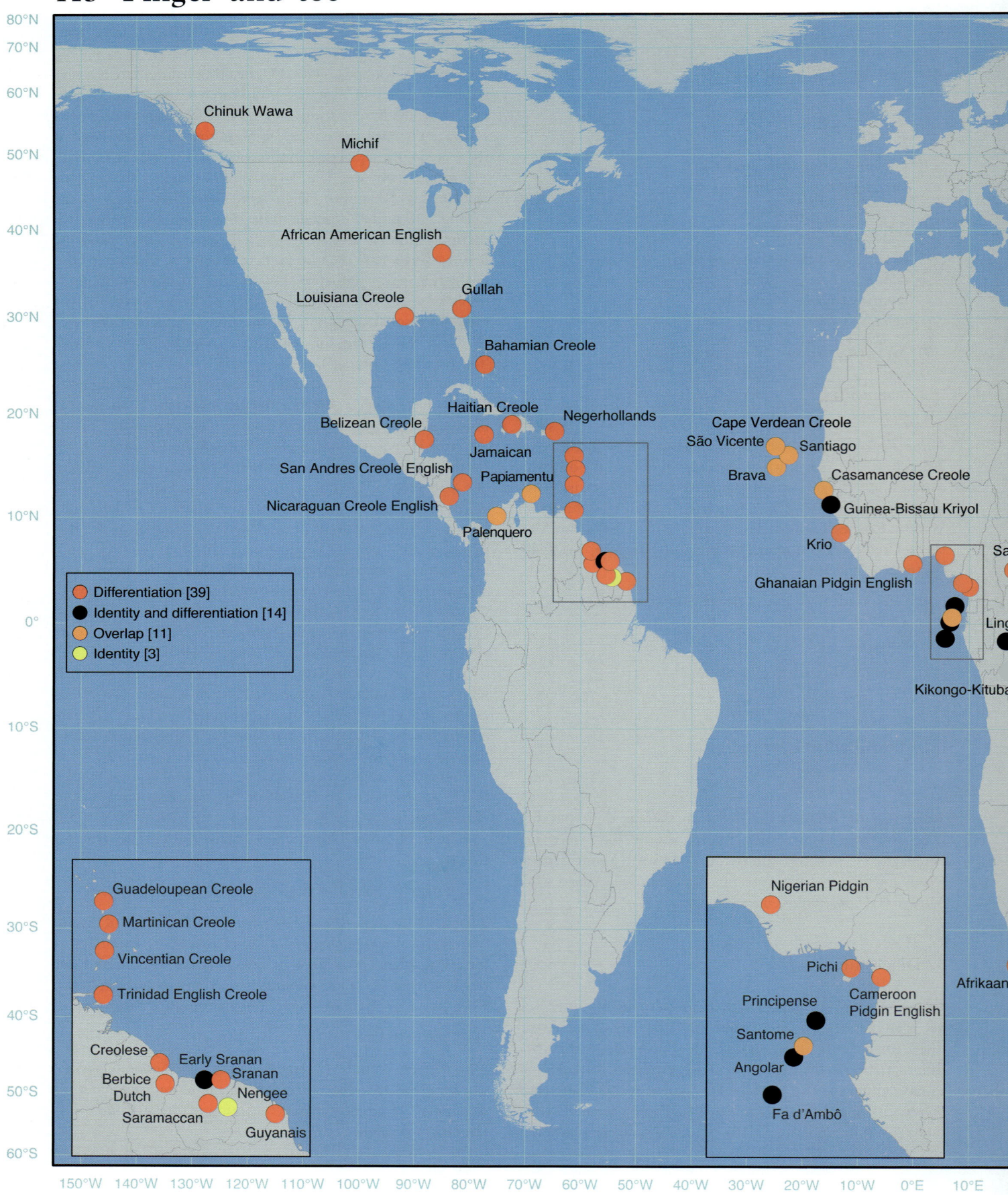

Chapter 114
'Body hair' and 'feather'

MAGNUS HUBER AND THE *APiCS* CONSORTIUM

1. Feature description

●	1. Differentiation	43
●	2. Identity	7
●	3. Overlap	14
●	4. Identity and differentiation	5

This feature considers the formal identity or differentiation between the terms referring to (body) hair and feather. Some languages differentiate between the hair of the head and body hair, as in Principense *pene* 'body hair' vs. *kabelu* 'hair of the head'. In such cases, contributors were asked to base their judgements on the expression for body hair. Thus, since *pene* also refers to 'feather', Principense was classified as an identity language.

Almost two-thirds of the *APiCS* languages have separate expressions for '(body) hair' and 'feather'. The rest have a polysemous expression meaning (body) hair or feather (referred to as 'hair/feather' identity in the following). When such polysemous terms are used, disambiguation depends on the context, but a number of languages with 'hair/feather' identity can also resort to additional words or phrases with the particularized meanings '(body) hair' or 'feather'.

For the purposes of this feature, we assume that all the expressions provided by the contributors are conventional rather than ad hoc creations for disambiguation. In addition, no difference is made between words, compounds, and phrases. This means that the Ternate Chabacano phrase *pilyého del páhro* (lit. 'hide of bird') is considered equivalent to the Sranan compound *fowru-wiwiri* (lit. 'bird hair') and the Norf'k monomorphemic *feather*. Also, words/phrases referring to (body) hair and feather are counted as separate expressions even if there is formal overlap between them, as in Kinubi *su-rás* 'hair' (lit. 'hair head') and *su-téri* 'feather' (lit. 'hair bird'). Further, the fact that a language may have several synonyms referring to (body) hair or feather is irrelevant for this feature. For example, in addition to the forms just cited, Kinubi has the synonyms *su* for 'hair' and *ris* for 'feather'. Nevertheless, since there is no semantic overlap between the expressions for 'hair' and 'feather', Kinubi is classified as a differentiating language.

2. The values

The *APiCS* languages show four patterns with regard to the identity or differentiation of '(body) hair' and 'feather':

Value 1. '(Body) hair'–'feather' **differentiation** means that there is one word that refers to '(body) hair' and another word that refers to 'feather'. As already mentioned, this includes cases of formal overlap as evidenced by Kinubi *su-rás* 'hair' and *su-téri* 'feather'. Differentiation is the most frequent value in the *APiCS* sample, 43 languages (62%) relying on this strategy. Thirty-seven of these are lexified by European languages, two are mixed languages partially lexified by European languages (Gurindji Kriol by English, Michif by French), and the other four are the African contact languages Fanakalo, Kikongo-Kituba, Kinubi, and Mixed Ma'a/Mbugu. Examples are:

(1) Vincentian Creole (Prescod 2013)
    hei 'hair'
    feda 'feather'

(2) Fa d'Ambô (Post 2013)
    xabelu 'hair'
    péna 'feather'

(3) Tayo (Ehrhart & Revis 2013)
    feve 'body hair'
    plim 'feather'

(4) Cavite Chabacano (Sippola 2013a)
    pelo 'hair'
    pluma 'feather'

(5) Berbice Dutch (Kouwenberg 2013a)
    hari 'hair'
    plim 'feather'

(6) Mixed Ma'a/Mbugu (Mous 2013)
    ahlú 'hair'
    lu-zoyá 'feather'

Value 2. In the **identity** constellation, there is a general expression for '(body) hair/feather' but there is no term that denotes only '(body) hair' or only 'feather'. Seven languages (10%) show 'hair/feather' identity without separate words for '(body) hair' or 'feather' – Ambon Malay (*bulu*), Belizean Creole (*hɛ*), Juba Arabic (*suf*), Lingala (*súki*), Principense (*pene*), Saramaccan (*puuma*), and Singapore Bazaar Malay (*bulu*).

Value 3 subsumes cases of semantic overlap. There are two different words, one of which denotes '(body) hair/feather' and the other only '(body) hair' or only 'feather'. Of the 14 languages (20%) in *APiCS* showing overlap, five are lexified by French (the creoles of Guadeloupe, Haiti, Martinique, Reunion, and the Seychelles), three by English (Bahamian Creole, Sranan, Trinidad English Creole), two by Spanish (Ternate and Zamboanga Chabacano), one by Portuguese (Santome), and the other three by non-European languages (Chinuk Wawa, Pidgin Hawaiian, Sri Lankan Malay).

(7) Martinican Creole (Colot & Ludwig 2013b)
 chivé 'hair/feather'
 pwel 'feather'

(8) Trinidad English Creole (Mühleisen 2013)
 feaders 'body hair/feather'
 hair 'hair'

(9) Zamboanga Chabacano (Steinkrüger 2013)
 pélo 'hair/feather'
 pélo de páharo 'feather'

(10) Santome (Hagemeijer 2013)
 pena 'body hair/feather'
 kabelu 'hair'

(11) Chinuk Wawa (Grant 2013)
 típsu 'hair/feather'
 yáksu 'hair'

Value 4. In **identity and differentiation** there are at least three words; one denotes '(body) hair', one denotes 'feather', and the third denotes 'hair/feather'. This pattern is found in only five languages (7%) of the *APiCS* sample. Three of these are English-lexified (Early Sranan, Nengee, Tok Pisin), one is Portuguese-lexified (Angolar), and Sango is lexified by Ngbandi, a northern Volta-Congo language:

(12) Tok Pisin (Smith & Siegel 2013)
 gras 'hair/feather'
 gras bilong bodi 'body hair'
 gras bilong pisin 'feather'

(13) Angolar (Maurer 2013a)
 pena 'hair/feather'
 pena ôngê 'body hair'
 pena situ 'feather'

(14) Sango (Samarin 2013)
 kwa 'hair/feather'
 kwa (*ti*) *li* 'hair'
 kwa (*ti*) *ndeke* 'feather'

3. Discussion

The *APiCS* languages can be classified into two broad categories: 26 languages have a 'hair/feather' identity expression (values 2–4) and 43 do not (value 1). 'Hair'–'feather' is a cross-linguistically common semantic association, with no areal "hotspot" and found in 35 per cent of Urban's (2012: 451) convenience sample of 148 languages.

It is significant, however, that 'hair/feather' identity is not found in the Germanic and Romance lexifiers of the languages in *APiCS*. Of the 56 *APiCS* languages with a European lexifier considered here, only one-third (18) have an identity expression (values 2–4), and only three (Belizean Creole, Principense, and Saramaccan) rely exclusively on 'hair/feather' identity (value 2). The majority of these languages, however, categorically differentiate between '(body) hair' and 'feather'. The reason for this may be that the European lexifiers also have different words for '(body) hair' and 'feather' and that the contact languages tended to inherit this distinction with the lexicon, even if the substrates had 'hair/feather' identity.

On the other hand, the *APiCS* languages with a non-European lexifier have a somewhat stronger tendency to rely on identity expressions (10 of 15 languages), for the most part mirroring 'hair/feather' identity in the lexifiers. Compare, for instance, Ambon Malay, Singapore Bazaar Malay, and Sri Lankan Malay, which all have identity words derived from Malay *bulu* 'hair/feather'.

All 'hair/feather' identity words recorded in *APiCS* are monomorphemic and the following observations can be made regarding their etyma: *APiCS* contact languages that draw the bulk of their lexicon from English show the highest variation, which may be partially due to the high number of these languages in our sample. They derive their 'hair/feather' identity words from *weed* (Early Sranan, Nengee, Sranan) or *grass* (Tok Pisin), from *feather* (Bahamian Creole, Trinidad English Creole) or the Portuguese *pluma* 'feather' (Saramaccan), or from *hair* (Belizean Creole).

Three French-lexified *APiCS* languages derive their 'hair/feather' word from *plume* 'feather' (the creoles of Haiti, Reunion, and the Seychelles) and two derive it from *cheveu* 'head hair' (the creoles of Guadeloupean and Martinique).

The etymon of the 'hair/feather' word in three Portuguese-lexified *APiCS* languages is *pena* 'feather', while for two Spanish-lexified creoles it is *pelo* 'hair'.

The majority of the non-European lexifiers have a 'hair/feather' word, and this appears to have been adopted by the respective contact languages, for example, Ambon Malay, Singapore Bazaar Malay, and Sri Lankan Malay (< Malay *bulu* '(body) hair/feather') and Pidgin Hawaiian (< Hawaiian *hulu* 'body hair/feather').

114 'Body hair' and 'feather'

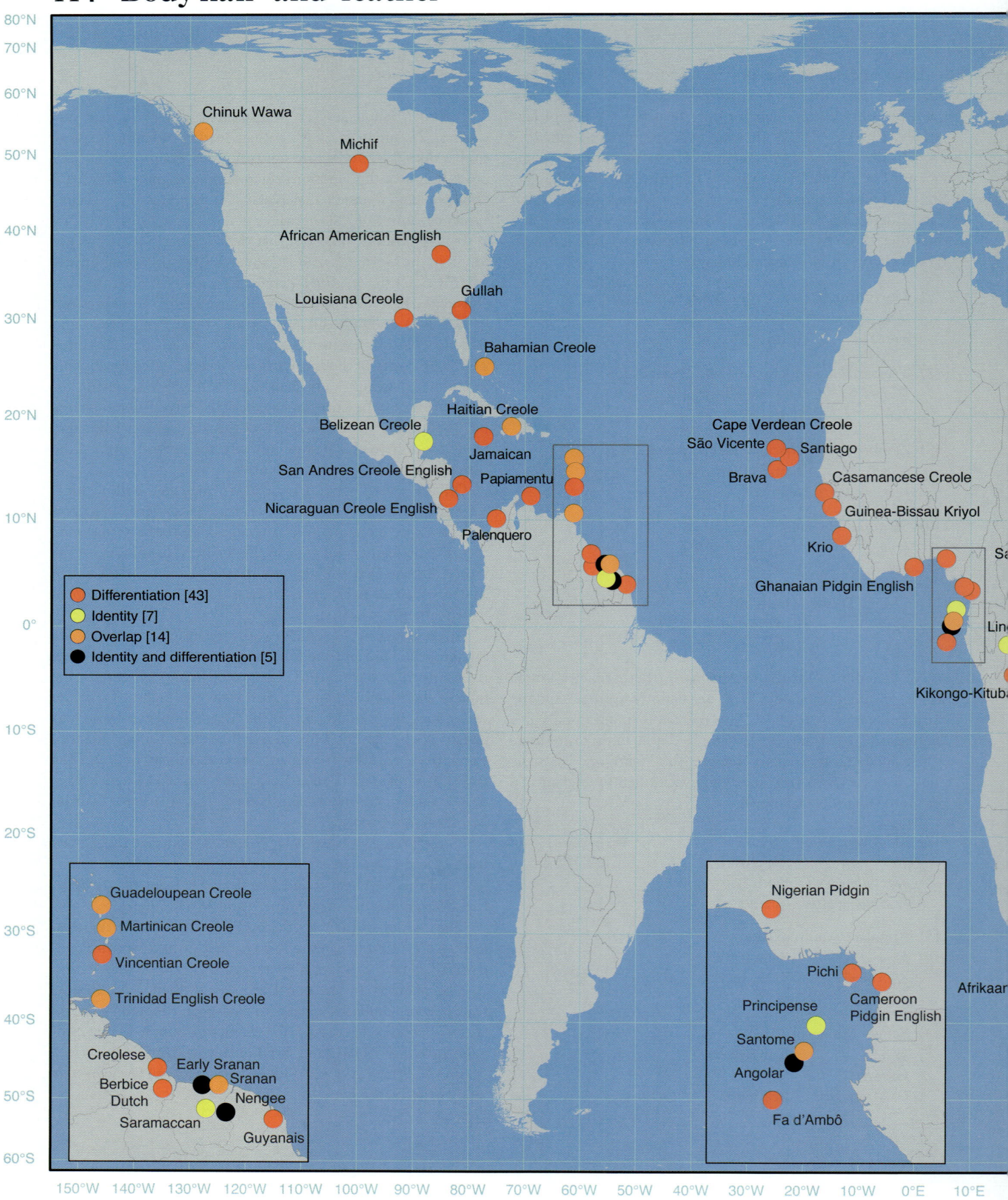

Chapter 115
'Hear' and 'smell'

MAGNUS HUBER AND THE *APiCS* CONSORTIUM

1. Feature description

Map 115 shows the identity or differentiation of the words expressing the meanings 'to hear' and 'to smell', the latter used transitively.

In many languages of the world, one or several sense perceptions and/or processes of cognition are expressed by the same verb (see Evans & Wilkins 2000, Vanhove 2008). Compare, for example, French *entendre*, which means both 'to hear' and 'to understand', and *sentir*, which can mean 'to feel', 'to smell', 'to taste', or more generally 'to perceive'. Such formal identity in the semantic domains of sense perception and cognition is also common among the *APiCS* languages. For example, Bislama *harem* and Kinubi *ásma* both mean 'to hear' and 'to feel', while Tayo *sa:(ti)* and younger generation Principense *xintxi* mean 'to smell' and 'to feel'. A very common case of identity is that between 'to hear' and its metaphorical extension 'to understand', as found, among others, in Eskimo Pidgin *tusar-*, Ghanaian Pidgin English *hiɛ*, Guinea-Bissau Kriyol *obi*, Palenquero *kuchá*, and Sango *ma*. Some contact languages have a general verb of sense perception, like Nigerian Pidgin, where "*hyar* 'hear' can be used to refer to stimuli detected by any of the senses" (Faraclas 2013).

The present feature explores the extent of overlap in the area of sense perception by focusing on the words meaning 'to hear' and 'to smell'.

2. The values

This feature has four values:

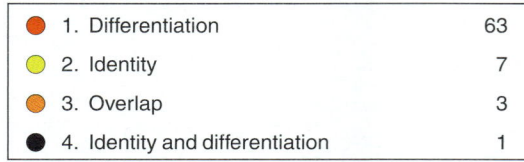

● 1. Differentiation		63
● 2. Identity		7
● 3. Overlap		3
● 4. Identity and differentiation		1

Value 1. We speak of **differentiation** if one word denotes 'to hear' and another word denotes 'to smell'. Note that this value also covers cases of (accidental) phonological overlap, as illustrated by Pidgin Hindustani *suno* 'to hear' vs. *suŋo* 'to smell', because they constitute separate words even though they are partially identical.

Differentiation of 'to hear' and 'to smell' is by far the most common value in *APiCS*: 85 per cent of the contact languages in our sample use different words to encode 'to hear' and 'to smell', as illustrated by Norf'k:

(1) *ya* 'to hear'
 smael 'to smell' (Mühlhäusler 2013)

Value 2: There is **identity** if a single word is used to express 'to hear' or 'to smell' and no word exists that denotes only 'to hear' or only 'to smell'.

This is the case in Fanakalo, where *izwa* means both 'to hear' and 'to smell' and where there is no other word whose meaning is restricted to either 'to hear' or 'to smell'. A number of *APiCS* contributors point out that the verb used has an even more general meaning, covering more sense perceptions than just 'to hear' and 'to smell'. In Kikongo-Kituba, for example, "the basic meaning of *wa* is 'perceive'" (Mufwene 2013).

Because of the semantic indeterminacy of the verb, the context plays a crucial disambiguating role. The particular interpretations of 'to hear' or 'to smell' arise in the context and/or are created only in conjunction with the other constituents that the general verb of sense perception combines with. Most often this is the object expressing the perceived entity, as in (2):

(2) Kikongo-Kituba (Mufwene 2013)
 Mono mene wa makelele.
 1SG PRF perceive noise
 'I have heard noise.'

 Mono mene wa nsudi.
 1SG PRF perceive smell
 'I have smelt (sth.).'

In one *APiCS* language, however, the disambiguation is achieved not by the object of perception but by a prepositional phrase referring to the organ of sense perception:

(3) Chinuk Wawa (Grant 2013)
 kámtaks kápa q'walên
 know PREP ear
 'to hear'

 kámtaks kápa nus
 know PREP nose
 'to smell'

It could be argued that the constructions illustrated by (2) and (3) actually present cases of differentiation rather than identity since in addition to the (identical) verb other (different) sentence constituents are necessary to generate the semantic concepts of 'to hear' and 'to smell'. Following this argumentation, the particularized meaning 'to hear' in Kikongo-Kituba is represented by *wa makele* and 'to smell' by *wa nsudi*. Seen this way, while there is formal overlap between the constructions expressing the two sense perceptions (*wa*), we are dealing with essentially different forms because the two constructions are not identical (*makele* vs. *nsudi*). However, this line of argumentation presupposes that the constituents form part of the verb, which they do not, or that *wa makele* and *wa nsudi* are fixed expressions, for which there is no evidence. Also, perception verbs are explicitly or implicitly transitive and thus usually require an object, no matter whether or not a language has an abstract perception verb ('to perceive') or particularized perception verbs ('to hear' and 'to smell'). Since this object is necessarily different for hearing and smelling, both in languages assigned to value 1 (differentiation) and to value 2 (identity), they cannot form the basis of classification. This leaves us with the verbs only, which seems to correspond to the intuition of the speakers of "identity" language: at least for Kikongo-Kituba the contributor's "native speaker intuition is that the SAME form is being used in all these constructions, *pace* the English translation" (Mufwene, p.c.).

Identity between 'to hear' and 'to smell' is reported for earlier stages of some *APiCS* languages. For example, Bislama *harem* and the related Tok Pisin *harim* covered both meanings in earlier times (Meyerhoff 2013, Smith & Siegel 2013). It seems that this identity was broken up through pressure from the lexifier English, whose *smell* was borrowed to cover the olfactory perception. As a consequence, the meaning of *harem/harim* was narrowed to auditory perception, just as in English.

Value 3. **Overlap** refers to cases where there are two different (possibly related) words, but one of them denotes 'to hear' and 'to smell', and the other one denotes only 'to hear' or only 'to smell'.

There are only three languages in the sample where this is the case, all belonging to the West African Krio–Pidgin English continuum. In Krio, Ghanaian Pidgin English, and Nigerian Pidgin the word derived from English *hear* means 'to hear' and 'to smell', while the word derived from *smell* means 'to smell' only. This overlap is probably an intermediary stage between identity and differentiation, in which an older word covering both hearing and smelling (identity) coexists with the newly borrowed English *smell* (incipient differentiation). For full differentiation to develop, the more general older word will have to undergo semantic narrowing to refer to auditory perception only.

Value 4. The **identity and differentiation** constellation is a combination of values 1 and 2: there are at least three (possibly related) words; one denotes only 'to hear' and another denotes only 'to smell' (differentiation), and the third denotes 'to hear' or 'to smell' (identity).

Casamancese Creole (Biagui & Quint 2013) is the only language in the *APiCS* sample that fulfils these criteria: *wobí* means 'to hear' (4a) and *kerá* 'to smell' (4b), while *sintí*, with a generalized meaning 'to feel', is used for both hearing (5a) and smelling (5b):

(4) Differentiation: *wobí* 'to hear' vs. *kerá* 'to smell'
 a. *N   ∅   wobí añju na   corá fora.*
    1SG.SBJ PFV hear child PROG cry outside
    'I hear the child crying outside.'
 b. *I   ∅   kerá   keru   di tabaku.*
    3SG.SBJ PFV smell[verb] smell[noun] of tobacco
    'S/he smelt a/the smell of tobacco.'

(5) Identity: *sintí* 'to hear' or 'to smell'
 a. *N   ka ∅   sintí wora ku   mininu ∅ kordá.*
    1SG.SBJ NEG PFV feel hour REL.OBJ child PFV wake.up
    'I did not hear when the child woke up.'
 b. *Mininu ta sintí keru di si   mamé.*
    child HAB feel smell of POSS.3SG mother
    'A child is able to recognize (smell) its mother's smell.'

3. Distribution

Values 2 (identity), 3 (overlap), and 4 (identity and differentiation) all involve identity, that is, a word that covers both auditory and olfactory perception. In this respect, these values contrast with value 1 (differentiation), where there is no word that means both 'to hear' and 'to smell'. The map shows that with one exception (Chinuk Wawa) all value 2, 3, and 4 languages are located in Africa and on the Gulf of Guinea islands. Since these languages have diverse lexifiers—African (Fanakalo, Kikongo-Kituba, Lingala, Sango), English (Ghanaian Pidgin English, Krio, Nigerian Pidgin), and Portuguese (Angolar, Casamancese Creole, Principense)—and English and Portuguese do not have a 'hear'–'smell' identity, this suggests that it must be due to African substrate and/or adstrate influence. Indeed, Viberg (1984: 141–2) and Welmers (1973: 476) report a wide distribution of 'hear'–'smell' identity in sub-Saharan languages. However, the absence of identity in the African diaspora creoles on the other side of the Atlantic remains a puzzle. More research is clearly needed, including a comprehensive worldwide typological study on perception verbs and an analysis of perception verbs in earlier stages of contact languages.

115 'Hear' and 'smell'

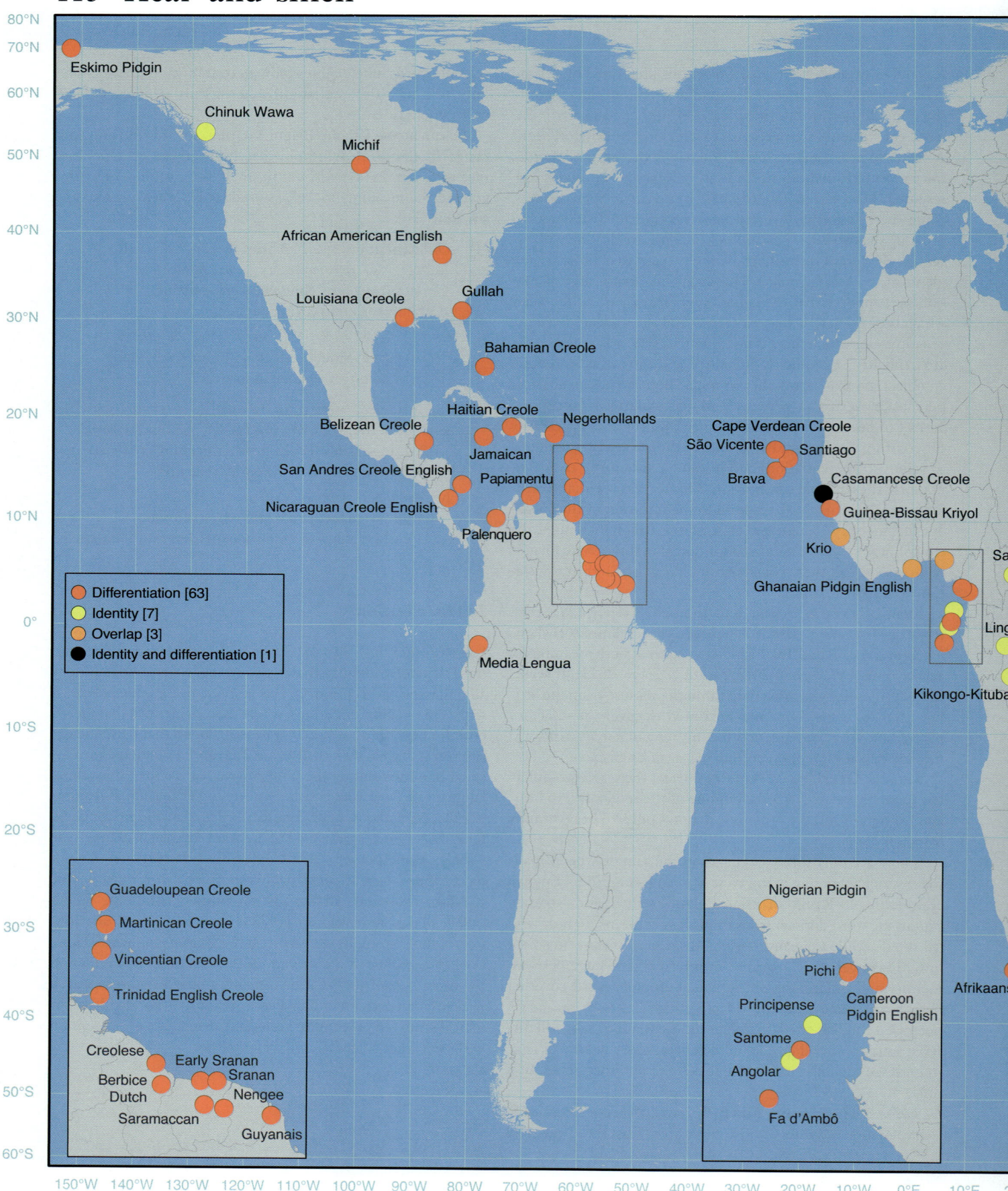

Chapter 116
'Green' and 'blue'

MAGNUS HUBER AND THE *APiCS* CONSORTIUM

1. Feature description

Map 116 is about the lexical choices that *APiCS* languages make when referring to the "cool" colour sensations green and blue, specifically, whether the **basic colour terms** for green and blue are identical or different. The map is based on the corresponding *WALS* chapter by Kay & Maffi (2005), who follow Hering (1964) in proposing a universal of six primary colour categories (black, white, red, yellow, green, blue). Languages differ as to how the psychological colour space is covered by their basic colour terms, that is, words whose "meaning is not predictable from the meaning of [their] parts", whose "signification is not included in any other color term", whose "application must not be restricted to a narrow class of objects", and which are "psychologically salient for informants" (Berlin & Kay 1969: 6).

The data for the *World Color Survey* (see Kay et al. 2010, http://www1.icsi.berkeley.edu/wcs) that form the basis of Kay & Maffi's (2005) *WALS* contribution were collected using objective psychological methods (to elicit colour terms, a set of 330 Munsell colour chips were shown to native speakers). It should be pointed out that the *APiCS* data are more impressionistic and results should thus be treated with some caution: the contributors had not been provided with standardized colours to show to speakers of the contact languages, and in many cases the questionnaire answers are based on the contributor's *post-hoc* interpretation of field recordings and may therefore be influenced by the colour system of the contributor's language. Nevertheless, Map 116 shows some interesting results that call for further research.

Note that Kay & Maffi's (2005) "Green and blue" map includes information on whether these colour terms cover black or yellow as well. This is not the case in *APiCS*, which considers the terms for green and blue only, regardless of whether they also refer to other colours. From the comments of some *APiCS* contributors it is clear, however, that in contact languages the terms referring to green and blue cover other colour sensations too. For example, Sango *vuko/voko* means 'be dark/black/blue/green/etc.' (Samarin 2013) and Korlai *pret*, in variation with Marathi-derived *shahi* 'blue', refers to 'black, (dark) blue' (Clements 2013). That the same term refers to black and blue is a common phenomenon in the world's languages and is found in the first four of the five evolutionary stages of basic colour term systems proposed by Kay & Maffi (1999: 748); see also §3.

2. The values

We distinguish between four values for this feature:

●	1. Differentiation	60
●	2. Identity	6
●	3. Overlap	3
○	4. Not applicable	3

Value 1. In **differentiation** one basic colour term refers to green and another to blue. This is attested in African-American English, for instance:

(1) green referring only to green
    blue   referring only to blue (Green 2013)

With 83 per cent of the languages in our sample showing differentiation, this is the most frequent value.

Value 2. **Identity** refers to a colour system where one basic colour term covers both green and blue, and no word exists that denotes only 'green' or only 'blue'. A minority of six *APiCS* languages (8%) have such a system, as illustrated by Fa d'Ambô:

(2) *vedyi* referring to green or blue (Post 2013)

The other languages with green–blue identity are Angolar, Casamancese Creole, Chinuk Wawa, Sango, and Saramaccan.

Value 3. In the situation called **overlap** there are two different basic colour terms. One refers to the green and the blue sensation, and the other only to green or blue. Fanakalo, Nigerian Pidgin, and Pidgin Hawaiian are the three contact languages in our sample (4%) that have green–blue overlap:

(3) Nigerian Pidgin (Faraclas 2013)
    grin referring to green or blue
    blu referring only to blue

Value 4. The last value, **not applicable**, contains the three interesting cases of so-called non-partition languages (Kay & Maffi 1999: 744–5, 751–3), which do not have a basic colour term that covers blue and/or green. The basic colour terms of non-partition languages do not completely partition up the psychological colour space. Kikongo-Kituba, Lingala, and Mixed Ma'a/Mbugu have terms for black, white, and red, but the other colour sensations are referred to by fixed phrasal expressions (e.g. *kuler ya saka~saka* 'colour of cassava leaves' in 4a) or sometimes by loans from languages that do have a basic term for the colour in question (e.g. *bule* < French *bleu* 'blue' in 4b):

(4) Kikongo-Kituba (Mufwene 2013)
   a. *lele   ya   kuler   ya   saka~saka*
      garment CONN colour CONN cassava.leaf
      'green garment' (lit. 'colour of cassava leaf garment')
   b. *lele   ya   bule*
      garment CONN blue
      'blue garment'

In fact, the three value 4 languages look exactly like the only non-partition language in the *World Color Survey*: Yélîdnye, a non-Austronesian language of Rossel Island (Papua New Guinea), has basic terms for black, white, and red, but uses fixed phrasal expressions to refer to the other colours (Kay & Maffi 1999: 751–3).

3. Discussion

Numerical distribution. Values 2 (identity) and 3 (overlap) both involve identity in that there is a basic colour term that covers both the green and the blue sensations. Even though Kay & Maffi's (2005: 542–3) *WALS* sample is biased in that Meso and South America are over-represented and Sub-Saharan Africa and Asia are under-represented, a comparison with the *APiCS* sample may be enlightening. In the *WALS* map, language systems relying on some kind of green–blue identity form a great majority (85 languages, 71%), so the fact that only nine *APiCS* languages (13%) have such systems needs an explanation.

There is a strong tendency for *APiCS* languages to derive the terms for both green and blue from their lexifiers. Only three languages derive one of the colour terms from a substrate/adstrate: Fanakalo (*luhlaza* 'green/blue' < Zulu, *bluwan* 'blue' < English; Mesthrie 2013), Korlai (*verd* 'green' < Portuguese, *shahi* 'blue' < Marathi; Clements 2013), and Sri Lankan Malay (*ijo* 'green' < Malay, *niila* 'blue' < Tamil; Slomanson 2013). Some contact languages have colour terms from two European languages, such as Papiamentu *bérdé* 'green' from Portuguese or Spanish and *blau* 'blue' from Dutch (Kouwenberg 2013b). Similarly Pichi, which has *grin* and *blu* from English as well as *verde* 'green' and *azul* 'blue' from Spanish (Yakpo 2013).

In the vast majority of cases, the meanings of the lexifier colour terms remain unchanged in the contact language, so that the colour systems are the same as those of the lexifier. Since there is a strong bias in *APiCS* towards European-lexified contact languages (60 of 76 languages have a European lexifier) and all European lexifiers are value 1 (differentiation) languages, the proportion of differentiation languages is much higher in *APiCS* than in Kay & Maffi's (2005) sample—of the 60 European-lexifier *APiCS* languages, only five are value 2 (identity) or value 3 (overlap) languages: Angolar, Casamancese Creole, Fa d'Ambô, Saramaccan, and Nigerian Pidgin.

Geographical distribution. With the exception of Chinuk Wawa and Saramaccan, the value 2 (identity) and value 3 (overlap) languages are all located in Africa, as are the three non-partition languages (value 4). As far as the European-lexified contact languages among these are concerned, this points towards strong substratal/adstratal African influence, a point that could also be made with regard to the "radical" creole Saramaccan across the Atlantic. With regard to the African-lexifier *APiCS* languages, this seems to be simply a case of the transfer of the lexifier colour systems to the contact languages, just as with the transfer of green–blue differentiation to the European-lexifier contact languages, discussed above.

The evolution of colour term systems. Kay & Maffi (1999, 2005) propose a five-stage model of the evolution of colour term systems in the world's languages. The model is concerned only with the six primary colour categories (black, white, red, yellow, green, blue) and basically predicts a development from a hypothesized two-term Stage I to Stage V, where each of the six categories has its own distinct basic colour term.

Diachronic evidence in *APiCS* supports the Kay & Maffi model. For example, Early Sranan *blakka/brakka* covered both black and blue (van den Berg & Bruyn 2013), while in Modern Sranan, *blaka* 'black' no longer refers to blue (Winford, p.c.). That is, Modern Sranan has entered the last evolutionary stage, where all six primary colour categories are referred to by separate basic colour terms.

Diachronic evidence in *APiCS* also suggests that in terms of the feature values, the evolution of colour systems may develop from identity (value 2) via overlap (value 3) into differentiation (value 1). Nigerian Pidgin, for example, has moved from identity to overlap, probably under lexifier influence: "Formerly, the stative verb *blak* was used to refer to the spectrum from black to purple to blue to green, but now the separate stative verbs *blu* 'be blue' and *grin* 'be blue/green' are much more commonly used" (Faraclas 2013). Similarly, Fanakalo started out with the Zulu-derived *luhlaza* covering green and blue (identity), then added English-derived *bluwan* 'blue' (overlap) (Mesthrie 2013), and may at some point end up with *luhlaza* 'green' and *bluwan* 'blue' (differentiation). This last stage seems to have been reached by Principense, presumably via the same trajectory: "Modern Principense differentiates between 'green' and 'blue'; however, only blue has a corresponding ideophone, which suggests that formerly, *zulu* [now 'blue'] might have referred to 'blue' as well as to 'green'" (Maurer 2013c). To what extent these developments are influenced by lexifier/adstrate pressure is a matter for future research.

116 'Green' and 'blue'

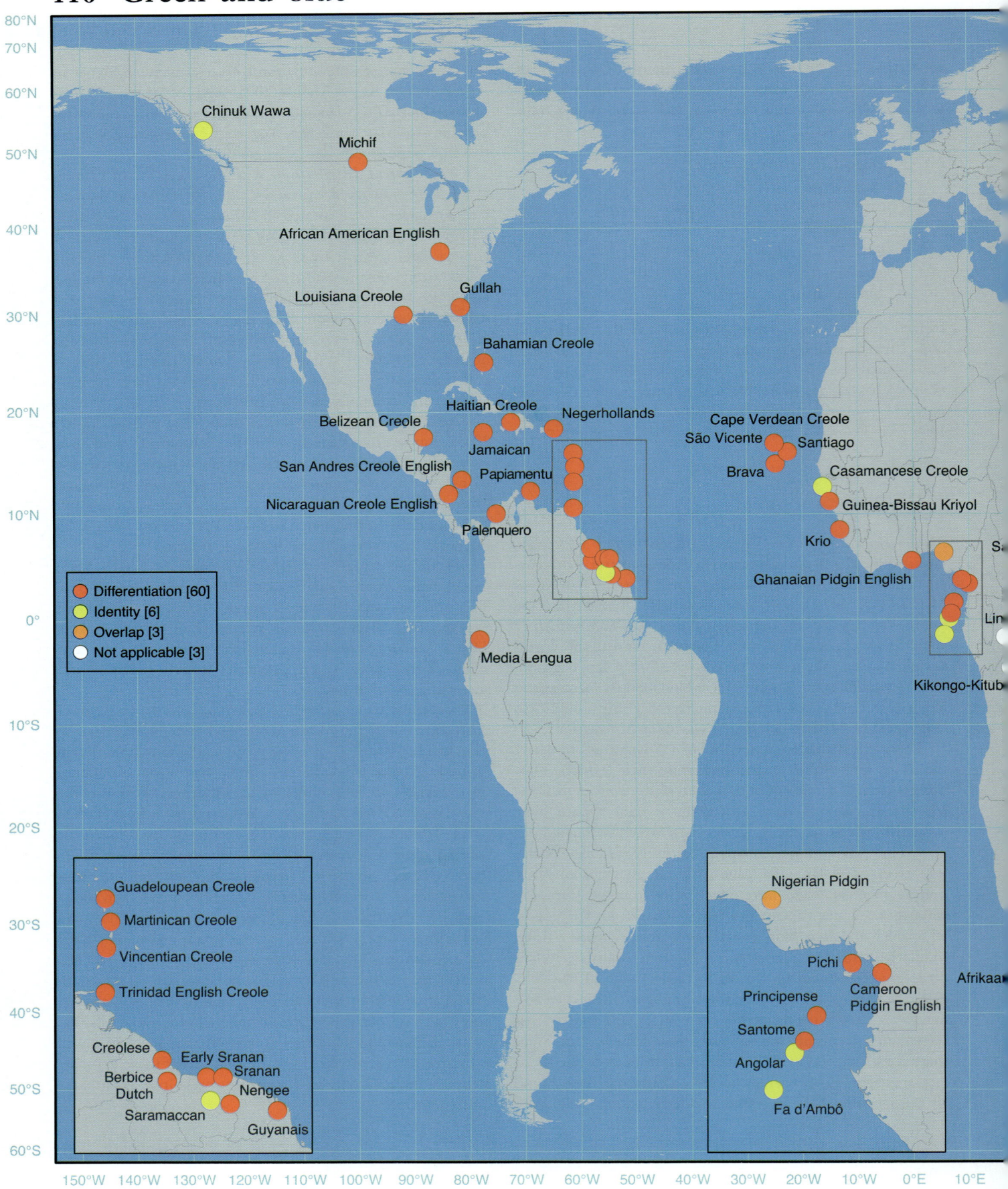

Chapter 117
Female and male animals

MAGNUS HUBER AND THE *APiCS* CONSORTIUM

1. Feature description

Map 117 shows the strategies in contact languages that specify whether animals are female or male. Only morphologically productive, non-lexicalized, patterns like *lion–lioness* are considered here. Lexicalized pairs such as English *bull–cow* are disregarded, as are unproductive patterns like *fox–vixen*, even if they are etymologically related. Thus, Guadeloupean Creole *poul* 'hen' and *kòk* 'cock' (Colot & Ludwig 2013a) do not count as words with sex-denoting elements for the present purposes.

The question whether the base word, apart from the generic meaning, can also denote only the female or only the male animal (like English *tiger* meaning 'male and female tiger' or only 'male tiger') is irrelevant for this feature. Thus, Seychelles Creole—where *bourik* 'donkey' "refers to both sexes, but one can distinguish the two sexes by adding *femel* and *mal*" (Michaelis & Rosalie 2013)—is classified as a language with sex-denoting elements. For this reason, only when a language does not have a single sex-denoting element is it classified as not sex-denoting (value 5 "No sex-denoting element").

Also irrelevant for this feature is the token frequency of the element, that is, sex-denoting elements for animals that are rarely referred to count the same as those for animals that speakers talk about more frequently. As to the type frequency, as long as there is at least one word among all the words for animals that can receive a sex-denoting element, this suffices for a value to be "true", the actual frequency of the particular pattern in comparison to other patterns attested in the same language is indicated in the relative importance field in the *APiCS* database.

2. The values

We distinguish between sex-denoting words (values 1 and 2) and affixes (values 3 and 4), which can either be preposed (values 1 and 3) or postposed (values 2 and 4). Sex-denoting words can include third-person-singular pronouns ('he', 'she'), nouns ('man', 'woman') or adjectives ('male', 'female').

Value 1. **A preposed sex-denoting word** is the most frequent value in our sample, 31 languages (44%) relying exclusively on this strategy, and another 7 (10%) along with other strategies. Many *APiCS* languages have a preposed word for both male and female animals:

		excl	shrd	all
●	1. Preposed sex-denoting word	31	7	38
●	2. Postposed sex-denoting word	23	7	30
●	3. Sex-denoting prefix	1	0	1
●	4. Sex-denoting suffix	3	1	4
●	5. No sex-denoting element	6	0	6

(1) San Andres Creole English (Bartens 2013b)
shi daag   *hi daag*
3SG.F dog   3SG.M dog
'bitch'   'male dog'

(2) Sri Lanka Portuguese (Smith 2013)
maaci pavaam   *fɛɛmiya pavaam*
male peafowl   female peafowl
'peacock'   'peahen'

(3) Reunion Creole (Bollée 2013)
en mal lapen   *en femel lapen*
INDF male rabbit   INDF female rabbit
'a male rabbit'   'a female rabbit/doe'

(4) Sri Lankan Malay (Slomanson 2013)
klaki-kucing   *pompang-kucing*
male-cat   female-cat
'tom-cat'   'female cat'

Contact languages can have different preposed elements to denote the same sex. These can be nouns that are inherently male or female, as shown in (5), or items from different word classes, for example, a pronoun and a noun, as in (6), or a pronoun and an adjective, as in (7):

(5) Guyanais (Pfänder 2013)
mouché chyen   *mal chyen*
mister dog   male dog
'male dog'   'male dog'

manman poul   *fimèl chat*
mother hen   female cat
'hen'   'female cat'

(6) Bahamiam Creole (Hackert 2013)
he cat   *man cat*
3SG.M cat   man cat
'tomcat'   'tomcat'

(7) Hawai'i Creole (Velupillai 2013)
 ʃi-gɔt   fimæɔ laɪan
 3SG.F-goat   female lion
 'she-goat'   'lioness'

The elements can also derive from different lexifiers, as seen in Chinuk Wawa, where the male-denoting word derives from English *man* and the female-denoting word from Nootka/Nuuchahnulth *ɬoːcsma* 'woman'. The latter was remodelled in Chinuk Wawa by analogy with English *wo-man* (Grant 2013):

(8) Chinuk Wawa (Grant 2013)
 tlúčman kámuks   *man kámuks*
 woman   dog   man dog
 'bitch'   'male dog'

Value 2. Twenty-three *APiCS* languages (32%) exclusively rely on **postposed sex-denoting words**, and another 7 (10%) have this along with other values. Again, many languages have words for both female and male animals:

(9) Casamancese Creole (Biagui & Quint 2013)
 karnedu macu   *karnedu fémiya*
 sheep   male   sheep   female
 'ram'   'ewe'

(10) Tok Pisin (Smith & Siegel 2013)
 dok man   *dok meri*
 dog man   dog woman
 'male dog'   'bitch'

(11) Mauritian Creole (Baker & Kriegel 2013)
 en   sat mal   *en   kabri femel*
 INDF.ART cat male   INDF.ART goat female
 'a tomcat'   'a female goat'

(12) Kinubi (Luffin 2013)
 korú mária   *korú rági*
 sheep woman   sheep man
 'ewe'   'ram'

Value 2 also contains the interesting cases of Kikongo-Kituba and Lingala, where the sex of the animal is not expressed by a single element but a connectival ('of') phrase:

(13) Lingala (Meeuwis 2013)
 sósó ya mobáli   *sósó ya mwási*
 chicken of man   chicken of woman
 'cock'   'hen'

Interestingly, in Sango, which in many respects patterns like Kikongo-Kituba and Lingala, "*Ti* 'of' is never used in [such] constructions" (Samarin 2013). Rather, Sango uses preposed sex-denoting words (value 1).

Value 3. **Sex-denoting prefixes** are found in only one language, Sranan, where it is the exclusive strategy:

(14) *man-doksi*
 man-duck
 'drake' (Winford & Plag 2013)

Note, however, that the status of *man-* 'man' and *uma-* 'woman' as prefixes or words is controversial (Braun 2009), so Sranan could possibly be another candidate for value 1.

Value 4. Only three languages (4%) have **sex-denoting suffixes** and another one (Afrikaans) shares this with other strategies:

(15) African American English and Singlish
 lion-ess (Green 2013, Lim & Ansaldo 2013)

(16) Fanakalo (Mesthrie 2013)
 inja   *inja-kazi*
 dog   dog-woman
 'male dog'   'bitch'

The presence of *-ness* in African American English and Singlish may be explained by their rather close proximity to Standard English.

Value 5 subsumes languages that have **no productive sex-denoting elements**: Media Lengua, Mixed Ma'a/Mbugu, Norf'k, Palenquero, Tayo, and Ghanaian Pidgin English.

3. Distribution by lexifier

For the majority of European-lexified languages in *APiCS*, the syntax of the lexifier seems to have provided the model for the order of the animal term and its sex-denoting element. Of the 27 English-lexified contact languages, 20 (or 21, including Sranan) have preposed sex-denoting words, which are either adjectives or nouns. These languages follow the English ADJ N or right-headed compound order. The Portuguese-lexified languages also appear to have adopted the Portuguese model: 12 of 13 have postposed sex-denoting words, following the predominant postnominal position of adjectives and left-headedness of compounds in Portuguese. Interestingly, although French compounds are also predominantly left-headed and most adjectives follow the noun, 8 of 10 French-lexified *APiCS* languages have PREPOSED sex-denoting words. The explanation could be that this reflects the more common prenominal adjective position in earlier French (Boucher 2004: 53–4). Three of the five contact languages with African lexifiers have no sex-denoting strategy (Kikongo-Kituba, Lingala, Mixed Ma'a/Mbugu). Fanakalo is rather like these, as its suffix is rarely used, and it has no other strategy. Only Sango has a common preposed sex-denoting word.

117 Female and male animals

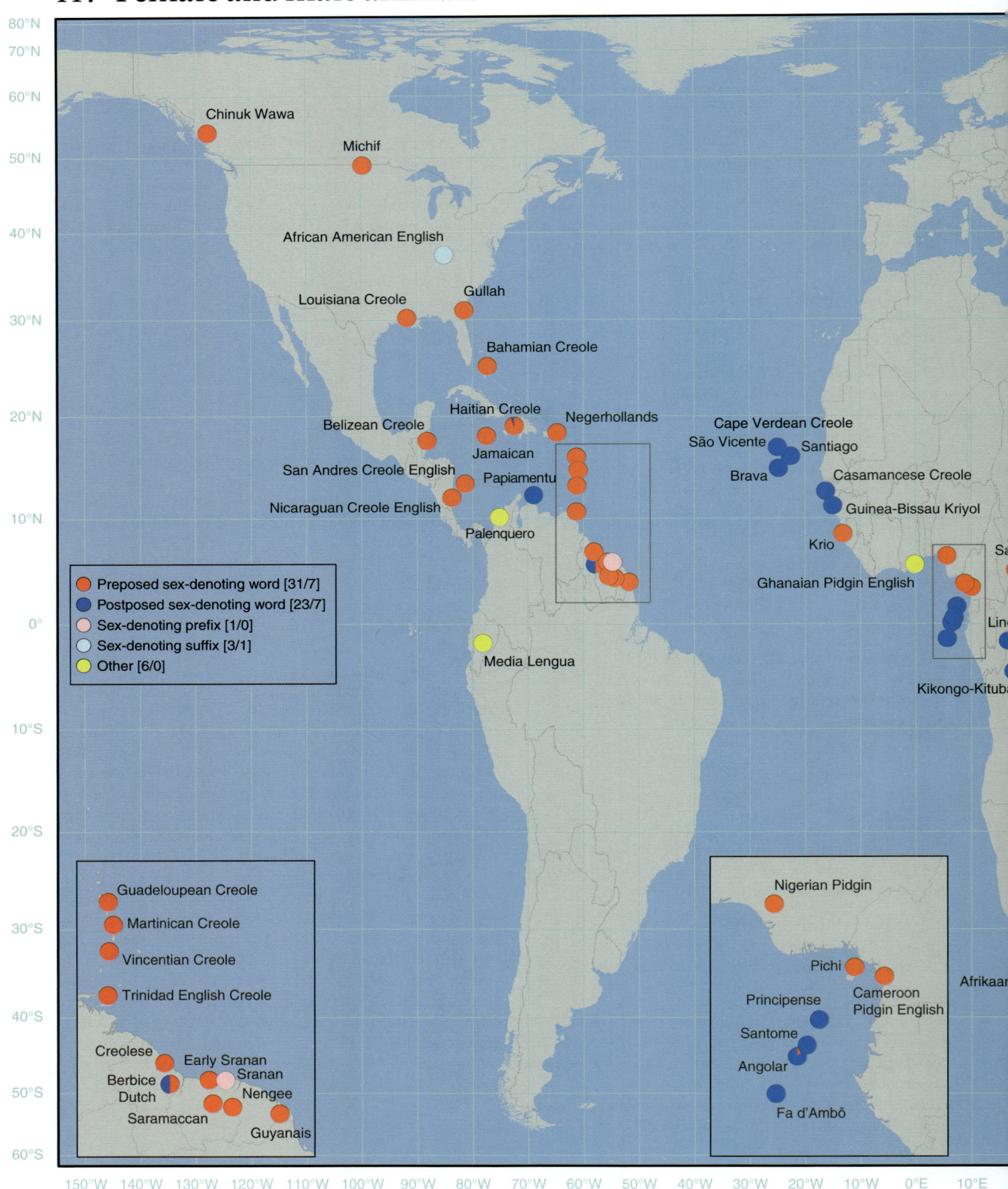

PHONOLOGY

Chapter 118
Syllable onsets

PHILIPPE MAURER AND THE *APiCS* CONSORTIUM

1. Introduction

Syllable onsets—the initial parts of syllables which precede the vowel—may show different degrees of complexity. The three values assigned to this feature represent the increasing complexity of syllable onsets. On an implicational scale, languages with more complex onset types seem to also have all the less complex types (see Blevins 1995 and Carlisle 2001). An example is Afrikaans, which has *straf* 'punishment' (complex syllable onset) but also *kry* 'get' (moderately complex syllable onset) and *kat* 'cat' (simple syllable onset).

No distinction is made in this feature as to whether the syllable occurs word-initially or word-internally, and recent unassimilated loans have been ignored.

A comparison with *WALS* feature 12, 'syllable structure' (Maddieson 2005b), is not possible because in the *WALS* feature, syllable onsets (this chapter) and syllable codas (Chapter 119) are conflated.

2. The values

We distinguish the following three values:

○	1. Only simple onsets	10
○	2. Onsets at most moderately complex	25
○	3. Onsets may be complex	41

Value 1 (**only simple onsets**) indicates that a language has only syllables without onsets and syllables with one consonant in onset position, such as *a*, *sa*, and *ka* in Principense *a.sa.ka* 'kind of ant', a prenasalized consonant as in Sango *mbo* 'dog', or an affricate such as *tʃ* in Singapore Bazaar Malay *ba.tʃa* 'read'. Further examples of simple onsets are Angolar *ô.u* 'thread' and *n.tê* 'head', Juba Arabic *sa.ba.lú.ka* 'gutter', and Chinese Pidgin Russian *wu.tʃi.la* 'yesterday'.

Value 2 (**onsets not more than moderately complex**) refers either to the combination of an obstruent and a liquid or glide, such as *gr* in Diu Indo-Portuguese *gray* 'crow' and *pl* in Jamaican *plaa.tn* 'plantain', or it refers to the combination of *s* and another consonant, such as *st* in Trinidad English Creole *stap* 'stop' and *sk* in Cameroon Pidgin English *skul* 'school'.

Further examples of moderately complex onsets are Guyanais *pre.myè* 'first', Kinubi *stá.gal* 'to work', Yimas-Arafundi Pidgin *trəŋ* 'tooth', and Media Lengua *prish.ta* 'to loan'.

Value 3 (**onsets may be complex**) is represented by those syllables that consist of

(i) s + obstruent + sonorant, as *str* in Negerhollands *strom* 'current, waves';
(ii) obstruent + nasal, as *km* in Sranan *kmo.po* 'to come from';
(iii) obstruent + obstruent, as *bz* in Cape Verdean of São Vicente *bzot* 'you (pl.)' or *pt* in Reunion Creole and Seychelles Creole *pti* 'small'.

Further examples of complex onsets are Santome *stlu.vi.su* 'job', Berbice Dutch *spring.han* 'grasshopper', Batavia Creole *in.stru.men.tu di skri.bang* 'writing materials', Ambon Malay *strep* 'stripe', and Bislama *splin* 'spleen'.

None of the *APiCS* languages shows more than three consonants in syllable onsets. However, other languages allow for more consonants in this position, as for example Russian *vstr* in *vstreča* 'meeting'.

In only 13 per cent of the *APiCS* languages are syllable onsets restricted to the simplest single-consonant type; in the overwhelming majority of the *APiCS* languages (87%), syllable onsets are non-simple, and more than 50 per cent have complex onsets.

True pidgins, that is, non-extended pidgins, have simple as well as complex syllable onsets. Simple syllable onsets occur in Singapore Bazaar Malay, in Chinese Pidgin Russian, and in Pidgin Hawaiian. Moderately complex syllable onsets are found in Chinese Pidgin English, Pidgin Hindustani, Yimas-Arafundi Pidgin, and Eskimo Pidgin, while complex syllable onsets occur in Chinuk Wawa and Fanakalo. Since these pidgins are not spoken natively, their syllable onset values vary according to the onset values of the speakers' native languages.

3. Areal distribution

Simple syllable onsets (value 1) are virtually absent from the Caribbean, the Indian Ocean, South Asia, and Southeast Asia, but the other two values (moderately complex and complex syllable onsets) are found in all regions. See also Chapter 119 on syllable codas.

Chapter 119
Syllable codas

PHILIPPE MAURER AND THE *APiCS* CONSORTIUM

1. Introduction

Syllable codas are the final parts of syllables which follow the vowel. The four values assigned to this feature are ordered according to the increasing complexity of syllable codas. On an implicational scale, languages with more complex coda types seem to have all the less complex types as well (see Blevins 1995 and Carlisle 2001). An example is Jamaican, which has *mamps* 'fat woman' (value 4, complex coda), but also *rent* 'rent' (value 3, moderately complex coda), *skyan.dal* 'scandal' (value 2, simple coda), or *ma.ka* 'thorn' (value 1, no coda)

In this feature, no distinction is made as to whether the syllable occurs word-finally or word-internally, and recent unassimilated loans have been ignored.

A comparison with the *WALS* feature 12, 'syllable structure' (Maddieson 2005a), is not possible because in the *WALS* feature, syllable onsets (Chapter 118) and syllable codas (this chapter) are conflated.

2. The values

We distinguish the following four values:

○	1. No syllable codas	7
●	2. Only simple codas	32
●	3. Codas at most moderately complex	30
●	4. Codas may be complex	6

Value 1 (**no syllable codas**) is found for example in Pidgin Hawaiian *ba.lo.ta* 'vote'.

Value 2 (**only simple codas**) refers to a single liquid, a nasal, or an obstruent in the coda, as in Louisiana Creole *bal* 'dance', Media Lengua *ri.sin* 'recently', and Michif *ka.yaash* 'long ago'.

Value 3 (**codas at most moderately complex**) refers to the combination of two consonants, either of a liquid/nasal + obstruent in coda, as *ld* in Korlai *kald* 'broth' and *nk* in Afrikaans *dink* 'to think', or of two obstruents in coda, such as *kt* or *ks* in Kinubi *wakt* 'hour' and Belizean *aks* 'ask'.

Value 4 (**codas may be complex**) refers to combinations of three consonants in the coda, such as *mps* in Vincentian Creole *glimps* 'glimpse'.

3. Distribution

The most widespread value is value 2 (43%, simple codas), followed by value 3 (40%, moderately complex codas), value 1 (9%, no codas), and value 4 (8%, complex codas).

The areal distribution of the values shows that simple and moderately complex codas (values 2 and 3) occur in all regions, but that the absence of a coda and complex codas is mostly restricted to a particular area.

Value 1 (no coda) occurs almost exclusively in Africa (Kikongo-Kituba, Lingala, Mixed Ma'a/Mbugu, Sango, Principense, Santome), with the exception of Pidgin Hawaiian. It seems that the absence of a coda has been retained from the lexifier languages, the exceptions being the Portuguese-based creoles Principense and Santome, where this value is without doubt due to the influence of the African substrate languages.

Value 4 (complex coda) occurs in the Atlantic (Cape Verdean Creole of São Vicente, Jamaican, Vincentian Creole), in North America (Chinuk Wawa, African American English), and in Southeast Asia (Batavia Creole), but is absent from continental Africa, South Asia, and the Pacific.

4. Comparison with Chapter 118

The following table compares the values which may occur in syllable onsets (Chapter 118) and in syllable codas (this chapter). Since there are no *APiCS* languages lacking onsets, values 1 and 2 of Chapter 119 (no syllable codas and only simple codas) have been conflated here.

	onset (%)	coda (%)
no or simple	13	52
moderately complex	33	40
complex	54	8

The table shows that there are considerably more languages with no or simple codas than languages that have simple onsets, and, inversely, that there are many more languages having complex onsets than complex codas. The number of languages with moderately complex onsets corresponds more or less to the number of languages having moderately complex codas.

118 Syllable onsets

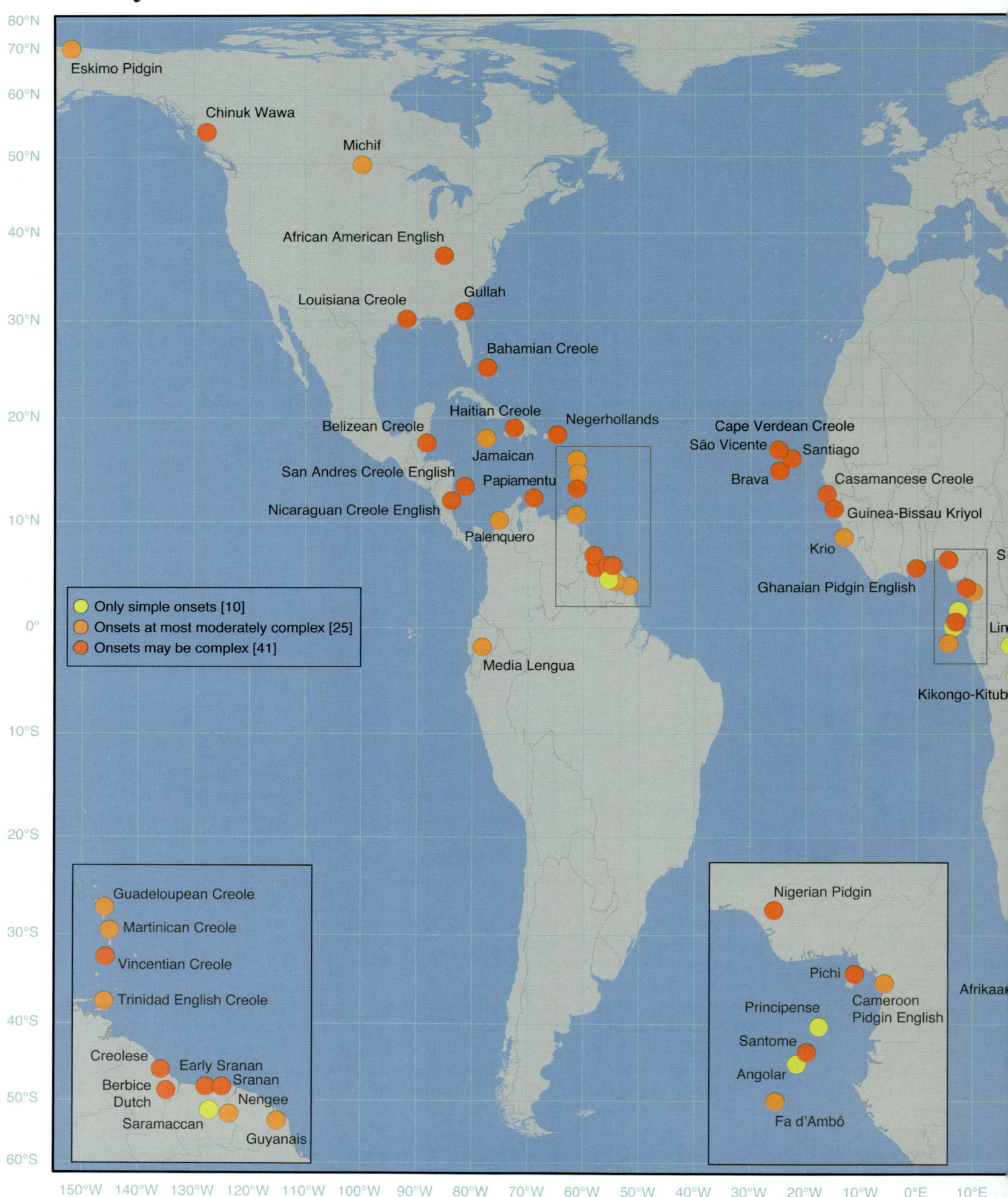

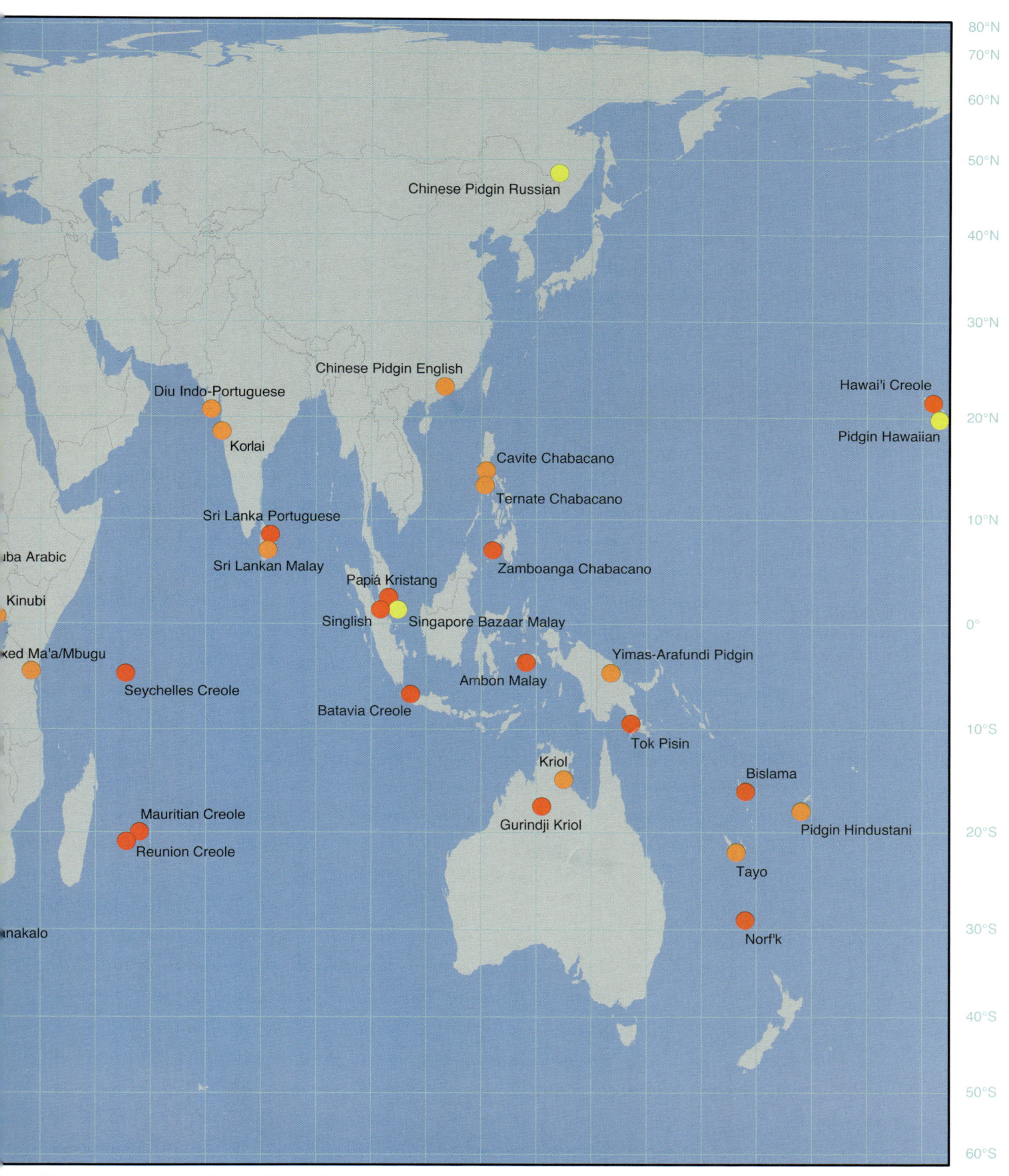

119 Syllable codas

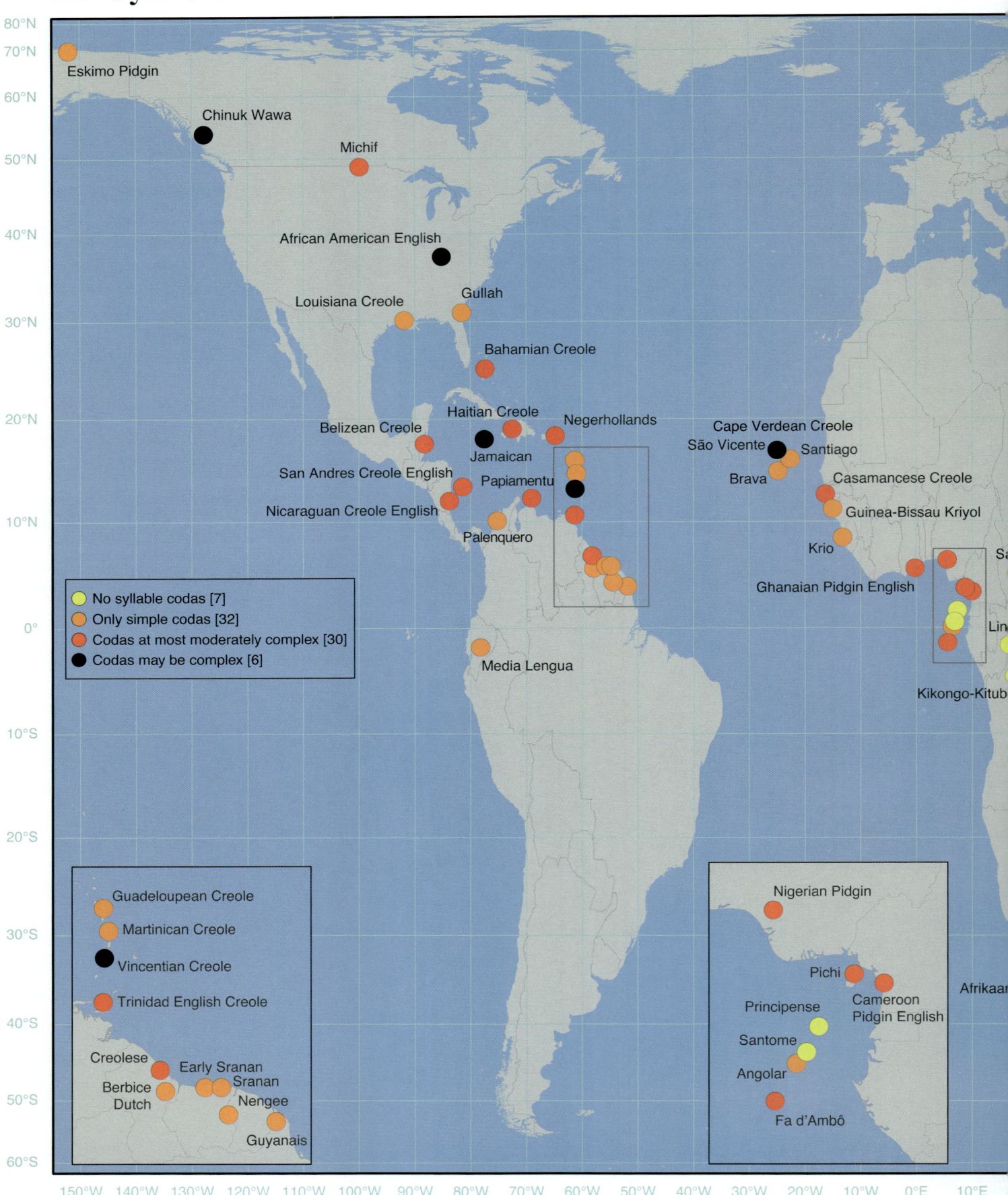

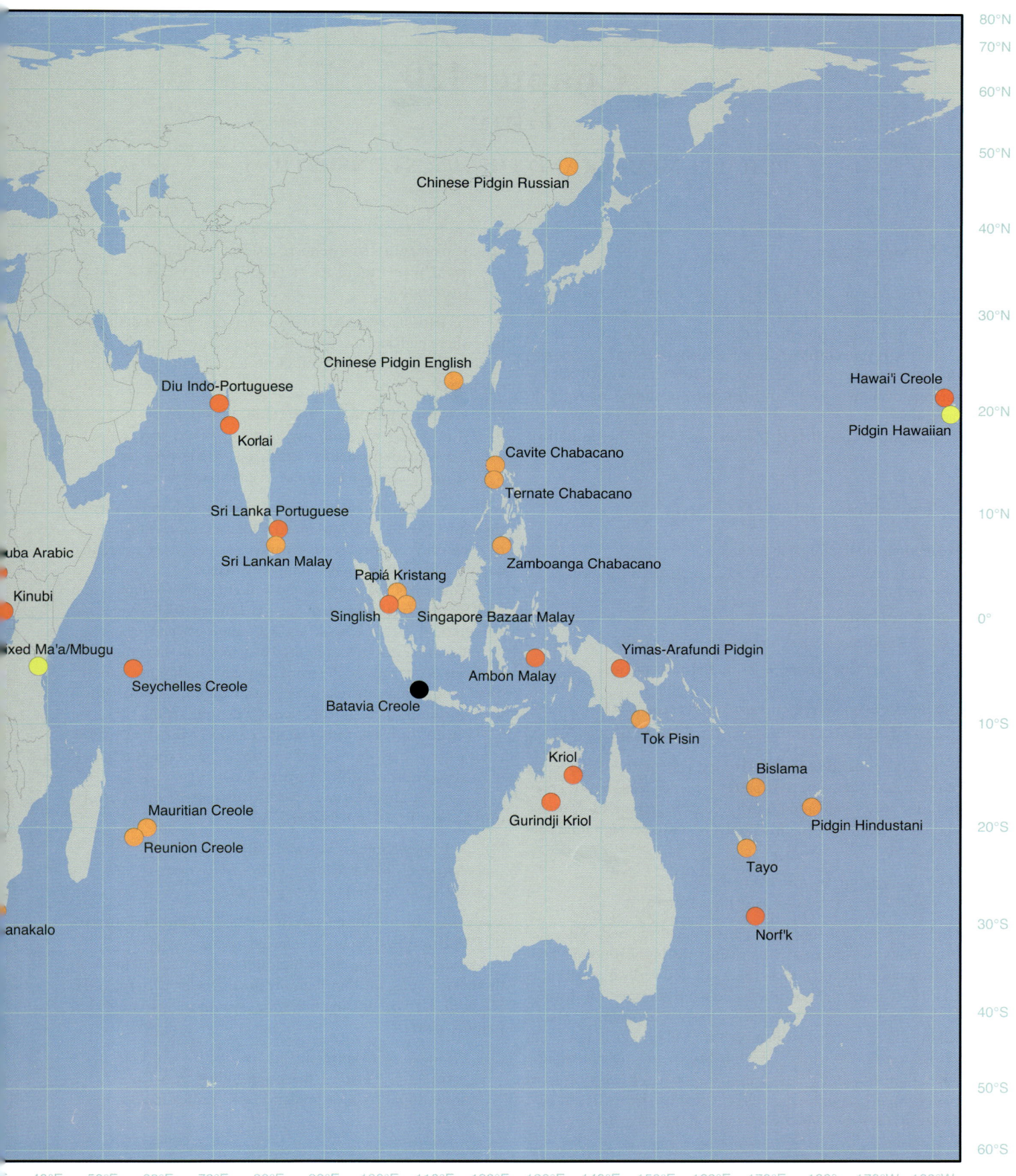

Chapter 120
Tone

PHILIPPE MAURER AND THE *APiCS* CONSORTIUM

1. Introduction

Tone refers to pitch contrasts that distinguish different words, either different lexeme stems or different grammatical forms, such as singular vs. plural, or different tenses of the verb.

In the great majority of the *APiCS* languages (52 languages), the contributors report that no tonal distinctions exist, but future research may well show that some of these languages do have tone.

This feature parallels *WALS* feature 13 (Maddieson 2005a).

2. The values

We distinguish the following values:

○	1. No tone distinctions	52
●	2. Reduced tone system	9
●	3. Simple tone system, for lexical distinctions only	3
●	4. Simple tone system, for lexical and grammatical distinctions	9
●	5. Complex tone system, for lexical and grammatical distinctions	1

Value 2 (a **reduced tone system**) is a system where only some of the logically possible tone patterns are realized. Several possibilities occur. Papiamentu distinguishes high and low tones, but in disyllabic words, only high–low and low–high tone patterns occur:

(1) Papiamentu (Kouwenberg 2013b)
káskà 'peel' (noun) vs. *kàská* 'peel' (verb)

High–high and low–low tonal patterns are excluded. Since Papiamentu's two-tone patterns mainly distinguish nouns from verbs (nouns having in most cases HL and verbs in most cases LH), tone is used almost exclusively for grammatical distinctions (syntactic categories). Exceptions are, for example, *mùchá* 'child' and *tàmbé* 'also', which both are LH in spite of not being verbs, or *fángù* 'to catch', which is HL in spite of not being a noun. Note that in Papiamentu, stress too plays a major role, as can be seen in example (2), where the first two items are stressed on the first syllable, and the last item on the last syllable.

(2) Papiamentu (Kouwenberg 2013b)
'*mátà* 'plant (noun)' vs. '*màtá* 'kill (verb)' vs. *mà'tá* 'killed (participle)'

Another case of a reduced tone system is Ghanaian Pidgin English, where high and low tone are used to distinguish two grammatical categories or to distinguish lexical from grammatical categories.

(3) Ghanaian Pidgin English (Huber 2013)
if jù **go** *si mà haus, ju jɔsɛf jù* **gò** *sɔri*
if 2SG go see my house 2SG 2SG.REFL 2SG FUT be.sorry
'If you go and see my house, even you will be sorry.'

In this example, the main verb *go* carries a high tone, whereas the future marker *gò* is low-toned. Other examples are *dé* 'locative copula' vs. *dè* 'progressive marker', *bí* 'bee' vs. *bì* 'existential copula', and *wé* 'way' vs. *wè* 'completive aspect'.

Creolese has, for example, *flówà* 'flour' vs. *flòwá* 'flower' and *ánsà* 'answer (verb)' vs. *ànsá* 'answer (noun)', and Nengee has *bùkú* 'mould' vs. *búkù* 'book' and *nà* 'copula' vs. *ná* 'negator'.

Yet another case is represented by Fanakalo, where tonal distinctions occur only in the word *lo*. With a high tone, it means 'that' or functions as a relativizer, with a low tone it means 'this'; with no tone it fulfils the function of a definite article.

Simple tone systems (values 3 and 4) exhibit a two-way contrast (e.g. high–low or high–neutral), and exploit all or almost all logically possible tone patterns.

Value 3 (a **simple tone system for lexical distinctions only**) can be found in Kikongo-Kituba:

(4) Kikongo-Kituba (Mufwene 2013)
màlémbè 'slow', *mùnòkò* 'mouth', *dìlálá* 'orange', *pòló-pòló* 'indiscrete', *pètè-pètè* 'soft'

Value 4 (a **simple tone system for lexical and grammatical distinctions**) occurs in nine languages.

Principense distinguishes high and low (or neutral) tones; in disyllabic nouns, the four logically possible tone patterns (HH, HL, LH, LL) occur. The following examples illustrate lexical minimal pairs:

(5) Principense (Maurer 2013c)
máká 'litter' vs. *màkà* 'mark', *ótó* 'other' vs. *òtò* 'neck', *bóbó* 'stupid' vs. *bòbó* 'mulatto', *átxì* 'profession' vs. *àtxí* 'you (sg)'

In addition to this, Principense also uses tone for grammatical distinctions, in the sense that tone distinguishes between syntactic categories (nouns vs. verbs):

(6) Principense (Maurer 2013c)
fálá 'speech, talk' vs. fàlà 'to speak, to talk'
myánsá 'threat' vs. myànsà 'to threaten'

Similar distinctions can be found in two other Gulf of Guinea creoles, namely in Santome and Angolar.

In Krio, there is a difference between fǎdá 'God', fǎdà 'father', and fàdá 'Catholic priest'; in the grammatical domain we find gó 'to go' vs. gò 'future marker', as in Ghanaian Pidgin (see ex. 3).

In Pichi, four different tone patterns occur in disyllabic nouns:

(7) Pichi (Yakpo 2013)
fíbà 'fever', wɔ̀tá 'water', nyóní 'ant', bàtà 'buttocks'

Furthermore, tone may be used for grammatical distinctions, as in dé 'locative copula' vs. dè 'progressive marker'.

In Saramaccan, we find jàà 'scatter', jáá 'year', jàá 'you have', and jáá 'you haven't'.

Lingala has four tonal patterns with disyllabic nouns, with the following minimal pairs:

(8) Lingala (Meeuwis 2013)
ngàmbò 'difficulty' vs. ngámbò 'opposite side of a river or a street', mòtò 'person' vs. mòtó 'head', sàngò 'news' vs. sángó 'priest'

In the grammatical domain, subjunctive is distinguished from present perfect:

(9) Lingala (Meeuwis 2013)
ná-li-a   vs. na-li-á
1SG.SBJV-eat-FV   1SG-eat-PRS.PRF
'that I eat'   'I have eaten'

Value 5 (a **complex tone system**) is a system that shows more than two tone contrasts; this is found in only one language: Sango. This language displays a three-tone system (high, middle, low). Lexical minimal pairs are given in (10).

(10) Sango (Samarin 2013)
kwá 'death, corpse' vs. kwā 'hair, feather' vs. kwà 'work', mènè 'to swallow' vs. ménē 'blood'

In the domain of grammatical distinctions, there is only one case, namely lo 'he, she, it'. If lò has a low tone, the verb gets something like an indicative reading; if it has a high tone, the verb gets a subjunctive interpretation. However, this distinction is restricted to a small number of speakers.

3. Areal distribution

All languages with a reduced or a simple tone system belong to the Atlantic area and to continental Africa; in Asia, no *APiCS* language is reported to have a tone system.

Some tonal languages are Iberio-Romance based (Angolar, Fa d'Ambô, Principense, and Santome in the Gulf of Guinea, and Papiamentu in the Caribbean); some are English-based (Cameroon Pidgin English, Ghanaian Pidgin English, Krio, Nigerian Pidgin English, and Pichi in West Africa, as well as Creolese, Nengee, San Andres Creole English, and Saramaccan in the Caribbean); but no tonal distinctions are reported for French-, Dutch-, Arabic-, or Malay-based languages. However, all African-based *APiCS* languages exhibit tonal features: Fanakalo, Kikongo-Kituba, Lingala, and Mixed Ma'a/Mbugu.

4. Comparison with *WALS*

According to Yip (2002: 1), up to 60–70 per cent of the world's languages are tonal, but in the *WALS* sample (Maddieson 2005a) only 42 per cent of the languages display tone distinctions.

The vast majority of the *APiCS* languages show no tone distinctions (70%), which is probably due to the fact that many languages, especially the European languages, that were involved in creolization and similar phenomena are not tonal, or had more influence than the tonal languages involved in the contact situation. However, the Portuguese-based creoles of the Gulf of Guinea, for instance, show that creole languages may have a simple tone system in spite of the fact that their European lexifier (in this case Portuguese) is not tonal.

Only 22 *APiCS* languages (30%) possess some kind of tonal distinctions. The most common types are reduced tone systems (nine languages), and simple tone systems for lexical and grammatical distinctions (also nine languages). Note that in most cases, grammatical distinctions are limited to differentiation in syntactic categories, mainly V vs. N, or to differentiation of grammatical markers, such as copula vs. progressive marker, or differentiation of lexemes and grammatical markers like 'to go' vs. future marker. Simple tone systems for lexical distinctions only occur in Fa d'Ambô, Kikongo-Kituba, and Trinidad English Creole.

120 Tone

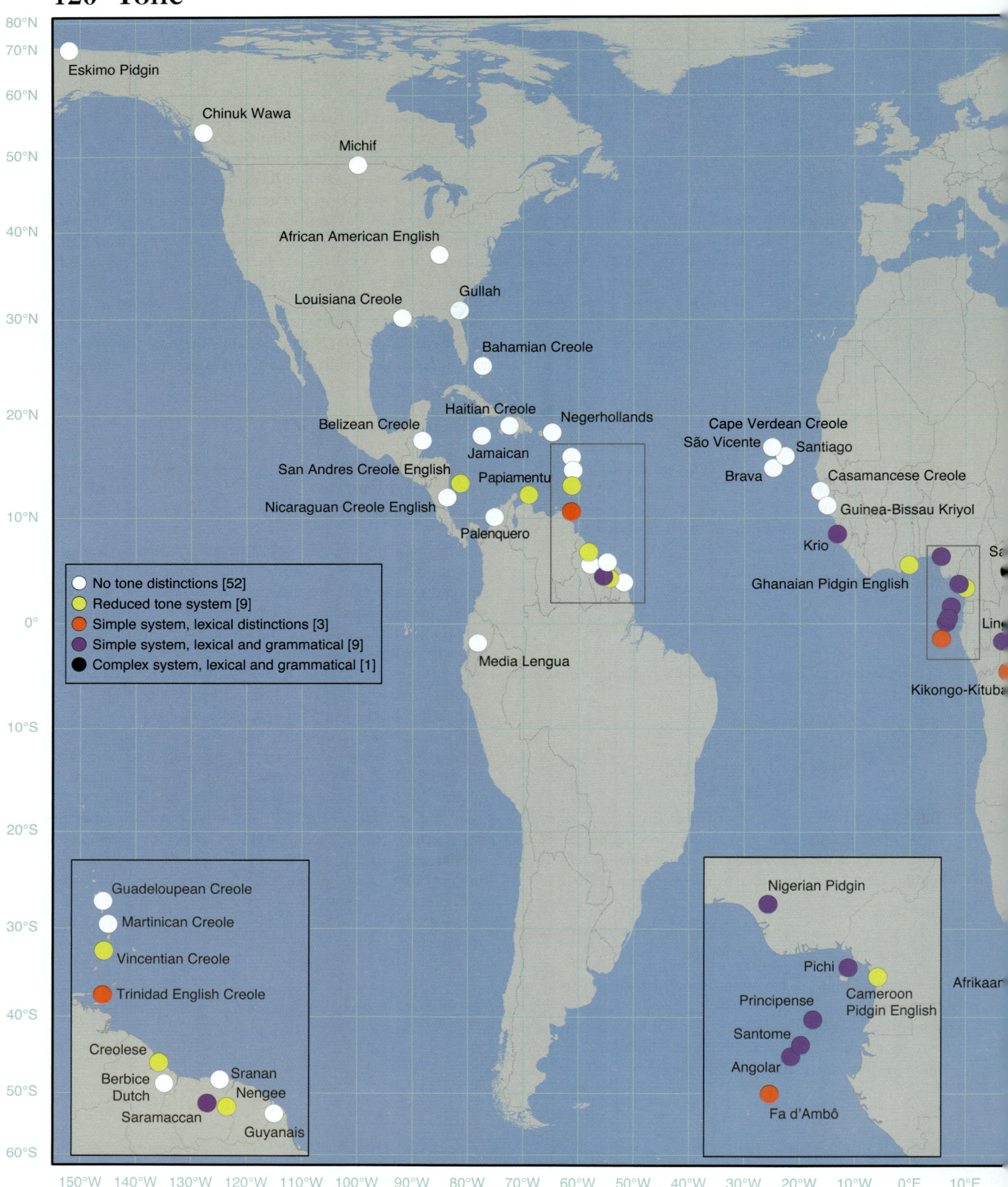

INTRODUCTION TO THE SEGMENT CHAPTERS

1. Basics

Distinctions between the vowel systems and the consonant systems of the *APiCS* languages were treated in a different way from the morphosyntactic and lexical features in our questionnaire. While we had no choice but to make a specific selection of 120 morphosyntactic and lexical features—because there is an indefinitely large number of them—the segment inventories of languages are relatively small, allowing us to ask the contributors to supply all of them.

Thus, our questionnaire for the segment features consisted of another 93 features, the segment types that are the most frequent in the world's languages (according to Maddieson 1984). If a language had segments that do not fall into any of these 93 types, the contributors were asked to add a new segment type. In the end, we had 177 different segment features. The segment features were filled in using a database layout in the form of the IPA chart (Figure 1).

The values were quite uniform:

1. Exists (as a major allophone)
2. Exists only as a minor allophone
3. Exists only in loanwords
4. Does not exist

In addition, the contributors were asked to provide an example word with gloss and were allowed to include a comment.

The information that we have on segments is thus very rich, but it would of course be too much to show another 177 world maps, one for each segment type. Thus, we have selected ten segment features (Chapters 121–30) which are particularly interesting because they show substantial variation across the *APiCS* languages. In *APiCS Online*, the complete information on all the segment features is given.

2. Segments vs. phonemes, major allophones and minor allophones

In descriptive grammars, the segment inventories (i.e. inventories of consonants and vowels) are usually described as "phoneme inventories". We avoid the term "phoneme" here, because a classification of segments into phonemes requires an abstract analysis, and analyses may differ significantly depending on the assumptions. Phonemes may subsume allophones with rather different phonetic properties, so comparing phonemes across languages is difficult. Phonemes are descriptive categories, but for our purposes we just need segment types as comparative concepts (Haspelmath 2010). Thus, we left aside phoneme status and just asked our contributors about the segments that are found in their language. We wanted to know whether they exist as major allophones, as minor allophones, or only in loanwords.

By **major allophone**, we mean an allophone (i.e. a phonetic realization) that occurs in about half the tokens of a phoneme or more often, while a minor allophone is an allophone that occurs in less than half of the tokens. For example, in Principense, the phoneme /s/ has two allophones: [ʃ] (before a high front vowel) and [s] (elsewhere). Thus, [s] is a major allophone, and [ʃ] is a minor allophone (see Chapter 125).

Our definition of major and minor allophone allows for a situation where a phoneme has two major allophones (namely when there are exactly two allophones, and they both occur equally frequently). It also allows a situation in which a phoneme has no major allophones, for example, when it has five allophones, each of which occurs about one-fifth of the time. Note that we did not ask the contributors to specify which phoneme a segment belongs to.

In practice, our contributors seem to have chosen "minor allophone" also in situations where the segment in question does not occur in complementary distribution with another segment and thus would strictly speaking qualify as a contrastive segment (a phoneme), but where the segment occurs under quite restricted circumstances. Thus, "exists as a major allophone" can also be interpreted as "exists in a prominent way" and "exists as a minor allophone" as "exists in a limited way". We did not make a serious attempt to distinguish the various subtypes of prominent and limited existence, as the major focus of the *APiCS* questionnaire was on the 120 morphosyntactic features.

One frequent issue for phoneme systems is the extent to which diphthongs, long vowels, and geminate consonants are included. We did not provide specific guidelines for these special cases, and as a result our database is probably less than fully consistent with respect to these kinds of segments.

Introduction to the segment chapters

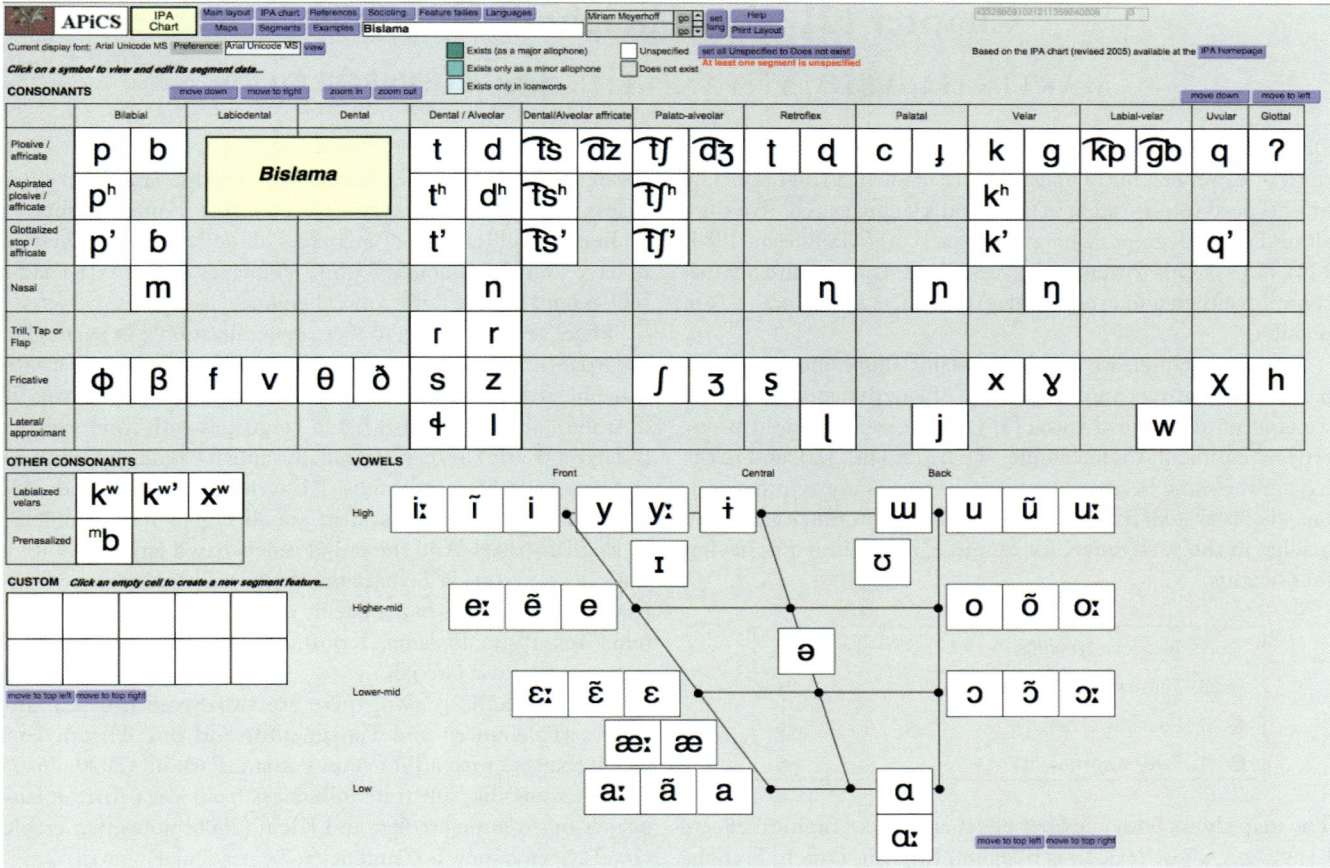

Figure 1. The *APiCS* database interface

3. Distribution of segment features

Of the 177 segment types in our database, only six exist in all 76 languages: [n], [m], [s], [p], [t], and [k]. But only two (n and m) exist as major allophones in all languages. The voiceless stops [p], [t], and [k] are not the major allophones in Kriol, where there is no voicing contrast in plosives, and where their most common realization is as voiced plosives. Moreover, [p] has a very limited distribution in Kinubi and Juba Arabic (it does not exist in Arabic at all), and [t] has a limited distribution in Pidgin Hawaiian (it does not exist in Hawaiian). Thus, there is a lot of variation.

However, especially for the consonants there is a clear tendency to be either common or very uncommon: 21 consonants occur in 52 or more languages (at least two thirds of the languages), and 97 consonants occur in 25 languages or less (i.e. less than one third). Only 3 consonants occur in the intermediate range. The 21 most common consonants are given in (1) in decreasing order of commonness, and the three intermediate consonants are given in (2).

(1) n, m, s, t, k, p, d, g, b, l, j, w, ŋ, f, ʃ, z, v, tʃ, dʒ, h, ɲ
(2) r, ʒ, ɾ

Seventy-one consonants occur five times or less frequently.

4. The ten segment chapters chosen for this atlas

While we asked our contributors for individual segments, languages of course typically show segment classes. Thus, six of our ten segment features are aggregate features that subsume information from several different segment features: vowel height distinctions ([e] vs. [ɛ] etc.) (121), nasal vowels (122), labiodental fricatives [f] and [v] (124), palato-alveolar sibilants [ʃ] and [ʒ] (125), interdental fricatives [θ] and [ð] (127), and prenasalized segments [ᵐb], [ⁿd], etc. (129).

Only four of our features are direct reflections of the individual segment features in the database: the schwa vowel (123), the voiced sibilant [z] (126), the palatal nasal (128), the segment [h] (130).

Chapter 121 Vowel height distinctions

MARTIN HASPELMATH AND THE *APiCS* CONSORTIUM

One interesting question in vowel systems is how many distinctions of vowel height (or aperture) are made in a language. The most typical vowel system in the world's languages has five vowels and three degrees of height (i, e, a, o, u) (Maddieson 1984: 126), but systems with four degrees (i, e, ɛ, a, ɔ, o, u) are not uncommon either, and even five degrees (i, ɪ, e, ɛ, a, ɔ, o, ʊ, u) are possible.

For this chapter, we took only major allophones and non-nasal vowels into account, regardless of length distinctions, and we ignored the central vowel [ə] (schwa), whose height properties are difficult to determine. We treated [a], [æ], and [ɑ] as having the same height. Most vowel systems are symmetrical, but when a system has four heights in the front range and three heights in the back range, for example, it is counted as having four heights.

○	1. Two vowel heights	3
●	2. Three vowel heights	31
●	3. Four vowel heights	36
●	4. Five vowel heights	6

The map shows both a lexifier effect and a geographical effect: Languages whose lexicon is based on English, Dutch, French, or Portuguese show a clear tendency to have four or even five vowel heights (like the lexifier), while the other languages show a clear tendency to have three or even just two vowel heights.

In geographical terms, languages of the Atlantic region tend to have four vowel heights, while languages of the Asia-Pacific region tend to have fewer vowel heights.

There are exceptions to these generalizations; in particular, the Atlantic region has three Portuguese-based languages with three heights (Casamancese Creole, Guinea-Bissau Kriyol, Fa d'Ambô), and six English-based languages with three heights (Nengee, (Early) Sranan, Trinidad English Creole, Nicaraguan and San Andres Creole English). But the languages outside this region with a four-level system are all Portuguese-, French-, or English-based. And the only French-based language with a three-level system is Tayo (in the Pacific). There are three English-based languages in the Pacific region with a three-level system (Tok Pisin, Bislama, Kriol), and one Portuguese-based language (Batavia Creole).

In the Atlantic region, there are two Spanish-based languages (Palenquero and Papiamentu) and one African language (Sango) with a four-level system. Parkvall (2000: 25–7) discusses possible substrate influences from West African languages on Atlantic creoles, and Klein (2006) notes that creole vowel systems show no tendency to be particularly small.

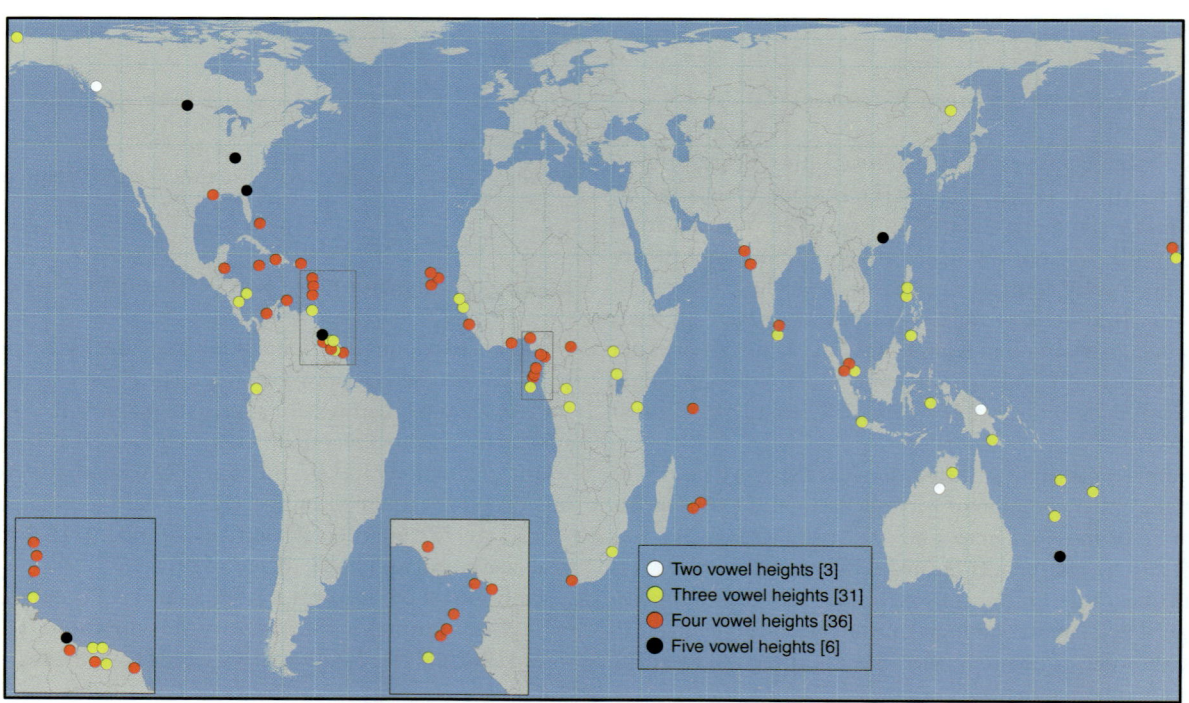

Chapter 122 Nasal vowels

MARTIN HASPELMATH AND THE *APiCS* CONSORTIUM

According to Hajek's (2005) worldwide survey, contrastive nasal vowels are found only in about a quarter of the world's languages, with a heavy areal concentration in equatorial South America and West Africa. Among the *APiCS* languages, 34 are reported to have some nasal vowels:

●	1. Present in a prominent way	14
○	2. Present in a limited way	9
○	3. Present only as minor allophones	11
○	4. No nasal vowels exist	42

Thus, it is not surprising that almost all of the languages with nasal vowels in *APiCS* are spoken in the Atlantic region. There seems to be a clear substrate effect here, with nasalization of vowels in African languages influencing the creoles (Boretzky 1983: 53–6, Parkvall 2000: 30–1). *APiCS* has nasal vowels also in South Asia and in the Indian Ocean, which again fits with Hajek's observations, as he finds a local concentration of languages with vowel nasalization in South Asia.

But the lexifier languages, too, have a strong influence on the distribution of nasal vowels. French and Portuguese have nasal vowel phonemes, so nasal vowels are particularly prominent in languages with these lexical bases.

Nasal vowels are said to be **present in a prominent** way if there are nasal vowels as major allophones in at least three different heights (e.g. ĩ, ɛ̃, ã; see Chapter 121 on vowel height). Of the 14 languages in this category, eight are based on Portuguese, which has three heights of nasal vowels. Four are English-based languages, where the nasal vowels are clearly secondary, deriving from sequences of vowel + syllable-final nasal, for example:

Ghanaian Pidgin English		Jamaican		
bĩ	'bean'	*suhn* [sũ]	'soon'	
tɛ̃	'ten'	*sohn* [sɔ̃]	'some'	
kã	'come'	*pahn* [pã]	'(up)on'	

Nasal vowels are **present in a limited way** if there are some nasal vowels as major allophones, but at most in two vowel heights. This is the pattern of French (which only has [ã], [ɛ̃], [ɔ̃]), and almost all French-based creoles are represented in this value. (Tayo in New Caledonia is the only French-based creole that lacks nasal vowels, evidently because the Austronesian substrates lack them.)

Another 11 languages have nasal vowels **only as minor allophones**. Since vowels are always to some extent phonetically nasalized in front of nasal consonants, more languages could probably be categorized in this way.

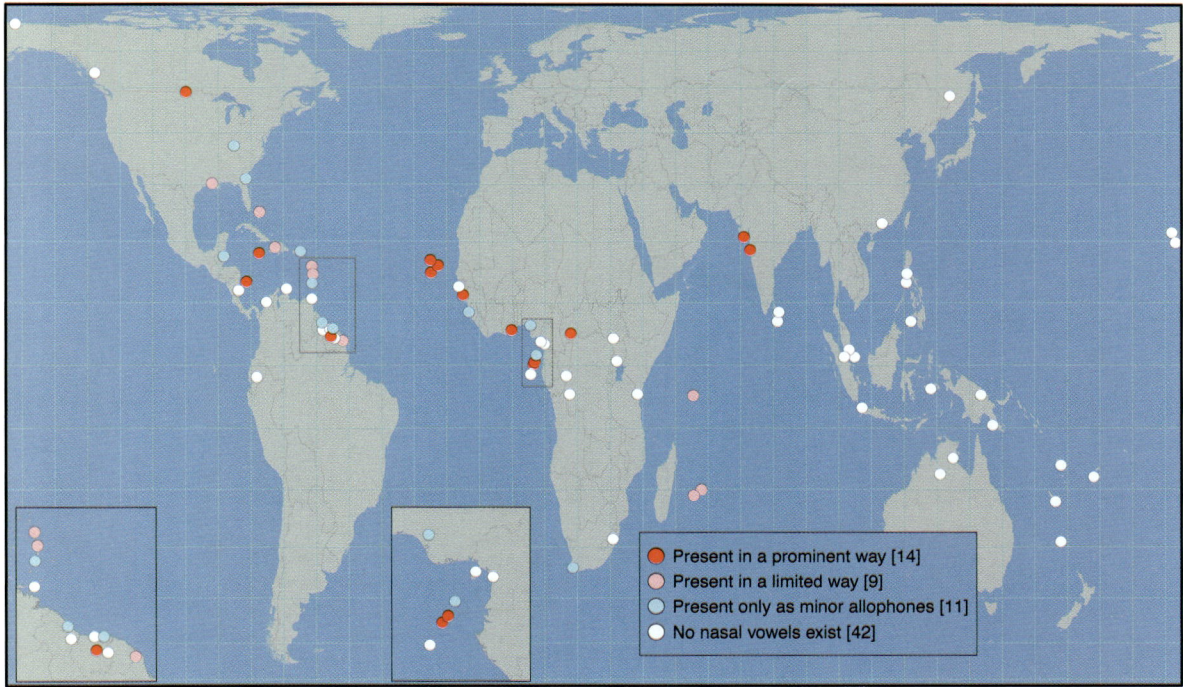

Chapter 123 The schwa vowel

MARTIN HASPELMATH AND THE *APiCS* CONSORTIUM

The schwa vowel, generally written as [ə], occurs frequently in unstressed syllables in English, Dutch, and French, as well as in European Portuguese (though not in Spanish). This sound is interesting in the present context because its distribution in the pidgins and creoles is much more limited. It occurs in less than half of the *APiCS* languages:

●	1. [ə] exists as a major allophone	18
●	2. [ə] exists as a minor allophone	13
●	3. [ə] exists only in loanwords	2
○	4. [ə] does not exist	43

Schwa occurs in the three Dutch-based languages, as well as in ten English-based languages, which tend to be less basilectal, and in the Cape Verdean Creole varieties, which are less basilectal than the other Portuguese-based varieties of Africa. The more basilectal English-based Atlantic creoles (such as Pichi, Ghanaian Pidgin English, Sranan, and Saramaccan) lack schwa. In the French-based languages, schwa is generally absent (with the exception of a few words from French in Mauritian Creole).

Schwa from the lexifier was widely replaced by other vowels, especially [i] and [a]. For example, French [ə] becomes [i] in Michif (e.g. *fimel* 'female', from French *femelle*) and Haitian Creole (*vini* 'come', from French *venir*) and [e] in Seychelles Creole (*letan* 'time', from French *le temps* 'the time'), and the second vowel of *fashion* is transcribed as [ɑ] in Chinese Pidgin English.

While African languages tend to have rich vowel systems (see Chapter 121), they typically have symmetrical five-vowel or seven-vowel systems lacking schwa (Holm 1988: 116), so the relative scarcity of schwa in Atlantic pidgins and creoles may be due to the influence of the indigenous African languages.

In the European languages, schwa is generally restricted to unstressed syllables. The situation is similar in many Malay varieties (e.g. Singapore Bazaar Malay *belúm* 'not yet'), as well as in Malay-influenced languages such as Papiá Kristang (e.g. *rëdónu* 'round') and Batavia Creole *ótër* 'other' (from Portuguese *outro*; schwa is written as *ë*). But in South Asian languages, [ə] may also occur as the main vowel of a monosyllabic word, for example, Sri Lanka Portuguese *capa* 'hat' (schwa may be written as *a* in these languages).

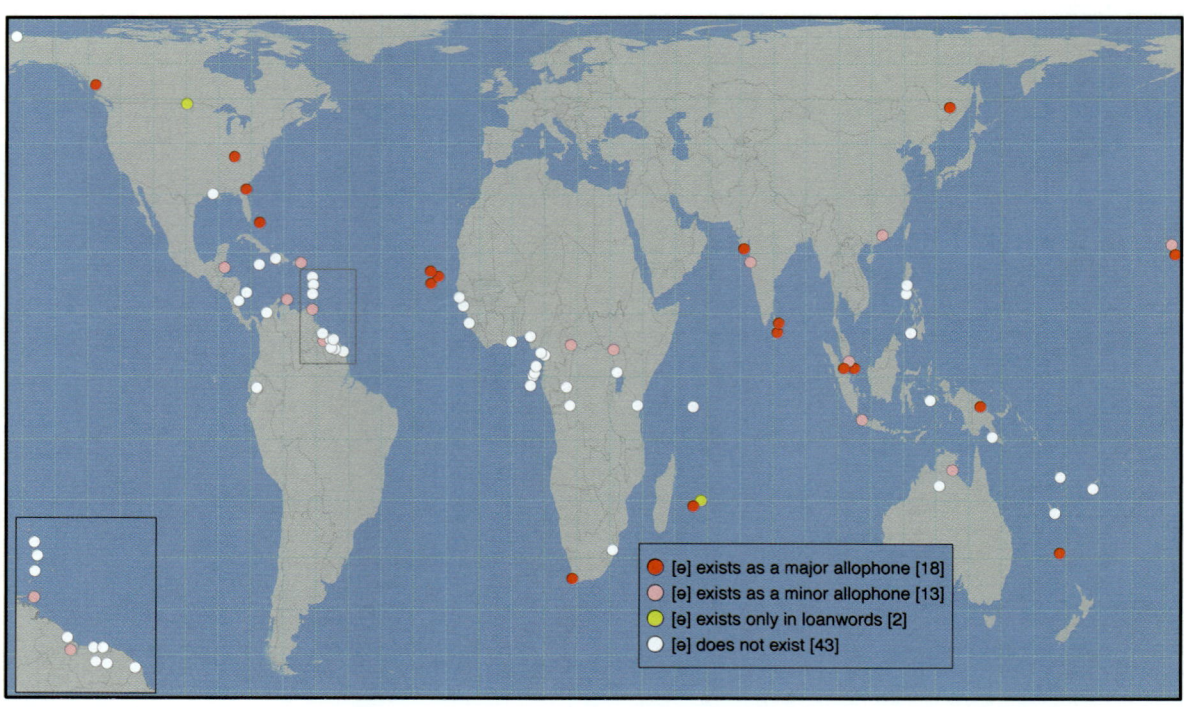

Chapter 124 Labiodental fricatives

MARTIN HASPELMATH AND THE *APiCS* CONSORTIUM

The labiodental fricatives [f] and [v] have a more limited distribution in the world's languages than the labial plosives [p] and [b], so we expect to find some interesting variation in their occurrence across *APiCS*. Here we consider both [f] and [v] and ask to what extent they occur in our languages.

●	1. Both [f] and [v] exist as major allophones	45
●	2. [f] and [v] exist in a limited way	12
●	3. Only [f] exists	12
●	4. Only [v] exists	3
○	5. Neither [f] nor [v] exists	4

Thirty-one languages do not have both [f] and [v] as major allophones, and as in the pair [ʃ/ʒ] (Chapter 125), it is the voiceless fricative ([f]) that has the wider distribution, lacking only in seven languages, while [v] is absent from 16 languages.

[f] is lacking (values 4–5) in some Southeast Asian and Pacific languages with Austronesian and Papuan substrates, as well as in Eskimo Pidgin and Chinese Pidgin Russian. Lexifier words with [f] are normally replaced by [p], as in Ternate Chabacano *plor* 'flower' (Spanish *flor*), *pamilia* 'family'; Tok Pisin *lip* 'leaf', *pret* 'afraid'.

[v] is lacking (values 3 and 5) in a number of Atlantic creoles (Berbice Dutch, Palenquero, Sranan), though not in the French-based creoles. In other Atlantic creoles it occurs in a limited way, for example, in Casamancese Creole, Pichi, Gullah, Nengee. In the Spanish-based creoles, the absence or restricted occurrence of [v] is not surprising, because Spanish has no contrast between [v] and [b]. But in the Dutch-, English-, and Portuguese-based languages it is less expected, and Parkvall (2000: 47–50) discusses possible West African substrate influences leading to the common replacement of [v] by [b].

Quite a few Atlantic creoles have remnant forms from earlier stages where replacement of [v] by [b] was more common, e.g. older African American English *nebber* 'never', or Cape Verdean Creole *bo* 'you' (from Portuguese *vós*). Saramaccan has [v] in words of Portuguese origin such as *véntu* 'wind', but words of English origin regularly have [b], for example *libi* 'live' (Holm 1988: 137). See also Chapter 110.

In non-Atlantic languages, [v] is sometimes replaced by [w], as in Norf'k (*wekels* 'victuals') and in Chinuk Wawa. And a few languages (especially in South Asia) have the labio-dental approximant [ʋ] instead (Korlai, Diu Indo-Portuguese, Sri Lanka Portuguese).

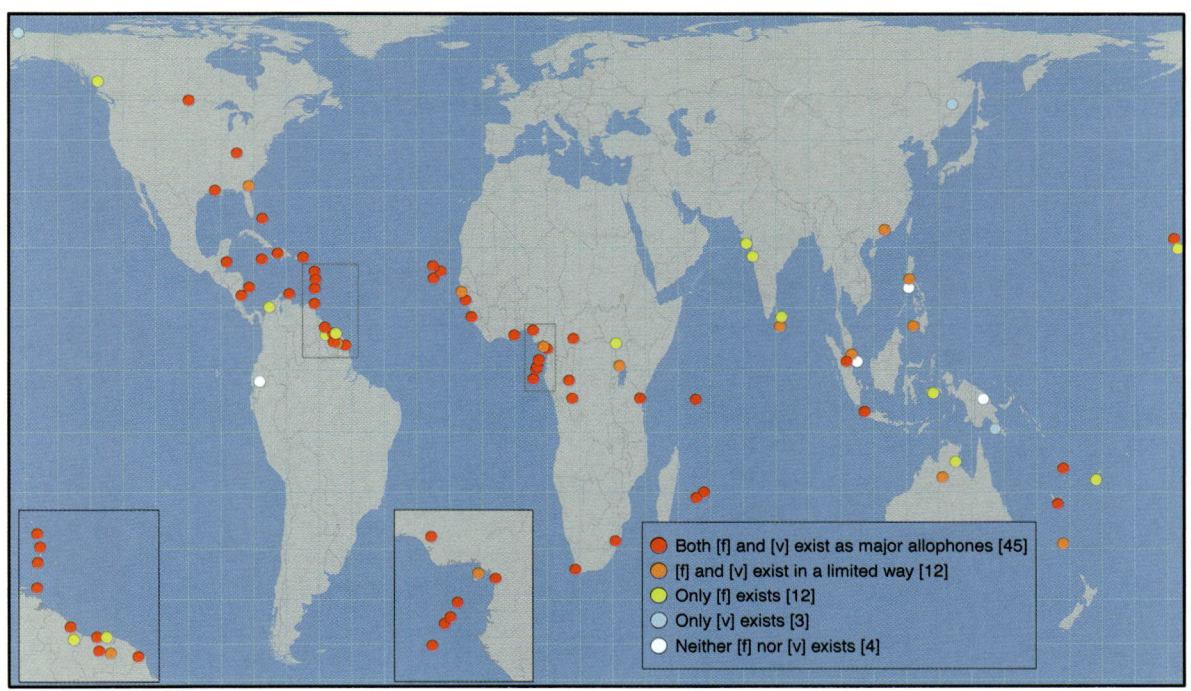

Chapter 125 Palato-alveolar sibilants

MARTIN HASPELMATH AND THE *APiCS* CONSORTIUM

The palato-alevolar ("hushing") sibilants [ʃ] and [ʒ] are much less common in the world's languages than the (dental or) alveolar sibilants [s] and [z], so it is not surprising that there is interesting variation in their occurrence across *APiCS*. Here we consider both [ʃ] and [ʒ] and ask to what extent they occur in our languages.

- 1. Both [ʃ] and [ʒ] exist as major allophones — 17
- 2. [ʃ] and [ʒ] exist in a limited way — 20
- 3. Only [ʃ] exists — 25
- 4. Neither [ʃ] nor [ʒ] exists — 14

The 17 languages where both [ʃ] and [ʒ] exist as major allophones are almost all languages with a European (English, Portuguese or French) lexifier.

In another 20 languages both [ʃ] and [ʒ] exist, but at least one of them is either a minor allophone or occurs only in loanwords. For example, in Principense [ʃ] and [s] do not contrast, but [ʃ] is an allophone of /s/ that occurs before [i]. In Zamboanga Chabacano, [ʃ] occurs in words such as *informasyón* (alternating with [sj]). In Lingala, [ʃ] occurs only in loanwords and placenames such as *Kinshása*. In Bislama, the pronunciation of [ʃ] in words such as [ʃus] 'shoes' "indexes higher education, or greater exposure to English or French" (Meyerhoff 2013).

There are 25 languages where only [ʃ] exists (as a major or minor allophone or only in loanwords), but the converse language type, with only a [ʒ] sound and no [ʃ], is not attested. This is in line with the general tendency for fricatives to be voiceless. Examples of such languages are Bislama, Gullah, Korlai, and Tayo.

Finally, 14 languages lack [ʃ] and [ʒ] entirely. This type is found particularly among the Asian and Pacific languages, as well as in the Indian Ocean and only in a few Caribbean languages. In French-based languages such as Seychelles Creole, French [ʃ] and [ʒ] are reflected by [s] and [z]:

(1)
s*y*en	dog	French *chien*
sov *s*ouri	bat	French *chauve souris*
*z*arden	garden	French *jardin*
*z*enn	young	French *jeune*

Parkvall (2000: 43–5) notes that [ʃ] and [ʒ] are lacking in many West African languages, so he regards substrate influence on the Atlantic creoles as quite likely. In the Indian Ocean, Malagasy influence may play a role.

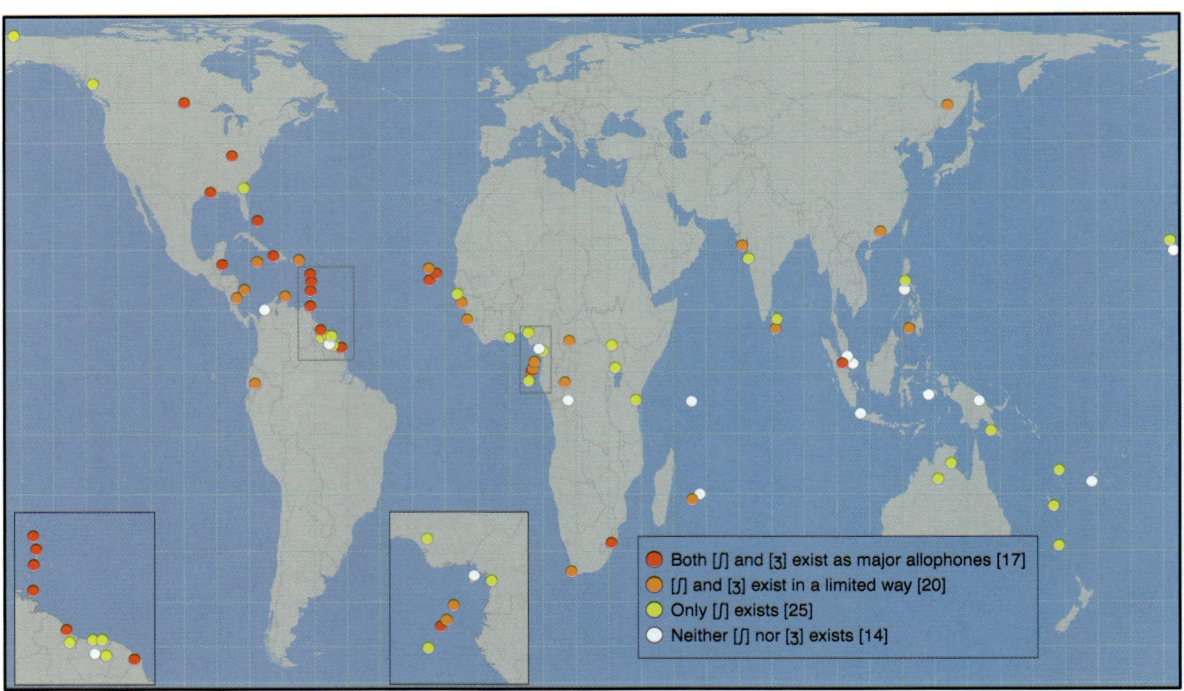

Chapter 126 The voiced sibilant [z]

MARTIN HASPELMATH AND THE *APiCS* CONSORTIUM

Like other voiced fricatives (see Chapters 124–5), the voiced dental/alveolar fricative sibilant [z] occurs less widely than its voiceless counterpart [s]. In fact, [s] is one of the few segment types that occurs in all 76 languages.

The voiced sibilant [z] is a separate phoneme in English, Dutch (though to a limited extent), French, and Portuguese, but it does not occur as a phoneme in Spanish (only as an allophone in front of nasals, such as *mismo* 'self').

🔴	1. [z] exists as a major allophone	47
🌸	2. [z] exists as a minor allophone	7
🟡	3. [z] exists only in loanwords	6
⚪	4. [z] does not exist	16

The *APiCS* languages that lack [z] are mostly the Asian languages with a strong influence of Austronesian languages. But of course, in the Chabacano varieties the absence of [z] is also due to its absence in the Spanish lexifier. Batavia Creole, Tok Pisin, and Tayo are likely to have lost the [z] of their (Portuguese, English, and French) lexifiers due to the influence of Austronesian. Normally the [z] in lexifier-derived words is replaced by [s], but in Batavia Creole it is replaced by [dʒ], for example *medja* 'table' < Portuguese *mesa*.

The Malay varieties and Pidgin Hawaiian have Austronesian lexifiers lacking [z]. In addition, [z] is missing in the northern pidgins Chinuk Wawa and Eskimo Pidgin.

In the languages of the Atlantic region, [z] is mostly present, even in the Spanish-based Papiamentu and Media Lengua. In the French-based languages, it occurs very prominently in word-initial position in words such as Seychelles Creole *zannimo* 'animal', Guyanais *zwazo* 'bird', Michif *zitwel* 'star', *zaanfaan* 'child'. This derives from the French plural form, where vowel-initial words have the article [lez] or [dez], whose last consonant is interpreted as a root consonant (*les animaux* 'animals', *les oiseaux* 'birds', *les étoiles* 'stars', *les enfants* 'children').

[z] is missing in (Early and modern) Sranan and in Berbice Dutch, as well as in Pichi, and it only occurs as a minor allophone in Nengee (where it is found mostly in ideophones and tends to be replaced by [s]). Words from English and Dutch with [z] tend to undergo devoicing in the Guianas, which Parkvall (2000: 31–2) attributes to Akan influence.

In Angolar, [z] occurs only in front of [i], but this is because it has shifted to [ð] in all other positions (see Chapter 127).

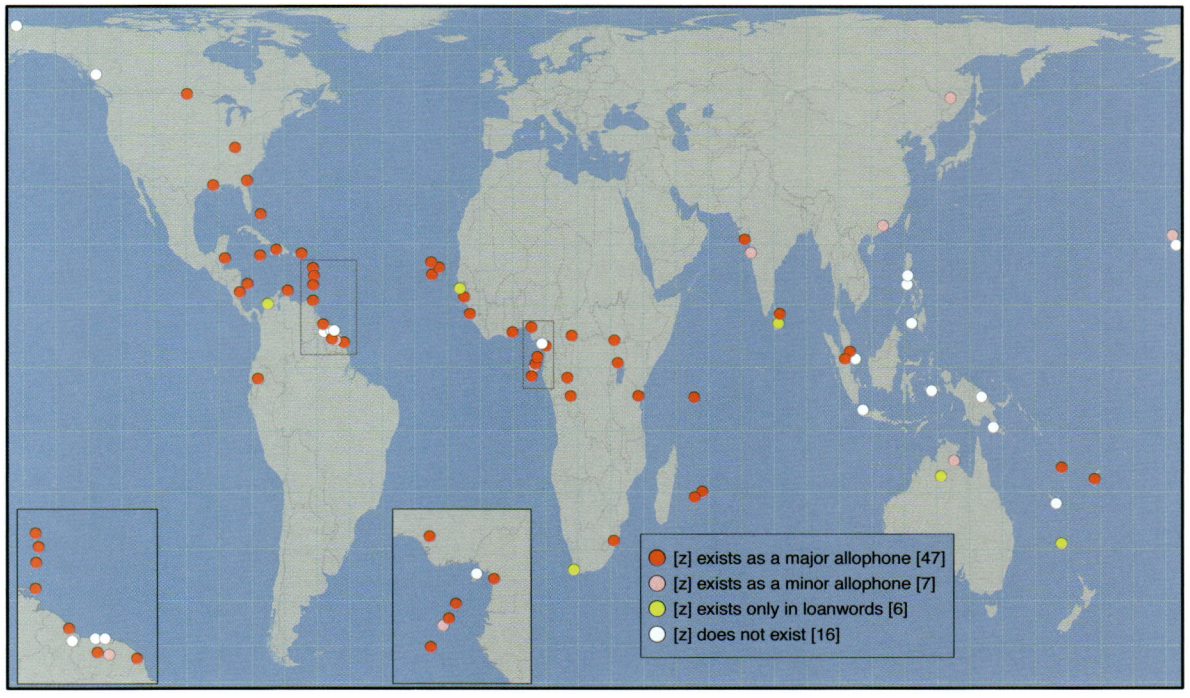

Chapter 127 Interdental fricatives

MARTIN HASPELMATH AND THE *APiCS* CONSORTIUM

The sounds [θ] and [ð] (as in English *thick* and *this*, respectively) are commonly called interdental fricatives, though Maddieson (2005c: 83) calls them dental nonsibilant fricatives. They represent a less loud and lower-pitched sound than the sibilants [s] and [z]. In Maddieson's (2005c) worldwide sample, they occur only in about 8 per cent of the languages, so they are quite uncommon. But they are found sporadically on all continents.

Among the languages of *APiCS*, interdental fricatives are found in 16 languages:

●	1. [θ] and [ð] are major allophones	3
●	2. [θ] and [ð] are minor allophones	6
●	3. [θ] and [ð] exist only in loanwords	3
●	4. Only [ð] exists, as a minor allophone	3
●	5. Only [θ] exists, in a limited way	1
○	6. Neither [θ] nor [ð] exists	60

Eleven of these languages are English-based, and they inherited their [θ] and [ð] sounds from English. But the majority of English-based languages have replaced these sounds by [t] and [d], respectively. This can be seen easily for the demonstratives *this* and *that*, which appear in the following ways in typical English-based pidgins and creoles:

(1) Hawai'i Creole   *dæd*   that
    Jamaican   *dis-ya* this
    Saramaccan   *dɛ*   there

[θ] and [ð] are major allophones in African American English and in Norf'k. They are found as minor allophones in Bahamian, Belizean, and Nicaraguan Creole (three less basilectal Caribbean English Creole varieties). In addition, they are found in the Asian varieties Singlish and Chinese Pidgin English. In other English-based varieties, they are only found in loanwords, or only [θ] or only [ð] are found.

The most striking case of a non-English-based variety with [θ] and [ð] is Portuguese-based Angolar in the Gulf of Guinea, where the former [s] and [z] sounds turned into [θ] and [ð] (except in front of [i]). For some discussion of Angolar interdentals, see Maurer (1992) and Parkvall (2000: 32).

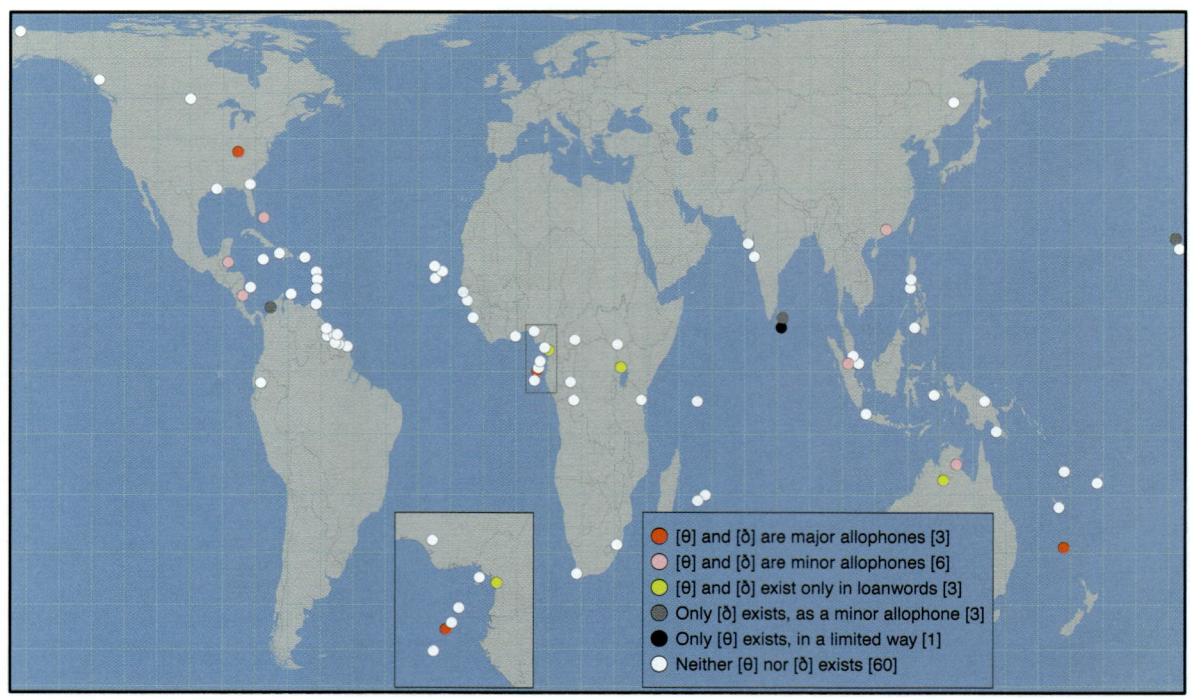

Chapter 128 The palatal nasal

MARTIN HASPELMATH AND THE *APiCS* CONSORTIUM

While all *APiCS* languages have the widespread nasal consonants [m] (bilabial nasal) and [n] (dental/alveolar nasal), there is much more variation in the occurrence of the palatal nasal [ɲ], the sound in Spanish *señor*, Portuguese *senhor*, and French *seigneur* ('lord, sir').

●	1. [ɲ] exists as a major allophone	34
●	2. [ɲ] exists as a minor allophone	12
●	3. [ɲ] exists only in loanwords	6
○	4. [ɲ] does not exist	24

One would expect that [ɲ] is found primarily in the Romance-based languages, and indeed most Spanish-, Portuguese-, and French-based languages have this sound:

Ternate Chabacano	*sunyá*	dream (*soñar*)
Palenquero	*año*	year (*año*)
Papiamentu	*ñetu*	grandchild (*nieto*)
Cape Verdean of Brava	*vizinhu*	neighbour (*vizinho*)
Santome	*panha*	catch (*apanhar*)
Batavia Creole	*finyu*	fine (*fino*)
Reunion Creole	*manyer*	manner (*manière*)
Tayo	*swaɲe*	take care (*soigner*)

However, three Portuguese-based languages lack [ɲ] (Angolar, Diu Indo-Portuguese, Korlai), and in the French-based creoles, the counterpart of French [ɲ] is often regarded as a kind of nasalized [j̃] (this sound also exists in Papiamentu and the Portuguese-based Gulf of Guinea creoles).

In the English-based creoles, [ɲ] is often said to be found in loanwords from African languages such as Jamaican and Nicaraguan Creole English *nyam* 'eat', Nengee *nyan* 'eat', and Ghanaian Pidgin English *nyama* 'spoilt'. But in some languages, [ɲ] is also described for examples such as Gullah *ɲu* 'new', Cameroon Pidgin English *nyus* 'news'. On the other hand, Mesthrie (2013) describes Fanakalo *nyama* 'meat' as having an initial cluster [nj-]. Thus, some of the apparent differences are due to different descriptions of the languages.

[ɲ] exists in Malay (e.g. Singapore Bazaar Malay *banyak* 'much'), but not in Arabic, so in Juba Arabic and Kinubi it is found only in loanwords (from Bari and Swahili, respectively).

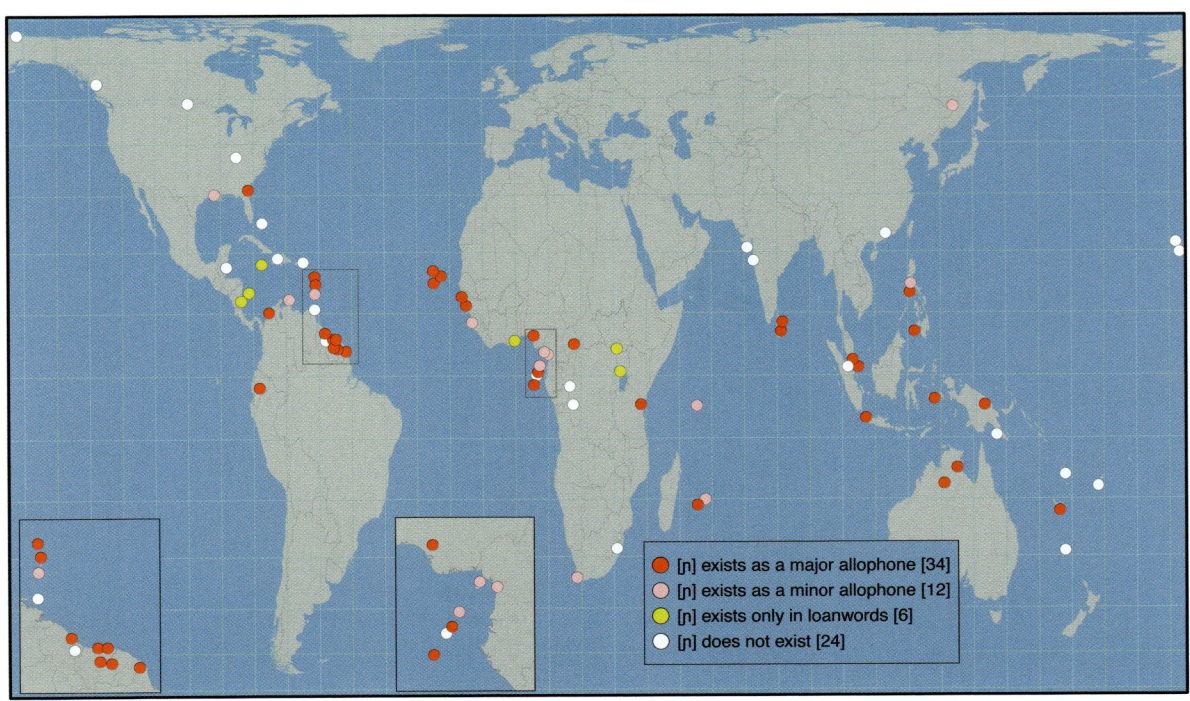

Chapter 129 Prenasalized consonants

MARTIN HASPELMATH AND THE *APiCS* CONSORTIUM

Quite a few *APiCS* languages have prenasalized segments, this is, homorganic sequences of nasal and nonnasal consonants which function as single segments in the languages (see Herbert (1986: 10) for discussion of the definition of prenasalized consonants). The most common types are prenasalized voiced plosives. Some examples of [ᵐb], [ᵑg], [ⁿd], and [ⁿdʒ] are given in (1)–(4).

(1) voiced bialbial plosive [ᵐb]
    Lingala   *mbóka*   village
    Santome   *mblôlô*   (a fish species)
    Tayo   ᵐ*boku*   much

(2) voiced velar plosive [ᵑg]
    Palenquero   *ngato*   cat
    Casamancese Creole   *ŋgratu*   ungrateful
    Cameroon Pidgin English ᵑ*gmbi*   spirit

(3) voiced dental/alveolar plosive [ⁿd]
    Mixed Ma'a/Mbugu   *ndaté*   stick
    Angolar   *ndatxi*   root

(4) voiced palato-alveolar sibilant affricate [ⁿdʒ]
    Angolar   *ndjibela*   pocket

In one-quarter of the *APiCS* languages, there is at least one prenasalized sound:

- ● 1. Prenasalized segments exist — 19
- ○ 2. No prenasalized segments — 57

Consonants other than voiced plosives are more rarely prenasalized in our data (e.g. [ⁿt] in Santome *ntenu* 'pan', [ⁿs] in Cameroon Pidgin English ⁿ*sɔ* 'Nso (place)').

Prenasalization is generally not common in the world's languages, but in sub-Saharan Africa it is fairly widespread (though not in Kwa and Kru languages, see Parkvall 2000: 39–43). Thus, the concentration of prenasalization in the African *APiCS* languages is not surprising. In some languages, only words taken from the indigenous African languages have prenasalized segments, while in others, lexifier-derived words also show prenasalization, for example, Palenquero *ngato* 'cat'. Word-medially it is often difficult to tell whether a prenasalized sequence is a single segment or a sequence (cf. Holm 1988: 127–30), so the examples here all show word-initial prenasalization.

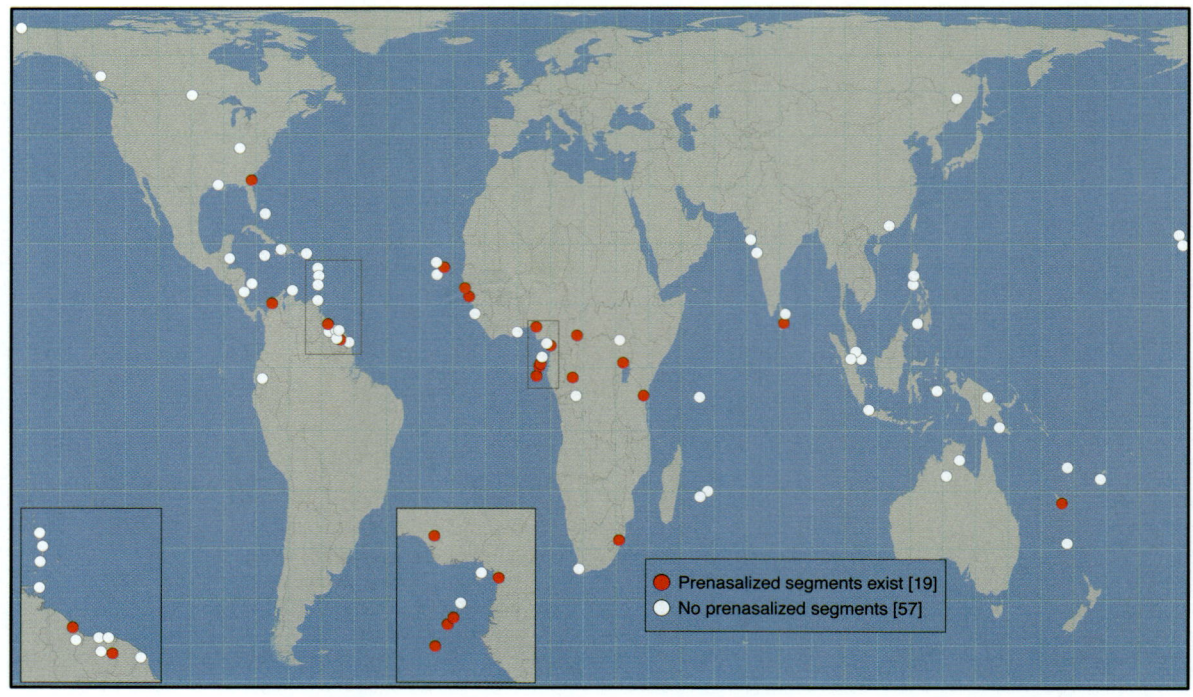

Chapter 130 The segment [h]

MARTIN HASPELMATH AND THE *APiCS* CONSORTIUM

The sound [h], variously described as a voiceless glottal fricative or a whispered approximant, tends to have a restricted distribution. It occurs in English and Dutch, but only in syllables that carry stress, i.e. primarily in word-initial position. In most contemporary varieties of the Romance languages French, Spanish, and Portuguese, it does not occur, though some varieties have a secondary [h] (in Spanish, deriving from *j* [x], and in Brazilian Portuguese, deriving from *rr*).

In Spanish and French, there used to be an [h] sound (written *h*) that was lost fairly recently, and that still existed in many varieties in the colonial era, in words such as Spanish *hecho* 'done' (from Latin *factum*) and French *haler* 'pull' (a loanword from Franconian). (The older, Latin-derived [h] was lost early in all Romance languages.)

●	1. [h] exists as a major allophone	48
●	2. [h] exists as a minor allophone	6
●	3. [h] exists only in loanwords	2
○	4. [h] does not exist	20

In the *APiCS* languages, the presence or absence of [h] appears to depend primarily on the lexifier: Portuguese-based languages generally lack [h], and the French-based creoles of the Indian Ocean do not have any instances of [h] inherited from older French. By contrast, almost all of the English-based languages have [h], even though this is sometimes unstable and tends to get lost (much as in southern British English varieties).

The Spanish-based creoles generally have [h] deriving from Spanish [x] (written *j* or *g*), e.g. Ternate Chabacano *hugá* 'play' (Spanish *jugar*), Zamboanga Chabacano *hénte* 'person' (Spanish *gente*), Cavite Chabacano *ohas* 'leaves' (Spanish *hojas*), Papiamentu *muhé* 'woman' and Media Lengua *muhir* 'woman' (Spanish *mujer*). In Palenquero, Schwegler (2013) reports that [h] is preserved from earlier or dialectal Spanish in words like *hecho* 'done'.

Similarly, in the French creoles of the Caribbean, [h] is preserved from earlier French in words such as *halé* 'haul, pull' (in Guadeloupean, Martinican, and Louisiana Creole). In Haitian Creole, it occurs in loans such as *hoholi* 'sesame' (cf. Spanish *ajonjolí*), but it is marginal and has phonemic status only in the south of Haiti (Fattier 2013). Earlier French [h] is also preserved in Michif, as in *dahor* 'outside'. In the Indian Ocean varieties Mauritian and Seychelles Creole, a secondary [h] has developed in the demonstrative/article *sa*, which is often pronounced [ha].

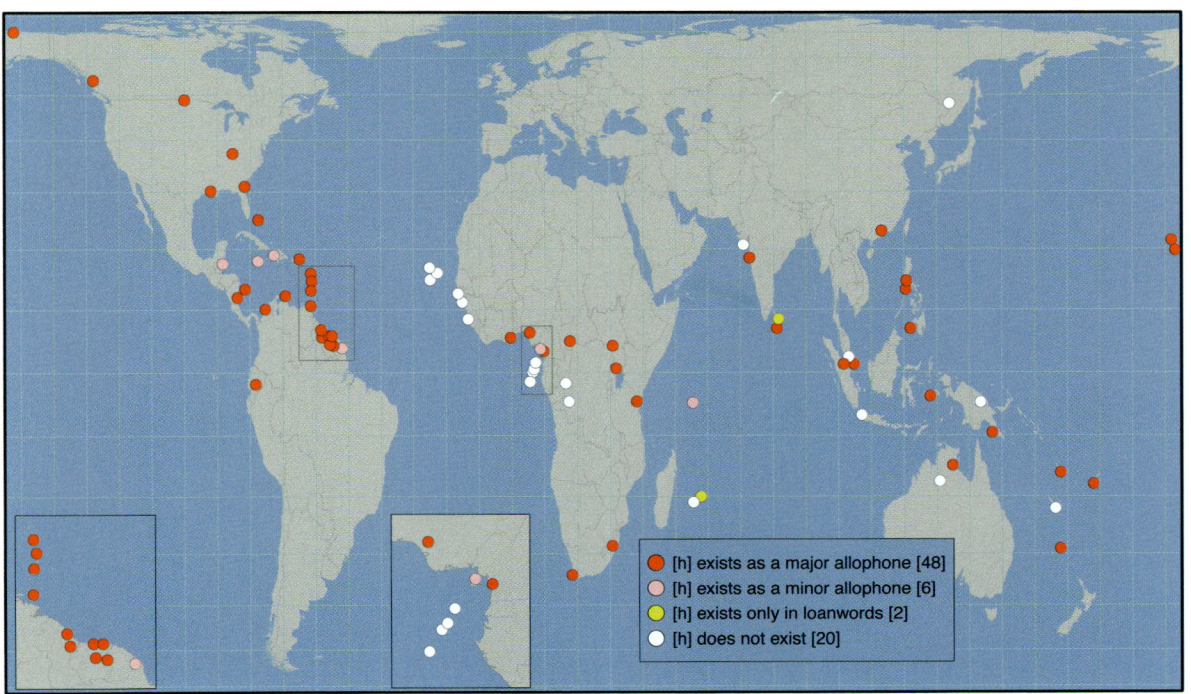

REFERENCES

Aboh, Enoch O., Smith, Norval & Zribi-Hertz, Anne. 2012. Reduplication beyond the word level: A cross-linguistic view. In Aboh, Enoch O., Smith, Norval, & Zribi-Hertz, Anne (eds.), *The morphosyntax of reiteration in creole and non-creole languages*. Amsterdam/Philadelphia: Benjamins, 1–26.

Aboh, Enoch O., Veenstra, Tonjes, & Smith, Norval S. H. 2013. Saramaccan structure dataset. In *APiCS Online* (apics-online.info).

Aikhenvald, Alexandra. 2006. Serial verb constructions in typological perspective. In Aikhenvald, Alexandra & Dixon, R. M. W. (eds.), *Serial verb constructions: A cross-linguistic typology*, 1–68. Oxford: Oxford University Press.

——Dixon, R. M. W. (eds.), 2006. *Serial verb constructions: A cross-linguistic typology*. Oxford: Oxford University Press.

Aissen, Judith L. 2003. Differential object marking: Iconicity vs. economy. *Natural Language and Linguistic Theory* 21(3). 435–83.

Ameka, Felix. 1990. The grammatical packaging of experiencers in Ewe: A study in the semantics of syntax. *Australian Journal of Linguistics* 10(2). 139–81.

APiCS = Michaelis, Susanne Maria, Maurer, Philippe, Haspelmath, Martin, & Huber, Magnus (eds.), *The atlas of pidgin and creole language structures*. Oxford: Oxford University Press, 2013.

APiCS Online = Michaelis, Susanne Maria, Maurer, Philippe, Haspelmath, Martin, & Huber, Magnus (eds.), *The atlas of pidgin and creole language structures online*. Leipzig: Max Planck Institute for Evolutionary Anthropology. Available online at http://apics-online.info, 2013.

Arends, Jacques, Muysken, Pieter, & Smith, Norval (eds.), 1995. *Pidgins and creoles: An introduction*. Amsterdam/Philadelphia: John Benjamins.

Baker, Philip. 1995. Some developmental inferences from historical studies of pidgins and creoles. In Arends, Jacques (ed.), *The early stages of creolization*, 1–24. Amsterdam/Philadelphia: John Benjamins.

——Huber, Magnus. 2001. Atlantic, Pacific, and world-wide features in English-lexicon contact languages. *English World-Wide* 22(2). 157–208.

——Kriegel, Sibylle. 2013. Mauritian Creole structure dataset. In *APiCS Online* (apics-online.info).

—— —— 2013a. Mauritian Creole. In Michaelis, Susanne Maria, Maurer, Philippe, Haspelmath, Martin, & Huber, Magnus (eds.), *The survey of pidgin and creole languages*. Vol. II, 250–60. Oxford: Oxford University Press.

Bakker, Dik. 2011. Language sampling. In Song, Jae Jung (ed.), *The Oxford handbook of linguistic typology*, 100–27. Oxford: Oxford University Press.

Bakker, Peter. 1997. *A language of our own: The genesis of Michif, the mixed Cree-French language of the Canadian Métis*. Oxford: Oxford University Press.

——2008. Pidgins versus creoles and pidgincreoles. In Kouwenberg, Silvia & Singler, John Victor (eds.), *The handbook of pidgin and creole studies*, 130–57. Chichester: Wiley-Blackwell.

——2013. Michif structure dataset. In *APiCS Online* (apics-online.info).

Bao Zhiming. 2005. The aspectual system of Singapore English and the systemic substratist explanation. *Journal of Linguistics* 41(2). 237–67.

Baptista, Marlyse. 2013. Cape Verdean Creole of Brava structure dataset. In *APiCS Online* (apics-online.info).

Bartens, Angela. 2004. A comparative study of reduplication in Portuguese- and Spanish-based creoles. In Fernández, Mauro, Fernández-Ferreira, Manuel, & Vázquez Veiga, Nancy (eds.), *Actas del III Encuentro de ACBLPE*. (Lingüística Iberoamericana, 24.) Madrid/Frankfurt: Iberoamericana/Vervuert. 239–53.

——2011. Substrate features in Nicaraguan, Providence and San Andrés Creole Englishes: A comparison with Twi. In Lefebvre, Claire (ed.), *Creoles, their substrates, and language typology*, 201–24. Amsterdam/Philadelphia: John Benjamins.

——2013a. Nicaraguan Creole English structure dataset. In *APiCS Online* (apics-online.info).

——2013b. San Andres Creole structure dataset. In *APiCS Online* (apics-online.info).

Baxter, Alan N. 1988. *A grammar of Kristang (Malacca Creole Portuguese)*. Canberra: Australian National University.

——2013. Papiá Kristang structure dataset. In *APiCS Online* (apics-online.info).

Berlin, Brent & Kay, Paul. 1969. *Basic color terms: Their universality and evolution*. Berkeley: University of California Press.

Biagui, Noël Bernard & Quint, Nicolas. 2013. Casamancese Creole structure dataset. In *APiCS Online* (apics-online.info).

Bickerton, Derek. 1980. Creolization, linguistic universals, natural semantax and the brain. In Day, Richard R. (ed.), *Issues in English creoles*, 1–18. Heidelberg: Julius Groos.

——1981. *Roots of language*. Ann Arbor: Karoma.

Bisang, Walter. 1992. *Das Verb im Chinesischen, Hmong, Vietnamesischen, Thai und Khmer: vergleichende Grammatik im Rahmen der Verbserialisierung, der Grammatikalisierung und der Attraktorposition*en. Tübingen: Narr.

Blevins, Juliette. 1995. The syllable in phonological theory. In Goldsmith, John (ed.), *The handbook of phonological theory*, 206–44. Cambridge, MA: Blackwell.

Bollée, Annegret. 2000. La restructuration du pluriel nominal dans les créoles de l'Océan Indien. *Études Créoles* 23(2). 25–39.

——2013. Reunion Creole structure dataset. In *APiCS Online* (apics-online.info).

Boretzky, Norbert. 1983. *Kreolsprachen, Substrate und Sprachwandel*. Wiesbaden: Harrassowitz.

Bossong, Georg. 1998. Le marquage différentiel de l'objet dans les langues d'Europe. In Feuillet, Jacques (ed.), *Actance et valence*

References

dans les langues de l'Europe, 193–258. Berlin/New York: Mouton de Gruyter.

Boucher, Paul. 2004. Perfect adjective positions in French. A diachronic perspective. In Coene, Martine et al. (eds.), *Current studies in comparative Romance linguistics*, 41–61. Antwerp: Antwerp Papers in Linguistics.

Braun, Maria. 2009. *Word-formation and creolisation: The case of Early Sranan*. Tübingen: Niemeyer.

Bril, Isabelle. 2002. *Le nêlêmwa (Nouvelle-Calédonie): Analyse syntaxique et sémantique*. Paris: Peeters.

Brown, Cecil H. 2005. 'Hand' and 'arm'. In *WALS*, 522–5.

Bruyn, Adrienne, Muysken, Pieter, & Verrips, Maaike. 1999. Double-object constructions in the creole languages: Development and acquisition. In DeGraff, Michel (ed.), *Language Creation and Language Change*, 329–73. Cambridge, MA: MIT Press.

Bybee, Joan L. 1985. *Morphology: A study of the relation between meaning and form*. Amsterdam/Philadelphia: John Benjamins.

——Perkins, Revere, & Pagliuca, William. 1994. *The evolution of grammar: Tense, aspect and modality in the languages of the world*. Chicago: University of Chicago Press.

Carden, Guy. 1993. The Mauritian creole "lekor" reflexive: Substrate influence on the target-location parameter. In Byrne, Francis & Holm, John (eds.), *Atlantic meets Pacific: A global view of pidginization and creolization. Selected papers from the Society for Pidgin and Creole Linguistics*, 105–17. Amsterdam/Philadelphia: John Benjamins.

——Stewart, William A. 1988. Binding theory, bioprogram, and creolization: Evidence from Haitian Creole. *Journal of Pidgin and Creole Languages* 3(1). 1–67.

Cardoso, Hugo C. 2012. Luso-Asian comparatives in comparison. In Cardoso, Hugo C., Baxter, Alan N., & Pinharanda Nunes, Mário (eds.), *Ibero-Asian Creoles: Comparative perspectives*, 81–124. Amsterdam/Philadelphia: John Benjamins.

——2013. Diu Indo-Portuguese structure dataset. In *APiCS Online* (apics-online.info).

Carlisle, Robert S. 2001. Syllable structure universals and second language acquisition. *International Journal of English Studies* 1(1). 1–19.

Chaudenson, Robert. 1974. *Le lexique du parler créole de la Réunion*. Paris: L'Harmattan.

Chimpanzee Sequencing and Analysis Consortium. 2005. Initial sequence of the chimpanzee genome and comparison with the human genome. *Nature* 437(7055). 69–87.

Clements, J. Clancy. 2013. Korlai structure dataset. In *APiCS Online* (apics-online.info).

——Mahboob, Ahmar. 2000. WH-words and question formation in pidgin/creole languages. In McWhorter, John H. (ed.), *Language change and language contact in pidgins and creoles*, Vol. 21, 459–97. Amsterdam/Philadelphia: John Benjamins.

Colot, Serge & Ludwig, Ralph. 2013a. Guadeloupean Creole structure dataset. In *APiCS Online* (apics-online.info).

—— ——2013b. Martinican Creole structure dataset. In *APiCS Online* (apics-online.info).

Comrie, Bernard. 2005. Alignment of case marking. In *WALS*, 398–405.

——Kuteva, Tania. 2005. Relativization strategies. In *WALS*, 494–501.

——Smith, Norval. 1977. Lingua descriptive studies: Questionnaire. *Lingua* 42. 1–72.

Corbett, Greville. 2000. *Number*. Cambridge: Cambridge University Press.

——2005a. Number of genders. In *WALS*, 126–9.

——2005b. Sex-based and non-sex-based gender systems. In *WALS*, 130–3.

——2005c. Systems of gender assignment. In *WALS*, 134–7.

Corne, Chris. 1988. Mauritian Creole reflexives. *Journal of Pidgin and Creole Languages* 3(1). 69–94.

——1989. On French influence in the development of Creole reflexive patterns. *Journal of Pidgin and Creole Languages* 4(1). 103–15.

Creissels, Denis. 2005. A typology of subject and object markers in African languages. In Voeltz, F. K. Erhard (ed.), *Studies in African linguistic typology*, 43–70. Amsterdam/Philadelphia: John Benjamins.

——2010. Benefactive applicative periphrases: A typological approach. In Zúñiga, Fernando & Kittilä, Seppo (eds.), *Benefactives and malefactives: Typological perspectives and case studies*, 29–68. Amsterdam/Philadelphia: John Benjamins.

——2011. Control and the evolution of possessive and existential constructions. Paper read at the Workshop 'Variation and Change in Argument realization', Naples and Capri, 27–30 May 2010, revised August 2011.

Croft, William. 2003. *Typology and universals*. 2nd edn. Cambridge: Cambridge University Press.

Cysouw, Michael. 2003. *The paradigmatic structure of person marking*. Oxford: Oxford University Press.

——2005. Inclusive/exclusive forms for 'we'. In *WALS*, 162–9.

Daniel, Michael & Moravcsik, Edith. 2005. The associative plural. In *WALS*, 150–3.

——Spencer, Andrew. 2009. The vocative: An outlier case. In Malchukov, Andrej & Spencer, Andrew (eds.), *The Oxford handbook of case*, 626–34. Oxford: Oxford University Press.

Déchaine, Rose-Marie & Manfredi, Victor. 1994. Binding domains in Haitian. *Natural Language and Linguistic Theory* 12. 203–57.

DeGraff, Michel. 1994. To move or not to move? Placement of verbs and object pronouns in Haitian Creole and in French. In Beals, Katharine, Denton, Jeannette, & Knippen, Robert (eds.), *Papers from the 30th Regional Meeting of the Chicago Linguistic Society*, 141–55. Chicago: University of Chicago.

——1997. Verb syntax in, and beyond, creolization. In Haegeman, Liliane (ed.), *The new comparative syntax*, 64–94. London: Longman.

——2005. Morphology and word order in "creolization" and beyond. In Cinque, Guglielmo & Kayne, Richard S (eds.), *The Oxford handbook of comparative syntax*, 293–372. Oxford: Oxford University Press.

den Besten, Hans & Biberauer, Theresa. 2013. Afrikaans structure dataset. In *APiCS Online* (apics-online.info).

Déprez, Viviane. 2007. Implicit determination and plural. In Baptista, Marlyse & Guéron, Jacqueline (eds.), *Noun phrases in creole languages: A multi-faceted approach*, 301–36. (Creole Language Library, 31.) Amsterdam/Philadelphia: John Benjamins.

Devonish, Hubert & Thompson, Dahlia. 2013. Creolese structure dataset. In *APiCS Online* (apics-online.info).

Diessel, Holger. 1999. *Demonstratives: Form, function, and grammaticalization*. Amsterdam/Philadelphia: John Benjamins.

——2005a. Distance contrasts in demonstratives. In *WALS*, 170–3.

——2005b. Pronominal and adnominal demonstratives. In *WALS*, 174–7.

References

Diki-Kidiri, Marcel. 1977. *Le sango s'écrit aussi-- : Esquisse linguistique du sango, langue nationale de l'Empire centrafricain*. Paris: Société d'études linguistiques et anthropologiques de France.
Dixon, R. M. W. 1994. *Ergativity*. Cambridge: Cambridge University Press.
——2004. Adjective classes in typological perspective. In Dixon, R. M. W. & Aikhenvald, Alexandra Y. (eds.), *Adjective classes: A cross-linguistic typology*, 1–49. Oxford: Oxford University Press.
do Couto, Hildo Honório. 1996. *Introdução ao estudo das línguas crioulas e pidgins*. Brasília: Editora Universidade de Brasília.
Dryer, Matthew S. 1989. Plural words. *Linguistics* 27. 865–96.
——1991. SVO languages and the OV: VO typology. *Journal of Linguistics* 27(2). 443–82.
——2005a. Coding of nominal plurality. In *WALS*, 138–41.
——2005b. Definite articles. In *WALS*, 154–7.
——2005c. Indefinite articles. In *WALS*, 158–61.
——2005d. Order of subject, object and verb. In *WALS*, 330–3.
——2005e. Order of adposition and noun phrase. In *WALS*, 346–9.
——2005f. Order of genitive and noun. In *WALS*, 350–3.
——2005g. Order of adjective and noun. In *WALS*, 354–7.
——2005h. Order of demonstrative and noun. In *WALS*, 358–61.
——2005i. Order of numeral and noun. In *WALS*, 362–5.
——2005j. Order of relative clause and noun. In *WALS*, 366–9.
——2005k. Order of degree word and adjective. In *WALS*, 370–3.
——2005l. Position of interrogative phrases in content questions. In *WALS*, 378–81.
——2005m. Expression of pronominal subjects. In *WALS*, 410–13.
——2005n. Negative morphemes. In *WALS*, 454–7.
——2005o. Polar questions. In *WALS*, 470–3.
——2011a. Order of adjective and noun. In Dryer, Matthew S. & Haspelmath, Martin (eds.), *The world atlas of language structures online*. Munich: Max Planck Digital Library. Available online at http://wals.info. Accessed 30 Nov. 2011.
——2011b. Order of negative morpheme and verb. In Dryer, Matthew S. & Haspelmath, Martin (eds.), *The world atlas of language structures online*. Munich: Max Planck Digital Library. Available online at http://wals.info. Accessed 5 Jan. 2012.
——2011c. Order of subject, object and verb. In Dryer, Matthew S. & Haspelmath, Martin (eds.), *The world atlas of language structures online*. Munich: Max Planck Digital Library. Available online at http://wals.info. Accessed 5 Jan. 2012.
——2011d. Order of genitive and noun. In Dryer, Matthew S. & Haspelmath, Martin (eds.), *The world atlas of language structures online*. Munich: Max Planck Digital Library. Available online at http://wals.info. Accessed 13 Jan. 2012.
——2011e. Order of adposition and noun phrase. In Dryer, Matthew S. & Haspelmath, Martin (eds.), *The world atlas of language structures online*. Munich: Max Planck Digital Library. Available online at http://wals.info. Accessed 15 May 2012.
Ehrhart, Sabine. 1993. *Le créole français de St-Louis (le tayo) en Nouvelle-Calédonie*. Hamburg: Buske.
——Revis, Melanie. 2013. Tayo structure dataset. In *APiCS Online* (apics-online.info).
Eriksen, Pål, Kittilä, Seppo, & Kolehmainen, Leena. 2010. The linguistics of weather. In *Studies in Language* 34(3). 565–601.
————————2012. Weather and language. In *Language and Linguistics Compass* 6(6). 383–402.

Escure, Geneviève. 2013. Belizean Creole structure dataset. In *APiCS Online* (apics-online.info).
Evans, Nicholas & Wilkins, David. 2000. In the mind's ear: The semantic extensions of perception verbs in Australian languages. *Language* 76. 546–92.
Faraclas, Nicholas. 1984. *A grammar of Obolo*. Bloomington: Indiana University Linguistics Club.
——2013. Nigerian Pidgin structure dataset. In *APiCS Online* (apics-online.info).
Farquharson, Joseph T. 2013. Jamaican structure dataset. In *APiCS Online* (apics-online.info).
Fattier, Dominique. 1996. Regards sur les pronoms personnels de l'haïtien (dans une perspective comparative). In Véronique, Daniel (ed.), *Matériaux pour l'étude des classes grammaticales dans les langues créoles*, 213–42. Aix-en-Provence: Publications de l'Université de Provence.
——2005. Remarques sur l'interrogation en créole haïtien. *La linguistique* 41(1). 41–56.
——2013. Haitian Creole structure dataset. In *APiCS Online* (apics-online.info).
Ferguson, Charles. 1971. Absence of copula and the notion of simplicity. In Hymes, Dell (ed.), *Pidginization and creolization of languages*, 141–50. Cambridge: Cambridge University Press.
Filimonova, Elena (ed.), 2005. *Clusivity: Typology and case studies of inclusive-exclusive distinction*. Amsterdam/Philadelphia: John Benjamins.
Finney, Malcolm Awadajin. 2013. Krio structure dataset. In *APiCS Online* (apics-online.info).
Foley, William. 1991. *The Yimas language of New Guinea*. Stanford: Stanford University Press.
——2013. Yimas-Arafundi Pidgin structure dataset. In *APiCS Online* (apics-online.info).
Fortescue, Michael. 1984. *West Greenlandic*. London: Croom Helm.
Gast, Volker & van der Auwera, Johan. 2011. Scalar additive operators in the languages of Europe. *Language* 87(1). 2–54.
Gil, David. 2005a. Distributive numerals. In *WALS*, 222–5.
——2005b. Sortal numeral classifiers. In *WALS*, 226–9.
——2005c. Para-linguistic usages of clicks. In *WALS*, 572–5.
Goodman, Morris. 1964. *A comparative study of Creole French dialects*. The Hague: Mouton.
Grant, Anthony. 2013. Chinuk Wawa structure dataset. In *APiCS Online* (apics-online.info).
Green, Lisa. 2013. African American English structure dataset. In *APiCS Online* (apics-online.info).
Greenberg, Joseph H. 1963. Some universals of grammar with particular reference to the order of meaningful elements. In Greenberg, Joseph H. (ed.), *Universals of language*, 73–113. Cambridge, MA: MIT Press.
——1966. *Language universals, with special reference to feature hierarchies*. The Hague: Mouton.
Güldemann, Tom. 2008. *Quotative indexes in African languages: A synchronic and diachronic survey*. Berlin/New York: Mouton de Gruyter.
——2012. Thetic speaker-instantiating quotative indexes as a cross-linguistic type. In Buchstaller, Isabelle & van Alphen, Ingrid (eds.), *Quotatives: Cross-linguistic and cross-disciplinary perspectives*, 117–42. Amsterdam/Philadelphia: John Benjamins.

References

Hackert, Stephanie. 2013. Bahamian Creole structure dataset. In *APiCS Online* (apics-online.info).

Hagemeijer, Tjerk. 2007. *Clause structure in Santome*. Doctoral dissertation, University of Lisbon.

——2013. Santome structure dataset. In *APiCS Online* (apics-online.info).

——2013a. Santome. In Michaelis, Susanne Maria, Maurer, Philippe, Haspelmath, Martin, & Huber, Magnus (eds.), *The survey of pidgin and creole languages*. Vol. II, 231–24. Oxford: Oxford University Press.

Haiman, John. 1983. Iconic and economic motivation. *Language* 59(4). 781–819.

Hajek, John. 2005. Vowel nasalization. In *WALS*, 46–9.

Hall, Robert A. Jr. 1944. Chinese Pidgin English grammar and texts. *Journal of the American Oriental Society* 64. 95–113.

Hammarström, Harald. 2008. Complexity in numeral systems with an investigation into pidgins and creoles. In Miestamo, Matti, Sinnemäki, Kaius, & Karlsson, Fred (eds.), *Language complexity: Typology, contact, change*, 287–304. Amsterdam/Philadelphia: John Benjamins.

Haspelmath, Martin. 1990. The grammaticization of passive morphology. *Studies in Language* 14(1). 25–72.

——1997. *Indefinite pronouns*. Oxford: Oxford University Press.

——2001. Non-canonical marking of core arguments in European languages. In Aikhenvald, Alexandra Y., Dixon, R. M. W. and Onishi, Masayuki (eds.), *Non-canonical marking of subjects and objects*, 53–83. Amsterdam/Philadelphia: John Benjamins.

——2002. *Understanding morphology*. London: Arnold.

——2005a. Occurrence of nominal plurality. In *WALS*, 142–5.

——2005b. Indefinite pronouns. In *WALS*, 190–3.

——2005c. Nominal and verbal conjunction. In *WALS*, 262–5.

——2005d. Ditransitive constructions: The verb 'give'. In *WALS*, 426–9.

——2005e. Negative indefinite pronouns and predicate negation. In *WALS*, 466–9.

——2005f. 'Want' complement clauses. In *WALS*, 502–5.

——2007. Coordination. In Shopen, Timothy (ed.), *Language typology and syntactic description*. Vol. II: *Complex constructions*, 1-51. 2nd edn. Cambridge: Cambridge University Press.

——2008a. A frequentist explanation of some universals of reflexive marking. *Linguistic Discovery* 6(1). 40–63.

——2008b. Frequency vs. iconicity in explaining grammatical asymmetries. *Cognitive Linguistics* 19(1). 1–33.

——2010. Comparative concepts and descriptive categories in crosslinguistic studies. *Language* 86(3). 663–87.

——2011a. On S, A, P, T, and R as comparative concepts for alignment typology. *Linguistic Typology* 15(3). 535–67.

——2011b. The indeterminacy of word segmentation and the nature of morphology and syntax. *Folia Linguistica* 45(2). 31–80.

——2013a+. Argument indexing: A conceptual framework for the syntax of bound person forms. Max Planck Institute for Evolutionary Anthropology.

——2013b+. On the cross-linguistic distribution of same-subject and different-subject "want" complements: Economic vs. iconic motivation. *SKY Journal of Linguistics*, to appear.

——Matthew S. Dryer, David Gil, & Bernard Comrie (eds.). 2005. *The world atlas of language structures*. Oxford: Oxford University Press.

Haviland, John. 1979. Guugu Yimidhirr. In Dixon, R. M. W. & Blake, Barry J. (eds.), *Handbook of Australian languages* 1, 27–180. Amsterdam/Philadelphia: John Benjamins.

Hawkins, John A. 1999. Processing complexity and filler-gap dependencies across grammars. *Language* 75. 244–85.

Heine, Bernd. 1997. *Possession: Cognitive sources, forces and grammaticalization*. Cambridge: Cambridge University Press.

——2005. On reflexive forms in creoles. *Lingua* 115. 201–57.

——König, Christa. 2010. On the linear order of ditransitive objects. *Language Sciences* 32(1). 87–131.

Helmbrecht, Johannes. 2005. Politeness distinctions in pronouns. In *WALS*, 186–9.

Herbert, Robert K. 1986. *Language universals, markedness theory, and natural phonetic processes*. Berlin: de Gruyter.

Hering, Ewald. 1964. *Outlines of a theory of the light sense* [Original 1920: *Grundzüge der Lehre vom Lichtsinn*]. Translated by L. M. Hurvich, & Dorothea Jameson. Cambridge, MA: Harvard.

Holm, John. 1978. *The Creole English of Nicaragua's Miskito Coast: Its sociolinguistic history and a comparative study of its syntax and lexicon*. Ph.D. dissertation, University of London.

——1984. Variability of the copula in Black English and its creole kin. *American Speech* 59. 291–309.

——1988. *Pidgins and creoles*. Vol. 1: *Theory and structure*. Cambridge: Cambridge University Press.

——2004. *Languages in contact: The partial restructuring of vernaculars*. Cambridge: Cambridge University Press.

——Michaelis, Susanne (eds.), 2008. *Contact languages: Critical concepts in language studies*. London: Routledge.

——Patrick, Peter (eds.). 2007. *Comparative creole syntax. Parallel outlines of 18 creole grammars*. London: Battlebridge.

Huber, Magnus. 2013. Ghanaian Pidgin English structure dataset. In *APiCS Online* (apics-online.info).

Hurch, Bernhard (ed.), 2005ff. *Graz Database on Reduplication*. Graz: University of Graz. Online at http://reduplication.uni-graz.at/redup, accessed 20 March 2013.

Idiatov, Dmitry. 2007. *A typology of non-selective interrogative pronominals*. Ph.D. dissertation, University of Antwerp.

Ihemere, Kelechukwu Uchechukwu. 2006. A basic description and analytic treatment of noun clauses in Nigerian Pidgin. *Nordic Journal of African Studies* 15(3). 296–313.

Intumbo, Incanha, Inverno, Liliana, & Holm, John. 2013. Guinea-Bissau Kriyol structure dataset. In *APiCS Online* (apics-online.info).

Janson, Tore. 1984. Articles and plural formation in creoles: Change and universals. *Lingua* 64. 291–323.

Kay, Paul & Maffi, Luisa. 1999. Color appearance and the emergence and evolution of basic color lexicons. *American Anthropologist* 101(4). 743–60.

—— —— 2005. Colour terms. In *WALS*, 534–45.

—— —— Berlin, Brent, Merrifield, William R., & Cook, Richard. 2010. *World color survey*. Stanford, CA: CSLI Publications. (See also http://www1.icsi.berkeley.edu/wcs/.)

Keenan, Edward. 2003. An historical explanation of some binding theoretic facts in English. In Moore, John & Polinsky, Maria (eds.), *The nature of explanation in linguistic theory*, 153–89. Stanford: CSLI Publications.

Keesing, Roger M. 1988. *Melanesian Pidgin and the Oceanic substrate*. Stanford: Stanford University Press.

Kemmer, Suzanne. 1993. *The middle voice*. Amsterdam/Philadelphia: John Benjamins.

Khin Khin Aye. 2013. Singapore Bazaar Malay structure dataset. In *APiCS Online* (apics-online.info).

———2013a. Singapore Bazaar Malay. In Michaelis, Susanne Maria, Maurer, Philippe, Haspelmath, Martin, & Huber, Magnus (eds.), *The survey of pidgin and creole languages*. Vol. III, 86–93. Oxford: Oxford University Press.

Kiyosawa, Kaoru & Gerdts, Donna B. 2010. Benefactive and malefactive uses of Salish applicatives. In Zúñiga, Fernando & Kittilä, Seppo (eds.), *Benefactives and malefactives: Typological perspectives and case studies*, 147–83. Amsterdam/Philadelphia: John Benjamins.

Klein, Thomas B. 2006. Creole phonology typology: Phoneme inventory size, vowel quality distinctions and stop consonant series. In Bhatt, Parth & Plag, Ingo (eds.), *The structure of creole words*, 3–21. Tübingen: Niemeyer.

———2013. Gullah structure dataset. In *APiCS Online* (apics-online.info).

König, Ekkehard. 1991. *The meaning of focus particles: A comparative perspective*. London: Routledge.

———Gast, Volker. 2006. Focused assertion of identity: A typology of intensifiers. *Linguistic Typology* 10(2). 223–76.

———Siemund, Peter. 2000. The development of complex reflexives and intensifiers in English. *Diachronica* 17(1). 39–84.

——— ——— with Töpper, Stephan. 2005. Intensifiers and reflexive pronouns. In *WALS*, 194–7.

Koopman, Hilda. 1986. The genesis of Haitian: Implications of a comparison of some features of the syntax of Haitian, French, and West African languages. In Smith, Norval & Muysken, Pieter (eds.), *Substrata versus universals in creole genesis*, 231–58. Amsterdam/Philadelphia: John Benjamins.

———2000. Prepositions, postpositions, circumpositions and particles: The structure of Dutch PPs. In Koopman, Hilda (ed.), *The syntax of specifiers and heads*, 204–60. London: Routledge.

Kortmann, Bernd & Lunkenheimer, Kerstin (eds.), 2011. *The electronic world atlas of varieties of English*. Leipzig: Max Planck Institute for Evolutionary Anthropology. http://www.ewave-atlas.org.

Kouwenberg, Silvia (ed.), 2003. *Twice as meaningful: Reduplication in pidgins, creoles and other contact languages*. London: Battlebridge.

———2013a. Berbice Dutch structure dataset. In *APiCS Online* (apics-online.info).

———2013b. Papiamentu structure dataset. In *APiCS Online* (apics-online.info).

Kriegel, Sibylle. 1996. *Diathesen im Mauritius- und Seychellenkreol*. Tübingen: Narr.

———2000. Distribution fonctionnelle des morphèmes réfléchis en créole mauricien et seychellois. *Etudes Créoles* 23(2). 66–78.

———Michaelis, Susanne & Pfänder, Stefan. 2003. Modalité et grammaticalisation: Le cas des créoles français. In Kriegel, Sibylle (ed.), *Grammaticalisation et réanalyse: Approches de la variation créole et française*, 165–92. CNRS Editions, collection Langage.

Kuteva, Tania & Comrie, Bernard. 2005. The typology of relative clause formation in African languages. In Voeltz, F. K. Erhard (ed.), *Studies in African linguistic typology*, 209–25. Amsterdam/Philadelphia: John Benjamins.

——— ———. 2012. The evolution of language and elaborateness of grammar: The case of relative clauses in creole languages. In Comrie, Bernard & Estrada-Fernández, Zarina (eds.), *Relative clauses in languages of the Americas: A typological overview*, 27–46. Amsterdam/Philadelphia: John Benjamins.

LaCharité, Darlene & Wellington, Jean. 1999. Passive in Jamaican Creole: Phonetically empty but syntactically active. *Journal of Pidgin and Creole Languages* 14(2). 259–83.

Lang, Jürgen. 1990. A categoria número no crioulo caboverdiano. *Papia* 1(1). 15–25.

———1991. Die Kategorie Numerus im kapverdischen Kreol. *Neue Romania* 10. 1–19.

———2013. Cape Verdean Creole of Santiago structure dataset. In *APiCS Online* (apics-online.info).

Lanz, Linda A. 2010. *A grammar of Iñupiaq morphosyntax*. Ph.D. dissertation, Rice University.

Lawal, Adenike S. 1989. The classification of Yoruba serial verb constructions. Unpublished Ms.

Lazard, Gilbert. 1998. *Actancy*. Berlin/New York: Mouton de Gruyter.

Leeding, Velma J. 1976. Garawa. In Dixon, R. M. W. (ed.), *Grammatical categories in Australian languages*, 382–90. Canberra: AIAS.

Lefebvre, Claire. 1998. *Creole genesis and the acquisition of grammar: The case of Haitian creole*. Cambridge: Cambridge University Press.

———2011. The problem of the typological classification of creoles. In Lefebvre, Claire (ed.), *Creoles, their substrates, and language typology*, 3–33. Amsterdam/Philadelphia: John Benjamins.

———Brousseau, Anne-Marie. 2002. *A grammar of Fongbe*. Berlin/New York: Mouton de Gruyter.

———Ritter, Elizabeth. 1993. Two types of predicated doubling adverbs in Haitian Creole. In Byrne, Francis and Winford, Donald (eds.), *Focus and grammatical relations in creole languages*, 65–91. Amsterdam/Philadelphia: John Benjamins.

Levin, Beth & Rappaport Hovav, Malka. 1995. *Unaccusativity: At the syntax-lexical semantics interface*. Cambridge, MA: MIT Press.

Li, Michelle & Matthews, Stephen. 2013. Chinese Pidgin English structure dataset. In *APiCS Online* (apics-online.info).

Lichtenberk, Frantisek. 2000. Inclusory pronominals. *Oceanic Linguistics* 39(1). 1–32.

Lim, Lisa & Ansaldo, Umberto. 2013. Singlish structure dataset. In *APiCS Online* (apics-online.info).

Lord, Carol. 1993. *Historical change in serial verb constructions*. Amsterdam/Philadelphia: John Benjamins.

Luffin, Xavier. 2005. *Un créole arabe: Le kinubi de Mombasa*. Munich: Lincom.

———2013. Kinubi structure dataset. In *APiCS Online* (apics-online.info).

McWhorter, John H. 2001. The world's simplest grammars are creole grammars. *Linguistic Typology* 5(2–3). 125–66.

Maddieson, Ian. 1984. *Patterns of sounds*. Cambridge: Cambridge University Press.

———2005a. Tone. In *WALS*, 58–61.

———2005b. Syllable structure. In *WALS*, 54–7.

———2005c. Presence of uncommon consonants. In *WALS*, 82–5.

Malchukov, Andrej, Haspelmath, Martin, & Comrie, Bernard. 2010. Ditransitive constructions: A typological overview. In Malchukov, Andrej L., Haspelmath, Martin, & Comrie, Bernard (eds.), *Studies in ditransitive constructions: A comparative handbook*, 1–64. Berlin/New York: De Gruyter Mouton.

Manessy, Gabriel. 1985. Remarques sur la pluralisation du nom en

References

créole et dans les langues africaines. *Études Créoles* 8. 129–43.

Manfredi, Stefano & Petrollino, Sara. 2013. Juba Arabic structure dataset. In *APiCS Online* (apics-online.info).

Maslova, Elena & Nedjalkov, Vladimir P. 2005. Reciprocal constructions. In *WALS*, 430–3.

Matras, Yaron & Bakker, Peter (eds.), 2003. *The mixed language debate: Theoretical and empirical advances*. Berlin/New York: Mouton de Gruyter.

Maurer, Philippe. 1988. *Les modifications temporelles et modales du verbe dans le papiamento de Curaçao (Antilles Néerlandaises): Avec une anthologie et un vocabulaire papiamento-français*. Vol. 9. Hamburg: Buske.

——1992. L'apport lexical bantou en angolar. *Afrikanistische Arbeitspapiere* 29. 163–74.

——1995. *L'angolar. Un créole afro-portugais parlé à São Tomé. Notes de grammaire, textes, vocabulaires*. Hamburg: Buske.

——2003. Procès de grammaticalisation dans le système TAM du papiamento de Curaçao. In Kriegel, Sibylle (ed.), *Grammaticalisation et réanalyse: Approches de la variation créole et française*, 233–47. Paris: CNRS-Editions.

——2009. *Principense (Lung'Ie): Grammar, texts, and vocabulary of the Afro-Portuguese Creole of the island of Principe, Gulf of Guinea*. London: Battlebridge.

——2011. *The former Portuguese Creole of Batavia and Tugu (Indonesia)*. London and Colombo: Battlebridge.

——2013a. Angolar structure dataset. In *APiCS Online* (apics-online.info).

——2013b. Batavia Creole structure dataset. In *APiCS Online* (apics-online.info).

——2013c. Principense structure dataset. In *APiCS Online* (apics-online.info).

——2013d. Papiamentu. In Michaelis, Susanne Maria, Maurer, Philippe, Haspelmath, Martin, & Huber, Magnus (eds.), *The survey of pidgin and creole languages*. Vol. II, 163–81. Oxford: Oxford University Press.

Meakins, Felicity. 2011. *Case-marking in contact: The development and function of case morphology in Gurindji Kriol*. Amsterdam/Philadelphia: John Benjamins.

——2013. Gurindji Creole structure dataset. In *APiCS Online* (apics-online.info).

Meeuwis, Michael. 2013. Lingala structure dataset. In *APiCS Online* (apics-online.info).

Melzian, Hans. 1937. *A concise dictionary of the Bini language of Southern Nigeria*. London: Kegan Paul, Trench, Trubner & Co.

Mesthrie, Rajend. 2013. Fanakalo structure dataset. In *APiCS Online* (apics-online.info).

——Surek-Clark, Clarissa. 2013a. Fanakalo. In Michaelis, Susanne Maria, Maurer, Philippe, Haspelmath, Martin, & Huber, Magnus (eds.), *The survey of pidgin and creole languages*. Vol. III, 34–41. Oxford: Oxford University Press.

Meyerhoff, Miriam. 2000. The emergence of creole subject–verb agreement and the licensing of null subjects. *Language Variation and Change* 12(2). 203–30.

——2013. Bislama structure dataset. In *APiCS Online* (apics-online.info).

Michaelis, Susanne. 1994. *Komplexe Syntax im Seychellen-Kreol*. Tübingen: Narr.

——2008. Valency patterns in Seychelles Creole: Where do they come from? In Michaelis, Susanne (ed.), *Roots of creole structures: Weighing the contribution of substrates and superstrates*, 226–51. Amsterdam/Philadelphia: John Benjamins.

——Haspelmath, Martin. 2003. Ditransitive constructions: Creole languages in a cross-linguistic perspective. *Creolica* (creolica.net).

——Rosalie, Marcel. 2000. Polysémie et cartes sémantiques: Le relateur *(av)ek* en créole seychellois. *Etudes Créoles* 23(2). 79–100.

—— ——2013. Seychelles Creole structure dataset. In *APiCS Online* (apics-online.info).

Miestamo, Matti. 2005. *Standard negation: The negation of declarative verbal main clauses in a typological perspective*. Berlin/New York: Mouton de Gruyter.

Migge, Bettina. 2003. *Creole formation as language contact: The case of the Suriname creoles*. Amsterdam/Philadelphia: John Benjamins.

——2013. Nengee structure dataset. In *APiCS Online* (apics-online.info).

Miller, George A. 1993. Images and models, similes and metaphors. In Ortony, Andrew (ed.), *Metaphor and thought*. 2nd edn., 357–400. Cambridge: Cambridge University Press.

Miller, Philip H. 1992. *Clitics and constituents in phrase structure grammar*. New York: Garland.

Moravcsik, Edith A. 1978. Reduplicative constructions. In Greenberg, Joseph H. (ed.), *Universals of human language*. Vol. 3: *Word structure*, 297–334. Stanford: Stanford University Press.

——2003. A semantic analysis of associative plurals. *Studies in Language* 27(3). 469–503.

Mous, Maarten. 2013. Mixed Ma'a/Mbugu structure dataset. In *APiCS Online* (apics-online.info).

Mufwene, Salikoko S. 2013. Kikongo-Kituba structure dataset. In *APiCS Online* (apics-online.info).

——2013a. Kikongo-Kituba. In Michaelis, Susanne Maria, Maurer, Philippe, Haspelmath, Martin, & Huber, Magnus (eds.), *The survey of pidgin and creole languages*. Vol. III, 3–12. Oxford: Oxford University Press.

——Dijkhoff, Marta B. 1989. On the so-called "infinitive" in Atlantic creoles. *Lingua* 77(3). 297–330.

Mühleisen, Susanne. 2013. Trinidad English Creole structure dataset. In *APiCS* Online (apics-online.info).

Mühlhäusler, Peter. 1981. The development of the category of number in Tok Pisin. In Muysken, Pieter (ed.), *Generative studies on creole languages*, 35–84. Dordrecht: Foris.

——2013. Norf'k structure dataset. In *APiCS Online* (apics-online.info).

——2013a. Norf'k. In Michaelis, Susanne Maria, Maurer, Philippe, Haspelmath, Martin, & Huber, Magnus (eds.), *The survey of pidgin and creole languages*. Vol. I, 232–40. Oxford: Oxford University Press.

Muysken, Pieter. 1981. Halfway between Quechua and Spanish: The case for relexification. Highfield, Arnold & Valdman, Albert (eds.), *Historicity and variation in creole studies*, 52–78. Ann Arbor: Karoma.

——1993. Reflexes of Ibero-Romance reflexive clitic + verb combinations in Papiamentu: Thematic grids and grammatical relations. In Byrne, Francis & Winford, Donald (eds.), *Focus and grammatical relations in the creole languages*, 285–301. Amsterdam/Philadelphia: John Benjamins.

———2013. Media Lengua structure dataset. In *APiCS Online* (apics-online.info).

———Smith, Norval. 1990. Question words in pidgin and creole languages. *Linguistics* 28(4). 883–904.

——— ——— 1994. Reflexives. In Arends, Jacques, Muysken, Pieter, & Smith, Norval (eds.), *Pidgins and Creoles. An introduction*, 271–88. Amsterdam/Philadelphia: John Benjamins.

Nedjalkov, Vladimir P. (ed.), 2007. *Reciprocal constructions.* 5 vols. Amsterdam/Philadelphia: John Benjamins.

Neumann-Holzschuh, Ingrid. 1985. *Le créole de Breaux Bridge, Louisiane: Étude morphosyntaxique, textes, vocabulaire.* Hamburg: Buske.

———Klingler, Thomas A. 2013. Louisiana Creole structure dataset. In *APiCS Online* (apics-online.info).

Nichols, Johanna. 1986. Head-marking and dependent-marking grammar. *Language* 62(1). 56–119.

———Bickel, Balthasar. 2005. Locus of marking in possessive noun phrases. In *WALS*, 102–5.

Nordhoff, Sebastian. 2009. *A grammar of upcountry Sri Lanka Malay.* Utrecht: LOT.

———2012. Establishing and dating Sinhala influence in Sri Lanka Malay. *Journal of Language Contact* 5(1). 23–57.

Osumi, Midori. 1995. *Tinrin grammar.* Honolulu: University of Hawai'i Press.

Paauw, Scott. 2013. Ambon Malay structure dataset. In *APiCS Online* (apics-online.info).

Parkvall, Michael. 2000. *Out of Africa: African influences in Atlantic creoles.* London: Battlebridge.

Perekhvalskaya, Elena V. 2008. *Russkie pidžiny.* St Peterburg: Aletejja.

———2013. Chinese Pidgin Russian structure dataset. In *APiCS Online* (apics-online.info).

Peterson, David A. 2007. *Applicative constructions.* Oxford: Oxford University Press.

Pfänder, Stefan. 2013. Guyanais structure dataset. In *APiCS Online* (apics-online.info).

Plag, Ingo. 1998. The syntax of some locative expressions in Sranan: Preposition, postposition, or noun? *Journal of Pidgin and Creole Languages* 13. 335–53.

Polinsky, Maria. 2005. Applicative constructions. In *WALS*, 442–5.

Pollock, Jean-Yves. 1989. Verb movement, Universal Grammar, and the structure of IP. *Linguistic Inquiry* 20(3). 365–424.

Post, Marike. 2013. Fa d'Ambô structure dataset. In *APiCS Online* (apics-online.info).

Prentice, David John. 1990. Malay (Indonesian and Malaysian). In Comrie, Bernard (ed.), *The world's major languages*, 913–35. Oxford: Oxford University Press.

Prescod, Paula. 2013. Vincentian Creole structure dataset. In *APiCS Online* (apics-online.info).

Rickford, John R. 1998. The creole origins of African-American Vernacular English: Evidence from copula absence. In Mufwene, Salikoko S., Rickford, John R., Bailey, Guy, & Baugh, John (eds.), *African-American English: Structure, history, use.* London: Routledge.

———1999. *African American vernacular English: Features, evolution, educational implications.* Malden, MA: Blackwell.

———Rickford, Angela E. 1976. Cut-eye and suck-teeth: African words and gestures in New World guise. *The Journal of American Folklore* 89(353). 294–309. (Reprinted in Rickford 1999).

Rivierre, Jean-Claude. 1980. *La langue de Touho. Phonologie et grammaire du cèmuhî (Nouvelle-Calédonie).* Paris: SELAF.

Roberts, Ian G. 1997. *Comparative syntax.* London: Arnold.

Roberts, Sarah J. 2013. Pidgin Hawaiian structure dataset. In *APiCS Online* (apics-online.info).

———2013a. Pidgin Hawaiian. In Michaelis, Susanne Maria, Maurer, Philippe, Haspelmath, Martin, & Huber, Magnus (eds.), *The survey of pidgin and creole languages.* Vol. III, 119–27. Oxford: Oxford University Press.

Rounds, Carol. 2001. *Hungarian: An essential grammar.* London: Routledge.

Rowlands, E. C. 1969. *Teach yourself Yoruba.* London: Hodder and Stoughton.

Rubino, Carl. 2005. Reduplication. In *WALS*, 114–17.

Samarin, William J. 2013. Sango structure dataset. In *APiCS Online* (apics-online.info).

———2013a. Sango. In Michaelis, Susanne Maria, Maurer, Philippe, Haspelmath, Martin, & Huber, Magnus (eds.), *The survey of pidgin and creole languages.* Vol. III, 13–24. Oxford: Oxford University Press.

Schachter, Paul & Otanes, Fé T. 1972. *Tagalog reference grammar.* Berkeley: University of California Press.

Schladt, Mathias. 2000. The typology and grammaticalization of reflexives. In Frajzyngier, Zygmunt & Walker-Curl, Traci S. (eds.), *Reflexives*, 103–24. Amsterdam/Philadelphia: John Benjamins.

Schröder, Anne. 2013. Cameroon Pidgin English structure dataset. In *APiCS Online* (apics-online.info).

Schultze-Berndt, Eva & Angelo, Denise. 2013. Belizean Creole structure dataset. In *APiCS Online* (apics-online.info).

Schwegler, Armin. 2002. El vocabulario africano de Palenque (Colombia). Segunda Parte: Compendio de palabras (con etimologías). In Moñino, Yves & Schwegler, Armin (eds.), *Palenque, Cartagena y Afro-Caribe: Historia y lengua*, 171–227. Tübingen: Niemeyer.

———2007. A fresh consensus in the making: Plural MA and bare nouns in Palenquero. In Baptista, Marlyse & Guéron, Jacqueline (eds.), *Noun phrases in creole languages: A multi-faceted approach*, 205–22. Amsterdam/Philadelphia: John Benjamins.

———2013. Palenquero structure dataset. In *APiCS Online* (apics-online.info).

Seuren, Pieter & Wekker, Herman. 1986. Semantic transparency as a factor in creole genesis. In Muysken, Pieter & Smith, Norval (eds.), *Substrata versus universals in creole genesis*, 57–70. Amsterdam/Philadelphia: John Benjamins.

Sharma, Devyani & Rickford, John R. 2009. AAVE/Creole copula absence: A critique of the imperfect learning hypothesis. *Journal of Pidgin and Creole Languages* 24(1). 53–90.

Siegel, Jeff. 2008. *The emergence of pidgin and creole languages.* Oxford: Oxford University Press.

———2013. Pidgin Hindustani structure dataset. In *APiCS Online* (apics-online.info).

Siewierska, Anna. 2004. *Person.* Cambridge: Cambridge University Press.

———2005a. Gender distinctions in independent personal pronouns. In *WALS*, 182–5.

———2005b. Alignment of verbal person marking. In *WALS*, 406–9.

———2005c. Verbal person marking. In *WALS*, 414–17.

———2005d. Passive constructions. In *WALS*, 434–7.

References

Silverstein, Michael. 1976. Hierarchy of features and ergativity. In Dixon, R. M. W. (ed.), *Grammatical categories in Australian languages*, 112–71. Canberra: Australian National University.

Singer, Ruth J. 2001. The inclusory construction in Australian languages. *Melbourne Papers in Linguistics and Applied Linguistics* 1(2). 81–96.

Sinnemäki, Kaius. 2010. Word order in zero-marking languages. *Studies in Language* 34(4). 869–912.

Sippola, Eeva. 2013a. Cavite Chabacano structure dataset. In *APiCS Online* (apics-online.info).

——2013b. Ternate Chabacano structure dataset. In *APiCS Online* (apics-online.info).

Slomanson, Peter. 2013. Sri Lankan Malay structure dataset. In *APiCS Online* (apics-online.info).

——2013a. Sri Lankan Malay. In Michaelis, Susanne Maria, Maurer, Philippe, Haspelmath, Martin, & Huber, Magnus (eds.), *The survey of pidgin and creole languages*. Vol. III, 77–85. Oxford: Oxford University Press.

Smith, Geoff P. & Siegel, Jeff. 2013. Tok Pisin structure dataset. In *APiCS Online* (apics-online.info).

—— ——2013a. Tok Pisin. In Michaelis, Susanne Maria, Maurer, Philippe, Haspelmath, Martin & Huber, Magnus (eds.), *The survey of pidgin and creole languages*. Vol I, 214–22. Oxford: Oxford University Press.

Smith, Ian R. 2013. Sri Lanka Portuguese structure dataset. In *APiCS Online* (apics-online.info).

Smith, Norval. 1994. An annotated list of creoles, pidgins and mixed languages. In Arends, Jacques, Muysken, Pieter, & Smith, Norval (eds.), *Pidgins and creoles: An introduction*, 331–74. Amsterdam/Philadelphia: John Benjamins.

——1999. Pernambuco to Surinam 1654–1665? The Jewish slave controversy. In Huber, Magnus & Parkvall, Mikael (eds.), *Spreading the word: The issue of diffusion among the Atlantic creoles*, 251–98. London: Westminster University Press.

Smith-Stark, Cedric. 1974. The plurality split. *Chicago Linguistic Society* 10. 657–71.

Stassen, Leon. 2005a. Noun phrase conjunction. In *WALS*, 258–61.

——2005b. Predicative possession. In *WALS*, 474–7.

——2005c. Nominal and locational predication. In *WALS*, 482–5.

——2005d. Zero copula for predicate nominals. In *WALS*, 486–9.

——2005e. Comparative constructions. In *WALS*, 490–3.

——2005f. Predicative adjectives. In *WALS*, 478–481.

——2009. *Predicative possession*. Oxford: Oxford University Press.

Steinkrüger, Patrick O. 2007. Notes on Ternateño (A Philippine Spanish Creole). *Journal of Pidgin and Creole Languages* 22(2). 367–77.

——2013. Zamboanga Chabacano structure dataset. In *APiCS Online* (apics-online.info).

Stolz, Thomas. 2006. (Wort-)Iteration: (k)eine universelle Konstruktion. In Fischer, Kerstin & Stefanowitsch, Anatol (eds.), *Konstruktionsgrammatik: Von der Anwendung zur Theorie*, 105–32. Tübingen: Stauffenburg.

——2008. Total reduplication vs. echo-word formation in language contact situations. In Siemund, Peter & Kintana, Noemi (eds.), *Language contact and contact languages* (=Hamburg Studies on Multilingualism 7), 107–32. Amsterdam/Philadelphia: John Benjamins.

——Veselinova, Ljuba N. 2005. Ordinal numerals. In *WALS*, 218–21.

——Stroh, Cornelia, & Urdze, Aina. 2005. Comitatives and instrumentals. In *WALS*, 214–17.

Swolkien, Dominika. 2013. Cape Verdean Creole of São Vicente structure dataset. In *APiCS Online* (apics-online.info).

Tepowa, Adebiyi. 1904. Notes on the (Nembe) Brass language. *Journal of the Royal African Society* 4. 117–33.

Tesnière, Lucien. 1951. Le duel sylleptique en français et en slave. *Bulletin de la Société de Linguistique de Paris* 47(1). 57–63.

Thomas, Charles W. 1860. *Adventures and observations on the West Coast of Africa, and its islands* [. . .]. Vol. 1. New York: Derby & Jackson.

Urban, Matthias. 2012. *Analyzability and semantic associations in referring expressions: A study in comparative lexicology*. Ph.D. dissertation, University of Leiden.

van den Berg, Margot C. & Bruyn, Adrienne. 2013. Early Sranan structure dataset. In *APiCS Online* (apics-online.info).

van der Auwera, Johan & Ammann, Andreas. 2005. Overlap between situational and epistemic modal marking. In *WALS*, 310–3.

——Lejeune, Ludo (with Valentin Goussev). 2005. The prohibitive. In *WALS*, 290–3.

van der Voort, Hein. 2013. Eskimo Pidgin structure dataset. In *APiCS Online* (apics-online.info).

——2013a. Eskimo Pidgin. In Michaelis, Susanne Maria, Maurer, Philippe, Haspelmath, Martin, & Huber, Magnus (eds.), *The survey of pidgin and creole languages*. Vol. III, 166–73. Oxford: Oxford University Press.

van Sluijs, Robbert. 2013. Negerhollands structure dataset. In *APiCS Online* (apics-online.info).

——2013a. Negerhollands. In Michaelis, Susanne Maria, Maurer, Philippe, Haspelmath, Martin, & Huber, Magnus (eds.), *The survey of pidgin and creole languages*. Vol. III, 265–74. Oxford: Oxford University Press.

——2013b. Afrikaans. In Michaelis, Susanne Maria, Maurer, Philippe, Haspelmath, Martin, & Huber, Magnus (eds.), *The survey of pidgin and creole languages*. Vol. III, 285–96. Oxford: Oxford University Press.

Vanhove, Martine. 2008. Semantic associations between sensory modalities, prehension and mental perceptions. A crosslinguistic perspective. In Vanhove, Martine (ed.), *From polysemy to semantic change. Towards a typology of lexical semantic associations*, 341–70. Amsterdam/Philadelphia: John Benjamins.

Velupillai, Viveka. 2013. Hawai'i Creole structure dataset. In *APiCS Online* (apics-online.info).

Verma, Manindra & Mohanan, K. P. (eds.). 1991. *Experiencer subjects in South Asian languages*. Stanford: CSLI Publications.

Veselinova, Ljuba N. 2005. Suppletion according to tense and aspect. In *WALS*, 322–5.

Viberg, Åke. 1984. The verbs of perception: A typological study. *Linguistics* 21. 123–62.

Voorhoeve, Jan. 1957. The verbal system of Sranan. *Lingua* 6. 374–96.

Wälchli, Bernhard & Zúñiga, Fernando. 2006. Source-Goal (in)difference and the typology of motion events in the clause. *STUF-Language Typology and Universals* 59(3). 284–303.

WALS = Haspelmath, Martin, Dryer, Matthew S., Gil, David & Comrie, Bernard (eds.), *The world atlas of language structures*. Oxford: Oxford University Press.

Weber, David John. 1989. *A Grammar of Huallaga (Huánaco) Quechua*. Berkeley: University of California Press.

References

Welmers, William E. 1973. *African language structures*. Berkeley: University of California Press.

Wendeland, Wilhelm. 1939. *Im Wunderland der Papuas: Ein deutscher Kolonialarzt erlebt die Südsee*. Berlin: Verlag für Volkstum, Wehr und Wirtschaft.

Winford, Donald. 1993. *Predication in Caribbean English creoles*. Amsterdam/Philadelphia: John Benjamins.

——Plag, Ingo. 2013. Sranan structure dataset. In *APiCS Online* (apics-online.info).

Yakpo, Kofi. 2009. *A grammar of Pichi*. PhD dissertation Radboud, Universiteit Nijmegen. http://webdoc.ubn.ru.nl/mono/y/yakpo_k/gramofpi.pdf.

——2013. Pichi structure dataset. In *APiCS Online* (apics-online.info).

Yip, Moira. 2002. *Tone*. Cambridge: Cambridge University Press.

Zúñiga, Fernando. 2011. Why should beneficiaries be subjects (or objects)? Affaction and grammatical relations. In Kittilä, Seppo, Västi, Katja, & Ylikoski, Jussi (eds.), *Case, Animacy and Semantic Roles*, 329–48. Amsterdam/Philadelphia: John Benjamins.

SUBJECT INDEX

ability 216, 217, 399
accusative 226, 227, 265
accusative alignment 230, 231, 232, 233
acrolectal 89, 359, 423, 437
additive focus particle 422
addressee 127, 220, 236, 240, 410, 429
address form 428
adjacent 26, 27, 41, 65, 69, 89, 130, 131, 159, 168, 172, 173, 177, 394, 419, 422, 423, 422, 428
adjective xxxvi, xl, xli, xlii, xlvi, xlviii, 7, 10, 11, 30, 31, 35, 38, 39, 89, 101, 154, 155, 158, 159, 162, 204, 268, 290, 294, 295, 299, 436, 437, 468, 469
adjoined relative clause 26, 27
adnominal xl, xli, 18, 34, 72, 73, 114, 115, 118, 122, 123, 126, 127, 130, 131, 134, 135, 142, 151, 154, 155, 307, 350
adnominal demonstrative xli, 18, 34, 118, 122, 123, 126, 127
adposition xli, xlv, 14, 15, 135, 142, 143, 142, 146, 226, 230, 261, 272, 273, 314, 315, 318, 319, 322, 323, 330, 331, 330, 335, 339, 342, 366, 370, 375
adpositional phrase 142, 143, 142, 272
adverbial element 40
adversity 358
affactive 363, 432, 433, 432
affirmative 196, 197, 220, 221, 291
affix xl, 6, 14, 59, 64, 88, 106, 131, 134, 135, 142, 143, 146, 176, 180, 226, 244, 245, 265, 319, 351, 355, 359, 362, 366, 367, 370, 371, 383, 387, 386, 398, 399, 402, 403, 422, 468
affixation 131
agent 2, 226, 230, 232, 236, 240, 244, 260, 268, 359
agreement xxxvi, xxxvii, xl, xli, 85, 154, 155, 226, 245, 335, 391, 433
agreement marker 245, 335, 391
alienable 142
alignment xli, 230, 231, 230, 232, 233, 236, 240
allophone 484, 485, 486, 487, 488, 489, 490, 491, 492, 493, 495
alternation 241, 441
ambitransitive 359
analogy 44, 89, 347, 469
analysable/analysability 73, 81, 347
anaphoric 19, 34, 106, 346, 347, 350, 351
anaphoric function 19
anaphoric pronoun 346, 347, 350, 351
anaphoric situation 34, 106
animacy xl, 84, 127
animal 88, 89, 93, 432, 468, 469, 491
animate 50, 51, 84, 119, 138, 226, 227
A-not-A question 411
antecedent 150
antidual 104, 105
aperture 486

applicative xlii, 362, 363
areal 11, 19, 31, 51, 115, 123, 135, 163, 169, 173, 185, 189, 201, 221, 244, 249, 311, 319, 457, 474, 475, 481, 487
areal clustering 311
areal pattern 169, 249
argument 35, 40, 64, 150, 217, 226, 227, 230, 232, 236, 240, 244, 245, 252, 253, 257, 260, 265, 268, 269, 272, 319, 334, 338, 339, 358, 362, 399, 461
argument index 64
argument position 150
aspect xl, xli, xlvi, xlviii, 26, 168, 172, 173, 176, 177, 184, 188, 192, 193, 196, 197, 200, 201, 204, 205, 208, 209, 212, 213, 217, 249, 294, 334, 335, 338, 339, 342, 402, 410, 419, 445, 480
aspect change 208, 209
aspect marker xli, 172, 173, 177, 184, 188, 192, 193, 197, 200, 204, 217, 294, 334, 338, 402
associative plural xli, 92, 93
associative relationship 34
at-rest 314, 326, 327, 326, 330, 331, 330
attenuating 100, 101
attributive 6, 10, 14, 31, 101, 205
attributive adjective 10, 101
attributive possessive construction 6, 14
atypical passive 358, 359
auxiliaries 399, 403
auxiliary 169, 177, 180, 355, 358, 359, 398, 399

background clause 414, 415, 418, 419
bare plural noun phrase 114, 115
bare singular noun phrase 114, 115
basilect(al) 69, 89, 233, 253, 354, 437, 488, 492
benefactive 342, 362, 363
bimorphemic 277, 444, 445
bipartite negative marker 398
body-part 6, 102, 104, 105, 142, 146, 260, 261, 268, 269, 272, 346, 347
body-part relation 6
body-part term 104, 105
borrowed 41, 45, 58, 61, 135, 185, 284, 355, 359, 461
bound person form 232

cardinality 110
cardinal numeral xli, 22, 134, 135
case affix 14, 146, 226, 265
case marker 146, 272, 273, 318, 319, 327
case suffix 143, 146, 233, 241, 261, 307, 315
causal 395
circumlocution 444, 445
circumposed 19, 34, 35, 158

507

Subject index

circumposition 14, 15, 314, 315, 318, 319, 327, 326, 331, 330, 383
class-inclusion 290
clause-second position 176, 177
cleft construction 44, 414, 415, 414, 418
click xlii, 432, 433, 432
clitic 14, 64, 65, 233, 245, 319, 411
coda 474, 475, 479
cognitive experience 260
collective 84
colour (term) xxxvi, xliii, xlv, 464, 465
comitative xli, 76, 276, 277, 280, 281, 285, 306, 307, 379
companion 354, 355
comparative concept xxxviii, xl, xlviii, 290, 319, 484
comparative construction 150, 158, 159, 162, 163
comparative degree 158
comparative marker 158, 159
comparee 158, 162
complementary distribution 119, 484
complement clause 248, 291, 295, 382, 386, 390, 391
complementizer xlii, 163, 378, 379, 382, 383, 387, 390, 391
completive 168, 192, 197, 204, 205, 480
compositional 80
compound interrogative 72, 73
conjoined marking 162, 163
conjunct(ion) xli, 76, 97, 280, 281, 284, 285, 379, 460
consonant 65, 441, 474, 475, 484, 485, 487, 491, 493, 494
constituent negation 402
constituent order xlv
coordinate xlviii, 76, 208, 209, 245, 338
coordinator 76, 284, 285
copula xl, 44, 45, 204, 217, 252, 268, 290, 291, 290, 294, 295, 298, 299, 302, 303, 310, 414, 415, 414, 418, 419, 440, 480, 481
coreferential 64, 346, 347
correlative relative clause 26, 27, 367
counterfactual 172, 173
count noun 110, 138
country boundaries xlv
creolization 65, 253, 315, 481
cross-referencing 226
current state 184, 185, 184, 188, 189, 192

database xxxi, xxxii, xl, xliii, xliv, xlvi, xlvii, xlviii, 335, 437, 468, 484, 485
dative 162, 241, 260, 261, 264, 265, 268, 269, 307
dative alternation 241
dative subject construction 261, 265
declarative 2, 44, 45, 196, 220, 221, 402
declarative clause 2
decreolization 399
definite xl, xli, xlvi, 34, 35, 38, 39, 61, 84, 85, 89, 97, 106, 107, 110, 111, 114, 115, 118, 119, 197, 226, 227, 290, 394, 395, 480
definite article xl, xli, xlvi, 34, 35, 38, 39, 85, 89, 106, 107, 110, 111, 114, 115, 118, 119, 394, 395, 480
definiteness 34, 84, 85, 97, 106
degree word xl, xli, 30, 31, 158, 159
deictic expression 18, 126
demonstrative xl, xli, 10, 18, 19, 27, 34, 35, 85, 97, 106, 107, 110, 118, 119, 122, 123, 126, 127, 248, 252, 253, 492, 495
dependent person form 64, 65, 232, 245
determiner 6, 84, 97, 114, 154, 155, 362
diachronic xxxviii, xxxix, xl, 81, 134, 163, 173, 185, 212, 233, 311, 343, 379, 465
dialect atlas xxxvii
differential object marking 226
differentiation xlv, 58, 96, 97, 196, 276, 277, 280, 281, 284, 285, 302, 303, 310, 315, 322, 323, 350, 351, 448, 449, 452, 453, 452, 456, 457, 456, 460, 461, 464, 465, 481
diminutive 101, 436, 437
direction xlii, 61, 334, 335
directional serial verb construction xlii, 334
directive modality 378
disambiguation 452, 453, 456, 460
discontinuous 159
distributive xli, 22, 101, 130, 131
distributive numeral xli, 22, 130, 131
distributivity 100, 101, 130, 131
ditransitive construction xli, 226, 236, 237, 240, 265, 269
ditransitive verb 236, 240, 261, 265
dominant word order 3
double-object construction 236, 237, 241
dual 54, 55, 58, 59, 76, 85, 104
duplifixation 93, 100
dynamic verb xli, 200, 201, 205, 213, 298

echo compound 100
echo question 45
echo word 100
elliptical answer 50, 54, 64, 150
embedded clause 382
emotion 260, 264, 265, 268, 269
emphasizer 346, 347
epistemic possibility 216, 217
ergative alignment 230, 231, 232
etymology/etymological 45, 105, 143, 169, 185, 217, 342, 436, 437, 440, 441, 468
exclusive xxxv, xli, xlii, xliv, 3, 7, 11, 15, 19, 31, 44, 50, 51, 58, 59, 76, 89, 97, 104, 135, 151, 169, 184, 193, 204, 205, 209, 213, 221, 248, 249, 256, 257, 269, 272, 273, 276, 277, 299, 303, 306, 307, 315, 319, 327, 343, 351, 379, 383, 419, 422, 441, 457, 468, 469, 475, 480
existential xlii, 80, 81, 80, 248, 252, 253, 257, 298, 307, 310, 311, 406, 407, 480
existential argument 252, 253
existential construction 80, 81, 80, 248, 252, 253, 311, 406, 407
existential verb xlii, 252, 253, 257, 298, 307, 310
experiencer 248, 249, 260, 261, 264, 265, 268, 269
experiencer construction 260, 261, 264, 265, 268, 269
expletive 248, 249, 252, 253, 256, 257, 310
expletive subject 248, 249, 252, 253, 256, 257, 310

factive verb 382
family xxxvii, 54, 68, 92, 93, 143, 232, 276, 307, 342, 489
fear 189, 209, 260, 268, 269, 285, 347, 406
feminine 50, 51, 60, 69, 135

focus xxxv, xxxviii, xlii, 2, 40, 44, 64, 72, 76, 100, 142, 154, 236, 240, 256, 260, 264, 290, 298, 338, 342, 350, 354, 394, 402, 406, 414, 415, 414, 418, 419, 422, 423, 422, 460, 484
focus clause 414
focus construction 342, 414, 415, 422
focus marker 290, 354, 418
focus operator 422
focus(ing) particle 290, 350, 414, 415, 414, 422, 423
free morpheme 319
free word 14, 402
frequency adverb 30, 40, 41
fronting 45, 414, 415, 414, 418, 419
full noun phrase xli, 2, 76, 146, 226, 230, 232, 236, 244
full reduplication 100
full verb 189
future xxxv, xxxvi, xlviii, 169, 172, 173, 184, 185, 184, 188, 189, 193, 196, 197, 217, 273, 299, 367, 465, 480, 481
future marker 169, 172, 173, 193, 196, 197, 217, 480, 481
future situation 184, 193

Gall–Peters projection xlv
gap 366, 367, 370, 371, 374, 375, 374
gender xxxvi, xl, xli, 50, 51, 60, 85, 135, 146, 154, 155, 253
gender agreement xxxvi, xl, xli, 154, 155
gender syncretism 60
genealogically balanced sample xxxvii
general imperfective marker 185
generic xli, 35, 72, 73, 80, 81, 80, 97, 106, 107, 114, 115, 359, 406, 468
generic noun xli, 72, 73, 80, 81, 114, 115, 406
genitive xliii, xlviii, 6, 135, 143, 146, 306, 307
genitive adposition 135
geographical distribution 45, 97, 163, 181, 217, 265, 343, 433, 465
gloss xxxvi, xlv, xlvii, xlviii, 151, 366, 370, 374, 386, 484
gradable property 158, 162
gradable word 101
grammatical aspect 192
grammaticalization/grammaticalized 14, 15, 35, 55, 59, 173, 180, 185, 311, 342, 378, 440, 441
grammatical gender 154
grammatical marker xxxix, 176, 180, 181, 362, 481
grammatifier 227
grande 154, 253, 436, 440
grooming verb 346, 347
Groupe Européen de Recherche en Langues Créoles xlvi
Gulf of Guinea xlv, 7, 22, 23, 41, 69, 81, 122, 123, 142, 151, 173, 200, 256, 257, 314, 319, 323, 327, 331, 335, 355, 403, 407, 429, 437, 441, 461, 481, 492, 493

habitual xli, 176, 180, 184, 185, 184, 186, 188, 189, 192, 193, 196, 200, 204, 335, 441
habituality 188, 189
habitual situation 184, 200
headache 110, 260, 261, 268, 269
head noun xxxvi, xl, 6, 23, 26, 27, 367
hierarchy 84, 453
highlighter 414, 415, 414, 418, 419
homonymy 60, 61

homorganic sequence 494
horizontal pattern 230
hushing sound 490

iconic function 100, 101
identification function 290
identity xlv, 73, 89, 93, 96, 97, 111, 276, 277, 280, 281, 284, 285, 302, 303, 310, 311, 322, 323, 350, 351, 354, 386, 448, 449, 452, 453, 452, 456, 457, 456, 460, 461, 464, 465
ideophone 437, 465, 491
idiomatic xlvii, 347
imperative 220, 221, 245, 335, 386, 402
imperfective 168, 169, 172, 176, 185, 192, 193, 204, 208, 213, 217
imperfective aspect 172, 192, 208
imperfective marker 169, 172, 185, 192, 193, 204, 217
implicational relationship 232
implicational scale 84, 474, 475
implicit subject 386
inalienable 142
inanimate xxxvii, 50, 51, 84, 85, 93, 97, 127, 138, 227, 237
inceptive 209
inchoative xli, 192, 201, 204, 205, 294
inclusive xxxv, xli, 58, 59, 411
inclusory construction 76, 77
incorporation 261
indefinite article xli, 22, 38, 39, 81, 85, 106, 107, 110, 111, 114, 115, 154, 291
indefinite pronoun xli, xlii, 80, 406
independent personal pronoun xli, 51, 54, 58, 60, 61, 64, 150, 232
independent pronominal possessor xli, 142, 150, 151
independent pronoun 51, 64, 65, 233, 363
indexing 143, 146, 147, 146, 226, 362
indirective construction 236, 241
indirect object 236, 237
indirect question 382
inequality 158, 162
infinitive 185, 209, 386, 391, 419, 440
inflectional morphology 40
inflectional properties 122, 123
inposition 14
inset map xlv, xlvi
in situ 44, 45, 414, 415, 414, 484
instrumental xli, 14, 272, 273, 276, 277, 280, 338, 339
instrument relative clause xlii, 26, 366, 367, 370, 374, 375
intensifier xlii, 347, 350, 351, 422
intensity 100, 101
interdental fricative 485, 492
interjection 428, 432
interlinear word-by-word gloss xlv
internally headed relative clause 10, 27
interrogative xli, 44, 45, 72, 73, 80, 81, 80, 410, 411
interrogative intonation 410, 411
interrogative phrase xli, 44, 45, 410
interrogative pronoun xli, 45, 72, 73, 80
intertwined language xxxv
intransitive verb 334
irregularity 212

Subject index

isolating language 154
iteration 100, 101

juxtaposition 76, 77, 146, 147, 284, 285, 444

kinship relation 6, 142, 146
kinship term 69, 92, 93, 428

labiodental 441, 485, 489
labiodental ingressive fricative 433
language bioprogram hypothesis 172, 200
language name xxxvii
lect xxxvi, xlvi, xlvii, 15
leftward position 168
legend xliv, xlv, 18, 30, 58, 212, 314, 318, 322, 342, 444, 492
Leipzig Glossing Rules xlv
lexicalized 163, 249, 468
lexical semantics 154
lexicon-provider xxxvi
liking 260
locational adverb 18, 126
locational meaning 162
locative xlii, 15, 19, 34, 35, 295, 298, 299, 302, 303, 307, 310, 311, 335, 363, 480, 481
locative demonstrative 34, 35
logical 40, 172, 230, 236, 432, 433, 432, 448, 480
lower numeral 22, 23
low tone 65, 221, 480, 481

macrofunctionality 61
main clause 2, 27, 196, 291, 390, 402, 403
major allophone 484, 485, 486, 487, 488, 489, 490, 491, 492, 493, 495
malefactive 363
map caption xlv
map projection xlv
masculine 50, 51, 60, 69, 135
matrix clause 390, 418
Max Planck Institute for Evolutionary Anthropology xxxi, xlvi, xlix
mensural numeral classifier 138
mental participant-internal ability 216
metaphorical 256, 460
meteorological event 256
minor allophone 484, 487, 488, 490, 491, 492, 493, 495
mixed language xxxi, xxxiii, xxxv, xxxvi, xlix, 2, 10, 11, 23, 26, 34, 41, 54, 59, 72, 84, 85, 93, 114, 119, 122, 123, 131, 134, 155, 168, 177, 180, 184, 188, 220, 226, 227, 230, 233, 245, 261, 265, 273, 276, 281, 295, 307, 310, 311, 314, 315, 319, 327, 331, 334, 335, 339, 343, 346, 362, 407, 422, 433, 452, 453, 456
modal verb 184, 217, 398
monoclausal 236, 240, 334, 338, 342
monomorphemic 72, 277, 444, 445, 452, 453, 456, 457
monotransitive 2, 230, 232, 236, 237, 260, 268
mood xli, 168, 172, 173, 196, 197, 216, 217, 245
mood marker xli, 168, 172, 173, 196, 197, 217
morph xxxi, xxxvii, xl, xlii, xlv, xlvii, 34, 38, 40, 51, 73, 100, 106, 110, 158, 192, 298, 319, 331, 358, 366, 370, 374, 398, 399, 402, 403, 410, 411, 468, 484

morpheme xlii, xlv, xlvii, 34, 38, 100, 106, 110, 192, 298, 319, 331, 366, 370, 374, 398, 399, 402, 403
morphological xl, 51, 73, 358, 468
morphological expression xl
morphological reduction 51
motion construction 314, 318, 322, 326, 327, 331
motion-from xlii, 314, 315, 318, 319, 322, 323, 326, 330, 331, 330
motion-to xlii, 314, 315, 318, 319, 322, 323, 326, 327, 326, 331
multiple-choice feature xlii, xliii, xliv, xlvii, 2, 6, 10, 162

named place 314, 315, 318, 319, 322, 334
nasal xlii, 474, 475, 485, 486, 487, 491, 493, 494
nasalization 487
nasal vowel xlii, 485, 486, 487
national language xxxvi
native-speaker linguist xlvii
naturalistic spoken example xlvii
negation xxxviii, xlii, 196, 249, 291, 398, 399, 402, 403, 406, 407, 432, 433
neuter 50, 60
neutral alignment 230, 232, 233, 236
nominalization 395
non-default lect xxxvi
non-reduction 366, 367, 370, 371, 374
non-referential 290
non-specific 114
notional head 27
noun-class system 50
noun phrase conjunction xli, 280, 281
null-subject 245
number syncretism 60
numeral xli, 10, 22, 23, 31, 38, 39, 55, 76, 77, 81, 84, 101, 110, 111, 130, 131, 134, 135, 138, 139, 154, 355

object xli, xlii, xliii, xlv, 2, 3, 6, 7, 26, 40, 41, 44, 64, 65, 105, 142, 162, 168, 169, 177, 196, 226, 227, 232, 233, 236, 237, 240, 241, 248, 252, 257, 260, 261, 264, 265, 268, 269, 306, 318, 323, 338, 339, 346, 355, 358, 359, 362, 363, 366, 367, 370, 371, 374, 375, 379, 395, 399, 402, 403, 441, 460, 461, 464
objective genitive 6
object relative clause xlii, 26, 366, 370, 371, 374, 375
obligatory person form 244
oblique 248, 264, 268, 269, 307, 358, 359, 362, 374, 375
obstruent 474, 475
obviative 227
older generation xxxvi, 299
onset 474, 475, 477
ontological categories 72, 80
ontological category
open-class item 169, 176, 177, 180, 181
optional person form 244
ordinal numeral xli, 22, 134, 135
orientation xxxvi, xlv, 314, 315, 318, 322, 323, 326
overlap xlv, 96, 97, 123, 208, 216, 276, 277, 280, 281, 284, 285, 302, 303, 310, 311, 322, 323, 350, 351, 448, 449, 452, 453, 452, 456, 457, 456, 460, 461, 464, 465
ownership 6, 142, 146

Subject index

palatal nasal 485, 493
palato-alveolar sibilant 485, 490, 494
paradigm frequency xliii
para-linguistic 432
paratactic 208, 209
P argument 358, 362
partial reduplication 100, 130
participant-external possibility 216
participle 169, 358, 480
passive xlii, 358, 359, 358
passive participle 358
past marker xli, 168, 169, 172, 173, 176, 177, 197, 335
patient xlvii, 2, 226, 227, 230, 232, 233, 236, 237, 358
pequenino xl, 436, 437
perfective xli, 168, 172, 176, 177, 192, 193, 196, 197, 200, 201, 205, 208, 213, 217, 335
perfective dynamic situation 201
permanent possession 306
personal name 76, 428
personal pronoun xli, 50, 51, 54, 55, 58, 60, 61, 64, 76, 84, 85, 96, 107, 142, 143, 146, 147, 150, 226, 230, 232, 233, 236, 244, 253, 347, 350, 351, 428
person form 54, 58, 59, 61, 64, 65, 68, 69, 147, 232, 233, 244, 245
person-indexing construction 147
person syncretism 60, 61
phoneme 432, 484, 487, 491
phrasal expression 249, 444, 445, 464, 465
phrase xl, xli, xlii, xlv, 2, 6, 14, 15, 22, 30, 31, 34, 35, 38, 40, 44, 45, 55, 72, 76, 77, 80, 84, 85, 88, 97, 100, 101, 106, 107, 110, 111, 114, 115, 118, 122, 142, 143, 142, 146, 147, 154, 155, 159, 162, 169, 209, 226, 227, 230, 232, 236, 244, 252, 253, 264, 272, 273, 280, 281, 284, 290, 291, 294, 295, 298, 299, 302, 303, 306, 307, 311, 358, 359, 374, 375, 379, 399, 410, 414, 415, 422, 428, 429, 444, 445, 452, 453, 456, 460, 469
physical-effect verb 230
physical or mental transfer 236, 240
physical participant-internal ability 216
piccaninny 436, 437
pidginization 65, 315
pie chart xliii, xliv, xlv
pied-piping construction 367, 371
plantation 3, 11, 84, 119, 445
plural xxxix, xli, 35, 38, 50, 51, 54, 55, 58, 59, 60, 61, 60, 68, 69, 76, 84, 85, 88, 89, 92, 93, 96, 97, 100, 101, 104, 105, 107, 114, 115, 119, 123, 253, 359, 440, 480, 491
plural article 89, 97
plural marker xxxix, xli, 35, 84, 85, 88, 89, 92, 93, 96, 97, 107, 114
plural marking 84, 85, 88, 89, 93, 96, 97, 104, 114
plural word 85, 88, 89, 96, 97, 105
polarity 298, 334, 338, 342
polar question xlii, 410, 411, 433
politeness xli, 68, 69
possession xlii, 6, 142, 146, 151, 252, 306, 307, 310, 311
possessive preposition 146, 151
possessive pronoun 142, 143, 147, 150, 151, 261, 346
possessor xli, xlii, xliii, 6, 7, 35, 106, 142, 143, 146, 147, 150, 151, 260, 269, 306, 307, 346, 444

possessum xli, xlii, xliii, 6, 7, 142, 143, 142, 146, 147, 146, 151, 306, 307, 444
possibility xlvi, 76, 89, 97, 118, 151, 172, 173, 208, 216, 217, 221, 230, 264, 277, 306, 318, 327, 339, 354, 366, 370, 374, 387, 403, 410, 414, 418, 444
postposition 14, 15, 143, 146, 147, 233, 241, 272, 276, 314, 315, 318, 319, 323, 327
predicate negation 406, 407
predicative xl, xli, xlii, 10, 31, 142, 150, 154, 290, 291, 294, 295, 298, 299, 302, 303, 306, 310, 311
predicative adjective xlii, 10, 31, 154, 294, 295, 299
predicative locative phrase xlii, 298, 299, 302, 303, 311
predicative noun phrase xli, xliii, 290, 291, 294, 295, 298, 299, 302, 303, 311
predicative possession xlii, 142, 306, 310
prefix 11, 65, 85, 88, 89, 122, 123, 143, 142, 221, 245, 253, 310, 398, 419, 469, 468
prenasalized 474, 485, 494
preposition 14, 15, 77, 143, 146, 147, 150, 151, 162, 226, 227, 233, 236, 237, 240, 241, 261, 264, 265, 272, 276, 285, 307, 314, 315, 318, 319, 322, 323, 326, 327, 326, 330, 331, 330, 342, 359, 362, 367, 370, 371, 374, 375, 374, 386, 445, 460
present state 201
primary surpass marking 162
pro-drop 245, 248, 249
pro-drop parameter 249
progressive xli, 168, 169, 172, 173, 176, 180, 181, 184, 185, 184, 188, 189, 193, 196, 197, 204, 205, 208, 209, 217, 335, 480, 481
progressive affix 180
progressive aspect 184, 197, 204
progressive function 184, 185, 184, 208
progressive marker xli, 168, 169, 172, 173, 176, 180, 181, 184, 185, 184, 188, 193, 196, 204, 205, 209, 480, 481
prohibitive xli, 220, 221, 402
pronominal demonstrative 122, 123
pronominal possessor xli, 6, 142, 143, 150, 151, 346
pronoun xxxviii, xxxix, xli, xlii, 2, 45, 50, 51, 54, 55, 58, 60, 61, 64, 65, 68, 69, 72, 73, 76, 77, 80, 84, 85, 89, 92, 93, 96, 97, 107, 111, 122, 123, 142, 143, 146, 147, 150, 151, 163, 168, 169, 177, 221, 226, 230, 232, 233, 236, 241, 244, 245, 248, 249, 252, 253, 257, 261, 290, 310, 338, 339, 342, 346, 347, 350, 351, 350, 354, 355, 359, 363, 366, 367, 370, 371, 374, 375, 374, 399, 406, 418, 428, 468, 495
proper name 69, 93
proper noun 6
purely aspectual system 177, 192, 193
purely temporal system 192, 193

quantificational 253
quantifier 89, 97, 130, 169
questionnaire xxxi, xxxii, xlvi, xlvii, xlviii, 260, 464, 484
question particle 410, 411

raining construction 256, 257
reanalysis 147
recipient 226, 236, 237, 240, 241, 240, 261, 265, 269, 342, 343, 379
reciprocal construction xlii, 354, 355
reduplication 88, 89, 96, 100, 101, 130, 131, 394, 418, 419

511

Subject index

reflexive construction 346, 351, 354
reflexive pronoun xlii, 346, 347, 350, 351, 350
relative clause xli, xlii, 10, 11, 26, 27, 35, 81, 97, 291, 366, 367, 370, 371, 374, 375
relative importance xliii, xlvii, 10, 468
relative particle 366, 367, 370, 371, 374, 375, 374
relative pronoun 163, 366, 367, 370, 371, 374, 375, 374, 418
reported-speech construction 378
resultative 168, 192
resumptive pronoun 27, 290, 338, 339, 366, 367, 370, 371, 374, 375, 374
retention 35, 315, 347
rightward position 168, 169
rigid order 40
rising intonation 410
role-marking 230

savvy xl, 440, 441
schwa 485, 486, 488
secondary-object construction 236, 237
secondary surpass marking 162
secundative construction 236
semantic role 26, 366, 370
semi-creole xxxv
sensation 260, 464, 465
serialized verb 14
serial verb xlii, xlvi, 159, 162, 163, 208, 237, 241, 265, 272, 273, 276, 281, 314, 315, 318, 319, 323, 326, 327, 326, 331, 330, 334, 335, 338, 339, 342, 362, 378, 379, 382
serial verb construction xlii, 159, 162, 163, 208, 237, 272, 273, 276, 315, 326, 327, 326, 331, 330, 334, 338, 339, 342, 362, 378, 382
sex-denoting word xliii, 468, 469, 468
sibilant 485, 490, 491, 492, 494
simplification 291, 299, 315, 319
singular 50, 51, 54, 58, 60, 61, 65, 68, 69, 76, 77, 84, 85, 104, 105, 110, 114, 115, 220, 233, 245, 248, 253, 468, 480
sonorant 474
sortal numeral classifier 138
speech act participant 127
standard marker 159, 162, 163
standard negation xlii, 398, 402
standard negator 196
standard NP 158
standard of comparison 162
state word 204, 205
stative situation 290
stative verb xli, 184, 192, 196, 200, 201, 294, 465
stem 88, 89, 96, 122, 123, 212, 261, 362, 378, 386, 480
stem change 88, 89, 96
stimulus 264, 265, 268
strong suppletion 212, 213
structural feature xxxi, xxxvii, xl, xliv
structure dataset xxxi, xlv
student assistant xlvi, xlviii
subject xxxviii, xli, xlii, xliii, 2, 3, 6, 7, 10, 26, 40, 41, 44, 64, 65, 114, 142, 154, 169, 173, 208, 221, 232, 233, 240, 241, 240, 244, 245, 248, 249, 252, 253, 256, 257, 260, 261, 264, 265, 268, 269, 290, 294, 298, 299, 302, 306, 307, 310, 334, 335, 338, 343, 346, 350, 355, 358, 359, 366, 367, 370, 371, 374, 375, 386, 387, 386, 390, 391, 394, 398, 399, 402, 406
subject relative clause xlii, 26, 366, 367, 370, 371
subset NP 76, 77
substrate xxxi, xlvi, 3, 7, 11, 15, 19, 22, 23, 26, 31, 35, 45, 51, 58, 59, 72, 77, 80, 89, 100, 123, 131, 138, 143, 163, 193, 201, 205, 226, 237, 244, 245, 257, 260, 261, 265, 269, 281, 285, 291, 295, 299, 303, 307, 315, 319, 323, 327, 331, 335, 343, 347, 354, 359, 367, 379, 387, 395, 419, 422, 429, 433, 436, 440, 444, 449, 457, 461, 465, 475, 486, 487, 489, 490
subvarieties xxxvi, xlvi
suck teeth 432, 433
suffix 23, 84, 85, 88, 89, 96, 135, 143, 142, 146, 151, 158, 193, 205, 221, 233, 241, 261, 276, 307, 315, 346, 358, 362, 363, 398, 419, 422, 469, 468
suppletion xli, 212, 213
suppletive 88, 134, 135, 158, 212, 233, 398
surpass marker 162
syllable 65, 88, 89, 100, 410, 437, 474, 475, 477, 479, 480, 487, 488, 495
symmetrical verb 354
synchronic feature xxxviii
syncretism 60, 61, 60
syntactic categories 480, 481
syntactic category 342

TAM marker 168, 169, 172, 173, 177, 181, 196, 197, 200, 201, 249, 290
temporal adverbial 40, 41
tense xli, 19, 168, 169, 172, 173, 176, 177, 180, 185, 188, 192, 193, 196, 197, 200, 201, 205, 209, 212, 213, 217, 273, 290, 291, 294, 298, 299, 334, 335, 338, 342, 394, 399, 402, 419, 480
tense–aspect system 177
theme 236, 237, 240, 241, 240, 330, 334, 338, 339
third-person-plural pronoun xxxix, xli, 61, 85, 89, 93, 96, 97
tightness of the link xli, 168, 172, 176, 180
title xxxv, xli, 68, 69, 428
token frequency xliii, 14, 468
tone xlii, 65, 88, 89, 221, 480, 481
tone change 88
topical 2, 265, 290, 298, 307, 359
topicalization 2
topic xlii, 2, 19, 138, 142, 146, 227, 265, 290, 298, 306, 307, 359, 432
trade xxxv
transitive clause 2, 226
transitive motion verb 326, 330, 331
transitive possession verb xlii, 252, 306, 310, 311
transitive possessive construction 306, 311
transparent structure 72
transposition 101
tripartite pattern 230
triplication 101
truth value 216
typical action verb 264

uniquely identifiable 38, 106, 110
universal trend xlvi, 422
University of Giessen xlvi

value box xl, xliii, xliv, 2, 6, 50, 84, 88, 104, 334, 386, 406, 432
verbal/clausal conjunction 284, 285
verbal conjunction xli, 284, 285
verbal person marker 64
verb chain 208, 209
verb doubling xlii, 394, 418, 419
verb-doubling construction 394, 395, 418
verb inflection 40
verb movement 40
verbs of knowing xlii, 382, 383
verbs of speaking xlii, 378, 379, 383
vocative xlii, 97, 428, 429
vocative marker xlii, 428, 429
vocative phrase 428, 429
voiced sibilant 485, 491
voiceless 485, 489, 490, 491, 495

voiceless glottal fricative 495
vowel xlii, 65, 88, 89, 221, 295, 398, 474, 475, 484, 485, 486, 487, 488, 491
vowel height 485, 486, 487

weak suppletion 212, 213
whispered approximant 495
wh-phrase 44
word-class-changing 100, 101
word order xliii, xlv, 2, 3, 6, 23, 38, 40, 41, 146, 147, 155, 226, 236, 241, 265, 406, 410
word-order typology 143
World Color Survey 464, 465

zero xxxvii, 184, 188, 192, 200, 201, 205, 208, 230, 236, 244, 291, 299, 302, 303, 315, 318, 319, 322, 323, 335, 354, 366, 367, 370, 371, 374, 375, 374, 379, 383, 391, 444
zero anaphora 244
zero-copula 291
zero-marking 318, 322, 354, 371, 379

AUTHOR INDEX

Aboh, Enoch O. xviii, xxxiii, xxxv, 100, 119, 127, 209, 213, 216, 241, 298, 311, 318, 327, 350, 354, 359, 382, 387, 419, 436, 445
Aikhenvald, Alexandra xlviii, 208, 334, 338, 342
Aissen, Judith 226
Ameka, Felix 260, 261, 265
Ammann, Andreas 216
Angelo, Denise xviii, xxxii, xxxiii, xxxiv, 23, 27, 54, 77, 85, 92, 115, 119, 143, 146, 163, 173, 204, 240, 241, 253, 257, 299, 383, 398, 399, 423, 428, 436, 440
Ansaldo, Umberto xviii, xxxii, xxxv, 22, 30, 180, 257, 291, 299, 323, 334, 342, 469
Arends, Jacques xlix, 302

Baker, Philip xviii, xxxii, xxxiv, 7, 19, 35, 61, 104, 105, 126, 131, 158, 172, 177, 197, 249, 256, 291, 314, 323, 359, 383, 423, 437, 469
Bakker, Dik xxxvii
Bakker, Peter xviii, xxxii, xxxv, xlviii, xlix, xxxiv, 3, 10, 11, 15, 26, 27, 41, 127, 151, 155, 169, 181, 227, 261, 272, 362, 383, 387, 407, 411, 415
Bao Zhiming 205
Baptista, Marlyse xviii, xxxii, xxxiv, 106, 131, 181, 189, 212, 226, 264, 269, 280, 290, 294, 306, 355, 383, 453
Bartens, Angela xviii–xix, xxxii, xxxiv, xxxv, 44, 100, 107, 130, 142, 150, 176, 197, 213, 244, 253, 314, 335, 379, 382, 391, 394, 406, 423, 429, 433, 436, 440, 468
Batt, Oleg xvii
Baxter, Alan xix, xxxii, xxxiv, 34, 76, 189, 192, 197, 227, 237, 244, 248, 285, 334, 343, 355, 358, 359, 371, 391, 436
Berlin, Brent xlix, 464
Biagui, Noël Bernard xix, xxxii, xxxiii, xxxiv, 19, 88, 115, 159, 163, 177, 181, 185, 188, 205, 221, 244, 248, 256, 264, 277, 335, 370, 402, 433, 440, 448, 461, 469
Biberauer, Theresa xix, xxxii, xxxiv, 45, 69, 93, 101, 107, 111, 115, 177, 193, 220, 227, 245, 252, 269, 284, 315, 319, 327, 331, 390, 403, 410, 444
Bibiko, Hans-Jörg xvii
Bickel, Balthasar 146
Bickerton, Derek xxxvii, 172, 173, 200, 201, 204, 302
Bisang, Walter 379
Blevins, Juliette 474, 475
Bollée, Annegret xix, xxxii, xxxv, 19, 50, 77, 85, 89, 104, 105, 126, 197, 212, 241, 277, 285, 318, 330, 331, 367, 374, 403, 440, 441, 468
Boretzky, Norbert 60, 163, 295, 299, 303, 331, 379, 487
Bossong, Georg 226, 260
Boucher, Paul 469
Braun, Maria 469
Bril, Isabelle 323
Brousseau, Anne-Marie 387
Brown, Cecil H. 448, 449

Bruyn, Adrienne xix, xxxii, xxxiii, xxxiv, 15, 18, 27, 31, 110, 115, 119, 134, 147, 163, 173, 177, 181, 185, 217, 237, 252, 264, 315, 343, 418, 429, 436, 465
Bybee, Joan 176, 185

Carden, Guy 347
Cardoso, Hugo C. xix, xxxii, xxxiv, 15, 18, 22, 41, 65, 93, 114, 130, 143, 154, 163, 176, 233, 241, 261, 269, 294, 326, 370, 436, 441, 444
Carlisle, Robert S. 474, 475
Chaudenson, Robert 105
Clements, J. Clancy xix–xx, xxxii, xxxiv, 27, 50, 72, 100, 147, 159, 180, 205, 213, 227, 233, 260, 265, 273, 375, 378, 383, 419, 440, 464, 465
Colot, Serge xx, xxxii, xxxiv, 30, 45, 64, 72, 73, 76, 96, 118, 126, 143, 151, 162, 185, 209, 217, 253, 268, 280, 284, 291, 294, 299, 302, 306, 322, 342, 355, 359, 367, 371, 375, 394, 411, 414, 419, 440, 441, 452, 457, 468
Comrie, Bernard xvii, xli, xlvi, xlix, 230, 231, 232, 314, 366, 367
Corbett, Greville 54, 84, 92, 154
Corne, Chris 347
Creissels, Denis 244, 245, 311, 362
Croft, William 60
Cysouw, Michael 54, 58, 61

Daniel, Michael 92, 93, 428
Davey, John xvii
Déchaine, Rose-Marie 347
DeGraff, Michel 40, 41
den Besten, Hans xx, xxxii, xxxiii, xxxiv, 45, 69, 93, 101, 107, 111, 115, 177, 193, 220, 227, 245, 252, 269, 284, 315, 319, 327, 331, 390, 403, 410, 444
Déprez, Viviane 84
Devonish, Hubert xx, xxxii, xxxiii, xxxiv, 19, 31, 45, 104, 122, 130, 143, 172, 209, 237, 264, 272, 299, 311, 339, 355, 374, 429, 433, 436, 441, 445
Diessel, Holger 118, 122, 123, 126
Dijkhoff, Marta B. 391
Diki-Kidiri, Marcel 61
Dirksmeyer, Tyko xvii
Dixon, R.M.W. xl, xlviii, 208, 232
do Couto, Hildo Honório 208
Dryer, Matthew S. xli, xliii, xlviii, xlix, 2, 3, 6, 7, 10, 11, 14, 15, 18, 22, 23, 26, 27, 30, 31, 35, 41, 44, 45, 88, 89, 106, 110, 244, 398, 399, 402, 403, 410, 411

Ehrhart, Sabine xx, xxxii, xxxiii, xxxv, 10, 38, 44, 55, 59, 115, 126, 143, 181, 237, 294, 307, 318, 371, 379, 433, 444, 453, 456
Eriksen, Pål 256, 257

Author index

Escure, Geneviève xx, xxxii, xxxiv, 35, 96, 119, 126, 184, 200, 290, 306, 310, 330, 399, 402, 428, 432, 436
Evans, Nicholas 460

Faraclas, Nicholas xx, xxxii, xxxiv, 41, 45, 92, 130, 177, 181, 188, 248, 269, 273, 281, 339, 371, 387, 391, 399, 410, 414, 419, 433, 445, 460, 464, 465
Farquharson, Joseph xxi, xxxii, xxxiv, 18, 31, 38, 44, 65, 105, 205, 236, 248, 252, 272, 302, 323, 347, 379, 386, 441
Fattier, Dominique xxi, xxxii, xxxiv, 19, 31, 35, 60, 80, 88, 101, 104, 114, 118, 123, 126, 177, 188, 240, 256, 257, 334, 342, 347, 351, 375, 387, 394, 419, 429, 433, 441, 448, 495
Ferguson, Charles 291
Filimonova, Elena 58
Finney, Malcom A. xxi, xxxii, xxxiv, 19, 147, 168, 172, 184, 226, 236, 252, 253, 280, 322, 342, 371, 378, 440, 445
Foley, William xxi, xxxii, xxxv, 2, 14, 23, 54, 122, 127, 143, 168, 181, 192, 294, 298, 315, 334, 449
Forkel, Robert xvii
Fortescue, Michael 23

Gast, Volker 350, 422
Gerdts, Donna B. 362
Gil, David xli, xlix, 130, 131, 138, 432, 433
Gleixner, Lea xvii
Goodman, Morris 60, 61
Grant, Anthony xxi, xxxii, xlvi, xxxiv, 126, 131, 147, 181, 241, 269, 303, 311, 322, 339, 371, 407, 422, 440, 445, 457, 460, 469
Green, Lisa xxi, xxxii, xlv, xxxiv, 6, 18, 176, 188, 284, 311, 326, 334, 378, 399, 432, 464, 465, 469
Greenberg, Joseph H. 60, 143
Güldemann, Tom 378

Hackert, Stephanie xxi, xxxii, xxxiv, 22, 64, 65, 69, 85, 92, 101, 114, 386, 402, 432, 436, 468
Hagemeijer, Tjerk xxi–xxii, xxxii, xxxv, 23, 45, 64, 73, 85, 96, 101, 110, 122, 130, 146, 173, 252, 257, 295, 334, 346, 355, 387, 403, 411, 418, 433, 436, 445, 457
Haiman, John 347
Hajek, John 487
Hall, Robert 410
Hammarström, Harald 22
Haspelmath, Martin xxii, xl, xli, xlvi, xlviii, xlix, 22, 26, 30, 34, 38, 40, 44, 54, 58, 60, 64, 68, 72, 76, 80, 84, 88, 92, 100, 106, 110, 118, 142, 146, 147, 150, 204, 226, 230, 232, 236, 237, 240, 244, 245, 252, 260, 284, 285, 319, 323, 346, 347, 350, 354, 358, 359, 362, 366, 370, 374, 386, 387, 394, 398, 402, 406, 410, 422, 428, 432, 484, 486, 487, 488, 489, 490, 491, 492, 493, 494, 495
Haviland, John 76
Hawkins, John A. 367, 371, 375
Heine, Bernd 241, 311, 346
Helmbrecht, Johannes 68
Herbert, Robert K. 494
Hering, Ewald 464
Holm, John (member of author group Intumbo et al.) xxii, xxxii, xxxiv, xxxv, xxxvi, xxxvii, xli, xliii, xliv, xlvi, xlix, xxxiv, 45, 65, 93, 169, 173, 209, 233, 237, 253, 142, 163, 302, 326, 351, 358, 366, 379, 390, 394, 399, 411, 419, 423, 488, 489, 494
Huber, Magnus xxii, xxxii, xlvi, xxxiv, 2, 6, 10, 14, 18, 31, 34, 88, 162, 181, 193, 233, 237, 253, 261, 295, 371, 391, 436, 437, 440, 444, 448, 452, 456, 460, 464, 468, 480
Hurch, Bernhard 100

Idiatov, Dimitry 72
Ihemere, Kelechukwu Uchechukwu 391
Intumbo, Incanha xxii, xxxii, xxxvi, xxxiv, 45, 65, 93, 142, 169, 173, 209, 233, 237, 253, 326, 351, 358, 366, 390, 399, 411, 419, 423
Inverno, Liliana (member of author group Intumbo et al.) xxii, xxxii, xxxiv, 45, 65, 93, 142, 169, 173, 209, 233, 237, 253, 326, 351, 358, 366, 390, 399, 411, 419, 423

Jahraus, Alexander xvii
Janson, Tore 84, 89
Jung, Hagen xvii

Kahrel, Peter xvii
Kay, Paul 382, 414, 464, 465
Keenan, Edward 350
Keesing, Roger M. 58
Kemmer, Suzanne 347
Khin Khin Aye xxii, xxxii, xxxv, 11, 19, 26, 50, 158, 168, 220, 241, 245, 249, 272, 335, 342, 379, 411, 415, 440, 444
Kiyosawa, Kaoru 362
Klein, Thomas B. xxii, xxxii, xxxiv, 50, 111, 138, 146, 147, 159, 268, 295, 314, 371, 382, 399, 410, 415, 440, 486
Klempel, Christina xvii
Klingler, Tom xxii, xxxii, xxxiii, xxxiv, 35, 115, 119, 126, 155, 163, 169, 204, 237, 253, 269, 299, 358, 386, 403, 428, 441
König, Christa 241
König, Ekkehard 241, 350, 422
Koopman, Hilda 15, 257
Kortmann, Bernd xxvii, 158, 367
Kouwenberg, Sylvia xxiii, xxxii, xxxiv, 6, 15, 18, 41, 50, 69, 73, 85, 89, 100, 107, 115, 119, 127, 130, 147, 158, 169, 177, 180, 184, 196, 216, 220, 237, 241, 245, 256, 268, 298, 302, 335, 339, 342, 358, 386, 394, 403, 407, 414, 415, 418, 436, 440, 444, 456, 465, 480
Kriegel, Sibylle xxiii, xxxii, xxxiv, 7, 19, 35, 61, 104, 126, 131, 158, 172, 177, 197, 217, 249, 256, 314, 323, 347, 359, 383, 423, 469
Kuteva, Tania 366, 367

LaCharité, Darlene 359
Lang, Jürgen xxiii, xxxii, xxxiv, 10, 40, 45, 69, 84, 89, 119, 131, 184, 204, 294, 338, 359, 371, 394, 407, 423, 436, 437, 440, 444, 445
Langbein, Sven xvii
Lanz, Linda A. 23
Lawal, Adenike S. 327
Lazard, Gilbert 64
Leeding, Velma 230
Lefebvre, Claire 35, 61, 143, 257, 299, 347, 387, 394, 395
Levin, Beth 359
Li, Michelle xxiii, xxxii, xxxiv, 3, 18, 19, 31, 34, 50, 60, 61, 65, 111, 114, 127, 131, 138, 163, 169, 172, 181, 184, 197, 226, 227, 233, 244, 249, 257, 261, 272, 277, 294, 298, 306, 331, 334, 347, 350, 351, 374, 383, 410, 429, 441, 457, 481, 490

Author index

Lichtenberk, Frantisek 76, 77
Lim, Lisa xxiii, xxxii, xxxv, 22, 30, 180, 257, 291, 299, 323, 334, 342, 469
Lord, Carol 146, 379, 493
Ludwig, Ralph xxiii, xxxii, xxxiv, 30, 45, 64, 72, 73, 76, 96, 118, 126, 143, 151, 162, 185, 209, 217, 253, 268, 280, 284, 291, 294, 299, 302, 306, 322, 342, 355, 359, 367, 371, 375, 394, 411, 414, 419, 440, 441, 452, 457, 468
Luffin, Xavier xxiii–xxiv, xxxii, xxxiv, 22, 30, 35, 38, 51, 88, 100, 154, 168, 172, 181, 189, 193, 212, 221, 264, 281, 307, 314, 391, 411, 414, 469
Lunkenheimer, Kerstin xxxvii, 158, 367

McWhorter, John 142
Maddieson, Ian 474, 475, 480, 481, 484, 486, 492
Maffi, Luisa 464
Mahbood, Ahmar 72
Malchukov, Andrej 236
Manessy, Gabriel 84, 89
Manfredi, Stefano xxiv, xxxii, xxxiii, xxxiv, 19, 45, 88, 101, 111, 114, 169, 177, 220, 241, 252, 260, 294, 311, 318, 330, 347, 367, 415, 429, 433, 445
Maslova, Elena 354
Matras, Yaron xxxv, xlix
Matthews, Stephen xxiv, xxxii, xxxiv, 111, 138, 163, 244, 257, 261, 294, 298, 306, 334, 350, 410, 441
Maurer, Philippe xxiv, xxxii, xliv, xlvi, xxxiv, xxxv, 7, 18, 23, 30, 38, 50, 69, 73, 77, 85, 92, 96, 97, 111, 114, 122, 126, 127, 130, 134, 138, 143, 147, 151, 154, 158, 163, 168, 169, 172, 173, 176, 180, 184, 185, 188, 192, 196, 200, 205, 208, 209, 212, 216, 217, 220, 227, 233, 240, 244, 252, 260, 261, 272, 273, 276, 280, 291, 295, 303, 319, 331, 334, 338, 339, 342, 343, 347, 355, 359, 366, 375, 379, 386, 387, 403, 407, 414, 415, 418, 419, 429, 436, 437, 441, 445, 452, 457, 465, 474, 475, 480, 481, 492
Meakins, Felicity xxiv, xxxii, xxxiv, xxxv, 14, 18, 19, 23, 54, 77, 93, 123, 150, 177, 201, 230, 232, 273, 276, 307, 319, 327, 331, 338, 347, 354, 371, 410, 433, 436, 444, 448, 453
Meeuwis, Michael xxiv, xxxii, xxxiv, 19, 22, 45, 51, 64, 77, 88, 146, 162, 168, 189, 221, 253, 264, 307, 363, 371, 378, 387, 419, 429, 469, 481
Melzian, Hans 123
Mesthrie, Rajend xxiv, xxxiii, xxxiv, 2, 30, 115, 127, 131, 159, 169, 173, 176, 291, 318, 330, 362, 366, 436, 437, 465, 469, 493
Meyerhoff, Miriam xxiv, xxxiii, xxxiv, 11, 27, 44, 45, 54, 68, 77, 93, 96, 110, 115, 126, 131, 150, 169, 245, 277, 335, 355, 390, 399, 415, 432, 440, 441, 461, 490
Michaelis, Susanne Maria xxiv–xxv, xxxiii, xxxv, xliv, xlvi, xlix, xxxv, 18, 22, 26, 30, 34, 58, 77, 92, 104, 111, 126, 147, 154, 158, 162, 201, 204, 216, 236, 237, 248, 256, 260, 264, 268, 272, 285, 290, 294, 298, 302, 306, 310, 314, 318, 322, 323, 326, 330, 331, 334, 335, 355, 362, 366, 370, 374, 375, 378, 382, 383, 386, 390, 391, 394, 398, 402, 407, 415, 422, 428, 432, 444, 468
Miestamo, Matti 196, 398, 402
Migge, Bettina xxv, xxxiii, xxxiv, 14, 61, 68, 81, 104, 107, 119, 122, 127, 130, 204, 205, 265, 269, 285, 295, 315, 319, 334, 375, 448
Miller, George A. 453
Miller, Philip H. 245
Mohanan, K. P. 265

Moravcsik, Edith A. 92, 93, 100
Mous, Maarten xxv, xxxiii, xxxiv, 14, 105, 127, 155, 200, 217, 221, 253, 256, 303, 311, 314, 363, 382, 398, 414, 444, 456
Mufwene, Salikoko S. xxv, xxxi, xxxiii, xxxiv, 10, 22, 44, 92, 126, 131, 143, 244, 294, 363, 366, 379, 391, 406, 411, 415, 419, 433, 444, 453, 460, 461, 465, 480
Mühleisen, Susanne xxv, xxxiii, xxxv, 51, 97, 105, 119, 158, 252, 299, 358, 375, 399, 418, 433, 441, 457
Mühlhäusler, Peter xxv, xxxiii, xxxiv, 7, 55, 59, 84, 89, 163, 257, 290, 318, 398, 423, 444, 452, 460
Muysken, Pieter xxv, xxxiii, xlix, xxxiv, 72, 100, 162, 168, 176, 180, 193, 227, 245, 265, 273, 276, 315, 346, 347, 371, 383, 387, 403, 411, 440

Nedjalkov, Vladimir P. 354
Neumann-Holzschuh, Ingrid xxii, xxv–xxvi, xxxiii, xxxiv, 35, 115, 119, 126, 155, 163, 169, 204, 237, 253, 269, 299, 358, 386, 403, 428, 441
Nichols, Johanna 146, 147
Nordhoff, Sebastian 39, 395

Osumi, Midori 323
Otanes, Fé T. 76

Paauw, Scott xxvi, xxxiii, xxxiv, 10, 23, 30, 138, 143, 181, 192, 196, 232, 256, 257, 260, 268, 343, 391, 411, 429, 432
Parkvall, Michael 163, 347, 379, 486, 487, 489, 490, 491, 492, 494
Patrick, Peter xxxvii, xli, xlii, xlvi
Perekhvalskaya, Elena V. xxvi, xxxiii, xxxiv, 2, 10, 19, 27, 41, 50, 106, 126, 147, 169, 273, 277, 302, 327, 402, 407, 411, 428
Peterson, David A. 362
Petrollino, Sarah xxvi, xxxii, xxxiii, xxxiv, 19, 45, 88, 101, 111, 114, 169, 177, 220, 241, 252, 260, 294, 311, 318, 330, 367, 415, 429, 433, 445
Pfänder, Stefan xxvi, xxxiii, xxxiv, 14, 118, 142, 181, 290, 315, 335, 343, 355, 374, 423, 440, 441, 445, 468
Pietzner, Verena xvii
Plag, Ingo xxvi, xxxiii, xxxv, 15, 61, 101, 107, 110, 118, 126, 146, 173, 261, 295, 331, 339, 378, 411, 433, 469
Polinsky, Maria 105, 362, 363
Pollock, Jean-Yves 40
Post, Marike xxvi, xxxiii, xxxiv, 11, 23, 38, 40, 41, 177, 237, 264, 327, 342, 347, 362, 382, 398, 423, 436, 437, 440, 453, 456, 464
Prentice, David John 7
Prescod, Paula xxvi, xxxiii, xxxv, 6, 97, 100, 104, 131, 159, 181, 291, 294, 299, 335, 347, 375, 383, 414, 445, 456

Quint, Nicolas xxvi–xxvii, xxxii, xxxiii, xxxiv, 19, 88, 115, 159, 163, 177, 181, 185, 188, 205, 221, 244, 248, 256, 264, 277, 335, 370, 402, 433, 440, 448, 461, 469

Rappaport Hovav, Malka 359
Revis, Melanie xvii, xxvii, xxxii, xxxiii, xlvi, xlviii, xxxv, 10, 38, 44, 55, 59, 115, 126, 143, 181, 280, 294, 307, 318, 371, 379, 433, 444, 453, 456
Rickford, Angela E. 432, 433
Rickford, John R. 299, 302, 303, 432, 433

Author index

Ritter, Elizabeth 394, 395
Rivierre, Jean-Claude 323
Roberts, Ian 248
Roberts, Sarah J. xxvii, xxxiii, xxxiv, 54, 55, 93, 107, 159, 169, 227, 249, 273, 335, 367, 402, 415, 436, 437, 448
Rosalie, Marcel xxvii, xxxiii, xxxv, 18, 26, 30, 34, 77, 92, 104, 111, 126, 147, 154, 201, 204, 216, 236, 272, 285, 310, 326, 335, 355, 375, 383, 391, 407, 415, 428, 432, 444, 468
Rounds, Carol 104
Rowlands, E.C. 429
Rubino, Carl 100

Samarin, William xxvii, xxxiii, xxxv, 11, 22, 31, 61, 80, 110, 122, 126, 131, 188, 189, 200, 217, 265, 269, 280, 307, 338, 375, 382, 418, 419, 428, 433, 448, 457, 464, 469, 481
Schaber, Sandy xvii
Schachter, Paul 76
Schladt, Mathias 347
Schmidt, Claudia xvii
Schmortte, Eva-Maria xvii
Schneider, Ulrike xvii
Schröder, Anne xxvii, xxxiii, xxxiv, 30, 96, 101, 107, 119, 130, 154, 193, 205, 315, 323, 351, 354, 366, 370, 407, 418, 445
Schultze-Berndt, Eva xxvii, xxxii, xxxiii, xxxiv, 23, 27, 54, 77, 85, 92, 115, 119, 143, 146, 163, 173, 204, 240, 241, 253, 257, 299, 383, 398, 399, 423, 428, 436, 440
Schwegler, Armin xxvii–xxviii, xxxiii, xxxiv, 55, 65, 85, 89, 143, 151, 169, 200, 204, 284, 350, 354, 374, 403, 423, 433, 441, 453, 495
Seuren, Pieter 72
Sharma, Devyani 299, 302, 303
Siegel, Jeff xxviii, xxxiii, xxxv, 6, 11, 18, 22, 27, 30, 31, 54, 58, 59, 64, 77, 92, 96, 101, 111, 126, 127, 130, 146, 162, 181, 237, 284, 290, 298, 319, 327, 334, 350, 354, 370, 379, 402, 423, 433, 441, 457, 461, 469
Siemund, Peter 350
Siewierska, Anna 50, 51, 64, 65, 232, 244, 358, 359
Silverstein, Michael 232
Singer, Ruth J. 77, 290
Sinnemäki, Kaius 226
Sippola, Eeva xxviii, xxxiii, xxxiv, xxxv, 2, 19, 27, 38, 55, 60, 81, 115, 127, 143, 150, 151, 189, 201, 216, 227, 237, 241, 249, 253, 268, 298, 310, 314, 343, 355, 359, 411, 423, 440, 444, 449, 452, 456
Slomanson, Peter xxviii, xxxiii, xxxv, 11, 26, 39, 41, 80, 93, 107, 127, 150, 176, 196, 217, 227, 257, 261, 265, 273, 276, 307, 323, 327, 394, 398, 415, 444, 453, 465, 468
Smith, Geoff P. xxviii, xxxiii, xxxv, 11, 31, 54, 64, 77, 92, 96, 101, 111, 126, 130, 181, 237, 327, 334, 350, 354, 370, 379, 423, 433, 441, 457, 461, 469
Smith, Ian R. xxviii, xxxiii, xxxv, 44, 106, 123, 138, 139, 176, 197, 216, 227, 233, 241, 265, 272, 206, 387, 440, 444, 449, 468
Smith, Norval S. H. (member of author group Aboh et al.) xxviii, xxxii, xxxiii, xxxv, xlix, 7, 15, 72, 100, 119, 127, 209, 213, 216, 241, 298, 311, 314, 318, 327, 346, 347, 350, 354, 359, 382, 387, 419, 436, 445
Smith-Stark, Cedric 84

Spencer, Andrew 428
Stassen, Leon 162, 163, 280, 281, 290, 295, 302, 303, 306, 307, 311
Steinkrüger, Patrick O. xxviii, xxxiii, xxxv, 19, 35, 41, 44, 55, 107, 118, 155, 163, 180, 192, 227, 233, 291, 367, 382, 398, 407, 444, 457
Stewart, William A. 347
Stolz, Thomas 5, 100, 134, 276
Surek-Clark, Clarissa xxxiv, xxxv, 437
Swolkien, Dominika xxviii–xxix, xxxiii, xxxiv, 6, 115, 126, 177, 209, 213, 249, 257, 260, 264, 269, 281, 351, 418, 429, 444, 449

Taylor, Bradley xvii
Tepowa, Adebiyi 15
Tesnière, Lucien 77
Thomas, Charles W. 441
Thompson, Dahlia xxix, xxxii, xxxiii, xxxiv, 19, 31, 45, 104, 122, 130, 143, 172, 209, 237, 264, 272, 299, 311, 339, 355, 374, 429, 433, 436, 441, 445

Urban, Matthias 445, 457

van den Berg, Margot C. xxix, xxxii, xxxiii, xxxiv, xxxv, 15, 18, 27, 31, 110, 115, 119, 134, 147, 163, 173, 177, 181, 185, 217, 252, 264, 315, 343, 418, 429, 436, 465
van der Auwera, Johan 216, 220, 422
van der Voort, Hein xxix, xxxiii, xxxiv, 2, 23, 81, 107, 273, 314, 383, 403, 436, 437
van Sluijs, Robbert xxix, xxxiii, xxxiv, xxxv, 15, 34, 96, 126, 147, 154, 177, 181, 185, 212, 217, 253, 281, 326, 334, 343, 370, 383, 386, 418, 437, 452
Vanhove, Martine 460
Veenstra, Tonjes (member of author group Aboh et al.) xxix, xxxii, xxxiii, xxxv, 100, 119, 127, 209, 213, 216, 241, 298, 311, 318, 327, 350, 354, 359, 382, 387, 419, 436, 445
Velupillai, Viveka xxix, xxxiii, xxxiv, 41, 115, 146, 197, 212, 256, 280, 284, 310, 398, 418, 441, 469
Verma, Manindra 265
Veselinova, Ljuba N. 134, 212, 213
Viberg, Åke 461
Voorhoeve, Jan 172

Wälchli, Bernhard 323
Weber, David John 230
Wekker, Herman 72
Welmers, William E. 461
Wendeland, Wilhelm 441
Widlitzki, Bianca xvii
Wilkins, David 460
Winford, Donald xxix–xxx, xxxiii, xxxv, 61, 101, 107, 110, 118, 126, 146, 162, 173, 261, 295, 302, 331, 339, 378, 411, 433, 465, 469

Yakpo, Kofi xxx, xxxiii, xxxiv, 26, 41, 55, 96, 105, 107, 150, 159, 221, 248, 264, 273, 295, 339, 367, 390, 391, 399, 429, 465, 481
Yip, Moira 481

Zúñiga, Fernando 363

LANGUAGE INDEX

African American English xx, xxi, xxix, xxxii, xxxiv, xxxv, 6, 72, 89, 151, 158, 176, 180, 188, 213, 257, 284, 302–3, 311, 326, 378, 432, 437, 469, 475, 489, 492

African-based languages 81, 465

African languages xxvi, 22, 31, 34, 35, 45, 55, 61, 86, 89, 123, 201, 245, 257, 295, 303, 314, 347, 354, 367, 378, 395, 419, 422, 429, 445, 449, 486–8, 490, 493, 494

African Portuguese-based languages 40–1, 189

Afrikaans xix, xx, xxxii, xxxiv, xxxv, 7, 11, 15, 45, 60, 69, 72, 81, 85, 93, 101, 107, 111, 122, 135, 142, 146, 147, 150, 151, 169, 177, 181, 184, 188, 193, 213, 220, 221, 227, 241, 245, 252, 253, 257, 269, 284, 303, 315, 327, 331, 355, 390, 403, 410, 414, 423, 437, 444, 469, 474, 475

Akan 15, 91, 378, 491

Algonquian 362

Ambon Malay xxxiii, xxxiv, 10, 11, 23, 30, 59, 61, 69, 72, 88, 89, 101, 130, 134, 135, 138, 139, 143, 146, 168, 177, 181, 188, 192, 201, 232, 233, 249, 256, 257, 260, 268, 284, 302, 343, 346, 351, 355, 383, 390, 391, 411, 414, 429, 432, 449, 452, 456, 457, 474

Angolar xxiv, xxxii, xxxiv, 18, 72, 73, 85, 88, 89, 91–2, 100, 111, 123, 127, 130, 134, 143, 147, 151, 158, 181, 189, 240, 256, 260, 261, 269, 295, 303, 311, 323, 327, 331, 335, 338, 339, 366, 367, 375, 379, 383, 386, 387, 407, 415, 429, 436, 437, 452, 453, 457, 461, 464, 465, 474, 491, 492, 493, 494

Arabic xxiii, xxiv, xxxiii, xxxiv, 7, 11, 19, 22, 35, 45, 51, 54, 72, 84, 88, 89, 101, 111, 118, 122, 135, 143, 146, 151, 168, 169, 173, 177, 184, 188, 189, 201, 220, 221, 241, 249, 252, 260, 284, 285, 290, 291, 294, 303, 311, 330, 335, 351, 355, 367, 407, 411, 415, 422, 429, 433, 445, 453, 456, 474, 485, 493

Arabic-based/-lexified languages 7, 38, 51, 54, 72, 122, 135, 173, 177, 201, 335, 422

Arabic vernacular 146

Atlantic creoles 7, 31, 81, 163, 201, 205, 244, 252, 253, 261, 265, 291, 295, 299, 323, 343, 347, 378, 379, 394, 395, 419, 486, 488, 489, 490

Atlantic English-based languages 72, 73, 93, 233, 354, 391

Australian languages 23, 27, 54, 55, 58, 163, 230, 354

Austronesian languages 26, 54, 58, 81, 245, 347, 465, 487, 489, 491

Bahamian Creole xxi, xxxii, xxxiv, xxxvii, 22, 64, 65, 68, 69, 73, 85, 89, 92, 158, 180, 185, 189, 257, 265, 291, 311, 323, 386, 402, 432, 436, 437, 445, 449, 457

Balanta 335

Bantu-based languages 22, 81, 85, 134, 135, 146, 168, 176, 201, 245, 265, 285, 335, 362, 363, 422

Bantu languages 3, 7, 11, 22, 35, 50, 51, 58, 65, 81, 85, 88, 93, 105, 134, 135, 146, 168, 176, 201, 226, 245, 253, 257, 265, 285, 299, 323, 331, 335, 355, 362, 363, 422, 437, 452

Bantu lexifier 362

Bari 493

Batavia Creole xxxii, xxxiv, xxxvi, 30, 73, 81, 89, 119, 122, 127, 139, 143, 177, 185, 189, 208, 227, 233, 244, 252, 273, 295, 303, 323, 338, 339, 343, 355, 383, 415, 436, 445, 452, 474, 475, 486, 488, 491, 493

Belizean Creole xxxii, xxxiv, 35, 81, 88, 96, 119, 126, 150, 184, 185, 188, 200, 221, 290, 306, 310, 323, 330, 343, 402, 414, 428, 432, 436, 445, 456, 457

Berbice Dutch xxiii, xxxii, xxxiv, xxxvi, 6, 7, 15, 31, 41, 50, 73, 89, 100, 123, 134, 147, 158, 177, 180, 185, 189, 209, 220, 245, 268, 285, 298, 311, 327, 335, 338, 339, 342, 355, 379, 383, 391, 394, 403, 414, 415, 418, 444, 449, 452, 453, 456, 474, 489, 491

bilingual mixed language xxv, 131, 134, 168, 177, 184, 188, 220, 273, 281, 334, 335, 339, 343, 415

Bininj Gun-wok 58

Bislama xxiv, xxxiii, xxxiv, xxxvii, 7, 11, 27, 34, 44, 45, 54, 55, 58, 68, 73, 89, 93, 96, 97, 110, 126, 131, 134, 150, 158, 169, 177, 185, 189, 217, 249, 257, 269, 281, 285, 298, 315, 322, 331, 335, 351, 355, 379, 390, 415, 449, 460, 461, 474, 486, 490

Bobangi xxxiv

Brava *see* Cape Verdean Creole of Brava

Cameroon Pidgin English xxxiii, xxxiv, 30, 73, 81, 96, 101, 107, 119, 123, 130, 134, 135, 184, 188, 193, 205, 217, 265, 303, 315, 323, 351, 354, 366, 370, 407, 418, 429, 445, 474, 493, 494

Cape Verdean Creole xviii, xxviii, 6, 7, 10, 40, 41, 45, 51, 68, 69, 72, 81, 89, 96, 106, 119, 123, 126, 131, 135, 146, 151, 176, 177, 181, 185, 189, 204, 209, 212, 213, 220, 226, 249, 253, 256, 257, 260, 264, 265, 269, 280, 281, 285, 290, 294, 295, 303, 306, 323, 335, 338, 339, 351, 355, 371, 383, 394, 395, 407, 414, 415, 418, 423, 429, 436, 437, 444, 445, 449, 453, 474, 475, 488, 489, 493

Cape Verdean Creole of Brava xxxii, 51, 69, 81, 106, 131, 135, 176, 181, 189, 212, 226, 256, 264, 269, 280, 290, 306, 355, 383, 453, 493

Cape Verdean Creole of Santiago xxxii, xxxiv, 10, 40, 45, 51, 69, 119, 131, 135, 176, 181, 185, 189, 204, 294, 338, 339, 371, 394, 407, 423, 436, 437, 444, 445

Cape Verdean Creole of São Vicente xxxiii, xxxiv, 6, 51, 68, 69, 96, 126, 135, 151, 177, 185, 189, 209, 213, 249, 257, 260, 264, 265, 269, 281, 285, 351, 414, 415, 418, 429, 444, 445, 449, 474, 475

Caribbean English-based languages xix, xxvii, xxxii, 143, 151, 162, 233, 299, 314, 323, 354, 407

Casamancese Creole xxxiii, xxxiv, 19, 68, 69, 88, 123, 135, 159, 163, 169, 177, 181, 185, 188, 205, 213, 220, 221, 244, 248, 249, 256, 257, 264, 265, 281, 303, 323, 335, 339, 355, 367, 370, 375, 402, 415, 429, 433, 448, 453, 461, 464, 465, 469, 486, 489, 494

Cavite Chabacano xxxiii, xxxiv, xxxvi, 2, 60, 69, 81, 88, 127, 134, 135, 150, 151, 177, 185, 189, 212, 216, 217, 220, 227, 249, 310, 314, 343, 407, 423, 444, 449, 452, 453, 456, 495

Chabacano xxviii, xxx, xxxiv, xxxvi, 2, 3, 19, 27, 35, 41, 44, 55, 58, 59, 60, 68, 69, 80, 81, 89, 101, 107, 118, 119, 127, 134, 135, 143, 146, 150, 151, 162, 163, 177, 180, 185, 189, 192, 201, 212, 216, 217, 220,

Language index

227, 233, 241, 249, 253, 268, 284, 291, 298, 310, 314, 315, 322, 323, 343, 355, 366, 367, 382, 402, 407, 411, 423, 444, 449, 452, 453, 456, 457, 489, 490, 491, 493, 495; *see also* Cavite, Ternate, Zamboanga

Chinese Pidgin English xviii, xx, xxiii, xxiv, xxviii, xxxii, xxxiv, 18, 65, 107, 111, 134, 135, 138, 139, 142, 163, 181, 184, 193, 244, 245, 257, 260, 261, 273, 285, 291, 294, 295, 298, 306, 323, 334, 335, 339, 350, 410, 411, 410, 415, 437, 449, 474, 488, 492

Chinese Pidgin Russian xxxiii, xxiv, xxxvi, 2, 10, 15, 19, 26, 27, 35, 41, 50, 65, 68, 80, 85, 105, 106, 107, 122, 126, 147, 168, 169, 177, 181, 184, 193, 201, 213, 220, 245, 273, 302, 327, 402, 407, 411, 428, 449, 474, 489

Chinook xxxiv

Chinuk Wawa xxxii, xxxiv, 3, 35, 80, 85, 122, 126, 131, 147, 169, 177, 181, 184, 193, 201, 217, 241, 269, 284, 303, 311, 314, 322, 339, 351, 371, 407, 422, 445, 452, 457, 460, 461, 464, 465, 469, 474, 475, 489, 491

Classical Arabic 54

Cree xxiv, 11, 51, 59, 143, 151, 261, 355, 362, 363, 407

Creolese xxxii, xxxiii, xxxiv, 19, 31, 41, 45, 73, 88, 101, 104, 105, 111, 122, 130, 134, 135, 143, 172, 185, 189, 209, 213, 233, 249, 264, 265, 272, 299, 311, 323, 339, 351, 355, 374, 429, 432, 433, 436, 445

Cushitic xxxiv

Dahalo 444

Diu Indo-Portuguese xxxii, xxxiv, 7, 15, 18, 22, 41, 65, 81, 85, 89, 93, 101, 107, 130, 135, 143, 163, 176, 185, 189, 227, 233, 241, 249, 261, 269, 285, 294, 295, 326, 327, 370, 383, 433, 436, 444, 449, 474, 489, 493

Dutch 346, 355, 406, 407, 444, 465, 486, 488, 491, 495

Dutch-based xxvi, 15, 34, 50, 51, 97, 111, 131, 142, 168, 177, 188, 212, 216, 253, 257, 386, 414, 453, 481, 488, 489

Early Sranan xxix, xxxii, xxxvi, 7, 15, 18, 27, 31, 61, 110, 119, 134, 135, 147, 163, 173, 177, 181, 185, 189, 217, 264, 285, 315, 322, 331, 343, 418, 429, 436, 437, 445, 452, 453, 457, 465

East African languages 35

Eastern Ijo 444

Egyptian Arabic 118

English xxii, xxx, xxxiii–xxxiv, xxxv–xxxvii, xl, xliii, xlvi–xlvii, 2–3, 6–7, 10–11, 15, 18–19, 23, 30–1, 34–5, 40, 44–5, 50–1, 54–5, 58, 60–1, 65, 68, 72–3, 80–1, 84–5, 88–9, 93, 96–7, 101, 104–7, 110–11, 118–19, 122–3, 126–7, 130–1, 134–5, 138–9, 142–3, 146–7, 150–1, 158, 162–3, 168–9, 172–3, 176–7, 180–1, 184–5, 188–9, 192–3, 201, 205, 209, 212–13, 216–17, 220, 226, 230, 233, 241, 244–5, 248–9, 252–3, 256–7, 260–1, 264–5, 268–9, 273, 280–1, 284–5, 291, 294–5, 298–9, 302–3, 306, 310–11, 314–15, 322–3, 326–7, 330–1–334, 335–8, 339, 342–3, 347, 350–1, 354–5, 366–7, 370–1, 375, 378–9, 382, 386, 390–1, 394, 402, 406–7, 410–11, 414–15, 418, 422–3, 428–9, 432–3, 436–7, 444–5, 449, 452–3, 456–7, 460–1, 464–5, 468–9, 474, 486–95

English-based languages xxvi, xxxvii, xl, xlv, 19, 31, 34, 35, 50, 51, 55, 58, 61, 68, 72, 73, 81, 89, 93, 97, 105, 106, 110, 111, 118, 119, 122, 123, 126, 127, 130, 131, 134, 135, 143, 146, 147, 151, 158, 162, 168, 172, 173, 176, 177, 180, 181, 184, 185, 188, 189, 192, 201, 205, 209, 212, 216, 217, 220, 233, 241, 248, 249, 252, 253, 256, 257, 265, 281, 284, 295, 299, 302, 303, 314, 323, 327, 331, 338, 339, 342, 343, 347, 350, 354, 355, 367, 371, 375, 378, 379, 386, 391, 402, 407, 410, 414, 415, 422, 423, 429, 432, 433, 486, 487, 488, 492, 493, 495

Eskimo xxxiv

Eskimo Pidgin xxxiii, xxxiv, xxxvi, 2, 23, 35, 65, 81, 84, 107, 169, 181, 184, 193, 197, 201, 245, 273, 291, 314, 383, 403, 436, 437, 460, 474, 489, 491

European languages xxv, 14, 50, 58, 84, 89, 92, 201, 209, 245, 253, 260, 284, 315, 350, 367, 386, 406, 407, 410, 419, 422, 429, 432, 433, 452, 456, 457, 465, 488

Ewe 15, 260, 261, 265, 269

Fa d'Ambô xxvi, xxxiii, xxxiv, xxxvi, 22, 23, 123, 151, 177, 184, 264, 303, 307, 311, 323, 327, 335, 339, 342, 346, 347, 382, 423, 436, 437, 452, 453, 456, 464, 465, 486

Fanakalo xxxiii, xxxiv, 2, 11, 22, 30, 34, 65, 73, 122, 127, 130, 131, 135, 146, 159, 168, 169, 173, 176, 181, 184, 249, 285, 291, 298, 303, 323, 330, 351, 362, 363, 366, 436, 437, 445, 449, 452, 456, 460, 461, 464, 465, 469, 474, 493

Fante 429

Fongbe 35, 61, 257, 299, 387, 395

French xxvi, xxxvii, xlvi, xxxiv, xxx, 2, 3, 7, 10, 11, 18, 19, 30, 31, 34, 35, 40, 50, 54, 55, 60, 61, 65, 68, 72, 73, 81, 84, 85, 89, 97, 105, 106, 110, 111, 118, 122, 126, 127, 131, 134, 135, 142, 146, 147, 151, 158, 162, 163, 168, 172, 173, 177, 180, 181, 184, 188, 189, 201, 209, 212, 216, 217, 226, 233, 244, 245, 249, 252, 253, 256, 257, 261, 268, 269, 273, 284, 285, 291, 295, 299, 302, 303, 307, 310, 311, 314, 315, 322, 323, 327, 330, 338, 339, 342, 343, 347, 350, 355, 379, 394, 403, 407, 410, 414, 415, 423, 429, 437, 444, 445, 449, 452, 453, 456, 457, 460, 465, 469, 486, 487, 488, 489, 490, 491, 493, 495

French-based languages xxvi, xxxvii, xlv, 19, 34, 50, 55, 61, 68, 72, 73, 81, 85, 89, 97, 105, 111, 118, 122, 126, 127, 131, 134, 135, 142, 147, 151, 158, 163, 168, 172, 173, 177, 181, 184, 188, 189, 201, 209, 212, 216, 217, 233, 245, 249, 252, 253, 257, 273, 284, 291, 295, 299, 302, 303, 307, 314, 323, 330, 338, 339, 342, 343, 355, 379, 394, 403, 407, 410, 414, 415, 423, 429, 486, 487, 488, 489, 490, 491, 493, 495

Garrwa 230

Gbe 205, 395

German 2, 3, 6, 11, 68, 127, 130, 184, 201, 216, 220, 347, 350, 406, 407, 410, 457

Ghanaian Pidgin English xxii, xxxii, xxxiv, 15, 18, 31, 34, 73, 88, 89, 123, 134, 162, 177, 181, 185, 189, 193, 217, 233, 253, 261, 265, 269, 294, 295, 331, 339, 351, 371, 391, 436, 449, 460, 461, 469, 487, 488, 493

Guadeloupean Creole xx, xxxii, xxxiv, 30, 45, 64, 68, 72, 118, 126, 135, 159, 181, 185, 189, 209, 217, 253, 291, 294, 299, 302, 303, 306, 338, 354, 367, 375, 394, 415, 444, 452, 468

Guinea-Bissau Kriyol xxii, xxxii, xxxiv, xxxvi, 45, 65, 69, 73, 89, 93, 123, 127, 135, 142, 146, 150, 151, 169, 173, 177, 181, 185, 189, 209, 220, 233, 249, 253, 256, 257, 269, 303, 314, 323, 326, 335, 351, 355, 366, 378, 390, 411, 419, 423, 452, 453, 460, 486

Gulf of Guinea creoles 7, 22, 23, 41, 69, 81, 122, 123, 142, 151, 173, 200, 256, 257, 314, 323, 327, 331, 335, 355, 403, 407, 429, 437, 461, 492, 493

Gullah xxii, xxv, xxxii, xxxiv, 3, 50, 72, 73, 89, 111, 135, 138, 146, 147, 151, 159, 177, 185, 189, 233, 268, 295, 314, 323, 371, 382, 410, 411, 415, 437, 445, 489, 490, 493

519

Language index

Gurindji xxiv, xxxiv, 54, 59, 93, 119, 230, 436, 444, 448, 449, 452
Gurindji Kriol xxiv, xxxii, xxxiv–xxxvi, 7, 14, 18, 19, 23, 54, 55, 59, 77, 93, 114, 119, 123, 134, 150, 168, 177, 180, 184, 188, 201, 220, 230, 232, 273, 276, 295, 307, 315, 319, 327, 331, 338, 339, 347, 354, 371, 410, 415, 433, 436, 444, 448, 449, 452, 453, 456
Guyanais xxiii, xxxiii, xxxiv, 14, 34, 68, 85, 118, 134, 142, 173, 181, 188, 285, 290, 298, 303, 311, 314, 315, 335, 343, 355, 374, 423, 429, 445, 468, 474, 491

Haitian Creole xxi, xxxii, xxxiv, xxxvi, 19, 31, 34, 35, 40, 41, 60, 61, 65, 80, 81, 88, 89, 101, 104, 105, 118, 123, 126, 143, 146, 177, 181, 185, 188, 189, 200, 221, 240, 249, 256, 257, 281, 285, 299, 302, 303, 322, 334, 346, 347, 351, 387, 394, 395, 419, 423, 429, 433, 448, 452, 453, 488, 495
Hawai'i Creole xxiii, xxviii, xxix, xxxiii, xxxiv, 7, 89, 142, 146, 151, 180, 188, 212, 249, 256, 284, 298, 310, 383, 415, 437, 469, 492
Hiligaynon 59
Hindustani *see* Pidgin Hindustani
Hokkien (Chinese) 205, 335

Ibero-Romance-based xxiv, xlvi, 30, 34, 122, 127, 134, 135, 168, 169, 177, 180, 181, 184, 185, 188, 189, 205, 209, 212, 216, 220, 249, 295, 335, 338, 414, 415
Igbo 60, 61
Ijo 7, 15, 444, 449
Imbabura 68
Indian Ocean creoles 3, 7, 34, 35, 61, 89, 93, 105, 127, 131, 142, 151, 163, 173, 201, 204, 209, 241, 244, 245, 249, 257, 273, 291, 294, 299, 323, 335, 339, 474, 487, 490, 495
Indo-Aryan languages 27
Indonesian 23, 58, 139
Iñupiaq (Eskimo) 23

Jamaican xxi, xxv, xxix, xxxii, xxxiv, 18, 31, 44, 65, 81, 101, 105, 111, 143, 151, 185, 189, 205, 248, 252, 261, 265, 272, 273, 302, 303, 315, 323, 347, 379, 386, 429, 437, 474, 475, 487, 492, 493
Jaminjung 58
Juba Arabic xxiv, xxxii, xxxiii, xxxiv, 11, 19, 35, 45, 88, 89, 101, 111, 135, 143, 146, 151, 168, 169, 177, 184, 188, 189, 220, 221, 241, 249, 252, 260, 284, 294, 303, 311, 330, 351, 355, 367, 407, 414, 415, 429, 433, 445, 453, 456, 474, 485, 493

Khoekhoe 15
Kikongo-Kituba xxv, xxxiii, xxxiv, 10, 11, 22, 44, 50, 51, 72, 81, 85, 88, 92, 122, 126, 131, 135, 143, 176, 184, 188, 244, 256, 285, 294, 303, 307, 314, 315, 323, 338, 339, 355, 362, 363, 366, 379, 406, 410, 411, 414, 415, 419, 433, 444, 445, 452, 453, 456, 460, 461, 464, 465, 469, 475
Kimanyanga xxxiv, 444
Kimbundu 201
Kinubi xxiii, xxxiv, 11, 22, 30, 34, 35, 51, 88, 89, 100, 134, 135, 143, 168, 172, 173, 181, 185, 189, 193, 212, 220, 221, 249, 264, 281, 285, 307, 314, 351, 355, 391, 411, 414, 429, 456, 460, 469, 474, 475, 485, 493
Korlai xix, xxxii, 3, 7, 27, 35, 50, 68, 69, 73, 84, 93, 100, 135, 147, 159, 176, 180, 205, 208, 213, 227, 233, 249, 260, 261, 265, 269, 273, 295, 303, 307, 375, 378, 383, 415, 419, 452, 453, 464, 465, 475, 489, 490, 493

Krio xxi, xxxii, xxxiv, 19, 97, 123, 135, 147, 168, 172, 173, 184, 185, 189, 217, 226, 236, 252, 253, 280, 315, 319, 322, 331, 342, 371, 378, 440, 445, 461, 481, 499
Kriol xxviii, xxxii–xxxv, 7, 11, 14, 18, 19, 23, 27, 54, 55, 58, 59, 77, 81, 85, 88, 89, 92, 93, 101, 114, 115, 119, 123, 134, 143, 146, 150, 163, 168, 169, 173, 177, 180, 184, 188, 196, 201, 204, 220, 230, 232, 233, 240, 241, 253, 257, 273, 276, 291, 295, 299, 302, 307, 315, 319, 323, 327, 331, 338, 347, 354, 371, 383, 398, 399, 410, 415, 423, 428, 433, 436, 440, 444, 448, 449, 452, 453, 456, 485, 486, 502
Kru 494
Kwa 3, 261, 395, 494

Latin 81, 110, 226, 366, 406, 407, 495
Lingala xxiv, xxxii, xxxiv, 11, 19, 22, 45, 50, 51, 64, 65, 73, 81, 85, 88, 123, 134, 135, 143, 146, 162, 168, 176, 181, 184, 188, 189, 200, 201, 216, 221, 245, 249, 253, 264, 265, 285, 307, 315, 323, 346, 351, 355, 363, 371, 378, 387, 403, 415, 419, 423, 429, 445, 452, 453, 456, 461, 464, 469, 475, 490, 494
Louisiana Creole xxiii, xxvi, xxxii–xxxiv, 34, 35, 68, 81, 85, 89, 111, 119, 126, 151, 163, 168, 169, 185, 189, 204, 205, 217, 233, 249, 253, 269, 299, 314, 323, 343, 386, 391, 403, 415, 428, 444, 475, 495

Malagasy 35, 105, 490
Malay *see* Ambon Malay, Singapore Bazaar Malay
Malay-based languages 35, 59, 80, 89, 122, 134, 168, 177, 184, 188, 192, 220
Malayo-Portuguese 273
Mandarin 205
Marathi 135, 464, 465
Martinican Creole xx, xxxii, xxxiv, xxxv, 19, 34, 73, 81, 85, 96, 126, 143, 151, 162, 181, 185, 189, 204, 249, 268, 280, 284, 302, 322, 342, 355, 371, 394, 411, 414, 419, 429, 444, 452, 457
Massai xxxiv
Mauritian Creole xviii, xxxii, xxxiv, xxxvii, 3, 7, 19, 35, 61, 68, 85, 88, 104, 111, 126, 130, 131, 135, 158, 172, 177, 181, 188, 209, 217, 249, 256, 257, 285, 299, 302, 314, 323, 347, 351, 354, 383, 411, 414, 415, 423, 429, 453, 469, 488, 495
Media Lengua xxxiii–xxxv, 11, 26, 68, 100, 122, 162, 168, 176, 180, 185, 189, 193, 227, 233, 245, 265, 273, 285, 303, 315, 323, 355, 371, 383, 387, 403, 410, 411, 415, 422, 449, 469, 474, 475, 491, 495
Michif xviii, xxxii, xxxiv–xxxvi, 2, 10, 11, 14, 15, 26, 27, 34, 41, 50, 51, 59, 72, 80, 81, 85, 88, 89, 111, 119, 122, 127, 134, 143, 151, 168, 169, 176, 181, 184, 188, 220, 221, 227, 233, 241, 245, 261, 272, 273, 281, 314, 331, 351, 355, 362, 383, 387, 407, 411, 415, 453, 456, 475, 488, 491, 495
Mixed Ma'a/Mbugu xxv, xxxiii–xxxv, 11, 14, 22, 72, 81, 85, 88, 89, 122, 127, 135, 143, 146, 168, 176, 180, 184, 188, 200, 201, 216, 217, 221, 233, 245, 253, 256, 285, 303, 310, 311, 314, 322, 351, 355, 362, 363, 382, 414, 444, 445, 453, 456, 464, 469, 475, 494
Modern Standard Arabic 54

Negerhollands xxix, xxxiii, xxxiv, 7, 15, 34, 88, 89, 96, 97, 122, 126, 134, 135, 147, 177, 181, 185, 189, 212, 217, 253, 281, 303, 314, 326, 334, 335, 343, 370, 383, 386, 418, 452, 474
Nengee xxxiii, xxxiv, 14, 15, 31, 61, 68, 81, 101, 104, 105, 107, 119, 122, 127, 130, 134, 135, 173, 185, 189, 204, 205, 217, 233, 261, 265,

Language index

269, 285, 295, 315, 331, 334, 351, 375, 429, 437, 448, 453, 457, 486, 489, 491, 493
Ngbandi xxxv, 11, 457
Nicaraguan Creole English xxxii, xxxiv, xxxvii, 107, 111, 130, 135, 142, 151, 176, 180, 213, 253, 257, 351, 394, 414, 423, 436, 437, 486, 492, 493
Nigerian Pidgin xxxii, xxxiv, xxxvi, 41, 45, 88, 92, 96, 119, 123, 130, 134, 177, 181, 184, 188, 217, 248, 265, 273, 281, 285, 295, 339, 371, 387, 391, 410, 414, 415, 419, 433, 445, 452, 453, 460, 461, 464, 465
Nootka 469
Norf'k xxxiii, xxxiv, xxxvi, 7, 55, 59, 97, 101, 163, 180, 212, 217, 257, 290, 407, 411, 423, 437, 444, 452, 456, 460, 469, 489, 492
Nuuchahnulth 469

Obolo 387
Oceanic languages 54, 55, 58, 226, 323
Old English 54, 110

Pacific English-based languages 146
Palenquero xxvii, xxxiii, xxxiv, 35, 55, 65, 68, 85, 88, 89, 135, 142, 143, 151, 169, 181, 200, 201, 204, 212, 221, 249, 257, 284, 285, 295, 314, 323, 350, 354, 374, 403, 423, 433, 453, 460, 469, 486, 489, 493, 494, 495
Papiá Kristang xxxii, xxxiv, xxxvi, 11, 34, 73, 88, 89, 100, 107, 134, 135, 139, 147, 177, 189, 192, 227, 244, 248, 249, 273, 285, 303, 315, 323, 334, 339, 343, 355, 371, 383, 391, 436, 452, 453, 488
Papiamentu xxiii, xxiv, xxvii, xxxii, xxxiv, xxxv, xxxvii, 7, 18, 50, 69, 73, 81, 85, 88, 89, 101, 107, 118, 119, 126, 127, 135, 147, 169, 173, 181, 184, 185, 189, 208, 212, 216, 217, 220, 233, 241, 245, 249, 256, 257, 295, 302, 323, 335, 338, 343, 347, 350, 355, 386, 394, 407, 414, 415, 436, 445, 453, 465, 486, 491, 493, 495
Philippine languages 3, 45, 335, 355, 423
Pichi xxx, xxxiii, xxxiv, 26, 41, 55, 65, 73, 81, 96, 105, 107, 123, 135, 150, 159, 181, 185, 189, 217, 221, 248, 256, 264, 265, 273, 285, 294, 295, 306, 315, 331, 339, 343, 367, 390, 391, 429, 445, 465, 488, 489, 491
Pidgin Hawaiian xxiii, xxxiv, 3, 34, 54, 55, 59, 65, 93, 107, 122, 135, 143, 159, 168, 169, 177, 181, 184, 193, 201, 220, 227, 249, 273, 291, 315, 322, 335, 367, 402, 415, 436, 437, 448, 457, 464, 474, 475, 485, 491
Pidgin Hindustani xxviii, xxxiii, 6, 15, 18, 22, 27, 30, 65, 81, 122, 127, 134, 146, 162, 169, 177, 181, 184, 193, 272, 284, 290, 291, 295, 298, 303, 314, 323, 402, 423, 460, 474
Portuguese xxii, xxxiii, xxxvi, xxxvii, xxxiv, xxxv, xl, 3, 7, 11, 15, 18, 19, 22, 23, 26, 27, 30, 31, 35, 40, 41, 44, 50, 51, 58, 64, 65, 68, 69, 72, 73, 80, 81, 84, 85, 89, 93, 97, 100, 101, 106, 107, 111, 122, 123, 130, 131, 134, 135, 138, 142, 143, 147, 151, 163, 169, 173, 176, 180, 185, 189, 192, 201, 205, 208, 209, 213, 216, 217, 220, 226, 227, 233, 241, 244, 245, 248, 249, 252, 253, 257, 261, 265, 268, 269, 272, 273, 285, 291, 294, 295, 303, 306, 307, 310, 314, 315, 322, 323, 326, 327, 331, 335, 338, 339, 342, 343, 346, 347, 350, 355, 367, 370, 379, 383, 387, 402, 403, 406, 415, 423, 429, 433, 436, 437, 444, 445, 449, 452, 453, 457, 461, 465, 468, 469, 474, 475, 486, 487, 488, 489, 490, 491, 492, 493, 495
Portuguese-based languages xxvi, xxvii, 19, 22, 27, 31, 35, 40, 41, 50, 51, 68, 69, 72, 84, 85, 89, 97, 122, 123, 130, 142, 151, 163, 173, 176, 180, 189, 201, 213, 220, 227, 244, 245, 248, 249, 253, 257, 265, 273,

285, 294, 303, 314, 323, 331, 338, 339, 342, 343, 347, 367, 402, 403, 415, 429, 475, 486, 488, 489, 492, 493, 495
Principense xxiv, xxxii, xxxv, xxxvi, 23, 69, 72, 81, 85, 97, 123, 151, 163, 169, 172, 173, 181, 189, 205, 209, 213, 233, 248, 249, 256, 272, 280, 291, 295, 303, 306, 323, 327, 335, 339, 342, 347, 351, 355, 375, 403, 415, 419, 429, 436, 437, 452, 453, 456, 457, 460, 461, 465, 474, 475, 484, 490

Quechua 11, 227, 230, 265, 355, 403, 422

Reunion Creole xix, xxxii, xxxv, 3, 7, 19, 34, 50, 61, 68, 72, 73, 81, 104, 105, 126, 172, 176, 181, 188, 212, 213, 217, 233, 241, 249, 285, 295, 303, 322, 330, 331, 367, 374, 403, 415, 452, 453, 457, 468, 474, 493
Río de la Plata Spanish 226
Romance-based languages lvi, 30, 34, 81, 110, 111, 122, 127, 135, 147, 184, 185, 188, 189, 201, 205, 212, 216, 220, 233, 249, 295, 335, 338, 415, 422, 493
Russian xxvi, xxxiv, 2, 10, 15, 19, 26, 27, 35, 41, 50, 65, 68, 80, 85, 105, 106, 107, 122, 126, 147, 168, 169, 177, 181, 184, 193, 201, 213, 220, 245, 249, 273, 290, 291, 302, 327, 350, 402, 407, 411, 428, 449, 474, 489

San Andres Creole English xxxii, xxxv, 73, 135, 150, 213, 233, 244, 253, 257, 314, 335, 379, 382, 391, 406, 415, 429, 433, 437, 468, 486
Sango xxvii, xxxii, xxxv, 11, 22, 31, 34, 61, 69, 80, 81, 88, 89, 110, 111, 119, 122, 123, 126, 130, 131, 134, 143, 146, 177, 185, 188, 189, 193, 200, 216, 217, 249, 265, 269, 280, 284, 295, 307, 338, 339, 354, 375, 382, 383, 403, 415, 418, 419, 428, 429, 433, 445, 448, 457, 460, 461, 464, 469, 474, 475, 486
Santome xxi, xxxii, xxxv, 23, 45, 64, 69, 73, 85, 96, 97, 101, 107, 110, 122, 123, 130, 135, 146, 172, 173, 189, 252, 253, 256, 257, 295, 303, 306, 323, 327, 334, 335, 339, 346, 355, 387, 403, 411, 418, 429, 433, 436, 445, 453, 457, 474, 475, 493, 494
Saramaccan xix, xxxii, xxxiii, xxxv, xxxvi, 81, 88, 101, 119, 127, 135, 146, 185, 189, 209, 213, 216, 217, 241, 253, 285, 298, 303, 311, 315, 322, 323, 327, 350, 354, 382, 387, 394, 410, 411, 419, 436, 437, 445, 453, 456, 457, 464, 465, 488, 489, 492
Seychelles Creole xix, xxv, xxvii, xxxiii, xxxv, xxxvii, 3, 7, 18, 26, 30, 34, 60, 61, 73, 85, 92, 101, 104, 107, 111, 126, 147, 151, 158, 181, 188, 201, 204, 205, 216, 217, 233, 249, 261, 269, 272, 273, 290, 299, 302, 310, 322, 326, 335, 339, 355, 375, 379, 383, 391, 402, 407, 415, 428, 429, 432, 444, 457, 468, 474, 488, 490, 491, 495
Shuswap 362
Singapore Bazaar Malay xxxii, xxxv, 11, 19, 26, 50, 59, 68, 96, 107, 134, 135, 139, 142, 143, 151, 158, 168, 177, 184, 205, 220, 241, 245, 248, 249, 272, 302, 335, 338, 339, 342, 343, 355, 379, 411, 415, 444, 449, 452, 457, 474, 488, 493
Singlish xxiii, xxxii, xxxv, 22, 30, 72, 89, 101, 142, 146, 151, 176, 180, 184, 188, 205, 249, 253, 257, 291, 295, 299, 303, 323, 334, 335, 342, 343, 407, 423, 437, 469, 492
Sinhala 26, 139, 395
Sinitic languages 139, 343
Southeast Asian Portuguese-based languages 343
Spanish xxvii, xxx, xxxiv, 11, 61, 68, 69, 72, 80, 81, 84, 85, 106, 107, 111, 118, 119, 127, 131, 134, 135, 142, 146, 151, 185, 192, 226, 227, 233, 241, 245, 248, 249, 253, 257, 261, 268, 269, 284, 285, 310, 311,

521

Language index

Spanish (*cont.*)
 314, 315, 327, 335, 343, 347, 350, 403, 406, 423, 433, 436, 437, 444, 445, 449, 452, 453, 457, 465, 486, 488, 489, 491, 493, 495
Spanish-based languages xxvi, 68, 72, 107, 118, 131, 135, 192, 233, 241, 245, 249, 253, 311, 314, 327, 335, 343, 350, 423, 486, 489, 491, 495
Sranan xix, xxvi, xxix, xxxiii, xxxv–xxxvii, 7, 15, 18, 27, 31, 59, 61, 73, 85, 101, 107, 110, 118, 119, 126, 134, 135, 146, 147, 163, 173, 177, 181, 185, 189, 217, 252, 253, 261, 264, 285, 295, 311, 315, 322, 323, 331, 339, 343, 346, 347, 355, 378, 411, 418, 429, 433, 436, 437, 445, 452, 453, 456, 457, 465, 469, 474, 486, 488, 489, 491
Sri Lankan Malay xxiii, xxx, 7, 15, 26, 41, 58, 59, 80, 85, 89, 93, 107, 115, 127, 134, 135, 139, 143, 146, 150, 176, 188, 216, 217, 227, 257, 261, 265, 273, 303, 307, 315, 323, 327, 331, 338, 339, 343, 394, 395, 410, 415, 444, 449, 452, 453, 457, 468
Sri Lanka Portuguese xxiii, xxxiii, xxxv, 3, 7, 15, 26, 44, 51, 58, 69, 80, 89, 100, 106, 123, 134, 135, 138, 139, 147, 163, 176, 180, 216, 227, 233, 241, 261, 265, 272, 291, 306, 315, 323, 346, 379, 383, 387, 415, 444, 449, 453, 468, 488, 489
Standard French 403, 407
Sudanese Arabic 445
Swahili 226, 493

Tagalog 54, 58
Tahitian 7
Tamil 11, 26, 58, 106, 139, 227, 346, 444, 465
Tayo xx, xxxii, xxxiii, xxxv, xxxvi, xxxvii, 10, 44, 55, 59, 68, 85, 88, 89, 126, 134, 143, 146, 168, 177, 181, 188, 193, 201, 217, 245, 249, 257, 261, 265, 269, 280, 294, 298, 303, 307, 323, 351, 371, 379, 415, 433, 444, 453, 456, 460, 469, 486, 487, 490, 491, 493, 494
Ternate Chabacano xxviii, xxxiii, xxxv, 2, 19, 27, 55, 68, 80, 101, 119, 127, 134, 135, 143, 151, 177, 185, 189, 201, 241, 253, 268, 298, 315, 322, 355, 411, 452, 453, 456, 489, 493, 495
Tok Pisin xxviii, xxxiii, xxxv, 3, 7, 11, 23, 31, 34, 54, 55, 58, 64, 73, 85, 88, 89, 92, 93, 96, 97, 101, 111, 126, 130, 134, 146, 162, 169, 180, 181, 189, 217, 245, 249, 291, 298, 315, 322, 327, 331, 334, 350, 354, 370, 379, 415, 423, 433, 445, 453, 457, 461, 469, 486, 489, 491

Tolai 3, 7, 11, 58
Trinidad English Creole xxxiii, xxxv, xxxvii, 51, 97, 104, 119, 158, 252, 299, 323, 367, 375, 418, 432, 445, 457, 474, 486
Tugu Creole 273
Twi 429

Ubangian languages 22, 88
Ungarinjin 58

Vanuatu languages 7, 432
Vincentian Creole xxxiii, xxxv, 6, 73, 81, 97, 100, 104, 127, 131, 151, 158, 159, 181, 185, 189, 249, 291, 294, 299, 303, 335, 339, 347, 375, 383, 414, 429, 437, 445, 456, 475
Visayan languages 444
Volta-Congo 457

West African languages 35, 40, 41, 51, 55, 58, 61, 85, 123, 147, 189, 201, 205, 244, 245, 257, 260, 291, 295, 299, 303, 323, 331, 343, 354, 367, 387, 407, 419, 461, 486, 489, 490
West African substrate languages 201, 205, 244, 260, 291, 299, 331, 343, 387, 419, 489
Wolof 335

Xwela Gbe 205

Yélidnye 465
Yimas xxii, xxxv
Yimas-Arafundi Pidgin xxxii, xxxv, 2, 3, 7, 14, 15, 23, 54, 65, 111, 122, 127, 143, 168, 177, 181, 184, 192, 201, 217, 272, 291, 294, 295, 298, 315, 334, 338, 339, 379, 422, 449, 474
Yoruba 201, 327, 335, 429

Zamboanga Chabacano xxviii, xxxiii, xxxv, 19, 35, 41, 44, 58, 69, 88, 107, 118, 127, 135, 146, 162, 163, 177, 180, 185, 189, 192, 227, 233, 284, 291, 323, 367, 382, 407, 444, 452, 453, 457, 490, 495
Zulu xxi, 11, 362, 449, 465